Sixth Edition

TERRORISM TODAY
THE PAST, THE PLAYERS, THE FUTURE

Jeremy R. Spindlove

Clifford E. Simonsen

Pearson

330 Hudson Street, NY, NY 10013

—This edition is dedicated to Evan in the hope that you will grow up in a safer and kinder world

Vice President, Portfolio Management: Andrew Gilfillan
Portfolio Manager: Gary Bauer
Editorial Assistant: Lynda Cramer
Senior Vice President, Marketing: David Gesell
Field Marketing Manager: Thomas Hayward
Product Marketing Manager: Kaylee Carlson
Senior Marketing Coordinator: Les Roberts
Director, Courseware and Content Producers: Brian Hyland
Managing Producer: Cynthia Zonneveld
Managing Producer: Jennifer Sargunar
Content Producer: Ruchi Sachdev

Manager, Rights Management: Johanna Burke
Manufacturing Buyer: Deidra Smith, Higher Ed, RR Donnelley
Cover Design: StudioMontage
Cover Art: Bottom: Lane V. Erickson/Shutterstock; Top: Lakeview Images/ Shutterstock; Inset: By Aaron Tang [CC BY 2.0 (http://creativecommons. org/licenses/by/2.0)], via Wikimedia Commons
Full-Service Project Management: Manas Roy
Composition: iEnergizer Aptara®, Ltd.
Printer/Binder: LSC Communications/Willard
Cover Printer: Phoenix Color/Hagerstown
Text Font: Times LT Pro 10/12

Library of Congress Cataloging-in-Publication Data
Names: Spindlove, Jeremy R., author. | Simonsen, Clifford E., author.
Title: Terrorism today : the past, the players, the future / Jeremy R. Spindlove, Clifford E. Simonsen.
Description: Sixth Edition. | Hoboken : Pearson, [2018] | Revised edition of the authors' | Includes index.
Identifiers: LCCN 2016039412 | ISBN 9780134549163 | ISBN 0134549163
Subjects: LCSH: Terrorism. | Terrorism—History. | Terrorism—Prevention.
Classification: LCC HV6431 .S53 2018 | DDC 363.325—dc23 LC record available at https://lccn.loc.gov/2016039412

1 16

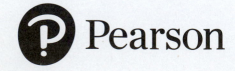

ISBN 10:   0-13-454916-3
ISBN 13: 978-0-13-454916-3

CONTENTS

List of Maps   viii

Preface   ix

About of Authors   xv

Part 1   The Definitions and History of Terrorism   1

Chapter 1   IN SEARCH OF A DEFINITION FOR TERRORISM   2

Overview   2

Terrorism: Searching for a Definition   4

Some Approaches to Defining Terrorism   5

The FBI Construct   8

The U.S. Department of Defense (DOD) Constructs   8

The United Nations—Actions to Counter Terrorism   10

Structures of Terrorist Groups   12

Common Terrorist Qualities   12

Terrorism as Criminal Behavior   15

Hostage Taking   15

Legal Issues in Hostage Taking   16

Assassination   16

Constitutional Rights   17

The USA Patriot Act: Preserving Life and Liberty   19

Summary • Review Questions • End Notes

Chapter 2   A BRIEF HISTORY OF TERRORISM   24

Overview   24

Violence and Terrorism   24

When Did Violence Become Terrorism?   26

State-Sponsored and Religious Terrorism   27

The Turks and the First Crusade   29

Islam   31

Jihad   33

Jihadization   35

The Media and Terrorism   35

State Terror and Genocide   39

Cyclical Nature of Terrorism   40

Contemporary Events: Historical Roots   40

The Lone Wolf   41

Summary • Review Questions • End Notes

Part 2   Global Terrorism   45

Chapter 3   THE UNITED STATES OF AMERICA   46

Overview   46

Connecting the Dots   47

Domestic Terrorism and Extremism   50

The Black Panthers and Nation of Islam   53

The Ku Klux Klan   53

Osama Bin Laden and Al Qaeda Threat to America   54

Preparations For 9-11   55

The Aftermath   57

Radical Islam and the United States   59

Pre-Radicalization   59

Self-Identification   59

Indoctrination   60

U.S. Foreign Policy—Challenges and Opportunities   61

Watch Lists   63

Extraordinary Rendition   64

Religious Extremism   66

Summary • Review Questions • End Notes

Chapter 4   CANADA AND THE CARIBBEAN   74

Overview   74

Puerto Rico   75

Canada   76

Immigration and Canada   78

Canada's Domestic Terrorism   80

International Terrorism—Sikh Terrorism   80

The Bombing of Air India Flight 182   83

Liberalism and Refugees   84

The Islamist Threat to Canada and Lone Wolf Attacks   85

Cuba   88

The Dominican Republic and Haiti   89

Summary • Review Questions • End Notes

Chapter 5   GREAT BRITAIN AND NORTHERN IRELAND   93

Overview   94

Ireland's Civil War   94

Irish War of Independence, 1919–1921   95

"The Troubles," 1968–1998   96

Political Objectives   97

Financing Terror   100

The Irish Republican Army and Provisional Irish Republican Army   101

Continuity Irish Republican Army   102

Direct Action Against Drugs   103

Republican Sinn Féin   103

Real Irish Republican Army   104

Other Irish Terrorist Groups   104

Turf Wars   108

Northern Ireland's Protestant Marching Season   111

The Pira and International Terror   113

The Northern Ireland Peace Process   114

Power-Sharing Executive   118

Countering Irish Terrorism   119

State-Sponsored Terrorism—Libya   120

Domestic Terrorism in Mainland Britain   123

Islamic Extremism   124

Hizb ut-Tahrir (The Islamic Liberation Party), al-Muhajiroun, and Islam4uk   125

Tablighi Jamaat   126

London—July 7, 2005   129

Operation Crevice   131

Murder of Lee Rigby—May 22, 2013   133

Extreme Right-wing Groups   138

Summary • Review Questions • End Notes

Chapter 6   WESTERN EUROPE   140

Overview   140

Spain   141

Spain's 9-11   147

France   148

Al Qaeda in France   152

Attacks on Paris, 2015—Charlie Hebdo and Bataclan   153

Germany   156

Terrorism and the Olympic Games Movement   160

Al Qaeda in Germany   161

Italy   165

The Red Brigade   166

GAP and NAP   167

Greece and Turkey   169

Greece   169

Cyprus   172

Turkey   173

Al Qaeda in Turkey   177

Belgium   178

Timeline—Brussels Attack   180

Netherlands   182

Danish Cartoons—Freedom of the Press   183

Sweden and Norway   183

Summary • Review Questions • End Notes

Chapter 7   EASTERN EUROPE AND THE BALKANS   188

Overview   188

Russia and the Soviet Union   189

Russia's Free-Market Economy and the Russian Mafla   194

Uzbekistan and Kyrgyzstan   195

Chechnya   197

Doku Umarov—The Chechen bin Laden   198

Ukraine   201

Georgia   202

Yugoslavia   203

Bulgaria   207

Czech Republic   208

Summary • Review Questions • End Notes

Chapter 8   NORTH AFRICA AND THE MIDDLE EAST   211

Overview   212

Israel and Its Right to Exist   212

The Stern Gang   214

Haganah, Irgun Zeva'i Le'umi, National Military Organization   215

Mossad   216

The Palestinian Liberation Organization   217

Political Considerations—Hamas, Fatah, and the Palestinian Authority   218

Al-Fatah   219

Operation Bayonet   219

Abu Nidal Organization   219

Significant Incidents   220

Al-Aqsa Martyrs Brigades   221

Hamas   223

Izz ad-Din al-Qassam Brigades   226

Hamas–Fatah Disunity   227

Weaponry   229

Fatah and Hamas—Unity Government   229

Jordan   233

Lebanon   235

Hezbollah   237

Hezbollah—War with Israel   239

Syria   240

Morocco   243

Egypt   244

Anwar Sadat, 1919–1981   245

Egypt's Islamic Extremists   245

Libya   247

Colonel Muammar El-Qaddafi   247

Operation El-Dorado Canyon   248

Islamic State—Threat to Libya   251

Tunisia   254

Sudan   255

Algeria   256

Al Qaeda in the Land of the Islamic Maghreb, Formerly GSPC   260

Summary • Review Questions • End Notes

Chapter 9   THE PERSIAN GULF   263

Overview   263

Saudi Arabia   264

From the Palestinians to Riyadh   266

Al Qaeda and the Saudi Kingdom   266

Wahhabi Islam   266

Sayyid Qutb (1906–1996)   268

Saudi Hezbollah—Khobar Towers   269

Islamic State—Threat to Saudi Arabia   271

Kuwait   272

Iraq   273

Saddam Hussein (1937–2006)   274

Operation Iraqi Freedom   277

Iraqi Insurgency   281

Al Qaeda—Islamic State in Iraq and Levant (ISIL)   282

Weapons of Mass Destruction   286

Support for International Terrorism   287

Bahrain   287

Oman   288

Iran   290

The Shah of Iran   291

Iran and Nuclear Weapons   294

Sponsoring Terrorism   295

Yemen   297

Summary • Review Questions • End Notes

Chapter 10   NORTHEAST, CENTRAL, AND SOUTHERN AFRICA   302

Overview   302

Ethiopia   303

Somalia   304

Piracy—A Somali Issue   308

Uganda   309

The Lord's Resistance Army   312

Zimbabwe   314

Unilateral Declaration of Independence   314

Zanu-PF 5 Brigade   316

South Africa   317

Afrikaner Nationalism   318

Islam in South Africa   321

Qibla Movement   322

Kenya   323

International Terrorism in Central Africa   324

Angola   326

Mozambique   327

Rwanda   328

Democratic Republic of Congo, Formerly Zaire   330

Nigeria   332

Summary • Review Questions • End Notes

Chapter 11   SOUTHERN AND SOUTHEAST ASIA   338

Overview   338

India   339

India's Political Assassinations   340

Special Economic Zone   341

Islam and India   341

Mumbai Attacks, November 2008   342

The Punjab and Sikhism   343

Pakistan   344

U.S. Navy Seals Kill Osama bin Laden—May 2011   344

Benazir Bhutto   345

Sikh Terrorism   349

Kashmir   350

Islamic Militancy   352

Nepal   352

Sri Lanka   353

Liberation Tigers of Tamil Eelam—LTTE   353

Afghanistan   356

Al Qaeda (The Base)   357

Taliban-Linked Insurgents—Haqqani Network   359

Islamic Emirate of Afghanistan   360

Burma (Myanmar)   362

Cambodia   364

Thailand   366

Thailand's Insurgency   367

Vietnam   368

Summary • Review Questions • End Notes

Chapter 12   THE PACIFIC RIM   372

Overview   372

China   373

Pan-Turkic Movement—Uighurs   374

Hong Kong   378

Taiwan (Republic of China)   378

Japan   379

Japanese Red Army   381

The Two Koreas   382

The Philippines   384

Indonesia   387

Jemaah Islamiyah (JI)   390

Australia   393

International Terrorism   394

Summary • Review Questions • End Notes

Chapter 13   LATIN AMERICA AND SOUTH AMERICA   399

Overview   400

Latin American Terrorism   401

Mexico   401

Guatemala   407

Honduras   408

El Salvador   409

Nicaragua   410

Sandinista National Liberation Front   411

Contras   411

Panama   412

Central American Gang Problems   413

Colombia   415

National Liberation Army   418

Right-Wing Death Squads   418

Peru   421

Bolivia   423

Brazil   424

Uruguay and Paraguay   426

Argentina   428

Chile   429

Military Dictatorship   430

Venezuela   432

Ecuador   433

Summary • Review Questions • End Notes

Part 3   The War on Terror   437

Chapter 14   COUNTERING TERRORISM   438

Overview   439

The Roles for Counterterrorism   439

Northern Ireland   442

Terrorism and Aviation   443

Operation Bojinka   448

Liquid Bomb Plot   449

Passenger Terminal Attacks   450

Combating Terrorists   455

UN Security Council Resolution 1373   458

The Patriot Act   459

U.S. Naval Station—Guantánamo Bay—Cuba   462

International Policing   463

Intelligence Gathering   463

Intelligence Services   465

Counterterrorism Units   467

Hostage Rescue Units   473

Canada   474

Piracy   475

Chemical and Biological Weapons   479

Biological Weapons   482

Dirty Bombs   485

Summary • Review Questions • End Notes

Chapter 15   THE FUTURE—WHAT NEXT FOR TERRORISM?   489

The Past and the Future   489

Al Qaeda and Islamic State   490

Aviation   491

Terrorism Larger Stage   492

Weapons of Mass Destruction   493

The Future Threats from WMD   494

Holy Terror   495

Suicide and Religious Terrorism   496

Technology and Countering Terrorism   498

Summary • End Notes

Chapter 16   RISK MANAGEMENT, INCIDENT MANAGEMENT, AND BUSINESS CONTINUITY MANAGEMENT   501

Overview   501

What Is a Risk Assessment?   501

Purpose   503

Executive Summary (Sample Document)   503

Sample Risk Assessment   503

Security Management Plan (Sample)   518

Overview   519

Business Continuity Management and Incident
   Management   520

Incident Management   522

World Health Organization   523

Incident Awareness   526

Managing Information   528

Testing Your Organizational Response   529

Exercise Objectives   529

Why Continuity and Disaster Recovery
   Planning?   529

Incident Management Exercise   530

Summary • End Notes

Glossary   535
Index   544

LIST OF MAPS

FIGURES

FIG 3-1   Map of the United States   47
FIG 4-1   Map of Puerto Rico   75
FIG 4-2   Map of Canada   77
FIG 5-1   Map of Great Britain and Northern Ireland   94
FIG 6-1   Map of Spain   141
FIG 6-2   Map of France   148
FIG 6-4   Map of Germany   157
FIG 6-6   Map of Italy   165
FIG 6-7   Map of Greece   170
FIG 6-8   Map of Turkey   173
FIG 6-11   Map of Belgium   178
FIG 6-12   Map of the Netherlands   182
FIG 6-13   Map of Sweden   184
FIG 6-14   Map of Norway   185
FIG 7-1   Map of Russia   189
FIG 7-3   Map of Kyrgyzstan   196
FIG 7-4   Map of Uzbekistan   196
FIG 7-9   Map of Ukraine   201
FIG 7-10   Map of Georgia   202
FIG 7-11   Map of Bosnia and Herzegovina   204
FIG 7-12   Map of Bulgaria   207
FIG 7-13   Map of Czech Republic   208
FIG 8-1   Map of Israel   212
FIG 8-5   Map of Gaza Strip   223
FIG 8-11   Map of Jordan   233
FIG 8-12   Map of Lebanon   235
FIG 8-13   Map of Syria   240
FIG 8-14   Map of Morocco   243
FIG 8-15   Map of Egypt   244
FIG 8-16   Map of Libya   247
FIG 8-17   Map of Tunisia   254
FIG 8-18   Map of Sudan   255
FIG 8-19   Map of Algeria   257
FIG 9-1   Map of Saudi Arabia   264
FIG 9-6   Map of Kuwait   272
FIG 9-8   Map of Iraq   274
FIG 9-16   Map of Bahrain   287
FIG 9-17   Map of Oman   288
FIG 9-18   Map of Iran   290
FIG 9-20   Map of Yemen   297
FIG 10-1   Map of Ethiopia   303

FIG 10-2   Map of Somalia   304
FIG 10-11 Map of Uganda   309
FIG 10-13 Map of Zimbabwe   314
FIG 10-14 Map of South Africa   318
FIG 10-15 Map of Kenya   323
FIG 10-20 Map of Angola   326
FIG 10-21 Map of Mozambique   327
FIG 10-22 Map of Rwanda   329
FIG 10-23 Map of Nigeria   332
FIG 11-4   Map of India   340
FIG 11-5   Map of Pakistan   344
FIG 11-12 Map of Nepal   353
FIG 11-13 Map of Sri Lanka   353
FIG 11-15 Map of Afghanistan   356
FIG 11-16 Map of Burma   363
FIG 11-17 Map of Cambodia   364
FIG 11-18 Map of Thailand   366
FIG 11-19 Map of Vietnam   368
FIG 12-1   Map of China   373
FIG 12-2   Map of Hong Kong   378
FIG 12-3   Map of Japan   379
FIG 12-5   Map of North Korea   382
FIG 12-6   Map of South Korea   383
FIG 12-7   Map of the Philippines   384
FIG 12-10 Map of Indonesia   387
FIG 12-14 Map of Australia   393
FIG 13-1   Map of Mexico   401
FIG 13-2   Map of Guatemala   407
FIG 13-3   Map of Honduras   409
FIG 13-4   Map of El Salvador   410
FIG 13-5   Map of Nicaragua   410
FIG 13-6   Map of Panama   413
FIG 13-7   Map of Colombia   415
FIG 13-8   Map of Peru   421
FIG 13-9   Map of Bolivia   424
FIG 13-10 Map of Brazil   425
FIG 13-11 Map of Uruguay   426
FIG 13-12 Map of Paraguay   427
FIG 13-13 Map of Argentina   428
FIG 13-15 Map of Chile   430
FIG 13-16 Map of Venezuela   432
FIG 13-17 Map of Ecuador   433

PREFACE

When we first contemplated a text on terrorism in its very broad scope, very little of that focus was on the United States. Texts on terrorism are not new, and prior to 9-11 they focused quite naturally on left- and right-wing groups and paramilitaries in Europe, Asia, and South America. The concept of terrorism includes such a wide range of activities that the most difficult task was how to make a text short enough to be effective for instructors, casual readers, and students, but long enough that it adequately covers an acceptable depth into this discipline. The rapidly changing world we now inhabit has become preoccupied with terrorism and the threats posed to our daily lives, and we admit that, at times, it seemed like we were trying to paint a moving bus—the players, organizations, and operations often changed faster than the speed at which we could write the words, and this continues to be the case!

We are grateful to those professors who have used and reviewed our previous texts and made valuable suggestions for additional material and information as well as correcting factual errors.

"What is terrorism?" As you read this book, it will become apparent that most terrorism actions are committed by groups of fanatics, some religious some not, dissidents and lone wolves, often with conflicting goals and little interface; but that has changed with the use of the Internet to spread global jihad. Many of these groups are continuing their plans to upset security and safety in Western democracies. We hope that the knowledge we have assembled in this book will stimulate students and others to seek out ways to offer better safety and security to all persons worldwide.

Your authors have attempted to provide a clear overview of many of the sectors and operations that comprise the broad terms *terrorism* and *counterterrorism*. We explore some specific subjects and locations in greater depth than others, reduce redundancy, and cover as many differences and similarities as possible. We present this edition with the belief that any learning experience should be enjoyable as well as educational. We offer instructors a text that we have organized and written with the goal of making teaching and the learning experience as interesting and effective as possible. We cover the essentials of the subject and include a large array of pedagogical tools in each chapter.

Security is an ancient need for humans—a basic rung on the ladder of Maslow's hierarchy of needs. The twenty-first century dawned and we awoke to a decade of unspeakable terrorist atrocities—attacks in New York, London, Washington, Madrid, Stockholm, and Bali, to name but a few. The second decade has proved to be no less deadly than the first with lone wolf attacks and commando style attacks in Europe, Asia, Africa, and the United States. Terrorism remains an elusive term to define; and we have presented an array of material to include opinion and theories on terrorist events.

THE TRADITION CONTINUES

The methodology for textbook development, which we have used successfully in the past, continues to be the foundation and cornerstone for this edition of *Terrorism Today*. We have built on the comments of readers, instructors, and students to the book's previous editions:

- An engaging writing style, resulting in a book that is highly readable and effective as an informational, teaching, and learning tool.
- A balanced treatment of practical examples, technology, history, and data from available documents and academic research.
- A systems approach to exploring the varied elements of terrorism, terrorists, and the various motives for terrorist groups as a potentially integrated and interrelated series of subsystems.
- An unbiased presentation of a wide range of topics, making for a text suitable for instructors and students from many disciplines and points of view.
- In-chapter and end-of-chapter materials that augment the textual materials with examples of events, persons, stories, terms to remember, maps, graphs, and photographic illustrations.

NEW TO THIS EDITION

Comprehensively updated to keep pace with today's fast-moving world of terrorism:

- **Up-to-date Terror Attack Briefs** detail specific attack incidents and provide examples of terror attack methodology by specific groups.
- **New statistical charts and information** on suicide attacks help students appreciate that the scale of terror attacks has not diminished with a War on Terror.
  - Data catalogued by the University of Chicago Project on Security and Terrorism provides insight on the value placed by the terrorist and the effectiveness of this method of attack.
  - For example, Figure 2.1 charts the number of terrorist attacks in 2015 and which countries had the most attacks, and Chapter 10 presents suicide attacks by location, year, target type, religion and weapon.
- **A new Chapter 16, "Risk Management, Incident Management, and Business Continuity Management,"** helps prepare students for the real world of terrorism and shows how to take a proactive approach to security and risk mitigation in the business, organization, or operation where they will work.

ORGANIZATION OF THE TEXT

This edition has again been divided into three major parts and sixteen chapters that build from historical backgrounds to predictions about terrorism in the twenty-first century. The addition of the sixteenth chapter discusses the practicality of risk management in a security environment and how to build an effective program that also addresses incident management and business continuity management. Each chapter begins with a set of Learning Outcomes, which should be accomplished after completion of the text. Information on specific terror events of note is included in the body of the text to illustrate and frame each chapter. Extensive endnotes, placed at the end of each chapter, provide helpful content and applicability to the subject matter. These should be considered as important as the textual materials themselves for presentation and study. The materials we have selected come from what we hope are the best and most currently available sources in the field. We presented them in their original form, or blended them into our own writing to minimize confusion.

Part One: The Definitions and History of Terrorism

Part One offers a historical look at terrorism's origins. Learning about the types of terror and their history will provide the student/reader with the background necessary to understand the evolution of terrorism in the present and into the future.

CHAPTER 1: IN SEARCH OF A DEFINITION FOR TERRORISM   Chapter 1 presents some basic definitions for terminology used throughout the following chapters. The information will allow the student to understand and differentiate between terrorist acts and ordinary criminal acts. The chapter presents defining issues, operational terms, useful typologies, as well as forms and tactics of terrorism in today's troubled world. Terrorism as criminal behavior and its use as a method for change are detailed. Such acts as ambush, assassination, arson, bombing, hijacking, hostage taking, kidnapping, blackmail, and protection are included. The initiation and development of the Patriot Act are covered in detail.

CHAPTER 2: A BRIEF HISTORY OF TERRORISM   Chapter 2 describes an act of violence as a logical progression, but one that can take place in microseconds within a single individual. Violence perpetrated for ideological reasons and for a systematically organized cause or complaint is shown to be much different. Chapter 2 also explores the motives and methods employed by individual terrorists or groups and state sponsors with some perceived agenda as compared to the motives of a state for suppressing dissent and revolution. The student/reader is introduced to the concept of state-sponsored terrorism, a concept that supports terrorist groups and individual terrorists with weapons, money, and supplies to achieve a government's goals. Discussions range from the Crusades to the continuing frictions between major religions around the world today. Islam, jihad, media, and social media involvement in terrorism are broadly reviewed.

Part Two: Terrorism Around the World

Part Two brings the reader to terrorist events—both left-and right-wing—of the twentieth and early twenty-first centuries. We examine the right-wing factions in various countries and regions, their similarities and differences, and their goals and objectives. We also look at the left-wing factions in various countries and regions, using a similar methodology, and we contrast the two. Part Two covers regions and nations in the investigation of terrorism, its many different forms and factions, and their interrelationships.

CHAPTER 3: THE UNITED STATES OF AMERICA   We examine the events leading up to 9-11 and the so-called intelligence "dots" that were never connected to prevent that cataclysmic event. We examine what has happened since 9-11 in the U.S. War on Terror. We examine and analyze "homegrown" terrorism in the United States to see how it compares with terrorism in other parts of the world. The United States is no longer free from the violent terrorist actions that have been plaguing the rest of the world. Defending the Homeland, the Patriot Act coupled with rendition tactics and how Americans are being radicalized will also be discussed.

CHAPTER 4: CANADA AND THE CARIBBEAN   We now examine the problems of immigration, illegal aliens and refugees, and the threat posed not just to Canada but also to the United States. Canada has for several decades expounded on its program of "multiculturalism," and this chapter reviews how Canada became a haven for fund-raising activities for terror groups including the Tamil Tigers and Sikh extremists. Canada suffered one of the worst terrorist attacks prior to 9-11, namely the downing of Air India Flight 182 in the Irish Sea, and this chapter examines that case in detail.

CHAPTER 5: GREAT BRITAIN AND NORTHERN IRELAND   Sectarian violence and terrorism associated with a long-enduring fight typifies Northern Ireland for much of the last century, and we examine the background to the "Irish Problem" and bring the reader up to date with examples of friction and terrorism on both sides of the issues; "the Troubles," as they have been termed, lasted for more than forty years and have only now reached the final, almost peaceful chapter. This chapter provides a model for examining other terror spots of the world. It shows similarities and differences in the use of terrorism in meeting political or religious goals. Ireland and mainland Britain have been embroiled in terrorism for more than four decades. Here, we examine the current political processes and the methods employed to reach a solution to the violence. We discuss the concerns of security forces and the export of terror knowledge to other international terror groups. The rise of Islamic extremism and suicide attacks by young British-born men on the London transport system and lone wolf attacks by jihadists are also discussed.

CHAPTER 6: WESTERN EUROPE   Chapter 6 examines terrorism, past and present, in Western Europe. The rise and fall of the ETA movement is tracked and draws comparisons with Ireland's Republican terrorist movement. We look at the turbulent history of Spain—from the inquisition to the fascist reign of terror under Franco, to the many terrorist activities in Spain, especially those involving the Basque separatists and Islamic extremists. In the twenty-first century, Europe is the target for international terror cells plotting and planning mayhem in other regions as well as their adopted homelands. Europe is witnessing the arrival of and threats from homegrown terrorism with commando style attacks in Paris and Brussels as western Europe struggles to contain the threats posed by refugees and migrants from the conflicts raging in Syria and Iraq.

CHAPTER 7: EASTERN EUROPE AND THE BALKANS   Chapter 7 recounts the sad history of the multiracial, multireligious region formerly known as Yugoslavia, from the partisan terrorism and German terrorism in World War II to the divided state that has seen constant interracial and interreligious fighting since its breakup. Terrorism and even genocide will be the main weapons in these battles for ethnic purity. We discuss the tensions between Uzbeks and Kyrgyz and the presence of Islamic radicals that will try and dictate outcome following decades of cultural repression under the Soviet boot. We examine the Russians and their long history of national terrorism to keep the populace under control, from the Czars, to the Soviet Union, and Stalin's murder of

50 million of his countrymen. The role of the ICTY in bringing war criminals who have committed crimes against humanity to justice is also reviewed.

CHAPTER 8: NORTH AFRICA AND THE MIDDLE EAST   Chapter 8 examines this most complex region of the world, where terrorism is a way of life in both local and international conflicts. We realize that all of the conflicts are similar in this region and terror is the primary weapon used by all sides. From the Ottoman Empire to the creation of the State of Israel to an Arab Spring, and the bloodshed that is Syria; the region has been subjected to wars, internal battles involving nationhood, religion and ethnic conflicts that have seen methods of terrorism, and the creation of terror groups that have spread throughout the world.

CHAPTER 9: THE PERSIAN GULF   Chapter 9 explores the Persian Gulf states, an area rich with oil and gas deposits and also the presence of diverging religious beliefs of Islam. We discuss the persecution of the Kurds in Iraq, the use of oil revenue to sponsor worldwide terrorism, and the threat of the use of nuclear, biological, and chemical weapons stirring the pot of terrorism in this area. The second Gulf War, the fall of Saddam Hussein, the U.S. military presence, and the rise of Islamic State have had a destabilizing effect on the entire region

CHAPTER 10: NORTHEAST, CENTRAL, AND SOUTHERN AFRICA   Chapter 10 examines the Dark Continent, from the long struggle for freedom from apartheid in South Africa to a quite different struggle in Robert Mugabe's dictatorship in Zimbabwe. We explore the genocide in the Congo, Uganda, and Rwanda and tribalism that divides most of these regions. We examine the presence of al Qaeda and groups pledging allegiance to Islamic State in Kenya and the atrocities of Boko Haram in Nigeria.

CHAPTER 11: SOUTHERN AND SOUTHEAST ASIA   Chapter 11 looks at past and present terrorism in southern and southeast Asia. India has a long history of terrorism; also, it possesses nuclear weapons. Following independence, India has had to combat attacks from religious factions and rebel causes. Pakistan and India maintain a tense relationship, with sporadic border violence bringing both countries to the brink of all-out war. The 2008 attack by extremists in Mumbai is also reviewed as having relevance for destabilizing the region. We re-examine Afghanistan, the first battlefield of the post-9-11 War on Terror. This chapter covers a long, ongoing war suffered by Sri Lanka (formerly Ceylon) with the Tamil Tigers and their eventual surrender. From the Khmer Rouge in Cambodia to the guerrilla fighters in the jungles of Malaysia and Indonesia, terrorism has seemed to find a long-term home in Southeast Asia.

CHAPTER 12: THE PACIFIC RIM   Chapter 12 explores the countries of the Pacific Rim. We examine China, which has moved past its terror-filled period following the ascension of Communism. Terror as a philosophy can be traced back through Chinese history as a viable means to control that vast nation. From the fighters against the government at the turn of the twentieth century to World War II and the Japanese occupation and to the terrorist tactics of the Marcos regime, the history of the Philippines has also shown that terror can be a useful tool in controlling a large, scattered, and very poor country. We explore the "successful" deployment of a weapon of mass destruction (WMD) by a Japanese cult/terror group, which stands as an example of the threat such weapons pose to the West in the twenty-first century. Indonesia with its vast Muslim population has encountered Islamic extremism with links to both al Qaeda and Islamic State.

CHAPTER 13: LATIN AMERICA AND SOUTH AMERICA   Chapter 13 discusses Latin America's struggles with terrorism. The so-called banana republics have long suffered from dictators who used terrorism against their people as well as rebels who used terrorism against governments. We examine major conflicts in terms of past history and present status and the roles of Mexico and Cuba in these struggles. Mexico has a long history of terrorism and revolution. The "other America" has been rife with terrorist activities for a long time, from The Shining Path of Peru to the "disappeared" in Brazil and Argentina. We discuss the drug cartels in Colombia that have led to political upheavals. The violence and danger of this region, as well as suppressive Latin American governments, invite terrorist organizations to emerge.

Part Three: The War on Terror

Part Three discusses the varying efforts of nations around the world to detect or defeat terrorism, to find other ways to deal with it, and to manage the threats of terrorism in the post 9-11 era. We will examine what the future of terrorism might be.

CHAPTER 14: COUNTERING TERRORISM Chapter 14 examines the world of counterterrorism—both politically and operationally. We determine which methods are effective and which have failed. These range from national paramilitary groups to local activities by regular citizens. We study in detail the importance of intelligence gathering, the cycle of intelligence, and the proper uses of intelligence against terrorism. The threats to aviation from acts of terror, along with maritime piracy, are discussed. The chapter examines worldwide counterterrorist groups and strategies, from the Delta Force in the United States, Delta 88 in Indonesia and to the Mossad in Israel, to the Special Air Service in the United Kingdom, and many other highly organized and effective groups both police and military. We discuss the strategies of the United Nations and regional governments and their successes and failures. The threats posed by chemical and biological agents have to be considered as the world prepares for the unexpected and the possibility of attack with WMDs.

CHAPTER 15: THE FUTURE—WHAT NEXT FOR TERRORISM? Chapter 15, as in the words of Pogo Possum, *"predicting stuff is difficult, especially if it's in the future"*. In looking forward we have to look back, and looking back at the last half-century we can possibly get a better understanding of terrorism and the future trends in terrorist activity. We will also look at the methods that we will need to employ to deter future terror actions wherever they might spring from.

CHAPTER 16: RISK MANAGEMENT, INCIDENT MANAGEMENT, AND BUSINESS CONTINUITY MANAGEMENT Chapter 16 gives students some insight and information on risk management principles and how to conduct a risk assessment. We live in a world of uncertainty which means we need to be capable of assessing risk and threats, and determining what needs to be done in mitigation. How will your business or organization function in the event of disaster—here we take a look at the models for Business Continuity and how to manage and train for incident management.

INSTRUCTOR SUPPLEMENTS

Instructor's Manual with Test Bank Includes content outlines for classroom discussion, teaching suggestions, and answers to selected end-of-chapter questions from the text. This also contains a Word document version of the test bank.

TestGen This computerized test generation system gives you maximum flexibility in creating and administering tests on paper, electronically, or online. It provides state-of-the-art features for viewing and editing test bank questions, dragging a selected question into a test you are creating, and printing sleek, formatted tests in a variety of layouts. Select test items from test banks included with TestGen for quick test creation, or write your own questions from scratch. TestGen's random generator provides the option to display different text or calculated number values each time questions are used.

PowerPoint Presentations Our presentations are clear and straightforward. Photos, illustrations, charts, and tables from the book are included in the presentations when applicable.

To access supplementary materials online, instructors need to request an instructor access code. Go to **www.pearsonhighered.com/irc**, where you can register for an instructor access code. Within 48 hours after registering, you will receive a confirming email, including an instructor access code. Once you have received your code, go to the site and log on for full instructions on downloading the materials you wish to use.

ALTERNATE VERSIONS

eBooks This text is also available in multiple eBook formats. These are an exciting new choice for students looking to save money. As an alternative to purchasing the printed textbook, students can purchase an electronic version of the same content. With an eTextbook, students can search the text, make notes online, print out reading assignments that incorporate lecture notes, and bookmark important passages for later review. For more information, visit your favorite online eBook reseller or visit www.mypearsonstore.com.

ACKNOWLEDGMENTS

Trying to acknowledge all those who have provided help and advice will make a long list, and here I must start with our families who have provided endless support together with our close personal friends, then our colleagues and international friends in academia, as well as professionals and practitioners in terrorism at the international, federal, state, and local levels. To each of them we extend our deepest appreciation and gratitude for encouraging and assisting us in putting together a text about this important topic that seems to work. We would, however, like to thank the special people at Pearson Education, in particular Jennifer Sargunar who was always available either online or via phone call to help, direct, and guide us, and Gary Bauer who helped turn our prose, ideas, and concepts for a book about terrorism into a textbook that will greatly assist students, readers, and instructors alike. I would also like to thank the reviewers for their valuable feedback: David MacDonald, Eastfield College; Thomas O'Connor, Austin Peay State University; P.J. Verrecchia, York College of Pennsylvania; and Stephen Wofsey, Northern Virginia Community College.

Special thanks to Mike McGuire for his constant support in all matters related to combat and counterterror exercises, and to Gary Wilson, a good friend, colleague, and former Royal Ulster Constabulary Police officer, to Tony Forward, retired Chief Superintendent, Surrey Constabulary, for their photography skills; and to David Loban, CEO of Vigil Technology for assisting and guiding me through developing Chapter 16. To my friends at Global News, and in particular to Steve Darling, co-anchor at Canada's *Global News Morning*, for his ongoing support of this text. Thanks also for the research being done with CPOST under the direction of Professor Robert Pape, Professor of Political Science at the University of Chicago Project on Security and Terrorism. Last, but by no means least, thanks to my wonderful wife Esther, my two sons Tim and Peter and their beautiful wives Laura and Ashley, without their constant cheerful support this sixth edition may not have happened. Cliff and I both found that writing can be a lonely task, especially when it involves such a specific and rapidly changing field. It is not easy to discuss the book with anyone else, while in the frantic throes of creation and revision. At this point I should point out that my coauthor and longtime friend has passed away after losing his battle with Alzheimer's disease. To those of you who knew Cliff you know what a big presence and kind heart he had. Cliff realized early on that he had this terrible disease and did everything in his power to fight it which he did with the support of all his family members. He had an extraordinary mind and a capacity for learning, and this terrible disease has deprived not only his family but also his many friends around the world. I personally will miss not only his friendship, knowledge, and insight but also his rampant good humor and terrible golf game!

ABOUT THE AUTHORS

Jeremy R. Spindlove retired from his position as Director of Safety and Business Continuity Management North America for DHL Supply Chain in May 2015, a global leader in supply chain management. Based in Vancouver, Canada, his responsibilities extended throughout Canada and the United States. He is now a principal in LLA Technologies Inc., a company developing state-of-the-art mesh networked security and life safety systems deployable in almost any environment. He has had firsthand experience in terrorism—first, through his service in the Surrey Constabulary (the United Kingdom) as a first responder on the scene in 1974 when a Provisional Irish Republican Army cell detonated two bombs, one in the Horse and Groom and the second in the Seven Stars pub in Guildford, which killed six and wounded more than sixty. Jeremy went on to be recruited by British Airways as an overseas security officer to supervise air terminal security operations for the airline in Baghdad, Iraq, for two years; in Amman, Jordan, for three months; and in Beirut, Lebanon, for six months. He traveled globally throughout the network conducting airport risk assessments for BA. On his return to the UK, Jeremy set up a fraud investigation unit, tracking and intercepting illegal immigrants transiting the UK en route to North America on forged passports and travel documents. He has been assigned to security duties escorting H.M. Queen Elizabeth to the Far East in 1987 and to Rome in 1988. Jeremy immigrated to Canada in 1988 and holds dual Canadian/British citizenship. He has held critical security leadership positions as Manager of Security and then Director of Airport Security at Vancouver International Airport. He is a qualified Passenger Screening Instructor and, during his airport tenure in 1994, served on a Canadian Advisory Board reviewing airport and aviation security regulations. In 1996, he moved to the Tibbett and Britten Group North America as Manager and, later, Director of Loss Prevention, Health and Safety for Western Canada and the United States, advancing to a senior position with broader responsibilities. Jeremy Spindlove was presented the Royal Humane Society Award by Britain's Queen Elizabeth in 1976 for his courage in saving a woman's life. He is a longtime member of ASIS International and the Academy of Criminal Justice Sciences and the coauthor of the five successful previous editions of *Terrorism Today: The Past, The Players, The Future*. He is a frequent guest commentator on airport security and terrorism for Canada's Global News Network. He has also authored a contributory text on victims of terrorism entitled *Victimology—A Study of Crime Victims and Their Roles*, edited by Judith M. Scarzi and Jack McDevitt.

Clifford E. Simonsen, Ph.D. (deceased) (August 1933–July 2013): Formerly President of Criminology Consultants Inc., Clifford E. Simonsen had an extensive background and education related to the topics of terrorism, crime, and criminal behavior.

His extensive education included B.S., University of Nebraska at Omaha, Law Enforcement and Corrections; M.S., Florida State University, Criminology and Corrections; MPA, the Ohio State University, Correctional Administration; and Ph.D., the Ohio State University, Administration of Criminal Justice and Deviant Behavior. Cliff retired after 32½ years as a Military Police Colonel. His extensive education in the military includes the Military Police Officer Basic Course; the Military Police Officer Advanced Course; the Advanced Police Administration Course; the U.S. Army Command and General Staff College; the OR/SA Executive Course; the Industrial College of the Armed Forces; and the U.S. Army War College.

Cliff had been an active member and supporter of many prestigious professional associations, including American Correctional Association (ACA) International Committee, Washington State Correctional Association (WCA), American Society for Industrial Security (ASIS) (lifetime award), Certified Protection Professional CPP (lifetime award), The International Association of Professional Security Consultants (IAPSC), International Academy of Criminology (IAC), Academy of Criminal Justice Sciences (ACJS), and The Retired Officers Association (TROA).

His honors and awards include two Meritorious Service Awards, U.S. Army; Legion of Merit, U.S. Army; Korean National Police Medal of Merit, Korean government; Outstanding Service International Association of Halfway Houses; Outstanding Achievement as a Scholar, Washington State Council on Crime and Delinquency; Fellow of the International Institute for Security and Safety Management, IISSM, New Delhi, India.

He has authored *Corrections in America: An Introduction*, 11th ed., Prentice Hall Publishing Co., NJ (2006); *Juvenile Justice Today*, 4th ed., Prentice Hall Publishing Co., NJ (2003); *Terrorism Today: The Past, the Players, the Future*, 5th ed., Prentice Hall Publishing Co., NJ (2006).

The Definitions and History of Terrorism

In Search of a Definition for Terrorism

LEARNING OUTCOMES

After studying this chapter, students should be able to:

1. Summarize the historical roots of the term terrorism and the difficulty of arriving at an all-encompassing definition.

2. List some of the approaches to defining terrorism.

3. Analyze the structures of terrorist groups and their possible common qualities.

4. Apply the FBI construct to a prominent terror event.

5. Compare and contrast the existing definitions as detailed in this chapter.

KEY WORDS TO NOTE

Assassination—The targeted killing of an important person for political or ideological reasons

Hague Conventions—International treaties first negotiated at The Hague in the Netherlands pronouncing formal statements on the laws of war

Islamic Sharia—Islamic law that influences legal process and codes in most Muslim countries

Jihad—Islamic term used to describe a holy war against religious or political oppression

Prescribed—To establish rules, laws, and direction

Proscribed—To outlaw and ban terror organizations

Water Boarding—A form of water torture where a captive is restrained and water poured over a cloth on the face forcing a gagging reflex—has the sensation of being drowned

VBIED—Vehicle-borne improvised explosive device

OVERVIEW

Terrorism constitutes one of the most serious threats to global security. Universal acceptance of a definition that fits every terrorist event and meets every country's political need, as well as that of the United Nations, has not been achieved. Terrorism has been around for centuries. Since 2001, when hijackers flew commercial airliners into New York's World Trade Center Towers and the Pentagon in Washington, DC, and the subsequent attacks in London, Madrid, and Mumbai, the fear of terrorism has spawned a global response led primarily by the United States and strongly supported by Great Britain. This became the now-familiar "War on Terror," a phrase coined by then U.S. President George W. Bush in the aftermath of 9-11. With the prospect of the next attack taking place in Chicago, Delhi, Singapore, or Melbourne, the specter of a feared but unknown doom has required the expenditure of huge sums of money to protect us from the threat of dangerous, threatening fanatics we call, for lack of a better title, "terrorists." The prospect of more attacks has become an everyday reality to Western nations. This threat has forced airlines and the aviation industry to make drastic changes in their methods for securing thousands of flights each day as well as the hardening of terminal facilities and operations. The Internet and other media streams respond and immediately inform and frighten the public about terrorist acts from around the globe. We also need to realize that there is no globally accepted definition of terrorism.

This chapter examines and asks several key questions: Just who is this larger-than-life monster that we call a "terrorist?" What are terrorist acts? Can we protect ourselves against them? How do we define "terrorism"? Combs, discussing this problem, says, "Terrorism is a political as well as a legal and military issue; its precise definition in modern terms has been slow to evolve. Not that there are not numerous definitions available—there are hundreds! But few of them are of sufficient legal scholarship to be useful in international law, and most of those which are legally useful lack the necessary ambiguity for any political acceptance."[1] The 9-11 attacks provided a wake-up call for the U.S. government, which quickly passed the USA Patriot Act of 2001.

We now begin the exercise of trying to define "terrorism" and/or "terrorist behavior." The terms must be carefully constructed so that they project the precise meanings intended. A terrorist incident is any violent act that can become a broader threat as the purpose and intention for such action becomes clearly known, and the act is clearly of a criminal nature. What it is (and is not) called hinges on finding a commonly understood meaning for the term "terrorism." This chapter will lay a foundation for the reader/student to use throughout the rest of this text.

To better understand these concepts, we must explore some historical context and the specific rules that society has developed over time to define the use of criminal and antisocial acts to meet political or social goals. Behavior in social groups, whether they are for primitive tribes or complex modern nation-states, can be regarded as points on a simple continuum.

Changes in Behavioral Definitions

In even the most primitive societies, certain acts or groups of acts have been universally forbidden, discouraged, or **proscribed**. Such acts include murder, rape, kidnapping, incest, and treason (or some form of rebellion affecting the entire social group's safety and the leadership's authority). By contrast, most societies have encouraged, sponsored, or **prescribed** behaviors such as marrying, having children, hunting, growing food, and other actions that clearly benefit the group's or tribe's common social welfare and survival.

Terrorism will inevitably fall into the range of behaviors that are not only a violation of laws but also a violation of politics and practices (mores) of a social group or tribal organization. Often the violation of codified law requires that a person must call a public safety officer to make an investigation or an arrest. All of these behaviors are related to the ways that social groups or subcultures chose to respond to transgressions that violate their mutually agreed standards. What is considered right or wrong has been shown capable of being placed on a behavior continuum from prescribed to proscribed (see Figure 1-1). The balance point of the behavioral continuum is not constant and

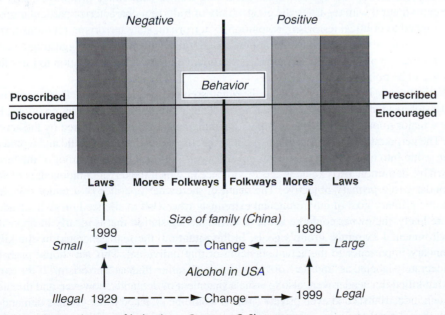

FIGURE 1-1 The continuum of behavior. *Courtesy:* C. Simonsen.

often changes over time, at different times, and in different societies. The values of the society as a whole are continuously subjected to challenges that test the limits of taste and acceptance. A clear example is the widespread growth of the Internet and social media in the twenty-first century.

TERRORISM: SEARCHING FOR A DEFINITION

It is perhaps too easy to use terms such as "terror," "terrorism," and "terrorist" for acts and persons that shock the senses of most reasonable people. The Reign of Terror, which took place in France from 1792 to 1794, is generally accepted by most as the first event to be commonly called "terrorism." During the French Revolution, those who resisted the dictums of the revolutionaries faced arrest, imprisonment, and death by the guillotine. Most convictions were made without the benefit of trials or legal due process. The revolutionary groups went to extreme lengths to eliminate every possible threat, eventually seeking out those with even moderate-to-mild opposition to their cause. Those who considered themselves to be possible targets of the revolutionaries finally decided to adopt countermeasures for their self-preservation. On July 27, 1794, members of the Jacobin dissenters murdered Robespierre and his council of supporters. The Reign of Terror, in which over 400,000 "suspects" (including children and women) had been imprisoned, hanged, or beheaded, finally came to an end. But the seminal concepts of terror tactics as a part of a political strategy grew directly out of this bloody episode. From a devastating beginning, terrorism and terrorist acts became defined as "the systematic application of violence to establish and maintain a new political or religious system." Such a definition may be difficult to use today, primarily because it fails to separate terrorism from other acts of aggression that use terror as only a small component, not the primary objective, of such behavior. For example, terror in conventional warfare between nation-states is a natural by-product of the violence and confusion of combat. Military objectives and tactics are usually chosen in order to effect the quickest elimination of an enemy's force, its morale, and its will to fight through the destruction or disruption of its command, control, communication, and support and supply networks. Victory is decided by force of numbers, skill at arms, weapon superiority, strategy and tactics, or a combination thereof. Terror is not intended to be a primary factor or function in such military actions.

Trained soldiers or citizens frightened into surrender or compliance but not physically injured are the most logical and realistic targets of terrorism; other casualties are easily classified according to the way they were injured or killed. Rosie offers a tentative definition of terrorism for our consideration: "The use and/or threat of repeated violence in support of, or in opposition to, some authority, where violence is employed to induce the fear of similar attack in as many non-immediate victims as possible so that those so threatened accept and comply with the demands of the terrorists."[2]

Within this awkward definition, we can perhaps work out a methodology for describing the variety of behaviors springing from terrorists acting from a wide range of motives. This definition remains neutral with regard to the great variety of traits that characterize particular groups. It can be applied to political terrorism, revolutionary terrorism, state terrorism, religious terrorism, insurgencies, and all the many other variations. It eliminates the need for suggesting a particular type of motivation as part of the definition of terrorism and creates a temptation to infer that terrorism has to be politically motivated.

Is the twenty-first-century assassin the quintessential suicide bomber? The suicide bomber regardless of gender calculates his or her acts to induce extreme fear in a wider populous, hoping to have a major impact on a far larger population than those likely to be injured by the acts themselves. The perpetrators would most likely believe that these drastic means could and would coerce a wider group into abandoning a political or military agenda that lies at the root of the terrorists' actions. This definition also excludes acts of violence in which the terror component is incidental, or secondary, to a primary objective. The death of the owner operator of a major oil company may be the primary goal of environmental extremists who wish to silence him or his leadership. Or, more likely, the owner could be about to influence legislation that is clearly in opposition to the environmental extremist group's goals. In this situation, the fear generated by the killing is of secondary importance to the actual silencing of that individual. This act should probably be more accurately labeled as "murder" or "assassination," rather than as "terrorism." If the extremist group that killed this leader were also to issue a statement of demands, however, and threaten that more such industrialists and even private citizens would be attacked if the group's demands were not met, then it would be more accurate to refer to the group's actions as "terrorism."

Labeling persons or groups as terrorists does not preclude also categorizing those same persons or groups as "guerrillas," "ideologues," or "revolutionaries." An example could go as follows: "A grocery store owner, who plays baseball on weekends, might be sometimes referred to as a 'baseball player.' But he has not, however, stopped being a grocer." Members of the IRA (Irish Republican Army), PLO (Palestine Liberation Organization), or ETA (Euskadi Ta Askatasuna) may be revered as freedom fighters by their subgroups of the local political system. But, to others they clearly continue to be seen as "terrorists." Without some recourse to established definitional parameters, these kinds of labels are just a matter of value judgment. If the person making the judgment does not agree with the objectives of the group using such methods to gain some goal, they will be called (with very few exceptions) terrorists. The group thus categorized immediately denies this, of course, and calls itself a National Liberation Army, or a "Workers Army," or some similar identifying term. The conclusion is that a terrorist group invariably has no legitimacy and therefore its goals have no validity. The label of "terrorist" then becomes a catchall term of derision and, thus, obscures whatever legitimate complaints the group may have had. In order to understand the phenomenon of terrorism, one must always assess the divergent views of what precisely constitutes terrorism and then ask, "What is the current definition in use?" Reaching a general consensus on a universal definition of terrorism has generated many debates in the social sciences. No single definition seems to satisfy every terrorist or act of terrorism, and there is no "one-size-fits-all" for terrorist/terrorism situations.

Terrorism is clearly a very special type of violence. It is a tactic used in many situations—peace, conflict, and even war. The threat of terrorism can be ever-present, and an attack, such as the one on the World Trade Center in 2001, can occur when least expected. The 9-11 attacks were the kind of events that almost always force a transition from peaceful coexistence to conflict—or war. As an example of a terrorist act, the assassination of Archduke Franz Ferdinand in 1914 led to the outbreak of World War I in Europe.

Combating terrorism is a factor that must be considered in all military plans and operations. Combating terrorism requires a continuous state of intelligence gathering and awareness, and should be a constant practice, rather than a particular type of military operation. Terrorism is also a criminal offense under nearly every national and international legal code. With few exceptions, acts of terrorism are forbidden in war—just as they are in times of peace.[3]

SOME APPROACHES TO DEFINING TERRORISM

The following diverse definitions are also used to describe terrorism:

Simple: Violence or threatened violence intended to produce fear or cause change.

Legal: Criminal violence violating legal codes and punishable by the state.

Analytical: A specific political and/or social factor behind individual violent acts.

State sponsored: National or other groups used to attack Western or other vested interests.

State: Power of the government used to repress its people to the point of submission.[4]

In his book *Political Terrorism* (1983), Alex Schmid surveyed 100 scholars and experts in the field and asked for their definition of terrorism. This analysis found two constant characteristics:

1. An individual is being threatened.
2. The terrorist act's meaning is derived from the choice of target and victims. Schmid's analysis concluded that the following elements are common throughout the 100 definitions surveyed:
   - Terrorism is an abstract concept with no real essence.
   - A single definition cannot account for all the possible uses of the term.
   - Many different definitions often share common elements.
   - The meaning of terrorism derives from the victims or targets.[5]

Schmid also provided the following from his research of those 100 definitions:

Terrorism is an anxiety inspiring method of repeated violent action, employed by (semi-) clandestine individual, group or state actors, for idiosyncratic, criminal or political reason, whereby—in contrast to assassination—the direct targets of violence are not the main target.

The perpetrators of terrorism may truly believe that their cause is altruistic and that it serves for the betterment of society. In Bruce Hoffman's (1998) *Inside Terrorism*, he states that the terrorist is fundamentally a violent intellectual who is prepared to use and, indeed, is committed to using force in the attainment of perceived goals.

Hoffman also adds that by distinguishing terrorists from other types, such as thugs or common criminals, we come to appreciate that terrorism is

- primarily political in aims and motives;
- violent or—equally important—threatens violence;
- designed to have far-reaching psychological repercussions, beyond the immediate victim or target;
- conducted by an organization with an identifiable chain of command or conspiratorial cell structures (whose members wear no uniform or identifying insignia); and
- perpetrated by a subnational group or non-state entity.[6]

Can we accept that "terrorism" is simply a means to an end—nothing more and nothing less? Can we apply the term to an event without the inclusion of moral beliefs and sociological–political mumbo jumbo? The operatives of the PLO are clearly terrorists. But that fact alone does not mean that their aims and objectives are not without some validity. Provisional IRA members might be described as "freedom fighters"; even if they do not accept the label of terrorist, they would almost always be labeled so by those whom their actions affect, be they the general public, government, or specific individuals. Militant groups, particularly those like the Irish terror groups and Spain's ETA, whose *modus operandi* includes bombings in public places and targeted assassinations, are universally condemned and labeled terrorists.

It is often easier for one to perceive a long-established, freely elected (even dictatorial, religious, or royalist) regime as "legitimate" than it is to accept that a handful of individuals with views significantly different from the majority might deserve the same classification. This holds true if the individuals use methods that provoke moral indignation against a sanctioned, "legitimate" target, such as the government. When an indiscriminate "enemy" label is applied to those not actually supportive of a dissenting aggressor's objective, the situation becomes far more disturbing, even more so because the aggressors frequently use violence as a means to their ends. Wearing no uniforms, they employ weapons that may not need to be personally fired or activated (e.g., letter bombs, improvised explosive devices (IEDs), vehicle-borne improvised explosive devices (**VBIEDs**), and time bombs). Likewise, unknown aggressors kill unknown victims for reasons that are seldom made clear until after the attack.

There will always be "bottom-line" considerations, of course, even when the targets are considered "acceptable enemies" in the eyes of many. Violence against the former Soviet-backed regimes, for example, finds more favor among Western observers, even when such strikes could be clearly defined as terrorist actions. But if the nature of the assault transgresses certain unwritten, but widely accepted, boundaries of decency or fair play, then condemnation is more likely to be applied. The downing of a Russian helicopter gunship by Chechen rebels is more likely to be interpreted (except by supporters of the Russians) as acceptable, than would be the downing of a civilian airliner by the PLO. The deliberate slaughter of armed soldiers in an ambush is more easily accepted than is the slaughter of small children. In descending order, "fair game" for terrorists or dissenters might be depicted as follows:

- Military personnel
- Government officials
- Civilians unconnected in any way with the continuance of the policy against which the terrorist is fighting

This same attenuated sample list might constitute the basis of a target selection for almost any military offensive. However, a terrorist group would consider the following order to be more appropriate for maximum impact:

- Civilians unconnected in any way with the continuance of the policy against which the group is fighting
- Government officials
- Military personnel

This second, seemingly illogical, order is the one that is very logical for terrorists because maximum fear can be generated by attacks against non-combatants. This prioritizing demonstrates to the populace as a whole that the targeted regime is clearly unable to protect them. Such actions are generally a far safer technique—for the terrorist group—than trying to prove that the regime cannot protect itself. Terror groups will choose to cause outrage and revulsion in their target audience in order to maintain the required level of terror, fear, and anger against government agencies. You should now have a clearer basis for understanding that while strategies incorporating acts of terrorism in the past centuries have changed in delivery and methods, the primary aims of terrorist acts have always remained generally constant:

- To bring attention to perceived grievances or causes by some act or acts.
- To use media coverage of such acts in order to get the widest possible dissemination of their message.
- To contain reaction by the public at large through fear and intimidation.
- To coerce change and destabilize opponents through the threat of further and continued use of such acts until the grievances or causes are recognized and acted upon.

Over a quarter of a century ago, Jenkins argued that "terrorism is theatre; therefore, terrorists do not want a lot of people dead … they want a lot of people watching and listening."[7] In recent years, that rationale has significantly diminished with the advent of Islamist terror attacks. This watching and listening has been used over the centuries—from a few villagers who stood by while terrorists acted out or gave their speeches up to today's instant and live worldwide television coverage by all of the major networks of the vilest acts, piped directly into millions of homes. It is seldom that one hears much about the barbarous acts committed in Third World countries, such as Rwanda, Congo, Zimbabwe, Burma, and Sudan, on the evening news in other than a quick sound bite. But let a few armed attackers take over a commercial airliner from a developed country, with 150–300 or so paying passengers, and the media flocks to stand by and listen to the demands of the terrorists and broadcast them around the globe.

Following the London subway suicide attacks, the British government sought to define terrorism as it might apply to the current threat and attack scenarios. At the time, the existing legislation, the Prevention of Terrorism Act of 1989, which had been formulated to deal with Irish nationalist terrorism, defined terrorism as "the use of violence for political ends, and includes any use of violence for the purpose of putting the public or any section of the public in fear." As it is written, this is obviously a very broad definition of terrorism and excludes violence for religious ends or for a non-political ideological end. Subsequently, the Terrorism Act 2000 was developed to remedy the defects of the 1989 definition. In the United States, the Homeland Security Act of 2002 defines terrorism as "any activity that involves an act that is dangerous to human life or potentially destructive of critical infrastructure or key resources; and is a violation of the criminal laws of the United States or of any State or other subdivision of the United States and appears to be intended to intimidate or coerce a civilian population; to influence the policy of a government by intimidation or coercion or to affect the conduct of a government by mass destruction, assassination, or kidnapping."

Another current UK definition for terrorism can be found in the Reinsurance (Acts of Terrorism) Act 1993, section 2(2), which states: "In this section 'acts of terrorism' means acts of persons acting on behalf of, or in conjunction with, any organization which carries out activities directed towards the overthrowing or influencing, by force or violence, of Her Majesty's government in the United Kingdom or any other government de jure or de facto."

This chapter just begins our study of the topic "terrorism" and examines the difficulty in deciding just what that term really means. Author George Rosie further highlights this difficulty as follows:

Terrorism is a complex, multifaceted, and often baffling subject. The organizations involved have a way of emerging, splintering, disappearing and then reappearing, which makes it very difficult for the average person to follow. Individuals come and go, are jailed, die, go underground, or apparently vanish. Counter terror bureaucracies are formed then reformed, names are changed, and leaders are shuffled around, like deck chairs on the Titanic, as they are promoted, demoted, forced to resign, or put out to pasture. Incidents proliferate across the world, some of which can trigger a chain of events that will destabilize a whole region and bring nations and governments to the edge of ruin. At the same time, major terrorist actions can shock for a short while, and then be quickly forgotten (except by those who were directly affected by the inevitable tragedy). Treaties are written, theories propounded, grievances aired, tactics discussed, occasionally to some effect, but usually not. Causes are picked up by the world's media, examined, probed, and then all too soon often overlooked, until the next explosion occurs, or the next airliner is hijacked.[8]

We now continue our examination of what terrorism is (and what it is not) with a few more commonly used definitions. Acts of terrorism conjure emotional responses in the victims (those hurt by the violence and affected by the fear) as well as in the practitioners. Even the U.S. government cannot agree on one, single definition. Following are a few more common definitions of terrorism:

- Terrorism is the use or threatened use of force designed to bring about political change—Brian Jenkins.
- Terrorism constitutes the illegitimate use of force to achieve a political objective when innocent people are targeted—Walter Laqueur.
- Terrorism is the premeditated, deliberate, systematic murder, mayhem, and threatening of the innocent to create fear and intimidation in order to gain a political or tactical advantage, usually to influence an audience—James M. Poland.
- Terrorism is the unlawful use or threat of violence against persons or property to further political or social objectives. It is usually intended to intimidate or coerce a government, individuals, or groups, or to modify their behavior or politics—U.S. Vice President's Task Force, 1986.
- Terrorism is the unlawful use of force or violence against persons or property to intimidate or coerce a government, the civilian population, or any segment thereof, in furtherance of political or social objectives—FBI definition.
- Terrorism is the calculated use of violence or the threat of violence to inculcate fear; intended to coerce or to intimidate governments or societies in the pursuit of goals that are generally political, religious, or ideological—Department of Defense definition.[9]

THE FBI CONSTRUCT

The FBI seems to have developed a very useful construct of what is to be considered terrorism in the United States. This issue concerns foreign power–sponsored or foreign power–coordinated activities that

1. Involve violent acts that are dangerous to human life and a violation of the criminal laws of the United States or any state, or that would be a criminal violation if committed within the jurisdiction of the United States, or any state.
2. Appear to be intended to
   - intimidate or coerce a civilian population;
   - influence the policy of a government by intimidation or coercion; and
   - affect the conduct of a government by assassination or kidnapping.
3. Occur totally outside of the United States, or transcend national boundaries in terms of the means by which they are accomplished, the persons they appear intended to coerce or intimidate, or the locale in which their perpetrators operate or seek to find asylum.

Investigating acts of terrorism overseas includes interviewing victims, collecting forensic evidence, and apprehending terrorist fugitives. The FBI coordinates all overseas investigations with the U.S. Department of State and the host foreign government.[10]

THE U.S. DEPARTMENT OF DEFENSE (DOD) CONSTRUCTS

Christopher G. Essig stated at the United Nations, quoting from his paper *Terrorism: Is It a Criminal Act or an Act of War?*:

This is discussed in depth at the Army War College at Carlisle Barracks, Pennsylvania, and its implications for National Security in the twenty-first century, but there is no single determination for classifying all acts of terrorism, neither as acts of war, nor criminal acts. In light of a predicted terrorist threat significant enough to threaten the survival of the nation (catastrophic terror), this determination is less a legal or academic exercise and more practically one based on how such a determination governs this situation (law enforcement or national security?) to respond to the threat. More important is how that response protects our nation's interests and our status in the world community. Catastrophic terror makes relying solely on a law enforcement response a dangerous option. Yet, reflecting on the changing strategic environment, an act of war determination, in a classical legal sense, is equally impractical. A new determination, carrying the same weight as an act of war must be developed and accepted, domestically and internationally, to provide legal response options offering greater latitude to law enforcement and national security forces. This latitude will provide the means to better meet threats to national security in the twenty-first century.

Terrorism, as further defined by the DOD, is usually considered to be calculated, and the selection of a target preplanned and rational. The perpetrators know the effect they seek. Terrorist violence is considered to be neither spontaneous nor random. Terrorism is intended to produce fear in someone other than the victim. In a layperson's terms, "Terrorism is a psychological act conducted primarily for its impact on a specific audience." In the decade since 9-11, the Islamist threat has hardened against Western democracies as well as secular Middle East regimes. Many believe that the 9-11 attacks and the subsequent invasions of both Iraq and Afghanistan were exactly what the Islamists hoped to achieve. For the Islamists, the presence of foreign troops in the Middle East gives them the excuse they so dearly need to extend, prolong, and widen their **jihad** to global proportions.

The DOD definition also addresses goals. Terrorism may be motivated by political, religious, or ideological objectives. In one sense, terrorist goals are invariably political—extremists are driven by religious or ideological beliefs and usually seek political power to compel the general society to conform to their views. The objectives of terrorism distinguish it from other violent acts aimed at personal gain, such as criminal violence. However, the definition permits including violence by organized crime when it also seeks to influence government policy. Some drug cartels and other international criminal organizations engage in political action when their activities influence governmental functioning. As noted previously, the essence of terrorism is the intent to inculcate fear into persons other than its direct victims in order to make a government or other audience finally change its political behavior.

Terrorism is common practice in insurgencies, but insurgents are not necessarily terrorists; especially if they comply with the rules of war and do not engage in forms of violence that could be clearly identified as terrorist acts, then they should probably not be termed as "terrorists." Insurgents can be defined as those who rebel against leadership and authority and could well be termed as "rebels" or "rebellious." Insurgents may resort to tactics that are by their very act considered acts of terrorism. The terms "terrorist" and "terrorism" are so widely used by politicians and commentators alike that being able to discern who is a terrorist and how to define the term becomes markedly complex. Terrorists are rarely inhibited with their attacks and actions, convincing themselves their actions are justified by an even higher law or principle. Their single-minded dedication to a goal, however poorly it may be articulated, renders legal sanctions ineffective. By contrast, war is subject to the rules of international law and of course the terrorists recognize no rules. No person, place, or object of value is immune from terrorist attack; there are no innocents.

The U.S. Department of State

Office of the Coordinator for Counterterrorism—Section 2656f(a) of Title 22 of the U.S. Code states as follows:

The term "international terrorism" means terrorism involving citizens of the territory of more than one country.
- The term "terrorism" means premeditated, politically motivated violence perpetrated against non-combatant targets by subnational groups or clandestine agents.
- The term "terrorist group" means any group practicing, or which has significant subgroups which practice, international terrorism.

INTERPRETATION AND APPLICATION OF KEY TERMS The terms "international terrorism," "terrorism," and "terrorist group" have the definitions assigned to them in 22 U.S.C. 2656f(d) (see above). The term "non-combatant," which is referred to but not defined in 22 U.S.C. 2656f(d)(2), is interpreted to mean, in addition to civilians, military personnel (whether or not armed or on duty) who are not deployed in a war zone or a warlike setting.

The definition allows for military targets or personnel to be included in the definition of terrorism; thus, the U.S. Department of State considers attacks against non-combatants as terrorism, and this encompasses not only the general public but also the military personnel who are unarmed or off duty. This would apply to attacks in which military personnel have been targets in civilian locations, such as the Berlin disco bombing in 1986, which resulted in the deaths of two U.S. servicemen. Also, the bombing of the USS *Cole* in the port of Aden in 2000 is an event that by definition is considered by the United States as a terrorist attack. This suicide attack resulted in the death of seventeen U.S. servicemen. The above-mentioned U.S. definition considers it to be terrorism when acts of terror target military installations or personnel when a state of military hostilities does not exist at a specific site or location.

THE UNITED NATIONS—ACTIONS TO COUNTER TERRORISM

The League of Nations, the forerunner organization to the United Nations and formed after the Great War of 1914–1918, in its attempt to bring a measure of world stability defined terrorism as follows:

> All criminal acts directed against a State either intended or calculated to create a state of terror in the minds of particular persons or a group of persons or the general public.

The United Nations General Assembly continues to struggle defining terrorism and between 1963 and 1999 has come up with thirteen international conventions aimed at terrorist actions and, in particular, outlawing airline hijackings and diplomatic hostage taking. The UN came up with a draft, which still remains contentious to many member states—however, the General Assembly has resolved to fight "terrorism," even if it has failed to adequately define the term. The UN General Assembly's Ad Hoc Committee (AHC) on Measures to Eliminate International Terrorism concluded its Fourteenth Session on April 16, 2010, without reaching agreement on the draft Comprehensive Convention on International Terrorism (CCIT).

The United Nation's Global Counterterrorism Strategy was adopted by member states on September 8, 2006. The strategy—in the form of a resolution and an annexed plan of action—is a unique global instrument that enhances national, regional, and international efforts to counter terrorism. This was the first time that all member states agreed to a common strategic approach to fight terrorism, even if they couldn't agree to a definition, not only sending a clear message that terrorism is unacceptable in all its forms and manifestation but also resolving to take practical steps individually and collectively to prevent and combat it. These steps include a wide array of measures ranging from strengthening state capacity to counter terrorist threats to better coordinating United Nation's counterterrorism activities. The adoption of the strategy fulfilled the commitment made by world leaders at the 2005 September Summit, and the strategy built on many of the elements proposed by the Secretary-General in his May 2, 2006, report entitled *Uniting Against Terrorism: Recommendations for a Global Counterterrorism Strategy.*[11]

The Arab Convention for the Suppression of Terrorism

Unofficial translation from Arabic by the United Nations English translation service.

Preamble

The Arab states signatory hereto,

Desiring to promote mutual cooperation in the suppression of terrorist offences, which pose a threat to the security and stability of the Arab Nation and endanger its vital interests, being committed to the highest moral and religious principles and, in particular, to the tenets of the **Islamic Sharia**, as well as to the humanitarian heritage of an Arab Nation that rejects all forms of violence and terrorism and advocates the protection of human rights, with which precepts the principles of international law conform, based as they are on cooperation among peoples in the promotion of peace, being further committed to the Pact of the League of Arab States, the Charter of the United Nations and all the other international convents and instruments to which the Contracting States to this Convention are parties.

Affirming the right of peoples to combat foreign occupation and aggression by whatever means, including armed struggle, in order to liberate their territories and secure their right to self-determination, and independence and to do so in such a manner as to preserve the territorial integrity of each Arab country, of the foregoing being in accordance with the purposes and principles of the Charter of the United Nations and with the Organization's resolutions.

The Arab States have agreed to conclude this convention and to invite any Arab State that did not participate in its conclusion to accede hereto.

Part One: Definitions and General Provisions

Article 1

Each of the following terms shall be understood in the light of the definition given:

1. **Contracting State**
    Any member State of the League of Arab States that has ratified this Convention and that has deposited its instruments of ratification with the General Secretariat of the League.

2. **Terrorism**
    Any act or threat of violence, whatever its motives or purposes, that occurs in the advancement of an individual or collective criminal agenda and seeking to sow panic among people, causing fear by harming them, or placing their lives, liberty or security in danger, or seeking to cause damage to the environment or to public or private installations or property or to occupying or seizing them, or seeking to jeopardize national resources.

3. **Terrorist Offence**
    Any offence or attempted offence committed in furtherance of a terrorist objective in any of the Contracting States, or against their nationals, property or interests, that is punishable by their domestic law. The offences stipulated in the following conventions, except where conventions have not been ratified by Contracting States or where offences have been excluded by their legislation, shall also be regarded as terrorist offences:

    *   The Tokyo Convention on Offences and Certain Other Acts Committed on Board Aircraft, of 14 September 1963.
    *   The **Hague Convention** for the Suppression of Unlawful Seizure of Aircraft, of 16 December 1970.
    *   The Montreal Convention for the Suppression of Unlawful Acts against the Safety of Civil Aviation, of 23 September 1971, and the Protocol thereto of 10 May 1984.
    *   The Convention on the Prevention and Punishment of Crimes against Internationally Protected Persons, including Diplomatic Agents, of 14 December 1973.
    *   The International Convention Against the Taking of Hostages, of 17 December 1979.
    *   The provisions of the United Nations Convention on the Law of the Sea, of 1982, relating to piracy on the high seas.

The League has twenty-two current members and includes the following states:

Egypt, Sudan, Algeria

Morocco, Iraq, Saudi Arabia

Yemen, Syria, Tunisia

Somalia, Libya, Jordan

United Arab Emirates, Lebanon, Palestine

Mauritania, Kuwait, Oman

Qatar, Djibouti, Bahrain, and Comoros

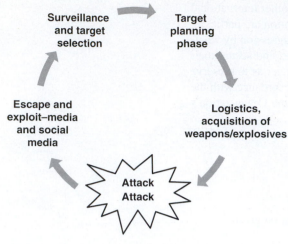

FIGURE 1-2   Terrorist attack cycle.

STRUCTURES OF TERRORIST GROUPS

Terrorists tend to organize themselves all over the world in ways that enable them to function well in the specific environment in which they are located and then be able to carry out the acts of terrorism. We shall now discuss some general organizational principles for terrorists that shed insight into how a terrorist thinks. Above all else, the most important thing to a terrorist is tight security. Why? Because they are always operating in a hostile environment!

It does not matter if the terrorists are in Europe, Asia, or the Americas, as wherever they are is a hostile environment. Their safety and security is best provided by what is called a "cellular structure." This is primarily most important because the structure ensures that not one of them can identify any more terrorists than those in their specific cell of operation. It is like a safety net for them. Terrorist groups—those that are not supported by a specific government or are not state sponsored—always create what is called a tight support structure of "sympathizers" or many other people who may have been coerced into supporting or helping them for various reasons. Such a support system can be either active or passive. By that we mean intelligence collection, recruiting, monetary support, logistics, dissemination of propaganda, or, worse, a young person strapped up with explosives and sent to a specific target for self-destruction (see Figure 1-2). This is clearly despicable, but it is a reality in terrorism just as is the use of women and children as human shields for covert operations. It is a fact in the lifestyle of terrorism and terrorists, wherever they are to be found.

COMMON TERRORIST QUALITIES

What qualities does a terrorist leader look for when selecting his followers for an operation? It is difficult to give a categorical or simple answer to this question. However, certain qualities separate terrorists who form the "hard core" of terrorist organizations from those who comprise the peripheral elements, whose activities are mostly seen in a supportive role.

First, they must believe passionately in the justness of their cause! This is a most important quality, because this is also the motivating factor for all their subsequent actions. The obvious example of this is the radicalization of young Muslim men and women over the last decade being drawn by calls for global jihad either from jihadist websites or from actually immersing themselves in self-styled training camps.

Second, they must possess a "killer instinct," in other words, a predilection to kill, not in anger, not in the heat of the moment, not during a fight or a battle, but kill at anytime, anywhere, in absolute cold blood, and without any pangs of conscience or feelings of pity and remorse for the targeted victims.

Third, they must possess an ability to act effectively as loners, if circumstances so warrant, even though in their private lives they may not be loners. Members of conventional armies, and insurgent and guerrilla organizations, train, live, and move together. They normally operate in groups, although there may be circumstances when individual members may have to operate totally alone. On the contrary, in the case of terrorist organizations, they may train and occasionally live together, but more often their members operate as loners unless they are tasked for specific operations, such as the hijacking of an aircraft, a kidnapping, a coordinated series of suicide attacks as took place in London in 2005, and the 2008 attacks on hotels and train stations in Mumbai, India.

About 60 percent of the terrorist incidents reported every year are operations in which the terrorists acted as loners for assassinations, sniper missions, throwing of hand grenades, planting of explosives, IED, or VBIED, suicide bombings, and so on. Thus, operating as a loner requires greater physical and mental courage and individual determination and even greater dedication and loyalty than operating in groups. Independent groups that have been inspired by al Qaeda and the Islamist extremist preaching of Osama bin Laden have seen a level of "religious" violence and considerable bravery on behalf of the autonomous cell members, unmatched by the likes of European groups such as ETA and the Irish terrorist groups.

Fourth, they must have a very high degree of physical courage, because a terrorist risks not only death but even worse than death—capture, physical torture, and long imprisonment—if caught.

The development of bureaucratic states led to a profound change in terrorism. Modern democratic governments have continuity that older, charismatic, royal, religion-based, or inherited governments do not. Terrorists soon found that the death of a single individual, even a monarch, did not necessarily make a great enough impact to produce the policy changes they had sought. Terrorists reacted by turning to an indirect method of attack. By the early twentieth century, terrorists began to attack people who were previously considered "innocents" to generate political pressure from and by the public. These indirect attacks managed to create a public atmosphere of anxiety, fear, and an undermining of confidence in government. Their very unpredictability, and apparent randomness, makes it virtually impossible for governments to protect all potential victims. The public then cries out for safety and protection that the state cannot give. Frustrated and fearful, the people then demand that the government make concessions to the terrorists in order to stop the attacks.

Modern terrorism behavior and philosophy offers its practitioners many advantages. First, by not recognizing innocents, terrorists can acquire and attack an infinite number of targets. They can select their target and then determine when, where, and how to attack. This range of choices gives terrorists a high probability of success with minimum risk. If the attack goes wrong, or fails to produce the intended results, they can simply deny responsibility.

Ironically, as democratic governments become more common, it may be getting even easier for terrorists to operate. The first terrorist bombing of the World Trade Center in New York City, the Oklahoma City Federal Building truck bombing, the bombing of the two U.S. embassies in Kenya and Tanzania, and the suicide attack on the USS *Cole* in Yemen all were *dots* that were never connected, culminating in the hijacked aircraft attacks on the World Trade Center on 9-11! Such "follow-the-dots roadmaps" proved how easy it could be for terrorists to operate in a free or democratic society. Authoritarian governments, whose populace may have even better reasons to revolt, may also be less constrained by requirements for due process and impartial justice when combating terrorists. As national leaders and politicians address terrorism, they must consider several relevant characteristics:

1. Anyone can be a victim. Some terrorists may still operate under certain cultural restraints, such as a desire to avoid harming women, but essentially there are no more innocents these days.
2. Attacks that may appear to be senseless and random may not be senseless or random to the perpetrators/terrorists. Their attacks have made perfect sense. Acts such as suicide bombings in public places of assembly or shooting into crowded restaurants are guaranteed to heighten public anxiety. This is always the terrorists' immediate objective.
3. The terrorist or terrorist group needs to publicize the attack. If no one knows about it, it will not generate the desired fear and pressure on government. The need for publicity often drives target selection—the greater the symbolic value of the target, the more publicity the attack brings to the terrorists and the more fear it generates. The media often provide the notoriety, intentionally or inadvertently, that the terrorists desire, simply by just covering the terrorist event.
4. Any leader planning for effective ways to combat terrorism must understand that nothing can protect every possible target all the time. It must be seen clearly that terrorists would most likely just change their attack tactics from more protected targets to less protected ones. This is the key to defensive measures.[12]

Motivations for Terrorists

Terrorists are inspired by many and diverse motives. One can even classify them into three distinct categories: *rational*, *psychological*, and *cultural*. Many combinations and variations of these factors may shape a terrorist. Rational terrorists will think through their goals and options, often conducting a sort of "cost/benefit analysis" of expected results. They seek information to determine whether there are less costly or more effective ways with which to achieve their individual or group objectives. To assess the risk, they weigh the target's defensive capabilities against their own offensive abilities to accomplish an attack. They analyze the terrorist group's capabilities to sustain the effort. The essential question is whether terrorism will probably work and accomplish the desired goals, given societal conditions at the time. The terrorist's rational analysis is similar to that of a military commander or a business entrepreneur considering available resources and courses of action. Groups considering terrorism as an option always ask a crucial question: "Can terrorism induce enough anxiety to attain their goals without causing a backlash that will destroy the cause and perhaps even the terrorists themselves?" To misjudge the answer to that question is to court disaster. After 9-11, the backlash was the "War on Terror." Psychological motivations for resorting to terrorism usually derive from the terrorist organizations' or individuals' personal depth of dissatisfaction with their life and accomplishments. Individuals find a reason to be involved in a dedicated terrorist action. Although no clear psychopathy can always be found among terrorists, there is a nearly universal element in them that can be described as the "true believer." Terrorists seldom even attempt to consider that they may be wrong or that other views might have some merit. Terrorists tend to project their own antisocial attitudes and motivations onto others, creating a polarized "us-versus-them" outlook. They attribute evil motives to anyone outside their own group. This enables the terrorists to dehumanize their victims and removes any sense of ambiguity from their minds. The resulting clarity of purpose appeals to those who crave and need the use of violence to relieve their constant anger.

Another common characteristic of the psychologically motivated terrorist is the desperate need to belong to a like-minded group. With some terrorists, group acceptance is a stronger motivator than the stated political objectives of the organization. Such individuals define their social status by group acceptance.

Terrorist groups with strong internal motivations find it necessary to justify the group's existence continuously. A terrorist group must, as a minimum, commit some violent acts to maintain group self-esteem and legitimacy. Another result of psychological motivation is the intensity of the group dynamics among terrorists. They tend to demand unanimity and are intolerant of any dissent or different opinions. With the enemy clearly identified and determined to be unequivocally evil, pressure to escalate the frequency and intensity of operations is ever present. The need to belong to the group discourages any possible resignations, and the fear of compromise disallows their acceptance; compromise is also usually rejected. Terrorist groups lean toward inflexible positions. Having placed themselves "beyond the pale" (forever unacceptable to ordinary society), they cannot consider any compromise. They can then expect any negotiation to be dishonorable, even treasonous. Such dynamics also make any announced group goal nearly impossible to achieve. By definition, a group that has achieved its stated purpose is no longer necessary. As a result, success threatens the psychological well-being of its members. Therefore, when a terrorist group approaches its stated goal, it is inclined to pause and redefine it. The group may reject the achievement as false or inadequate, or the result of the duplicity of the unknown, unnamed "them." Terrorist groups also often suffer from a nagging fear of success. One effective psychological defense against success is to define goals so broadly that they are impossible to achieve. Even if the world proclaims the success of a political movement, the terrorists can deny it and fight on. Cultural concepts also shape values and motivate people to actions that seem unreasonable to outside observers. For example, Americans are often generally reluctant to appreciate the intense impact that cultural factors have on behavior. They too often easily accept the myth that rational behavior guides all human actions. It is easy to reject as unbelievable such things as vendettas, martyrdom, suicide bombers, and self-destructive group behavior when Americans observe them in others. There is disbelief that such things as the destruction of a viable state can be done just for the sake of ethnic purity, especially when the resulting state becomes economically or politically unstable.

The treatment of life, in general, and individual life, in particular, is a cultural characteristic that has a tremendous impact on terrorism. In societies in which people identify themselves in terms of group memberships (family, clan, or tribe), there may be a willingness to accept levels of self-sacrifice seldom seen elsewhere. At times, terrorists seem to be eager to give their lives for their organization or cause. The lives of "others," even strangers, whom they perceive as being totally evil by their terrorist value system, can therefore be snuffed out without any sense of remorse. Other factors include the manner in which aggression is channeled and the concepts of social organization. In many political systems, there are effective, non-violent means for succession to power. A culture may have a high tolerance for non-political violence, such as banditry or ethnic turf battles, and remain relatively free of political violence. The United States, for example, is one of the most violent societies in the world, yet political violence remains a rare aberration. By contrast, both France and Germany, with low tolerance for violent crime, have had long histories of political violence.

A major cultural determinant of terrorism is the perception of "outsiders" and anticipation of their threat to long-held ethnic values or to a terrorist group's survival. Fear of cultural dilution or extermination leads to violence that, to someone who has not experienced it, seems irrational. All human beings are sensitive to threats to their personal values and beliefs, those with which they identify themselves. These include language; religion; tribal, racial, or group membership; and a sense of homeland territory. The possibility of losing any of these can trigger defensive, even xenophobic, reactions.

Religion may be the most volatile of cultural identifiers because it encompasses values and beliefs deeply rooted in a long-standing and ancient cultural paradigm. A threat to one's religion puts not only the present at risk but also one's entire cultural past, present, and future. Many religions, including Christianity and Islam, are so confident they are right that they have often used force to make converts or to eliminate non-believers. Terrorism in the name of religion can be especially violent, and will be discussed in detail in Chapter 2. Like all terrorists, those who are religiously motivated view their acts with moral certainty and even divine sanctions. What would otherwise be extraordinary acts of desperation becomes a religious duty in the mind of the religiously motivated terrorist. This helps explain the high level of commitment among religious extremist groups and suicide bombers and their willingness to risk their own deaths.

TERRORISM AS CRIMINAL BEHAVIOR

The broad range of violent activities that are often labeled as "terrorism" can now be seen as difficult, even impossible, to define in a simplistic and universal way. There are some specific acts that seem to straddle the behavioral continuum in such a way so as to cloud the effort to somehow distinguish between criminal acts and terrorist acts. Some so-called terrorist acts are as specific and localized as to be outside the scope of the broader definitions. We shall now examine a few of those that seem especially relevant as we examine crime and terror in the twenty-first century.

HOSTAGE TAKING

Taking hostages, whether for political reasons or for extortion of funds to support terrorist groups, is an often-used tactic. The policy of the United States is to make no concessions to terrorists who hold official or private U.S. citizens as hostages. The United States will not pay ransom, release prisoners, change its policies, or agree to other acts that might encourage terrorism. At the same time, the United States will use every available and appropriate resource to gain the safe return of American citizens who are being held hostage by terrorists. Hostage taking is defined under international law (the International Convention Against the Taking of Hostages, adopted December 17, 1979) as "the seizing or detaining, threatening to kill, injure, or continue to detain a person in order to compel a third party to do, or abstain from doing, any act as an explicit or implicit condition for the release of the seized or detained person. Such activity is also considered a criminal act in most countries around the world, as a part of extortion or kidnapping for profit." It is generally accepted in the international community that local governments are responsible for the safety and welfare of persons within the borders of their nations. Terrorist threats and public safety shortcomings in many parts of the world have caused the United States to develop enhanced physical and personal security programs for U.S. citizens and to establish cooperative arrangements with the U.S. private sector to help warn and protect business travelers. The United States has established bilateral counterterrorism assistance programs and close intelligence and law enforcement relationships with many nations to help prevent terrorist incidents, or to resolve them in a manner that will deny the terrorists political or financial benefits from their actions. The United States also seeks to employ adequate and effective judicial prosecution and punishment for terrorists who seek to victimize the U.S. government, or its citizens, and will use all appropriate legal methods toward these ends, including extradition alone and/or, hopefully, with appropriate cooperation from the other governments. After many serious incidents, the United States has finally concluded that paying ransom or making other concessions to terrorists in exchange for the release of hostages only increases the probability and danger that others will then be taken hostage—*ad infinitum*. A good example of hostage taking and ransom and the overall ineptitude of international response is well documented in relation to acts of piracy (see Chapter 14). In some very poor nations, kidnapping and ransom are considered growth industries. The Horn of Africa and Nigeria are good examples of Third World countries where hostage taking and piracy are growth industries. U.S. policy strongly encourages U.S. companies and private citizens not to respond to terrorist ransom demands. It believes that good security practice, relatively modest security training and expenditures, and continual close cooperation with embassy and local authorities will lower the risk to Americans abroad who are living and working in such high-threat environments.

Although the United States is concerned for the welfare of its citizens, it cannot support requests from private companies that host governments should violate their own laws or abdicate their normal law enforcement responsibilities. On the other hand, if the employing organization or company of a hostage works closely with local authorities and follows U.S. policy, U.S. Foreign Service posts can be involved actively in efforts to bring such stressful incidents to a successful conclusion. This includes providing reasonable administrative services and, if desired by the local authorities and the American organization, full participation in strategy sessions. Requests for U.S. technical assistance or expertise are considered on a case-by-case basis. The full extent of U.S. government participation must await an analysis of each specific set of circumstances. This again demonstrates the problems involved with making precise definitions of who can do what in a situation that may or may not be terrorism.

LEGAL ISSUES IN HOSTAGE TAKING

Under current U.S. law (18 U.S.C. 1203, Act for the Prevention and Punishment of the Crime of Hostage-Taking, enacted in October 1984, on implementation of the UN convention on hostage taking), seizure of a U.S. national as a hostage anywhere in the world is a crime, as is any hostage taking in which the U.S. government is a target or the hostage taker is a U.S. national. Such acts are, therefore, subject to investigation by the FBI and to prosecution by U.S. authorities.

ASSASSINATION

On September 11, 2001, Osama bin Laden and his al Qaeda cohorts struck a blow against Western social values and have, by these acts, created a lingering and justifiable fear that they will attempt to strike at the United States again. This fear increased pressure on U.S. officials, and around the talk-show circuit, to perhaps reconsider **assassination** as a method of solving problems with world leaders whom we consider to be dangerous. The old argument still remains, "How many lives would we have saved if Hitler had been assassinated in 1938?" This argument is strong, and for a long time, many countries have ordered and approved using "extreme sanction" against leaders of unfriendly countries or against leaders of criminal or terrorist organizations. "Cut the head off the snake" was considered a good response to perceived danger. But, ordering an assassination today would mean moving away from long-established policy and practice.

Time will tell whether or not the United States can ever accumulate the needed backing of the international community to head into a "sure-to-spiral upward" path of assassinations adopted to meet perceived solutions to growing problems. The problem is similar to that of euthanasia— "Who decides when a person is so evil, or in such bad health, that their elimination is the only alternative?" This issue will have a long discussion period, in times when cooler emotions may eventually prevail. The situation in Iraq showed what methods had to be used to oust Saddam Hussein—and his trial and execution will help to clarify whether such actions were justifiable or considered too extreme. Bin Laden's killing or assassination by U.S. Navy SEALs in May 2011 did not raise the ire or angst of many countries, and the U.S. military action authorized by President Obama was supported by both the UN and NATO. The fact that bin Laden was possibly unarmed at the time of his death was raised as an issue by groups such as Amnesty International.

Examples of Past Hostage Crises

Lebanese Hostage Crisis—1982–1992   Lebanon was in complete turmoil by 1981, and the kidnapping most effectively conducted by organizations fronting for Hezbollah saw some ninety-six foreign hostages being kidnapped mostly from Western countries and primarily journalists, diplomats, or teachers from the American University in Beirut. The majority of those kidnapped were from the United States, France, West Germany, Great Britain, and Switzerland. Captive Terry Waite, a special envoy of Britain's Archbishop of Canterbury, was in Beirut negotiating independently for the release of other kidnap victims when he was seized and remained in almost solitary confinement from the time of his capture in January 1987 until his ultimate release in November 1991. The longest-held hostage was U.S. citizen and the senior Middle East correspondent for the Associated Press, Terry Anderson, who was kidnapped by elements of Hezbollah in March 1985 and was not released until December 1991.

Black September—Munich Olympic Games, September 1972   A group of eight Palestinian terrorists entered the Athlete Village and took eleven Israeli athletes and some of their trainers hostage. Their demands were simple; the release of some 200 Palestinians held by the Israeli government. The standoff with West German Police lasted around eighteen hours, and on the evening of September 5, 1972, the hostages and their kidnappers were ferried by helicopter to Fürstenfeldbruck Airport. West German Police attempted a rescue mission that resulted in all eleven hostages being killed. This single event prompted the West German Police to develop a counterterror force to combat terrorist events, and ultimately the crack force **GSG-9** came into being.

Japanese Ambassador's Residence, Lima, Peru—December 1996   Members of Peru's Tupac Amaru Revolutionary Movement seized the ambassador's residence during a Christmas reception and took Peruvian government officials, foreign diplomats, and Japanese businessmen hostage while demanding the release of Tupac Amaru members in Peruvian prisons. A majority of the foreign diplomats were released, but the hostage crisis continued for nearly four months and ended only when Peruvian "special forces" tunneled into the compound and successfully rescued the remaining eighty hostages.

ISIL Kidnappings—Syria, November 2012   Islamists kidnapped Western journalist James Foley. Foley was a U.S. citizen who was working in Syria for Agence France-Presse covering the Syrian civil war. He was held captive and undoubtedly subjected to various forms of torture, including starvation, beatings, mock executions, and **water boarding**, a tactic used by the CIA on detainees at Guantanamo Bay. He was either sold or handed over by his original captors to the fledgling ISIL and his beheading in August 2014 by ISIL was videoed and posted on the Internet. It is understood that he was beheaded in retaliation for U.S. airstrikes in Iraq and the U.S. refusal to pay over $100 million in ransom.

Kidnapping for ransom or political gain remains a global issue. Some of the most significant countries and the elements most likely to engage in kidnapping of Westerners are primarily as follows:

- Mexico—drug cartels and associated gangs
- Lebanon—elements sponsored by Hezbollah
- Iraq and Syria—Islamic State
- Algeria and Niger—al Qaeda-inspired al Qaeda in the Islamic Maghreb (AQIM)
- Nigeria—Boko Haram—al Qaeda inspired and possibly sponsored by affiliated al Qaeda groups

CONSTITUTIONAL RIGHTS

Finally, we raise the question of subversion of constitutionally guaranteed federal rights. The Fourteenth Amendment of the U.S. Constitution defines "residents" as being citizens of both the federal government and the state in which they reside. It expressly forbids states from making any ordinance, law, or regulation that abridges the federal rights of citizens. If there is a constitutional right to abortion, and the effects (whether by "color" or "usage") of local, county, or state government clearly abridge that right, is that right an issue that might be considered by federal courts? If one defines antiabortion terrorism as an effort to impose a set of religious beliefs on others, is there a colorable question of separation of church and state? Students of constitutional history may later consider these early years of this millennium as an odious period of challenge to and denial of their liberties.

Clearly, terrorism is a complex, multifaceted, and often baffling subject to define. The players involved have a way of rising to prominence, splintering, disappearing for years, and then suddenly reappearing. Counterterrorism bureaucracies are formed and then reformed, names are changed, and leaders are shuffled around as they are promoted, demoted, killed, or forced to resign. Incidents proliferate across the world, some of which can trigger off a chain of events that will destabilize a whole region and bring nations to the edge of ruin. At the same time, major terrorist actions can shock for a short while and then be eventually forgotten by all except those seriously impacted by the tragedy. Treatises are written, theories propounded, grievances aired, and tactics discussed, occasionally, to some effect, but more often, not. Causes are picked up by the world media, examined, probed, and then all too often overlooked in the rush to cover some new breaking story—until the next bomb explodes, or the next airliner is hijacked or downed, like those in Russia in 2004, or another cataclysmic event, like the 9-11 attacks, happens in some major city, as London experienced in July 2005, the bungled attacks on Glasgow Airport, Scotland, in July 2007, and the Mumbai attacks in 2008.

With the various definitions of terrorism and their application to specific events, you should have a good foundation for the study of terrorism and terrorist acts. Terrorism drastically shocks the senses and promotes fear and concern around the world. In the next chapter, we shall review state-sponsored and religious terrorism from several viewpoints. Terrorist causes are often looked upon as bizarre or weird in the context of the present. But most issues (political, religious, racial, or ethnic) have a long, historic pattern that always needs to be discovered and examined in a particular context. We believe that those who understand the historic foundations of these issues that have shaped the free world, since the attacks of 9-11, will never again be able to view the evening news in the same way ever again.

You can now appreciate that there is neither a universally accepted nor a simple definition of terrorism. According to acknowledged terrorism expert Walter Laqueur, "the only characteristic generally agreed upon is that terrorism involves violence and the threat of violence." This criterion alone does not produce a useful definition as it includes many acts not usually considered terrorism, such as war, organized crime, revolution, or even a simple riot. *Asymmetric warfare* and *low-intensity operations* are military terms for tactics that sometimes include terrorism. At its core, the definition of terrorism is not so much a description of a particular kind of violence, like bombing or assassination, but a way to characterize an act of violence relative to terrorists and their point of view.

"Terrorism," then, is a term that attempts to define, as a separate phenomenon, a philosophy of coordinated violence that tends to have a high degree of social impact on a targeted society. Rebels in opposition to an established social order may perpetrate terrorist violence, or a state may inflict it upon its own citizens or those of another state. One study by the U.S. Army discovered over 100 definitions that have been used. A few more of such examples will highlight and emphasize the problem of settling upon any precise definition:

U.S. Code of Federal Regulations   "The unlawful use of force and violence against persons or property to intimidate or coerce a government, the civilian population, or any segment thereof, in furtherance of political or social objectives" (28 C.F.R. Section 0.85).

Current U.S. National Security Strategy   "Premeditated, politically motivated violence against innocents."

U.S. Department of Defense   The "calculated use of unlawful violence to inculcate fear; intended to coerce or intimidate governments or societies in pursuit of goals that are generally political, religious, or ideological."

The U.S. Department of Justice   "The unlawful use of force or violence committed by a group or individual against persons or property to intimidate or coerce a Government, the Civilian population or any segment thereof in furtherance of political or social objectives."

A 1984 U.S. Army Training Manual   "Terrorism is the calculated use of violence, or the threat of violence, to produce goals that are political or ideological in nature."

European Union   There are currently twenty-eight member states in the EU also comprising countries from the former Soviet bloc. Each member state may have its own definition of terrorism that defines such incidents as criminal. The EU created a framework document for member states to align their legislation with the EU directives; in conclusion, the EU accepts that in International Law there is no generally accepted definition, so it states that "terrorism" can be defined as the intentional and systematic use of actions designed to provoke terror in the public as a means to certain ends. As is so often the case, a planned series of attacks by any disparate group will cause governments to establish emergency and often far-reaching legislation aimed at protecting the nation. After the 9-11 suicide attacks, the U.S. government moved quickly to pass the Patriot Act, which addressed and formalized into law the U.S. response to how terrorism would be combated from within.

THE U.S. CODE, TITLE 18 PART I CHAPTER 113B SEC 2331

Sec 2331—Definitions:

(1) "International terrorism" means activities that -
   (a) involve violent acts or acts dangerous to human life that are a violation of the criminal laws of the United States or of any State, or that would be a criminal violation if committed within the jurisdiction of the United States or of any State;
   (b) appear to be intended -
      (i) to coerce or intimidate a civilian population;
      (ii) to influence the policy of a government by intimidation or coercion; or to affect the conduct of a government by mass destruction, assassination, or kidnapping; and
      (iii) to affect the conduct of a government by mass destruction, assassination, or kidnapping;
   (c) occur primarily outside the territorial jurisdiction of the United States, or transcend national boundaries in terms of the means by which they are accomplished, the persons they appear intended to intimidate or coerce, or the locale in which their perpetrators operate or seek asylum;
(2) the term "national of the United States" has the meaning given such term in section 101(a)(22) of the Immigration and Nationality Act;
(3) the term "person" means any individual or entity capable of holding a legal or beneficial interest in property;
(4) the term "act of war" means any act occurring in the course of -
   (a) declared war;
   (b) armed conflict, whether or not war has been declared, between two or more nations; or
   (c) armed conflict between military forces of any origin; and
(5) the term "domestic terrorism" means activities that -
   (a) involve acts dangerous to human life that are a violation of the criminal laws of the United States or of any State;
   (b) appear to be intended -
      (i) to intimidate or coerce a civilian population;
      (ii) to influence the policy of a government by intimidation or coercion; or to affect the conduct of a government by mass destruction, assassination, or kidnapping; and
   (c) occur primarily within the territorial jurisdiction of the United States.[13]

Immediately following the attacks on the United States on September 11, 2001, the Department of Homeland Security was created by merging twenty-two separate agencies into one cohesive department with the goal of protecting the homeland.

THE USA PATRIOT ACT: PRESERVING LIFE AND LIBERTY

(Uniting and Strengthening America by Providing Appropriate Tools Required to Intercept and Obstruct Terrorism)

Congress enacted the Patriot Act by overwhelming, bipartisan margins, arming law enforcement with new tools to detect and prevent terrorism: The USA Patriot Act was passed nearly unanimously by the Senate 98-1, and 357-66 in the House, with the support of members from across the political spectrum.

The Act Improves Our Counterterrorism Efforts in Several Significant Ways:

1. **The Patriot Act allows investigators to use the tools that were already available to investigate organized crime and drug trafficking.** Many of the tools the Act provides to law enforcement to fight terrorism have been used for decades to fight organized crime and drug dealers, and have been reviewed and approved by the courts. As Sen. Joe Biden (D-DE) explained during the floor debate about the Act, "the FBI could get a wiretap to investigate the mafia, but they could not get one to investigate terrorists. To put it bluntly, that was crazy! What's good for the mob should be good for terrorists" (Cong. Rec., 10/25/01).

   - **Allows law enforcement to use surveillance against more crimes of terror.** Before the Patriot Act, courts could permit law enforcement to conduct electronic surveillance to investigate many ordinary, non-terrorism crimes, such as drug crimes, mail fraud, and passport fraud. Agents also could obtain wiretaps to investigate some, but not all, of the crimes that terrorists often commit. The Act enabled investigators to gather information when looking into the full range of terrorism-related crimes, including: chemical-weapons offenses, the use of weapons of mass destruction, killing Americans abroad, and terrorism financing.

   - **Allows federal agents to follow sophisticated terrorists trained to evade detection.** For years, law enforcement has been able to use "roving wiretaps" to investigate ordinary crimes, including drug offenses and racketeering. A roving wiretap can be authorized by a federal judge to apply to a particular suspect, rather than a particular phone or communications device. Because international terrorists are sophisticated and trained to thwart surveillance by rapidly changing locations and communication devices, such as cell phones, the Act authorized agents to seek court permission to use the same techniques in national security investigations to track terrorists.

   - **Allows law enforcement to conduct investigations without tipping off terrorists.** In some cases if criminals are tipped off too early to an investigation, they might flee, destroy evidence, intimidate or kill witnesses, cut off contact with associates, or take other action to evade arrest. Therefore, federal courts in narrow circumstances long have allowed law enforcement to delay for a limited time when the subject is told that a judicially approved search warrant has been executed. Notice is always provided, but the reasonable delay gives law enforcement time to identify the criminal's associates, eliminate immediate threats to our communities, and coordinate the arrests of multiple individuals without tipping them off beforehand. These delayed notification search warrants have been used for decades, have proven crucial in drug and organized crime cases, and have been upheld by courts as fully constitutional.

   - **Allows federal agents to ask a court for an order to obtain business records in national security terrorism cases.** Examining business records often provides the key that investigators are looking for to solve a wide range of crimes. Investigators might seek select records from hardware stores or chemical plants, for example, to find out who bought materials to make a bomb, or bank records to see who's sending money to terrorists. Law enforcement authorities have always been able to obtain business records in criminal cases through grand jury subpoenas, and continue to do so in national security cases where appropriate. These records were sought in criminal cases, such as the investigation of the Zodiac gunman, where police suspected the gunman was inspired by a Scottish occult poet, and wanted to learn who had checked the poet's books out of the library. In national security cases where use of the grand jury process was not appropriate, investigators previously had limited tools at their disposal to obtain certain business records. Under the Patriot Act, the government can now ask a federal court (the Foreign Intelligence Surveillance Court), if needed to aid an investigation, to order production of the same type of records available through grand jury subpoenas. This federal court, however, can issue these orders only after the government demonstrates the records concerned are sought for an authorized investigation to obtain foreign intelligence information not concerning a U.S. person or to protect against international terrorism or clandestine intelligence activities, provided that such investigation of a U.S. person is not conducted solely on the basis of activities protected by the First Amendment.

2. **The Patriot Act facilitated information sharing and cooperation among government agencies so that they can better "connect the dots."** The Act removed the major legal barriers that prevented the law enforcement, intelligence, and national defense communities from talking and coordinating their work to protect the American people and our national security. The government's prevention efforts should not be restricted by boxes on an organizational chart. Now police officers, FBI agents, federal prosecutors, and intelligence officials can protect our communities by "connecting the dots" to uncover terrorist plots before they are completed. As Sen. John Edwards (D-N.C.) said about the Patriot Act, "we simply cannot prevail in the battle against terrorism if the right hand of our government has no idea what the left hand is doing" (Press release, 10/26/01).

   • Prosecutors and investigators used information shared pursuant to section 218 in investigating the defendants in the so-called "Virginia Jihad" case. This prosecution involved members of the Dar al-Arqam Islamic Center, who trained for jihad in Northern Virginia by participating in paintball and paramilitary training, including eight individuals who traveled to terrorist training camps in Pakistan or Afghanistan between 1999 and 2001. These individuals are associates of a violent Islamic extremist group known as Lashkar-e-Taiba (LET), which operates in Pakistan and Kashmir, and that has ties to the al Qaeda terrorist network. As the result of an investigation that included the use of information obtained through FISA, prosecutors were able to bring charges against these individuals. Six of the defendants have pleaded guilty, and three were convicted in March 2004 of charges including conspiracy to levy war against the United States and conspiracy to provide material support to the Taliban. These nine defendants received sentences ranging from a prison term of four years to life imprisonment.

3. **The Patriot Act updated the law to reflect new technologies and new threats.** The Act brought the law up to date with current technology, so we no longer have to fight a digital-age battle with antique weapons—legal authorities leftover from the era of rotary telephones. When investigating the murder of *Wall Street Journal* reporter Daniel Pearl, for example, law enforcement used one of the Act's new authorities to use high-tech means to identify and locate some of the killers.

   • **Allows law enforcement officials to obtain a search warrant anywhere a terrorist-related activity occurred.** Before the Patriot Act, law enforcement personnel were required to obtain a search warrant in the district where they intended to conduct a search. However, modern terrorism investigations often span a number of districts, and officers therefore had to obtain multiple warrants in multiple jurisdictions, creating unnecessary delays. The Act provides that warrants can be obtained in any district in which terrorism-related activities occurred, regardless of where they will be executed. This provision does not change the standards governing the availability of a search warrant, but streamlines the search-warrant process.

   • **Allows victims of computer hacking to request law enforcement assistance in monitoring the "trespassers" on their computers.** This change made the law technology-neutral; it placed electronic trespassers on the same footing as physical trespassers. Now, hacking victims can seek law enforcement assistance to combat hackers, just as burglary victims have been able to invite officers into their homes to catch burglars.

4. **The Patriot Act increased the penalties for those who commit terrorist crimes.** Americans are threatened as much by the terrorist who pays for a bomb as by the one who pushes the button. That's why the Patriot Act imposed tough new penalties on those who commit and support terrorist operations, both at home and abroad. In particular, the Act:

   • **Prohibits the harboring of terrorists.** The Act created a new offense that prohibits knowingly harboring persons who have committed or are about to commit a variety of terrorist offenses, such as destruction of aircraft; use of nuclear, chemical, or biological weapons; use of weapons of mass destruction; bombing of government property; sabotage of nuclear facilities; and aircraft piracy.

   • **Enhanced the inadequate maximum penalties for various crimes likely to be committed by terrorists,** including arson, destruction of energy facilities, material support to terrorists and terrorist organizations, and destruction of national-defense materials.

- **Enhanced a number of conspiracy penalties,** including for arson, killings in federal facilities, attacking communications systems, material support to terrorists, sabotage of nuclear facilities, and interference with flight crew members. Under previous law, many terrorism statutes did not specifically prohibit engaging in conspiracies to commit the underlying offenses. In such cases, the government could only bring prosecutions under the general federal conspiracy provision, which carries a maximum penalty of only five years in prison.
- **Punishes terrorist attacks on mass transit systems.**
- **Punishes bioterrorists.**
- **Eliminates the statutes of limitations for certain terrorism crimes and lengthens them for other terrorist crimes.**[14]

Civil libertarians were less than happy about the sweeping powers of the Patriot Act, particularly sections that authorized roving wiretaps, which effectively allowed police to obtain a wiretap warrant on *any* phone used by a *suspected* terrorist. Prior to the Patriot Act, police would have to seek judicial approval/authorization for each individual phone. Lawmakers sought to minimize the effect on civil liberties by including a sunset clause, which would cause the act to expire at the end of four years. In even the most primitive societies, certain acts or groups of acts have been universally forbidden, discouraged, or proscribed. Such acts include murder, rape, incest, kidnapping, and treason (or some form of rebellion affecting the entire social group's safety and the leadership's authority). In contrast, most societies have encouraged, sponsored, or prescribed behaviors such as marrying, having children, hunting, growing food, and other actions that clearly benefit the group's or tribe's common social welfare and survival. Terrorism often falls into the range of behaviors that are not only a violation of laws but also a violation of the politics and practices (mores) of a social group or tribal organization. Often, the violation of codified law requires that a person must call a public safety officer to make an investigation or an arrest. All of these behaviors are related to the ways that social groups or subcultures choose to respond to transgressions that violate their mutually agreed-to standards of conduct. In 2001, shortly after 9-11, the U.S. Department of Homeland Security was born out of public outrage and the aftereffects of the attacks. Terrorism from abroad had struck at the United States and awakened a "sleeping giant," one that realized that the world had changed. Something had to be done quickly to assure Americans that the government was going to respond strongly and would not allow something terrible like this to happen again at the hands of foreign terrorists. As the horrific attacks of September 11, 2001, recede into time, only the lasting effects of security are clear to us all. The world certainly has not become a safer place, particularly for citizens from Western countries and in particular those from the United States and Great Britain traveling abroad; the United States is engaged in a conventional war against insurgents in both Iraq and Afghanistan and is still a target for the hatred and ire of Islamist terror cells, be they foreign or home grown.

Summary

Finding a complete, all-encompassing, and generally accepted definition for terrorism continues to elude us all; definitions exist, and more will be forthcoming over the years. Terrorism is used daily to describe all manner of atrocities, many related to global events and others totally unconnected to conventional terrorism. This chapter has taken a broad approach to looking at some but not all the various definitions that are currently favored by government, academia, and the judiciary, and though each of the definitions listed has some descriptive bearing on the word "terror" as we observe it today, definitions will ultimately change with the types of terror events we become exposed to. The world is changing, and the definition for terror will also change. Legislation has been enacted to combat and

prevent terrorism and definitions have been applied in a variety of regions around the world. The various definitions go a long way in assisting us to understand not only what terrorism is but how it is viewed by nation-states and organizations such as the UN. We will see in the next chapters that although al Qaeda and its dominant successor Islamic State and their affiliates persist in having designs on a global jihad, global terrorism has been fought by a large number of nations on a global scale for decades, and in this we will consider the European, Middle East, and Central American terrorist organizations. Although this chapter will give the student pause for thought on how best to create a definition for terrorism, it will, we believe, continue to be elusive as the nature of terrorism constantly changes.

Review Questions

1. Discuss the geopolitical conditions that make the task of defining terrorism complicated for the UN General Assembly.
2. Discuss similarities and contrasts between what has taken place with Islamic State atrocities in the twenty-first century and that perpetrated in the seventeenth century during the French Revolution.
3. Create your own definition of terrorism, based on an actual terrorist event that has recently taken place in your country.
4. Discuss hostage taking as a criminal incident as opposed to a terrorist event and what elements may complicate the determination.
5. Determine the similarities between the U.S. definitions of terrorism and those of the Arab League.

End Notes

1. Cindy C. Combs. *Terrorism in the Twenty-First Century* (Upper Saddle River, NJ: Prentice Hall, 1997).
2. George Rosie. *International Terrorism: A New Mode of Conflict* (Los Angeles, CA: Crescent, 1975, p. 4).
3. The Hague Regulation of 1907 and the Geneva Conventions of 1949.
4. George Rosie. *The Directory of International Terrorism* (New York: Paragon House, 1987).
5. *U.S. Army Field Manual 100-20*, "Combating Terrorism." Stability and Support Operations (Washington, DC: Department of Defense, U.S. Government Printing Office, 1993), Chapter 8.
6. Editors: "FBI Counterterrorism Responsibilities." *FBI Website*, see Internet index (Washington, DC: U.S. Government Printing Office, Department of Justice, 1996).
7. *U.S. Army Field Manual.* "Combating Terrorism."
8. Ibid.
9. Jonathan R. White. *Terrorism: An Introduction* (Pacific Grove, CA: Brooks/Cole Publishing, 1991, p. 13).
10. Alex P. Schmidt. *Political Terrorism* (Cincinnati, OH: Transaction Books, Anderson Press, 1983, p. 107).
11. United Nations General Assembly Adopts Global Counterterrorism Strategy (September 8, 2006), www.UN.org.
12. Bruce Hoffman. "Defining Terrorism." *Inside Terrorism* (New York: Columbia University Press, 1998, p. 19).
13. Cornell University Law School: Legal Information Institute, http://www.law.cornell.edu/uscode/text/18/2331, retrieved March 2011.
14. U.S. Department of Justice. https://www.justice.gov/archive/ll/highlights.htm.

A Brief History of Terrorism

LEARNING OUTCOMES

After studying this chapter, students should be able to:

1. Describe how violence becomes terrorism and its historical roots.

2. List the five areas where state-sponsored terrorism can achieve its ends.

3. Describe how social media and Internet resources have become the modern communication tools for sophisticated terror groups.

4. Compare and contrast Islamism with jihad.

5. Summarize how media and modern media models work for and against terrorists.

KEY WORDS TO NOTE

Ayatollah Khomeini—Iranian Grand Ayatollah, leader of the revolution against the Shah of Iran in 1979

Ethnic cleansing—Depopulation or deporting (war crime) often during wartime and associated with genocide (crime against humanity)

Grand Mufti of Jerusalem—The Muslim cleric in Jerusalem responsible for Muslim holy sites, including the Al Aqsa Mosque

Hashish eater—Origin of the word "assassin" in ancient times

Inspire—An English online magazine published by al Qaeda in the Arabian Peninsula aimed at influencing jihad and targeting young men and women to take action

Khalid Sheikh Mohammed—Al Qaeda's Number 3 man who claimed responsibility for Daniel Pearl's death

Mujahideen—An Arabic term for an Islamic guerilla fighter

Zealots—A person(s) who is uncompromising and fanatical in pursuit of their religious, political, or other ideals

OVERVIEW

The term "terrorism" was coined during the French Revolution and the Jacobean reign of terror. However, that does not mean that individual and group acts—what we might classify as today's terrorism—cannot be traced back to the earliest activities of humankind. This chapter will briefly examine human violence and how it evolved into the label of "terrorism" in the twenty-first century. We shall examine the evolution of human behavior into what we have attempted to define (with considerable difficulty) in Chapter 1. This viewpoint will provide the reader with a different perspective on the behavioral aspects of violence.

VIOLENCE AND TERRORISM

What conditions generate violence? What are the justifications for using violence as a stepping-stone to terrorism? What allows a person or a group to apply violence to a specific situation, complaint, or event and believe it to be a logical, or natural, response? Violence is the application of destructive and harmful power that results in measurable damage caused by a conscious decision by an individual, or individuals, to apply it. Violence in this sense has had broad usage throughout history, demonstrated by the application of great force to achieve specific short-term goals by persons acting alone, or in mobs, or even as part of an organized group of like-minded individuals.

If we think about the paradigm of violence as seen in the fury of a wounded or humiliated animal, we can readily see that violence, or something very much like it, is not even a uniquely *human* behavior. Animals also release their energies in violent and destructive ways. In fact, it is the very similarity of such behavior by brutes that makes violence so distasteful to a rational human mind.[1]

In the earliest social groups, or tribes, violence could be identified, controlled, or quickly dealt with by either individual or group retaliation. Violent people were considered to be behaving like animals and banished to the wilds; they were forced to live as "outlaws," those who chose to operate outside the rules/laws of the group. Probably the earliest examples of what might be called terrorist behaviors were those actions intended to frighten another group into running away or surrendering by threat of violence. Individuals took actions such as painting themselves in bright patterns and colors, brandishing weapons and shouting threats, killing enemies and placing their heads on poles, and perhaps wearing the skins, teeth, and claws of violent animals. The goal was to shock or frighten the "enemy" so badly that it would either run away in fear or finally submit and surrender to the will of its adversaries.

Modern societies are composed of diverse religious, ethnic, and racial groupings that often seem out of context or not in sync with the ruling structures. Use of one-on-one violence as a way to draw attention to an individual (or group) and grievance becomes more difficult. When public officials seem to be inaccessible, a natural temptation for a frustrated constituent is to burst into their office, pound on the desk, or perhaps even wave a weapon, or stalk the officials and then attack them verbally or physically at an open-air market or other public place. At the extreme, some may even attempt to seriously injure or even kill. When a bureaucracy refuses to respond to a perceived grievance, it can result in spectacular and destructive behavior. Shooting a politician or destroying public property is not always a rational choice for the aggrieved person's situation. The motivation is often to not just stand there but also "do something" out of anger, frustration, fear, and a deep sense of hopelessness. The self-perceived hapless "victim(s)" begins to see all of society as a monstrous machine, out to get him or her or them! It is against this background that the distraught and frustrated person begins to believe that some kind of a serious "payback" blow must be struck. In today's global societies, there is a definite tendency to consider violence as an attractive, attention-getting solution, as most actions are social in nature. There are very few constructive, autonomous, and well-thought-out actions open to those who are not writers, doctors, or self-employed professionals. The doing of virtually anything worthwhile usually requires cooperation with, and actions of, others. Violence and destruction, however, are among a small number of things that are easily available to a single individual. The aggrieved needs no assistance to shoot at drivers from a freeway overpass or to drive a car into a group of pedestrians. But this "natural" desire to "do something" can often easily be channeled into a "violent" something. The fast-moving pace of modern society may make one feel that it is critical to do something—anything—whether it is bad or good! The catchy phrase is relevant here: "Don't just stand there . . . do something!" Violence, precisely because it is usually structured as an individual decision, leaves an individual with a feeling of actually having active involvement.

An act of violence can be described as a logical three-step progression:

1. Formation of intent
2. Execution
3. Immediate consequences

All can take place in microseconds. The feeling that whatever we do is not caused by something of our own design has been verified and replaced by thoughts that are all unique and individually formed in regard to one's own action(s).

Violence perpetrated for ideological reasons, and for a systematically promoted cause or complaint, is significantly different. Organizations in the business of doing such things frequently suffer from too much thinking and discussion and very little action. In the mind of an individual person, being told to do something does not nearly match the satisfaction of an act both conceived and performed by that specific person. Individuals who take violent action on their own, on the other hand, can take satisfaction in the self-empowered nature of their individually conceived act. They then can both claim and accept responsibility for their acts: "I did that, and I'm proud of it." Acts of violence planned and executed by a group, on the other hand, always have to share diluted credit. As a result, the blame or credit is spread so broadly it fails to satisfy anyone.

For example, Lachs presents a thoughtfully surprising positive side of the horrors of war: "Many people report that great danger leads to an exhilaration that renders an experience vibrant. Some say they can never recapture the keen sense of being totally alive that they felt in battle, or even when they merely supported the war effort."[2] The often dull and predictable regularity of most individuals' daily lives seems to validate such claims as just believable and natural. Living in a boring routine, in a cocoon-like, safe society, eventually makes life dull. War makes one begin to contemplate one's death and life—up close and personal—feeling and living the moment with crystal clarity. Something akin to this effect happens in connection with violence. In these outbursts, the adrenaline flows in great quantities, the eyes focus tightly into "tunnel vision," and blood rushes to the brain and other vital organs. Any soldier in combat, or police officer who has been involved in a street shootout, can describe that effect absolutely clearly. This is a drug that is not available on the street or in a pharmacy but, once experienced, can be just as addictive.

WHEN DID VIOLENCE BECOME TERRORISM?

By definition, the assassination of Julius Caesar, in 44 B.C., was an act of terrorism. This holds true as well when a modern political assassination is defined as terrorism.[3] Most modern political scientists generally treat assassination as a terrorist act, whether by an individual acting alone (as John Hinckley did when he shot President Ronald Reagan) or in concert with a group (as with Charles Manson's "groupies" in the attempted shooting of President Ford).

Group terrorism became common in as early as the Middle Ages. In fact, the word "assassin" comes from the Arabic term *hashashin*, which literally means **hashish eater**. It was used to describe a sectarian group of Muslims who were employed by their spiritual and political leader (the local Caliph) to spread terror in the form of murder and destruction among their religious enemies, with the promise of instant acceptance, of being directly transported to paradise, if they were killed themselves.[4] This promise is similar to the incentives claimed for suicide bombers in the Israel–Palestinian ongoing cycle of violence throughout the 1990s and the current suicide bombings that have been occurring with groups and individuals in Iraq and Afghanistan and, of course, the hijackers of the four civilian aircraft used in the 9-11 attacks. Marco Polo's travel journals included lurid tales of murder committed by these assassins. These early terrorists were motivated not only by promises of eternal reward in the "afterlife" but also by unlimited access to sex, hashish, and other drugs. Even the Crusaders made mention of this group of fanatics and the terror they inspired.[5]

The region from which the original assassins emerged was then known as Persia (the present-day Iran). In recent times, the **Ayatollah Khomeini** became the religious leader of the Shi'ites in Iran during its religious revolution in the late 1970s. It is widely believed and accepted that the young men in the Iran–Iraq War had been told that they would go directly to paradise if they fought bravely and died fighting for Allah. Reports from that war claimed that fifteen- and sixteen-year-olds were walked into the guns of their enemies, the Iraqis, in waves, unarmed and unafraid. Islam, Christianity, Judaism, and Hinduism are not, by doctrine, violent religions; neither are most of the other religions. It is the mixture of religion and politics that has often resulted in violence, frequently against innocent victims, which clearly makes it, according to the definition we suggested in Chapter 1, "terrorism." The Middle East, as the home of three major world religions, has been plagued by a variety of violent sects and religions. The creation of violent sects, and the blending of religion and politics, are similar to the Brotherhood of Assassins, and continue to fan the flames of violence. Religion is a special kind of "narcotic" that can both motivate terrorist actions in its name and deaden consciences to the slaughter inflicted on innocent people.

If terrorist acts were perceived as the proper way to "right the wrongs" committed by government, then the use of political assassins would not always be looked upon with disfavor.

Vidal, a leading French legal scholar, has noted that, whereas formerly the political offender was treated as a public enemy, he or she is today considered a friend of the public good—a person of progress, desirous of bettering the political institutions of his country, having laudable intentions, hastening the onward march of humanity. His only fault is that he wishes to go much too fast and then employs, attempting to realize the progress that he desires, irregular, illegal, and violent means.[6]

Not until the middle of the twentieth century was the murder of a head of state, or any member of his family, formally designated as terrorism. Even today, those who commit the "political" crime of murdering a head of state can often enjoy a type of special protection in the form of political asylum.[7]

More than 2,000 years ago, the first known acts of what we now call terrorism were perpetrated by a radical offshoot of the Zealots, a Jewish sect active in Judea during the first century A.D. The **Zealots** resisted the Roman Empire's rule of what is today Israel through a determined campaign primarily involving assassinations. Most of the violence perpetrated occurred in broad daylight with the intent to inculcate fear into the local as well as the wider community. They acted like our twentieth- and twenty-first-century terrorists, sending their open message to the Romans and any of the local population that may have considered siding with the Roman occupation.

We have seen many instances of suicide attacks used by Islamic extremists in the twenty-first century, and this was also evident in early history when an Islamic movement called the Assassins used the same type of tactic. Between the tenth and twelfth centuries, the Assassins waged numerous suicide attacks against the Christian Crusaders who had invaded parts of the area we now refer to as the Middle East. The Assassins embraced the same notions of self-sacrifice and suicidal martyrdom evident in Islamic extremist ideology today. The Assassins, 800 years ago, believed that violence was a divine act that assured their ascendancy to heaven, should they perish during the task.

STATE-SPONSORED AND RELIGIOUS TERRORISM

State terrorism, whether internal (against its own people or dissenters) or external (using or funding outside terrorist groups or individuals), offers a real threat to international stability and security. Internal terrorism can often inspire the formation of resistance movements, which then may resort to revolutionary or terror tactics. This cycle of terror and violence can result in a whirlwind that can suck in all sanity within its reach—innocent or guilty. Exportation of the support for external terror, sponsored by rogue states, has resulted in a proliferation of terrorist attacks worldwide. Even nations whose official policy specifically rejects the use of terror have been guilty of providing financial and operational aid, often clandestinely, to those who would promote and perform their terrorism. Early attacks on Jews in what is now Israel were sponsored and supported by religious leaders, such as Haj Mohammed Amin al-Husseini (1893–1974), the **Grand Mufti of Jerusalem** who dedicated his entire life to forcibly removing Jews from Arab land. After his death in 1974, his dedication to the Arab cause was carried on by his nephew Yasser Arafat.

State-Sponsored Terrorism as Warfare in the Twenty-First Century

There is no global consensus as to a definition of state-sponsored terrorism. During the second half of the twentieth century, various countries began to use terrorist organizations to promote state interests in the international domain. In some cases, states have established "puppet" terrorist organizations, whose purpose is to act on behalf of the sponsoring state, to further the interests of the state, and to represent its positions in domestic or regional fronts. The patron state provides its beneficiary terrorist organization with political support, financial assistance, and the sponsorship necessary to maintain and expand its struggle. The patron uses the beneficiary to perpetrate acts of terrorism as a means of spreading its ideology throughout the world or, in some cases, the patron ultimately expects the beneficiary to gain control of a state or impart its ideology to the general public. There are currently only three countries designated by the United States as "state sponsor," Iran, Sudan, and Syria, with Cuba having been removed from the list in 2015. Iran, besides sponsoring insurgent acts in Iraq, has

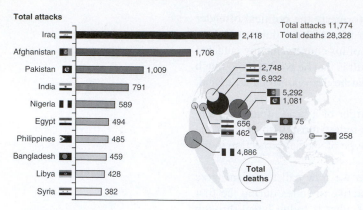

FIGURE 2-1 Countries with the most terrorist attacks and total deaths worldwide in 2015. *Source:* Statista.com and U.S. Department of State.

ongoing association with and provides support to Hezbollah, Hamas, Palestinian Islamic Jihad, and al Qaeda. Hezbollah, the Lebanese-based terrorist organization formed in 1982 by Iranian Revolutionary Guards Corps is closely allied to the Syrian Ba'ath Party regime. With Iran and Syrian support, it is accountable for the 1983 suicide bombing of the U.S. Marine Corps barracks in Beirut, the 1982 Israeli embassy bombing in Argentina, the bombing of the Jewish Cultural Center in Buenos Aires, and the 1996 Khobar Towers bombing in Saudi Arabia. Hamas, based in the Palestinian territories, also sponsored by Iran, and its terror wing, the Izz ad-Din al-Qassam Brigades, are involved in suicide attacks primarily against Israeli targets. Hamas was formed in 1987, and since 2000 has conducted over 425 attacks, with 377 killed and 2,070 injured. Hamas is also responsible for the 2002 suicide bombing at Netanya, which killed twenty-three people (Figure 2-1).

State Sponsor: Implications

Designating countries that repeatedly provide support for acts of international terrorism (i.e., placing a country on the terrorism list) imposes four main sets of U.S. Government sanctions:

1. A ban on arms-related exports and sales.
2. Controls over exports of dual-use items, requiring a thirty-day congressional notification for goods or services that could significantly enhance the terrorist-list country's military capability or ability to support terrorism.
3. Prohibitions on economic assistance.
4. Imposition of miscellaneous financial and other restrictions, including
   • Requiring the United States to oppose loans by the World Bank and other international financial institutions;
   • Lifting diplomatic immunity to allow families of terrorist victims to file civil lawsuits in U.S. courts;
   • Denying companies and individuals tax credits for income earned in terrorist-listed countries;
   • Denial of duty-free treatment for goods exported to the United States;
   • Authority to prohibit any U.S. citizen from engaging in a financial transaction with a terrorist-list government without a Treasury Department license; and
   • Prohibition of Defense Department contracts above $100,000 with companies controlled by terrorist-list states.[8]

State-sponsored terrorism can achieve strategic ends where the use of conventional armed forces is neither practical nor effective. The high costs of modern warfare and concern about non-conventional escalation have turned terrorism into an efficient, convenient, and generally discrete weapon for attaining sponsor state interests in the international realm. Some specific advantages are as follows:

• **Low cost—financially:** Terrorism offers a relatively inexpensive method of making a point for insurgent groups who lack the finances, personnel, or armaments to win against a nation's army on a conventional battlefield. Terrorist tactics also can provide small non-"superpower" nations a low-cost way to wage war, whether overtly or clandestinely, on a hostile state whose resources provide a serious obstacle to waging a full-scale war.

• **Low cost—politically:** For states, particularly those that can successfully provide and hide clandestine support for terrorist groups, the political cost can be quite low as long as such support remains secret. On the other hand, profit in arms sales might become temptingly high.

• **High yields—financially:** States that are arms dealers to terrorists can usually profit quite handsomely, with little or no political, military, or economic impact. Sometimes being

caught results in the recall of a couple of ambassadors, but seldom is there any impact on diplomatic or trade relations.
- **High yields—politically:** For dissenters who decide to use terrorism as a political weapon, the political currency can be very large in value. This is especially true when the targeted government's reactions are not supported by citizens in the middle and could lead to a regime being ousted from power. Major concessions can then be "bought" when a successful terrorist incident shocks the populace too much.
- **Low risk—politically and financially:** The costs of financing terrorist operations can be much less than those of maintaining a fully equipped and trained army. And the individuals carrying out these operations are not subjected to as much risk as there would be in conventional warfare. In a successful terrorist operation, the rewards are often very big. For a failed operation, the losses are generally small, unless the failure can be traced back to a state sponsor. The finding of these linkages has become very costly in financial and, more importantly, political terms.[9]

Iran under the leadership of President Hassan Rouhani is a prime example of a state sponsor of terrorism. His predecessor Mahmoud Ahmadinejad joined the Revolutionary Guards in 1986, and there have been reports, denied by Iran, that he was one of the student leaders who held Americans hostage in the U.S. embassy in Tehran. He is virulently anti-Semitic, denies that the Holocaust took place, and wants to see Israel wiped off the face of the earth. His involvement in supporting the insurgency in Iraq is well documented, and much of the weaponry being used and the fighters involved have been both trained and funded by his regime.

In May 2002, Colin Powell, the then U.S. secretary of state, clearly designated the governments that are supporting terrorism. Those named were Cuba, Iran, Iraq, Libya, North Korea, Sudan, and Syria. Since the U.S.-led invasion, Iraq is no longer on that list, and Libya is making moves to be fully accepted back into the "international community." By and large, these governments have continued to provide support to international terrorism, either by engaging in terrorist activity themselves or by providing arms, training, safe havens, diplomatic facilities, financial backing, logistics, and/or other support to terrorists. The U.S. policy of bringing maximum pressure to bear on state sponsors of terrorism and encouraging other countries to do likewise has paid dividends. There has been a clear decline in state-sponsored terrorism in recent years. A range of bilateral and multilateral sanctions serves to discourage state sponsors of terrorism from continuing their support for international acts of terrorism, but continued pressure is essential. In January 1991, President George Herbert Bush informed Congress that he was continuing sanctions against Libya as the "Libyan government continues to employ international terrorism and to support it, in violation of international law and international rules of conduct." Currently, Libya has become cooperative with both the United Kingdom and United States in extraditing terrorist suspects, and in 2006, signed a treaty to that effect with the UK government. The United States continues to designate Iran, Syria, and Sudan, as states sponsoring terrorism.

THE TURKS AND THE FIRST CRUSADE

The Turks were not originally from Turkey as most people think—they were a nomadic people from Central Asia, known today as Turkmenistan ("Land of the Turks"). One Turkish tribe, the Seljuks, began moving into the Anatolian peninsula, or the area we now call Turkey. These Turks were Muslims, but a Christian emperor, Michael VIII, controlled the peninsula. The emperor appealed to Pope Urban II to help him rid Anatolia of "unbelievers." The Pope received Michael's call for assistance but decided to use the situation to advance a more ambitious plan. Jerusalem was considered Holy Land to Christians, Jews, and Muslims, but in 1095, Muslims controlled the city. The message from Emperor Michael VIII presented Pope Urban II with an opportunity to justify and wage a "War of the Cross," or Crusade, retake the Holy Lands, and eradicate the unbelievers.

Pope Urban II persuaded the knights of Europe to join in the Crusade, by appealing to their religious convictions. They were told that Muslim Turks were robbing, raping, and killing Christian pilgrims journeying to Jerusalem. The Pope suggested that the knights fight Muslims instead of continuing to fight one another. Crusaders left their homes and families for a long journey into the unknown. While they did not succeed in ridding the Holy Lands of non-believers, the Crusaders found other, more worldly benefits:

- An increase in trade with Europe
- Travels to new lands and learning about new and interesting cultures
- Spices that allowed food to last longer and taste better
- Fine cloths manufactured in the Middle East

The Christians had recaptured the Holy Lands by the end of the Second Crusade, but a Muslim general named Saladin launched a jihad (an Islamic holy war) and recaptured Jerusalem. Saladin was neither an Arab nor a Turk—he was Kurdish. The Kurds lived between the Turks and Arabs in the mountainous lands of northern Iraq and eastern Turkey, even as they do to this day. When Saladin recaptured Jerusalem in 1187, the Christians launched a Third Crusade, perhaps the most famous, led by "King Richard the Lion-Hearted" of England. The Christians fought hard in the Third Crusade, but Saladin was able to hold Jerusalem for the Muslims. The two warriors agreed to a truce that left the Muslims controlling the Holy Lands, but with Christians free to visit their shrines. Although many other so-called Holy Wars have taken place over countless centuries, the Crusades are considered to be the eight campaigns into the Holy Lands that occurred from 1095 to 1291 A.D. The following is a listing of those eight major campaigns:

- The First Crusade, 1095–1099
- The Second Crusade, 1147–1149
- The Third Crusade, 1189–1192
- The Fourth Crusade, 1202–1204
- The Fifth Crusade, 1218–1221
- The Sixth Crusade, 1228–1229
- The Seventh Crusade, 1248–1254
- The Last Crusade, 1270–1291

Hundreds of wars and attempts at extermination of certain groups of people have stemmed from religious, ethnic, racial, and tribal differences since the Crusades, and even before—Catholics against Protestants, Jews against Arabs, Sikhs against Hindus, Hindus against Muslims, Tutsis against Hutus, Communists against Democracies, Kosovo against Serbia, Khmer Rouge against Republicans, Shiites against Sunnis. The list goes on and on, all with the same religious fervor. The main weapon in these latter-day attempts at **ethnic cleansing** has been terrorism, using broad tactics from abductions, forced religious conversion, slavery, rape, mass executions, and beheadings. From the inquisition to ethnic cleansing, the resulting terror has created deep splits among religions, tribes, and ideologies throughout the world.

RELIGIOUS TERRORISM   Were the Crusades simply a form of terrorism in the name of religion? One definition of "genocide" is as follows: "A conspiracy aimed at the total destruction of a group and thus requires a concerted plan of action. The instigators and initiators of a genocide are cool-minded theorists first, and barbarians only second. The specificity of genocide does not arise from the extent of the killings, nor their savagery or resulting infamy, but solely from the intention: the destruction of a group."[10]

Terrorist acts in the name of religion have been more frequent in the latter part of the twentieth century. Many groups like to link their grievances to religion when in fact they are in reality concealing a political agenda or motivation. There are many books and reports covering the topic of suicide and terrorism but little empirical research on the people who carry out these attacks and why. After the event takes place, there is in-depth coverage of the individual participant but no real understanding of the motivation. Families often report they had no prior knowledge that their family member was intent on blowing himself or herself to kingdom come in the name of religion! Obviously those recruiting for the suicide mission remain as instructors and would never consider the act for themselves. So the recruiter must target those who may already be susceptible to the idea of suicide. Research being conducted with failed suicide bombers has indicated that the young men in at least half of the cases were already depressed and "defeated" and may have considered suicide even if they had not been recruited to a suicide mission. Prior to the 1980s, there are no recorded cases of Islamic suicide bombers, and the first

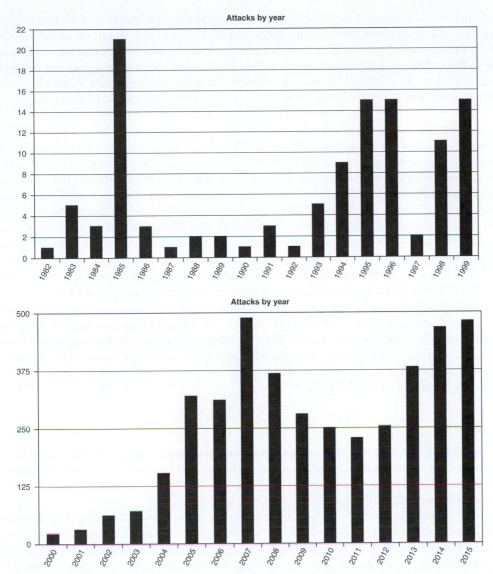

FIGURE 2-2 Suicide attacks worldwide 1982–1999 compared with 2000–2015. *Source:* Chicago Project on Security and Terrorism, http://cpost.uchicago.edu.

is most likely the truck bomb attack on the U.S. Marine Base in Beirut in 1983. In nearly all cases, the suicide bomber has no criminal record and is therefore difficult at best to track—but in general, they do not act alone and require a network to train them, acquire materials, and target selection. Of the more than 3,000 suicide bombers of the last thirty years, only four are believed to have been unaided (Figure 2-2). Suicide terrorism or martyrdom is efficient, inexpensive, easily organized, and extremely difficult to counter, delivering maximum damage for little cost. The shocking nature of a suicide attack also attracts public attention. Glorifying the culture of martyrdom benefits the terrorist organization and inspires more people to join the group or even consider independent action.

ISLAM

Twenty-first-century terrorism centers on fanatical elements preaching a firebrand and extreme version of Islam. Considered one of the oldest of religions, it refers to the doctrines of the Prophet Muhammad dating back to the sixth century. Muhammad was born in Mecca and is revered as God's representative, and in Islam, God is referred to as Allah. Muslim adherents can be found in vast numbers throughout the globe and number around one-fifth of the global population. At the dawn of the tenth century, Islam and the Caliphs held control over a vast section of the globe, stretching from India in the east to Spain in the west. Jerusalem was considered the Holiest of places not just by Christians but also by Muslims and Jews, and this brings us to the Crusades. During the Middle Ages, religion was at the forefront when it came to territorial conquest, and the kings of European countries, including France and England, mounted a series of campaigns, in fact, a total of eight between 1096 and 1270—the aim being not only the conquest of rich lands but also to establish their religious claim to Jerusalem. Control of Jerusalem changed numerous times during the Crusades. Islam itself has been consumed with internal battles over the centuries on the rightful succession of Caliphs (rulers). A split within the religion created two separate groups of adherents within the Muslim faith, Shia and Sunni; the Sunni Muslims have the larger following and dominate countries of the Middle East. Osama bin Laden's al Qaeda adherents are followers of the Sunni version of Islam who believe in and follow the teachings of the Prophet Muhammad. The Shiite sect believes that the rightful Prophet of Islam is Ali, a cousin of Muhammad. The Middle East conflict is currently drawn along religious lines in Iraq and Iran; both countries have Shia Muslims as the dominant sect within their respective nations. The former president of Iraq, Saddam Hussein, held power with a Sunni minority government and enforced his iron will not just against the Kurds but also against any and all Shia opponents of his totalitarian regime for over a quarter of a century. Since the attacks against the United States on 9-11, the Madrid trains bombings in Spain, the London tube train and bus bombings of 2005, and the wave of Islamic violence sweeping across European nations, many in both the media and general discussion have quite naturally linked Islam with extreme violence and fanaticism. Politicians have even referred to Islamist fascism as having declared war on the West.

Islamism

Islamism is an ideology that demands an individual's complete adherence to the sacred law of Islam and rejects as much as possible outside influence. It is imbued with a deep antagonism toward non-Muslims and has a particular hostility toward the West. It amounts to an effort to turn Islam, a religion and civilization, into an ideology.

Islamism is yet another twentieth-century radical utopian scheme. Like Marxism–Leninism or fascism, it offers a way to control the state, run society, and remake the human being. It is an Islamic-flavored version of totalitarianism. Islamism is also a total transformation of traditional Islam. Islamism is not a medieval program but one that responds to the stress and strains of the twentieth century.

Islamism is a huge change from traditional Islam. One illustration: Whereas traditional Islam's sacred law is a personal law, a law a Muslim must follow wherever he is; Islamism tries to apply a Western-style geographic law that depends on where one lives. Take the case of Sudan, where traditionally a Christian was perfectly entitled to drink alcohol, for he is a Christian, and Islamic law applies only to Muslims. But the current regime has banned alcohol for every Sudanese. It assumes Islamic law is territorial, because that is the way a Western society is run.

Islamism has few connections to wealth or poverty; it is not a response to deprivation. There is no discernible connection between income and Islamism. The ideology appeals primarily to modern people; so it is fascinating to note how many Islamist leaders (e.g., in Turkey and Jordan) are engineers.

Islamism is a powerful force. It runs governments in Iran, Sudan, and under the Taliban, Afghanistan. It is an important force of opposition in Algeria, Egypt, Turkey, Lebanon, and the Palestinian authority. Islamists are also present in the United States and, to a stunning extent, dominate the discourse of American Islam.

The Islamists' success in Iran, Sudan, and Afghanistan shows that were they to come to power elsewhere, they would create enormous problems for the people they rule, for the region, and for the United States. Their reaching power would lead to economic contraction, the oppression of women, terrible human rights abuses, the proliferation of arms, terrorism, and the spread of a viciously anti-American ideology. These are, in short, rogue states, dangerous first to their own people and then to the outside world.[11]

JIHAD

"Jihad" is a term that the West has come to know and fear. It dates back to the Middle Ages. In the linguistic sense, the Arabic word "jihad" means struggling or striving and applies to any effort exerted by anyone. In this sense, a student struggles and strives to get an education and pass course work; an employee strives to fulfill his or her job and maintain good relations with his or her employer; a politician strives to maintain or increase his or her popularity with his or her constituents and, so on. The terms "strive" and "struggle" may be used for/by Muslims as well as non-Muslims; for example, Allah, the One and Only True God, says in the Qur'an:

> We have enjoined on people kindness to parents; but if they strive (Jahadaka) to make you ascribe partners with Me that of which you have no knowledge, then obey them not . . .
>
> (THE HOLY QURAN, 29:8; also see 31:15)

In the above verse of the Qur'an, it is non-Muslim parents who strive (*jahadaka*) to convert their Muslim child back to their religion. In the West, jihad is generally translated as "holy war," a usage the media have popularized. According to Islamic teachings, it is unholy to instigate or start war; however, some wars are inevitable and justifiable.

If we translate the words "holy war" back into Arabic, we find *harbun muqaddasatu*, or for "the holy war," *al-harbu al-muqaddasatu*. We challenge any researcher or scholar to find the meaning of jihad as holy war in the Qur'an, or authentic Hadith collections, or in early Islamic literature. Unfortunately, some Muslim writers and translators of the Qur'an, the Hadith, and other Islamic literature translate the term "jihad" as "holy war" because of the influence of centuries-old Western propaganda.

This could be a reflection of the Christian use of the term "Holy War" to refer to the Crusades of a thousand years ago. However, the Arabic words for "war" are *harb* or *qital*, which are found in the Qur'an and Hadith.

For Muslims, the term "jihad" is applied to all forms of striving and has developed some special meanings over time. In its defense of Islam, Allah declares in the Qur'an:

> To those against whom war is made, permission is given (to defend themselves), because they are wronged—and verily, Allah is Most Powerful to give them victory—(they are) those who have been expelled from their homes in defiance of right—(for no cause) except that they say, 'Our Lord is Allah' . . .
>
> (THE HOLY QURAN, 22:39–40)

> Fight in the cause of Allah against those who fight against you, but do not transgress limits. Lo! Allah loves not aggressors. . . . And fight them until persecution is no more, and religion is for Allah. But if they desist, then let there be no hostility except against transgressors.
>
> (THE HOLY QURAN, 2:190, 193)[12]

In trying to understand the modern-day applications of jihad, the following from the Ontario Consultants on Religious Tolerance is perhaps easier to comprehend:

A small percentage of Muslims who are from the extreme, radical, and violent wing of Islamic fundamentalism, and who are "passionate, [deeply] religious and anti-Western"[13] might dwell on passages or verses dealing with conflict, war, and resistance to oppression. Many conclude that the Qur'an expects them to engage in acts of terrorism, assassinations, suicide bombings, armed aggression against persons of other religions, oppression of women, executing innocent persons, and so on.

Those Muslim fundamentalists who are not extreme, violent, and radical, and those Muslims from mainline or liberal wings of the religion, might concentrate on passages and themes of spirituality, justice, personal struggle, peace, freedom, and so on.

They are consulting the same book with a different emphasis and achieve very different results. We see the same split among Christians as they study Islam and the Qur'an.

Some emphasize the earlier passages in the Qur'an, which stress on cooperation with the Jews and Christians—the *People of the Book*. They tend to interpret jihad in terms of personal struggle toward purity.

Others emphasize later passages of the Qur'an, which were received during a time of conflict. They tend to interpret jihad as holy war.

They come to opposite conclusions about whether Islam is a religion of peace or war.[14] Jihad came to us in the twenty-first century from Osama bin Laden, who claimed that God not men make laws, understanding and interpreting God's laws is the role of religious scholars, while not believing in legislators, and all law is eternal. He had no possible need of legislators. His view was that Sharia law is absolute, and this vision underpinned his hatred of secular regimes in the Muslim world, whether democratic or dictatorial. He at best took a cynical view of the United Nations, or any world body that would support not only the presence but also the original creation of Israel in 1947 on Palestinian territory. Bin Laden's position maintained that when Islam is threatened, the correct course taken is to struggle in its defense and it is the duty of Muslims everywhere to defend Islam; this struggle is termed "jihad."

In February 1998, bin Laden, together with Muslim fundamentalists from Pakistan, Bangladesh, and Egypt, declared jihad on the United States, benefactor of Israel and of the tyrants who rule the Islamic birthplace in Saudi Arabia. The four fundamentalists pronounced the following:

> To kill the Americans and their allies—civilians and military—is an individual duty incumbent upon every Muslim in all countries, in order to liberate the al-Aqsa Mosque and the Holy Mosque from their grip, so that their armies leave all the territory of Islam, defeated, broken and unable to threaten any Muslim. This is in accordance with the words of God Almighty: 'Fight the idolaters at any time, if they first fight you.'

Since September 11, 2001, the global jihad and, probably in more particular terms, the war against the United States, can be easily witnessed in the hatred we see in the media. The media are strong communicators, particularly in the Middle East, with a diet of hate being spewed forth by religious leaders calling for death to Americans, Jews, Israelis, and Britons. Not only is the insidious nature of their broadcasts abhorrent, but they are also educating their children on a diet of jihad to become suicide bombers and murderers.

Following the attacks in London in July 2005, there was considerable revulsion at the fact that young British Muslims were responsible for the attacks. The original thought was that these were marginalized youth who had some axe to grind, but the truth here is that all came from good backgrounds and were well educated and part of mainstream society. However, the Muslim Councils in Great Britain, far from denouncing the perpetrators, claimed that it was the Muslim community that was under attack and that the young men were not Muslims. This was a claim voiced by Mohammed Naseem, chairman of the Birmingham Center Mosque. Blaming the attacks squarely on Tony Blair (former Labor Party prime minister) for his government's support of the U.S.-led war in Iraq, Dr. Azzam Tamimi from the Muslim Association of Britain stated in the *London Evening Standard*: "and God knows what will happen afterwards, our lives are in real danger and it would seem, so long as we are in Iraq and so long as we are contributing to injustices around the world, we will continue to be in real danger. Tony Blair has to come out of his state of denial and listen to what the experts have been saying that our involvement in Iraq is stupid." Among those experts would have to be included the leader of the Muslim Council of Britain, Sir Iqbal Sacranie, who has labeled Israel a "Nazi state" responsible for the "ethnic cleansing" of Palestine.[15] The defensive nature of Islam's religious leaders became more evident when Sir Iqbal's comments during a televised BBC Panorama program in August 2005 colorfully compared suicide bombers from Hamas with Mahatma Gandhi and Nelson Mandela. He went on to state that those fighting oppression and occupation were in fact freedom fighters, not terrorists. He referred to Sheikh Yassin, the former leader of Hamas, as a "renowned Islamic scholar." The attacks in Paris, in November 2015, carried out in the name of ISIL or Islamic State and accounted for the largest number of deaths from any such attack since the end of World War II, were carried out by returning radicalized EU citizens of Middle East decent, five French, two Belgian, and two Iraqis. These citizens were able to take advantage of the mayhem surrounding the mass influx of refugees from Syria and Iraq and to take advantage of the borderless nature of the EU.

JIHADIZATION

This is the phase in which the group members accept their individual duty to participate in jihad and self-designate themselves as holy warriors, or **mujahideen**. Ultimately, the group will begin operational planning for a terrorist attack. These activities include planning, reconnaissance, preparation, and execution. While the previous phases can take months or even years to reach "jihadization," this final phase can be a very rapid process taking only a few months or weeks to run its course.[16]

The far-reaching inspiration of Osama bin Laden and his al Qaeda terrorist organization has resulted in attempts by self-styled jihadists to attack U.S. targets. One such attack that was disrupted by the FBI in early 2007 was that of a group of Islamists who planned to attack the Fort Dix Army camp. Six men began practicing with semiautomatic weapons in rural Pennsylvania, and in January 2006, a video tape of their activities that they had taken to a local store to have it transferred into a DVD format raised the clerk's suspicion, who contacted the FBI. During the ensuing investigation, the FBI successfully infiltrated the group. All the members of the group held down normal jobs throughout the planning phases. The six conspirators, four ethnic Albanians from the former Yugoslavia, a Turkish immigrant, and a U.S. citizen from Jordan, planned to buy M16's AK-47s as well as rocket-propelled grenades and mount an attack on the New Jersey Army Base at Fort Dix and kill as many service personnel as they could. The far-reaching tenets of Osama bin Laden's jihadist ideology come from the belief that:

- This is a clash of civilizations. Militant jihad is a religious duty before God. The clash is necessary for the salvation of one's soul and to defend the Muslim nations.
- Only two camps exist, and there can be no middle ground in an apocalyptic showdown with both the West and the Muslims who do not agree with al Qaeda's vision of "true Islam."
- Violence is the only solution; peace is an illusion.
- Many of the theological and legal restrictions on the use of violence by Muslims do not apply to this war.
- The United States' power is based on its economy and, thus, large-scale mass-casualty attacks, especially focused on the United States and Western economic targets, are a major goal.
- Muslim governments that are religiously unacceptable and cooperate with the West must be violently overthrown.[17] The U.S. government has been steadfast on its position relative to enemy combatants that now reside at Guantanamo Bay. The United States has also adopted tactics that have been broadly criticized by such groups as Amnesty International for its actions.

THE MEDIA AND TERRORISM

At the dawn of the twenty-first century, the media in North America would not be concentrating that much on terrorism as a daily topic, but since 9-11, terrorism has become the number one topic for every news media outlet. Although we could consider the 9-11 attack as a single and one-off event, the speculation about what will come next consume the media. Everything that has the possibility of being terrorist-related now gets ample and even excessive media coverage. The media are sometimes at fault for glamorizing a terrorist event, and one such event is the hijacking of an Israeli airliner over Europe, in 1970, by a Palestinian group led by a vivaciously portrayed Leila Khaled. The media created an impression that she was an adventurer to be admired, while at the same time ignoring her criminal acts. Scant coverage was provided to the Israeli security officer who shot and killed her colleague. Terrorists need publicity if they are to inspire fear and respect, and secure favorable understanding of their cause, if not their act itself. The first airliner attack on the World Trade Center was not caught on news media film, but the second airliner hitting the Twin Towers most certainly was—whether the terrorists intended this or not, the coverage they received and the fear, panic, and attention they got has created a frenzy of news coverage ever since. Margaret Thatcher's metaphor that publicity is the oxygen of terrorism underlines the point that public perception is a major terrorist target, and the media are central in shaping and moving it. For terrorism, the role of the media is critical.[18]

Terrorists' Needs and the Media

- Prior to the advent of "social media" terrorists were not in the market to go out and buy media space; so publicity, free publicity that a group could generate was a definite asset. From the terrorist perspective, an unedited interview with Osama bin Laden by CNN in May 1997 was an enormous coup for al Qaeda. For news networks, access to a terrorist will always be a coup and a hot story and is treated as such.
- The sympathetic ear of the media and a modicum of editorial spin may turn a media event to the terrorists' advantage. One may not agree with terrorist acts, but this does not preclude being sympathetic to their plight and cause. Terrorists believe that the public needs to be educated that their cause is just and terrorist violence is the only course of action available to them.
- Terrorist organizations may also seek to court or place sympathetic personnel in press positions—particularly in wire services. The Al-Jazeera news network in the Middle East continues to be a particular favorite news wire service of terrorists as its avenue to information sharing with the public.
- Legitimacy—Terrorist causes want the press to give legitimacy to what is often portrayed as ideological or personality feuds, or divisions between armed groups and political wings. For the military tactician, war is the continuation of politics by other means; for the sophisticated terrorist, politics is the continuation of terror by other means. IRA and Hamas are examples of groups having "political" and "military" components. Musa Abu-Marzuq, for example, who was in charge of the political wing of Hamas, is believed to have approved specific bombings and assassinations.[19] Likewise, the "dual hat" relationship of Gerry Adams of Sinn Féin—the political wing of the IRA—to other IRA activities is subject to speculation. Distinctions are often designed to help people join the ranks or financially contribute to the terrorist organization.

They also need the press to provide a level of legitimacy to the findings and viewpoints of specially created non-governmental organizations (NGOs) and study centers that may serve as covers for terrorist fund-raising, recruitment, and travel by terrorists into the target country. The World and Islam Studies Enterprise funded and controlled by the Palestinian Islamic Jihad is but one known example.[20] In hostage situations, terrorists need to have details on identity, number, and value of hostages, as well as details about pending rescue attempts and details on the public exposure of their operation. Particularly where state sponsors are involved, they want details about any plans for military retaliation.

- Terrorist organizations seek media coverage that causes damage to their enemy. This is particularly noticeable when the perpetrators of the act and the rationale for their act remain unclear. Terrorists need the media to spread and magnify the panic and fear on their behalf, to facilitate economic loss (like scaring away investment and tourism); one example of this comprised the threats proclaiming that a summer bombing campaign of tourist locations along the Spanish coast by ETA would take place. The locals and the visiting tourists would then lose faith in their governments' ability to protect them, and to trigger government and popular overreaction to specific incidents and the overall threat of terrorism.

Internet use to spread the message of jihad is not particularly new and has been available since the mid-1990s to globally reach and radicalize impressionable minds. Internet accessible magazines such as **Inspire** were produced by al-Malahem Media, the branch of al Qaeda in the Arabian Peninsula in July 2010. The U.S. government believes that *Inspire*, which is in English, was produced by a Saudi-born U.S. citizen, Samir Khan, who left the United States for Yemen in 2009. Khan has a history of producing jihadist publications so it seems likely that he is involved in this venture. The magazine editor also clearly states that *Inspire* is an effort by al-Malahem Media to reach out to, radicalize, and train the millions of English-speaking Muslims in the West, Africa, South Asia, and Southeast Asia. *Inspire* follows the trend of AQAP publications and leaders in praising Fort Hood shooter Maj. Nidal Hasan and failed Christmas Day bomber Umar Farouk Abdulmutallab and lifting them up as examples for all jihadists to follow. While 'Inspire' is the method of delivery to reach the intended convert we should look at the man behind the 'messages' that Nidal was receiving. Anwar al-Awlaki an American born Muslim cleric with dual U.S. Yemeni citizenship, who soon after 9-11 was preaching in a mosque in Washington D.C. at that time was considered moderate in his preaching's and teaching on Islam – this attitude began to change and he became more radical in his views and no longer posted internet sermons that preached a peaceful coexistence between the religions of Islam and Christianity. He would leave the U.S. and become convinced that the war on Islam was being waged by the west. He joined al Qaeda in the Arabian Peninsula (AQAP) and was probably the best known of the group with a worldwide following for his radical ideology and of his inspirational calls for jihad via the internet sermons he posted. Awlaki was based in the Middle East and AQAP has consistently targeted U.S. interests both in the Saudi peninsula and in the U.S.

What Government Leaders Want from the Media

Governments seek understanding, cooperation, restraint, and loyalty from the media in efforts to limit terrorist harm to society. In the West, where there is freedom of the press to a great extent, governments need cooperation from the press to push their agenda in efforts to punish or apprehend those responsible for terrorist acts, specifically the following:[21]

- Both governments and terrorists want to advance their agendas but, of course, from completely different perspectives. From their perspective, the media should support government courses of action when operations are under way and disseminate government-provided information when requested. This includes understanding of policy objectives, or at least a balanced presentation (e.g., why governments may seek to mediate and yet not give in to terrorist demands).
- An important goal is to separate the terrorist from the media to deny the terrorist a platform, unless doing so is likely to contribute to his or her imminent defeat.[22]
- Another goal is to have the media present terrorists as criminals and avoid glamorizing them; to foster the viewpoint that kidnapping a prominent person, blowing up a building, or hijacking an airplane is a criminal act regardless of the terrorists' cause.
- In hostage situations, governments often prefer to exclude the media and others from the immediate area, but they want the news organizations to provide information to authorities when reporters have access to the hostage site.
- They seek publicity to help diffuse the tension of a situation, not contribute to it. Keeping the public reasonably calm is an important policy objective.
- It is generally advantageous if the media, especially television, avoid "weeping mother" emotional stories on relatives of victims; as such coverage builds public pressure on governments to make concessions.
- During incidents, they wish to control terrorist access to outside data to restrict information on hostages that may result in their selection for harm; government strongly desires the media not to reveal planned or current antiterrorist actions or provide the terrorists with data that may help them.
- After incidents, they want the media not to reveal government secrets or detail techniques on how successful operations were performed and not to publicize successful or thwarted terrorist technological achievements and operational methods so that copycat terrorists do not emulate or adapt them.[23]
- They want the media to be careful about disinformation from terrorist allies, sympathizers, or others who gain from its broadcast and publication. Many groups have many motives for disseminating inaccurate or false data, including, for example, speculation as to how a plane may have been blown up or who may be responsible.
- They want the media to boost the image of government agencies. Agencies may carefully control leaks to the press, giving scoops to newsmen who depict the agency favorably and avoid criticism of its actions.
- They would like journalists to inform them when presented with well-grounded reasons to believe a terrorist act may be in the making or that particular individuals may be involved in terrorist activity.

- In extreme cases, where circumstances permit, vital national security interests may be at stake, and chances of success high, they may seek cooperation of the media in disseminating a ruse that would contribute to neutralizing the immediate threat posed by terrorists. In common criminal investigations involving heinous crimes, such media cooperation is not uncommon, when media members may hold back on publication of evidence found at a crime scene, or assist law enforcement officials by publishing misleading information or a non-promising lead to assist authorities in apprehending a suspect by, for example, lulling him or her into a false sense of security.

Although the media have a duty to report responsibly and track down the next biggest news scoop, the reporters themselves have become targets for terrorists in the modern era; the case of Daniel Pearl from the Wall Street Journal in 2002 is a case in point. Many, if not all, journalists view getting to the story a primary objective over their own personal safety. Pearl, aged thirty-eight, the *Wall Street Journal*'s South Asia bureau chief, was taken hostage in Pakistan in January 2002. At the time, he was attempting to track down and interview the leader of Jamaat ul-Fuqra; after meeting a go-between at a Karachi restaurant, he was taken to a house, where two weeks later his execution by beheading was videotaped and broadcast for the world to see. Al Qaeda's Number 3 man, **Khalid Sheikh Mohammed**, claimed responsibility for Pearl's death. With their ability to manipulate their audience through the medium of the Internet, is there necessity to set any specific code of conduct on mainstream news coverage while attempting to preserve the independence of the media's role? This is a hotly debated topic, and although there may be voluntary guidelines, there are four other policy decisions that may help preserve that independence and overcome some objections to their treatment of terrorism:

1. To consider matters relating to the timing of news. Temporary withholding of news may be legitimate in some instances such as a kidnapping.
2. To make deliberate attempts to balance coverage (an extremely difficult goal to attain) may counteract some of the negative effects of terrorism.
3. To acknowledge that news tailoring is a fact of everyday news production and focus on reporting that might be expected to lessen tensions and aid the negotiating process.
4. To accept that the media have an important role to play in public education and, at times other than during terrorist incidents, to feature items regarding the ethics of using violence for political ends, the legitimate needs of law enforcement in a democratic society, the non-romantic side of terrorism, and the existence of avenues of dissent. Part of this role must also encompass a vigorous determination to investigate and report on the injustices and inequalities in society that, if left to fester, may be the cause of acts of terrorism.[24]

Social Media in Twenty-First Century

The ability to communicate with supporters and like-minded affiliates is crucial to the success and advancement of any group or organization. In the terrorist theater, Islamic State (ISIL) would seem to lead the way in creating its own media front and image. Not only does ISIL occupy physical territory it also occupies and to a certain extent dominates areas of the Internet. In 2014, it seemed impossible that ISIL would be equipped to attack and take Mosul, the second largest city in Iraq. However, ISIL embarked on an online campaign aimed exclusively at the residents of Mosul and what they should expect from ISIL and bombarded the residents with hideous videos and text messages. Not surprisingly the campaign worked—we need to bear in mind that the majority of the Iraqi military in Mosul gave up without a fight as most were Shia, and the Mosul inhabitants predominantly Sunni. ISIL as a growing enterprise uses all the available tools of the Internet utilizing Zello, WhatsApp, Kik, Wickr as well as private chat rooms and using encrypted messaging. Their messaging is able to reach hundreds of thousands of supporters anywhere on the globe—providing information on and disseminating instruction. It would appear that ISIL is highly proficient, well organized, and sophisticated in its use of online technologies (Figure 2-3).

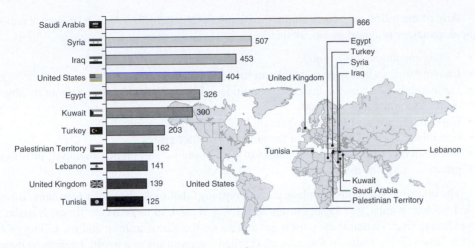

FIGURE 2-3   ISIS supporters tweeting.   *Source:* Statista.com.

STATE TERROR AND GENOCIDE

State-approved use of power and resources to terrorize and attempt to liquidate a specific group of citizens, immigrants, and religious or ethnic groups has created some ambivalence about what to label as a proper designator. Raphael Lemkin, in his 1944 book, *Axis Rule in Occupied Europe*, coined the word "genocide." He constructed this term from the Greek word *genos* (race or tribe) and the Latin suffix *cide* (to kill). At the end of World War II, the War Crimes Tribunal in Nuremberg was at a loss as to what this crime should be called. History was of little use in finding a proper word to fit the nature of the crimes that Nazi Germany had engaged in at its extermination and concentration camps. "Ethnic cleansing" has been used in recent years to soften the term for eradication of specific groups of people. But hard or soft, the word "genocide" better describes "the destruction of a nation or an ethnic group." It implies the existence of a coordinated plan, aimed at total extermination, to be put into effect against individuals selected as victims purely, simply, and exclusively because they are members of some target group.[25]

"Mass murder," the term that was often used at the time, is an inadequate description of the atrocities committed in Nazi-occupied territories. It could not account for the motives, which arose solely from "racial, national, homosexual, gypsy, or religious" considerations, not the conduct of the war. Genocide required a separate definition, as it was clearly not just against the rules of war, but also a crime against humanity. Raphael Lemkin was the first person to put forward the theory that genocide is not a war crime and that the immorality of genocide should not be confused with the amorality of war.[26]

Terrorist acts have too often created a vicious "cycle of violence," with those against whom the terror violence is first carried out becoming so angered that they themselves resort to terrorism in response. This is clear in the present situation in the Israel-Palestine disputes in the Middle East and the Northern Ireland troubles, which have resulted in the deaths of thousands of innocent people by countering "their" violence with "our" violence in an endless cycle of "tit-for-tat" attacks. Each violent action calls for an equal or greater violent reaction—*ad infinitum*. When the violence is non-selective, and innocent people are killed by car bombs and purely random acts of violence, the reaction of the victims is likely to "break all the rules" in their selection of targets and become terrorist violence itself. "Round and round it goes and where it stops nobody knows" becomes the theme song of terrorism. In the same way as in a case of homicide, the natural right of the individual to exist is implied, so in the case of genocide as a crime, the principle that any national, racial, or religious group has an equal right to exist is then clearly evident. Attempts to eliminate such groups violate this right to exist and to develop within the international human community. Lemkin's efforts and his single-minded perseverance brought about the Convention for the Prevention and the Punishment of the Crime of Genocide, which was voted into existence by the Convention of the General Assembly of the United Nations in 1948. After stating in Article I that genocide is a crime under International Law, the convention laid down the following definition:

Any of the following acts committed with intent to destroy, in whole or in part, a national, ethnical, racial, or religious group, as such:

- Killing members of the group;
- Causing serious bodily or mental harm to members of the group;
- Deliberately inflicting on the group conditions of life calculated to bring about its physical destruction in whole or in part;
- Imposing measures intended to prevent births within the group;
- Forcibly transferring children of the group to another group;
- A criminal act . . . with the intention of destroying . . . an ethnic, national, or religious group . . . targeted as such.[27]

The controversial thousand-plane carpet bombings that took place over Germany; incendiary and nuclear bombs over Japan during World War II; and, in more recent times, Napalm and Agent Orange over Vietnam; the poison gas attacks on the Kurds in Iraq; and the killing of over 500,000 Tutsis by the Hutus in Rwanda, all claimed their victims in a totally haphazard manner. Intrinsic meaning is lost when words like "genocide" or "holocaust" are used loosely to describe any human disaster with a large number of victims, regardless of the cause. It would be hard to deny that some form of evil has always existed in the world. But if such evil is seen in general impersonal terms such as "barbarism," human's inhumanity to human, chance circumstance, or plain hatred, then there are no individual culprits toward whom an accusing finger can be pointed. So-called collective blame is just another way of denying the facts.

CYCLICAL NATURE OF TERRORISM

Perhaps the most prominent proponents of individual and collective violence as a means of destroying governments and social institutions were the Russian anarchists. These were revolutionaries within Russia who sought an end to the Tsarist state of the late nineteenth century. "Force only yields to force," and terror would provide the mechanism of change, according to the Russian radical theorist Alexander Serno-Solovevich.[28]

In the writings of two of the most prominent spokesmen for revolutionary anarchism, Mikhail Bakunin and Sergei Nechaev, one finds philosophies often echoed by modern terrorists. Bakunin, for example, advocated in his *National Catechism* (1866) the use of "selective, discriminate terror." Nechaev, in his work *Revolutionary Catechism*, went further in advocating both the theory and practice of pervasive terror violence. He asserted of the revolutionary: "Day and night he must have one single thought, one single purpose: merciless destruction. With this aim in view, tirelessly and in cold blood, he must always be prepared to kill with his own hands anyone who stands in the way of achieving his goals."[29]

This is surely a very large step in the evolution of a terrorist from the use of a lone political assassin in earlier centuries. Even the religious fanatics of the Assassins were arguably less willing to kill "anyone" to achieve a political objective. But this difference may well have existed more on paper than it did in practice. In spite of this written willingness to "kill anyone" who stood in the way, even the Socialist Revolutionary Party resorted primarily to selective terror violence and took special pains to avoid endangering innocent bystanders. The Union of Russian Men, which formed to combat the growing revolutionary movement "by all means," was not only sanctioned by the Tsar but also granted special protection by him. This reactionary group engaged in a variety of terrorist activities, including, but not limited to, political murders, torture, and bombing. The Okhrana (the Tsarist secret police) used vicious counterterror against the militant revolutionaries in an unabated attack until World War I began. John Thompson, commenting on the rising tide of "terrorism" in Russia during the last half of the nineteenth century, explained the relationship of state and revolutionary terrorism in this way: "Wrong a man . . . deny him all redress, exile him if he complains, gag him if he cries out, strike him in the face if he struggles, and at the last he will stab and throw bombs."[30]

CONTEMPORARY EVENTS: HISTORICAL ROOTS

If contemporary terrorism is somehow different from historical terrorism, how is it different? One reason for briefly reviewing the historical pattern and roots of terrorism is to be able to discover whether that pattern still remains accurate in the contemporary world. If terrorism today is just like the terrorism of previous centuries, but with better weapons, then we can use historical patterns to more accurately predict behavior. Then we can construct responses based on successful attempts that were used to combat this phenomenon in the past. If terrorism today is actually different, however, historical patterns are less useful in designing responses, although such patterns may still be of use in understanding the dynamics of such a phenomenon. Terrorism has clearly existed for centuries. What we need to know, as we move ahead in the twenty-first century, is whether these new forms of terrorism are actually that much different from their historical counterparts.

Related to the differences between historical and modern terrorism are important developments in the contemporary world. Modern methods of travel, for example, make it possible to carry out an assassination in the morning in country "X" and be halfway around the world from that nation within a matter of hours. Modern communications, too, have created a "smaller world." Events in places like Nigeria, Cape Town, or Sri Lanka, for instance, are immediately transmitted in a dozen ways around the world. Such rapid communications, too, have served to expand the theater and enlarge the audience to which the terrorist plays out the drama of death and violence. To catch the attention of America, the Third World terrorists need not hijack airliners, fly to New York City and Washington DC, and crash them into the World Trade Center Towers and the Pentagon.

The dramatic increase in the arsenal of weapons available to today's terrorists is also worthy of consideration. The would-be assassin need not rely on a rifle or a handgun to eliminate his victim. A letter bomb, an envelope containing anthrax, or explosives can do the job without endangering the perpetrator, as the Unabomber in the United States has demonstrated (Figure 2-4). The potential for destruction through chemical and biological weapons has not yet been fully field-tested either (see Chapter 14), although the sarin toxin attacks in subways in Japan in 1995 gave ample evidence of the potential for such biochemical weapons when used on the vulnerable mass transit system of a modern city. Perhaps, until recently, the consequences of using such weapons were too dramatic for most groups to contemplate. But modern technology has certainly put at the terrorist's disposal a vast array of lethal and largely indiscriminate weapons, of which the sarin toxin apparently used in Japan represents only a very simple example. With this arsenal, the selection of victims has become devastatingly indiscriminate.

We hope the student can now see that, as historical precedents for terrorism grow, it becomes very hard to distinguish between legitimate and illegitimate violence. As nations born out of a climate of violence, such as Ireland and Israel, become themselves illegitimate, it is increasingly difficult to condemn the terrorist for using such methods, also employed in the struggles for independence and survival. The longer the history of terrorism, the harder it is to make the label of "terrorism" stick to the actions of any group or nation.

THE LONE WOLF

One aspect of twenty-first-century terrorism is the "lone wolf," a male or female who seemingly acts independently of a terrorist organization but has established sympathies or been radicalized by online social media or other modes of communications, but is not being handled or directed

TERRORIST ATTACK BRIEF

Theodore KACYZNSKI Kaczynski aka The Unabomber

The man that the world would eventually know as Theodore Kaczynski came to our attention in 1978 with the explosion of his first, primitive homemade bomb at a Chicago university. Over the next 17 seventeen years, he mailed or hand delivered a series of increasingly sophisticated bombs that killed three Americans and injured 24 twenty-four more. Along the way, he sowed fear and panic, even threatening to blow up airliners in flight.

On April 3, 1996, FBI investigators arrested Kaczynski and combed his cabin. There, they found a wealth of bomb components; 40,000 handwritten journal pages that included bomb-making experiments and descriptions of Unabomber crimes; and one live bomb, ready for mailing.

Kaczynski's reign of terror was over. His new home, following his guilty plea in January 1998: an isolated cell in a "Supermax" prison in Colorado.

FIGURE 2-4   The Unabomber.   *Source:* Federal Bureau of Investigation.

by a terror group. While we have no set definition of what a lone wolf is, there is an example in Gus Martin's text which is helpful—*Lone Wolves*—"have a vague and sometimes delusional assumption that their actions will further a greater cause against a corrupt or evil social order."[31] All too often, these attacks are being carried out by people often with a criminal past with an antisocial behavior problem; they are misfits. In the current trend, most attacks from 2014 to 2016 have been carried out in the name of Islamic State (IS) but in fact have no discernable ties to the organization. This is an aspect of terrorism that is part of the IS arsenal which openly encourages its supporters and sympathizers around the world to attack and as we are now seeing individuals and small groups of individuals have been motivated into attacking random targets. In almost all cases, these attackers believe that they are righting wrongs perpetrated against Islam and are fighting a just cause in defending their religion. In August 2016, a young Canadian took just this route to destruction—having converted to Islam he was intent on supporting the Islamic State. There are many examples of lone wolf attacks, particularly in Europe with the July attack on a Catholic church where two declared IS supporters cut the priest's throat in front of his congregation; other lone wolf attacks:

- 2001—Richard Reid—shoe bomber (airliner)
- 2009—Major Nidal Hasan—Fort Hood shooting (military base)
- 2009—Northwest Airlines—Umar Farouk Abdulmutallab—Underwear bomber (airliner)
- 2013—Boston marathon bombing—(sporting crowd, public venue)
- 2014—Parliament Hill shooting Ottawa, Canada—Michael Zehaf-Bibeau (War Memorial)
- 2015—San Bernardino, California—shooting (public health facility)
- 2016—Nice, France—truck attack on Bastille Day (National Holiday)
- 2016—Strathroy, Ontario, Canada—Aaron Driver (failed suicide attacker)

In most of the above cases, each one displayed or came to the authorities' attention due to radicalization, criminal activity, or online social media activity. The objectives of the attackers seem mostly symbolic as well as random with the result that the attack instills fear in a much wider community than just the area that was attacked. The lone wolf poses a challenging problem as they are difficult to detect and infiltrate. Community involvement and police interaction with communities at the grassroots level will bring some of these to the authorities' attention. Radicalization and being radicalized is not a criminal activity and monitoring of large numbers of radicalized young men and women by security services is almost impossible. The lone wolf will continue to be one of the most serious risks in the coming years.

Summary

We have seen in this chapter how violence evolves into terrorism and how not only individuals and groups but states also sponsor involvement in terrorism. Terrorism is a centuries old issue and religion has played its prominent part in it. Radicalization, Islam, Islamism, and Jihad are all terms that are now common place and will be used numerous times throughout the following chapters. We have seen how modern media play a crucial role in presenting terror events to the masses. In this technological era where everyone has a device to record and film, these devices and technologies have been picked up and adopted by sophisticated terrorist organizations to show the brutality of their specific terror agenda.

Review Questions

1. Explain how social media play a role in recruiting terrorist sympathizers and the areas of the Internet where recruiting may take place.
2. Describe the difference between Islam and Islamism.
3. Compare recent terror attacks and determine whether they would be classified as low cost or high cost operations financially.
4. Analyze a recent terrorist incident in the West and discuss whether these perpetrators were radicalized homegrown terrorists and how they might have been prevented from taking such action.

End Notes

1. John Lachs. "Violence as Response to Alienation." *Alienation and Violence* (Middlesex, UK: Science Reviews Ltd., 1988, pp. 147–160).

2. *The Relevance of Philosophy to Life* by John Lachs. Published by Vanderbilt University Press, © 1995.

3. Cindy C. Combs. *Terrorism in the Twenty-First Century* (Upper Saddle River NJ: Prentice Hall, 1997).

4. Ibid., p. 21.

5. See Marshall G.S. Hodgson. *The Order of the Assassins* (London, UK: The Institute of Ismaili Studies, 1960); Bernard Lewis. *The Assassins: A Radical Sect in Islam* (London, UK: The Institute of Ismaili Studies, 1968).

6. Bernhardt J. Hurwood. *Society of the Assassin: A Background Book on Political Murder* (London, UK: International Institute for Strategic Studies, 1996).

7. Political asylum is sanctuary or refuge for a person who has committed a crime such as assassination of a political figure. It is granted by one government against requests by another government for the extradition of that person to be prosecuted for this "political" crime. *Funk and Wagnall's Standard Dictionary*, Comprehensive International Ed., vol. 1, p. 86, col. 3.

8. *Country Reports on Terrorism—Released by the Office of the Coordinator for Counter Terrorism* (April 28, 2006), http://www.state.gov.

9. Funk & Wagnalls New Comprehensive International Dictionary Of The English Language, vol. 1—Deluxe Edition. Published By International Press, © 1980.

10. U.S. Department of State. *Patterns of Global Terror Report* (2002–2003).

11. Distinguishing between Islam and Islamism. Reprinted with permission of Center for Strategic and International Studies.

12. "Jihad Explained." The Institute of Islamic Information and Education. Brochure No. 18. Chicago.

13. Craig Branch. *Act of War—Jihad*. Apologetics Resource Center. http://www.apologeticsresctr.org/act_of_war.htm.

14. B.A. Robinson. Ontario Consultants on Religious Tolerance. Originally written (March 28, 2003), http://www.religioustolerance.org/isl_jihad.htm.

15. Jewish Chronicle, May 27, 2005.

16. Mitchell D. Silber and Avril Blatt. *NYPD Radicalization in the West: Senior Intelligence Analysts* (New York Police Department: NYPD Intelligence Division).

17. Raphael F. Perl. *CRS Issue Brief*. Specialist in international affairs in Foreign Affairs and National Defense Division, Congressional Research Service (October 22, 1997).

18. Steven Emerson. "Islamic Terrorism from Midwest to Mideast." *Christian Science Monitor* (August 28, 1996).

19. *Terrorism and the Middle East Peace Process: The Origins and Activities of Hamas in the United States*, testimony by international terrorism consultant, Steven Emerson, before the Senate Subcommittee on the Near East and South Asia (March 19, 1996, p. 11).

20. *Impact of Television on U.S. Foreign Policy*, 1994, U.S. Congress, House Committee on Foreign Affairs, 103rd Congress, 2nd Session, GPO, Washington (April 26, 1994, p. 53).

21. In the case of the anonymous "Unabomber," it was publication of a manifesto in the New York Times and Washington Post that triggered the leads and actions by the suspect's family, which resulted in an arrest.

22. John F. Burns. "Spiriting Off of Fugitive by U.S. Irks Pakistanis." *New York Times* (June 23, 1997, p. A9).

23. Grant Wardlaw. *Political Terrorism, Theory, Tactics and Counter Measures* (Melbourne, Australia: Cambridge University Press, 1989, p. 85).

24. The U.S. Central Intelligence Agency, *World Fact Book*.

25. Ibid.

26. Ibid.

27. Ibid.

28. U.S. Department of State, *Country Reports on Human Rights Practices*, 1998.

29. Ralph Lemkin. *Axis Rule in Occupied Europe* (Warsaw, Poland: University of Stockholm, 1944).

30. Convention for the Prevention and Punishment for the Crime of Genocide; General Assembly of the United Nations, 1948.

31. Gus Martin. *Understanding Terrorism Challenges, Perspectives and Issues* (Sage Publications Inc. 2016, p. 270).

PART TWO

Global Terrorism

3

The United States of America

LEARNING OUTCOMES

After studying this chapter, students should be able to:

1. Recall that connecting the dots was a failure in intelligence gathering and application.
2. Summarize the various groupings that make up left-wing and right-wing hate groups in the United States.
3. Restate the stages to radicalization.
4. Analyze the planning stages for the 9-11 attacks.
5. Relate how the Patriot Act is designed to fight terror.
6. Compare the Fort Hood attack and the Boston marathon bombings.

KEY WORDS TO NOTE

Anwar al-Awlaki—Anwar al-Awlaki was an American-born imam who later became the most influential English-language recruiter for the cause of violent jihad

Bojinka plot—Serbian word meaning "big bang" was a plot hatched by Ramzi Yousef to smuggle bomb making materials in liquid form on to a number of aircraft and detonate them in mid-air

Domestic terrorism—Groups of individuals who are based and operate entirely in the United States and Puerto Rico without foreign direction and whose acts are directed at elements of the U.S. government or population

God Father of Jihad—Nickname for the Palestinian cleric, Abdullah Yusuf Azzam who was the central figure in the global development of the militant Islamist movement

Hizb ut-Tahrir—A global Islamic political party whose goal is to unite all Muslim countries to unify as an Islamic Caliphate

Jamaat ul-Fuqra—Terrorist group established in Pakistan and with operations inside the United States—considered a probable al Qaeda affiliate

Radicalization—Process by which an individual or group adopts increasingly extreme political, social, or religious ideals

Umar Farouk Abdulmutallab—aka the Underwear Bomber—with explosives in his underwear attempted to blow up a flight to the United States on Christmas Day 2009

U.S. Patriot Act—Law passed in 2001 following the 9-11 attacks in the United States; uniting and strengthening America by providing appropriate tools required to intercept and obstruct terrorism

OVERVIEW

Unable to achieve their unrealistic goals by conventional means, international terrorists attempt to send an ideological or religious message by terrorizing the general public. Through the choice of their targets, which are often symbolic or representative of the targeted nation, terrorists attempt to create a high-profile impact on the public of their targeted enemy or enemies with their act of violence, despite the limited material resources that are usually at their disposal.[1] So what role has U.S. foreign policy or lack thereof played in raising the foreign terror threat levels in the United States? This will be discussed for a broader understanding of issues around global terrorism.

"Jihad," "**radicalization**," and "homegrown terrorists" were terms or words unheard of in the United States before the attacks on the World Trade Center in New York on September 11, 2001, but now form part of daily discussions on protecting the homeland. Since 9-11, the threat from terror attacks from both external and internal forces has not diminished. Al Qaeda and more recently Islamic State followers, be they in the Arabian Peninsula or regions of Africa, the Indian subcontinent, or in the United States, continue to pose threats to the safety of U.S. citizens and interests globally. During the last thirty years of the twentieth century, most terror groups and subgroups operating throughout the world had their specific stated political agenda; al Qaeda and its inspired followers appear to have no political agenda in mind but simply death and destruction of Western democracies. Islamic State goes further than that of al Qaeda and has proclaimed a Caliphate in the regions of northern Iraq and parts of Syria. In attacking the West, their prime agenda is to set up Islamic Caliphates and overthrow Western democracies and secular states, and the challenge now is to not only understand the threat but also track down those radicals who are planning on striking against the United States and beyond. It is important to note that there is nothing illegal about becoming radicalized and as such the freedom of speech and association to a great degree is protected under the Constitution. The actions taken after radicalization become the threat. In Britain, the attacks in 2005 were the work of "homegrown terrorists." The same threat exists in the United States either from radicalized citizens or visitors to the United States on visas, and of course those entering illegally through international borders. In this chapter, we will review the events of the last two decades with obvious emphasis on jihad in America. The following "failure to connect the dots" indicates that although the indications were all there, connecting the so-called dots either was beyond the intelligence community's ability or the unspeakable events coming were too unfathomable to be credible (Figure 3-1).

CONNECTING THE DOTS

Dot No. 1—1993: World Trade Center Bombing in New York City

A car bomb exploded underneath the World Trade Center in New York, killing six people and injuring more than a thousand others. The bombing shocked the United States, which had not suffered from the terrorist acts that had plagued other parts of the world. Mario Cuomo, then New York State governor, said: "No foreign people or force has ever done this to us. Until now, we felt invulnerable." At approximately 12:18 P.M. February 26, 1993, an improvised explosive device in the back of a rental vehicle detonated on the second level of the parking basement.

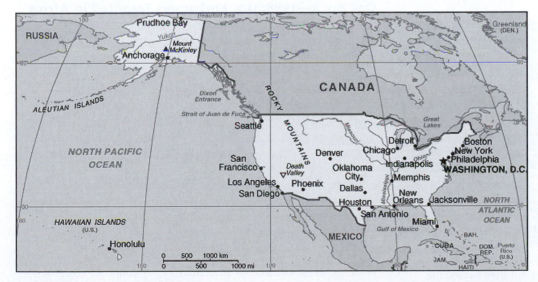

FIGURE 3-1 Map of the United States. *Source:* Central Intelligence Agency, *The World Factbook*, 2008.

The resulting blast produced a crater approximately one hundred fifty feet in diameter and five floors deep in the parking basement. That structure consisted mainly of steel-reinforced concrete, twelve to fourteen inches thick. The epicenter of the blast was approximately eight feet from the south wall of World Trade Center Tower One, near a support column. The device had been placed in the rear-cargo portion of a one-ton Ford F350 Econoline van, which had been rented from a Ryder Rental agency in Jersey City. Approximately six thousand eight hundred tons of concrete and steel were displaced by the massive blast. The main explosive charge consisted primarily of approximately one thousand two hundred–one thousand five hundred pounds of homemade (nitrogen fertilizer-based) explosive and urea nitrate. The fusing system was made from twenty, two hundred and twenty-minute lengths of nonelectric, burning-type fuses. The fuse material ended up in lead azide acting as the terminator/initiator. Also, incorporated into this thrown-together homemade device, and placed under the main explosive charge, were three large metal cylinders of highly compressed hydrogen gas. The resulting massive explosion killed six people and injured more than a thousand. Over fifty thousand people were evacuated from the huge World Trade Center complex during the hours immediately following the blast. The initial inspection, on February 27, was described as a scene of "massive devastation, almost surreal in appearance." There were small pockets of fire, electrical sparks arcing from damaged wiring, and dozens of parked automobile alarms whistling, howling, and honking. The explosion ruptured two of the main sewage-removal lines from both of the World Trade Center towers and the Vista Hotel, plus several water mains from the air-conditioning system. In all, more than two million gallons of water and sewage drained into the tower and was then pumped out of the crime scene.

Dot No. 2—1995: The Oklahoma City Bombing

According to a classified Pentagon study, the Oklahoma City bombing was caused by more than one bomb. Two independent Pentagon experts concluded that five separate bombs caused the destruction of the Oklahoma City Federal Building in April 1995. A huge truck bomb destroyed most of that building, leaving one hundred sixty eight people dead and more than five hundred others injured. Preliminary reports indicated that the bomber might have been from the Middle East. After many more unconfirmed rumors, prejudice and public anger rose to a fever pitch. The arrest of Timothy McVeigh and his subsequent trial, conviction, and execution, as well as the arrest and conviction of his friend and accomplice, Terry Nichols, grated on the already-raw nerves of an entire nation. When it was revealed that both were members of local right-wing militias, it became clear that American and not foreign, domestic terrorists had planned and committed this terrible act. Those two events and many others since have caused officials and security and law enforcement agencies in the United States to rethink and reorganize their perceptions of where serious terrorist threats might really lie. But the dots still had not yet been connected, and the general public soon slipped back into their everyday lives.

FIGURE 3-2 The bombing of U.S. Embassy in Nairobi, Kenya— 207 Kenyans and twelve U.S. citizens lost their lives in the explosion. *Courtesy:* Federal Bureau of Investigations

Dot No. 3—1998: U.S. Embassies Targeted in Africa

On August 7, 1998, very powerful, almost simultaneous, explosions rocked two U.S. embassies in East Africa. The blasts took place at almost the exact same time, 10:30 A.M. in Kenya and Tanzania. Embassy officials confirmed that the explosions were the result of car bombs detonated near the two embassies, one in the capital of Kenya, Nairobi, and the other in Dar es Salaam, the capital of Tanzania. In Kenya, the explosion toppled the tall Ufundi Cooperative Bank building over onto the U.S. embassy (Figure 3-2). The blast occurred shortly after the U.S. ambassador, Prudence Bushnell, had met with the Kenyan Trade Minister at the nearby bank. She was taken from the site on a stretcher, feared to be badly injured, but later found to have sustained only minor wounds from flying glass and debris. The bank building, located between the trade center and the embassy, was leveled almost to the ground. Apparently, the bomb had been placed there, rather than at the embassy itself, because of the embassy's bombproof construction. In Tanzania, another massive explosion left a large crater outside of the U.S. embassy. An eyewitness stated: "The people at the front of the building didn't stand a chance." The blast occurred near the spot where a gasoline tanker truck had been observed parked in the embassy parking lot. The attack took the lives of two hundred and seven Kenyans and twelve Americans. Ahmed Khalfan Ghailani who was sentenced to life in prison on January 25, 2011, was an al Qaeda operative and Tanzanian national who conspired with Osama bin Laden to attack both embassies. Each embassy was attacked by a suicide bomber driving large truck bombs packed with approximately one thousand pounds of TNT. Ghailani purchased the truck as well as tanks of oxygen and acetylene gas that were used in the bombing of the U.S. embassy in Tanzania. He also stored detonators that were used in the bomb at his residence.[2]

FIGURE 3-3 USS COLE. *Courtesy:* Federal Bureau of Investigations

Dot No. 4—2000: The Suicide Bombing of the USS *Cole*

A gaping hole in the hull of the USS *Cole* testified to the force of the suicide terrorist bombing that killed seventeen sailors as the U.S. Navy vessel was docked in Yemen in October 2000 (Figure 3-3). The ship was attacked in a suicide mission by a small inflatable boat packed with explosives that rammed into the port side of the ship just above the waterline. This was not the first such attempt to attack a U.S. naval vessel—a similar attack planned to coincide with the new millennium on January 3, 2000, also in the port of Aden, on the USS *The Sullivans* had failed as the heavily laden boat carrying the explosives capsized.

Dot No. 5—2009: The Underwear Bomber, Detroit

The attempt to blow up an airliner over Detroit on Christmas Day by **Umar Farouk Abdulmutallab** with a hidden explosive device in his underpants was a significant blow to the American psyche, a blow to the international traveler, and not the least to the intelligence community. There has been much discourse from both the United States and Great Britain as to where exactly he had received his radical indoctrination. Although the British contend it was not until he was out of the country and in Yemen, there are, of course, telltale snippets that indicate that he had already been a target of Britain's security service M-15 for his radical activities at University College London (UCL). Abdulmutallab had attended this institution from 2005 to 2008 and was president of the UCL Islamic Society (ISOC) and during the academic year 2006–2007 organized a controversial "War on Terror" week. Extremist speakers have regularly spoken at UCL, including supporters of the terrorist group Hamas and members of **Hizb ut-Tahrir**, and those who have spoken in support of the Taliban warned Muslims not to integrate into Western societies, argued in favor of domestic violence, and advocated the destruction of Israel.

There is an accepted perception in government and particularly in the United Kingdom that Islamic extremism deserves special consideration, which again hinges on a false belief that the experience of poverty and exclusion can create specific grievances, which may then lead to radicalization. Further study of recent and well-publicized attacks, for instance the 9-11 attacks, the London tube train bombings, and the Glasgow airport attacks, quickly dispels any rational belief that poverty plays any part on the perpetrators' side.

Timothy McVeigh—Oklahoma City Bombing, 1995

In 1995, homegrown terrorism surfaced in the United States when McVeigh bombed the Alfred P. Murrah Federal Building in Oklahoma City, killing 168 people (Figure 3-4). This was notably the most vicious attack by an American citizen on fellow Americans. McVeigh was a member of the Patriot movement that developed in the early 1990s, a group that believed in the true American ideals of individualism, armed citizens, and minimum interference from governments. McVeigh used a rented Ryder truck packed with ammonium nitrate, fuel oil, and Tovex high explosive. Most counterterrorism experts were candid in stating that they had not predicted the

FIGURE 3-4   The bombing of Alfred P. Murrah federal building, 1995. *Courtesy:* Federal Bureau of Investigations

sort of attack that was carried out in Oklahoma. In 1995, there were a considerable number of right-wing "militia" groups, rabidly anti-establishment and antigovernment, stemming not from social injustices but more likely from proposed gun control legislation. After the Alcohol, Tobacco and Firearms (ATF) raid on the Waco compound of the Branch Davidians, there was notable unrest and disillusionment from "patriot," "militia," and "constitutionalist" groups who believed that the attack at Waco was a massacre by the authorities. The early 1990s were not a time when U.S. terrorism experts were paying much, if any, attention to Islamists and in the mid-1990s, international terrorism within the United States was generally not considered a major threat. Nevertheless, there were indications that if some foreign terrorist group became disgruntled enough at the United States, and was determined to act out that anger, it could create major problems to U.S. commerce, infrastructure, and population, given leadership and financing.

The levels of terrorism experienced in places like Beirut, Belfast, Paris, London, Madrid, Kabul, Islamabad, and Palestine did not carry much impact in the United States except as a news item; nor did terrorism create major nervousness or any impact on the American lifestyle.

The United States, after all, had never been subjected to as much political violence or international terrorism as the likes of Europe, the Balkans, the Middle East, Northern Ireland, the Persian Gulf, Africa, or South and Southeast Asia. A few exceptions come to mind—the Symbionese Liberation Army (SLA), the Black Panthers, the Weathermen, the Unabomber, and even single issue groups such as Animal Liberation Front (ALF)—but such domestic terrorist acts had been few and far between. On the other hand, the IRA's ongoing slaughter in Northern Ireland with car bombs (as the reader will learn about in Chapter 5) continued to be frequent and unremitting. After August 7, 1998, the United States was slowly awakening to the fact that it was no longer immune to larger-scale attacks, clearly identifiable as foreign terrorist acts. The first World Trade Center explosion became (perhaps) a significant marker of the first salvo by foreign terrorists using politically motivated actions that attack random victims. The bombing was intended to incite fear as well as add a determined and well-planned external terrorist signature to an act of violence.

But terrorism in the United States was not to be limited to those with external agendas from foreign sources, as demonstrated by the attack on the Federal Building in Oklahoma City, Oklahoma. The terrorists in this case were Americans, members of a paramilitary survivalist militia from Michigan. They had responded to a long-festering anger over the U.S. government's actions involving the "Waco Massacre" of the Branch Davidians, a fringe religious group headed by David Koresh.

DOMESTIC TERRORISM AND EXTREMISM

The face of domestic terrorism continues to change. The FBI has defined **domestic terrorism** "as groups of individuals who are based and operate entirely in the United States and Puerto Rico without foreign direction and whose acts are directed at elements of the U.S. government or population." This definition is suitably wide enough to class terror events from both the ideological left and right. If we study traditional attacks in the United States, we can see that domestic issue terror can then be categorized accordingly as

- Revolutionary nationalist groups
- Extreme right-wing ideological groups (Ku Klux Klan)
- Extreme left-wing ideological groups (Weather Underground)
- Foreign groups operating in the United States
- Religious extremist groups

The Southern Poverty Law Center that tracks and monitors all hate groups has established that there has been an increase in recent years; in 2015, there existed 998 antigovernment "patriot" groups, 190 KKK groups, and a forty-two percent rise in the number of anti-Muslim hate groups up from 2014. The definition used to determine a hate crime comes close enough to be almost indistinguishable with terrorism: "A hate crime, also known as a bias crime, is a criminal offence committed against a person, property, or society that is motivated, in whole or in part, by the offender's bias against a race, religion, disability, sexual orientation or ethnicity/national origin." Militia groups have been a part of U.S. history since the revolutionary wars against the British, and they make a resurgence, particularly at times like the present, with a severely depressed economy, a total collapse and loss of faith in the financial system, and the first African-American president in power. Militia groups are not alone in fermenting violent response to social or political problems. Militias tend to attract those whose focus is political, whereas hate groups such as the racial purists of the Supreme White Alliance or the Christian fundamentalist Army of God are similarly frequent advocates of violence. Where is the line drawn between hateful speech and inciting violence and between a militia group and a terrorist organization? Was the act of the shooter at Fort Hood the work of a "lone wolf" or because he was of Muslim faith and possibly radicalized over the Internet he would therefore be classified as a terrorist? The **U.S. Patriot Act** allows U.S. law enforcement significant leeway in dealing with terrorist investigations and rarely if ever has the term "terrorism" been applied to militia or extremist groups. The arrest in March 2010 of nine Hutaree militia members for "conspiracy to levy war" against the U.S. government and "being an antigovernment organization which advocates violence against local, state, and federal law enforcement" questions whether the charges should have been for terrorist panning and activity. They were charged with seditious conspiracy and attempts to use weapons of mass destruction, but there was no mention of terrorism in the charges.[3]

The Weather Underground

The 1960s was a decade of change around the world. In the United States, the war in Vietnam was beginning and so too were movements and activists challenging the respected norms and values particularly in areas of human rights. The Weather Underground is one activist group worthy of mention. Formed originally as a splinter group that believed that peaceful protests were ineffective, they began advocating violence as a means to social and political change. In early March 1970, one of its mainstream leaders, Bernardine Dohrn proclaimed a declaration of war, and days later, three Weathermen were killed by one of their own bombs that accidentally detonated in their basement apartment in Manhattan. The bomb had been intended for a dance at a military base. Reaching the point where violence takes the place of peaceful protest may have been brought about by actions of the Chicago Police Department in a shootout with members of the Black Panther movement that saw Mark Clark and Fred Hampton shot to death. Many believed this to be a government-sanctioned hit to wipe out militant groups such as the Panthers, making this a pivotal moment in the Weather Underground's history. Most of the members found themselves on the FBI's Ten Most Wanted list for at least the next decade. Their activities continued until the late 1970s, at which time the leaders had come out of hiding and begun serving terms of imprisonment. The movement came to an unofficial end in 1981 when Kathy Boudin from the Weathermen resurfaced to participate in an armed robbery in New York, which resulted in the shooting deaths of three men. Boudin was sentenced to twenty-two years in prison and released in 2003.[4]

Left-Wing Terrorism

Over several decades, left-wing-oriented extremist groups posed the predominant domestic terrorist threat in the United States. In the 1980s, however, the FBI neutralized many of these groups by arresting key members who were conducting criminal activity. The failure of Communism and the fall of the former Soviet Union in 1989 deprived many leftist groups of a coherent ideology or tangible support. As a result, membership and belief in the "cause" in these groups have waned.

The United States still faces a threat from some left-wing extremists, including a few Puerto Rican terrorist groups and a Cuban group. Although Puerto Rico voted to remain within the U.S. Commonwealth in 1993, some extremists still plan and conduct minor terrorist acts to draw attention to their support for independence.

Right-Wing Terrorism

Right-wing extremist groups, located at the opposite end of the political spectrum, generally adhere to an antigovernment or racist ideology. These groups still continue to attract some followers. Many of these recruits feel disenfranchised by rapid changes in the U.S. culture and economy or are seeking some form of personal affirmation. As American social structures continue to change, the potential for escalating hate crimes by extremist right-wing groups is an increasingly valid concern. Of particular note, many state and local law enforcement organizations, consider a broader range of activities and acts as terrorist, or potentially terrorist, than does the FBI. The official FBI statistics do not count many threatening acts by organizations, such as the skinheads, street gangs, and drug dealers, as terrorist acts. States and municipalities are equally adamant in identifying right-wing (neo-Nazi, the KKK, anti-Semitic, anti-federalist, and militias) and issue-specific (antiabortion, animal rights, and environmentalist) organizations as major potential sources for supporters of terrorism in the United States.

The burgeoning militia movement in the United States was placed under the spotlight on the admissions by Timothy McVeigh and Terry Nichols. Such paramilitary, rabid, antigovernment groups will continue to attract supporters. Several factors have contributed to the increase of this generally antigovernment mood. In a changing political and economic environment, issues such as gun control legislation, the United Nations' involvement in international affairs, U.S. efforts around the world seemingly unsupported by its former allies, and clashes between dissidents and law enforcement are cornerstones of militia ideology. When tied into neo-Nazi zeal and radical philosophies, you have an explosive situation. Some militia members firmly believe that the U.S. government is deeply involved in a conspiracy to create a "New World Order." According to their adherents and radical believers, international boundaries will be dissolved and the United Nations will be allowed to become the ruling power in the world. Other militia advocates believe that the federal government has gotten either too powerful or simply illegal and out of control. Many of these militants continue to conduct paramilitary training and stockpile illegal weapons in preparation for an armed Armageddon-type of confrontation with the government. A few of these extreme militia members could pose a serious terrorist threat.

Revolutionary Nationalist Groups

The U.S. government's experience with the Puerto Rican nationalist group, Los Macheteros, dates back to an armed robbery on September 12, 1983, at an armored car depot in West Hartford, Connecticut. After the day's pickups were done, a guard named Victor M. Gerena suddenly turned on his two comrades. He then restrained them at gunpoint, injected both with an unknown substance, and began packing blocks of currency into his rented car.

Authorities eventually determined that Gerena's robbery had been planned by Los Macheteros, a group founded in the 1970s by Ojeda Rios, a musician who had turned communist and Puerto Rican revolutionary. Using bombings and attacks on police officers and U.S. government personnel, the group pushed for an end to U.S. control of the island.

The FBI caught up with the leader of this group in Puerto Rico in September 2005; Filiberto Ojeda Rios was tracked to a farmhouse, which was then surrounded by agents, and during the ensuing shootout, Rios died of a single gunshot wound.[5]

Left-Wing Aggression

The radical student movements, civil rights marches, and anti-Vietnam war demonstrations of the 1960s galvanized a large number of student organizations to frame their struggles around an antiestablishment theme. As the Vietnam War intensified, so too did the attitudes and activities of the growing student movements. One such group that supported the use of terrorism and violence was the Weather Underground Organization (Weathermen), which had its roots within the Students for Democratic Society and aimed at a revolutionary overthrow of the United States government. The group engaged mainly in sporadic bomb attacks at police stations and at the Pentagon. However, when the Vietnam War ended in 1973, the Weather Underground began to dissolve.

THE BLACK PANTHERS AND NATION OF ISLAM

The New Black Panther Party for Self-Defense takes its name from the original Black Panther Party, formed by Huey Newton and Bobby Seale in Oakland, California, in 1966. The original Panthers combined militant Black Nationalism with Marxism and advocated black empowerment and self-defense, often through violent confrontation. By 1969, the group had an estimated five thousand members spread through twenty chapters around the country. In the early 1970s, however, the group lost momentum and most of its support due to internal disputes, violent clashes with police, and infiltration by law enforcement agencies. Despite the collapse, the group's mystique continued to influence radicals, and by the early 1990s, a new generation of militant activists began to model themselves after the original Panthers. Essentially, a black supremacist movement but with anti-Semitic undertones, the Nation of Islam has been around since the 1930s and became more prominent with notorious speeches from NOI national spokesman Malcolm X until his assassination in 1965.

THE KU KLUX KLAN

Ku Klux Klan (KKK) has its beginnings in small-town America and was born out of boredom and small-town life by six Confederate veterans, in December 1885. The Klan began life as a social club in Pulaski, Tennessee, not far from the Alabama border. As a means of distraction, the members began to ride around town at night wearing white sheets, and then extended this to pointed hats; they adopted this bizarre costume as their official regalia (Figure 3-5). They formed up like a college fraternity and began to hold elaborate initiation ceremonies for new members, with a form of hazing rituals. The KKK would likely have faded away as quietly as they had been formed, but in 1886, the membership expanded to other towns, and activities became more sinister and violent toward the black communities. As the KKK expanded and developed, it engaged in some of the most brutal terror attacks over the early decades of the twentieth century. It was well known for decades as the major advocate for white supremacy and power, and segregation of the races is foremost among its agenda. KKK members allege there was a conspiracy between Jewish people, white liberals, blacks, and other minorities to take over the United States.

Since 1865, KKK has provided a vehicle for racial hatred in America, and its members have been responsible for atrocities that are difficult for most people to even imagine. Although the membership and actions of the traditional and historical KKK declined in the last half of the twentieth century, there are too many other groups that go by a variety of names and symbols that have been at least as dangerous as the KKK ever was.

Some of these comprise teenagers who shave their heads and wear storm trooper jackboots, display swastika tattoos, and call themselves "skinheads" or "neo-Nazis." Some of them are young men who wear camouflage fatigues and practice guerrilla warfare tactics at secret locations for training in weaponry and violence. Some of them are conservatively dressed professionals who publish materials filled with their bizarre beliefs—ideas that range from denying that the Nazi Holocaust against the Jews in WW II had ever happened, to those with the conviction that the federal government is an illegal body and that all governing power should rest with county sheriffs or militias. Despite their peculiarities, they all share the deep-seated hatred and resentment that had given life to the Klan and terrorized racial minorities, the weak, and Jews in this country for almost a century and a half.

The Klan itself has had three periods of significant strength in American history: first, in the latter half of the nineteenth century, then again in the 1920s, and, more recently, during the 1950s and early 1960s, when the Civil Rights Movement was at its height. The Klan finally experienced a small resurgence in the 1970s, but it never again approached its past level of influence. Since then, with open and universal access to the Internet, the Klan has become just one element in a much broader spectrum of white supremacist and hatred activity. It is important for the student/reader to understand, however, that violent prejudice is not limited to the KKK or any other white supremacist organization. People who have no ties to any organized group, but who share their virulent hatred, commit bombings, assaults, murders, and arsons every year.

FIGURE 3-5   KKK marching on Pennsylvania Ave, Washington.
Courtesy: Federal Bureau of Investigations

Historical research explains the roots of racism and prejudice, which sustains the KKK beliefs even into the twenty-first century. As for current events, that is an even easier lesson for most minorities who grew up in the racially torn years of the 1950s. Young civil rights activists, working alongside John Lewis, Andrew Young, the late Dr. Martin Luther King, Jr., Julian Bond, and many others, saw the KKK as an all-too-visible power in many of the places they went to organize voter registration and protest segregation. They knew what the Klan was and often had a pretty good idea of who its members were. They also knew what Klan members would happily do to them if they thought they could get away with it.

You can read in almost any news media stories about crosses being burned in the yards of minorities or mixed-race couples, and it seems as if we are suddenly thrust back into the 1960s. Some claim the Klan today should just be ignored and it will fade away. Past history, however, will not let us ignore current events. Those who would use violence to deny others their rights cannot be ignored. The background of the KKK and its battles with the law illustrate why hate groups cannot be ignored. It is unattractive part of American history—some of the things you read here will make you angry or ashamed; some will turn your stomach and make you sick at heart. But it is important that we try to understand the villains as well as the heroes in our past if we are to continue building a nation where equality, freedom, and democracy are preserved.

Victims of the Klan

The image of a black man hanging lifeless by a rope from a tree limb has become a symbol for the worst of Klan violence. Between 1889 and 1941, three thousand eight hundred and eleven black people were lynched for "crimes" such as threatening to sue a white man, attempting to register to vote, joining labor unions, being "disrespectful" to a white man, even looking at a white woman, or just for no reason at all. During the American Revolution, the term Lynch Law described an informal court run by Colonel Charles Lynch of Bedford County, Virginia, who tried Tories and criminals in an effort to restore law and order to the frontier. Lynch's punishments consisted generally of fines or an occasional whipping. In the 1850s, the KKK used "Lynch Law." Later, the term was used to commonly describe a quick finding of guilty and the hanging of one of a group's objects of hate.

Today, there is a trend to spread hate and racism by forming so-called militias that freely use the Internet through social media to spread their twisted messages of hatred and intolerance. In the late 1920s, during the years of prohibition, gangs and mobsters preyed on society and each other with deadly violence. Mobsters gunned down those who opposed or interfered with their bootlegging and traumatized all those who witnessed or heard of such carnage. Terror strikes at the public's basic need for safety. Serial killers are unwitting terrorists when their deeds are publicized, and street gangs in American cities today use drive-by shootings as a tactic for creating fear and terror in their "hoods." These demonstrations keep their rivals in check and neighborhood citizens afraid to report these and other crimes against their own communities to the police. The same kinds of fear-inducing methods have long been the favorite tactics of the Mafia, or "Cosa Nostra" ("Our Thing"). From killings in schools and fast-food places to motorcycle gangs terrorizing an entire town, all forms of violence can be utilized as a means to incite terror.

With a population rapidly approaching over three hundred million, the United States remains a "nation of immigrants," people who came to a great and prosperous land, legally and illegally, from the four corners of the earth. As far as terrorism is concerned, many of these immigrants escaped from various forms of it, leaving their home countries to come to a place where such actions were unthinkable. As we have now seen, the history of the United States does not support that premise, and many forms of terror have scarred its brief but bloody past—and even now sometimes mar its present.

A growing terrorism threat in the United States is not only from foreign sources but also from dissatisfied, domestic purveyors of violence, hate, and terror.

OSAMA BIN LADEN AND AL QAEDA THREAT TO AMERICA

Osama bin Laden, the planner behind the 9-11 attacks and prior attacks on the USS *Cole* in Yemen and the embassy bombings in Nairobi and Dar es Salaam, announced a fatwa, an interpretation of an Islamic law, in a London Arabic newspaper in 1998. In this proclamation, he stated that the United States had declared war against God and His messenger. Bin Laden called for the killing of Americans anywhere as being a sacred duty of all Muslims. In a television interview with ABC in Afghanistan, bin Laden expounded even further on this theme by stating the importance for Muslims to kill Americans more so than other infidels.

Bin Laden was one of the many sons of a Saudi construction magnate—a wealthy son who went to Afghanistan to fight against the Soviet invasion in 1980. Arabs from the Middle East, Africa, and Asia headed to Afghanistan to wage jihad against the Soviets. Bin Laden's actual involvement in the fighting has never been established. However, his role became that of a financier for the movement in Afghanistan. When bin Laden was in Afghanistan, the United States and Saudi Arabia supplied him with hundreds of millions of U.S. dollars in secret aid and support to the jihad against the Soviet invasion. The ultimate defeat and the full pullout of the Soviet forces in 1988 left bin Laden with an interesting dilemma—what to do next? Bin Laden and his Islamic fighters had managed to defeat the Soviet Army and, in doing so, had set up a base for their operations in Afghanistan. A literal translation of "al Qaeda" is "the base," or "the foundation." The al Qaeda of the 1980s was a far cry from what it is today. In those post-Soviet months, the group developed and organized along corporate structures, complete with departments that dealt with arms procurement, media relations, and propaganda and intelligence. In Afghanistan, bin Laden worked closely with a Palestinian cleric, Abdullah Yusuf Azzam, who was nicknamed the "**Godfather of Jihad**." During the 1980s, Azzam was the central figure in the global development of the militant Islamist movement. He built a scholarly, ideological, and practical paramilitary infrastructure for the globalization of Islamist movements, which, until then, had been focused on separate national, revolutionary, and liberation struggles. Azzam envisioned a Pan-Islamic transnational movement that would transcend the political map of the Middle East drawn by non-Islamic colonial powers.[6] Azzam traveled throughout Europe, the Middle East, and North America, where he visited more than fifty cities to raise money and preach jihad. His belief was that Afghanistan was a model for future struggles with the objective of establishing an Islamic Caliphate across all Muslim lands under foreign occupation. Azzam's radical ideology, combined with his skill at organizing paramilitary training for more than twenty thousand Muslim recruits from about twenty countries around the world, created an international cadre of highly motivated and experienced militants, intent on perpetuating his vision of global Islamic revolution. In his book, *Join the Caravan*, Sheik Azzam implored Muslims to rally in defense of Muslim victims of aggression, restore Muslim lands from foreign domination, and uphold the Muslim faith.[7]

Azzam's success, and that of his fighters in Afghanistan, was solidified with the support of the CIA and Saudi Arabia. When the CIA began supplying Azzam's fighters with FIM-92 Stinger man-portable, surface-to-air missiles, the conventional military superiority of the Soviet MI-24 helicopters was neutralized, deeply demoralizing the Soviet troops and hastening victory for the Mujahideen fighters.

Azzam and his two sons were killed in a car bomb attack in Peshawar, Pakistan, in November 1989. His radical thoughts and ideology live on, however, through his related paramilitary manuals and a London-based media organization, Azzam Publications.

Azzam combined hatred for the West, Christians, and Jews, whom he routinely accused of carrying out diabolical conspiracies against Islam, with nostalgia for the days of the Islamic Caliphate, when non-Muslims were still treated formally as second-class citizens. It was the United States that seemed to epitomize for Azzam the ongoing Jewish–Christian conspiracy. Ironically, it was in the United States that Azzam was able to raise huge amounts of money, enlist new fighters, and, most important, provide the political freedom to freely coordinate with other top radical Islamic movements. Azzam helped bring about the mobilization of the Muslim Brotherhood movement more than any other leader did. Today, the military wing of Hamas in the West Bank is called the Abdellah Azzam Brigades.[8]

PREPARATIONS FOR 9-11

Germany was the major launching pad for the four primary members of the 9-11 suicide plot developed by Osama bin Laden in Afghanistan. The recruits were well versed in Western society and held fervently anti-West ideologies and would suit bin Laden's needs for the attack on America. Mohamed Atta, Hani Hanjour, Marwan al Shehhi, and Ziad Jarrah completed their foundational training in Kandahar in 1999 and came to the United States in early 2000 to begin flight training. By now, al Qaeda possessed leaders who were able to evaluate, approve, and supervise the planning and direction of a major operation; a personnel system that could recruit candidates, indoctrinate them, vet them, and give them the necessary training; communications sufficient to enable planning and direction of operatives and those who would be helping them; an intelligence effort to gather required information and form assessments of enemy strengths and weaknesses; the ability to move people great distances; and the ability to raise and move money necessary to finance an attack.[9]

The planning stage inside the United States involved financing and training operatives for the 9-11 attack. The team members began training at flight schools in Florida and Oklahoma. All of the students were in the United States on "visitor" visas. According to the 9-11 Commission Report, the flight training was paid for by funds wired from Dubai between June and September 2001. Al Qaeda had assembled pilots but determined they would also require other teams to assault the cockpits and subdue the crews of the targeted flights. Twelve of the thirteen who were selected for this task came from Saudi Arabia; the thirteenth came from the United Arab Emirates. In assessing these teams, a Saudi investigation noted that members came from a variety of backgrounds:

- All were between twenty and twenty-eight years old.
- Most were unemployed.
- Most had little more than high school education.
- Most were probably unmarried.
- Four came from a cluster of towns in an isolated and underdeveloped region of Saudi Arabia.

All of the hijackers who made the trip to the United States were not hindered by immigration or customs. None had arrived through Canada, as originally thought. Al Qaeda trained all of these terrorists in Afghanistan for this specific operation.

Throughout the summer months of 2001, the hijackers, including the trained pilots, undertook surveillance flights across the United States in the types of aircraft that they planned to hijack. At the same time, they tested the security system by carrying box cutters either on their person or in carry-on baggage.

Following the 9-11 attacks on the United States, there was an immediate outcry for a response in kind and to determine where to direct such a response. Osama bin Laden and his support network in Taliban-controlled Afghanistan came quickly to the forefront of targets. A meeting was held on September 13, 2001, between Richard Armitage, deputy secretary of state; Maleeha Lodhi, Pakistan's ambassador to the United States; and Mahmud Ahmed, the head of Pakistan's intelligence service. The deputy secretary stated that the United States wanted Pakistan to take the following steps:

- Stop al Qaeda operatives at its border and end all logistical support for bin Laden.
- Give the United States blanket overflight and landing rights for all necessary military and intelligence operations.
- Provide territorial access to the United States and allied military intelligence and other personnel to conduct operations against al Qaeda.
- Provide the United States with intelligence information.
- Publicly condemn the terrorist acts.
- Cut off all shipments of fuel to the Taliban and stop recruits from going to Afghanistan.

The United States also wanted Pakistan to break relations with the Taliban government if the evidence implicated bin Laden and al Qaeda, and the Taliban continued to harbor them. The following month the United States began its assault on Afghanistan in its response to the 9-11 attacks.

Combined and improved dissemination of intelligence has been credited for many successes in the aftermath of 9-11, and Britain and Europe have been in the forefront of information sharing and cooperation. The British experience with homegrown terror and the openness of the threat posed by Islamic clerics, such as the hook-handed Abu Hamza al-Masri, a credible cleric yet, alone, was not immediately recognized, as a security threat to either Britain or its allies. Al-Masri openly praised the success of the 9-11 attacks, and one of his young and impressionable students at his London mosque was Richard Reid, the shoe bomber. Al-Masri was extradited from the United Kingdom to the United States of America and was convicted and sentenced in federal court in Manhattan, in January 2015, to life in prison for aiding kidnappers during a 1998 hostage-taking in Yemen, sending a young recruit to jihadi training in Afghanistan in 2000, violating U.S. sanctions against the Taliban, and attempting to establish an al Qaeda-style training camp in Bly, Oregon.

The threat from within the United States will continue to focus on the minds of the security and intelligence community. Attempts by citizens to assemble and procure items to make bombs, both conventional and nonconventional, such as that by U.S. citizen Jose Padilla, will remain a high priority. He was arrested at Chicago O'Hare Airport on suspicion of plotting a dirty bomb attack. With the U.S. ability to hold such persons as "enemy combatants" continuing to be challenged, he was eventually indicted in 2005 and, although not charged with plotting to detonate a dirty bomb, was convicted along with three others in 2007. The fact remains that he is in prison and also cooperating with the FBI about any involvement he may have had with al Qaeda while outside of the United States.

THE AFTERMATH

There have been many questions on whether the U.S. authorities could have prevented the attacks on 9-11. However, the training for the crews operating on those flights worked against them and in the hijackers' favor, in that the crews did what they were trained to do—keep the passengers calm and do as the hijackers instructed. Unfortunately, they were never to know the true intentions of the hijackers, until it was too late.

The intelligence community knew that Osama bin Laden had threatened to "cut off the head of the serpent" (the United States) and cause mass casualties; it also knew that bin Laden was planning to do something with aircrafts. An FBI Field Office knew that several pilots were in training, but even with all of this information, the "dots were never connected." Could we have then expected anything else? Hindsight is always 20/20, and intelligence gathering is not a finite art, and it is invariably the case that after an event takes place, previously gathered information contributes a substantial evidence trail to the terrorist. In 2001, passenger screening was one of the lowest-paid and most menial tasks at airports, particularly in the United States. Aviation security suffered a major blow to its performance and credibility—and rightly so. For more than two decades, the industry has lacked any desire to beef up security—a fact clearly laid bare on 9-11. Airline crew training programs had never covered how to tackle determined terrorists, and the cockpits had an almost "open-door" policy for visitors. No one suspected that dedicated terrorists would commit mass suicide in such a ghastly manner as occurred on 9-11. Historical terror events and "dots" pointed clearly to a buildup by internationalized terror fanatics from the Islamic world, with serious planning for inflicting attacks against U.S. targets. So, it was purely a matter of *when* and not *if* an attack would come to the U.S. shores. However, the United States and the rest of the world were not prepared for the outcome or the reaction to it. The failure of the intelligence communities to correctly intercept the 9-11 operatives could be blamed on historical events. Since the end of the Cold War, the need for covert operatives had been in decline. Many CIA specialists were moved to different areas of activity, such as the Balkans or Africa. Further, the levels of new recruits to the CIA continued to decline. By the end of the last decade of the twentieth century, the CIA was virtually stripped of any incoming new recruits. Recruits to the CIA typically took a period of seven years of training to become fully effective.

Chronology of Events of September 11, 2001

08:46:40	Hijacked American Airlines Flight 11 flew into the upper portion of the North Tower of New York's World Trade Center. The aircraft cut through floors 93–99.
09:03:11	Hijacked United Airlines Flight 175 flew into the South Tower of the World Trade Center. The aircraft cut through floors 77–85.
09:37	Hijacked American Airlines Flight 77 crashed into the west wall of the Pentagon in Washington DC.
09:40	The FAA suspends all U.S. air traffic. This is the first time that this drastic action has been undertaken.
09:58:59	In a period of ten seconds, the South Tower of the World Trade Center collapses.
10:10	A portion of the west side of the Pentagon collapses.
10:10	United Airlines Flight 93, also hijacked, crashes in Shanksville, Somerset County, Pennsylvania.
10:28	The North Tower of the World Trade Center collapses.

FIGURE 3-6 Hijacked American Airlines Flight 77 crashed into west wall of the Pentagon at 09:40 on September 11 2001. U.S. military Service members and recovery personnel work at the collapsed section of the Pentagon in Arlington, Va., Sept. 12, 2001. *Source:* Department of Homeland Security

More than two thousand six hundred people died at the World Trade Center; one hundred and twenty-five died at the Pentagon; and two hundred fifty-six died on the four aircraft. The death toll on 9-11 surpassed that of the surprise Japanese attack on Pearl Harbor in December 1941.[10]

The War on Terror materialized through a pre-9-11 directive concerning al Qaeda and evolved into National Security Presidential Directive 9 entitled, "Defeating the Terrorist Threat to the United States." This directive would extend to a global war against terrorism—not just aimed at al Qaeda but also at nations that harbored terrorists and terror groups and organizations.

In October 2001, U.S. forces began their attack on Afghanistan, along with a coalition of forces, aimed at dislodging the Taliban and capturing Osama bin Laden. In August 2006, the U.S. government issued its National Strategy for Combating Terrorism document. The document makes its central platform that to win the War on Terror, the United States must

- advance effective democracies as the long-term antidote to the ideology of terrorism;
- prevent attacks by terrorist networks;
- deny weapons of mass destruction to rogue states and terrorist allies who seek to use them;
- deny terrorists the support and sanctuary of rogue states;
- deny terrorists control of any nation they would use as a base and launching pad for terror; and
- lay the foundation, and build the institutions and structures needed to carry the fight forward against terror, and help ensure ultimate success.

The next step is to understand how the radicalization of Muslims has taken place and how that threatens the United States. The 2005 attacks in the United Kingdom were carried out by radicalized young men who were either born in the United Kingdom or immigrated at a young age. The fact that all were unremarkable and had drawn little or no attention to themselves is something that the United States and other western democracies will have to consider when attempting to define how the next attack will materialize from inspiration and ideology—inspiration gathered from the spectacular events of 9-11 and ideology from the al Qaeda leader Osama bin Laden preaching a global jihad, turning young men into inspired "Holy Warriors." One of the main perpetrators captured by the United States as one of the masterminds of the 9-11 attacks was Khalid Sheikh Mohammed (KSM). Born in Kuwait, he attended and graduated from North Carolina A&T State University in 1986 with a degree in mechanical engineering. He spent time in Afghanistan fighting the Soviets and joined with Ramzi Yousef in the Philippines in 1994 to organize the **Bojinka plot**, which was to target at least a dozen commercial airliners with simultaneous bombings over the Pacific Ocean. Intelligence agencies disrupted the planning for this attack, and Yousef was subsequently captured in 1995. Between 1995 and 2001, KSM was in hiding but had persuaded Osama bin Laden to provide him with operatives and logistical support for a new airliner attack. The culmination of the planning was the attacks on New York and Washington on September 11, 2001. KSM headed the al Qaeda Media Committee from 2000 and helped build ties and close operational support between al Qaeda and Jemaah Islamiyah (JI), which was plotting against U.S. and Israeli targets in Southeast Asia.

Terrorists will take every opportunity to exploit deficiencies in security systems, and it is particularly so when it comes to aviation. The terrorists have a particular fascination for attacking both airliners and airports. The "Bojinka II" plot stands out as a more sophisticated version of the plot to detonate bombs on airliners over the Pacific in the mid-1990s; it was foiled in Britain with the arrest of twenty-four British-born Muslims in August 2006. Although it has never been determined exactly how many aircraft were to be targeted in this attack, the explosives were to be brought onto aircraft in liquid form and disguised as sport drinks. These improvised explosive devices (IEDs) would then be assembled and detonated in mid-air believed to be on aircraft departing the Great Britain for the United States. It is obvious that had the plot succeeded, the death toll could well have reached the number of deaths witnessed on 9-11. The plot was far reaching with terrorist planning and operational cells spread around the world and is believed to have originated in Pakistan.[11]

RADICAL ISLAM AND THE UNITED STATES

Jihad is a flourishing ideology, and while it thrives, those wishing to embrace such an ideology continue to pose a threat. The experiences in Britain and Europe from radicalized Muslims could well be the example for further attacks in the United States. Governments cannot protect every building and every citizen and therefore cannot protect every target. The threat from the home-grown jihadist comes from a reality that those trying to enter the United States will use whatever legal and illegal means they can employ, whether they originate from countries in the U.S. Visa Waiver Program or have entered illegally through either Canada or Mexico; they may also be current U.S. citizens presently conspiring to attack the country from within. It is a tactical reality that these individuals are already on U.S. soil.

In review of the terrorist attacks by homegrown terrorists in the United Kingdom in 2005, we can begin to get a picture of a radicalized jihadist. He is invariably the child of moderate Muslim immigrants and aged under thirty-five. The jihadist comes from a varied ethnic back-ground and, contrary to popular belief, is not economically destitute, but rather has a full-time job and is well educated. There is little evidence to suggest that they have any criminal background, therefore making them more unremarkable! Mohammad Sidique Khan, one of the 2005 London bombers, was in fact a family man; he had studied business at Leeds Metropolitan University from 1998 to 2001 and was working as a teaching assistant with young children. So what transforma-tion did this young man undergo that lead him to become a suicide bomber in his country of birth?

The Jihadi–Salafi ideology is the driver that motivates young men and women, either born or living in the West, to carry out "autonomous jihad" via acts of terrorism against their host countries. Salafi–jihadists employ religious rhetoric and symbols to advance their cause. Although they selectively pick from the Islamic tradition only those elements that advance their narrow agenda, they nevertheless draw from the same religious sources that inform the lives and practices of more than a billion other Muslims.[12] This ideology has served as the inspiration for groups such as those that carried out the Madrid train attacks in 2004, the Dutch Hofstad Group, the 2005 London bombers, the Toronto 18 in 2006, (see Chapter 4) and more recent events in San Bernardino, CA. The New York Police Department (NYPD) Intelligence Division undertook a review of radical Islam to better understand the phases that went into the process of radicaliza-tion, and their review paper identified four specific phases in the process:

1. Pre-radicalization
2. Self-identification
3. Indoctrination
4. Jihadization

Although the NYPD model is sequential, individuals do not always follow a perfectly linear progression; however, those who do pass through the entire process are quite likely to become involved in the setup and organization of terror attacks.

PRE-RADICALIZATION

This is the point of origin for individuals before they began this progression. It is their life situ-ation before they were exposed to and adopted Jihadi–Salafi Islam for their own ideology. The majority of the individuals involved in plots came from unremarkable backgrounds and jobs and lived seemingly normal crime-free lives. The Toronto 18 terror suspects reportedly were well integrated into Canadian society.

SELF-IDENTIFICATION

This is the phase where individuals, influenced by both internal and external factors, begin their exploration of Salafist Islam, gradually gravitate away from their old identity and begin to associ-ate themselves with like-minded individuals and adopt this ideology as their own. In the Toronto case, the suspects had struggled with their identity, and some had formed a religious club and chat groups; they had also adopted the traditional Muslim style of dress, and some grew beards. The catalyst for this religious seeking is a cognitive opening or crisis, which shakes one's certitude in previously held beliefs and opens an individual to be receptive to new worldviews. What those worldviews are and what specific event sparks the religious changes could be many varied events, be it social, economic, or world events involving Muslims, or even a family member's death.

INDOCTRINATION

This is the period when the individual progressively intensifies his beliefs and wholly adopts Salafist teachings and ideology and concludes that the conditions and circumstances exist for action to further and support the cause of jihad. In most events, this phase is driven by a "spiritual sanctioner." While the initial self-indoctrination process may be an individual act, association with like-minded individuals is an important factor as the process deepens. By the indoctrination phase, this self-selecting group becomes increasingly important as radical views are encouraged as well as reinforced by the religious sanctioner.

Another example of homegrown threats against the United States, successfully investigated by FBI, is the "Lackawanna Group," a reference to the working class town of Lackawanna, south of Buffalo, where the Islamist conspirators came from, and is home to three thousand Muslim Americans, whose families come from the Republic of Yemen, on the Arabian Peninsula. The inspirational leader of the Lackawanna Group was Kamal Derwish who, although born in Buffalo and raised in Saudi Arabia, is steeped in that country's fundamentalist breed of Islam, known as Wahhabism. Derwish had trained in al Qaeda camps in Afghanistan and fought with Muslims in Bosnia. After returning to Saudi Arabia in 1997, he had been jailed for extremist activities. He returned to the United States in 2001 and began to inspire a group of like-minded young Muslims at his local mosque. This can be likened to the events that happened at London's Finsbury Park mosque, where Abu Hamza al-Masri preached his hatred of the West. In the spring of 2001, the following group members flew to Afghanistan for training: Mukhtar al-Bakri, Sahim Alwan, Jaber Elbaneh, Faysal Galab, Yahya Goba, Shafal Mosed, and Yasein Taher. Juma al-Dosari, who it is believed had fought with other Muslim fighters alongside Kamal Derwish in Bosnia, arrived in the United States in early 2001 and joined the Lackawanna Group. The Buffalo FBI Field Office was alerted to the Yemeni group via an anonymous letter, and, although the group was investigated, no charges could be substantiated. Following the 9-11 attacks, al-Dosari left to fight with the Taliban in Afghanistan and was captured while doing so sometime in the fall of 2001.

He was declared an enemy combatant and sent to the U.S. Naval Base on Guantanamo Bay, Cuba, where he was questioned. Al-Dosari's interrogation confirmed that the Lackawanna suspects were the targets of an al Qaeda recruitment operation. Mukhtar al-Bakri was arrested by Bahraini Police in September 2002 and subsequently interviewed by the CIA. He revealed the names of the other members of the Lackawanna Group; Sahim Alwan, Faysal Galab, Yahya Goba, Shafal Mosed, and Yasein Taher were arrested. In early November 2002, Kamal Derwish was killed in Yemen by a CIA Predator Drone while tracking the al Qaeda plotters of the USS *Cole* attack. Although Derwish was an American citizen, the government would not discuss his death or any connections he may have or have had with al Qaeda. This very brief example indicates the very real problems that exist within the Muslim communities in the United States. The Lackawanna Group was sentenced to between seven and ten years in prison in 2003 and has been cooperating with the government.

How Muslims integrate and how they view themselves not only in the United States but also in other Western countries is an ongoing concern not just to religious groups but to governments as well. The overwhelming view from research companies, such as Pew Research, point out that many Muslims feel better off in Western society, although their standard of living is often not comparable to that of the general population in the host country.

The widespread appeal of Islamic extremism in the United States is certainly being taken seriously—the problem applies to many European countries as well as the United States. The ability of young Muslim men to become influenced through Internet chat rooms as well as travelling to areas of North Africa and Afghanistan will continue to pose a security threat to the homeland. The list below typifies the activities that are taking place and the very real threats they pose:

- July 2009: Daniel Patrick Boyd—conspiracy to commit murder. From North Carolina along with his two sons was accused of discussing violent jihad and possession of weapons. The U.S. Marine Corps Base at Quantico Virginia was the suspected target.
- September 2009: Najibullah Zazi from Denver—plotting to set off a bomb on the New York subway system.
- October 2009: Colleen LaRose from Philadelphia—online name Jihad Jane, allegedly agreed to kill a Swedish artist who drew a picture of the Prophet Muhammad with the body of a dog.

TERROR ATTACK BRIEF

Plot to Assassinate Saudi Ambassador to the United States.

Between spring and October 2011, Iran through its Quds Force plotted to murder the Saudi Ambassador on American soil. The plan was to plant a bomb in a Washington DC restaurant frequented by the ambassador. The plan was disrupted by U.S. agents who were alleged to have infiltrated the group in Mexico. According to the criminal complaint, the IRGC is an arm of the Iranian military that is composed of a number of branches, one of which is the Quds Force. The Quds Force conducts sensitive covert operations abroad, including terrorist attacks, assassinations, and kidnappings and is believed to sponsor attacks against Coalition Forces in Iraq. In October 2007, the U.S. Treasury Department designated the Quds Force for providing material support to the Taliban and other terrorist organizations.

A criminal complaint filed today (October 11, 2011) in the Southern District of New York charges Manssor Arbabsiar, a 56-year-old naturalized U.S. citizen holding both Iranian and U.S. passports, and Gholam Shakuri. In a July 14, 2011 meeting in Mexico, CS-1 allegedly told Arbabsiar that he would need to use four men to carry out the Ambassador's murder and that his price for carrying out the murder was $1.5 million. Arbabsiar allegedly agreed and stated that the murder of the Ambassador should be handled first, before the execution of other attacks. Arbabsiar also allegedly indicated he and his associates had $100,000 in Iran to pay CS-1 as a first payment toward the assassination and discussed the manner in which that payment would be made. During the same meeting, Arbabsiar allegedly described to CS-1 his cousin in Iran, who he said had requested that Arbabsiar find someone to carry out the Ambassador's assassination. According to the complaint, Arbabsiar indicated that his cousin was a "big general" in the Iranian military; that he focuses on matters outside Iran; and that he had taken certain unspecified actions related to a bombing in Iraq. According to the complaint, Arbabsiar also admitted to agents that in connection with this plot, he was recruited, funded, and directed by men he understood to be senior officials in Iran's Quds Force. He allegedly said these Iranian officials were aware of and approved of the use of CS-1 in connection with the plot as well as payments to CS-1; the means by which the Ambassador would be killed in the United States; and the casualties that would likely result.

Both defendants are charged with conspiracy to murder a foreign official; conspiracy to engage in foreign travel and use of interstate and foreign commerce facilities in the commission of murder-for-hire; conspiracy to use a weapon of mass destruction (explosives); and conspiracy to commit an act of international terrorism transcending national boundaries. Arbabsiar is further charged with an additional count of foreign travel and use of interstate and foreign commerce facilities in the commission of murder-for-hire.

FIGURE 3-7 Plot to assassinate the Saudi Ambassador to the United States.

- November 2009: Eight Somali Americans charged with attending camps and training with al-Shabaab in Somalia.
- November 2009: A man of Palestinian descent but born in the United States, Major Nidal Malik Hasan, a U.S. Army psychiatrist sentenced to death in the killing of thirteen people at Ford Hood, Texas.
- December 2009: Five men from Alexandria arrested in Pakistan charged in an extensive plot that included possible attacks in the United States and fighting troops in Afghanistan.
- May 2010: Faisal Shahzad, born in Pakistan but became a U.S. citizen, allegedly tries to set off a car bomb in Times Square, New York.[13]
- October 2011: Manssor Arbabsiar, a 56-year-old naturalized U.S. citizen plotted to assassinate Saudi Ambassador to the United States (Figure 3-7).

U.S. FOREIGN POLICY—CHALLENGES AND OPPORTUNITIES

The United States is a world super power and between WWII and 9-11 managed to control by foreign policy and diplomacy the region of the Middle East. After WWII, the Arab states had shed their colonial restraints and adopted their own monarchies and dictatorships. Arab economies were heavily dependent on oil drilling and supply which brought untold wealth and with it institutionalized corruption which did little for indigenous people as a whole. The Arab model that existed to the end of the twentieth century was kept in place by the wealth from oil meaning that their traditional sociocultural systems remained in tack. The Middle East is no stranger to uprisings and terror over the last fifty years of the last century, but by the early 1990s, mistrust and discontent had risen and with it emerged the coalescing force of the Muslim Brotherhood which had created numerous franchises that became political forces and opposition to Arab regimes. Widespread Arab frustrations lead us to the 2011 Arab Spring. The Arab Spring saw uprisings in almost all regions of the Middle East with violent uprisings in Libya, Egypt, Yemen, and Syria. The nature of civil wars as seen in the Middle East is that they also destabilize the neighboring states.

So what of U.S. foreign policy in the region? The region has always had a strong outside representative dating back to the Ottoman conquests in the sixteenth century. That strong presence had been a constructive force that was able to mitigate widespread conflict and the various Arab states were accustomed to a strong third party presence. U.S. policy under the Obama administration has been "hands off" or "disengagement." The earlier U.S.-led invasion of Iraq and the ground war created no significant change or benefit for the good of that country and the "disengaging" and its troop withdrawal led to the reawakening of al Qaeda proxy ISIL and the bloodletting between Shiites and Sunni.

With a lack of direct political influence from the United States in the Middle East, civil wars continue to rage more than five years post Arab Spring and the U.S. administration's inaction has failed to put in place any coherent strategy to deal with them. Even two years after President Obama had claimed that the U.S. administration would help the region to develop a new Arab state system, it has not happened. In addressing the region's civil war, the United States has been focusing on ISIL as the cause and the symptoms for the civil wars. The ongoing civil war in Syria has spread to Iraq and the two combined have sucked in neighboring regions in Turkey. Civil war in the destabilized region of North Africa, primarily Libya, is seeing the spread of unrest to its neighbors in Tunisia, Mali, and Egypt. Both the civil wars in Syria and Yemen have led to engagement from Iran, Saudi Arabia, and the Gulf States and in a broader context, this has become a clash of religion with Sunni against Shia and their respective supporting nation-states. The al Qaeda and ISIL factions have not yet found a fertile ground in the stronger regional states, including Palestinian territories and Jordan. A spillover of the civil war into Jordan will ultimately come closer to Israel. In spite of the War on Terror and the damage inflicted by the United States on al Qaeda in Afghanistan, the rise of militant Islam and Salafi–jihad has grown out of all magnitude. The stabilization (to a degree) of Iraq in 2007 pushed the al Qaeda and their proxies to the edge of extinction. But having created a level of stability, the United States did not stay around to make it enduring and by 2011, the complete withdrawal of its forces had allowed proxy groups such as the fledgling Islamic State of Iraq and the Levant to fill the void.

ISIL had been able to proclaim a caliphate in parts of Iraq and Syria.

In his essay to Foreign Affairs magazine in April 2016, Kenneth M Pollock clearly lays out the strategy based on historical facts on the way forward for super powers to intervene and end civil wars.

- Firstly, military dynamics must change such that none of the warring parties believes that it can win a military victory and none fears that its fighters will be slaughtered if one side lays down its arms.
- Power-sharing agreement is paramount so that all groups are fully invested in a new governing body.
- Institutions must be in place that assure all parties that the first two above conditions endure—unknowingly, this is precisely the path taken by the NATO in Bosnia 1994–1995 and the United States followed in 2007–2010.[14]

A 2015 report by the U.S. Department of State, *Country Reports,* stated that the ongoing civil war in Syria has been a significant factor in driving worldwide terrorism events. In 2014 alone, the rate of foreign terrorist fighters who traveled to Syria—totaling more than sixteen thousand foreign terrorist fighters from more than ninety countries—exceeded the rate of foreign terrorist fighters who traveled to Afghanistan, Pakistan, Iraq, Yemen, or Somalia at any point in the last twenty years. Many of those foreign terrorist fighters joined ISIL, which has seized contiguous territory in western Iraq and eastern Syria for a self-declared Islamic caliphate.

U.S. foreign policy will need to see some significant change in order to be seen as a global leader that can influence change in the Middle East. The current civil wars have created millions of refugees mostly Muslims and those refugees are flooding the West, and with them foreign fighters will return to their countries and begin the recruiting and the circle of violence that is terrorism. The United States will not be immune to the threats from ISIL and affiliates posed by leaving the Middle East to fester indefinitely.

WATCH LISTS

Testimony Before the Committee on Homeland Security and Governmental Affairs, U.S. Senate, October 2007

Pursuant to Homeland Security Presidential Directive 6, the Attorney General established Terrorist Screening Centers (TSCs) in September 2003 to consolidate the government's approach to terrorism screening and provide for the appropriate and lawful use of terrorist information in screening processes. TSC's consolidated watch list is the U.S. government's master repository for all records of known or appropriately suspected international and domestic terrorists used for watch list-related screening.

- When an individual makes an airline reservation, arrives at a U.S. port of entry, or applies for a U.S. visa, or is stopped by state or local police within the United States, the frontline screening agency or airline conducts a name-based search of the individual against applicable terrorist watch list records. In general, when the computerized name-matching system of an airline or screening agency generates a "hit" (a potential name match) against a watch list record, the airline or agency is to review each potential match. Any obvious mismatches (negative matches) are to be resolved by the airline or agency. Page 3, GAO-08-194T.

  The National Counterterrorism Center and the FBI rely upon standards of reasonableness in determining which individuals are appropriate for inclusion on TSC's consolidated terrorist watch list. In general, individuals who are reasonably suspected of having possible links to terrorism—in addition to individuals with known links—are to be nominated. As such, inclusion on the list does not automatically prohibit an individual from, for example, obtaining a visa or entering the United States. As of May 2007, TSC's watch list contained approximately 755,000 records.

- From December 2003 (when TSC began operations) through May 2007, agencies encountered individuals who were on the watch list about 53,000 times. Many individuals were encountered multiple times. Actions taken in response included arresting individuals and denying others entry into the United States. Most often, however, agencies questioned and then released the individuals because there was not sufficient evidence of criminal or terrorist activity to warrant further legal action. Nevertheless, such questioning allowed agencies to collect information on the individuals, which was shared with law enforcement agencies and the intelligence community.

- Screening agencies do not check against all records in the consolidated watch list, partly because screening against certain records (1) may not be needed to support the respective agency's mission or (2) may not be possible owing to the requirements of computer programs used to check individuals against watch list records. Not checking against all records may pose a security risk. Also, some subjects of watch list records have passed undetected through agency screening processes and were not identified, for example, until after they had boarded and flew on an aircraft. Federal agencies have ongoing initiatives to help reduce these potential vulnerabilities.

- The federal government has made progress in using the consolidated watch list for screening purposes, but it has not (1) finalized guidelines for using watch list records within critical infrastructure components of the private sector or (2) identified all appropriate opportunities for which terrorist-related screening should be applied. Further, the government lacks an up-to-date strategy and implementation plan—supported by a clearly defined leadership or governance structure—which are important for enhancing the effectiveness of terrorist-related screening.

Several actions have been recommended to promote a more comprehensive and coordinated approach to terrorist-related screening. Among them are actions to monitor and respond to vulnerabilities and to establish up-to-date guidelines, strategies, and plans to facilitate expanded and enhanced use of the list. The Department of Homeland Security and the FBI generally agreed with GAO findings and recommendations.[15]

EXTRAORDINARY RENDITION

In the United States, the question of dealing with terrorists and the need to gather much needed intelligence became a major priority for the former Bush Administration (2001–2009). The U.S. government did not recognize those captured in both Afghanistan and Iraq as being prisoners of war, but rather as "enemy combatants." This led to speculation surrounding treatment of the detainees in Guantanamo Bay, as well as the well-documented 2006 abuses at Abu Ghraib prison near Baghdad by U.S. Military Police and other agencies of the U.S. Government. The stories of abuse became front-page media stories in the Middle East with You Tube videos depicting military personnel engaging in degrading and abusive attacks on Iraqi prisoners.

Back home, the need for solid intelligence continued. Complaints have been made by Amnesty International and others that the United States, in its race and determination to go to extraordinary lengths to gather information, is violating both U.S. and international laws. By categorizing detainees as enemy combatants, the United States does not apply the rigorous standards required under the Geneva conventions. What is taking place and being driven in secret, presumably by the CIA, is an activity referred to as extraordinary rendition, which has been defined as "the transfer of an individual, with the involvement of the United States or its agents, to a foreign state in circumstances that make it more likely than not, that the individual will be subjected to torture, or cruel, inhuman, or degrading treatment."[16] This practice has not had much press in the United States, likely because of the secret manner in which it is being conducted. However, there are cases of "rendition" that took place prior to 9-11, and certainly the practice has been even more widespread since that attack. Specifically, critics claim the United States is violating international conventions that ban the use of torture. Since 9-11, dozens of "enemy combatants" have been sent to third-party countries, such as Morocco, Saudi Arabia, Yemen, Egypt, and Jordan. All of these countries—in particular, Egypt and Jordan—have close ties to the CIA, and all have been cited by the U.S. State Department as using torture in interrogations. Detainees have been taken often under cover of darkness and transported by private jet to these countries for interrogation. The interrogation tactics used would be illegal if conducted inside the United States. The Convention against Torture prohibits torture carried out at the "instigation of or with the consent or acquiescence" of officials. Handing someone over to a foreign intelligence service with the knowledge that the person will be tortured fits within the prohibitions of the convention. It also appears that U.S. officials engage in the treatment of detainees that may include torture. Witnesses have reported that captives are "softened up" by the U.S. military. The detainees are said to have been blindfolded and thrown into wells, bound in painful positions, subjected to loud noises, and deprived of sleep. There is growing resistance to the use of torture even from law enforcement officials.[17] Article 3 of the United Nations Convention against Torture, to which the United States is a signatory, states that "no party shall expel, return ('refouler') or extradite a person to another State where there are substantial grounds for believing that person would be in danger of being subjected to torture. For the purpose of determining whether there are such grounds, the competent authorities shall take into account all relevant considerations including, where applicable, the existence in the State concerned of a consistent pattern of gross, flagrant, or mass violations of human rights."

Maher Arar—Canadian Citizen

While the number of cases and the extent to which the government is involved in rendition is uncertain, there is a significant case that has embarrassed both the U.S. and Canadian governments for the manner in which a Canadian citizen, transiting through JFK en route back into Canada, was detained and sent on to Syria. Arar came to Canada with his family and had no intention, according to him, of returning to Syria. In the wake and paranoia of 9-11, it is entirely probable that mistakes were made in targeting individuals for this form of treatment. Failings by the Canadian intelligence service and the RCMP led to an individual being forcibly removed from an in-transit location to Syria, where he remained incarcerated and, according to Amnesty International, was severely tortured. He was released on October 5, 2003, three hundred seventy-four days after first being deported to Syria. No charges have been brought against him by Syria, the United States, or Canada even though it was alleged that he had contact with al Qaeda sympathizers.

USA Patriot Improvement Act

On March 9, 2006, President Bush signed the USA Patriot Improvement and Reauthorization Act of 2005. Since its enactment in October 2001, the Patriot Act has been vital to the War on Terror and protecting the American people. The legislation allows intelligence and law enforcement officials to continue sharing information and using the same tools against terrorists already employed against drug dealers and other criminals. While safeguarding Americans' civil liberties, this legislation also strengthens the U.S. Department of Justice (DOJ) so that it can better detect and disrupt terrorist threats, and it also gives law enforcement new tools to combat threats. America still faces dangerous enemies, and no priority is more important to the U.S. president than protecting the American people without delay.

THE PATRIOT ACT CLOSES DANGEROUS LAW ENFORCEMENT AND INTELLIGENCE GAPS

The Patriot Act Has Accomplished Exactly What It Was Designed to Do

- It has helped us detect terrorist cells, disrupt terrorist plots, and save American lives.
- The Patriot Act has helped law enforcement break up terror cells in Ohio, New York, Oregon, and Virginia.
- The Patriot Act has helped in the prosecution of terrorist operatives and supporters in California, Texas, New Jersey, Illinois Washington, and North Carolina.

The Patriot Act Authorizes Vital Information Sharing to Help Law Enforcement and Intelligence Officials Connect the Dots Before Terrorists Strike

The Patriot Act enables necessary cooperation and information sharing by helping to break down legal and bureaucratic walls separating criminal investigators from intelligence officers.

The Patriot Act Eliminates Double Standards by Allowing Agents to Pursue Terrorists with the Same Tools They Use Against Other Criminals

Before the Patriot Act, it was easier to track a drug dealer's phone contacts than a terrorist's phone contacts, and it was easier to obtain a tax cheat's credit card receipts than to trace the financial support of an al Qaeda fund-raiser. The Patriot Act corrected these double standards—and America is safer as a result.

The Patriot Act Adapts the Law to Modern Technology

The Patriot Act allows Internet service providers to disclose customer records voluntarily to the government in emergencies involving an immediate risk of death or serious physical injury and permits victims of hacking crimes to request law enforcement assistance in monitoring trespassers on their computers.

The Patriot Act Preserves Our Freedoms and Upholds the Rule of Law

The legislation signed today adds over thirty new significant civil liberties provisions.

THE PATRIOT ACT REAUTHORIZATION SAFEGUARDS OUR NATION

The Patriot Act Reauthorization Creates a New Assistant Attorney General for National Security

By creating a new Assistant Attorney General for National Security, this legislation fulfills a critical recommendation of the Commission on the Intelligence Capabilities of the United States regarding Weapons of Mass Destruction. This allows the Justice Department to bring its national security, counterterrorism, counterintelligence, and foreign intelligence surveillance operations under a single authority.

The Patriot Act Reauthorization Tackles Terrorism Financing

This bill enhances penalties for terrorism financing and closes a loophole concerning terrorist financing through "hawalas" (informal money transfer networks) rather than traditional financial institutions.

The Patriot Act Reauthorization Protects Mass Transportation

This bill provides clear standards and tough penalties for attacks on our land- and water-based mass transportation systems, as well as commercial aviation.

THE PATRIOT ACT REAUTHORIZATION COMBATS METHAMPHETAMINE ABUSE

The Patriot Act Reauthorization Includes the Combat Methamphetamine Epidemic Act of 2005

This bill introduces commonsense safeguards that will make many ingredients used in methamphetamine manufacturing more difficult to obtain in bulk and easier for law enforcement to track. For example, the bill places limits on large-scale purchases of over-the-counter drugs that are used to manufacture methamphetamines and requires stores to keep these ingredients behind the counter or in locked display cases. It increases penalties for smuggling and selling methamphetamines.[18]

RELIGIOUS EXTREMISM

Jamaat ul-Fuqra

There resides, somewhat eerily, a network of possible terrorists-in-waiting within a little-known organization called **Jamaat ul-Fuqra**, which has the literal translation, "community of the impoverished." This group's Islamic roots in the United States date back as far as 1980, when it was founded by Sheikh Mubarak Ali Gilani, a Pakistani cleric, who incorporated the group under the name of "Muslims of America." The organization has tax-exempt status in the United States and an educational section that supports student training in Pakistan. The group has done little to draw attention to itself in mainstream United States and all but denies its very existence. One of ul-Fuqra's first members was Stephen Paul Paster, who had converted to Islam and was convicted of bombing a hotel that was owned by an Indian cult in Portland, Oregon, in 1983. On his release from prison, Paster went to Pakistan, where he joined Gilani and other instructors teaching advanced courses in Islamic military warfare. On a broader scale, ul-Fuqra members are believed to have been involved in fighting in Chechnya, Bosnia, Afghanistan, Kashmir, and Lebanon. U.S. sources believe some of its members are affiliated with the al-Kifah Refugee Center in Brooklyn, New York. Following the first attack on the World Trade Center in 1993, the FBI determined that Muslim men, including participants in the attack, had been recruited at the al-Kifah refugee office in Brooklyn and sent to training camps in Afghanistan—first to fight the Soviet army and later to engage in a jihad against the United States. In 1993, the FBI also learned of a plot to blow up bridges, tunnels, and landmarks in New York. That investigation led to the conviction of Omar Abdel Rahman, the "Blind Sheikh," for soliciting others to commit all of those acts of terrorism in 1993. A further connection linked the infamous "shoe bomber," Richard Reid, to the Brooklyn office. Moreover, *The Wall Street Journal* reporter Daniel Pearl was investigating Gilani in Pakistan when he was kidnapped and murdered (Figure 3-8).

Islamic Extremism—A U.S. Military Case

The Fort Hood shooting in November 2009 could have been put down to a workplace violence incident or as is often referred to as someone "going postal." The alleged perpetrator was a serving military officer and psychiatrist Major Nidal Malik Hasan. His activities and possible disillusionment with not just the military but also his adopted country first surfaced in 2008 when he came to the attention of the Joint Terrorism Task Force (JTTF). So what was it that could have turned this professional soldier and doctor against his country? To many observers,

TERROR ATTACK BRIEF

Wall Street Journalist—Daniel Pearl

Daniel Pearl, 38-year-old reporter and chief of the Wall Street Journal's South Asia bureau for two years, was kidnapped in Karachi, Pakistan, on January 23, 2002. He had been researching a story linking the alleged shoe-bomber Richard Reid with al Qaida and various Islamic radical groups in Pakistan. His kidnappers sent email messages accusing Pearl of being a spy and listing numerous demands.

For weeks Daniel Pearl's fate was unknown. President Bush and President Musharraf condemned the kidnapping and stated that no concessions would be made to terrorists.

Pakistani law enforcement officials worked tirelessly to locate Pearl and his abductors, and U.S. Embassy officials cooperated closely in the investigation. On February 21 it was learned that Mr. Pearl was murdered by his captors.

Police in Karachi made several arrests in the case, including Ahmed Omar Sheikh. Sheikh spent five years in prison on charges of kidnapping three British citizens and one U.S. citizen in 1994. In 1999, hijackers took over Indian Airlines flight 814 en route from Nepal to India and forced the plane to land in Kandahar, Afghanistan. In exchange for the 155 persons aboard, they demanded the release from an Indian prison of Sheikh and Masood Azhar, founder of the Jaish-e-Mohammed, which the United States designated a Foreign Terrorist Organization in 2001. The Government of India released them.

President Bush said: "Those who threaten Americans, those who engage in criminal barbaric acts, need to know that these crimes only hurt their cause, and only deepen the resolve of the United States of America to rid the world of these agents of terror." The Department of State called the murder of Mr. Pearl "an outrage" and said the United States and Pakistan "are committed to identifying all the perpetrators in this crime and bringing them to justice."

"His murder is an act of barbarism that makes a mockery of everything Danny's kidnappers claimed to believe in," read a statement by Peter Kann, publisher of the Wall Street Journal, and Paul Steiger, the newspaper's managing editor. "They claimed to be Pakistani nationalists, but their actions must surely bring shame to all true Pakistani patriots."

Daniel Pearl leaves behind his wife, French journalist Marianne, who at the time of his murder was seven months pregnant with their first child.

The murder of Daniel Pearl underscores the importance of not making concessions to terrorists, the dangers faced by journalists around the world, the nature of the current terrorist threat, and the need to maintain vigilance and take appropriate security precautions.

FIGURE 3-8   Terror Attack Brief—Wall Street journalist—Daniel Pearl.   *Courtesy:* U.S. Department of State.

this was a case of terrorism but maybe that oversimplifies the issues. We find the following testimony provided by Brian Jenkins before the Senate Homeland Security and Governmental Affairs Committee on November 19, 2009, to be both intuitive and instructive in evaluating terrorist incidents.

Again, based solely upon what has been publicly reported, the path that takes Hasan to the Fort Hood slayings includes many of the signposts identified in the radicalization process: his search for meaning and spiritual guidance, his engagement via the Internet with jihadist ideology, his adoption of the jihadist view that the West and Islam are irreconcilably opposed, the broadening of his sense of grievance from the personal to what he saw as a besieged Muslim community, his reported online encounter with an enabler—a jihadist imam whose writings would morally validate and reinforce Hasan's own feelings of anger and aggression, his expression of extremist views, and at some point, his decision to kill. If some of the markers of radicalization and recruitment are missing, it is because, except for Hasan's reported correspondence with the imam, Anwar al-Awlaki, his journey may have been entirely an interior one.

Fort Hood Attack

Fort Hood, Texas—November 5, 2009

Subject—Major Nidal Malik Hasan

Career—15 year U.S. Military–Army Psychiatrist

Work Location—Walter Reed Army Medical Center

Attack Location—Soldier Readiness Processing Center, Fort Hood, Texas

FIGURE 3-9 Fort Hood, Texas.   *Courtesy:* US Army

CONVICTED: August 23, 2013—Tried under The Uniform Code of Military Justice and convicted by a jury at a military court-martial of thirteen counts of premeditated murder and thirty-two counts of attempted murder and was sentenced to death—he is currently in military prison at Fort Leavenworth, Kansas.

Soft target-U.S. servicemen and women on bases in the United States would not be carrying loaded weapons—these would only be available for live fire training, so this location has to be viewed as a "soft target." The only personnel carrying loaded weapons would be military and civilian police. The attack took place in a crowded area that was packed with soldiers and in a matter of seconds he had killed twelve soldiers and one civilian and wounded a further thirty-two others (Figure 3-9).

The Investigation

For more than a decade, the FBI has forecast the dangers posed by "lone wolf" terrorists both domestic and international, and in 2007, it published its own model of violent radicalization that seems to parallel the understanding in the psychiatric community. The FBI describes violent radicalization as the "way stations"—four incremental stages of development:

PRERADICALIZATION - IDENTIFICATION - INDOCTRINATION - ACTION

Lone actors can pass through the four stages with little or no contact from a leader or another violent radical and in the case of Major Hasan, he did have some minor contact in the year preceding his Fort Hood attack with **Anwar al-Awlaki**, the U.S. born imam who was killed in Yemen by a U.S. drone strike in 2011. Between 2008 and 2009, approximately eighteen emails were sent by Hasan to al-Awlaki, not all of them being responded to. Awlaki was educated in the United States and obtained his B.Sc. in Civil Engineering at Colorado State University in 1994. He subsequently spent time in San Diego where he served as imam from 1995 to 2000 and then to Falls Church Virginia and on to England where he reportedly lectured youth groups on jihad. Although he was being monitored by the FBI and JTTF, there was nothing to signal any involvement in international terrorism, however, he becomes a prime example of a radicalization leader. He established and sustained an international reputation as a charismatic imam who provided Islamic guidance in English through sermons, lectures, publications, recordings, and a website. He managed to successfully blur his anti-Western rhetoric with mundane religious observations and advice. His rhetoric increasingly included public statements and exhortations to violence against the United States. Lectures and Internet audios in support of jihad provided the needed stimulus for radicalization. What role he played in Hasan's radicalization is not determined. Their contact and reviews of emails did not suggest that Hasan was a terror threat. Hasan had subscribed to al-Awlaki's web page and was receiving and retained at least twenty-nine email updates from al-Awlaki. The subjects covered were varied but the following is a short list of examples:

- December 2009 email titled "Salutations to al-Shabaab of Somalia" offered congratulations to al-Shabaab "for your victories and achievements," asked Allah to "guide you and grant you victory"
- January 2009 email provided Word and pdf copies of Awlaki's "44 Ways of Supporting Jihad"
- July 2009 email discussed "Fighting against Government Armies in the Muslim World," challenging the Muslims fighting on behalf of America against the Mujahideen in Pakistan, Somalia, and the Maghrib…. What kind of twisted fight is this? The blame should be placed on the soldier who is willing to follow orders.

Although there was no established connection between the mass emailing and the ones sent to Hasan personally, it definitely shows how difficult the decision making becomes and although al-Awlaki was at some point under scrutiny from federal agencies, it did not signify enough to trigger concerns about his connection to a serving Muslim military officer.

During his trial for murder Hasan defended himself and in 2014 wrote that he wanted to join Islamic State. Following the trial, the William H Webster Commission on the FBI Investigations,

Counter Terrorism Intelligence, and the Events at Fort Hood report made some interesting finding in regard to issues of information, failure to follow up on leads, computer and technology issues, and failure of the FBI Headquarters to coordinate two field offices working on leads that were related to Hasan.

The failure in connecting the 'dots' as we saw in 2001 has appeared again, but given the nature of this attack and who executed it, should we be surprised—another question remains that this was a case that was handled and taken to trial by the military and Hasan was not prosecuted in federal court for terrorism offences.

A second case where previous information sharing involved United States and Russia will now be reviewed:

The Boston Marathon Bombing

Boston—April 15, 2013

> **Subjects**—Dzhokhar Tsarnaev and his brother Tamerlan Tsarnaev
>
> **2002–2003**—Immigrated with parents from Kyrgyzstan
>
> **Attack Location**—finish line 2013 Boston marathon, Boston, Massachusetts

On April 15, 2013, two pressure cooker bombs placed near the finish line at the Boston marathon detonated within seconds of each other, killing three and injuring more than two hundred people. Law enforcement officials identified brothers Tamerlan and Dzhokhar Tsarnaev as primary suspects in the bombings (Figure 3-10). After an extensive search for the then unidentified suspects, law enforcement officials encountered Tamerlan and Dzhokhar Tsarnaev in Watertown, Massachusetts. Tamerlan Tsarnaev was shot during the encounter and was pronounced dead at the scene. Dzhokhar Tsarnaev, who fled the scene, was apprehended the following day. A decade earlier, the two brothers immigrated to the United States from Kyrgyzstan with their parents Anzor Tsarnaev and Zubeidat Tsarnaeva. Anzor Tsarnaev, an ethnic Chechen, his wife Zubeidat Tsarnaeva, and their son Dzhokhar Tsarnaev arrived in the United States from Kyrgyzstan in 2002. They applied for and received an immigration benefit. The elder son, Tamerlan Tsarnaev, and his sisters, Bella and Ailina Tsarnaeva, arrived in the United States in 2003 and also received an immigration benefit. In the years that followed, all six family members became Lawful Permanent Residents of the United States.

Two years before the Boston marathon bombings, Tamerlan Tsarnaev and Zubeidat Tsarnaeva came to the attention of the Federal Bureau of Investigation (FBI) based on information received from the Russian Federal Security Service (FSB). In March 2011, the FBI received information from the FSB alleging that Tamerlan Tsarnaev and Zubeidat Tsarnaeva were adherents of radical Islam and that Tamerlan Tsarnaev was preparing to travel to Russia to join unspecified underground groups in Dagestan and Chechnya. The FBI-led Joint Terrorism Task Force in Boston (Boston JTTF) conducted an assessment of Tamerlan Tsarnaev to determine whether he posed a threat to national security and closed the assessment three months later having found no link or "nexus" to terrorism. In September 2011, the FSB provided the Central Intelligence Agency (CIA) information on Tamerlan Tsarnaev that was substantively identical to the information the FSB had provided to the FBI in March 2011. In October 2011, the CIA provided information obtained from the FSB to the National Counterterrorism Center (NCTC) for watch listing purposes, and to the FBI, Department of Homeland Security (DHS), and the Department of State for their information. Upon NCTC's receipt of the information, Tamerlan Tsarnaev was added to the terrorist watch list. Three months later, Tamerlan Tsarnaev traveled to Russia, unfortunately his travel movements did not prompt additional investigative steps to determine whether he posed a threat to national security. The FBI closed the assessment on June 24, 2011, having found no link or nexus between Tamerlan Tsarnaev and terrorism. On January 12, 2012, Tamerlan again traveled to Russia returning in July and the investigation is unclear as to whether that travel plan was disseminated to the FBI.

FIGURE 3-10 Boston marathon bomb suspect. *Source:* FBI Photo/Alamy Stock Photo

Tsarnaev was active online as well and the investigation uncovered from Dzhokhar's personal computer his viewing of *Inspire* Magazine and the posting of jihadi themed videos in late 2012. There was also one of these issues that contained an article titled "Make a bomb in the kitchen of your mom" which included the instructions for assembling the pressure cooker bombs used in this attack.

APRIL 8, 2015   Dzhokhar Tsarnaev is found guilty of carrying out the 2013 bombing at the finish line of the Boston marathon and sentenced to death.

In many ways, this attack although nothing like as deadly as 9-11 shows the complexity of decision making on how long and how far to track, investigate, watch, and monitor possible or probable jihadists within the United States.[19]

Some analysts say that al Qaeda and others are currently following a strategy of "leaderless resistance." Leaderless resistance envisions an army of autonomous terrorist operatives, united in a common cause, but not connected organizationally. Although it is difficult for authorities to destroy a leaderless enterprise, leaderless resistance is a strategy of weakness. Outside of Pakistan and Afghanistan, its leaders can do little other than exhort others to violence. However, leaderless resistance does enable terrorist leaders to assert ownership of just about every homicidal maniac on the planet, thus projecting an illusion of strength. Major Hasan's Internet imam was quick to praise the Fort Hood murders as another jihad victory. At least sixty Islamist-inspired terrorist plots against the homeland since 9-11 illustrate the continued threat of terrorism against the United States. Fifty-three of these plots were thwarted long before the public was ever in danger thanks to law enforcement and intelligence. This total includes plots to carry out attacks in the United States or abroad, as well as support for foreign terrorist organizations. Although not all of the plots, if undiscovered, are likely to have resulted in successful attacks, very little separates the ambitions of jihadist wannabes from a deadly terrorist assault. The essential ingredient is intent. Domestic intelligence collection remains a necessary and critical component of homeland security. Apart from common inspiration, there is no evidence of any organizational connection between these events. They appear to be individual responses to jihadist propaganda in the context of U.S. policy decisions. American foreign policy should not be determined by a handful of shooters and would-be bombers, but we must accept the fact that what America does or does not do in the Middle East, Afghanistan, and Pakistan may provoke terrorism in the United States (Figure 3-11).

Six of the plots since 9-11 targeted American soldiers or military facilities in the United States: (Torrance, 2005; Fort Dix, 2006; New York City, May 2009; Arkansas, 2009; North Carolina, 2009; Fort Hood, 2009), which could reflect in part jihadist exhortation and in part the plotters' own perceptions that attacking military targets is more legitimate than attacking civilians. However, the majority of the plots appear to have been aimed at causing mass civilian casualties, especially in public transportation venues. What does the Hasan case tell us about the radicalization of Muslims in America? Not a lot. In all, roughly 100 individuals in these plots have been charged with crimes related to terrorism. These include Muslim immigrants, native-born Muslims, and converts to Islam. It is interesting to note that in the Fort Hood case Hasan was not charged in federal court but under military law with murder. Almost all actors were here legally, most being U.S. citizens. A few, like Nidal Hasan, were veterans of military service. Some of the terrorist plotters uncovered in the United States began to radicalize before 9-11, while others, like Hasan, are more recent converts to jihadist worldviews. The Boston bombers were immigrants from a war-torn conflict in the Balkans. Almost all were recruited locally and in the Boston case there involved travel back to the Balkan region in the months prior to that attack—we have no evidence of terrorist sleeper cells being established in this country.

The plots show that radicalization and recruitment to terrorist violence is occurring in the United States and remains a security concern. With roughly 3 million Muslims in America, although some estimates run much higher, 100 terrorists represent a mere 0.00003 percent of the Muslim population—fewer than one out of 30,000.

FIGURE 3-11   The author discussing the Boston marathon bombing on Global News.   *Source:* Global News - Canada

Lone Wolf Extremism

On December 2, 2015, in San Bernardino, California just north of Los Angeles, a young married couple conducted an assault on the workplace of one of the attackers—it was at first thought to be yet another in an unending stream of mass killings that are characteristic of the United States— the investigation indicates this is a "lone wolf" attack where the attackers have not sought direction or likely been controlled by an external group or entity but have become extremist in their views and attitudes through online association. Syed Rizwan Farook, a Pakistani, held permanent U.S. residency. Farook worked at the location he and his wife targeted so it was first thought to be a workplace violence attack and not specifically terror-related. The following is an analysis conducted by Stratfor.com in the early stages of the investigation detailing the workplace relationship with the attacker Syed Farook:

San Bernardino: Workplace Violence or Terrorism?

Syed Rizwan Farook got into an altercation at his office holiday party December 2, after which he and his wife, Tashfeen Malik, conducted a sophisticated attack on the event. Though many details of the attack remain unclear and the motive is still being investigated, the incident seems to be a prime example of the blurred line that sometimes exists between international ideologically driven terrorism and violence perpetrated by lone assailants. Farook was a twenty eight-year-old public health employee for San Bernardino County, where he had worked for the past five years. According to witnesses, he began to argue with another employee at the office holiday party. He then left the party and retrieved his wife, and both returned around 11 A.M. armed with assault rifles and semi-automatic handguns and dressed in black tactical gear. The two shot indiscriminately at the employees of the Inland Regional Center in San Bernardino, killing fourteen people and wounding twenty-one, before fleeing in a black SUV. Police eventually caught up with the SUV in a chase and shootout that left Farook and Malik dead and two officers wounded. Later, investigators found a failed explosive device that used the remote control from a car as the command detonator at the scene of the attack and, at the couple's home, twelve pipe bombs, ample material to construct bombs, and two thousand rounds of ammunition for a .223.

Neither Farook nor Malik were known to the FBI, but investigators are searching for potential links to international terrorist groups. The key to establishing these links will be found on the couple's technological devices. And according to initial searches, Farook does seem to have been in touch by phone and through social media with at least one international terrorism suspect on the FBI watch list. Moreover, the failed explosive device at the scene seems to be similar to one featured in the jihadist magazine Inspire.

As the FBI takes over the investigation and more details about Farook and Malik emerge, we will begin to get a better understanding of who the two were and what their seemingly mixed motives were for the attack. It will be particularly important to note whether Farook and Malik operated alone or whether they were part of a larger grassroots cell, which poses a much bigger threat from a law enforcement perspective.

In the meantime, discussions about the role of the authorities and the individual in ensuring safety will be prominent. When thinking about personal protection, it is important to remember that the brain is the most important weapons system—even for armed individuals. When people have the proper mindset, practice good situational awareness, and recognize a problem while it is still developing, they put themselves in a much better position to effectively deploy and employ their body, knife, gun or whatever secondary weapon they have access to. If the brain is not effectively and actively engaged, a person is left relying on luck, happenstance and the ineptitude of the criminals—these are not things prudent people should trust their lives to.

Moreover, as more details emerge on just what happened in San Bernardino the morning of December 2, it is important that individuals and policymakers keep a cool head. Terrorism is a fact of life and will continue to be so. This is because there is a wide variety of groups that practice it and seek to use violence as a means of influencing the behavior of a government—either their own or another. Terrorist attacks are also easy to conduct, especially if the assailant is not concerned about eluding capture. Finally, it is impossible to protect everything, so there are a large number of vulnerable targets in every country. This means that some terrorist attacks will invariably succeed.

The way in which people react to successful attacks—whether with a sober, measured response or with hysteria—defines whether an attack has been successful as an act of terrorist theater. Making sure that response is measured will help guard against costly and ineffective policy decisions.[20]

Along with its immigrant communities, the United States has imported numerous terrorist campaigns. Cuban, Puerto Rican, Croatian, Serbian, Palestinian, Armenian, Taiwanese, and Jewish extremists have all carried out attacks on U.S. soil, in addition to the homegrown terrorist campaigns of the far left and far right. In fact, the level of terrorist violence was greater in the United States in the 1970s than it is today. The lack of significant terrorist attacks on the United States since 9-11 suggests not only intelligence and investigative success but also an American Muslim community that remains overwhelmingly unsympathetic to jihadist appeals. However, radicalized Muslims do exist in the United States and we have covered several such examples in this chapter. Security threats from the border regions of the United States require some discussion. Canada has one of the longest "undefended" borders in the world running from the Pacific Ocean to the Atlantic and while the majority of the Canadian population resides roughly within hundred miles of the border with the United States, more recent concern in the United States is the threat from its southern border with Mexico. There are estimates that each year between four hundred thousand and one million undocumented migrants cross the border into the United States and these may not necessarily be Mexicans. U.S. Border Patrol estimates they apprehend one in four illegal border crossers. Even as early as 2000, the number of illegals gaining access who were other than Mexican jumped from twenty-eight thousand in 2000 to nearly sixty-nine thousand in 2004. An increasing threat is from radicalized Islamists wanting to enter the United States to set up terror cells and conduct operations, arriving from central and South American countries where they have learned to speak Spanish and to blend in with the masses that regularly cross the border. While drugs smuggling remains the focus along the border and numerous tunnels have been discovered along the two thousand-mile border; these are obvious locations to also smuggle people as well as drugs and weapons. Building a physical barrier may not necessary resolve the underlying issue of jihadists who are already present in the United States. Americans strongly affirm religious freedom and tolerance but there is a widespread discomfort with Islam and a reluctance to accept Muslims, based on perceptions about their views on Sharia Law and extremism primarily. In 2015 and 2016, the upsurge of migrants into Europe from the Middle East conflicts in Syria and Iraq coupled with the attacks centered on European capitals of France and Belgium is making the United States fearful not only of immigrants but Muslims in general. This is very much an unfounded fear as Muslims are spread throughout U.S. society and can be found in all walks of life—unlike Europe where integration has failed; high unemployment has marginalized an entire generation of Muslims, living in ghettos they become ripe for plucking by the radicals.

Summary

Terrorism is not a new phenomenon for the United States—it has been and continues to be at risk from jihadists either from planned or lone wolf style attacks—as this chapter relates, and can be traced back to the first attack on the New York World Trade Center (planned) and followed by the well-planned and executed 9-11 attacks. Other less sophisticated but nonetheless devastating were the attacks in Boston and Fort Hood by seemingly unlikely suspects. It is overly simple to suggest that U.S. foreign policy is somehow at fault or the cause of the problem. Al Qaeda under its leader was intent on a spectacular attack against the United States on U.S. soil and it took a further ten years to track down and kill the mastermind, Osama bin Laden. All terror groups undergo change and this is the case with al Qaeda, with its central leadership in disarray it has been usurped by Islamic State, a group that has declared a self-proclaimed caliphate in parts of Syria and Iraq. The United States

introduced the Patriot Act and Homeland Security to facilitate and reorganize its asset and intelligence sharing structure which has unearthed and prevented multiple attacks. Unfortunately, if only one attempt in a hundred gets through the damage can be substantial. Intel sharing and organization is still problematic and miss steps will often come down to human failings. The threat posed by Islamist jihadists has not diminished with the death of bin Laden but now comes from Islamic State which has eclipsed al Qaeda in its operations and sophistication. Islamic State, similarly, has aspirations for spectacular attacks against the United States and other Western states and uses the Internet to inspire its radical elements to mount attacks in the United States. The radicalization and use of immigrants through the radicalization process supported by a tranche of media from chat rooms, videos, and social media remains an unsolvable problem. The threat remains and we have seen from Fort Hood to Boston to San Bernardino, the opportunity to strike with lone wolf style attacks poses an intelligence nightmare in attempts to uncover these plots and prevent them coming to fruition. This chapter also discussed the historical roots of internal domestic terror groups and these will not be deterred so long as Muslims within the United States are perceived as a threat. Other extremist groupings look at the government with fear and loathing and that has spiked a revival of militia and survivalist groups.

Review Questions

1. Define the failings of the intelligence community that led to the events on 9-11.
2. What political and economic circumstances do you consider may give rise to the increased number of right-wing militias in the United States?
3. Evaluate the impact of social media in recruiting and enabling homegrown terrorists.
4. Analyze why homegrown terrorist or lone wolf attacks are so difficult to detect and prevent.
5. Demonstrate how the PATRIOT Act has helped close the intelligence gaps.
6. List the stages of radicalization.

End Notes

1. Rex A. Hudson. *The Sociology and Psychology of Terrorism*: *Who becomes a Terrorist and Why?* A report prepared under an Interagency Agreement by the Federal Research, Library of Congress (September 1999).
2. Department of Justice News Release. United States Attorney Southern District of New York (November 17, 2010).
3. Amir Lechner. "Home Grown Radicals." *Intersec, The Journal of International Security*, vol. 20, no. 5 (Chertsey, UK: Albany Media Ltd., May 2010, p. 13).
4. *The Movement*. http://www.pbs.org/independentlens/ weatherunderground/movement.html.
5. *Washington Post*. www.washingtonpost.com/wpdyn/content/ article/2005/09/28/AR.htm.
6. Sheikh Abdullah Azzam. *Defence of the Muslim Lands*. www. religioscope.com/info/doc/jihad/azzam_defence_1_table.htm.
7. Clark Staten. *Domestic Terrorism: The Enemy from Within*. www.emergency.com/domsterr.htm.
8. Steve Emerson. *Abdullah Assam: The Man before Osama bin Laden*. www.iacsp.com/itobli3.htm.
9. Executive Summary 9-11 Commission Report (July 22, 2004).
10. 9-11 Commission Report and Executive Summary of the 9-11 Commission Report (July 22, 2004).
11. Report #15 in a NEFA series. "Target America." *Bojinka II: The Transatlantic Bomb Plot* (April 2008). http://www.nefafoundation. org/newsite/file/FeaturedDocs/Bojinka2LiquidBombs.pdf.
12. Assaf Moghadam. "The Salafi–Jihad as a Religious Ideology." *CTC Sentinel*, vol. 1, no. 3 (February 2008, pp 14–16).
13. Homegrown Terror. http://www.washingtonpost.com/wp-dyn/ content/article/2010/06/06/AR2010060603996.
14. Kenneth M. Pollack. "Fight or Flight: America's Choice in the Middle East." *Foreign Affairs,* vol. 95, no. 2 (The Council on Foreign Relations, March/April 2016).
15. U.S. Government Accountability Office.
16. Association of the Bar of the City of New York and Center for Human Rights and Global Justice. *Torture by Proxy: International and Domestic Laws applicable to "Extraordinary Renditions"* (New York: ABCNY and NYU School of Law, 2004).
17. Michael Ratner. *War on Terror: The Guantanamo Prisoners, Military Commissions and Torture* (February 2005). www.ccr-ny.org/v2/viewpoints/viewpoint.asp.
18. The White House. www.whitehouse.gov/news/releases/2006/03/ 20060309–7html.
19. This is part of report of an unclassified summary of a 168-page classified report that was also issued, April 10, 2014, by the Inspectors General for the Intelligence Community, Central Intelligence Agency, Department of Justice, and Department of Homeland Security.
20. www.stratfor.com—This article was originally published by stratfor.com, a leading global intelligence and advisory firm based in Austin, Texas.

Canada and the Caribbean

LEARNING OUTCOMES

After studying this chapter, students should be able to:

1. List and explain the events that led to the destruction of Air India Flight 182.

2. Describe Canada's liberal attitude to immigration and how it has helped spread the threat of terrorism.

3. Summarize the events that were lone wolf attacks in Quebec and Ottawa.

4. Explain how terrorism has been exported from Canada.

5. Compare the lone wolf attacks in Canada with those discussed in Chapter 3 (United States of America).

6. Relate the means by which Papa Doc was able to control his country with statewide terror tactics.

KEY WORDS TO NOTE

Ahmed Ressam—Migrant caught crossing into the United States with bomb making equipment aimed at bombing Los Angeles International Airport—known as the Millennium Plot

Air India Flight 182—Flight originating in Vancouver was destroyed off the coast of Ireland by a bomb placed in a bag in the hold of the aircraft

Babbar Khalsa International (BKI)—A Sikh terrorist group sponsored by expatriate Indian Sikhs demanding an independent Sikh state called Khalistan (Land of the Pure) from Indian territory

Canadian Security and Intelligence Service (CSIS)—Investigates and reports on threats to Canada's national security

Multiculturalism—Official Canadian government policy since its introduction in the 1970s on the social importance of immigrants and their integration

Omar Khadr—A Canadian of Pakistani origin captured in Afghanistan and detained in Guantanamo; tried, convicted, and sentenced under U.S. Military Commissions Act 2009 after pleading guilty to killing U.S. serviceman Christopher Speer

Papa Doc—Francois Papa Doc Duvalier—notorious ruler of Haiti throughout the 1960s

Talwinder Singh Parmar—Considered part of the plot group that bombed Air India Flight 182 in 1985, killing over three hundred—also leader of the Babbar Khalsa terrorist organization. Killed by Indian police while in custody in 1992

Tonton Macoutes—Haitian Secret Police—used to spread fear and terror among the populace

OVERVIEW

Canada is associated with terrorist activity and has been a home base for terrorist organizations dating as far back as the 1980s. The country's first experience with terror was strictly a home-grown affair with the French separatist movement in Quebec in the 1970s, but a much more violent form of terrorism during the 1980s was a direct result of events taking place on the Indian subcontinent. This chapter looks at the Sikh terrorist movement that downed an Air India Boeing 747 aircraft off the coast of Ireland and Canada's inability at the time to recognize the threats being posed by external forces. After 9-11, there was considerable criticism from politicians in the United States concerning the porous border between the two countries. The Canadian government has always fostered a liberal approach to immigration policy in contrast to the United States. In a 2002 security report by Canadian Security and Intelligence Service, it was stated that there were more terrorist organizations active in Canada, with the possible exception of the United States, than anywhere else in the world. There were believed to be more than forty such organizations, although not directly involved with violence within Canada, that were involved in terror-related activities, including fund-raising; lobbying through front organizations; providing support for terrorist operations abroad; procuring weapons and material; intimidating and manipulating immigrant communities in Canada, such as Tamil/Sri Lankan migrants in Toronto and Somali migrants in Edmonton, Alberta; and, the obvious concern to the United States, the facilitating of access to the United States.

PUERTO RICO

Puerto Rico is closely aligned with the United States, and the island's inhabitants possess all the rights and obligations of U.S. citizens, except for the right to vote in U.S. presidential elections. The United States also governs the Virgin Islands, Guam, and American Samoa. Puerto Rico is slightly less than three times the size of Rhode Island (Figure 4-1). The Taino Indians, who inhabited the territory originally, called the island Boriken, or Borinquen (a word that, with various modifications, is still popularly used to designate the people and the island of Puerto Rico). The Taino Indians, who came from South America, inhabited a portion of the island when the Spaniards arrived. While the post-Colombian native language is Spanish, the status of official languages has been a central issue in Puerto Rican education and culture since 1898. Until 1930, U.S. authorities insisted on making English the primary language of instruction in the schools, the intent being to produce English-speaking persons of American culture. But strong resistance to the policy finally brought about a change to the use of Spanish as the basic school language, with English becoming a second language studied by all students. In 1991, the Puerto Rican legislature, following the lead of the pro-Commonwealth Popular Democratic Party and Governor Hernandez Colon, endorsed a bill that made Spanish the island's official language, thus reversing a 1902 law that gave Spanish and English official recognition. In 1993, pro-statehood Governor Pedro J. Rosello signed legislation restoring equal status to English and Spanish for a population of close to 3.9 million.

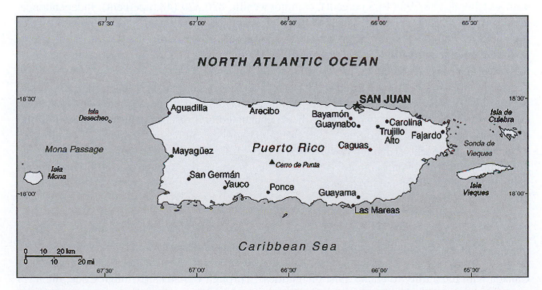

FIGURE 4-1 Map of Puerto Rico. *Source:* Central Intelligence Agency, *The World Factbook, 2008.*

It is estimated that some two million Puerto Ricans have migrated to the United States over the years and had they remained in Puerto Rico, the island would be so densely populated that there would be virtually no room for people to live. Because of massive migration to the United States, more Puerto Ricans are now said to live in New York City than in San Juan.

Besides slaves from Africa (Sudan, Congo, Senegal, Guinea, Sierra Leone, and the Gold, Ivory, and Grain coasts), other ethnic groups brought to work on the plantations joined the island's rich racial mix. Fleeing Simón Bolívar's independence movements in South America, Spanish loyalists fled to Puerto Rico, a fiercely conservative Spanish colony, during the early 1800s. French families flocked to Puerto Rico from both Louisiana and Haiti. As changing governments or violent revolutions depressed the economies of Scotland and Ireland, many farmers from those countries also journeyed to Puerto Rico in search of a better life.

While Puerto Ricans have had a fairly peaceful existence, they have seen some incidents that were considered terrorism in nature, or close to it. In January 1981, the most notable incident occurred when a quasi-terrorist group, the Macheteros, blew up eleven jet fighters of Puerto Rico's National Guard near San Juan. Ronald Fernandez, professor of sociology and author of *Los Macheteros: The Violent Struggle for Puerto Rican Independence*, has spent many years researching Puerto Rico. He writes of the Macheteros' frustrations and susceptibility to lashing out:

> On August 25, 1989, Filiberto Ojeda Rios, acting as his own attorney, gave his closing argument to the jury in a U.S. court in San Juan. The indictment, drawn in the name of the United States of America, charged that Ojeda Rios had shot at and assaulted agents of the Federal Bureau of Investigation. President Reagan had appointed the prosecutor, and President Carter, the American flag standing in the courtroom, had appointed the judge, but the jury was all Puerto Rican.
>
> Far from denying his actions, Ojeda Rios embraced them, and asked the jury to uphold the right of the Puerto Rican people to use force in self-defense against the unwanted, foreign presence of the United States. There are no American heroes (in this story), nor is there a happy ending. Yet, it is imperative for Americans to know our own contribution to the perpetuation of colonialism. When the sun rose on October 12, 1992, marking five hundred years of colonialism, Americans would have done well to take a look at Puerto Rico and the destruction wrought there in the name of "democracy."
>
> The island today has a per-capita income less than one-half that of Mississippi, the poorest state in the United States. Its rates of suicide, mental illness, drug addiction, crime, alcoholism, and sterilization of women are among the highest in the world.[1]

The hotly contested issue of the eventual status of Puerto Rico continues. In 1991, in an islandwide vote, Puerto Ricans rejected an amendment that would have "reviewed" their commonwealth status. In the referendum, commonwealth status was reaffirmed by a very close vote, with statehood, 788,296 (46.3 percent); commonwealth, 826,326 (48.6 percent); independence, 75,620 (04.4 percent); and nulls, 10,748 (00.7 percent). This issue has caused tempers to flare up, but those in opposition fall short of forming newer terrorist groups.

We have seen that the United States still seems to be "the land of the free and the home of the brave." But its very freedom, in a world of terrorism, can be an "Achilles' heel." As the world economic situation continues to destabilize and the American economy has gone into steady decline, the gap between those who can get ahead (haves) and those who cannot (have-nots) continues to widen. As that gap widens, the disenchanted and disenfranchised of both left and right movements in the United States, and around the globe, will become a more active threat to its peace and tranquility. Chapter 15 will discuss U.S. efforts to provide coordinated and effective homeland security to a nation that has felt too secure and, for too long, protected by two oceans had no fears of international terrorism.

CANADA

In November 2002, Osama bin Laden listed Canada as a state to be attacked by his followers. Bill C-36 of Canada's Anti-Terrorism Act and its amended version C-51 provides the Government of Canada with the ability to create a list of "entities." Through Canada's Criminal Code, the term *entity* is defined as a person or group, trust, partnership, or fund, or an unincorporated association or organization. The government can therefore list an entity as a terrorist organization if it satisfies the following legal test that there are reasonable grounds to believe the entity

- has knowingly carried out;
- has attempted to carry out;
- has participated in, or facilitated, a terrorist activity; or
- is knowingly acting on behalf of, at the direction of, or in
- association with an entity that has knowingly carried out, attempted to carry out, participated in, or facilitated a terrorist activity.[2]

Canada has a Criminal Code and defined terrorism within that Code to be "terrorist activity to include an act or omission undertaken either in or outside Canada for a political, religious or ideological purpose, that is intended to intimidate the public with respect to its security, including economic security, or to compel a person, government or organizations to do or refrain from doing any act, and that intentionally causes one of a number of specific forms of serious harm."

Canada shares with the United States one of the longest "undefended borders" in the world, but that may not be the case any longer (Figure 4-2). After the United States declared War on Terror in 2001, it realized that its northernmost neighbor could pose a threat to U.S. national security—from terrorist groups within Canada. The United Nations Human Development Agency heralds Canada as one of the best countries in which to live. That said, the country has become a haven for terror groups actively campaigning and fund-raising for terrorism around the globe. Historically, they have not acted against their host. The undefined border between Canada and the United States no longer exists, and since 9-11, the United States no longer believes the border with Canada can continue to remain undefended. After the attacks, U.S. National Guardsmen were rushed to the border, and the number of border control officers along the 4,000-mile border has more than tripled.[3]

Juliet O'Neill, of the *Ottawa Citizen*, said in 1996, "You're more likely to be struck down by lightning or die in a car crash than find yourself victim of a terrorist attack in Canada."[4] Although that remark might have seemed appropriate at the time that is certainly not the case over twenty years later. Canada remains a target for terrorist attacks even if that premise is based solely on a decade-old edict from Osama bin Laden. The Front de Liberation du Quebec (**FLQ**) crisis in 1970 was the first time that Canada came face-to-face with terrorist violence. Then, the mid-1980s Armenian attacks on Turkish diplomats in Ottawa occurred followed by Sikh extremists in western Canada involved in the bombing of an Air India jet that blew up over the coast of Ireland, killing three hundred and twenty-nine passengers, mostly Canadians. This incident occurred in June 1985 on the same day as an explosion in the baggage collection hall at Tokyo airport from a bag arriving on a Canadian Pacific airliner from Vancouver.

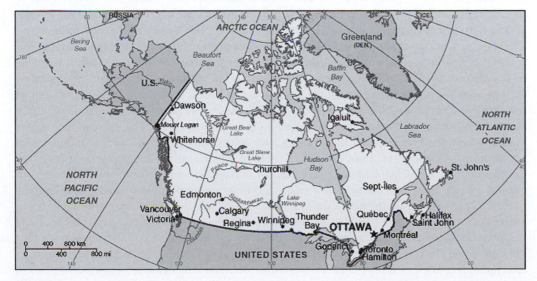

FIGURE 4-2 Map of Canada. *Source:* Central Intelligence Agency, *The World Factbook, 2008.*

Canada is a nation founded on immigration, and tolerance as well, and, as such, admits more than three hundred thousand immigrants plus twenty-five thousand asylum seekers a year. With the Syrian and Iraq refugee crisis in Europe, Canada has taken in over twenty-five thousand refugees since December 2015 and this in certain circles is viewed as a possible threat to national security. Given the liberal attitude to immigration policy, time will tell whether any of the incoming refugees are actually involved in supporting terrorist organizations. However, most of the incoming Syrians had arrived from camps in Lebanon where they had resided for many months before being vetted for entry.

A concern is that Canada is being used as a base for organizing, fund-raising, consciousness-raising, transport, and logistics for international terrorists from among the many refugees as well as honest immigrants there. These groups have ranged from the Tamil Tigers and Islamic extremists to Protestant and Irish Catholic paramilitaries in the 1980s and 1990s and even Latin American, African, and Asian extremists are present. Canada stays on the alert for homegrown terrorism from a list that is referred to as "issue group extremists." Examples of these are animal rights extremists, armed Indians, antiabortion radicals, neo-Fascists, bikers, and skinheads.

IMMIGRATION AND CANADA

The opportunity for terrorists to sneak into the country under the guise of refugees has distinct concerns for **Canadian Security and Intelligence Service (CSIS)**. A report issued by CSIS in 2002 stated, ". . . there were more international terrorist organizations active in Canada than anywhere in the world. This can be attributed to Canada's proximity to the United States . . . and to the fact that Canada is a country built upon immigration, represents a microcosm of the world . . . terrorist groups are present here whose origins lie in regional, ethnic, and nationalist conflicts, including the Israeli-Palestinian one as well as those in Egypt, Algeria, Sudan, Afghanistan, Lebanon, Northern Ireland, the Punjab, Sri Lanka, Turkey, and the former Yugoslavia."

Among tactics used by low-level terrorist groups in recent years are consumer-scare threats, mail bombs, shootings, and vandalism. Canada has major problems with illicit production of cannabis for the domestic and U.S. drug market. Use of hydroponics technology permits growers to plant large quantities of high-quality marijuana indoors. With its links to the Far East and a long coastline, Canada has a continuing and growing role as a transit point for heroin and cocaine entering the U.S. market. There are many connections between organized crime and terrorism—while high-quality Canadian hash travels south to the vibrant California markets, the return route brings weapons and cocaine, and thus links to terrorism. The trade in illegal drugs between Canada and the United States is significant, and the terrorist group that may be involved in this trade would likely be the Tamil Tigers with bases of operation in Toronto and Montreal; however, the trafficking of people, which gets little news coverage, is of more concern to Homeland Security in the United States. Canada's liberal attitude to immigration sets the stage for a two-tier system of legality and illegality. Few of the people who traveled here through the conventional system should be regarded with suspicion (although this system is in desperate need of reforms), while the refugee system is subjected to considerable and unending abuse. Canada's immigration and refugee system needs a radical overhauling, and the Canadian government appears to recognize that, but few changes have been made to make it happen. Evidence of frontline corruption has been evidenced in Hong Kong and Eastern Bloc countries where Canadian authorities have "failed" to properly verify the backgrounds of immigrant applicants. As the past is always so often an indicator of what may happen in the future, we need only look at the threats posed from the failure to check student visas and the abuse that they are subject to in the United States. The abuse of the refugee system is one that Canada is currently living with, and yet seems ill prepared to combat with any degree of diligence. During the 1980s, a surge in illegal immigrant activity from India, Sri Lanka, Vietnam, and Cambodia saw the Canadian immigration and refugee system under continuous assault. False and counterfeit documentation is a central process in people-smuggling operations. Groups of up to twenty travel through major international airports, possibly being escorted. After they have managed to successfully get by the airline's cursory passport check, the passports or immigration documents are returned to the escort during flight for reuse on the next mission, or are flushed down the aircraft toilets; on arrival in Canada, the undocumented traveler then presents himself or herself to be a refugee claimant. Your authors spent a number of years in the United Kingdom intercepting a large number of these illegal immigrants/refugees during the

1980s, the majority originating from Sri Lanka, Afghanistan, Saudi Arabia, Somalia, Algeria, and Sudan. A number of terrorists have been caught entering Canada with false passports—Mokhtar Haouari and **Ahmed Ressam** both did that in February 1994 (Ressam had arrived in France with a fake Moroccan passport in the name of Nasser Ressam in 1993 and arrived in Montreal with an altered French passport in the name of Tahar Mejadi). Mohamed Zeki Mahjoub, a Toronto-area convenience store clerk, who is also suspected of being a major "fixer" for Islamic jihad, came to Canada with a doctored passport. Aynur Saygili, a PKK member, who came to Canada to take over a Kurdish cultural organization, also had a doctored passport when entering Canada.

Terrorists Returning?

As of early 2014, the Government knew of more than one hundred and thirty individuals with Canadian connections who were abroad and who were suspected of supporting terrorism-related activities.

Canada is aware of about 80 individuals who have returned to Canada after travel abroad for a variety of suspected terrorism-related purposes. Those purposes varied widely. Some may have engaged in paramilitary activities. Others may have studied in extremist schools, raised money or otherwise supported terrorist groups. Some had their travel interrupted by financial issues, injuries, or outside intervention and may plan to travel again. Some extremist travelers never achieved their goals and simply returned to Canada. Canada has created legislation in its attempt to combat this issue:

The Combating Terrorism Act came into force in July 2013 creating four new offences to prevent and deter persons from leaving Canada for terrorism-related purposes. An individual commits an offence by leaving or attempting to leave Canada for the purpose of:

- knowingly participating in or contributing to any activity of a terrorist group for the purpose of enhancing the ability of any terrorist group to commit a terrorist activity. This includes providing training, receiving training, or recruiting a person to receive training;
- knowingly facilitating a terrorist activity;
- committing an indictable offence on behalf of, at the direction of or in association with a terrorist group;
- committing an indictable offence that constitutes a terrorist activity.

Babbar Khalsa International (BKI) member Iqbal Singh arrived in Canada in 1991 as an undocumented refugee (after hopping through several countries with false documentation).[5] He was subsequently removed from Canada in 2000. Another notable refugee was Ahmed Ressam who came into Canada in 1994—he was of Algerian descent and arrived in Montreal on a crudely doctored false passport. He was allowed to remain in Canada following his claim for political asylum as he claimed that he was accused of weapons offenses and that he would be tortured if returned to Algeria. He failed to attend his subsequent refugee hearing and an arrest warrant was issued. Ressam was able to change his name using a stolen baptismal certificate and created his new identity as Benni Antoine Noris; this allowed him to apply for a Canadian passport. Ressam lived for some time in a Montreal apartment with links to the Algeria's Armed Islamic Group (GIA)—Algeria's Armed Islamic Group. In 1996, following the groups involved in hijacking of an Air France aircraft to Marseilles—the follow-up raid on the group in Roubaix uncovered details of an address and phone number in Montreal, the apartment occupied by Ressam. CSIS were alerted and actively seeking Ressam—he subsequently left Canada for training in Afghanistan in 1998 returning the following year. Returning to Canada as Benni Noris did not bring him to the attention of CSIS or the Canadian Immigration Service. He hatched his plan for an attack on Los Angeles International Airport (LAX) using a suitcase bomb—he had conducted surveillance of the airport on his return from Afghanistan. In November 1999, he moved to Vancouver and set up a bomb making factory in an east side Vancouver motel. On December 14, he took the BC Ferry Service to Vancouver Island and then to Port Angeles, in Washington State—he had hidden a large quantity of explosives in the trunk of the vehicle he was driving which he was planning to take to LAX. In Port Angeles, he aroused the suspicions of the U.S. Customs and was subsequently arrested when the suspicious substance was discovered. Ressam became known as the Millennium Bomber and was initially sentenced to over twenty years in prison in April 2001, but was resentenced in 2012 to thirty-seven years.

CANADA'S DOMESTIC TERRORISM

Front de Liberation du Quebec

Liberal and extreme-thinking young Quebecers were eager for change and to establish a separate, French-speaking sovereign state within Canada. Terrorism in such a liberal country as Canada has been rare, but the turbulent days of the radical 1960s saw terrorism come to Central Canada in the shape of a separatist movement, the Front de Liberation du Quebec (FLQ). From early in 1963, its goal was the separation of Quebec from the rest of English-speaking Canada. Canada is part of the British Commonwealth, and in the 1960s, French-speaking Quebec wanted separation to create its own sovereign state within Canada. A somewhat muted debate on separation and sovereignty continues to this day. The left-wing FLQ espoused a workers' revolution as a means of achieving its goal of separation. They along with many French-speaking Canadians strongly resented the control that English Canada exerted on both politics and the economy in Quebec. The Parti Quebecois, still a political party today, has actively pursued an agenda of separation.

The political boost that the FLQ needed came from an unexpected direction. On a visit to Montreal in 1967, the French President General Charles De Gaulle, in what has become a famous speech, ended with the phrase, "Vive le Quebec Libre" (Long live free Quebec). Throughout the 1960s, the FLQ targeted Anglophile areas of Montreal for bomb attacks.[6]

More than two hundred explosions took place between 1963 and 1970, with both Federal and Provincial governments seemingly powerless to intervene. They used robberies in the traditional fashion for financing their operations and also as a reason to hit any Anglophile businesses. The major terrorist event that spelled the end for the FLQ was the kidnapping of the British trade commissioner James Cross and the Province's labor minister Pierre Laporte. The kidnapping produced little value to the FLQ but gave the prime minister, Pierre Trudeau, the reason he needed to use a firmer hand against all subversive elements, not only in Quebec but also throughout the rest of Canada. The two were kidnapped in October 1970 and the dead body of Laporte was found days later in the trunk of a car. Canadians were appalled that the FLQ would go to such drastic lengths, and Laporte's brutal murder turned public and political opinion sharply against them. James Cross was located in a suburb of Montreal by the Royal Canadian Mounted Police (RCMP). After protracted negotiations, the kidnappers were allowed to fly to Cuba in exchange for the release of James Cross. They had also demanded the release of colleagues serving prison sentences for FLQ offenses, but these demands were never met. One of the founder members of the FLQ, Raymond Villeneuve, was convicted of planting a number of bombs and was sentenced to twelve years in prison. A national referendum in October 1995 saw a narrow defeat for the separation movement; however, by then, Villeneuve had been released from prison and was again assisting with a new, younger breed of Quebec separatists, also hell-bent on tearing up the Canadian Constitution. The Mouvement de Liberation Nationale du Quebec is deemed extremely small with only a couple of dozen die-hard activists and consists of some former militant members of the defunct FLQ.[7] This terrorist movement, the only one of note in normally reserved and peaceful Canada, has shown that this country is not immune to such social violence.

INTERNATIONAL TERRORISM—SIKH TERRORISM

Canada has had an official multicultural policy since 1971, which in so many regions has had the negative effect of ghettoizing non-English-speaking communities in the major Canadian cities of Montreal, Toronto, and Vancouver. Canada has been home to numerous generations of hardworking Sikh immigrants for most of the twentieth century, but it was political events and actions of Indian Prime Minister Indira Gandhi that were to have a profound effect on Sikhs and Canadian security services. Gandhi had been convicted of corruption in 1975, but had steadfastly refused to resign. Following more than a year of emergency rule, Gandhi was defeated in the country's next General Election. By using dirty politics to aid her return to politics, Gandhi needed to target the alliance between the party that represented Sikh interests and the Hindu party in the Punjab region. Akali Dal (AD), which represented those Sikh interests, had to be seriously undermined by Gandhi's political machine. Financing of all Sikh temples in India was controlled by the Shiromani Gurdwara Prabandhak Committee (SGPC), an organization that was also backing the AD party. The temples were fabulously wealthy, and influential, and having control and influence with the temples meant power. Gandhi and her political party determined to undermine the AD by supporting and promoting a more radical Sikh movement. The intent of Gandhi's Congress Party was to show AD simply as soft supporters of Sikh ideals. The man targeted to lead the political embarrassment of AD was the now infamous Jarnail Singh Bhindranwale, at the time a relatively unknown but nonetheless a popular religious leader. The Congress Party helped promote a new Punjab-based Sikh party, the Dal Khalsa (Party of the Pure), for Bhindranwale. The Congress Party was also aware that Bhindranwale was a powerful advocate for an independent Sikh homeland and was not immune from using violence to achieve his goals. Bhindranwale quickly established his religious standing and manipulated the various Sikh teachings to his own ends, and through this evolved a dedicated armed following of his ideals. By the start of the 1980s, the Dal Khalsa movement was implicated in several murders of religious opponents, and it was now clear to most political observers that Indira Gandhi and the Congress Party had lost what little control they thought they may have exercised over Bhindranwale and his Dal Khalsa movement. Dal Khalsa had begun to establish training camps at some of the Sikh temples and formed an alliance with the All India Sikh Students Federation, which had a violent history in its own struggle to determine a separate Sikh state.

Numerous failed attempts by the Indian government's intelligence service to infiltrate Dal Khalsa accounted for the deaths of more than one hundred operatives from the security services. Subsequently, the central government took control of the state of Punjab, and in retaliation, the Dal Khalsa movement took control of the Golden Temple, with several hundred of its armed militants. The Sikhs hold the Golden Temple as their holiest of temples and central to the religion. Indian security police surrounded the temple in an operation named Operation Blue Star in June 1984 and demanded that Bhindranwale surrender. He refused and was killed during the fierce assault that followed. The number of those killed in the assault included many innocent pilgrims, and although the death toll has never been confirmed, it is believed to have run to several thousand. Bhindranwale's Dal Khalsa movement had attracted global support in Sikh communities that were in favor of an independent Sikh homeland and none more so than Dal Khalsa members in British Columbia. The assault on the Golden Temple in Amritsar gave the Sikh radical element all the legitimacy they required. The temple storming gave rise to Sikh extremism in Canada and many street protests in Vancouver; Canada's Pacific coast turned violent. Moderate Sikhs within the Sikh community were attacked and beaten, and although demonstrations were observed by the police, they failed to take any actions or sanctions, and the beatings went unprosecuted. On October 31, 1984, two of Indira Gandhi's Sikh bodyguards attacked and killed her, blaming her for the desecration of the Golden Temple. Rioting ensued throughout India, and many Sikhs fled to the safer Punjab area. In Western Canada, among the BKI movement, there was elation. However, the Sikh extremists were planning another attack against the Indian government.

Babbar Khalsa

The Babbar Khalsa (BK) was founded in India in 1978. Originally, its founder, Sukhdev Singh Dasuwal, was a follower of Bhindranwale, but he broke away to form his own group and later tried to kill Bhindranwale. Within several years, branches of the BK were established in a number of Western countries, being most active in Canada and Britain. Outside India, they operate as the BKI. The BK was present at the Golden Temple in June 1984 with Bhindranwale and his armed followers. A number of Babbars left only days before the assault on the holy complex, putting intergroup rivalries above the defense of the temple.

Philosophically, the Babbars concentrated on changing or, more accurately, controlling the lifestyles of individual Sikhs and were never hesitant about using violence and murder as a way of enforcing a strict fundamentalist code of discipline. So strict are they in the interpretation of Sikh doctrine and practices that observers have often noted their similarity to a religious cult. By the early 1990s, the Canadian-based Talwinder Singh Parmar had broken away from the BKI and formed the Azad Babbar Khalsa ("Independent Babbar Khalsa").[8]

Sikh extremists were to become a major concern to CSIS. The Air India bombing, which claimed more than 300 lives, was the single-largest loss of life to aircraft terrorism prior to the attacks on September 11, 2001. Of those who were killed, one hundred and fifty-four were Canadians.

Sikh extremism was not new to Canada, and CSIS was actively watching the various Sikh extremists, particularly in Toronto and Vancouver. Sukhdev Singh Babbar and Talwinder Singh Parmar founded BKI. The first cell or unit of BKI, led by Talwinder Parmar, was discovered in Canada in 1981. BKI has branches in not only Canada but also the United States, France, Germany, Switzerland, and Pakistan. The group's objective is for an independent Sikh state that would be named Khalistan. Parmar was a prime suspect in the Air India bombing, and his associate, Inderjit Singh Reyat, the bomb maker, indicated under interrogation that he had been making a bomb for Parmar for an attack in India. Parmar's rise to significance came after he returned from a trip to India in May 1982. The Indian government requested his extradition for the murder of two police officers in Punjab in November 1981. Parmar remained out of Indian custody, but was detained in Europe in May 1984 just as Operation Blue Star was being mounted by government troops against the Golden Temple in Amritsar. Followers of Sikh separatist Jarnail Singh Bhindranwale had occupied the temple, and when negotiations between police and the separatists failed, Prime Minister Indira Gandhi ordered troops to clear the temple. The resulting loss of life accounted for eighty-three soldiers and four hundred and ninety Bhindranwale followers. Indira Gandhi was to die soon after at the hands of her Sikh bodyguards. Almost as if it were a war cry, the attack on the Golden Temple generated significant support across Canada for the Sikh separatist movement, and demonstrations were coordinated from Montreal to Vancouver.

Speaking Out Against Sikh Terrorism

Apart from some very diligent members of the local press, some influential Sikhs have stood up to the extremist Sikh movements in Western Canada—unfortunately, the fight has been taken straight to them with devastating consequences. Tara Singh Hayer, Order of British Columbia (OBC), was one such Vancouver businessman who was outspoken against the extremist movement. As a symbol of the struggle for human rights, peace, and freedom of expression, Mr. Hayer paid an enormous personal price for his beliefs. Aware that discrimination thrives on ignorance, Mr. Hayer worked tirelessly to promote understanding between ethnic and cultural groups.

After immigrating to Canada in 1970, he worked as a miner, teacher, truck driver, and a manager of a trucking firm before becoming a full-time journalist. In 1978, he established the community newspaper *The Indo-Canadian Times* and has built it into the leading Punjabi language newspaper in North America.

In August 1988, he survived an attempt on his life, which left him in a wheelchair. Despite this attack, Mr. Hayer has never wavered in his commitment to tolerance, peace, and understanding between cultural communities.

In 1992, he was honored with the Commemorative Medal for the 125th anniversary of Canada and a Certificate of Appreciation from the RCMP among his other awards, Mr. Hayer received the Journalist Award from the Municipality of Surrey, a city just south of Vancouver, for courageous and outstanding contribution to Punjabi journalism in Canada. He also received the International Award of Distinction for Journalism from the International Association of Punjabi Authors and Artists.

Tara Singh Hayer continued, even when faced with violence, to be a voice of moderation and reason.

In the early and mid-1980s, Hayer was affected by the "nationalist fervor" of Sikhs. The aftermath of Operation Blue Star at the Golden Temple in Amritsar made an indignant Hayer a Khalistan supporter. But his mental makeup and liberal mind-set did not allow him to remain a Khalistan supporter for long. He was revolted by the violence and mayhem associated with the movement. He returned to the path of moderation. The 1985 explosion on an Air India plane drew fearless criticism from Hayer. Thereafter, Hayer remained estranged from the Sikh extremists and their supporters in Canada. Tara Hayer was shot to death as he got out of his vehicle and into his wheelchair at his home in Surrey, British Columbia, on November 18, 1998.[9]

Talwinder Singh Parmar

News reports showed Parmar inciting crowds in Vancouver with his rhetoric and threats of death to Rajiv Gandhi. By 1985, reports and intelligence from CSIS indicated that a Sikh backlash for the Amritsar attacks was probable but could not specifically identify a target. What was to become the target was the Boeing 747, **Air India Flight 182** from Montreal to London, which had originated in Vancouver. Parmar returned to India in 1988 and was subsequently shot by Indian police in 1992. After the Air India bombing, Parmar was the prime suspect in the downing of Air India Flight 182 as revenge for the Golden Temple attack by the Indian government.[10]

In November 2007, a prominent Liberal politician, Ujjal Dosanjh, called for tougher laws to combat the rise of extremism in Canada. Dosanjh, a former attorney general and premier of British Columbia, had himself been the victim of Sikh extremism before and after the Air India bombing. Moderate Sikhs residing in British Columbia endured death threats, physical attacks, and fire bombings from the extreme Sikh movement throughout the 1980s and 1990s. The resulting climate of fear and intimidation was not taken seriously enough by the police or politicians, which paved the way for the Air India bombing. Dosanjh believes that if the authorities had taken action, more witnesses would likely have come forward with more information.[11]

In March 1984, the Indian government appealed for the extradition of **Talwinder Singh Parmar** from Canada. The request was refused on the technicality that Canada could not extradite fugitives to a country that did not recognize the Queen as its head of state. In November 1985, the RCMP conducted a raid on the homes of suspected Sikh radicals, Talwinder Singh Parmar, Inderjit Singh Reyat, Surjan Singh Gill, Hardial Singh Johal, and Manmohan Singh. Following the sweep, Parmar and Reyat were arrested on weapons, explosives, and conspiracy offences. The charges against Parmar were dropped owing to lack of evidence. Reyat paid a fine for the weapons' offences, but investigators initially failed to link him to the Air India bombing. Reyat then moved to Coventry, England.[12]

THE BOMBING OF AIR INDIA FLIGHT 182

Two Canadian Sikhs—Ripudaman Singh Malik, a fifty-seven-year-old millionaire businessman, and Ajab Singh Bagri, a Sikh preacher and sawmill worker from the British Columbia interior—were charged with eight counts, including conspiracy to murder, for the downing of Air India. The third conspirator and confidant to Talwinder Parmar was Inderjit Singh Reyat, who pleaded guilty in 2003 to manslaughter for supplying the bomb-making materials that destroyed the Air India flight. The court sentenced Reyat to a term of five years in prison following his plea bargain. The Air India investigation and trial has lasted over twenty years. On March 16, 2005, both men were found not guilty on all eight counts in British Columbia Supreme Court and, as a result, were set free. The verdict stunned the British Columbia Sikh community and divided it as well. This was considered the worst act of terrorism in Canadian history: three hundred and thirty-one people were killed in two decisive and deliberate explosions—one in a Japanese airport, another aboard Air India Flight 182. When Air India was downed, Canada relied on the newly created CSIS for its intelligence gathering, and in the twenty-plus years since then, the Canadian Security Intelligence Service has been at the forefront of this investigation along with the RCMP. There have been claims of interference and total mismanagement of the entire case, and for over twenty years, Canadians have grappled with this unsolved crime for which no one has yet been brought to justice (Figure 4-3).

TERRORIST ATTACK BRIEF

Terrorist Group: Sikh Extremists (Khalistan)

Case Facts: A suitcase containing an explosive device was loaded onto an Air India flight—the passenger was not on board the aircraft. The bomb detonated at around 0700 off the southern coast of Ireland. The flight data recorder and voice recorder were subsequently recovered from the ocean bed.

Investigation: The bombing of Air India Flight 182 on June 23, 1985, represents the worst terrorist attack in Canadian history. The attack planned and executed in Canada by Sikh extremists claimed the lives of 329 innocent people—280 of them Canadian. In the immediate aftermath of the bombing, and in the years that followed, the largest, most complex and expensive investigation in Canadian history failed to bring those responsible for the bombing to justice. Subsequent reviews also failed to provide answers to the families of the victims on how this tragedy could have been prevented.

FIGURE 4-3 Bombing of Air India Flight 182—June 23, 1985. *Source:* The Government of Canada Response to the Commission of Inquiry into the investigation of the bombing of Air India Flight 182. publicsafety.gc.ca.

Only one person has so far been sentenced for involvement in this bombing. What went wrong? How did these two men manage to be found not guilty? In his six hundred pages of judgment, presiding judge Justice Ian Josephson, pointed to evidence that was "markedly short" of reasonable doubt. Much of the evidence presented against Malik and Bagri came down to evidence provided by unreliable and often unbelievable witnesses supplying hearsay evidence. There was also condemnation for the actions of CSIS, who had the main suspects under surveillance when they were testing the explosives. CSIS subsequently destroyed surveillance tape evidence. Judge Josephson singled this out as "unacceptable negligence." In addition to the problems of lack of physical evidence, the prosecution called Reyat as one of its star witnesses. The judge found him to have "patently and pathetically fabricated" his testimony. At the end of twenty years, Canada, unfortunately, has little to show for this investigation. The immediate effect of the 1985 disaster was the introduction of the requirement to match passengers with their bags. Of course, where a human element is involved, there is always room for error. The terror scenario played out again in the 1980s with the bombing of a Pan Am 747 over Lockerbie, Scotland, by agents of Colonel Qaddafi's Libyan regime.

LIBERALISM AND REFUGEES

How Canada accommodates its refugee problems is well documented, and many take extreme advantage of the liberal program that allows convicted terrorists to remain within this safe haven. One example of abuse of the refugee system is the case of Mahmoud Mohammad, who immigrated to Canada in 1987 with his family from Lebanon. Mohammad is a former member of the Popular Front for the Liberation of Palestine (PFLP) who, in 1968, attacked an El Al aircraft on the tarmac at Athens International Airport. Mohammad and an accomplice fired more than eighty rounds and threw six hand grenades at the aircraft, killing one passenger in the attack. He was sentenced to eighteen years in jail but released after only two years when Palestinian terrorists hijacked a Greek airliner and demanded his release. Since then, Mohammad has resided in southern Ontario, having lied on his immigration application. The Canadian Immigration Service finally deported him to Lebanon in 2013, some twenty-six years after his illegal entry to Canada. His lawyers argued that he should not be deported owing to his poor health.

The story of Mahmoud Mohammad is a classic example of why Canada is often seen as a liberal haven for organizations looking to raise funds without government interruption. Canada is one of the few Western governments that did not recognize and list the Tamil Tigers from Sri Lanka as a terrorist organization until a change in government in 2006 saw as one of its first acts a Conservative government listing the Tigers as a "terrorist organization." Thousands of Sri Lankan refugees and immigrants have come to Canada over the last few decades. As we noted earlier, Canada tends not to incarcerate refugees but rather allows them into society until their status hearings take place. In many instances, this can take several years and often results in an amnesty and the granting of landed immigrant status. With Canada's vast numbers of illegal/refugee entrants/claimants, it is virtually impossible to check backgrounds to find out how bona fide the claims really are.

The Liberation Tigers of Tamil Eelam (LTTE) is a violent separatist organization that had been fighting in Sri Lanka for nearly four decades until the death of their leader Velupillai Prabhakaran and subsequent defeat by the Sri Lankan military in May 2009. The government of Sri Lanka believes that of all funds raised by the LTTE annually (Canadian $120 million), twenty-five percent originated through funding from front organizations, proceeds of crime, and drug activity, as well as from Tamil residents located in Canada. The LTTE has been associated with trafficking people into Canada on forged travel documents for more than two decades. The influx into Canada has meant that a huge Tamil community has built up, allowing LTTE to levy war taxes on Tamils. On arrival in Canada, many Tamils find that much of their community life is controlled by LTTE front organizations. In Canada, the term **multiculturalism** is used to define almost anything that is not white and Anglo Saxon to such an extent that the government has unwittingly funded many of the Tamil Tiger front organizations involved in immigrant settlement services, as well as Tamil media and housing. From a fund-raising perspective, Canada must be viewed as a choice destination because any opposition voiced publicly is invariably met with claims of racism and intolerance. In 2000, two Liberal Cabinet members, including the finance minister and former Liberal Prime Minister Paul Martin, attended a fund-raising event for a group identified as a front for the Tamil Tigers. When opposition members questioned the pair about the event in Parliament, the Liberal response was to smear the questioners as racists.[13]

THE ISLAMIST THREAT TO CANADA AND LONE WOLF ATTACKS

The Toronto 18—this is the name given to a large group of immigrants that were either born in Canada or migrated there as children with their families and were responsible for plotting a series of attacks against train stations and other public facilities, storming the Parliament Buildings and taking hostages, and intending to behead the Prime Minister. Their case came to court in 2007, in Ontario. The group was infiltrated by undercover police in 2005 and from then was constantly monitored. Their activities included setting up a training camp in the Ontario countryside where they learned how to fire weapons. The group was preparing to attack specific targets in Southern Ontario, including CSIS Headquarters and the Canadian Broadcasting Center. As the planning phase moved along the group were looking to acquire ammonium nitrate, the same material used in the 1995 bomb attack in Oklahoma City by Timothy McVeigh. The group wanted to acquire around six thousand pounds of this material which was made harmless through the "sting" operation. The Toronto eighteen is another example of youth involvement in radicalization—four of the eighteen were below the age of eighteen and the remainder not much more than teenagers. Members of the group were charged with knowingly participating in a terrorist group—nearly all pleaded guilty to the charges. Radicalization in this case was due to the influence of chat rooms and the internet played a major role—the group had watched videos from Anwar al-Awlaki (see Chapter 3) which inspired them to jihad.

Project Souvenir—Amanda Korody and John Nuttall—Homegrown Terror Plot

Canada's RCMP successfully disrupted a bombing of the Provincial Legislature Building in Victoria, BC on Canada Day July 1, 2013, coming just two months after the Boston marathon bombings. Amanda Korody and John Nuttall, who both lived in British Columbia in a suburb of Vancouver had plotted to detonate pressure cooker type devices on the outside of the building—their intent was to cause mass casualties as crowds gathered for the traditional Canada Day celebrations. The homemade bombs were packed with nails and bolts to cause widespread injury. The two had branded themselves as "al Qaeda Canada" and their goal was to convince Canadians to stop sending troops to Muslim countries.

The two Canadians were recent converts to Islam and had been radicalized over the internet. They came to the attention of the Canadian Security Intelligence Service in February of 2013 as a result of a tip-off. The Federal Police (RCMP) mounted an undercover "sting" operation to track and monitor their actions. They were successful and rendered the devices inert prior to them being deployed. There has been no evidence to suggest that these two had a wider organization that they belonged to or that they were being supported by funds from external sources. Their trial concluded in June 2015 when both were convicted of conspiracy to murder. The follow on from this has been an appeal that the RCMP exceeded their powers and acted inappropriately in the undercover sting operation bringing into question the whole legality of this operation and the case. The case is before a judge, in camera mostly, as the Intelligence Service provides documents to the judge hearing the appeal that the RCMP acted in aiding and abetting the activities of Korody and Nuttall and that they were effectively entrapped. In July 2016, the Supreme Court of British Columbia overturned the convictions of both Korody and Nuttall as the court determined that they had been entrapped by the RCMP. In this case, the judge believed that the RCMP had gone to extraordinary lengths to assist the couple in planning, funding, and going to such lengths that the couple had been propelled into the bomb plot. The mental capacity of both suspects also comes into play here; were they ever capable of creating and carrying out such an act—clearly the prosecution at appeal believed they were, however, the judge did not and both had their convictions and sentences overturned. In a 2014 Human Rights Watch Report which discussed entrapment in the United States using undercover operatives in sting operations similar to the Korody and Nuttall case, a former FBI agent Michael German told Human Rights Watch:

"Today's terrorism sting operations reflect a significant departure from past practice. When the FBI undercover agent or informant is the only purported link to a real terrorist group, supplies the motive, designs the plot and provides all the weapons, one has to question whether they are combatting terrorism or creating it. Aggrandizing the terrorist threat with these theatrical productions only spreads public fear and divides communities, which doesn't make anyone safer"[14].

Lone Wolf Attacks in Quebec and Ottawa—October 2014

By October of 2014, the RCMP and Intelligence Service were believed to be monitoring a large number of Canadians planning to join up with factions in Syria and Iraq, namely, ISIL. One such person being looked at and was interviewed by police was Martin Couture-Rouleau aged 25, and this came about from his public Facebook posting that appeared to show that he was becoming radicalized. As no other activity or threat was uncovered there was no further action taken. Four months later on October 20, 2014, Couture-Rouleau was in the Quebec township of Saint-Jean-sur-Richelieu. He waited in a strip mall parking lot for two hours and when he saw two Canadian soldiers he deliberately drove his vehicle at them, striking both men and killing one of them. In the subsequent police chase, his car crashed into a ditch and he was shot by local police as he exited the damaged car carrying a knife. This is yet another of those cases where a young man living on the fringes of society has sought out an avenue for his anger and frustrations at perceived injustices perpetrated by government policies. He had converted to Islam in 2013 and was a staunch supporter of ISIL. He had attempted to travel to Syria a year earlier; however, his passport was revoked preventing him from travelling.

On October 22, two days after this attack, a young Canadian of Libyan descent calmly walked up to a soldier on ceremonial guard duty at the Canadian National War Memorial in Ottawa and shot him three times in the back at close range. Corporal Nathan Cirillo of the Argyll and Sutherland Highlanders Regiment of Canada died where he fell; other soldiers attempted to stop the young man but took cover when they were shot at—soldiers on ceremonial guard carry only unloaded weapons. The perpetrator Michael Zehaf-Bibeau aged thirty-five then drove a short distance to the Parliament Buildings. Parking his vehicle outside the perimeter fence, he then went on foot and car-jacked an official limousine and drove directly to the main entrance of the Parliament Building. He entered the building and encountered security staff where after a struggle he shot one in the foot. He ran further into the building and by this time was being pursued by members of the RCMP. A shoot out ensued and Zehaf-Bibeau was shot fifteen times by members of the RCMP and the Sergeant-at-Arms of the House of Commons. Zehaf-Bibeau converted to Islam some ten years prior to this attack and had been involved with drugs and numerous run-ins with law enforcement. He was yet another individual lured by the online propaganda and extreme interpretation of the Quran. He was intending to travel to a location in the Middle East, possibly Syria or Saudi Arabia and had come to Ottawa and applied for a Canadian passport, which at the time of the attack his application was ongoing. The RCMP uncovered a video tape in Zehaf-Bibeau's vehicle that appears to have been shot the day of the attack and in it, he criticizes the Canadian Prime Minister and government and that he is retaliating for Canada's attack on innocent Muslims in their homeland. Whatever the state of mind was of this young man and his perception of Canada's involvement in supporting the attacks on ISIL, it leads us to realize that young and impressionable men and women living on the fringes of society are being drawn in and snared by the huge propaganda machine that spreads the extreme ideologies of Islam. Zehaf-Bibeau had likely been radicalized online and that coupled with obvious problems with drugs may have led him to act in this manner.

The Canadian government immediately moved to strengthen its anti-terror legislation giving intelligence and police broader powers by introducing the Security of Canada Information Sharing Act, aimed at ensuring a broader sharing of information between government agencies; the Secure Air Travel Act aimed primarily at those intending to use air travel to commit acts of terrorism elsewhere; and amended Canada's Criminal Code and the Canadian Security Intelligence Service Act, the latter permitting the intelligence service to take measures both inside and outside of Canada to reduce the security threat to Canada. While the government had support from the Liberal Party it was not unanimously supported by all parties in government. With a change of government in the fall of 2015, the incoming Liberal government had pledged to make amendments to the far reaching sections of the Act.

The Lone Wolf—Aaron Driver—August 2016

Canada had a further near miss with a lone wolf when a youth named Aaron Driver came to the attention of security services in 2014 after complaints about his online support for ISIS. There followed a period of time when his online activity made it such that police were able to place Driver under a Peace Bond, which is a court order to keep the peace and be on good behavior for a period of time. This essentially means that the person must not be charged with a criminal offence. Peace bonds often have other conditions too, such as not having any weapons or staying away from a person or place. Peace bonds are usually for one year, but sometimes they are shorter. One year is the maximum length. In Driver's case, the police had wanted to electronically tag and monitor him but this was subsequently denied by the court. The twenty-four-year-old was very keen to move to the Middle East in support of ISIS. Canada unlike the United States does not have the same capacity or extensive capability to monitor online activity of suspects although it is believed that currently Canada is tracking more than three hundred extremists but Aaron Driver not being one of them. Driver had relocated from the prairie city of Winnipeg to the Toronto region of Canada and it was there that he began to act on his radical and extreme beliefs. Like in so many instances, we see suicide bombers posting their martyrdom video online for the world to see after their act has been committed, Aaron Driver posted just such a video in early August 2016 and his posting was picked up by the monitoring services of intelligence agencies in the United States which alerted Canada to the imminent threat posed by Driver. Although the online video shows much of his face covered, security agencies and police in Canada identified the male in the video as Aaron Driver. Driver was preparing to leave his home in taxi with a bomb in his possession as police arrived at his address—there immediately followed a shoot-out in which Driver was killed and his bomb detonated, slightly injuring the cab driver. Where Driver was going to deliver his bomb is unclear but what is clear is that even though he was known to the police he did not create the impression that he would be an imminent threat. The aim of the lone wolf by using a dramatic attack of violence on an unsuspecting public audience apart from the immediate damage inflicted, is the much broader psychological damage that has even greater impact. In this case, the sharing of intelligence between countries with mutual interests in security was paramount in preventing the attack.

The Case of Omar Khadr

Terrorist organizations require the support of networks able to fund activities in other theaters of conflict—Canada is seen by a host of organizations as a rich breadbasket in which to gather funds, and al Qaeda's support network had been operating effectively through the Khadr family in Ontario, close to the U.S. border. It is believed that millions of dollars have been accrued for the al Qaeda network from within Canada. When the Soviet Union invaded Afghanistan in 1980, Khadr (senior) went to Afghanistan, where he met Osama bin Laden. Injured by a land mine, he returned to Canada in 1992 for medical aid. Upon recovery, he returned to Pakistan. There, police arrested him in 1995 for his part in the car bombing of the Egyptian Embassy in Islamabad. Fortune was on Khadr's side—Canada's prime minister, Jean Chretien, interceded personally with the Pakistanis on his behalf. Khadr was released and returned to Canada. After the 9-11 attacks, Khadr disappeared. Khadr was believed killed in Afghanistan in 2002 during a gun battle. His fourteen-year-old son Omar was captured after that action in which the younger Omar mortally wounded a U.S. Army medic.[15]

Related activities of the immediate family include the following:

- Wife Maha Elsamnah took son Omar from Canada to Pakistan in 2001 and enrolled him in al Qaeda training.
- Daughter Zaynab, twenty-three, was engaged to one terrorist and married another al Qaeda member in 1999. Osama bin Laden was present at the nuptials. Zaynab endorses the 9-11 atrocities and hopes her infant daughter will die fighting Americans.
- Son Abdullah is an al Qaeda fugitive constantly on the move. Canadian Intelligence states he ran an al Qaeda training camp in Afghanistan during the Taliban period, something Abdullah denies.
- Son Abdul Karim, half-paralyzed by wounds sustained in the October 2002 shootout that left his father dead, is presently a prisoner in a Pakistani hospital.[16]

Omar Khadr was captured and sent to the Guantanamo Bay detention camp where he was eventually tried by a Military Commission Tribunal after a plea agreement. In October 2010, he pleaded guilty to murder in violation of the laws of war, attempted murder, conspiracy, and two counts of providing material support to terrorism and spying. His plea deal meant that he would spend the following year in prison and was repatriated to Canada in 2012 to serve the remainder of his eight-year sentence there and following a Supreme Court of Canada ruling was released on bail in May 2015. He is the youngest prisoner to have been held at Guantanamo Bay and the first since World War II to be prosecuted by a military commission for war crimes while a minor.[17]

Canadian authorities believe more than two hundred young men and women have gone to the Middle East and joined up with Islamist groups, principally Islamic State, over the past three to four years and while there is now legislation aimed at preventing travel for purposes of terrorism, the question about what happens to these men and women should they return is a difficult one. Those that are not killed or used as suicide bombers may well return as fully trained jihadists now competent to carry out attacks as witnessed in France (Paris) in 2015. The threat remains high from the lone wolf and poses a threat to both Canada and its neighbor to the south.

Refugee System under Pressure

The Canadian refugee claimant system is under considerable strain, not to mention abuse from those countries' citizens seeking to implant terrorist sleepers in Canada. Notable examples follow. Mohamed Harkat arrived in Canada from Malaysia on a forged Saudi passport. He was initially unassuming and found casual work in the Ottawa region of Ontario once his refugee application was granted in 1997. He later wed a Canadian woman. Since 1997, CSIS has scrutinized Harkat and claims he was involved with al Qaeda in Pakistan and also other Islamist terror groups before coming to Canada. In 1994, Abdul Jabarah arrived as a refugee claimant with his family from Kuwait. Said to have been recruited by al Qaeda in 1990, he was killed in a police raid in Saudi Arabia in 2003 after his terror cell was involved in truck bombings. Nizar Ben Muhammed Nawar was one of 1,300 Tunisian students who entered Montreal in 1999. He and 100 others dropped from sight after the 9-11 attacks. A suspected al Qaeda recruit, he has returned to Tunisia, where he is actively involved in terror attacks. A member of Hezbollah, Omar el-Sayed was arrested in Edmonton, Alberta; he had entered Canada on a forged Dutch passport in 1998. He was arrested for possession of fake identification papers and was wanted on drugs and weapons charges in Germany. A judge granted bail in 2002, and el-Sayed vanished.

Canada lacked a defined policy on refugees until the late 1960s. It had expected a dwindling number of refugees, chiefly Europeans, following World War II. However, Canada accepted around three thousand refugees per year between 1960 and 1979, and from 1979 to 1998 that figure changed to almost twenty-five thousand accepted refugee claims per year. Canada sees itself as a predominantly liberal state founded on immigration. Thus, Canada's approach and its almost open-door policy on refugees opened the flood gates—while the vast majority settled well in Canada, some refugees came for different reasons and used Canada's liberalism to help fund their stay in the country. In "Regina versus Singh" in 1985, the defendant, facing deportation for ties to Sikh terrorism, successfully argued Canada's Charter of Rights and Freedoms extended to applicants such as him, and he was entitled to the same rights and freedoms as any Canadian citizen.

CUBA

The Republic of Cuba is the largest country in the Caribbean. It is located between the Caribbean Sea and the North Atlantic Ocean, just ninety miles south of Florida, and is slightly smaller than Pennsylvania. The United States leases the U.S. Naval Base at Guantanamo Bay. The base remains a geographical part of Cuba, and only mutual agreement of the two nations or U.S. abandonment of the area can terminate the lease. This has been a contentious issue in U.S.-Cuban relations for decades. The population is almost eleven million with fifty-one percent being Mulatto, thirty-seven percent white, eleven percent black, and one percent Chinese.

Fidel Castro

Kim Il-Sung, Deng Xiaoping, Peron, Khrushchev, Kadar, Franco, and Tito are all famous dictators, long departed. Castro had all but destroyed his country with iron-fisted leadership, yet managed to stay in power until his resignation due to ill-health in February 2008. Born on August 13, 1926, Fidel Castro led a revolt against the Batista dictatorship and became the president of Cuba in 1959.

Castro was the "classic" dictator in that he emerged not from the historical center of his society but from its physical and moral peripheries. His father was a rough and deceitful "Gallego" from the impoverished north of Spain. Like Napoleon the Corsican, Hitler the

Austrian, and Stalin the Georgian, who came from similar backgrounds, Castro has a perversely captivating combination of seductiveness and violence. As a boy, he tried to burn down his parents' house and burn up his father's car. Legend says that young Fidel would regularly hang over a canyon while the trains thundered by. Above all, he was always the perfect Machiavellian, naturally mastering every technique of political, physical, and psychological manipulation over the Cuban people, his troops, and leaders around the world.

When he was at the Jesuit high school, Castro was fascinated with reading about the European fascists. From Mussolini, he took the Italian's hysterical rhetorical gestures. From Hitler, he borrowed his lessons in the sociology of revolution. Hitler had created a power base from the alienated and devastated German lower classes. Castro created his own base from poor workers and farmers. When he marched into Havana in January of 1959, he immediately began using his unique system of revolutionary control. He brought down the upper classes, and the middle classes, by seizing their lands and removing their privileges, or by simply terrorizing them. He removed any and all of his competitors to either by sending them to places where they would surely die (Che Guevara in Bolivia, 1967; Frank Pais on the streets of revolutionary Santiago de Cuba, 1957) or, when that did not work, by executing them (General Ochoa in Havana, 1989). His military and intelligence organizations assured, and still assure, control over the island. Castro has been extraordinarily adept at using the traditional Cuban fear of the "Miami Cubans" and the hated "Americanos" to hold his own people ignorant and in check.[18]

"Hatred is an element of struggle; relentless hatred of the enemy that impels us over and beyond the natural limitations of man and transforms us into effective, violent, selective, and cold killing machines. Our soldiers must be thus; a people without hatred cannot vanquish a brutal enemy."

Thus spoke Che Guevara in 1967. Guevara was one of the most radical of Castro's entourage who was, as mentioned earlier, sent by Fidel to die in Bolivia. Guevara used hatred or, as he put it, "relentless hatred" to "impel us over and beyond the natural limitations of man." This use of hatred to encourage the dehumanization of one's enemy is but another manifestation of the doctrine found throughout the centuries to justify mass murder and torture. It has been used to apparently great success in Cuba, keeping Castro in power for more than forty years.

A State Sponsor of Terrorism

Cuba has been on the U.S. Department of State list of State Sponsors of Terrorism since 1982 but with softening relations between U.S and Cuba president, Obama had Cuba removed from the list of state sponsors in May 2015. Castro had stated that the September 11, 2001, terrorist attacks in the United States were in part a consequence of the United States having applied "terrorist methods" for years[19]. The Castro regime has been a supporter of revolutionary groups in Latin America for the past thirty years. Most notably with regard to Colombian guerrilla group members in Cuba, the State Department annual reports on global terrorism for 2002 and 2003 acknowledged that Colombia acquiesced to the presence of Colombian guerrillas in the country and has publicly said that it wants Cuba's continued mediation with the ELN in Cuba. The Cuban government maintains that it has been actively involved in hosting peace talks and that its contributions to peace talks have been acknowledged by Colombia and the United Nations[20].

THE DOMINICAN REPUBLIC AND HAITI

These two small countries share an island and have been involved in strife, war, rebellion, and terrorism in the Caribbean to some extent, although minor. We shall examine them briefly as a possible source of future problems in that region.

The Dominican Republic

Noted more for its major league baseball players in the United States, the Dominican Republic is located on the eastern two-thirds of the island of Hispaniola, between the Caribbean Sea and the North Atlantic Ocean. It is slightly more than twice the size of New Hampshire, with a population of about 7.9 million. The ethnic mix is a reflection of past developments, with whites, sixteen percent; blacks, eleven percent; and mixed races, seventy-three percent. The population is ninety-five percent Roman Catholic.

Economic reforms launched in late 1994 contributed to exchange rate stabilization, reduced inflation, and strong GDP growth in 1995–1996. In 1996, there was increased mineral and petroleum exploration; a new investment law that allows for repatriation of capital dividends has drawn more investment to the island. President Leonel Fernandez Reyna, who came to power in August 1996, inherited a trouble-ridden economy hampered by a pressured peso; a large external debt; nearly bankrupt, state-owned enterprises; and a manufacturing sector hindered by daily power outages. The Dominican per capita purchasing power is $3,670—three times that of its neighbor, Haiti. The Dominican Republic has been very quiet in the wake of the events of 9-11 and seems to be satisfied with staying out of the kinds of conflicts it has engaged in the past.

The Republic of Haiti

The Republic of Haiti occupies the western one-third of the island of Hispaniola, bordering on the west of the Dominican Republic. It is slightly smaller than Maryland and has a population that is predominately black (ninety-five percent), with mulattos and whites making up five percent. These more than 6.5 million people are crowded into one-half the land space of their neighbor, the Dominican Republic. Haitians are predominately Roman Catholic (eighty percent), and an overwhelming majority also practices voodoo.

Haiti is one of the poorest countries in the world. About seventy-five percent of the Haitian population lives in poverty. Nearly seventy percent of all Haitians depend on the agriculture sector, which consists mainly of small-scale, subsistence farming and employs about two-thirds of the country's workforce. Haiti has experienced little or no job creation since President Rene Preval took office in February 1996. Failures to reach agreements with international sponsors have denied Haiti badly needed budget and development assistance. Meeting aid conditions in 1997 was especially challenging in the face of mounting popular criticism of reforms.

François **Papa Doc** Duvalier was the absolute dictator of Haiti from 1957 to 1971. His nickname came from his career as a physician. He became director general of the Haitian National Public Health Service in 1946 and, subsequently, served as minister of health and of labor. After opposing Paul Magloire's coup in 1950, he hid in the interior, practicing medicine, until he was granted a general political amnesty in 1956. In 1957, with army backing, "Papa Doc" was overwhelmingly elected president. Re-elected in a sham election in 1961, he declared himself "President for Life" in 1964. His regime, the longest in Haiti's history, was a brutal reign of terror; political opponents were summarily executed, and the notorious **Tonton Macoutes** (secret police) kept the populace in a state of abject terror and fear. Under Duvalier, the economy of Haiti continued to deteriorate, and the illiteracy rate remained at about 90 percent. Duvalier nevertheless maintained his hold over Haiti. His practice of voodoo encouraged rumors among the people that he possessed supernatural powers. He died in 1971, after arranging for his son, Jean-Claude ("Baby Doc"), to succeed him.

Jean-Bertrand Aristide became president of Haiti in December 1990, only to be ousted seven months after taking office. He went into exile in Venezuela and later the United States. In 1993, a twenty thousand-member U.S.-led multinational force intervened to forcibly disband the army and restore Aristide to power.

Aristide was a radical Catholic priest who defended liberation theology. He worked among Haiti's poor and was part of a group of progressive priests who opposed the Duvalier dictatorship. Expelled from his religious order in 1988 because of his revolutionary teachings, he became the candidate of a coalition of leftist parties in the 1990 presidential elections and was elected with an overwhelming majority. Party infighting plagued Aristide toward the end of his five-year term, however, and continued for the new administration of Rene Preval, who took over in February 1998.[21] In the relative safety of the new UN-protected Haiti, Aristide launched a new umbrella movement to invigorate and unify the governing Lavalas coalition. Many Haitians had hopes of seeing Aristide back in the National Palace in 2000. He has insisted that his latest efforts are not a challenge to Preval, a friend and activist whom he belatedly endorsed for president in 2002. By law, Aristide could not seek a consecutive term as president of Haiti.

To emphasize that the appearance of safety in this battered nation is not necessarily reality, in 1998 unknown gunmen opened fire on the National Palace and police headquarters in the latest apparent effort to try to destabilize Haiti's government. At least one person was killed, a civilian working at the police station, and a policeman was slightly injured. UN soldiers and Haitian police officers returned fire, but no casualties were reported. UN helicopters also took to the air and patrolled the city. There have been death threats against Preval, former President Aristide, and several liberal Haitian legislators.

Preval has blamed the attacks on soldiers from the army that ousted Aristide in 1991. The army was reformed after an American-led military intervention restored the exiled Aristide in October 1994. Preval has also speculated that the subversion could be connected to his controversial plan to privatize some state-owned enterprises. The fate of this beleaguered, poor, and downtrodden country is far from settled. The state terrorism created by the two despotic Duvaliers, and a combination of violence and voodoo, has left a legacy of former state terrorists ready to leap into the vacuum created by the departure of the UN operation. Time will tell if this dire prediction will come to pass.[22] The twenty-first century has not been kind to Haitians: first the devastating earthquake and then the sudden return in January 2011 of "baby-doc" Duvalier after twenty-five years of exile in France. Exactly what effect his presence will have is yet to be seen, and it must be borne in mind that nearly 50 percent of Haitians are under the age of eighteen and would likely have no knowledge of the man and his notorious TonTon Macoutes. Human rights groups such as Amnesty International and Human Rights Watch urged Haiti to prosecute Mr. Duvalier, saying he should be held accountable for the torture and killing of civilians under his rule[23]. Like so many dictators, the Duvaliers used their own personal militia who were directly responsible only to Duvalier; they were given virtual license to torture, kill, and extort. They murdered hundreds of Duvalier's opponents, sometimes publicly hanging the corpses as warnings. After Papa Doc's death in 1971, his son changed their name to the National Security Volunteers, though they continued to terrorize the citizenry. After the overthrow of Baby Doc (1986), although officially disbanded, the group continued to spread terror. It remains to be seen as to whether any remnants remain.

Summary

Approximately ninety percent of Canada's population lives within one hundred miles of the border with the United States. The downing of an Air India Boeing 747 off the southern coast of the Republic of Ireland on June 22, 1985, was the worst ever single terrorist attack prior to 9-11. Most of the people on board Air India Flight 182 were Canadian citizens. Canada's only previous brush with an organized attack using terror tactics had been Quebec's experience with the FLQ. Lone Wolf attacks in Quebec and Ottawa highlighted the ease with which a single terrorist can wreak havoc on society. These attacks outline the concern over Internet inspired jihad being pulsed into the minds of young and impressionable men and women. Canada has a large number of its citizens fighting with factions in Syria and Iraq and their eventual return will be a security nightmare for both Canada and the United States. Canada does a good job at integration and is currently accepting thousands of refugees from the Syria and Iraq conflicts but will this lead to problems of radicalization in years to come from some of these new Canadians? Sporadic problems in the Caribbean and in Cuba continue to flare. Most of the terrorist and insurgent problems in the islands have been as a result of economic downturns and inefficient and corrupt governments. Cuba remains firmly under the control and dictates of the Castro family, and their power continues to dominate in the region as well as covertly influence Latin American states. As the events of 9-11 recede to form part of history, we must expect the new generation of terrorists to come from the ranks of extreme Islam—those terrorists with designs on launching jihad against both Canada and the United States will very likely come from within our own borders. Britain, as we shall see in Chapter 5, has experienced and suffered from attacks by homegrown terrorists, those who immigrated to a new homeland only to repay their adopted country with terror and death.

Review Questions

1. Evaluate how homegrown terrorism has led to changes in Canadian terror legislation.
2. Describe how immigration and refugees have played a role in evolving terror trends in Canada.
3. Describe how terrorists were able to bomb an Air India flight.
4. List the elements of the lone wolf attacks in Ottawa and Quebec.
5. Describe methods used by Cuban and Haitian dictators to control their populace and to ensure their political office.

End Notes

1. U.S. Department of State. *Background Notes: Geographic Entities and International Organizations.* http://www.state.com.
2. Courtesy of Public Safety Canada.
3. John Bissett. "Troubled Borders; Canada, The United States and Mexico." John Bissett, former Executive Director Canadian Immigration Services speaking at the 2nd North American Meeting on the Trilateral Commissions New York (November 14–16, 2003).
4. Juliet O'Neill. *The Ottawa Citizen* (August 3, 1996).
5. *The Mackenzie Institute: The Sub Committee on Immigration and Claims* (January 2000).
6. George Rosie. *The Directory of International Terrorism* (New York: Paragon House, 1987, p. 123).
7. Canadian Press. "Neo-FLQ Group to Fight for Breakup." (December 3, 1995).
8. John Thompson is President of the Mackenzie Institute "Overseas Terrorism in Canada" *Terrorism in Canada's History*, Chapter 2. www.mackenzieinstitute.com.
9. Government of British Columbia (2004). www.protocol.gov.bc.ca.
10. Stewart Bell. *Cold Terror, How Canada Nurtures and Exports Terrorism Around the World* (Etobicoke, ON: John Wiley & Sons, 2004, p. 19).
11. Kim Bolen. "MP calls for Tougher Laws to Deal with Extremists." *The National Post* (November 22, 2007).
12. CBC archives. www.cbc.ca.
13. John Thompson. "How the Tigers Came to Canada." *The National Post* (February 28, 2005).
14. Email from Michael German, fellow at the Brennan Center for Justice, to Columbia Law School's Human Rights Institute, April 8, 2014.

15. Human Rights Watch, 2014—Illusion of Justice, p. 22 (220 pages). *Human Rights Abuses in Terrorism Prosecutions*, Columbia Law School Human Rights Institute.
16. Daniel Pipes. "The Khadrs: Canada's First family of Terrorism." *New York Sun* (March 11, 2004).
17. The Khadrs: Canada's First Family of Terrorism by Daniel Pipes. Copyright © 2004 by Daniel Pipes. Reprinted with permission of Author.
18. Jane Sutton. "Guantanamo Canadian to Serve Eight More Years in Prison." (November 1, 2010). Reuters. http://uk.reuters.com/article/idUKTRE69R01Q20101101.
19. Santo Domingo. "Offices of the General Customs Receivership" (Courtesy National Archives, 1907).
20. Andrew Cawthorne. "Cuba's Castro Urges U.S. to Keep Calm." *Reuters* (September 11, 2001).
21. Cuban Ministry of Foreign Relations. "Declaration by the Ministry of Foreign Affairs: Cuba Has Nothing to Hide, and Nothing to Be Ashamed Of." (May 2, 2003).
22. *The Columbia Encyclopedia*, 5th ed. (New York: Columbia University Press, 1993). Licensed from Inso Corporation. Aristide, Jean-Bertrand. http://bartleby.com.
23. Michael Norton. Associated Press Writer (Port-au-Prince, Haiti, August 19, 1996).
24. Ingrid Arnesen and Jose Cordoba. "Haiti: Ex-Dictator Duvalier Returns." *Wall Street Journal* (January 17, 2011), http://online.wsj.com/article/SB10001424052748704511404576086631400208152.html. Retrieved February 27, 2011.

Great Britain and Northern Ireland

LEARNING OUTCOMES

After studying this chapter, students should be able to:

1. Describe the incidents and events that characterized the "Troubles."

2. Analyze the structures of the Catholic and Protestant terrorist organizations operating in Northern Ireland.

3. List the political objectives of Sinn Féin.

4. Describe how Islamist radical organizations have operated in a liberal society.

5. Summarize the value and effectiveness of the Diplock Commission.

6. Discuss how UK's Counterterror legislation has evolved to control the radical jihadist threat to the United Kingdom.

KEY WORDS TO NOTE

Abu Hamza al-Masri—Radical Egyptian Sunni Muslim cleric who preached at London's Finsbury Park Mosque

Active Service Units (ASUs)—Small and secretive terror cells that operate autonomously

Decommissioning—Provision in the Northern Ireland Peace Agreement that puts weapons beyond the use of Irish terror organizations

Diplock Commission—Set up in 1972 to consider legal measures against terrorism in Northern Ireland, which led to the establishment of courts without jury; named after Kenneth Diplock

Good Friday Agreement—Plan for devolved government in Northern Ireland signed on April 10, 1998; included terms of early release of prisoners and decommissioning of weapons

Ian Paisley—Protestant minister who became the public face of opposition to the Republican movement

Internment—Confinement, often used in wartime; in this case, used in Northern Ireland during the 1980s to combat Irish republican terrorism

Lee Rigby—Unarmed soldier from 2nd Battalion Royal Regiment of Fusiliers, run down and beheaded in London by jihadists

Orange Order—Originating in the seventeenth century, this is the largest Protestant organization in Northern Ireland and regards itself as defending civil and religious liberties of Protestants and seeks to uphold the rule and ascendancy of a Protestant monarch in the United Kingdom

SAS—Special Air Service—British Army Regiment heavily involved in counterterror operations

Sinn Féin—Led by Gerry Adams—left-wing Irish republican political party that seeks an end to British rule in Northern Ireland

FIGURE 5-1   Map of Great Britain and Northern Ireland.
Source: Central Intelligence Agency, *The World Factbook, 2008.*

OVERVIEW

Britain is no stranger to acts of domestic terrorism from Irish terror groups during the last thirty years of the twentieth century. Successive British governments have allowed an influx of Islamic extremists into the country, who have inspired, trained, and funded radical elements to fight *jihad* abroad and at home. We examine what is still considered to be one of the most successful and logistically well-organized terror groups of the modern era—the Provisional Irish Republican Army (PIRA)—as well as other factions operating in both Northern Ireland and mainland Britain. Attempts to disarm Irish terror groups continued to be a major political challenge for the Labor government of former Prime Minister Tony Blair. The Good Friday Agreement, or Belfast Agreement, signed on Friday, April 10, 1998, came as a major sticking point in achieving a measure of independence for Northern Ireland. We examine how Irish terrorists have turned away from the gun and toward political strategies to attain their goals (Figure 5-1).

In 2005, the Irish Republican Army (IRA) formally renounced violence and instructed its active units and volunteers to cease all activities and "assist the development of purely political and democratic programs through exclusively peaceful means." The long-term effects of this on Northern Ireland will be apparent only with the passage of time. Of concern to Britain in particular but also the rest of Europe has been the growth of "homegrown" terror cells inspired by radical Islamists. Since the terror attacks of 9-11, Britain has gone to draconian lengths to deter and defeat the rise of Islamic extremism. This chapter examines the rise of Islamic extremism in Britain, reviewing the measures being taken to limit and track down those that have become involved with suspected al Qaeda terrorist operations. The bomb attack outside the British Embassy in Turkey in 2004 was al Qaeda's first specific, targeted attack against British interests abroad. New laws aimed at curbing terrorism have meant a tenuous return to an internment-type process used unsuccessfully in Northern Ireland in the 1970s and 1980s. Britain struggled with the realization that Islamic terror had come to its shores, and Britons were ill prepared for the reality that the attacks were the work of young British men who were educated and raised in England. The type of terror they were now witnessing was more commonly associated with terror attacks in the Middle East rather than London!

IRELAND'S CIVIL WAR

Michael Collins, an Irishman born in the south, entered the British Civil Service and joined the Postal Office in London in 1906. About this time he joined the secretive Irish Republican Brotherhood (IRB). In 1912, the British government introduced an Irish Home Rule Bill giving Ireland a separate parliament but with limited autonomy. The Catholic Irish nationalists welcomed the proposed bill, but Protestant unionists in the north saw it as a threat. With the outbreak of World War I in August 1914 and the passing of the act in September, the IRB saw this as an ideal opportunity to strike at the British while they were focused on war with Germany. The act was not implemented due to the outbreak of war.

Germany saw an opportunity to destabilize the British by providing support to the Irish independence movement. While the German offer was readily accepted by members of the movement, little of material assistance actually reached Ireland. In 1916, Michael Collins returned to Ireland and joined the Irish Volunteers, the nationalist's paramilitary wing. On Easter Monday 1916, the IRB made its move. Led by Padraic Pearse and James Connolly, one thousand six hundred Irish rebels, mostly members of the Irish Volunteers, rose up in Dublin and seized key points in the city. The rebels proclaimed an independent Irish republic but failed to garner popular support. The rebellion lasted for five days and resulted in the destruction of large portions of the city before it was crushed by the British military. Fifteen of its leaders were arrested, summarily tried, and sentenced to death. All were executed by firing squad. Widely reviled during and after the failed rebellion, the dead men quickly became martyrs to the Irish, with their executions turning popular sentiment against the British. Michael Collins participated in the Easter Rising and was subsequently interned at Frongoch Prison Camp, Wales. He returned to Ireland after his release and began setting up an underground intelligence organization. In 1918, the Sinn Féin political movement received strong support, winning seventy-three of the one hundred and five allotted seats for Ireland. None of those elected including Michael Collins took their seat in the House of Commons in London and, instead, pledged to constitute themselves as the legislature of an independent Ireland. Twenty-seven of the elected members met in Dublin and declared the first Irish Assembly (Dáil Éireann). It declared itself as the sole law-making authority for the Irish people and demanded that Britain leave the country.

IRISH WAR OF INDEPENDENCE, 1919–1921

British attempts to subvert and destroy the **Sinn Féin** government were the starting point for the Anglo-Irish War of 1919–1921 (also known as the Irish War of Independence) and led to the formation of the IRA, the Dáil Éireann's militia. Collins was made commander of the new force. Collins' success in infiltration of British security services was combated by a group of British intelligence agents dubbed the "Cairo Gang." Collins' Irish forces executed nineteen British agents (the "Cairo Gang") on November 20, 1920, placing him at the top of Britain's most wanted list, with a £10,000 reward on his head. At the end of the year, the British Parliament passed the Government of Ireland Bill, separating the six predominantly Protestant counties in the north (Northern Ireland) from the remaining twenty-six counties in the Catholic south. As a means of combating the growing dissention in Ireland, the British established a militia force known infamously as the Black and Tans. They were best described as an auxiliary to the Royal Irish Constabulary and staffed by soldiers returning from the war in Europe. They symbolized the harsh and repressive British rule over the country. When Michael Collins' men killed the nineteen British undercover agents, the Black and Tans by way of reprisal surrounded a Gaelic football match in Croke Park Dublin, and when shooting broke out, twelve spectators and players were killed and a further sixty injured. This became known as the First Bloody Sunday.[1] The Black and Tans got their nickname from the mixed style of uniform they wore that comprised khaki trousers and dark vest and shirts. This militia organization were given free license as they rampaged through Irish villages and towns; but their actions so outraged the British public that they were recalled and subsequently disbanded in 1921.

While the Government of Ireland Act 1920 was welcomed in the north, the south continued to call for full independence from Britain. By July 1921, a truce was in place and Collins was part of the negotiating delegation sent to London to discuss peace. On December 6, the Anglo-Irish Treaty was signed and established the Irish Free State as a dominion within the British Commonwealth and partitioned Northern Ireland from the rest of the country, leaving it as part of the United Kingdom and with limited self-government. The treaty granted the twenty-six counties greater independence than Ireland had enjoyed in over 700 years, and most impartial observers regarded it as a stepping stone to full independence within a generation or two. Compared to the modest Home Rule Act of 1914, the treaty was a gigantic step forward for Republicans. But the true hard liners—including the IRA's Cathal Brugha—found three fatal flaws:

1. It excluded six counties in Ulster, thereby abandoning Catholics and nationalists in that part of Ireland;
2. It did not establish a truly independent Republic, only a semiautonomous state in which Britain controlled harbors in times of emergency; and
3. It required an oath of fidelity to the Crown from elected officials.

The treaty was ratified by the Dáil Éireann on January 7, 1922, by a vote of 64–57. Pro-treaty candidates won 92 out of 128 seats in the Free State general elections held in June. A provisional government was formed with Collins as chairman, but effective administration was obstructed by the anti-treaty faction, which formed a rival government led by Eamon de Valera.

Some IRA units supported the treaty and transformed themselves into the army of the new Irish Free State, giving up the name *IRA*. Other IRA units were anti-treaty and, under Brugha, continued to function under the name *IRA*. They promptly commandeered the Four Courts building as IRA headquarters. Five months later, another election was held and the pro-treaty faction received a safe majority (58–36). They immediately formed a permanent "Irish Free State" government.

The Irish Civil War began almost immediately. Using artillery borrowed from Britain, the Free State government, which proved to be highly authoritarian, bombarded IRA headquarters (the Four Courts building) with artillery fire, killing Cathal Brugha in the process. Then, with military assistance from Britain, it brutally and methodically set about destroying the rebellious opposition. The government used the same tactics that had been most effective against them when they were rebels. It executed seventy-seven anti-treaty advocates, some with cause, and some without. It burned down homes and imprisoned over eleven thousand anti-treaty citizens. Eventually, the numerically superior Free State Army overwhelmed the IRA.

Collins took command of the army in mid-July and was replaced by William Thomas Cosgrave as chairman of the government. In August, Collins visited his troops in the South and, on his return, was killed during an ambush at Béal na Bláth (Mouth of Flowers) in West Cork on August 22, 1922. Collins was the only fatality and is believed to have died from a ricochet bullet.

In 1937, a new constitution drafted by de Valera was adopted, and the name of the state was changed from "Irish Free State" to "Eire." In 1948, Republicans attained their 150-year-old dream, at least for the twenty-six counties: In name as well as in substance, the twenty-six counties became a full Republic outside the Commonwealth, pursuant to legislation sponsored by John A. Costello (1891–1976), a Fine Gael leader who succeeded de Valera as prime minister in a coalition government. The same legislation renamed the state from "Eire" to the "Republic of Ireland," its current name.[2]

"THE TROUBLES," 1968–1998

In the early days of "The Troubles" (the term for fighting between Catholics and Protestants), the PIRA was considered to be more of a nuisance than a terrorist threat to the security of Ireland. "The Troubles" began with civil rights marches in Northern Ireland. In October 1968, the newly formed Northern Ireland Civil Rights Association organized a march in Londonderry demonstrating its strength and frustration at the discrimination of Catholics by a Protestant majority. The Catholics in the North, probably in copycat fashion of the civil rights marches in the United States led by Dr. Martin Luther King, Jr., demanded better access to jobs, housing, and a fairer share of the economy; the marches and marchers quickly turned violent, and, in an attempt to quell the situation, the British government urged the Northern Ireland Prime Minister Terrence O'Neill to make far-reaching reforms to prevent further outbreaks. The British Home Secretary James Callaghan later wrote, "Ulster had arrived in the headlines."[3] Without the ability to sway the Unionist politicians, however, reforms were doomed to failure. Rioting again broke out in the summer of 1969, and this time troops were sent in to restore order and protect the Catholic enclaves. The end of 1970 would count the triggering of one hundred and fifty-three bombs and incendiary devices against Protestant businesses in Northern Ireland.

In the thirty-plus years of "The Troubles," more than three thousand people on both sides of the religious divide have been killed. To place some meaning and dimension to that figure—if one were to do a comparison-based population size with a comparable terrorist campaign in the United States, the resulting death toll would have reached over six hundred thousand! The enormity of "The Troubles" should not be minimized for its effect on several generations of Irishmen and women. The first Catholic death of the "Troubles" was a teenager, struck on the head by a baton wielded by a member of the Royal Ulster Constabulary (RUC) during street demonstrations and violence on July 14, 1968.

Religion and discrimination have been the battleground, stemming from centuries of social injustice—a region divided by a dominant Protestant presence over a Catholic minority. This led to discrimination against Catholics in almost every facet of everyday life, from finding employment to housing. For instance, almost exclusively, Protestant members staffed the RUC. (It is important to note that the service was always open to the Roman Catholic minority, but those who chose to join were, along with their families, victims of intimidation from within their own community.)

The Independent Commission on Policing for Northern Ireland set up in 1998 (more commonly known as the Patten Report), an act of Parliament—the Police (Northern Ireland) Bill of May 2000—led to a rebirth of the RUC as the Police Service of Northern Ireland (PSNI) on November 4, 2001. Divested of its antiterrorism role, it was to be brought back into a more all-encompassing community-style policing role.

Other changes finally came into effect at the end of the twentieth century, including the removal of the word "Royal" from the police department's title, as well as other recommendations unpopular with the Unionists, who viewed the change as pandering to the Republican movement.

Much criticism was leveled at the RUC; however, the sacrifice made by the men and women who served in the force cannot be overlooked. During the Troubles, three hundred and two officers lost their lives, and many thousands were injured; the force received a vast number of awards and commendations:

- 16 George Medals
- 103 Queens Gallantry Medals
- 111 Queens Commendations

On April 12, 2000, Her Majesty, the Queen, in presenting the force with the George Cross (awarded for acts of great heroism or for the most conspicuous courage in circumstances of extreme danger) said in part of her speech:

Due, in no small measure, to the bravery and dedication over the years of the men and women of the Royal Ulster Constabulary, Northern Ireland is now a much more peaceful and stable place in which to live.

The 1960s were a decade of change, with the British Empire seen to be giving up its colonies without a fight. Britain had just withdrawn from one of its last colonies—Aden, in the Persian Gulf—after a total breakdown of law and order achieved through terrorist violence. The IRA concluded that it could topple the British government, which it thought would back down if confronted by the kind of violence that had occurred in Aden. As a result of a split in the ranks of the IRA, the Provisional IRA was formed in 1969 as the clandestine armed wing of Sinn Féin, a legal democratic socialist political movement dedicated to the removal of British forces from Northern Ireland. The Official IRA, which had been in existence for more than forty years, declared a ceasefire in 1972. A further split in the Provisional Movement resulted from the policies of the Sinn Féin leader Gerry Adams between 1994 and 1998. In the fall of 1997, one faction accepted the **Good Friday Agreement**, and the other, a newly formed splinter of PIRA, the Real IRA (RIRA) (or New IRA, as it is sometimes called), continued armed resistance against British occupation of Northern Ireland. Together with the civil rights issues, and the American debacle in Vietnam, the PIRA aimed to make good use of what it considered positive factors. To the PIRA, Northern Ireland was seen as just another British colony, waiting its turn for independence. With this and recent history in mind, they believed that the killing of British soldiers would quickly influence the decision-making processes of the British government and public opinion.

POLITICAL OBJECTIVES

In order to appreciate and understand the kinds of terror campaigns that have been waged by both Republican and Loyalist paramilitaries in the province, it is important to acquire a basic understanding of the political goals of these groups. The IRA of the 1920s demanded, and continues to demand, one united Ireland, and separation from the United Kingdom. In support of this, the Nationalists turned to using campaigns of terror. The Easter Uprising was among the first in a long chain of terrorist incidents conducted throughout the twentieth century. In the early 1920s, bands of IRA men were relentlessly pursued by the Black and Tans. In the 1960s, Cathal Goulding, the Army Council's Chief of Staff for the IRA, considered and then established a position toward shifting the IRA away from violence as the only means to achieve its ends. His idea was the formation of both a Catholic and a Protestant workers group, aimed at the overthrow of capitalism and achieving a united Ireland. As a result, the end of 1969 found a situation rampant with internal disarray and a split in the IRA ranks. Goulding's ideas offended many Catholics who saw themselves as the defenders of the Catholic enclaves of the North, as well as IRA members. When renewed fighting broke out in 1969, following the civil rights marches, the IRA's lack of weaponry rendered it incapable of protecting the northern Catholics. At a special IRA convention held in Dublin in August 1969, it was voted, predominantly by the southerners, to adopt a policy of political activism. Further, it allowed election of Sinn Féin members to both the Dublin and British parliaments. To the men of the North, this was viewed as recognition of partition, or "sleeping with the enemy." Led by Sean MacStiofain, the PIRA was formed the following month. Rory O'Brady, Leo Martin, Billy McKee, Francis Card, and Seamus Twomey led the PIRA in 1969. They believed that violence could solve their political problems. Splinter groups were formed from the ranks of the IRA. The PIRA was formed as a splinter group from the IRA as well as a smaller group, the Irish National Liberation Army (INLA).

Sinn Féin,[4] the name of the political party representing the original IRA, was adopted by the splinter Provisionals as their "political wing." Gerry Adams, a prominent civil rights advocate, had long been suspected of being involved directly with the PIRA Council; however, he was responsible for Sinn Féin's rise to power over the past three decades as the political party that would achieve the goal of separation. A sense of fear surrounded the Sinn Féin party, in truth, because so many of its members had gravitated from the ranks of the PIRA and its **active service units (ASUs)**. The PIRA had effectively used terror campaigns in Northern Ireland against its Protestant neighbors, members of British Army units, and the mostly Protestant RUC. Sectarian reprisals by Loyalist paramilitaries had targeted Catholic families, mainly in Belfast and Londonderry, with Protestant groups targeting innocent civilians purely on the grounds that they were Catholics. PIRA carried out indiscriminate attacks on the British mainland against a broad array of targets. Many were military and government establishments, but the brutal sophistication and indiscriminate nature of the attacks caused widespread death and destruction. Targets ranged from pubs frequented by soldiers, to shopping centers, business districts, airports, and the official London residence of the British prime minister—10 Downing Street. The objective was to successfully attack British military, political, and economic targets with the aim of undermining the political will of the government, frightening the citizens, and sapping the British economy. They also attacked prominent British subjects and, in 1975, assassinated Ross McWhirter, the coauthor of the *Guinness Book of Records*, who had offered a reward for the capture of IRA terrorists.

The political aims of Sinn Féin/Irish Republican groups continue to be the complete removal of British rule and the establishment of a united Ireland. How could that objective be achieved? In their minds the only way to reach their goal was to wage war. After more than thirty years of "The Troubles," the bombs and guns had the effect of motivating the political leaders on all sides toward a peace agreement. This has been achieved—but, again, at what cost? As noted, more than 3,600 people, both military and civilian, have died during the long course of "The Troubles." Groups that have split away from the IRA to form the Provisional IRA, the Continuity IRA (CIRA), and the Real IRA cannot be seen as having lost contact with the political organization, Sinn Féin.

Protestants believe that both Gerry Adams (President of Sinn Fein 1983–present) and Martin McGuiness formerly a member of the PIRA and currently the Deputy First Minister of Northern Ireland and a member of Sinn Fein; they have had a long association with the IRA and PIRA and view them as terrorists-turned-politicians. The political "end game" has seen the prominent rise to political power of both Adams and McGuiness. Both men held positions of considerable influence during the negotiations with Britain's Labour government. Both men have been elected to sit in the British House of Commons. However, neither has taken his seat to date, as that would require the men to swear an allegiance to Her Majesty, the Queen—an act they view as repugnant. A landmark date for these two men came on January 21, 2002, when they were greeted in London by British Prime Minister Tony Blair and then occupied their new offices in the Palace of Westminster. Although the peace process has achieved a lot, the PIRA has never really "gone away." The tenuous ceasefire has been breached time and again by both the Loyalists and the Republicans, with punishment beatings and attacks. Sinn Féin continues to be seen as the party that can make significant inroads in Westminster. However, during the period since the signing of the peace accord, the Loyalist paramilitaries have not moved their political base and have no real representation in the political arena.

Other paramilitary players have stood for government election in Northern Ireland; during the hunger strikes in 1981, Bobby Sands, a Republican prisoner in the Maze Prison, began his hunger strike "until death." The press coverage that the prisoners garnered allowed his name to become so prominent that he was nominated to run in a local by-election; however, he died in prison in May the same year, three weeks after being elected as MP for Fermanagh and South Tyrone. A further nine hunger strikers would die in the Maze Prison.

Internment

Modern-day **internment** relates to the attempts to contain the fervent Irish Republican movement. However, this style had previously been tested from 1939 to 1945 and again from 1956 to 1962. For terrorist organizations to have success, they must first achieve political recognition, or at least gain some kind of special status. When reintroduced on August 9, 1971, it resulted in the rounding up of three hundred and forty-two mainly Republican sympathizers drawn from a list supplied by the RUC Special Branch. They were placed in detention indefinitely without trial (ability afforded to the Unionist government of the time under the Special Powers Act, 1922) in an old and disused former Royal Air Force base at Long Kesh outside Belfast. Internment failed to decrease the levels of violence in Northern Ireland; in fact the violence escalated. The rounding up of civilians from Republican areas of Belfast and Londonderry placed more than 400 persons in detention in August 1971, and those numbers swelled to over nine hundred by 1972. What was remarkable was that no Loyalist suspects were rounded up for internment, but neither were many members of the Provisional IRA, the majority of whom had fled south. The effectiveness of this process was soon questioned when it was clear that no significant Republicans were among those interned; however, this may, in part, have been due to poor and outdated intelligence. The deteriorating events in the North led the British government to suspend the Northern government in Stormont Castle and use direct rule from London. Housed in Long Kesh (renamed the Maze Prison), detainees were incarcerated with convicted paramilitary prisoners. Paramilitary prisoners began demanding 'special status', which, at the time, was applied only to internees. The Republican prisoners viewed themselves as political prisoners and demanded to be recognized as such. In 1974, the British government, under the direction of the secretary of state for Northern Ireland William Whitelaw, granted Special Category Status to paramilitary prisoners as well as the internees. Special Category Status gave prisoners the following privileges:

- Freedom of association with others in the prison (previously available only to internees).
- One prison visit per week.
- The option of wearing prison uniforms.
- Weekly food parcels.
- No requirement to perform prison work.

The Maze Prison became a training ground for Republicans, and with more than one thousand Special Category prisoners, the ability of prison staff to control their activities soon became questionable. Special Category Status was ended in 1976 by Merlyn Rees, the Secretary of State. The Maze Prison had constructed new blocks to house Republican prisoners. Their design in the shape of an "H" had them aptly named as *H-Blocks*. Those prisoners moved to the H-Blocks claimed they were political prisoners and not criminals and therefore had a right to Special Category Status. Their demands were not met, and they escalated their action by refusing to wear prison clothes or to wash. If one looks at the hypocrisies of terrorism (which is mostly oppression committed in the name of freedom), we will see there are several:

- Terrorists unilaterally suspend democracy for their own acts.
- Terrorists expect democratic principles to be fully applied to them if they are captured.
- Terrorists seek special recognition from governments they do not recognize.
- Terrorists avoid mentioning violation of their victims' human rights.[5]

With their status now revoked, the Republican prisoners took internal action by refusing to wear prison clothing and wearing only a prison blanket. The prisoners' actions fell on deaf ears of the British government, led by "the Iron Lady," Margaret Thatcher. The culminating events of the protests were the hunger strikes and the associated deaths, which made headline news around the world. The hunger strikes ended in October 1981, after which the British government allowed the prisoners to wear their own clothes.

After the 1998 Good Friday Agreement, when more than 400 paramilitary prisoners—both Republican and Loyalist—were released, the remaining half-dozen were scattered to different prisons. During the period of internment—August 9, 1971–December 5, 1975—1,981 people had been detained: 1,874 were Catholic/Republican, and the remaining 107 were Protestant/Loyalist.

By 1970s, the PIRA campaign was operating at full capacity; one of the most violent days was in July 1972, when they detonated a total of twenty-seven bombs in Belfast, killing seven and wounding one hundred and thirty others. The bombs were indiscriminate and injured both Catholics and Protestants.

FINANCING TERROR

For the PIRA of the 1970s and beyond to have any success against the British Army, it had to establish an arsenal of weaponry to fight its campaign. The obvious method of raising funds for terrorist activities had often been bank robberies. While this method was used in the early days of the campaign, it was not the PIRA's only avenue for funds. Terrorism is clearly not just a cost-effective means of political representation at a broad level, but terrorist tactics can be inexpensively implemented in terms of finance. Fertilizers and other commercially available chemical compounds found in household products will, for the foreseeable future, remain part of the basic arsenal of even the most powerful terrorist groups.[6]

The PIRA has been successful in raising funds by committing armed robberies, kidnappings, extortion, money laundering, smuggling, and drug dealing. It also raises funds through foreign aid and legitimate business ventures. The most spectacular robbery, and possibly the largest in Northern Ireland's history, involved the Northern Bank of Ireland and the theft of more than £20 million in December 2004. Intelligence pointed toward this being a PIRA operation owing to its sophistication and the logistics required to carry it out. Indications are that armed backup units were in place, should police units stumble onto the raid. Why would PIRA risk this kind of activity while delicate talks were ongoing with respect to the Peace Accord? From a historic point of view, the PIRA had previously carried out spectacular operations when events such as peace talks involving the British government had to be disrupted or otherwise stalled. For example, shortly after a breakout from the Maze Prison, one of the escapees was part of a PIRA cell that detonated a bomb in the Grand Hotel in Brighton on October 12, 1984, the location for the Conservative Party Conference. The nighttime bombing (when the explosive was planted at least a month before the event and placed on a long-term timer) was aimed at Margaret Thatcher's Conservative Cabinet. Patrick McGee was convicted of planting the bomb in the Grand Hotel three weeks earlier (McGee was released in 1999 as part of the Good Friday Peace Agreement). The explosion killed five people and injured more than thirty.

Revenues generated from illegitimate sources have funded legitimate business interests in the North, from nightclubs to taxi companies and security companies. Broadening the scale of legitimate business interests allows the terrorists the opportunity to permeate all levels of Northern Ireland society.

Extortion was an early method employed by PIRA in the 1970s. They demanded money "with clear menace" from local clubs, pubs, and businesses. This evolved into more sophisticated applications when PIRA established legal security companies that businesses would need to hire to protect themselves from threats by Loyalist terror groups. As the years have rolled by, PIRA has managed to skillfully continue less overt forms of extortion in such a way as to distance itself from the thuggery image, often seen as the hallmark of Loyalist groups. The Ulster Defense Association (UDA) and its methods are often reviled for their thuggery. The public image of this group is that of thugs out for easy money to fund a lavish lifestyle rather than support a political campaign.

It remains unclear just how involved the terrorist groups, both Republicans and Loyalists in the North, have been in the drug trade. Certainly, the PIRA has acted as escorts to certain international drug shipments, but its involvement in the supply chain remains unclear. Anyone wishing to buy drugs in PIRA-controlled neighborhoods would likely need approval from the PIRA leadership. There have certainly been punishment beatings, and even killings of citizens, both for drug use and for selling drugs. It is safe to assume that if there is an abundant supply of drugs, this kind of activity will finance terrorist activity.

Weapons procurement has been a major project for the PIRA. Its accumulations of weaponry are largely owing to the support it has received from rogue states, none more so than Libya, enabling the PIRA to stockpile considerable quantities of weapons, ammunition, and explosives over the last thirty years. Libya under Colonel Qaddafi was drawn toward the PIRA most likely as a result of the hunger strike deaths of the ten PIRA members. Libya saw itself as a country emerging from colonialism and had considerable sympathy for the Revolutionary Movement in Northern Ireland. Libya's support in the early 1970s is believed to have been about $3 million in hard currency, including weapons and explosives. One notable incident involved a shipment containing at least five tons of Russian-made weapons that was intercepted by Irish authorities in 1974. The shipment was destined for the PIRA and was hidden in the hold of the freighter *Claudia*. Authorities intercepted her off the coast of Ireland. The number of prior shipments has never been fully confirmed, but sources believe at least three others successfully reached the terrorists.[7]

Although the PIRA had a representative in Tripoli, the relationship began to sour, the amount of the funds dwindled with the seizure of the *Claudia*, and arms shipments from Libya ceased. Libya's interference was seen by both the U.S. government of Ronald Reagan and the British government of Margaret Thatcher as acts of a state that clearly sponsored terrorism.

In August 1979, in one of their more sensational attacks, the PIRA targeted the British Royal family, detonating a bomb in a small fishing vessel being operated by Lord Louis Mountbatten, the last Viceroy and first Governor General of India, and cousin to the Duke of Edinburgh, husband of Queen Elizabeth II. The bomb also killed eighty-two-year-old Lady Brabourne, mother-in-law to Mountbatten's daughter, and three teenage boys, one of them his grandson. Lord Mountbatten was seventy-nine years old. On the same day, the PIRA also killed a patrol of eighteen British soldiers in a roadside bombing at Warrenpoint, County Down.

THE IRISH REPUBLICAN ARMY AND PROVISIONAL IRISH REPUBLICAN ARMY

Official records do not indicate the exact membership numbers of the many Northern Ireland paramilitary groups, but it is widely believed that the number of IRA members reached a peak of around one thousand five hundred–two thousand active members in the war-torn years of the 1970s. Membership declined over the next fifteen years until the announced ceasefire in 1994, at which point membership was probably only three hundred–five hundred. Still one of the most powerful and effective terror organizations of the last century, the IRA traces its roots to the Easter Rebellion of 1916 in the Republic of Ireland and gets its name from the first "volunteers" who fought for a free Irish State. The birth of the Provisional IRA came with the IRA split in December 1969, between the "Officials" and the "Provisionals." Confusion was rampant, as both organizations had a military wing, the "Official" and "Provisional" IRA, and both had a political wing, the "Official" and "Provisional" Sinn Féin. It was the "Official" IRA that declared a ceasefire in the summer of 1972, and, from then on, the term *IRA* was used for the organization that had developed from the "Provisional" IRA. From a splinter group of a small and badly equipped paramilitary grouping, the "Provisional" IRA developed into a well-financed, well-equipped guerilla/terrorist organization that was involved in what it called "an armed campaign" for almost three decades. The IRA's development of wider connections in countries like Libya, Spain, North America, and South America for logistical and weaponry support expanded it into a truly international terrorist organization.

The IRA has been known to conduct activities outside of Northern Ireland and mainland Britain. It has been active in Europe and had set up safe houses during the early 1990s for operations aimed at military and government targets in the Netherlands, France, and West Germany. Ease of movement and lack of border controls in the Benelux countries made opportunities just that much simpler. Weapons seizures in Europe in the early 1990s and two ASU arrests likely slowed down any advances that PIRA may have contemplated for extensive operations in Europe. The PIRA has more or less observed the ceasefire put in place since the end of the 1990s. In August 2001, the credibility of the PIRA and Sinn Féin was brought into question when Colombian security forces arrested PIRA's head of engineering while he was developing mortars for the Revolutionary Armed Forces of Colombia (FARC) guerillas. Three suspected members of PIRA were arrested on August 11, 2001, at Bogotá's El Dorado International Airport, charged with training FARC in explosives handling and urban terrorist tactics. Of the three Irishmen arrested, one was identified as Niall Connolly, who had been in Latin America for at least a decade, according to Colombian and British officials.

Since 1996, however, Connolly had lived in Havana under the pseudonym David Bracken and acted as the Sinn Féin ambassador to the Fidel Castro government. He reportedly traveled frequently to Venezuela, Panama, Nicaragua, and El Salvador, where he is believed to have established contacts interested in arms smuggling, drug trafficking, and supporting the FARC's expanding insurgency in Colombia. Sinn Féin denied having any relationship with Connolly or knowledge of his activities in Latin America, but Cuba's foreign ministry released a statement on August 17, 2001, stating that Connolly had lived in Cuba for five years as Sinn Féin's Latin American representative.[8] Ulster unionists feared that the IRA was, on one hand, talking peace and **decommissioning**, while on the other, conducting training and seeking high-powered weapons. The other two suspects were identified as James "Mortar" Monaghan and Martin McCauley. Monaghan was a former member of Sinn Féin's ruling executive body and according to Garda Commissioner Pat Byrne, both were experts in the design and manufacture of increasingly effective homemade mortars. The two were also skilled in the use of mercury-tilt switches designed to blow up people in cars and radio-controlled "command" bombs for use against armored vehicles. These are technologies that would have significantly enhanced FARC's explosive-handling capabilities. Remote-controlled explosive devices have been a key feature of terrorist operations in Northern Ireland, particularly in the border regions.

The U.S. Central Intelligence Agency reportedly supplied the Colombian government with satellite footage of the three suspects training FARC rebels inside a demilitarized zone. Colombian officials have described the FARC–PIRA link as a "business relationship," in which the PIRA trades advanced explosives-handling techniques for illegal drugs, cash, or weapons. The three PIRA men spent three years in jail and were released on condition that they remain in Colombia pending an appeal from the Colombian government of their convictions. They were convicted of training Marxist rebels, in December 2004. Both have since returned to Ireland but with no extradition treaty between Colombia and Ireland they are unlikely to ever be returned. The PIRA members most likely schooled FARC rebels in how to mix high-powered synthetic explosives to extend the range of homemade gas cylinder mortars. The FARC needed to extend the roughly 400-meter range of its homemade mortars because of better defenses at military compounds built with American assistance.

It is no surprise that the PIRA is one of the most ruthless and well-organized terror groups in history. It has achieved success against significant odds, and by the late 1960s and early 1970s, it had changed dramatically in its makeup. By the end of the 1960s, the Catholic minority was under increasing pressure and assault from Protestant gangs. Catholic enclaves needed protection from Protestant gangs who were burning, shooting, and bombing Catholic housing districts. Out of necessity and pressure from the authorities, the PIRA evolved from a loosely knit organization to one with a military structure, employing geographically based brigades, battalions, and companies. The PIRA reorganized to form cells based on the continental cellular structure and better adapted to modern-day terrorist activities. Autonomous ASUs were formed within these cells, becoming almost impossible to penetrate or identify, as each cell had only three to four members. They were given code names and directed by controllers. It was difficult to operate in the Catholic housing districts of Belfast and Londonderry, as everyone knew everyone else. The PIRA owed much of its success to the effectiveness of the cell system.

As part of its mainland campaign after the collapse of the 1974–1975 ceasefires, it centered its attacks on London. Londoners were unfazed by the bombing campaign and stoically went about their business. The PIRA was always concerned about the activity of the British Special Air Service Regiment (**SAS**), and in one now-famous incident, the Balcombe Street siege, the PIRA cell gave up without a fight when news was leaked that the London Metropolitan Police were handing over to the SAS. What had started out as a botched raid on a London restaurant saw the four-man PIRA team chased down by uniformed police officers. The gang holed up in a residential area, Balcombe Street, and took an elderly couple hostage for six days before surrendering peacefully. The gang was also responsible for the death of Ross McWhirter, co-founder of the Guinness Book of Records and an outspoken conservative who wanted restrictions on the Irish population living in England (Figures 5-2 and 5-3).

CONTINUITY IRISH REPUBLICAN ARMY

The CIRA was a breakaway, or splinter, group of Republicans from the mainstream Provisionals. CIRA may have been in existence in the South for several years. In 1986, some of those Republicans attending the Sinn Féin Ard Fheis (party conference) walked out in protest, but they never presented the threat to the organization posed by the dissidents in 1969. The group

FIGURE 5-2 and FIGURE 5-3   Pictured at Gough Barracks, Armagh in 1991, the bullet ridden Toyota Hiace van used by the East Tyrone Brigade of the Provisional Irish Republican Army in the May 8, 1987, attack on the RUC station in the village of Loughgall, County, Armagh. The eight PIRA gunman involved in the attack were engaged by members of the SAS (Special Air Service) regiment in a furious firefight that resulted in the deaths of all eight terrorists and one civilian. *Courtesy:* Gary Wilson.

was led by Ruairí Ó Brádaigh, who went on to form the Republican Sinn Féin, and other veteran activists. Despite the purity of their beliefs, the Ó Brádaigh wing failed to persuade enough Provisionals to join them. The split was small and contained. The fear of reprisals from PIRA was ever present, and it was years before the CIRA revealed its existence. That, in itself, was a comment on the group's frailty.[9]

DIRECT ACTION AGAINST DRUGS

Sometimes PIRA used the name Direct Action Against Drugs (DAAD) when it wanted to claim responsibility for certain operational activities in Northern Ireland. It is basically a cover name for the Provisionals and not a separate or distinct terror group in the North.

REPUBLICAN SINN FÉIN

The Republican Sinn Féin (RSF) is a breakaway group from Sinn Féin, formed in 1986. The party decided to end its traditional abstention policy, and those who opposed the move walked out to form the RSF. The group was led by Ruairí Ó Brádaigh, former president of Sinn Féin, and Dáithí Ó Conaill, former chief of staff of the IRA. At the 1988 RSF Ard Fheis, or annual conference, the party reaffirmed its support for the "armed struggle." RSF rejected the 1993 Downing Street declaration and was also squarely against the peace process.[10] RSF saw itself as forming part of a wider Republican Movement with a number of organizations sharing similar ideological and political perspectives including the CIRA, Cumann na mBan,

Fianna Éireann, Cabhair, the National Commemoration Committee, and the Republican Prisoners Action Group. RSF strenuously rejected the allegation that it was the "political wing" of the CIRA, as it denied any assertion that the latter was its "military wing."

REAL IRISH REPUBLICAN ARMY

The Real IRA split from the Provisional IRA in 1998 over political differences, forming an armed counterpart to the political 32-County Sovereignty Movement (32CSM). The group shares the common IRA goal of reunifying Northern Ireland and Ireland, but rejects the PIRA ceasefire and the Belfast Agreement, continuing to direct violence against the British government in Northern Ireland.

Viewed as one of the most dangerous groups in existence after the Good Friday Agreement, one of its most devastating accomplishments was the bomb attack of the town center of Omagh on August 15, 1998. Twenty-nine civilians were killed in this bombing, and more than two hundred were wounded. It was, singly, the worst terrorist attack in Northern Ireland history. Following this atrocity, the group was forced to call a ceasefire. In spite of this, the group remains in existence and gets its support from those not aligned with the peace process. As long as there is a modicum of deadlock and lack of progress, this group is likely to continue to try to sway support away from the PIRA. The Real IRA 2008 New Year's Statement published in the Sovereign Nation newspaper was very clear about their intent moving forward:

> The Irish Republican Army will continue to carry out armed attacks against the British military and political apparatus in Ireland, and those who assist in anyway their illegal occupation. Once again the constitutional nationalist and establishment parties are attempting to sell the lie that the RUC/PSNI are a civic police force, and this has been borne out by recent events, that the RUC/PSNI are primarily a political police force whose primary function is to protect British interests in Ireland. It is for this reason that the IRA have carried out a number of attacks against the British police in Ireland, these attacks will continue.

RIRA operates in the same way as does the PIRA, with bomb attacks on security forces and commercial locations and targeting mainland Britain. Its leadership includes Bernadette Sands Mckevitt, the sister of Bobby Sands, a PIRA member who died from a hunger strike, and Francie Mackey, a one-time Sinn Féin counselor for Omagh. Its weapons and explosives likely come from PIRA sources, and there is concern that the group is purchasing weapons through Balkan states (Figure 5-4).

FIGURE 5-4 Mural commemorating the death of Bobby Sands who died during a hunger strike. *Courtesy:* Chief Superintendent Tony Forward.

OTHER IRISH TERRORIST GROUPS

Irish National Liberation Army

Also called People's Liberation Army (PLA), People's Republican Army (PRA), and Catholic Reaction Force (CRF), this small group is an offshoot of the breakup of the IRA in the late 1960s. They reject the ideology of both the official IRA and the Provisional IRA and are considered more Marxist in orientation than the PIRA. Formed in the early 1970s with a small membership of about thirty, it is headquartered in Dublin. Its goals and activities have centered in the Belfast and Londonderry areas. Their political objectives being the formation of a thirty-two-county Socialist Republic in Ireland, the forced removal by any means, including violence, of British troops from Northern Ireland, and the overthrow of the elected government of the Republic of Ireland. They express solidarity with other national liberation and terrorist organizations around the world. Its leadership consisted of Harry Flynn, Gerard Steenson,

Thomas Power, and Dominic McGlinchey. McGlinchey, Steenson, and Power were all killed in bitter feuding between INLA and the PIRA in the late 1980s. Their most audacious act of terror remains the 1979 assassination of Airey Neeve, the British Conservative Party spokesman on Northern Ireland. Neeve was killed when a powerful bomb destroyed his car as he was leaving the Houses of Parliament in London. A highly decorated World War II veteran, he wrote a study of the Nuremberg trials. In his study's final chapter, he was to reflect on the impact the Nuremberg trials had had on his life and the fight between good and evil.

This assassination marked INLA's first operation outside Ireland. The group was decimated in the 1980s as a result of the "Supergrass" trials. The word *supergrass* is an outgrowth of an eighteenth-century slang term, *copper* (meaning *informer*), which rhymed into *grasshopper*, later shortened to just "grass." "Super" was added to precede "grass" in the late-twentieth century to imply informing on a truly grand scale. In the context of Northern Ireland, the Supergrass strategy involved "reforming" terrorists by allowing them to divulge information in court about fellow terrorists and current prisoners in exchange for a new identity in a new country. Police in Northern Ireland used this strategy, and the evidence at that time was admissible in court. Supergrasses were responsible for a number of arrests and convictions of Irish terror suspects; the evidence provided was not required to be corroborated. Uncorroborated testimony is among the more dubious practices in a court of law. These Supergrassers were designated as such by INLA and PIRA militants for those who informed on their former comrades. By the end of the decade, the problems with admission of Supergrass evidence as part of the court process led to the release of many imprisoned INLA and PIRA members. The result—a bloody feud between the INLA and PIRA militants. INLA still remains brutal and unpredictable. The organization was responsible for the murder of Billy Wright, a Loyalist Protestant and Maze Prison militant, on December 27, 1997. The result of this assassination was a spate of sectarian attacks, in which eight Catholics were murdered. The INLA has been observing a ceasefire since August 1998.

Ulster Volunteer Force

A loyalist paramilitary group that also operated under the names *Protestant Action Group* and *Protestant Action Force* in the 1970s with around 1800 members. By 2006, that number had dwindled to a hard core of several hundred supporters. Ulster Volunteer Force (UVF) was considered to be the largest of the Loyalist paramilitary organizations. Formed at the outset of "The Troubles" in 1966, it takes its name from its Irish forefathers—the original UVF was formed in 1912 to oppose, by force, the Home Rule Bill for Ireland. In 1914, the volunteers smuggled thirty five thousand rifles into Larne, County Antrim. Later, men of the UVF joined the British Army en masse as the 36th Ulster Division, which suffered huge losses at the Battle of the Somme. As they went over the top that day and charged the enemy lines, the Ulster soldiers shouted, "No surrender," echoing the same cry used by the apprentice boys in the siege of Londonderry of 1688. Its limited goals are aimed at securing the North's constitutional position within the United Kingdom and to aggressively defend its Protestant heritage.

The endless cycle of violence that has typified Northern Ireland life for more than a quarter of century can be laid squarely at the doorsteps of both Protestant and Catholic paramilitaries. On many occasions, these groups use different names of ally groups to claim responsibility for attacks. The Loyalist paramilitary groups invariably did not claim specific responsibility for their murders—they moved and operated under various subgroups in their terrorist structure.

The UVF has been responsible for scores of assassinations in Northern Ireland, mostly of innocent Catholics. The UVF leader in the 1960s was Augustus (Gusty) Spence, who killed a Catholic man in a pub on the Shankill Road, Belfast, in June 1966 and was sentenced to life in prison. They are also credited with the simultaneous bombings of Dublin and Monaghan on May 17, 1974, killing thirty-three civilians (Figure 5-5).

FIGURE 5-5 Chelsea Street, Belfast decorated with Loyalist murals and flying the Union Jack (Since this photograph was taken Chelsea Street has been completely redeveloped). *Courtesy: Gary Wilson.*

FIGURE 5-6 Loyalist mural of the Ulster Volunteer Force (UVF) insignia (the original would have traditionally featured the Red Hand of Ulster in the center).   *Courtesy:* Gary Wilson.

Throughout the 1970s, their main battleground was the Shankill Road area of Belfast and parts of County Antrim. The group was proscribed in 1974, making it an illegal organization. They continued their bloody sectarian attacks, killing twelve people in October 1975. Raids by security forces in 1977 saw twenty-six suspects arrested for the killings. Their convictions resulted in a total of seven hundred years imprisonment. Their decline came about mostly from informers, whom the British security services were able to skillfully manipulate for information on past attacks, resulting in further arrests and convictions throughout the 1990s. In spite of these setbacks, the UVF continued sectarian attacks against Catholics throughout the 1990s. In 1996, a number of disaffected members of their mid-Ulster brigade formed the Loyalist Volunteer Force (LVF). For its political influence, the Progressive Unionist Party (PUP) is considered as its front in much the same way as Sinn Féin and PIRA (Figure 5-6).

Along with many other paramilitary groups, the UVF did declare a ceasefire in 1994. Later in the decade, the UVF was frequently accused of violating the ceasefire agreement. As late as August 2005, the UVF continued its sectarian attacks. Gusty Spence announced that the UVF and the Red Hand Commando would "assume a nonmilitary, civilianized role." The UVF continued to feud with other loyalist groups, which caused the British government to announce in 2005 that it no longer recognized the UVF's 1994 ceasefire. Since 2005, the group's leadership has attempted to distance the UVF from criminal activities, although with very questionable results. The Independent Monitoring Commission, formed in 2004 to monitor paramilitary organizations in Northern Ireland, in its April 2006 report stated that the UVF remained an active and violent paramilitary organization. By May 2007, with most other groups either out of commission or having declared a permanent ceasefire, they declared that they were renouncing violence and ending their terror campaign. They also stated that UVF was not disarming but, like the PIRA, was simply putting their weapons and explosives beyond reach.

Ulster Democratic Party

The Ulster Democratic Party (UDP) also uses the name Ulster Loyalist Democratic Party. The group was formed in 1989 as a political front for the UDA. The ULDP was the original political mouthpiece of UDA in 1981. This organization had little or no political gains and successes. PIRA assassinated its leader John McMichael with a car bomb at his Lisburn home in December 1987. The UDP strategy was to outwardly portray itself as a distinct political movement and was not aligned with the UDA; we have seen this with PIRA and Sinn Féin. The government banned membership of UDP in 1992. Under the terms of Section 30(3) of the Northern Ireland Emergency Provisions Act of 1996, the following Loyalist groups were proscribed:

- The Red Hand Commandos
- The Ulster Freedom Fighters
- The Ulster Volunteer Force
- The Ulster Defense Association

The following are the proscribed Republican groups:

- The Irish Republican Army
- The Irish National Liberation Army
- The Irish Peoples Liberation Organization
- Women's Wing of the Irish Republican Army (Cumann na mBan)
- Youth Wing of the Irish Republican Army (Fianna na hEireann)
- Saor Eire (Free Ireland)

The UDP was finally dissolved in November 2001. It seems logical that infighting and disagreement over the Good Friday Agreement was the cause of the disbandment of the organization.

Ulster Defense Association/Ulster Freedom Fighters

The UDA is also one of the largest Loyalist paramilitary groups in Northern Ireland. They also use the name *Ulster Freedom Fighters* (UFF) as a cover for terrorist actions. An abundance of Loyalist defense associations sprang up in the first years of "The Troubles," which saw numerous attacks in the 1970s on Catholics. Members of the UFF claimed responsibility for these attacks, but they were effectively being conducted by UDA members. The two groups should be viewed as one and the same, and it is difficult to understand why the UDA was not proscribed until August 1992. Along with the UVF, the UDA had significant numbers located in Belfast and was a commanding force to either attack Catholics or challenge the British army presence.

Their aim was to create an independent Northern Ireland, both within the European Union and the Commonwealth. To create the correct political mind-set, it needed to create a viable political forum and thus formed the New Ulster Political Research Group (NUPRG) in 1978. In June 1981, the Ulster Loyalist Democratic Party (ULDP) was established, replacing the NUPRG. The ULDP also proposed independence for Northern Ireland within the British Commonwealth. The UDA was politically savvy and was able to create a document by 1987 that set out its vision for a new political settlement and structure for the North. In spite of UDA's obvious links with terrorism, the proposal document did receive some favorable reviews from politicians and the British Government's Northern Ireland Office. UDA leader, John McMichael was killed by a PIRA bomb, but the UDA/UFF continued its attacks on Catholics and Republican supporters into the 1990s. The UDA/UFF joined in the 1994 ceasefire, and members of the UDP were involved in the multiparty talks in 1996. The Good Friday Agreement remained a political football throughout the remainder of the century. Many groups on both sides were opposed to various sections of the agreement, particularly policing and power sharing.

UDA/UFF continued to feud with other loyalist groups and also maintained its campaign of attacks on Catholics. The ongoing feud and the attacks forced the government to announce that UDA/UFF, the UVF and the LVF had ended their ceasefires. Sporadic feuding continued within the UDA, and on February 22, 2003, the UDA declared a ceasefire. The LVF was formed in 1996 as a breakaway group from the Loyalist UFF. LVF is a violent, anti-Catholic movement, strongly opposed to the 1994 ceasefire agreement. Its membership is likely small and accounts for maybe three dozen active members. The British government proscribed the LVF in 1997. Its leader Billy Wright was murdered inside the Maze Prison by members of the Republican Irish National Liberation Army (INLA) in December 1997. As has been the case throughout "The Troubles," no terror act by one side goes without retaliation from the other. In the two weeks following Billy Wright's death, sectarian violence accounted for the murders of eight Catholics by members of the LVF and UFF.

The LVF agreed to a ceasefire in May 1998, but continues to oppose the peace process. In 1998, under the auspices of the Independent International Commission on Decommissioning (IICD), it began to decommission some of its arsenal of weapons. Any weapons and explosives it may have limited access to are likely under the control of other Loyalist groups. It is believed that no other Loyalist groups have decommissioned any weapons or explosives; however, the UVF has claimed to put their weapons "beyond reach."

The LVF, at its peak, had around three hundred members, and the group has not been credited with carrying out any attacks since February 2003. Billy Wright was "succeeded" by Mark Fulton, a close acquaintance who reportedly idolized the founder of the LVF; Fulton has been described as Wright's hit man and is thought to be personally responsible for over a dozen sectarian murders. While in jail, awaiting trial on charges of conspiracy to murder a rival loyalist, Fulton died of strangulation on June 9, 2002, in an apparent suicide. He was found in his jail cell in the isolation wing of the prison with a belt wrapped around his neck.[11]

Red Hand Defenders

The Red Hand Defenders (RHD) formed in late 1998 from a group of Loyalist paramilitaries disaffected by the Good Friday Agreement. There has been speculation that RHD is simply a cover name for UDA and LVF members to carry sectarian violence. This would be to their benefit, as only those paramilitaries on formal ceasefire were able to benefit from the early prison-release program within the Good Friday Agreement. If this is the case, clearly the RHD is established as a cover and has no real existing members as they would be considered members of either the UDA or the LVF.

During the 1998 marching season, RHD conducted what seems to be a revenge bomb attack, killing an RUC officer. This attack followed the RUC decision to restrict the Orange Order from marching along the Garvaghy Road in Portadown, County Armagh. They had also claimed responsibility for the killing of Rosemary Nelson, a Catholic human rights lawyer, in Lurgan in March 1999. RHD and the Orange Volunteers (OV) seemed to surface around the same period, and it is thought that the OV may be another cover for Loyalists.

Orange Volunteers

The OV is a Protestant Loyalist paramilitary with ties to the Orange Order. The group originated at the outset of "The Troubles." It was at that time second only to the UDA and the UVF in size and support. The group was believed to be inactive by the end of 1980, but its name came up once again in 1998 at the same time as the RHD. Like other paramilitaries of the time, OV was made up of those disaffected by the Good Friday Agreement and is likely closely linked with the same membership as the RHD. The operational effectiveness of this "new" group is unsophisticated and has utilized homemade blast bombs (pipe bombs) and hand grenades. It may be that this small group of dissidents is also involved in crime, most particularly drug dealing.

TURF WARS

The early 1970s could be described as turf wars among the warring factions of the IRA, the INLA, the UFF, and the UVF. Tit-for-tat murders and revenge killings of both Catholics and Protestants were common, driven mostly by pure hatred.

This was epitomized by the infamous "Shankill Butchers," a gang of UVF members led by "The Master Butcher" Lenny Murphy, operating in West Belfast and intimidating the Catholic community and carrying out merciless, cutthroat killings. In those early days, there was a struggle for supremacy in the housing districts and ghettos of West Belfast. The feuding was partly ideological and partly material in that they were fighting for control of the criminal rackets in Belfast and Londonderry. Since the Good Friday Agreement came into force, much of the continued violence has related to criminal activities within the paramilitaries, both Protestants and Catholics.

One Protestant fighter stands out among all others for his audacious attacks against Republicans. In March 1988, the crack British counterrevolutionary warfare unit from the SAS Regiment killed three PIRA members on the island of Gibraltar (Figure 5-7). At their funeral in Milltown Cemetery, with the world's press watching, a man approached from the road and hurled grenades at the assembled Republicans, including Gerry Adams. In the ensuing mayhem, the Protestant Michael Stone was arrested; he was charged and sentenced and was subsequently released in 2000 under the terms of the Good Friday Agreement. His actions did not end there; in 2006, he single-handedly stormed into the foyer of the Northern Ireland Assembly, carrying a bomb and waving a handgun and knife, before being tackled by security staff.

FIGURE 5-7 Wall mural commemorating the deaths of Dan McCann and Sean Savage—killed by SAS in Gibraltar—March 1988. *Courtesy:* Chief Superintendent Tony Forward.

Civil Liberty and Human Rights

Civil rights, human rights, and civil liberty issues have aided and confused the processes of both peace and terror. The British government has used human rights violations as a tool, both legislatively and as a method of controlling the violence in Ulster.

The Catholic marches of the late 1960s sparked the rioting and bloodshed that led to larger and larger troop deployments in Ulster. Internment was introduced in the 1970s by the British government to curtail the actions of the paramilitary groups. Internment had little strategic effect, but provided PIRA members with significant public sympathy—they were seen as "martyrs for the cause."

With the increase in sectarian violence, judges and juries also became targets for the terrorist groups. The **Diplock Commission**[12] was set up to look at ways of dealing with the legal aspects of controlling a terrorist in a democratic society. Ensuring the safety and integrity of the security forces and giving them the unfettered ability to bring the terrorists before the courts, the Northern Ireland Emergency Provisions Act was passed in 1973. The measures, seen as draconian, served the security services well. The act provided for terrorist offenses to be listed as "scheduled" offenses:

- Scheduled offenses were to be tried by a senior judge sitting alone, with more than the rights of appeal.
- Bail was prohibited for scheduled offenses unless granted by the High Court, with stringent conditions attached.
- Persons could be held on police arrests without warrant for seventy-two hours.
- Suspects arrested by the military could be held for four hours.
- Security forces had extensive powers for search and seizure.
- Those arrested for weapons and explosives offenses had the onus of proof reversed for them to prove their innocence.
- The secretary of state could issue detention orders from information gathered if the security forces believed the information and evidence to be valid.[13]

Nonjury trials were introduced in Northern Ireland in 1972 as a response to witness intimidation by paramilitary groups. The introduction of "Diplock Courts" was opposed by civil liberty organizations and both nationalists and Republicans. At their peak, more than 300 trials per year were held without a jury. Some of those operating the system were targeted by the IRA and, in 1987, Lord Justice Maurice Gibson and his wife were killed by a bomb. The government technically abolished Diplock courts in 2007, but nonjury trials can be used if jurors are believed to be at risk of intimidation. Between August 1, 2008 and July 31, 2009, thirteen nonjury trials were held, down from twenty-nine in the previous year.

With many convictions for terrorist offenses gathered through this sweeping legislation, the PIRA still managed to make both political and publicity points for its predicament. Once in prison, the terrorist took control and intimidated prison officers both inside and outside the confines of jail. These laws were adopted in the early 1970s and since then have undergone frequent reviews and amendments. In 1988, fifteen years after it was enacted, the Prevention of Terrorism Act, providing sweeping powers to security forces in Britain, was challenged in the international court. The provision within the act to detain terrorist suspects for up to seven days was determined to have violated the European Convention on Human Rights. In 1999, the Home Secretary announced the establishment of a review group comprising representatives of the Northern Ireland Office, the Northern Ireland Court Service, the Attorney General's Office, the Director of Public Prosecutions (Northern Ireland), and the then RUC. Underlying the work of the review group was the general consensus that normalization should occur as soon as possible and that the restoration of jury trial would be seen as a normalizing event. In a report to the secretary of state for Northern Ireland in May 2000, the review concluded that the time was not yet right for an immediate return of jury trial. The principal reason for this was the conclusion that the risk of jury intimidation remained significant.[14]

The Terrorism Act of 2000 reformed much of the mechanisms and powers dealing with terrorism. The provisions of this act extended to all forms of domestic and foreign terrorism within the United Kingdom. Certain provisions of previous terrorism legislation, applicable only to Northern Ireland, could be extended for a maximum of five years. The act broadened the definition of terrorism to include actions or threats of action that are designed to

- influence the government;
- intimidate the public;
- advance a political, religious, or ideological cause;
- involve serious violence against a person or serious damage to property;
- endanger a person's life;
- create a serious risk to the health or safety of the public; or
- interfere with an electronic system.

Special powers within the act include special entry, arrest, and search and seizure authority without a warrant under certain circumstances.

Periodic reviews of the emergency powers specifically relating to Northern Ireland have been undertaken. While the perception may well be that life has returned to a level of normalcy, this is not necessarily expressed by the judiciary in its reviews. Examples of the powers available to both police and military forces came from Schedule 5, Sections 81–88 of the act. Lord Berriew, in his review, concluded that Section 81 allows a police officer to enter and search any premises if he or she has reasonable suspicion that a person is or has been concerned in the commission, preparation, or instigation of acts of terrorism. Section 82 provides that any police officer

> may arrest, without warrant, any person he or she has reasonable grounds to suspect is committing, has committed, or is about to commit a scheduled offense, or an offense under the Act that is not a scheduled offense, and may enter and search any premises or other place for that purpose.

Section 82(3) empowers a police officer to seize and retain anything that he or she suspects is being, has been, or is intended to be used in the commission of a scheduled offense. Section 83 provides a power of arrest and detention for a period not exceeding four hours to a member of Her Majesty's Forces on duty who reasonably suspects that a person is committing, has committed, or is about to commit any offense, together with corresponding powers of entry and seizure.

This act was further supported with the enactment of the Anti-terrorism Crime and Security Act of 2001, which addressed terrorism and foreign nationals. Civil rights movements have objected to provisions in both of these acts, specifically in sections where the burden of proof is reversed in suspected terrorism cases. In reflecting on 9-11, the legislation was also aimed at those Britons involved with attacks overseas. For instance, the British press reported that in December 2000, a British Muslim from Birmingham, England, was alleged to have conducted a suicide attack on an Indian army barrack in Srinagar; in another, a Briton was reportedly plotting a terrorist attack, earlier the same year, against Israel.

One topic not often discussed is the human rights abuse record of the paramilitaries in Northern Ireland before and after the Good Friday Peace Agreement. Both loyalist and republican communities were literally controlled by their respective paramilitaries and justice (summary) was meted out by punishment squads and this practice has been going on for more than forty years! What is troubling about the abuse is that little has been done to stop or prevent it from official channels. The loyalists and republican groups continue to rule with a rod of iron and speaking about past atrocities by any member of the respective community is liable to result in punishment. A code of silence continues to exist that protects the punishments squads from ever being brought to justice. A large number of young men and women as young as twelve years of age have been subjected to punishment beatings over the years for a variety of offenses mostly for antisocial behavior, including substance abuse, joy-riding or anything that may have offended the paramilitary hierarchy. The target group on both sides of the sectarian divide was almost all working class. The punishments meted out with iron bars, clubs spiked with nails were often done in front of parents to witness the 'punishment'; on other occasions families were delivered a note instructing them to take their son or daughter to a location to be shot—the shooting in the knee (knee capping) or ankle were favored locations.

Child abuse by paramilitaries is covered under the UN Convention on the Rights of the Child. Part of Article 37 of the Convention states: "No child shall be subjected to torture or other cruel, inhuman or degrading treatment or punishment." Clearly that does not seem to have much weight in Northern Ireland. Aside from beatings there are numerous instances where children and their entire families were banished from the area and had to relocate either to different regions of Ireland or to mainland Britain; returning to Ireland could mean a death sentence.

Between 1990 and 2013:

- 94 children were shot by loyalist paramilitaries.
- 73 children were shot by republican paramilitaries.
- 166 children were beaten-some badly mutilated—by loyalist paramilitaries.
- 178 children were beaten by republican paramilitaries.
- In total, more than 500 children were abused by the IRA, UVF, UDA, etc.[15]

These figures are clearly not the full story as many assaults were never reported. The code of silence among the communities in the north still exists and the hard men of the paramilitaries are well protected by their political masters. There are many incidents that can be related but here we will give two such examples of the brutality, fear, and terror inflicted on Irish families and that fear and terror for speaking out is still very present today.

The Case of the McConville Family—Michael McConville

The case of Michael McConville is one that typifies the brutality of the punishment squads. Michael's mother Jean was abducted by the IRA and taken across the border to the Republic where she was beaten to death after being interrogated.

The IRA came to the McConville home and forcibly abducted the mother. She had been beaten the night before by the IRA. Michael McConville was just eleven years old when his mother was taken. The abductors were wearing masks when she was forcibly taken and the following day they returned to the home and handed over her purse and rings—it was then that the family realized she was dead.

The following week, the IRA grabbed Michael McConville, put a hood over his head, and took him to a house. He was tied to a chair and beaten repeatedly for around three hours. He was threatened with death if he said anything to anyone about the IRA.

With his mother dead, the allegation by the IRA that his mother was an informant has never been substantiated.[16]

The aftermath of the case reveals that the republican movement, including Sinn Féin, has a poor track record when it comes to revealing the truth about activities most would regard as total disregard for human life.

The Case of Anthony O'Neill

The next subject is also treated severely and this time by the INLA.

Anthony O'Neill, described by his family as "no angel," was taken from his bed, tied up, and thrown into a manhole where he was beaten about the head in an INLA punishment attack last year. The INLA left the eighteen-year-old boy there for seven hours before he chewed through his restraints and escaped. He had been accused of joyriding, which he denied.

Unable to deal with the depression and paranoia caused by the attack, Anthony killed himself last week. "The INLA are bully-boys who threaten and humiliate kids," his sister Patricia O'Neill, 18, said. "Because there is no war these paramilitaries are turning on their own people.

The community is too scared to say anything. The young people are more afraid in the community because they feel they are on their own and have no one to turn to."[17]

The organized and systemic abuse of children was conducted by both Protestant and Catholic paramilitaries both before and after the 1998 Peace Agreement. A vast number of the injuries were life threatening and life changing in nature leaving permanent psychological and physical damage. All those who were victims were fully aware that by speaking out to the police or health authorities would only make certain of further punishment being given to either themselves or their families.

NORTHERN IRELAND'S PROTESTANT MARCHING SEASON

The Reverend Ian Paisley (April 1926–September 2014)

Ian Paisley had been the public face of Protestant reaction to Republicanism (Catholics). Paisley was the leader of the Democratic Unionist Party of Northern Ireland and moderator of the Free Presbyterian Church. As the mouthpiece of the Unionist movement, he was often sentenced for unlawful assembly as he conducted marches and protests around the province in the years leading up to the "Troubles." He even coined a battle cry first heard at the siege of Londonderry in 1688, "No surrender," when thirteen apprentice boys closed the gates of the city on the Jacobite army. In his hard-line Protestantism, he loudly proclaimed opposition to any and every concession offered to the Catholic community. He was an outspoken opponent of the Good Friday Agreement. However, in 2007, Ian Paisley was sworn in at Stormont Castle as Northern Ireland's First Minister and was photographed alongside the other senior member of the power-sharing executive and his old archenemy, Martin McGuiness from Sinn Féin. With the guns silent and politics, the order of the day, Paisley stepped down from politics as leader of the DUP and First Minister in 2008 and left politics altogether in 2011.

The Loyalists, including the entire Orange Order, were determined not to be part of any Republic. It seems almost incredible to people outside of Northern Ireland that the act of marching, seemingly so irrelevant to most, should cause such widespread anger and revulsion. Marching in military style has been a part of Protestant history for over 200 years. The lore and beliefs have been passed down from generation to generation. To understand what motivates such sectarian hatred between the Catholics and Protestant communities requires a review of the historical roots of marching.

Marching season falls between Easter Monday and the end of September, when more than 2,000 marches are held throughout the North. There are, however, specific march dates in history that create more flashpoints on the calendar than do other marches. The Protestants celebrate the victory of Protestant King William over Catholic King James I at the Battle of the Boyne, on July 12, 1690. But this is more than just the celebration of a victory; for Protestant Orangemen, it is the need to display their allegiance to the Crown and Protestantism. Sometimes referred to as "Orangeism," it could also be described as Ulster Unionism on the march. The **Orange Order** and the Ulster Unionist Council constitute an integrated political movement that is determined that Northern Ireland will remain within the United Kingdom along with England, Scotland, and Wales and will never be absorbed by a Catholic-dominated, all-Ireland republic.[18] Both the Orange Order and the Apprentice Boys say that marching is an essential part of their Protestant culture. The Apprentice Boys is a Loyalist organization similar to the Orange Order. This group annually commemorates the ending of the 105-day siege of Londonderry in 1688. They march with a crimson flag first carried by Protestant supporters of William of Orange who were besieged in Londonderry by an Irish Jacobite army.

The challenges to peace during marching season are many, as the marchers wind their way through long-established routes in Catholic enclave such as the Garvaghy Road in Portadown and the Lower Ormeau Road in Belfast. Both areas have been rife with outbursts of violence in recent years. The Independent Commission on Policing in Northern Ireland made a recommendation in 1998 that it should be a condition for the approval of a parade that the organizers provide their own marshals. This should include, as appropriate, representatives of the neighborhoods involved along the parade route. The Catholic communities, through which Protestants demand the right to march, have so much hostility to marching because it would take but one small incident to provoke an outbreak of serious sectarian violence.

The Loyal Orange Institution, or Orange Order, was founded in 1795 after a Protestant victory at Loughgall, County Armagh. This is referred to as the "Battle of the Diamond." In September 1795, several hundred Defenders (Catholics) assembled at a crossroads called the Diamond, near Loughgall in County Armagh. They had come to attack the house of one Dan Winter, where they were convinced the "peep-o-day boys" (Protestants) stored their guns and met to conspire against Catholics. The Battle of the Diamond, on Monday, September 21, lasted a brief fifteen minutes. The "peep-o-day boys" suffered no losses, but as many as forty-eight Defenders were said to have been killed. The first Orange Lodge was established that evening. One James Sloan, an innkeeper, became the first grand secretary, with power to issue warrants to whichever group of Protestants that wanted to follow his rule and set up Orange Lodges. They were required to swear an oath of allegiance to "His Majesty, King George III, and his successors so long as he and they support the Protestant ascendancy."[19]

Sectarian Violence

The terror groups on both sides of this complex situation have targeted the police and the military as their legitimate targets. The long-established hatred and revulsion of some Catholics for Protestants, and vice versa, has caused the senseless deaths of many innocent civilians. People have been killed purely for their religious affiliations, whether they are from PIRA or a Loyalist paramilitary. Tit-for-tat killings have been a hallmark of Northern Ireland's history through most of the twentieth century and into the twenty-first. (An obvious parallel is the conflict between the Israelis and Palestinians.) This dates back as far as June 17, 1922, when the IRA issued an order for the destruction of property owned by Orangemen. According to police reports, at 2:30

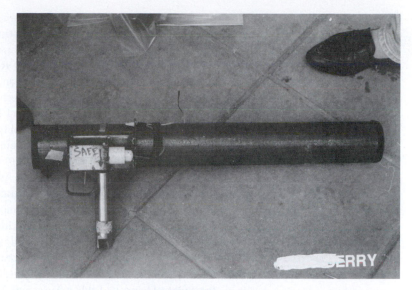

FIGURE 5-8 and FIGURE 5-9   IED Circa 1991/1992, a PRIG (Projected Recoilless Improvised Grenade) pictured at the scene of an unsuccessful attack on a joint RUC/Army patrol in Londonderry City Centre. The PIRA member, concealed in an alleyway, fired the launcher but missed the patrol completely. The projectile landed harmlessly in an office. *Courtesy:* Gary Wilson.

that morning, IRA men executed six unarmed Protestants and a policeman. The attack was motivated purely along religious lines and had no significance in the struggle for the IRA. Five decades later in 1976 a similar, but far more gruesome, attack took place in the Kingsmills area in South Armagh and claimed the lives of ten Protestant workers, who were stopped on their bus ride home from work and executed in a hail of bullets by members of the PIRA. Marching season is the time of year when sectarianism comes into play. Protestants have viewed the treatment of Sinn Féin and the Republican movement as an erosion of their own political and economic power base. As they lose ground, this violence, sectarian in nature, has begun to spread. In 2001, in the weeks leading up to the 9-11 attacks in the United States, Protestants pelted Catholic primary schoolchildren with rocks and verbal abuse as they made their way to school through the Protestant Ardoyne district of Belfast. These scenes were more reminiscent of an earlier age in the southern United States involving bussing of black students to school. The Holy Cross School in Ardoyne district has existed for more than thirty years, but the demographics of the area around it have changed. Mainly a Protestant area when "The Troubles" began, many of the middle-class Protestants moved away throughout the 1990s, and more Catholic families have moved into the area, to the chagrin of Protestants (Figures 5-8 and 5-9).

THE PIRA AND INTERNATIONAL TERROR

The Sinn Féin and Irish Republican terror groups had a problem, and that problem was credibility. The Peace agreement required weapons to be decommissioned and although some decommissioning had taken place, there was a double standard—the PIRA turned in the old weapons, but then actively pursued acquiring new ones. In May 2002, the PIRA purchased a quantity of Russian-made AN-94 assault rifles. In April 2002, the Israelis identified pipe bomb devices made by PIRA terrorists in the hands of Palestinian terrorists. Paul Collinson, a former officer with the Royal Engineers Bomb Disposal, who worked for the Red Cross at the Jenin refugee camp in Palestine, commented, "The pipe bombs I found in Jenin are exact replicas of those in Northern Ireland. The size of bomb, the way they put the nail in, the way of igniting it with a light bulb filament, where they drilled the holes through, the use of a command wire and the means of initiating the bomb; these are all the same."[20] As we can tell from this report, the PIRA continues to ply its terrorism trade on an international scale not only in the Middle East but also, as mentioned earlier, in South America. This broader involvement of the PIRA on the international stage was also a focus of the U.S. House of Representatives International Relations Committee. This committee concluded that Irish, Iranian, Cuban, and Spanish terror groups had probably been sharing techniques and honing their terror skills, while using illicit drug proceeds for payment. Gerry Adams, as the president of Sinn Féin, not surprisingly turned down an invitation to testify before the congressional committee on the topic.

How closely linked are Sinn Féin and the Irish terror groups? There is little doubt that Adams and McGuiness have the ability to exert significant pressure, whether direct or implied, on the workings of the PIRA and the Army Council. In early 2002, a daring raid was made on the Northern Ireland Police Special Branch offices at Castlereagh. The PIRA managed to seize highly confidential documents that named police informants and undercover operations. To most observers in the security services, it is highly probable that the PIRA Army Council ordered and conducted this seizure. Most, if not all, terror groups come to the table to talk peace only when they are in such a desperate situation that signing a deal or calling a ceasefire is all that is left to them. In 1994, the PIRA called a ceasefire—not when they were winning the battle, but when they were losing it. Both Adams and McGuiness are survivors, and to control the dissidents within the Republican movement, it would seem wholly logical for the PIRA to continue as before, but allowing Sinn Féin the freedom to express concern, sometimes outrage and, more frequently, denial of knowledge of PIRA activities when it comes to the thorny topics of bomb making and weapons acquisition.

There are many differences between the struggle for peace in Northern Ireland and the struggle for peace in the Middle East. In Northern Ireland, there are still many political problems to be resolved, as well as centuries of fear and distrust standing between Catholics and Protestants. However, for Northern Ireland there is a tunnel, and there even appears to be some light at the end of it.

THE NORTHERN IRELAND PEACE PROCESS

It is generally agreed that the peace process was developed from a combination of factors. A realization, by both the PIRA and the British Army, that the war could not be won militarily, and the decision by the PIRA to develop political strategies through Sinn Féin, as an alternative way to fight for its goals:

- The willingness of the Social Democratic Labour Party (SDLP) to engage with Sinn Féin in pursuing common nationalist political goals by peaceful means.
- A changing social and economic context in which many of the discriminations against Catholics was addressed and in which a legal and social infrastructure to address issues of inequality, equality, and respect for diversity began to be developed.
- An increased willingness by many within civic society, for example, among businesses, trade unions, and community groups, to actively engage in the process of contact and political leverage for peace.
- The development of some new (albeit small) political parties by the Loyalists, and by the Women's Coalition, which enabled some new thinking on the political landscape.
- A changing international context, including proactive involvement from the U.S. government, and many U.S. businessmen and politicians, as well as assistance with developing peace processes from South Africa.[21]

In August 2001, just a few weeks before 9-11, the Good Friday Agreement was on the verge of collapse and PIRA had failed to decommission its weapons. The events of 9-11 appear to have had a sobering effect on the men of violence in Northern Ireland. With endless bombings and more than three thousand six hundred killed in sectarian violence, both main players—the British government, which has endured with an occupying army for over three decades, and the Irish terror organizations—eventually came to the conclusion that the fighting must end. From the terrorist standpoint, the use of the gun, albeit used to good effect, has not had its desired effect of removing British occupying forces from Northern Ireland. Early attempts at peace settlements in the two decades preceding the Good Friday Agreement were doomed to failure. Events that would hinder any lasting peace have principally been the decommissioning of weapons in the possession of the paramilitary groups and the PIRA's foreign involvement in Colombian and Middle East terrorism. For many decades, the romantic image of Irish freedom fighters taking on the British was lore in the Irish-American communities of New York and Boston. Media coverage of terrorism—played out on U.S. television screens—has required a fundamental shift in the PIRA's attitude toward decommissioning of weapons. The PIRA has received significant amounts of financial aid from U.S. organizations and support groups; however, in the aftermath of 9-11, the romantic view of the cause for most Americans faded quickly.

Decommissioning

The decommissioning of weapons was a central issue in the peace deal/accord.

In September 1997, the IICD was established to oversee the decommissioning of paramilitary weapons from both sides.

The 1998 Belfast Agreement committed all participants to the total disarmament of all paramilitary organizations. The agreement called on all sides to work constructively with the decommissioning teams to use any influence they may have to achieve the decommissioning of all paramilitary arms within two years of the referendum, in May 1998. Although this target was never met, progress was nonetheless made. The first act of decommissioning was witnessed by the IICD in December 1998, when the LVF decommissioned a quantity of weapons.

Caches of weapons and explosives have been stockpiled through the last two decades of the twentieth century. These arms shipments came from state sponsors of terrorism, specifically Colonel Qaddafi of Libya. This support would surely be repugnant to the American public still recovering in the aftermath of 9-11.

In October 2001, the PIRA, under the scrutiny of IICD, "put beyond use" (a term used by the PIRA to signify destruction) a large quantity of weapons and explosives. The first round of PIRA decommissioning was orchestrated shortly after the arrest in Colombia of two senior members of the Republican movement and FARC guerillas. This can only have been an embarrassment to the Sinn Féin leadership and something that would likely damage relations between the Republicans and their U.S. support networks. On the other side of the equation, the Ulster Democratic Unionist Party, led by the Reverend Ian Paisley, was not satisfied with the manner in which the destruction of the weapons and explosives had taken place and was demanding a full listing of weapons destroyed. However, the decommissioning was viewed as a landmark event that gave the British government a further opportunity to announce the removal and closure of the network of army watchtowers along the border with the Republic.

On October 23, 2001, the IRA issued the following statement on the BBC regarding the subject of disarmament:

> The IRA is committed to our republican objectives and to the establishment of a united Ireland based on justice, equality, and freedom. In August 1994, against a background of lengthy and intensive discussions involving the two governments and others, the leadership of the IRA called a complete cessation of military operations in order to create the dynamic for a peace process. "Decommissioning" was no part of that. There was no ambiguity about this. Unfortunately, there are those within the British establishment and the leadership of Unionism who are fundamentally opposed to change. At every opportunity, they have used the issue of arms as an excuse to undermine and frustrate the process. It was for this reason this decommissioning was introduced to the process by the British government. It has been used since to prevent the changes that a lasting peace requires. In order to overcome this and to encourage the changes necessary for a lasting peace, the leadership of Oglaigh na hEireann (IRA) has taken a number of substantial initiatives. These include our engagement with the Independent International Commission on Decommissioning (IICD) and the inspection of a number of arms dumps by the international inspectors, Cyril Ramaphosa and Martti Ahtisaari. No one should doubt the difficulties these initiatives cause for our volunteers, our supporters, and us. The political process is now on the point of collapse. Such a collapse would certainly, and eventually, put the overall peace process in jeopardy. There is a responsibility upon everyone seriously committed to a just peace to do our best

to avoid this. Therefore, in order to save the peace process, we have implemented the scheme agreed with the IICD in August. Our motivation is clear. This unprecedented move is to save the peace process and to persuade others of our genuine intention.

SIGNED: P. O'NEILL.[22]

The PIRA's reluctance for verification of arms decommissioning continued to be a stumbling block for Republicans and Loyalists.

Further decommissioning took place in 2003 and 2004, but the PIRA still retained the ability to use force. While they may have decommissioned all of their arms, they had not actually disbanded, and no one except the PIRA has any definitive knowledge as to the number and types of weapons that remain cached. This being said, in 2005 PIRA issued the following statement:

The leadership of Oglaigh na hEireann (IRA) announced on 28 July that we had authorized our representative to engage with the IICD to complete the process of verifiably putting arms beyond use. The IRA leadership can now confirm that the process of putting arms beyond use has been completed.

SIGNED: P. O'NEILL.

(Ret) General John de Chastelain (IICD Commission Chairman) has indicated that the following estimates are an accurate representation of the PIRA arsenal that was decommissioned:

- 1,000 rifles
- 2 tonnes of Semtex
- 20–30 heavy machine guns
- 7 surface-to-air missiles (unused)
- 7 flame throwers
- 1,200 detonators
- 11 rocket-propelled grenade launchers
- 90 handguns
- 100+ grenades[23]

The peace process, starting with the Good Friday Agreement, has stumbled along for more than half a decade. The aim of a coalition of parties was to lead what might be termed a "joint assembly" made up of all "interested parties," including Sinn Féin. The inclusion of Sinn Féin, and the perception that its leaders still have links and influence over PIRA activities, has had a definite impact on the power-sharing process. Unionist parties were adamant that they could not work out a government with Sinn Féin so long as the Provisionals retained possession of their weapons and munitions. But, with the final decommissioning of the PIRA arms, a power-sharing government for Northern Ireland has become a reality. In May 2007, Ian Paisley and Martin McGuiness were sworn in at Stormont Castle as Northern Ireland's First Minister and Deputy First Minister, respectively, and both Republican groups (Catholics) and the Unionists (Protestants) now make up the power-sharing executive in Northern Ireland.

The "Agreement" is a document that goes a long way in addressing political, social, economic, and judicial inequalities that, to many, would seem to have been root causes of the thirty years of "The Troubles." Three of the most common points, decommissioning, security and policing, and justice have been cause for not just debate, but at times the near breakdown of the whole Agreement. The following sections taken from the Agreement form some of the most contentious points:

PRISONERS

1. Both governments will put in place mechanisms to provide for an accelerated program for the release of prisoners, including transferred prisoners, convicted of scheduled offenses in Northern Ireland or, in the case of those sentenced outside Northern Ireland, similar offenses (referred to hereafter as qualifying prisoners). Any such arrangements will protect the rights of individual prisoners under national and international law.
2. Prisoners affiliated to organizations that have not established or are not maintaining a complete and unequivocal ceasefire will not benefit from the arrangements. The situation in this regard will be kept under review.

3. Both governments will complete a review process within a fixed time frame and set prospective release dates for all qualifying prisoners. The review process would provide for the advance of the release dates of qualifying prisoners, while allowing account to be taken of the seriousness of the offenses for which the person was convicted and the need to protect the community. In addition, the intention would be that, should the circumstances allow it, any qualifying prisoners who remained in custody two years after the commencement of the scheme would be released at that point.

4. The governments will seek to enact the appropriate legislation to give effect to these arrangements by the end of June 1998.

5. The governments will continue to recognize the importance of measures to facilitate the reintegration of prisoners into the community by providing support both prior to and after release, including assistance directed toward availing of employment opportunities, retraining and/or re-skilling, and further education.

As mentioned earlier, the decommissioning of weapons by paramilitaries has been a major stumbling block for politicians, particularly from the Unionists.

Decommissioning

1. Participants recall their agreement in the Procedural Motion adopted on September 24, 1997, "that the resolution of the decommissioning issue is an indispensable part of the process of negotiation," and also recall the provisions of paragraph 25 of Strand 1 above.

2. They note the progress made by the Independent International Commission on Decommissioning and the governments in developing schemes that can represent a workable basis for achieving the decommissioning of illegally held arms in the possession of paramilitary groups.

3. All participants accordingly reaffirm their commitment to the total disarmament of all paramilitary organizations. They also confirm their intention to continue to work constructively and in good faith with the Independent Commission and to use any influence they may have to achieve the decommissioning of all paramilitary arms within two years following endorsement in referendums North and South of the agreement, and in the context of the implementation of the overall settlement.

4. The Independent Commission will monitor, review, and verify progress on decommissioning of illegal arms, and will report to both governments at regular intervals.

5. Both governments will take all necessary steps to facilitate the decommissioning process to include bringing the relevant schemes into force by the end of June.

Security

1. The participants note that the development of a peaceful environment on the basis of this agreement can and should mean a normalization of security arrangements and practices.

2. The British government will make progress toward the objective of a return as early as possible to normal security arrangements in Northern Ireland, consistent with the level of threat and with a published overall strategy, dealing with
   i. The reduction of the numbers and role of the Armed Forces deployed in Northern Ireland to levels compatible with a normal peaceful society;
   ii. The removal of security installations;
   iii. The removal of emergency powers in Northern Ireland;
   iv. Other measures appropriate to and compatible with a normal peaceful society.

3. The Secretary of State will consult regularly on progress and the response to any continuing paramilitary activity with the Irish government and the political parties, as appropriate.

4. The British government will continue its consultation on firearms regulation and control on the basis of the document published on April 2, 1998.

5. The Irish government will initiate a wide-ranging review of the Offences Against the State Acts 1939–85 with a view to both reform and dispensing with those elements no longer required as circumstances permit.[24]

The power base for the PIRA and Sinn Féin had rested as much on the gun and the bomb as it did on the vote. The governments of both Dublin and London have believed that terrorism cannot be defeated but must be appeased, and this has caused them to waver in negotiations—first, demanding concessions from the PIRA, next backing down or withdrawing the demand, and then pressuring the democratic parties not to make the same demands. Success in the elections has gone to those parties that have openly opposed serving in government assemblies with armed terrorists. Appeasement will surely win in the end!

POWER-SHARING EXECUTIVE

The peace process has been long and protracted and has at times almost crashed and burned! The appetite for a power-sharing government follows nearly forty years of sectarian violence and political posturing and squabbling. In the history of Northern Ireland's "Troubles," May 8, 2007, was a landmark day—a power-sharing local authority had been brokered and recognized by the governments of both the Republic of Ireland and the United Kingdom. The Reverend Ian Paisley, leader of the dominant party among Northern Ireland's Protestant community, and Martin McGuiness, the deputy head of Sinn Féin Republican Party, were both sworn in as leader and deputy leader, respectively, to lead the new Northern Ireland government. The events would end political and direct rule from London, which had been in effect since the Northern Ireland Assembly was suspended in 2002. Looking back over the last thirty-five years, it's almost inconceivable that these two men, Paisley and McGuiness, would ever speak to each other let alone form the leadership nuclei of a new power-sharing government—in the past, Paisley had long accused McGuiness of being an IRA terrorist and that he had acquired the nickname of "Dr. No" for his continued rejection of the Good Friday Agreement. The May 8 oath that both men took also included a commitment to the Northern Ireland Police, something the Republicans had long resisted as the police were viewed as part of the Union enemy. The "Troubles" are officially over in Northern Ireland, but what remains of the men of violence? They have certainly not disappeared but have continued to act as organized crime units, controlling drugs and other illegal activities. It is hoped that with cooperation, with the police now enshrined in the new government approach to business, the police service will be able to curb the actions of former terrorists now engaged in criminal activity.

The Police Service of Northern Ireland

The Police Service of Northern Ireland—historically, the RUC—has long been composed disproportionately of Protestant and Unionist members. The total percentage of Catholics within the force is only about seven percent. Over the last three decades, the RUC has been identified with political control, formerly from the Unionist government in Stormont and latterly during the periods of Direct Rule from Westminster, not as upholders of the law, but seen as defenders of the state, and the nature of the state itself has remained the central issue of the political argument.

In 1998, the British government appointed the former governor of Hong Kong, Chris Patten, to head the Independent Commission on Policing in Northern Ireland. The commission's report made one hundred and seventy-five recommendations for change. When the recommendations were presented, the Sinn Féin party was adamant that the only way forward for the peace accord was a full implementation of all the recommendations, including the striking of the word "Royal" from the police title. The police force has always had a predominantly Protestant flavor and has lost some three hundred officers, who were killed in terrorist acts, and over nine thousand injured during the "Troubles." Policing in the North cannot be likened to the work of any other police force operating in a Western democracy. In 1985, INTERPOL stated that the RUC was the most dangerous force anywhere in the world in which to serve, even surpassing that of Colombia. The Patten Report, entitled "A New Beginning: Policing In Northern Ireland," covered every region of the force from recruitment, IT, size of force, composition by religious affiliation, culture and ethos, public order policing, and human rights. The aim of the recommendations was to attract and sustain support for the new organization from the entire community. The problems faced by the police service in Northern Ireland are, in a sense, unique in a divided society, each side with its own particular history and culture. But many problems are similar to those confronting police services in democratic societies elsewhere. The Independent Commission studied policing in other countries, and while it could discover no model that could simply be applied to Northern

Ireland, it was able to find plenty of examples of police services wrestling with the same challenges. The challenge for the police service in the North was how it could be accountable to the community it serves if its composition—in terms of ethnicity, religion, and gender—is vastly different to that of its society. In the words of the founder of the British police service, Sir Robert Peel, the police service's main objective is the prevention of crime rather than the detection and punishment of offenders. The end of the 1990s saw a debate in Britain on policing as it affected ethnic minorities and communities and the police service's relationship with those communities. There is obviously no perfect model for Northern Ireland, and there is no example of a country that, to quote one European police officer, "has yet finalized the total transformation from force to service." The commitment to a fresh start gives Northern Ireland the opportunity to take best practices from elsewhere and to possibly lead the way in overcoming some of the toughest challenges of modern policing.[25]

COUNTERING IRISH TERRORISM

Through necessity the British government developed wide-scale antiterrorist and counterterrorist measures against the terror groups in Northern Ireland. Never before in its history had a British government to deal with internal terrorist activities on the scale that emerged from Northern Ireland. On many occasions, Britain has met violence with violence and has had some innovative ideas to counter the terrorists. Among those innovations are its reputed shoot-to-kill policy, internment, removal of a defendant's right of silence during judicial proceedings, and the prohibiting of news media broadcasting statements of PIRA and Sinn Féin. With the "Irish question" appearing now to be answered after a near century of political and sectarian violence, one has to question how effective the countermeasures really were. The hostility shown by and to Prime Minister Margaret Thatcher helped to fuel the terror campaign against British economic, military, and political targets. She constantly reiterated that she would "never give in" to the IRA. Each side's inability to achieve a military victory should be obvious to the other. The lessons for the rest of the world from Northern Ireland's conflict would seem to be the following:

- Authorities must pursue every effort to make political compromises with dissidents before violence becomes institutionalized.
- Authorities cannot achieve a military victory over terrorists and still maintain civil liberties and democratic institutions.
- Counterterror techniques by authorities that kill, injure, or frighten non-combatants provide support for terrorist groups. Indeed, revolutionary terrorist groups depend on the authorities to perpetrate provocation and outrages against non-combatants.
- Terrorist groups can be devastatingly effective with very few members, given the worldwide availability of sophisticated weapons and explosives.
- Terrorist groups can sustain community support by using both the latent sympathy of citizens, as well as intimidation.
- Even the most technologically sophisticated, well-organized, well-financed, and highly motivated counterterrorist methods can be frustrated by a small group of terrorists that have some community support.[26]

Britain's counterterrorism organizations have had notable successes. The SAS Regiment, which continued to thwart and strike at Republican terrorists through the 1980s and 1990s, was instrumental in preventing terrorist attacks and setting up offensive traps, resulting in the capture and often the death of terrorists. The SAS has had significant success against the PIRA and has been responsible for a number of successful ambushes against them. Many ambushes, spectacular in nature, resulted in heavy loss of life to the terrorists. Most notable was an ambush in March 1988 on the island of Gibraltar of an unarmed ASU that British and Spanish intelligence had determined was about to carry out an attack on the British colony. The terrorists' target was the ceremonial band of the 1st Battalion Royal Anglian Regiment, which had arrived in Gibraltar after a tour of duty in Northern Ireland. Army intelligence officers have been expecting a PIRA attack on a military target for some months. The SAS unit gunned down the PIRA cell in broad daylight; killed were Daniel McCann, thirty, and Sean Savage, twenty-four, both known PIRA activists, and Mairead Farrell, thirty-one, the most senior member of the gang who had served ten years for her part in the bombing of a hotel outside Belfast in 1976.

A car used by the PIRA cell was found two days later containing 140 lbs of Semtex with a device timed to detonate during the "changing of the guard" ceremony. An inquest the same year concluded the three had been lawfully killed; but in 1995 the European Court of Justice ruled that the SAS soldiers had violated the fundamental right to life of the PIRA members.

Britain was widely criticized at the time for this action. In the post 9-11 environment, one wonders whether the same criticism would be applied now.

Judicial process was the primary weapon against the terror groups in Northern Ireland, and Britain's early response in sending in troops to protect Catholics from Protestants did not have its desired effect. The PIRA was up against the entire intelligence resources of a major Western government. The brigade and battalion structures of the PIRA, established at the latter end of the 1960s, became targets for penetration by the RUC. Informants were placed within the organization, and several senior PIRA members were arrested. As noted previously, the PIRA remodeled its battalions into smaller cells where only a minority of people knew who was who. The British government was prepared to meet violence head-on with its special counterrevolutionary warfare force, the British SAS Regiment.[27]

STATE-SPONSORED TERRORISM—LIBYA

Diplomatic Immunity

To circumvent the interference of foreign customs officials, Qaddafi used diplomatic privileges to move contraband weapons into and out of diplomatic missions in Europe. By the 1980s, Qaddafi had renamed the Libyan embassies as the Libyan People's Bureaus. The problems faced by the British government of Margaret Thatcher and public protests outside the Libyan People's Bureau in St. James's Park, London, would result in the severing of diplomatic ties between the two countries. The following are extracts from the Vienna Convention on Diplomatic Relations, 1961:

ARTICLE 22

1. The premises of the mission shall be inviolable. The agents of the receiving state may not enter them, except with the consent of the head of the mission.
2. The receiving State is under a special duty to take all appropriate steps to protect the premises of the mission against any intrusion or damage and to prevent any disturbances of the peace of the mission or impairment of its dignity.
3. The premises of the mission, their furnishings and other property thereon and the means of transport of the mission shall be immune from search, requisition, attachment or execution.

ARTICLE 29

The person of a diplomatic agent shall be inviolable. He shall not be liable to any form of arrest or detention. The receiving State shall treat him with due respect and shall take all appropriate steps to prevent any attacks on his person, freedom or dignity.

ARTICLE 31

1. A diplomatic agent shall enjoy immunity from the criminal jurisdiction of the receiving State. He shall also enjoy immunity from its civil and administrative jurisdiction.
2. A diplomatic agent is not obliged to give evidence as a witness.

ARTICLE 45

If diplomatic relations are broken off between two States, or if a mission is permanently or temporarily recalled:

a. the receiving State must, even in case of armed conflict, respect and protect the premises of the mission, together with its property and archives;
b. the sending state may entrust the custody of the premises of the mission, together with its property and archives, to a third State acceptable to the receiving State;
c. the sending State may entrust the protection of its interests and those of its nationals to a third State acceptable to the receiving State.

On April 17, 1984, news networks in London showed the dramatic turn of events when gunfire erupted from the Libyan People's Bureau onto the demonstrators outside. The demonstrators were mainly exiled Libyan students protesting against Qaddafi. The gunfire killed a Metropolitan policewoman, Yvonne Fletcher. Intelligence intercepts of messages between Tripoli and the London Libyan People's Bureau revealed that those inside were ordered to fire on the demonstrators. On the home front, the Libyan-controlled press released a different story about the incident, stating that the police had stormed the building and described the episode as a "barbarous outrage." The standoff at the Libyan People's Bureau ended on April 27, when the occupants agreed to be taken to the Civil Services College in Berkshire to be interviewed by police. Under diplomatic privilege, they refused to help in the investigation and were returned to Libya. The events at St. James's Square were the culmination of a series of bombings and attacks against dissident Libyans in London and the northwest of England.

PAN AM FLIGHT 103—LOCKERBIE, SCOTLAND   One of the most significant terrorist attacks of the last fifty years has been the destruction of a Pan Am 747–200 over Lockerbie, Scotland, on December 21, 1988. The trial and conviction of a mid-level Libyan intelligence officer still leaves the obvious question as to the complicity of the leader of the Libyan government. In 1999, Libya fulfilled one of the requirements of the United Nations Security Council Resolutions (UNSCR) by surrendering two Libyans suspected in connection with the bombing for trial before a Scottish court in the Netherlands. One of these suspects, Abdelbaset al-Megrahi, was found guilty; the other was acquitted. Al-Megrahi's conviction was upheld on appeal in 2002. In August 2003, Libya fulfilled the remaining UNSCR requirements, including acceptance of responsibility for the actions of its officials and payment of appropriate compensation to the victims' families. UN sanctions against Libya were lifted on September 12, 2003. In August 2009, al-Megrahi was released by Scottish authorities on compassionate grounds based on his apparent illness from terminal cancer. Al-Megrahi died May 20, 2012, nearly three years after his release on compassionate grounds (Figures 5-10 and 5-11) .

FIGURE 5-10   On December 21, 1988, Pan Am Flight 103 exploded over Lockerbie, Scotland, killing all 259 people on board as well as eleven on the ground. Though it was almost immediately evident that a bomb had caused the disaster, it took more than eleven years to bring anyone to trial. The nose of the airplane landed mostly intact in a field about four miles from the town of Lockerbie. The wreckage was strewn over 50 square miles. Twenty-one of Lockerbie's houses were completely destroyed and eleven of its residents were dead.   *Source:* Federal Bureau of Investigations.

TERRORIST ATTACK BRIEF

Terrorist Group: Syrian Intelligence Operation

Case Facts: An early attempt at a proxy suicide bombing involves the case of Nazer Hindawi, a Jordanian Palestinian who with the support of Syria, had spent a considerable amount of time in Ireland and befriended a young Irish girl whom he managed to get pregnant. On August 17, 1986, he sent her back to the Middle East to meet his family via an El Al flight to Tel Aviv. At mid-morning, with the El Al 747 at departure Gate 23, Terminal One, passengers for that flight began to come through the pre-boarding security checks. All passengers leaving the United Kingdom in 1986, and specifically those with checked baggage, were asked a series of questions:

- Is this your baggage?

- Did you pack it yourself and are you taking any packages for somebody else?

- Have you left your baggage unattended at any time?

The pregnant girl from the Republic of Ireland answered all the questions. Her passport was checked and her hand luggage and hold baggage were screened by X-ray. The girl proceeded to the El Al boarding gate with her single piece of carry-on baggage. The bag was of nylon construction with an expanding compartment at the base, a type of bag used by millions of travelers. El Al is one of the most secure airlines in the world; it always conducts its own secondary security checks and questioning of every passenger. The pregnant girl was going to visit her boyfriend's family in the Middle East; he, however, was not traveling. The El Al security staff thought this was an unusual story, and while doing the physical check on the bag, noticed that even when empty it seemed overly heavy for its construction. At that point, a police explosive search dog reacted to the bag. Further inspection revealed several sheets of plastic explosive wired to a calculator and battery. The bomb was in a false bottom of the bag. The bomb was set to detonate approximately two hours after departure.

On further examination of her hand luggage, it was found to contain a Semtex bomb (see drawing below).

Investigation: Hindawi had been in the pay of the Syrian intelligence service and had agreed for a sum of money to place a bomb on an El Al flight. He was provided with a safe house in London and also with a Syrian passport. After the bomb was discovered, Hindawi panicked and was concerned that he may be killed by his Syrian minders. He contacted his brother, who called the police. At his subsequent trial in 1986, he was sentenced to forty-five years in prison.

Blue "Trolley Bag"

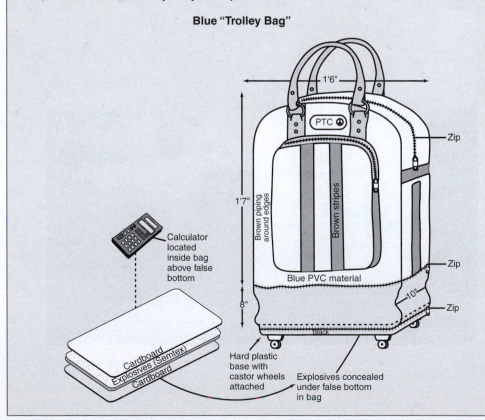

FIGURE 5-11   Trolley bag bomb—Attempted bombing of El Al Flight, at London's Heathrow Airport April 17th, 1986. *Courtesy:* J. Spindlove.

On December 19, 2003, Libya announced its intention to rid itself of WMD and medium-to close-range (MTCR) class missile programs. Since that time, it has cooperated with the United States, the United Kingdom, the International Atomic Energy Agency, and the Organization for the Prohibition of Chemical Weapons toward these objectives. Libya also signed the IAEA Additional Protocol and became a State Party to the Chemical Weapons Convention. In response, the United States terminated the applicability of the Iran-Libya Sanctions Act to Libya and then President Bush signed an Executive Order on September 20, 2004, terminating the national emergency with respect to Libya and ending IEEPA-based economic sanctions. This action had the effect of unblocking assets blocked under the Executive Order sanctions. Restrictions on cargo aviation and third-party code sharing were lifted, as were restrictions on passenger aviation. Certain export controls remained in place and Libya remained on the state sponsors of terrorism list. U.S. diplomatic personnel reopened the U.S. Interest Section in Tripoli on February 8, 2004. The mission was upgraded to a U.S. Liaison Office on June 28, 2004. Libya re-established its diplomatic presence in Washington, DC, with the opening of an Interest Section on July 8, 2004, which was subsequently upgraded to a Liaison Office in December 2004.[28]

DOMESTIC TERRORISM IN MAINLAND BRITAIN

The Angry Brigade

Totally forgotten by many, however, is a small terror group that came to life in the 1960s—the decade that saw the Beatles, widespread drug use, and fundamental changes in societal views and values. The Angry Brigade was Britain's only noteworthy, homegrown terror group.

Their members were dissimilar in almost every way to the Irish terrorists and had no clearly defined enemy to focus on, other than wealthy, middle-class Conservatives running business corporations. Unlike the terrorists in both Northern Ireland and the mainland, the Angry Brigade was a loosely formed group of Communist-style workers' party members. Angry Brigade was a left-wing revolutionary movement, militant and pro-labor. They came to some prominence in the late 1960s. With no military knowledge or background, the Angry Brigade espoused Marxist theories in the hope that workers would find them acceptable in the 1960s. Britain was a changing society with a strong Conservative government under Alec Douglas Hume. Modernization and growth in the factories, particularly in the auto industry and the dockyards, were the order of the day. The leaders of the Angry Brigade sought to change government policy and usher in a new era of socialism by murdering politicians and bombing public buildings.

Activist or Terrorist

As activists in a workers' party struggle against the state and big business, the Angry Brigade issued communiqués and proclamations stating their cause. The brigade hoped to gain recognition by professing support for the Irish Nationalist Movement and such mirror-image revolutionaries as the Symbionese Liberation Army (SLA) in the United States. Closer to home, the group espoused support for the activities of the Red Brigade in Italy and the German Red Army faction. There is no recorded information that the group received any support, either financial or militarily, from either of these terrorist organizations. What is certain is that the brigade caused explosions aimed primarily at political and business figures. The group was tracked down by London's Metropolitan Police and prosecuted for its terrorist and criminal acts. The Angry Brigade's members believed that they were engaged in a workers' struggle that could only come to fruition if the working masses rebelled against their masters. This altruistic goal was never realized, however, possibly owing to the atrocious nature of the brigade's attacks. Little has been heard of the group since the main protagonists were jailed in 1972. They could be termed a "copycat," as they likened themselves to the Weathermen in the United States and, in a later period, to the German terrorist group Baader-Meinhof gang. The ringleaders, who became known as the Stoke Newington Eight, were sent to prison for long terms in 1972.

Angry Brigade Terrorist Acts

The Angry Brigade is believed to have been involved in a number of bombings in London aimed at banks, corporations, and foreign interest businesses, such as the Bank of Bilbao. The Brigade supported the Basque separatists in Spain. It is unclear what this group hoped to achieve by attacking the homes of the commissioner of the Metropolitan Police and a member of parliament. Certainly, these actions demonstrated an ability to coerce and intimidate, but their overall effectiveness can be dismissed as having minimal effect in making any changes in the political arena. Unlike the PIRA, the Brigade had no political machinery similar to that of Sinn Féin, or any media support.

Animal Rights Militia

Animal rights activists have been prevalent in Great Britain for several decades, but the Animal Rights Militia is the only one of their many groups to have moved toward terror tactics aimed at companies and research institutes. In 1986, bombs were planted under cars, and at the homes of prominent research scientists and animal importers. Although adequate warnings were given, this marked the group's trend toward violent action. This group, while perhaps using what could be terrorist tactics, is still considered more like criminals than true terrorists. The Terrorism Act of 2000, although aimed at curbing Northern Ireland terror groups, could also be focused on the Animal Liberation Front, an activist organization that is believed responsible for a number of bomb attacks against animal research establishments and the agricultural industry. Attacks on fast food establishments in Belgium appear to have been the work of the same group.

ISLAMIC EXTREMISM

Islam and Christianity continue to collide and the rise of Islamic extremism in the United Kingdom has not receded and will likely increase with the numbers of migrants coming across Europe from the regions of Syria and Iraq—in 2010, there were roughly 40 million Christians and some 3 million Muslims in the United Kingdom. Over the last three decades, Islamic groups have managed to relocate to the United Kingdom as a sanctuary or base for various activities for fund-raising, and primarily to escape their own repressive regimes. Britain's liberal policies made it easy for Islamic groups to set up official charities to raise funds for their own causes. Terrorists wanted in other countries were given safe haven in the United Kingdom and left free to foment hatred against the West. Extremist groups such as Hizb ut-Tahrir remained legal despite being banned in many European and Muslim countries. Radicals such as Abu Qatada, was extradited to Jordan on terrorist charges in 2012 was subsequently tried and released by a court in Amman, Jordan in September 2014; Omar Bakri Mohammed, who left the UK for Lebanon in 2010 has not been allowed back in; and Abu Hamza, after eight years of fighting extradition to the United States was finally extradited in 2012 on terrorism charges and convicted and sentenced to life in prison in January 2015. As early as 1998, Osama bin Laden was quoted in *Time* magazine: "Our work targets world infidels. Our enemy is the crusader alliance led by America, Britain, and Israel. It is a Crusader–Jewish alliance." Britain's military presence in Afghanistan also makes the country a prime target. The Muslim population in Britain runs to just over two million and a constant inflow of refugees—both legal and illegal—crosses into the country from Europe on an almost daily basis. So, how deeply entrenched were Muslim fanatics within the Muslim faith in Britain? The answer is quite startling; according to British officials, up to sixteen thousand British Muslims are either actively engaged in or support terrorist activities, while up to three thousand are estimated to have passed through al Qaeda training camps, with several hundred thought to be primed to attack the United Kingdom.[29]

Islamic groups operating within mainland Britain are often from terrorist organizations that appear on the U.S. State Department list of overseas terrorist organizations. These groups include Gama'a al-Islamiyya, Hamas, Shining Path, the Liberation Tigers of Tamil Eelam, Hezbollah, and the Kurdistan Workers' Party. All of these groups had been actively recruiting and raising funds freely in the United Kingdom until September 11, 2001.

The West began to take serious note of al Qaeda in the days after the 1998 attacks on the U.S. embassies in Nairobi and Dar es Salam and the waterborne suicide attack in 2000 on the USS *Cole* in Yemen. It became clear that the reach and spread of al Qaeda and its ideology throughout the world, and particularly in Europe, would pose one of the most significant risks to Western democracies.

Britain was long viewed as one of Europe's most liberal societies but that view may be changing following the introduction of tough antiterrorism legislation in 2001.

London remains a haven for young Muslim immigrants and asylum seekers, and with diminishing prospects for work, they have managed to adapt to the generosity of a welfare state that provides for their physical well-being. Many resorted to attending institutions such as the Finsbury Park Mosque, where many observers would say that they were brainwashed into global movements such as al Qaeda and then sent throughout the world to carry out jihad. Evidence has been uncovered linking Richard Reid, who attempted to detonate an explosive device in his shoes on board a U.S. trans-Atlantic flight in December 2001, Zacarias Moussaoui, the so-called twentieth hijacker (9-11), as well as the millennium bomber, Ahmed Ressam. The Finsbury Park Mosque on St. Thomas's Road, Finsbury Park, was among London's first purpose-built mosques when it was opened in 1993. It was managed by a registered charity but due to disagreements among the trustees, the institution became poorly managed. In the resulting vacuum, one **Abu Hamza al-Masri**—a disabled Afghan war veteran—through intimidation and strong-arm tactics was able to take over the mosque in 1996, creating no-go zones for the trustees and physically removing them from the building. Abu Hamza al-Masri collected around him supporters, including those dabbling in petty crimes and forgeries. The trustees pressed the charity commissioners to intervene, but action became protracted over the years. Legal moves failed to dislodge Hamza and his band. The mosque was subject to an early morning raid in January 2003. The police did not take action when Abu Hamza al-Masri and his supporters commenced conducting prayers on the street outside.

The one-eyed, hook-handed Imam continued to be outspoken in his support for Osama bin Laden. In a television interview, he made no apologies and showed no remorse for the 9-11 attack on the World Trade Center. So, was Finsbury Park Mosque a fertile and covert breeding ground for al Qaeda? The mosque itself attracted many Muslims from the London area, namely, Pakistanis, Bengalis, Egyptians, and Algerians. Abu Hamza, himself an Egyptian, had been in the United Kingdom for more than twenty-five years. His presence was imposing—a missing eye and a hook in place of his right hand—to young and impressionable Muslims who would see little future for themselves in the Western democracies and be easily indoctrinated by the Imam and his cohorts. A Canadian Broadcast Corporation (CBC) documentary on recruiting al Qaeda in Britain focused squarely on the Finsbury Park Mosque. Their exposé included hidden video-taping of recruiting activities inside the mosque, as well as videos of terrorist training tactics, even how to slit a person's throat. The problem for British police lay in its inability to pinpoint any crime that the Imam may have committed. When the mosque was forcibly closed in 2002, that did not stop the one-eyed Abu Hamza from preaching on the street outside the mosque, with dialogue such as, "Seek the way of death ... if you die to defend your religion, you are a martyr... die honorably, don't die humiliated."[30] He was also charged in the United States with conspiracy for his involvement with an Islamic group in Yemen that took sixteen tourists as hostage in 1998. It's alleged that he provided a satellite phone to the Islamic Army of Aden and spoke to the conspirators before the attack. On May 27, 2004, British police arrested Abu Hamza. He was charged and convicted in October 2004 on ten counts ranging from inciting racial hatred to soliciting or encouraging the murder of others—"namely, a person or persons who did not believe in the Islamic faith, in particular the Jewish people." Al-Masri facing eleven charges in the United States, including charges related to a 1998 kidnapping in Yemen and the formation of a terrorist training camp in Oregon in 1999, was extradited in 2012 and convicted in 2015.

HIZB UT-TAHRIR (THE ISLAMIC LIBERATION PARTY), AL-MUHAJIROUN, AND ISLAM4UK

Hizb ut-Tahrir (HT) is a global organization that is banned in numerous countries. From 1986 to 1996 the group was led by Omar Bakri Mohammed. The organization is antidemocratic and strives to make Islamic caliphates. While despising the democracy of the United Kingdom, its leaders have been more than content to relish the rights, freedoms, and latitude provided under just such a democracy, and with a UK location, they also take advantage of the world press availability. In viewing their website, they define a clear message to the politicians—even with events unfolding in Libya in the spring of 2011, they called for the intervention to be by Muslim countries and not from the empire seeking countries of Europe. A 2010 assessment made by the government of this organization determined that individuals who were members did not necessarily progress to violence. The Cabinet Home Affairs Committee stated, "*We do not believe that it is accurate to regard radicalization in this country as a linear 'conveyor belt' moving from grievance, through radicalization, to violence … . This thesis seems to both misread the radicalization process and to give undue weight to ideological factors."* Before government considers the legitimacy of such groups, it is also worthy of note that at least nineteen terrorists convicted in Britain have had links with al-Muhajiroun, including Omar Khyam, sentenced to life imprisonment as leader of the "fertilizer bomb" plot, and Abdullah Ahmed Ali, the ringleader of the airliner "liquid bomb" plot, who is serving a life sentence. HT also like to debate their side of the political spectrum in the United Kingdom, specifically when it comes to labeling Muslims as moderates or extremists.

HT says it opposes terrorism and condemned the 9-11 and 7-7 attacks. However, it regards integration as "dangerous," orders all Muslims to keep apart from non-believers, and says that "those [Muslims] who believe in democracy are Kafir," or apostates. A British would-be suicide bomber, Omar Sharif, was radicalized partly by HT activists at his London University.[31] In 1996, Omar Bakri Mohammed split away from HT in disagreement of policy and direction and formed al-Muhajiroun (AM). Omar Bakri came to Britain when the Saudi Arabian government banned AM in 1986 and lived on government handouts throughout his time in the United Kingdom. He left to go to his native Lebanon in 2005, and the government Home Secretary took immediate steps to ban his return as it was alleged that his presence was "not conducive to the public good."

AM provided backing to Abu Hamza, at the Finsbury Park mosque, and in advertising a conference held in the mosque in 2002, AM leaflets described the 9-11 hijackers as the "magnificent 19." AM was also known for its intimidation of Jewish university students with inflammatory leaflet drops and radical campaigns that included distributing posters nationwide in 2000 claiming: "The last hour will not come until the Muslims fight the Jews and the Muslims kill the Jews." As a result, it was outlawed on campuses by the National Union of Students in 2001.

AM disbanded in 2004 when Mohammed shut it down fragmenting into two smaller groups, the Saviour Sect and al-Ghurabaa, both later proscribed by the home office for the "glorification of terrorism." AM probably still exists but under different colors as its supporters simply set up new groups, some overt and some covert, and not yet proscribed by the government. Islam4UK is one such group to emerge and being run by Mohammed's former AM cohort Anjem Choudary. Its public appearances have not endeared them to the wider British public for their attempts to march in Wootton Bassett to disrupt the funeral processions for fallen UK soldiers returning from Afghanistan. Anjem Choudary has been an avid supporter of extreme Islam for years and has been linked to many extremists in the United Kingdom including the killers of Lee Rigby, but has always managed to operate just beyond the reach of British law; however, in 2015, he was arrested and charged with being a supporter of IS by promoting the terror group in his lectures and online, and telling his supporters to follow the orders of the caliph Abu Bakr al-Baghdadi and if necessary, travel to the Middle East and support IS. Choudary was convicted in July 2016 and could face a sentence up to ten years in prison. His presence in prison will pose more headaches as he will then have a ready audience of imprisoned extremists to continue to radicalize.

TABLIGHI JAMAAT

Tablighi Jamaat, an Islamic revivalist organization that has spread from its origins in India in the 1920s to the broader Muslim world is believed to have many thousands of members in the United Kingdom.

Considered an extreme Islamist movement, its European headquarters in the northern English town of Dewsbury has been *in situ* since 1978. It has its own extreme views on Islam's place in the world and is considered by British security experts to be the leading force in Islamic extremism and a fertile recruiting ground for young men—Mohammed Siddique Khan, the leader of the London bomb plot in July 2005, has links to Jamaat. The number of adherents that come to the Dewsbury mosque is quite startling—they come from all over England and Western Europe to meet and be preached to in Dewsbury. To the many law-abiding Muslims in Britain, it is fair to say that their religion is often hijacked by those with an extremist agenda, and it is unfortunate that the voices of moderate Muslims are seldom heard, let alone listened to. With the influx of Muslims in the 1970s came their highly traditional faith influenced by Sufism, passive and quiescent. Over the years, theirs became an increasingly activist faith centering on the mosques that were now generating a highly radicalized ideology, and according to the Pakistani Bishop of Rochester (Christian), a whole generation of Muslim children was indoctrinated with a set of inflammatory ideas about the need for Islam to achieve primacy over the non-Islamic world.[32] The fuel for the radicalization process came from two important events in the 1980s and 1990s. First, the Soviet invasion of Afghanistan, which saw British forces training and equipping Afghan fighters (mujahideen) against the Soviets whom they eventually drove out of their homeland; these Muslim fighters found a cause and a vocation—holy war. Second, the Bosnian war in which a steady media stream depicted the massacres of Muslims by Christian neighbors. Thousands of Islamic fighters from both Afghanistan and Bosnia found their way West.

The Prevention of Terrorism Act 2005

Britain, thanks in part to the onslaught of Irish terrorism in Britain since the 1970s, has developed a cohesive and effective counterterrorism posture—it is no coincidence that Britain as yet has not been attacked on the massive scale as its neighbors in France since the London bombings in July 2005. The United Kingdom is the intelligence powerhouse in the region with its close ties to the U.S. intelligence community. The United Kingdom has a cutting edge team that is more than double the size of its European counterparts in the area of digital intelligence.

There exists strong cooperation between all branches of the security, intelligence, and police communities in the United Kingdom which has led to more than 220 terrorism-related arrests between March 2015 and March 2016 and this has been achieved without significantly infringing civil liberties.[33]

A system of control orders under the Prevention of Terrorism Act 2005 has replaced the Part 4 powers under the Anti-terrorism, Crime, and Security Act 2001. The Prevention of Terrorism Act allows for control orders to be made against any suspected terrorist, whether a UK national or a non-UK national, or whether the terrorist activity is international or domestic. The home secretary is required to report to Parliament as soon as reasonably possible after the end of the relevant three-month period on how control order powers have been exercised during that time.

The Facts about Control Orders

- Control orders enable the authorities to impose conditions upon individuals ranging from prohibitions on access to specific items or services (such as the Internet) and restrictions on association with named individuals, to the imposition of restrictions on movement or curfews. A control order does not mean "house arrest."
- Specific conditions imposed under a control order are tailored to each case to ensure effective disruption and prevention of terrorist activity.
- The home secretary must normally apply to the courts to impose a control order based on an assessment of the intelligence information. If the court allows the order to be made, the case will be automatically referred to the court for a judicial review of the decision.
- In emergency cases, the home secretary may impose a provisional order, which must then be reviewed by the court within seven days.
- A court may consider the case in open or closed session—depending on the nature and sensitivity of the information under consideration. Special advocates will be used to represent the interests of the controlled individuals in closed sessions.
- Control orders will be time limited and may be imposed for a period of up to twelve months at a time. A fresh application for renewal has to be made thereafter.
- A control order and its conditions can be challenged.
- Breach of any of the obligations of the control order without reasonable excuse is a criminal offense punishable with a prison sentence of up to five years, or an unlimited fine, or both.
- Individuals who are subject to control order provisions have the option of applying for an anonymity order.
- To date, the government has not sought to make a control order requiring derogation from Article 5 of the European Convention on Human Rights.

Terrorism Act 2006

The Terrorism Act contains a comprehensive package of measures designed to ensure that the police, intelligence agencies, and courts have all the tools they require to tackle terrorism and bring perpetrators to justice.

The act was not a direct response to the July 2005 attacks on London, as new terrorism legislation had already been planned.

After the attacks, consultations with law enforcement and intelligence agencies were held to make sure that their views were considered when developing new legislation.

Content of the Terrorism Act

The act specifically aims to make it more difficult for extremists to abuse democratic freedoms and encourage others to commit terrorist acts.

It created a number of new offenses:

- **Acts preparatory to terrorism**—This aims to capture those planning serious acts of terrorism.
- **Encouragement to terrorism**—This makes it a criminal offense to directly or indirectly incite or encourage others to commit acts of terrorism. This will include the glorification of terrorism, where it may be understood as encouraging the emulation of terrorism.
- **Dissemination of terrorist publications**—This will cover the sale, loan, or other dissemination of terrorist publications. This will include those publications that encourage terrorism and those that provide assistance to terrorists.

- **Terrorist training offenses**—This makes sure that anyone who gives or receives training in terrorist techniques can be prosecuted. The act also criminalizes attendance at a place of terrorist training.

The act also makes amendments to existing legislation, including

- introducing warrants to enable the police to search any property owned or controlled by a terrorist suspect;
- extending terrorism "stop and search" powers to cover bays and estuaries;
- extending police powers to detain suspects after arrest for up to twenty-eight days (though periods of more than two days must be approved by a judicial authority);
- improved search powers at ports; and
- increased flexibility of the proscription regime, including the power to proscribe groups that glorify terrorism.

Laws in Britain have been created and amended to accommodate acts of terrorism, and those laws have been subject to Human Rights challenges. In 2006, the Law Lords issued a declaration that Section 3 of the Terrorism Act 2005 was incompatible with the right to a fair trial under Article 6 of the European Convention on Human Rights. In 1989, the European Court of Human Rights had extended the scope of the provision in the European Convention on Human Rights that prohibits torture and degrading treatment. For Western countries attempting to deport illegal immigrants, including suspected terrorists, they were now prohibited from doing so if the judge thought that abuses might be practiced in the country to which the suspect was being deported. The very liberal interpretation by British judges has made removal from Britain an onerous prospect and ultimately playing into the hands of the terrorists wishing to seek out a safe haven.

The government believes it is under attack from Islamic extremists and has gone to unprecedented lengths to inform the public that it is not a case of *if* an attack will happen, but *when*. The government's resilience has relied on draconian measures to hold at bay those it feels have been or may likely be involved or connected to terrorism. To get a greater understanding of how widespread the threat of radical Islam is to the social fabric of Britain, one needs to also appreciate that immigration has played a major part in all this. Travel the streets of London and you will witness a melting pot of languages and people from around the world that have made not only London but also provincial towns and cities their home. But immigration does not always translate into integration. Britain has long been referred to as a multicultural society, but the official view on that is changing in the most part due to radical Islamic extremism in Britain. For years, proponents of multiculturalism have branded their critics as racists, but radical Islam has managed to shock to consciousness Europe's brain-dead politicians, and now the insidious multicultural model is open to public scrutiny. During a February 2011 security conference in Munich, Germany, Prime Minister David Cameron declared Britain's long-standing state-sponsored policy of multiculturalism an abysmal failure. The British government is responsible for creating a generation of global citizens who thoroughly despise their nation's heritage and have no loyalty to their country what-soever. Even if the government would abandon its multicultural policy tomorrow, it would take at least a decade to negate multiculturalism's deadly, divisive effects. David Cameron stated, "We've allowed the weakening of our collective identity. Under the doctrine of state multiculturalism, we have encouraged different cultures to live separate lives, apart from each other and the main-stream. We have failed to provide a vision of society to which they feel they want to belong."[34]

To many observers, Britain became a target for Islamic extremists only after its support for the U.S. campaign in Iraq. In reality, Muslims from around the globe have relocated to the United Kingdom and have been doing so for more than forty years. In Britain, hundreds of thousands of Muslims lead law-abiding lives and live and work in peace and harmony. Nevertheless, moderation among the majority appears to be a highly relative concept consider-ing their widespread hostility toward Israel and the Jews, for example, or the way the very con-cept of Islamic terrorism or other wrongdoing is automatically denied.[35] Long before the events of 9-11 unfolded, and the coalition invasion of Taliban-controlled Afghanistan, and then Iraq, the United Kingdom was home to radical Muslims. One example is the case of Dhiren Barot, who, as far back as 1999, was plotting an attack on London's Heathrow airport. Barot was an airline ticket agent, and his plans included detonating a bomb on a bus in the tunnel connecting the arterial roads to the center of the airport, and exploding a bomb in a tube train under the River Thames with the intent to flood the underground chamber and cause an untold number of deaths as a result. Barot was grammar school educated, and had converted from Hinduism to Islam, and in 1995, long before George Bush became president he attended a training camp in Kashmir. He is a staunch believer that terror works, and that it is a religious duty of all Muslims. So, if we believe that foreign policy can dictate a sea change in Muslim terrorist actions, we need to think again. It is purely a convenient excuse for the Muslim extremists to use and cite both Iraq and Afghanistan.

LONDON—JULY 7, 2005

As previously noted, London has become home to a network of extreme Islamist groups that have consistently used the liberal society in Britain to preach hatred abroad. The mass immi-gration of Muslims to Europe was an unintended consequence of the post-World War II guest worker programs. Backed by friendly politicians and sympathetic judges, foreign workers, who were supposed to stay temporarily, benefited from family reunification and became permanent residents. Muslims now constitute the majority of immigrants in most Western European coun-tries. Jihadist networks span Europe, thanks to the spread of radical Islam among the descendants of guest workers. The threat of an attack on the British capital has been an increasing security concern since the invasions of Afghanistan and Iraq. Britain is one of the core groups of coun-tries that bin Laden and his fanatics listed for an attack, so it was no surprise to authorities when it eventually came. However, the method of delivery in the London subway attacks was what most disturbed the authorities.

July 7, 2005, heralded the start of the G8 Economic Summit in Edinburgh, Scotland, which was attended by world leaders and the world's press. Thursday, July 7, was the day after London had been awarded the 2012 Summer Olympic Games, and most Londoners were in a celebratory mood. That would all change at 8:50 A.M. at the height of "rush hour."

Terror Attack Timeline—July 7, 2005

08:50—A bomb with approximately 10 pounds of high explosives is detonated by a sui-cide bomber aboard a westbound Circle Line Underground train about 100 yards into a tunnel after departing Edgware Road station.

08:50—A second explosive device detonates on a Piccadilly Line Underground train just after it left Kings Cross Station. This bomb was also estimated to contain approximately ten pounds of high explosives.

08:50—A third explosion occurs on a Circle Line Underground train as it approaches Liverpool Street Station. This device is also believed to have contained about ten pounds of high explosive.

09:47—A fourth explosion takes place on the upper deck of a Number 30 London Transport bus traveling from Hackney Wick to Marble Arch. The bus had been diverted from its normal route, and the explosion occurred outside the offices of the General Medical Council in Russell Square. The blast destroyed most of the upper deck, killing thirteen people.

The bombings from all four attacks left fifty-seven dead and more than seven hundred injured. The timing of the attacks shows that this was well planned and scripted and intended to cause maximum casualties and make the statement that Islamist extremists have the capability to strike at the heart of the British capital. This may have been a symbolic gesture on the part of the bombers, as it has become clear that all four attacks were the acts of suicide bombers. The motivations for the attacks will be the subject of months of analysis and investigation; however, it is clear that the bombers were all male, and three of the four were born in the United Kingdom and were of Pakistani descent. The fourth, who came to Britain from Jamaica with his parents when he was a baby, had been a recent convert to Islam. All four fit into the age and education level characteristic of Hamas bombers in Israel. In London, unlike the United States and Canada, the motorway system, the streets of most major cities, and the transportation systems are lined with closed-circuit television (CCTV) cameras. Shortly after these attacks, CCTV footage showed the bombers gathering as a group at a regional train station before embarking on their journey to London. The vehicle they traveled in was recovered and valuable evidence gathered. It now seems that the intelligence community had identified at least one of the bombers as a potential Islamic extremist; however, a risk assessment did not determine that this target was a sufficient risk to warrant in-depth surveillance. This might seem strange, but we believe this is all part of connecting the dots. Does this possible miss indicate a tactical error on the part of Britain's security services? The sheer numbers of British-born Muslims now make the task of identifying those who may pose a risk far more complex than simply keeping close tabs on foreign nationals visiting the country. The fairly lax U.S. Visa Waiver program allows virtual unrestricted access by British and other European nationals to the United States. This attack would likely have been organized by external forces that supported the cell by providing the ingredients for the bomb, timing devices and detonators, as well as the expertise to construct such a device. Tracking down the support network will be the main role for the police investigators. The British police have a wealth of experience in dealing with terrorism through their activities with Irish terror groups, but this is the first instance of a terror attack carried out by suicide bombers and marks a dramatic turn in events. If suicide missions have the aim of disrupting transportation and sending fear through the traveling public, then the events that took place exactly two weeks after these attacks are worthy of discussion. On July 21, 2005, reports came in around 12:30 in the afternoon of more bomb attacks on the London Underground system and bus transportation. In similar circumstances, three backpack bombs were left on trains at the Oval Kennington, Shepherd's Bush, and Warren Street Underground stations. A small detonation appeared to have taken place in each case, but no injuries were reported. The fourth bomb went off on the top deck of a Number 26 bus in Hackney, again without causing injury. This second round of attacks is likely to have been the work of al Qaeda-inspired Islamist sympathizers willing to make the statement that the threat remains and that the security and police service are powerless to prevent future attacks.

The July 21, 2005 Failed Bomb Attack Timeline

- **12.25 P.M.**—Mukhtar Said Ibrahim, Yassin Hassan Omar, and Ramzi Mohammed are believed to have entered Stockwell tube station.
- Yassin Hassan Omar traveled north on the Victoria Line.
- Mukhtar Said Ibrahim traveled to Bank station on the Northern Line.
- **12.34 P.M.**—Ramzi Mohammed went north on the Northern Line attempting to detonate his improvised explosive device before reaching the Oval Kennington station; he ran out of the station.
- Yassin Hassan Omar attempted to detonate his improvised explosive device (IED) on the Victoria Line train as it approached Warren Street Station; he too ran out of the station.

- **1.06 P.M.**—Mukhtar Said Ibrahim left Bank Station and boarded Number 26 bus to Hackney Wick and attempted to detonate his device as he disembarked at Harrow Road.
- Hussein Osman is believed to have embarked at Westbourne Park onto a Hammersmith and City Line train heading west. He attempted to detonate his device near Shepherds Bush Station; he ran from the station.
- **July 23**—Unexploded device is found in Little Wormwood Scrubs Park.
- **July 25**—Yassin Hassan Omar is arrested in Birmingham.
- **July 29**—Said Ibrahim and Ramzi Mohammed are arrested in West London.
- Hussein Osman is arrested in Rome by Italian police.

The bombs all failed to detonate and, this, as it turned out, was more owing to luck than ineptitude on the part of the terrorists. The bombs consisted of hydrogen peroxide mixed with chapatti flour, and detonators created out of high-strength hydrogen peroxide, acid, and acetone, which were placed in tubes of cardboard with light bulbs wired to batteries. UK forensic experts believe that they failed to detonate because the initiator was not sufficiently powerful to set off the main charge.

In July 2007, four men were jailed for forty years each for attempting to carry out suicide bomb attacks on London's transport system. Mukhtar Said Ibrahim, the group's leader, had traveled to Pakistan in December 2004 to hone and learn his bomb-making skills at the same time as two of the July 7 bombers, Mohammed Siddique Khan and Shehzad Tanweer, were there. There was no evidence that the two attacks in London were linked, but the judge believed that both attacks were masterminded in Pakistan.

OPERATION CREVICE

In April 2007, five men were convicted of conspiracy to cause explosions using homemade devices, and although the group had discussed many targets and had acquired the fertilizer base for their bomb, they appeared not to have formulated a target or a defined target plan for their operation. Operation Crevice was a combined operation between the British, U.S., Canadian, and Pakistani security services, which ultimately led to the arrest of the five men. All were born and raised in Britain and had become radicalized in local mosques and had then traveled to Pakistan for training. The convicted men, Salahuddin Amin, 32; Omar Khyam, 25; Anthony Garcia, 25; Jawad Akbar, 23; and Waheed Mahmood; all received life sentences. The group came together in 2002, and several of them traveled back and forth between the United Kingdom and Pakistan to facilitate training. Following training, they began to focus on assembling an explosive device, but appear to have abandoned the idea of smuggling components for their bomb in favor of a homemade version. In September 2003, Anthony Garcia purchased six hundred kilograms of ammonium nitrate, which they kept in a self-storage lockup in West London. In February 2004, staff at the depot notified police of the suspicious amount of fertilizer being stored. It appears that at this time several of the conspirators were already under surveillance. Members of the group were bugged, and conversations about target selection were recorded. Waheed Mahmood had previously worked for the National Grid and had stolen discs detailing the location of high-pressure gas pipelines. Having decided to use fertilizer, the group was having difficulty acquiring detonators, and it is alleged that they contacted a Canadian citizen, Mohammad Momin Khawaja, to supply them. Khawaja flew to the United Kingdom and met with Khyam; he did not bring detonators with him, but they discussed using remote long-range detonators for their attack. The group then bought airline tickets to Pakistan, and it was at that juncture that the group was arrested as the police and security services feared that the plot to detonate a bomb was now at an advanced stage. The authorities had in fact exchanged the fertilizer for another inert substance. This conspiracy was being hatched at the same time as the July 7, 2005, attack on the London Underground system was taking place. It seems quite remarkable that this group that had traveled to Pakistan, and had actively trained and were highly motivated to carry out a mission, had only received rudimentary training and little or no direction from al Qaeda about how and where to target their attack. It became clear at their trial that Omar Khyam was training in Pakistan at the same time as the July 7 bomber, Mohammed Siddique Khan who, together with Shaheed Tanweer (July 7), were picked up on surveillance in the UK meeting with Khyam and Garcia.[36]

Shoot to Kill Policy

This was mentioned earlier in relation to an SAS assault on a PIRA ASU in Gibraltar in the 1980s. Now, some two decades later, we are witnessing police on the streets of London carrying automatic weapons. They have the authority to shoot first if a suspect fits a profile of a suicide bomber and to ask questions afterward. The danger in this is that innocents can and do get killed—in the SAS case, the ASU in question was known to the security services; however, they were not armed. In London, on Friday, July 22, 2005 (as Scotland Yard detectives were still investigating the failed suicide bombs of July 21 in London), a young, olive-skinned man ran from police in Stockwell after being repeatedly ordered to stop. He was wearing a heavy overcoat in 70-degree temperatures and ran down into the Underground station and onto a waiting train. Police officers shot him in the head a total of seven times and once in the shoulder (according to autopsy reports). Later, it was determined that the man was not a suicide bomber, but a Brazilian electrician Jean Charles de Menezes, who had no connection to any ongoing terrorist investigation or activity. Life on the streets of London has changed. Our archetypical view of the friendly British Bobby is now gone. In November 2007, the London Metropolitan Police were found guilty of endangering the public over the shooting death of Menezes and fined £175,000 with £385,000 in costs. The London Metropolitan Police Commissioner, Sir Ian Blair, was forced to resign in September 2008 by the Lord Mayor of London, who informed Sir Ian that he had lost confidence in him to continue in his position as Commissioner.

Points for Consideration

While the scheduling of the G8 Summit, with world media attention, may be significant in the timing of the London attacks, the announcement of London's selection to host the Olympics would be far too recent an event for the terrorists to have planned for. It did, however, give added opportunity to the attackers. The complete lack of a specific, credible threat for another attack, either in the United Kingdom or Europe, does little to alleviate the threat. The London Underground and bus attacks are shown to be consistent with al Qaeda's approach to taking traditional terror tactics and using them on a scale not seen before. Consistent with current insurgent attacks in Iraq, the bus bombing may have been a required element in order to video the actual attack sequence. This attack has the hallmarks of an al Qaeda or al Qaeda-inspired attack, as at the time that was the only group executing this type of atrocity on a global scale.

An Ongoing Threat

We have detailed some of the major events that have involved radical homegrown Islamists; however, the threat has not diminished. At the end of June 2007, a car bomb was detected by authorities in the heart of London; before it could explode, a second vehicle was found a few hours later—the treasure trove of evidence that these unexploded vehicle bombs were able to put the police hot on the trail of resident Islamists. Within twenty-four hours, another attack took place at the International Airport in Glasgow, Scotland. At around 3.00 p.m., two men in a Jeep SUV rammed the entrance doors to the terminal; they had soaked themselves in gasoline, and the rear of the Jeep contained propane tanks. The driver and passenger were Bilal Abdullah and Kafeel Ahmed, respectively, both twenty-seven-year-old doctors. Kafeel Ahmed died from 90 percent burns to his body in August 2007. The terrorists were highly qualified and respectable doctors; a third doctor was arrested the following day. Although the attack and the improvised bombs were crudely made, there was the possibility that had all three vehicles detonated as planned, there would have been a significant injury count. There is speculation that due to the failure of the two bomb-laden vehicles in London, the Jeep (used in the Glasgow attack) may have been at a third unknown location, somewhere in London. When the two primary vehicles failed to detonate, it's probable that the cell decided to relocate away from London and aim at a softer but nonetheless spectacular target. At the time, the Labor Party had a new prime minister in Gordon Brown, a Scotsman; so this may have been an attempt to send the new prime minister a harsh message. As for the perpetrators, it seems that the reach of extreme Islam knows no bounds in its ability to radicalize even these professional young men. It could also be that they were inspired and not directed by al Qaeda and had no organizational links to transnational jihadist networks. If it is determined that they did have jihadist links, it seems clear that the organization is incapable of supplying skilled terrorists, which in part will likely be because of counterterror activities of the security services. The threat to the United Kingdom is definitely not from external forces but from internal, and the comment by Prime Minister Gordon Brown that Britons face a threat that is "long-term and sustained" in nature would seem appropriate.

MURDER OF LEE RIGBY—MAY 22, 2013

Since 2010 and the emergence of the Islamic State in Iraq and Syria, a large number of young British men and some women have been indoctrinated and radicalized and gone to the Middle East and joined IS. On the home front in 2013, there were many who still espoused radical views and some turned them into actions. What happened in May 2013 was one of the most vicious and very public attacks on a member of Britain's military. It was at first thought to be a random act but the calculated manner in which the two attackers behaved and their actions after the attack tell a different story.

In the early afternoon of May 22, **Lee Rigby**, a member of the 2nd Battalion Royal Regiment of Fusiliers was returning to his barracks in Woolwich. He was returning from duties at the Tower of London and was wearing civilian clothes, carrying a military backpack over his shoulder and wearing a Help for Heroes sweat top.

Michael Adebolajo and his accomplice Michael Adebowale were both born in the United Kingdom of Nigerian descent and the previous day had been to a shop in south London and purchased a butcher's knife and a meat cleaver. They spent the day of the attacking driving around the area of Woolwich Barracks waiting their opportunity to attack a soldier. Lee Rigby was unfortunate to be crossing the street near the barracks when he was spotted by the two men.

They drove their car across the street striking him down and colliding with a bollard. Both men then dragged the severely injured soldier to the middle of the street then attacked him with the butcher knife and meat cleaver in what appeared to an attempt to behead the young Fusilier. Interviewed by police, Adebolajo stated that after having run Lee Rigby down, they did not want to inflict him much pain and that the most humane way to kill a creature is to cut the jugular. Adebolajo also stated that "he may be my enemy but he is still a man."(Figure 5-12).

Unlike most attacks of any violent nature—this was in broad daylight in the English capital, both assailants remained at the scene. Passersby at first thought that this was a serious car accident and passersby stopped to provide first-aid assistance. In this instance, they were not attacked by the two men, rather Adebolajo engaged in conversation with the public attempting to explain their actions for killing the soldier. We have seen in past terror attacks by al Qaeda inspired individuals their goal being to kill as many people as possible, in this attack the two men made no attempt to attack bystanders and they had every opportunity to do so. Michael

FIGURE 5-12   Video grab taken from ITV News of a man holding weapons by the scene in John Wilson Street, Woolwich where off-duty soldier Lee Rigby was murdered.   *Source:* National News/ ZUMA Press/Newscom.

Adebolajo engaged in discussions with members of the public, justified his actions, and criticized the government for actions in Afghanistan and Iraq.

The London Metropolitan Police arrived on the scene some ten minutes after the attack along with armed officers. The two men had waited patiently for them to arrive and had even warned bystanders to keep back when the police arrived. This was a clear intention that they expected to be confronted by armed officers and the military and expected to be shot and to die as martyrs. The police did shoot both men but only injuring them. In the following investigation both men stated that they were soldiers and killing an enemy soldier was their duty whether he be in Iraq or London. Both were charged with Lee Rigby's murder.

In the years leading up to this attack, Adebolajo had been involved in London gangs which has for many years been the fertile recruiting ground for Islamic extremists. Both were involved in spending time under the influence of Omar Bakri, Anjem Choudary, and Abu Hamza. Both men came from respectable middle class backgrounds with both sets of parents in professional careers. Both drifted towards the gang cultures of south London and then to the extreme teachings of radical Islamists. Like so many radicalized young men their desire was to fight for al Qaeda overseas. Adebolajo got as far as Kenya in his attempt to join al Qaeda but was intercepted and turned back to the United Kingdom. This may have driven him to consider how to attack at home if he could not do so abroad.

At their trial, a considerable assessment was done on both men to determine their mental state and fitness to stand trial. Adebowale, the twenty-two-year-old had mental issues; as a teenager he had witnessed a particularly brutal murder and since then suffered from depression and said he often heard voices; he was also a user of street drugs. Adebolajo was deemed completely competent and sane—both were fit to stand trial. Both men stated their innocence at trial and stated that they were soldiers and had a duty to kill. They both were of the belief that their actions would please God.

Woolwich Attack Timeline

2006 Michael Adebolajo is arrested with Ibrahim Hassan, during a protest against cartoons of the Prophet Muhammad. He first comes to the attention of MI5.

2007 Arrested by police under the Firearms Act for carrying CS spray and it emerges that he has previous arrests for assault.

May–September 2008 MI5 opens a surveillance file on him following the high-priority Operation Ash, which was focusing on several terrorist targets. He is also linked to an investigation into the activities of extremist group al-Muhajiroun.

October 2008 Operation Ash is closed and Adebolajo's file is transferred to Program Amazon, a joint operation run by the police and MI5. At some stage during this year MI5 links him to a network trying to acquire "items for a terror attack." The network was disrupted by police with Adebolajo listed as "contact" of the main suspect.

November 2010 He is arrested in Kenya in an operation in which a British special forces team was involved.

November 25, 2010 He is questioned by anti-terror SO15 police officers after his return from Kenya. He is categorized as a "low-risk" target.

Spring 2011 After a four-month delay, a file into his activities in Kenya is opened by MI5.

May 2011 MI5 makes an urgent application for further intrusive surveillance of Adebolajo.

August 2011 MI5 passes information to the police about his "possible intention to be involved in the London riots."

Late 2011 Following an investigation into a possible attack linked to al-Qaeda in the Arabian Peninsula, he is listed as a "high-priority" suspect.

October 2012 Surveillance on him is about to be cancelled when new information comes to light suggesting he may be acting as a contact for East Africa-based terrorist group al-Shabaab.

April 11, 2013 Surveillance on him is cancelled weeks before Fusilier Lee Rigby's murder.

May 22, 2013 Adebolajo and his accomplice Michael Adebowale murder Rigby near the Royal Artillery Barracks in Woolwich. They are both shot and arrested.

May 31, 2013 Adebolajo is released from hospital and taken into police custody.

December 19, 2013 Along with Adebowale, he is found guilty of murdering Rigby.

February 26, 2014 Adebolajo is handed a whole-term life sentence, while Adebowale is given a forty-five-year minimum term.[37]

This was a very successful operation from the terrorist standpoint. There was mass media coverage from start to finish and was being broadcast live before the police had even reached the scene. Although only one died in this attack, the scale of savagery that took place is almost indescribable and without doubt the worst terrorist attack on British soil. Sentencing Adebolajo to a 'whole-life term' means that he spends the rest of his life in prison; Adebowale received forty-five years and will be able to apply for parole when he is seventy-seven years old.

In the aftermath, many questions have been asked of the security service about how these men managed to escape being more closely monitored than they were, and could this attack have been prevented or stopped. From the above timeline it is clear that there was a level of monitoring and an attempt to turn Adebolajo into an informant for the security services. Given that a total of six years had elapsed, it is problematic to assume that one or both of these men could have been closely watched for that amount of time. An attack of this nature against a randomly selected soldier with little planning required is almost impossible to predict let alone prevent.

The United Kingdom continues to upgrade and improve its response to terrorism and has probably the best example of legislation aimed at curbing, controlling radicalization, and deterring returning jihadists. The Counterterrorism Bill sought to make inroads into preventing the United Kingdom from attacks such as Woolwich and the London Underground attacks. However, success in defending the United Kingdom will also depend on intelligence sharing with its European Union partners and as we will see in Chapter 6, Belgium is challenged in this area. The UK strategy is detailed in the below high points of their most current counterterror legislation (2015) (Figure 5-13).

FIGURE 5-13 On August 3rd 2016 the Commissioner, Sir Bernard Hogan-Howe and the Mayor of London, Sadiq Khan announced the start of Operation Hercules in which additional firearms officers will be deployed in visible roles in the capital.

Hercules is part of the Met's commitment to delivering extra armed officers to protect London against the threat of terrorism. The Mayor has welcomed the Commissioner's increase of 600 additional firearms officers to protect London against any attack. The first are now fully trained and operationally ready. *Source:* Courtesy of Mayor's Office for Policing and Crime.

Background Counterterrorism and Security Bill

The terrorism threat to the United Kingdom is considerable. It is as bad as any time since 9-11. We need to act to ensure that our law enforcement and intelligence agencies have the powers they need to keep us safe.

The Bill will:

- give the police new powers to disrupt people travelling abroad to fight for a terrorist organization, and manage their return to the United Kingdom;
- strengthen law enforcement agencies' ability to monitor and control the actions of those in the United Kingdom who pose a terrorist threat; and
- enhance the Government's ability to combat the underlying ideology that feeds, supports, and sanctions terrorism.

These new powers will ensure that our law enforcement and intelligence agencies have the powers they need to stop people travelling to fight for terrorist organizations overseas, and to deal decisively with those already here who pose a risk to the public.

The collapse of Syria and the emergence of the Islamic State of Iraq and the Levant (ISIL), not only threatens the stability of the Middle East, but presents a clear danger here in the United Kingdom. On August 29, 2014, the independent Joint Terrorism Analysis Centre raised the UK national terrorist threat level from SUBSTANTIAL to SEVERE, meaning that a terrorist attack is 'highly likely'. Approximately five hundred individuals of interest to the security services have travelled to the region from the United Kingdom since the start of the conflict. A number of these individuals have joined terrorist organizations, including ISIL, and it is estimated that half of them have returned to the United Kingdom. This legislation has been brought forward at the earliest opportunity to respond to this increased threat. The new powers in the Bill will help to stop people travelling overseas to fight for terrorist organizations or conduct terrorist-related activity, and deal with individuals already in the United Kingdom who pose a risk to the public. This new legislation will sit alongside the existing suite of powers that is already used extensively to combat the terrorist threat: pursuing prosecution against those suspected of terrorism-related activity; using the Royal Prerogative to remove the passports of those who want to travel abroad to engage in terrorism; barring foreign nationals from re-entering the United Kingdom, where they are suspected of terrorism-related activity; stripping British citizenship from those who have dual nationality; working with the Internet industry to remove terrorist material hosted in the United Kingdom or overseas; and enacting recent emergency legislation to safeguard the retention of communications data and ensure a firm legal basis for our interception powers, both of which are crucial in the investigation of those involved in terrorist activity, in this country and overseas (Figure 5-14).

What is in the Bill?

Measures to disrupt travel to and from Syria and Iraq

- Providing the police with a power to seize a passport at the border temporarily, during which time they will be able to investigate the individual concerned (Part 1 Chapter 1).
- Creating a Temporary Exclusion Order that can temporarily disrupt the return to the United Kingdom of a British citizen suspected of involvement in terrorist activity abroad and ensure that they return in a manner which we control (Part 1 Chapter 2).

TERROR BYTE

500 Britons Joined Conflict in Syria/Iraq

UK experts estimate that at least 500 Britons joined the conflict in Syria and Iraq and around twenty-seven have allegedly died in those countries. According to the Met, about fifty people per week are referred to de-radicalization programs. Police prevention is at its highest since the aftermath of the July 7, 2005 attack on London's transport system. Police made over 200 terrorism-related arrests in 2014, a significant increase, as a result of conducting high numbers of counterterrorism investigations. Police charged at least sixteen people for terrorism-related offenses after returning from Syria and Iraq.

FIGURE 5-14   500 Britons joined conflict in Syria/Iraq.   *Source:* U.S. Department of State.

TERROR BYTE

Bomb Plotter Sentenced to 40 Year Jail Term

Abid Naseer aged 29 was sentenced for his role in planning to bomb a shopping center in Manchester, England as part of an al Qaeda operation. He was convicted in March 2015 of *providing material support to al Qaeda, conspiring to provide material support to al Qaeda and conspiring to use a destructive device in relation to a crime of violence.* "This al Qaeda plot was intended by the group's leaders and Naseer to send a message to the United States and its allies," said U.S. Attorney Robert L, Capers in a statement. "Today's sentence sends an even more powerful message in response; terrorists who target the U.S. and its allies will be held accountable for their violent crimes to the full extent of the law."

FIGURE 5-15   U.S. versus Naseer, U.S. District Court for the Eastern District of New York, No.10-cr00019, 2015.   *Source:* U.S. Department of Justice.

- Enhancing our border security for aviation, maritime, and rail travel, with provisions relating to passenger data, authority-to-carry ('no fly') lists, and security and screening measures. These will help us to enforce our security requirements with carriers that provide transport to and from the United Kingdom (Part 4).

Measures to deal with people in the United Kingdom who pose a terrorism threat

- Enhancing existing Terrorism Prevention and Investigation Measures, including stronger locational constraints on subjects and a power to require them to attend meetings as part of their ongoing management, e.g. with the probation service or Job Centre Plus staff (Part 2).

Measures to disrupt the activities of terrorist organizations

- Enabling the retention of additional information by communications service providers in order to attribute an Internet Protocol address to a specific individual, enhancing vital investigative capabilities (Part 3).
- Explicitly prohibiting insurers from reimbursing a payment that has been made in response to a terrorist demand (Part 6).

Measures to support people at risk of being drawn into radicalization

- Creating a general duty on a range of organizations to have due regard to the need to prevent people being drawn into terrorism.
- Putting the voluntary program for people at risk of radicalization on a statutory basis.[38] (Figure 5-15).

Cold War Returns to Britain—Death of Alexander Litvinenko

In November 2006, a former Russian spy, Alexander Litvinenko, died an agonizing death in a central London hospital from radiation poisoning. It was determined that Litvinenko had been exposed in some manner to Polonium-210. The dose he was administered could only have been prepared or manufactured in a nuclear facility and given to him through his food in a lethal dose. The radiation killed his cells causing his organs to shut down. According to a 2000 database produced by Stanford University's Institute for International Studies, approximately 88 pounds of radioactive material including weapon-usable uranium and plutonium were removed without authorization from nuclear facilities in the former Soviet Union. While on his deathbed, Litvinenko, an outspoken critic of Russian leader Vladimir Putin, accused Putin of being complicit in his poisoning. Polonium poisoning is a very unusual method of assassination unless it was intended to send a message to the wider expatriate Russian community in London. While the Russian leader and his government have strongly rebuffed any suggestion of government involvement, the British authorities believe Litvinenko was killed by a former KGB agent, Andrei Lugovoi, and have unsuccessfully sought his extradition from Russia to stand trial in the United Kingdom—a request that has been denied by Russia.

EXTREME RIGHT-WING GROUPS

The issues of immigration and violence by right-wing groups against immigrants are not new phenomena for Britain. Hate crimes have been prevalent throughout the twentieth century. The British National Party has a political agenda that demands Britain become independent from Europe and stop the influx of immigrants. The party also calls for the deportation of criminal and illegal immigrants. While this party maintains this stance, it has attracted a hooligan element that attacks indiscriminately persons of foreign origin. The loosely knit group at the center of these attacks—the Skinheads—is associated with football violence. Skinheads first appeared in Britain around the early 1970s and could be found in almost every city in the country. This group is definitely a cult rather than an organization with any political aspirations. Skinhead youths have changed little since those early days of the 1970s: shaved heads, Nazi insignias, tattoos, checked shirts, blue jeans, and steel-toed "bovver" boots in the Doc Martens style. They were easily spotted as angry young men who symbolized a tough, working-class background. The Skinheads were known for their violent rampages and became synonymous with extreme nationalism. Their favored targets for violent attacks were Jews, homosexuals, and Asians. Their style of dress soon went out of fashion; however, a small hard-core movement along the lines of neo-Nazi exists today. Their hate attacks target Jewish cemeteries and Asian shopping areas. Many of the attacks appear random in nature, but there is a belief that some attacks involving English soccer clubs are planned in advance. They are often seen at marches and parades with the British National Party (BNP), although there is no evidence to suggest that any Skinheads are members. The ebb and flow of this cult-like movement has endured for almost thirty years and has spread its aggressive attitudes toward Jews and immigrants across Europe and North America.[39] With the large number of migrants of all nationalities flooding into Britain from EU countries and former Eastern Bloc countries and refugees from Iraq, Syria, and Afghanistan has given groups like the BNP a significant platform for their grievances—receiving little or no attention from the media, the police have managed to uncover dangerous elements planning terror attacks against migrants particularly from the Middle East. There has been little reported about extreme right-wing elements apart from demonstrations seen outside courts where Muslims are on trial. There remains a threat from British extreme right-wing groups and in the last ten years there have been several cases where white British males have been charged with possession of weapons and explosives.

Summary

The ongoing threats from Islamic extremists have pushed Irish domestic terrorism threats out of our focus, but the threat to security both in Northern Ireland and the British mainland from Irish terrorists has not gone away, it still exists. This chapter has charted the birth and rise of Irish terrorism from the 1920's to the present—a long and complex history involving sectarian violence and the emergence of the PIRA, one of the most sophisticated and successful terrorist organizations.

The suicide attacks by al Qaeda-inspired Islamic extremists in 2005 on the London Underground and subsequent attempts in 2007 to suicide bomb Glasgow airport are an indication of the lengths to which these committed individuals will go to prosecute their cause. While the attack in Glasgow was far less sophisticated and well planned out, it leads observers to the belief that good intelligence is disruptive to their cause. Britain views itself in the forefront of threats from al Qaeda and now Islamic State and other like-minded jihadist groups, whether from Islamist groups for its Afghanistan involvement or from resident Islamists with aims to turn the country into an Islamic Caliphate. The horrific attack and murder of Lee Rigby is but one example of the atrocities they will go to in the name of religion.

Review Questions

1. Describe the conditions that led to the "Troubles" in Northern Ireland.
2. Analyze the various methods employed by the British government to stem the tide of terrorism.
3. Describe the importance of "marching season" and its historical context.
4. List and explain the application of the Diplock Commission and Scheduled Offenses in efforts to bring terrorists to trial.
5. Explain how extreme Islamic ideology has been able to flourish in the United Kingdom.
6. Summarize the content of the Terrorism Act 2006.

End Notes

1. *The World Book Encyclopaedia*, vol. 10, S.V. "Home Rule."
2. Ibid.
3. Quote taken from *The Troubles—The Background to the Violence in Northern Ireland*, Edited by Taylor Downing, a Channel Four Book.
4. Strategic Forecasting. http://www.stratfor.com/standard/analysis_view.php.
5. Paul Medhurst. *Global Terrorism* (New York: United Nations Institute for Training & Research Program of Correspondence and Instruction, 2002, p. 70).
6. John Horgan and Max Taylor. "Playing the Green Card—Financing the IRA." *Terrorism and Political Violence*, vol. 11, no. 2 (Summer 1999, pp. 1–38).
7. U.S. Department of State. Libya/PIRA background paper (July 1998).
8. "Strategic Forecasting." http://www.stratfor.com/standard/analysis_view.php.
9. Ed Moloney. *A Secret History of the IRA* (Toronto, ON: Penguin Books, 2002, p. 289).
10. Gayle Olsen-Raymer. *Terrorism: A Historical and Contemporary Perspective* (New York: American Heritage Custom Publishing, 1986, p. 197).
11. *MIPT Terrorism Knowledge Base*. http://www.mipt.org/
12. *The Diplock Report: Report of the Commission to Consider the Legal Procedure to Deal with Terrorist Attacks in Northern Ireland.* Cmnd.5185 (London: HMSO, 1972, p. 13).
13. Jim Smyth. "Stretching the Boundaries: The Control of Dissent in Northern Ireland." *Terrorism: An International Journal*, vol. 11, no. 4 (Queens University, Belfast; Taylor and Francis, 1988, pp. 289–295).
14. *Report on the Operation in 2003 of Part VII of the Terrorism Act 2000*, sec. 5, Nonjury Trial Section, 74, 75.
15. They shoot children, don't they? Part 1 of report on paramilitary attacks on children in Northern Ireland from 1990 to 2013. By Michael Nugent, Nov 10, 2014—downloaded March 18, 2016. http://www.michaelnugent.com/2014/11/10/they-shoot-children-dont-they-part-1/
16. http://www.thejournal.ie/michael-mcconville-jean-mcconville-murder-gerry-adams-ira-1442811-May2014/#comments—Christina Finn, May 1, 2014.
17. Youngsters who paid the price for insulting paramilitaries by Thomas Harding. Copyright © by 2004 by Telegraph Group Limited. Reprinted with permission of Telegraph Group Limited (UK).
18. Andrew Boyd. *The Orange Order, 1795–1995* (1995), www.history.com.
19. Ibid.
20. *The Weekly Telegraph*, London (May 7, 2002, p. 13).
21. CAIN. http://cain.ulst.ac.uk.
22. IRA Statement on Decommissioning. www.cnn.com/world.
23. Force Estimates—Janes Intelligence Review.
24. Extract Northern Ireland Peace Agreement. http://www.nio.gov.uk/agreement.htm.
25. *A New Beginning in Northern Ireland*, Extract 1.3 and 1.4 London: 2, 3.
26. John W. Soule. "Problems in Applying Counterterrorism to Prevent Terrorism: Two Decades of Violence in Northern Ireland Considered." *Terrorism: An International Journal*, vol. 12, no. 1 (1989).
27. Jonathan R. White. *Terrorism: An Introduction* (Pacific Grove, CA: Brooks/Cole Publishing, 1991, pp. 220–221).
28. U.S. Department of State.
29. *Draft Report on Young Muslims and Extremism*, UK Foreign and Commonwealth Office, 2004; Robert Winnett and David Leppard. *Sunday Times* (July 10, 2005).
30. Mathew Mcallester. "Islamic Radicals draw Attention in Great Britain." (May 23, 2004), www.startribune.com.
31. Andrew Gilligan. "Hizb ut-Tahrir is not a gateway to terrorism." *Claims Whitehall Report—Telegraph* online. http://www.telegraph.co.uk/journalists/andrew-gilligan/7908262/Hizb-ut-Tahrir-is-not-a-gateway-to-terrorism-claims-Whitehall-report.html.
32. Ibid, p. 9.
33. David Omand. "Keeping Europe Safe." David Omand is visiting Professor in the Department of War Studies at King's College, London and at Sciences Po, in Paris. He served as the United Kingdom's Security and Intelligence Coordinator from 2002–2005. (Foreign Affairs September/October 2016, vol 95, No. 5, p.88).
34. Jerry Kane. "The Milestone Dairies," *Britain's Prime Minister calls for an end to Multiculturalism* (February 10, 2011). http://imkane.wordpress.com/2011/02/10/britains-prime-minister-calls-for-an-end-to-multiculturalism/
35. Melanie Phillips. *Londonistan* (London: Encounter Books, 2007, p. 6).
36. Janes. "Terrorism and Security Monitor." (June 2007).
37. "Lee Rigby murder: Were we told the whole truth?" New claims suggest omissions in what MPs were told of plan to recruit young extremist as double agent. Jamie Merrill, Jane Merrick, Serina Sandhu, Mike Glover. Saturday 29, November 2014—downloaded March 18, 2016. http://www.independent.co.uk/news/uk/crime/lee-rigby-murder-were-we-told-the-whole-truth-9893247.html.
38. https://www.gov.uk/government/collections/counter-terrorism-and-security-billOpen Government Licence v3.0.
39. Anti-Defamation League. *The Skinhead International, A Worldwide Survey of Neo-Nazi Skinheads* (New York: Anti-Defamation League, 1995). ADL, 823 UN Plaza New York. http://www.nizkor.org/hweb/orgs/american/adl/skinhead-international.

Western Europe

LEARNING OUTCOMES

After studying this chapter, students should be able to:

1. Restate the rise and decline of the ETA in Spain.

2. Describe the rise of right- and left-wing terrorist movements in Europe.

3. Analyze the rise of Islamic extremism linked to al Qaeda in Europe.

4. Describe the role played by al Qaeda in Germany in the build up to the 9-11 attacks on the United States.

5. Discuss the threat from Muslims returning from Syria and Iraq to mainland Europe.

6. Discuss how the Schengen Agreement helps facilitate attacks such as those that took place in Paris (2015) and Brussels (2016).

KEY WORDS TO NOTE

Anders Behring Breivik—A Norwegian citizen and far-right Fascist responsible for the 2011 massacre in Oslo

Armenian Secret Army for the Liberation of Armenia (ASALA)—A Marxist-Leninist extremist organization that operated from 1975 to 1986

Charlie Hebdo—French weekly satirical magazine

Dev Sol—Revolutionary People's Liberation Front, formed in 1978 following a split with the Turkish People's Liberation Front, is a Marxist organization that is violently anti-NATO and anti-USA

Euskadi Ta Askatasuna (ETA)—Founded by young nationalists in 1952, it is a Basque separatist group fighting for independence from Spain

Ilich Ramirez Sanchez—"Carlos, the Jackal"—led the 1975 assault on the OPEC HQ in Vienna

Jyllands-Posten—Danish morning newspaper that published cartoons of the Prophet Muhammad

RAF—Red Army Faction—left-wing German militant group that morphed from the Baader–Meinhof gang in the 1960s

Schengen Agreement—Treaty of 1985 that laid the foundation for a Europe free of borders

TATP—Tri-acetone Tri-peroxide (TATP)—Ingredient for IED

Theo Van Gough—Dutch filmmaker murdered on the street in Amsterdam

OVERVIEW

Europe's experience with terrorism has been significant and continues to have major problems with homegrown terrorists—the unstable situation in the Middle East, and in particular, Syria and Iraq has drawn large numbers of second and third generation young men from France,

Germany, Spain, and others to take advantage of the open borders between European nations and the porous border between Turkey and Syria to go to the Middle East and join groups such as Islamic State. The threat of terrorism facing European countries now comes from the many hundreds of returning jihadists with designs on targeting their host countries. This chapter will chart the rise and course of the various terror groups that have operated in Europe over the past fifty years and the obvious changing nature of the terror threat. Information sharing between nations on terror suspects and their movements presents challenges as well as opportunities. We have witnessed commando-style attacks by well-armed and trained terrorists attacking civilian targets in Paris in 2015—these attacks mirror the events that took place in Mumbai in 2008 when terrorists attacked hotels and train stations killing one hundred and sixty-four people and wounding hundreds more. France, Spain, Italy, and Germany have all seen external terror attacks from both right- and left-wing groups.

SPAIN

Spanish Nationalism and the Basques

The Basque region spills north across the Pyrenees and into southern France, with an estimated half a million Basques living on French soil, and approximately 2.5 million living within the borders of Spain (Figure 6-1). The origins of the Basque people are uncertain; however, they have been living in this region since long before the Gauls and Iberians settled in Spain and France. They have their own language called Euskera that is not derived from any other European language or dialect. With the size of the region's population, it would be logical to expect that Basque territory might be a self-governing principality, similar to Monaco. The Basque people do not have their own homeland and, in similar fashion to the Irish Republican movement, have been fighting for self-government and their own homeland since the first quarter of the twentieth century. General Francisco Franco came to power during the Spanish Civil War of 1936–1939 and ruled Spain as an iron-fisted dictator until his death in 1975. In the intervening years, Spain achieved rapid economic growth and prosperity.

FIGURE 6-1 Map of Spain. *Source:* Central Intelligence Agency, *The World Factbook, 2008.*

Basque Separatism

As the twentieth century drew to a close, there were only two European regions of nationalist conflict. The most notable nationalist conflict and the most documented has been the terrorist campaign waged in Northern Ireland. The Basques of the Pyrenean region of Spain have waged their own internal struggle for a national identity and have not enjoyed a separate homeland or autonomy since the twelfth century. They have indeed managed to maintain and protect their own language and culture over the centuries. General Franco's approach to dealing with the Basque nationals was to suppress them at all costs by incorporating the Basque region into Spain at the end of the Spanish Civil War and outlawing both their culture and their unique language. Franco's actions led to a rebirth of Basque nationalistic fervor in the late 1950s. Spain continued to suffer from the scourge of terror attacks perpetrated by **Euskadi Ta Askatasuna (ETA)** into the twenty-first century. In 1999, ETA broke its "unilateral and indefinite" ceasefire and recommenced a bombing and assassination campaign. Since the turn of the century, attacks have increased and, like the attacks by Irish Republicans, the Basque separatists favor the indiscriminate use of remotely detonated bombs in public places, as well as assassination of local and state officials. Following the 9-11 attacks in the United States, the U.S. government, which re-designated ETA every two years as a Foreign Terrorist Organization, went one step further in October 2001 and designated ETA under former president Bush's September 23, 2001, Executive Order 13224, as a "Specially Designated Global Terrorist Organization." Executive Order 13224 was specifically aimed at those persons and groups that provide financial support and assistance to terrorist organizations. More specifically, the order further blocked property and prohibited transactions with persons who commit, threaten to commit, or support terrorism. In February 2002, under Executive Order 13224, the U.S. Department of the Treasury designated twenty-one Spanish nationals as members of, assisting in, sponsoring, or providing financial, material, or technological support for, or financial and other services to, or in support of ETA's acts of terrorism, and are otherwise believed to be acting for, or on behalf of them. These twenty-one individuals were identified by the European Union on December 21, 2001, for their involvement in terrorist acts.[1]

Euskadi Ta Askatasuna

In 1959, the Basques formed the ETA (Basque Fatherland and Freedom). It was dedicated to promoting Basque independence. ETA was not originally formed as a terrorist group but following General Franco's vicious oppression of the Basques, the group was left with no option but violent retaliation. ETA, much like the Republican IRA, gathered its support from the working classes. Their members come from regions that identify with the strong and unique ethnic identity of the Basque people. They are invariably young, frustrated nationalists with deep anger against their lack of autonomy. The majority of Basques favors nationalism, but do not support the terrorists' violent "any means to an end" approach to resolve a political goal of self-government and determination. ETA has, over the past twenty-five years or more, been a fragmented organization that has seen many offshoots of the original group formed, disbanded, and re-formed again.

A political report, commissioned in 1986 by the Basque regional government, described the region as being amenable to political solutions. It also described ETA as "an unfortunate child of the Franco Dictatorship." Much of the report suggested political solutions such as how to accommodate Basque Nationalism within the framework of Spain and the European Economic Community (EEC). One of the recommendations was that Basque terrorists, who under Spanish law were tried in Madrid's "special courts," should instead be tried in their Basque courts. And further, they recommended that policing of terrorists should come under the control of Basque police and not Spain's national police.[2]

Since the 1950s, ETA has been riddled with internal squabbling, bitter dissension, and discontent. The group split in 1966, into what was known as ETA-Zarra (or old ETA) and ETA-Berri (or young ETA). ETA-Zarra was further divided into two subgroups: ETA-5 and ETA-6. The subgroup ETA-5 was then divided further into ETA-Military and ETA-Politico Military, and the most hardened and seasoned campaigners for armed action come from the subgroup ETA-Military.[3] These splits have caused confusion and consternation among the Basque people as to which of these proliferating schisms to support or oppose. "Actions Unite–Words Divide" is the slogan adopted by ETA-Military, and their terrorist members adopted the same cell-like structure as that used by the Provisional IRA. ETA-military commandos, or irurkos, were made up of three-man cells called "Sleeping Commandos" and were organized in the late 1970s by the ETA-Military commander, Miguel Apalategui.[4] The "sleepers" were to be called up from the Basque community to perform a single terrorist act and then return to their jobs under relative anonymity. To finance its campaign, ETA used robbery and extortion.

Development of the ETA Organization

ETA's growth, and its Youth Movement, is traced back to the Basque Nationalist Party (PNV). The party had been in exile since Franco's defeat of Spain's Republicans in the 1939 Civil War. The Basque Youth Movement was determined to ensure that the Basque's unique language and culture would not die. ETA's political position was purely democratic and in 1957, a group of young Basques traveled to France to convince the exiled PNV government to organize and lead an armed struggle against General Franco. PNV leader, Jose Maria Leizaola, and his government, flatly rejected the idea. ETA's First Assembly came about in May 1962 when a small group of university students and activists gathered to discuss how to go forward and gain support for their ideals. Much of what they discussed at that First Assembly was the example set by other groups struggling for a national identity against such regimes as Fidel Castro in Cuba and others struggling against colonial rule in Africa and the Middle East. These became the first few steps along ETA's path toward terrorism. Determined not to be captured by the police, they set up their own three-man cell structure and defined ETA as a "Revolutionary Movement for National Liberation."

The works and writings of Mao Tse-tung played a significant role in ETA's development. Impressed by Mao, a young Basque, Jose Ortiz, studying in Paris, attempted to rouse others in ETA to the same level of understanding that he had found in his readings of Mao. The Second ETA Assembly, in 1963, set about attempting to rid itself of Maoist influences. No split occurred after the Second Assembly, but shortly thereafter, the Maoist militants within produced their own mini-manual, *Insurrection in Euskadi*. The tract brought forth the Basque determination to embark on a war of revolution. A Third Assembly in 1964 broke away from the old, established Nationalist PNV and, influenced by the Maoists, redefined the group as being anti-capitalist and anti-imperialist. An ETA leader defined the new direction as follows: "The primacy of the human person and of his rights is the basis for any political action." As ETA ideology veered toward the left, the French government took action against ETA founder members on French territory and removed them from the frontier region with Spain.

Eustakio Mendizabal Benito headed up ETA at the start of 1970. Benito's group was known as the "Military Front of ETA." He believed passionately in securing a homeland for the Basque people and preserving their language and had a deep concern about the future. Benito financed his terrorist operations by resorting to criminal activities including armed robbery, extortion, and kidnappings. They had no training in the art of weaponry or the use of explosives while members actively purchased arms through the underground arms networks and bought, as their first consignment, 500 new, 9-mm Firebird Parabellum pistols. They also stole explosives from local factories and quarry operations.

ETA members are known to have received training from the Popular Front for the Liberation of Palestine (PFLP) at its base in South Yemen. One of ETA's most audacious acts was the assassination of Luis Carrero Blanco on December 20, 1973. From 1967 till his death, Carrero Blanco served as the vice president of Spain under General Franco. When General Franco stepped down from office in June 1973, Carrero Blanco succeeded him as Spain's prime minister. ETA has become more advanced and well equipped, and has formed alliances with the Revolutionary Armed Forces of Colombia (FARC) terrorists and members of the PIRA (Northern Ireland). With the peace process holding firm in Northern Ireland, ETA may be hard-pressed for support from the Irish republican movement. In prior times, they would have traded explosives to the PIRA in exchange for training in bomb making.

New Century—New Campaign

The previously mentioned ceasefire, which ended in 1999, had probably been misread and likely misunderstood by both the Spanish government and the media. It was widely reported that ETA was severely weakened and ready to capitulate. At a secret meeting between ETA and the Spanish government in 1999, the government presumed that ETA was ready to deal. What actually took place at that meeting has never been revealed; in fact, ETA quickly resumed hostilities against the Spanish government. Similar ceasefires had taken place in Northern Ireland, and many observers have felt that these ceasefires, far from being the death knell for ETA, were a time for covert rebuilding and recruiting. The Basque Socialist Coalition, known as the Herri Batasuna (Peoples Unity) Party led by Arnoldo Ortiz, officially denies any links or involvement with ETA. Throughout the spring and early summer of 2002, ETA engaged in a prolonged campaign targeting Spain's lucrative tourist industry. The ebb and flow of terrorist success is most often measured by the organization's ability to remain at large and to function in a cohesive manner. Spanish authorities, in a cooperative effort with France, have had some spectacular successes in capturing ETA's leadership. In October 2004, French police arrested seventeen Basque separatists in the Pyrenees region of France. Not only were the arrests a blow to ETA, but at the same time, they uncovered caches of arms and more than seven hundred kilograms of explosives, including potassium chlorate, an ingredient used in the manufacture of bombs. Subsequently, the Spanish government passed legislation that made political parties that supported terrorism illegal. Following this through, the government officially declared the Herri Batasuna Party illegal in 2003. The law also ensured that there could be no resurgence under a new name, so that when former members of the banned group reappeared with the intention of running in local elections in 2003 under the name Autodeterminaziorako Bilgunea (AuB), these lists were determined to be nothing more than Batasuna in a new guise and were similarly banned by Spain's Constitutional Court. ETA continued to seek out new targets to attack and one such target was the lucrative Spanish holiday market, and in its effort to attack the tourists visiting Spain during summer months, it planned a bombing attack on a cross channel ferry; fortunately, the authorities disrupted these plans and no attack has taken place yet. The group also attacked Madrid airport over Christmas season in 2006.

On November 4, 2004, Ortiz attended a mass in San Sebastian and called for an end to the violence. The War on Terror had caught up with Batasuna, and by June 2003, the organization's name appeared on both the European and U.S. Department of State lists of terrorist organizations.[5] Although Batasuna does have considerable Basque support, the appearance of Islamic extremism in Europe no doubt had a significant effect on the Spanish population and particularly since the bombings of the Madrid train stations in March 2004. The president of the mainstream Nationalist Party and also one of the fathers of Basque Nationalism, Xabier Arzalluz, commented publicly, "The time has come to fight for the independence of the Basque region in the streets!" Ostensibly, the appeal that set the Herri Batasuna Party apart from others was that it conjured up memories of the repressive regime of General Franco. The legislation may have had the markings of a bygone era, but Herri Batasuna's political influence would continue to exist in some format and, along with it, some two hundred thousand voters, many of whom could become willing supporters of a separatist movement. Many observers compare the ETA movement to the Irish Republican Army and Northern Ireland "Troubles." ETA's campaign was actually markedly different from the PIRA's, as it specialized in kidnappings and extortion. This had rarely been a trademark of the PIRA.

In spite of the fact that large numbers of the Herri Batasuna Party had been arrested for their involvement and support of ETA attacks, the party continued to maintain its position by publicly stating that it had no ties, neither institutional nor political, to ETA. Spanish Judge Baltazar Garzon has stated that Herri Batasuna was inextricably linked to legal groups and organizations that continued to provide economic and political support to ETA. From these groups it finds new recruits for the possibly ailing ETA ranks. Although there are no valid estimates of ETA strength, it still continues to use indiscriminate bombings.[6]

Similar to its Irish counterparts, ETA has not been able to maintain a long and lasting peace accord. The five-decade-old battle for a Basque homeland has cost more than eight hundred and fifty lives, and the ceasefire proclaimed in the summer of 2006 came to an end within six months—with an ETA bomb attack on Madrid Airport on December 30, and although they did not declare the ceasefire over, the Spanish government most certainly considered it over. Formal notification by ETA came on June 5, 2007, with an announcement that their "permanent ceasefire" was over, stating "minimum conditions for continuing a process of negotiations that do not exist."[7] The Spanish, who may have had some lingering sympathy toward ETA's struggle, were turned away with the diet of violence that was unleashed in the Madrid railway attacks of 2004, and although the ETA organization has not been as active as in pre-Madrid or 9-11 years, they still pose a threat. For a peace process to evolve, the same conditions as in Northern Ireland would likely be required to include a cessation of violence and a verified decommissioning of weapons and explosives. The parallels to Irish terror are quite often drawn, but in essence there are fundamental differences between the two conflicts. There is no equivalent sectarian divide of Catholics and Protestants and neither is there dual involvement of the two governments, the British in London and the Republic of Ireland in Dublin.

While ETA sporadically returned to violence, the Irish issue is settled with a power sharing administration between the two major protagonists. The Basque region has had more power devolved to it than Northern Ireland, and current attitudes to any separation of any region of Spain is pathologically opposed by politicians in Madrid, while at the same time the democratic processes in the United Kingdom, which frequently debates the separation of Scotland and Wales, are based on the wishes of the general public.

Opposition to ETA

Accion Nacional Española (ANE), Spanish National Action, was a right-wing terror movement that targeted Basque separatists. ANE was formed in the 1970s and operated against the Basques in northern Spain. It is known to be responsible for reprisal killings of many ETA terrorists and sympathizers, and has also been active in bombings on both sides of the Spanish border. A joint Spanish and French operation in 2001 led to the arrests of thirty-seven ETA members residing in France. Going along with the United States in its war against terror, the French agreed to extradite immediately to Spain any ETA members who had warrants issued against them. In the past, the stumbling block for the French had been the political issue surrounding nationalism, which invariably led to interminably long delays in the extradition process.

Spain has combated terrorism with its paramilitary Special Operations Group, Grupo Especial de Operaciones (GEO). GEO is part of Spain's national police and is stationed in Guadalajara, near the capital, Madrid. It has special response capabilities and is responsible for VIP protection duties, as well as countering and responding to terrorism. It was designed along the lines of many other European specialist counterterrorism units and is specifically focused on dealing with aircraft hijackings, maritime threats, and hostage taking. The GEO can also be utilized in a support role for Spanish police operations outside the realm of terrorism and is trained and active in protecting visiting heads of state and providing security for high-profile events such as the Olympic Games held in Barcelona in 1992.

GEO has had some noteworthy successes and was responsible for foiling the assassination attempt on King Juan Carlos in 1995 and an attempt by ETA to attack the Barcelona Olympics in 1992. GEO remains the foremost threat to terror cells and activity on the Spanish mainland.

ETA History Timeline

1959—Euskadi Ta Askatasuna (ETA), or Basque Homeland and Freedom, founded during dictatorship of General Franco to fight for self-determination.

1968—Police chief murdered in ETA's first planned killing.

1973—Franco's prime minister, Luis Carrero Blanco, killed when his car passes over ETA explosives in Madrid.

1980—ETA's bloodiest year. Almost one hundred killed, despite Spain's return to democracy.

1985—First ETA car bombing in Madrid. American tourist killed while jogging and sixteen civil guards wounded.

1987—ETA supermarket bomb attack in Barcelona—twenty-one shoppers killed. ETA apologizes for "mistake."

1995—The Popular Party opposition leader, Jose Maria Aznar, later prime minister, escapes ETA bomb. Saved by vehicle's armor plating.

1998—ETA announces truce. It lasts fifteen months.

2000—A former Socialist health minister, Ernest Lluch, shot dead in Barcelona.

2004—Al Qaeda train bombings in Madrid kill one hundred and ninety-one people and reinforce Spanish revulsion against violence. ETA's suspected leader and twenty-one suspects arrested.

2005—Spain's parliament gives government permission to open peace talks with ETA if the group lays down its arms.

2006—Permanent ceasefire announced, lasts approximately six months.

2006—December—ETA sets off car bomb at Madrid's newly opened International Airport Terminal killing two.

2007—ETA ceasefire at an end.[8]

2009—ETA fiftieth anniversary—celebrated with bombs in northern city of Burgos and on the Island of Majorca.

2010—ETA again announces another ceasefire.

2011—ETA announces a permanent and general ceasefire.

ETA's declaration of an end to hostilities on January 10, 2011, recognizes that the solution to the Basque conflict will come "though a democratic process that takes the will of the Basque people as its maximum point of reference, and dialogue and negotiation as its tools." And by noting that the ceasefire will be verifiable, it seems to be opening the door for outside observers to confirm that it is no longer making or purchasing weapons or engaging in the extortion it has used in the past to raise funds. Since 2011, ETA has not conducted any further attacks—it has not disbanded either.

Frente Revolucionario Anti-Fascista Y Patriotico

Although little remembered today, Spain suffered from other terror groups, one of which was the left-wing Maoist group, Frente Revolucionario Anti-Fascista Y Patriotico (FRAP).[9] In an ironic twist, FRAP received worldwide recognition when members were sentenced to death in 1975 for killing a Spanish policeman in Madrid. The worldwide outcry led to demands for Spain to be thrown out of the United Nations. Unmoved by these outbursts for clemency, the Spanish government followed through with the executions as planned on September 27, 1975.

Grupa De Resistencia Antifascista Primo Octobre

The First of October Anti-Fascist Resistance Group (GRAPO)[10] was another left-wing terror group active in the 1970s at about the same time as FRAP. Four Spanish police officers were killed in a retaliatory action over the execution of five left-wing terrorists. The group takes its name from this action on October 1, 1975. GRAPO was also responsible for at least one attempt on the life of King Juan Carlos. Juan Carlos Delgado de Codex led the group until his death in 1979, while attempting to evade arrest.

Islamists and Spain

After 9-11, Spain embraced the global assault on international terrorism and strongly supports mutual assistance as a strategy to deny safe haven to terrorists. Mutual agreements and cooperation with the French have enabled both countries to root out ETA suspects on the French side of the border. Spain has also been responsible for the break-up and arrest of two suspected al Qaeda-affiliated cells in late September and November 2001. In July 2002, Spanish police continued disrupting suspected al Qaeda members operating on the Spanish mainland. In July 2002, the Spanish police arrested three men who were alleged to be of Syrian origin: two were naturalized and the third held Spanish residency. The police found videotapes from a 1997 visit to the United States in the suspects' possession. The footage shows various angles of the New York World Trade Center towers. Spain's interior minister, Angel Acebes, stated that the footage "was obviously not what a tourist would make." In addition, other high-profile locations had been taped, including San Francisco's Golden Gate Bridge, the Sears Tower in Chicago, the Empire State Building, and the Disneyland theme park in California. While this footage was filmed some four years prior to the 9-11 attacks, it gives considerable weight to the theory that al Qaeda in the late 1990s was very well organized and meticulously planned its attacks down to the smallest detail. Photos of the bridges focused on the construction of the bridge supports, while another two videos showed violent mujahideen "terrorist training," fighting, and suicide bombers.[11]

The suspected cell leader was Syrian-born Imad Barakat Yarkas, also known as Abu Dahdah. Yarkas is believed to be an organizer and financer for Islamic extremists operating in

Spain. Along with two other suspects charged in connection with the 9-11 attacks are Moroccan-born Driss Chebli and Syrian, Ghasoubun. Spanish prosecutors are seeking seventy four thousand years of jail time for each of the accused and fines of €893 million.[12] The wider prospects for international terrorism in Spain have focused mainly on Algerian nationals residing in or visiting the country. Since 9-11, Spanish authorities have made significant headway in this respect when Mohammed Atta, one of the 9-11 suicide pilots, met with an Islamic cell operating in Madrid in the summer of 2001. Atta's motives and his activities in Spain have not been established, but one may draw the inference that he was meeting and strategizing for terrorist attacks. Spain has established that Atta tried to visit an Algerian who was serving a prison term for forgery. In trying to determine how widely spread the Osama bin Laden network is, Atta would seem able to give the most direct evidence of links among activities in France, Spain, and the United States. Atta was present in Spain at the same time as Tunisian immigrant and former pro soccer player Nizar Trabelsi, who was later arrested in a plot to bomb the U.S. embassy in Paris. If Atta met with Trabelsi, the next rational conclusion would be that the attacks in New York and Washington, DC, were to be coordinated with bombing attacks in Europe.[13] As the investigation and links continue to be investigated, the widespread nature of the cell structure in Europe appears to infect France, Spain, Italy, Germany, the Netherlands, as well as Eastern European countries. Spain's significance also indicates that Ahmed Ressam visited Spain prior to his arrest in the plot to blow up the Los Angeles International Airport on New Year's Eve in 1999.

SPAIN'S 9-11

The characteristics of the attack on Madrid's rail system on March 11, 2004, bear further discussion. First, this was the worst act of terrorism on Spanish soil since the end of its civil war more than sixty years ago. Second, the Conservative government was quick to blame ETA for this attack. History tells us the United States made a similar quick response when it initially blamed Islamic extremists for the attack on the Alfred P. Murrah building in Oklahoma City in April 1995, and it was later determined to be the work of homegrown terrorists. The Madrid bombs bore none of the similarities of ETA's previous attacks and for the following reasons:

1. ETA has usually claimed responsibility for its attacks, but did not do so on this occasion.
2. ETA has invariably given advance warnings of its attacks, often to minimize civilian casualties.
3. The leader of the banned Batasuna Party publicly denied any ETA involvement and indicated an Arabic involvement (this was considered an unusual comment on Batasuna's part).

The ten, almost simultaneous, attacks in Madrid were immediately blamed on ETA, which would have meant that ETA had changed its targets away from the police, judiciary, and politicians, and was now targeting the public in general. It was not long before authorities found a videotaped message outside a mosque and, thus, the wider political implications for both Spain and the rest of Europe were about to be realized.

Up until the Madrid bombings, Spain's ruling Conservative government led by Jose Maria Aznar was a committed ally and supporter, not just of the U.S. and British War on Terror but also of deploying Spanish troops to the war in Iraq. To the Spanish voter, the realization was clear—three days before a general election an Islamic extremist cell had detonated bombs in Madrid, killing one hundred and ninety-one. A disillusioned public that did not support the war in Iraq was now going to turn what was likely to have been a Conservative victory into a stunning defeat. Spain returned the Socialist Party under the control of Jose Luis Rodriguez Zapatero to power. The power to openly change the direction of a nation was about to be shown to the men of terror. The first act by the Socialist government was to pull Spanish troops out of Iraq. Many Spaniards viewed this as a cowardly reaction to terrorism. What is also becoming apparent is that the Islamic extremists who attacked the Spanish public were supporters of the al Qaeda movement. This devastating attack changed the political will and direction of a nation, and its effects caused Spain to turn its back on a previously stated commitment in Iraq. Does Spain's about-turn mean that the country is bending to the will of the terrorists? Some would say yes; however, since the Madrid attacks, the Spanish have managed to unearth a considerable number of Islamic extremists operating within its borders. Iraq aside, the threat is clear and the cause is also clear: Islamic extremism is not on the decline, but is increasing and particularly so in Europe.

MADRID—MARCH 11, 2004   The fanaticism of the terrorists and their will to destroy not only innocents but also themselves was evidenced in the Madrid suburb of Leganes in April 2004. The group that had claimed responsibility for the Madrid train station bombing had stated that it would turn Spain into an inferno if it did not pull its troops out of Iraq and Afghanistan and cease its support for the United States. The letter containing this threat was supposedly from a group calling itself "Abu Dujana Al Afghani" (Ansar Group, al Qaeda in Europe). Concern for Europe, and not just Spain, is the link believed between this group and Abu Musab al-Zarqawi, the Jordanian terrorist conducting his insurgency campaign in Iraq at the time. While this may be speculation, what is known is that Ansar al-Islam is an extreme Islamic terrorist organization that has been responsible for numerous attacks in Iraq, Turkey, and Jordan. The Spanish police cornered the main suspects in the Madrid train station bombings in an apartment in Leganes. Before the raid could begin, the terror cell in the apartment building detonated a bomb that destroyed part of the building. In the ensuing confusion, several of the suspects may have fled the area. The explosion killed three people. To Spaniards the term "11M" is as significant and distressful as 9-11 is profoundly disturbing for Americans. It symbolizes the March 11, 2004, Madrid station bombings that killed 191 and injured nearly 2,000 other commuters. The culmination of the investigation saw a number of radical Islamists in a Madrid court in October 2007. The three lead suspects convicted of murder and attempted murder, each received sentences of 34,000–40,000 years in prison; however, Spain does not have death penalty and the longest a prisoner can serve is forty years, so the 34,000-year term was largely symbolic. A total of twenty-one out of twenty-eight defendants were convicted of the lesser charge of belonging to a terrorist organization.

FRANCE

A Long Acquaintance with Terrorism

On the face of it, France had not seen the same level of terrorist activity as have, perhaps, other major European countries but with its large immigrant population that situation and threat level changed dramatically with the attacks in Paris in 2015 (Figure 6-2).

FIGURE 6-2   Map of France.   *Source:* Central Intelligence Agency, *The World Factbook, 2008.*

European terrorists and Middle Eastern terror groups have always needed bases, not only safe houses but also safe countries from which to mount their terror campaigns without too much political or police interference. Until the Madrid bombings, Europe was perceived to be a logistics base for terror groups and cells. The twenty-first-century reality is that Europe (France included) has become a fertile recruiting ground for the likes of Abu Musab al-Zarqawi, the Jordanian who led the insurgent attacks in Iraq. The country of choice for many terrorist groups and terrorists has often been France. From a strategic point of view, terror groups have considered the country an ideal location from which to strike and then return to hide. It has borders with Spain, Italy, Germany, Switzerland, Belgium, and Luxembourg, plus an efficient transportation network of roads, air, sea, and rail systems.

France has not been immune to terror. History books are full of atrocities perpetrated during the French Revolution. (The word "terrorism" was born from that time.) What needs more consideration and discussion surrounds the type of terror groups that utilize France for their base of operations and their reasons for doing so. The next section discusses some specific groups that have successfully used France as a base to mount terror operations and even to carry on turf wars outside their own countries.

The Popular Front for the Liberation of Palestine (PFLP) in France

In the late 1960s and 1970s, France became the European safe haven for the beleaguered PFLP organization. The PFLP was one of the most militant and aggressive Palestinian groups linked to the Palestine Liberation Organization (PLO). Wadi Haddad controlled and led the "external" operations from a secure base, in Aden, now South Yemen, and directed PFLP operations in Europe. They had set up safe houses in Paris for planned attacks in Europe. The audacious attacks carried out by the group include some of the most spectacular attacks in recent history: the attacks at Zurich Airport in 1969, the Dawson Field hijackings in 1970, and the attack on the Organization of Petroleum Exporting Countries (OPEC) headquarters in Vienna in 1975, led by Ilich Ramirez Sanchez, better known as Carlos the Jackal,[14] who now resides in a French prison cell. The Jackal was linked to the following attacks:

- **1972**—Massacre of eleven Israeli athletes by Palestinian gunmen at the Munich Olympic Games.
- **1973**—Edward Sieff, whose family owned Marks and Spencer's department stores, was attacked and wounded.
- **1974**—Armed assault and takeover of the French Embassy in The Hague by members of the Japanese Red Army.
- **1975**—Two French intelligence agents were killed while investigating the Orly Airport attack on an Israeli airliner.
- **1975**—Attack on the OPEC headquarters in Vienna in which three people died and eleven were taken hostage.
- **1976**—Air France, airliner hijacked to Entebbe, Uganda.
- **1982**—Bombing attack on the Paris–Toulouse Express.
- **1983**—Bombing attack on Marseille's main railway terminal killing five people.

The justification for terrorism has been argued vigorously. However, since the end of World War II, the use of terror as a means to an end has had several primary benefits: (1) to receive local and, in most cases, worldwide attention for a specific cause or causes; (2) as an outlet for political impotence and frustration; and (3) to carry out combative measures for countries or states not in the financial position to take direct action themselves. In the political arena, the latter would occur where a state did not wish to take direct confrontational action but rather use the cloak of terror, for which it could always deny any involvement in the aftermath of the event. The Palestinian cause will be dealt with under a separate chapter; however, many organizations like the PLO, and various offshoots, used France in the 1960s and 1970s as a friendly base for operations.

Japanese Red Army

The Japanese Red Army (JRA) terror group was also prominent in France in the 1970s. This group was pledged to a worldwide Marxist revolution and actively supported and was very much involved in the Palestinian struggle in the Middle East.[15] The group was formed in the early 1970s based on feudal Japanese Samurai warrior traditions, as well as Marxism. The JRA operated globally and has been involved in major international terror attacks in support of the Palestinian cause. They participated in the ferocious attack on Lod Airport in Israel,[16] killing Puerto Rican pilgrims in the departure lounge. The group also murdered two U.S. sailors in Italy in 1988. In continuous worldwide support of its Palestinian brethren, the group also hijacked an airliner and held the passengers hostage, demanding the sum of US$6 million in ransom.

Action Direct

France is a center of operations for international terrorism, but it also has had its own brand of internal terrorists. Action Direct (AD) was a Marxist terrorist group unlike many of its other European and Middle Eastern counterparts. It evolved, not out of the 1960s, but the late 1970s and early 1980s. Considered a left-wing revolutionary group, it began as a Communist revolutionary organization and limited its focus to virulent anti-American sentiment. One of its more audacious attacks was a raid on the Goldenberg Restaurant in Paris in August 1982 when gunmen opened fire, killing six patrons and injuring a further twenty-two other diners.

With its strong views on American interference in European affairs, it adopted the anti-American rhetoric of the Palestinian cause and began attacking Israeli and Zionist targets and those associated with capitalism and imperialism, such as the North Atlantic Treaty Organization (NATO). As AD evolved, it began to build a network of other left-wing terror groups operating in Europe, particularly in Germany, France, and Belgium. The Communist Combatant Cells (CCC) in Belgium,[17] the Red Brigade (RB) in Italy, and the German-based Red Army Faction supported AD's campaign against NATO. With its original base in Paris, AD also became an international terror organization.

There is skepticism in official quarters that this group had to feed off and be supported by the other left-wing groups. Since the unification of East and West Germany, the level of left-wing violence and terror has decreased. This, however, does not indicate that the group has split up or disintegrated, and AD will most likely continue, in some form, to espouse and support its philosophical goals.

Alien Invaders

In recent times, France has been the breeding ground for unwelcome guests from the European and Middle East theaters of terrorist conflict. On the home front, there has been the Front de la Liberation Nationale de la Corse (FLNC), a group of Corsican separatists, as well as the extreme left-wing AD group. Another is the Armee Republicaine Bretonne (ARB). The ARB and the FLNC are distinct in their aims as compared to the AD. They are purely regional French factions with the goal of local autonomy. AD, on the other hand, has somewhat fuzzy international ideological goals. Confusingly, to the casual or the uninformed observer, AD has gone after anti-Jewish interests, which, one would normally associate with the extreme right wing as opposed to the extreme left. France's tolerance for the number of groups active within its borders is probably born out of its own realization of how the French Republic was created. This tolerance has led many other groups to use Paris as a primary base for internal and external operations. The Corsican Army (Armata Corsa) set up in 1999 to oppose links between nationalists and the Corsican Mafia on the other hand, has its roots in the criminal classes of Corsica and seems to function partly on the nationalist scene and partly on the criminal side of life. It does, however, denounce the Mafia-style activities that have plagued the island of Corsica. Its attacks have been mostly symbolic as Armata Corsa seeks to create an island state independent from France, and also the return of Corsican terrorists imprisoned in mainland France. The group has been mainly involved in attacks against public figures and buildings as well as tourist locations, and has concentrated on nearly all the attacks on Corsica.

With the disintegration of the empire of the Shah of Iran, students in Paris took control of the Iranian Embassy to show their support for Ayatollah Khomeini. The city was a tolerant host to both sides, with both pro- and anti-Khomeini supporters making their protests public. Both groups clashed during a street protest.

The **Armenian Secret Army for the Liberation of Armenia (ASALA)** represents another region of Europe. This French group of exiled Armenians was intent on promoting its cause and airing its grievances against the government of Turkey. ASALA's grievances go back in history to 1915–1922, when the Turks massacred more than 1 million Armenians headquartered in the Middle East; its actions are aimed at securing a homeland of its own. Most Armenians lived within former Soviet Bloc countries.

The most aggressive groups operating out of Paris have been the PLO and the Algerian Islamic terrorist group known as the Armed Islamic Group (GIA). The PLO's headline-catching events included the rocket attack at Orly Airport, when in broad daylight two Lebanese Palestinians calmly parked their car near the runway and, armed with a RPG-7 rocket launcher, fired at an El Al flight taxiing for take-off. Fortunately, the rocket missed the El Al aircraft and hit an empty Yugoslav jetliner.[18] The two terrorists escaped capture at the airport. Not to be outdone by the failure, another attack was scheduled for Orly Airport six days later. By this time, the airport was strongly protected by military security. The group entered the airport with an assembled bazooka, much to the astonishment of the armed police, and a furious gun battle between police and terrorists ensued amid hundreds of passengers and spectators in the airport building. As for the GIA, their actions in France in the mid-1990s included attacks on the Paris Metro subway system. Approximately five million Muslims live in France out of a total population of 58 million. GIA's actions in France resulted in bombings throughout 1995, and, in July of that year, a gas canister bomb exploded in the subway, killing seven and injuring eighty-six. Algeria, a former French colony, had been fighting a rising tide of Islamic radicalism. Rather than accede to it, the Algerian government, at that time under Liamine Zeroual, used military force to repress GIA. Because of its support for the Algerians, the French became a legitimate target for the GIA, who hoped France would withdraw its support for Algeria. Aircraft hijackings, by GIA terrorists, seem to be almost a prediction of the tragic events of 9-11. In December 1994, armed terrorists disguised as police officers boarded an Air France jet in Algiers and hijacked it to France. The aircraft was reportedly packed with explosives to be detonated over the capital city of Paris. The aircraft landed in Marseilles and was stormed by members of the crack anti-terror group Groupe d'Intervention de la Gendarmerie Nationale (GIGN), which ended the fifty-four-hour siege that culminated in the death of three of the hostages and all of the terrorists.

In April 2001, Fateh Kemal an Algerian-Canadian who had been arrested in Jordan and extradited to France was sentenced in Paris for operating a support network believed to be linked to al Qaeda. He was sentenced to eight years in jail. The French were able to establish links between Kemal's operatives and Ahmed Ressam, the millennium bomber arrested by U.S. Custom agents when he was crossing from Canada into Washington State with a bomb intended for a terrorist attack at the Los Angeles International Airport. On the day before the 9-11 attacks, French authorities began to investigate a group linked to al Qaeda that planned to attack U.S. targets in France. The group's leader, Djamel Beghal, was extradited from the United Arab Emirates (UAE) to France in October 2001 as part of that investigation. It was very patient intelligence work that revealed that Kemal was an expert document forger, head of the network of which the Roubaix gang was a part, and had also spent time in Afghanistan, where he'd been in contact with bin Laden. The French authorities believe it is clear that in the decentralized, compartmentalized, and intersecting root system of Islamic networks, Kemal had been given the responsibility for creating and transporting false ID documents to be used by militants being assembled in Turkey, Bulgaria, Belgium, France, Bosnia, and North America.

Kemal and twenty-three associates were convicted for activities related to association with terrorist enterprises. There was no demonstrative proof of their service or allegiance to bin Laden, although such links would be impossible to verify given the dispersed, cellular nature of these operations (thus organized precisely to prevent police from following a linear trail back to the top) and their vague hierarchy and direction.[19] Kemal was released from prison in 2005 and deported to Canada, where proceedings were launched to have his citizenship revoked and for his deportation back to his native Algeria. That attempt failed however and Kemal sought and applied for a Canadian passport—that request has been continually denied.

Although France has been a strong UN ally, the U.S. desire to seek death penalty for Zacarias Moussaoui, the only man arrested in connection with the 9-11 attacks, has meant a lack of cooperation between the French intelligence services and those of the United States. Both the French and German governments have been supplying evidence to the United States concerning Moussaoui, but not material that could lead to his execution. In spite of this, the French have been party to counterterrorism discussions at the G-8 summit meetings.[20]

AL QAEDA IN FRANCE

With France's close ties to the North African continent during its colonial era, it is not surprising that many immigrants from Morocco and Algeria migrate to France. The planning and recruiting for the 9-11 attack did not take place in Muslim countries, but mainly on the continent of Europe—in Germany, France, and England in particular. The security and intelligence failures can be linked back to Europe and a failure to follow up on specific intelligence reports from the French security services.

As for al Qaeda, most of its French cells were made up of second-generation immigrants, and as investigations have shown, most of the combatants showed little or no interest in Islam in their own countries. It seems the seeds of Islamic radicalism may have been planted in the mosques of Europe. Radical Islamic beliefs are not the sole domain of Muslims. Richard Reid, the infamous "shoe bomber," and two French-native brothers, David and Jerome Courtailler, are converts to Islam. Lionel Dumont, a French citizen from the northern French town of Roubaix, and also a convert to Islam, saw military service with the French in Somalia. In the early 1990s, he went to the former Yugoslavia and joined a mujahideen group, the Takfir wal-Hijra, in Bosnia. He returned to France and formed an organization with others from the North African communities, called the Gang of Roubaix, which was involved in several terrorist attacks. His links to al Qaeda have never been confirmed, and so far he has evaded arrest from French authorities.[21]

During former president Bush's re-election campaign in 2004, he commented, "More than three quarters of al Qaeda have been brought to justice." This may well have sounded great for the electorate, but, as we have seen, al Qaeda is becoming a rallying cry movement for young and impressionable Muslims around the globe, more particularly those in Western countries such as France, Germany, and the Netherlands. The first prominent example is British citizen Richard Reid, who boarded an American Airlines flight in Paris bound for Miami on December 22, 2001, and attempted to detonate a bomb hidden in his shoes. Richard Reid may have seemed an unlikely candidate for an Islamic convert—nevertheless his troubled youth brought him into contact with those who would ultimately set him on a path to terrorism.

1992–1994—The British Home Office says Richard Reid was twice incarcerated at Feltham (Middlesex) Young Offenders Institution in West London—for ten days in 1992 and a month in 1994. It was not known what charges led to Reid's incarceration there.

Late 1998 and early 1999—Brixton Mosque chairman Abdul Haqq Baker says Reid and Zacarias Moussaoui—the only person so far charged with conspiracy in the 9-11 terrorist attacks on the United States—attended the same South London mosque during this period, though it is not known if they were there at the same time.

July 2001—Israeli government officials say Reid traveled to Israel for "around ten days" before traveling by land to Egypt.

August to December 2001—Reid reportedly lives in Amsterdam, working in restaurants.

Early December 2001—Reid allegedly spends ten days in Brussels, Belgium, staying at the Dar Salam hostel in an Arab and North African neighborhood.

December 5 and 6, 2001—Reid tells Belgian authorities he'd lost his British passport. The British Embassy issues him a new one.

December 15, 2001—Reid reportedly checks out of the Brussels hostel and arrives in Paris, France, the next day.

December 17, 2001—Reid buys round-trip ticket from Paris to Miami, Florida, to Antigua. Police say he appears to have spent his entire time in the area around the Gare du Nord, one of the city's major train stations.

December 21, 2001—French authorities question Reid after a security agent becomes suspicious because Reid is traveling without checked luggage. Authorities eventually say Reid can board his flight, American Airlines Flight 63, but by then it has already left Paris.

December 22, 2001—Reid boards American Airlines Flight 63, which is following the same route as the flight he'd missed a day earlier. Ninety minutes later, he allegedly tries to use a match to light explosives hidden in his shoes and is subdued when passengers and crew jump on him and strap him to his seat. Doctors aboard the aircraft sedate him. Plane diverts to Boston, Massachusetts, and Reid is arrested and charged with interfering with a flight crew.

December 28, 2001—A federal judge denies Reid's bail and remands him to jail in Plymouth, Massachusetts.[22]

January 30, 2003—Reid is sentenced in Federal Court to life in prison.

Richard Reid has been cast as a bungling amateur when in fact the opposite is the case, as there is ample evidence that he had been in contact with other jihadists and had received terror training. With respect to Moussaoui, the intelligence sources on both sides of the Atlantic should have picked up on his activities. French intelligence tracks nearly all North Africans traveling from France to Pakistan and/or Afghanistan. British newspapers reported that the French Directorate of Territorial Security repeatedly informed its counterparts in Britain that Zacarias Moussaoui, who was residing in London in the early 1990s, had made trips to both Afghanistan and Pakistan. Further, he was considered to be involved in terrorism. As part of the investigation into the murder of three French Consular staff in Algeria, Moussaoui's name was found in an address book that was seized. Unfortunately, information provided to the British appears to never have been acted upon.[23]

The FBI had been warned in advance of the 9-11 attacks, and that Moussaoui was associated with Osama bin Laden. Moussaoui was arrested on an immigration violation; the French intelligence report was never acted upon.[24] Zacarias Moussaoui was born in France and, like other suspects arrested in Germany, was not known as an Islamic extremist. In 1992, he went to England and shared an apartment with the French Courtailler brothers while he studied for a degree. Sometime during this period he came under the spell of the fanatical Muslim cleric, Abu Qatada.

Europe is currently the recruiting haven for Islamic militants and social media are fast becoming the route extremists are using to spread their message and recruit jihadists. In 2011, we saw how effective the use of the Internet and social media forums can be in rallying popular support for uprisings as evidenced in Egypt, Tunisia, Libya, Yemen, and Syria. Terrorists and radical Islamist groups continue to use the Internet as a recruiting tool, and social media forms part of their arsenal. In a message posted to the Shumukh al-Islam jihadist forum, a forum member called for supporters of al Qaeda to prepare attacks, including assassinations, suicide bombings, and chemical and bio-weapons attacks, against French individuals in retaliation for enforcing the law banning face veils. The April 13, 2011, poster encouraged forum members to "annihilate them and extirpate them, horrify and terrorize them, do not leave them one place without terrorizing them and making them horrified by you."[25]

Europe is suffering from the worst migrant crisis since World War II. Primarily, refugees are arriving by sea to the Greek Islands and by land through Turkey. More than a million arrived by sea alone in 2015, with the principal countries that they represent being Syria, Afghanistan, and Iraq. This mass movement of migrants across the European continent is most certainly sprinkled with jihadists making the journey as refugees and hiding in the confusion. The ease with which the borders of Europe can be breeched is being exploited by adherents to the radical ideologies of IS/al Qaeda.

ATTACKS ON PARIS, 2015—CHARLIE HEBDO AND BATACLAN

In 2015, the horrors of this threat were realized in graphic detail with commando-style attacks in the capital city of Paris. Both attacks were planned, directed, and well-coordinated. The operatives involved in the November 13, 2015, attacks in Paris, who were trained and directed by the Islamic State were able to conduct a far deadlier attack in contrast to the Woolwich attack in London in 2013, where the two individuals were radicalized and inspired but had not undergone external training and were not being directed by external groups such as Islamic State.

The attack was against **Charlie Hebdo** offices in January 2015. Charlie Hebdo is a weekly satirical magazine that is more attuned with anti-religious sentiment, has a strong left-wing bias, and regularly ridicules Jews, Christian Catholics, and Muslims in its magazine articles. The magazine had attracted attention, particularly in the Muslim world for its cartoon depictions of the Prophet Muhammad, unfazed by threats of violence and demonstrations against

Jyllands-Posten, the newspaper which had given its support to the publishing of depictions of the cartoon illustration. Al Qaeda in Yemen named the editor of Charlie Hebdo, Stephane Charbonnier on their most wanted hit list. It is most certainly the case that in liberal western countries press freedoms are recognized while the same style of reporting would be unacceptable in Muslim nations. In France, as in many western states there is an inherent right for authors of magazines, newspapers, etc. to have freedom of speech and expression and that means they can criticize, characterize, and satirize public figures, institutions such as the church, and in the case of Charlie Hebdo cartoons relating to Islam. There are also laws of defamation available for redress to such publications.

This attack was carried out by three well-armed and trained men who forced their way into the offices and went directly to the second floor offices having first sprayed the entrance reception area with gunfire killing the receptionist. On the second floor an editorial meeting was in progress with fifteen staffers present—the two terrorist shouted for "Charb," short for Charbonnier, the editor who was in the meeting room to identify him for execution. They shot nearly all their targets with head shots in execution style. It has been estimated that they were in the building for around ten minutes. As they left the premises, they made their way along the street and were confronted by a police officer who was injured in an exchange of gunfire with the two men. They then went to the police officer and shot him in the head. From video footage, it was clear that these men were well trained and well prepared for the actions they were taking; they moved in support of one another and fired in short bursts or single shot. They escaped from the scene in a hijacked vehicle. In the three days following the attack on Charlie Hebdo, one terror suspect surrendered to police while the remaining two, brothers Saïd and Chérif Kouachi were killed in a shootout with French police. France has a population of around 7 million Muslims and a large number have gone to Syria and Iraq—the exact numbers are vague but believed to be in the thousands. The numbers of those who have returned are believed to be in several hundreds.

Coordinated Attacks in Paris—November 13, 2015

The attacks in Paris were a multipronged attack against "soft targets," a soccer stadium, a series of restaurant, cafes and bars, and a concert hall. They were well planned and executed to cause maximum confusion, panic, fear, devastation, and loss of life.

The first target was the Paris soccer stadium Stade de France where France was playing Germany, the first bomb detonated at around 9.20 P.M. local time but as the attackers all wearing suicide vests had arrived late, they had missed the tightly packed crowd trying to enter the stadium. When they spotted police they detonated their bombs—all were killed along with one civilian. The next attack came around five minutes later at 9.25 on the rue Bichat and rue Alibert when attackers shot at people outside Le Carillon, a café and bar with automatic weapons killing fifteen and wounding many more. The next attack approximately seven minutes later on the rue de la Fontaine au-Roi was carried out by a lone attacker with a Kalashnikov who fired at restaurant guests at the Bonne Briere killing five and injuring eight; this was quickly followed by another restaurant attack on the rue Charonne—the two attackers targeted guests seated on the outside patio of La Belle Equipe killing nineteen. At 9.45 P.M. a lone male wearing a suicide vest sat down in the Comptoire Voltaire café and placed his order at which point he detonated his bomb killing himself and wounding fifteen others (Figure 6-3).

The final attack was mounted by a three-man team at the Bataclan Theater at 9.40 P.M. where the American band, Eagles of Death Metal, was playing to a packed audience. The three attackers entered the theater and began to systematically kill every civilian they could find. One attacker was shot by police, detonating his suicide vest—the remaining two took hostages to the second floor and the French police stood back until the special force units arrived. The Research Assistance Intervention Deterrence (RAID) team from the French National Police took command and stormed the building—when the siege was over all

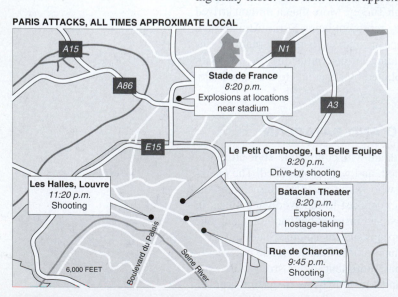

PARIS ATTACKS, ALL TIMES APPROXIMATE LOCAL

FIGURE 6-3 Map of Paris showing attack locations.
Courtesy: www.Stratfor.com.

three attackers were dead. A total of one hundred and thirty-two people were killed in the attacks and more than three hundred and fifty were injured. The seven attackers were two from Belgium and five from France, all were citizens of their respective countries.

The attackers were set up in three teams of three—a total of seven died in the Paris attacks and the remaining two were killed five days later in French Police raid in Saint Denis. Several of the attackers had been to Syria and Yemen between 2012 and 2014 and had fought with AQ in Yemen and ISIS in Syria. The ringleader and probable mastermind for this attack was identified as Salah Abdeslam, a Belgian national. He was arrested three days before the Brussels bombings in March 2016.

Europe—Current Affairs

What Europe is experiencing from jihadists is far more serious and sinister than a 'lone wolf' attack—from the amount of planning and coordination that went into the Paris attack, it is certain that the cellular network from which they operated had a sophisticated support network to allow the perpetrators locations to hide and prepare for this attack. The current thinking puts to rest the theory that these are single jihadists returning but are part of multiple attack groups that are supported by a network of friends who may not necessarily be radicalized but are sympathetic to Islam at the very least. The threat to Europe is significant from radicalized young men and women. Many are second generation immigrants who have grown up in the Muslim neighborhoods of Paris and Brussels in areas where they have been marginalized and where unemployment rates are very high—this makes them a target for those offering them a way out through radicalization.

A 2015–16 study on jihadi militants returning to the west has been compiled from research done by the New America think tank and the following statistics give us pause for thought:

Western fighters in Syria and Iraq represent a new demographic profile, quite different from that of other Western militants who had fought in Afghanistan in the 1980s or Bosnia in the 1990s.

- Women are represented in unprecedented numbers. One in seven of the individuals in New America's dataset are women. Women were rarely if at all represented among militants in previous jihadist conflicts.
- They are young. The average age for individuals in New America's dataset is twenty-five. For female recruits, the average age is twenty-two. Almost one-fifth of New America's samples are teenagers, of whom more than a third are female.
- They are active online. Over a quarter of the Western militants in New America's dataset were reported either to have been active in online jihadist circles or to have radicalized via interaction online. However, there continue to be cases of physical in-person recruitment.
- Many have familial ties to jihadists. One-third of the Western militants have a familial connection to jihad, whether through relatives currently fighting in Syria or Iraq, through marriage, or some other link to jihadists from prior conflicts or attacks. Of those with a familial link, over half have a relative fighting in Iraq or Syria, while almost one-third are connected through marriage, many of them new marriages conducted after arriving in Syria.
- The Americans drawn to the Syrian jihad—two hundred and fifty have tried or have succeeded in getting to Syria, according to official estimates—share the same profile as the Western fighters overall: women are well-represented, and the volunteers are young, they are active online, and many have family ties to jihad. More than one in seven of the Americans who traveled, attempted to travel, or supported others' travel to Syria are women. The average age of American militants is twenty-five, with one-fifth still in their teens. Eight out of ten of the Americans are active in online jihadist circles.
- Only six American militants have returned from fighting or training with militant groups in Syria and been taken into custody, while another American militant returned to the United States and then left for Syria again where he conducted a suicide attack in 2014.
- This makes a total of seven American "returnees" to the States who have trained with militant groups in Syria. The numbers of returnees to European countries are orders of magnitude greater.

Any assessment of the threat to the West posed by Western fighters drawn to the Syrian conflict must begin with an examination of who those fighters are. New America gathered names and information for six hundred and four Western fighters from twenty-six Western countries:

Albania (4), Australia (35), Austria (6), Belgium (111), Bosnia (5), Canada (26), Denmark (14), Finland (4), France (63), Germany (38), Ireland (7), Italy (6), Kosovo (4), Luxembourg (2), Macedonia (4), Montenegro (1), Netherlands (29), New Zealand (1), Norway (13), Portugal (3), Serbia (2), Spain (3), Sweden (24), Switzerland (2), the United Kingdom (165), the United States (30), and two other Westerners whose country affiliations are unknown.[26]

France as a secular nation also has Europe's largest Muslim community and faces a dilemma between accommodating Islam and maintaining secularism. In 2004, it passed a law banning headscarves or any other "conspicuous" religious symbols in schools to uphold a separation between church and state. France is currently the only state in Europe to have such a ban. In April 2011, it banned the wearing of the Muslim veil in public places, which provided a focus for al Qaeda-inspired groups to target French interests.

In Paris during November 2005, two Muslim youths died while being chased by French police, which sparked a week of rioting. Many Muslim migrants live in slum areas of the major cities and finding work is difficult at best. The presence of so many disgruntled youth, both immigrant and second generation, provides ample fodder for radical Muslim extremists to recruit from. The attacks in the French city of Toulouse in March 2012 showed how the intelligence community is often unable to prevent what on the surface appears to be a "lone wolf" attack from a committed jihadist. This was low-cost terrorism involving either a small cell of dedicated jihadists or an individual radicalized and trained for such an attack; the attacks saw three French paratroopers gunned down in a street by a lone gunman, to be quickly followed by the daytime massacre at a Jewish school where the same gunman killed the head teacher and three children. The perpetrator was alone for the attacks but was a committed jihadist who had traveled extensively to Asia and like his counterparts in the United Kingdom received training in the tribal regions of Pakistan's border area. Such was the premeditated nature of the attacks that the assailant Mohammed Merah even used a camera to record his killings and post them on the Internet. His attacks were calculated and well planned, and he was well known in jihadist circles in France. Also, he undoubtedly received material support from other jihadists in this operation. Merah was known to French intelligence and also was on a No-Fly list and still managed to execute this attack.

GERMANY

A Mixed History of Fascism, Terrorism, and Democracy

Germany has survived two world wars, was divided into two nations, paid the price of Nazism as well as Communism, and, at the end of the twentieth century, rose as a major industrial power in Europe. History clearly describes the years between the two world wars as being economically harsh for Germany. However, it is important to look back at some significant periods of the twentieth century that affected the German people as well as neighboring countries (Figure 6-4). Between the two world wars, Germany saw the rise of the Nazi Party and the ultimate power of its leader, former Austrian corporal, Adolf Hitler. Humbled by its reparation payments and crippled by the devastation of the Great Depression of 1929, the Germans faced unemployment and starvation. The reparation repayment was renegotiated under the terms of the Young Plan, against which Adolf Hitler campaigned long and hard throughout Germany. By July 1932, the Nazi Party held 38 percent of the seats in the German Parliament (Reichstag).[27] Hitler's passionate, self-appointed mission was to lead a depressed Germany back to greatness, rid it of Communist and other influences, and purge the society of its ills. To achieve this, he had to gain absolute power and control. In 1933, Paul Von Hindenburg, president of Germany, proclaimed Hitler as chancellor (prime minister). With total control, Hitler proclaimed his government as the "Third Reich." With that, Germany's dictator began his own reign of terror on Germany. By the end of July 1933, through legal processes, Hitler had destroyed the German constitution and outlawed freedom of the press, unions, and all political parties with the exception of the National Socialist Party (the "Nazi" Party). His own breed of police, the Gestapo, hunted down all opponents of his government. Many were arrested on suspicion alone and, more often than not, were jailed or shot.

The Nazis used terror tactics to gain control over the populace. All German children, boys and girls, were required to join the Hitler Youth or the Society of German Maidens. These children of Germany were indoctrinated into the Nazi philosophy and military discipline and were used as spies to inform on family members who did not embrace National Socialism. A

FIGURE 6-4 Map of Germany. *Source:* Central Intelligence Agency, *The World Factbook, 2008.*

sophisticated network of spies monitored and reported on the German people and fostered an atmosphere of physical and psychological terror.

Germany's New Order

There have been hundreds of accounts about Hitler's "Final Solution" for the "Jewish problem." He believed that the German people were a genetically superior race and that his country had to be purged of the impure, non-Aryan peoples. Those groups singled out for special treatment were Jews, Gypsies, Poles, homosexuals, and Slavs. The term Holocaust is widely used to define the mass murder of over six million Jewish people. Hitler and his Nazi Party members began their reign of terror on the Jews as early as 1933 and by the latter half of that decade had solidified enough power to begin "cleansing" the Jewish population. Sometime in early November 1938 (the date has never been precisely confirmed), beginning around the ninth of the month and lasting for about forty-eight hours, Nazi Party members destroyed thousands of Jewish businesses and synagogues throughout Germany, killed dozens of Jews, and sent almost forty thousand to concentration camps. The night is referred to as *Kristallnacht* (night of the broken glass).

When German armies rolled across Europe, a similar fate awaited Jews in those countries that Germany had conquered. The names of the camps still strike terror into many communities: Belsen, Auschwitz, Buchenwald, Dachau, and others. Hitler's brand of terror, which accounted for the mass murder of millions of Jews and others considered non-Aryan or those who did not fit his Aryan picture of perfection, was a simple means to an end. The Nazi leadership saw it as the cleansing of a nation and those it had conquered. Such use of political terrorism was considered a weapon of psychological warfare.

Post-World War II Germany and Terrorism

After World War II, a long period of rebuilding and healing took place. By the 1960s, the Federal German Republic was experiencing three different types of terrorism:

1. **Left-wing** terrorism came from the imported views of radical students and their opposition to the U.S. war in Vietnam.

2. **Right-wing** terrorists opposed the left-wing radicals in a continuation of the anti-Communist past.
3. **Criminals** also adopted the terror group's actions and copied and mimicked their attacks for personal criminal gain.

The 1960s were the decade of widespread student unrest, although in Germany there was no real catalyst to take the protests to the next stage. Student protests were prevalent on many university campuses in Europe as a platform for anti-Vietnam War protests. Modern terrorism, in Germany's case, has been typified by indiscriminate violence, sensationalized by the murder of innocents.

The student left-wing radicals at the Berlin Free University, in a somewhat copycat style, protested against American involvement in Vietnam. The protests were restricted mainly to marches and the distribution of leaflets, but there was no catalyst in place to take any serious action at a higher level of violence. Two main protagonists came to the forefront of the student protests: Andreas Baader and Gudrun Ensslin.[28] As in many university campuses of the 1960s, both Communism and Marxism were prevalent in the Berlin Free University. Baader, Ensslin, and, later, Meinhof were all committed Marxists. The German **Red Army Faction** was formulated at Berlin University led by Gudrun Ensslin and by the freewheeling Andreas Baader, who presented more of a playboy image than that of a terrorist.

Kidnapping for ransom was a hallmark of many of the terrorist groups operating in Europe and the Middle East during the 1960s and 1970s. The kidnapping of a prominent German industrialist Herr Hanns-Martin Schleyer by the Red Army Faction is an example of how desperate the various groups were for media and government attention. Schlayer and his entourage were attacked in a Cologne suburb and his bodyguards were killed.

Red Army Faction

This group of committed Marxists sought to engage the United States in a combative role by extending the Vietnam War to German soil. They achieved this by attacking U.S. interests in West Germany, and particularly U.S. servicemen and military bases. Many books describe Andreas Baader as more of a delinquent and a follower than a committed terrorist. He seemed, in many accounts, to draw pleasure from being at the center of an infamous criminal network. To finance its program of violence, the group resorted to a series of bank robberies and other crimes.

The igniting factor that sparked this group into action on a grand scale was, in fact, an eloquent German lawyer, Horst Mahler, who joined the student movement to give it impetus toward a violent action. In 1968, Ensslin and her boyfriend Baader attempted to destroy two Frankfurt department stores with firebombs. They were both captured and sentenced and, a year later, temporarily released during an amnesty for political prisoners. When the amnesty was over, they fled to France as fugitives. They returned to West Germany to join with Horst Mahler, but Baader was again arrested. At this point in the group's development, Ulrike Meinhof came into the picture.

Meinhof was the editor of an underground newspaper called *Konkert*.[29] The paper had been launched in the 1950s, sponsored and supported by Communist groups in East Germany. Meinhof is reputed to be a close friend of Gudrun Ensslin, and it was Ensslin who persuaded Meinhof to assist in Andreas Baader's prison breakout. The jailbreak on May 14, 1970, resulted in changing the name of the group to the Baader–Meinhof Gang (Figure 6-5). Over the following two years, Meinhof spent time in Jordan not far from the capital, Amman, and received training in weaponry from the Palestinians. Meinhof and colleagues became skilled in the use of their favorite weapon, the Russian Kalashnikov (the AK-47 assault rifle). After training with the PLO, the group was involved in the attack on the OPEC headquarters in Vienna, Austria, on December 21, 1975. At this point, the Red Army Faction (RAF) joined forces with a group that called itself the "Arab Revolution," a cover name for the PFLP.[30]

Ilich Ramirez Sanchez, better known as "Carlos the Jackal," led the assault on the OPEC building in Vienna in 1975 that targeted the oil-producing countries and was more a case of raising money than having a significant political impact. The Saudi Arabian and Iranian governments are believed to have paid a ransom of $50 million for the safe return of their nationals. Among the five strong groups that attacked the building were two German terrorists—Gabrielle Tiedemann and Hans-Joachim Klein. During a gun battle with Austrian security officers, Klein was captured and seriously injured. No political demands were made except the demand that the Austrians broadcast a political statement for the Baader–Meinhof

TERRORIST ATTACK BRIEF

A combo of three photos taken May 1977 shows, from left, Jan-Carl Raspe, Gudrun Enslin and Andreas Baader, three of the leading figures of the German terrorist group RAF (Red Army Faction). Wednesday September 5, 1977; the start of a 44-day terror campaign by the left-wing Red Army Faction—an ordeal that began with the kidnapping of a top industrialist and ended in bloody defeat for the terror group, whose leaders killed themselves in prison. The so-called "German Autumn" was a test of will for Chancellor Helmut Schmidt, who recently admitted he still felt personal guilt toward the family of murdered hostage Hanns-Martin Schleyer. (AP Photo)

FIGURE 6-5 Red Army Faction—Baader–Meinhof Gang. *Courtesy:* AP files/AP Images.

group. The Austrians allowed the terrorist and a number of the hostages to fly to Algiers and then to Tripoli. The large amount of ransom money was transferred to a bank in Aden to bank-roll further terrorism.

German authorities arrested the principals of the Baader–Meinhof Gang, which numbered about one hundred active supporters. In May 1972, Baader, Gudrun Ensslin, Holger Meins, and Jean-Carle Raspe placed three pipe bombs near the entrance to the I.G. Faben building, which housed the U.S. Army Corps. Both bombs detonated within minutes of each other. The officers' mess was destroyed, and Lt Colonel Paul Bloomquist, a decorated Vietnam War veteran, died from his injuries. The Baader–Meinhof Gang, calling themselves the Petra Schlem Commando, claimed responsibility for the attack and demanded an end to the U.S. mining of Vietnam harbors. Baader and others of the group were captured and sentenced in 1972.

The group was housed in the maximum security Stammheim Prison. Ulrike Meinhof, suffering from acute depression, hanged herself in her prison cell on May 9, 1976. As for the remainder of the group's members, it is something of a controversy as to how they met their ends. On the night of October 18, 1977, several members of the Baader–Meinhof group died from self-inflicted gunshot wounds in their prison cells.[31] Many have asked how guns could have been smuggled into a top-security prison. The most likely answer to that is lawyers for the group brought in the weapons to attempt a breakout.

The deaths coincided with news of a dramatic rescue by the antiterrorist group Grenzschutzgruppe-9 (GSG-9) in October 1977. The GSG-9 stormed a Lufthansa aircraft at Mogadishu, Somalia, killing three hijackers and rescuing the ninety passengers. It would seem to be entirely logical that the RAF, or as it was usually called, the "Baader–Meinhof Gang," would cease to exist. However, it exists to this day and its growth has not been stemmed by arrests of prominent members over the past two decades. With arrests of successive leaders and gang members, the RAF has continued to rise like a phoenix from its own ashes. It is believed that its growth in the 1970s and 1980s was due, in part, to an elaborate communications system and network set up among the imprisoned terrorists, their lawyers, and the activists still working for the cause. Public opinion soured toward the RAF in 1977, an opinion that had generally held them up as romantics fighting for a misunderstood cause. This was naturally embellished by the popular press, which continued to sensationalize the group's criminal activities and misdeeds. However, the previously mentioned hijacking of a Lufthansa airline to Mogadishu, Somalia, by terrorists supported by the RAF resulting in the murder of the aircraft's pilot, Jurgen Schumann, was the single act that helped turn public opinion against the group.

TERRORISM AND THE OLYMPIC GAMES MOVEMENT

The 1972 Olympic Games were held in Munich—this would be the first time in Germany since the 1938 Berlin Games—but the 1972 games will not be remembered for the seven Gold Medals in swimming by Mark Spitz of the United States but for a barbaric terrorist attack against Israeli Olympic athletes. In the early hours of September 5, 1972, eight members of the Palestinian Black September terrorist group entered the village and after a fight with members of the wrestling team managed to secure a total of nine Israeli hostages—then began a tense standoff with negotiations throughout the day—the terrorists were demanding the release by Israel of over two hundred Palestinian prisoners and by Germany the release of Andreas Baader and Ulrike Meinhof plus safe passage out of Germany. The German Border Police were dispatched to handle any rescue/assault mission. At the time there were no recognized anti-terror operation specialists in the German Police—this event would establish the GSG-9 force as a specialist unit for counterterrorism operations. The plan by the Germans was, at some point in the movement of the athletes and the terrorists to mount an attack on the terrorists and to free the Israeli hostages. The group of athletes and terrorists took off in two helicopters to Furstenfeldbruck NATO airbase a short distance from the Games Village. As they arrived and were about to inspect a waiting aircraft to take them out of Germany, sniper fire from the terminal building commenced—in the ensuing confusion all the athletes were killed along with five of the attackers with three being captured. The three captured terrorists were released after a Lufthansa airliner was hijacked the following month. The Olympic Games attack were a watershed for security realizing that a new era in terrorism was at hand, and states made determined efforts to establish counterterror police/military units ready to respond to such attacks and hostage takings. This event was to establish the GSG-9 as Germany's elite counterterror unit.

The **RAF** reached the pinnacle of their existence toward the end of the 1970s. The group was responsible for the assassination of the West German attorney general, Siegfried Buback, and Hanns-Martin Schleyer. They went so far as to attempt to murder the head of NATO in Europe—U.S. Army Four-Star General Alexander Haig. They remained active into the 1980s and by then had joined forces with a little-known German terror unit called the June Second Movement and another called the Red Cells. Little is known of their members or numbers; it seems likely that the groups continue to operate independently of each other. The significance of the date June 2, 1967, is in remembrance of Benno Ohnesorg, who was killed on that day during a student protest that turned into a riot. RAF's most notorious act was the abduction of Peter Lorenz, a candidate for the post of mayor of West Berlin. The ransom paid was for the release of four of the group's compatriots who were then flown to South Yemen.

A Reawaking of Germany's Past

Germany had relied on an influx of foreign immigrant workers for the post-World War II rebuilding of its destroyed infrastructure. The *Gastarbeiter* program, in which Turkish immigrants were brought into Germany strictly for use as menial laborers, celebrated forty years of its introduction in 2011. Some Germans continue to be openly hostile to immigration policies, especially since the events of 9-11. Integration by large numbers of immigrants to German society over the last three decades has clearly failed.

Anti-Semitic behavior still lurks as a haunting reminder from Germany's past. Invariably, the message and threats of belligerent intolerance continue to come from radical German Skinhead and neo-Nazi factions. It would be incorrect to label every Skinhead as a racist, as many are from varying religious denominations that are non-racist and are not purveyors of hate crimes. Much of the bigoted violence in Germany has been directed against foreign workers, particularly poor and desperate Turkish immigrants. However, throughout the 1990s and into the new millennium, Jews and Turks became the Skinheads' target of choice. Year after year since, starting in 1990, there has been a steady increase in the number of hate crimes associated with Skinheads and attacks on members of Jewish and Turkish communities. They are most likely to be in their teens and early twenties. Skinheads usually operate in gangs and much of their hatred and violence is spewed after bouts of binge drinking. The gangs roam the streets looking for likely victims to attack. The collapse of the Communist regime in East Germany significantly affected the Skinhead situation. The emergence of the eastern Skinheads radicalized the movement in both numbers and militancy. Skinheads tended to move in with the extreme right-wing movements in Germany, namely Michael Swierczek's National Offensive, Frank Huebner's German Alternative, The National Front, and Christian Worch's National List.

German authorities were originally either slow or reluctant to respond to the right-wing threats being posed by the Skinhead's hate movement and propaganda; however, in the last decade or so, German authorities have banned some of the neo-Nazi groups and confiscated their propaganda materials. Skinheads have traditionally not aligned themselves with any particular political party, as they view the parties as being part of the "system."

Skinheads also view imprisonment as a badge of honor. Evidence indicates that Skinheads are receiving a thorough indoctrination in neo-Nazi ideology at "comradeship evenings" held in prison. Much of this is provided by the Relief Agency for National Political Prisoners and their Dependents, a right-wing group that sends a steady stream of propaganda to incarcerated neo-Nazis and Skinheads.[32]

Germany in the Twenty-First Century

The unification of Germany, was one of the most unexpected turning points in Germany's modern history, brought with it doubts about a new Germany's ability to cope with the depression and despair suffered by its people in the former East Germany. By the end of 1997, there were growing signs in German cities of right-wing neo-Nazi groups (Skinheads) fostering hate campaigns against immigrants living in Germany. With most European communities lowering the barriers on movement between countries and with the fall of the Soviet Union, many thousands of ethnic groups surged westward for a "better life." What they found in Germany was a growing resentment, mainly by extreme right-wing groups, to the rising tide of ethnic groups seeking jobs in a struggling economy. Skinheads and others saw the immigrants as responsible for the high rate of unemployment and the economic conditions. In many cities, extremists took the law into their own hands and, in shows of nationalist strength, began abusing and intimidating immigrants.

By the spring of 1998, immigrants had virtually disappeared from some cities, having been frightened away by the fearsome onslaughts of neo-Nazists. No specific group or organized terror campaign is being sustained, although special police units are being utilized to break up obvious gangs of Skinheads. No one can predict how far—or if—Germany will regress toward a neo-Nazi influence, or whether this type of incident has been a mere pothole in the rough road to unification. What most observers are watching for from the German government is a signal that it fervently opposes the nationalist movements. With a growing number of incidents involving ethnic groups and neo-Nazi influences at various levels inside Germany's military, it is no surprise that there is a feeling of unease and terror in those who see the unsettling prospect of a rise in the nationalist movement yet again. Since the civil war began in Syria vast numbers of migrants have settled in Germany from Syria, Iraq, and other states in North Africa and the Middle East. This has had an effect on the political landscape and the influx is pushing right-wing groups to the forefront. With terror attacks taking place in Belgium and France, Germany and other states within the EU are fearful as to which country will be attacked next.

AL QAEDA IN GERMANY

Since 9-11, Germany has come to the realization that it has become not only a safe haven but also a recruiting country for radical dissident Muslim youths. Imams in Germany's mosques were calling for a jihad against the United States. Students from North African and Middle Eastern countries were studying in university campuses throughout the country. Evidence points to Germany as being a staging post for Islamic extremists wanting to gain access to North America via forged travel documents, either directly or through Canadian ports of entry. This is a practice that has been ongoing for more than two decades. Many questions still remain, one of the most baffling being, "Why did the intelligence communities fail to detect the planning and steps toward 9-11?" Undoubtedly a very difficult question, as we can now see that all the signs were there and the intelligence on certain individuals were available. Clearly, it simply was not recognized as significant or it was ignored. *The 9-11 Commission Report*, published in 2004, makes considerable mention of the involvement of the Hamburg cell and its growth and training in Afghanistan, its members' ability to move around Europe and the United States, and ultimately, its ability to plan and carry out, undetected, the largest terrorist event in recent history. A successful attack on the

United States involving the members of the Hamburg cell would require complex planning and exceptional execution. *The 9-11 Commission Report* puts forward the following list, which it believed al Qaeda would have required to fulfill:

- Leaders who were able to evaluate, approve, and supervise the planning and direction of the operation.
- Communications sufficient to enable planning and direction of the operatives and those who would be helping them.
- A personnel system that could recruit candidates, vet them, indoctrinate them, and give them necessary training.
- An intelligence effort to gather required information and form assessments of enemy strengths and weaknesses.
- The ability to move people.
- The ability to raise and move the necessary funds.

The information on the planes operation presented in *The 9-11 Commission Report* shows that by the spring of 2000, al Qaeda was able to meet these requirements. By late May 2000, two operatives assigned to the planes operation were already in the United States. Three of the four Hamburg cell members would arrive soon after.

Intelligence gathering and covert activities by Western governments was not at Cold War levels, and, although the intelligence community and security services recognized the threat of al Qaeda, they undoubtedly underestimated the tactical capabilities of the group to strike deep into the heart of America. Germany had been more preoccupied with domestic issues and the revelation that planning for 9-11 had taken place within their country came as a shock to most Germans. Two prominent members of the 9-11 hijackers, Mohamed Atta and Marwan al-Shehhi, who are believed to have been the pilots who flew the aircraft into the two World Trade Center towers, spent a significant amount of time in Germany. Atta had studied at the Hamburg University for eight years; it appears that he attracted no suspicions from German authorities. He was not openly hostile and did not espouse radical or extreme Islamic views, at least not publicly. Since the fall of the Third Reich and Germany's rebuilding, the German government has been reluctant to interfere with individual rights and civil liberties. In Atta's case, subsequent investigations have revealed that he developed a small religious studies group that is now suspected of being a cover for his principal terrorist planning operations. In Germany, a religious freedom law forbids the government from banning or restricting any group that it recognizes as a religious group. Scientology is restricted under this law, as Germany has ruled that this is, in fact, a commercial enterprise, not a religion. As in the United States, German prosecutors must overcome a high standard of evidence to effect a prosecution. Germany's ability to gather and disseminate intelligence within its borders is also somewhat self-defeating.

The third pilot involved in the 9-11 attacks also spent considerable time in Germany. Ziad Zamir Jarrah was born in the Bekka Valley in Lebanon, a stronghold of Hezbollah extremists. Jarrah and his immediate family were not religious fanatics by any means. His parents appeared genuinely shocked and surprised that their son would be involved in a suicide attack on the United States. Jarrah received a monthly allowance from his father that was more than adequate. However, Jarrah's involvement may have stemmed from his friendship with local radical Muslims in Aachen. Jarrah's transformation from an easygoing youth to an Islamic fanatic is puzzling to many. It appears that he drank alcohol and partied at college in Germany. His transformation to more radical ways evidently began around 1996 after he returned from a trip to Lebanon. He changed course in 1997 from dentistry to aircraft engineering for no specifically identified reason. At the same time, he was becoming more steeped in traditional Islamic ways. He grew a full beard and avidly read about jihad and debated the merits of Holy War with his friends. During the latter months of 1999, he told his girlfriend that he was planning to wage a jihad because there was no greater honor than to die for Allah. Radical Muslims in Aachen were involved in fund-raising through local mosques for the Hamas terror group to aid suicide missions in the Middle East.[33]

As part of the coalition against terrorism, Germany has also banned a network of radical Islamic groups centered on the Kaplan organization based in Cologne. German police raided some two hundred residences in seven separate German states in connection with the ban and seized the headquarters of the Kaplan group. Metin Kaplan, the Caliph of Cologne, is served a prison sentence for calling for the murder of a rival religious leader. German authorities have characterized the Kaplan group as being anti-Semitic and antidemocratic and have also banned Kaplan's associated foundation, the "Servants of Islam," as well as other groups totaling one thousand one hundred members.[34]

Kaplan was extradited to Turkey in November 2004 and convicted in 2005 of attempting to overthrow the Turkish constitution and treason—he was sentenced to aggravated life imprisonment.

However, another more diverse group may well be a wolf in sheep's clothing. The Milli Görüs, which has a translation meaning of "National Vision," is the largest Muslim organization in Germany, with over twenty seven thousand members. Its influence is felt within the tight-knit Muslim communities, particularly in the Turkish-Muslim areas. German authorities believe that the group is the foreign wing for Islamist leader and former Turkish premier Necmettin Erbakan and that it secretly seeks to dismantle Germany's democratic structures. Milli Görüs, however, describes itself as an apolitical, unaffiliated lobby for the interests of Muslims living in Germany. German domestic intelligence believes that despite all the public posturing from Milli Görüs to show that it is apolitical and seeks to help Muslims to integrate into German society, the group is in fact indoctrinating Muslim youth. In an August 2007 interview, Erbakan made the following statement:

> When we look at the map of the world, we see about two hundred countries painted in colors, and we think that there are many races, religions, and nations. The fact is that for three hundred years, all these [200 nations] have been controlled from one center only. This center is the racist, imperialist Zionism. Unless you make this correct diagnosis for the illness, you cannot find the cure to it. You will ask, 'What is this belief, this racist imperialism that destroys happiness in this world?'
>
> 'Do you know what the safety of Israel means?' It means that they will rule the twenty-eight countries from Morocco to Indonesia. Since all the Crusades were organized by the Zionists . . . since it was our forefathers the Seljuks who stopped them, according to the Kabbala there should be no sovereign state in Anatolia. This is these people's [i.e. the Jews'] religion, their faith. You can't argue or negotiate with them. This is their religion, and it comes from the Kabbala.[35]

The activities of Milli Görüs have attracted the attention of Germany's Office for the Protection of the Constitution (BFV), one of three national intelligence services in Germany that is charged with gathering information on domestic as well as foreign extremist and terror groups. BFV considers Islamic terrorism poses the biggest security threat to Germany in modern times.[36] Islam is the third-largest religious denomination in Germany, but because it lacks a centralized structure like the Catholic and Protestant churches, it doesn't have the same rights and privileges as the Christian churches. Milli Görüs wants to be recognized as an Islamic church and, thus, unite the splintered Islamic community in Germany. The group has neither been banned nor been identified as being involved in crime and terrorism. The German intelligence agencies will, no doubt, continue to monitor the group's activities and development. Germany has also become a fertile recruiting ground for homegrown converts to Islam to wage jihad. In late 2006, a man was spotted carrying out a surveillance operation on U.S. military installations in and around the city of Hanau. For almost a year German authorities kept the suspect under surveillance, which also led them to other conspirators. The Germans were convinced that an attack was being planned against a U.S. or British installation in Germany. The operation culminated in September 2007, when the German GSG-9 counterterror force raided a house in Oberschledorn and arrested the suspects who were planning to move a large quantity of hydrogen peroxide. The cell had been trained in Pakistan and had amassed almost 700 kilograms of chemicals to make explosives. On March 2, 2011, Arid Uka an Albanian Muslim boarded an American military bus carrying soldiers to the Frankfurt airport and opened fire, killing two and injuring an additional two soldiers who were on their way to Afghanistan. There are indications that Uka, an ethnic Albanian Muslim from Kosovo, who was born and raised in Germany, had recently become radicalized and sought to carry out a terrorist attack against American forces in retaliation for the American presence in Afghanistan; his motivation remains unclear. Regardless of whether or not Uka is revealed to have been motivated by jihadist sympathies, small-scale attacks by individual Muslims against American and Western targets, of the type that Uka carried out, have been strongly encouraged by leading jihadist ideologues and on English-language jihadist forums for jihadist sympathizers in the West.

Islamic Jihad Union and German Mujahideen

For Germany, the growth of the Salafist movement may pose significant threat to its internal stability. Records of the numbers of Salafists in Germany range up to about 5,000. Those Germans who joined al Qaeda and IJU in Pakistan began their radical road in Salafist mosques. This is where they were radicalized and recruited. Visiting the al-Nur Mosque in Berlin, the al-Quds Mosque in Hamburg, or the multicultural house in Neu-Ulm was the first step toward jihad.

A large group of radicals have now received their training and are returning to Europe to carry out lone wolf attacks. The fear from a security perspective is a Mumbai/Paris or Brussels style of attack happening on German soil. Official sources indicate over two hundred Germans may have received training in bomb making and weapons training at camps in Pakistan and Afghanistan. The popular use of social media better defines the activities of the German Mujahideen (Taliban) providing a stream of propaganda. It is an offshoot of the IJU and formed in 2009 after an increasing number of Germans arrived at IJU in Mir Ali, North Waziristan. However, the organization never consisted of more than a dozen. Some were killed and some joined the IJU, with some returning to Germany. Their remaining activists are likely situated in Berlin area.

France and Belgium have banned the burqa; Germany, the United Kingdom, and Italy all took part in Afghanistan occupation; Denmark and Sweden appear to have insulted the prophet; the Netherlands is home of Geert Wilders; France has been targeted by Islamic State and so too has Belgium—the list of reasons for al Qaeda influenced jihadists to attack the European Union countries is growing and so too is the number of terror recruits returning from Syria and Iraq.

Under the Council of Europe Framework Decision of June 13, 2002, on combating terrorism, terrorist offenses are international acts, which, given their nature or context, may seriously damage a country.

Terrorist offenses are committed with the aim of

- Seriously intimidating a population or
- Unduly compelling a government or international organization to perform or abstain from performing and act or
- Seriously destabilizing or destroying fundamental political, constitutional, economic, or social structures of a country or international organization.

Terrorist offenses include

- Attacks upon a person's life that may cause death.
- Attacks upon the physical integrity of a person.
- Kidnapping or hostage taking.
- Causing extensive destruction to a government or public facility, a transport system, an infrastructure facility, including an information system, a fixed platform located on the continental shelf, a public place or private property likely to endanger human life or result in major economic loss.
- Seizure of aircraft, ships, or other means of public or goods transport.
- The manufacture, acquisition, possession, transport, supply, or use of weapons, explosives, or nuclear, biological, or chemical weapons, as well as research into and development of biological and chemical weapons.
- The release of dangerous substances, or causing fires, floods or explosions, the effect of which is to endanger life.
- Interfering with or interrupting the supply of water, power, or any other fundamental natural resource, the effect of which is to endanger human life.
- Threatening to commit any of the acts listed above.[37]

The German government continues to target persons supporting terrorist networks, and this is exemplified in the 2011 conviction of the wife a jihadist. The German-Turkish wife of convicted terrorist Fritz Gelowicz was found guilty of collecting up to $4,000 for terrorist groups, the Islamic Jihad Union, the German Taliban Mujahideen, and al Qaeda, between November 2009 and February 2010. She was also convicted of publishing propaganda texts on the Internet that solicited members for terrorist groups. German prosecutors had characterized the woman as a "fanatical militant" who labeled "infidels" as enemies of Islam and called for their "annihilation." Her husband had been arrested in 2007 while preparing eight-hundred pounds of explosives to detonate at the German parliament as it voted on its NATO force in Afghanistan the following month; he was sentenced to twelve years in prison in March 2010.

ITALY

By 1954, under Mussolini, Italy was the most likely Western country to turn Communist. Following World War II and the formation of a democratically elected government in Italy, the opportunity naturally presented itself for the Communists to come to the fore. A strong, Communist-indoctrinated, left-wing group with some fairly imaginative goals to steer Italy onto a different path than that established by the allied powers rose up. As the new millennium arrived, the transnational terrorism from al Qaeda and its associated cells became a frustrating reality for the Italian government and security services. Terrorist plots would be planned and executed by foreign terror operatives residing in Italy (Figure 6-6).

Terrorism and Italy

The only significant terrorist movement to emerge from Italy has been the RB, which has its origins in the early 1970s and grew out of an established left-wing political party, The Metropolitan Political Collective. They aimed to bring about a Communist revolution in Italy, which it believed would spread throughout Europe. At the other end of the spectrum was a smaller and little-known group, the Ordine Nuove (New Order), an extreme right-wing and Fascist movement. Like the RB, Ordine Nuove embarked on a campaign of terror to establish its goal of a strong Italian state, supported by a powerful Fascist structure. Throughout the 1970s, both groups used bombings and assassinations as their modus operandi, and it was not often evident which group was responsible for what specific attacks. Italy, like Germany, France, and Spain, is also contending with Islamist threats.

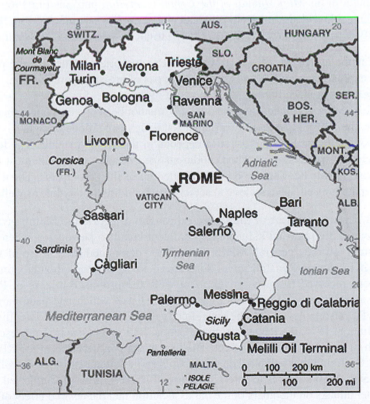

FIGURE 6-6 Map of Italy. *Source: Central Intelligence Agency, The World Factbook, 2008.*

THE RED BRIGADE

The left-wing Red Brigade (RB), like its German compatriots in the RAF, had its origins on the Italian university campuses in the latter half of the 1960s. The group might be considered as a fledgling of the World War II Volante Rosse, formed during the campaign against Nazi Germany as a Communist resistance movement. It continued its campaigns until the end of 1949 and had ongoing links to the Italian Communist Party, no doubt spawning the next generation of left-wing extremists to emerge on the campuses of the 1960s.

After World War II, Italy moved toward a governing style modeled on the political and economic example of the United States. Between 1950 and 1962, the industrial growth and success of the Italian government lay in the hands of coalitions of political parties—the Republicans, Liberals, Social Democrats, and Christian Democrats, all apparently trying to move beyond the Fascist past. While exploiting the need for industrial growth and foreign trade, Italy had neglected the social structure of the country. The bubble burst in 1968 with a cultural-style revolution in the universities and schools and was quickly followed in 1969 with the worst union unrest in the industrialized north that Italy had ever experienced. The unions could not be placated and factories were seized and occupied by both workers and student demonstrators. Workers and management were intimidated and attacked. All of this became the fertile ground for the emerging RB.

The founding members of the RB, Renato Curcio and Margherita Cagol, came from the sociology department of Trent University.[38] They began to target the symbolic nature of the Italian state by attacking senior executives, politicians, and parts of Italian society perceived as being repressive by nature. RB did not burst onto the Italian scene but rather confined itself to incubation, largely in Milan's industrial heart. The period from 1969 to 1972 was a time of building, training, and testing of the RB's objectives. Minor firebombings and destruction of property were the order of the period. Their support structure outside of Milan at this time was considerably weak. From 1972 to 1974, the RB entered a new phase of expanding to the adjacent areas of Turin and Genoa while experimenting in kidnapping and extortion. During this same time frame, Italian security forces were able to capture Renato Curcio after a gun battle in which his wife, Margherita Cagol, was killed. Observers predicted the imminent demise of the RB, but that was far from reality. The next generation of RB was on the scene and ready to continue the fight with the Italian government and society in general. The RB has, to some length, emulated the tactics laid out by Carlos Marighella in his *Mini Manual of the Urban Guerrilla*, published in 1969. Attention to detail and technical knowledge, as well as logistical and intelligence information, became a hallmark of the RB. Contained in the *Mini Manual* is Marighella's definition of assaults:

- Assault is the armed attack, which we make to expropriate funds, liberate prisoners, and capture explosives, machine guns, and other types of arms and ammunition.
- Assaults can take place in broad daylight or at night.
- Daytime assaults are made when the objective cannot be achieved at any other hour, as, for example, the transport of money by the banks, which is not done at night.
- Night assault is usually the most advantageous to the urban guerrilla. The ideal is for all assaults to take place at night when conditions for a surprise attack are most favorable and the darkness facilitates flight and hides the identity of the participants. The urban guerrilla must prepare himself, nevertheless, to act under all conditions, daytime as well as nighttime.

The RB perfected the art of kidnapping throughout the 1970s. Mainly symbolic in its action, the group did go beyond kidnapping prominent business personages when it kidnapped Genoa's assistant attorney general, Mario Sossi. They demanded the release of RB prisoners from jail and, in particular, Renato Curcio. Sossi was held captive for a month before his release. The concessions received from the government were the promised release of RB members. However, the attorney general would not permit the release, which had been bargained under duress.[39] The RB also believed that the concessions they received had sufficiently undermined the state. On June 8, 1974, the RB struck down Genoa's Attorney General Francesco Coco in an armed ambush, which had a twofold effect. The first was a confirmation of the RB's retaliatory ability against the figure that had blocked the group's earlier attempts to free its colleagues; and, the second was that RB's threats to selected jurors in the Turin trial of Curcio led to a delay in the trial. Further attacks on members of the bar association had the desired effect of delaying the trial. The intimidating effect of terrorism was working well.

RB Structure

The RB utilized the tried-and-tested cell structure to prevent infiltration and detection. Working from large industrial areas, it had widespread support among the working classes, who provided logistical support to the group.

At its peak, it is believed there were more than five hundred active members, with a support structure possibly in the thousands. It seems likely that by the last decade of the twentieth century, the RB was reduced down to around fifty active members.

As the twenty-first century dawned, it was not clear that the movement had not undergone resurgence as in late 2003, more than two-hundred pounds of high explosives and detonators were discovered during a police raid of a known RB house. The police discovered documents claiming responsibility for several attacks including the assassination of a government consultant in 2002. Some one hundred and forty of the original RB activists are still sought by Italy, many thought to be living in France.

With its Communist Marxist/Leninist ideology, its early support would have come from the Soviet Union, which in the Cold War years would have provided support for such organizations operating in the West.

Kidnapping

Italian terrorists perfected the art of kidnapping and, in fact, enhanced it. It enabled corporations to get kidnap insurance, turning the crime into a growth industry. This short-sighted provision made it possible for kidnappers to get their money and, for those who were kidnapped, to be released. The RB, on the other hand, kidnapped for different reasons and rarely for money. Two kidnappings stand out for their sheer audaciousness and the brutality with which they ended. These two kidnappings were significant watersheds for the RB. The first, which resulted in nothing more than the symbolic execution of the president-elect, Aldo Moro, was to turn public opinion against the RB. Several communiqués were issued prior to his murder, and the RB made every effort to exploit the media coverage of this atrocity. During Aldo Moro's captivity, the RB showed its strength of purpose and its ability to continue with other operations and carried out two murders and six shootings in Rome, Turin, Milan, and Genoa, in spite of the massive police search and crackdown on the RB and any known members.[40] It was a significant demonstration of the RB's ability to conduct several simultaneous operations.

The second was the release of General James Dozier, the Italian police force's first successful rescue of a kidnap victim from the RB. By the mid-1980s, the number of terrorist incidents committed by RB was down significantly, following a decline in support from the left. By the mid-1990s, RB was distributing communiqués to indicate a cessation of all operations.

GAP AND NAP

Two other groups on the fringes of the Italian terrorism scene in the 1970s modeled themselves on the same style of clandestine activities and systematic violence as the RB. The Partisan Action Group (GAP) originated in Milan at about the same time (1969) as the RB. Their inception is believed to have involved the wealthy Italian publisher Giangiacomo Feltrinelli, who was the group's paymaster and sponsor. Feltrinelli believed that right-wing extremism was on the rise and a return to Fascism was a real possibility. He believed that the only way to confront the risk was to form an urban guerrilla movement. His approach was to form the GAP, a resistance/partisan movement modeled on the resistance fighters of World War II. This model differed from that of the RB, which probably accounts for the non-merging of the groups in the early days.[41] In the days of student and union unrest, which had also spread to Italy's prison system, another movement sprang up. The Armed Proletarian Nuclei (NAP) came to life from a left-wing prison movement—the Movement of Proletarian Prisoners and the Ongoing Struggle (Lotta Continua).[42] Unlike the RB, this group gained little acknowledgment. Coming from the ranks of Naples prison inmates, the membership immediately began the "armed struggle," financing its movement primarily by robbing banks. Its main base of operation started in Naples and spread to Rome. The group used explosives to bomb prisons and also attacked prison officials. Unlike the RB, all NAP members were easily traceable from their criminal records. Their modus operandi, coupled with their lack of attention to their own security, resulted in numerous arrests. With no ideological base, NAP'S recruitment of criminal elements led to its eventual downfall. The remainder of the group's membership joined the ranks of the RB. Throughout the terror campaigns, the majority of NAP targets were either political or paramilitary by nature. Indiscriminate attacks against the Italian populace were uncommon.

The Mancino Law

In 1993, the Italian government issued Decree No. 122 as an emergency measure to control, restrict, and limit attacks of a racial nature. Two months later, it was transformed into Law No. 205 by the then interior minister Nicola Mancino. The law enabled the state to prosecute individuals for "incitement to violence for a broad range of hate crimes" that included the use of symbols of hate.[43] Hundreds of youths have been charged under this legislation. Two Italian names have become associated with hate crimes in Italy: Maurizio Boccacci, a Skinhead organizer, and Dr. Sergio Gozzoli, an outspoken anti-Semite and a Holocaust denier.

Skinhead Organizations

The Italian Skinheads, following the example of the Germans, had by the early 1990s, organized themselves under the leadership of the Movimento Politico Occidentale (MPO, Political Movement of the West), founded by Maurizio Boccacci and headquartered in Rome. The group had links to other far-right Skinhead groups in France, Germany, and Great Britain. A notable incident that was bound to become a flash point was the painting of yellow stars on more than one hundred Jewish businesses and shops in Rome. Jews attacked MPO skins as a result. The MPO has been banned by the government but has since renamed itself with the Fascist trappings of "I Camerati," a term used by Mussolini to address his fascist followers.[44]

In its effort to become more politically acceptable, delegates at a convention of the neo-Fascist Movimento Sociale Italiano (MSI, Italian Social Movement) voted to move toward the mainstream political parties and to dissolve the MSI. They merged with Alleanza Nazionale (National Alliance), and it was hoped this would make the overall far-right movement more respectable. The delegates also agreed on a strong position against anti-Semitism. The extremists in the organization—many of them Skinheads—broke away from the alliance and reestablished their own version of the MSI.

Ideology

The Italian Skinhead ideology and that of the far-right extremists echo the sentiments of a past generation of neo-Fascists. Their ideology is loosely based:[45]

- The denial of Nazi genocide against the Jews; "historical revisionism."
- Fear and hatred of foreigners, based on the myths of Aryan purity and supremacy.
- The fear and demonization of the Jews in a context of a sinister plot to rule the world.

With the breakdown of the symbolic, and all-too-real Berlin Wall, the influx of Russian and Eastern nationals to the west—particularly Germany and Italy—has fueled the far-right into action.

International Terrorism

Italy has been no stranger to acts of terrorism, with the result that post-9-11 Italy, with its excellent police and intelligence services, has not only aided the U.S.-led War on Terror with its strong military contributions, but has had successes in tracking down and arresting suspected al Qaeda cells. International terrorism requires funding, and in the weeks after 9-11, the Italian government established the Financial Security Committee. This group comprised senior ministry officials from finance, justice, and foreign affairs, whose aim was to stem the flow of funding to terrorist groups in Europe. Even prior to 9-11, Italian security services had targeted such institutions as the Islamic Cultural Center in Milan because they suspected that an al Qaeda lieutenant, Sami Ben Khemais Essid, who had spent time training as a terrorist recruiter in Afghanistan, was active in Italy. The Italians were monitoring the Cultural Center to discover evidence of traffic in arms and explosives and discovered that Ben Khemais was, in fact, in contact with other extreme terrorist groups throughout Europe.

Among those seen at the Cultural Center were terrorists associated with the New York World Trade Center bombing in 1993 and the bombings of the U.S. embassies in Tanzania and Kenya in 1998. The apparent ease with which international terror groups, and particularly those associated with Osama bin Laden, have been able to operate with comparative freedom in Italy is a lesson that security services are now beginning to appreciate. Ben Khemais was sentenced to eight years in prison for his activities. His activities also give us an insight to what may be al Qaeda's next style of terror attack. During their investigation, Italian police intercepted Khemais' conversation with another terrorist, which detailed the use of a deadly poison gas attack. Al Qaeda sympathizers and Euro converts to radical Islam will continue to attempt attacks. With a vast population of immigrant workers throughout Europe and with no solid border defenses, the movement between countries by al Qaeda-inspired cells will be a challenge for the foreseeable future. The presence of extreme thinking imams has also been at issue for Germany as it has been for the British authorities. In June 2003, the imam of the Rome mosque began inciting his own congregation to jihad in much the same manner as has taken place at London's Finsbury Park Mosque.

GREECE AND TURKEY

Terrorism is no stranger to these two countries; however, the actions of respective indigenous terrorist groups are restricted for the most part to actions within their countries, rather than out in the international arena. Both countries have had their own regional differences over the years and at times have come close to all-out war—both countries are members of NATO. Their differences centered on territorial claims to a group of islands in Aegean Sea and the divided status of Cyprus, occupied by both Greeks and Turks. Turkey aspired to join the European Union, and its application was actually supported by the Greek government. Their belief being that if Turkey could change its attitude and be accepted into "Europe," it would no longer pose a threat to Greece; however, Turkey's likelihood of joining all but vanished when Cyprus joined the EU in 2004 and with its veto could effectively prevent Turkey from joining. The two are not currently in open conflict and that is probably because of two eastern bloc countries joining the European Union, Bulgaria and Romania. This means that Greece now has a land link to the rest of "Europe" without worrying about a hostile Turkey. To cement a lasting peace between them, the Greek prime minister Costas Karamanlis visited Turkey officially in January 2008—the first visit by a Greek minister to Turkey in almost fifty years.

GREECE

Revolutionary Organization November 17

After twenty-eight years, twenty-three assassinations, three hundred and forty-five bombings, and no arrests, the rest of the West viewed the Greek attitude and its inability to prevent and deter terrorism with a modicum of cynicism (Figure 6-7). The EU placed considerable pressure on the Greek government for the security of the Olympic Games, held in Athens in 2004. Reacting to fears that Greek authorities could not prevent another Olympic Games attack, the Greek government arrested almost seventy-five percent of the believed membership of the November 17 group. In December 2003, fifteen members were convicted and sentenced: five members received life sentences, and imposed sentences on the others totaled two hundred and forty-four years.

The November 17 group had operated in Greece with almost total immunity until the arrests and convictions in 2003. Police and security services had been unable, or unwilling, to identify or arrest any members of November 17. This group of left-wing extremists is considered Marxist-Leninist, anti-imperialist, anti-United States, anti-Europe, and anti-NATO. Their first terrorist action was the assassination of U.S. diplomat, Richard Welsh, in 1975. They have their origins in the university campuses of Greece, much like other left-wing groups in the 1970s. The group's name, November 17, commemorates the date of the attack on the students, NTUA (National Technical University of Athens), on November 17, 1975. Greek military and police, under the control of the ruling colonels, killed several student activists and captured and tortured many more.

The Greek Military Junta was overthrown a few short months after the university incident. November 17's actual membership number is not known, but it can be assumed that it is a small

FIGURE 6-7   Map of Greece.   *Source:* Central Intelligence Agency, *The World Factbook, 2008.*

group, with approximately twenty to thirty hard-core members. It did not participate in low-level operations to test its own ability; rather, it burst onto the world stage with a high-visibility terrorist attack on a U.S. diplomat.

In its early years, they committed relatively few attacks; in fact, between 1975 and 1985, November 17 carried out only six attacks. Perhaps the length of time between operations was relative to the fact that police arrested no one. One of its earliest attacks was on the CIA station chief Richard Welsh, who was shot outside his Athens residence several weeks after his identity had been published in the press.

The failure to track down November 17 was a sad reflection on the internal workings of the Greek government and its security services. Over the last twenty years, the group has carried out three hundred and forty-five bombings, resulting in sixty-one deaths and two hundred and fifty injuries. Until 2003, no November 17 terrorist had ever been arrested and charged with offenses in connection with those incidents.

They did expand operations after 1985 and, by 1990, had carried out about forty attacks including bombings, assassinations, and shootings, often targeting U.S. military personnel stationed at NATO bases in Greece, Greek industrialists, and politicians. They have been critical of the Greek government for its position in respect to U.S./NATO bases in Greece as well as Greece's membership of the EEC. The largest number of attacks carried out by the group was directed at internal targets and foreign targets residing on Greek soil. To ensure that no other group claimed responsibility for November 17's terror acts, the group used handguns of the same caliber in consecutive attacks against Greek targets.

They viewed themselves as the people's vanguard and protector . . . to lead the working class in an armed struggle. It makes its point with ideological communiqués and actions in support of its cause. Attacks are geared to making the subverted classes more abstractly aware of what is taking place in the political and economic processes in the country. The group fervently holds the United States responsible for complicity with Turkey over the Cyprus crisis, thus making the United States a legitimate military target in its war for the oppressed. Their early attacks were primarily symbolic; the first was against the United States, and subsequent attacks were against the Greek police hierarchy and representatives of the Greek Military Junta. An example of the group's hatred toward the United States can be seen from the content of one of the November 17 communiqués: "The American military forces in our country are an occupation force, and we are going to hit anybody who is a member of it or an agent of its secret services. These actions are going to continue and are going to increase until the last Turkish soldier leaves Cyprus and the last American soldier leaves our country."[46]

In Greece's internal struggle with domestic terrorism, the break for Greek authorities came in 2002, with a botched bombing attack that seriously injured a terrorist bomber. As strange as this may seem, this was the first November 17 terror suspect that Greek authorities have been able to apprehend. The bomber in this instance was Savas Xiros, who was carrying a device that detonated prematurely as he approached the ticket office of a hydrofoil company in Piraeus. In the explosion, Xiros lost a hand and was blinded. The ensuing investigation found a 38 Smith and Wesson revolver in his possession, which had never been fired, but its rightful owner was a Greek police officer who was killed in a 1984 robbery. The bomber's fingerprints also matched those on the getaway car used in the assassination of a British/Greek tycoon. Greek police have had, and continue to have, a mutual assistance program with both the British police and the U.S. FBI as a result of the Greek government's signing of a joint memorandum on combating crime.

Epanastatikos Laikos Agonas

The second-most destructive group operating on Greek soil, Epanastatikos Laikos Agonas (ELA, Revolutionary Peoples Struggle), is also committed to the overthrow of the Greek system and is a violent Marxist-Leninist organization. That is where any similarity between it and November 17 probably ends. It also grew out of the university campuses of the 1960s and early 1970s. Its fundamental aims and philosophy were directed at the state, imperialism, and capitalism. Most, if not all, of its targets for terror were of a symbolic nature. Unlike the secretive nature of November 17, which seeks to communicate its positions via communiqués or email, ELA actually utilizes and operates an underground newspaper to forward its aims and political viewpoint. In May 1990, ELA announced that it had merged with another left-wing group, the revolutionary organization May 1. Up to this point the strategy of the ELA had been to avoid death and injury to Greeks as well as foreigners on Greek soil. It had conducted a low-level style of campaign and had not ventured into the more dangerous world of remotely detonated bombs. A communiqué to the Greek government in 1993 appeared to be the turning point in ELA's violent methods in its dealings with the state. It perceived all police officers to be the "local representatives of the CIA."[47]

On September 19, 1994, the ELA remotely detonated a bomb alongside a police bus, killing one officer and injuring ten others, as well as a passerby. The ELA gave no warnings, which had previously been a signature for the group. Detonating the bomb without prior warning signaled a new and more virulent strain in Greek terrorist behavior. Successive and continuous failures by the Greek government to effect any cohesive response to domestic terror has allowed the organizations to continue to operate with impunity. While neighboring countries in Europe, Germany, Italy, France, and Belgium, had, for the most part, decisively dealt with left-wing violence and terrorist threats with a strong and dedicated response force established by powerful political mandate, it seemed to be lacking in Greece until 2001.

Much of the blame for the lackluster efforts of the Greek police must rest on the shoulders of those in political circles.

Revolutionary Cells/Revolutionary Nuclei

Revolutionary Cells, also known as Revolutionary Nuclei (RN), has its beginnings from a wide spectrum of anti-NATO, anti-United States, and anti-European Union left-wing groups in the mid-1990s. The group is believed to be the successor to the ELA. ELA has not been credited with any attacks since 1995, and many believe that RN (from the manner and style of its communiqués showing much of the same style as used by ELA) has now taken its place. RN's attacks in the 1990s were considered low level and were aimed mainly at companies that had NATO defense contracts as well as Greek government buildings. The RN has been most active in the Athens area and has also targeted European banks. The size of this terror group is believed to be relatively small, drawing support mainly from the Greek militant left.

Minor Terrorist Groups

The number of terrorist actions in Greece increased in 1998, not only against the state but also aimed at Jewish and anti-Semitic groups, foreigners, as well as politicians. The source of the terror appears to be previously unheard-of organizations operating in Greece. Firebombing has been the hallmark of the attacks, which have been aimed at vehicles and buildings. The government of Greece has indicated that these attacks are coming from various quarters—the New Group of Satanists, the Children of November, Anarchist Street Patrol, and Conscientious Arsonists, all previously unknown before 1998. With the ineptitude of the Greek security services already a well-established fact, only time will tell if their newly formed special task force of more than one thousand undercover police officers will be effective. As Greece depends heavily on its tourist trade for much-valued foreign currency, this style of attack, which seems so indiscriminate, will do a lot to drive that trade elsewhere.

CYPRUS

Situated in the Eastern Mediterranean Sea, this small island has a population of some six hundred fifty thousand people and consists of seventy-eight percent Greek-Cypriots, eighteen percent Turkish-Cypriots, and four percent Maronite and Latin-Cypriots. The Turks and Greeks have lived together on the island for the last five centuries, and mosques and churches can be found almost side by side in many communities.

National Organization of Cypriot Combatants

Cyprus had long been under the control of the British Empire, which by the 1950s was well into its decline. The vast majorities of Cypriots were of Greek origin and, in the 1950s, were under the leadership of the Greek Cypriot Archbishop Makarios. Similar to the operations of the Stern Gang in Palestine, the **National Organization of Cypriot Combatants (EOKA)** terrorist organization and its followers began to strike at the occupying influences of Great Britain. EOKA was established in 1954 as an underground movement with the blessing and approval of Makarios. The revolt began in earnest with the bombing of the Cyprus Broadcasting Station on April 1, 1955. The British government had declared a state of emergency on the island and the Archbishop went into exile in the Seychelles. Makarios returned to Cyprus in 1959 and was elected president of the Cyprus Republic; the Founding Agreements made Turkey, Greece, and Great Britain "guarantor states" for Cyprus. Both the Turkish and Greek communities reached an agreement on a constitution for Cyprus, resulting in a Greek-Turkish Republic. Great Britain retained sovereignty over two military bases on the island. Within three years, Archbishop Makarios was preparing constitutional changes that would abrogate the power-sharing agreements that were contrary to the Constitution. The resulting intercommunal violence was to have a lasting effect on the island.

On July 20, 1974, Turkey invaded the island to "protect" the minority Turkish-Cypriot community. The international community quickly condemned the action. UN Resolution 353, adopted on the day of the invasion, called for all states to respect "the sovereignty, independence and territorial integrity of the Republic of Cyprus." It further demanded an immediate end to foreign military intervention in the Republic of Cyprus. Turkey ignored the United Nations and the international community and seized control of at least one-third of the Republic's territory and since then has engaged in a type of terrorism that we now refer to as "ethnic cleansing." More than one thousand six hundred Greek Cypriots are still unaccounted for, following the invasion, and more than twenty thousand lost their homes and possessions. This was a constant and festering sore for the November 17 terrorist group, which continued to blame the United States for failing to act on behalf of the Greek Cypriots. Turkish forces enforced a partition of the island, and Turkish Cypriots fled to the north into Turkish-occupied Cyprus, while Greek Cypriots fled south to the Greek side of the line. Since the 1970s, there has been little terrorist activity and plenty of political posturing with both Greece and Turkey claiming their side of the island as the legitimate Republic of Cyprus. In December 2004, Turkey agreed that it would recognize Greek Cyprus as a European Union (EU) member; however, the Turkish prime minister warned the EU that the Cyprus problem must be solved justly for both sides.

TURKEY

The history of the Turkish Ottoman Empire stretches back to when the Ottoman Turks invaded and captured Constantinople in 1453, bringing an end to the Byzantine Empire. The Ottoman Empire stretched across Eastern Europe and into regions of the Middle East, as we know it today (Figure 6-8). It stretched as far south as the western reaches of Saudi Arabia and to Yemen at the southern end of the Red Sea. Its conquests stretched through North Africa, from Cairo in the east and Algiers in the west. By the dawning of the eighteenth century, the Turkish Empire was commonly termed "the Sick Man of Europe" and was beginning to lose its huge territorial gains of the previous centuries. The empire lost Algeria to French rule in 1830, and by the end of 1880, Great Britain had taken control of Cyprus and Egypt. France seized Tunisia in 1881. With its empire crumbling, the Turks had to contend with disruptions on the home front as well, ruled by the dictatorship of Sultan Abdul-Hamid II. His rule was one of fear and violent repression of religious groups and stimulated the first covert organization set up to oppose the dictator. The Young Turks, as they were known, were dissatisfied students and disaffected military personnel opposed to Hamid. The group staged a successful coup in 1908 with the aim of restoring democracy to Turkey. The replacement for Abdul-Hamid was his brother, Mohammad V. The Young Turks had envisioned returning the Ottoman Empire to its former greatness; however, the populace was less concerned with aspirations toward empire building and more concerned with its own democratic rights and freedoms. With the empire crumbling, Turkey entered World War I on the side of Germany in the hopes that it would win back much of its losses of the past half century.

Kemal Ataturk

As has been witnessed throughout history, many inspirational freedom fighters and military heroes with nationalist aspirations have risen to take control over and to form popular governments. Mustafa Kemal was one such leader. Kemal's origins in the Turkish military and his exploits as a natural leader of men brought him to the forefront of politics in Turkey. He formed the provisional government in 1920 after the invasion of the country by forces from Britain, France, and Greece. The Ottoman government was unable to protect the country, so the country turned to its nationalist leader, Kemal. The Sultan's powers weakened and the nationalists grew stronger and were able to forcibly evict the Greeks from Turkish soil. Turkey today is formed around the boundaries outlined in the Treaty of Lausanne signed by the nationalists in 1923. The word "Ataturk" is the surname given to Kemal and means "Father of the Turks."[48]

FIGURE 6-8 Map of Turkey. *Source:* Central Intelligence Agency, *The World Factbook, 2008.*

Separating religion from state has been a hallmark of Turkish politics, and Atatürk nearly removed Islam from public life in the period 1923–1938. Over the decades, however, Islamists fought back, and by the 1970s, they formed part of a ruling coalition; in 1996–1997, they even headed a government. They took power following the elections of 2002, when winning a third of the vote secured two-thirds of the parliamentary seats. Ruling with caution and competence, they got nearly half the vote in 2007, at which point their gloves came off and the bullying began, from a wildly excessive fine levied against a media critic to hare-brained conspiracy theories against the armed forces. The ruling party handily won the 2011 elections returning Recep Erdogan who began his politics as an Islamist in the 1990s, and under his tenure, the once all-powerful military has yielded to civilian politicians.[49] That Turkey is close not only in proximity but also in step with Iran is disquieting—Turkey is showing signs of moving along the same ghastly path as Iran—introducing strict adherence to Sharia law. In the coming years, Turkey may pose a significant threat to peace in the region.

Revolutionary Left (Dev Sol)

A left-wing Marxist group that has its origins in the Turkish Peoples Liberation Army split off in the late 1970s to form **Dev Sol**. This group is vehemently anti-NATO and anti-United States. The aims of this group are to foster an uprising or popular national revolution among the Turkish working classes. The group is financed primarily from armed robberies and extortion from businesses carried out in Turkey.

During the 1980s, the group restricted its area of operation to the domestic scene, mainly in Izmir, Istanbul, and Ankara. With the Middle East crisis and the Desert Storm Operation against Iraq, the group began attacks on the U.S. military personnel. The group launched a rocket attack at the U.S. Consulate in Istanbul in 1992. Since the early 1980s, the group has suffered from internal factional fighting and has carried out limited operations at home. From the training perspective, it is believed that the membership, which is considered to number several hundred, received training and indoctrination at radical Palestinian camps. By the end of 1998, this group was not particularly active in Turkey, but there are indications that it is beginning to resurface and may threaten U.S. commercial interests and Turkish government figures. Unlike PKK it has carried out limited operations and in early 2016 conducted just two minor attacks aimed at police and government installations. In one attack, two female attackers fired on and threw hand grenades at a police transport in Istanbul. Both women were killed in the ensuing gun battle.

Kurdistan Workers Party and Kurdistan Freedom Falcons

The leadership and organization of the Kurdistan Workers Party (PKK) originated from the student movement at Ankara University. Abdullah Ocalan, the leader—now behind bars in Ankara but still the leader—set up the organization with the specific aim of liberating the Kurds. Ocalan was considerably brutal in his methods and used his version of terrorism on his own followers and fellow Kurds. By executing the dissenters, any dissent in the group was put down. It is believed that Ocalan killed more than ten thousand Kurds during the 1980s. His actions had some sobering effects on the Kurdish people—they showed them that PKK was strong and that the people should side with PKK in the struggle for freedom from Turkey. Any failure to actively support the movement was perceived as siding with the Turks. Operating in southeastern Turkey, this Kurdish terror group seeks to set up a Kurdish state fashioned on Marxist lines. Mainly composed of Turkish Kurds, PKK has been in operation since 1974.

Large numbers of Turks migrated to Germany during the last half century, and this, has added to the financial viability of the PKK, an organization responsible for the death of at least forty five thousand people since 1984. Turkey, home to twelve million Kurds; the neighboring countries of Iraq, Syria, and Iran have substantial but smaller Kurdish populations. To finance operations, PKK uses a variety of tried-and-tested methods. It is involved in the lucrative trade in illegal immigrants from Iraq into European centers. PKK also controls a lucrative portion of the drug traffic from the East into Europe. Its other levels of fund-raising include extortion from Kurds residing in France, Germany, Belgium, and Romania. PKK also receives aid from state sponsors, such as Iran and Syria. From Syria's perspective, the destabilization of the Turkish regime plays an important economic role.

It had been felt that the group was trying to become more mainstream politically, and has reformed itself with name changes—from the Kurdistan Freedom and Democracy Congress (KADEK) in 2000, and then to the People's Congress of Kurdistan (KONGRA-GEL). From a wider viewpoint, Turkey's support for the U.S. War on Terror has not endeared it to the Syrian regime, nor has its support of Israel. As the War on Terror continued, PKK was declared a "terrorist organization" by the EU in May 2002. PKK continues to receive support from Iran and also maintains bases in the Bekka Valley, Lebanon. Abdullah Ocalan, imprisoned under sentence of death in a Turkish prison, declared in 2000 that his group, the PKK, which has for so long sought an independent Kurdish state through violent struggle, had changed its stance and would now seek, through a political campaign, only guarantees of Kurdish political, economic, social, and cultural rights in a democratic Turkey. PKK membership, which probably ran to more than five thousand in 1999 at the time of Ocalan's capture, was diminished down to around one thousand, with Kurdish fighters moving to neighboring Iraq following the U.S. invasion there. Small pockets of PKK members, who had by spring of 2005 changed the name back to PKK from KONGRA-GEL, became active in southeastern Turkey. With the United States occupied in Iraq and Turkey acting a role of neutrality in the region, the United States was faced with Iraqi Kurds that actually supported the invasion. The Kurds' designs for an autonomous region adjacent to the Turkish border area were a matter of national security for Turkey. The United States most certainly wanted to protect the Kurds against any aggression from Turkey's military in the border region. The fact remains that the Kurds have been sheltering PKK separatists.

PKK launched its first attacks in 1984: the more than thirty-year conflict has caused about forty six thousand casualties. However, the turmoil caused by Operation Iraqi Freedom in 2003 provided a safe environment for PKK to regroup and reorganize. Since then, it has gained new strength and power—extending its network on European soil, creating broadcasting platforms for propaganda purposes, and securing new means of funding. In 2010, it launched an impressive number of effective attacks against Turkish troops, infrastructures, and cities. At the peak of its eight-month-long campaign, PKK declared a unilateral ceasefire at the beginning of Ramadan, subsequently extending it until 2011's Turkish general elections—the ceasefire ended in 2015 and attacks by PKK and its urban proxy, the Kurdistan Freedom Falcons (TAK) continue. TAK is believed to be an active part of the PKK using a different name to carry out attack so that the PKK can effectively carry on its political agenda. TAK did not conduct any actions during the PKK ceasefire and has now resumed activities and successfully targets primarily the police and military. Two significant attacks have been claimed by TAK—the December 2015 attack of the international airport that damaged the buildings and several aircraft, and a suicide bomb attack on a military convoy bus in Ankara that killed twenty-nine and wounded many more. With their proximity to Iraq it came as no surprise that PKK perfected the use of IED's against military patrols with over a dozen of such attacks. PKK also began attacking strategic infrastructures such as gas and oil pipelines. They carried out one attack on the Kirkuk–Ceyhan pipeline, carrying crude oil from Iraq to Turkey followed by the Tabriz–Ankara pipeline, which transports natural gas from Iran to Turkey. Although the attacks caused minor damage and inconvenience, the intent of the attacks may have been to embarrass Turkish efforts to become an energy hub within the EU-funded Nabucco project. The Nabucco consortium comprises leading European energy companies from Austria, Hungary, Germany, Bulgaria, Romania, and Turkey. Unlike attacks by Islamist militants in Europe the PPK/TAK have minimized attacks that involve civilian casualties and focus mainly on military and police. The end game is to garner publicity and support for their cause for an independent Kurdish region.

Islamic State

Operations by Islamic State have so far been limited and poorly planned and unsophisticated. First operation in 2015 involved a pregnant Chechen woman detonating a bomb at a police check point killing herself and one police officer. As 2015 progressed, ISIS attacks became more sophisticated and targeted. Toward the end of 2015 and into 2016, ISIS began to target and disrupt Kurdish demonstrations to stir up unrest between Turkey and the Kurds. A double suicide bomb attack at an outdoor rally of the Kurdish People's Democratic Party left over one hundred dead in October 2015. In 2016, ISIS began to target Turkey's tourism locations. Two suicide bomb attacks in January and March killed German and Israeli tourists. With its proximity to the

FIGURE 6-9 Dead bodies lie on the ground after two explosions in the Turkish capital of Ankara killed nearly 100 people on October 10, 2015. The bombs went off near the main train station in the city. *Courtesy:* Newzulu /Alamy Stock Photo.

Iraq/Syrian crisis ISIS will likely expand operations in this region by using the mass exodus of Syrians and Iraqis flooding into Europe to hide trained jihadists to operate in Turkey. The sophistication of these attacks is fairly low but with willing suicide bombers available and what would appear to be a ready supply of weapons and explosives we should expect to see similar attacks as those that took place in Brussels and Paris. It is estimated that around two million Syrian refugees have sought shelter in Turkey (Figure 6-9).

Turkey would seem to be at crossroads and is increasingly being drawn into a spiral of international violence and tension around the conflicts in neighboring Syria and Iraq. Turkey's policy on ISIS had long been ambivalent, but there were signs that Turkey was actually combating the ISIS threat, for example by countering the ISIS presence in Turkey more actively by monitoring the border with the ISIS-controlled area in Syria more strictly and making Turkey's Incirlik air base available for coalition airstrikes against ISIS. In response to the attacks in Istanbul in January 2016, there was a new wave of arrests and Turkey carried out artillery bombardments of ISIS areas in Syria and Iraq. Since October 2015, a series of arrests have been made of ISIS supporters. Stricter checks were also introduced at airports, and more jihadist travelers, including those from the Netherlands, were stopped. It is still unclear how far these steps are effectively preventing ISIS from operating in Turkey.[50]

Turkish Hezbollah

The Turkish Hezbollah should not be confused with Hezbollah in Lebanon as it has no known alliance with or connection to that organization. The group established its name in 2004, more or less as a pseudonym while defending propaganda around its terror campaigns.

The group was founded in the 1980s by student activists of Kurdish origins and led by Hüseyin Velioğlu. In the early 1908s, members traveled to Iran and were supported by elements of the Iranian government and learned their terror trade that way. There is no evidence to suggest that the Iranians used Hezbollah as its proxy for operations in Turkey. In fact, Velioğlu appears to have run the organization as a highly centralized autocracy, making every decision himself and insisting that his subordinates present him with detailed reports on all of their activities.

During the late 1980s and early 1990s, Turkish authorities ignored the organization's propaganda activities in the Kurdish areas of southeastern Turkey. At the time, the first insurgency of the Kurdistan Workers Party was at its height and the Turkish security forces appear to have regarded the propagation of any form of Islam as providing an ideological bulwark against the PKK's atheistic Marxism. They did not react when Velioğlu decided to initiate the jihad by targeting rival organizations in the region, starting with the PKK. In the early 1990s, Hezbollah is estimated to have killed over four hundred PKK militants and played an important role in preventing the organization from supplementing its rural insurgency by establishing an effective urban cell network in southeastern Turkey. Many mainstream Turks have long believed the Turkish Hezbollah to be an instrument of the state that was being used as its clandestine security force to tackle PKK.[51]

Hezbollah had a three-stage phase to their overall plans:

- Phase 1: Communication—period of propaganda and indoctrination
- Phase 2: Community—establishing a popular base within society
- Phase 3: Jihad—overthrow of the secular government and establishment of an Islamic state

After a series of raids on Hezbollah safe houses in southeastern Turkey in 1999, Velioğlu and the rest of the organization's leadership relocated to Istanbul. On January 17, 2000, Velioğlu was killed during a police raid on a Turkish safe house in Beykoz, a suburb on the Asian shore of Istanbul.[52]

Assassination has been Hezbollah's most common tactic, usually involving a daylight attack, often by pairs of young assassins using pistols of Eastern European manufacture.[53] The numbers killed in such attacks between 1992 and 1995 amount to over one thousand. Not only did Hezbollah attack the PKK, but by the end of the last decade it was targeting specific senior security officials who were responsible for arresting Hezbollah members. Hezbollah, apart from its normal tactic of assassination, had also resorted to extreme levels of torture, including burning and burying its targets while they were still alive. Turkey continues to view PKK as a threat far greater than Hezbollah; however, a crackdown did eventually materialize and more than one thousand Hezbollah members have been arrested. In concluding the future of terrorism in

TERRORIST ATTACK BRIEF

Suicide Bombing and Attack—Istanbul, Turkey—June 28, 2016

An attack on one of the world's busiest international airports, Istanbul's Ataturk International Airport was a scene now becoming all too familiar in Europe. Three male attackers were almost apprehended by security police but managed to gain entry to the airport and fired indiscriminately in the terminal building. The attack left forty-four people dead and over two hundred injured. The attack was carried out by Islamic State. IS is targeting Turkey, a Muslim majority country for its close ties to the United States and support for military attacks against IS in Syria. CCTV footage inside the terminal shows gunman rampaging through the facility firing at passengers before being shot. Officials believe the men were from Russia, Uzbekistan, and Kyrgyzstan and entered Turkey about a month prior to the attack, from Raqqa, bringing with them the suicide vests and bombs used in the attack.

FIGURE 6-10 Suicide attack—Ataturk International Airport—June 28, 2016. *Courtesy:* CNN— http://www.cnn.com/2016/06/30/europe/turkey-istanbul-ataturk-airport-attack/index.html downloaded June 30, 2016.

Turkey, the answers to its spread lie clearly with the government and its ability to improve the social–economic well-being of young Turkish Islamists. In January 2011, Turkish Hezbollah members were released from custody following a new law that limited the term of detention to ten years. Eighteen were released from custody after having been arrested following the mutilation assignation of Kurds in the south back in 2000.

Armenian Terrorism

Like the Kurds, the ethnic Armenians of northeastern Turkey have, since 1974, been fighting for their own homeland and autonomy in the region. Two terror groups have come to the fore: the ASALA and the Justice Commandos of the Armenian Genocide. Both groups have targeted diplomats from Turkey in Europe and the United States as part of their terror campaign. Their attacks became more violent when they started to detonate bombs at airports in the 1980s. They set off a bomb at Orly Airport in France adjacent to the Turkish Airlines check-in counters, killing ten and wounding more than seventy in the process. The leader of ASALA, Hagop Hagopian, was shot to death on an Athens street in 1988, and since then the group has been silent (Figure 6-10).[54]

The Nationalist Threat

The Turkish Revenge Brigade is a previously unknown group that sprang up in 1998, in opposition to Kurdish movements. Considered to be ultranationalist, the group has targeted Kurdish and left-wing journalists who support the Kurdish movement. In May 1998, two members of the group attempted to assassinate a leading Turkish human rights activist, Akin Birdal. The motive for the attack is uncertain, but the head of the Human Rights Association claimed at the time that Birdal had received prior death threats and had asked for protection from the government, but to no avail. How the nationalist movement will develop and who is backing and financing its operations is unclear. No doubt, previous reports of Turkish death squads and their involvement earlier in the decade come back into question.

AL QAEDA IN TURKEY

Al Qaeda's presence in Turkey was likely a foregone conclusion after U.S. and British forces invaded Iraq. Both Britain and the United States are obvious and defined targets for al Qaeda and its splinter groups. In the first direct attack against Great Britain, an al Qaeda cell based in Turkey attacked the British Embassy compound in Istanbul in November 2003. In determining that al Qaeda was responsible, authorities looked at what was spread before them—simultaneous attacks, within seconds of each other; and the targets, the British Embassy and the HSBC Bank in Istanbul.

The method of attack in both instances was by suicide bombing. One has to speculate on what the terrorist cell hoped to gain by attacking during the holy month of Ramadan and killing mostly Muslims. Could it be that the cells involved believed that such an attack would radicalize the Muslim population and encourage others to join their apocalyptic fight against the Western democracies so long hated by al Qaeda? Or was this the start of a broader campaign being waged by al Qaeda against British interests in Europe? For the last two decades, Turkish authorities have concentrated almost exclusively on the PKK and more recently on Turkish Hezbollah and al Qaeda. The week prior to the British Embassy blast had seen suicide bombers target two synagogues in Istanbul. Authorities identified the bombers as Turks from Bingol. Al Qaeda and its affiliates will continue to threaten U.S. interests in the region, given its continued use of a Turkish Air Force base outside Adana. In April 2011, Turkish Intelligence authorities uncovered a plot to use rockets to attack U.S. military aircraft at the base in southeastern Turkey. According to the General Directorate of Security (Emniyet Genel Mudurlugu), the plot was to be carried out by two Syrian members of al Qaeda identified as Abu Muhammad al-Kurdi and Salih Battal.

BELGIUM

Belgium, and its involvement with terrorism, was of considerable internal concern during the 1970s and 1980s. In a country with a population of only 10 million, political violence had been unheard of compared to the troubles besieging its neighbors (Figure 6-11). Belgian terrorism was not widely publicized by the world press and probably received little or no mention in the U.S. press. However, terrorist incidents have taken place on Belgium soil from external terror groups. These attacks dating back to the 1970s and 1980s were basically anti-capitalistic in nature. Palestinian terrorists, from the Black September group, hijacked a Belgium state (Sabena) airliner to Israel in 1972, and PLO terrorists also attacked the Iraqi Embassy in Brussels in 1978.

Belgium's internal troubles in the 1980s came from the direction of neo-Fascist terror gangs, who up until then had not been active but had aligned themselves with other terror groups in Europe. Considered more of a criminal gang element on the outer fringes of violent political struggle was the right-wing DARE, the New Force Party, and the West New Post. All were considered extreme

FIGURE 6-11 Map of Belgium. *Source:* Central Intelligence Agency, *The World Factbook, 2008.*

Fascist movements, but they had been non-violent in comparison to the activities of such groups in the rest of Europe.

Ongoing criminal terror attacks were causing a crisis in the government and panic in the country, with innocent bystanders being killed. By the mid-1990s, Belgium became one of those EU countries favored by migrants from Turkey and North Africa who brought with them their own brand of Islamic extremism. In Belgium today, some 50 percent of newborns are Muslim—a third of Muslims in the United Kingdom and Belgium are under fifteen versus a fifth of the native population. Counting all age groups, they're a minority. But in generational demographics, Muslims are swiftly becoming a majority.

The country began its flirtation with extremism when an Algerian terror cell of GIA was discovered in the mid-1990s. During the 1970s, members of the Muslim Brotherhood had fled from North Africa and the Middle East and were comfortably residing in European countries including Belgium. Mainly focused on propaganda and fund-raising they would form part of what would become a global jihad movement in the new millennium. In 1998, a jihadist network known as the Mellouk Network and led by Fared Mellouk was broken up in a coordinated crackdown by EU intelligence agencies. The period 1998–2001 represented the apex of al Qaeda-dominated jihad; with cells Europewide, the movement was led by the two main protagonists, Osama bin Laden and Ayman al Zawahiri. However, that would soon change with the U.S.-led attack on Afghanistan and the Iraqi invasion following 9-11 and the obvious disintegration of the al Qaeda, centralized style of administration. Many of its members fled Afghanistan and its veterans took up station in Europe. Once in Europe, they launched their local jihad on European soil, creating and maintaining sleeper cells, recruiting, preparing and plotting terror attacks. Most of the cells and activists were not necessarily directly linked to but were inspired by the potent al Qaeda mythology.[55] While Belgium may seem to be well advanced in its recognition of the threats posed by jihadist organizations, it is not going to be immune from the global threats that they pose. In 2003, Belgium authorities arrested and sentenced Nizar Trabelsi, a thirty-seven-year-old Tunisian, to ten years in prison for planning to drive a car bomb into the cafeteria of a Belgian air base where about 100 U.S. military personnel were stationed. Trabelsi claims to have met Osama bin Laden and been trained in an al Qaeda camp in Afghanistan in the months prior to the 9-11 attacks.

In May 2014, the threat from jihadists returning to European countries was not fully recognized to be that serious a threat and the attack on the Jewish Museum of Brussels in May 2014 illustrates how difficult it becomes to secure and safeguard "soft targets," whether they are single "lone wolf" attacks or ones of a more planned and structured format. A twenty-nine-year-old Mehdi Nemmouche, born in France and likely radicalized in one of his prison stints had been to Syria in 2012 and then to the Far East before returning to Germany. He walked into the Jewish Museum and fired an AK-47 before escaping. He was subjected to a random check by security police at a Marseille Bus Depot the following week and was found in possession of an AK-47 which subsequently linked him to the Museum attack the week before.

Coordinated attacks—Brussels—March 2016

From the above attack, we now move fast forward to Brussels in March 2016, where we witness an attack that appeared to be well planned but subsequent investigations show that the terrorists were originally planning to execute this attack in France and due to the pressure from police aborted that plan and improvised by attacking targets in Belgium. We can attribute this to the arrest of the last known attacker from the November Paris attack on the Bataclan Theater. The single terrorist still unaccounted for named Salah Abdeslam was captured alive on March 18. The fact that he had managed to escape from France back to Brussels was one aspect; the fact that he was actively engaged in the planning and execution of further plots shows how the authorities have miscalculated the ability of the returning jihadist; far from being considered 'lone wolf' these attackers have a broad network or cellular support structure for their specific targets. Several suspects were still at large when two suicide bombers detonated their bombs near the security screening area at Brussels' Zaventem International Airport on March 22, 2016, and approximately an hour later at 0910 a bomb explodes at the Maelbeek Metro Station. The three bombs claimed a total of thirty-five lives including three of the bombers; a third suspect appears not to have detonated his bomb and left the suitcase bomb behind before escaping from the airport.

TIMELINE—BRUSSELS ATTACK

- **7:55** —Three suspected attackers arrive by taxi with three suitcases.
- **7:58** —Two explosions occurred in the airport's check-in area ten seconds apart.
- **8:20** —Police close roads and all rail transport to the airport is stopped.
- **9:05** —The Belgium government elevates the terror threat level to its highest level.
- **9:10** —Explosion in Brussels Maelbeek Metro Station kills at least twenty people.
- **9:27** —All public transport in Brussels is suspended.
- **17:14** —Belgian police detonate a third bomb at Brussels Airport.
- **19:30** —A police raid in Schaerbeek uncovers a nail bomb and an Islamic State flag.

Soft Targets

Airports are hardened targets but only in specific locations and most particularly around the passenger screening area, boarding gates, and restricted access points to the airfield—that leaves the entire reception concourse at most airports as a juicy target for terrorists to attack. Attacks on airports are not uncommon. Rome's Leonardo da Vinci Airport and Vienna Airport were simultaneously attacked by members of the Abu Nidal group in 1985.

In the case of the Brussels attack, one has to consider some probable missed opportunities on behalf of the security structure in Belgium. The police service is somewhat fractured in the capital and communication or lack of it failed to identify one of the airport bombers who had been released from prison in 2014—Ibrahim el-Bakraoui had served a reduced term for armed robbery and was released on license with the proviso that he not leaves the country. He then appears to have been arrested in Turkey in June 2015 as a suspected terrorist—he was held and then deported to the Netherlands—it is understood that this was made aware to Belgian authorities who failed to act on the information. Subsequent to his deportation he was released by the Netherlands for lack of any material information coming from Brussels. His brother Khalid was killed when his device exploded at the metro station—the two were of Moroccan descent but born and raised in a suburb of Brussels. It is highly probable that the two were radicalized in the Belgian prison system where so many other young men are radicalized.

BOMB CONSTRUCTION   The bombs used in both the Paris attacks of November 2015 and in the Brussels attack used **Tri-acetone Tri-peroxide** (**TATP**). This is a very difficult, mixture to build into a large IED such as a vehicle borne IED but has been perfected for suicide vests and suitcase bombs. To construct a weaponized device using TATP requires the acquisition of acid and peroxide in large quantities, if handled and assembled without caution it becomes extremely unstable, it can degrade quickly and can detonate prematurely. TATP was nicknamed the Mother of Satan by Hamas due to its potent behavior! TATP was the material used in the London Underground (subway) attacks in 2005. Batches of TATP would need to be used within a few days of manufacture so in both Paris and Brussels attacks a bomb maker and factory was in play.

Information gathering and sharing is a major issue for the EU. Aside from Britain, Germany, and the Netherlands most all other countries refuse to share information and as we have seen in Brussels sharing that information internally is also an issue. Now, some fifteen years after the 9-11 attacks on the United States the same information gathering and sharing problems is happening in Europe. With porous borders and thousands of Europeans being recruited by Islamic State and hundreds of thousands of refugees flooding to EU countries from the crisis in Syria and Iraq, the EU will need to take urgent steps and radically adjust its outlook particularly on border controls and information sharing. While the systems implemented in the United States following 9-11 may not be perfect they are a vast improvement on what went before.

Europe's Muslim Population—Schengen

Muslims have been a part of the fabric of European countries for centuries—it is only in the last thirty years that problems have surfaced. The young fanatics that we are witnessing in terror attacks after often third, fourth, or fifth generation migrants. The **Schengen Agreement** which is the backbone of the borderless states of Europe was signed by five of ten member states in 1985. In 1990, the Schengen Convention proposed a common visa policy among member states and the abolition of border controls within those states. The Schengen Area operates very much like a single state for international travel purposes with external border controls for travelers entering and exiting the area, and common visas, but with no internal border controls. It currently consists of twenty-six European countries covering a population of over 400 million people and an area of 4,312,099 square kilometers (1,664,911 square miles). The only two EU states operating outside of this convention is the United Kingdom and the Republic of Ireland. As far back as 2002, the Belgian government was concerned with the number of radical imams preaching jihad within its borders—at that time Belgium had a population of around 350,000 Muslims but by 2014 that number had risen to just under 650,000. Germany and France have the largest populations of Muslims than other EU countries with roughly 4.7 million in each country. For the past decade the EU has been on a severe economic decline and this has had a marked effect on Muslims in general with high unemployment within that socio-religious group. In the large European cities like Paris, Brussels, and Munich there is frequent discrimination within the job market against Muslims so the unemployment rate is alarmingly high. Add that to the welfare state system that allows them to survive on state handouts without the need to work makes them an ideal target for radicals to turn them to jihad and the promise of a better life than the one they are experiencing. With so many young men feeling disenfranchised and alienated from society it is hardly surprising that they are easily persuaded to join in the radical discourse and get involved in militant activities.

The area of Brussels where these men hailed from was Molenbeek. The police thought they had disrupted terror operations with the 2014 arrest and sentencing of Khalid Zerkani. Zerkani's involvement in the Paris and Brussels attacks is only now being realized. The authorities had seized his computer which contained a treasure trove of material. At his trial he denied any links to terrorism. Court documents and interviews with Molenbeek residents and security officials indicate he had direct involvement with several crucial figures who are now dead or under arrest in connection with the November 2015 massacre in Paris and the Brussels bombing in March 2016. Belgian investigators have stated that Abdelhamid Abaaoud, a Molenbeek resident who led the November attacks in Paris was a disciple of Zerekani. How many others have fallen for Zerkani's indoctrination to terrorism is not yet known.[56]

Revolutionary Front for Proletarian Action

The terms *revolutionary* and *proletarian* are often used as much by European neo-Nazis as they are by leftist groups. Contemporary Nazis also hate European links to the United States. The Revolutionary Front for Proletarian Action (FRAP) conducted its first action on April 20, 1985, a date universally celebrated by European Nazis as the birthday of Adolf Hitler. This was a bombing attack on the North Atlantic Assembly (NAA) in Brussels and was followed the next day by an attack against the offices of AEG-Telefunken. The first reaction by authorities to these attacks and also from the media was that it was the work of an ultra-leftist group. The initial arrests were made from among members of leftist groups in Belgium. The attacks on these two establishments suggested that FRAP was as likely to be have been rightist as Communist, although the ambiguous circumstances of these attacks meant that it would be the left that would be stigmatized.[57]

Communist Combatant Cells

Pierre Carette was the leader of the Belgian Communist Combatant Cells (CCC) group and became politically active when establishing a committee to gain the release of imprisoned members of the German RAF. In October 1984, CCC conducted a series of attacks on political and military targets, and Carette was subsequently arrested the following year. He was sentenced to life in 1988 for an attack on the Federation of Belgian Enterprises in Brussels in 1985, which resulted in the death of two firefighters. He was released after fifteen years in 2003.[58]

Carette and the CCC began their short-lived campaign in October 1984. They attacked offices belonging to Litton Data Systems and two months later attacked a NATO oil line near Brussels. Other attacks took place against symbolic property targets in Brussels and Antwerp. Carette's 1985 arrest spelled the end of the CCC. It is still not clear who or what was involved in the destabilizing attempt of Belgium. Was it all an attempt by the left, or was it some other form of terrorism with an as-yet undefined rationale? Whatever the case, there are some underlying aspects to the Belgium political structure that are relevant. One should not dismiss a theory that an agent provocateur may have been involved in the Belgian experience.

NETHERLANDS

The perceived threat that overpopulation from immigration may have on a liberal society is evidenced in the assassination of Pim Fortuyn and **Theo Van Gough**. Fortuyn was a blunt-speaking, anti-Muslim politician, who became better known in death than in life. His comment, "The Netherlands is full," was one of his famous slogans (Figure 6-12). His viewpoint criticized the fact that the Netherlands was home to one million Muslims, the vast majority from Turkey and Morocco. He referred to Islam as a "backwards" religion that censored freethinkers and mistreated homosexuals and women. His assassination, the first in Holland in three hundred years, generated widespread sympathy for freedom of speech. Perhaps, surprisingly, it was not at the hands of a fanatical Muslim extremist that he met his death in a hail of bullets. His murderer was Volkert van der Graaf, an animal rights activist; however, van der Graaf's motives for the assassination are not readily clear. The wake-up call for the Netherlands, and the knowledge of the presence of Islamic extremism there, was brought home with the broad-daylight assassination in Amsterdam of Theo Van Gough on November 2, 2004. Mr. Van Gough, an avid and public critic of Islam—using his position as a filmmaker, columnist, and television talk-show host as his platform—was attacked by a Moroccan with dual Dutch–Moroccan citizenship. The attacker, a member of an extreme Islamic group that has been named by the Dutch Intelligence Service as the Hofstadgroep, repeatedly shot Mr. Van Gough and then proceeded to stab him and slash his throat, to the point where his head was almost severed. The Netherlands was shocked by this public display of Islamic fanaticism on its streets, in a country where radical extremists account for a very small minority of the 1 million Muslims living there. The assassin, Mohammed Bouyeri, was sentenced to life in prison on July 26, 2005. After the killing, Bouyeri attached a note and his knife to the body of Van Gough. The note stated: "I surely know that you, Oh Europe will be destroyed." The Hofstadgroep is also believed to be linked through its wider network with al Qaeda.[59] Soon after the attacks on 9-11, the Dutch Intelligence Service noted that the global recruiting of young Muslims was moving ahead in the Netherlands. The service believed that several dozen Muslims had been recruited for suicide missions in the Middle East.

Dutch teenager Samir Azzouz was cleared of planning attacks on Amsterdam's Schiphol Airport, a nuclear reactor, and government offices. He had been found in possession of machine

FIGURE 6-12 Map of the Netherlands. *Source:* Central Intelligence Agency, *The World Factbook, 2008.*

gun cartridges, mock explosive devices, electrical circuitry, maps and sketches of prominent buildings, and chemicals that could be bomb ingredients. Such cases raise a difficult question: In the absence of an actual attack, how close must a suspect be to detonating a bomb before prosecutors can demonstrate guilt?[60]

DANISH CARTOONS—FREEDOM OF THE PRESS

The publication of a dozen cartoons depicting the Prophet Muhammad in the Dutch national paper *Jyllands-Posten* resulted in at first localized protest and then open street riots. The violence might have been contained in Holland if it had not been for imams taking a tour of the Middle East and stirring up Islamic fervor by distributing the same cartoons. The press will and do argue that political satire is what they do and many cartoons are seen in national papers on a regular daily basis. Islam forbids any depiction of the Prophet Muhammad; so when these cartoons appeared in 2005, the tensions in the European Muslim communities were raised. The rioting and deaths that ensued seemed totally out of context from any message the cartoons may have been intending to portray to a wider audience. The Netherlands has a large Muslim immigrant population not dissimilar to other European countries, but it seems that any newspaper that prints any controversial commentary does so at its own risk.

Insulting a religion is despicable if that is what this is—or is it freedom of the press; however, in February 2006, more than three months after the original publication, the imam of the Peshawar mosque in Pakistan, one Mohammed Yousef Qureshi, offered 1.5 million rupees (US$30,000) reward for killing one of the cartoonists who portrayed the Prophet Muhammad. There was no outcry from Western democracies or from the Dutch government for that matter. The way to resolve differences with the press has, in Western society, rested with the courts. In October 2006, a Danish court dismissed a lawsuit brought by a group of Muslim organizations against *Jyllands-Posten.* "It cannot be ruled out that the drawings have offended some Muslims' honor, but there is no basis to assume that the drawings are, or were conceived as, insulting or that the purpose of the drawings was to present opinions that can belittle Muslims," said the city court in Aarhus. *Jyllands-Posten* called the decision a victory for freedom of the press, while the Muslim groups who jointly filed the lawsuit said they planned to launch an appeal.[61] The integration of Muslims has not been helped by the growth of Islamophobia in the Netherlands due to the many acts of jihadist violence around the world. This has led the non-Muslim population to distance itself. This, in turn, has led many Muslims to reorient themselves toward their own communities and cultural and religious backgrounds. As a result, polarization between Muslims and non-Muslims has been on the rise for the past few years, a trend that can accelerate radicalization processes.[62] Jihadists see the Netherlands as a legitimate target. ISIS leaders have repeatedly called for attacks in the West. ISIS has warned that it will mainly carry out attacks in the countries participating in the anti-ISIS coalition. Dutch participation in airstrikes against ISIS and in Syria could raise the Netherlands' profile among jihadists. The number of Dutch jihadist travellers to Syria/Iraq is continuing to rise steadily by around four or five per month. By March 1, 2016, according to the information available, a total of some two hundred and forty people had gone to jihadist conflict zones, forty-two had been killed, and around forty had returned. Around one hundred and sixty people are therefore still in Syria, some forty percent of whom are women. At the end of February 2016, media reported about the execution by ISIS of eight Dutch jihadists and the imprisonment of seventy-five others. Although there may be a conflict between ISIS members in which Dutch jihadists are involved and although ISIS is known to regularly execute members from its own ranks, the execution and imprisonment of Dutch jihadist in such great numbers is for the time being considered to be improbable. The number of confirmed jihadist travelers rose by fifty-six in 2015. In 2014, there were seventy confirmed instances of jihadist travel, compared with seventy-six in 2013. Almost all Dutch jihadist travelers known to have reached Syria/Iraq end up in areas controlled by the ISIS.[63]

SWEDEN AND NORWAY

Neither of these two countries is synonymous with terrorism, but by Christmas 2010 and July 2011 both came to terms with bombings and massacres. In both countries, it would assume the form of a "lone wolf" attack: in Stockholm, on shoppers in early December 2010, and in Oslo, a bomb attack against the government buildings in the center of the city, and a massacre on an island retreat for Youth Party members on the same day claiming over eighty lives. Sweden's only prior association to a major terror event dates back to the February 1986 assassination of Swedish Prime Minister Olof Palme. He was shot in the back by a lone gunman while walking with his wife on a Stockholm street. His attacker has never been identified and motive for the attack not clarified (Figure 6-13).

In the December 2010 Stockholm attack, an online jihadist forum, Shumukh al-Islam, was first to identify the Stockholm suicide bomber Taimour Abdulwahab al-Abdaly. Al-Abdaly, a twenty-nine-year-old Iraqi from Baghdad with a wife and two daughters, had moved to Sweden but was currently living in England. In a message left behind, he stated "Briefly, to Sweden and the Swedish people, because of Lars Vilks and his drawings of the Prophet Muhammad, Allah's peace and prayer be upon him, your soldiers in Afghanistan, and your silence over all this, your sons and daughters and brothers and sisters will die just as our brothers, sisters and children are dying. Now the Islamic State has fulfilled what it had promised you, for now we are here in Europe and Sweden, and we are a fact, and not a mirage." The investigation linked his comments to those made by Abu Omar al-Baghdadi in 2007, when he broadcast a threat against specific European companies including Scania, Volvo, IKEA, and Electrolux, as well as threats against Lars Vilks. Al-Abdaly had left Iraq in 1991 and lived in Stockholm and the United Kingdom

FIGURE 6-13 Map of Sweden. *Source:* Central Intelligence Agency, *The World Factbook.*

and was studying at a university. He frequented the Luton Islamic Centre where he was vociferously outspoken in his views. How and when he became radicalized has not been determined. His explosive device malfunctioned, which accounted for him being the only fatality. In the Oslo attacks, jihadi forums were praising the executers and warning other European countries including France and England that this was what they should expect as well—in this instance, the jihadi forums were well wide off the mark, as the suspect was a right-wing extremist who wanted to create a new order and purify Europe of immigrants, hardly something for jihadists to cheer about.

The Norway attacks were apparently the work of an extreme right-wing Christian and vehemently anti-immigration Norwegian named **Anders Behring Breivik**. On July 22, 2011, he was able to mount two almost simultaneous attacks—one a large car bomb detonated outside government offices in the center of Oslo killing eight people. He made his way dressed as a police officer to a resort island of Utoya, which was hosting the youth movement of the (left-wing) Norwegian governing party. He was able to get on the island in disguise and then calmly executed as many men of the youth movement as he could; his rampage was not stopped for over an hour—the time it took the Norwegian police to acknowledge the attack and get a response team to the island. Breivik killed sixty-nine people on the island. He was convicted of terrorism and premeditated murder and sentenced to twenty-one years in imprisonment (Figure 6-14).

FIGURE 6-14   Map of Norway.   *Source:* Central Intelligence Agency, *The World Factbook.*

Before the attacks were credited to this extreme right-wing Norwegian, the jihadist websites were glorying the action in the belief that it was carried out by an Islamist group, but on this occasion, the killer is best described as a somewhat deranged individual—Breivik had written his own manifesto—"*2083. A European Declaration of Independence*"—which provided insight into his motivations. His ideology appears to be a form of reactionary Christian fundamentalism, fueled by hatred of Islam, Marxism, and non-whites. He posted his manifesto on the Internet just prior to the attacks—the details describe his attack plan as being a number of years in the making, and he subscribed to many far-right Islamophobia websites and forums. Far-right extremists have kept a low profile in Norway. Norway's intelligence services have warned of potential problems from far-right extremists, but the population and the media were more focused on the possibility of Islamist violence. Breivik was also able to remain under the intelligence radar by owning his own farming company, which allowed him to purchase large amounts of commercially available fertilizer that was used to manufacture his car bomb. Publishing the manifesto only on the day of the attack gave scant opportunity for the intelligence services to react.

Summary

Terrorism has been synonymous with Europe for more than fifty years and, discounting the levels of genocide practiced by the Nazis in World War II, has been the battleground for both the right and the left-wing extremists. While anti-capitalist terrorism marked much of the 1960s era with Baader–Meinhof and RAF, and the 1970s and 1980s with November 17, ETA, and PKK, a transformation has taken place. With the fall of Communism came the influx of migrants from the former Soviet republics to Germany, Italy, France, the Netherlands, and Spain. From North Africa, the influx came from the Muslim countries of Morocco, Tunisia, and Algeria, with universities accepting students from the wider swath of Islam from the oil-rich Persian Gulf states. The second decade of the millennium sees mass migration from the Syrian civil war, as well as from Iraq and Afghanistan. The War on Terror firmly rooted in a Western attack on the Islamic nations of Iraq and Afghanistan has led to young, disaffected migrants, many of whom are second generation, taking up calls to jihad. These immigrants may have had no prior interest in their own Muslim faith, but were drawn back into it by skilled Islamic recruiters for a worldwide Jihad against Western democracies. The United States and Great Britain are prime targets, but European nations will also have to contend with the broad specter of jihad in such metropolitan centers as Paris, Berlin, Brussels, Amsterdam, Madrid, and Rome, as the second generation of marginalized youths from Islamic countries become the suicide bombers and terrorists of tomorrow. Europe's future security relies heavily on the network of security and intelligence agencies and their ability to identify the threats from Islamic extremism and the capacity and capability to pre-empt attacks. There can be no doubt that Europe is a target for Islamic extremism for recruiting, training, organizing, and spreading jihad. The Madrid train bombings of 2004, the attempt to destroy a flight from Amsterdam to Detroit in 2009, Paris in 2015, Brussels in 2016, and lone wolf attacks in Sweden and France are but a harbinger of more attacks to come. In Chapter 7, we will again see the threat of al Qaeda and Islamic State as radical Islam takes its toll in the east in Chechnya and the former Soviet Republics.

Review Questions

1. Explain why the Basque separatist campaign may have failed to achieve its goals.
2. List the reasons for the collision of religion with freedom of speech and expression in Western Europe.
3. Describe the conditions that led to the creation and rise of Germany's Red Brigade.
4. Describe how the Schengen Agreement has aided the facilitation of mass migration and opportunities for terrorists.
5. Apply the attack cycle for both the Paris and Brussels terror attacks in 2015 and 2016.
6. Recount the Munich Olympic Games attack that led to the creation of the counterterror group.
7. Summarize the extreme right-wing attacks in Norway that were at first thought to be that of Islamists.

End Notes

1. U.S. Department of State Information Programs (2009). www.usinfo.state.gov.
2. Intel Brief, courtesy U.S. Department of State (2009) archives on ETA, http://www.state.gov/s/ct/nls.
3. William Gutteridge, Ed. "Contemporary Terrorism," an article by Peter Janke, (The Institute for the Study of Conflict, 1986, p. 152). Facts on File, Inc.
4. George Rosie. *The Directory of International Terrorism* (New York: Paragon House, 1987, p. 111).
5. http://en.wikipedia.org/wiki/Batasuna.
6. "Spain: Move to Outlaw Separatist Party May Fail." *Strategic Forecasting* (July 5, 2002), www.stratfor.com/premium/analysis.
7. "BBC World News." *ETA Declares Ceasefire* (2007). http://search.bbc.co.uk/cgi-bin/search/results.pl?q=eta+ceasefire.

8. "A History Written in Blood." http://www.telegraph.co.uk/news/main.jhtml?xml=/news/2006/03/23/weta223.xml.

9. Rosie. *The Directory of International Terrorism*, p. 135.

10. Pino Arlacchi. *Men of Dishonor* (New York: William Morrow and Co. Inc., 1993, p. 27).

11. Disk News Service. *Spain Arrests al Qaeda Suspect with WTC Footage* (July 16). http://news.bbc.co.uk.

12. Reuters Madrid. *Prosecutor Seeks 220,000 Years for al Qaeda Suspects* (February 14, 2005).

13. ZDF (German TV). Elmar Thevessen and Ulf Roller, "Das Netzwerk des Terrors." (October 24, 2001).

14. David Yallop. *Tracking the Jackal* (New York: Random House Inc., 1993, pp. 48–49).

15. Philip Jackson. "Under Two Flags: Provocation and Deception in European Terrorism." *Terrorism: An International Journal*, vol. 2 (New York: Taylor and Francis, 1988, p. 280).

16. Grant Wardlow. *Political Terrorism, Theory, Tactics and Counter-measures* (London: Cambridge University Press, 1982, p. 38).

17. Philip Jenkins. "Strategy of Tension: The Belgian Terrorist Crisis 1982–1986." *Terrorism: An International Journal*, vol. 13 (New York: Taylor and Francis, 1990, p. 299).

18. Yallop. *Tracking the Jackal*, p. 98.

19. *Fighting Terrorism: Lessons from France*. http://www.time.com/time/nation/article/0,8599,176139,00.html.

20. U.S. Department of State Web site, Patterns of Global Terrorism. http://www.state.gov.

21. *TF1.Fr (French TV)*. "Gang de Roubaix: La Jeunesse de Dumont a l'Etude." (October 4, 2001); "Bin Laden's Invisible Network." *Newsweek*, International edition (October 29, 2001, p. 50).

22. "Timeline—The Shoe Bomb Case." (July 1, 2002). http//edition.cnn.com/2002/us/01/07/reid.timeline/index.html.

23. Adam Sage and Daniel McGory. "French Agents Knew of Hijack Suspect in 1994," *The London Times* (October 3, 2001, p. 4).

24. *BBC World* "Moussaqoui" (December 13, 2001); *CNN Inside Europe* (December 16, 2001).

25. SITE Monitoring Service—Jihadist Threat. "Forum Member Calls for Chemical and Biological Attacks in France." (April 2011). https://news.siteintelgroup.com/

26. "ISIS in the West." (March 2016). http://www.newamerica.org/ Creative Commons 4.0 International license

27. *The World Book Encyclopedia*, vol. 9, S.V. "Reichstag." (1990, p. 254).

28. Richard Huffman. "Motivations from an Internet Article." *Terrorist motivations* (1997). www.Baader-meinhof.com.

29. Ibid.

30. Rosie. *Directory of International Terrorism*, p. 220.

31. Ibid.

32. Anti-Defamation League Website, *The Skinhead International*: A Worldwide Survey of Neo-Nazi Skinheads (New York: Anti-Defamation League, 1995). www.Nizkor.org.

33. Emerson Vermaat. "Occasional Paper" (Toronto: The Mackenzie Institute, 1993, pp. 129–131).

34. U.S. Department of State, *Patterns of Global Terrorism*, released by the Office of Coordinator for Counterterrorism (May 21, 2002), Europe Overview.

35. Antisemitism and the Turkish Islamist "Milli Gorus" Movement: Zionists/Jews "Bacteria," "Disease". Published by The Middle East Media Research Institute, © 2007

36. "German Intelligence says Islamists Present Major Threat." http://www.dw-world.de/dw/article/.

37. EUROPOL—TE-SAT 2010 EU Terrorism Situation and Trend Report. www.europol.europa.eu.

38. William Gutteridge, Ed. *Contemporary Terrorism. A Challenge to Italian Democracy*, by Vittorfranco S. Pisano (London: The Institute for the Study of Control, 1986, p. 167).

39. Ibid.

40. Ibid.

41. Ibid.

42. Ibid.

43. Anti-Defamation League Website, *The Skinhead International*.

44. Ibid.

45. Ibid.

46. Andrew Corsun. "Revolutionary Organization November 17 in Greece." *Terrorism: An International Journal*, vol. 14, no. 2 (London: Taylor and Francis, 1991, p. 86).

47. G. Kassimeris. "Greece: Twenty Years of Political Terrorism." *Terrorism and Political Violence,* vol. 7 (London: Frank Kass, 1995, p. 81).

48. *World Book Encyclopedia*, vol. 19, S.V. "Kemal Ataturk," p. 511.

49. Barin Kayaoglu. "London School of Economics: Election 2011, The More Turkey Changes, The More its Political Parties Stay the Same." (June 1, 2011). http://blogs.lse.ac.uk/ideas/2011/06/election-2011-the-more-turkey-changes-the-more-its-political-parties-stay-the-same/

50. "Terrorist Threat Assessment." (Summary DTN41. 17 Mar 2016)—National Coordinator for Security & Counterterrorism, Ministry of Security and Justice, The Netherlands. https://english.nctv.nl/publications-products/Terrorist-Threat-Assessment-Netherlands/ downloaded March 29, 2016.

51. Gareth Jenkins. "Back with a Vengeance—Turkish Hezbollah—Global Terrorism Analysis." *The Jamestown Foundation Terrorism Monitor*, vol. 6, no. 2 (January 25, 2008). www.jamestown.org.

52. Ibid.

53. Human Rights Watch. "What is Turkey's Hizbollah?" (February 2000). http://www.hrw.org.

54. Ibrahim Cerrah and Robert Peel. "Terrorism in Turkey," *Intersec*, vol. 7 (West Byfleet, England: West Byfleet, 1997, p. 19).

55. Rick Coolsaet and Tanguy Struye de Swielande. "Belgium and Counterterrorism Policy in the Jihadi era (1986-2007)." *Working Paper 40*. http://www.docstoc.com/docs/40615492/Belgium-and-Counterterrorism-Policy-in-the-Jihadi-Era-(1986-2007), retrieved April 22, 2011.

56. "A Mentor Mingled Crime and Religion." New York Times, April 12, 2016.

57. Philip Jenkins. "Strategy of Tension: The Belgian Terrorist Crisis 1982–1986." *Terrorism: An Inter-national Journal* (London: Taylor and Francis, 1990, p. 304).

58. http://en.wikipedia.org/wiki/Pierre_Carette.

59. Daniel Pipes. "Theo Van Gough and Education by Murder in Holland." *The New York Sun* (November 16, 2004).

60. http://www.reuters.com (April 8, 2005).

61. CBC News Online. October 26, 2006: Muhammad cartoons: A Timeline. http://www.cbc.ca/news/background/islam/muhammad_cartoons_timeline.html.

62. "Home-Grown Terrorism and Radicalisation in the Netherlands Experiences, Explanations and Approaches." Testimony by Lidewijde Ongering, Deputy National Coordinator for Counterterrorism: U.S. Senate Homeland Security and Governmental Affairs Committee (June 27, 2007).

63. "Terrorist Threat Assessment." (Summary DTN41. 17 Mar 2016)—National Coordinator for Security & Counterterrorism, Ministry of Security and Justice, The Netherlands. https://english.nctv.nl/publications-products/Terrorist-Threat-Assessment-Netherlands/ downloaded March 29, 2016.

Eastern Europe and the Balkans

LEARNING OUTCOMES

After studying this chapter, students should be able to:

1. Recount the events in early twentieth-century Russia that led to the Great Terror.

2. Cite how the United Nations defines crimes against humanity and how it has been applied in the former Yugoslavia.

3. Show how the breakup of the former Yugoslavia led to a period of genocide.

4. Summarize how the two Chechen wars have led to a significant Islamist threat to Russia from its former republics.

5. Illustrate how state-sponsored assassination may be a problem in Bulgaria.

KEY WORDS TO NOTE

Boevaya Oranisatsia (BO)—"The Fighting Organization"; terror suborganization within the Russian Social Revolutionary Party; given autonomy under the party

Bolsheviks—Extreme left-wing radicals, who favored revolution

Cheka—Communist secret police organization established during the Russian Revolution in 1917

Doku Umarov—Islamist leader described as the Chechen bin Laden

HEU—Highly enriched uranium

International Atomic Energy Agency—Agency responsible for monitoring nuclear stock piles

International Criminal Tribunal for the Former Yugoslavia (ICTY)—United Nations court of law handling war crimes

Kosovo Liberation Army (KLA)—A Kosovar Albanian group that sought to break away from the Federal Republic of Yugoslavia in the 1990s

Radovan Karadzic—Bosnian Serb leader convicted in 2016 by ICTY of genocide

OVERVIEW

Terrorism in the former Eastern Bloc and the now Soviet Republics is not a new phenomenon. Repression by the former Soviet Union, with its pitiful and sad history, was depicted by famous novelists of the nineteenth century. Tolstoy, author and creator of *War and Peace* in 1869, captured the horrors of the French invasion of Russia in 1812. Reforms by Czar Alexander II were strongly opposed by his son Alexander III, who succeeded him after his assassination. It was this repressive approach that slowly nurtured the seeds of revolution, which were at first written about as themes of desperation, discontent, and bitterness by the many great intellectuals of that era.

This chapter reviews those early terror theories that were at work in Russia and the Slavic states and also examines how the Soviet Union promoted state-sponsored terrorism. Many of the nineteenth-century Russian writers, such as Maxim Gorky, wrote short stories and plays that reflected the theories of a Communist state in Russia. The early seeds of terrorism grew out of the appalling conditions in which the people of Russia existed under the Czars and out of a need for social and political change. After the breakup of the Soviet Union in 1991, the new millennium continued to witness unrest and the relentless abuses of human rights by Chechen rebels and Russian security forces.

We begin with a review of well-known historic events, and then examine others that occurred in the central and eastern Europe. We will find how the War on Terror has played out in the Chechen Republic and how actions of Chechen rebels are labeled as terrorism by Russia. The availability of nuclear weapons, and their accessibility to terrorists through the Czech Republic, will also be carefully considered.

RUSSIA AND THE SOVIET UNION

Narodnaya Volya (NV) (1878–1881)

Roughly translated Narodnaya Volya[1] means "the people's will." NV was a highly effective terrorist organization that existed for only four years. NV grew out of other clandestine Russian movements and had been formed by the intelligentsia. Hard-liners from several of these groups formed the NV. Like other terrorist organizations, the NV used terrorism as a means to a political end. It aimed to cause the ruling Romanovs so much distress and turmoil that their actions would shake the Russian Empire's political foundation (Figure 7-1). Surprisingly, its membership was drawn from the Russian elite, and numbered probably no more than five hundred, with some fifty or more extremists. It set out to overthrow the tyranny of the Czars and declared a death sentence on Czar Alexander II. The group made several unsuccessful attempts upon his life.

One of its most fanatical members was twenty-seven-year-old Sophia Perovskaya, who succeeded in planting a bomb that killed Czar Alexander II in 1881. A fanatic, as well as the daughter of a Russian General, she was arrested along with five others and publicly executed. The NV was also responsible for the death of General Mezentsev, head of the Third Section of the Czarist OKHRANA (secret police) and also the Governor-General of Saint Petersburg. NV members were hunted down and arrested by Czarist authorities, and terrorism in Russia diminished significantly over the next twenty years.

The inspiration for Lenin to form the Social Democratic Labor Party was born from NV's theories. Lenin's views of, and appreciation for, NV had taught him important lessons—that a revolutionary organization cannot be limited to terrorism, but must seize total autocratic and bureaucratic power. The NV symbolized the general social crisis that existed in nineteenth-century Russia, and later during the **Bolshevik** Revolution, which replaced the old order in Russia. Terrorism faded quickly with the passing of the NV until the formation of the Social Revolutionary Party at the turn of the twentieth century. Members of NV took extreme care in

FIGURE 7-1 Map of Russia. *Source:* Central Intelligence Agency, *The World Factbook, 2008.*

planning and carrying out their assassinations to avoid killing innocent citizens. Targets for retribution were those deemed guilty of acts of corruption and offenses against the people.

Terror and revolution are two words that would be used frequently and interchangeably for Russians over the first twenty years of the twentieth century. The prime objective for terrorism in early twentieth-century Russia was to awaken the masses to the potential for sociopolitical change. The philosophical view of this approach is seen today by events unfolding in North Africa and the Middle East with the masses attempting to overthrow existing authority.

Within the Social Revolutionary Party was a terrorist subgroup that was given autonomy under the party—**Boevaya Oranisatsia (BO)**, or the Fighting Organization. Whereas the NV was more aligned with the educated Russian hierarchy, the BO appealed to a wider Russian audience than just the elite. Within the revolutionary movement, widespread dissent continued over the use of terror tactics, and with the emergence of the class struggle, terrorism as a weapon of that period became redundant.

Russian orator Mikhail Bakunin traveled widely throughout Europe promoting his revolutionary ideals. His ideals were based on the destruction of the prevailing social order, as it existed. His approach to anarchy conflicted greatly with that of Karl Marx, and the two were bitter rivals. Bakunin put forward no useful or thoughtful ideas for a future social order. Marx saw him as a dangerous fanatic. Bakunin's view was that the state had to be overthrown, but Marx believed that it was capitalism that had to be purged. Marx's theory and ideology were that violence was necessary to transform the nature of the working class and that violent insurrection was the only means to change society.

Opposition to the Bolsheviks' rule came from the intelligentsia, as well as from opposition newspapers. The Russian Republics were deeply involved in a civil war in the years from 1918 to 1921. In March 1918, Lenin dissolved the constituent assembly when it failed to recognize the leadership of the Bolshevik government. The protests from the socialist left went unheeded by Lenin, so much so that the group withdrew from the coalition. The Bolsheviks then began a period of terror and repression against all groups that voiced opposition. Hundreds of artists and intellectuals were arrested, who were simply aghast at the attitude of the Bolsheviks and had expected a society based on freedom in the wake of the overthrow of the Czarist government. The Bolsheviks dealt with nationalists, social revolutionaries, as well as members of the intellectual levels of society (professors, writers, and artists) in the harshest of manners. The church in Russia also became a target of Communist terror and oppression. A systematic campaign by the Communists to deny the Russian Orthodox Church any voice in the Soviet Union started in the 1920s, and by 1939, all the clergy, and many of the church's followers, had been shot or sent to forced labor camps. Of the fifty thousand churches in Russia, only about five hundred remained open.

Joseph Stalin

To many, the name "Stalin" conjures up scenes of sheer despotic terror. In the first quarter of the twentieth century, his name was synonymous with the word "terror." This chapter is not presented to teach the student the fundamentals of the Russian Revolution, but to explain that the intricate use of terror tactics, practiced by Lenin's Bolsheviks, had the unspoken, unanimous support of the Communist Party. Were the Bolsheviks considered to be terrorists, or were they revolutionaries fighting for their political beliefs for a new Soviet Republic? In hindsight, and because popular movies such as *Doctor Zhivago* seemed to glorify the hostility and man's inhumanity to his fellow man, should we consider the Russian Revolution a result of effective terrorism? In later years, and specifically during the Cold War, the United States and NATO allies viewed the Soviet Union as the prime exporter and sponsor of modern-day terrorism. The terrorist "Carlos the Jackal" is believed to have received his indoctrination, training, and funding in the Soviet Union. Although there is some evidence that he did receive part of his university education there, no substantive evidence has ever been unearthed that shows the Soviet Union did, in fact, sponsor him.

Josef Vissarionovich Dzhugashvili adopted the name "Stalin," a Russian word meaning "steel." Following Lenin's death, Stalin became the "Absolute Ruler" of the Soviet Union, from 1929 until he died in 1953. As a young man, he earned a scholarship to study theology but was subsequently expelled for preaching Marxist ideologies. He was a strong political supporter of Bolshevism throughout Europe and is credited with being the first editor of *Pravda*, the newspaper voice of the Communist Party. Stalin used extreme measures on the Russian populace to ensure absolute and blind obedience to his will. Anyone who opposed him was summarily dealt with and either shot or sent to labor camps (Gulags) in Siberia. This form of state terrorism was carried out by his head of the secret police, Laurenty Beria.

The Secret Police

Many states where suppression of the masses takes place require a sanctioned police force or security apparatus to do the bidding of a cruel regime. Apart from Adolf Hitler, there have been few other world leaders who have slaughtered and sent to labor camps so many of their own countrymen. The Communist regime under Stalin viewed dissent against the party as a repudiation of the proletarian struggle and a violation of Marxist–Leninist ideology. Any threat to the ideology was a threat to the authority of Stalin and the state. The Bolsheviks, and then the Communists, relied heavily on strong, political secret police force to secure their rule. The original secret police, the "**Cheka**," was formed in 1917, with the intention that it would be disbanded after the Bolsheviks under Lenin had consolidated power. The first chief of this secret police force was Feliks Dzerzhinsky, who had the power under the Bolsheviks to investigate all or any "counter-revolutionary crimes."

Much has been written of the Russian Revolution, and few would argue that the results of the October 1917 Revolution would surely be felt for decades to come. Even though the Soviet Union has disappeared into history, the difficulty of defining what actions were terrorism becomes problematic. There is no doubt that the Social Democrats of the Lenin era were terroristic in attitude and nature. However, when reviewed and portrayed as a class struggle for worker rights, why are these struggles now termed as "revolutionary actions"? Is it the popular belief that where a common populace supports a cause, whether it is righteous or not, these activities are no longer referred to as merely terrorist acts, but rather a full-blown "popular resistance" or "revolution"?

Western governments have criminalized terrorism and created legislation to deal with specific "acts of violence" against the state, including the banning of terrorist-linked, backed, or supported groups. Is it reasonable to rationalize that a popular revolution existed within the borders of Spain (ETA) or in Northern Ireland (IRA)? As we strive to understand what terrorism means in each specific category and, indeed, each country, it becomes less easy to define. In Afghanistan, following the Soviet invasion in 1979, no doubt the rebels fighting for the freedom of their country out of the mountains around Kabul would most likely be termed as "terrorists" by the Soviet Union. It is equally fair to believe that to the Afghans these "terrorists" are better described as "freedom fighters." It is ironic that one of those freedom fighters, who were provided support in the form of training from both the United States and Great Britain, would turn and bite the hands that fed him. We are referring to Osama bin Laden. U.S. Special Forces and Britain's Special Air Service Regiment (SASR) trained Afghan freedom fighters and equipped bin Laden and his followers for covert-style operations against their new "enemies" in the West. Some of those fighters, no doubt, were eventually involved in fighting alongside the Taliban and al Qaeda against coalition forces in Afghanistan.

The Great Terror

Throughout modern history, there have been many dictators who have purged their respective societies of all opposition, both from within and outside their own political structures. The murder of a senior Politburo member on December 1, 1934, was to set in motion a chain of events that resulted in the "great terror." Sergei Kirov was leader of the Communist Party in Leningrad and an influential member of the ruling elite. Popular as he was in Leningrad, in support of workers' welfare, he disagreed with Stalin's policies. Although he was not thought to be a threat to Stalin, he had been approached by some party members to take over as general secretary.[2]

Did Stalin, who was having doubts about the loyalty of the Leningrad apparatus, perceive Kirov as a threat? It seems entirely possible that the People's Commissariat for Internal Affairs (NKVD) could well have planned Kirov's murder on Stalin's instructions. Using the murder of Kirov as the excuse he needed to crack down hard and to purge the Leningrad party structure, Stalin introduced wide-sweeping laws that resulted in millions of Russians being arrested. This purge lasted for approximately four years and Stalin never again visited Leningrad. That four-year period saw millions of Russians sent to labor camps as well as summary executions and show trials. To say the Russian populace was terrified would be an understatement! In view of Stalin's terror tactics, his complete and total domination of the Russian people was further enforced by forcibly resettling more than 1 million people, primarily Muslims from the Northern Caucasus region and the Crimea. Ethnic Tartars, Chechens, Meskhetians, and Kalmyks, as well as Bulgarians, Greeks, and Armenians from the Black Sea coast, were deported.

These deportations took place during and after World War II, with the excuse that all of these deportees were collaborators with the German occupying forces. The forced deportations took place with the use of cattle cars, reminiscent of German deportations of Jews and gypsies to forced labor and extermination camps. The destination for the deportees was Uzbekistan, Siberia, and Kazakhstan—names that today have a ring of familiarity. By the mid-1950s, Nikita Khrushchev denounced the forced deportations. However, many deportees were still not permitted to return to their native homelands until after the collapse of the USSR in 1991.

Estonian Guerrilla Movement, 1944–1955

One guerrilla group that existed after the collapse of the German Axis was an Estonian movement called the Metsavennad, which means "guerrilla fighters." With the retreat of the German army, Estonian soldiers who had been drafted into the German army attempted to escape Stalin's discipline, either by leaving the country or fleeing to the forests of Estonia. These men were known as the "forest brethren." German deserters also joined this movement. It formed a protective band around Estonians to prevent violence meted out by the Soviets. The group was well-equipped militarily and was also supported by those who sought revenge against the Soviet Union for previous forced deportations associated with collectivization in March 1949. Their cause was the ultimate independence of Estonia, and, although this was a fruitless gesture against the might of the Soviets, they hoped for some relief and withdrawal of the Soviets, possibly with another European theater of war. A post-Stalin amnesty in 1955 saw the movement disappear.

School for Terrorism

The Patrice Lumumba University, also known as "Killer College,"[3] was located near Moscow and established in 1961 as the Soviet Union's educational contribution to the Third World countries of Africa and Asia. It was at this university that the terrorist Ilich Ramirez (Carlos the Jackal) received his postsecondary education. The Venezuelan Communist Party sponsored Ilich's admission and that of his brother Lenin's to this secretive university. Partying played a big part in their curriculum while they were in Moscow and, on several occasions, they ran afoul of their Soviet army and KGB minders. Ilich was arrested while demonstrating for the cause of thirty Iranian students who had lost their passports in a seizure by the Shah's government. Although sponsored by the Venezuelan Communists, neither Ilich nor Lenin were Communist party members, and their ongoing confrontations with the orthodox members of the Venezuelan Communist youth movement at the university finally led to their grants being suspended and their expulsion. Although there have been many books and articles written about Carlos the Jackal, whether or not the KGB recruited him during the period he spent in Moscow will probably never be known. On his own admission, after leaving the Soviet Union in 1970, his next stop was the destination of choice for many international terrorists—Beirut, Lebanon.

Into the Millennium

With the breakup of the Soviet Union, and with many of the Russian republics seeking to go their own way, separate from the new Russian Federation, Russia found itself in somewhat unfamiliar waters at the end of 1998. No longer controlled by the Communists, and with its people now sampling capitalism, Russia began to see many disaffected youths leaning toward right-wing nationalism. In the summer of 1998, Boris Yeltsin was openly commenting in press reports about the right-wing nationalist threat. What was already surfacing in Russia, now experiencing rampant unemployment, had already surfaced in a unified Germany. Russian youth were even beginning to blame immigrants and Jews for the lack of jobs and the country's other woes. Hate crimes and other violent actions were now commonplace in Russia. Had Russia gone full circle in the last one hundred years? At the turn of the twentieth century, Russia was in turmoil with the uprising of the worker classes. By 2006, the threat was clearly being seen from Islamic groups, many living in Russia's neighboring republics (Figure 7-2).

TERRORIST ATTACK BRIEF

Terrorist Group: Caucasus Dissidents (Ingushetia)

Case Facts: A suicide bomber detonated around 15 lbs of explosives inside the arrivals area of the airport killing thirty-six and injuring almost two hundred.

Investigation: The bombing had the hallmarks of extremists from the Caucasus region and the investigation began to focus on the North Caucasus region of Ingushetia. In March 2011, two young brothers from Ingushetia were arrested for their part in the bombing as well as for assisting the bomber make his way to the airport.

FIGURE 7-2   Suicide Bombing—Domodedovo International Airport—Moscow—January 24, 2011. *Source:* Based on Russian court issues arrest warrant for suspected accomplices of Domodedovo bomber. Published by Sputnik, © 2011.

Russia now allows the press more freedom to report on events as they occur in everyday life than ever before. This new freedom may become part of the lifeblood of any terrorist group starting up in Russia. Under Communist domination, the government-controlled media rarely reported on any anti-Soviet acts. However, since 9-11, there has been a crackdown on what is published and what is disseminated to the worldwide media. This is probably a direct consequence of President George W. Bush's tacit support for Russian president Putin to fight terrorism in the Caucasus. Without these restrictions, a key component in any terrorist arsenal is the ability to present such activities to a broad audience. In the democracies of the West, the suicide bombings in Moscow and the Beslan School attack in 2004, with the resulting loss of life, have made banner headlines. There has been little press freedom to report the true extent of military activities by Russian forces in Chechnya. Russia continues to blame Chechen rebels for bomb attacks in Moscow and continues to use this as a valid reason to carry out military operations against the Chechen state. Chechnya is a small, landlocked state with a predominantly Muslim population of approximately 1 million people. Russian President Vladimir Putin was quick to support President Bush and his declaration of a War on Terror. In dealing with the breakaway Republic of Chechnya, Putin and his government seemed to take the U.S. War on Terror as tacit approval to continue legitimized attacks on Chechnya.

Vladimir Vladimirovich Putin, President of the Russian Federation

Putin was born in Leningrad on October 7, 1952, and after university he worked at the Foreign Intelligence Service and served in Germany. After his return to Leningrad, Putin became an aide to the vice-president of the Leningrad State University in charge of international issues. Putin held several key positions until 1997 when he worked as head of the president's Main Audit Directorate and Presidential Deputy Chief of Staff. From July 1998 to March 1999, he was Director of the Federal Security Service. Between March 1999 and August 1999, Putin combined his job as Federal Security Service director with his work as Security Council Secretary. On August 9, 1999, he was appointed First Vice-Prime Minister and, later, Acting Prime Minister. On March 26, 2000, he was elected to the presidency of the Russian Federation.[4]

To ensure support for the U.S. role in attacking terrorism, the Bush administration had essentially ignored the issues surrounding the Russian actions in the south Caucasus region. With the Cold War over, the enemy was no longer the Soviet Union. Times had changed dramatically, and the threat now came from worldwide terrorism, advanced through the hate and malice of fighters immersed in the Muslim faith, with extremist Islamic justification for their actions. The regions of Dagestan and Chechnya are home to countless Muslims; however, the threat perceived by Russia was vastly different than for that of Western democracies and Islamic extremists. Chechens were fighting for their independence from their former Russian masters, and Russia continued to use its military to maintain control of the region. Chechnya remains an unsettled region, and Russia can continue to expect the unexpected from the Islamic fighters in Chechnya, and perhaps the many other Islamic provinces of Russia. Strange-sounding names like Ingushetia and Beslan are a world away from major urban U.S. cities, and perhaps that is why so little of what exactly is going on in this region gets widely reported. Many observers believe that the Russian security forces are doing little to prevent the spread of terror and—in fact, from their brutal responses—are likely furthering that cause. This observation and criticism continue to be aimed at the U.S. government and its failure to clearly define any foreign policy for the region.

RUSSIA'S FREE-MARKET ECONOMY AND THE RUSSIAN MAFIA

Russia became a "democracy" following the breakup of the Soviet Union. What, one must ask, happened to the KGB after the breakup? The answer to that is, "more of the same—under a different title." The KGB is called the Federalnaya Sluzhba Bezopasnosti Rossiyskoy Federatsii (FSB). From July 1998 until August 1999, Vladimir Putin was the head of the FSB. Over the last thirteen years, the FSB has undergone several structural changes as a result of political power struggles and was changed to reflect five separate departments and eight directorates:

- Counterintelligence Department
- Antiterrorist Department
- Strategic Forecasting and Analysis Department
- Personnel and Management Department
- Operational Support Department
- Directorate of Analysis and Suppression of the Activity of Criminal Organizations
- Investigations Directorate
- Operational–Search Directorate
- Operational–Technical Measures Directorate
- Internal Security Directorate
- Administration Directorate
- Prison System Directorate
- Scientific–Technical Directorate

Organized crime was on the rise in the Russian Federation but the police force was ill-equipped to respond. Interpol, on the other hand, was hard at work, tracking the exploits of more than four hundred Russian international criminals. The Office of International Criminal Justice estimated that at least four thousand organized crime syndicates were operating in the Russian Federation by 1996.

With the breakup of the Soviet Union came the dissolution of the Soviet's intelligence service (KGB). Its agents, however, did not fade into oblivion. Scratching the surface of Russian bureaucracy will uncover layers, like the little Russian dolls, of control dominated by former KGB operatives, many in local government. Organized crime syndicates in the Russian Federation, in collaboration with former KGB officers, is probably a major factor in a booming trade in former Soviet-made weaponry, not the least of which are nuclear capability products.

The "Russian Mafia's" links with former KGB operatives have led to the escalation of weapons sales to terrorist groups. The Mafia has moved from purely internal criminal activities to the exporting weapons to terrorist groups, some with the potential of mass destruction capability. Weapons of mass destruction have been placed on the market for sale to the highest bidder, and some of these sophisticated weapons have ended up in the hands of Third World countries. The potential for global conflict from these sales, while yet to be realized, should not be ignored or minimized.

Russia continues to be at the crossroads on the road to reform—or possibly is taking the long and winding path to anarchy and corruption. Its near neighbors have been embroiled in revolutions throughout the first decade of the twenty-first century; however, a new era of Russian dominance in the region is beginning to assert itself. This lawless society in Russia has led criminal elements to feed on the possibilities of controlling the state and reaping the rewards from corrupt politicians. With the criminal element playing so large a role in the proceedings of daily life in Russia, it is no wonder that these elements will stop at nothing to achieve their goals. On November 22, 1998, the staunch, pro-democracy parliamentarian, Galina Starovoitova, a vocal campaigner for human rights and against political corruption, was murdered in a scene reminiscent of a James Bond movie. She was shot three times in the head at close range as she entered her apartment building. Her campaign had exposed corrupt local politicians, and it is believed that this led to her assassination. Starovoitova was well respected but was among a minority of democracy reformers. The professional hit had all the hallmarks of a gangland-style execution. In a country where few women rise to the heights of local or national politics, her passing was something of a watershed for Russian politics. "Democracy, free-market economy, and the rule of law" are not words or statements that go hand in hand when describing the Russian Federation. Widespread corruption continues to manifest itself in both private and public organizations, and organized crime covers vast areas of the economy, from diversion of collected revenues, a form of money laundering, to the defrauding of overseas aid donors. The illegal trade in arms dealing, and the concern that al Qaeda followers would like to acquire nuclear capability, suggests that Russia may be a prime source for such weaponry. The threat of nuclear terrorism from terror groups, in particular al Qaeda and its global affiliates, to fashion a nuclear weapon requires discussion in relationship to the available materials needed to support such an operation. The Russian states have many sites that produced nuclear material during the Cold War years and beyond. Observers and politicians, particularly those in the U.S. administration, believe the only probable method for a group such as al Qaeda to acquire material for such a weapon is through a rogue or hostile state. The U.S. policy is fashioned to continuously target hostile states that pose a nuclear supply threat. Maybe this is a sound policy, or maybe it is not. What need concern the world at large are the nuclear stockpiles around the globe and the poor security and accountability that characterize a great many of these sites. To consider fashioning a nuclear bomb, terrorist organizations and nations have different requirements. Nuclear weapons development requires facilities for research and development in the manufacture, control, development, and deployment for conventional means. For the terrorist, the word should be "unconventional." For al Qaeda and its affiliated terror network, using a boat, truck, plane, or car as the means of delivering a nuclear weapon would be their conventional method. The fatwa bin Laden sought and received from a Saudi cleric in 2003 for the use of a nuclear bomb would be permissible under Islamic law, indeed even mandatory, if it were used as a means to stop U.S. actions against Muslims. "If a bomb that killed ten million of them and burned as much of their land as they have burned Muslims' land was dropped on them, it would be permissible," the ruling held.[5]

According to the **International Atomic Energy Agency (IAEA)**, since 1993 there have been one hundred and seventy-five cases of trafficking in nuclear material and two hundred and one cases of trafficking in other radioactive sources (medical, industrial, etc.). However, only eighteen of these cases have actually involved small amounts of highly enriched uranium or plutonium, the material needed to produce a nuclear weapon. IAEA experts judge the quantities involved to be insufficient to construct a nuclear explosive device. However, Mr. El Baradei, Director General of the IAEA, said: "Any such material being in illicit commerce and conceivably accessible to terrorist groups is deeply troubling." There has been a sixfold increase in nuclear material in peaceful programs worldwide since 1970. According to IAEA figures, there are four hundred and thirty-eight nuclear power reactors, six hundred and fifty-one research reactors (of these, two hundred and eighty-four are in operation), and two hundred and fifty fuel cycle plants around the world, including uranium mills and plants that convert, enrich, store, and reprocess nuclear material. Additionally, tens of thousands of radiation sources are used in medicine, industry, agriculture, and research.[6] In respect to Russia in particular, the threat of theft of weapons-grade material such as highly enriched uranium (**HEU**), the compound needed to make a nuclear weapon, is still a major cause for concern. While treaties have been drawn up between the United States and Russia, much work in destroying the stockpiles and securing the existing ones must be addressed. The material for the terrorist to build his bomb is available and currently not that secure. This has been the case since the early 1990s, and either the West has been fortunate or the terrorists have not yet acquired the skill level to manage deploying some form of nuclear strike; a more likely scenario would be a "dirty bomb" or radiological dispersion devices (RDD). The materials for these are more readily available from commercial, industrial, and medical facilities around the world. In 1995, Chechen nationalists placed one such device made up of Cesium 137 and dynamite in Moscow's Ismailova Park. Fortunately, it failed to detonate.

UZBEKISTAN AND KYRGYZSTAN

This little understood and recognized region has suffered massively since the breakup of the Soviet Union and is currently threatened by ethnic issues and violence and the obvious reawakening of the threats from Islamic extremism in the region (Figures 7-3 and 7-4). Violence erupted in Kyrgyzstan in summer 2010 resulting from government largess and corruption. How the violence began and who orchestrated the ethnic attacks has not been determined, but after President Kurmanbek fled the country, the capital Bishkek was looted. Tensions continue between Uzbeks and Kyrgyz, and what will be problematic for the region is the Islamic radicals that will try and dictate outcome following decades of cultural repression under the Soviet boot. These two countries are inadequately equipped to handle any levels of terror activity. The spread of militant Islam to the region is reflected in Afghanistan. In 1996, Russia, Tajikistan, Kyrgyzstan, and

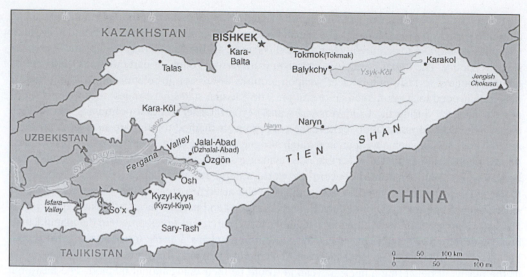

FIGURE 7-3   Map of Kyrgyzstan.   *Source:* Central Intelligence Agency, *The World Factbook.*

FIGURE 7-4   Map of Uzbekistan.   *Source:* Central Intelligence Agency, *The World Factbook.*

Kazakhstan signed the Shanghai Treaty with China, designed to demilitarize their mutual borders, and the following year they signed a follow on treaty demilitarizing the 4,300-mile former Soviet-Chinese border. This did not solve the problem, which still exists a decade later of the vast and largely unpoliced borders with Afghanistan.[7]

Islamic Movement of Uzbekistan

Uzbekistan eventually became a Soviet republic in 1926 following stiff opposition to the Red Army after World War I. By the twenty-first century, since the end of Soviet control in the 1990s, the Uzbek government had considerably alienated its Muslim population. This may have partly attributed to the rise of the Islamic Movement of Uzbekistan (IMU), renamed the Islamic Movement of Turkestan (IMT), in the mid- to late 1990s, against government actions. The government's response to the terrorist attacks in March 2004 generated a wide negative reaction from the West. Closely affiliated with al Qaeda, IMU is best described as a coalition of Islamic militants from Uzbekistan and other Central Asian states. The group is led by Tohir Yuldashev, a strong anti-Western supporter. The group changed its name in 2001 to the Islamic Party of Turkestan and expanded its goal to that of making Central Asia into an Islamic Caliphate. IMU activities have mainly been against Uzbek targets and the IMU is also supporting actions against foreign troops in Afghanistan.

CHECHNYA

A Mixed Background of Terror and Warfare

In 1991, the presidents of Russia, Ukraine, and Belarus joined together and signed a pact, the Minsk Treaty, which formally broke up the Soviet Union and created in its place the Commonwealth of Independent States. The Muslim states within the former Soviet Union were never consulted and were largely left to fend for themselves. Uzbekistan, Tajikistan, and Kyrgyzstan, or the "Stans," as they are called, have suffered from lack of strong political leadership and over the last twenty years ethnic tensions have come to a head.

After winning the Caucasian War (1817–1864), the Russians deported hundreds of thousands of Chechens. In 1877, 1920, 1929, 1940, and 1943, the Chechens made unsuccessful attempts to topple first the Czars and then the Communists. While most of the Chechen males were fighting against Hitler in the winter of 1943–1944, Stalin ordered that Chechnya be obliterated. Villages were burned, half a million people were deported to Kazakhstan and Siberia, and their land was given to non-Chechens. In 1957, the Chechens were allowed to return to their homeland. Dzhokhar Dudayev seized power in Chechnya in August 1991, after a popular vote elected him president that November. Dudayev declared independence from the Soviet Union just a month before its collapse.

Problems in the Caucasus

In February 1994, Russian President Boris Yeltsin and president of the Republic of Tatarstan, Mintimer Shaimiev, initialed a treaty delineating a division of powers between the Russian national government and the government of Tatarstan. The treaty afforded Tatarstan a considerable amount of autonomy and was welcomed by Yeltsin's Nationalities Minister, Sergei Shakhrai, as a "breakthrough." Kabardino-Balkaria and Bashkortostan followed in short order. These treaties represented a fine-tuning of Russia's evolving federation relations, the basic framework of which had been established by the new Russian Constitution of December 1993. The consolidation of Russia's territorial integrity was essential to prevent another Afghanistan failure. The control of the vast group of Islamic states within and without the vast Russian borders was imperative. Above all, there was the explosive situation in the North Caucasus. There, among other problems, the breakaway republic of Chechnya continued to refuse to consider itself a part of the new Russian Federation.

Moscow's previous response to Chechnya's challenge amounted to a policy of benign neglect toward both the republic and its president, Dzhokhar Dudayev. Moscow allowed the republic to go its own way and even attempted periodically to enter into negotiations with Dudayev. The Russian government repeatedly asserted that under no condition would force be used to resolve its differences with the republic and expressed the hope that these treaties would serve as a model for finding a negotiated solution with Chechnya.

Moscow began stepping up financial and military support for opposition forces to the government in Chechnya. Fighting in the republic intensified over the summer, leading to a major attack on Grozny by the combined forces of the Chechen opposition in an effort to overthrow Dudayev. Despite support from helicopters and aircraft with Russian markings, the attack failed. A week later, President Yeltsin decreed the government and military will take all necessary steps to disarm "illegal armed formations" in the republic. Subsequently, forty thousand Russian troops poured into Chechnya. It was a debacle, and the Chechen rebels were able to send the demoralized Russian Army home in defeat.[8] In August 1994, the Russian government began military action to stop Chechnya's secession. Russian troops began aerial bombing and attacked the capital of Grozny in December and again in February 1995. The rebel Chechen government fled to the hills, and Chechnya was put under armed Russian occupation.

Regardless of whether Russia had a right to use force to defend its territorial integrity against Chechen secession, in hindsight the invasion was a tactical error. The war made it inconceivable that Chechnya would ever become a "normal" member of the Russian Federation, even if it was granted considerable autonomy and a treaty-based relationship with Moscow, like that with Tatarstan. The hostility of the Chechen people toward Russia, deeply rooted before the conflict, has been immeasurably intensified by the brutality of the war and will not be ameliorated by Moscow's promises of financial aid to reconstruct the republic. The Chechen republic will remain a burden on the Russian people, a political nightmare for whatever party is in power in Moscow, and a major and possibly decisive impediment to the preservation of Russian democracy.[9]

Current Situation

The Russian military, in May 2002, openly proclaimed that it was clamping down on the vicious attacks of its soldiers against Chechens; however, this proclamation seems not to have been heeded by the soldiers themselves. Two weeks later, Russian soldiers seized five young men and methodically knifed them to death.[10]

The Russian army has managed to fight two separate wars in Chechnya, the last ending in 2000. Chechens remained undaunted and throughout 2000, the war was still being taken to the Russian public. Bomb attacks continued in Moscow—in the Pushkin Square bombing on August 8, 2000, the bomb was detonated at the height of the evening rush hour, injuring more than ninety and killing twelve. Suicide attacks continued in 2004, with the simultaneous downing of two Russian passenger aircraft and train station attacks in Moscow. Chechnya suffers from a ferocious economic embargo from Russia, which has caused most of its infrastructure to be either destroyed or decaying; thus, Chechnya is barely functioning.

DOKU UMAROV—THE CHECHEN BIN LADEN

Doku Umarov, a Chechen Islamist, has called for jihad, but it is somewhat surprising that this group is not engaged in a global jihad but one aimed solely at Russia. Attacks including bombings, suicide attacks, and assassinations have been the hallmark of the campaign of retribution against Russia for its attacks on Chechnya. In March 2010, a suicide attack on Moscow's metro system claimed forty lives and injured over a hundred in two separate suicide attacks. Umarov claimed responsibility and also that the attacks would continue as indeed they have. Further smaller-scale attacks continued in 2010. A Chechen Islamist group claimed credit for the September 9, 2010, bombing in Vladikavkaz, North Ossetia, which killed eighteen people and wounded one hundred and forty. The Riyadus Salikhin Martyrs' Brigade issued a statement on a website affiliated with Chechen rebel groups saying the attack was part of its jihad in the northern Caucasus. In January 2011, a suicide bomber detonated a suicide vest in the arrivals area of Moscow's Domodedovo Airport, which killed thirty-five and injured dozens more, and again this attack was claimed by Umarov.

Assassinations

Akhmad Kadyrov, the Kremlin-backed president of Chechnya, was killed in a bomb attack in May 2004, along with twenty others when an explosion ripped through a VIP section of a stadium where he was celebrating the defeat of the Nazis in World War II. He was named as the head of Chechnya's civil administration in 2000, and the Kremlin had entrusted him with organizing a 2003 referendum that would approve a constitution, cementing Chechnya's status as an inseparable part of Russia. Kadyrov was accused of siphoning funds destined for Chechen reconstruction. A former Imam, he had fought on the side of the Chechen separatists but later switched sides in an attempt to lead the republic to some sort of stability following two wars (Figure 7-5).

TERRORIST ATTACK BRIEF

Terrorist Group: Islamist Militants

Case Facts: Three heavily armed men managed to access the compound housing the Parliament building and stormed the building killing four and injuring at least twenty others.

Investigation: After gaining entry and killing a handful of people, the terrorists sprayed the building with automatic weapons and one terrorist blew himself up—the remaining terrorists also detonated devices killing themselves as Chechen Security Police stormed the building. The tension in the region remains, and although there are almost daily attacks by Islamists focused against the military and police, this was a well-planned attack—although no government deputies were injured in the attack.

FIGURE 7-5 Attack—Chechen Parliament Building—Grozny, Chechnya—October 19, 2010. *Source:* Based on Magnitude of deadly Chechen parliament attack rattles Russia. by Tom A. Peter. Published by CS Monitor, © 2010.

The Beslan school attack in North Ossetia in September 2004 was an operation by Basayev, but was more likely to have been promoted and supported by former Chechen president and war-lord Aslan Maskhadov. Maskhadov was killed by Russian forces in a shootout in March 2005. He was elected president of Chechnya during its brief period of independence in the mid-1990s.

Shamil Salmanovich Basayev (January 14, 1965–July 10, 2006) was the right-hand man of the former Chechen President Dzhokhar Dudayev who was elected following the breakup of the Soviet Union, in 1991. Basayev was to the Russians what Osama bin Laden was to the Americans. He was responsible for numerous guerrilla attacks on security forces in and around Chechnya as well as terrorist attacks on Russian civilians, including the Russian Theater siege in Moscow and the Beslan School massacre, which resulted in three hundred deaths of mostly school children.[11]Most Chechens believed themselves to be Russian and found it difficult to determine exactly how they should react. Terrorist actions led by Basayev were to have an immediate effect in ending the First Chechen War. In June 1995, Basayev led an eighty-plus team of Chechen fighters into Russia and attacked the southern city of Budyonnovsk where they stormed the police station, government buildings, and the city hall. When Russian reinforcements arrived, Basayev and his group retreated and took over a thousand hostages at the local hospital—the ensuing battle resulted in the death of thirty hostages unable to escape the grenades being thrown into the hospital by the special force. The unsuccessful attempt led to an eventual ceasefire—Basayev managed to negotiate his way out. In exchange for the hostages, the Russian government agreed to halt military actions in Chechnya—on June 18, 1995, Viktor. S. Chernomirdin, Prime Minister of the Russian Federation, issued the following statement.

To release the hostages who have been held in Budenovsk, the Government of Russian Federation:

1. *Guarantees an immediate cessation of combat operations and bombings in the territory of Chechnya from 05 AM, 19 June 1995. Along with this action, all the children, women, elderly, sick and wounded, who have been taken hostage, should be released.*

2. *Appoints a delegation, authorized to negotiate the terms of the peaceful settlement of conflict in Chechnya, with V.A. Mihailov as a leader and A.I. Volsky as a deputy. Negotiations will start immediately on the 18th June 1995, as soon as the delegation arrives in Grozny. All the other issues, including a question of withdrawal of the armed forces, will be peacefully resolved at the negotiating table.*

3. *After all the other hostages are released, provide Sh. Basayev and his group with transport and secures their transportation from the scene to the Chechen territory.*

4. *Delegates the authorized representatives of the Government of the Russia Federation A. V. Korobeinikov and V. K. Medvedickov to deliver this Statement to Sh. Basayev.*

Prime Minister of the Russia Federation

V. S. Chernomirdin

18.06.95

However, by the time of the second Chechen war, the stark brutality of the Russian troops toward the civilian population—which has seen more than two hundred fifty thousand killed, including around forty five thousand children—the options became clear: stay in the towns and be rounded up, kidnapped, or murdered or head for the forests and take up arms. A huge number chose the latter. As a Muslim population, Chechnya has been involved with affiliated terror groups from Muslim countries trained in Afghanistan during the Taliban regime. The Riyadus Salikhin group, under Shamil Basayev, claimed responsibility for the Dubrovka Theater attack in 2002, which led to the deaths of more than 100 civilians. Basayev claimed responsibility for all five major suicide bombings in Russia in 2004 and had stated that he reserved the right to use chemical and toxic substances and poisons against the Russians. As part of its political endgame with the Russians, the United States, through its then secretary of state Colin Powell, made the following comment in 2003 in regard to Basayev: "He has committed, or poses a significant risk of committing, acts of terrorism that threaten the security of U.S. nationals, or the national security, foreign policy, or economy of the United States." This kind of response for a warlord/terrorist who had not likely left Chechnya in the previous ten years may seem somewhat bewildering and confusing (Figure 7-6).

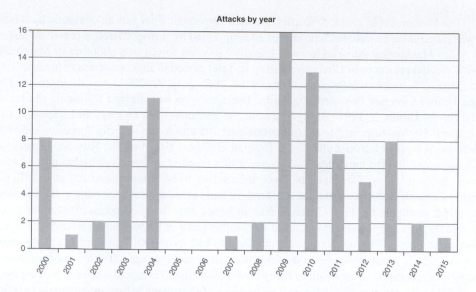

FIGURE 7-6 Suicide attacks between 2000–2015—Russia and Eastern Europe. *Source:* Chicago Project on Security and Terrorism, http://cpost.uchicago.edu.

To ensure that Chechnya stayed compliant to Russia, the installation of Ramzan Kadyrov, the son of the assassinated Akhmad Kadyrov, by Russia's President Putin was designed to ensure that Chechnya would remain compliant and subdued. The Russian authorities were considerably concerned as to what might befall the 2014 Sochi Winter Olympic Games as Umarov had urged his fellow Islamist militants to target the games that he had dubbed the "satanic games." Umarov had been responsible for many terror atrocities targeting Russian public areas, including the 2009 bomb attack on the Moscow–St Petersburg Express killing twenty six, the 2010 Moscow Metro suicide bombings (thirty nine dead and over eighty injured), and the 2011 Moscow Domodedovo Airport bombing (thirty six dead and over one hundred injured). There have been several reports over the years detailing Umarov's death but in late March 2014, a report from the Russian Islamist website the Kavkaz Centre stated that the self-styled Caucasus Emirate had died. Details on how he died are unclear. Umarov and his Emarat Kavkaz joined the IMU and the Riyadus-Salikhin Reconnaissance and Sabotage Battalion of Chechen Martyrs. Currently Chehcen Islamists are now engaged in fighting in the Syrian civil war and no doubt the Russians are more content to be able to target them in Syria than in their home states (Figure 7-7).

The Criminal Code of Russia defines terrorism as "any action endangering the lives of people, causing sizable property damage, or entailing other socially dangerous consequences; for the purpose of violating public security, frightening the population, or exerting influence on decision-making."

Russia has continued tightening its antiterrorism and other national security legislation since 2006, leading to concerns that some of the reforms infringe on human rights. The provision banning jury trials for terrorism suspects was approved by Russian President Dmitry Medvedev at the beginning of 2009. The Federal Law on Counteracting Terrorism (2006) targets ideologies as well as practices by including them in the definition of terrorism and terrorist activity.

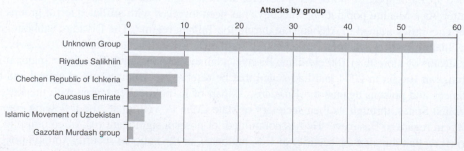

FIGURE 7-7 Suicide attacks by terror groups between 2000–2015. *Source:* Chicago Project on Security and Terrorism, http://cpost.uchicago.edu.

Attacks by location

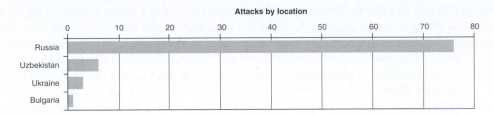

FIGURE 7-8 Suicide attacks by location. *Source:* Chicago Project on Security and Terrorism, http://cpost.uchicago.edu.

The law defines terrorism not only as "practices of influencing the decisions of government, local self-government or international organizations by terrorizing the population or through other forms of illegal violent action" but also as any "ideology of violence." One would suspect this is aimed at Chechnya. The definition of terrorist activity, which complements the definition of terrorism, is even broader. The 2006 law includes the following in the definition of such activity: propaganda information that calls to terrorist activity, information that justifies or supports the need for such terrorist ideas, dissemination of materials or activity, and also "informational or other types of aiding and abetting with regard to planning, preparation or implementation of a terrorist act."

This definition can easily be interpreted to include any "alien" or "offensive" ideology or political agenda (e.g., communist) or dissent (e.g., opposition to the Russian government's policies in the North Caucasus) (Figure 7-8).[12]

UKRAINE

Ukraine declared its independence in 1991 after decades of rule by the Soviet Union and the Czars before that. The former Soviet states of Ukraine and Kyrgyzstan have both experienced political unrest and felt the interfering hand of Russia in its attempt to steer both states away from democracy and a return to Communist ideals (Figure 7-9). Intelligence sources suggest that Russia used every means at its disposal to prevent the election of the pro-democracy, pro-West candidate Viktor Yushchenko from succeeding in the Ukraine. Political and outspoken pressure was placed on the Ukrainian public with strongly worded support for the Russian favorite, Viktor Yanukovych. Russia reverted to its old tactics, not of invasion, which it has used so unsuccessfully in recent history, but of assassination. In this case, the popular Yushchenko was the target. Reports indicate that the Russian secret police was involved in supplying the dioxin poison that made the candidate so ill in September 2004. On September 27, 2009, Yushchenko said in an interview

FIGURE 7-9 Map of Ukraine. *Source:* Central Intelligence Agency, *The World Factbook, 2008.*

aired on Channel 1+1 that the testimony of three men who were at a dinner in 2004 at which he believes he was poisoned is crucial to finishing the investigation, and he claimed these men were in Russia. Ukrainian prosecutors said Russia has refused to extradite one of the men, the former deputy chief of Ukraine's security service Volodymyr Satsyuk, because he holds both Russian and Ukrainian citizenship.[13] Ukraine remains an unstable fault line between the East and the West with pro-Russian separatists aggressively destabilizing the country with aid from Russian forces. The separatists saw how easily the Crimea was assimilated back in to the Russian fold and wanted the same for Ukraine. With the Ukrainian government looking to the West for support has made this region a frontline for political posturing between Russia and the West (United States).

GEORGIA

Georgia's Pankisi Gorge area is best described as a lawless region, home to refugees as well as Arab and Chechen terrorists. Successive Georgian leaders have been unable to exert control over this region that has likely been a fertile training ground for Chechens to launch attacks at Russian targets. British authorities suspect Ricin production is established in this region. Controlling terrorism and the scourge of the Pankisi Gorge is a problem not easily solved. The mere threat and obvious presence of Islamic extremist terrorists functioning in the area do nothing to assist the United States in its wider War on Terror. As time passes, the government attempts to crack down on this region have, at best, been weak and, at worst, totally inadequate (Figure 7-10).

In the summer of 2002, Shevardnadze announced that his security forces would be cracking down on terrorists and others in the region of the Gorge; following that announcement, troops moved into the region. A further proclamation from the ministry of the interior was released that simply stated, "The information about the presence of a large number of armed terrorists is invalid." Human intelligence coming from this region indicates significant numbers of Islamic extremists operating in the Pankisi Gorge, so the Georgian claims may be out of line with the reality for this area. The presence of Islamic militants, particularly Chechens, has been an ongoing issue since the mid-1990s. On March 22, 2002, Georgian ethnic Chechen journalist, Islam Saidaev of the Caucuses Committee and fellow Chechen, Zurab Khangoshvili were arrested on the basis of suspected al Qaeda connections. Their arrests were prompted by a letter from the U.S. Embassy to Georgian authorities that they were the only two people from Georgia to have performed the pilgrimage to Mecca, Islam's holiest city, that year. This religious act alone was sufficient to raise the suspicion of al Qaeda sympathies, a surreptitious argument used by the United States to justify an enlarged military presence in Georgia.[14] The national TV station in Georgia announced in August 2002 that the Pankisi region was home to a few al Qaeda sympathizers, criminals, and bandits.

FIGURE 7-10   Map of Georgia.   *Source:* Central Intelligence Agency, *The World Factbook, 2008.*

After 9-11, Georgia supported the U.S.-led War on Terror, and following that support, the United States sent special operations troops to Georgia to ensure that local forces were able to respond to and root out terrorists in the Pankisi region. What has now turned out to be a fiasco can be blamed on many variables, including corrupt officials and the fear of reprisals from Chechen crime groups who are somewhat aligned with the Chechen extremists, and who are certainly capable of targeting officials in Georgia for reprisals.

With no serious outcome to the attempt by the Georgian security forces to crack down or otherwise disperse any terrorists, the region has become a prime location for Islamic militants to continue to regroup and train for future operations. The reality appears to be that al Qaeda can operate with impunity in the republic of Georgia.

YUGOSLAVIA

From World War I to Ethnic Cleansing

Yugoslavia was established by the League of Nations out of the union of territories dating back to the end of World War I in 1918. Bordering the Soviet Bloc countries of Romania, Hungary, and Bulgaria, the Communist state of Yugoslavia encompassed six separate republics mainly founded on their ethnic or religious background. The area in question has been populated for at least 100,000 years.[15] The first Slavs moved to the area in around the fifth century migrating from regions of southern Poland and the Russian republics. Differing groups of Slavs formed their own enclaves and independent states. Serbians founded Serbia and Croats founded Croatia; however, from about 1400 onward, the southern Slavs were ruled by foreign powers.

The Turkish Empire controlled Serbian areas, while Hungary and Austria ruled Slovenia and Croatia, respectively. As the centuries moved by, the desire for a united region became a goal of Slovenia and Croatia. The movement to unite sparked an incident that was to change the destiny of Europe and the fate of millions. On June 28, 1914, in Sarajevo, Gavrilo Princip, a Bosnian Serb terrorist, assassinated Archduke Franz Ferdinand of Austria-Hungary, which led to the outbreak of the Great War of 1914–1918. Yugoslavia was so named by King Alexander I, in 1929. The king ruled briefly as an absolute dictator; however, dissident Croat terrorists assassinated him in 1934.

To say that modern-day terrorism played a part in the structure of a nation such as Yugoslavia would not be far from the truth. Two resistance groups fought against each other, as well as against the occupying Germans during World War II. The partisans were led by Josip Tito and his Communist Party and the Chetniks who supported the monarchy under King Peter.

By the end of World War II, the partisans under Tito established a Communist government and on November 29, 1945, the region became the Federal People's Republic of Yugoslavia, thus abolishing the monarchy and sending King Peter into permanent exile. As will be seen throughout this sad tale, many dictators have felt the need to dominate and destroy all opponents of the regime. Yugoslavia under Tito was no different, with many opponents of the Communist government being imprisoned, killed, or exiled. Tito declared a one-party Communist state, but Yugoslavia was not to be a puppet of the Soviet Union. In the late 1940s, Yugoslavia severed all ties with the Soviet Union and became a moderate voice in the region during the Cold War years (Figure 7-11).

Modern-Day Problems

The people of Yugoslavia were split along ethnic lines into six republics, with Slovenia in the north and Croatia on its southern border. To the south of Croatia was the often-disputed land of Bosnia-Herzegovina. Immediately to the east are Serbia and Montenegro. Civil strife among these ethnic regions has not, until recently, been cause for serious concern. Although nationalist tendencies have been in the forefront of Yugoslavia's political history for the last quarter of the twentieth century, they had not erupted into violent conflict until the civil war of the 1990s. Under Tito's rule, the republics had been forced to keep their nationalist feelings in check. Tito's aim was to eliminate old ethnic divisions and create a united social revolution. When Tito died in 1980, the old nationalist desires of the various republics were reborn. Up to this time Serbs, Croats, and Muslims had lived side by side in a form of peaceful coexistence.

When tough economic times befell them, the Yugoslavs protested Communist Party policy and began to demand changes to a political system that had failed to permit any other political parties to participate. Nationalism was therefore again on the rise in the six republics of Yugoslavia.

FIGURE 7-11   Map of Bosnia and Herzegovina.   *Source:* Central Intelligence Agency, *The World Factbook*.

Acts of political terrorism have been mostly nonexistent. What had been occurring was a bloody civil war, pitching neighbor against neighbor—almost a Balkanized version of Northern Ireland. All sides in this conflict, however, have used different tactics from those used in the Northern Ireland conflict. Reports out of the various regions cite incidents of "ethnic cleansing," a sanitized term for such extreme measures as the extermination of whole villages (genocide).

The United Nations defines crimes against humanity as crimes committed in armed conflict, whether international or internal in character, and directed against any civilian population:

   a. murder;
   b. exterminations;
   c. enslavement;
   d. deportation;
   e. imprisonment;
   f. torture;
   g. rape;
   h. persecutions on political, racial and religious grounds;
   i. other inhumane acts.[16]

Article two of the United Nations Convention on the Prevention and Punishment of the crime of genocide states:

Genocide means any of the following acts committed with intent to destroy, in whole or in part, a national, ethical, racial or religious group, as such:

   a. Killing members of the group;
   b. Causing bodily or mental harm to members of the group;
   c. Deliberately inflicting on the group conditions of life calculated to bring about its physical destruction in whole or in part;
   d. Imposing measures intended to prevent births within a group;
   e. Forcibly transferring children of the group to another group.[17]

In Bosnia-Herzegovina, the exact number of Muslims killed and displaced remains practically impossible to ascertain. But, by January 1993, between two hundred and two hundred fifty thousand people, ten percent of the Muslim population, are thought to have died, and by early 1994, almost 2 million people were displaced.

Nationalist conflict and resulting civil war have not had the hallmark of terrorist activity as has occurred in other areas, like Palestine and Israel. One exception was the attempted assassination by bombing of Kiro Gligorov, the president of Macedonia, an event that had the clear markings of terrorist action.

Ethnic violence between Albanians and Serbs was illustrated by atrocities committed by both sides. In all respects, the conflict had turned into a regional war. The lightly armed "freedom fighters" were fighting against tanks and heavy artillery. Through the last decade of the twentieth century, Slobodan Milosevic's government had been criticized for its treatment of ethnic minorities, especially in the areas of Vojvodina, Sandak, and Kosovo.[18] Milosevic came to power in 1989 and played a dominant role in the conflict in both Bosnia and Croatia, supplying military and financial support to the Serb nationalist campaigns. He supported proposals from the international community for a brokered peace plan in 1994; however, it was not well-received by the Bosnian Serb leadership. This failure prompted Milosevic to close the border between the two republics. In 1995, he signed the Dayton Peace Accord with Bosnian President Alija Izetbegovic and Croatian President Franjo Tudjman. Full diplomatic relations were restored the following year between the former Yugoslavia, now the Federal Republic of Yugoslavia (FRY), and Bosnia-Herzegovina. As for Kosovo, it had resisted the Serbian government since losing its autonomy, and the formation of the **Kosovo Liberation Army (KLA)** in the mid-1990s began attacks on the Serbian police. The response was swift, as the Serbian police and Yugoslav military attacked the ethnic Albanian community in early 1998, forcing a quarter of a million people to flee from their homes. At this juncture, the North Atlantic Treaty Organization (NATO) threatened to use force to curb the assaults by Yugoslavian forces against the ethnic Albanians. Throughout much of 1998 and into early 1999, peace talks were attempted but failed, resulting in a U.S.-led NATO bombing campaign against Yugoslav military targets. This had the opposite effect on the Milosevic government, which hardened its position and intensified its campaign by burning entire villages and forcing the ethnic Albanians in Kosovo to flee to Albania, Montenegro, and Macedonia. Six hundred and fifty thousand people were forced from Kosovo between March 1998 and April 1999.[19] Many unsubstantiated reports of brutal treatment, rape, and torture of civilians in the Albanian region of Kosovo were beginning to emerge when, by June 1999, the Serbian government agreed to a peace plan for Kosovo. NATO's bombing campaign was suspended on June 10, 1999, and the United Nations Security Council authorized peacekeepers to enter the province. Milosevic lost the federal presidential election in September 2000 to a coalition of opposition parties called the Democratic Opposition of Serbia (DOS). In December 2000, DOS won 176 of the 250 seats in Serbia's National Assembly. In March 2001, the Serbian government arrested Milosevic on charges of abuse of power and embezzlement and in June 2001, following pledges of economic support to the tune of $1 billion by Western governments, Milosevic was extradited to the **International Criminal Tribunal for the Former Yugoslavia (ICTY)** in the Hague, the Netherlands, to stand trial for war crimes.[20] The actions of the Serbian government mirror those of the Nazis during World War II, with the rounding up and arrest of those who have given, or were suspected of giving, any assistance to the so-called rebels. Those arrested were doctors, aid workers, lawyers, and journalists. In March 2016, the Bosnian Serb leader Radovan Karadzic was convicted by the ICTY for his role in the massacre at Srebrenica in 1995; he was found guilty of war crimes, crimes against humanity, and genocide. His followers were responsible for the massacre of thousands of Bosnian Serbian civilians. He had evaded arrest for more than a decade and his sentence at the age of 70 to 40 years in prison should mean he never again sees freedom again.

Kosovo remained a UN protectorate state; but, in March 2004, there were widespread ethnic clashes across the region. For more than five years, the region has made progress, but the violence certainly laid bare inadequacies of the UN-led mission to Kosovo (UNMIK) and the NATO Peacekeeping Force (KFOR). Much of the violence returned the region to the levels not seen since 1999. Much of this was apparently orchestrated simultaneously by ethnic Albanian groups, possibly with the guidance or control of the Albanian

National Army (AKSh), which is known to have launched attacks against ethnic minorities and security forces.

Since NATO intervened in 1999, Kosovo has become the crime capital of Europe. The illicit sex trade is flourishing and has become a major transit point for drugs en route to Europe and North America from Afghanistan. The demobilized KLA has not been disbanded or eliminated and is heavily involved in organized crime as well as political intrigue.[21] The majority of Kosovo Albanians saw UN involvement as the major obstacle to independence from Serbia. The geopolitics of the region has changed significantly since 1999—at that time there was no risk involved for a NATO and U.S.-led attack on Yugoslavia—Russia was not a force and was easily ignored. Russia was weak and in no position to challenge the United States and NATO. Putin was rebuilding the Russian sphere of influence in the former Soviet Union. He was meeting with the Belarusians over reintegration and at the same time warning Ukraine not to flirt with NATO membership. He was reasserting Russian power in the Caucasus and Central Asia. His theme was simple: Russia is near and strong; NATO is far away and weak. He was trying to define Russian power in the region.

Kosovo declared its independence on February 18, 2008, and immediately the United States acknowledged Kosovo as an independent state. As of February 2011, seventy-five countries had recognized Kosovo's independence, including twenty-two of twenty-seven EU member states, all of its neighbors (except Serbia), and other states from the Americas, Africa, and Asia.

Notwithstanding the geopolitics of the region, Kosovo is made up of about two million people of whom only one hundred and twenty thousand are ethnic Serbs, the rest are ethnic Albanians. Kosovo is cherished by Serbs as home to celebrated Serb Orthodox monasteries and as the site of the battle of Kosovo in 1389, which resulted in the Serbs being defeated by the Ottoman Empire—the likelihood is that Serbia would retaliate but with political and economic sanctions only. While a majority of EU countries led by Britain, France, and Germany support the Kosovo independence move, some countries such as Spain and Greece are somewhat concerned with recognizing Kosovo as they have their own breakaway groups within their countries. The short term is uncertain, and Kosovo is in much need of support from the EU countries at a time where unemployment is running near forty percent. It is possible that the declaration could be the cure for the outstanding issue of the Yugoslavia collapse and the signal for economic expansion in the Balkans; alternatively, Kosovo's independence could again stir up conflict between the Albanians and Serbs and result in the destruction of Bosnia.

The International Criminal Tribunal for the Former Yugoslavia

The following is an extract from the indictment against Slobodan Milosevic before the International Criminal Tribunal for the former Yugoslavia:

> Beginning on or about 1 January 1999 and continuing until the date of this indictment, forces of the FRY and Serbia, acting at the direction, with the encouragement, or with the support of **Slobodan MILOSEVIC**, **Milan MILUTINOVIC**, **Nikola SAINOVIC**, **Dragoljub OJDANIC**, and **Vlajko STOJILJKOVIC**, have murdered hundreds of Kosovo Albanian civilians. These killings have occurred in a widespread or systematic manner throughout the province of Kosovo and have resulted in the deaths of numerous men, women, and children. Included among the incidents of mass killings are the following:
>
> **a.** On or about 15 January 1999, in the early morning hours, the village of Racak (Stimlje/Shtime municipality) was attacked by forces of the FRY and Serbia. After shelling by the VJ units, the Serb police entered the village later in the morning and began conducting house-to-house searches. Villagers, who attempted to flee from the Serb police, were shot throughout the village. A group of approximately twenty five men attempted to hide in a building, but were discovered by the Serb police. They were beaten and then were removed to a nearby hill, where the policemen shot and killed them. Altogether, the forces of the FRY and Serbia killed approximately forty five Kosovo Albanians in and around Racak.[22]

Milosevic conducted his own defense against the charges. He suffered from blood pressure and heart problems and died during the proceedings at The Hague on March 11, 2006.

BULGARIA

State-Sponsored Terrorism

The debate on Moscow's level of effort in the arena of state-sponsored terrorism can be theorized at length; however, there is considerable belief that its Communist neighbor, Bulgaria, is active in this area, possibly on Russia's behalf. The extent of Bulgaria's involvement in state-sponsored terrorism is an issue worth discussion (Figure 7-12). During the Cold War, Moscow's attempts to destabilize the Western democracies involved the use of terror tactics against not only nations but also symbolic personages. In Rome, Italy, on May 13, 1981, a Turkish nationalist attempted to assassinate Pope John Paul II in St. Peter's Square. The Pope was shot and his would-be assassin arrested. The ensuing investigation uncovered a link to Bulgaria. The Pope's assailant, Mehmet Ali Agca, is believed to have had an accomplice in place to aid in his escape from Italy. The accomplice, Oral Celik, escaped capture by leaving Italy in a Bulgarian Embassy diplomatic truck. The following year, a Bulgarian State Airline official was charged in Rome in connection with the assassination attempt.[23] Further evidence of Bulgaria's complicity to export terror is seen in the actions of Sallah Wakkas, a Syrian national operating out of Athens. He had purchased more than $50 million worth of Soviet-made weapons and ammunitions from a Bulgarian weapons company, KINTEX.[24]

Further Bulgarian involvement was uncovered when Greek customs seized a ship en route to North Yemen in 1984. The contents of a consignment of oil tankers revealed huge quantities of weapons and ammunitions. The ship's cargo of trucks had been consigned by the Bulgarian State cargo agency, Bulfracht, while the paperwork for the consignment was produced by Inflot, the Bulgarian state shipping agency. It must be assumed that this arms shipment was destined for the Palestine Liberation Organization's training camps in North Yemen. One must deduce that this is just an example of many other shipments that had not been intercepted. In addition, Bulgaria's involvement in drug trafficking has been fairly well documented. Drugs, of course, can be used in the sale or barter for weapons and explosives. KINTEX of Bulgaria has also been known to be a supplier of heroin and morphine to Kurdish dissidents in Turkey, and these drugs have been used as trade for weapons.[25]

FIGURE 7-12   Map of Bulgaria.   *Source:* Central Intelligence Agency, *The World Factbook, 2008*.

Further evidence of Bulgarian attempts at destabilization revolves around the Red Brigade's shadowy involvement in the kidnapping of the American NATO general James Dozier. From evidence deduced by the examining judge at the trial of the Red Brigade ringleader, Antonio Savasta, Bulgaria played a part in the interrogation of the general and offered logistical and training support to the Red Brigade.

Bulgaria's Muslim community has also come under scrutiny since 9-11, in particular the Salafist group Al Waqf al Islami, which has its origins in Eindhoven in the Netherlands. There have been crackdowns by the Bulgarian Police on this group, but so far there has been no indication that Bulgaria is becoming a hotbed of Islamic radicalism.

Bulgaria may seem to be free of terrorism but not foreign terrorists. One case in particular is that of Palestinian Naif Hassan Omar Zayed who had been sentenced and imprisoned in Israel in 1986 for killing an Israeli. He subsequently escaped from prison and fled to Bulgaria where he has lived a relatively simple and peaceful existence. The fact that he was a member of a Palestinian revolutionary group did not stop him being a focus for Israel to recapture even twenty years later. Israel had requested his extradition causing Zayed to flee his home for the protection of the Palestinian mission in Sofia, a well-guarded and protected facility. However, on February 26, 2016, he was found lying dead on the back lawn of the diplomatic mission. Who and how he was killed and how the assailant or assailants gained access has not been determined and if Israel is involved in any way it is likely that we will never know that answer. Israel invariably exacts revenge for those that attack its citizens wherever they chose to hide. This may have been a state-sanctioned assassination by Israel, Bulgaria, or even the Palestinians themselves.

CZECH REPUBLIC

The Czech Republic and, formerly, Czechoslovakia were well known for being the central clearing point for the arms trade of Eastern and Western Europe (Figure 7-13). Although the republic is not synonymous with terrorism, its long-standing involvement in the arms business makes its exports very appealing to terrorist groups. Its Communist past and ties with the Soviet KGB allowed it to have extensive networks throughout the world, where it plied the arms trade effectively. The Czech Republic became a full member of NATO in 1999, but this did not necessarily curtail its

FIGURE 7-13   Map of Czech Republic.   *Source:* Central Intelligence Agency, *The World Factbook, 2008.*

arms disposal business to countries such as Yemen, which divert their weapons to third countries. The tracking of munitions across international borders, both legally and illegally, continues. *Jane's Intelligence Digest* reported in July 2004 that the Swedish defense ministry had shipped 328 ton of surplus plastic explosives. The material was similar to Semtex. The twenty-trailer convoy had traveled across Denmark and Germany before being intercepted by Czech Customs. What is disturbing about this single shipment was that the material was unmarked (unscented), which would easily allow for it to be smuggled aboard a commercial airliner. Since 9-11, the Czech Republic has raised its voice in the UN to better define terrorism. In 2001, the Czech Republic stated in the UN General Assembly (GA) that the GA could make an enormous contribution if it provided a general definition of terrorism, as this was a missing element in the international legal and political framework. The Czech Republic seemed to believe that when terrorism was defined, the international combat of terrorism was likely to be more successful with abuses of this combat prevented.[26]

Summary

Russia and the former Soviet republics have undergone enormous changes. No longer is Russia a Communist-dominated federation; no longer is it the "Great Bear of the East" that wielded so much power and influence in the world due to military strength and nuclear weapons. Russia is experiencing terrorism from Islamist extremists from Chechnya—not just in the streets of Moscow but also in the air and in its neighboring republics. Organized crime infects Russian society; Russian Mafia-style syndicates permeate all levels of the Russian society. Chechnya remains an ongoing threat to the region's stability as Islamic extremists spread out to neighboring republics. Certainly, since the events of 9-11, Russia has seized the opportunity to use military excesses to press home any advantages it can against the rebel state, under the banner of "War on Terror." The region of Macedonia has been devastated by sporadic wars within its borders; the term *ethnic cleansing* (genocide) is now used again to describe the mass murder of a particular ethnic group. Only now, nearly a quarter of a century later, are those responsible for that genocide being brought to justice. For the future, the regions of the North Caucasus may continue to pose a threat as Islamist groups profess their allegiance to the Islamic State that is still rampant in the Middle East and Europe. Russia continues to have designs on its former republics to wrest them away from Western influences.

Review Questions

1. Describe the methods of state terror used by Stalin to control the former USSR.
2. Analyze how ethnic cleansing and genocide in the former Yugoslavia was able to flourish and subsequently prosecuted.
3. List and explain the reasons for the upsurge in Islamist terror attacks from Chechnya.
4. Compare and contrast the attack by Mehmet Ali Agca with the attack on Palestinian Naif Hassan Omar Zayed.

End Notes

1. *The New Encyclopaedia Britannica*, vol. 8 (1985, p. 298).
2. "Secret Police." Revelations from the Russian Archives, Library of Congress (1996). http://leweb2.loc.gov/cgi-bin/query.
3. David Yallop. *Tracking the Jackal* (New York: Random House, 1993, p. 20).
4. Courtesy Russian Leadership Directory.
5. Mathew Bunn and Anthony Weir. *The Seven Myths of Nuclear Terrorism* (Philadelphia, PA: Current History, Inc., 2005, p. 153).
6. International Atomic Energy Agency.
7. Anthony Tucker-Jones. "'Flare Up in the Stans' INTER-SEC." *The Journal of International Security*, vol. 20, no. 8 (Chertsey, UK: Albany Media, September 2010).
8. Edward Walker. "The Crisis in Chechnya." *Center for Slavic and Eastern European Studies Newsletter* (Spring 1995).
9. Edward Walker. "What's Next in Chechnya." *Association for the Study of Nationalities*. http://www.nationalities.org.
10. "Putin's War." *U.S. News & World Report* (May 27, 2002, p. 26).
11. *BBC News online* (July 10, 2006), www.bbc.co.uk.
12. Lev Levinson. "Submission to the Eminent Jurists Panel in Connection with Public Hearings on Terrorism, Counter-Terrorism and Human Rights in Russia." *Human Rights Institute Governance as a Counter-Terrorist Operation* (Moscow, January 2007). http://ejp.icj.org/IMG/Levinson.pdf.
13. Viktor Yuschenko. http://www.absoluteastronomy.com/topics/Viktor_Yushchenko.
14. "The Plight of Chechen Refugees in Georgia," (March 21, 2005). www.ihrc.org.uk, retrieved May 1, 2011.
15. Araminta Wordsworth. "Sinking Further in a Morass of Brutality." *Canada's National Post* (December 10, 1998, p. A15).
16. "The United Nations and Human Rights 1945–1995." *UN Blue Book Series*, vol. 7 (1995, p. 424).
17. Ibid.
18. Norman L. Cigar. *The Policy of Ethnic Cleansing* (College Station, TX: A&M University Press, 1995, p. 9).
19. Serbia History-Encarta online Encyclopedia. http://encarta.msn.com.

20. Ibid.

21. Ibid.

22. United Nations. www.un.org/icty/indictment/english/mil-ii990524e.htm.

23. Major General Lewis Mackenzie, former commander of UN troops in Kosovo, 1992. "We Bombed the Wrong Side." *The National Post* (April 6, 2004). The prospects for the region under the auspices of the UN are not exceptionally high.

24. Clare Sterling. "Bulgaria Hired Agca to Kill Pope." *The New York Times* (June 10, 1984).

25. Philip Sherwell. "NATO Planes Strike on Kosovo." *The Weekly Telegraph*, Issue #359 (The Telegraph Group Ltd., June 9–15, 1998, p. 19).

26. Jorri Duursma. "Definition of Terrorism and Self Determination." *The Harvard Review* (December 20, 2008). http://hir.harvard.edu/definition-of-terrorism-and-self-determination?page=0,0.

North Africa and the Middle East

LEARNING OUTCOMES

After studying this chapter, students should be able to:

1. Recount the political steps in the creation of the Jewish State in Palestine.
2. Summarize the differences between Hamas, Fatah, and the PLO.
3. Review the structure of Hamas and its long-term goals.
4. Demonstrate how the Hashemite Kingdom of Jordan has managed to stay relatively immune from Islamic extremism and terrorism.
5. Identify the methods used by ISIS to gain a foothold in Libya and the threats it poses to stability in the region.
6. Examine the reasons for the rise of Islamic State in Libya.

KEY WORDS TO NOTE

Al-Fatah—A left-wing nationalist Palestinian political party and largest member of the Palestine Liberation Organization (PLO). It has supported a wide variety of European terrorist groups through the 1960s and 1970s

Ariel Sharon—Israel's eleventh Prime Minister and former Israeli Army general

Balfour Declaration—1917 declaration pledging British support to a Jewish homeland in Palestine

Black September—A Palestinian terror group that takes its name from the bloody month that saw hijackings of airliners and fighting with Jordanian troops leading to the expulsion of Palestinians from Jordan

Fedayeen—An Arab commando or guerilla unit

Hamas—An offshoot of the Islamic Brotherhood and an acronym for the Islamic Resistance Movement

Hezbollah—Also known as Party of God—a Shia Muslim militant group based in Lebanon

Izz ad-Din al-Qassam Brigades—The military functioning wing of Hamas in Gaza

Jabhat al Nusra—Islamist group fighting against the Syrian regime—established in 2012 as al Qaeda's proxy in Syria

Palestine Liberation Organization (PLO)—Established by Yasser Arafat in 1964 as a political body representing the Palestinian people

Rejectionist—A Middle East political term meaning the unilateral refusal of any peaceful settlement with Israel

Sheikh Ahmed Yassin—Muslim cleric and founder of Hamas—assassinated by Israel

Terry Waite—Special Envoy of Britain's Arch Bishop of Canterbury—captured and held hostage by Hezbollah from 1987 to 1991

U.S. Marine barracks in West Beirut—October 1983—A Hezbollah suicide bomber drove an explosive laden truck into the barracks killing 241 U.S. Marines

OVERVIEW

The late Yasser Arafat stated, "Peace for us means the destruction of Israel. We are preparing for an all-out war which will last for generations." The Peace Accords, and the innumerable sessions proclaiming a new round of talks to resolve the question of Palestinian statehood/homeland and Israeli security, will be examined in detail in this chapter. Resistance to the presence of Israeli settlers in Palestine, the effect this has on Israel's security, and the response by the men of terror in Palestine will also be discussed. Israel's right to exist, and the threats and assaults it has had to withstand, form much of the basis for terror attacks and extreme Islamic movements bent on the ultimate goal—the destruction of the Jewish state.

Palestinians have been depopulated and, for all intents and purposes, terrorized out of their homes to make room for Jewish settlers. This has persisted, contrary to international law, for over half a century. Syria has a role in this problem, under the relatively inexperienced son of the late president Assad. The Gaza Strip and the West Bank have become a flash point for internal fighting between **Al-Fatah** and **Hamas** since the death of Yasser Arafat. The Arab Spring has now embroiled a vast region and brought super powers on a collision course. Islamic State is ever present across Iraq, Syria, the Palestinian territories, Lebanon, Libya, Algeria, Tunisia, and Egypt and continues to spread to sub-Saharan Africa and so too is al Qaeda although the latter no longer gets front page headlines, it is still a force in the region.

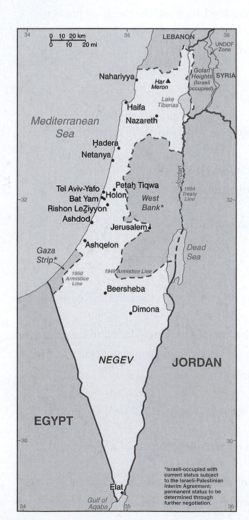

FIGURE 8-1 Map of Israel. *Source: Central Intelligence Agency, The World Factbook, 2008.*

ISRAEL AND ITS RIGHT TO EXIST

"The Middle East Crisis" focuses on the issues of "security" of the State of Israel and "hope" for the Palestinians for their own homeland with ultimate international recognition (Figure 8-1). Pro-Israel lobbyists in the United States contend that "U.S. aid to Israel enhances American national security interests, by strengthening our only Middle East ally in an unstable, dangerous, and vital region of the world." The ongoing issue surrounding the Israeli settlements in the Palestinian Authority (PA) areas continues. Since 1967, Israel has continued to create settlements in these territories. "The creation of a viable Jewish state, in an adequate area of Palestine instead of in the whole of Palestine would be acceptable," stated then President Harry S. Truman in 1946.[1] The questions regarding Israel's inflexibility, and the Palestinian refugees' having a safe homeland, clearly cannot be viewed as a new phenomenon. As far back as the creation of Israel, the United States has been fielding the criticism, and often the blame, for Israel's intransigence, her belligerence, and her arrogance for cold-bloodedness in her attitude toward refugees.[2] The quest for a separate Palestinian state remains as much in focus today as it was over a half-century ago. In 1948, the United States and Britain appreciated that the 1947 UN partition plan had failed. They concluded that their best political solution was to deny the Palestinians a state of their own. Under this strategy, the Palestinians would simply be absorbed into the neighboring Arab states mainly Transjordan, as it was then known, now the Hashemite Kingdom of Jordan.[3] Land is not the only issue surrounding the Middle East crisis, but the retention of land seized by Israel beyond the UN mandate of 1947, and following the Six-Day War of 1967. This issue is still as relevant today as it was after the Six-Day War. In May 2011, Israel's Prime Minister Benjamin Netanyahu argued that Israel is ready to make painful concessions in any peace deal but insisted that Jerusalem will not be divided nor will it make concessions on its border security or on the border of a future Palestinian state. In effect, Israel will make no concessions relative to the 1967 borders. Netanyahu refers to Hamas as the Palestinian version of al Qaeda and that for any peace deal to be formulated Fatah would need to rip apart its agreement with Hamas in order to facilitate any Israeli settlement.

Political Considerations

To understand the complexities of the Middle East and North Africa region, we first look at the imperialist influences and designs on this region at the time of World War I. By the latter part of the 1800s, the Ottoman Empire was in total disarray and internal factional disturbances were continuing within the realm as Turkey's influences waned.

The dwindling Turkish Ottoman Empire comprised a significant section of the Arab territories of the Middle East, and this area was, by 1914, an area ripe for the plucking. Britain, France, and Russia all had designs on the Arab lands. Turkey was fighting on the side of the German Empire against Britain and France, so it suited Britain to turn the Arabs against the Turks. To sustain the Jews on the side of Britain, the British government issued the "**Balfour Declaration**," named after the highly respected British Foreign Secretary, Sir Arthur James Balfour. The Declaration read as follows: "*His Majesty's Government views with favor the establishment in Palestine of a national homeland for the Jewish people, and will use their best endeavors to facilitate the achievement of this objective, it being clearly understood that nothing shall be done which may prejudice the rights of non-Jewish communities in Palestine, or the rights and political status enjoyed by Jews in any other country.*"

This declaration sought to win both financial and political support for the war from Jews in Europe and the United States. The Jews viewed this as tacit agreement for having their own homeland in Palestine. The Arabs, however, read a different meaning into the wording. They believed that they had been forced to agree to any terms put forward, before an agreement on self-determination of lands for the Jews had been realized. The Arabs fought in the belief that they were assured independence; the Jews in Palestine offered to raise troops to fight on the side of the British.

Promising independence to both Zionists and Arabs alike, the British government had unwittingly sown the seeds for an endless succession of wars. In the following decades, the Jews and Arabs would fight conventional wars that would turn into what is now called "modern-day terrorism," a situation that endured for the remainder of the twentieth century. With Arabs and Jews focused on fighting the Turks, Britain achieved its immediate aim of controlling the region and assured support from both. Albeit a short-sighted political decision, it left the Middle East with the distinction of becoming a breeding ground for future generations of terrorists.

The very name "Palestinian" was often seen as synonymous with "Terrorism." This view adequately portrays the problems that beset this area of the Middle East. British strategic aims, at the end of World War I, were to solidify a friendly presence in Palestine to ensure protection of its shipping routes into Africa and to the east into India. Of major importance in this plan would be the Suez Canal and the major shipping route from the Indian Ocean to the Mediterranean. After World War I, Britain set up the Arab kingdoms of Saudi Arabia, Iraq, and Syria in such a fashion that only strong and traditional, family groups controlled them.

The influx of Jewish refugees escaping Europe at the end of the 1930s and during and after World War II was staunchly opposed by the British Conservative Government of Winston Churchill. Despite the desperate need to find a haven for refugees, the doors of Palestine remained shut. The Zionist leadership met in the Biltmore Hotel in New York City in 1942 and declared that it supported the establishment of Palestine as a Jewish Commonwealth. This was a restatement of Zionist aims that went beyond the Balfour Declaration and a determination that the British were, in principle, an enemy to be fought, rather than an ally.

Settlements and Terror

Israel's history is founded on its struggle to exist in a hostile environment, surrounded by unfriendly Arab neighbors and Arab refugees. Since the 1948 Arab-Israeli war, the areas that were occupied by Israel have seen countless incursions by Arab refugees and particularly from Jordan and Egypt. Many of these incursions were raids by "foraging Arabs" returning to their home villages and stopping en route to rob and steal. Many attacks on civilians in Jewish-occupied regions resulted, and it is from these early incursions that the Israelis initiated various response mechanisms. To combat these attacks, the Israelis adopted a policy of destroying abandoned Arab villages along the border region and establishing Israeli settlements in their place. Hundreds of Israeli civilians had been killed by 1953, when the Israeli government established "Unit 101," a special operations/commando unit. Ariel Sharon led this unit in August 1953, on orders from former Prime Minister David Ben-Gurion. The unit drew much criticism due to its killing of innocent civilians, and in particular the Qibya operation, which left almost seventy civilians dead. However, its extreme methods of attack would eventually form the cornerstones for the development of the Israeli Defense Force (IDF). The brutal nature of the unit's attacks against civilian targets eventually led to its abandonment in 1954, integrating it into the 202nd Paratroop Brigade.

THE STERN GANG

The "Stern Gang" was an extreme, right-wing organization, founded by Avraham Stern in 1940 as a split-off group from the Irgun. Irgun was a Jewish terrorist group organized in the 1930s to defend the Jewish settlers from Arab attacks and, after World War II, used its skills to attack the British in Palestine. Irgun's attacks culminated in the massacre of two hundred and fifty Arab civilians at the settlement of Deir Yassin, outside Jerusalem in 1948. This action prompted Israeli former Prime Minister David Ben-Gurion to call for the Irgun to be disbanded and absorbed into the Haganah Army, the forerunner to the IDFs. Stern was killed by British forces in 1944, but the gang continued under the leadership of Israel Eldad, Natan Yellin-Mor, and Yitzhak Shamir, who would become Israel's Prime Minister forty years later. Two notable assassinations are credited to the Stern Gang. On November 6, 1944, they killed the British resident minister for the Middle East, Lord Moyne, and on September 17, 1948, the then UN special mediator for Palestine, Count Folke Bernadotte. The Deir Yassin massacre, in 1948, also involved the Stern Gang, but the much larger Irgun was the main perpetrator of that massacre. Both Stern and Irgun were in existence prior to the formation of the State of Israel, and both sought the formation of the Jewish state through actions that are considered terrorism and were mainly directed against the British mandate in Palestine. The Stern Gang's attacks were against the British, not the Arab communities. Discussion of Stern's approaches to the Nazis is controversial due to their very abhorrent nature; maybe it was a case that, in 1939, "his enemy's enemy was therefore Stern's friend." Stern could likely only consider this in terms of the total liberation of the region from British control.

Under the 1947 UN Partition Plan, Israel's original size had been limited to 5,900 square miles. Following the fighting in 1948, Israel's land total became 7,800 square miles. The 1967 Six-Day War dramatically altered the borders of Israel. After this brief war, Israel controlled some 20,870 square miles of newly acquired territory . . . nearly five times its original size.[4] Settlements continued to be created, and Palestinians were being dispossessed of their land as Israel's expansion continued. Condemnation of Israel came from United Nations resolutions, which, in most cases, were vetoed by the United States. However, in March 1976, the United States finally condemned these settlements as being both illegal and an obstacle to peace. By the time of the U.S. declaration, there were already about sixty-eight settlements in the territories, not counting Jerusalem. William W. Scranton, the former U.S. Ambassador to the United Nations, informed the Security Council,

> Next, I turn to the question of Israeli settlements in the occupied territories. Again, my government believes that international law sets the appropriate standards. An occupier must maintain the occupied areas as intact and unaltered as possible, without interfering with the customary life of the area, and any changes must be necessitated by the immediate needs of the occupation and be consistent with international law. The Fourth Geneva Convention now speaks directly to the issue of population transfer in Article 49. Clearly then, substantial resettlement of the Israeli population in the occupied territories, including East Jerusalem, is illegal under the convention and cannot be considered to have prejudged the outcome of future negotiations between the parties or the location of the borders of states of the Middle East. Indeed, the presence of these settlements is seen by my government as an obstacle to the success of the negotiations for a just and final peace between Israel and its neighbors.[5]

Israeli expansionism continued in spite of these words spoken forty years ago. In February 1989, former Israeli Prime Minister Yitzhak Rabin assured a "Peace Now" delegation that negotiations (with the Palestinians) were nothing but some "low-level discussions" that avoided any serious issues and granted Israel "at least a year" to resolve the problem (presumably by force). Rabin further stated, "The inhabitants of the territories are now subject to both harsh military and economic pressure; in the end they will be broken."[6]

The Oslo Peace Accords of the 1990s have been so encumbered as to make it impossible to determine what concessions, if any, Israel has made. This is due to the Israeli conditions, entailments, and qualifications, which were so one-sided that Palestinians felt no semblance of self-determination. It is not difficult to see why Palestinians then see terrorism as a tool—and likely their only tool—to make their claims clear to the world at large. The actions of suicide terrorists on 9-11 may have been seen as an opportunity for the Israeli government to bury the Intifada once and for all. In the week following 9-11, the Israelis took their War on Terror directly into Palestinian territory.

The Israeli army killed twenty-eight Palestinians and mounted sixteen incursions into PA areas. The response to the swiftness of the Israeli incursion forced Arafat to declare a cease-fire on all fronts and express readiness to enlist in America's coalition for "ending terrorism against unarmed innocent civilians." Following this, the PA leader warned Islamic Jihad, Hamas, and others not to give "pretexts" that would aid Mr. Sharon's designs. Although these groups heeded the call from Arafat and ended the firing on Jewish settlements from Palestinian areas, they did not agree to end armed actions in their own defense of Palestinian towns still under occupation. These groups also affirmed that they would respond if Israel acted against them or their people. On September 24, 2001, the Israeli army established a twenty-mile "closed military zone" along the West Bank's northern border with Israel. This was ostensibly established to prevent suicide bombers from infiltrating any Israeli territory.[7] A test of Israel's will, came in the subsequent surprising events, which triggered the Second Intifada uprising: attacks by suicide bombers and rioting that continued off and on through 2002. Israeli Prime Minister Ehud Barak dispatched a military force, led by then Defense Minister Ariel Sharon, to the Al-Aqsa Mosque compound. Sharon strode into the *Haram al-Sharif* (The Noble Sanctuary) in what was designed to be a gesture to assert his rights as an Israeli to visit this Muslim holy place. This single act sparked the beginning of the Second Intifada. Sharon cannot be described as a statesman whose actions were likely to endear him to Palestinians in general. His reputation was mainly due to his checkered career, in particular his questionable involvement in the Sabra and Shatila refugee camp massacres that took place in Beirut in 1982.

Throughout the latter half of 2001 and 2002, the Israeli government held the Palestinian Authority's leader, Yasser Arafat, "personally responsible" for terrorist and suicide attacks against Israel. Israel adopted the military option to attack specific "Terror" targets inside the Palestinian-controlled areas. In January 2002, the Israeli Air Force used U.S.-made F-16s to drop bombs on Arafat's compound in Ramallah. Most military actions had been in response to Palestinian suicide attacks against Israeli targets. Israel also used targeted assassinations to deter, destroy, and remove Hamas militant leaders.

HAGANAH, IRGUN ZEVA'I LE'UMI, NATIONAL MILITARY ORGANIZATION

The Haganah (Hebrew—defense) were established as a Jewish defense force in the 1920's as a response to the lack of protection offered to local Jewish communities by the British from attacks by Arabs. They had no central command in the beginning and were made up mainly of farmers who were poorly equipped. Haganah underwent a quick transformation following riots in 1929 and saw its numbers swelled with Jewish youth from the countryside and the cities. With the British Mandate firmly in place, Haganah participated in actions in defense of British interests to suppress the growing Arab revolts. The British forces in Palestine were actively supporting if not officially recognizing the Haganah. In 1939, the British began to severely restrict all forms of Jewish migration to Palestine, and this would have been a turning point for Haganah and its leadership. The main method of smuggling refugees from Europe was by ship, and although many were intercepted and returned, a large number succeeded in reaching Palestine, thanks to the Haganah organization.

National Military Organization (NMO), a Jewish underground organization, was founded in 1931 by a group of Haganah commanders who left the Haganah in protest against its defense charter. In April 1937, during the Arab riots, the organization split—about half its members returned to the Haganah. They carried out reprisals against Arabs, which were condemned by the Haganah. The term "Special Night Squads" originates from an invention of the British Army in Palestine in 1938 when Orde Wingate set up plans using British soldiers, members of Haganah, and the Jewish Settlement Police to combat nighttime incursions by Arabs into northern Palestine. Irgun operated exclusively in Palestine as a Jewish group for the establishment of a modern-day Israel. Their main targets were the resident Arab Palestinians and the occupying British Army in Palestine. Bombings were the order of the day, and the two-pronged attacks were designed to have two legitimate aims for the Jews. The first was to destabilize the British presence in the region and make it costly for the British to retain a presence. With the agreement on partition by the United Nations formally granted in 1948, the terrorists of the Irgun began to immediately attack and kill Arab families and individuals who remained in the Jewish sector. The effect on the demoralized Palestinians was to produce a mass exodus from the area. Several notable members of Irgun played an important role over the following years in the development and political status of Israel. Menachem Begin led Irgun activities during the 1940s, and when the State of Israel was official, he entered politics and founded the right-wing Herut Party and became leader of the Israeli opposition party from 1948 to 1967. He became Prime Minister in 1977 of the right-wing coalition government and took a very hard line against the Arabs. In spite of that he began talks with Egypt in 1977, mediated by then U.S. President Jimmy Carter in the peace treaty of 1979, winning him a share of the Nobel Peace Prize with former Egyptian President Anwar Sadat. Following the Israeli invasion of Lebanon in 1981 to rid the region of burgeoning terrorist threats to Israel, Begin would resign in 1983 following worldwide condemnation for the invasion.

Hosni Mubarak, Sadat's successor, would hold that peace in place until the spring revolutions that swept the Middle East and North Africa in 2011.

Ariel Sharon

Until his sudden illness, which has kept him in a virtual coma since 2006, **Ariel Sharon** was viewed with passion by Israelis. He joined the Haganah and, later, the IDF. After college studies he returned as a major to head up the IDF's Unit 101. The unit was criticized for targeting civilians, resulting in the widely condemned Qibya Operation in the autumn of 1953. More than sixty Jordanian civilians were killed in an ambush of Arab Legion forces. Shortly afterward, Unit 101 was merged into the 202nd Paratroop Brigade.

Sharon was a member of the Israeli Knesset from 1973 to 1974 and, again, from 1977 to 2006. He served as the security adviser to Prime Minister Yitzhak Rabin and as Minister of Agriculture (1977–1981) and Defense Minister (1981–1983) in Menachem Begin's Likud government. During the Israeli invasion of Lebanon in 1982, while Ariel Sharon was defense minister, a massacre of several hundred Palestinians in Sabra and Shatila refugee camps in Beirut was carried out by the Phalanges, a Lebanese-Christian militia allied with Israel. It has been speculated that Ariel Sharon played a significant part in allowing the Christian militia a free hand in the camps and by security the perimeter for them to conduct atrocities within the two Palestinian camps. He was elected Prime Minister in February 2001 soon after the collapse of Barak's government. His former deputy Prime Minister Ehud Olmert assumed the role of Prime Minister on a permanent basis on the declaration of Sharon's permanent incapacity in April 2006.

MOSSAD

The Israeli Secret Intelligence Service

In July 1949, Reuven Shiloah, a close associate of David Ben-Gurion, proposed establishing a central institution for organizing and co-coordinating intelligence and security service. The object was to enhance interservice coordination and cooperation. On December 13, 1949, Ben-Gurion authorized the establishment of the "Institution for Co-ordination" to oversee the political department and to coordinate the internal security and military intelligence organizations. The institution, Mossad, was born on that day.

The Mossad started out under foreign ministry auspices. In March 1951, with a view to enhancing its operational capabilities and to unifying all overseas intelligence gathering, Ben-Gurion authorized its final reorganization. An independent, centralized authority was set up to handle all overseas intelligence tasks. This was called the "Authority" and formed the major part of the Mossad. It included representatives of the other two services at HQ and field echelons. The Mossad broke free of the foreign ministry and reported directly to the Prime Minister, thus becoming part of the Prime Minister's office. The Mossad eventually adopted the following verse from the Book of Proverbs as not only its motto, guide, creative awakener, and ideology but also as a dire warning: "*Without guidance do a people fall, and deliverance is in a multitude of counsellors*" Proverbs XI/14.[8]

THE PALESTINIAN LIBERATION ORGANIZATION

In May 1964, four hundred and twenty-two Palestinian national figures met in Jerusalem under the chairmanship of Ahmad Shuqeiri and, following an Arab League decision, founded the **Palestinian Liberation Organization (PLO)**. They laid the foundations and structure of the PLO and, in the early years, followed Pan-Arabic ideology. They set up as an umbrella movement for a large number of varied Palestinian interest groups and were regarded by many, the Israelis in particular, as a terrorist organization. The early PLO was not a cohesive organization and contained a broad spectrum of moderate to extremely radical viewpoints. The militant members of PLO were known as **Fedayeen** (warriors), prepared to die for Allah. With such diverse opinions, the PLO became splintered and factional. This internecine struggle was much like the many Republican factions in Northern Ireland.

Their driving philosophy was the restoration of Palestine, the destruction of Israel, and the re-creation of an Arab state in Palestine. The PLO was loosely organized under three headings: the Executive Committee, the Central Committee, and the Palestine National Council. The Executive Committee coordinated the major terror activities, and the Central Committee acted as an advisory structure to the Executive Committee. During the 1960s, PLO guerrilla groups carried out sporadic attacks against Israel. However, the organization lacked strong leadership, and during this period, they operated from bases inside the Hashemite Kingdom of Jordan, ruled by British-educated King Hussein. In Jordan, Yasser Arafat laid the groundwork for his operations among the Palestinians. In 1964, Arafat took control of the PLO and turned it from a feeble political movement to one that would be recognized as the only one to represent all the Palestinian people. By 1974, the Arab nations had recognized the PLO as "the sole, legitimate representative of the Palestinian people." In the same year, the United Nations (excluding Israel) similarly recognized the PLO.

Like all good political and terrorist organizations, Arafat's PLO had a senior security advisor, Ali Hassan Salameh (aka Abu Hassan), the "Red Prince." The Israeli intelligence agency, Mossad, believed Salameh to be the PLO member responsible for planning the Munich Olympic Games massacre. Golda Meir, then Prime Minister of Israel, gave Mossad the task of tracking down the man responsible for the attack. The search lasted seven years. In their attempts to assassinate Salameh, Mossad killed an innocent Moroccan bartender in Lillehammer; such was their fervor to exact retribution on the PLO. Salameh was killed by a remote-controlled bomb, in January 1979, detonated in a stationary vehicle as he drove by with his bodyguards. Arafat worked tirelessly to steer the PLO toward political legitimacy and, in 1988, took the monumental step of announcing the right of Israel to exist and renouncing the further use of PLO terrorism. This commitment, from the man who then spoke for the displaced Palestinians, moved Israel toward discussions on Palestinian self-rule. Young Palestinians, who were frustrated with the slow progress toward self-rule in a homeland of their own, then turned to Hamas or Hezbollah for their leadership.

On September 13, 1993 (in Oslo), the Declaration of Principles between the Israelis and the Palestinians was signed. Palestinian groups formerly under the umbrella of the PLO, such as the Popular Front for the Liberation of Palestine (PFLP) and also the Democratic Front for the Liberation of Palestine-Hawatmeh (DFLPH), suspended their participation in the PLO in protest and continued their campaigns of violence against not only the Israelis but also Americans and members of Arafat's PLO. Arafat remained as the PLO leader until his death in 2004. He had been the specific target of Israel almost unceasingly since 9-11. He endured house arrest in his own compound for much of 2002–2004. Israeli raids into Palestinian areas such as Ramallah and Jenin, to root out terrorists who were targeting civilians, still continued unabated in spite of international condemnation for the use of military hardware in the West Bank and Gaza regions. By the middle of 2002, Arafat was clinging on to the leadership of the PLO, but faced a mounting challenge from Hamas militants.

The likelihood that a Palestinian/Israeli accord could be brokered between Sharon and Arafat was always questionable. Both had a long history of mistrust for each other. Sharon's long-remembered direct or indirect involvement with Christian militias in the Sabra and Shatila camp massacres did nothing to ease the dangers for peace in the region.

Arafat operated more as a dictator than a democratic leader, and some two years after an agreed deadline for democratic elections to be held, Arafat blamed the delay on the Israeli occupation. He stated frequently that this must end before elections could take place.

The world held its collective breath following Arafat's death in a Paris hospital in 2004. Without any viable successor, the vacuum could well have been filled with warring factions that would have done nothing to promote peace in the region. By 2006, the warring and infighting between the various factions of Hamas and the PLO/Fatah became a long-awaited reality. Arafat had been the main player in Palestinian politics and terror for over forty years and held a stranglehold on the PLO and its activities.

Arafat had been chairman of the Palestine Liberation Organization, the titular head of Fatah, then president of the PA, and president of the State of Palestine as declared by the PLO in 1988. Fatah is the name used to describe the Palestinian National Liberation Movement and is the largest constituent within the PLO. The elections held in 2005 to elect Arafat's successor saw the ascension of Mahmoud Abbas (aka Abu Mazen). Elected on January 9, 2005, as president of the PA, Abbas and then Israeli Prime Minister Sharon faced some daunting challenges on both sides of their collective boundaries. Abbas had opposed the Intifada that had lingered since 2000 and aimed to support the U.S.-brokered "road map" to a peace settlement for the region. At an executive meeting on January 16, 2005, the PLO appealed for an end to armed attacks because they would provide excuses to the Israeli position of undermining Palestinian stability. With more than five thousand deaths since the start of the 2000 Intifada, and two-thirds of that number being Palestinians, the hope was that Abbas would get much-needed support of the Arafat factions within the Fatah movement so that he would eventually have sufficient clout to control the various factions that sought only armed conflict with Israel.

POLITICAL CONSIDERATIONS—HAMAS, FATAH, AND THE PALESTINIAN AUTHORITY

In 2015 and into 2016, saw a rise in attacks against Israelis—these were "lone wolf" attacks carried out usually with knives killing over twenty civilians in 2015. What precipitated these attacks and were they part of a wider plan by a broader group such as Hamas or the PA to pressure Israel? Some observers have started calling these attacks the start of the Third Intifada or the Intifada of Knives. However, to become an uprising or awakening which is the meaning of the Arabic word intifada, we would expect to see a possibly more defined series of attacks, whether these continue to evolve and spread farther afield only time will tell. What is important in this is the political end game for both Hamas and the PA leadership. The first two intifadas were the direct provocation viewed by the Palestinians of Israeli encroachment and action at the Temple Mount and as recent as the fall of 2015, there were rumors that Israel was planning to change the status quo that bans non-Muslim prayer at the Temple. So a third intifada is not out of the question. These random knife attacks would seem to be out of the control of the Palestinian leadership.

For the PA to maintain its somewhat tenuous hold on power in its territory, it does require a measure of conformity with the Israelis as well as support from them—their main rival for the hearts and minds of the Palestinians remains Hamas. In order to maintain its position, it has the political and economic support from Israel and by doing so is often viewed as too weak even by moderate Palestinians. Support for the PA is waning and support for Hamas is on the rise. If the PA were viewed as supporting and motivating a third intifada in efforts to shore up its support, it would have a negative effect on its Israeli relationship. Hamas, on the other hand, which is committed to the destruction of Israel is not currently equipped for a long drawn out military campaign. Much of its military arsenal is depleted specifically its long range rocket capability. The security barriers between Israel, Gaza, and the West Bank have been effective in halting Hamas' ability to tranship weapons and explosives. Both Hamas and the PA need also to be mindful of Islamic State. More so Hamas who are being challenged for power by both IS and Islamic Jihad who want a much more aggressive approach to achieve change for the Palestinians. In October 2015, Mahmoud al-Zahar, a senior official with Hamas said it was necessary to turn the attacks against Israelis into a full-fledged intifada. The Israelis on their part could forestall any possibility of a third intifada by offering concession to the PA in the form of increased work permits for Palestinians. The violence will continue and with IS and Islamic Jihad in the not too distant background, we expect greater violence to come regardless of Israeli concessions.

AL-FATAH

Al-Fatah (or *Al-Asifa*), the fighting organization within the PLO, actually predated the PLO by six years. Under the leadership of Yasser Arafat, it took total control of the PLO after the debacle of the 1967 Six-Day War. It is considered the largest terrorist group under the PLO banner—estimated to have a force of up to fifteen thousand Fedayeen. The group is financed mostly by wealthy Arab states.

Al-Fatah, however, has never managed to prove itself as a military machine against the Israelis in spite of its size and support structure, not even in the occupied territories of the Gaza Strip and the West Bank region of Jordan. Fatah was not able to prevent the Jordanian army from forcibly removing the PLO from its Jordanian training camps around Ajloun and Jerash in 1970, nor could it prevent a repetition in Lebanon, when the PLO was swept out by an Israeli invasion force in 1982.

OPERATION BAYONET

In Chapter 6, we discussed how members of Black September had succeeded in breaching the Olympic Games security at the 1972 Munich Games and massacred eleven Israeli athletes. For the Israeli government there was to be retribution, and the then Israeli Prime Minister Golda Meir secretly ordered Mossad to track down and kill all those involved in the planning and execution of the raid in Munich. Mossad agents spread throughout Europe and the Middle East and tracked their targets and assassinated them; they made one error—in 1973, in Lillehammer, Norway, they killed an innocent Moroccan waiter who looked like their intended target Ali Salameh. Between 1979 and 1982, Mossad and Israeli military commandos killed more than a dozen members, effectively eradicating the entire group responsible for the Olympic Games attack.

Black September is the name of the Al-Fatah terror wing and takes its name from the month of the Palestinians eviction from Jordan; **Black September** is the operational military arm of Al-Fatah.

In spite of the extensive Mossad operation in Europe, Black September rebounded as the defense arm of Al-Fatah, protecting it and Arafat from the extremist groups sponsored by Syria and Iraq, who were funding Abu Nidal's Black June.

During the 1960s and 1970s, Al-Fatah offered training facilities to a wide range of the Middle Eastern, European, Asian, and African terrorist organizations, as well as insurgent groups. Reciprocal arrangements within these groups allowed for terror operations to be carried out in each other's names, throughout the world. The arrangements also helped with the financial support required to allow the groups to maintain their operations.

Like the Palestinian people, Al-Fatah is spread throughout the Middle East but is primarily headquartered in Tunisia. Al-Fatah has been provided with aid from Saudi Arabia, Kuwait, and some of the other Arab states in the Persian Gulf region. Al-Fatah members have likewise received training from the former USSR as well as other former Communist Bloc countries.

The tangled web of Middle East terrorism does not start and finish with the PLO. The PLO, like most organizations that are spread over a wide area, will have many different points of political view.

ABU NIDAL ORGANIZATION

Sabri al-Banna (1937–2002), also known as Abu Nidal, spent his teenage years in Saudi Arabia and became actively involved in Arab Nationalism by joining the Ba'ath Party. His activities resulted in his arrest and subsequent expulsion from Saudi Arabia. He would become Fatah representative in Khartoum Sudan in 1968 and then in Baghdad in 1970. At the height of his influence in the 1970s and 1980s, he was considered the world's most dangerous terrorist. He rejected any idea of peaceful settlement with Israel and split from Yasser Arafat Fatah faction within the PLO over that issue in 1974. He became increasingly dangerous not only to the West but also to Yasser Arafat's control of the PLO.

Abu Nidal is the cover name for Sabri al-Banna, and the organization uses the following names:

- Revolutionary Council
- Palestinian National Liberation Movement
- Black June

- Black September
- The Revolutionary Arab Brigades
- The Revolutionary Organization of Socialist Muslims
- The Egyptian Revolution; Revolutionary Egypt
- Al-Asifa (The Storm)
- Al-Iqab (The Punishment)
- The Arab Nationalist Youth Organization

The Abu Nidal Organization (ANO) was recognized as one of the bloodiest terror groups operating in the Middle East. It certainly became a truly international terror operation by expanding its horizons and ability to strike at its enemies wherever they might be throughout the globe.

Al-Banna was drawn to Baghdad due to its "rejectionist" approach to those Middle East countries that favored a peace deal with Israel. "**Rejectionist**" is a Middle Eastern political term meaning unilateral refusal of any peaceful settlement with Israel. Iraq would have been considered one of the most extreme rejectionist states and one that would not sanction any such deals with Israel. This also had the effect of alienating those states in favor of moderation, such as Jordan and Egypt. Al-Banna's goals can be summarized simply: first and foremost, the destruction of Israel; and second, control of the PLO with the support of the rejectionist Iraqi government. It seemed to suit Iraq to have a terrorist group within its boundaries that would do its bidding in return for bases and logistical support. Al-Banna, under the protection of Saddam Hussein, trained about two hundred fighters for their joint cause.

Al-Banna believed that by creating terror on a world stage—rather than just the Middle East—he could meet his goals. His ruthless approach to terrorist actions and atrocities focused the world media and political attention firmly on the regional problems. Abu Nidal has carried out attacks in at least twenty countries and is responsible for the deaths of over nine hundred people. The group has not just targeted Israel but also the United Kingdom, the United States, and France, and those moderate Palestinians with the temerity to seek a peaceful settlement with Israel have also been attacked. Many attacks were spectacular in their audaciousness. The ANO credits itself with the assassination attempt on the Israeli ambassador outside the Dorchester Hotel in London, in June 1982. Three men, Hussein Ghassan Said, Marwan al-Banna, and Nawaf al-Rosan approached Israel's then ambassador Shlomo Argov as he got into his car after a banquet at the Dorchester Hotel, in Park Lane, London. Said shot Argov in the head. Al-Banna was Abu Nidal's cousin, Said a Jordanian, and the third of Argov's would-be assassins, al-Rosan, was a Baghdad intelligence colonel.[9]

The ambassador, Shlomo Argov, was seriously injured. This single terrorist attack precipitated another "eye for an eye—tooth for a tooth" revenge response from the Israelis, the 1982 invasion of Lebanon.

The PLO, under Yasser Arafat, denied any involvement in the attack. However, from the Israeli viewpoint, this was sufficient cause to attack, as "terrorism begets terrorism." Israel's response was a military hard line. The Israeli Air Force mounted a bombing raid on Palestinian camps in Beirut, killing at least fifty, with two hundred injured. It has been speculated that this act provided the Israelis with the excuse to conduct a full-scale invasion of southern Lebanon to purge the region of PLO fighters. The invasion commenced two days after the attack on Argov and was termed "Operation Peace for Galilee." The action was aimed at destabilizing Lebanon and forcing the PLO to flee the country to Syria, Tunisia, and Iraq. As Abu Nidal's notoriety increased, so too did the international make-up of the training camps in and around Baghdad. These training camps attracted radical European elements wishing to learn the trade of terrorism.

SIGNIFICANT INCIDENTS

Abu Nidal was successful in attacking aviation targets. Two such attacks date back to 1985:

December 27, Rome Airport, 08:15—Leonardo Da Vinci Airport is situated on the outskirts of Rome and is the principal international airport in Italy. At 08:15, four young Arabs threw hand grenades at a line of passengers waiting in the check-in line for the El Al flight. El Al's check-in desks are flanked by those of Trans World Airlines (TWA). The four Arabs then opened fire with Kalashnikov AK-47 assault rifles on the American and Israeli passengers waiting in line. Other passengers, including Greeks, Mexicans, and two Arabs, were killed in the attack. El Al has a record of being proactive in aviation security, and at Rome airport, its armed security staff returned fire, along with Italian police, and killed three and injured one of the terrorists. Fifteen passengers were killed and seventy injured.

The terrorists were Arabs, so the PLO was immediately denounced as having orchestrated the attack. In fact, Abu Nidal was the likely culprit; however, the incidents in Rome and Vienna were most likely aimed at discrediting Arafat and the PLO. Both Austria and Italy were well disposed to the Palestinian cause, and this action would have been designed to turn those countries against Arafat.

December 27, Vienna Airport, 08:15—this airport attack was timed to coincide with the Rome attack. There were fewer casualties in Vienna than in Rome: two dead and forty-six injured. The terrorists used the same modus operandi as their colleagues in Rome. However, they were able to fight their way out of the airport and escape temporarily by car, pursued by Austrian police. A gun battle followed, and one of the terrorists was killed and the remaining two surrendered. Again, this attack is attributed to Abu Nidal and his attempt to discredit Arafat.[10]

The ANO has shifted bases periodically from Iraq to Syria and has also had bases in Lebanon, Libya, and the Sudan. Its support network and financial aid came primarily from Iraq and Syria and, more recently, from Libya. Reports of Sabri al-Banna's death came on August 19, 2002, through Middle East news reports that he died of gunshot wounds in Baghdad. He was reportedly suffering from leukemia, and it is not known whether his death was murder or suicide.

Popular Front for the Liberation of Palestine

The Popular Front for the Liberation of Palestine (PFLP) was founded under the umbrella of the PLO in 1967. Its cofounders were George Habash and Wadi Haddad. Habash was born in Lydda, Palestine, in 1925, of a wealthy family that followed the teachings of the Greek Orthodox Church. Wadi Haddad was born in Safad, Galilee, in 1939.[11]

When the British mandate on Palestine ended in 1948, Habash was studying medicine at the American University in West Beirut. He and his family became refugees overnight and fled to Jordan. After completing his studies, Habash set up a clinic with another Palestinian from the Greek Orthodox Church, Wadi Haddad, in Amman, Jordan. It might seem strange that two committed doctors trained to save lives should organize a terrorist group. Both were committed to the belief in the 1950s that Gamal Abdel Nasser (Egypt) was the best hope for the liberation of Palestine. Both were extreme left-wing Marxists. In 1957, Nasser's supporters came close to toppling the Hashemite Monarchy of Jordan; however, King Hussein was able to defeat the uprising. Habash and Haddad fled and relocated their base of operations to Syria. The PFLP sprang from the Arab Nationalist Movement, which the two men had set up. Both viewed Yasser Arafat with loathing for his involvement with the United States and for his efforts at appeasement of the Israelis. Their philosophy espoused terror and was born of the rationale that Israel won its prize by terror, so Arabs should gain Palestine back similarly with terror (Figures 8-2, 8-3, and 8-4).

AL-AQSA MARTYRS BRIGADES

This group, unlike Hamas, does not strive for an Islamic state in Palestine but rather uses Islam as a weapon to inspire its struggle for an independent Palestine. The movement is linked to Yasser Arafat's Fatah faction and is responsible for numerous attacks against Israelis, both in the occupied territories and in Israel.

The Brigade takes its name from the Al-Aqsa Mosque, one of the holiest of Muslim sites. Shortly after the death of Yasser Arafat, they renamed themselves, for a short time, as Brigades of Martyr Yasser Arafat. As a relatively new organization, it did not make it to the U.S. State Department's list of foreign terrorist organizations until after a deadly suicide bombing in Jerusalem in March 2002.

Total Attacks	174
Total Deaths	867
Total Wounded	5,433
Average Deaths per Attack	5
Average Wounded per Attack	31.2

FIGURE 8-2 General statistics for suicide attacks in 2000–2015. *Source:* Chicago Project on Security and Terrorism, http://cpost.uchicago.edu.

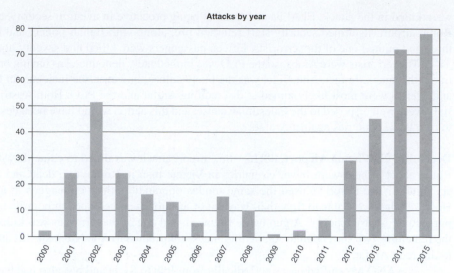

FIGURE 8-3   Suicide attacks by year in 2000–2015.   *Source:* Chicago Project on Security and Terrorism, http://cpost.uchicago.edu.

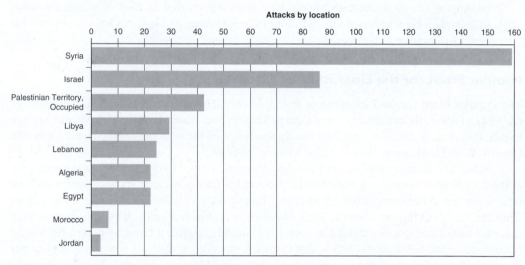

FIGURE 8-4   Suicide attacks by location in 2000–2015.   *Source:* Chicago Project on Security and Terrorism, http://cpost.uchicago.edu.

Denials of its links to the PLO and Fatah have been commonplace; however, investigative journalists from Britain's BBC exposed documents in November 2003 that showed that the Fatah organizations were, in fact, paying Al-Aqsa Brigades $50,000 a month. Further confirmation came in 2004 from the then Palestinian Prime Minister Ahmed Qurei, when he stated in an interview in *Asharq al-Awsat*, a London-based Muslim newspaper: "We have clearly stated that the Aqsa Martyrs Brigade are part of Fatah. We are committed to them and Fatah bears full responsibility for the group." Some of the group's more sensational attacks have been suicide attacks in Israel, most notably:

- **March 2, 2002**—Beit Yisrael suicide bomber kills eleven.
- **January 5, 2003**—Twenty-two killed in southern Tel Aviv bus depot.
- **April 17, 2006**—Two suicide bombers are believed to have carried out the attack at Tel Aviv's Old Central Bus Station. There were at least nineteen fatalities and one hundred and fourteen injured and nine in serious or critical condition.

The group's modus operandi is to employ a suicide belt for the individual bomber. The bomber wears a vest that covers the upper region of the body and is packed with explosives, bolts, nails, and ball bearings to inflict widespread injury. Hiding this style of bomb requires a heavy layer of outer clothing as the bomb belt will likely weigh between ten and forty pounds, depending on the size of the bomber. Al-Aqsa has been using young teenagers for this activity and, like Hamas, has also used female bombers.

The Gaza Strip

The Gaza Strip[12] is an area of 140 square miles (Figure 8-5). It is home to over 830,000 Palestinians and between 4,000 and 5,000 Israeli settlers. The Palestinian population is concentrated in four cities and eight refugee camps. Ninety-nine percent of the population is Sunni Muslim. Although Gaza City is one of the oldest cities in the world, the borders of the area we know as the Gaza Strip were only created in 1949. With the end of the British mandate in Palestine and the resulting Arab-Israeli battles, eventually two-thirds of this area was claimed by Israel. Egypt claimed the remaining third. After the creation of the Gaza Strip, more than 250,000 Palestinians escaped from the fighting in other areas of the Middle East and came to settle there. Since that time, Israel has refused to allow those Palestinians to return home, in defiance of UN Resolution 141. Most of the current inhabitants of the Gaza Strip are descendants of this group.

The Suicide Bomber

The Palestinian terrorists have successfully used suicide bombers to attack targets within Israel during the Intifada. The First Intifada (1987–1993), was a spontaneous explosion of popular resistance to the Israeli occupation. The Palestinians made a conscious and determined choice to consolidate their efforts in the struggle toward independence, regardless of the cost. Since the signing of the Oslo Agreements in 1993, Palestinian terrorist organizations have sent over seventy suicide bombers on missions against Israeli targets. *Yediot Aharonot*, the Israeli daily newspaper, presents a profile of the typical (Palestinian) suicide bomber:

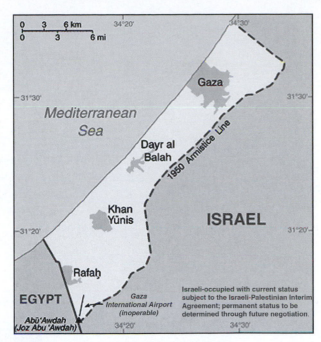

FIGURE 8-5 Map of Gaza Strip. *Source:* Central Intelligence Agency, *The World Factbook, 2008.*

- 47 percent of the suicide bombers have an academic education, and an additional 29 percent have at least a high school education.
- 83 percent of the suicide bombers are single.
- 64 percent of the suicide bombers are between the ages of eighteen and twenty-three; most of the rest are under thirty.
- 68 percent of the suicide bombers have come from the Gaza Strip.

In a column published in *The New York Times*, William Safire wrote that "the pride and joy of Arafat's arsenal was a weapon of mass terror that has no known defense: the human missile." Safire describes the suicide bombers as being "brainwashed" and considers the efforts necessary to enable the launching of these "missiles."[13] (Figures 8-6, 8-7, and 8-8).

HAMAS

Sheikh Ahmed Yassin

The central figure in the establishment of the Hamas organization was **Sheikh Ahmed Yassin**, a wheelchair-ridden "cleric," whose spiritual ideology fuels the current Palestinian terrorism. Many observers contend that Yassin preached only hatred and attacks on the Israeli state, whereas his comments and ideology would say otherwise. He continually called for suicide terrorism as part of a Muslim's religious obligation and stated in 1998 that "the day in which I will die as a shahid (martyr) will be the happiest day of my life." Yassin most certainly was an IDF target on more than one occasion. He was finally assassinated in a helicopter gunship attack by Israeli forces on March 22, 2004. Yassin had long called for Islamist terrorists to join with Hamas in global jihad and to strike at Western interests everywhere if Iraq were conquered. A global jihad involving young and impressionable Muslims from throughout Europe was responsible for the upsurge in suicide bombings in Israel and terrorist attacks and insurgency in Iraq. Yassin had the dubious distinction of providing the first female suicide bombers for his attacks against Israel. It was, in fact, a British suicide bomber who was responsible for the attack on Mike's Place in Tel Aviv in 2003. Although the crippled Sheikh was as much a symbol of Palestinian resistance as

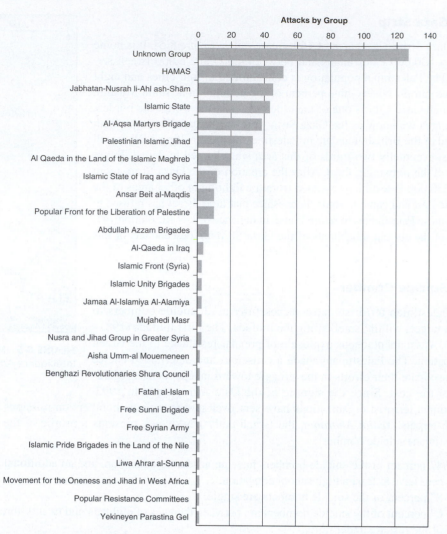

FIGURE 8-6   Suicide attacks by terror groups in 2000–2015.   *Source:* Chicago Project on Security and Terrorism, http://cpost.uchicago.edu.

Attacks and Casualties by Weapon			
Weapon Type	**attacks**	**killed**	**wounded**
Airplane	0	0	0
Belt Bomb	153	941	4,288
Car Bomb	231	2,184	5,433
Other	7	29	202
Unknown	2	19	50

FIGURE 8-7   Suicide attacks and weapons used in 2000–2015. *Source:* Chicago Project on Security and Terrorism, http://cpost.uchicago.edu.

Attackers, Attacks, and Casualties by Religion 2000–2015				
Religion	**Attackers**	**Attacks**	**Killed**	**Wounded**
Muslim (NA)	25	25	209	1,195
Muslim (Other)	1	1	19	70
Muslim (Sunni)	38	37	382	617
Unknown	306	294	2,553	7,970

FIGURE 8-8   Suicide attacks and attackers by religion in 2000–2015. *Source:* Chicago Project on Security and Terrorism, http://cpost.uchicago.edu.

was Yasser Arafat, Yassin was operating in a manner totally different from that of the Fatah organization. Yassin was active in sabotaging the peace accords of the 1990s and was hostile to the corrupt and secular PLO of Yasser Arafat. Under Yassin, Hamas aimed to replace the PLO with its own liberation of Palestine from the Jordan River to the Mediterranean Sea by means of violence and armed insurrection and establish an Islamic Palestinian State from the ruins of Israel.

Yassin joined the Muslim Brotherhood while studying at Cairo's Al-Azhar University and adopted the movement's belief that the rule of Islam should be imposed everywhere. After returning to Gaza, Yassin became actively involved in politics. In 1973, he founded the Islamic Center in Gaza, which soon controlled all religious institutions. In 1979, he founded the Islamic Organization; a body that Israeli military initially hoped would reduce the political influence of Yasser Arafat's Fatah movement. At the time, the Islamic Organization dealt mostly with welfare. But the ideology of the Muslim Brotherhood fueled Yassin's belief that the Israelis occupied an Islamic land whose ownership was not negotiable, and the sheikh gradually shifted from social and religious activity to clandestine activities against Israeli rule in the West Bank and Gaza.

Yassin was arrested in 1984 and sentenced to thirteen years in jail for possessing illegal arms, establishing a military organization, and calling for the annihilation of Israel. Yassin acknowledged that he founded an organization of religious activists with the goal of fighting nonreligious factions in the territories and carrying out "jihad" operations against Israel. This organization used monies from Islamic activists in Jordan to acquire large quantities of weapons. He was imprisoned until May 1985, when he was released in a prisoner exchange deal between Israel and the terrorist organization of Ahmed Jibril.

During the First Intifada in 1987, Yassin transformed his Islamic organization into a new body called Hamas. An acronym for the Islamic Resistance Movement, *Hamas* means "zeal" in Arabic. In Hebrew, it means evil.[14]

Ahmad Rashad, a research associate at the United Association for Studies and Research, attributes Hamas' popularity to several factors:[15]

- Its call for the liberation of all of Palestine.
- Its reputation as an efficient organization.
- Its honesty and lack of corruption.
- Its resilience to Israeli crackdowns.
- Its daring and successful attacks against Israeli military targets.
- Its home-based leadership within the occupied territories, as opposed to the PLO's expatriate direction.

The Hamas doctrine is a mixture of Palestinian nationalism mixed with Islamic fundamentalism and seeks to create an Islamic state from the Mediterranean Sea to the River Jordan. Hamas has for the last four decades received military and financial funding from Iran which like Hamas seeks the destruction of Israel. Hamas has in the past formed a unity government in Gaza with Al-Fatah but the two sides rarely came to agreement on any issues and open warfare erupted between the two in 2006 leading to Fatah's expulsion from Gaza in 2007, and since that time Hamas has governed the Gaza Strip. Being in government has not meant that Hamas has moderated its position on Israel and has launched hundreds of rockets both short and long range into Israel. Hamas likely supported the Egyptian uprising that overthrew the government of Hosni Mubarak in 2011; however, when in 2013, the Egyptian military removed the pro-Hamas Muslim Brotherhood President Mohammed Morsi, he was also suspected and investigated for his close ties to Hamas. The effect this had on Gaza and Hamas was that the Egyptian military destroyed nearly 90 percent of the tunnels connecting Gaza and Egypt. Hamas had invested a considerable amount of effort in their construction and accounted for a large portion of their annual budget. With the tunnel system all but destroyed, their annual budget shrank almost overnight. With the civil war raging in Syria, Hamas has been an open supporter of the Sunni groups against the Syrian Government—this has led to problems in getting funds from Iran which is backing and supporting the Syrian regime. Hamas had a political base in Damascus but relocated in 2012 due to the civil war. For its part Iran has viewed and continues to view Hamas as a "resistance movement."

Organization and Structure of Hamas

Hamas has been heavily involved in the local political scene in Gaza by putting up candidates for union representatives and the board of trade. Its political opponent is the PLO. Hamas dates back to the mid-1980s, when it identified itself as a wing of the Palestinian Muslim Brotherhood. The brotherhood had been seeking to establish a political wing for its organization, and in 1985 and 1986, it issued leaflets in Gaza to encourage a policy of civil disobedience. The leaflets were issued under names such as Harakat al-Kifah al-Musallah (Armed Struggle Movement), al-Murabitoon ala Ard al-Isra (The Steadfast on the Land of al-Isra), and Harakat al-Muqawama al-Islamiyya

(Islamic Resistance Movement, IRM). As the tensions grew in the mid-1980s, these communiqués became more and more politicized, and by 1988, the name "Hamas" began to appear.

IZZ AD-DIN AL-QASSAM BRIGADES

The **Izz ad-Din al-Qassam Brigades** were established in 1992 as the Hamas military wing, the numbers inside the wing may vary but are believed to be as many as twenty five thousand or more. Hamas likes to insist that the military wing is a separate entity and does not take direction from the political wing of Hamas. This can be likened to the Northern Ireland situation whereby the Provisional IRA have always stated that they have no connection or direction from the political wing Sinn Fein—we know this to be untrue and the same can be said for the Qassam Brigades and Hamas.

The military and intelligence wings of Hamas function independently; the intelligence wing gathers information and carries out surveillance operations on collaborators, drug dealers, and other antisocial activities and metes out punishments ranging from warnings to executions. It also distributes literature about Israeli recruitment policy and methods of collaboration and warns the populace about complicity. The intelligence wing also monitors crime in the region. The military wing has different, but well-defined, goals and objectives:

- Establish usar (families) and underground cells.
- Gather information on IDF activities for use in planned operations.
- Carry out training programs in hand-to-hand combat.
- Carry out military-style operations against the IDF.

Hamas military strikes have continued, predominantly against Israeli settlers in the territories, and suicide attacks mainly against civilian targets in Israel. Tactics are of a hit-and-run nature— planting a bomb or a suicide bombing in populated areas of Jerusalem, for example. Despite the PLO agreements with Israel, the Hamas movement declared Arafat a traitor for his agreements with the Zionist enemy. Hamas' response to these agreements has resulted in an increase in disputes with the PLO. Hamas receives its support from other Muslim countries, including Turkey, Iran, Afghanistan, Saudi Arabia and the Gulf States, Yemen, and even Malaysia. Hamas, although similar to the PLO, is willing to settle for a peace agreement with Israel, but has firm objectives that must be met before an agreement can be reached. In 1994, Hamas proclaimed that it was not opposed to peace; however, for it to ". . . cease military operations in Gaza and the West Bank . . ." the following conditions would have to be met:

1. Complete Israeli withdrawal from the occupied territories.
2. Disarm the settlers and dismantle the settlements.
3. Place international forces on the "green line" established in the occupied territories during the 1948 and 1967 wars.
4. Hold free and general elections to determine true representation of the Palestinian people.
5. The Council, which will be composed of electoral victors, shall represent the Palestinians in any negotiations that determine their future and that of the occupied territories.

Many Palestinians lauded the Gaza-Jericho Agreement of 1993, as they saw the new prospect of establishing their own legitimate Homeland. However, the slow progress since the agreement was reached and the continued development of the occupied territories by Israeli settlers has led to disillusionment by many Palestinians. This led to internal strife between PLO and Hamas, with pro-Arafat supporters being assassinated. Israel continued to wrangle over interpretation of sections in the agreement with the PLO throughout the remainder of the twentieth century. It is no surprise that acts of terror aimed at Israeli settlements and at targets in the West Bank and Gaza Strip continued unabated. Hamas has been able to retain sufficient military strength to protect its interests against the Israelis and has a broad political constituency, especially among the young, due to the combination of its fundamentalist religious message and social welfare programs.

Hamas' social programs, such as establishing clinics and schools, are an effective alternative to the PA's own social infrastructure, which was crumbling from corruption and mismanagement even before much of it was destroyed by the Israeli military. The current Intifada, which has continued remorselessly since September 2000, has enabled Hamas to garner and maintain support from other Palestinian factions including Fatah, in what is becoming an unshakeable national consensus.[16] The military wing of Hamas, the Izz ad-Din al-Qassam Brigades, has continued to carry out suicide attacks against Israel in spite of massive security operations to block all such attempts. Hamas declared an "all-out war" on Israel in January 2002 as a result of an Israeli incursion into the West Bank city of Tulkarem, which saw Israeli commandos shoot dead four Hamas bomb makers and the West Bank leader of Hamas, Yousef Soragji (Figure 8-9).

FIGURE 8-9 The military wing of the Palestinian Islamist movement Hamas takes part during a rally to mark the 12th anniversary of the death of assassinated Hamas spiritual leader Sheikh Ahmed Yassin. Izz ad-Din al-Qassam Brigades rally in Gaza City, Palestinian Territories—March 23, 2016. *Source:* ZUMA Press, Inc./ Alamy Stock Photo

The proximity of the Palestinians to the Israeli populous has made for somewhat easy pickings for the Hamas men of terror. Their targets have usually been civilian centers in Tel Aviv, Jerusalem, and other Israeli cities such as seaside resort towns like Netanya. Massive security clampdowns and numerous checkpoints on major arterial roads as well as street checks have not prevented repeated Hamas suicide missions. Each successful attack resulted in a swift and ferocious response by Israel targeting "suspected" militants in refugee camps in Palestinian territory. The cycle of violence prevailed throughout 2004 and up to the "truce" in early 2005. Israel also reverted to targeted assassination of "suspected" militants, mainly from Hamas. On the night of July 23, 2002, an F-16 fighter aircraft dropped a one-ton bomb on the Gaza home of a Hamas leader. The collateral damage was fourteen civilian deaths. This type of action by the Israeli forces could clearly be defined as a form of state terror. Israel claimed that it had not intended to kill innocent civilians; however, dropping a one-ton bomb in a residential neighborhood would likely have just that effect. In times of war, civilians are often involved in "mistakes." The direct targeting of civilians, as in the World War II German bombings of London and the allies' carpet bombing of Dresden, can be construed as atrocities or terrorism, as they have no specific military objective or significance. In targeting terrorists who hide or live in a civilian environment, such distinctions become blurred. From a Palestinian viewpoint, there is much to be gained in the propaganda war in showing dead civilians to eager news crews. What effect this style of reciprocal attack by Israel will have for peace is uncertain. Although calls for an investigation and wide criticism have ensued in the Israeli media, widespread condemnation has not been long lasting or particularly loud from the international community.

HAMAS–FATAH DISUNITY

When Hamas won the general election in March 2006, it set itself on a collision course with not only Israel but also Fatah. Hamas had managed through its grassroots social programs and community involvement to solidify its popularity in the Gaza Strip and have it recognized as a viable alternative to the corrupt Fatah-dominated West Bank. No doubt Hamas had watched and mirrored the Hezbollah approach to political power in Lebanon. The West's response to Hamas winning the election was the cessation of funds to the Palestinian National Authority. Hamas may have won the election; it had not won international recognition. Still listed as a terrorist entity, it was not going to be an easy transformation to an internationally recognized legitimate authority in the region. Hamas assumed far more political responsibility than it was capable of assuming, and with the rule of law on the streets effectively being the gun, internal battles followed. The Palestinian security apparatus has always been at the center of power in both Gaza and the West Bank and taking control of that apparatus sparked the start of violence in 2007. Fatah and Hamas sparred in the political arena over control and attempted to come up with a power-sharing agreement through the Saudi Arabia-brokered Mecca Agreement. The deal disintegrated with the battle over control of security forces. In its effort to effectively control Fatah, Hamas mounted an offensive in the Gaza Strip in June 2007.

Hamas believed by doing so, it would be able to negotiate from a position of strength with Fatah over the security forces. This had the effect of two separate states being controlled by warring Palestinian factions, something that Israel would be quick to take advantage of. Hamas gunmen, in one week of June 2007, tore down the portraits of Yasser Arafat from office walls and removed the Palestinian flag, replacing it with the green banner of Islam. Hamas forcibly removed Fatah from Gaza and executed many of its key representatives. Secular nationalism of the sort Fatah has stood for was beginning to look like the weak force and radical Islam as the strong force.[17] In January 2007, Hamas announced that it would never negotiate with Israel and would not be abiding by any of the treaties that Fatah had previously negotiated with the Israelis. The March 2007 kidnapping of a British Broadcasting Corporation (BBC) journalist

Alan Johnson in Gaza by members from the shadowy group calling itself the Army of Islam provided the opportunity for Hamas to demonstrate to the international community its ability not to act and control events in Gaza. The Army of Islam is made up of ex-members of Hamas, so it is very likely that Hamas would be able to exercise influence to have the journalist released unharmed. The Hamas-brokered release of Johnson in July 2007 did little to deter the Israelis from making inroads with the Fatah-controlled West Bank to further curtail Hamas in Gaza and prevent any reconciliation between Hamas and Fatah. The Israeli government of Ehud Olmert agreed to a meeting with Mahmoud Abbas and also granted a group of wanted exiled Palestinian leaders including the controversial figure, Nayef Hawatmeh, permission to enter the West Bank for the meeting. Hawatmeh had been the mastermind behind the 1974 Ma'alot massacre. Ma'alot is located in the Western Galilee, twenty-kilometers east of Nahariya. Ma'alot was founded in the 1950s when hundreds of thousands of immigrants came to Israel from North Africa, refugees from hostile Arab nations where they were no longer safe. The Israeli Government at that time decided to place new immigrants in development towns such as Ma'alot. On May 15, 1974 (Israel's Independence Day), a group of 11th grade students were on a field trip to the Golan. That night the children were housed at a school in Ma'alot where they slept on the floor. During the night, three Arab terrorists dressed as IDF soldiers attacked the school, killing the guard and some of the children. Some of the children escaped by jumping out of a window on the second floor and the rest were held as hostages.

The terrorists were identified as members of the Democratic Front for the Liberation of Palestine (DFLP) who had infiltrated from Lebanon. They demanded the release of Arab terrorists from Israeli prisons, or they would start to kill the children. The deadline was set at 6:00 P.M. the same day. Israel's policy forbade negotiation with terrorists; the plight of the children forced an exception. By 3:00 P.M., a decision was reached to negotiate, but the terrorists refused a request for more time. At 5:45 P.M., a unit of the elite Golani brigade stormed the building. All of the terrorists were killed in the assault, but not before they took the lives of twenty-one children. There were a total of twenty-six victims, including several people murdered by the terrorists on their way to the school the night before. In Beirut, demonstrations honoring the fallen fedayeen as noble martyrs of the cause were ordered by Nayef Hawatmeh, the DFLP leader.[18]

For the Israelis it was crucial to develop a dialogue of sorts with Fatah on the West Bank to prevent Hamas becoming the only Palestinian (Islamist) voice for the region. The Ma'alot massacre took place nearly a half century ago, but it is still fresh in Israeli memories and so is the name of the mastermind behind the attack, Marwan Bargouti. The other concern for Israelis is that any amnesty may also include demands for his release. The Palestinians wanted a large number exchanged for a captured Israeli soldier, Corporal Shalit. On June 25, 2006, Shalit—a corporal at the time—was captured in a cross-border raid near the Kerem Shalom crossing to the Gaza Strip by Hamas terrorists. The terrorists dug underneath the border from Gaza, emerged on the Israeli side and subsequently sprayed automatic fire and grenades toward Shalit's tank which had been on patrol. Two IDF soldiers (Pavel Slutsker and Chanan Barak) were killed in the attack, three others were wounded and Shalit, wounded as well, was abducted and forced back into Gaza. On October 11, 2011, Prime Minister Netanyahu announced the signing of an exchange deal for the release of Shalit. Assembled through German mediators and the Egyptian government, the deal stipulated that Israel would release one thousand and twenty-seven Palestinian prisoners in a staggered move over the coming months. In the early afternoon of October 18, 2011, Shalit was set free and returned to Israel after one thousand nine hundred and forty days in Hamas captivity.[19]

Marwan Bargouti was an early follower of Yasser Arafat. He was elected to the Palestinian Parliament in 1996 and was an outspoken opponent of Israel. He was a member of Fatah and leader of Tanzim, the military wing of Fatah. He was accused by Israel of founding the Al-Aqsa Martyrs and he became a target for both arrest and probably assassination by Israel. He survived a missile attempt on his life when his bodyguard's car was hit in 2001. He was subsequently arrested in Ramallah the following year by Israeli Special Forces and spirited back to Israel. He was sentenced to life in prison. He has been active in politics from his prison cell where he managed to help design the Mecca Agreement, which attempted to bring about a national unity government for the Palestinians in 2007. While he remains popular in the Palestinian territories he would appear to be solid bargaining chip for Israel. He was not released as part of the prisoner exchange for Corporal Shalit.

WEAPONRY

The ability to strike at Israeli settlements is far easier from the West Bank than it is from the Gaza Strip, which borders an area of Israel that is sparsely populated. The mini civil war that developed briefly over the summer of 2007 did not diminish Hamas's capabilities or their goals of attacking Israel. Hamas's arsenal contains assault rifles and AK 47s, but they have also built up an array of improvised rocket devices, considered highly unstable, which will only get to perfection with more practice. They have developed short-range rockets without any technical guidance system to support target identification. The rockets, named as "Qassam Rockets" after the Syrian Cleric Izz al-Din al-Qassam, have been used extensively by Hamas against Israeli civilian targets. These devices are steel tubes with their stabilizing fins welded to their side using potassium nitrate fertilizer and sugar as the main propellant with TNT as the warhead. The longest-range missile to have struck any target has been twelve kilometers. These missiles have a launch team of between five and ten people dependent on the type and size of the rocket being fired, and this brings the operators into considerable risk of being spotted by Israeli drones in the skies above, or unmanned aerial vehicles (UAVs).

FATAH AND HAMAS—UNITY GOVERNMENT

The Arab spring of 2011 saw widespread popular uprisings throughout the Middle East not least in Egypt. Both Hamas and Fatah met in Cairo in May 2011 and agreed to settle their hostilities—for the time being, but the long- and short-term results of this need further review. The complexity of Middle East politics now has Hamas and its Islamic extreme doctrines calling for the destruction of Israel supposedly aligned with a secular Fatah and the PA, which recognizes the right of Israel to exist. Just how these two groups can coexist and form a unity government is questionable. Maybe the levels of unrest in the Middle East are seen by Hamas as an opportunity for popular demonstrations against Israel. The peace treaty negotiated with Egypt could be in jeopardy—whatever brand of democracy surfaces in Egypt will have a bearing on how Hamas and the PA react. Hamas may not be as militant or as popular with Palestinians as it was six or seven years ago, so it may become a minority in any newly elected Palestinian government. The issues internally for both Fatah and Hamas will revolve around their internal security apparatus. In February 2007, they signed their first unity government agreement in Mecca which lasted less than four months, when in June 2007 Hamas took control of the Gaza Strip and forced Fatah representatives out. On June 14th President Mahmoud Abbas dissolved the Unity Government and declared a state of emergency. The territory is effectively split in two with Hamas controlling the government in Gaza and the West Bank under the control of the Palestinian National Authority. In early 2016, the Fatah movement and Hamas reached a new accord and a reconciliation agreement was established, at which point the Palestinian Prime Minister Rami Hamdallah announced that he would resign and form a new National Unity Government. A crucial element of the agreement was the deal on the control of the Rafah Crossing between Gaza and Egypt; it is the sole authorized crossing for Gazans to enter Egypt and is of key economic importance to Gaza. Under the control of Hamas, the crossing had been mostly closed by the Egyptians to prevent jihadists making moves into Egypt. The intention being that the Rafah Crossing will be controlled by Fatah which will make the Egyptians more amenable to opening this route to and from the Gaza Strip.

Palestinian Liberation Front

A group best known for pioneering and perfecting the art of international airline hijacking in the late 1960, they split from the PFLP General Command in the mid-1970s and then again into pro-Syrian, pro-Libyan, and pro-PLO factions. Its membership cadre is estimated to be between fifty and one hundred.[20] Palestinian Liberation Front (PLF) based its operations in Iraq, having moved there from Tunisia after the attack on the cruise liner *Achille Lauro* in October 1985 and the murder of a wheelchair-bound, U.S. citizen Leon Klinghoffer. Abu Abbas, a long-time supporter of Yasser Arafat, led the PLF. Abbas was born in a refugee camp in Syria in 1948. He was a long-time Palestinian terrorist with a price on his head after the murder of the *Achille Lauro* passenger, Leon Klinghoffer. Abbas rose to prominence in the PLO and was elected to the powerful and influential Executive Committee of the PLO in 1982. Until 1985, he operated from Tunisia. After the *Achille Lauro* incident, Italian authorities briefly detained him until he was flown to Yemen (Figure 8-10).

TERRORIST ATTACK BRIEF

Terrorist Group: Palestine Liberation Front (PLF)

Case Facts: On 7 October 1985, the *Achille Lauro*, an Italian luxury liner, with some 100 mostly elderly passengers on board, was hijacked in Egyptian waters by terrorists representing the Palestine Liberation Front (PLF). The ship's captain was ordered to sail for Tartus, Syria. That night, the hijackers informed Egyptian authorities of their action by radio and stated their demand for release of fifty Palestinian prisoners held by Israel. The next day, after being denied docking rights at Tartus by Syrian authorities, the terrorists decided to kill one of their hostages to prove their determination. Pushing the elderly, wheelchair-bound Jewish-American passenger Leon Klinghoffer to the side of the ship, the leader of the terrorists shot him in the head and chest and then threw his body overboard. The Syrians still continued to deny the ship docking rights, but before a second passenger could be killed, the terrorists received a radio message from PLF leaders directing them to leave the passengers unmolested and to head to Port Said, Egypt. Once there, the Egyptian government, unaware that Klinghoffer had been murdered, provided the hijackers with safe passage in exchange for freeing the ship and its passengers.

Investigation: Through clever intelligence work, the National Security Council staff determined that the terrorists were still in Egypt and were about to be flown to Tunisia on an Egypt Air 737 airliner. They reasoned that, with a lot of luck, the United States might be able to intercept the plane before it reached its destination. Saratoga (CV 60), with Commander Task Force (CTF) 60 on board, was steaming northward through the Adriatic Sea toward a port call at Dubrovnik, Yugoslavia, on the afternoon of October 10, following completion of a major North Atlantic Treaty Organization (NATO) exercise in the central Mediterranean.

Suddenly, the carrier received orders from Sixth Fleet headquarters to reverse course and to launch the alert combat air patrol. Despite the ship's "Alert 60" status, two F-14A Tomcats and an E-2C Hawkeye were airborne within twenty-two minutes. Apprised of the emerging situation by Sixth Fleet, Rear Admiral David Jeremiah, CTF 60, immediately alerted his staff that Saratoga was going after the hijackers, even though the plane's exact takeoff time from Egypt, the route it was flying to Tunisia, and its altitude were unknown.

FIGURE 8-10   Achille Lauro Hijacking—The Mediterranean—October 1985.   *Source:* Based on Achille Lauro hijacking ends, 1985. http://www.history.com/this-day-in-history/achille-lauro-hijacking-ends.

Israel remained the prime target of Palestinian terrorist attacks during 1990. Escalating tensions resulted in a number of serious incidents during the year. On May 30, Israeli forces foiled an attempted seaborne assault against the Tel Aviv beachfront. Four terrorists were killed and twelve captured. The attack was carried out by the Palestine Liberation Front, led by Abu Abbas, with substantial assistance from Libya. Former PLO chairman Arafat's failure to take concrete actions against the PLF, a constituent PLO member, led to the suspension of U.S. dialogue with the PLO.[21]

Abbas was an outspoken supporter of Saddam Hussein during the Gulf War and was subsequently captured by U.S. forces during the U.S.-led invasion of Iraq in 2003 He was never brought to trial and died of natural causes while in custody the following year.

The PLF has garnered material support from the Ba'athist regime in Syria and the Libyan regime of Colonel Qaddafi. It has a presence in Gaza and the West Bank as well as in Lebanon.

The Popular Front for the Liberation of Palestine—General Command

A secular Marxist group, The Popular Front for the Liberation of Palestine—General Command (PFLP-GC) traces its history back to 1959 and the formation of the PLF by former Syrian Army Captain Ahmed Jibril. The left-wing PLF led by George Habash merged with the PFLP in 1967. Ahmed Jibril was actively supported and sponsored by Syria, whereas Habash was seeking a political solution and negotiations with Egypt. The differences between the two were vast and never likely to be settled amicably. In 1968, Jibril split from George Habash and headquartered his new group the PFLP-GC in Damascus. Like its Syrian sponsors, the PFLP-GC wanted armed confrontation with Israel, and Syria was content for them to be their proxy in attacking Israeli interests. They launched attacks internationally to gain broader attention; in 1970, they detonated a bomb on board a Swiss Air flight between Munich and Tel Aviv killing over forty passengers. In 1974, suicide bombers were used for the first time in an attack on Israel, killing eighteen near Kiryat Shmona. While the wider Palestinian movement and groups sought to become more legitimate in dealing with Israel with the eventual goal of Palestinian statehood, the PFLP-GC under Jibril followed the direction of Syria and continued to target Israel. This led to bitter internal struggles and infighting. However, the PFLP-GC continued to openly oppose moves by the PLO to negotiate and make concessions to Israel, joining a rejectionist front of leftist Palestinian groups and resigning from the PLO Executive Committee and Central Council. In 1984, the PFLP-GC was evicted from the PLO and shifted further away from Palestinian interests. In 1986, the PFLP-GC and elements of Syrian military intelligence were implicated in the Hindawi affair—the attempted bombing of an Israeli El Al flight from London. Syria came under fire from the international community, and the United States withdrew its ambassador from Damascus. After that, Syria relied more and more on the PFLP-GC to carry out terrorist operations on its behalf. For a period of time in the 1980s, the group was set up in Tripoli and sponsored by the late Libyan leader Colonel Qaddafi. They remained somewhat marginalized in the mid-1990s as Arafat established the PA that controlled much of the West Bank and Gaza Strip. Since the second Palestinian Intifada in September 2000, PFLP-GC has tried to reassert itself by attacking Israel. The U.S. State Department classifies the PFLP and PFLP-GC as foreign terrorist organizations.

Democratic Front for the Liberation of Palestine

A strong and vocal opponent to the Israeli peace accord with the PLO; this Marxist group split from the PFLP in 1969.[22] DFLP believes the Palestinians can only achieve their goals by mass uprising. Its political position in the 1980s was somewhere in between those of Arafat and the rejectionists. DFLP again split into two more factions in 1991—one pro-Arafat and one hard-line group headed by Nayef Hawatmeh. This group was suspended from the PLO for opposing the 1993 Declaration of Principles. The DFLP is estimated to have a membership totaling about 500 activists across both groups and has carried out its terror campaign mostly in Israel and the occupied territories. Since 1988, the DFLP has been involved only in cross-border raids into Israeli areas. It received its funding and logistical support primarily from Qaddafi's Libyan regime and Syria's Assad government.

Palestinian Islamic Jihad

The **Palestinian Islamic Jihad (PIJ)** an Islamic nationalist group with roots among the Palestinian fundamentalists in the Gaza Strip dating back to the 1970s. The founders of the PIJ, Fathi Shaqaqi and Abd al-Aziz Awda, were students in Egypt and members of the Egyptian Muslim Brotherhood until the late 1970s when they decided that the brotherhood was becoming too moderate and insufficiently committed to the Palestinian cause. The PIJ emerged as a separate entity committed to the militant destruction of Israel and the reestablishment of a sovereign Palestinian state. The PIJ, despite being a Sunni group, took inspiration from revolutionary, theocratic Shia ideals espoused during the 1979 Iranian Revolution that established an Islamic regime. The group is much smaller than its Islamic brothers in Hamas and offers no political agenda or social programs. Its ideals continue to be the destruction of Israel and the establishment of a Palestinian state.

Ramadan Abdullah Shallah— Secretary General, PIJ

Ramadan Abdullah Shallah was born in the Gaza Strip and spent five years at Durham University in northern England, where he reportedly coordinated the activities of PIJ by sending and receiving orders to and from cells of the organization in Gaza and the West Bank. From 1990 to 1995, Shallah lived in Tampa, Florida, where he was a leading member of the Islamic Concern Project (aka the Islamic Committee for Palestine). The organization distributed official PIJ literature used to indoctrinate followers by glorifying PIJ suicide bombers as martyrs. After PIJ leader Fathi Shaqaqi's death in October 1995, Shallah became the new leader of PIJ and a member of its Shura (consultative) Council.[23] The PIJ strikes at both Arabs and Jews alike and has not limited its area of operation to the territories and the Gaza Strip, like Hamas. In 1991, the group attacked a tourist bus in Egypt, killing eleven passengers, nine of them Israelis. Its method of attack in Israel and the occupied territories has been suicide bombings of bus stations and markets.[24] PIJ continues to front attacks on Israeli targets in both Israel and the territories, although since the 9-11 attacks on the United States and Israel's erection of the security fence has limited its activities. With respect to any disengagement plan that the Israelis have envisaged, the PIJ network in Northern Samaria has emerged as one of the most tangible threats to the implementation of the disengagement plan, as its leadership questions the value of sticking to the policy of calm (tahadiyah). The PIJ network, encompassing Jenin and Tulkarm and all of the villages in between, was responsible for a major attack within Israel—the suicide bombing at the Stage Club in Tel Aviv on February 25, 2005, in which five Israelis were killed and fifty more were wounded. One of its senior commanders, Luay Saadi, one of Israel's "most wanted" terrorists was killed by the Israeli army in October 2005 in retaliation for his planning of the Stage Club bombing. After the attack, the PIJ leadership in Damascus engaged in evasive tactics designed to escape the Israeli response. Signs were accumulating that indicated that PIJ was back in action, but they were credited with only one attack in March 2007. Israeli intelligence sources also saw evidence that the military wing in the northern West Bank had resumed planning major attacks.[25]

Kach and Kahane Chai (Motto: Terror against Terror)

Kach is a Jewish ultranationalist group operating in Israel and founded by the late Rabbi Meir Kahane, founder of the Jewish Defense League (JDL), a U.S. organization dedicated to protecting American Jews. The JDL became increasingly militant, espousing violence and vigilantism to curb anti-Semitism. The Kach movement (Hebrew for "Thus") emerged from this international JDL office.

In 1984, the Kach and Kahane Chai organization was declared a terrorist organization by the Israeli government under the 1948 Terrorism Law.[26] Binyamin Kahane, the son of Rabbi Meir Kahane, who was assassinated in the United States in 1990, lead this group. They aim to restore the biblical state of Israel and purge the land of all Arabs. The Kach and Kahane was an outspoken supporter of the terrorist attack on the Ibrahimi Mosque by Dr. Baruch Goldstein in February 1994. On several occasions over the last thirty years it has attempted, unsuccessfully, to turn itself into a political movement by running candidates for the Israeli Knesset; however, after the Goldstein attack, the government banned the group from Israeli politics. The group has threatened and attacked Palestinians and Arabs in Hebron and the West Bank and is an embarrassment to the Israeli government. The group was violently opposed to Ariel Sharon's disengagement plan and the dismantling of Jewish settlements in both the Gaza Strip and the West Bank.

The 1993 Declaration of Principles—at its signing seen as breakthrough agreement—has staggered on with no outward resolution of the critical issues in the region; however, it is important to list its main points.

DECLARATION OF PRINCIPLES

Article VI: Preparatory Transfer of Powers and Responsibilities

1. Upon entry into force of this Declaration of Principles and the withdrawal from the Gaza Strip and the Jericho area, a transfer of authority from the Israeli Military Government and its Civil Administration to the authorized Palestinians for this task, as detailed herein, will commence. This transfer of authority will be of a preparatory nature until the inauguration of the Council.

2. Immediately after the entry into force of this Declaration of Principles and the withdrawal from the Gaza Strip and the Jericho area, with the view to promoting economic development in the West Bank and Gaza Strip, authority will be transferred to the Palestinians on the following spheres: education and culture, health, social welfare, direct taxation, and tourism. The Palestinian side will commence in building the Palestinian Police Force, as agreed upon. Pending the inauguration of the Council, the two parties may negotiate the transfer of additional powers and responsibilities, as agreed upon.[27]

The Declaration of Principles signaled a major breakthrough and a new hope for a definitive solution to the Palestinian question, even peace in the area that, of course, has not been realized.

The full text of the Declaration of Principles is not included in this chapter; however, its contents form the basis and fabric for both the Israelis and the Palestinians to move toward the goal of a homeland for the displaced Palestinians. It has been a very bumpy road since 1993, and whether the two sides are able to fulfill the contents of the declaration and meet all that is stipulated remains to be seen. There is considerable resentment in the territories and Gaza Strip of the slow pace toward meeting the goals of the principles.

It is worthwhile to note that the Oslo strategy was to redivide and subdivide an already fractured and fragmented Palestinian territory into three subzones: A, B, and C, in ways entirely devised and controlled by the Israeli side, because the Palestinians were, until very recently, a "map-less" society. At the negotiations, there were no Palestinian representatives with any geographical knowledge who could either argue or contest decisions.[28]

Recruitment and indoctrination into the terrorist cause is believed to continue unabated in the Gaza Strip as the next generation of terrorists are groomed and schooled in hatred aimed at their Israeli neighbors. Children as young as age seven are parading with automatic assault weapons and singing patriotic Palestinian songs that glory in the destruction of Israel.[29] This is hardly a harbinger of a peaceful settlement in the years to come. The core of mistrust between the Palestinians and the Israelis, in both words and deeds, runs deepest in the occupied territories.

JORDAN

The Hashemite Kingdom of Jordan has been a "refuge" for thousands of displaced Palestinians from West Bank villages for the last four decades and continues to receive a mass of refugees from the conflicts in Syria and Iraq (Figure 8-11). Current figures indicate that the kingdom has absorbed 1.7 million refugees, almost 13 percent of its total population. Considerable support and sympathy for the Palestinian cause probably exists among the Jordanian population. The current King Abdullah's wife Rania is Palestinian. Jordan became a safe haven for the Palestinians after Israel's creation, but problems arose with so many extreme elements actively embroiled in terrorist campaigns against Israel. The PFLP had training camps within striking distance of Jordan and for the leadership of the PFLP, the king of Jordan himself became a target. There were open confrontations in the streets of Amman between Fedayeen members and the late King Hussein's troops. Wadi Haddad and George Habash were desperate to get the "Palestinian question" into the focus of world attention. It is not certain whether the two men were actually in concert over the operation, but, in July 1970, Haddad was in Beirut with Leila Khaled, a committed member of PFLP, planning one of the most spectacular hijacking events of the twentieth century. The hijacking of international airliners to Dawson's Field in Jordan provoked a reaction around the world, and the traveling public experienced the start of passenger screening security at airports worldwide. King Abdullah inherited the Kingdom from his father and was educated in the United States and at Sandhurst, the British Military Academy. One might be tempted to think that Jordan would be in line for the next Arab Spring but King Abdullah appears to have been masterly in holding onto the reins of power and the people within the kingdom. He has funneled significant amounts of foreign aid into his military and police apparatus and in doing so has shown the United States that this is a stable and friendly regime—he has gone further by shifting on a regular basis those in senior military positions and given positions of high rank to Bedouin tribal members and conscripted many Bedouins into the armed forces. By maintaining his tight grip and control on his powerful military machine he has been able to maintain security overall and appease tribal unrest among the Bedouin.

Jordan's ties to other Arab states are also important; it has strong historic ties to Saudi Arabia and is viewed as a stable Sunni Muslim kingdom. Good relationships with the Gulf States as well as Egypt exist. King Abdullah's brother in law is Sheikh Mohammed bin Rashid al-Maktoum of the United Arab Emirates.

FIGURE 8-11 Map of Jordan. *Source:* Central Intelligence Agency, *The World Factbook, 2008.*

Hijacking of Airliners: A New Tactic?

Over the last half of the twentieth century, there have been so many terrorist attacks that it is sometimes hard to recall them. The spectacular ones seem to be held in our mind: the Munich Olympic Games massacre; the Iranian Embassy siege in London; the destruction of the U.S. Marine barracks in Beirut, Lebanon; the Oklahoma City bombing; Pan Am Flight 103 over Lockerbie; the Air India bombing off the coast of Ireland; and, of course, the New York World Trade Center and the Pentagon attacks are etched in our memories. The hijacking of airliners and hostage-taking has the immediate ability to focus world attention through media coverage.

The actions of the PFLP almost led to a civil war in Jordan and certainly led King Hussein to forcibly remove the PLO from the territory. The hijackings were audacious for their sheer nerve, daring, and lack of any respect for international convention.

The first hijacking took place on a TWA Boeing 707 at 11:50 A.M. on September 6, 1970. The plane was en route from Frankfurt, West Germany, to New York. The airliner had a full complement of crew and one hundred and forty-five passengers when it was seized in the skies above Belgium. The pilot was ordered to fly to Jordan. At about the same time, a Swissair DC-8 with a similar number of passengers and crew was seized over France and flown to the same location, Dawson Field, Jordan. At about 2:00 P.M., an attempt was made to hijack a third airliner, an El Al flight en route to Amsterdam from Tel Aviv. Due to confusion at check-in, the El Al hijack team was reduced to three members: Leila Khaled and Patrick Arguello and the third, an Arab. When the pilot refused to obey their instructions, a violent fight ensued and a flight attendant was shot. An Israeli sky marshal killed the Arab hijacker. Khaled and Arguello were overpowered, and the aircraft landed at London's Heathrow Airport, where they were both arrested. The remaining members of Khaled's group who had failed to make the flight hijacked a Boeing 747 operated by Pan American Airlines.

The airliner flew to Beirut, where it refueled and went on to Cairo. The PFLP blew the 747 up on the ground at Cairo Airport, after the crew and passengers were taken off. This action by the PFLP, though aimed at the international arena, was a statement to the Egyptian government about its acceptance of the Middle East peace agreement. With hostages numbering about 300 being held in Jordan, the PFLP laid out its demands to the international community. The hijackers demanded the release of the three members of the PFLP who had been jailed for an earlier attack on Zurich Airport, and who were presently languishing in a Swiss jail. They also demanded the same for terrorists being held in West Germany for the Munich Airport attack. Their third demand involved Leila Khaled's release from police custody for attempting to hijack an El Al airliner over Europe. The British government of conservative Prime Minister Edward Heath was in utter turmoil over how to deal with this problem, so the PFLP gave it another nudge by hijacking a BOAC VC-10 and adding one hundred and ten British passengers to the hostage list. After heavy pressure and diplomatic talks, the PFLP moved the hostages to the comfort of Amman, Jordan. Over the next two weeks, the hostages were moved around Amman in small groups before all were released on September 30, 1970. The PFLP destroyed the British, Swiss, and American airliners at Dawson Field before the watchful lenses of the world's media.[30]

The last British hostages were released on the same day that Leila Khaled was flown out of the United Kingdom and back to the Middle East. Israel has always steadfastly refused to negotiate with terrorists, and it strongly criticized the Western powers for giving in.

LOD (Israel) Airport Attack May 30, 1972

In May 1972, a daring attack led by Kozo Okomato, Yasuda Yasuki, and Okudeira Takushi from the Japanese Red Army, possibly acting on the behest of the Black September group, attacked Lod Airport. The team arrived at the airport near Tel Aviv and pulled from their luggage Czech-made 7.62 machine guns. They opened fire indiscriminately in the terminal building and killed twenty-four instantly and injured seventy-seven others. Two of the attackers were killed by Israeli security; Kozo Okomato was tried by Israel and sentenced to life in prison but was released in May 1985 in a prisoner exchange with the PFLP-General Command. Kozo fled to Libya. In February 1997, he was arrested again, this time in Lebanon, but was deported; he eventually disappeared. Today he is rumored to be living in North Korea.[31]

These events pushed the Middle East to the brink of war. The Bonn Summit conference of major Western powers met in 1978 and agreed to sanctions against states that aided and abetted the hijacking of aircraft. The countries agreeing were the United States, the United Kingdom, Canada, France, Italy, Japan, and West Germany.

Jordan in the Twenty-First Century

Jordan's wider role in Middle Eastern affairs is relevant for the Palestinian government of Mahmoud Abbas, who is considered to be pro-Jordanian. To assist in security, Jordan's King Abdullah has allowed Palestinian fighters to return to the West Bank. Most of these fighters have been trained by the Jordanian military and are pro-Jordan. Abdullah has also requested the Israelis to allow this action to take place. This is Jordan's opportunity to play a major role in the security of the West Bank, a region it considers part of its Hashemite Kingdom. At the same time, any attacks against the stability of the Abbas regime could be tempered with the presence of Jordanian-trained Palestinian fighters. Jordan shares land borders with Iraq, Syria, the Palestine territories, and Israel. One of its many notorious citizens is Abu Musab al-Zarqawi, born in Jordan in 1966 of Palestinian parentage. Zarqawi was al Qaeda's representative in Iraq and the founder of al Qaeda in Iraq, and subsequently the Islamic State in Iraq and the Levant. He had been involved with terrorist activities for many years and is thought to have been one of Osama bin Laden's chief supporters. He is believed to have been in Afghanistan in 1990–1991, and while the intervening years record little of his activities, he did surface again in 1999 when he planned the Millennium attack on the Radisson Hotel in Amman Jordan. The plot was discovered and so was his involvement—he was sentenced to fifteen years in prison in absentia. He returned to Afghanistan in 2000 and set up training camps that specialized in biochemical weapons training.

When the Taliban were routed in 2001, Zarqawi was suffering from a leg wound that took him to Iraq, where his leg was amputated. During his recovery in Iraq he set up a base for his training operations, presumably with the blessing of the Iraqi regime. Zarqawi was linked to the assassination of a U.S. official in Jordan in late 2002. He returned to northern Iraq in 2003, and the fruits of his training were discovered in Britain when several suspects, who had direct links to him, were arrested for plotting to put ricin toxin into the military food supply.

Zarqawi continued to focus attacks also on his homeland, Jordan. In November 2005, he dispatched suicide bombers to target three U.S.-owned hotels in Amman, killing fifty-seven and injuring hundreds; all the casualties were Jordanians. Zarqawi died in a targeted bombing by the United States in June 2006.

Jordan has managed to temper relations with Israel over the years and King Abdullah has allowed the influx of Palestinians to Jordan providing a safe haven yet again for stateless Palestinians. With more than half of its annual budget made up of foreign financial aid, this small relatively stable kingdom will continue to receive adequate support to maintain a balance of power in this turbulent region of the Middle East. Given its geographical position one would suspect that the kingdom would have collapsed and degenerated into a failed state and overrun by Islamic State. IS is certainly present but King Abdullah and his powerful security apparatus have so far managed to be an oasis of hope in an otherwise turbulent region.

LEBANON

Lebanon has been in existence for centuries and is occupied by both Christians and Muslims. The Christians settled mainly in the mountainous regions, while the Muslims inhabited the coastal region (Figure 8-12). Like most of the Middle East, the area was under the rule of the Turkish Ottoman Empire until the end of World War I. After the war, the French began to prepare the region for independent status. The French assisted in the creation of the Lebanese Constitution. Lebanon gained its full independence in 1943, and, like its population, the government was designed to reflect the two majority religions, Christian and Muslim. From its very early days as an independent state, Lebanon had close links to Western powers. In the 1950s and 1960s, Beirut was affectionately called the "Riviera of the Middle East." Its hotels and restaurants

FIGURE 8-12 Map of Lebanon. *Source:* Central Intelligence Agency, *The World Factbook, 2008.*

and vibrant market scene made it a popular spot for tourists and the wealthy. Its location on the Mediterranean Sea helped it flourish as a port as well as a business center. Significant incidents brought about drastic changes in the Lebanese way of life, beginning with what must be termed "an uprising." The first signs of trouble surfaced in 1958, when dissatisfied Muslims violently opposed the government's strengthening of ties to the West. The uprising was tempered when U.S. forces were sent to the aid of Lebanon, and all seemed to return to relative tranquility in short order.

Palestinians Come to Lebanon

With the PLO's reversal of fortunes in 1969—when it was forcefully evicted by King Hussein's Army—vast members spilled into Lebanon. King Hussein's actions were in response to the increasing number of confrontations between the PLO and the Jordanian military. Support for the embattled King came from regular monetary contributions from the United States.

The Arab Muslim population in Lebanon swelled, but its people were treated, at best, as fourth-class citizens. Many lived in the shabby refugee camps around Beirut International Airport. Sabra and Shatila refugee camps and areas of southern Lebanon that were within striking distance of Israel remain in infamy as testament to atrocities committed by Christian militias.

By 1975, the constant warring from the PLO incursions into Israel and the retaliatory strikes by the Israeli air force against Palestinian camps brought the country to civil war. The PLO in Lebanon was widely supported by the predominately Muslim Arabs, but was opposed by the Lebanese Christians. To the casual observer, Beirut and all of Lebanon have seen a never-ending cycle of violence perpetrated by warring factions from within the country's borders and from unsympathetic neighbors such as Syria, Iran, Iraq, and Israel. Lebanon had become a lawless society with a feeble government unable to restore order or control both internal and external elements bent on its destruction. The style and structure of terrorism to be played out in this theater of conflict can be viewed as political in nature. It is considered to be the oldest technique of psychological warfare—political terrorism may be defined simply as coercive intimidation. It is the systemic use of murder and destruction, or the threat of murder and destruction, in order to terrorize individuals, groups, communities, or governments into conceding to the terrorist's political demands.[32] While Syria had its own agenda to include Lebanon as a part of greater Syria, far more sinister notions were spreading outward from the Persian state of Iran.

The last decade of the twentieth century saw a relative calm return to the streets of Beirut. However, the city continues to echo the problems of a bygone decade. In January 2002, a car bomb killed a Lebanese Christian warlord, Elie Hobeika, who had a dubious past and was a militia leader, armed and equipped by the Israeli military under the control of Ariel Sharon. Hobeika may have led the assault on the refugee camps of Sabra and Shatila near Beirut International Airport in 1982, massacring Palestinian civilians. All of this occurred with the knowledge and connivance of the Israeli military.

Hobeika had served as a Lebanese government minister until 1988 and in 2001 had agreed to give evidence against Ariel Sharon at the Belgian war crimes inquiry. Hobeika's record of involvement in the massacres is somewhat incomplete. Some say he directed operations of Christian fighters from outside of the camps. A 1983 Israeli investigation into the massacres concluded that Sharon bore indirect responsibility and that Hobeika did not enter the camps. Who profits from the death of Hobeika? Many would wish him dead, and not least of all, Palestinians. But the finger could equally be pointed at Israel for the embarrassment his testimony in Belgium would have caused the Israeli government. The group claiming responsibility for his death calls itself the "Lebanese for a Free and Independent Lebanon." However, the group has not been identified by any mainstream opposition groups in the country and could well be a cover name for some other organization.[33]

Political Assassinations

Assassination of anti-Syria politicians in Lebanon has been a feature of the political landscape. Rafik Hariri, a former Lebanese Prime Minister and outspoken opponent of Syria was killed in a massive car bomb attack in February 2005, and in June of the same year a leading anti-Syrian journalist was killed in a similar fashion. George Hawi, the former Lebanese Communist Party leader, was killed in a car bombing in June 2005, and the following month the former defense minister Elias Murr was seriously injured in an assassination attempt. In September, an out-spoken journalist from Lebanese Broadcasting was also injured in an assassination attack. In December, another anti-Syrian Parliamentarian was killed in a car bomb attack, and in November 2006, Pierre Gemayel, a Maronite Christian and outspoken critic of Syria, was assassinated when his car was ambushed by gunmen.[34]

Sunni Muslims account for about ninety percent of the world's Muslim population; the remaining ten percent are Shia Muslims. Struggles between the two groups date back to the seventh century; both hold the Quran as their sacred text and Muhammad as the Last Prophet. The Shia sect have and believe in their own version of Islamic law and their own theology. The Shia believe in a chain of leaders, or Imams, who came after Muhammad, and in a structure of spiritual authority through mullahs and a religious establishment.[35] Iran has the largest population of Shia Muslims in the world.

So, with an unstable government and warring factions fighting openly in the streets of Beirut, the country was ripe for the radicals to move in. With the Shah of Iran deposed and an Islamic revolution underway, the actions of fundamentalists spread to the Middle East.

The Shia Sect in Lebanon

Imam Mousa el-Sadr, an Iranian-born cleric, was the undisputed leader of the Shia community in Lebanon by the end of the 1960s.[36] The Shia community was not, at this point, involved in any type of terrorist activity. Shiites were, however, aligned to politically defend and represent the poor of Lebanon. Together with Gregoire Haddad, a Catholic archbishop, they set up Haraket el-Mahroumeen, or Movement of the Deprived. This group aimed to work within the Lebanese political system to achieve its political objectives. With the passing of time, the Imam found it no easy task to help the poor and oppressed so he changed his doctrine and approach to the government. His party would become rejectionist and take up arms to fight the injustices. The group was known by the acronym AMAL. In stark contrast to its near neighbors in Iran, the Shia sectarian movement continued to operate within the political system after the civil war of 1975. The Lebanese Shia community saw a ray of hope with the formation of a government out of the Iranian Revolution, particularly given the background and birthplace of the Imam. His contacts and involvement with the Iranian movement, as well as the leadership of AMAL, was to end with his abduction and disappearance in 1978. A natural vacuum ensued and the AMAL became the Islamic AMAL, with headquarters in the Bekaa Valley of Lebanon under the auspices of Hussein el-Musawi. Islamic AMAL was now foundering. Musawi joined forces to bring AMAL under the umbrella of Hezbollah.

HEZBOLLAH

The origins of the Hezbollah movement in Lebanon represent the most important and successful example of Islamic Iran's efforts to export its Pan-Islamic brand of revolution beyond its border.[37] Hezbollah is also known as follows:

- *Islamic Jihad*
- *Ansarollah*
- *Organization of the Oppressed*
- *Party of God*
- *Revolutionary Justice Organization*

Hezbollah goal remains the establishment of an Islamic state in Lebanon.[38] Their presence in Lebanon was supported and financed by Iran's revolutionary government; and members of the Iranian Revolutionary Guard were sent to the Bekaa Valley to join with the training cadres. It is widely accepted that Hezbollah is controlled and directed by radical Shiite clerics under the central control of Iran through contacts in the Syrian capital of Damascus. Up until his death in 1989, the supreme guardian of revolutionary causes was Iran's Ayatollah Khomeini, who called on "all oppressed Muslims to replace their governments with Islamic Fundamentalist ones." His brand of terror stretched far and wide, and he used terror as his instrument of punishment. His continued diatribes against the "Great Satan,"[39] his term for the United States, and his religious fatwa (of death sentence) against the British author Salman Rushdie for writing a novel called the *Satanic Verses* constantly stirred the pot of the Middle East politics.

With Hezbollah's rise in 1982, the group became a further embarrassment to the Lebanese government. Prior to the Israeli invasion of southern Lebanon, which led to the PLO retreating to Tunis, the streets of Beirut were controlled by various militia groups. These included the indigenous Druze populace from the hills around Beirut airport. It was not uncommon for rockets and mortars to be fired over the airport at the Palestinian positions nearby, causing death and destruction.

Hezbollah's main targets are the Israeli Jews, but it has also targeted non-Islamic influences in Europe, the United States, and Latin America. Since the withdrawal of the Israeli army from southern Lebanon, Hezbollah has been able to build and recruit combatants for its "Holy War" against Israel. The Al-Manar TV network broadcasts a constant and objective view portraying the values of "martyrdom" (suicide). Al-Manar broadcasts to more than twenty five million viewers in the Arab world including Palestinians in Gaza and the West Bank. Their objective is ". . . to encourage people to martyr themselves," in the words of Nayef Krayem, chairman of the network.[40] Beirut streets are marked with flags displaying the images of martyrs who have completed their suicide missions. Nevertheless, Beirut is still the temporary home to thousands of Palestinian refugees who are denied the same rights as the indigenous population and continue to live in squalor. Hezbollah has managed to gain prestige from the Arab states by being responsible for the ultimate Israeli withdrawal from southern Lebanon. The messages being sent to Gaza through the Al-Manar network may sow the seeds for more martyrs from the Palestinian population, but unlike Hezbollah, the Palestinians are unable to retreat to the hills of Lebanon to escape the reach of the Israeli military.

Any discussion of geopolitics in the region will involve both Lebanon and Syria, as Syria has been involved in every aspect of Lebanon's existence for the last four decades. Both Syria and Iran have trained Hezbollah to be the best military force in Lebanon. Syria has always considered its presence in Lebanon a necessity to prevent civil war breaking out between Muslims and Christians.

Who Killed Rafik Hariri?

The February 14, 2005, bomb attack that killed the former Lebanese Prime Minister Rafik Hariri has been blamed on Syria and sometimes on Israel, and the investigation by the UN Special Tribunal has implicated Hezbollah in the assassination. Hariri had been outspoken of the Syrian presence and interference in Lebanon and had been instrumental in calling for a Syrian withdrawal from Lebanon. It is doubtful whether it will ever be established exactly who or which faction or state ordered the Hariri's assassination, but it was troubling to observe his bodyguard had been significantly reduced and along with it all his experienced protection specialists. Syria denied any involvement and instead pointed the finger at Israel. Syria has been losing its grip on Lebanon since the death of the former Syrian president Hafez al-Assad in 2000. Its attempt to trample the Lebanese constitution by extending the presidency of its hand-picked puppet, Emil Lahoud, by three years was greeted with outrage in Beirut. Syria's President Assad died just one month after the final Israeli withdrawal from southern Lebanon. The young son of the former president, and his successor, is not necessarily as competent to deal with his father's old guard, who would view any concessions as a sign of weakness. There is always the probability that, in a move to undermine the young Syrian president, forces from within the Syrian intelligence and security apparatus may have conspired to kill Hariri and set Assad up for the ultimate fall. There is no definite evidence to link the killing to Syria; however, the likelihood of it being any other is unlikely.

Kidnapping

The speed and ruthless efficiency with which Hezbollah conducted kidnappings and executions in Beirut took the world completely by surprise. The January 1987 kidnapping of **Terry Waite**, the Archbishop of Canterbury's special envoy to the Middle East, was remarkable in that it was carried almost live on the major news networks. Hezbollah believed, at the time, that Terry Waite was working for the CIA. However, news bulletins, which showed Waite leaving an aircraft in Cyprus several steps ahead of Colonel Oliver North, provided ample incitement for the kidnappers to justify their actions. The refusal of the British and the United States to deal with terrorists or their demands resulted in Terry Waite and others being incarcerated for several years in the suburbs of Beirut before their eventual release in 1991.

Hezbollah—Structure and Development

From its original inception, Hezbollah operated like a "halfway house" for terrorists receiving its guidance and direction from three different people within its hierarchy: Abu Musawi, Hassan Nasrallah, and Sheik Mohammed Hussein Fadollah, the last being Hezbollah's spiritual leader. As a former fighter with the Islamic AMAL, Nasrallah's role was to format a terrorist force for the southern Lebanon region.[41]

As noted earlier, Hezbollah was intent on establishing an Islamic state in Lebanon. This would undoubtedly not be welcomed by the style of government established with the creation of Lebanon in the first quarter of the century, which assured that government would predominantly be in the hands of the Maronite Christian majority. As no census had been taken in the country for decades, it was probable that the Maronite Christians were no longer in the majority, a fact not lost on the Beirut militia commanders. With so many different groups fighting for control of the streets and the government, Hezbollah was not content to act like the PLO—as an umbrella for other groups. With Musawi's death, Nasrallah turned his terrorist forces toward the same style of revolution as had occurred in Iran and effectively created a regional militia movement. Many other groups had, by 1991, laid down their arms and signed a peace accord. Hezbollah, on the other hand, remained the one major force against the Israelis in southern Lebanon and has been waging a terrorist campaign ever since.

Hezbollah has used the suicide bomber to great effect, as has Islamic Jihad. Hezbollah is blamed for the suicide bomb attack on the **U.S. Marine barracks in West Beirut** in October 1983, when a suicide bomber drove an explosive-laden truck and detonated it as he crashed into the camp. The bomb killed two hundred and forty-one U.S. Marines. The outcry in the United States was loud and clear: "What are our boys doing over there?" In spite of the outrage, the suicide attacks continued with spontaneous irregularity and with the same devastating results. Intelligence on Hezbollah was scant, and bringing any culprit to trial was almost impossible.

The terror tactics employed in Beirut significantly changed on March 28, 1986, when two British teachers were kidnapped in what had been considered the "safe" area of West Beirut. The following month, Brian Keenan, a British national with dual nationality in the Republic of Ireland, was abducted. The following week, one of the Muslim militia groups operating in West Beirut announced that it had executed a British journalist, Peter Collett. The next day, the three bodies of the Americans—Peter Kilburn, Leigh Douglas, and Philip Padfield—were discovered, and another journalist, John McCarthy, was kidnapped. Beirut had become an extremely hostile place for Westerners. Hezbollah is in fact, an international terrorist group with the ability to strike at targets throughout the world. Through local cell structures in South America, Hezbollah is believed to have been responsible for several large bomb attacks in Buenos Aires in 1994, and a car bombing in London.

Hasan Nasrallah, considered to be one of the shrewdest politicians in Lebanon as well as being the secretary general of Hezbollah, has declared that his movement will not give up its arms, but with the withdrawal of Syrian troops, Hezbollah will continue to defend the interests of Syria and Syria's withdrawal poses the most serious challenge to the Shiite movement since the end of the civil war. Nasrallah's ability to mobilize hundreds of thousands of Shiites, along with those from the thirty or so pro-Syrian factions in Lebanon, threatens to expose the deep rift within Lebanese society—the very crisis the Syrians always maintained their presence prevented. Lebanon's recent history has been one of constant bloodletting as well as of political opportunism by various sects, who have repeatedly hired themselves out to regional powers to advance their sectarian interests. Syria was the last to play such a game.[42]

HEZBOLLAH—WAR WITH ISRAEL

During the summer of 2006, Hezbollah fighters made an incursion into Israel and captured two Israeli soldiers, setting off a chain of events over the summer months that has had a lasting effect not only on the political fortunes of the Israeli government but also on the Lebanese. The naval blockade of Lebanon, which the Israelis initiated after the raid and bombings of suspected Hezbollah strongholds in Southern Lebanon and the Bekaa Valley, received a response that the Israeli's seemed ill-prepared to handle. The Israeli strategy was a bombing campaign followed up by a conventional ground war with Israeli forces advancing as far as the Litani River. It became apparent that the Israeli government may have severely underestimated

Hezbollah's military might as they were well trained, equipped, and entrenched for the Israeli attack. They possessed a huge arsenal of rockets with which they targeted Israel, even reaching the outskirts of Haifa. Although the Israeli response was probably not what the Hezbollah were expecting, while the Lebanese government were powerless to prevent it from happening. As long as Israeli troops are occupying southern Lebanon, there will continue to be a reason for Hezbollah to attack them. Hezbollah gained a certain notoriety and significant Arab sympathy and support for its actions. Hezbollah has a significant political foothold in Lebanon and is heavily involved in community programs. Any attempt by the Lebanese government to curtail the fighters would provoke the Shiite population and inflame many of the sectarian passions that were responsible for Lebanon's long civil war. For the West to have any effect curtailing Hezbollah's popularity in Lebanon, it will have to show and provide aid in significant proportions—as at the moment Hezbollah is filling that void exclusively.[43] What surprised most observers of the war with Israel was that Hezbollah was in a position to operate at will without hindrance from the Lebanese army. Additionally, they were able to prosecute a conventional war thanks to state-of-the-art weapons and supplies they had received from Iran, which included shoulder-launched antitank missiles as well as night vision equipment. Hezbollah was able to benefit from territorial control in southern Lebanon without having to be concerned with the obligations and vulnerabilities that come with governance. It used state-of-the-art missiles to target the Israeli military and Israeli towns and cities. This was the first time a guerrilla army had managed to keep up a sustained bombardment on its enemy's territory, and the psychological effect that this had on the Israeli public was enormous. Hezbollah had managed to maintain its foothold in the south after the Israeli withdrawal in 2000 and gave the rationale that it was the Lebanese resistance protecting the interests of the Shiite populous, and they based this on the fact that in their opinion the Israelis continued to occupy a tiny portion of Israel, the border region of Sheba Farm.

The western section of Beirut is the predominantly Sunni area of the city and since the assassination of al-Hariri in 2005, his son Saad al-Hariri has armed and led the Sunni militia with support from Jordan and Saudi Arabia. The Sunnis armed themselves out of a sense of preservation against Shiite aggression. During the Lebanese civil war, the Sunnis looked to the PLO for protection, and since the fighting between Hezbollah and Israel in 2006, the Sunnis have come to realize that they need their own militias for protection.

Hezbollah's successes are partly due to its charismatic leader, Sheikh Hassan Nasrallah, rather than any inspiration from Tehran, but Nasrallah's stature has far exceeded Iranian expectations and is viewed with some skepticism for his accommodating approach with the Lebanese government. Israel has long sought to have him and others of Hezbollah assassinated, and the death of Imad Mughniyah in February 2008 indicates that Nasrallah, although no longer openly appearing at public gatherings or party meetings, is considered a target for Mossad. Iran still holds the purse strings and has no doubt insisted that Nasrallah remain out of sight.

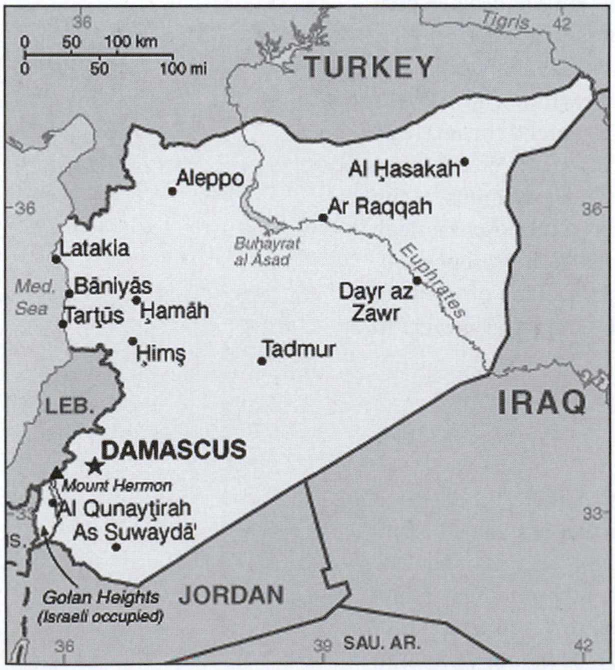

SYRIA

Syria has been a major player in the Israeli/Palestinian problems. This Muslim country has a population that is ninety percent Sunni Muslim. Syria gained independence from France in 1946, and by the mid-1960s, the Ba'ath Party rose to power with Hafez al-Assad as its president (Figure 8-13). For years, Syria had been dominated by a succession of military governments. Assad, a former Air Force colonel, died in 2001, and his power passed to his son, Bashar al-Assad, who continues much as his father did. Syria is a long-time supporter of the Palestinian cause and a sworn enemy of Israel. It has fought two unsuccessful campaigns against Israel and lost control of the Golan Heights on its southern border.

Although Syria has harbored and sponsored terrorists and terrorism, it is likely that any terrorist acts perpetrated on its soil would be quickly suppressed. Assad himself shied away from the public eye and quietly assisted groups such as Islamic Jihad and Hezbollah by

FIGURE 8-13 Map of Syria. *Source:* Central Intelligence Agency, *The World Factbook, 2008.*

allowing Iran to resupply them through Damascus. Assad's government was in open conflict with U.S. forces stationed in Lebanon and, in 1983, shot down an unarmed U.S. reconnaissance flight. Through the remaining two decades of the last century Syria maintained a thriving business in support of training camps for expatriate terror groups such as the PFLP-GC, led by Ahmed Jibril, the Palestine Islamic Jihad, and the Japanese Red Army.

Historically Syria does not permit homegrown terrorists to perpetrate actions against the state, and Assad's government violently suppresses any attempts, particularly by Islamic fundamentalists, to disrupt the workings of the state. Terrorists, fundamentalists, and other political factions are suppressed in the one-party state. Despite this, the Muslim Brotherhood has attempted to raise its banner in Syria.

In 1982, an open revolt in the city of Hama by Islamic fundamentalists resulted in the Syrian army taking decisive action to crush the uprising, which resulted in many deaths and casualties. Former U.S. President George Bush included Syria in his list of countries forming an "axis of evil" in 2002. Al-Assad had openly expressed support for the U.S. War on Terror, but he did little or nothing in support of it.

A Mossad-Targeted Assassination?

A car bombing in Damascus on February 12, 2008, claimed the life of the legendary Hezbollah leader Imad Mughniyah, nicknamed "The Wolf." He had managed to evade capture or death at the hands of the Mossad and the CIA for years. Mughniyah was the head of operations for Hezbollah and was killed after leaving a Syrian intelligence office in Damascus. Israel is obviously the prime suspect in his death but quite naturally is not claiming any responsibility for any action in Syria. Mughniyah had strong ties to the Iranian Intelligence Service and was responsible for a vast number of terrorist attacks including masterminding the U.S. Embassy bombing and numerous airline hijackings. He would have been a major target for the Israeli Mossad.

Syria's east borders Iraq and prior to the Iraq invasion by U.S. and allied troops, Syria was likely sending supplies and weapons into the region. Syria has long been a state sponsor of numerous terrorist groups throughout the last forty years and, with the presence of so many foreign troops on Muslim soil, Syria's willingness and ability to prevent insurgents going into Iraq would be questionable. The United States had three main issues with Syria during its presence in Iraq:

- Its ongoing support for Hezbollah.
- Border security, as it affects U.S. troop security within Iraq.
- Its support for Palestinian rejectionist groups.

Syria's close ties with Iran makes for complex problems in the region. Syria remains a constant threat to Israel while continuing its close relationship with both Iran and its regional proxy Hezbollah. Syria, which lies to the immediate south of Turkey, has managed to establish a relationship with that government as it sees the country's anti-U.S. stance as positive for its relationship with Turkey.

Syria expelled PKK leader Abdullah Ocalan in 1998 after threats of military intervention from Turkey. Relationships have changed dramatically between the two countries. In October 2007, Syria openly supported Turkey's decision to mount cross-border military operations to attack Kurdish rebels. The Syrians need the Turks more than Turkey needs Syria. Turkey, of course, has the respect of other Arab countries in the region and also Israel and the relationship with the United States will only be a temporary issue. Nevertheless, Syrian–Iranian relations remain a source of intense concern to Arab countries. Syria also considers itself to be the main power broker on issues relative to Lebanon. While Syria takes one step forward, it encumbers itself with two steps backward in its ongoing activities with Hezbollah. During the U.S.-led invasion of Iraq, the Syrians facilitated the free flow of Islamist fighters across its border and into Iraq to target American troops.

Syrian Unrest—Arab Spring

The unrest sweeping the Middle East and North Africa in 2011 has probably had the most serious effect on Syria—a country that has had to endure the same measures of repression as its neighbor Iraq suffered under Saddam Hussein. Unlike Egypt, where the protests were not supported by the military or secret police apparatus, the government forces of Bashar al-Assad went on the offensive. Although hollow promises for reforms were made, they were never likely to be fulfilled; and the Syrian crackdown showed how a dictatorship can engage in tactics to terrify and subdue its own people. During May 2011, the government arrested and tortured more than eight thousand protesters, cut roads and electricity to towns, and arrested journalists and restricted the freedom of the press. The Syrian leadership contended that its actions were to target Islamic extremist infiltrating the cities but the sheer scope of the crackdown along a crescent running from the coast to the Jordanian border suggests a leadership willing and content to use its military might against its own people. Syria's leadership continued to contend into 2012 that terrorist groups were to blame for the internal troubles afflicting the state rather than sweeping unrest from within, with government troops killing dissidents, including women and children.

Syrian Civil War Components

Trying to understand what is taking place and its broader effect not only for the Middle East but globally, it is necessary to break down the various sides involved in what the Arab Spring brought to Syria. The Syrian government maintains an active and well-supplied army, navy, and air force and is also supported by allied groups including the AMAL Movement, the Ba'ath Brigades, the Arab Nationalist Guard, the Palestine Liberation Army, and a large assortment of tribal groups. From a state perspective the Syrian government is also supported by elements of Hezbollah and Iran's Revolutionary Guards Quds Force. In 2015, Russia began to exert its influence in the region by providing military support with ground forces and air force support. Unfortunately, Russian air strikes against the Syrian opposition forces has targeted what may be considered more moderate groups at a time when moderate Syrian opposition is also battling against both al Qaeda and ISIS. As more and more foreign fighters have come to this region, so have the global powers begun to mobilize to exert influence in the region. Syria gets further logistical and hardware support from Russia, North Korea, and Iraq.

Opposition Groups

In opposition to the Syrian regime are three separate clusters, all with aims of toppling the regime but with different agendas. Firstly, the Syrian opposition fronted by al Qaeda and affiliated groupings. These would include such organizations as the Free Syrian Army which includes all its many named divisions, the Southern Front and the Northern Front but it is also supported by al Qaeda affiliates in a variety of different names. At this juncture and early on in the civil war the opposition received support from the United States and Britain as well as many EU countries, and as we recall the original premise was regime change and the removal of the Assad regime was probably foremost on U.S. and British politicians' minds. The problem with supporting a loosely formatted Free Syrian Army was that the West would be supporting and thus arming al Qaeda and its extreme jihadist cohort. Among this network of groups is the Nusra Front or **Jabhat al Nusra**. Al Nusra Front is considered an al Qaeda proxy in the region and takes direction from al Qaeda leadership. In 2015, al Qaeda leader Ayman al Zawahiri counselled al Nusra to adopt the following five goals:

- Better integrate the movement inside the Syrian revolution and its people.
- Coordinate more closely with all Islamic groups on the ground.
- Contribute towards the establishment of a Syria-wide sharia judicial court system.
- Use strategic areas of the country to build a sustainable al Qaeda power base.
- Cease any activity linked to attacking the West.

The al Nusra was established in 2012 and is composed mainly of Syrian jihadists with the intention to set up an Islamic emirate in place of the Syrian government and establish full sharia law. Currently the group differs significantly from its Islamic counterpart Islamic State. Al Nusra seems not to be following a global jihad but focusing squarely on gaining an advantage in Syria, and unlike IS it has not set up a caliphate and nor does it profess to control large swathes of territory. It does exert influence over the areas it subdues but not apparently as harshly as Islamic State has been known to do. Unlike IS it has not always imposed sharia law where there has been local opposition, also it has not been as blood thirsty as IS, which has demanded total allegiance and enforced it by mass beheadings. This may give the al Nusra Front an advantage in the long term in Syria as opposed to IS.

The second group against the Syrian regime comes from the Federation of Northern Syria and its allies—these allies include Kurdistan Workers Party (PKK) which is attempting to eke out a homeland of its own. Also supporting the North are the fighters from the Kurdish Peshmerga.

The third and final group is Islamic State which has spilled over from the Iraq theater into Syria and is confronting not just the Syrian government forces but also the opposition Syrian movements. As IS has already declared major portions of Iraq as its caliphate it now attempts to do the same in Syria. The Syrian government as mentioned earlier has widespread support from Russia and its air force has been successful in targeting IS within Syria.

MOROCCO

This North African country, neatly sandwiched between the Atlantic Ocean and Algeria, has been remarkably adept at keeping terrorism at bay. The Moroccan government has rigorously investigated all terrorist acts and threats and has been successful in countering any Islamic radicalism unrest within its borders (Figure 8-14). Morocco also arrested a member of the Algerian Islamic Salvation Front in December 1997.[44] Morocco gained its independence from French rule in 1955, after rioting broke out when the French sent the Sultan into exile. The uprising resulted in the Sultan being returned to his native Morocco. Sultan Muhammad V changed his title to that of "King" and established a constitutional monarchy to oversee and control all aspects of governing the country. On his death in 1961, his son Hassan assumed the mantle of King and also Prime Minister. Since its independence, Morocco has laid claims to regions of the Saharan Desert under Spanish mandate. Both Morocco and Mauritania had claims on the region and had to contend with the Polisario Front, an indigenous group operating in the Sahara region. The Polisario Front wanted self-determination and was not likely to accept being consumed by either Mauritania or Morocco. Mauritania dropped its claim to the desert region and, in its place, Morocco claimed the whole area. In its efforts to stave off Morocco, the Polisario Front received military support from Libya and Algeria.

On his death in 1999, Hassan was succeeded by his son King Mohammed VI who has been a strong U.S. ally in the War on Terror, and although many Moroccans have been involved in al Qaeda-style attacks in Europe, the Moroccan regime has hit hard at Islamic extremists attempting to upset the status quo within the country. An attack by Islamic extremists in Casablanca in May 2003 killed more than forty-two, mostly Moroccan civilians, even though the bomb attacks were at five different locations—a Spanish social club, the Belgian Embassy, a Jewish cemetery, a resort hotel, and a Jewish community center. These simultaneous attacks came close after a string of similar events in Saudi Arabia and were likely the work of al Qaeda operatives within Morocco. The important issue here is that al Qaeda is far from being harried and chased out of its support bases in the Middle East. It seems capable of planning and setting up attacks of this scale in two Muslim countries at a time when George Bush was informing the world that al Qaeda might be a spent force—the reality is quite the contrary. For its part, the Moroccan King and his government have hit hard at suspected Islamic extremists within Morocco. Although severely criticized for human rights abuses while doing so, Morocco seems determined to hold down the terror factions within its borders and assist in the U.S. War on Terror. There is growing evidence of increased jihadist activity by al Qaeda in the Islamic Maghreb (AQIM) and Islamic State in this region, and in spring 2007, a string of suicide attacks in Rabat had all the hallmarking of an al Qaeda-inspired campaign. Moroccan authorities have managed the disruption of multiple groups with ties to international networks that included AQIM and the Islamic State in Iraq and the Levant (ISIL). AQIM and ISIL continue to recruit Moroccans for combat in other countries,

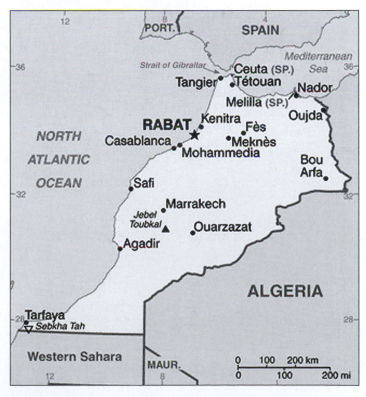

FIGURE 8-14 Map of Morocco. *Source:* Central Intelligence Agency, *The World Factbook, 2008.*

and there were reports of Moroccans attempting to join AQIM, ISIL, and other violent extremists in Iraq, Libya, and Syria. The Ministry of Interior (MOI) estimated that between one thousand and one thousand and five hundred Moroccans were fighting in the Syrian conflict, making them one of the largest foreign contingents in the conflict. The government was increasingly concerned about the potential return of veteran Moroccan foreign terrorist fighters from those conflict zones to conduct possible terrorist attacks at home, and Moroccans resident abroad becoming radicalized during their stays in Western Europe. AQIM and ISIL continue to call for attacks against the Moroccan monarchy and prominent Moroccan institutions and individuals. In July 2014, ISIL published a video online in which it promised to bring "jihad" to install the caliphate system in Morocco. The country appears to be making headway in its program to push back radicalization. It has a comprehensive strategy for countering violent extremism (CVE) that prioritizes economic and human development goals in addition to tight control of the religious sphere and messaging. Morocco has accelerated its rollout of education and employment initiatives for youth—the population identified as most vulnerable to radicalization and recruitment— and has expanded the legal rights and political and social empowerment of women. To counter what the government perceives as the dangerous importation of violent Islamist extremist ideologies, Morocco has developed a national strategy to affirm and further institutionalize Morocco's widespread adherence to the Maliki-Ashari school of Sunni Islam. In the past decade, Morocco has focused on upgrading mosques, promoting the teaching of relatively moderate Islam, and strengthening the Ministry of Endowments and Islamic Affairs (MEIA). The MEIA has developed an educational curriculum for Morocco's nearly fifty thousand Imams in its version of relatively moderate Sunni Islam.[45]

EGYPT

The history of Egyptian contributions to modern society is fascinating. Egypt's feat of civil engineering, craftsmanship, and overall attention to detail in developing a dynasty before most of the world became civilized is a matter of historic record (Figure 8-15). The influences of the Egyptian people and the Pharaohs swept through Africa, the Middle East, and Mesopotamia, dominating societies for centuries. Even now, the study of ancient Egyptian writings occupies the dedication of countless professors and universities. It is believed that the first Egyptian pyramid was built 2,500 years before the birth of Christ. Egypt became a part of the Roman Empire in 31 B.C., and Roman rule dominated Egypt until approximately 395 A.D., when the country was overrun and ruled by Muslims from the Arabian Peninsula.

Twentieth-Century Politics

History sometimes repeats itself and that is the case with Egypt, which had been a country within the Ottoman Empire. The Muslim Brotherhood, which comprises a large percentage of native Egyptians, played a major part in the assassination of then president Anwar Sadat in 1991. Sadat's readiness to make a peace deal with the Israeli government was as much about economics as anything else. Egypt was suffering from excessive military spending and Sadat had promised that this would be lessened with the signing of a peace treaty with the Israelis. At the latter part of the 1970s, Israel considered Egypt its most powerful enemy. A peace agreement between the two countries was being brokered by former U.S. president Jimmy Carter, and, on March 29, 1979, in Washington, DC, Menachem Begin and Anwar Sadat signed the accord. In hindsight, this may have been the political action that led to Sadat's untimely assassination. Immediately after the signing of the historic treaty, a summit of Arab League nations was held in Baghdad and Egypt was ostracized both economically and politically from the Arab world. Under the terms of the treaty, the Israelis gave up

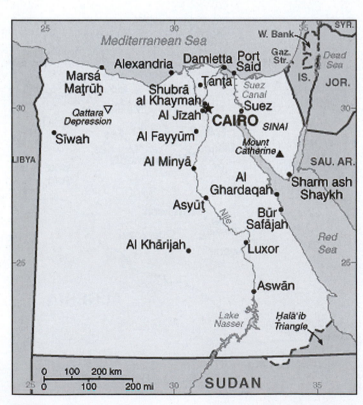

FIGURE 8-15   Map of Egypt. *Source:* Central Intelligence Agency, *The World Factbook, 2008.*

the Sinai in return for a peace deal and financial support from the United States. Egypt was now an outcast Arab state dependent on the United States for its aid. A large majority of Egyptians welcomed the accord.

ANWAR SADAT, 1919–1981

Over time, Anwar Sadat's style of government became increasingly autocratic. Although he had suggested that Egypt would benefit economically from the peace accord, there was no immediate change regarding military spending. In fact, spending in this area increased. Sadat was not gaining any allies among his Arab neighbors as he continued to attempt to keep the peace accord with Israel alive. Israel's attentions, by 1981, were diverted to the northeast and Lebanon. When the Israeli invasion of southern Lebanon began in 1982, the peace process with Egypt became mired in the sand. On the home front in 1981, Sadat was now facing increasing hostilities from the Muslim fundamentalists of the Brotherhood. Far from supporting Sadat, the Brotherhood was now actively challenging his rule. In June 1981, fighting erupted between Muslims and Christians in Cairo, which resulted in massive property damage and a large number of deaths. Sadat began to suppress the Brotherhood and arrested one thousand and five hundred members, including many of the organization's leaders.[46] Clearly out in the cold, Sadat's only close ally was the United States. This alliance fueled the Muslim Brotherhood's hatred of Sadat. This hatred was not aimed at the government, but at Sadat himself. Former president Nasser was, by all accounts, mourned by an entire nation; not so with the passing of Sadat. The Sadat government was seen as increasingly corrupt, with ordinary Egyptians suffering food shortages. Sadat's promise of a better life for Egyptians never seemed to materialize.

Following Sadat's assassination in 1981, there was no spontaneous eruption of violence, no revolution to carry the Muslim Brotherhood forward in Egypt, which had been the intention of the Muslim cell involved in the attack. Although Western world leaders and governments mourned his passing, Egyptians seemed to breathe a collective sigh of relief and, to some extent, regarded Lt. El-Sambouli as a hero. With Islamic fundamentalism on the rise throughout the Muslim world, it seemed probable that a revolt should occur, but this did not happen in Egypt for another thirty years. In elections in 1987, the Muslim Brotherhood allied with two political parties, won seventeen percent of the vote, which translated into fifty-six seats in the Egyptian National Assembly.[47] In April 1982, El-Sambouli and his five co-conspirators were found guilty of Sadat's assassination and executed for their crimes.

EGYPT'S ISLAMIC EXTREMISTS

Jamaat al-Islamiyya and Egyptian Islamic Jihad, both radical and extreme Islamic groups, advocate the violent overthrow of the secular Egyptian government and the establishment of an Islamist state. Members from both groups were known to have fought against the Soviet occupation of Afghanistan in the 1980s, and in Yemen's north-south civil war. The groups cooperated on the assassination of Egyptian President Anwar Sadat. The two groups gained much of their support from the slums of Cairo and the poorer regions of the state. Both have been responsible for attacks against foreign tourists in Egypt that decimated the lucrative Egyptian tourism economy. Both groups have their roots going back to the Muslim Brotherhood. They broke away from the MB due to its declaration of nonviolence.

Christians and Muslims have occupied Egypt for centuries. Egyptians who are born Christians are referred to as Copts, and number about five–six million. Formed in 1928 by Sheik Hassan al Banna, the Brotherhood stood solidly as then President Nasser's most vitriolic of opponents in Egypt. The Brotherhood would see an about-face by the presidential office with the arrival of Anwar Sadat, who overall only paid lip service to Sharia and at the same time released hundreds of Islamists from prison; and those factions of the Brotherhood willing to support Sadat against his extreme left opponents were themselves supported with large donations.

Following a violent campaign of attacks against the government, Christians, and other targets in Egypt, Jamaat al-Islamiyya has largely honored a March 1999 ceasefire with the Egyptian government. Exiled members of Jamaat al-Islamiyya are known to have joined al Qaeda and trained at its camps in Afghanistan.[48] The Islamic Jihad has close ties to bin Laden's al Qaeda and continues its assault on the Egyptian government. Due to the repressive nature of the Mubarak regime, the group had operated principally outside Egypt and had been turning its Islamic extremist campaign toward U.S. targets. Its philosophy is to overthrow the Egyptian government and to replace it with an Islamist government similar to the former Taliban regime in Afghanistan.

The Muslim Brotherhood is widely considered the world's most influential Islamist organization. The group earned legitimacy among its core constituency, the lower-middle class, as the most effective organized resistance against British domination (1882–1952). The Muslim Brotherhood joined with the Free Officers, nationalist military leaders who sought to wrest Egypt from the British-backed monarchy, but rivalry between the military and the Brotherhood ensued after King Farouk abdicated in 1952 and a military junta took charge with Gamal Abdel Nasser at the helm. At this juncture the military and the Brotherhood were at odds—as the military wanted a secular government and the Brotherhood a strict Islamist government. The attempted assassination of General Nasser in 1954 resulted in thousands of Brotherhood supporters being arrested including Banna's successor Sayyid Qutb. Qutb developed a doctrine of armed struggle against the regime in Egypt and beyond while writing from prison after his arrest for the assassination attempt. His work, particularly the 1964 manifesto *Milestones*,[49] has provided the intellectual and theological underpinnings for many militant Sunni Islamist groups, including al Qaeda and Hamas. Extremist leaders often cite Qutb, who was hanged in 1966, to argue that governments not based on sharia are apostate and, therefore, legitimate targets of jihad.

The Brotherhood emerged as a dominant political force in Egypt following Mubarak's removal from office amid mass protests in February 2011, in part because its organizational capacity was unmatched, but the group's electoral victories were tarnished by power struggles with the judiciary and the military. Battles over the drafting of a new constitution were a particular flash point. In the parliamentary elections in 2012, the Muslim Brotherhood's party the Freedom and Justice Party won half the seats in the People's Assembly and eighty-four percent of the seats in the Shura Council. Following a first round of voting in May, Muslim Brotherhood candidate Morsi won a narrow majority (51.7 percent)[50] in a June runoff against Shafiq.

Arab Spring—Egypt

The demonstrations in Cairo, in spring 2011, were not necessarily a popular revolution as the 300,000 demonstrators in Tahrir Square represented only a fraction of the population of Egypt. The media attention given to the demonstrations gave the Egyptian military the opportunity to carry out a bloodless coup and remove then President Mubarak from office. What was to follow was a remarkable quick change in democracy with the incoming Muslim Brotherhood government ultimately led by Mohammed Morsi.

Timeline

- **2011 November**—A result of the Arab Spring uprising spreading to Egypt—violence erupts in Cairo's Tahrir Square as security forces clash with protesters accusing the military of trying to keep their grip on power.
- **2011 December**—National Unity Government headed by new Prime Minister Kamal al-Ganzouri.
- **2012 January**—Islamist parties win big in parliamentary elections.
- **2012 June**—Muslim Brotherhood's Mohammed Morsi narrowly wins presidential election.
- **2012 August**—Prime Minister Hisham Qandil appoints a cabinet dominated by figures from the outgoing government, technocrats, and Islamists, but excluding secular and liberal forces.
- **2012 November**—Thousands of protesters take to the streets as President Morsi revokes the power of the judiciary's right to challenge his decisions and granting himself unlimited powers.
- **2013 January**—Huge protests against President Morsi across Egypt mark the second anniversary of the revolution—Army chief Abdel Fattah al-Sisi warns that political strife is pushing the state to the brink of collapse.
- **2013 June**—President Morsi appoints Islamists as regional leaders in thirteen of Egypt's twenty-seven governorships, including member of a former Islamist armed group Gamaa Islamiyya responsible for the massacre of tourists in Luxor in 1997.

- **2013 July**—In a coup d'etat Egyptian military deposes President Morsi following mass demonstrations calling on him to quit.
- **2013 August**—Hundreds killed as security forces storm pro-Morsi protest camps in Cairo.
- **2013 December**—Government declares Muslim Brotherhood a terrorist group.
- **2014 January**—New constitution bans parties based on religion.
- **2014 February**—Egyptian government resigns paving way for military leader to run for president.
- **2014 May**—Former Army chief Abdel Fattah al-Sisi wins presidential election.
- **2015 May**—Former President Morsi sentenced to death over 2011 mass breakout of Muslim Brotherhood prisoners, along with more than one hundred others. He was sentenced to twenty years in prison for the torture of protesters during his 2012–2013 rule.

In 2012, Morsi made a declaration that he, the Shura Council, and the Constituent Assembly were immune from any form of judicial review. His secular opponents were concerned about the role of Islam as the basis of law, feared insufficient protections for women's rights and freedoms of speech and worship, and distrusted the broad power accorded to the presidency. Morsi and his government's swift and heavy-handed approach was too much and too fast for the Egyptians and when in 2013 he appointed seventeen MB affiliated provincial governors, including a member of the former terrorist group Gamaa Islamiya as the governor of Luxor, where in 1997 the same group had massacred dozens of tourists, it became the tipping point for widespread protest. The powerful Egyptian military removed Morsi from power and he was subsequently sentenced to twenty years in prison. The Muslim Brotherhood is once again on the outside of the Egyptian political spectrum.

Sinai Province (SP)

This is an insurgent group that has already pledged its allegiance to the Islamic State and is continuing to cause major problems for the military government in Egypt. The group has carried out waves of attacks against military posts in and around the Sinai region. It has also moved into attacking airliners. In October 2015, it claimed responsibility for the bomb that destroyed a Russian passenger aircraft after leaving Sharm el-Sheikh—an Airbus A321, operated by Kogalymavia Airlines, which had taken off en route to St Petersburg, but crashed into the Sinai desert killing everybody on board. The authorities believe an explosive device was smuggled either into the cabin or the hold of the aircraft. As SP is aligned with IS, this had the almost immediate effect of Russia sending its military and air force to target IS in Syria.

LIBYA

Libya is situated at the northern tip of Africa and has a northern border on the Mediterranean Sea. Its nearest neighbors to the east are Egypt and the Sudan, with Chad and Niger to the south and Algeria and Tunisia to the west and northwest, respectively (Figure 8-16). The country is made up of ninety seven percent Sunni Muslims or Arabian Berber tribesmen. In the 1930s, under Italian dominance, there was discrimination against Libyan Jews, who have been persecuted in Libya ever since. Libyans attacked the Jewish sector of Benghazi during World War II and deported about two thousand Jews. By the time Libya had achieved independence in 1951, nearly all the remaining Libyan Jews had migrated to either Israel or Europe.[51]

COLONEL MUAMMAR EL-QADDAFI

Muammar el-Qaddafi was a man driven by hatred for the state of Israel, the United States, and foreign powers that support them. Up until the late 1990s, Libya did not limit itself to

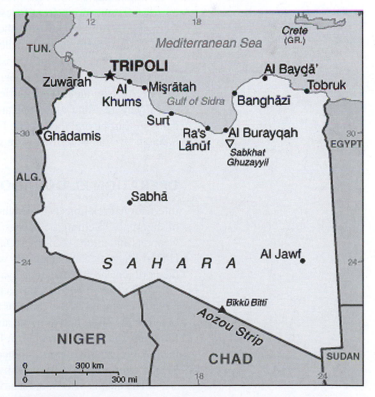

FIGURE 8-16   Map of Libya.   *Source:* Central Intelligence Agency, *The World Factbook, 2008.*

attacking foreign governments, but also sought out and assassinated Libyans opposed to the Libyan leader.

Qaddafi came to power following a military coup that deposed King Idris in 1969 and achieved dictatorial status as Libyan leader. Outspokenly anti-Israeli, anti-Zionist, and anti-Semitic in his public statements, he made no distinction among them. As a mark of his hatred for the Jewish people, he seized all Jewish-owned properties and businesses in 1971. He ruled with an autocratic style and ruthlessly "removed" all dissenters. His control of the government was absolute through the setup of people's committees. As a former military student and officer, he had never been cast in the secular role that he seemed to have adopted in the 1990s. With unrest of the Arab Spring sweeping across North Africa, his regime of terror ended ignominiously. The masses demanded democratic change and fighting broke out across the country. The fighters appealed for international intervention and were supported by NATO with air strikes against Libyan government strongholds. By the end of October 2011, Qaddafi and his hard-line loyalists were all but decimated. Qaddafi's convoy was bombed by NATO jets, and he took cover in a drainage tunnel only to be captured and shot by opposition fighters. The future for Libyans remains very uncertain. NATO support was provided, and Qaddafi was toppled and replaced by Islamists unfriendly to the West. The first pungent signs of disquiet came with the Benghazi desecration of British graves at the War Graves Commission Cemetery in Benghazi in February 2012, committed by an armed group of Salafists.

Support for Terror

The phenomenon of state-sponsored terrorism applies most appropriately to Libya, Iran, and Syria, and forms part of what George Bush termed the "Axis of Evil." The most outspoken of the Arab world leaders, Qaddafi embarked through the 1970s and 1980s on a reign of external terror against the United States and its citizens, specifically those in Europe. Qaddafi supported other terror groups in Europe and allowed them to train on Libyan soil. Qaddafi also provided weapons to such groups as the Provisional Irish Republican Army (PIRA). In one notable incident, Qaddafi supplied several tons of explosives and automatic weapons that were seized by security forces in the Irish Republic. To Qaddafi, the PIRA was fighting a guerrilla war of independence from the dominance of an imperialist power. Libya has been a home and terrorist training ground for more than thirty terrorist organizations, from Palestinian groups in the Middle East to the Red Army Faction from Germany to Abu Sayyaf from the Philippines. However, in order to get sanctions lifted (among other actions taken), Libya expelled members of the ANO in 1998.

There was sufficient opposition to the Qaddafi regime to prompt him to unleash internal assassins to track down and coerce the dissidents into returning to Libya. In 1984, more than thirty terrorist attacks were carried out by representatives of Libyan Revolutionary Committees on Libyans residing in Europe and the Middle East.[52] Not only did Qaddafi focus on his dissidents in Europe and the Middle East, he also sought them out in neighboring Chad and the sub-Saharan African states that were vociferously against his government.

OPERATION EL-DORADO CANYON

International relations between the United States and Libya were at an all-time low by the middle of the 1980s. Behind the scenes at this time was the Soviet Union, which had been supplying weapons and aircraft to Libya. On March 24, 1986, in an effort to make the Libyans lose face, the United States began maneuvers with its Sixth Fleet in the Mediterranean in the Gulf of Sirte off the north coast of Libya, in Libya's self-defined exclusion zone.

Libya responded with two terrorist attacks in Europe. In the first attack, on April 2, 1986, a bomb exploded in the cabin of a TWA passenger jet in Greek airspace. Four Americans were killed in the blast; however, the aircraft landed without further incident. Four days later, a powerful explosion ripped through La Belle discotheque in West Berlin, killing an American serviceman. American intelligence indicated that the disco bombing was planned and directed by "diplomats" from the East Berlin Libyan People's Bureau.

The deaths of U.S. citizens became the trigger the Reagan administration was searching for to launch a previously planned U.S. air strike in Libya. On April 14, 1986, aircraft from U.S. bases in the United Kingdom and aircraft carriers in the Mediterranean bombed targets inside Libya.

Over one hundred aircraft took part in the raid in and around Tripoli and Benghazi, causing heavy damage and loss of life. It is believed that then Colonel Qaddafi's adopted daughter was one of the fatalities. In all, more than one hundred lives were claimed. Was the attack sending a message to other state sponsors of terrorism or was this strike designed to help topple or kill the Libyan leader and allow for a more moderate government to be formed in its place? This was the first time the United States had launched such aggressive military action at a specific country in retaliation for terrorist attacks. Would other terrorist groups heed the example of the attack on Libya and cease activities against the United States? On the political front, members of the United Nations, including France and Italy, the two countries that had refused over flight clearances for strike aircraft from UK bases, condemned the United States. Did the French and Italian governments fear some form of reprisal attack from the Libyan leader? The UK government, on the other hand, the strongest American ally at the time, had already severed diplomatic ties with Libya over the death of Yvonne Fletcher. A far more serious terrorist attack was being planned, indicating that pre-emptive military actions may not be successful against determined and fanatical terrorist movements. Some thirteen years later, under a different U.S. administration, spy satellites and long-range smart bombs would again target terrorist sites this time, but in Sudan and Afghanistan.

During the last decade, with the mounting pressure on his country from UN sanctions that were not lifted until 1999, the colonel had to re-evaluate his position in the world. No longer did he have the support of the former Soviet Union. A period of appeasement was definitely necessary to Libya's survival. Libya has small stocks of biological agents and the risk that those could fall into the wrong hands or, to be more specific, into the hands of al Qaeda, has been a pressing issue for the United States. In May 2002, the U.S. State Department added Libya to the list of countries that were developing chemical and biological weapons of mass destruction (WMD). Certainly, Qaddafi had no love for the Islamic extremists or al Qaeda, and since 9-11 he had reportedly provided intelligence on Libyan militants outside of the country. This action benefitted Qaddafi as he maintained an iron-fisted approach to Islamic extremists inside Libya.

Libyan Islamic Fighting Group (LIFG)

Sunni Islamic militants have also been present in Libya but have not managed to engage any popular support for their cause. The Libyan Islamic Fighting Group (LIFG) has been in existence for several decades but only publicly announced its presence in a 1995 communiqué following a number of attacks against the Libyan regime. Over the course of 1995 and 1996, LIFG mounted assassination attacks against Colonel Qaddafi; all were unsuccessful. The LIFG leader and its founder, Salah Fathi bin Suleiman, was killed during a battle with Libyan military forces in September 1997. Unable to promote a popular uprising, the LIFG moved to exile in Sudan at a time when Osama bin Laden was setting up his organization in that country. The Libyan government brought significant pressure to bear on the Sudan government to kick out the LIFG members. Bin Laden, as a guest of the Sudan government, was compelled to remove the Libyan fighters from his camps. Many returned to Libya but did not stay long enough to be caught in Qaddafi's crackdown, but instead fled to Europe. Many rejoined al Qaeda in training camps in Taliban-controlled Afghanistan and since 9-11 went on to prosecute a global jihad. Recruits from Libya were heavily involved in the Iraq insurgency. In February 2006, the U.S. Treasury Department took significant steps aimed at nullifying LIFG's base in the United Kingdom, designating five individuals, three companies, and one charity as terrorists for their ties to LIFG. In addition to labeling Birmingham, U.K., resident Abdelrahman al-Faqih as a "senior leader for the LIFG" the Treasury Department also designated Midlands resident Mohammed Benhammedi as a "key financier for the LIFG" and "a member of . . . . the LIFG economic committee" who was "believed to provide funds for LIFG through Sara Properties Limited, Meadowbank Investment Limited, and Ozlam Properties Limited."[53]

The Sanabal Relief Agency was also described as a fund-raising front organization for the LIFG and was designated as a Specially Designated Global Terrorist (SDGT) entity.

Following the ousting of most elements of the former Qaddafi regime and being replaced by a transitional government, there have been moves to restore levels of justice and administration within Libya. Old foes have been hunted and foremost is the former intelligence chief Abdullah al-Senussi who is wanted not only for crime of embezzlement in Libya but also is subject to an arrest following his sentencing in absentia to life imprisonment for the September 19, 1989, terror attack on UTA Flight 772, killing one hundred and seventy people, including fifty four French nationals, when the French airliner exploded over Niger. He was extradited to Libya from Mauritania in 2012. Successive Libyan governments insisted on prosecuting Senussi on home soil. The International Criminal Court (ICC) ruled in 2013 that Libya was able and willing to prosecute Senussi and that it was no longer necessary to send him to The Hague to stand trial. Senussi was tried along with thirty six other Qaddafi government officials and in July 2015 was condemned to death by firing squad along with Qaddafi's son Saif al-Islam and seven other former officials.

Attack on Benghazi—U.S. Casualties—September 11, 2012

On the evening of September 11, 2012, a planned and coordinated attack by Islamic militants took place. They attacked the American diplomatic compound in Benghazi, Libya, killing U.S. Ambassador J. Christopher Stevens and U.S. Foreign Service Information Management Officer Sean Smith. Stevens was the first U.S. Ambassador killed in the line of duty since 1979. Several hours later, a second assault targeted a different CIA compound a mile away, killing CIA contractors Tyrone S. Woods and Glen Doherty. Ten others were also injured in the attacks.

Exactly which faction was responsible for the attacks has not as yet been determined—there were many factions in the Benghazi area at the time and hostile to the United States including AQIM. Much has been made of failures in this instance by the U.S. State Department and lax overall security support for these locations.

The following is a part of the unclassified report from U.S. Accountability Review Board:

The Accountability Review Board (ARB) report examines the circumstances surrounding the September 11-12, 2012, killings of four U.S. government personnel in Benghazi,

"In examining the circumstances of these attacks, the Accountability Review Board for Benghazi determined that:

1. The attacks were security related, involving arson, small arms and machine gun fire, and the use of RPGs, grenades, and mortars against U.S. personnel at two separate facilities—the SMC and the Annex—and en route between them. Responsibility for the tragic loss of life, injuries, and damage to U.S. facilities and property rests solely and completely with the terrorists who perpetrated the attacks. The Board concluded that there was no protest prior to the attacks, which were unanticipated in their scale and intensity.

2. Systemic failures and leadership and management deficiencies at senior levels within two bureaus of the State Department (the "Department") resulted in a Special Mission security posture that was inadequate for Benghazi and grossly inadequate to deal with the attack that took place.

   The short-term, transitory nature of Special Mission Benghazi's staffing, with talented and committed, but relatively inexperienced, American personnel often on temporary assignments of 40 days or less, resulted in diminished institutional knowledge, continuity, and mission capacity.

   Overall, the number of Bureau of Diplomatic Security (DS) security staff in Benghazi on the day of the attack and in the months and weeks leading up to it was inadequate, despite repeated requests from Special Mission Benghazi and Embassy Tripoli for additional staffing. Board members found a pervasive realization among personnel who served in Benghazi that the Special Mission was not a high priority for Washington when it came to security-related requests, especially those relating to staffing. In the weeks and months leading up to the attacks, the response from post, Embassy Tripoli, and Washington to a deteriorating security situation was inadequate. At the same time, the SMC's dependence on the armed but poorly skilled Libyan Martyrs' Brigade (February 17) militia members and unarmed, locally contracted Blue Mountain Libya (BML) guards for security support was misplaced. Post and the Department were well aware of the anniversary of the September 11, 2001 terrorist attacks but at no time were there ever any specific, credible threats against the mission in Benghazi related to the September 11 anniversary. Ambassador Stevens and Benghazi-based DS agents had taken the anniversary into account and decided to hold all meetings on-compound on September 11.

3. Notwithstanding the proper implementation of security systems and procedures and remarkable heroism shown by American personnel, those systems and the Libyan response fell short in the face of a series of attacks that began with the sudden penetration of the Special Mission compound by dozens of armed attackers.

   The Board found the responses by both the BML guards and February 17 to be inadequate. The Board's inquiry found little evidence that the armed February 17 guards offered any meaningful defense of the SMC, or succeeded in summoning a February 17 militia presence to assist expeditiously.

   The Board found the Libyan government's response to be profoundly lacking on the night of the attacks, reflecting both weak capacity and near absence of central government influence and control in Benghazi. The Libyan government did facilitate assistance from a quasi-governmental militia that supported the evacuation of U.S. government personnel to Benghazi airport. The Libyan government also provided a military C-130 aircraft which was used to evacuate remaining U.S. personnel and the bodies of the deceased from Benghazi to Tripoli on September 12.

4. The Board found that intelligence provided no immediate, specific tactical warning of the September 11 attacks. Known gaps existed in the intelligence community's understanding of extremist militias in Libya and the potential threat they posed to U.S. interests, although some threats were known to exist.

5. The Board found that certain senior State Department officials within two bureaus demonstrated a lack of proactive leadership and management ability in their responses to security concerns posed by Special Mission Benghazi, given the deteriorating threat environment and the lack of reliable host government protection. However, the Board did not find reasonable cause to determine that any individual U.S. government employee breached his or her duty."[54]

   It is probably noteworthy that the review board does not appear to have interviewed senior State officials about the incident and that includes Secretary of State Hilary Clinton.

Benghazi is located in eastern Libya and is the second largest city in the country. Since the fall of the Qaddafi regime it has been controlled by jihadist Islamist militias, some affiliated with al Qaeda, others with ISIS, and some independent. Benghazi is awash with armed militias fighting one another most of whom participated in toppling the Qaddafi regime. These militia factions are divided in their support of the two rival Libyan governments while waging power struggles with each other. The ISIS remains concentrated in a number of neighborhoods in the city, including the central district and the coastal region. IS has been bolstered by support from experienced commanders from the Syrian campaign—this they hope will bolster their presence in the rest of the country.

ISLAMIC STATE—THREAT TO LIBYA

Libya, much like Iraq and Syria has become mired in a civil war that has the potential to drag on for years to come. This results from the deep divisions between the various power centers and the access of the rival sides to military and economic assets like oil fields, the refugee-smuggling industry, and large stockpiles of weapons and ammunition from the Qaddafi era.

Inside Libya, ISIS is one of several organizations struggling for power and control. The establishment of ISIS in Libya increases the chaos and anarchy already plaguing the country, making it difficult to stabilize a central government (for various reasons not only connected to ISIS). Thus despite the efforts of the Tripoli and Tobruk governments to reach an agreement, in all probability in the coming years de facto Libya will be divided and suffer from war and turmoil, creating a governmental and security vacuum, and making it easy for ISIS to continue consolidating its power and making it difficult to uproot it.[55]

The overthrow of the Qaddafi regime left a political and security vacuum in the country that ISIS will seek to exploit. Qaddafi had established his regime based on traditional Islamic values as well as North African tribal values he added in new concepts (Pan-Arabism, Nasserism, African orientation). He set up a Libyan-wide system of institutions which, together with oppressive mechanisms and oil money, maintained his regime for a long time. The Arab Spring eroded the foundations of the Qaddafi regime and highlighted the tensions and contrasts, leading to chaos. Libya currently has no central and functioning government with which to fight ISIS. A great many tribal factions and loyalties come into play in Libya and IS will do its utmost to exploit the tribal differences. It has conducted activities in Libya in much the same manner as it did in Iraq and Syria. There exist two separate governments in Libya, one based in Tobruk and the other in Tripoli. The Tobruk regime is nationalist and strong anti-Islamist in design covering a swathe of the eastern region of Libya. In the west the Tripoli government is Islamist.

The international community recognizing the threat to stability in the region have helped broker a Government of National Accord which was formed in March 2016 with the intent to solidify all factions inside Libya and to work on the removal of Islamic State from its base at Sirte. While the Government of National Accord (GNA) has managed to gain international recognition and support, it remains fragile at best—as far as unity is concerned this government is made up of a collection of parties temporarily putting aside their deeply diverging interests. They do share a common enemy in the Islamic State, but will that be enough to hold them together in the long term?

Establishing a Base in Northern Libya

Islamic State collaborated with local jihadists in Barqa Province in eastern Libya in 2014 and gained its first foothold there. Many of the locals have experience fighting in the Syrian civil war and had returned to Libya. The central leadership at the time comprised foreign fighters who had moved to Syria in 2012 and had returned in 2014. One hard core group of foreign fighters the al-Battar Battalion had sworn their allegiance to the ISIS leader Abu Bakr al-Baghdadi. IS established its first base in Derna which was already Islamist under the Qaddafi regime[56]. They controlled the area in and around Derna until they were swept aside in the early summer of 2015 by a collaboration of al Qaeda affiliated groups and the Libyan Army under the control of the secular Tobruk government.

IS then set its sights on the coastal port of Sirte and as they had done in Iraq literally drove into town and took over control in early 2015. Site is located in the north central region of the country and here they have solidified their central base. It is a strategically important location not just for Libya but for ISIS. From this port a vast number of migrants have flocked to make the sea journey to Europe. These movements are facilitated by militias, criminal gangs, and ISIS. This is a lucrative trade in human capital and brings in millions of dollars a year.

ISIS, as of spring 2016, controls about one hundred and sixty miles of Libya's coastal road, effectively cutting Tripoli off from Tobruk and Benghazi. From Sirte, their goal is to reach the capital city of Tripoli in the west, Benghazi and Derna in the east, and the all-important oil fields in the south.

In and around Sirte and in other locations where ISIS established itself, it constructed a military infrastructure for terrorism and guerilla warfare against its many enemies inside and outside Libya:

1. Inside Libya ISIS directs its terrorism and guerilla warfare against the Tripoli and Tobruk governments, the Tobruk government-supporting Libyan army, and the many militias fighting against it. ISIS gives priority to carrying out attacks in the capital city of Tripoli and its surroundings to weaken the government and harm foreign representatives and citizens. In 2015, ISIS attacked the Corinthia Hotel (a diplomatic and governmental nerve center). It also carried out series of attacks on foreign legations and on oil fields east and south of Sirte (both series of attacks without significant results). It also carried out well publicized executions of so-called "infidels," Copts from Egypt, and Christians from Eritrea, to terrorize its enemies.

2. Outside Libya, ISIS directed most of its attacks against Tunisia, because of its relative weakness and its proximity to centers of ISIS control in Libya. During the past year, ISIS carried out a series of showcase terrorist attacks in Tunisia. They included an attack on the Bardo National Museum in Tunis, a shooting attack on a beach in Sousse, and an attack on a bus carrying members of the presidential guard. ISIS claimed responsibility in every instance and its Libyan infrastructure was reportedly involved in training, arming, and dispatching the terrorist operatives to Tunisia. ISIS in Libya also collaborates with jihadist operatives and organizations in northern Africa and sub-Saharan regions. Especially notable are the connections between ISIS in Libya and ISIS in the Sinai Peninsula, and between both of them and Boko Haram in Nigeria, which also swore allegiance to Abu Bakr al-Baghdadi.[57]

Territorial Methodology

In order for it to be successful, ISIS has established a system that has so far worked for them—they have succeeded by not working from a home base rather they parachute into regions in a clandestine manner and set up intelligence cells to determine which local actors are sympathetic to ISIS. They infiltrate local groups and create front organizations in preparation for their take-over of an area—the intelligence phase also allows them to identify those that are in opposition who will be targeted once ISIS gained control.[58]

Sometimes simultaneously with the intelligence phase, other times after it, ISIS begins to operate militarily in the specific area where it is attempting to gain influence. As seen with most insurgent factions, ISIS employs asymmetric warfare, with tactics that include hit and run attacks, sniper assassination operations, drive-by shootings, improvised explosive devices (IEDs), car bombs, and suicide attacks.[59]

In the same manner as they took control of cities and villages in Iraq and Syria, ISIS began reaching out to the local population as a propaganda exercise to show they are not as cruel and aggressive as media reports portray. Their strategy at this juncture is to win over the younger generation where the future of ISIS lies. They hold competitions, hand out food and school supplies, and also provide forums where they explain their version of Islam and the necessity for jihad. ISIS has a well-developed media machine able to quickly assemble information materials that are passed out at road blocks and check points. In the early stages this enables them to convince the populous that ISIS is good for them.

Last, IS seeks to gain support through its public relations office, where meetings and lavish meals are held with notable local clans and individuals to win over their support and gain buy-in for its program.[60]

Imposition of strict Sharia Law

Once they have gained total control and exerted their considerable influence they impose Sharia law or their strict interpretation of it. They root out their enemies and most all are executed either by a bullet to the head or beheading. Other forms of punishment include beating and whipping, caging, amputating hands and feet and even crucifixion. Homosexuals are also targeted and executed. Cigarettes, alcohol, and music materials are destroyed. Women are forced to wear veils at all times in public, coeducation in schools and universities is banned. In Sirte, the ISIS has been able to benefit from the defection of local jihadists, particularly from Ansar al-Sharia. Those that defect to ISIS must pledge their allegiance to Abu Bakr al-Baghdadi. The local and tribal links of both Ansar al-Sharia elements and ex-Qaddafi officials were a means for ISIS to gain information on possible new recruits in their community. Through these ties, ISIS has been able to set up a presence at the Ouagadougou Conference Center in Sirte[61], beginning in January 2015, despite still being weak at the time.

Atrocities against Christians

Public executions by ISIS are recorded and spread on social media for the sheer terror that they inflict on the global community—they are cruel and barbaric in nature. In February 2015, they beheaded twenty-one Egyptian migrant workers who were seized in Libya—they were believed to be Copts. The executions were followed up in April 2015 with a video produced by ISIS showing dozens of civilians in orange jumpsuits being marched along a beach and then having their throats slashed by black-clad ISIS members. The ISIS captives were Christians from Egypt and Ethiopia.

Strength of Islamic State

With the passage of time there will be fluctuations in the number of operatives in the IS camp—but as of spring 2016, there were in the region of two thousand–three thousand IS fighters in Sirte—whether that number is enough to ward off al Qaeda and the Libyan Army is questionable. But their strategic position does pose a threat to the oil fields which they have so far had little success in targeting. If they succeed in gaining control of Libyan oil fields and terminals it will be a blow to both Libyan governments. Additionally, ISIS is in a good position to threaten mainland Europe by moving IS fighters with migrants attempting to reach Europe through Italy. ISIS may seem somewhat entrenched in northern Libya but it is surrounded on all sides by unfriendly nations, Tunisia, Algeria, and Morocco to the west, Egypt to the east, and Sudan to the southeast.

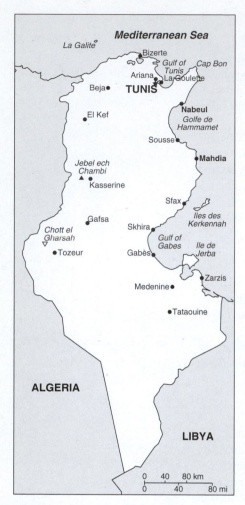

FIGURE 8-17 Map of Tunisia. *Source: Central Intelligence Agency, The World Factbook, 2008.*

None of these governments is pro-IS. Although IS may have Tunisia in its sights for a new territorial gain the likelihood of it making inroads there are considered low. If ISIS is successful in controlling Libya it will have a new base to export terror to sub-Saharan Africa and also north through Italy and into Western Europe. Libya will remain a key location for ISIS as it sees its positions weakening and loss of territory in both Syria and Iraq from both U.S. aerial bombardment and also from Russian attacks.

TUNISIA

Tunisia was, as we recall, the launch location for the popular Arab Spring uprisings in 2011. In Tunisia the populace toppled the hard man regime of Zine El Abidine Ben Ali (Figure 8-17). Since then this small nation to the northwest of Libya has managed to transition to a democratically elected and fully functioning government. Ben Ali's authoritarian rule and use of the Interior Ministry to control his people by restricting civil liberties and arresting opposition to his regime was a major factor in the popular uprising. Ben Ali had also imprisoned around ten thousand Islamists whom he feared would challenge his rule. That being said all the other ministries including the Interior Ministry and the Unions in Tunisia supported the uprising—there was no immediate civil unrest or civil war and there was no vacuum left by the removal of Ben Ali. Furthermore, the new government made an almost seamless transition to power keeping the existing ministries and staff in place. The new government did not sideline the Islamists rather it included the Islamist party into the new unity government.

Soft Targets

Tunisia has long had a thriving tourist industry attracting visitors from mainland Europe to its resorts and hotels. This alone makes Tunisia a target for IS and its affiliates. It has done so in 2015 to some effect. Tunisia continues to have internal security issues stemming mostly from the poorer regions of the country. The interior of Tunisia has high levels of unemployment and also literacy. These areas are also considered more religiously conservative making them attractive to jihadist groups anteing to infiltrate into Tunisia. In 2000, two militant groups formed the jihadist Tunisian Combatant Group which in 2006 was folded into al Qaeda in the Islamic Maghreb. The Arab Spring which brought about the Tunisian revolution enabled Islamist groups an opportunity to develop more freely than under the Ben Ali regime. Tunisia is not fully adept at challenging these threats and attacks by Islamist groups will continue to threat Tunisia's stability. Attacking soft targets such as tourist hotels, beaches, and resorts will have a significant effect on the Tunisian economy.

The unity government is fortunately united against the jihadist threat both internally and externally but the threat will persist in the interior with sporadic attacks against soft targets and government facilities in the cities.

Bardo National Museum—Tunis, March 18, 2015

Islamist fighters attempted a commando style attack on a government building in Tunis but were repelled by armed security—they then moved down the street to the neighboring Museum and took a number of hostages. Two men entered the museum and began to fire at tourists and succeeded in killing twenty-three—they were eventually overcome by Tunisian security after holding out for several hours.

Sousse Beach Resort—Tunisia, June 26, 2015

A lone gunman walked into the beach front hotel posing as a tourist and went through the hotel to the beach area where he began to systematically shoot civilians—he took the lives of thirty-nine tourists most of whom were British.

Tunisian Presidential Guard—Tunis, November 24, 2015

A suicide attack on a bus carrying members of the Tunisian Presidential Guard was carried out by an individual from ISIS—the bombing in the main street of Tunis killed twelve members of the Presidential Guard.

SUDAN

Sudan has been fighting an almost endless civil war between Muslims in the north and Christians in the south. Its government appears to have been devastated by the famine and poverty that have wrecked the nation (Figure 8-18). Sudan has, however, been on the U.S. State Department's list of countries that sponsor and support international terror groups. Safe haven and training grounds have been available to the ANO, Hezbollah, Hamas, and the PIJ. The UN Security Council passed several resolutions concerning the role of Sudan in sponsoring terror groups; not all have been complied with. One name stands apart from all others: Osama bin Laden. He was ordered to leave Sudan in 1997, but his legacy was to cause a military confrontation with the United States some twelve months later. Following the bombings of the U.S. embassies in the Kenyan and Tanzanian capitals, which claimed hundreds of lives, the United States struck back. In a reaction similar to that of Ronald Reagan, the Clinton administration retaliated on August 20, 1998. In his address to the nation then President Clinton stated, "Today I ordered our armed forces to strike at terrorist-related facilities in Afghanistan and Sudan because of the imminent threat they presented to our national security . . . In recent history they killed American, Belgian and Pakistani peacekeepers in Somalia. They plotted to assassinate the Pope and the president of Egypt. They planned to bomb six United States 747s over the Pacific . . . their (terrorist) mission is murder and their history

FIGURE 8-18 Map of Sudan. *Source:* Central Intelligence Agency, *The World Factbook, 2008.*

is bloody. The most recent terrorist events are fresh in our memory. Two weeks ago, twelve Americans and three hundred Kenyans and Tanzanians lost their lives. Another five thousand were wounded when our embassies in Nairobi and Dar es Salaam were bombed." The attack against a factory believed to be developing chemical weapons was carried out by a missile attack from U.S. naval ships in the Red Sea. The exact details of the strike were not confirmed; however, news reports seen on television indicated massive damage to the Al-Shifa Pharmaceutical Factory in Khartoum. Throughout the Middle East and Asia, there were spontaneous demonstrations against the United States, and the action probably gave impetus to the Islamic extremist movement in Afghanistan. As in the 1986 strike against Libya, this response is not seen as an effective deterrent for terrorism. To many analysts, it is seen as having precisely the opposite effect.

Darfur

Much is made of the term *genocide* and whether this is taking place in this region or not. What is definitely taking place is the total destruction of entire villages, including the rape and murder of women and children. As recently as the end of 2004, the Sudanese government made a peace deal with rebels it has been fighting in the southern part of the country for a quarter of a century. The region of Darfur has been in turmoil since 2003, likely as a result of the Sudanese government's fear of being unable to fight two separate insurgent uprisings at the same time and originating in far-flung, impoverished regions of the country.

The National Islamic Front government came to power through a military coup in 1989 and gets its support from Sudan's wealthy and economic interest groups, which reflect only a small minority of the Sudanese population. The peace deal brokered and then signed on January 9, 2005, with the southern rebels from the Sudan People's Liberation Movement/Army (SPLM), gave considerable power-sharing concessions to the rebel movement. The Comprehensive Peace Agreement provided for:

- A new constitution
- Power sharing
- Wealth sharing
- Security throughout the country

According to the agreement, new institutions would be created and a new government of National Unity installed once the constitution was ratified. SPLM Chairman John Garang would become the first vice president of Sudan and the new government of southern Sudan would be established. However, in Darfur, unlike the south, the problems began with the rise of two new movements to challenge the Khartoum regime—namely, the Sudan Liberation Movement/Army (SLA) and the Justice and Equality Movement (JEM). The region had been in conflict at both tribal and regional levels for decades and violent events were not uncommon, but the current levels of attack and counterattack by the government seem to be disproportionate to the problem. UN commissioners reported that the vast majority of attacks on civilians in villages have been carried out by government of Sudan armed forces and Janjaweed. The Janjaweed, or "evil horsemen," comprise mostly Arab ethnic militias. The attacks sponsored by the Khartoum government were aimed primarily at the African, rather than the Arab, population of Darfur.

The international legal definition of the crime of genocide is found in Articles II and III of the 1948 Convention on the Prevention and Punishment of Genocide. Article II describes two elements of the crime of genocide:

1. The mental element, meaning the "intent to destroy, in whole or in part, a national, ethnical, racial or religious group, as such," and
2. The physical element, which includes five acts described in sections a, b, c, d, and e. A crime must include both elements to be called "genocide."

Article III describes five punishable forms of the crime of genocide: genocide, conspiracy, incitement, attempt, and complicity.

EXCERPT FROM THE CONVENTION ON THE PREVENTION AND PUNISHMENT OF GENOCIDE

Article II

In the present Convention, genocide means any of the following acts committed with intent to destroy, in whole or in part, a national, ethnical, racial or religious group, as such:

(a) Killing members of the group;
(b) Causing serious bodily or mental harm to members of the group;
(c) Deliberately inflicting on the group conditions of life calculated to bring about its physical destruction in whole or in part;
(d) Imposing measures intended to prevent births within the group;
(e) Forcibly transferring children of the group to another group.

Article III: The Following Acts shall be Punishable

(a) Genocide;
(b) Conspiracy to commit genocide;
(c) Direct and public incitement to commit genocide;
(d) Attempt to commit genocide;
(e) Complicity in genocide.

It is a crime to plan or incite genocide, even before killing starts, and to aid or abet genocide. Criminal acts include conspiracy, direct and public incitement, attempts to commit genocide, and complicity in genocide.[62] What is clearly taking place in the Darfur region is state terrorism being inflicted on a subgroup and, in this instance, it is the non-Muslim population. The Janjaweed may or may not be practicing genocide, but perhaps the term "ethnic cleansing" could be used to describe the terrible events taking place. To date, we have witnessed that the international community under the auspices of the United Nations will pass resolutions, recommendations, and some sanctions against the government of the Sudan; however, the numbers killed run into the hundreds of thousands with over a million displaced.

ALGERIA

The People's Democratic Republic of Algeria (Algeria) emerged from its French colonial era through a nationalist movement that pitted the FLN (Front de Liberation Nationale) against French security forces, brutally aided by a pro-France terrorist organization known as the

Organisation armée secrète (OAS) (Figure 8-19). The terrorists' struggle lasted from 1954 to 1962; one million Algerians and seventeen thousand and five hundred French occupation forces were killed before the Evian Agreement of 1962 ended the FLN's campaign of assassination, bombing, and sabotage and the French's ferocious counterinsurgency campaign of torture, death, and repression.[63] The FLN emerged as victorious revolutionary heroes whose primary sense of political legitimacy lay in throwing out colonial suppressors. Algeria emerged from an effective, two-pronged FLN campaign against the French: the guerrilla war in the cities and rugged countryside of Algeria, and a diplomatic campaign in European and African capitals. France agreed to a plebiscite in 1962 on the issue of independence; ninety nine percent of the votes were cast in favor of Algerian independence. Ahmed Ben Bella, an FLN political leader during the war of independence, became the first president of independent Algeria. The FLN was in power from 1962 to 1992, when the civilian government was dissolved in a political coup.

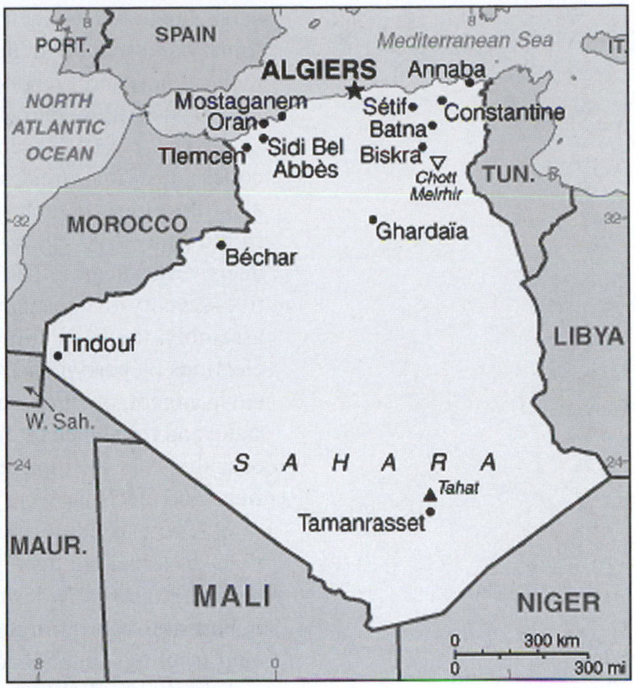

Algeria remained officially a one-party socialist country for the three decades of 1962 to 1992, assisted by the French in oil and gas technology, capital fusions, and foreign aid. Population growth increased the size of the nation from nine million in 1962 to more than twenty eight million in 1995; seventy five percent of Algerians are under the age of twenty-five.

The subsequent rise of a radical Islamic movement in Algeria, which won a round of the parliamentary elections in 1991, caused the FLN to abandon the election process and nullify the results. The party in question, the Islamic Salvation Front (FIS), was immediately banned by the FLN because of its radical Islamic goals. Following the ban, its military wing commenced a campaign of attacks against government and security forces.

FIGURE 8-19 Map of Algeria. *Source:* Central Intelligence Agency, *The World Factbook, 2008.*

Economic Crisis

It can be argued that the FLN was ineffective in governing Algeria from 1962 to 1992.[64] A rapidly growing number of young Algerians eager to secure economic positions and hoping for a brighter future encountered bureaucratic inefficiencies of a socialist state economy, coupled with corruption and rigid attempts to control entrepreneurship. A severe housing shortage emerged, along with declining agricultural and industrial production and a devastating drop in oil prices. The economic situation was complicated by a lack of consumer goods, high unemployment, and rising inflation. Servicing Algeria's huge foreign debt (more than $30 billion in 1995) requires almost all of the $9 billion in annual oil and gas revenues. In 1986, an austerity plan was imposed, in part to secure International Monetary Fund assistance.

October 1988 Riots

Algeria's deteriorating economic situation shattered social and economic expectations. Riots ensued and the military responded with excessive repression, firing on and killing hundreds of demonstrators. Thousands were arrested, and rumors began to circulate that security forces were torturing dissidents. Algeria's older citizenry, freedom fighters three decades before in the 1960–1962 era, equated the military's torture to that of the "Colons" (the sometimes-brutal French leaders of colonial days), a similarity that struck a chord and captured some Algerian hearts.

In late 1988, then President Chadli Bendjedid, undertook a democratic initiative. Referendums were held in 1988 and 1989, changing the constitution and including more respect for civil rights and a free press. Formation of political associations was permitted, and the one-party (FLN) system was abandoned. By February 1989, at least fifty new political parties were formed, including the Front Islamic du Salah (FIS), recognized as legal in September 1989 (Alexander). The FIS was organized through mosques and, by late 1989, had at least three million adherents. FIS political themes included criticizing the state bureaucracy, widespread corruption, and Western secular elites (French influences, primarily). Reflecting Islamic influences, subordination of women was advocated. The FIS sought an Islamic state governed by Islamic law; it proposed to discriminate against ethnic and other minorities (Berbers, Jews, Christians, polytheists, etc.) and French-speakers ("the enemies of God"). Religious extremists sought imposition of Sharia law into all aspects of politics and daily life in Algeria.

These earlier political pronouncements, especially the proposed imposition of puritan codes (drinking, dress, calendar, etc.), alarmed the educated, business people, and intellectuals. Minorities, French speakers, women, and the more educated staged counterdemonstrations. In the June 1990 elections for municipal, department, and provincial assemblies, the FLN was decisively defeated. The FIS won fifty-four percent of the popular vote cast, which totaled sixty-five–seventy-five percent of the eligible voters. Since no elections had been held for the national assembly, the FLN still controlled the national political scene and prepared for the June 1991 elections by gerrymandering to give more representation to FLN strongholds and districts. In this environment, one FIS leader (Abbassi Madani) called for a general strike, adoption of an Islamic state, and resistance through jihad and civil disobedience. The FIS was, interestingly, openly split over this call. Disruptive events occurred, but not mass revolution; the army declared a state of siege and elections were rescheduled for December.

There is some suggestion that the FIS might not have fared well in the fall 1991 elections, as it had not distinguished itself at local, urban, and municipal administration. It may have been that gerrymandering was an FLN provocation, and the FIS overreaction was triggered, in part, through infiltration of the FIS. In any event, the military declared a state of siege, banning meetings, publications, and demonstrations; suspending activities of political associations; and detaining civilian suspects. The military assumed local arrest authority and military tribunals conducted trials. FIS leaders were arrested en masse and detained in camps and jails. By fall 1991, the state of siege was lifted to permit elections, scheduled by Chadli Bendjedid for December 1991 and January 1992.

DECEMBER 1991 ELECTIONS   In the December phase of the national election, the FIS won 189 of 231 National Assembly seats with forty-seven percent of the eligible vote; the rejection of the FLN was obvious. Faced with a certain FIS victory, the military pressured the president to resign. The National Assembly was dissolved, and the Haut Comite d'Etat (HEC) imposed. On January 11, 1992, the military coup was affected. The HEC banned the FIS (its principal opposition party), jailed almost all the known leaders, detained some nine thousand–thirty thousand FIS members in five detention camps, and cracked down on the press. The latter included searching newspaper premises, expelling resident correspondents of European newspapers, arresting journalists writing for pro-fundamentalist papers, and jailing the editor of an independent weekly.

On January 22, authorities arrested the acting head of the FIS, radicalizing the movement and provoking widespread violence between FIS militants and security forces. A state of emergency was declared that continued until late 1995. By March 1992, the FIS leadership not in detention went underground or into exile, or migrated to adjacent countries. On May 5, military courts sentenced twelve FIS men to hang for the deaths of three army soldiers.[65] Five other Islamic extremist groups emerged and spread through Algeria: Armed Islamic Movement Group (an off-shoot of FIS), Armed Islamic Group, Hezbollah, Repentance and Emigration (*al-Takfir wa'l Hijra*), and Afghans (mostly veterans of the Afghanistan war). Actions were mostly decentralized acts of random terrorism and guerilla warfare. The volume of terrorist events increased sharply and included attacks on security forces, assault on the navy headquarters, and attacks on foreigners.[66] Bombings, assassinations, and attacks on government representatives expanded to include slitting the throats of captured foreigners, FLN members, and journalists. Disco dancers were killed by throat slitting and shooting. Petroleum workers were shot and plants were bombed. In the countryside, with its rugged terrain and desperately poor inhabitants, guerrillas controlled most of the mountain range. Satellite dishes were torn down, newspapers were banned, women were forced to wear traditional veils, men and women were segregated on buses, and Iranian-style enforcement of Islamic law prevailed. Eventually, an Air France airbus was hijacked, resulting in French security forces storming the plane, rescuing the hostages, and killing the hijackers.[67] Four nuns in Algiers were subsequently killed in retaliation. Iran and the Sudan provided arms and military training to the terrorists. To cut French support of the Algerian regime ($1.2 billion in annual aid to the Algerian government, intelligence, and training), a series of bombings in Paris in 1995 and other French cities was undertaken, resulting in deaths and casualties and putting a considerable dent in tourism.

Algerian military undertook brutal and repressive actions in response to Islamic terrorism and violence. Military courts began executing civilians convicted in the three courts that enforced the stringent antiterrorism law; and a strict curfew was declared. Pro-government death squads patrolled both rural and urban areas, and anti-FIS vigilantes took the law into their own hands. Villages formed self-defense groups to ward off FIS terrorism. Riots within prisons were fostered by FIS and other resistance members and were brutally repressed, along with the wholesale slaughter of detained FIS leaders.[68] The army was expanded through conscription, with mandatory military service of eighteen months. The military elite argued that Islamic extremism could be stopped only by force.

By 1994, foreign investment had dwindled to a trickle, families of diplomats were evacuated, embassies had been closed, the official unemployment rate had risen to 20 percent, the Algerian dinar (money) had been devalued by fifty percent, and servicing the international debt was consuming most of the petroleum-generated income. Efforts toward "national reconciliation" by national dialogue were made but failed, primarily by government intransigence in meeting directly with FIS leaders, or FIS boycotting of dialogues in other international sites. Even "secret meetings" appeared to have no appreciable ameliorative effect. It was in this environment that the military regime replaced the HEC with retired General Liamine Zeroual as president, signaling the direct movement of the military into the political arena. The rise of armed Islamic groups came to fruition in 1992 when the military government voided the victory of the FIS, the largest Islamic opposition party, in the first round of legislative elections held in December 1991. Islamists were aiming for a pure Islamic state and centered many of their attacks on the civilian population, inflicting countless massacres.

The Armed Islamic Group

The Armed Islamic Group (GIA) is an FIS splinter organization that continued the fight against the Algerian military regime in 1992. Since this North African country plunged into a civil war that year, the group has been linked to terrorist attacks in Europe and to the massacres of tens of thousands of civilians in Algeria. The government crackdown has been as fierce in Algeria as that witnessed in Egypt, and, in a similar vein, the GIA seeks to overthrow the current regime and replace it with a radical Islamic one. Many GIA members have joined other groups in Algeria to continue attacks against the secular government. GIA is also credited with the audacious hijacking of an Air France airliner from Algeria to France in 1994, in which the terrorists had planned to set off explosives over the French capital, Paris. The GIA has targeted ex-colonial rulers in particular and has carried out limited bombing campaigns in France. France became the natural target as the Algerian government sought support from France to clamp down on GIA activists operating and raising funds for the overthrow of the secular Algerian government.

Rais Massacre, Algeria

In 1997, Algeria was at the peak of a civil war that had begun after the military's cancellation of the 1992 elections, in fear that it would be won by the FIS. The farming village of Rais had been supporting Islamist guerrillas in the region over a period of time but had recently stopped providing them food and money. The attackers arrived at the village in the early morning hours, armed with shotguns, knives, axes, and bombs. They killed the village's men, women, children, and even animals, until dawn, cutting throats and taking the time to burn corpses. They mutilated and stole from the dead and committed atrocities against pregnant women. Estimates indicate more than four hundred were killed.[69]

The French government has continued to support the military government in Algeria, much to the opposition and ire of the GIA. Possible links to al Qaeda could relate to Ahmed Ressam, an Algerian national who attempted to cross from Canada to the United States with a bomb destined for Los Angeles International Airport in what is termed the "millennium plot." Although Ressam is Algerian and is believed to have met with al Qaeda operatives, this does not necessarily widen the ties between the two groups. The GIA's aims are purely internal, as the group advocates the removal of the secular government, whereas the al Qaeda objectives are clearly truly international.

Many Algerians, tired of the poor standards of living, yearn to leave their country. Most who have fled have gone to France, but many have fled to and sought refugee status in Canada. Their ability to speak French makes the Province of Quebec an ideal choice for settlement. The relentless killings and massacres bought little internal support for the GIA, and popular support diminished significantly by the end of the last decade of the twentieth century. The GIA officially rejected a 1999 amnesty law, but not so by its rank and file, who came down from their mountain hideouts, renounced their ways, and returned to their old lives after surrendering their weapons. Although this has meant a significant drop in GIA violence, with over eighty-five percent of its members deserting, it has likely been eclipsed by a new subgroup. The Salafist Group for Preaching and Combat (GSPC), together with the GIA, both denounce the amnesty of President Bouteflika. Unlike GIA, GSPC has not concentrated its attacks on the civilian population. GSPC has also pledged its allegiance to al Qaeda.

AL QAEDA IN THE LAND OF THE ISLAMIC MAGHREB, FORMERLY GSPC

On September 14, 2006, the GSPC formally swore its allegiance to Osama bin Laden and renamed the GSPC "al Qaeda in the Land of the Islamic Maghreb." With the demise of GIA, AQIM is taking the lead; however, there is again the probability that many within this movement, in similar fashion to the GIA, want to accept the government's amnesty proposals. This has led to factional fighting from within. In November 2004, the government proposed a new ceasefire for GSPC and its members, who total around five hundred, although significant losses suffered through the relentless actions of the Algerian security apparatus led to a slow but gradual collapse of this particular insurgency. GSPC had set up Islamic training camps in neighboring Chad, and, in 2004, one of the group's significant figures, Amari Saifi, a former Algerian paratrooper, was captured by rebels from the Movement for Democracy and Justice in Chad (MDJT).[70] The MDJT had offered to hand him over to the Algerians, but as time passed, he was handed over to the Libyan government and then to Algeria. Libya's involvement in this incident is probably a direct desire of the Qaddafi regime to show its commitment to the U.S. War on Terror. The Libyans had, in fact, threatened to launch military strikes against the rebels in Chad if Saifi was not handed over. In December 2006 and March 2007, the Islamic Maghreb launched its bombing campaign with roadside bomb attacks targeting foreign nationals in both attacks. This was a significant development and took the focus away from the internecine warfare attacks carried out in previous years and the senseless massacre of civilians. With the new focus on oil exploration and foreign workers, the newly improved and equipped GSPC were seeking to intimidate the West as did the insurgents in Iraq, by attacking oil and gas lines. While the West seeks oil farther away from the Middle East, attention has gravitated to oil rich areas in Africa. On April 11, 2007, the group launched a well-orchestrated suicide attack on the capital Algiers with suicide truck bombings killing thirty and injuring over two hundred. The attempt at destabilizing the government was the main goal here.

GIA/GSPC's operational presence in Europe is also a consideration, and this expansion was a result of the wave of crackdowns against Islamist militants by the Algerian government in the early 1990s. The Islamists spread to Spain, France, Italy, Britain, and Sweden and beyond. Large numbers of Algerian fighters have turned up in Chechnya and Bosnia as well as Iraq and Afghanistan and more recently in neighboring Libya. The unstable nature of Libya in 2011 posed significant political as well as security concerns for Algeria. The rebels in Libya could easily provide a safe haven for al Qaeda. The recent Arab unrest that swept Tunisia and Egypt and to a lesser extent Algeria did not have the same outcome as the latter two countries and that may be as a result of recent history. It is likely that memories related to the violence of the civil war are still too recent and represent a powerful deterrent to a full-scale revolt. An unstable Libya with a strong AQIM presence would likely engender groups within Algeria to move violently toward regime change. Only time will tell as to the effects of the Libyan uprisings on Algeria.

Summary

This chapter has covered the establishment of the State of Israel and the conflict it has faced from displaced Palestinians. The conflict has seen the rise of powerful terror groups sponsored by states with the ultimate destruction of the Jewish State. Hamas and Hezbollah are both working inside and supporting various factions in the Syrian Civil War and Iran in the background attempts to undermine and attack Israel. Israel may continue to remain the major power broker in the region and is prepared to use its military might whenever and wherever it sees fit to protect its nationhood. As for Palestine, how the unity government involving Hamas and Fatah will effectively operate will continue to focus our attention, as will the behavior of any new government in Egypt. Civil war and the presence of Islamic State, al Qaeda and others in Syria has brought in Russia, Iran, and the United States—the outlook for any peace in this region is bleak. While the United States and Europe continue to target ISIS in Syria, it is making inroads into Libya in the vacuum left there. The Muslim Brotherhood has been displaced from power in Egypt where its ever strong military controls events on the political landscape. Events in Libya and the rise of Islamic State attempting to gain a foothold from which to launch attacks and train fighters for jihad in western Europe and to export its brand of terror into sub-Saharan Africa will be ongoing for many years to come.

Review Questions

1. Describe the formation of the State of Israel and the methods employed by the young state to defend against external threats of violence and terror.
2. Define the principal difference separating Hamas and al Fatah.
3. Summarize the rise of the Muslim Brotherhood and its involvement in the political scene in Egypt.
4. Demonstrate how the Islamic State sets about gaining ground using Libya as an example.

End Notes

1. William Roger Louis. *The British Empire in the Middle East 1945–1951* (Oxford: Clarendon Press, 1988, p. 439).
2. Mark Ethridge. U.S. member of the Palestine Conciliation Report to State Department. Top Secret, NIACT (Beirut, March 28, 1949, FRUS 1949, pp. 876, 878).
3. Donald Neff. *Fallen Pillars: U.S. Policy towards Palestine and Israel since 1945* (Washington, DC: Institute for Palestine Studies, 1995, p. 83).
4. "The Foundation for Middle East Peace," Report on Israeli Settlement in the Occupied Territories, Special Report (July 1991); and Richard F. Nyrop, Ed., *Israel: A Country Study*, 2nd ed. (Washington, DC: U.S. Government Printing Office, 1979), XIX: Epilogue, p. 185.
5. Security Council. Published by United Nations, © 1976.
6. Noam Chomsky. *The New Intifada, Resisting Israel's Apartheid*, edited by Roane Carey (London: Verso, 2001, p. 13).
7. "The Beginning of the End of the Palestinian Uprising?" *The Economist* (September 29, 2001, p. 50).
8. Israel Secret Intelligence Service. http://www.mossad.gov.il/ Eng/About/History.aspx.
9. *Frosts Meditations*. http://www.martinfrost.ws/htmlfiles/ june2009/shlomo-argov.html.
10. George Rosie. *The Directory of International Terrorism* (New York: Paragon House, 1987, p. 290).
11. Ibid., p. 36.
12. "An Overview of the Gaza Strip." *Union of Palestinian Relief Committees Journal*, issue no. 25 (March 1997, p. 3).
13. *Israeli Insider*. http://israelinsider.com/home.htm.
14. Gil Sedan. "Over The Years, Sheik Yassin Grew In Status, Violence And Radicalism." PASSIA; IDF; Associated Press, and CNN.com (March 22, 2004); *Jewish Telegraphic Agency* (March 23, 2004).
15. This material was drawn from an article by Ahmad Rashad. "The Truth about Hamas." http://www.rjgeib.com/biography/ milken/crescent-moon/near-asia/palestine/palestine.htm.
16. "Hamas Has the Peoples' Heart." *The Economist* (December 1, 2001, p. 43).
17. "Martyrs and Traitors," *The Economist* (June 23, 2007).
18. http://www.palestinefacts.org/pf_1967to1991_terrorism_ 1970s.php.
19. Jewish Virtual Library. http://www.jewishvirtuallibrary.org/ jsource/biography/Gilad_Shalit.html, downloaded April 23, 2016.
20. MILNET. "Patterns of Global Terrorism." Articles maintained by George Goncalves. *United States Department of State Publications* 10321 (1997). http://www.state.gov/r/pa/ei/rls/dos/221.htm.
21. http://www.fas.org/irp/threat/terror_90/mideast.html.
22. MILNET. "Patterns of Global Terrorism." (1997).
23. MIPT. "Terrorism Knowledge Base." www.tkb.org.
24. MILNET. "Patterns of Global Terrorism." (1997).
25. http://www.haaretz.com/hasen/objects/pages/PrintArticleEn. jhtml?itemNo=568735.
26. MILNET. "Patterns of Global Terrorism." (1997).
27. Israeli Ministry of Foreign Affairs. "Main Points of the Declaration of Principles." (September 13, 1993). http://www. israel.org/MFA/Peace+Process/Guide+to+the+Peace+Process/ Declaration+of+Principles+_+Main+Points.htm.
28. Edward Said. "Palestinians Under Siege." *The New Intifada, Resisting Israel's Apartheid*, Ed. Roane Carey (London: Verso, 2001, p. 33).
29. Tom Gross. "Children Are Indoctrinated Into Terrorism." *The Weekly Telegraph*, issue no. 371. (London: Telegraph Group Inc., September 1, 1998, p. 20).
30. Richard Clutterbuck. *Guerrillas and Terrorists* (Athens, OH: Ohio University Press, 1980, p. 80).

31. Israeli Ministry of Foreign Affairs. www.mfa.gov.il.

32. Paul Wilkinson. *Terrorism and the Liberal State* (New York: New York University Press, 1979, p. 49).

33. Khaled Yacoub Oweis. "Slain Christian Warlord Had No Shortage of Enemies." Article by Reuters, *Daily Telegraph* (London January 25, 2002).

34. "London: Lebanon's Victims," *Daily Telegraph* (November 23, 2006).

35. "Sunnis and Shiites, the Great Schism." *Political Islam Glossary*, ibid.

36. Ayala Hammond Schbley. "A Study of Some of the Lebanese Shia's Contemporary Terrorism." *Terrorism: An International Journal*, vol. 12, no. 4 (Basingstoke, England: Taylor and Francis, 1989, p. 220).

37. Magnus Ranstorp. "Hizballah's Command Leadership." *Terrorism and Political Violence*, vol. 6, no. 3 (London: Frank Cass, 1994, p. 304).

38. Yonah Alexander. *Hizballah: The Most Dangerous Terrorist Movement*, vol. 4, no. 10 (New York: Intersec, Three Bridges Publishing Ltd., October 1994, p. 393).

39. Edgar O'Ballance. *Islamic Fundamentalist Terrorism*, vol. 5, no. 1 (New York Intersec, Three Bridges Publishing Ltd., January 1995, p. 14).

40. Guy Lawson. "A Few Good Martyrs." *Time* (January 2002, pp. 89–93).

41. "Patterns of Global Terrorism: 1997." *U.S. State department*, Hellenic Resources Network. http://www.hri.org/docs/USSD-Terror.

42. "Hezbollah: The Real U.S. Target in Lebanon." *Jane's Foreign Report* (Coulsdon, Surrey: Jane's Information Group, Sentinel House, March 10, 2005).

43. Hezbollah (Party of God), "In the spotlight" (August 24, 2006). www.cdi.org.

44. Jonathan R. White. *Terrorism: An Introduction*, 2nd ed. (Belmont, CA: Wadsworth Publishing Co., 1997, p. 141).

45. Country Reports on Terrorism. U.S. Dept of State. http://www.state.gov/j/ct/rls/crt/2014/239407.htm.

46. Heather Bleaney and Richard Lawless. *The Middle East since 1945* (London: B.T. Batsford Ltd., 1989, p. 37).

47. Ibid.

48. International Policy Institute for Counterterrorism. www.ict.org.

49. Zachary Laub. "Egypt's Muslim Brotherhood." CFR Backgrounders. http://www.cfr.org/egypt/egypts-muslim-brotherhood/p23991.

50. Ibid.

51. "Anti-Semitism World Report." (Libya, 1997). http://www.tau.ac.il/Anti-Semitism/annual-report.html.

52. "Patterns of Global Terrorism: 1984." *Terrorism: An International Journal*, vol. 9, no. 3 (Basingstoke, England: Crane Russak & Company Inc., 1987, p. 419).

53. U.S. Treasury Press Release (February 8, 2006). http://www.ustreas.gov/press/releases/archives/200602.html.

54. U.S. Department of State. U.S. Accountability Review Board Report on Benghazi Embassy Attack, dated December 2012. http://www.state.gov/documents/organization/202446.pdf.

55. *ISIS in Libya: A Major Regional and International Threat*. The Meir Amit Intelligence and Terrorism Information Center at the Israeli Intelligence and Heritage Commemoration Center. (January, 2016).

56. Ibid.

57. Ibid.

58. Aaron Y. Zelin. *The Islamic State's Territorial Methodology*. The Washington Institute for Near East Policy No.29, January 2016.

59. Ibid.

60. Ibid.

61. Ibid.

62. http://www.preventgenocide.org.

63. George Rosie. *Directory of International Terrorism* (New York: Paragon House, 1986).

64. Martha Crenshaw. "Political Violence in Algeria." *Terrorism and Political Violence*, vol. 6, no. 3 (1994, pp. 261–280).

65. Youssef Ibrahim. "Algeria Sentences 12 Militants to Hang," *The New York Times* (May 4, 1992, p. A-3).

66. Rachid Khiari. "Downtrodden Algeria Ruled by Death, Fear," *San Francisco Examiner* (April 4, 1994, p. A-9).

67. Thomas Sancton. "Anatomy of a Hijack," *Time* (January 9, 1995, pp. 54–57).

68. Jesse Birnbaum. "The Prison of Blood," *Time* (March 6, 1995).

69. Rais Massacre. http://en.wikipedia.org/wki/Rais_massacre.

70. *Jane's Intelligence Digest* (November 12, 2004).

The Persian Gulf

LEARNING OUTCOMES

After studying this chapter, students should be able to:

1. Summarize the role played by Saudi Arabia in balancing power in the Middle East.
2. Describe how Sunni groups have risen to prominence in sectarian fighting in Iraq.
3. Examine Iran's supporting and exporting terrorism in the Middle East.
4. Define the conditions that have allowed the rise of Islamic State in Iraq.
5. Describe the fundamental differences between al Qaeda and Islamic State.

KEY WORDS TO NOTE

Abu Bakr al-Baghdadi—Leader of the Islamic State—proclaimed the first emir of the Islamic Sate of Iraq and Levant in 2014

Abu Musab al-Zarqawi—Jordanian militant who ran terror training camps in Iraq and formed al Qaeda in Iraq—killed by U.S. forces in 2006

Amn al-Kharji—The little known foreign intelligence department for the Islamic State

Anwar al-Awlaki—A dual citizen (the United States and Yemen)—killed in a U.S. drone strike in Yemen in 2011, had acted as a planner and trainer for al Qaeda and affiliates

Arab Spring—A series of antigovernment protests, uprisings, and armed rebellions that spread across the Middle East in early 2011

Ba'athist Regime—Arab nationalist party with a mostly secular ideology that often contrasts with that of other Arab governments in the Middle East

Badr Brigade—Shiite militia group composed of Iraqi military officers who escaped, defected, or were captured during and after the Iran–Iraq war, 1980–1988

Islamic Revolutionary Guard Corps (IRGC)—Army of the Guardians of the Islamic Revolution—formed in Iran following the revolution to protect the Islamic regime

Mahdi Army—Formed in 2003, the Mahdi Army is an armed group loyal to Muqtada al-Sadr, a Shia leader from a family line of revered clerics persecuted under Saddam Hussein

Qods Force—Part of the Islamic Revolutionary Guard Corps (IRGC) responsible for extraterritorial operations, including terrorist operations. A primary focus is training Islamic fundamentalist terrorist groups

Sayyid Qutb—Egyptian and member of the Muslim Brotherhood

Sharia (Islamic Law)—The Islamic code or laws observed in many Muslim countries

OVERVIEW

Recent historic events in the Persian Gulf, the body of water that is surrounded by a number of Arab and Islamic states, is now well known to most students. The oil crises, the exile of the Shah of Iran, the Iraq–Iran war of the 1980s, the hostages at the U.S. Embassy in Iran, the Gulf

War of the early 1990s, the invasion of Iraq in 2003, and the Arab Spring, unrest in Bahrain, and civil war in Yemen have made the "Persian Gulf" a household term. Perhaps one of the most important areas of the world, especially when we consider state-sponsored terrorism, the Persian Gulf is surrounded by some of the biggest players on the field of terrorism. This chapter takes a fast-moving tour through the history and background of the major political and religious events in this region. We discuss how these countries are shaping the future of this region and how their past has influenced the present.

SAUDI ARABIA

The Kingdom of Saudi Arabia has borders with the Persian Gulf and the Red Sea, north of Yemen. The kingdom is slightly more than one-fifth the size of the United States, but only 2 percent of its land is considered arable (Figure 9-1). Bordering countries are Iraq, Jordan, Kuwait, Oman, Qatar, the United Arab Emirates, and Yemen. Its petroleum, natural gas, iron ore, gold, and copper have made Saudi Arabia and its ruling elite fabulously wealthy. The Saudis' extensive coastlines on the Persian Gulf and Red Sea provide leverage on shipping (especially crude oil) through the Gulf and the Suez Canal. Its population of only 20 million (which includes 5 million non-nationals) is able to build and support the infrastructure for the Kingdom in grand style. Ethnic groups are limited; 90 percent of the population is Arab and the remainder is Afro-Asian. One hundred percent are Muslim, and the official language is Arabic. As an Islamic monarchy, Saudi Arabia has no constitution. It is governed according to **Sharia (Islamic law)**; a literal translation of the word means the "path" and is also described by theologians as "God's Law." Sharia is supposed to be interpreted, and the law derived, from four sources:

1. The Quran, Islam's holy book, viewed by Muslims as the literal word of God;
2. The *hadith*, or record of the actions and sayings and preaching of the Prophet Muhammad;
3. The *ijma*, the consensus of Islamic scholars; and
4. The *qiyas*, a reasoning that uses analogies to apply precedents established by the holy texts in the Quran to problems not covered by them; for example, a ban on narcotics based on the Quranic injunction against wine drinking.

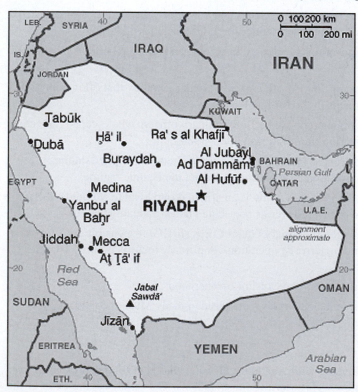

FIGURE 9-1 Map of Saudi Arabia. *Source:* Central Intelligence Agency, The World Factbook, 2008.

The Sharia governs all aspects of Muslim life, and some aspects of it have formed part of the current Islamic legal codes. Where there is opportunity to interpret laws, as is the case in democratic legal forums, Sharia has developed through five separate schools since the death of the Prophet Muhammad, four in the Sunni sect and one in the Shia sect.[1] Religious freedom is not recognized or protected under the laws, and basic religious freedoms are denied to all but those who adhere to the state-sanctioned version of Sunni Islam. The government limits the practice of all but the officially sanctioned version of Islam and prohibits the public practice of other religions.

King Abdul Aziz

The history of modern Saudi Arabia began in 1902, when Abdul Aziz Al-Sa'ud and a band of his followers captured the city of Riyadh, returning it to the control of his family. Abdul Aziz was born around 1880 and spent the early years of his life with his father in exile in Kuwait. After the capture of Riyadh, he spent the next twelve years consolidating his conquests in the area around Riyadh and the eastern part of the country, from where the Turks were expelled. The Arab tribes had never liked the Turks, and they were only too willing to listen to a new ruler, whose ambitions were assisted considerably by the troubles in the Ottoman Empire. In 1933, the lands under the control of Abdul Aziz were renamed the Kingdom of Saudi Arabia, and in 1936 a treaty was signed with Yemen marking it as the southern borders of the Saudi Kingdom.

Abdul Aziz's main preoccupations were the consolidation of his power and the restoration of law and order to all parts of his recently created kingdom. To these ends, he developed a system whereby every sheikh was responsible for his own tribe under the authority of the King, who was empowered to intervene to impose law and order. It was clearly understood that internal anarchy within the kingdom could quickly lead to foreign intervention. All agreed that this was unacceptable. King Abdul Aziz died in 1953, after more than half a century as leader, and King Saud bin Abdul Aziz, his eldest son, succeeded him to the throne. After eleven years, King Saud abdicated in favor of his brother, Faisal, the crown prince. In March 1975, King Faisal was assassinated in Riyadh by one of his nephews. The transfer of power, however, went smoothly, and King Khalid bin Abdul Aziz took power, with Fahad bin Abdul Aziz being made crown prince. King Khalid continued most of King Faisal's popular policies. It was during King Khalid's reign that Saudi Arabia enjoyed the prosperity and enormous wealth of the "petrodollar" boom years.

King Khalid died in June 1982 and was succeeded by Crown Prince Fahad bin Abdul Aziz. King Fahad was well versed in the art of governing, as he had served as the country's first minister of education. King Khalid had been in poor health for much of his reign, so Fahad ruled in all but title. Continuing development within the country and the infrastructure marked King Fahad's reign. On the political front, Iran's open hostility toward Saudi Arabia led the government to strengthen its ties of defense with the United States, Britain, and France.

Within days of Iraq's invasion of Kuwait in 1990, King Fahad allowed U.S. troops into the kingdom to help defend the country. In November 1990, he announced that plans were being made for the formation of a consultative council; there was some feeling that this was done in response to criticism that he had not consulted widely enough before allowing foreign troops into the kingdom. In any case, in March 1992, the king announced that the consultative council would be appointed by year's end, and he made its duties clear. Like other such creations in the Gulf States, the council is a purely consultative body with no legislative powers. Its formation, however, simply put an official stamp on the long-standing system of consultation, which has long been a mark of Arab politics and society. King Fahad suffered a stroke in 1995 and died on August 1, 2005. He was succeeded by his half-brother, Crown Prince Abdullah who died at the age of 90 in early 2015—the kingdom is currently ruled by King Salman. He has continued his predecessor's reforms and for the first time women were allowed to vote and stand for office with several being elected in the December 2015 elections.

The George W. Bush administration had a primary mission in the region, that of hunting down al Qaeda in the Gulf States. President George W. Bush made some tough statements on June 24, 2002, when he outlined the new U.S. plan for peace in the Middle East and set specific terms for dealing with the Palestinians. He again called on Palestinians to reform and promised that when the Palestinian people have new leaders, new institutions, and new security arrangements with their neighbors, the United States would approve and support the creation of a Palestinian State, whose borders and certain aspects of its sovereignty will be provisional until resolved as part of a final settlement in the Middle East. Since that statement, little has changed, although some positive recognition has come to the Palestinians, they remain mired in conflict between Hamas, controlling the Gaza Strip, and the Fatah-dominated region of the West Bank.

Demanding that the Palestinians essentially replace Yasser Arafat, Washington had substantially improved Arafat's position. Anyone within the Palestinian community (at that time) who had demanded Arafat's resignation was open to the charge of collaborating with the Americans. The United States was aware of the consequences of its demand. By making reform and new leadership prerequisites for further American participation in a peace process, the United States created the framework for its withdrawal from that process.

The U.S. president was, in effect, washing his hands of trying to solve the Israeli-Palestinian conflict. Washington's challenge, however, was not aimed at the Palestinians but at the country that pushed for greater U.S. involvement in the peace process—Saudi Arabia.

FROM THE PALESTINIANS TO RIYADH

Saudi Arabia inserted itself in the peace process when Crown Prince Abdullah used a column written by the *New York Times* writer Thomas Friedman, earlier in 2002, to publicize his own newly created Middle East peace proposal. Abdullah offered Israel complete normalization of ties with all the Arab States in exchange for Israel's full withdrawal to the 1967 borders. Though this was a promise Riyadh actually could not deliver, the tactic worked to buy time and direct the U.S. focus away, albeit temporarily, from Iraq and al Qaeda.

President Bush's Middle East policy appeared to make the United States eager to expand its involvement in the Middle East conflict. It was clear that the Bush administration would be able to achieve reforms only if the Palestinians were willing to work with Washington. However, peace required a new and different Palestinian leadership, and with Arafat's death in 2004, the way should have been cleared for the "road map" to take shape. President Bush indicated that although Washington would continue to be engaged, its focus will change. Specifically, the Bush administration will try to segment its Middle East policy, placing the Israeli-Palestinian conflict in a box to freely adopt a policy to pursue its primary Middle Eastern goals of destroying the al Qaeda and its wider plans of establishing democracy in Iraq and the region. Containing Iran and its designs on nuclear weapons also figures into U.S. strategy for the region. The single most important piece of any U.S. strategy to annihilate bin Laden's terrorist network is to do something about Saudi Arabia. Since Riyadh continues to be a key U.S. ally in the Gulf, whereas the other regional power, Iran, is decidedly anti-American, Washington has resisted placing any blame for 9-11 squarely on the Saudis. Under the Obama administration the Saudis have become increasingly frustrated with the U.S. foreign policy or lack thereof. Firstly, Saudi Arabia, which supports the opposition groups lined up against President Assad in Syria, felt betrayed when President Obama backed off promises to aid the opposition; it was further angered when President Obama decided on diplomacy over a military strike on Syria for its use of chemical weapons. In addition, Saudi Arabia continues to feel threatened by the warming of relations between the U.S. and Iran.

AL QAEDA AND THE SAUDI KINGDOM

Immediately after the events of 9-11, the United States considered that the efforts by the Saudi regime to track down supporters of al Qaeda were insufficient. It is important to note that the Saudi Royal family has over six thousand princes, including forty-five ruling princes, and it should be no surprise to discover that there are splits within the family as to the support being given and offered to the United States. The ruling princes are mostly progressive in their attitudes toward the West, but there are a growing number within the family who are more conservative. Strong anti-Western sentiment, not just in the Middle East but also in Saudi Arabia, will pose difficulties for the dictatorial governance of the king. The decade of the 1980s was characterized by the rise of ultraconservative, politically activist Islamic movements in much of the Arab world. These Islamist movements, labeled *fundamentalist* in the West, sought the government institutionalization of Islamic laws and social principles. Although Saudi Arabia already claimed to be an Islamic government whose constitution is the Quran, the kingdom has not been immune to this conservative trend.[2]

WAHHABI ISLAM

The term *Wahhabism* is a designation for the religious movement within Islam founded by Muhammad ibn Abd al-Wahhab (1703–1792). Members describe themselves as muwahhidun ("unitarians"), those who uphold firmly the doctrine that God is one, the only one (tawhid). This self-designation points to the movement's major characteristic—its opposition to any custom or belief threatening and jeopardizing the glorification of the one God. Wahabbiyyah is not a new sect within Islam but a movement whose purpose is to purify Islam of perceived heretical accretions. The Wahhabis base their doctrines on the teachings of the fourteenth-century scholar Ibn Taymiyyah and of the Hanbali School of Law, the strictest of the four recognized in the Sunni consensus. They believe that all objects of worship other than Allah are false, and anyone who worships in this way deserves to be put to death. To introduce the name of a prophet, saint, or angel into a prayer or to seek intercession from anyone but Allah constitutes a form of polytheism. Attendance at public prayer is compulsory, and the shaving of the beard and smoking are forbidden. Mosques should be architecturally simple, not luxurious or ornate. Prohibited are the celebrations of the Prophet's birthday, making offerings at the tomb of saints, and playing music. The injunctions of the Quran are to be taken literally.[3]

Osama bin Laden came from a wealthy Saudi background and yet spent little time immersed in the teachings and preaching of the strict adherence to Wahhabism. From his behavior and comments, it would be more likely to assume he accepted the ideology of Sayyid Qutb. Qutb is considered by many Muslims to be one of the most influential Muslim thinkers of the twentieth century. He studied briefly in the United States in the early 1950s and was appalled by what he saw as the debased nature of society. He has written many books which have influenced Islamists and nurtured the rise of groups such as al Qaeda. Bin Laden believed that the Saudi Royal family's support for Western interests was a betrayal of Islam. Although the strict adherence to Wahhabism continues in the kingdom, the Saudi approach had always been to encourage those who wanted to spread the word of Islam, and violent jihad to do so elsewhere—but not at home within the Saudi Kingdom. This strategy worked well, with the Saudis exporting militants to Bosnia, Afghanistan, and Iraq. Attacks on Western interests in the Kingdom indicate clearly that the influences of the al Qaeda network are no longer confined to remote locations in Afghanistan and the Russian Republics. Fighters are returning to Saudi Arabia and are targeting the Western influences within the Kingdom. Al Qaeda's ultimate goals for the kingdom remain the:

- removal of the Royal family and
- removal of all Western influences in the Kingdom.

Owing to the U.S. presence in Iraq, anti-Western sentiment grew quickly in Saudi Arabia. To effectively deal with al Qaeda operatives and sympathizers, the Saudis needed to rely on their own security apparatus. Although Saudi security services have arrested many terror suspects, they had been unable to infiltrate al Qaeda, garnering most of their intelligence from arrested suspects. Throughout 2003 and 2004, in almost every shootout that took place, involving attacks against Western targets and Saudi security forces, al Qaeda members were able to escape to fight another day. The availability of well-trained bomb makers returning from Iraq to set up operations in Saudi Arabia has had the desired effect on Western companies. So many had been targeted during the last decade that it had a negative effect on the oil economy of the Saudi Kingdom, which is almost totally reliant on Western expertise for its oil production. Al Qaeda's actual strength in the kingdom may be small and limited in number, but it has the sympathy of about fifty percent of the population. This sympathy, coupled with any possible power struggle within the Saudi Royal family, could lead to an eventual collapse of the existing pro-Western regime.

At the end of 2004, bin Laden was calling openly for attacks against his Saudi homeland. However, security forces in the kingdom have been cracking down hard since the string of bomb attacks in 2003. Al Qaeda's leader on the Saudi Peninsula, Fahd bin Faraj al-Juweir, is on record threatening Westerners and also the Saudi regime itself. He led a failed suicide attack on the Abqaiq Oil Refinery on February 24, 2006, and was subsequently killed three days later in a two-hour shootout with Saudi security forces. Two suicide attackers, both on a list of wanted militants, were killed in the refinery attack, which was the first significant strike by al Qaeda militants on oil facilities in the region (Figure 9-2).

Arab Spring—Saudi Arabia

The 2011 **Arab Spring** did actually resonate in the Saudi Kingdom and was in part led by the Shiite cleric Sheikh Nimr Baqir al-Nimr. He emerged as a figurehead in the protests that began in 2011 inspired by the Arab Spring. Here was a prominent, outspoken cleric who articulated the feelings of those in the country's Shia minority who feel marginalized and discriminated against. This was a figure active on the sensitive Sunni-Shia sectarian fault line that creates tension in the Kingdom and far beyond. Nimr has been portrayed by Saudi Arabia as a violent radical with loyalties to Iran. Nimr has been a stern and outspoken critic of the Saudi ruling family. He returned to Saudi Arabia in the mid-1990s following a period in exile.

General Statistics	
Total Attacks	1,920
Total Deaths	19,185
Total Wounded	45,254
Average Deaths per Attack	10
Average Wounded per Attack	23.6

FIGURE 9-2 General statistics for suicide attacks 2000–2015. *Source:* Chicago Project on Security and Terrorism, http://cpost.uchicago.edu.

He was arrested and imprisoned several times and was again arrested by Saudi security forces in 2012, after being shot in the legs during a car chase. He had been charged with "instigating unrest and undermining the kingdom's security," as well as delivering speeches against the government and defending political prisoners.[4] Saudi Arabia announced that the cleric had been executed along with forty-six others on January 2, 2016. Almost all those executed were for al Qaeda linked terror offences. One of those executed is believed to be a man convicted of shooting dead a freelance cameraman on an assignment for the BBC, Simon Cumbers, in 2004. Adel al-Dubayti was sentenced in November 2014 for his role in multiple al Qaeda attacks including the one in the capital Riyadh in which Cumbers was killed and which also left reporter Frank Gardner critically injured.[5]

SAYYID QUTB (1906–1996)

Sayyid Qutb joined the Muslim Brotherhood (MB) in 1951 and is probably the one man who could be considered the ideological grandfather of Osama bin Laden and the other extremists who surrounded him. Sayyid Qutb became radicalized on a trip to the United States back in the early 1950s. As Qutb traveled through America, he was shocked at the moral and spiritual degeneracy he observed, stating that "no one is more distant than the Americans from spirituality and piety."

In his home country of Egypt, his outspoken behavior brought him into direct conflict with the pro-Western government. Like so many other young radicals, he was imprisoned for his membership in the banned MB. One of the most important things Sayyid Qutb wrote during his incarceration was his explanation of how a Muslim might justly assassinate a ruler. For a long time, killing political rulers was expressly forbidden in Islam—even an unjust ruler was regarded as better than the anarchy of no ruler. Instead, the religious leaders of the *ulama* (Islamic scholars) were expected to keep the rulers in line. Qutb was hanged in Egypt in 1966.[6] Throughout the discussion in this text, we refer to Islamic extremists and also Islamism, and Islamism can be defined as being extremist political ideologies based on the Muslim religion and claiming that Islam must be the basis of political life. Islamists believe that Islamic law (Sharia) must be the basis for all statutory laws and that Muslims must return to the original teachings and the early models of Islam; and that Western military, economic, political, social, or cultural influence in the Muslim world is un-Islamic. Radical Islamists wish to restore and expand the Muslim Caliphate. Islamism developed originally in the context of the Ottoman Empire, the British Raj in India, and British and Turkish rule in Egypt and was therefore in part a reaction to colonialism. The basis of Islamism as developed by Qutb is virulently anti-Semitic, independent of any issues related to Israel or Zionism. This may also explain the targeting of Jews in attacks by al Qaeda, such as the one in Mumbai in November 2008.

The Saudi wing of al Qaeda has been waging a violent campaign aimed at toppling the pro-U.S. Saudi monarchy and expelling Westerners from the birthplace of Islam. Its most successful year would appear to be 2003, when suicide bombers attacked three Western housing complexes in Riyadh, but since then al Qaeda has been relatively contained. Throughout 2007 and into 2008, al Qaeda's relevance in Saudi Arabia was insignificant, especially by bin Laden's standards. In 2007, al Qaeda attacks were limited to just a single attack on February 26, allegedly by Walid Mutlaq al-Rashidi, one of Saudi Arabia's most wanted terrorists. This was an attack against French and Belgian citizens traveling by car in the northwest of the country, killing four Frenchmen. In April 2007, the Saudis announced that they had arrested one hundred and seventy-two suspected militants, forty foreign nationals and one hundred and thirty-two Saudi citizens. Historically, arrests by the Saudi security forces have involved shootouts and invariably loss of life to one or more of the militants. The likelihood is that this latest batch of militant arrests were part of the logistics and planning for a series of attacks and most likely none were frontline actors—so no last-stand shootout or heroics. Looking forward, it seems at the present that al Qaeda is having a difficult time trying desperately to maintain some level of relevance in Saudi Arabia. It has tried to appeal to all levels of society, including the security forces, with little or no success. Al Qaeda's leadership is clearly struggling to remain relevant in the ideological realm, a daunting task for an organization that has been rendered geopolitically and strategically impotent on the physical battlefield.[7]

SAUDI HEZBOLLAH—KHOBAR TOWERS

Saudi Hezbollah first came to light in 1987 and was established in the Kingdom's eastern province—it was established in retaliation for the Kingdom's heavy-handed handling of the Mecca riots when Saudi riot police killed 400 Iranian pilgrims at the annual Hajj. The group was supported and sponsored by Iranian elements.

At about 10:00 P.M. on June 25, 1996, a tanker truck loaded with at least five thousand pounds of plastic explosives was driven into the parking lot in front of the Khobar Towers residential complex in Dhahran (Figure 9-3). Moments later a massive explosion sheared the face off of Building 131, an eight-story structure which housed about one hundred U.S. Air Force personnel. Although rooftop sentries were immediately suspicious of the truck—parked some eighty feet from the building—and attempted an evacuation, few escaped. Comparable to twenty thousand pounds of TNT, the bomb was estimated to be larger than the one that destroyed the federal building in Oklahoma City a year before, and more than twice as powerful as the 1983 bomb used at the Marine barracks in Beirut (Figure 9-4).

The FBI indictment details the attack as follows: On the evening of June 25, 1996, Al-Mughassil, Al-Houri, Al-Sayegh, Al-Qassab, Al-Jarash, and Al-Mughis finalized plans for the attack that night. Shortly before 10 P.M, Al-Sayegh drove a Datsun, with Al-Jarash as his passenger, as a scout vehicle into the public parking lot in the front of Khobar Towers Building 131. Behind them was the getaway car, a white Chevrolet Caprice that Al-Mughis had borrowed. When the Datsun signaled that all was clear by blinking its lights, the bomb truck, driven by Al-Mughassil and with Al-Houri as a passenger, entered the lot and backed up against a fence in front of Building 131. Al-Mughassil and Al-Houri then exited the truck and entered the back seat of the Caprice for the getaway, driving away followed by the Datsun. In minutes, the blast devastated the north side of the building (Figure 9-5).

Immediately following the terrorist attack, the leaders fled the Khobar area and Saudi Arabia using fake passports. Only Al-Jarash and Al-Mughis remained behind. Al-Sayegh reached Canada in August 1996 where he was arrested by Canadian authorities seven months later. In May 1997, Al-Sayegh requested to meet with American investigators and denied knowledge of the Khobar attack. He also falsely described an estrangement between the Saudi Hezbollah and elements of the Iranian government. He was later removed to the United States based on a promise to cooperate. Instead, he reneged on the promise and unsuccessfully sought political asylum in the United States. The indictment charges that the defendants first conspired to kill

FIGURE 9-3 The truck bomb at Khobar Towers, Dhahran, Saudi Arabia caused a crater 185 wide by 35 feet deep—the Jersey Barrier in front of the Towers helped deflect the blast upwards. *Courtesy: US Air Force Photo/Alamy Stock Photo.*

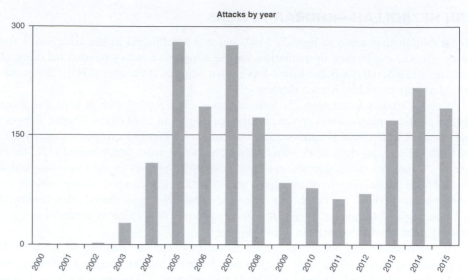

FIGURE 9-4   Suicide attacks by year 2000–2015.   *Source:* Chicago Project on Security and Terrorism, http://cpost.uchicago.edu.

FIGURE 9-5   Nineteen Airmen died and hundreds were injured in the terrorist attack on June 25, 1996, at Khobar Towers in Dhahran, Saudi Arabia. The facility housed U.S. service members and served as the headquarters for the U.S. Air Force's 4404th Wing (Provisional), Southwest Asia. At the time, it was the worst terrorist attack against the American military since the bombing of Marine Corps barracks in Beirut, Lebanon, in 1983.   *Courtesy:* U.S. Department of Defense.

Americans since at least 1988, when several of the group joined the Saudi Hezbollah, and later, in the Khobar attack, carried out the murders of American military personnel who were serving in their official capacity in Saudi Arabia.[8]

The ring leader of the once active terror group Saudi Hezbollah Ahmed al-Mughassil was arrested in Beirut and spirited back to Saudi Arabia in August 2015. He was arrested in a region that is heavily populated with Iranian Hezbollah and it is interesting to note that there has been no retaliation by Hezbollah for his arrest.

Saudi Counterterrorism

Nineteen of the 9-11 terrorists who attacked New York City and Washington DC were born in Saudi Arabia, and it is also the birthplace of Osama bin Laden. Not unnaturally the kingdom had to literally come into the twenty-first century and reform its approaches to terrorism and extremism. It has achieved that by forming liaisons and intelligence-sharing initiatives with Great Britain and the United States.

On a more advanced, focused level, Saudi Arabia has also been conducting two different, yet complementary, programs: "Counter-Radicalization" and "Rehabilitation." Whereas the broader public programs are preventative in nature, each of these programs goes directly to the active source of extremism propagation and serves to neutralize it. In creating these programs, Saudi Arabia's ministry of interior drew on the expertise of a group of international social scientists, psychiatrists, psychologists, and other physicians and experts to create strategies tailored to radicalism. In addition, the ministry has been working in conjunction with King Fahad Security College and Naif Arab University for Security Sciences to develop and refine the training activities for public security professionals.

- **Counter-Radicalization Program**: The purpose of the program is to combat the spread and appeal of extremist ideologies among the general populous. It strives to instill the true values of the Islamic faith, such as tolerance and moderation. Central to this effort is education about the dangers of radical Islam—consisting of school and religious programs and popular pronouncements, and the provision of positive, alternative outlets for at-risk groups—such as encouraging participation in sporting events and athletic programs, social outings, and so on.
- **Rehabilitation Program**: The rehabilitation program is intended to reintegrate deviants/extremists back into society, change their behavior (disengage them), and change their beliefs (deradicalize them). It is designed to target deviants who have completed their prison sentences. The program re-educates violent extremists and extremist sympathizers through intensive religious debates and psychological counseling. The goal is for them to renounce ideologies that espouse terrorism. Any individual who has committed or participated in a violent crime, constituting murder, will not be released following completion of the course.[9]

It is also worth noting that although these programs have the possibility to "softly" change the approach to extremism within the kingdom, their security services are continuously criticized for the length of detention without trial and the numerous allegations of ill-treatment and torture of suspects and detainees that pose a threat to the normalcy of the kingdom. The government also operated a rehabilitation program designed to re-educate those arrested for supporting extremism or terrorism, including Saudis formerly held at the Guantanamo Bay detention facility. The program was designed to reintegrate individuals into society and includes educational, social, and religious components to undermine extremist messages and foster a more tolerant attitude. The program builds on family and tribal relations to reinforce the message and speed the reintegration process. Those who complete the program and show evidence of having been rehabilitated are eligible for consideration for release from custody, though not before they have served any prison sentence for their previous crimes. The long-term effects of this program have yet to be evaluated to determine if any "graduates" have returned to their old activities or whether the actual program may be a recruiting area for Islamic extremist.[10]

ISLAMIC STATE—THREAT TO SAUDI ARABIA

It is certain that a large number of Saudis have participated in the civil war in Syria and likely further afield in Iraq. In 2016, with the Islamic State losing ground in Syria and attempting to gain footholds and influence elsewhere, the Saudi regime needs to be fully aware of the threat posed by returning jihadists as well as core IS activities. Currently, the Saudi security services have a relatively secure hold on militant activities but since the end of 2014 there has been an increase in IS activity from an IS affiliate naming itself Wilayat Najd. This affiliate group has carried out low-level attacks against military and police targets to date but also have attacked Shiite mosques, killing twenty-one in an attack on the al-Qudaih mosque in May 2015. The targeting of mosques is an IS trait that dates back to Iraq where the intent is to whip up sectarian conflict that can easily escalate out of control. While this has not happened in Saudi Arabia as yet, it is a troubling trend. From the security standpoint Saudi forces have uncovered numerous plots to attack both in Riyadh and the oil rich eastern province. In July 2015, the security services arrested over four hundred people as suspected IS members plotting bombings and shootings in the Kingdom. However, mass arrests of suspects which is so common in Saudi Arabia will have the desired effect for IS recruiters by alienating sections of the community and driving disgruntled Sunnis toward IS. IS has also used a social media and Twitter campaigns in 2014 to gather intelligence information on Saudi intelligence officers. In April 2016, IS gunman assassinated a Saudi Army Colonel from the Saudi Internal Security department. IS continues to focus its destabilizing tactics, particularly in the Shiite dominant eastern regions of the kingdom.

KUWAIT

The State of Kuwait, a nominal constitutional monarchy, is slightly smaller than New Jersey and lies between Iraq and Saudi Arabia, bordering the Persian Gulf (Figure 9-6). While its primary natural resource is petroleum, fish, shrimp, and natural gas are also plentiful. It is another Persian Gulf country with almost no arable land and no permanent crops (about seventy-five percent of its potable water must be distilled or imported). Kuwait has strategic value in its location at the entrance to the Persian Gulf. The small population of only 1,834,269 includes 1,381,063 non-nationals. The ethnic mix is forty-five percent Kuwaiti, thirty-five percent other Arab, nine percent South Asian, four percent Iranian, and seven percent other. Muslims make up eighty-five percent of the religious followers, but are split: Shia thirty percent, Sunni forty-five percent, and other ten percent. Christians, Hindus, Parsis, and others make up the remaining fifteen percent.

The chief of state is Amir Sheikh Saad Al-Abdullah Al-Sabah (since January 2006), and the head of government is the prime minister. While there are no official political parties and leaders, several political groups act as de facto parties (e.g., Bedouins, merchants, Sunni and Shia activists, and secular leftists and nationalists).

Kuwait has a small and relatively open economy with proven crude oil reserves of about ninety-four billion barrels, or roughly ten percent of world reserves. Kuwait has rebuilt its war-ravaged petroleum sector; its crude oil production averages two million barrels per day. Petroleum accounts for nearly half of its GDP, ninety percent of export revenues, and seventy-five percent of government income. Because of its high per capita income, comparable with Western European incomes, Kuwait provides its citizens with extensive health, educational, and retirement benefits. The bulk of the workforce is non-Kuwaiti, and they have a considerably lower standard of living than Kuwaitis. Per capita military expenditures are among the highest in the world. The World Bank has urged Kuwait to push ahead with privatization, including in the oil industry, but the government will move slowly on opening up the petroleum sector. The present Al-Sabah dynasty was established in Kuwait in the mid-eighteenth century, about 1760. Kuwait was nominally a province of the Ottoman Empire, ruled from Constantinople. This was observed on paper but seldom in fact. In 1899, when the Turks threatened to take actual control of the country, the ruling sheikh sought and received British protection.

The Kuwait Oil Company discovered oil in Kuwait in 1938, but because of World War II it was not exported until 1946, after which time Kuwait's economy flourished. Kuwait remained a British Protectorate until 1961, when it became independent under Sheikh Abdullah Al-Salem Al-Sabah. However, when Iraq claimed the emirate in the early 1960s, it once again received British protection. In July 1961, Kuwait joined the Arab League and in 1963 became a member of the United Nations. In February 1963, the first legislative elections were held, and Sheikh Abdullah, the Emir of Kuwait, inaugurated the first National Assembly.

During the 1980s, Kuwait experienced several terrorist attacks by Shiite Muslim extremists, including one in 1985 that attempted to assassinate the emir. Kuwait, like most Arab States, supported Iraq in the Iran–Iraq war (1980–1988). Kuwait played a major role in establishing the Gulf Cooperation Council (GCC) in 1981, consisting of Saudi Arabia, Kuwait, Bahrain, Qatar, the United Arab Emirates, and the Sultanate of Oman. The council held a firm position during Iraq's invasion of Kuwait on August 2, 1990, and its seven-month occupation of the Emirate.

FIGURE 9-6   Map of Kuwait.   *Source:* Central Intelligence Agency, The World Factbook, 2008.

Rather than befriend a tyrant, or surrender to Iraq's Saddam Hussein in the Gulf War, Kuwait stood firm in the heat of all the battles it faced. During the Iraqi occupation, from August 2, 1990, to Kuwait's liberation on February 26, 1991, the Kuwaitis once again gave evidence of their strength and fierce determination. After a decade, a whole generation is growing up with the memory of the Iraq invasion of Kuwait, but the younger teenage generation, with more fundamental, even radical views, seems to be sympathetic to the cause of the jihad in Iraq. Kuwait has a land border with Iraq, and it was one of the main staging points for U.S. troops en route to Iraq. It was also likely a returning point for insurgents escaping from areas such as Fallujah. Kuwait's proximity to the war zone—Iraq—has led to a spread of al Qaeda influence in the country and also those groups affiliated with Islamic State. There are indications that Kuwaitis have been involved in suicide missions in Iraq against U.S. targets. It is also clear that Kuwaiti extremists were training in camps in Afghanistan during the Taliban regime, and the likelihood is that some may have returned to Kuwait to further attack U.S. interest there. Taped messages from the number one terrorist in Iraq, al Zarqawi, called on fighters in 2005 to return to Kuwait and attack not only U.S. interests but also Kuwaiti government officials.[11] Many Muslim groups, particularly those in Kuwait, are still smarting from the 2004 Abu Ghraib prisoner abuse scandal and view it as part of the United States' overall plan to attack Islam and Muslims. Attacks in Kuwait, in comparison to those in Saudi Arabia, have been relatively minor.

During Ramadan in late June 2015, a suicide bomber walked into the center of the Shiite mosque in the capital city and blew himself up, killing twenty-five and wounding over two hundred worshippers. This again mirrors the strategy that IS uses elsewhere and this attack is also claimed by Wilayat Najd, the Saudi IS affiliate. Since the attacks in Saudi Arabia on Shiite mosques, security had been stepped up but this was not the case in Kuwait where the bomber was allowed freedom of access without any preliminary search protocols in place. IS continues the trend to attempt to spark a popular sectarian uprising between Sunni and Shia Muslims with this targeted assault (Figure 9-7).

The Arab Gulf states, including Kuwait, rely on foreign military support for their defense—as we saw in 1990 when Saddam Hussein invaded and occupied Kuwait. Kuwait's ruling family fled to the sanctuary of neighboring Saudi Arabia. That being said, we need to appreciate that these states need to contain the Shiite political influence in Iraq and prevent the spread of the Shiite militia groups, and they do this by providing a robust Sunni presence in the region. Iraq's Shiite militias are well trained and equipped by Iran's Revolutionary Guard Corps. The other factor that is in the hands of the Gulf States is the control of the world's oil distribution and increasing the amount of oil being produced that could seriously damage the Iranian oil industry, which utilizes outdated technology. The Sunni/Shia ethnic divide is a topic to be exploited by both the Saudi influence in the Gulf region and Iran. Iran has gone one up on the Saudis in this regard and has appealed to all Muslims (not only Shiites) to rise above nationalistic and sectarian divisions and called for Pan-Islamic unity. This has not become a reality, but it does make the Saudi regime extremely cautious in its dealings with Iran. Saudi Arabia has always seen itself as the leader of the Islamic world and has on many occasions attempted to use the ethnic card to create a rift between Iranian Shia and those in the Gulf States.

IRAQ

The Shia and Sunni divide has been clearly demonstrated in Iraq. Both Shia and Sunni are from the same religious order. Both are Muslim adherents to the Muslim faith founded by Prophet Muhammad (Figure 9-8). In the Shia sect, their beliefs are founded on the premise that following

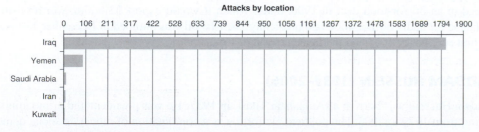

FIGURE 9-7 Suicide attacks by location 2000–2015. *Source:* Chicago Project on Security and Terrorism, http://cpost.uchicago.edu.

FIGURE 9-8 Map of Iraq. *Source:* Central Intelligence Agency, The World Factbook, 2008.

Muhammad's death in the seventh century his leadership passed to his cousin and son-in-law Imam Ali and then onto Ali's son Imam Hussein. In opposing this theory, the Sunni sect believes that following his death the leadership was passed to three caliphs chosen by Muhammad's followers. Sunni Arabs account for twenty percent of the population of Iraq and under Saddam Hussein's government they were favored while the Shia had their political rights and freedoms diminished. In the vacuum that the removal of Saddam Hussein created, we are now witnessing an ethnic and religious battle between Shia and Sunni groups. With its proximity to Iran that country has been supporting and funding the Shia militias in Iraq while the Sunni militias are mostly derived from the numerous and various Sunni Arab tribes. Of the total population, the Kurds who occupy the north-east of Iraq account for around eighteen percent of the overall population and have long sought total independence from Iraq. They have their own language.

The battle against the Islamic State has masked the deep divide within Iraq. In order to defeat IS many ethnic and religious groups, the Kurdish Peshmerga, Sunni Arab militias and Shia militias, and Iraqi government forces have worked somewhat cohesively to battle IS for territory but beneath that veneer of cooperation is deep mistrust as each has desires to increase political influence, social and economic gains, and establish territorial controls all of which will ultimately lead to infighting once IS is no longer a threat. Iraq will need a strong government to be able to satisfy all the varying demands for territory and autonomy but that will not happen until IS has been defeated.

The Ba'athist regime, held power over the last three decades of the twentieth century, engaged in extensive central planning and management of industrial production and foreign trade while leaving some small-scale industry and services and most agriculture to private enterprise. Iraq's economy has been dominated by the oil sector, which has traditionally provided about ninety-five percent of foreign exchange earnings. In the 1980s, financial problems were caused by massive expenditures in the eight-year war with Iran and damage to oil export facilities by Iran. This led the government to implement austerity measures and to borrow heavily and later reschedule foreign debt payments. Iraq suffered economic losses of at least $100 billion from the war. After the end of hostilities in 1988, oil exports gradually increased with the construction of new pipelines and restoration of damaged facilities. Iraq's invasion of Kuwait in 1990, and subsequent international economic embargoes and military action by an international coalition beginning in January 1991, drastically changed its economic picture. Industrial and transportation facilities, which suffered severe damage, have been partially restored. Oil exports were at only twenty-five percent of the pre-war level because of implementation of UN Security Council Resolution 986 in December 1996. The UN-sponsored economic embargo had reduced exports and imports and contributed to a sharp rise in prices. The Iraqi government had been unwilling to abide by UN resolutions so that the economic embargo could be removed. The government's policies of supporting large military and internal security forces and of allocating resources to key supporters of the regime had exacerbated shortages. In accord with a UN resolution, Iraq agreed to an oil-for-food deal in 1996, under which it would export $2 billion worth of oil in exchange for badly needed food and medicine. The first oil was pumped in December 1996, and the first supplies of food and medicine arrived in 1997.

SADDAM HUSSEIN (1937–2006)

Saddam Hussein was born in al-Auja, near Tikrit, in 1937. He was president and prime minister of Iraq from 1979 to 2003. His political platform was a combination of moderate social democracy, close to the European model, amid a struggle to keep the country of various ethnic and religious groups together. In the West, the image of Saddam Hussein went through a dramatic change, from being one of Europe's and the United States' favorites into the most negatively presented dictator in the world. He ran Iraq as his personal fiefdom eradicating all opposition to him and his party—he was brutal in the extreme with thousands of secret police in every level of society, he would likely rival the brutality of Josef Stalin! He was responsible for the torture and murder of likely hundreds of thousands of Iraqis during his twenty-three-year reign.

UN officials confirmed that Iraq had contravened the Geneva Convention by using chemical weapons against Iran. Iraq also used "mustard gas" from 1983 and the nerve gas "Tabun" from 1985, as it faced attacks from "human waves" of Iranian troops and poorly trained but loyal volunteers. Tabun can kill within minutes. In 1988, Iraq turned its chemical weapons on Iraqi Kurds in the north of the country. Saddam Hussein's invasion and occupation of Kuwait would cast him as a pariah in the region. At home, he presided over a secular state with relative freedom for the economic sector and freedom for women; there was also free education. He adopted a widespread and intricate system of secret police and spies to keep control on his people. Saddam was a Sunni Muslim, and the minority Sunnis enjoyed benefits and positions in Iraqi society, but other groups, especially Shia, were denied these benefits. After the U.S.-led invasion of Iraq, Saddam was captured, tried, convicted, and executed by an Iraqi court for crimes against humanity and his own people, the Kurds, the Marsh Arabs, and thousands of others who suffered under his rule. He was hanged on December 30, 2006. One of his most senior officials, Ali Hassan al-Majid, his first cousin, acquired the name "Chemical Ali" as well as the "Butcher of Kurdistan" for his role in the al-Anfal Campaign, during which he ordered a toxic gas attack on the Kurdish town of Halabja that resulted in the deaths of thousands of Kurds. He was the regional commander in southern Iraq and was responsible for suppressing the southern uprising of the Shiites. Ali was captured on August 21, 2003, and convicted of crimes against humanity and was executed in February 2010.

Iran and Iraq restored diplomatic relations in 1990 but were still trying to work out written agreements settling outstanding disputes from their eight-year war concerning border demarcation, prisoners of war, and freedom of navigation and sovereignty over the Shatt al-Arab waterway. In November 1994, Iraq formally accepted the UN-demarcated border with Kuwait that had been spelled out in Security Council Resolutions. This formally ended Iraq's earlier claims to Kuwait and to Bubiyan and the Warbah Islands. There is still dispute over Turkey's water development plans for the Tigris and Euphrates Rivers. Ironically, the area of the Middle East we now call Iraq, which we have seen in recent decades as a major source for state-sponsored terrorism and constant wars, is also where, many scholars agree, recorded history as we know it began.

Hammurabi was the Sixth king of the First Babylonian Dynasty (1810 B.C.–1750 B.C.). Hammurabi was the great lawgiver of the Old Babylonian (Amorite) Dynasty. His legal code was produced in the second year of his reign. Many new legal concepts were introduced by the Babylonians, and many have been adopted by other civilizations. These concepts included the following:

- Legal protection should be provided to lower classes.
- The state is the authority responsible for enforcing the law.
- Social justice should be guaranteed.
- Punishment should fit the crime.

A copy of the code is engraved on a block of black diorite nearly eight feet high. A team of French archeologists at Susa, Iraq, formerly ancient Elam, unearthed this block in 1901. The block, broken in three pieces, has been restored and is now in the Louvre Museum in Paris.

Abu Ja'far Muhammad ibn Musa al-Khwarizmi (680–750 A.D.), a great scholar and mathematician, originated algebraic equations. Some credit him with the invention of the concept of "zero." Al-Khwarizmi wrote ten math textbooks that have survived the test of time. His *Kitab hisab al'adad al-hindi* was an arithmetic textbook that introduced Hindu numbers to the Arab world; now they are generally known as Arabic numbers. Christian Europeans at first rejected the Arabic numbers and declared them the work of Satan. His major work is entitled *Kitab (al-jabr) w'al-muqabalah*, whose title gives us the word "Algebra."

In 1936, King Ghazi I formed the Pan-Arab movement with the other Arab States, promising kinship and non-aggression. The first coup d'état in the modern Arab world came in 1936, led by General Bakr Sidqi. This marked a major turning point in Iraq's history, opening the door for further military involvement in politics. In 1945, Iraq became a founding member of the Arab League and joined the United Nations.

Iraq joined in the war with Israel in 1948, in alliance with Jordan, according to a treaty signed by the two countries the previous year. The war had a negative impact on the Iraqi economy. Oil royalties paid to Iraq were halved when the pipeline to Haifa was cut. The war led to the departure of most of Iraq's prosperous Jewish community. About 120,000 Iraqi Jews immigrated to Israel between 1948 and 1952. In 1961, Kuwait gained its independence from Britain, and Abdul-Karim Qasim immediately claimed the Emirate as originally part of the Ottoman province of Basra. Britain reacted by dispatching a brigade to the country to deter Iraq. Qasim backed down. In 1963, Iraq finally recognized the sovereignty and borders of Kuwait.

Leading up to 1979, Saddam Hussein was the power base behind the ailing President General Ahmed Hassan al-Bakr. Bakr had appointed Saddam as his vice president, and when he stepped down due to ill-health, Saddam Hussein took full control as president of Iraq. He immediately began a sustained purge of all his and the Ba'ath Party's political rivals to assure his position and total control of Iraq. Once more, the political situation flared into hostilities with Iran. The Iran–Iraq war, which began in 1980, lasted for eight years and had a crippling effect on the economies of both countries. Neither side gained any territory but an estimated one million lives were lost. In July 1988, Iran accepted the terms of UN Resolution 598, and military actions ceased. Before Iraq had a chance to recover economically, Saddam once more plunged into war, with the invasion of Kuwait in 1990.

The United States declared its interest in protecting Kuwaiti sovereignty. In the ensuing months, the UN Security Council passed a series of resolutions condemning the Iraqi occupation of Kuwait and applied total, mandatory economic sanctions against Iraq. In November 1990, the UN Security Council adopted Resolution 678, permitting member states to use all necessary means, authorizing military action against the Iraqi forces occupying Kuwait, and demanding Iraq's complete withdrawal by January 1991.

Saddam Hussein failed to comply with this demand, and the Gulf War, Operation Desert Storm, began on January 17, 1991. Allied troops from twenty-eight countries participated. The combined air forces of Great Britain and the United States launched an aerial bombardment on Baghdad to start the battle. The war, which proved disastrous for Iraq, lasted only six weeks, but one hundred and forty thousand tons of munitions were dropped on the country, and as many as one hundred thousand Iraqi soldiers were killed. Coalition air raids destroyed roads, bridges, factories, and oil industry facilities and disrupted electric, telephone, and water service. Finally, a ceasefire was announced on February 28, 1991. Iraq agreed to UN terms for a permanent ceasefire in April of that year, and strict conditions were imposed, demanding the disclosure and destruction of all stockpiles of weapons, including weapons of mass destruction (WMD).

Insurrections quickly broke out in southern Iraq and in Kurdistan in the north, where rebels took control of most of the region's towns. Units of Saddam's elite Republican Guard that had survived the conflict suppressed protest with extreme brutality to gain control in the Basra, Najaf, and Karbala regions. In the southern cities, rebels killed Ba'athist officials, members of the security service, and other supporters of the Saddam regime. In Kurdistan, Iraqi helicopters and troops regained control of the cities taken by the rebels, and there was a mass exodus of Kurds to the Turkish and Iranian borders, fleeing from a possible repeat of the 1988 deadly chemical attacks. By the end of April 1991, 2.5 million refugees had fled from Iraq.

The United States, attempting to prevent the genocide of the Marsh Arabs in southern Iraq and the Kurds to the north, established air exclusion zones north of the 36th parallel and south of the 32nd parallel. The attempted assassination of former President George Bush in Kuwait prompted a swift military response on June 27, 1993. The Iraqi Intelligence Headquarters in Baghdad was targeted by twenty-three Tomahawk cruise missiles, launched from U.S. warships in the Red Sea and Persian Gulf.

In October 1994, Iraq again moved some Republican Guard units toward Kuwait, an act that provoked large-scale U.S. troop deployment to deter an Iraqi attack. The move was interpreted as a sign of Saddam's frustration with the continuation of stiff UN sanctions, but he backed down (establishing a pattern of behavior he continued using until the U.S. invasion of Iraq in 2003). He agreed to recognize the existence and borders of Kuwait. In the months that followed, Hussein's position appeared to become more precarious as dissatisfaction with his rule spread in the army and among the tribes and clans at the core of his regime.

In May 1995, Saddam fired his half-brother, Wathban, as interior minister and, in July, demoted his notorious and powerful defense minister, Ali Hassan al-Majid, to give more power to his two sons, Uday and Qusay. It became clear that Saddam felt more secure when protected by his immediate family members. Major General Hussein Kamil Hassan al-Majid, his minister of military industries and a key henchman, defected to Jordan, together with his wife (one of Saddam's daughters) and his brother, Saddam (also married to one of Saddam's daughters), and called for the overthrow of the regime. In response, Saddam promised full cooperation with the UN commission that was disarming Iraq (UNSCOM) in order to pre-empt any revelations that the defectors might make. Not surprisingly, when Saddam forgave the defectors and they returned to Iraq, other clan members murdered them both, soon after they crossed the border.

The weakening of the internal position of the regime occurred at a time when the external opposition forces were as weak as ever—too divided to take any effective action. At the same time, France and Russia were pushing for an easing of sanctions. The United States and Britain's determination to keep up the pressure on Iraq had prevailed, however. The apparent weakening of the regime was illusory. In fact, during 1996, the regime's grip on power seemed to have significantly strengthened despite Saddam's inability to end the UN sanctions. There was yet another major buildup of U.S. forces in the Gulf, as a result of Saddam's refusal to allow unrestricted UN inspections of suspected sites for storing WMD. In May 2002, on the eve of signing a historic U.S.–Russian nuclear arms reduction treaty, President Bush spoke strongly to President Putin of the Russian Republic, "If you arm Iran, you're liable to get the weapons pointed at you." Bush considered Russia's dealings with Iran the single, greatest proliferation threat on the globe at the time. On a day that took him from the old East–West divide of Berlin to the heart of the former Soviet Union, a defiant Bush answered critics of his expanding antiterrorist war plans. He denounced anyone who would appease terrorists or ignore threats to Europe.

OPERATION IRAQI FREEDOM

Saddam Hussein's reign came to an end in March 2003 following a demand by U.S. President George W. Bush that he and his two sons, Uday and Qusay, leave Iraq immediately. Bush promptly provided a forty-eight-hour deadline for compliance. No one expected the Iraqi dictator to comply with such a demand, and the following day, U.S. spokesman Ari Fleischer announced that the United States would invade Iraq whether Saddam and his sons left Iraq or not. Fleisher stated that "the bottom line is, a coalition of the willing will disarm Saddam Hussein's Iraq, no matter what." The U.S. justification for the invasion has been widely debated and challenged. Most importantly, the United States and Britain's action did not have the explicit endorsement of the United Nations. Most scholarly and legal authorities have concluded that the action violated the UN Charter. With the invasion by land and attacks from the air, the Iraqi military machine crumbled, and, on May 1, 2003, George Bush announced an end to major combat. Most of the Iraqi military and the well-trained and well-equipped Iraqi Republican Guard had not fought or been captured, but had simply "gone home." They took their weapons and munitions with them. This would be the starting point for the years of insurgency to follow. Apart from the regular conscript army of Iraq and the Republican Guard, there was a third and vitally important paramilitary group that had been established in the mid-1990s—namely, the Fedayeen Saddam. This organization numbered around 40,000–50,000 members and was staffed by Sunnis and supporters of the Ba'ath Party regime of Saddam Hussein. This group had been variously under the control of both Uday and Qusay Hussein for periods of time. The Fedayeen was responsible for some of the most atrocious acts against Ba'athist opponents. It conducted widespread campaigns of assassination but was loyal to the party. With the removal of Saddam Hussein, this force of fighters was adequately prepared and would have little to lose in fighting the United States and any Shiite-dominated government that came to power.

Deaths of Uday and Qusay Hussein—July 22, 2003

Lt. Gen. Ricardo Sanchez, Commander, Combined Joint Task Force Seven (CJTF-7) said:

> Today our coalition forces, associated with the 101st Airborne Division, Special Forces and Air Force assets, conducted an operation against suspected regime members. An Iraqi source informed the 101st Airborne division today that several suspects, including Qusay and Uday, numbers two and three on the U.S. Central Command's most-wanted list, were

hiding in a residence near the northern edge of the city. The six-hour operation began when the division's Second Brigade Combat Team approached the house and received small-arms fire. The division subsequently employed multiple weapons systems to subdue the suspects, who had barricaded themselves inside the house and continued to resist detention fiercely. Four persons were killed during that operation and were removed from the building, and we have since confirmed that Uday and Qusay Hussein are among the dead. The site is currently being exploited.[12]

The minority Sunnis had controlled Iraq for the last four decades of the twentieth century and had kept the large Shia majority in check. Saddam's security apparatus—and it was a well-organized one—melted away in the face of the U.S.-led invasion. It has been able to immerse itself back into society to carry on attacks against both the invading coalition forces and the Iraqi Shiites. The numbers of insurgent organizations operating in Iraq have multiplied since the official end to hostilities in 2003. Both sides—Sunni and Shia— developed fronts and insurgent forces to attack each other, the U.S. and coalition troops (Figure 9-9). The Sunni Islamists are similar to the Wahhabi sect in Saudi Arabia and composed of Iraqis belonging to the Salafi branch of Sunni Islam advocating a return to the pure Islam preaching's of the Prophet Muhammad and opposes any foreign non-Muslim influence. Hard-line Iraqi clerics and members of the MB in Iraq have helped support the militant Islamist movement. The Sunni groups include the following:

The Iraqi National Islamic Resistance: This group wants to establish an Islamic Iraq free from external interference and the forcible removal of U.S. forces. Its activities have centered on Baghdad, and its attacks have been primarily launched against military targets in areas west of Baghdad. It takes account of its activities by distributing information outside mosques at Friday prayers. It has also called on Arab states to send troops to help them in Iraq. In 2004, reports indicated that they were mounting around ten attacks a day, mainly against the U.S. and coalition forces.

The National Front for the Liberation of Iraq: This organization was formed soon after the invasion in 2003, and its influence is spread throughout the country. It consists of Islamists and nationalists and carries out attacks similar to those of the Iraqi National Islamic Resistance. In a statement sent to IslamOnline.net, the Front revealed that "after intensive contacts with a number of armed Iraqi groups and Arab volunteers who flocked to the country ahead of the U.S.-led invasion, a unified resistance command has now been forged." It indicated that the contacts made also included elements from Saddam Fedayeen and Ba'athists who were not loyal to Saddam Hussein.

The Iraqi Resistance Islamic Front (JAAMI)/Salah al-Din Brigades (SDB): This group, which formed in mid-2004, brings together a small coalition of resistance fighters. It formed a political party with SDB in 2004, and although it opposes the current political process, it is viewed as a moderate Islamic jihadist movement. Its operations take place mainly in Sunni regions of Iraq and are more military in style of attack; their leader Saif al-Din Mahmoud has pledged that his group will not use booby-trap bombs in cities or engage in the killing of hostages. The group tends to cooperate with all other jihadist groups with the exception of al Qaeda. It takes the stand that by declaring jihad it has the duty to fight the invaders. According to statements issued by the front, JAAMI's military wing, the Salah-al-Din and Sayf-Allah al-Maslul Brigades, has carried out dozens of operations against the U.S. occupation forces.

Imam Ali Bin-Abi-Talib Jihadi Brigades: This Shiite group appeared for the first time on October 12, 2003. It vowed to kill the soldiers of any country sending its troops to support the coalition forces and threatened to transfer the battleground to the territories of such countries if they were to send troops. The group also threatened to assassinate all the members of the Interim

Attackers, Attacks and Casualties by Religion				
Religion	Attackers	Attacks	Killed	Wounded
Muslim (NA)	15	15	223	692
Muslim (Shia)	1	1	4	0
Muslim (Sunni)	20	20	232	458
Secular	1	1	3	6
Unknown	1,920	1,885	18,723	44,099

FIGURE 9-9 Suicide attacks and attackers by religion. *Source:* Chicago Project on Security and Terrorism, http://cpost.uchicago.edu.

FIGURE 9-10   Live fire training for security contractors before deployment to Iraq.   *Courtesy:* Mike McGuire.

Governing Council and any Iraqi cooperating with the coalition forces. The group also announced that Al-Najaf and Karbala were the battlegrounds in which it would target the U.S. forces.

In addition to the groups resisting occupation, other armed groups emerged and resorted to operations of abducting and killing foreigners as a method, to terrorize the enemy and as a political pressure card to achieve specific demands (Figure 9-10).

The Islamic Army in Iraq: combines Islamism with Iraqi nationalism. It is made up primarily of former Ba'athists and is likely the largest active group; they target Iraqi police and military as well as members of the Shiite **Mahdi Army** and Badr groups.

Ansar al-Islam/Ansar al-Sunnah: Led by Mullah Krekar, this group is based in northern Iraq near the Iranian border and follows a strict form of Sunni Islam similar to Wahhabism. The group grew from the Islamic Movement of Kurdistan and comprises Afghan veterans and foreign fighters. Their aims are to rigorously enforce the concept of Sharia law in Iraq's northern provinces. When in control of villages, the group mandates strict religious observance, destroying a girls' school, outlawing "vice," and enforcing daily prayers at mosques.

Al Qaeda in Mesopotamia (AQM), aka Al Qaeda in Iraq: The most well-known and publicized group, led by Abu Musab al-Zarqawi—was the second-most-wanted terrorist on the planet after Osama bin Laden. Jama'at al-Tawhid wa'l-Jihad (Monotheism and Jihad Group) was the group's original name; it started operations in Iraq immediately following the coalition invasion. Zarqawi pledged support to bin Laden and renamed the group al Qaeda in Iraq, eventually forming the central core of the Islamic State of Iraq and Levant (ISIL).

Roadside bombings and beheadings, and posting gruesome videos of his atrocities on the Internet, were the hallmark of his insurgency operations (Figures 9-11 and 9-12). AQM attempted to bring other jihadist groups under its sphere of control and influence during 2006. However, this led to confrontation with other groups, most notably the Islamic Army in Iraq. The group is skilled at IED deployment, kidnapping, and assassination. It has kidnapped and executed numerous Western hostages since 2004. AQM rejects the political process, and any groups working with the government are considered legitimate targets for AQM. AQM's founder, the late **Abu Musab al-Zarqawi**, was born in 1966 a Palestinian Jordanian and had been sentenced to seven years in jail in Jordan in 1992 for plotting to overthrow the Hashemite Monarchy. He was killed on June 7, 2006, when U.S. forces bombed his safe house near the city of Baquba. On June 15, 2006, it was confirmed that Egyptian Islamic Jihad militant Abu Ayyub al-Masri would succeed Zarqawi as head of al Qaeda in Iraq. It has been claimed that at that time Iranian influence was being brought to bear, which precipitated attacks against other Iraqi insurgent groups. Al-Masri died in a coordinated attack by U.S. and coalition forces on a house near Tikrit. The

TERRORIST ATTACK BRIEF

Nick Berg – US Citizen and private contractor – Beheaded by al Qaeda in Iraq May 2004

Nick Berg went missing in Baghdad April 2004. On May 11th a video was posted to an Islamist web site showing Berg and five men standing over him. Wearing an orange jumpsuit, he identified himself as Nick Berg from Philadelphia. One of the men behind him believed to be Abu Musab al Zarqawi using a knife beheads Berg. Bergs killers are all shouting Allah akbar (God is great) during his brutal murder. It is believed that his death was in retaliation for abuses of Iraqi prisoners by US forces. Courtesy Strafor – Situation Report - **Iraq: American Civilian Beheaded May 11**th **2004,** www.stratfor.com

FIGURE 9-11   Nick Berg beheading.   *Courtesy:* www.stratfor.com—Situation Report—Iraq: American Civilian Beheaded, May 11, 2004.

coalition forces believed al-Masri to be wearing a suicide vest and proceeded cautiously. After the exchange of gunfire and bombing of the house, the Iraqi troops stormed the building and found two women still alive, one of whom was al-Masri's wife. Also killed was the second in command to al-Masri, Abu Abdullah al-Rashid al-Baghdadi.

Among AQM's many targets include the bombing of the Jordanian Embassy and the UN headquarters in Baghdad; the Najaf bombings on August 29, 2003, that killed Shiite leader Muhammad Baqir al-Hakim; and the bombing of the Italian military headquarters in al-Nasiria.

Mujahideen Shura Council

In early 2006, al Qaeda in Iraq posted an Internet statement saying it had joined five other insurgent groups in Iraq to form a new umbrella organization, the Mujahideen Shura Council. Two of these groups—the Victorious Sect Army and the Islamic Jihad Brigade—were known, while three were apparently new groups. The Mujahideen Shura Council issues statements and posts videos on a website—including a video showing the executions of two Russian hostages in June 2006. Its leader until his death was Abu Musab al-Zarqawi. The group functioned as an umbrella for Sunni insurgent groups. As of late 2006 it has absorbed into the Islamic State (IS).

Mahdi Army

The Mahdi army is a Shia militia movement led by Moqtada Sadr, a radical Shiite cleric, well supported by weapons plundered during the initial weeks of the U.S.-led invasion from Iraq's enormous weapons' stockpile. Analysts also believe that the movement is financed by Iran and also with training from the Shia group Hezbollah in Lebanon.

Sadr's brand of Shia nationalism, opposition to the U.S. presence in Iraq and hostility toward the powerful established Shia political parties, has proved popular among poor, disenfranchised Shia communities, and his key stronghold is the slum district of Sadr City, named after his father, a revered cleric murdered by Saddam Hussein's security forces. Mahdi fighters staged uprisings against U.S.-led forces in April and August 2004.

As insurgent attacks increasingly targeted Shia areas, the Mahdi Army became one of the major armed forces on the ground in Baghdad, controlling and protecting Shia areas. The Shia population in the Baghdad neighborhoods at first welcomed the Mahdi army as the national police and municipal officials were feeble at best, but they soon changed and began to display a serious appetite for sectarian violence as well as corruption and extortion. Whole areas were "cleansed" of Sunni civilians with many being summarily executed. The Mahdi army took over gas stations and mosques and extorted protection money from businesses. Al-Sadr was unable to control the rogue element within his movement, and they began to lose their grassroots support. The 2007 surge by the U.S. military further loosened the Mahdi army's control of the streets. Al-Sadr's reputation was severely damaged in August 2007 by fierce fighting

FIGURE 9-12   Photo from Internet video of Nick Berg and his murderers.   Site no longer operational—Jihadi webposting. *Source:* Roger Bacon/Reuters/Alamy Stock Photo.

in the holy city of Karbala when his men fought pitched battles and were fended off by the Badr Brigade militias of the Islamic Supreme Council of Iraq. While the two main Shia factions were fighting, this was not in the grand scheme of operations for the Iranians who want to have a united Shia movement, not a fractured one. The Sadr movement was pivotal to events, both political and military. By the end of 2011, and with the withdrawal of U.S. troops, militia members of the Mahdi Army loyal to Shiite cleric Moqtada al-Sadr were integrating into positions of influence within the Iraqi security apparatus. Al-Sadr had been instrumental in supporting the Shia Prime Minister Nouri al Malaki but was by 2015 one of his fiercest critics. Al-Sadr would appear to have the support of Iran in all that he does but keeping a strong hand at the helm in Baghdad with Shia dominance is one thing and sectarian violence quite another. History has shown that in the last decade his Mahdi Army have acted as death squads against the Sunni minority and although the Mahdi Army may have been renamed and rebranded as a Peace Battalion, their presence makes the statement that the Iraqi Army is not well enough suited to protect all the Shia interests particularly in Southern Iraq.

Badr Brigade/Corps

The Badr Brigade, a Shiite militia similar to the Mahdi army, composed of Iraqi military officers who escaped, defected, or were captured during and after the Iran–Iraq war, 1980–1988. The movement is supported by the Supreme Council for the Islamic Revolution in Iraq (SCIRI), the most powerful Shiite party in Iraq. The Iraqi Ba'ath Government began its reign with a brutal suppression of the religious leadership of Grand Ayatollah Sayyid Muhsin al-Hakim who was put under house arrest. His son Sayed Mahdi al-Hakim was accused of being a traitor who fled the country and was assassinated in Sudan in 1988. The Badr Brigade waged a low-level war of ambushes, sabotage, and assassinations against the regime, using undercover cells in Iraq and bases in Iran when Saddam Hussein was still in control in Iraq. In 1977, there was a popular uprising when the regime prevented the people from visiting the Shrine of Imam Hussein in the holy city of Karbala. Sayed Mohamad Baqir al-Hakim, the leader of SCIRI and the son of Grand Ayatollah Sayyid Muhsin al-Hakim, was arrested, tortured, and sentenced to life imprisonment without a trial. In 1980, Ayatollah Muhammad Baqir al-Sadr, who became the religious leader after the death of Sayyid Muhsin al-Hakim, was executed with his sister Amina al-Sadr. Saddam's regime issued a decree to execute all the members of the Islamic Movement. After Iraqi forces were removed from Kuwait in 1991, the popular uprising in the south of Iraq was partly coordinated by the secret cells and elements connected to Badr corps and took part in launching and spreading the uprising from the south to other parts of Iraq.

Its members were funded, trained, and equipped by the Iranian Revolutionary Guard Corps. During the U.S.-led-occupation government's crackdown on militia groups in 2003, the ten thousand-strong militia changed its name from the Badr Brigade to the Badr Organization of Reconstruction and Development. The group operates mainly in the southern Iraq region, in and around Basra, where a number of regional governments are dominated by SCIRI representatives. SCIRI wants to create a separate Shiite-run region comprising nine provinces in southern Iraq.

IRAQI INSURGENCY

The Iraq insurgency began shortly after Iraq was invaded by U.S. and coalition forces in 2003 and has continued through to 2011. The first phase of insurgency began shortly after the 2003 invasion and prior to the establishment of the new Iraqi government. The insurgency was aimed primarily at U.S. and coalition forces but rapidly expanded into a sectarian "war" with Sunni Muslim groups pitted against Shia groups. The invasion of Iraq and the bombing campaign that preceded it had devastated the infrastructures. Having put boots on the ground, the United States and its allies were unprepared to rebuild the devastation they had caused and over a period of time this was to create resentment against the occupying forces. The installation of a Shia dominated government in Baghdad would further alienate the Sunni minority who under Saddam Hussein were the dominant factor in all facets of the government, military, and secret police. As listed above, many different insurgent groups were formed to fight each other and the coalition forces. Many of the insurgent Sunni groups were under intense pressure until the U.S. withdrawal in 2011. Al Qaeda in Iraq, the forerunner to IS was established by Abu Musab al-Zarqawi and at the time (2006) with the endorsement of al Qaeda leadership with the aim of creating a sectarian divide in Iraq. Osama bin Laden's endorsement of the activities of Zarqawi as an affiliate of al Qaeda was also representative of al Qaeda's need for a presence in Iraq. Bin Laden also encouraged Muslim Iraqis and non-Iraqis of all ethnicities to cooperate in opposing the Iraqi government. His preferred method of attack on both coalition forces and government was the use of "martyrdom operations," or suicide attacks. Bin Laden and Zarqawi had based their calls for revolutionary change in Islamic societies on a stated belief in a model of governance where Muslim citizens would be empowered to choose and depose their leaders according to strict Islamic principles and traditions of consultation, or shura.[13]

AL QAEDA—ISLAMIC STATE IN IRAQ AND LEVANT (ISIL)

The Islamic State in Iraq and the Levant was the creation of Abu Musab al-Zarqawi and the al Qaeda presence in Iraq. IS is a global jihad organization with a Salafist–jihadi ideology. Salafism is an extremist Sunni Islamist school which aspires to restore the glory Islam had in the era of the Prophet Muhammad and the First Caliphate. This will be accomplished through jihad (holy war) considered as the duty of every Muslim. Zarqawi moved al Qaeda Iraq further than bin Laden's al Qaeda leadership had wanted. His successor Abu Bakr al-Baghdadi would go on to declare a Caliphate in Iraq and Syria and thus the Islamic State of Iraq and then Syria (ISIS) was realized. Since its inception the IS has been referred to as the most ruthless and well-funded terrorist organization. It is far more than that; IS by declaring itself as a state has thus far employed terror tactics and operations, suicide bombings, vehicle bombings etc. (Figure 9-13). It has also used conventional warfare to attack and overwhelm its opposition. It is more than just a terrorist group but rather a full blown insurgency. When it was first established in 2006 following Zarqawi's death, it had been pushed almost to the point of extinction with the U.S. troop surge and the corresponding Anbar Awakening in the Sunni regions of Iraq; so by 2010 just before the U.S. withdrawal they were nearly an extinct Sunni grouping. IS in spite of this still held onto their true beliefs and goals which were along the lines that al Qaeda leadership has espoused. The differences between the two, IS and al Qaeda relates to IS announcing a Caliphate, from al Qaeda's viewpoint a Caliphate will be declared only after the United States and its allies in Europe are defeated in so much as they no longer interfere in Muslim lands. Al Qaeda has always believed that attacking the United States was primary in its objective and then to focus on the overthrow of local governments. When ISIS in the summer of 2014 achieved significant military victories, the most spectacular being the capture of Mosul, the second largest city in Iraq, it was accompanied by the declaration of the founding of the IS (the Islamic Caliphate) by **Abu Bakr al-Baghdadi**, its charismatic Islamic jihadist leader in Iraq. Baghdadi has spoken on camera only once. But his Address, and the Islamic State's countless other propaganda videos and encyclicals, are online, and the caliphate's supporters have toiled mightily to make their project knowable. We know that their state rejects peace as a matter of

FIGURE 9-13   Vehicle bomb found by U.S. forces in Baghdad.   *Source:* U.S. Department of Defense.

Attackers, Attacks and Casualties by Target Type			
Target Type	Attacks	Killed	Wounded
Security	1,261	9,471	20,789
Political	232	2,186	6,840
Civilian	423	7,518	17,578
Unknown	4	10	47

FIGURE 9-14 Suicide attacks and casualties by target type.
Source: Chicago Project on Security and Terrorism,
http://cpost.uchicago.edu.

Suicide Attacks and Casualties by Weapon			
Weapon	Attacks	Killed	Wounded
Airplane	0	0	0
Belt Bomb	535	6,615	14,314
Car Bomb	1,342	12,279	30,494
Other	29	150	365
Unknown	14	141	81

FIGURE 9-15 Suicide attacks and casualties by weapons used.
Source: Chicago Project on Security and Terrorism,
http://cpost.uchicago.edu.

principle; that it hungers for genocide; that its religious views make it constitutionally incapable of certain types of change, even if that change might ensure its survival; and that it considers itself a harbinger of—and headline player in—the imminent end of the world (Figures 9-14 and 9-15).

IS became increasingly unpopular with the other Iraqi insurgent groups for its brutality towards Sunnis. By declaring a Caliphate Baghdadi was also stating that he was caliph and that Muslims of the world must conform to his edicts. Since becoming leader of IS Baghdadi has replaced many of the leadership that had been killed, with former Sunnis from Saddam Hussein's Ba'ath Party—many from the ranks of his intelligence organization and others with extensive military experience.

IS follows its own strict interpretations of Islamic law and enforces it in all regions that it overruns. ISIL aims to return to the early days of Islam, rejecting all innovations in the religion, which it believes corrupts its original spirit and anyone disagreeing with its interpretations is considered an apostate or infidel and subject to punishment, usually execution. Unlike other Islamist groups IS continues to emphasize the coming apocalypse and the final Judgment day. William McCants, Fellow and Director at the Brookings Institution's project on U.S. relations with the Islamic world noted that:

References to the End Times fill IS propaganda. It is a big selling point with foreign fighters, who want to travel to the lands where the final battles of the apocalypse will take place. The civil wars raging in those countries today [Iraq and Syria] lend credibility to the prophecies. The IS has stoked the apocalyptic fire. For Bin Laden's generation, the apocalypse wasn't a great recruiting pitch. Governments in the Middle East two decades ago were more stable, and sectarianism was more subdued. It was better to recruit by calling to arms against corruption and tyranny than against the Antichrist. Today, though the apocalyptic recruiting pitch makes more sense.[14] Bin Laden viewed his terrorism as a prologue to a caliphate he did not expect to see in his lifetime. His organization was flexible, operating as a geographically diffused network of autonomous cells. The IS, by contrast, requires territory to remain legitimate, and a top-down structure to rule it. (Its bureaucracy is divided into civil and military arms, and its territory into provinces.)[15]

Foreign fighters from around the world have flocked to join Baghdadi's caliphate with fighters from Pakistan, Afghanistan, Chechnya, Dagestan, France, Germany, Great Britain, Finland, USA, and Africa. A large number have returned to their home countries and will undoubtedly carry on the cause at home. Both al Qaeda and IS use terrorism as a tactic, but these organizations are insurgencies that aim first to overthrow all existing governments in the Muslim world and replace them with their own, and later, to attack the West from a position of power to spread their ideology to all of humanity. Separating the elements of ISIS and al Qaeda that are actively working to attack the West from the main bodies of those groups fighting in the Middle East, Africa, and South Asia is impossible. All al Qaeda groups and ISIS affiliates seek to take the war into the West to fulfill their grand strategic objective of establishing a global caliphate, albeit according to different timelines.[16] That IS wants to dominate not just the Middle East but to create a global caliphate and destroy all other religions is a frightening prospect for governments. Islamist groups are pledging allegiance to Baghdadi as far afield as Abu Sayyaf in the Philippines and Boko Haram in Africa.

In 2013, the IS campaign moved into and joined the civil war in Syria—their goal was not to attack the Assad regime but to gain territory for its state-building purposes. When al-Baghdadi made his 2014 caliphate proclamation, IS was controlling and administering large portions of Iraq and Syria. While fighting in Syria it never lost sight of Iraq and continued to gather territory throughout 2014–2015. It continues to massacre Iraqi civilians namely Shiites to propel Shia militias to attack the minority Sunni clans thus driving them into the arms of IS.

Islamic State—Children

The use of children in times of conflict is not new and child soldiers have been a factor in wars for centuries. In the modern era they are used widely in Africa (Lord's Resistance Army) and were used by Saddam Hussein to prop up his regime.

IS' leaders pay particular attention to children in their territory because the future of any state lies with the next generation. Therefore, the "caliphate" is investing heavily in indoctrinating children with IS extremist ideology as early as possible. IS has been very successful at using social media as a powerful recruiting tool. Their recruitment methods cover a broad span of people, from the very young to the old—but their target to ensure their future is the young. They have employed a vast array of areas of social media including Twitter, Facebook, YouTube, Pinterest, Instagram, Myspace, Tumblr, Ask.fm, Sendvid, Just Paste.it, Manbar.me and a host of others. If you have access to Internet you have access to IS and vice versa!

The Islamic State's on-going campaign portraying "A Perfect Caliphate," is designed to portray life inside IS-controlled territory as an idyllic world. The propaganda works. Thousands of foreign fighters have already joined up, with more expected to make the journey. At the same time, a shift in the tone of the Islamic State's propaganda is designed to encourage other sympathizers to support them on home soil, whether in Europe, USA, or Eastern Europe and Indonesia.

It is teenagers who are generally most susceptible to the Islamic State's message. While it can be difficult for parents to know for sure, there are a few things to watch out for. No one item can confirm your fear, however, if you see a combination of the following traits, your concerns may be valid:

- Have your teenager's values changed? Specifically, are they now condemning everyday practices that they used to accept?
- Are they using phrases you have never heard?
- Are they avoiding typical slang?
- Have they changed the way they dress or groom?
- Pay attention to what they are doing with their money. Are they hoarding cash?
- Has their friend set narrowed? Life-long friends either replaced or removed from their social circle?
- Are they spending more time online than usual? Are they secretive of where they are going online?[17]

Having been introduced to ideology at a young age, children are more likely to consider it normal, and therefore defend its practices. Thus, the indoctrination has both tactical and strategic value for IS. Not only can children help meet the present needs of the "caliphate," once they grow up, they will continue to propagate its existence and expansion, thus securing its long-term survival. There exists, moreover, an external strategic element to IS' recruitment of children. It allows IS leaders to gain the psychological upper hand against their opponents because their videos of children performing brutal acts break the boundaries of international norms, thus drawing global attention and increasing global fear of the "caliphate."[18] Children are taught the rigid IS curriculum, and are encouraged to spy on their families and friends. Those who comply are deemed loyal, and often taken to IS training camps. Elements of this have been seen in Somalia, where schools in areas controlled by al-Shabaab are forced to adopt its strict interpretation of Islam. English, the sciences, and other subjects that are deemed improper are not taught, and severe restrictions are imposed on girls' clothing. Teachers who refuse to cooperate with this strict regime are threatened, and often killed.[19]

Persecution

IS in its relentless thirst for acquiring territory inflicts its brand of Islam on every region it takes, and persecution of minority religious groups is common place.

Direct coercion into joining IS generally occurs through abductions. For example, on May 11, 2015, IS soldiers in charge of recruitment entered various high schools in the Hay al-Tamin region of eastern Mosul and imposed compulsory recruitment of the children, refusing them the right to decline. It was also confirmed by local media that the group has established military training camps for the children in both Tal Afar and in Raqqa, Syria.[20] On May 14, 2015, fifteen IS fighters who had lost or retreated from previous battles were executed by child soldiers in the Hamdaniya district, in the Nineveh plains. In June 2015, the United Nations Assistance Mission for Iraq in conjunction with the Office of the United Nations High Commissioner for Human Rights (UNAMI/OHCHR) estimated that IS had abducted between eight hundred and nine hundred children ranging between the ages of nine and fifteen years from various regions of Mosul.[21]

The abuse of civilians is not restricted to adults—girls of all ages have been taken by IS and have been tortured and raped, forced as sex slaves for IS fighters and as young as nine years of age being sold and married off to IS fighters.

Yazidis are a people that populate northern region of Iraqi Kurdistan. As IS fighters spread north, they killed hundreds of Yazidis. The IS advance caused a humanitarian disaster as thousands fled to the mountains to escape the genocide. IS captured adult males and young men and simply executed them.

Christians have in some instances been offered a choice of paying a tax or converting to Islam and failure to do one or the other would incur instant death. That IS fighters have engaged in a campaign of genocide is irrefutable, but bringing any of those involved to justice may take years if it happens at all.

Weapons and Munitions

IS has been able to acquire vast stockpiles of conventional weapons in Iraq taken from Saddam Hussein's supporters. They have acquired surface-to-air missiles and a vast array of weaponry and this has enabled them to overrun large areas of Iraq. Most of the areas seized have been in the areas north of Baghdad that were traditionally Sunni enclaves. IS has also sought out chemical weapons and is reported to be building stockpiles of Mustard gas.

Propaganda

IS employs various methods of media to publicize, attract, recruit, and terrorize its global audience. It uses all forms of modern media including online chat forums, Twitter, and most likely the Dark Web for more nefarious activities. It seems that IS in 2016 is also reading online material and freely available information to counter the 2015–16 drone attacks being conducted against the insurgent groups by the United States. In May 2016, it announced via a Polish-based file-sharing site JustPaste.it, that it had gathered the names of U.S. drone operators and published their names, photos, addresses, and telephone numbers on the site. It encouraged jihadis "to kill them wherever they are, knock on their doors and behead them, stab them, shoot them in the face, bomb them." The clear intent is to continue a ground swell of attacks by lone wolf jihadis, particularly in the United States. Most drone operations covering the Middle East are from bases in Nevada and New Mexico. Rather than a material leak or hacking event it seems that IS operatives have painstakingly gleaned the names of Reaper and Predator drone operators from news articles and military newsletters, and probably matching them to addresses and other personal details from publicly available sources on the Internet.

Fundraising

Maintaining a terrorist organization or an insurgency costs a significant amount of money. Funding for the IS that is occupying large parts of Iraq and Syria comes to them from a myriad of sources. It uses looting and extortion which is common place. In Iraq, in cities it took over, it plundered the banks. It is also engaged in illicit trade in oil from the oil fields of Iraq and supports smuggling rings taking oil to Turkey on the black market. The amount being gleaned from this operation will only be speculative but estimates are that IS is gaining enough revenue to maintain operations. Of course, they also engage in kidnappings for ransom and no doubt have been paid huge sums for captives running into millions of dollars. As the battle to defeat IS continues, the amount of money in their hands and what is done with it in the future has to be of concern, as when military operations subside there becomes a need to relocate and refund terror cells outside of the Middle East.

External Operations and Intelligence

As we have seen in the chapter covering Europe the IS is capable of conducting operations outside its core areas in the Middle East. While IS spend a lot of time on their publicity campaign there is one area that remains in the deep shadows and intentionally so.

Amn Al-Kharji

IS' successes are the result of a complex strategy executed by officials in the **Amn al-Kharji**, a shadowy wing of IS' bureaucracy responsible for selecting and training external operatives and for planning terrorist attacks in areas outside of IS territory, including those within European borders.

Little is heard of or known about the Amn al-Kharji as it has largely remained in the shadows. This aversion to publicity is deliberate, and demonstrates the Amn al-Kharji's strategic importance to IS. While IS' military branches in Syria and Iraq readily advertise their exploits, the Amn al-Kharji is shrouded in secrecy, sometimes employing disinformation to mislead intelligence agencies. Nonetheless, enough information now has emerged in open-source reporting to paint a picture—however incomplete—of the Amn al-Kharji. The most detailed information on the Amn al-Kharji comes from an interview of an IS defector, known only as "Abu Khaled." According to Abu Khaled, the Amn al-Kharji is one of four agencies that fall under IS' security apparatus. The four agencies are:

- **Amn al-Kharji**—ISIS foreign intelligence, whose operatives are sent behind "enemy lines" to conduct espionage or plot and perpetrate terrorist operations.
- **Amn al-Dawla**—responsible for internal security within IS' territory.
- **Amn al-Dakhili**—likened to an interior ministry.
- **Amn al-Askari**—the military intelligence wing.[22]

WEAPONS OF MASS DESTRUCTION

It would be difficult to discuss the problems in Iraq without talking about WMD and possible links to the al Qaeda networks. The reason the United States and its allies were in the region in the first place was that Saddam Hussein was believed to have nuclear weapons capability. In the post-9-11 security environment, the Bush administration made the decision to assume the worst. Many have charged that the White House either inflated or manipulated weak and otherwise ambiguous intelligence that showed Iraq as an urgent threat and thus make an optional war a necessity. In the two years that U.S. troops had been in Iraq, no sign to support the previous certainty that there were WMD had been uncovered. Large stockpiles of conventional weapons were unearthed but none of the type that suggested there was any urgency in waging a war against Iraq. During the 1990s, when weapons inspection teams were attempting to uncover any evidence of a nuclear program, UN sanctions were in place and had a marked effect on the economy of the country. These sanctions also prevented any upgrade in conventional weapons, and that is likely one reason why the Iraqi army's resistance was so minimal in 2003. The Iraqi military and weapons program had, in fact, steadily eroded under the weight of UN sanctions. The unique synergy of sanctions and inspections eroded Iraq's weapons programs and constrained its military capabilities. These facts were contrary to the Bush administration's contention that Iraq was a "gathering" threat. The renewed UN resolve demonstrated by the Security Council's approval of a "smart" sanctions package in May 2002 showed that the system could continue to contain and deter Saddam Hussein.

Unfortunately, only when U.S. troops invaded in March 2003 did these successes become clear. The Iraqi military had, in the previous twelve years, been decimated by the strategy of containment that the Bush administration had called a failure in order to justify war in the first place.[23]

SUPPORT FOR INTERNATIONAL TERRORISM

Prior to the invasion of Iraq, there were a large number of very senior U.S. politicians who could not accept that Iraq was involved in sponsoring terrorism or, for that matter, was a threat to U.S. security. Obviously, the world is a better place without Saddam Hussein; however, it is history that has determined his involvement in sponsoring terror groups. Many dissidents who escaped from Iraq during Saddam's regime claimed that he maintained terrorist training camps outside Baghdad. He had entertained and provided safe haven to Abu Abbas, a former secretary general of the Palestine Liberation Front. It was Abbas who was responsible for the hijacking of the cruise ship *Achille Lauro* in 1985, in which an American citizen, Leon Klinghoffer, was killed. Abbas was briefly in Italian custody but was able to produce an Iraqi diplomatic passport, forcing the Italian authorities to release him. He may have arrived in Baghdad around 1995 and was caught there by U.S. forces in April 2003. He died while in U.S. custody in March 2004.

Saddam Hussein's support for the families of Palestinian suicide bombers is also well known and reasonably documented. Sabri al-Banna, the leader of Abu Nidal Organization (ANO) was supported by the Saddam regime as well as by Syria and Libya. ANO was responsible for terrorist attacks in more than twenty countries, the deaths of more than four hundred, and over seven hundred injured. Nidal's terror group carried out simultaneous attacks in Rome and Vienna airports on December 9, 1985, killing nineteen. Sabri al-Banna died under mysterious circumstances from gunshot wounds while in his Baghdad apartment in 2002.

BAHRAIN

The State of Bahrain is on a scattered archipelago in the Persian Gulf, east of Saudi Arabia. These landmasses are small, totaling only 3.5 times the size of Washington DC. Bahrain has resources of oil, natural gas, and fish. It is close to primary Middle Eastern petroleum sources and located in a strategic position in the Persian Gulf. It has a very small population of 603,318 (including 221,182 non-nationals). Bahrain gained independence from the United Kingdom in 1971 (Figure 9-16).

Bahrain's chief of state is Sheikh Hamad Isa bin Salman Al Khalifa (since 1961), and the head of government is Prime Minister Khalifa bin Salman Al Khalifa (since 1970). The cabinet is appointed by the Amir, who is a traditional Arab monarch. Political parties are prohibited. Political pressure groups and leaders comprise, and represent, several small, clandestine leftist and Islamic fundamentalist outfits. Following the arrest of a popular Shia cleric, Shia activists have fomented unrest sporadically since late 1994, demanding the return of an elected national assembly and an end to unemployment.

In Bahrain, petroleum production and processing account for about sixty percent of export receipts, sixty percent of government revenues, and thirty percent of GDP. Economic conditions have fluctuated with the changing fortunes of oil since 1985, for example, during and following the Gulf crisis of 1990–1991. The sultanate continued to be plagued by arson attacks and other minor security incidents throughout 1997, mostly perpetrated by domestic dissidents.

The State Security Court jailed thirty-six Shia Muslims accused of a pro-Iranian plot to topple the government by force, while acquitting twenty-three others. Unrest in Bahrain has led to at least twenty-eight deaths and hundreds of arrests since December 1994.[24] Shiites suffer from higher rates of unemployment and are barred from employment in the police or security services. The government maintains that the protests plaguing the country are organized by Hezbollah-Bahrain,

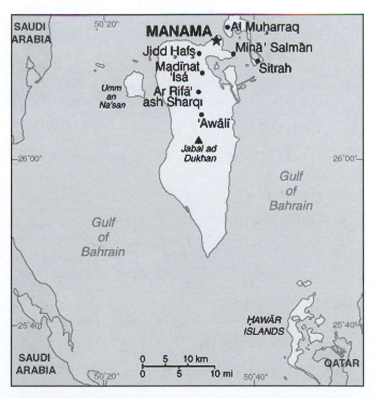

FIGURE 9-16 Map of Bahrain. *Source:* Central Intelligence Agency, The World Factbook, 2008.

allegedly backed by Iran.[25] Alleged members of the Bahraini Hezbollah were on trial. In all, fifty-four Shia Muslims in detention and twenty-seven others being tried in absentia are accused of fomenting violence and antigovernment activities.[26] The existence of Bahrain Hezbollah itself is questioned by some who accuse the government of fabricating its existence in order to blame outsiders for the political unrest. Their jail sentences range from five to fifteen years. Some Bahraini Hezbollah members reportedly underwent terrorist training in camps in Iran and Lebanon.

The Sunni Muslim-led government in Bahrain is reforming the political system to pacify a vocal and increasingly discontented Shiite majority. However, these measures are limited in substance and may end up fueling more dissent and unrest in the country.

In February 2002, Bahrain's leader, Sheikh Hamad Isa bin Al Khalifa, proclaimed himself king and declared his country a constitutional monarchy. Hamad also dissolved Bahrain's appointed consultative council, paving the way for the establishment of a bicameral parliament following elections scheduled for later in the year. Kuwait is currently the only Persian Gulf state with an elected parliament.

The government's transformation from the emirate system into a constitutional monarchy has been heralded as a step toward democracy. The feeling in the rest of the world is that it is not. Instead, it reflects the battle in an unresolved power struggle between Bahrain's minority Sunni Muslim-led government and the majority Shiite Muslim community. The Shia–Sunni imbalance in Bahrain and the unrest sweeping the Middle East during 2011 could impact security in the entire Persian Gulf region. The country is not a major oil producer but does have a vital refining industry that imports crude from neighboring states. It is also an important financial hub for the region, with many foreign banks located in the capital, Manama. Moreover, Manama is also headquarters for the U.S. Navy's Fifth Fleet and a center for U.S. military operations in the Gulf. Cooperation between Bahrain's two religious sects is critical to maintaining the island's calm. The situation in the country mirrors a historical contest between Islam's two largest sects throughout the Middle East, especially in the Persian Gulf. It also reflects the two distinct communities' struggle for control over Bahrain's valuable resources.

The 2011 Arab Spring uprisings also affected this small Arab nation—street protests and violence erupted and the ruling Sunni's were quick to call in help from Saudi Arabia to crush any opposition. The Shia Muslims are still waiting for the promised changes that the government has been promising and with dissident groups on the rise and gaining material support from Iran with weapons and explosives.

FIGURE 9-17 Map of Oman. *Source:* Central Intelligence Agency, The World Factbook, 2008.

OMAN

The Sultanate of Oman borders the Arabian Sea, the Gulf of Oman, and the Persian Gulf, between Yemen and United Arab Emirates. Although small, its natural resources include petroleum, copper, asbestos, some marble, limestone, chromium, gypsum, and natural gas. This parched nation has no arable land and no permanent crops. Oman is strategically located on the Musandam Peninsula and controls the Strait of Hormuz, a vital transit point for world crude oil. Seventy-five percent of Oman's two and a quarter million population is Sunni Muslim, with the remainder Shia Muslim and Hindu. Oman is a sultanate, a monarchy that has been independent since 1650, when it expelled the Portuguese (Figure 9-17).

On November 6, 1996, Sultan Qaboos issued a royal decree promulgating a new basic law, which clarified the royal succession, provided for a prime minister, barred ministers from holding interests in companies doing business with the government, established a bicameral Omani council, and guaranteed basic civil liberties for Omani citizens. The sultan is the chief of state, the head of government, and a hereditary monarch. Oman's economic performance is closely tied to the fortunes of the oil industry. Petroleum accounts for seventy-five percent of export earnings and government revenues, and roughly forty percent of GDP. Oman has proven oil reserves of 4 billion barrels, equivalent to about a twenty-year supply at the current rate of extraction. The earliest settlements in Oman, as in the Arabian Peninsula generally, date from some time in the third millennium B.C. At that time, and for some hundreds of years more, Oman was on the edge of the trade routes linking ancient Mesopotamia to the Indus Valley; however, it does not appear to have profited a great deal from its location.

The southernmost region of Oman, modern Dhofar, was responsible for the area's importance. It is one of the few spots in the world where frankincense trees grow. Frankincense is an aromatic gum from certain species of trees that grow only in southern Oman, the Wadi Hadhramaut in Yemen, and Somalia. The incense burns well because of its natural oil content. In addition, it has medicinal uses; these two factors, plus its relative scarcity, made frankincense an extremely sought-after substance in the ancient world. Frankincense was vital to the religious rites of almost every civilization in the ancient world. The great temples of Egypt, the Near East, and Rome itself were all major consumers of the scarce commodity, not to mention the thousands of other temples found in every city, town, and village. Indeed, the writer Pliny, in the first century A.D., claimed that control of the frankincense trade had made the south Arabians the richest people on earth.

In the second century A.D., at the height of the trade, some three thousand tons of frankincense were transported each year by ship from south Arabia to Greece, Rome, and the Mediterranean world. Although the trade went into a decline after the third century A.D., it still managed to keep south Arabia relatively wealthy for another three centuries.

The tribes in the northern part of Oman were converted to Islam during the first generation of the Islamic era, the middle of the seventh century A.D., and shortly thereafter came under the rule of the Umayyads, whose center was in Damascus. About a century later, the Omanis revolted against the Umayyads and expelled them from their country. The Umayyads themselves remained only a short time as the leaders of the Muslim world, for the Abbasids, whose capital was in Baghdad, soon overthrew them.

Oman managed to remain free of the Abbasids and continued its adherence to Ibadi Islam, which is still dominant in the country today. Because of Oman's remoteness from other Muslims, the Ibadis survived as a group long after they had vanished from other parts of the Muslim world.

By the end of the eighteenth century, the Omanis were in control of an extensive empire. At its height in the nineteenth century, the empire ruled both Mombasa and Zanzibar and had trading posts much farther down the African coast. (Oman's last colonial outpost—Gwadar, on what is now the coast of Pakistan—was not surrendered until September 1958, when Sultan Said bin Taimur allowed it to be reintegrated into Pakistan in return for a payment of £3 million.) In 1749, the first ruler of the present dynasty (Al-Busaidi) gained power, and in 1786, the capital was formally moved from the interior to Muscat. About this same time, Al-Busaidi adopted the title of "Sultan," which continues to this day.

The heyday of the Omani Empire occurred in the mid-nineteenth century under Sultan Said bin Sultan, who ruled from 1804 to 1856. He was responsible for bringing Dhofar under the Omani flag, and he also extended Omani influence and control down the East African coast. He had an army of six thousand and five hundred men and a navy consisting of fifteen ships. When he died, the empire split in two; one son became the sultan of Zanzibar and the other, the sultan of Muscat and Oman. In the very name of the latter, the perceived difference between the interests of the coast and those of the interior was acknowledged. In fact, they were regarded as two entities ruled by the same monarch, though the writ of the ruler in Muscat sometimes did not extend very far into the interior. Muscat's control depended very much on the regard for the Sultan held by the tribes of the interior. In the early twentieth century, the Sultan's power to control the interior of the country was felt to have decreased.

In February 1932, Sultan Said bin Taimur, father of the present ruler, came to power. When he tried to exercise his nominal control in the interior of the country in the early 1950s, the British, who believed the area had oil, backed him. And, in order to procure it, the British needed the Sultan to have control of the area and Oman's indefinite borders with Saudi Arabia and Abu Dhabi to be clearly drawn. The result was a territorial dispute over the Buraimi oasis involving Oman, Saudi Arabia, and Abu Dhabi. With British help and his own bravado, Sultan Said, in the end, was the winner, and the Buraimi oasis is today firmly within the borders of Oman.

Sultan Said bin Taimur was, in the words of one British writer, an arch-reactionary of great personal charm. He wanted no change of any sort in Oman and did all he could to isolate his country from the world. He issued all visas personally. He forbade travel to the interior by coastal residents and vice versa. Believing education was a threat to his power, he opposed it.

In general, Omanis were not allowed to leave the country, and those who did were seldom allowed to return. The sultan's only contact with the outside world was through his British advisers and Muscat's merchant families. He allowed the latter to establish enormously lucrative monopolies for the import of goods, which he saw as crucial to his survival. In exchange, the merchants stayed out of politics and imported nothing that Sultan Said felt reeked of progress or the West (radios, books, eyeglasses). Through their customs receipts, the merchants provided the Sultan with most of the country's income. Aside from a few rich merchants, most of the population relied on agriculture and fishing.

Oman has been Islamic since the seventh century. From 1932 to 1970, Oman was controlled by Sultan Said bin Taimur, a reclusive and repressive ruler whose policies finally resulted in revolt in Dhofar in 1965. In 1970, his son, the British-educated Qaboos bin Said, overthrew his father and embarked on an ambitious modernization program. This small and tightly controlled country has been bypassed by most of the terrorism and violence in the region and is almost totally unknown in the rest of the world.

Oman, a key U.S. ally in the Middle East, is adjusting its budget to reflect its assistance to the War on Terror, but the oil-rich sultanate is actually reducing defense funding and shifting the savings into social welfare programs. Unlike many other governments in the region, Oman's regime has faced relatively little domestic opposition to its relationship with the United States. This is largely due to strong oil revenues and an extremely tolerant local segment of Islam. Even so, it appears the Omani leadership is investing in preventative measures to keep a lid on unrest, knowing that Washington will guarantee its external security. By addressing domestic security before it becomes an issue, Oman hopes to avoid the problems faced by neighboring Saudi Arabia, where extremist Muslims actively oppose the basing of U.S. military forces there. A pacified population will allow the Omani government to deepen its involvement with the U.S. military, which is likely re-examining its options in the antiterrorism campaign.

The U.S. military currently uses at least three air bases in Oman as part of operations in Afghanistan. The Navy runs P-3 Orion aircraft patrols out of the Masirah air base, where at least one squadron of AC-130 gunships is based as well. Oman also hosts several Air Force pre-positioning sites, with enough equipment and fuel to maintain three air bases and twenty six thousand support personnel. Its continuing support of the United States makes Oman a key player in this global effort.

IRAN

One of the most controversial states in the Persian Gulf, the Islamic Republic of Iran borders the Gulf of Oman, the Persian Gulf, and the Caspian Sea, between Iraq and Pakistan. Iran is slightly larger than Alaska and has large resources of petroleum and natural gas (Figure 9-18). Its estimated population, 67,540,000, includes 917,078 non-nationals and a broad base of ethnic groups (Persian, fifty-one percent; Azerbaijani, twenty-four percent; Gilaki and Mazandarani, eight percent; Kurd, seven percent; Arab, three percent; Lur, two percent; Baloch, two percent; Turkmen, two percent; other, one percent) and religious affiliations (Shia Muslim, eighty-nine percent; Sunni Muslim, ten percent; Zoroastrian, Jewish, Christian, and Baha'i, one percent). This broad spectrum is reflected in languages as well (Persian and Persian dialects, fifty-eight percent; Turkic and Turkic dialects, twenty-six percent; Kurdish, nine percent; Luri, two percent; Balochi, one percent; Arabic, one percent; Turkish, one percent; other two percent). Iran is a theocratic republic, and its constitution codifies Islamic principles of government.

FIGURE 9-18 Map of Iran. *Source:* Central Intelligence Agency, The World Factbook, 2008.

Mujahedin-e-Khalq Organization

The Mujahedin-e-Khalq (MEK), also known as the National Liberation Army of Iran (NLA), the militant wing of the MEK, the People's Mujahedin of Iran (PMOI), and the Muslim Iranian Student's Society, was formed in the 1960s by a group of left-wing college radicals opposed to the Shah of Iran and became the largest and most militant group opposed to the Islamic Republic of Iran.

The MEK sought to counter what was perceived as excessive Western influence in the Shah's regime (1941–1979), and in the 1970s concluded that violence was the only way to bring about change in Iran. Since then, the MEK, following a philosophy that mixes Marxism and Islam, has developed into the largest and most active armed Iranian dissident group. Its history is studded with anti-Western activity and, most recently, attacks on the interests of the clerical regime in Iran and abroad. MEK was financed and supported through the Iraqi regime of Saddam Hussein and was actively supporting repression of Saddam's enemies within Iraq.

The MEK directs a worldwide campaign against the Iranian government that stresses propaganda and occasionally uses terrorist violence.

During the 1970s, the MEK staged terrorist attacks inside Iran to destabilize and embarrass the Shah's regime; the group killed several U.S. military personnel and civilians working on defense projects in Tehran and supported the 1979 takeover of the U.S. Embassy in Tehran. In April 1992, they carried out attacks on Iranian embassies in thirteen different countries, demonstrating the group's ability to mount large-scale operations overseas. Several thousand fighters with an extensive overseas support structure are based in Iraq. Most of the fighters are organized in the MEK's NLA.

In the 1980s, with the outbreak of war between Iran and Iraq, the group fled to Paris and most resettled back in Iraq by 1987. Their attacks were sporadic, and in 1999, they assassinated Iran's Army Chief of Staff Ali Shirazi and, in 2000, launched a rocket attack on the Presidential Palace. Until the U.S.-led invasion of Iraq, MEK had established numerous bases in the country, and these were overrun by the U.S. military in 2003, with the MEK surrendering peacefully and handing over their weapons and munitions. MEK continues to have supporters in Western Europe and also in the United States and Canada, but since its support structure and demise in Iraq, its membership has dwindled significantly.[27]

Maryam Rajavi and Massoud Rajavi have been the leaders of MEK since the early 1980s; they joined as students in the early 1970s. Massoud has been in charge of MEK's military wing operating in Iraq, and his whereabouts since the U.S. invasion are unknown. When Maryam Rajavi relocated with MEK to Paris in 1981, she was elected to the leadership position. Maryam was arrested by French police on a raid on the group's HQ near Paris in 2003.

Political pressure groups that generally support the Islamic Republic include Ansar-e Hezbollah, Mujahedin of the Islamic Revolution, Muslim Students Following the Line of the Imam, and the Islamic Coalition Association. Opposition groups include the Liberation Movement of Iran and the Nation of Iran party. Armed political groups that have been almost completely repressed by the government include Mujahedin-e-Khalq Organization (MEK), People's Fedayeen, Democratic Party of Iranian Kurdistan, and the Society for the Defense of Freedom.

In the early 1990s, Iran experienced a financial crisis caused by general financial mismanagement and an import surge that began in 1989. In 1993–1994, Iran rescheduled $15 billion in debt, with the bulk of payments due in 1996–1997. The strong oil market in 1996 helped ease financial pressures, however, and Tehran has so far made timely debt service payments. In 1996, Iran's oil earnings, which account for eighty-five percent of its total export revenues, climbed twenty percent from the previous year. Iran's financial situation remained tight through the end of the decade. Its continued timely debt service payments depended, in part, on persistent strong oil prices during the following years, a prediction that has failed badly as petroleum prices plummeted in 1998.

Iran is an illicit producer of opium poppy for the domestic and international drug trade. Iran continues to be a key transshipment point country for Southwest Asian heroin going to Europe.

THE SHAH OF IRAN

Mohammad Reza Pahlavi was restored to the Peacock Throne with the assistance of the Central Intelligence Agency in 1953. The CIA assisted in a coup against the left-leaning government of Dr. Mohammad Mossadegh, who had planned to nationalize Iran's oil industry. The CIA also provided organizational and training assistance for an intelligence organization for the Shah. With training focused on domestic security and interrogation, the intelligence unit was taxed with the mission to eliminate threats to the Shah. Formed under efforts of U.S. and Israeli intelligence officers in 1957, Sāzemān-e Ettelā'āt va Amniyat-e Keshvar (SAVAK) the National Organization for Intelligence and Security became an effective secret agency. General Bakhtiar was appointed its first director, only to be dismissed in 1961. He was assassinated in 1970 under mysterious circumstances. His successor, General Pakravan, was dismissed in 1966, failing to crush the opposition from the clerics in the early 1960s.

In 1961, Iran initiated a series of economic, social, and administrative reforms that became known as the Shah's White Revolution. The core of this program was land reform. Modernization and economic growth proceeded at an unprecedented rate, fueled by Iran's vast petroleum reserves, the third largest in the world. Domestic turmoil swept the country as a result of religious and political opposition to the Shah's rule and programs, especially SAVAK, the hated internal security and intelligence service.

The Shah turned to his childhood friend, General Nassiri, to rebuild SAVAK to properly serve the monarchy. Mansur Rafizadeh, the SAVAK director in the United States throughout the 1970s, claimed that General Nassiri's telephone was tapped by SAVAK agents reporting directly to the Shah, an example of the level of mistrust pervading on the eve of the revolution. SAVAK increasingly symbolized the Shah's rule from 1963 to 1979, a period of corruption, one-party rule, the torture and execution of thousands of political prisoners, suppression of dissent, and alienation of the religious masses. The United States reinforced its position as the Shah's protector and supporter, sowing the seeds of the anti-Americanism that later manifested itself in the revolution against the monarchy.

Accurate information concerning SAVAK has never been published. Pamphlets issued by the revolutionary regime after 1979 indicated that SAVAK had been a full-scale intelligence agency with more than fifteen thousand full-time personnel and thousands of part-time informants. SAVAK was attached to the office of the prime minister, and its director assumed the title of Deputy to the Prime Minister for National Security Affairs. Although officially a civilian agency, SAVAK had close ties to the military, and many of its officers served simultaneously in branches of the armed forces.

Another close confidant of the Shah, Major General Hossein Fardoust, was deputy director of SAVAK until the early 1970s, when the Shah promoted him to the directorship of the "Special Intelligence Bureau," which operated inside Niavaran Palace, independently of SAVAK.

Originally formed to round up members of the outlawed Tudeh (the Communist Party), SAVAK expanded its activities to include gathering intelligence and neutralizing the regime's opponents. An elaborate system was created to monitor all facets of political life. A censorship office was established to monitor journalists, literary figures, and academics throughout the country; it took measures against those who fell out of line. Universities, labor unions, and peasant organizations, among others, were all subjected to intense surveillance by SAVAK agents and paid informants. The agency was also active abroad, especially in monitoring Iranian students who opposed Pahlavi rule.

SAVAK contracted Rockwell International to develop a large communications monitoring system called IBEX. The Stanford Technology Corp. (STC), owned by Hakim, had a $5.5 million contract to supply the CIA-promoted IBEX project. STC had another $7.5 million contract with Iran's air force for a telephone monitoring system, operated by SAVAK, to enable the Shah to track his top commanders' communications.

Over the years, SAVAK became a law unto itself, having legal authority to arrest and detain suspected persons indefinitely. SAVAK operated its own prisons in Tehran (the Komiteh and Evin facilities) and others throughout the country. SAVAK's torture methods included electric shock, whipping, beating, inserting broken glass, and pouring boiling water into the rectum, tying weights to the testicles, and the extraction of teeth and nails. At the peak of its influence, SAVAK had at least thirteen full-time case officers running a network of informers and infiltrators covering thirty thousand Iranian students on U.S. college campuses. The head of the SAVAK agents in the United States operated under the cover of an attaché at the Iranian Mission, with the FBI, CIA, and State Department fully aware of these activities.

In 1978, the deepening opposition to the Shah erupted in widespread demonstrations and rioting. SAVAK and the military responded with widespread repression that killed between twelve and fifty thousand people and seriously injured another fifty thousand. Recognizing that even this level of state terrorism had failed to crush the rebellion, the Shah abdicated the Peacock Throne and departed Iran in 1979. Despite decades of pervasive surveillance by SAVAK, working closely with the CIA, the extent of public opposition to the Shah and his sudden departure came as a considerable surprise to the U.S. intelligence community and national leadership.

The SAVAK organization was officially dissolved by Ayatollah Khomeini shortly after he came to power. However, it was no surprise that SAVAK was singled out as a primary target for reprisals. Its headquarters were overrun and prominent leaders were tried and executed by Khomeini's representatives. High-ranking SAVAK agents were purged, and sixty-one SAVAK officials were among two hundred and forty-eight military personnel executed between February and September 1979.[28]

The 1979 Islamic revolution and the war with Iraq transformed Iran's class structure politically, socially, and economically. In general, however, Iranian society remains divided into urban, market town, village, and tribal groups. The clerics dominate politics and nearly all aspects of Iranian life, both urban and rural. After the fall of the Shah, much of the urban upper class of prominent merchants, industrialists, and professionals, favored by the former regime, lost influence to the senior clergy and its supporters. Bazaar merchants, who were allied with the clergy against the Pahlavi Shahs, also gained political and economic power since the revolution. The Shah went into exile and died in Cairo, in July 1980, where he was given a state funeral.

On February 1, 1979, exiled religious leader Ayatollah Ruhollah Khomeini returned from France to direct the revolution, resulting in a new, theocratic republic guided by Islamic principles. Back in Iran after fifteen years in exile in Turkey, Iraq, and France, he became Iran's national religious leader. Following his death on June 3, 1989, the Assembly of Experts, an elected body of senior clerics, chose the outgoing president of the republic, Ali Khamenei, to be his successor as national religious leader in what proved to be a smooth transition. In 1989, an overwhelming majority elected Ali Akbar Hashemi-Rafsanjani, the speaker of the National Assembly, president. He was re-elected in June 11, 1993, with a more modest majority of about sixty-three percent. Some Western observers attributed the reduced voter turnout to disenchantment with the deteriorating economy. Iran's post revolution difficulties included an eight-year war with Iraq, internal political struggles and unrest, and economic disorder. The early days of the regime were characterized by human rights violations and political turmoil, including the seizure of the U.S. Embassy compound and its occupants on November 4, 1979, by Iranian militants (Figure 9-19). By mid-1982, a succession of power struggles eliminated first the center of the political spectrum and then the leftists, leaving only the clergy. There has been some moderation of excesses, both internally and internationally, although Iran remains a significant sponsor of terrorism.

The Islamic Republican Party (IRP) was Iran's dominant political party until its dissolution in 1987; Iran now has no functioning political parties. The Iranian government is opposed by a few armed political groups, including the MEK (People's Mujahedin of Iran), the People's Fedayeen, and the Kurdish Democratic Party.

TERRORIST ATTACK BRIEF

Terrorist Group: Revolutionary Guards and Students

Case Facts: At the height of the Iranian Revolution that saw the overthrow of the Shah of Iran, a large group of students and part of a violent crowd stormed the U.S. Embassy—with the tacit support of the Revolutionary government of Ayatollah Khomeini.

Investigation: Iranian students stormed the embassy in response to U.S. support for the deposed Shah of Iran who had managed to escape to safe haven in the United States. The students were demanding his return. A stalemate ensued, and they held all fifty-five embassy staff hostage for 444 days. During this period, there was one failed attempt by U.S. Special Forces to release the hostages. The United States cut diplomatic relations with Iran following the embassy siege. The Shah died the following year in exile in Egypt, and at the same time Iraq invaded Iran. The hostages were released when President Reagan agreed to unfreeze Iranian assets in exchange for the safe return of the hostages.

FIGURE 9-19 Hostage Taking—U.S. Embassy Tehran, Iran—November 4, 1979.

Khomeini's revolutionary regime initiated sharp changes from the foreign policy pursued by the Shah, particularly in reversing the country's orientation toward the West. In the Middle East, Iran's only significant ally has been Syria. Iran's regional goals include its desire to establish a leadership role, curtail the presence of the United States and other outside powers, and build trade ties. In broad terms, Iran's Islamic foreign policy emphasizes the following:

- Vehement anti-U.S. and anti-Israel stances;
- Elimination of outside influence in the region;
- Export of the Islamic revolution;
- Support for Muslim political movements abroad; and
- A significant increase in diplomatic contacts with developing countries.

Despite these guidelines, however, bilateral relations are frequently confused and contradictory due to Iran's oscillation between pragmatic and ideological concerns. Iran's relations with many of its Arab neighbors have been strained by Iranian attempts to spread its Islamic revolution. In 1981, Iran supported a plot to overthrow the Bahrain government, and the unrest (Arab Spring) that swept the Middle East and Bahrain in 2011 would have been approved by Iran. In 1983, Iran expressed support for Shiites who bombed Western embassies in Kuwait and, in 1987 Iranian pilgrims rioted during the Hajj (pilgrimage) to Mecca in Saudi Arabia. Nations with strong fundamentalist movements, such as Egypt and Algeria, also mistrust Iran. Iran backs Hezbollah, Hamas, the Palestinian Islamic Jihad, and the Popular Front for the Liberation of Palestine-General Command—all groups violently opposed to the Arab–Israeli peace process.

Iran's relations with Western European nations have alternated between improvements and setbacks. French–Iranian relations were badly strained by the sale of French arms to Iraq. Since the war, relations have improved commercially but periodically are worsened by Iranian-sponsored terrorist acts committed in France. Another source of tension was Ayatollah Khomeini's 1989 call to all Muslims to kill Salman Rushdie, British author of *The Satanic Verses*. Many Muslims consider this novel blasphemous to their holy scriptures. The United Kingdom has sheltered Rushdie, and strains over this issue persist. There are serious obstacles to improved relations between the two countries. The U.S. government defines five areas of objectionable Iranian behavior:

- Iranian efforts to acquire nuclear weapons and other weapons of mass destruction;
- Its involvement in international terrorism;
- Its support for violent opposition to the Arab–Israeli peace process;
- Its threats and subversive activities against its neighbors; and
- Its dismal human rights record.

The United States believes that normal relations are impossible until Iran's behavior changes. The United States has made clear that it does not seek to overthrow the Iranian government but will continue to pressure Iran to change its behavior. Iran's continuing support of terrorists and terrorism creates continuing danger for Americans in Iran because of the generally anti-American atmosphere and the government's hostility to the U.S. government. American citizens traveling to Iran have been detained without charge, arrested, and harassed by Iranian authorities.[29]

IRAN AND NUCLEAR WEAPONS

The United States has cast Iran as being an integral part of the "axis of evil" and believes that it has been attempting to assemble the ingredients to manufacture weapons-grade nuclear material. This, of course, has not been confirmed. The Iranians can look at what has transpired since 9-11 and how the United States has reacted: The United States invades Iraq, which did *not* have nuclear weapons; the United States backed away from North Korea, which *does* have a nuclear weapons program. So, from a survivalist standpoint, the need for Iran to have an active nuclear program could be viewed as a method of restraining U.S. aggression. A nuclear Iran under the leadership of President Mahmoud Ahmadinejad pronounced in 2006 that the solution to the Middle East crisis would be the destruction of Israel.

Iran's connections with and sponsoring of terror groups is well known. Iran was intimately involved in the attack on the Khobar Towers complex in Saudi Arabia, and it has been supporting various Palestinian causes that hit at Israel's attempts at peace in the region. The obvious concern is that a nuclear Iran could supply the know-how to subgroups, or even the materials to construct a small nuclear device for delivery within Europe or the United States. Iran's nuclear program dates back to the days when the Shah was in control. By 2012, Iran was nuclear capable, and the control of the entire program rested in the hands of the president. Iran, against all opposition from external forces, continues to build and support the use of chemical, biological, and nuclear programs. The West views a nuclear Iran a threat to stability in the region, a region that descended into even more turmoil during 2011. A nuclear Iran and a nuclear Israel, does this mean equalization?

In January 2016, according to Secretary of State John Kerry, the world had become a safer place with the nuclear deal made with Iran. This deal resulted in sanctions being lifted against Iran as well as the release of more than $100 billion in frozen assets. In return Iran released five U.S. hostages and the United States returned twenty-one Iranians. Iran remains the number one sponsor of terrorism around the world and it has not moved away from its threatening stance towards both the United States and Israel. Iran poses a nuclear threat to the West and in particular to Israel—what it does with nuclear technology and who it shares it with will be more concerning. Iran has not changed its anti-American and anti-Israeli policy and has accelerated its illegal missile program. Iran has its long reach in the Shia militias in both Iraq and Syria is supporting destabilization in Bahrain and supporting the largely Shia dominated Houthis in Yemen's civil war. The late Ayatollah Ruhollah Khomeini referred to the West as "world devourers" who wish to stand against our religion, we will stand against their whole world and will not cease until the annihilation of all of them. Eighty-five percent of eighty-one million Shiites in Iran believe in Twelver Schism, the ideology espoused by Khomeini that embraces death.[30]

SPONSORING TERRORISM

Iran is considered by the U.S. State department to be the world's leading sponsor of terrorist groups and particularly those opposed to a Middle East Peace agreement. The Qods Force, the external operations branch of the **Islamic Revolutionary Guard Corps (IRGC)**, is Iran's primary mechanism for cultivating and supporting terrorists abroad. The IRGC has over a hundred thousand members and was originally formed after the revolution by Ayatollah Khomeini, who conscripted the most fanatical revolutionaries into the organization. He also amended Iran's constitution to give the IRGC the lawful right to "protect the spirit of the revolution," sending the corps to impose the regime's laws on Iranians through physical violence. The IRGC assassinated many key figures in the opposition during this time.[31] The IRGC are fiercely loyal to the clerical regime and also act as a counter to the military, which at the time of the revolution may have had loyalties to the Shah. As time passed, the IRGC and its structures operated totally independent of the Iranian military. Constructed along military lines with ground, sea, and air capability, the IRGC also controls the Iranian missile deployment program. The IRGC reports to and is accountable to the supreme leader and maintains complete political and social control and order over Iranian society.

Iran provided weapons, training, and funding to Hamas and other Palestinian terrorist groups, including Palestine Islamic Jihad (PIJ) and the Popular Front for the Liberation of Palestine-General Command (PFLP-GC), and has provided hundreds of millions of dollars in support to Lebanese Hezbollah at training camps in Iran. Since the end of the 2006 Israeli–Hezbollah conflict, Iran has assisted Hezbollah in rearming, in violation of UN Security Council Resolution 1701. Iran has equally interfered in Afghanistan and has provided training to Taliban forces, which has allowed them to promulgate successful attacks on U.S. and other forces in the region. The Qods Force, which is best described as a "Special Forces" unit that trains militant organizations and has been in Beirut, Sudan, and other troubled regions, also engages in espionage and assassination. Iran has continued to supply Iraqi militants with Iranian-produced advanced rockets, sniper rifles, automatic weapons, and mortars that have killed Iraqi and coalition forces. Iran was responsible for the increased lethality of some attacks on U.S. forces by providing militants with the capability to assemble explosively formed penetrators that were designed to defeat armored vehicles. The **Qods Force**, in concert with Lebanese Hezbollah, provided training outside of Iraq and advisors inside Iraq for Shia militants in the construction and use of sophisticated improvised explosive device technology and other advanced weaponry. The designation of countries that repeatedly provide support for acts of international terrorism as state sponsors of terrorism carries with it four main sets of U.S. government sanctions:

1. A ban on arms-related exports and sales.
2. Controls over exports of dual-use items, requiring thirty-day congressional notification for goods or services that could significantly enhance the terrorist-list country's military capability or ability to support terrorism.
3. Prohibitions on economic assistance.
4. Imposition of miscellaneous financial and other restrictions, including the following:

   - Requiring the United States to oppose loans by the World Bank and other international financial institutions;
   - Exception from the jurisdictional immunity in U.S. courts of state sponsor countries, and all former state sponsor countries (with the exception of Iraq), with respect to claims for money damages for personal injury or death caused by certain acts of terrorism, torture, or extrajudicial killing, or the provision of material support or resources for such acts;
   - Denial to companies and individuals tax credits for income earned in terrorist-list countries;
   - Denial of duty-free treatment of goods exported to the United States;
   - Authority to prohibit any U.S. citizen from engaging in a financial transaction with a terrorist-list government without a Treasury Department license; and
   - Prohibition of Defense Department contracts above U.S. $100,000 with companies in which a state sponsor government owns or controls a significant interest.

It is quite clear that designating Iran as a state sponsor of terrorism has done little to effect change in Iran or its attitude to the West and the Middle East.[32] Iran continues to threaten and call for Israel's destruction. It is intricately involved in propping up the Syrian regime of Bashar al-Assad and has sent fighters and Hezbollah into Syria to counter attacks by militias including IS. In May 2016, a key member of Hezbollah was killed in an explosion at Damascus airport. Mustafa Badreddine had been a leading figure and has been fighting in Syria in support of the Syrian regime. His credentials are impressive—he was being tried in a UN tribunal in absentia for his involvement in the assassination of former Lebanese Prime Minister Rafik Hariri in Beirut in 2005. He was a cousin and brother-in-law of Imad Mughniyah who was the head of Hezbollah military wing until he was killed in a car bombing in Damascus in 2008. Badreddine is believed to have had a hand in almost every major attack dating back to the 1980s and that includes the U.S. Marine Corps bombing in 1983 which killed over two hundred and forty people. His death will be a significant blow to the organization and also to Iran. Reports indicate that he died during an artillery barrage launched by Syrian opposition forces.

Al Qaeda and Iran

It is determined that there are links to the Iranian regime and al Qaeda stretching back to the early 1990s—Iran was a source of interest in the original 9-11 Commission Report on the attacks on New York and Washington. At the time there was apparently nothing to connect Iran to the 9-11 attacks. In December 2011, U.S. District Judge George B. Daniels ruled "that Iran and Hezbollah materially and directly supported al Qaeda in the September 11, 2001 attacks."[33] The 9-11 Commission reported that eight to ten of the 9-11 hijackers traveled through Iran between October 2000 and February 2001. They took advantage of an Iranian agreement to not stamp the passports of al Qaeda members going through the country. The travel of the hijackers appears to have been coordinated with Hezbollah, with one even boarding the same flight to Beirut as Hezbollah's operations chief, Imad Mughniyah.

The judge was also persuaded by testimony from three Iranian defectors, including a former intelligence officer named Hamid Reza Zakeri who defected in 2001 and claimed to have foreknowledge of the 9-11 attacks. Zakeri provided alleged top-secret intelligence documents proving that Iran and Hezbollah helped orchestrate the attacks. The public image of the Iranian President Hassan Rouhani is portrayed as being a moderate. We are not entirely in agreement with that being a correct characterization of him—his government continues to support terrorism and financial assistance continues to fund Hamas. He has also appointed those who have orchestrated terrorism against the United States. He also appointed numerous ministers with histories of supporting terrorism, extremism, and gross human rights violations. His Defense Minister was an orchestrator of the bombing of the U.S. Marine barracks in Lebanon in 1983 that killed two hundred and forty-one American troops. In 2012, the U.S. State Department reported a "clear resurgence" in Iranian terrorist activity and that Hezbollah's "terrorist activity has reached a tempo unseen since the 1990s." The IRGC and/or Hezbollah were linked to terrorist plots in Europe, Africa, the Middle East, South Asia, and the Far East.[34]

Iran's sponsorship of terrorist organizations is frequently mentioned in the context of other Middle Eastern regimes, which have supported various terrorist organizations for their own interests. However, this policy is not a mere tool in its strategic arsenal, but a fundamental element of the regime's identity. This is represented by two separate tenets of the regime's ideology: the duty of every Muslim to support jihad; and the mission of the Islamic regime in Iran to "propagate Islam" (tableegh-e-islami) or "export the Revolution."

These two pillars of Iranian doctrine are both characterized by support of proxy organizations that make use of terrorism. The former is exemplified by Iranian patronage of Hezbollah in Lebanon and of Hamas and Palestinian Islamic Jihad. The main theatres of the latter are Iraq and Lebanon, with lesser theatres among the Shiites of Saudi Arabia and Bahrain and radical Islamic movements in Africa and Central Asia.[35]

YEMEN

The modern Yemeni state was formed in 1990 with the unification of the U.S.- and Saudi-backed Yemeni Arab Republic, in the north, and the USSR-backed People's Democratic Republic of Yemen, to the south. The military officer Ali Abdullah Saleh, who had ruled North Yemen since 1978, assumed leadership of the new country (Figure 9-20).

The Republic of Yemen was established on May 22, 1990, with the merger of the Yemen Arab Republic (YAR; Yemen Sana'a or North Yemen) and the Marxist-dominated People's Democratic Republic of Yemen (Yemen Aden or South Yemen). The newly formed republic borders the Arabian Sea, the Gulf of Aden, and the Red Sea, between Oman and Saudi Arabia. Yemen is slightly larger than twice the size of Wyoming, with borders to Oman and Saudi Arabia. Estimates of its population run from 13.9 million to as high as 16.6 million people of Arab and Afro-Arab concentrations in western coastal locations, South Asians in the southern regions, and small European communities in the major metropolitan areas. Muslims, including Sha'fi (Sunni) and Zaydi (Shia), plus small numbers of Jews, Christians, and Hindus practice their brands of religion.

The former Aden (South Yemen) gained independence from the United Kingdom in 1967. The northern city Sana'a became the political capital of a united Yemen. The southern city Aden, with its refinery and port facilities, is the economic and commercial capital. Future economic development depends heavily on Western-assisted development of the country's moderate oil resources.

British and Turkish Domination

The British conquered Aden (Southern Yemen) in 1839, and it became known as the Aden Protectorate. The British made a series of treaties with local tribal rulers in a move to colonize the entire area of southern Yemen. British influence extended to Hadhramaut by the 1950s, and a boundary line, known as the Violet Line, was drawn between Turkish Arabia in the north and the South Arabian Protectorate of Great Britain, as it was then known. (This line later formed the boundary between northern and southern Yemeni states in the 1960s.)

Separate States and Unification

In the late 1960s, the British presence in southern Yemen was minimal, outside of Aden itself. In 1970, the republic's name was changed to the People's Democratic Republic of Yemen, or PDRY.

FIGURE 9-20 Map of Yemen. *Source:* Central Intelligence Agency, The World Factbook, 2008.

Mutual distrust between the two Yemens characterized the 1970s, and tensions flared into a series of short border wars in 1972, 1978, and 1979. Two presidents of the YAR were assassinated during this period. But under the presidency of Ali Abdullah Saleh of the Hashid tribe, in the late 1970s and early 1980s, the stability of the YAR steadily improved. By the end of 1981, a constitution had been drafted to implement a merger between the two states. Attempts to consolidate, however, were delayed by political instability in the PDRY, and it was not until 1990 that the merger was made official.

The new country was named the Republic of Yemen. The border was opened and demilitarized, and currencies were declared valid in both of the former countries. Sana'a took major steps during 1997 to improve control of its borders, territory, and travel documents. It continued to deport foreign nationals residing there illegally, including Islamic extremists identified as posing a security risk to Yemen. The interior ministry issued new, reportedly tamper-resistant passports and began to computerize port-of-entry information. Nonetheless, lax implementation of security measures and poor central government control over remote areas continued to make Yemen an attractive safe haven for terrorists. Moreover, Hamas and the PIJ maintain offices in Yemen. A series of bombings in Aden in July, October, and November 1997 caused material damage but no injuries. No group claimed responsibility. The Yemeni government blamed the attacks on Yemeni opposition elements that had been trained by foreign extremists and supported from abroad, possibly from Iran. Yemeni tribesmen kidnapped about forty foreign nationals, including two U.S. citizens, and held them for periods ranging up to one month.

Yemeni government officials frequently asserted that foreign powers instigated some kidnappings, but no corroborating evidence was provided. All were treated well and released unharmed, but one Italian was injured while resisting a kidnap attempt. The motivation for the kidnappings generally appeared to be tribal grievances against the central government. The government did not prosecute any of the kidnappers. At the end of 2007, there was a growing Shiite revolt against the Yemeni government, led by the Believing Youth Movement. Attacks from this group and open fighting with the military were primarily centered in the northern region of the country in the Province of Sana'a. The attacks seem to emanate from a complaint that the government had canceled a Shiite religious celebration.

Attacks against U.S. targets in the Gulf and surrounding states have been limited; however, the State of Yemen has experienced low levels of terrorism for some time. The al Qaeda attack on the USS *Cole* on October 12, 2000, in the Port of Aden, while on a refueling stop, appears to have been a protest against American presence in the Middle East; it was not directed at any particular aspect of U.S. policy, such as Palestine or Iraq (Figure 9-21).

FIGURE 9-21   USS Cole Yemen. On October 12, 2000, suicide terrorists exploded a small boat alongside the USS Cole—a Navy Destroyer—as it was refueling in the Yemeni port of Aden. The blast ripped a 40-foot-wide hole near the waterline of the Cole, killing seventeen American sailors and injuring many more.   *Courtesy:* Federal Bureau of Investigations.

The al Qaeda attack in the Port of Aden was the first successful suicide attack on a U.S. Naval craft by terrorists. Eyewitnesses said an inflatable speedboat helping the destroyer moor exploded alongside the ship, opening a twenty-foot by forty-foot hole at the waterline on the left side.

Seventeen American sailors were killed and thirty-nine injured in the seaborne suicide attack. The bomb is believed to have been made with a military grade C-4 plastic explosive, and around four hundred pounds or more were used in the attack. The investigation has shown that the attack group in this case contained not only Yemeni but also Muslims from other Middle Eastern countries.

Al Qaeda in the Arabian Peninsula

By the end of this first decade, the economy in Yemen was almost at the point of collapse, and the crackdown on al Qaeda in Saudi Arabia, in 2009, encouraged members to move to Yemen and forge alliances with militants in the country. By end of 2009, the al Qaeda migrants had merged to form al Qaeda in the Arabian Peninsula (AQAP). The primary goals of AQAP are consistent with the principles of militant jihad, which aims to purge Muslim countries of Western influence and replace secular "apostate" governments with fundamentalist Islamic regimes observant of Sharia. While Yemen remains on the brink of collapse and popular uprisings against the government continue, this allows AQAP to operate with little interference and to establish training facilities and support structures in Yemen. AQAP is hierarchical, compartmentalized, and highly decentralized, allowing it to withstand attacks and arrests and still continue to operate. The group has also mastered new recruitment, propaganda, and media campaigns, including a bimonthly AQAP magazine, *Sada al-Malahim* (the Echo of Battles), which offers theological explanations and praise for jihad fighters, tailored to appeal to its Yemeni audiences.[36] The presence of foreign fighters in Yemen and the proximity of other failed states in the Horn of Africa such as Somalia make Yemen a destination of choice for aspiring jihadists. The AQAP welcomed the presence of the American-born Yemeni-American cleric **Anwar al-Awlaki**, who gained several degrees at U.S. universities and is said to have provided spiritual guidance to the underwear bomber, Umar Farouk Abdulmutallab, and other suspected terrorists. Umar was a non-Arabic speaker so naturally was drawn to the writings of the U.S.-educated Anwar al-Awlaki. He later met al-Awlaki in Yemen and was recruited to al Qaeda. Umar Abdulmutallab, when arrested after his failed attempt to detonate a bomb in his underwear on board a Northwest flight over the United States, claimed that he had been given direction to do so by al-Awlaki. A month before the attack in November 2009, Abdulmutallab's father warned the U.S. Embassy in Nigeria that his son might be dangerous, a warning that officials failed to connect to other evidence that intelligence officials had gathered.[37] The bomb was made up of a highly explosive mixture of Pentaerythritol Tetranitrate (PETN) and Triacetone Triperoxide (TATP). TATP was also used by Richard Reid, the Shoe Bomber, in a similar plot to destroy a commercial airliner.

Yemen continues to be further destabilized with the civil war that has raged there since 2011 when the thirty-year regime of Ali Abdullah Saleh who was a Shiite with Sunni support within his government ended. The Houthi movement, whose base is among the Zaydi Shias of northern Yemen, rose up against Saleh's government six times between 2004 and 2010. The *Houthis* began in the late 1980s as a religious and cultural movement among practitioners of Zaydi Shi'ism in northern Yemen. The Zaydis are a minority in the majority-Sunni Muslim country, but predominant in the northern highlands along the Saudi border, and until 1962, Zaydi imams ruled much of the region. The Houthis became politically active after 2003, opposing Saleh for backing the U.S.-led invasion of Iraq. Houthis practice a religion closer to Sunni Islam than Shia Iran's dominant Twelver strain—have encroached into Sunni areas in Yemen. Houthis dominate northwestern Yemen and the capital, while AQAP is expanding its presence in southern and central provinces. The groups have clashed, and the Houthi advance can help AQAP find recruits and allies among Sunni tribes seeking to defend against what they view as a Shia and Iranian incursion. The Houthis repeatedly fought the Saleh regime—and, in 2009, an intervening Saudi force. In post-Saleh Yemen, the movement gained support from far beyond its northern base for its criticisms of the UN-backed transition. However, in its push to monopolize power, it has alienated one-time supporters. The Houthis have been supported by Iran and as a result Saudi Arabia sees their influence as destabilizing and views the Houthis primarily as proxies of Iran. President Abd Rabbuh Mansur Hadi, the internationally recognized president, returned to Yemen after eight months of exile in Saudi Arabia in November 2015, but he remains confined to the presidential palace in Aden and it is unclear whether he commands much authority beyond there.

Saudi Arabia has led the coalition air campaign to roll back the Houthis and reinstate Hadi's government. Riyadh perceives that Houthi control of Yemen would mean a hostile neighbor that threatens its southern border. It also considers Yemen a front in its contest with Iran for regional dominance, and losing Sana'a would only add to what it perceives as an ascendant Iran that has allies in power in Baghdad, Beirut, and Damascus. [38]

Muslim Population—Demographic

A comprehensive demographic study of more than two hundred countries finds that there are 1.57 billion Muslims of all ages living in the world today, representing twenty-three percent of an estimated 2009 world population of 6.8 billion.

While Muslims are found on all five inhabited continents, more than sixty percent of the global Muslim population is in Asia and about twenty percent is in the Middle East and North Africa. However, the Middle East-North Africa region has the highest percentage of Muslim-majority countries. Indeed, more than half of the twenty countries and territories in that region have populations that are approximately ninety-five percent Muslim or greater.[39]

More than three hundred million Muslims, or one-fifth of the world's Muslim population, live in countries where Islam is not the majority religion. These minority Muslim populations are often quite large. India, for example, has the third-largest population of Muslims worldwide. China has more Muslims than Syria, while Russia is home to more Muslims than Jordan and Libya combined.

Of the total Muslim population, ten to thirteen percent are Shia Muslims and eighty-seven to ninety percent are Sunni Muslims. Most Shias (between sixty-eight percent and eighty percent) live in just four countries: Iran, Pakistan, India, and Iraq.

Summary

The Arab Spring of 2011 and the declaration of an Islamic Caliphate in 2014 are two prime reasons that this region is in turmoil and will remain so for a long time—Iraq and its neighbor Syria under constant threats from Islamic State and escalating sectarian violence between Shia, Sunni, and Iraqi Kurds and no signs of a strong hand to steer and control the ethnic and religious elements in Iraq and Yemen mean further bloodshed. Major players seeking to exert their influence in this region see Iran using its proxies in failed state Yemen and Saudi Arabia using its powerful influence to counter Iran. The spread of extreme Islam in Iraq and consequences of its spread will have to be considered. Establishing democracies in parts of the world that have never experienced it may take many years, if ever, to reach fruition.

Review Questions

1. Describe how the Sunni and Shia elements in Iraq are fuelling sectarian violence.
2. List and explain why Iran supports the Houthis of Yemen and Saudi Arabia supports the current government.
3. Describe methods employed by Saddam Hussein to maintain his control over Iraq.
4. Compare the methods used by the Shah of Iran to control the populace with those used by the current regime.
5. Describe the type of support that Saddam Hussein provided to international terrorism.
6. Compare the stated goals of the Islamic State with those of al Qaeda.

End Notes

1. Sharon Otterman. "Islam: Governing under Sharia Law." Council on Foreign Relations. http://www.cfr.org/publications.
2. *Country studies—Saudi Arabia.* http://countrystudiesus/saudi-arabia.
3. General Information on Wahhabism. http://www.mb-soft.com/believe/txo/wahhabis.htm.
4. The Washington Post. "Saudi Arabia's Execution of Cleric Ignites Fury in Iran." www.washingtonpost.com. January 2, 2016.
5. BBC News. Sheikh Nimr Baqir al-Nimr: "Saudi Arabia Executes Top Shia Cleric." http://www.bbc.com/news/world-middle-east-35213244 downloaded April 30, 2016.

6. Austin Cline. *Your Guide to Agnosticism/Atheism.* http://atheism.about.com/od/islamicextremismpeople/a/qutb_p.htm.

7. Terrorism Intelligence Report: Fred Burton and Scott Stewart—Al Qaeda in 2008: the Struggle for Relevance—Stratfor.com.

8. FBI. "Terrorism Charges have been brought against 13 members of the pro-Iran Saudi Hizballah." https://www.fbi.gov/news/pressrel/press-releases/terrorism-charges-have-been-brought-against-13-members-of-the-pro-iran-saudi-hizballah. downloaded April 25, 2016.

9. *The Kingdom of Saudi Arabia Initiatives and Actions to Combat Terrorism.* (Washington, DC: Royal Embassy of Saudi Arabia Information Office, January 2011), www.saudiembassy.net.

10. U.S. Saudi Collaboration on Counterterrorism—Office of the Coordinator for Counterterrorism. U.S. State Department. http://www.susris.com/articles/2009/ioi/090502-saudi-collaboration.html.

11. *Arab Times* (February 15, 2005).

12. *U.S. Department of Defense: Press Briefing* (July 22, 2003).

13. *OSC Report GMP20041216000222* (December 16, 2004).

14. William McCants. *The ISIS Apocalypse: The History, Strategy, and Doomsday Vision of the Islamic State.* (St Martin's Press, 2015).

15. "What ISIS Really Wants." http://www.theatlantic.com/magazine/archive/2015/03/what-isis-really-wants/384980/ downloaded April 29, 2016.

16. "Al Qaeda and ISIS: Existential Threats to the U.S. and Europe." Institute for the Study of War. http://understandingwar.org/report/al-qaeda-and-isis-existential-threats-us-and-europe-0

17. Beacham Publishing's TRAC (Terrorism Research & Analysis Consortium); *Islamic State Propaganda Featuring Children*; Signs a Child is Being Targeted/Radicalized; http://www.trackingterrorism.org/article/islamic-state-propaganda-featuring-children/signs-child-being-targetedradicalized; accessed Tuesday, May 3rd, 2016.

18. Noman Benotman and Nikita Malik. *"Children of the Islamic State."* Quilliam Foundation London, March 2016.

19. Danielle Breitenbücher. *"Somalia: The Fate of Children in the Conflict."* International Committee of the Red Cross, 27 August 2015. https://www.icrc.org/casebook/doc/case-study/somalia-the-fate-of-children-in-the-conflict.htm.

20. "Report on the Protection of Civilians in the Armed Conflict in Iraq." 1 May–31 October 2015, Office of the United Nations High Commissioner for Human Rights and United Nations Assistance Mission for Iraq- Human Rights Office. http://www.ohchr.org/Documents/Countries/IQ/UNAMIReport1May31October2015.pdf.

21. Ibid.

22. The Daily Beast. *"How ISIS picks its Suicide Bombers."* http://www.thedailybeast.com/articles/2015/11/16/how-isis-picks-its-suicide-bombers.html.

23. George A. Lopez and David Cortright. "Containing Iraq, Sanctions Worked." George Lopez is Director of Policy Studies at the Joan B. Kroc Institute for International Peace Studies at the University of Notre Dame. David Cortright is president of the Fourth Freedom Forum and research fellow at the Kroc Institute. *Foreign Affairs* (July/August 2004).

24. www.cidcm.umd.edu/mar/chronology (Reuters, March 29, 1997).

25. www.cidcm.umd.edu/mar/chronology (Middle East Review of World Information).

26. www.cidcm.umd.edu/mar/chronology (AFP, March 6, 1997).

27. *Global Security.* http://www.globalsecurity.org/military/world/para/mek.htm.

28. Federation of American Scientists. www.fas.org.

29. U.S. Department of State. Public Affairs, Washington DC (July 1994). http://www.state.publicaffairs.gov.

30. "The Worst Foreign Policy Blunder in American History." The Philadelphia Trumpet. April 2016, vol. 24, No. 4.

31. Dr. Babek Ganji. "Iranian Strategy: Factionalism and Leadership." (Defence Academy of the United Kingdom: Conflict Studies Research Centre, March 2007).

32. State Sponsors of Terrorism. http://www.state.gov/s/ct/rls/crt/2009/140889.htm.

33. http://iran911case.com/

34. http://www.state.gov/j/ct/rls/crt/2012/209982.htm. "Middle East and North Africa Overview." Country Reports on Terrorism 2012. May 30, 2013.

35. Iranian Terrorist Policy and "Export of Revolution" (IDC Herziliya). http://www.herzliyaconference.org/_uploads/2903iranian.pdf.

36. Julie Cohn. "Islamist Radicalism in Yemen." Council on Foreign Relations. (June 29, 2010). http://www.cfr.org/yemen/islamist-radicalism-yemen/p9369.

37. "Abdulmutallab: Cleric Told Me to Bomb Jet." *CBS News* (February 2010). http://www.cbsnews.com/stories/2010/02/04/national/main6174780.shtml.

38. Zachary Laub. "Yemen in Crisis." Council on Foreign Relations, CFR Backgrounders. http://www.cfr.org/yemen/yemen-crisis/p36488. downloaded April 30, 2016.

39. "Mapping the Global Muslim Population." Pew Research Center, Religion & Public Life (October 7, 2009). http://www.pewforum.org/2009/10/07/mapping-the-global-muslim-population/#footnotes.

Northeast, Central, and Southern Africa

LEARNING OUTCOMES

After studying this chapter, students should be able to:

1. Describe how a failed state such as Somalia is a fertile region for Islamic extremism.
2. Discuss the spread of Islamic jihad across central Africa.
3. Recount how state terror in African countries continues into the twenty-first century.
4. Describe the funding mechanisms that are used by insurgent groups.
5. Restate how the UN failed to prevent genocide taking place in Rwanda.

KEY WORDS TO NOTE

Al-Shabaab—Islamic militant group based in Somalia seeking to create an Islamic caliphate in the region

Apartheid—A government policy of strict racial segregation once practiced in South Africa

Boko Haram—Nigeria-based Islamist terror group demanding imposition of Islamic law throughout the region

BOSS—South African state security apparatus first established by John Vorster in 1966 and set up to protect national security interests

Front for the Liberation of Angola (FNLA)—Guerilla organization that fought for independence from Portugal and became a political party in 1991

Front for the Liberation of Mozambique (FRELIMO)—Founded in 1962 as a liberation movement that fought for independence from Portugal

Mau Mau—A militant African nationalist movement active in Kenya during the 1950s whose main aim was to remove British rule and European settlers from the country

Omar Shafik Hammami—U.S. citizen who migrated to Africa and joined the al-Shabaab terrorist group

Unilateral Declaration of Independence (UDI)—A proclamation of independence for a newly formed country or state, in this case declared by the white minority in Rhodesia in 1965

Zakat Hawala—Islamic funding principle used to move vast sums of money undetected

OVERVIEW

In this chapter, we see the spread of support forming up with both al Qaeda and Islamic State from groups operating in central Africa—we will also review terrorism that evolves over time and turns a state against its ethnic, religious, and historic tribal enemies. Despotic leaders in the northeast, central, and southern regions of Africa have utilized measures they saw fit including genocide. We examine the rise and fall of some of the vilest despots and the terror tactics they employed, for example, Field Marshall and President for Life, Uganda's Idi Amin Dada. We shall also examine the historical roots of African terrorism and its progression to modern times, in places like Mozambique, Zimbabwe, the Republic of Congo, and South Africa. Each country has its own significant and unique history.

ETHIOPIA

Ethiopia has undergone dramatic changes since the 1974 overthrow of Emperor Haile Selassie, "The Lion of Africa." In 1935, Ethiopia became the object of Italian colonialism, and the Emperor fled the country to live in exile in England. During World War II, the British, with the help of the Ethiopians, evicted the Italians from the country and returned Emperor Haile Selassie to the throne (Figure 10-1).

Eritrea is a region of Ethiopia that lies to the north, along the Red Sea coast, which had been under Italian control and influence since the 1880s. The Ethiopian government took control of Eritrea in 1961, and ever since has been fighting an unending battle with Eritrean Nationalists seeking independence. Extremely poor living conditions, coupled with resentment of the Selassie regime's autocratic methods and corrupt government, resulted in a military coup led by Lt. Col. Mengistu Haile-Mariam in 1974. By 1977, he was the preeminent military ruler, seeking aid from the Soviet Union to establish a socialist People's Republic and was at first successful in fighting off incursions from Somali and Eritrean rebels. After he was elected to the presidency in 1987, Soviet aid along with the economy began to diminish. He abandoned socialism, and unable to mobilize the military resistance, he fled south to Zimbabwe. Trouble also flared up in the south of the country in the Ogaden, which was a disputed territory with neighboring Somalia. Many of the inhabitants are Somalis, and the resulting invasion of the region by Somalia's military in 1977 has been an ongoing and festering sore between the two nations.

By the end of the 1980s, the military rulers were turning toward elected civil government, under a new constitution. Although elections were held, the military leadership continued to control the country. On May 28, 1991, the Ethiopian People's Revolutionary Democratic Front (EPRDF) toppled the authoritarian government of Mengistu Haile-Mariam and took control in Addis Ababa.

A new constitution was promulgated in December 1994, and national and regional elections were held in May and June 1995. The main issue facing Ethiopia at the end of the decade was rebuilding the crumbling infrastructure of the country following years of civil war.

Ethiopia and Somalia still continue to squabble over the Ogaden region in the southern half of the country. The country is also a staging post for the transshipment of illicit drugs from Asia destined for Europe and North America and cocaine for the markets of South Africa.

The disputed Ogaden has seen the rise to prominence of the Ogaden National Liberation Front (ONLF). The group is a nationalist movement formed as far back as 1984 and seeks self-determination for the ethnic Somalis that inhabit this region. The ONLF formed in the wake of the Western Somali Liberation Front (WSLF), which lost the support of Somalis living in Ogaden after the 1977–1978 war in which Ethiopia crushed Somali government forces attempting to gain control of areas with large ethnic Somali populations. They had not been of particular concern to the Ethiopian government until the regime's military invasion of Somalia in 2006, which targeted the Somali Supreme Islamic Courts Council (SICC), which aspired to create a Greater Somalia in the disputed Ogaden. There was obvious collaboration between the SICC and members of the ONLF. Since that invasion, ONLF has come out and attacked government forces and foreign oil installations. The government responses to ONLF activity have been broad sweeps by its counterinsurgency troops and centering on villages that have supplied support to ONLF. The Ethiopian approach has seen its troops acting indiscriminately and has come under public pressure for its human rights abuses from the International Red Cross. Faced with mounting pressure to control the insurgency and to protect the oil resources in the Ogaden region, the Addis Ababa regime of Prime Minister Meles Zenawi must do all it can to destroy the ONLF. While the ONLF remains purely nationalist, there will only be concern for the U.S. interests should they become infiltrated

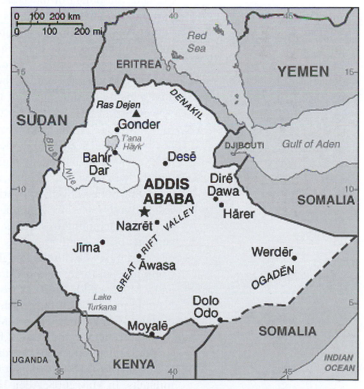

FIGURE 10-1 Map of Ethiopia. *Source:* Central Intelligence Agency, *The World Factbook, 2008.*

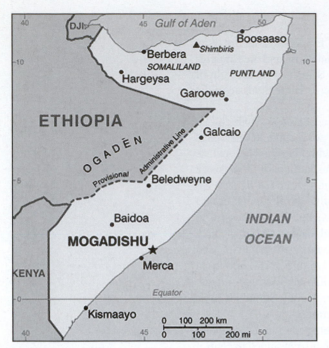

FIGURE 10-2 Map of Somalia. *Source:* Central Intelligence Agency, *The World Factbook, 2008.*

or aligned with al Qaeda. In Somalia, Ethiopian soldiers ensure the security of a secular government led by Abdullahi Yusuf, who would be unlikely to survive the onslaught from SICC and Islamist fighters. Ethiopia's fate and that of Somalia lay in the hands of dictators attempting to destroy an Islamist surge in the Horn of Africa.

SOMALIA

Ongoing inter-clan feuding and a weakened military from the fighting in Ethiopia had left Somalia in desperate straits. In 1969, the clans within Somalia felt that the distribution of wealth only resulted in benefits to very few people. The control of the beleaguered country reverted to military rule, under the banner of the Somali Revolutionary Socialist Party, led by Major General Siad Barre. The entire economy, that is, banks, schools, and land, came under the direct control of the military government. This action coincided with one of the major famines of the twentieth century, and the ruling party did essentially nothing to aid the sick, starving, and dying (Figure 10-2).

Resistance and uprisings finally came with the formation of the United Somali Congress (USC), which ousted Siad Barre on January 27, 1991. Since then, the country has deteriorated even further, with no functioning government, anarchy, and inter-clan fighting and banditry. This situation left one of the poorest countries in Africa to stumble around blindly with no functioning administration, as the various clans vied for power, until the transitional government of Ali Khalif Galaid was voted into power in 2000 . . . and just as quickly voted out by a no-confidence vote a year later. Somalia has been riven with inter-clan rivalries for several decades and various warlord factions have attempted reconciliation during those years. In the early 2000s, progress toward a centralized authority was made as some warlords participated in reconciliation talks that led to the development of the Transitional National Government. However, influential warlords, particularly Mohamed Aidid's son Hussein, refused to recognize any attempt at a central authority. After many failed attempts to establish a legitimate government at the center, a successful bargain was made in 2004 when the Somali Transitional Federal Government was formed, bringing various warlord clan factions together. This was created by an internationally supported peace process in Kenya that year. With the assimilation of warlords into the government and the spread of the Islamic Courts movement, the warlords' anarchical reign was effectively diminished for the first time in fifteen years.

After U.S. military intervention in Afghanistan, speculation was that its next target would be Somalia as it seemed to fit the bill of a lawless state that draws terrorists like a magnet. Sudan and Somalia remain the only regional countries not allied to the United States. Friendly relations with Kenya, Tanzania, Ethiopia, and Eritrea seem secure, despite some recent conflicts.

Since the U.S. missile strikes on Sudan—after the two U.S. embassy bombings (which resulted in Osama bin Laden being deported), and especially since 9-11, Africa's largest state has been attempting to shed its image as a "sponsor of terrorism," and thus cut back the U.S. support for the southern rebels. The defining moment in relations between the two countries occurred in 1993 with the slaughter of eighteen American Marines and the deaths of hundreds of Somalis in the capital of Mogadishu. The Clinton administration subsequently evacuated and withdrew all U.S. forces from Somalia. This was portrayed as Somali rejection of a peacekeeping mission but, in fact, the deaths were a direct result of a seventh botched attempt to capture the notorious warlord Mohamed Aidid. Aidid was killed several years later by a clan member. However, the hand of bin Laden was also at work as he had issued a "fatwa," calling for Muslims to attack the "soldiers of occupation." The United States has continued to strike at Somalia as it is viewed as a failed state, and this makes the country a refuge for al Qaeda militants. In May 2008, Aden Hashi Ayro, al Qaeda's commander in Somalia, was killed in a U.S. air strike. Ayro had trained in al Qaeda training camps in Afghanistan and was leader of the Islamist group al-Shabaab.

Al-Shabaab (aka Harakat Al-Shabaab al-Mujahidin, the Youth, Mujahidin al-Shabaab Movement, Mujahideen Youth Movement)

Objectives

- Removal of the Somali Government
- Removal of foreign influence in Somalia – particularly Ethiopia
- Establish Islamist emirate in Somalia

Roots and Ideology

- Group originates from the Islamic Courts Union
- Group is aligned with al Qaeda ideology
- Group mimics in some regards the Taliban movement
- Pledged allegiance e to al Qaeda in 2012

Tactics

- Suicide bomb attacks
- Car bombs (VBIED) and IEDs
- Media grabbing attacks such as Westgate Mall (Nairobi)

Size and Strength

At the end of 2015, the size of al-Shabaab was estimated to be approximately 5,000–10,000 fighters including foreign elements.

Originally the militant wing of the Islamic Courts Union, the group that controlled Somalia prior to the country's invasion by Ethiopian forces, al-Shabaab leaders have claimed affiliation with al Qaeda since 2007. Formed from clan members of the Hawiye clan, the organization consists of several thousand fighters. How closely aligned it is with al Qaeda is unknown even though they have pledged allegiance to al Qaeda. There have been instances of foreign fighters operating with al-Shabaab, including several who came from Europe and the United States. While al-Shabaab has controlled much of central and southern Somalia, it does not control the capital Mogadishu, and control of the capital Mogadishu is seen as pivotal to both al-Shabaab and Somalia's Transitional Federal Government (TFG). If the government were to lose control, then the jihadist movement would become de facto rulers of a large swathe of central and southern Somalia. The jihadists have used the conventional terrorist methods to attack government forces with IED and hit-and-run terrorist ambushes. To succeed in an environment where no central government has been in control for two decades requires a different approach. In 2008, al-Shabaab began to reach out to the Somali public with a series of town visits. A December 2008 International Crisis Group report describes these outings as "well-choreographed, with clerics addressing public rallies and holding talks with local clan elders." **Al-Shabaab** would hand out food and money to the poor, give criminals quick trials with "mobile sharia courts," and attempt to settle local disputes. As the group sought to take control of towns in southern Somalia, it began to use political strategies as well. Before a particular town was captured, insurgents had meetings with local clan leaders to convince them that their intentions were good.[1]

U.S. Connection

Appearing on the FBI Most Wanted Terrorist list is an American citizen **Omar Shafik Hammami**, a former resident of Daphne, Alabama, also known as Abu Mansoor al-Amriki, who provided material support to a designated foreign terrorist organization known as al-Shabaab. On February 26, 2008, al-Shabaab was designated as a foreign terrorist organization by the Secretary of State.

Hammami allegedly traveled to Somalia during 2006 and eventually joined al-Shabaab's military wing. In 2007, after Ethiopian forces invaded Somalia, Hammami joined the front lines as a fighter and eventually became a leader with al-Shabaab. On November 27, 2007, an indictment was returned in the United States Southern District of Alabama charging Hammami with 18 U.S.C. 2339A, providing material support to terrorists. On September 24, 2009, a superseding indictment charged Hammami with 18 U.S.C. 2339B, providing material support or resources to a designated foreign terrorist organization.[2] Sometime around 2002, Hammami had a falling out with his family and moved to Toronto, Canada and joined in with the Somali community. What precipitated his move to Somalia is not known. Once in Somalia, he quickly came to prominence

FIGURE 10-3 Omar Shafik Hammami aka Abu Mansoor al-Amriki was on the FBI's Most Wanted List with a reward of $5 million. Pictured in this undated photograph, Hammami had served as a commander and propogandist for al-Shabaab – his death in May 2013 was announced by senior members of al-Shabaab claiming that his death was at the hands of loyal al-Shabaab members. *Source:* Roger Bacon/Feisal Omar/REUTERS/Alamy Stock Photo.

and was active online in social media spreading his views on jihad. He was able to impress al-Shabaab leaders with his IT skills and climbed quickly within al-Shabaab's ranks. Between 2007 and 2010 he was involved in floggings, beatings, amputations, and executions and became one of the FBI's Most Wanted with a reward of $5 million on his head (Figure 10-3). In early 2012, he split from al-Shabaab claiming that the core of al-Shabaab was corrupt and that its leaders were only interested in their own self-promotion and moving away from the principles of their religion. Hammami was of the opinion that the jihadist movement is a global entity and cannot be reduced to local areas of combat. He warned that local jihadist states could lead to disunity because of local differences and contradictory local strategies that would counter achieving a world caliphate. He became a target of al-Shabaab for his outspoken comments and died in an attack in southern Somalia in September 2013. In January 2014, he was removed from the U.S. State Department's "Rewards for Justice" list.

Ethiopia has long been Somalia's primary rival in the region, and its foreign policy is aimed at keeping Somalia weak and divided. Ethiopia had been urging the United States to extend its War on Terror to Somalia since 9-11. Ethiopia invaded Somalia in 1996 and again in 1999 (capturing or killing hundreds of Somalis) and supported antigovernment rebels such as the Rahanweyn Resistance Army. In August 2000, a peace conference resulted in the closest thing that Somalia has had to a broad-based national government. However, Ethiopia, it seems, is actively trying to destabilize its neighbor. Somalia nevertheless continues to function and has established clans and sub clans with considerable inter- and sub clan rivalry. Somalia has been home to a key player for al Qaeda and one of the United States' Most Wanted Terrorists, Fazul Abdullah Mohammed; he was al Qaeda's longest-serving and highest-ranking operative in East Africa and was killed in a shootout with Somali forces at a checkpoint near Mogadishu on June 7, 2011. Mohammed was the mastermind of the 1998 bombings of two U.S. embassies in Nairobi and Dar es Salaam; he was also responsible for aligning al-Shabaab with al Qaeda and coordinating with the al Qaeda in Yemen (AQAP). His death came at a difficult time for al Qaeda, following the death of Osama bin Laden in May 2011, and replacing Mohammed with someone with his level of experience will be difficult. Following the death of Osama bin Laden, the al-Shabaab movement pledged its support to the new leader of al Qaeda, Ayman al-Zawahiri, in June 2011 (Figure 10-4).

Al-Shabaab's April 2, 2015, attack on Kenya's Garissa University College that killed 147 non-Muslim students was part of al-Shabaab's campaign to force Nairobi to order a withdrawal of the Kenyan Defense Force (KDF) from the Jubaland region of southern Somalia. The Kenyan government has presented an uncoordinated response that has largely focused on Islamist militancy as a foreign problem that is being imported across Kenya's porous border with Somalia.

KDFs began operations in the southern Somali region in 2011 aimed at stemming the tide of Islamists into Kenya. Their defense force also joined with the African Union Mission in Somalia to tackle al-Shabaab and have effectively created a buffer between the movement and Kenya. This however has not stopped the al-Shabaab from wanting to claim back territory taken by Kenyan forces. To that end, it has conducted a spectacular attack against the Garissa University.[3] There is ample evidence suggesting that global intelligence agencies had contacted their respective counterparts in Kenya in the days leading up to this attack and had warned the Kenyan government of an impending terrorist attack.

Somalia's location on the Indian Ocean gives it an easy launching platform to the Saudi peninsula. Somalia has a vast coastline, ideal for facilitating the movement of terrorists to operational hot spots in the Persian Gulf. Though mainly a Muslim nation, much of what transpires in that country is not due to religious infighting but inter-clan differences. The United States also declared the Somali Islamic Movement, al-Ittihad, a terrorist organization. Al-Ittihad emerged in 1991 as one of numerous warring militias; its aim was the establishment of an Islamic state. However, its military operations ended in defeat by invading Ethiopian troops in 1997 (Figure 10-5).

Somalia is traditionally Sunni Muslim and Islamic extremism is increasing rapidly. Al-Shabaab continues to face factional infighting and a rise in

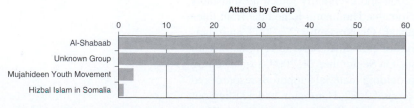

FIGURE 10-4 Suicide attacks by terror groups 2000–2015. *Source:* Chicago Project on Security and Terrorism, http://cpost.uchicago.edu.

TERRORIST ATTACK BRIEF

Laptop Computer Bomb—Daallo Airlines—Mogadishu, February 2016

On February 2, 2016, a Daallo Airliner took off from Mogadishu destined for Djibouti. Shortly after take-off there was an explosion that ripped a gaping hole in the aircraft fuselage just above the starboard wing of the aircraft. Aircraft fuel tanks are situated along the wings of aircraft. The explosion took place while the aircraft was at a relatively low level and the only death was the person holding the laptop bomb. Al-Shabaab claimed responsibility for the attack. Since the advent of modern day terrorism, the threat to civil aviation has continued to grow resulting in increased security measures in response to prior attacks. This has meant that attackers/bomb-makers must come up with more creative ways to circumvent security procedures and as we have seen since 9-11 that involves placing explosives in shoes (Richard Reid—December 2001) and the Underwear Bomber on Northwest Airlines flight to Detroit (December 2009). Bomb-makers are creating bombs from everyday objects including liquids, powders, and gels all with the aim of circumventing the established security procedures at airports.

FIGURE 10-5 Terrorist Attack Brief—Lap Top Bomb—Daallo Airlines, Mogadishu, February 2016
Source: www.Stratfor.com—Latest Airline Threat Suggests Limited Capabilities.

the significance of the Islamic State in Somalia. Al-Shabaab's foreign fighter elements have been rumored to want to pledge allegiance to IS rather than al Qaeda. Al-Shabaab has ruthlessly hunted down any of its members who attempt to defect to IS and executes them. In April 2016, a new jihadist group, Jahba East Africa, appeared in Somalia and pledged allegiance to the Islamic State. In a statement released, the group recognized Abu Bakr al-Baghdadi as the "rightful khalifa (leader) of all Muslims." It seems highly probable that this is part of a splinter group from al-Shabaab. Jahba East Africa claims to also have a presence in Kenya, Uganda, and Tanzania (Figures 10-6 to 10-10).

Suicide Attacks and Casualties by Location			
Country	**Attacks**	**Killed**	**Wounded**
Kenya	0	0	0
Somalia	90	769	936
Uganda	0	0	0

FIGURE 10-6 Suicide attacks by location 2000–2015. *Source:* Chicago Project on Security and Terrorism, http://cpost.uchicago.edu.

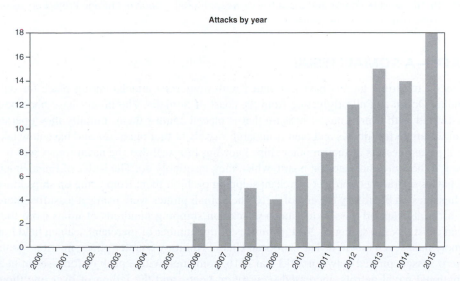

FIGURE 10-7 Suicide attacks by year 2000–2015. *Source:* Chicago Project on Security and Terrorism, http://cpost.uchicago.edu..

Suicide Attacks and Casualties by Target Type			
Target	Attacks	Killed	Wounded
Security	48	331	398
Political	38	415	519
Civilian	4	23	19
Unknown	0	0	0

FIGURE 10-8 Suicide attacks by target type. *Source:* Chicago Project on Security and Terrorism, http://cpost.uchicago.edu.

Suicide Attackers, Attacks, and Casualties by Religion				
Religion	Attackers	Attacks	Killed	Wounded
Muslim (NA)	4	4	65	115
Muslim (Sunni)	1	1	9	12
Unknown	91	86	695	809

FIGURE 10-9 Suicide attackers by religion. *Source:* Chicago Project on Security and Terrorism, http://cpost.uchicago.edu.

Suicide Attacks and Casualties by Weapon			
Weapon	Attacks	Killed	Wounded
Airplane	0	0	0
Belt Bomb	23	214	229
Car Bomb	67	555	707
Other	0	0	0
Unknown	0	0	0

FIGURE 10-10 Suicide attacks and casualties by weapon used. *Source:* Chicago Project on Security and Terrorism, http://cpost.uchicago.edu.

PIRACY—A SOMALI ISSUE

Attacks on maritime targets have continued with numerous attacks taking place far out into the Indian Ocean and all originating from the coast of Somalia. The pirates have become more sophisticated with every countermeasure that is placed against them. Initially they operated in coastal waters in fast dhows and then from large vessels farther out at sea and have now taken to using hijacked vessels as their mother ships knowing full well that the naval forces will not fire on them if they have hostages on board, which they invariably do. The Rules of Engagement for those navies operating to protect merchant shipping prohibit them from firing on ships known to have hostages on board. By the end of 2010, the Somali pirates were using at least five merchant ships as pirate support vessels to launch attacks on shipping hundreds of miles from the East African coast. By the spring of 2011, estimates of the number of merchant seamen held hostage was more than seven hundred. The European Union's military counter-piracy mission "Atalanta" saw zero vessels pirated between 2013 and 2016, compared with a peak of forty-seven in 2010. International naval patrols, increased security on boats, and the jailing of over one thousand pirates around the world have greatly reduced the threat.

UGANDA

Located in Central East Africa and bordering on Lake Victoria in the south, Uganda, as we know it today, went through a long and turbulent period in its history. Uganda gained its independence from Britain in 1962 and elected Milton Obote to be its first prime minister (Figure 10-11). In 1966, he was responsible for reordering the Constitution and replacing it with exclusive powers for the executive leadership. It was no surprise when the following year he declared himself president and Edward Mutesa, the country's first president, fled into exile in England. Obote placed most of Uganda under emergency laws and severely restricted the powers of the traditional tribes of Uganda's five tribal areas. Obote had extreme socialist views and was not popular with his people, and while at the Commonwealth Heads of State meeting in Singapore in 1971, his Army Chief Idi Amin led a coup against the government. Idi Amin Dada remained in power until 1979.

For Ugandans, the 1970s were horrific—a time when Uganda's self-proclaimed "President for Life," might well have coined the modern phrase "ethnic cleansing." The sheer scope of the terrorism against the Ugandan people during the very dark days from 1972 to 1979 is almost inconceivable. His praise of the work carried out by Adolph Hitler to exterminate the Jews, and his open hostility and demands for the destruction of Israel, spewed from the mind of this deranged psychopath! To try and understand any ideology that Amin may have had is incredibly difficult. He was extremely temperamental and prone to sudden changes of mind and irrational behavior.

What is not in question is the length he went to purge Uganda of any and all opponents, both political and social. His first move was to cleanse the country of any foreign influence and return Uganda and its wealth to the native Ugandans (primarily to himself). The son of a witch doctor, Amin's appetite for wealth knew no boundaries or the incredible lengths he would go to get it. Obote made him responsible for military control of the northern region of Uganda.[4] To achieve his wealth, he engaged in smuggling and murder or, to put it the old-fashioned way, "rape, plunder, and pillage."

Amin created a bureaucracy of state-sponsored terrorism to administer terror to Ugandans. He established two secret state police organizations, the Public Safety Unit and the Bureau of State Research. The Public Safety Unit was empowered to shoot to kill anyone—on just mere suspicion. The Bureau of State Research carried out interrogations and torture, usually also resulting in the death of any hapless prisoner. The actual number of Ugandan citizens killed during Amin's reign has never been accurately documented or accounted for, but it is believed to be as many as half a million.

As is too often the case in the African continent, tribal rivalries and old hatreds play a large part in the business of selective "genocide." Under Amin (a member of the Lugbara tribe), Uganda set in motion the calculated elimination of all the Lugbara's historical tribal enemies, especially the *Acholi* and *Langi* tribes. Handpicked secret police and vicious interrogation units from Amin's native *Lugbara* tribe were the implementers of this state-sponsored genocide.

On many occasions, Amin would observe or indulge in torture and other bizarre excesses personally. His presidential palace was linked by a series of tunnels connecting it to the Bureau of State Research in an adjoining building in the capital city of Kampala. He surrounded himself with a team of specially trained Palestinian bodyguards. When it came to executions, one of the methods employed was to provide a hammer to one prisoner who was then commanded, at gunpoint, to smash the skull of the prisoner next to him. This process of execution was then continued until the last prisoner was dispatched with a gunshot. The bodies of many executed prisoners were returned, in badly mutilated condition, to their families or dumped in rivers or in forests. Among other suspected atrocities practiced by Amin and his tribesmen was

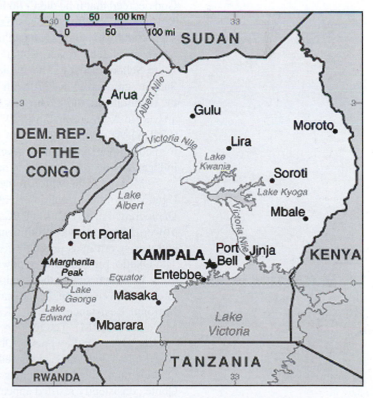

FIGURE 10-11 Map of Uganda. *Source:* Central Intelligence Agency, *The World Factbook, 2008.*

cannibalism. Killings by the army, where Amin's tribesmen were engaged in a systematic massacre of *Acholi* and *Langi* tribesmen, were the first signs to a watching public of the madness to follow. The expulsion of the Israelis, in 1972, was ultimately a result of their refusal to supply arms to Amin. The Asian exodus was one of the most significant events in Uganda's history. The reason for the expulsion is not clear; certainly Amin was under significant internal pressure to "deliver the goods" of postliberation euphoria and expectation, not just from the civilian population but also from his army. Uganda is only now beginning to heal, after over a third of a century.

Airline Hijacking to Entebbe

The 1970s saw an unprecedented number of airliner hijackings. One of the most notable was the hijacking of an Air France flight en route from Tel Aviv to Paris with two hundred and fifty passengers and crew. The hijackers consisted of both German and Arab members of the Popular Front for the Liberation of Palestine. The aircraft flew first to Benghazi, Libya, then to Entebbe, Uganda. After negotiations began, the hijackers released one hundred and forty-six hostages but held onto the remaining one hundred and six mainly Jewish passengers. They demanded the release of a large number of Arab terrorists being held in both Israeli and European prisons. As the negotiations dragged on it was clear to Israeli authorities that the Ugandan leader Idi Amin was helping the hijackers. The Israeli government quickly created a plan to rescue the hostages in Operation Jonathan. A force of Israeli commandos in three Hercules aircraft landed at Entebbe, much to the surprise of the hijackers and the Ugandan troops. The Israelis stormed the airport building killing seven of the eight hijackers as well as destroying Ugandan MIG aircraft on the ground. Three hostages were killed in the hour-long operation as well as the leader of the assault team Lt. Col. Jonathan Netanyahu. One hostage, an elderly English woman, Dora Block, who had previously been taken to a local hospital suffering from the effects of the hijacking was subsequently murdered by the Ugandans as a reprisal for the attack on Entebbe.

Asians and the British owned and controlled over half of Uganda's wealth, and expelling them was Amin's shortcut to achieving what was expected. In addition, Amin bore some motives for revenge on the British and wanted to teach them a lesson they would never forget. According to Amin, the reason for expelling the Asians was revealed to him in a dream, wherein God decreed that if he didn't do it, the country would be ruined. In 1978, Amin invaded Northern Tanzania in an effort to boost failing morale and wipe out more enemies. The retaliation was supported by expelled Ugandan troops, including the Front for National Salvation (FRONASA), which was led by Yoweri Kaguta Museveni. Museveni had been active since his student days at Ntare School, Mbarara; he studied political science and economics at the University of Dar es Salaam, graduating in 1970 with a Bachelor of Arts. The advance on Kampala was swift against the demoralized, though heavily armed, troops of Amin. The Tanzanian and Ugandan liberators arrived in Kampala in April 1979 under the banner of the Uganda National Liberation Army (UNLA). After a short period of indecision, the Uganda National Liberation Front (UNLF) was formed from an amalgam of several Ugandan political and military groups. Not for the first time in Uganda's history, the people had united against a common enemy.

Milton Obote, who had then returned from exile, would contest elections as leader of the Ugandan Political Coalition (UPC). A third major political party emerged to do battle with the Democratic Party (DP) and UPC. It was the Uganda Patriotic Movement (UPM) and, once more, Yoweri Museveni was prominent in Ugandan affairs. Milton Obote won the disputed election and was sworn in as president for his second term in 1980. Obote's army, under Major General Tito Okello, returned him to power, anxious for revenge on those who supported Amin in 1979.

Dissatisfied with the election results, Yoweri Museveni and twenty-six young men retreated into the Luwero Triangle and started what was to be a long campaign of guerrilla warfare. The National Resistance Army (NRA) was formed under the banner of the National Resistance Movement (NRM). The turning point in the long bush war was the death of the UNLA commander, Oyite-Ojok, who was Obote's cousin. Ojok was a powerful figure, and his death demoralized Obote's troops and caused a power struggle within the *Langi* and *Acholi* army factions. Obote's men rioted in the cities and towns, frustrated at the lack of success against the NRA. Obote consistently resisted appeals to negotiate with the NRA; he gradually alienated the *Acholi*, who felt they were fighting alone against the NRA. This up swell finally led to Obote being removed from power in 1985; he was granted political asylum in Zambia and died in exile in 2005.

The constitution was suspended, parliament dissolved, and Major General Tito Okello was sworn in as president in July 1985, but violence and lawlessness remained. Gradually, the NRA gained more support and more control in crucial areas. Museveni and Okello met in Kenya and signed peace agreements for a new, equally represented government. Within a month of the agreement, the war intensified and the NRA moved closer to Kampala. Then, on January 26, 1986, the NRA forces overran Kampala.

Yoweri Museveni was sworn in as president of Uganda on January 29, 1986, and announced that his takeover represented a fundamental change in the affairs of Uganda and not a "mere change of guards." He proclaimed a ten-point program wherein NRM would "usher in a new and better future for the people of Uganda." The ten points included issues ignored or maligned by the previous seven presidents, such as democracy, security, and elimination of corruption. To mixed reactions, a large, broad-based cabinet was appointed with friend and foe alike. In an effort to unite every corner of Uganda under one government, Museveni included representatives of previously antagonistic political parties, tribal groups, and religious factions in the government of the day.

Museveni extended personal invitations to exiled Ugandans, offering key government advisory or corporate positions. A significant brain drain had taken place during the war years and Museveni was anxious that these individuals help rebuild a fragmented and broken country. When the NRA arrived in Kampala, it encountered no serious resistance. The victorious soldiers were disciplined and friendly; this army was within the law, not above it.

The task that lay ahead in 1986 was immense. The violent policies of a whirlwind of governments had left Ugandans without belief in their leaders. National pride and identity were essential to rebuild the battered country. One of Museveni's most painful and arduous tasks was to convince the people that a democracy would emerge from a military takeover. The country was in a mess, and only a slow, systematic, and transparent examination of the damage might set wrongs to right again. The NRA re-established law and order everywhere in Uganda, except for the north and northeast, which had remained bastions of discontent and insecurity. The sporadic lawlessness in the north has been a constant problem to the NRA, and until a national identity emerges, the issue will remain.

Uganda's infrastructure, including its judicial system, the constitution, road construction, agriculture, health care, education, and tourism, had broken down and a system of locally elected government officials was put in place. Every Ugandan is a member of at least one legislative body that gives him or her voice in everyday affairs. This was to be the primary foundation on which a new national identity would be built. The personification of Uganda's malaise has been the magnitude of the AIDS crisis. Uganda was one of the first countries in Africa to recognize and begin to deal with this disease. The results have been very positive—education and awareness have been the key areas targeted.

Although Yoweri Museveni is a man with strong opinions and a keen sense of right and wrong, the reality of the chaotic situation he found in Uganda when he took power in 1986 meant that he had to accommodate people with views and attitudes that sometimes ran directly counter to his own.

In August 2002, humanitarian agencies and Ugandan authorities were working out an emergency plan following a Lord's Resistance Army (LRA) attack on a refugee camp in northern Uganda, which forced thousands of Sudanese refugees to flee into the bush. The office of the UN High Commissioner for Refugees (UNHCR) said plans were in hand to move at least twenty four thousand Sudanese refugees who had fled from the camp to a safer location, following an LRA attack on the Acholi-Pii refugee settlement in Pader District. UNHCR's information officer for Uganda reported that Ugandan authorities had, at an emergency meeting between humanitarian agencies and senior government officials, agreed to relocate the refugees to a safer location yet to be agreed upon, preferably in Yumbe, Hoima, or Nebii districts, all in western Uganda.

The International Rescue Committee (IRC) for Uganda said it was also planning a response, which would involve transporting food to Rachkoko from neighboring Kitgum District. This was the second LRA attack in a week on the Acholi-Pii Camp. The LRA group had first attacked the camp on July 31, 2002, but government soldiers repulsed the attackers, UNHCR said. Earlier, on July 8, LRA fighters had attacked the Maaji refugee settlement, in nearby Adjumani District, killing six refugees and putting another eight thousand into flight. The number of casualties incurred in the first attack remains unclear. Major Shaban Bantariza, the Ugandan army spokesman, told the BBC that about two hundred LRA fighters had killed four soldiers and eight civilians, losing eleven of their own in the process. The magnitude of the attack was an indication that the Ugandan government was no longer able to guarantee security in northern Uganda, where humanitarian assistance was becoming increasingly dangerous as a result. The IRC had earlier withdrawn most of its staff from the camp, following the first attack, but redeployed them there after receiving assurances from the Ugandan authorities guaranteeing their security. Since June 2001, the LRA has intensified attacks on northern Ugandan districts in response to the pressure exerted on it in southern Sudan. About half a million displaced Ugandans and some one hundred and fifty-five thousand Sudanese refugees live in camps in northern Uganda, according to the refugee agency.

THE LORD'S RESISTANCE ARMY

The Lord's Resistance Army (LRA) is one of the most ferocious organizations to have emerged in central Africa, yet few Westerners have ever heard of it, since nearly all its violence is perpetrated in the border region between Uganda and Sudan in East Africa.

On a continent plagued with guerrilla warfare, where war crimes are standard fighting fare, the LRA stands apart as an especially odious group. LRA crimes against humanity are so repulsive that its only former ally, the Islamic government of Sudan, jettisoned its relationship with the LRA to improve Sudan's international relations. What began in 1986 as a rebellion against the Ugandan government has metamorphosed into a military millenarian cult. Its reason for existence is to perpetuate the power of its leader, a ruthless witchcraft practitioner named Joseph Kony.[5] The LRA under Kony had a fearsome reputation for its brutality against the people of Northern Uganda, and it is believed the group has managed to abduct and indoctrinate over twenty thousand children into its ranks since it was first established in 1987.[6]

Since Museveni came to power in 1989, one of his most significant challenges has come from the LRA. The LRA has been led since its inception by Joseph Kony. Joseph, a member of the northern Acholi tribe was born in 1961 in the village of Odek in northern Uganda. He derived his original power base through his aunt who was the tribal mystic. The first movement in the development of the LRA was called the Holy Spirit Movement with the ideal of overthrowing the government in Kampala in retaliation for the collective violence meted out to the Acholi tribes. Kony had served in the Ugandan Peoples Democratic Army (UPDA) and described himself as a self-styled Prophet sent to save and avenge the Acholi. When the UPDA signed an accord with the Ugandan government in 1988, Kony refused to agree and splintered away with some other disgruntled troops. From this point in 1988, he established the LRA. With his military background and religious zeal, he created the Uganda Christian Democratic Army and began targeting the government. In 1991, he changed the name of the group to the LRA (Figure 10-12).

One of the more unsavory factors about the LRA is its propensity to forcibly recruit child soldiers as young as age twelve to either carry out attacks or be used as sex slaves. Human rights groups believe the LRA's ranks consist of 85 percent child soldiers. A large percentage of the children are kidnapped and forced to commit atrocities against their own families, and young girls are held as sex slaves and "wives" for local commanders. Recent attempts by the government to eradicate the LRA have included well-organized operations centered in southern Sudan, with the approval of the Sudanese government. However, there are claims that both sides have used extrajudicial methods to suit their needs. Ugandan People's Defense Forces (UPDF) is also reportedly using and abusing children. The operation inside Sudan, code named "Iron Fist," has displaced more than 1.2 million inhabitants from northern Uganda and seen over six hundred thousand children being used as soldiers. The phenomenon of "night commuters" has also emerged—an estimated twenty thousand children flee their homes each night in fear, seeking refuge from possible abduction by the LRA, and searching for places to sleep in churches and hospitals.[7] Uganda has deployed approximately eight thousand of its troops in the Democratic Republic of Congo (DRC). Again, this is a consequence of the rich reserves of timber and diamonds. A form of trade was developed in the border regions, with shipments transferred through Uganda under the control of the Ugandan military. There is no vested interest for the Ugandans to see any

FIGURE 10-12   In 2005, the International Criminal Court (ICC) issued arrest warrants for Joseph Kony—head of the Lord's Resistance Army (LRA)—and four other LRA leaders for crimes against humanity and war crimes.   *Source:* EPA/epa european pressphoto agency b.v./Alamy Stock Photo.

ceasefire or peace within the DRC. Much of the spoils in this conflict originate in the northern city of Kisangani. The LRA was funded and supplied by the government in Khartoum, and the Ugandan government was sponsoring attacks by the Sudan People's Liberation Army (SPLM); but since 2005, SPLM has been playing an official role in government, so the source of financial and material aid has dried up.

Museveni invited the International Criminal Court (ICC) to indict the LRA's leaders for war crimes, arguing that his country's own justice system was unable to deal with cases of such legal magnitude.[8] The warrants against Kony, Vincent Otti, Raska Lukwiya, Okot Odhiambo, and Dominic Ongwen were historic, since they were the first issued by the fledgling ICC, which began work in 2002. Lukwiya was killed in August 2006 during a fight between the LRA and Ugandan military forces. The LRA has suffered from regional political influences as it was often used as a pawn, particularly in the conflict between Sudan and Uganda. However, Sudan is more concerned with settling its grievances with Uganda rather than putting down the LRA. In 2008, Sudanese and troops from the Congo launched a joint operation, but with feuding and mistrust among the so-called allies, the operation named "Lightning Thunder" foundered. Although the campaign had some short-term successes, they never got near to capturing Kony and his lieutenants. The United States has for several years been training the Ugandan Special Forces; however, this will come to naught if the military is ill-supplied and poorly equipped for a counterinsurgency campaign that requires coordination and long-term commitment. Uganda would possibly need support from European nations and/or the United States to gain an upper hand on Kony and his gang; however, with so many other regional conflicts and uprisings taking place, it's hard to envisage any support coming to this area of central Africa. By the end of 2015, there had been many defections from Kony's despotic group and the probability that his end will likely be at the hands of one of his own should be contemplated. He has executed many of his high ranking officers over the past three years and those that have escaped tell stories of bloodshed of LRA members by Kony usually on a trumped up charge. The UN Secretary-General released a report on May 20, 2013, claiming that between 1987 and 2012, the LRA was "responsible for more than one hundred thousand deaths, that from sixty to one hundred thousand children are believed to have been abducted by the rebel group and that 2.5 million civilians have been displaced as a result of its incursions."

The Allied Democratic Forces (ADF)

The ADF is a coalition of Islamist sects and local opposition forces opposed to the Ugandan government. Originally based in Western Uganda, ADF now operates in the Democratic Republic of the Congo and is considered a terrorist organization. ADF was founded in Uganda in 1989 by Sheikh Jamil Mukulu, a radical Islamist who aimed to overthrow the government of President Yoweri Museveni and replace it with a loosely defined Islamist administration. It first came to attention in the 1990s and then has gone quiet. It is believed to be sponsored by the Sudanese secret service to wage a proxy war against Uganda (in response to the heavy support the SPLA had received from Uganda in South Sudan), the ADF promoted a heavily militarized Islamic agenda, conducting raids into southwest Uganda from bases in the Congolese Rwenzori Mountains. The ADF was pushed back from the borders of Uganda and by the new millennium was operating from the DRC. This group appears to be far less aggressive than the LRA and while it professes to be supporting the Muslims population against the tyranny of the Ugandan government it is not calling for an Islamic emirate.

ADF increases its numerical strength by abducting civilians from villages it attacks. Because of their socio-economic integration in the region, military action against them has largely been ineffective in the past. Their ties and networks in the borderland have been too strong to allow them to simply be thrown out of this area. Their ability to utilize the other side of the border in times of crisis has significantly helped them as well. Their borderland integration is also why the ADF's responses to disarmament and demobilization initiatives have generally been so lackluster. For a large part of the force, returning "home" to Uganda makes no sense, nor is it necessarily desirable.

The idea of the ADF serving as a proxy force for Sudan (in the group's earlier stages) and later for various extremist Islamic actors such as al-Shabaab, has been influential. The situation is clearly shaped by the global discourse on terrorism, and has received further encouragement from the Ugandan government.[9]

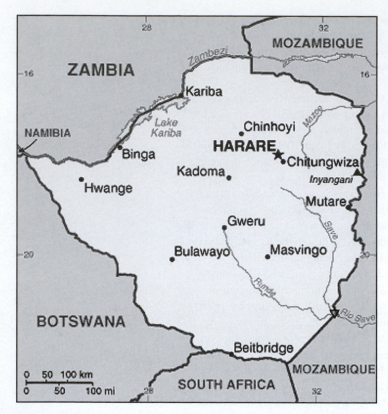

FIGURE 10-13 Map of Zimbabwe. *Source:* Central Intelligence Agency, *The World Factbook, 2008.*

ZIMBABWE

Many Black African states were looking to shed the yoke of the British Empire in the 1960s and 1970s. White rule in Rhodesia, under Ian Smith, ended in 1980, when the country gained its independence and Robert Mugabe became the country's first Prime Minister (Figure 10-13). However, Mugabe and his government faced violent opposition mainly from the region of Matabeleland. Mugabe's ruling party, the Zimbabwe African National Union (ZANU), was also strongly opposed by the Zimbabwe People's Revolutionary Army (ZIPRA) and the Zimbabwe African People's Union (ZANPU). Mugabe used what can easily be termed *state terror* on the peoples of Matabeleland to ensure his own position in Zimbabwe. To do this he used the Zimbabwe Army Fifth Brigade as a vehicle to control, repress, torture, interrogate, and execute all armed opponents in Matabeleland.

UNILATERAL DECLARATION OF INDEPENDENCE

November 11, 1965, is the date Ian Smith declared a **Unilateral Declaration of Independence (UDI)** for Rhodesia. If one were to look to the north about the same time, as scenes were being played out in the name of independence, the view was far from gratifying. Millions were dead in Nigeria and the Congo, more than half a million in the Sudan, and over two hundred thousand in Rwanda and Burundi. In nearly all instances, it was black man killing black man, and the countries were in the hands of blood-crazed dictators.[10]

Unfortunately for the rebel government of Ian Smith, the rest of the world, including Britain and the United Nations, would not recognize the new breakaway state and instead enforced strong economic sanctions on the country. In the years preceding the UDI, most forms of terrorism and violent criminal actions were well under the control of the authorities. In that era, when there was a perception of weakness and an opportunity arose to destabilize a region in Africa, the undertones of Communist involvement were never far away. So, too, it was with Rhodesia. Many of the young blacks were lured out of the country on promise of "scholarships" in Zambia and Tanganyika. In fact, these young men were being sent for Communist indoctrination and weapons training in camps in North Korea and the former USSR. They were returned via such ports as Dar es Salaam on the coast of Africa and then infiltrated back into Rhodesia to fight against the Smith government. Ian Smith was prime minister of Rhodesia and a powerful advocate of white minority rule; his unilaterally declared independence (UDI) from Britain in 1965 would result in a fifteen-year campaign against Communist-backed African nationalists fighting for an independent African state later to become Zimbabwe. The campaign would cost the lives of forty thousand people.

Smith never once backed down from his position that there should never be black majority rule in Rhodesia. The white South African government withdrew its support for Rhodesian UDI, and this was a turning point for Smith. By 1972, the armed African nationalists under Joshua Nkomo and Robert Mugabe were raiding white farms at will. Ian Smith died on November 21, 2007, aged eighty-eight.[11]

With so many ways to define terrorism, would the likes of Nkomo and Mugabe be viewed as terrorists, insurgents, freedom fighters, or just violent criminals? The answer to this question is not easy. From the Rhodesian standpoint, they were certainly seen as terrorists, so the Smith government used the Rhodesian Special Air Service Regiment to good effect in destroying these "terrorists." The task from the military standpoint was almost hopeless, given the makeup of the borders that surrounded the country. The only friendly region lay to the south with the South African government. The numbers of terrorists and insurgents continued to grow in the same manner as that faced by the United States when it fought an impossible-to-win war in Vietnam.

The politics of the day did nothing to inhibit the violence in Rhodesia. On the contrary, to most people in Rhodesia, both black and white, it seemed that the terrorist forces had the tacit support of the British government in the name of African nationalism. The two leaders of the terror groups, Joshua Nkomo and Ndabaningi Sithole, were openly supported in Britain even though they were leaders of the two parties banned by the Smith government. The black nationalists, Robert Mugabe being one of them, formed ZANU as a result of a split with the Nkomo leadership. Nkomo formed the opposing ZAPU movement. Formed along tribal lines, Nkomo's support came principally from the Ndebele tribes of Matabeleland in the west, while Mugabe's support lay in the tribes of Mashonaland in the east of the country.

Serious voting irregularities during the 2002 general election, witnessed by the Commonwealth observers, resulted in an announcement from London that Zimbabwe was to be suspended from the Commonwealth for twelve months. The leaders of South Africa, Australia, and Nigeria made the decision on behalf of the fifty-four-nation group, after studying an observer mission report on Zimbabwe's appalling presidential elections. Announcing the decision in London, former Australian Prime Minister John Howard said he hoped the international community would encourage reconciliation in Zimbabwe between the main parties. At a summit held before the Zimbabwe election, Howard and the presidents of South Africa and Nigeria, Thabo Mbeki and Olusegun Obasanjo, respectively, were appointed to decide what action, if any, the Commonwealth should take against Zimbabwe. The ballot in Zimbabwe saw the re-election of incumbent President Robert Mugabe amid allegations of violence, terrorism, and intimidation against the opposition, Movement for Democratic Change, led by Morgan Tsvangirai. Western governments severely criticized the fairness of the election, while African governments were less willing to condemn Mugabe.

The Commonwealth Observer Group accused Mugabe of using state powers and institutions to steal his victory. The United States, Britain, and the European Union condemned the elections as "unfair and not free." Before leaving Australia for London, Howard said, "This is quite a moment of truth for the Commonwealth . . . it's not something that can be swept under the carpet."

Mbeki and Obasanjo held talks with Mugabe to try and seek a compromise. Among the proposals speculated on was a government of National Unity, but both Mugabe and Tsvangirai cast doubt on the plan. Tsvangirai said: "We arrived at the conclusion that the objective conditions do not exist for meaningful discussion because Mugabe's party . . . ZANU-PF, is embarking on mass retribution against our members in the rural areas."

Mugabe, who has been in power since 1980, was sworn in for another six-year term. He took the victory as a mandate to pursue his land reform program. Zimbabwe's main Labor Federation called for a three-day general strike to protest what it called postelection harassment of workers.

The Harare meeting came on the same day that a white farmer was shot dead by suspected ruling party militants. Terry Ford was the first white farmer killed since Mugabe was reelected and the tenth killed since militants began often-violent occupation of white-owned land two years earlier. Denmark, which is not a member of the Commonwealth, announced it was closing its Harare Embassy and ending further developmental aid to the country and stated that reports from national and international observers clearly showed that the election was neither free nor fair. Denmark withdrew its embassy staff from Harare that summer.

Zimbabwe continues to reel under the effects of Mugabe's dictatorship, with millions facing certain death from disease, starvation, and state-sponsored violence, yet Mugabe's message to the nation was a promissory note for more misery and death. The annual National Heroes' Day in 2002 proved to be no exception. The illegitimate ZANU-PF government has routinely turned this somber national occasion into an indecent partisan junket to spread a message of violence and hatred.

Mugabe fails to connect with the primary concerns of the people of Zimbabwe, which are food, jobs, health, and an end to poverty. He instead concerns himself primarily with rhetorical nationalism. In fact, Zimbabwe now is a country where everything is in short supply except misery, starvation, and death. The regime has reduced innocent citizens to the levels of scavenging animals.

Where Zimbabweans expect a message of hope and decisive leadership to confront the problems bedeviling the country, they are told that their daughters and sons will be forcibly drafted into the so-called National Youth Service and be transformed into killing machines for the perpetuation of Mugabe's dictatorship. Change in Zimbabwe is inevitable, no matter how many innocent citizens are slaughtered by his regime. Evidence at hand demonstrates, beyond any reasonable doubt, the regime's culpability in widespread and systematic incidences of murders, tortures, rape, abductions, arsons, and many other forms of well-organized political violence that have taken place with impunity over the first decade of the twenty-first century. The partisan public media has never exposed nor condemned ZANU-PF violence, but has instead defended it. The police force, on the other hand, has mastered the art of selective harassment, arrests, and prosecution of the opposition, while ruling party criminals who are guilty of heinous crimes are walking scot free. As the 2008 elections came around, there was the real prospect that Mugabe now over eighty years old would relinquish his control and fade into obscurity. On the contrary, the March 2008 elections were a well-rigged affair by the dictatorship—thugs from Mugabe's ZANU-PF party roamed the countryside at will attacking and intimidating voters. True democracy is still not being felt in what was once the breadbasket of Africa.

In addition to the acts of barbarism that have been perpetrated with state sanction and impunity, the regime has sought to legalize the harassment of political opponents and to control what the people read, hear, and see through the enactment of legislation with severe democratic deficits, like Jonathan Moyo's Access to Information Act and John Nkomo's Public Order and Security Act. What is blatantly disturbing and unacceptable about the regime is that at a time when the nation has an avalanche of political and economic crises on its hands—for which the regime is responsible—its ministers, such as John Nkomo, Joseph Made, and Jonathan Moyo, are busy trying to outdo each other in their daily television appearances. The regime's ministers have become obsessed with little things at a time when they should be answering questions about more serious things, like the supplying of salt for Zimbabwean families.

The United Nations has condemned Zimbabwe, Uganda, and Rwanda for actions in the DRC. These three countries initially intervened in the DRC to stabilize the area in the aftermath of Laurent Kabila's overthrow of Mobutu Sese Seko and the subsequent chaos that took place in the eastern half of the former Republic of Zaire.

Both Uganda and Rwanda support the rebels in the east and Zimbabwe supports the government. However, the UN report accuses Zimbabwe, Uganda, and Rwanda of perpetuating the war for their own financial gain, as they exploit the country's rich mineral resources. The DRC is one of the richest countries in the world in minerals. It has gold, copper, diamonds, cobalt, Coltan (a metal ore for use in aerospace telecommunications industries), and timber.

In the rebel-controlled areas, Rwanda is accused of exporting Coltan mineral, which it mines inside the DRC; Uganda is accused of gold-smuggling activities; and Zimbabwe allegedly engages in joint ventures with DRC government officials, which benefit only the ruling elite back in Harare. The armed forces of the DRC have been pushed into the western half of the country, unable to penetrate the areas held by the Tutsi-backed rebels in areas where these three countries' armies are operating, despite receiving military aid from Zimbabwe, Angola, and Namibia.

The governments of Rwanda and Uganda reject the claims that they are prolonging the war for their own gain. Although UN-monitored ceasefire has been established, there is still fighting between rival armed groups. The result, as is the usual case in Africa, is paid for in civilian suffering and lives. Infant mortality stands at 40 percent. There are reportedly 2 million displaced persons and 16 million people classified as not receiving the basic nutritional levels as stipulated by the United Nations.

ZANU-PF 5 BRIGADE

The PF 5 Brigade came into existence under Prime Minister Mugabe's command. In October 1980, Mugabe signed an agreement with then North Korean president Kim II Sung that arranged for North Korean training of Zimbabwean troops. Koreans were sent to train this new brigade that Mugabe said would be used to "deal with dissidents and any other trouble in the country." The 3,500 ex-ZANLA troop members that made up the 5 Brigade were supplemented by some ZIPRA troops, which were withdrawn before the end of the training stage. The training lasted until September 1982. At deployment, the 5 Brigade was different from any other army units: it answered only to the prime minister and did not follow the standard military chain of command. It had unique codes, uniforms, radios, and equipment that were not compatible with standard-issue Zimbabwean army tools. The 5 Brigade's most distinguishing feature was their red berets.

The 5 Brigade was deployed twice into Matabeleland—once in Matabeleland North in late January 1983, then in Matabeleland South in January 1984. After this, they were retrained, deployed again, and then in 1986 finally withdrawn, to undergo a conventional training period under the British Military Advisory Team. In late 1986, the 5 Brigade was disbanded and its soldiers spread out between other regular army brigades.

The deployments of the 5 Brigade into Matabeleland in the early 1980s were marked with a reign of terror, with actions meant to draw out antigovernment "dissidents." Within the first weeks of the first deployments, 5 Brigade troops had murdered more than two thousand civilians; beaten thousands more, destroyed property, and burned houses. Civilians seemed to be specifically targeted during those weeks; hundreds of civilians were rounded up, marched at gun point to a central area, like a school or village well, beaten with sticks, and made to sing Shona songs praising ZANU-PF. These gatherings would then end with public executions.[12]

In the clinical sense, starvation has not yet set in Zimbabwe. But the signs are there—people with sticklike arms and legs and swollen bellies. AIDS is wiping out a whole generation of parents. Thousands upon thousands of small children barely exist with no food, no family income, no medicines, and no answers. Over a third of these children have HIV or AIDS. It is not life they are living—they are just waiting to die. Zimbabwe is now facing a major famine that may decimate half of the country's population.

Zimbabwe's 1992 Land Acquisition Act is at the heart of the redistribution of land owned by white farmers and arbitrarily handed over to blacks. The act was intended to speed up the land reform process by removing the "willing seller, willing buyer" clause. This empowered the government to buy land compulsorily for redistribution. From Harare, the word of Zimbabwean officials was that: "White Farmers will live to regret their defiance of government orders to abandon their land." This followed nearly three thousand white farmers being ordered to leave their property as part of a plan to seize white-owned lands and turn them over to poor blacks. No serious measures have yet been taken against farmers who have defied the deadline, which changes quickly and often. But, then Co-Vice President Joseph Msika, head of Zimbabwe's Land-reform Task Force, told state television about the farmers refusing to leave their land: "Those who are not going to work within the laws of Zimbabwe have nobody to blame but themselves. The law will take its course." A powerful local government minister said: "All the excuses by the farmers show what an arrogant and racist bunch they are. It shows they want to derail the land redistribution program by any means . . . they will not succeed," according to the state-run *Herald* newspaper. Former vice president Simon Muzenda warned that authorities would act firmly against farmers opposing the, "irreversible" land program. "You are told by government what we want done and you simply do that," he told state radio. In Washington DC, the U.S. State Department denounced Zimbabwe's attempt to evict the farmers and thousands of farm workers as "a reckless and reprehensible act."

While Robert Mugabe continues to rule supreme in Zimbabwe, he continues to target all opposition; in May 2005, he targeted the urban centers that failed to support him during his re-election campaign in March 2005. The country languishes in abject poverty and real fears of famine exist. In late May 2005, Mugabe ordered a "cleanup" that sparked rioting in Harare. Three thousand police supported by the Zimbabwe military destroyed informal settlements and street markets and arrested almost twenty thousand hawkers. The government-sanctioned destruction has left tens of thousands homeless with nowhere to repatriate. The opposition Movement for Democratic Change claims that this action is purely a pretext for the government to announce a "state of emergency." Today the Mugabe brand of politics, intimidation, murder, rape, and forced removals of Zimbabweans marks the standard for a failed state that the rest of the world, although condemning it, does little to correct.

SOUTH AFRICA

For the last half of the twentieth century, South Africa operated under a white-dominated apartheid government, using "**apartheid**" as an official method to control the actions, activities, and opportunities of native, black, colored, and African Asians in the Republic of South Africa. The main political party that was set up to fight apartheid was the African National Congress (ANC). Strangely,

FIGURE 10-14 Map of South Africa. *Source:* Central Intelligence Agency, *The World Factbook, 2008.*

that party started on a political platform and moved eventually toward armed confrontation with the South African government (Figure 10-14).

Color alone, by no means, carries with it a unity of belief, purpose, or ambition. The most virulent and persistent of hatreds in Africa is often those between people of the same color. The black population of South Africa is divided into at least seven distinct ethnic groups, each with its own written language and home area, and each resolved to retain its own identity. That way the groups could develop separately and still remain apart. In the forty years up to the early 1990s, the South African governments set out to regulate this "problem" by the establishment of separate, self-governing "homelands" for each group.[13] To most people, from the outside looking in, apartheid has always had an evil connotation. Although this text is not intended to be a forum for debating the pros and cons of segregation of ethnic groups in South Africa, it is relevant to the South African experience with terrorism.

Britain's involvement in the Cape colony dates back to over three centuries, when the region along the Cape was very important as a refueling and trading post for shipping to and from the Orient and India. The Cape colony was also home to Dutch migrants from Europe who had settled the Colony in 1652. From the middle of the sixteenth century, the Dutch East India Company had executive powers over the Colony, and all its inhabitants, but allowed Dutch settlers to leave the company and start their own farms. These people became known as "Boers." With the migration inland, the white farmers fought the tiny, "San Tribes," people (Bushmen) and either killed or enslaved them for work on their farms.

The Dutch government formally turned the Colony over to Britain in 1834. The first British settlers had arrived in the Cape in 1820, and with control going to Britain, an unpopular decision was made to end slavery. Britain established English as the official language of the Cape to the extreme resentment of the Boers living in the Colony. Unhappy with British rule, the Boers began to move north and settled in regions farther away in the Transvaal, the Orange Free State, and Natal. The move north became a historic event for the Boers and is generally referred to as the Great Trek.

With the discovery of diamonds in the Kimberley region, and gold in the Johannesburg areas, Anglos and Boers would eventually fight the first Anglo-Boer War. Overwhelming force of arms allowed the British to defeat the Boers by 1902, thus bringing about the Orange Free State, Transvaal, and Natal, all under firm British rule. This rule, not surprisingly, included all the Black tribes, most of which submitted peacefully to their new masters. As in most matters, there is always an exception to a rule, and the South African exception was the "Zulus." This warlike tribe would submit to nobody and, in 1879, defeated and destroyed a well-trained British regiment at Isandlwana. Overwhelming superiority of forces and firepower eventually defeated the Zulus, and by 1888, none of the black African tribes retained independence.

AFRIKANER NATIONALISM

Two famous Boer generals, Louis Botha and Jan Smuts, had a great part to play in the rise of Afrikaner nationalism in South Africa. General J. Hertzog formed the Nationalist Party, which had the ideology that the Boers had a right to rule South Africa and to unite the Anglos and Afrikaners. With a nationalist government coming to power in South Africa for the first time in 1922, nationalists began the changes that would shape the United South Africa of their dreams. This included the recognition of Afrikaans, alongside English, as the official language and also the development of industry less dependent on Great Britain. With the outbreak of World War II, South Africa was already an independent nation within the British Commonwealth, and there was considerable debate as to which side, if any, to support. Hertzog favored neutrality while the Boer General Smuts sided with the British against Germany.

Apartheid

During the war years, the Nationalist Party underwent a rebirth and change of direction under the inspiration of D. F. Malan, a strong supporter of the nationalist South African cause. Under his guidance, the adoption of segregation along racial lines (apartheid) was developed and instituted as part of government policy, with sweeping police powers of enforcement. The government had created the power to direct the masses as to where to live and where to work. The struggle against apartheid, or racism, as some observers prefer to call it, became a part of the South African struggle and terrorism for over fifty years. However, one significant incident in March 1960 marked the turning point in the attitude of the international community toward the apartheid government of South Africa and caused the sting of economic sanctions against it. One of the requirements of the apartheid laws was for all blacks to carry ID cards. In protest, blacks went to police stations without their cards and waited to be arrested. The same scene was played out in many locations; however, in Sharpsville, the police opened fire with automatic weapons, and killed sixty-seven and wounded over 200 blacks. From this one incident the ANC formed its military wing, the Umkhonto We Sizwe (Spear of the Nation).

Extreme Right-Wing Afrikaner Movement

Extremism in South African politics emerged at the end of the 1960s from splinter groups that broke off from the National Party and called themselves the Herstigte Nasionale Party (HNP). By 1971, all the hard-liners of Afrikaner Nationalism had been forced out from the National Party and thus formed the Afrikaner Weerstandsbeweging (AWB), The Afrikaner Resistance Movement. The AWB became known principally for its menacing, but flamboyant, leader, Eugene Terre'Blanche. Likened to Adolph Hitler, his speech-making skills were legendary, although his message was usually disjoined and with little meaning except to menace and threaten. This ability allowed Terre'Blanche to attract large crowds of supporters to his meetings. Not only was he a consummate politician and orator but also an accomplished sportsman. He served in the South African Police Service as a Warrant Officer. After leaving the police service, he went on to form the AWB in July 1973 with another former police colleague, Jan Groenewald. The early movement was extremely small, and the meetings were secret for fear of drawing the attention of the Bureau of State Security (**BOSS**).

BOSS, not surprisingly, portrayed all the same trappings and uniform style, complete with swastika, as the German Nazi Movement. Albert Hertzog, a former cabinet member of the National Party and founder of the HNP, was at this time outside of the party hierarchy, following the party's disastrous showing in the general election, and was looking for a cause to support. That support, together with his great business acumen, went to Terre'Blanche and the AWB. Although the 1970s were the formative years for the AWB, no specific acts of terror can be attributed to the organization. With the dismantling of the apartheid system in South Africa, that would change over the following seventeen years.

Many observers labeled the AWB as a neo-Nazi organization. Although the leadership of the AWB vehemently denied the label, the group's flamboyant uniforms did not easily dispel this viewpoint. Still searching for its true identity, the AWB went through several different scenarios, usually linked to storm trooper and motorcycle gang-style images with fearsome-sounding names like the Lightening Falcons or Storm Falcons. Most were burly and surly men outfitted with jackboots and helmets.

The first signs of violence came in 1985, when Terre'Blanche proclaimed that the AWB would form into units of guards. These groups were called the "Sentinels" or "Brandwag" and were formed up along the Northern Transvaal border with Zimbabwe. The white farmers in the border areas formed Brandwags to protect against incursions from across the border with Zimbabwe. The AWB equipped itself with its own bodyguard of heavies to "control" and monitor meetings. Most of the white farmers in the more remote regions of the Transvaal were also local commando (army) members, so it was not surprising that they would be well armed with sophisticated weapons. With the extreme right-wing's sympathy, and now sophisticated weapons in its members' hands, the aims of the AWB were to make sure black groups and political organizations would not become targets for action. What made the AWB so popular was its belief in preserving its claims to land and demands for an Afrikaner nation to be formed out of the former Boer Republics.

By the end of the 1980s, it became clear that the enemy of the AWB, apart from left-wing politicians, was also the ANC. Over the years that led up to the first ANC-elected government and the ending of the apartheid system in South Africa, AWB members and supporters carried out various terrorist acts to destabilize the ANC and the elected government. The AWB had hoped to escalate the violence into a full-scale civil war. As we now know, that was never to be the case. However, the bomb attacks were directed mainly at black civilian targets as were the indiscriminate use of bombs in the major cities. The bombing campaign resulted in many AWB arrests and convictions. In 1996, the AWB, still under the control of Terre'Blanche, announced that the movement would now operate underground.

The AWB symbol is the eagle. The group's official guidebook details that: "This emblem enables the AWB to give its full acknowledgement to the symbolism of the eagle which epitomizes the protection of the Lord: Like an eagle that stirs up its nest that flutters over its young, spreading out its wings, catching them, bearing them on its pinions" (*Deuteronomy* 32:11). Terre'Blanche was murdered in April 2010 by two of his farm workers while taking a nap at his ranch.

The Future

In April 1994, the ANC gained over sixty percent of the vote in the country's first free elections, bringing an end to apartheid and white minority rule. With the public's general acceptance of the new government, UN recognition, and the rapid lifting of international sanctions, it is difficult to see the AWB or a similar nationalist movement emerging in South Africa in any significant fashion for the near future. As long as Afrikaner nationhood is alive and well, however, there will always be the opportunity and threat for a different generation to take up where Terre'Blanche left off.

The African National Congress

The quasi-political African National Congress (ANC) movement dates as far back as 1912 and has consistently, along with other liberal groups, opposed the nationalists and their apartheid policies. Garnering support for any action, given the overwhelming numbers (seventy-five percent of the population is black and fourteen percent white, with the balance being made up of Asians), would not be difficult. Probably the most famous name connected to the movement is that of the first black president of South Africa, Nelson Rolihlahla Mandela. Born in 1918, the son of a tribal chief, Mandela received an excellent education and became a lawyer. Toward the end of World War II, he joined the ANC. Mandela, an outspoken opponent of apartheid, led protests and demonstrations against apartheid and police brutality during the 1950s, for which he was arrested and charged with treason. The charge was not proven, however, and he was acquitted. He was arrested again in 1962, charged with terrorist offenses, and sentenced to life in prison. His release thirty-two years later would become the harbinger and beginning of the new South Africa and a black majority government. The role of the ANC and various acts of terrorism in South Africa are intertwined. The ANC contention is that it had been driven to acts of criminal violence, bombings, shootings, and murder because it lacked any political alternative. With apartheid firmly in place and its leader firmly in jail, the ANC members embarked on a terror campaign aimed at the state, the white minority, and their own black brothers who failed to support them. Intertribal fighting has been a hallmark of fighting in the south. Some of the forms of brutality the ANC used are quite gruesome to describe. One favored method in killing recalcitrant blacks was the "rubber necklace"—a badly beaten victim was placed in a stack of used car tires and then set on fire.

The ANC received external support in its campaign from Communist sources outside South Africa's borders. This led to the government reducing and diminishing the effects of apartheid on the black and colored communities. The ANC had a military wing that advocated revolutionary violence. It further advocated the kind of Communist revolution that swept into Russia at the start of the twentieth century. A 1987 quote from Winnie Mandela, then wife of the imprisoned Nelson Mandela, clearly defined the Communist goals for the ANC: "The Soviet Union is the torchbearer for all our hopes and aspirations. In Soviet Russia, genuine power of the people has been transformed from dreams into reality." Since the middle of the 1980s, the Republic of South Africa has undergone drastic political changes, and with those changes came the fruition of the dream of the overthrow of the regime and the system of apartheid.

Having been banned since 1961, the ANC had been headquartered outside South Africa, in neighboring Zambia. To this extent, one may assume the Zambians gave material support to ANC terrorists crossing into South Africa. The South African police and military were very effective in patrolling and controlling border incursions from neighboring African countries, especially those hostile to the apartheid regime. The neighboring countries of Lesotho, Mozambique, and Botswana have been, at varying times, the locations for terrorist training bases for the ANC and were supported by Russian technicians. The external locations did not prevent the South African security forces from taking preemptive actions against the training base locations in those countries. The ANC also aided in defining the term *terrorism* by declaring in the 1980s that the South African government was a terrorist government and that the ANC was acting in self-defense.

Robben Island University (Isle of Purgatory)

Many historic landmarks have formed central points for penal servitude around the world. Well-known among those landmarks are Wormwood Scrubs in London, England; the Island of Elbe; Devil's Island; and Alcatraz. Not so well known to the world is Robben Island, situated off the southern coast of Africa at Cape Town, with a splendid view of Table Mountain. This island had served as a dropping-off point for Cape traders in the sixteenth century. It has been a leper colony, a hospital for the insane, an armed garrison, and the long-time residence of Nelson Mandela and other banned and convicted members of the ANC. Today it is a national monument and tourist attraction. The island was turned over to the South African Department of Prisons when the South African Artillery School vacated it in 1959. The first African political prisoners arrived at the prison to serve their sentences in 1962, along with members of the Pan-African Congress activists, as well as soldiers from an armed group called "Poqo." Members of the ANC, including Nelson Mandela, arrived soon afterward. Many arrived in a state of general illiteracy. However, "B Section," which housed Nelson Mandela and his cohorts, became known as Robben University. Here, many inmates were able to learn and further their political debates and beliefs. The ANC "students" observed a prison code that required they maintain their commitment to changing South African society, and to find positive development through their term of imprisonment. The code also required that none of them were to leave the prison without some education. The last prisoners left the island in 1991, after the ANC finally received political recognition.

Winnie Madikizela-Mandela

Winnie, the estranged wife of Nelson Mandela, the first black president of South Africa, has been described as the "Mugger of the Nation." During the political buildup to her husband's dramatic release from his life sentence on Robben Island, in true charismatic fashion, Winnie surrounded herself with a phalanx of bodyguards. As the ex-wife of the former president, her actions and those of her bodyguard have been questioned. Winnie Mandela, her bodyguards, and a group of tough youths from the Soweto Township became known as the Mandela United Football Club. Jerry Richardson, who was a convicted murderer, was the group's leader. They were involved in beatings of blacks in the townships. Winnie herself was convicted of kidnapping in 1991.[14]

Is South Africa out of the shadow of terrorism? Apart from the Planet Hollywood bombing in 1998, the country has been relatively free of terror attacks. The passage of time and the removal of the apartheid South African government have not seen any sudden improvement in everyday living conditions, hoped for by the millions of black South Africans. Questions are now coming to the table about corruption and incompetence of the highest order under the current government. Weak governments on the African continent have been susceptible to terrorism. However, until recently, South Africa had a strong democratic system of government and had control of its borders and an effective security force. It seems probable that the rainbow of nations in South Africa and their neighbors may someday pale. As whites leave the country in ever-increasing numbers for a safer life outside the Republic, the fabric and wealth of South Africa may suffer from instability.

ISLAM IN SOUTH AFRICA

People against Gangsterism and Drugs

People against Gangsterism and Drugs (PAGAD) was established in 1996 as a community anti-crime force. It originated in a network of hitherto disparate and isolated antidrug, anticrime groups and neighborhood watches frustrated by their inability to tackle problems whose roots extended far beyond their individual localities. Predominantly, but by no means exclusively,

Muslim, PAGAD began with a loose organizational structure and an informal, collective style of leadership. It was open to approaches from other anticrime groups and prepared, at least, to consider working with the police. Many of the more violent actions taken against drug dealers, such as the attack on Rashaad Staggie in August 1996, were neither planned nor formally sanctioned by the organization as a whole. PAGAD's development since these early days cannot be seen simply as the unfolding of a master plan conceived and executed by a small group of Islamic radicals. Rather, it has to be viewed as the outcome of the interplay between many internal and external forces . . . of action by PAGAD and its constituent elements and reaction by the state and its agencies in the specific political, social, and economic context of the Western Cape.

The state's view of PAGAD has changed dramatically over the last decade. From a popular anticrime movement, it has become first a violent, and therefore illegitimate, vigilante organization and then, since 1998, an urban terror group threatening not just the state's monopoly on the use of coercive force but the very foundations of constitutional democracy. In line with these altered perceptions, the state's response to PAGAD has changed from constructive engagement to demonization and repression.[15]

PAGAD has become rabidly anti-Western, as well as antigovernment in its activities. It views the current South African regime as a threat to Islamic values. The group is led by Abdus Salaam Ebrahim. PAGAD's G-Force (Gun Force) operates in small cells and is believed to be responsible for carrying out acts of terrorism and targeting mainly synagogues and nightclubs in the Cape region of South Africa.[16]

PAGAD's activities seem at odds with its value structure. The group's website lists the following as its goals:

- To propagate the eradication of drugs and gangsterism from society;
- To cooperate with and to coordinate the activities of people and people's organization having similar aims and objectives;
- To make every effort to invite/motivate/activate and to include those people and people's organizations that are not yet part of PAGAD;
- To raise funds to realize the foregoing aims; and
- PAGAD is a nonprofit-making movement. All its assets, income, and contributions shall be used to achieve these objectives of PAGAD.[17]

Boeremag (Boer Force)

Since the end of the apartheid regimes, South Africa has had to contend with a small outbreak of extreme right-wing nationalism in the form of the Boeremag movement. This group seeks to overthrow the current South African government and drive the black population north into central Africa and create a Boer (white) homeland. Boeremag's activities in the first four years of the millennium have been to place a number of bombs around buildings and bridges, most often where there is a large concentration of blacks. Bombs went off in the township of Soweto and the group expected the black population to rise up in a race war against the whites. Eighteen of the group's members have been arrested as it continues to demand a separate Afrikaner Homeland.[18]

Both the South African and U.S. governments have officially designated PAGAD as a terrorist organization. South African police efforts and court prosecutions severely damaged the group in the early 2000s. Since 2001, PAGAD has demonstrated a significantly weakened operational capability. Externally, the threat to the RSA comes from extreme jihadists who would focus on U.S. and Western interests in the state. However, RSA is considered somewhat neutral in the War on Terror and supports Palestinian rights.

QIBLA MOVEMENT

The threat comes from highly secretive groups such as Qibla, which was established among the Muslim immigrants in the 1980s and directed and supported by Iranian intelligence. Although Qibla is a purely South African organization, it is manipulated from a safe distance by the Iranian intelligence services, which use the organization not only to propagate the worldview of the Islamic Republic but also as a cover to conduct espionage in RSA.[19] As in other regions of the world, these Muslim movements have basically the same goal of creating an Islamic-controlled state. Qibla is also linked to PAGAD and infiltrates that movement in order to carry out its attacks.

KENYA

Myriad tribal groups, spread throughout the land, have populated Kenya for untold centuries. The Kikuyu is one of the largest tribes of the region, and it works the land alongside the Kamba, Masai, and Luo tribes. The beginnings of colonialism in the nineteenth century saw the erosion of the tribal rights in Kenya (Figure 10-15). Britain was granted title over the lands now called Uganda and Kenya. Uganda became a British Protectorate in 1885, and Kenya followed shortly after in 1893. Britain, in those days, was interested primarily in the rich natural resources of Uganda and constructed a railway system between Kampala and Mombasa. Much of the work was done by imported labor from the Indian subcontinent. Most of the merchants of Kenya and Uganda are the descendants of these railway workers. By 1915, British settlers had claimed the fertile highland regions for growing crops for export and displaced the tribes of those regions. Africans and Asians were prohibited from being landowners.[20] The British, unprepared to deal with the native issues in Kenya, permitted the growth of Black Nationalist movements, and, in 1929, one of the most prominent African leaders of the twentieth century, Jomo Kenyatta, went to England to negotiate for land rights on behalf of the Kikuyu Central Association. With the onset of World War II, Africans were conscripted, thus providing a trained cadre for what became the **Mau Mau** terrorist group.

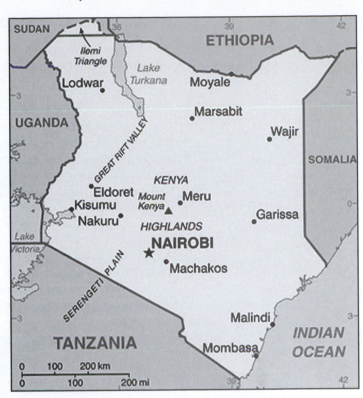

FIGURE 10-15 Map of Kenya. *Source:* Central Intelligence Agency, *The World Factbook, 2008.*

Unlike its near neighbors, the population of Kenya has been relatively free of terrorist activity and atrocities. Insurrections and uprisings in Kenya have been perpetrated in living memory by what is still considered one of the most shadowy and frightening organizations to gain a foothold on the African subcontinent, the Mau Mau. This almost mythical, shadowy, and mysterious organization in Kenya came to prominence again as a result of what may be construed as a colonial land grab. In fact, the tribes of Kenya were land farmers and cattle herders who considered the land "everyone's land." But much of their area was "owned" by white families. Kenya became part of Britain's far-flung empire, bringing with it taxation as well as education to the natives of the region. Britain and the settlers were of an unshakable belief that the land was the sole property of the tribal government, and therefore the colonial government had rights to the land. Naturally, such an assumption did not sit well with the tribes of Kenya. The land grab instigated a rebirth of the Mau Mau. Although the specific aims of the organization have never been detailed, the group flourished in the tribal lands of Kenya.

One of the best-educated tribes of the region was the Kikuyu, and it was from this environment that the Mau Mau found its roots. The Kikuyu, like the other tribes, had been reduced almost to the levels of third-class citizens or serfs in their own country. In a region of the world where superstitions and magic have a considerable foothold, the groundswell of support for a secret society, to fight for the people, quickly became apparent. The Mau Mau had taken an oath—that the Kikuyu took extremely seriously—for the total removal of all whites and those who had supported the colonial British government. In the early 1950s, the Mau Mau began attacking white settlers on their farms in Kenya. The attacks came to a full-scale rebellion in 1956 and were finally forcibly crushed by the British. Many tribesmen were sent to detention camps or were hunted and killed. The Mau Mau leader at the time was Dedan Kimathi, who was executed for leading the uprising. The Mau Mau campaign had a softening effect on the British and sincere efforts were made to stabilize the country; however, from 1956 to 1960, the country was under a "state of emergency." The Kenyan African Union (KANU), led by Jomo Kenyatta, sought independence for the country. In 1963, Britain granted full independence to Kenya. Kenyatta became the country's first president.

INTERNATIONAL TERRORISM IN CENTRAL AFRICA

With the emergence and spread of Islamic fundamentalism throughout the Middle East, and also into regions of Northern and Southern Africa, it is not surprising that a "soft" target, such as an embassy of a foreign superpower, would suffer the brunt of a terrorist attack.

That attack came against the U.S. embassy in Nairobi, Kenya, in early August 1998. The U.S. embassy in Nairobi certainly did not have the levels of security protection afforded to other U.S. legations, particularly in the Middle East. The embassy was considered below the acceptable standards for security, particularly after the bombing of the U.S. Marine Corps barracks in Beirut in 1984, which claimed the lives of two hundred and forty-two marines. Recommendations to tighten U.S. security had not included Kenya; presumably, the threat assessment was considered low for this region of the world. With lax security and the location of the building being in the center of Nairobi, it became too good a target for the determined terrorist to pass up. A massive car bomb decimated the embassy building and caused extensive damage to the surrounding buildings (Figure 10-16). The bomb claimed one hundred and seventy lives, mostly Africans, and wounded several thousands. The object of the attack was the U.S. administration, and not Kenya. The attack has been credited to bin Laden and also to Fazul Abdullah Mohammed—both now dead. Abdullah had operated in east Africa and found safe haven in the badlands of Somalia. He was fluent in five languages and was the master of disguise. His death in a shootout at a Somali

FIGURE 10-16   East African Embassy bombings—Nairobi and Dar es Salaam.   *Source:* Federal Bureau of Investigations.

Most Wanted Terrorists

MURDER OF U.S. NATIONALS OUTSIDE THE UNITED STATES; CONSPIRACY TO MURDER U.S. NATIONALS OUTSIDE THE UNITED STATES; ATTACK ON A FEDERAL FACILITY RESULTING IN DEATH

FAZUL ABDULLAH MOHAMMED

Aliases: Abdallah Fazul, Abdalla Fazul, Abdallah Mohammed Fazul, Fazul Abdilahi Mohammed, Fazul Adballah, Fazul Abdalla, Fazul Mohammed, Haroon, Harun, Haroon Fazul, Harun Fazul, Fadil Abdallah Muhamad, Fadhil Haroun, Abu Seif Al Sudani, Abu Aisha, Abu Luqman, Fadel Abdallah Mohammed Ali, Fouad Mohammed.

DESCRIPTION

Dates of Birth Used:	August 25, 1972; December 25, 1974; February 25, 1974;	Hair:	Black	
		Eyes:	Brown	
		Sex:	Male	
Place of Birth:	Moroni, Comoros Islands	Complexion:	Dark	
Height:	5'3" to 5'5"	Citizenship:	Comoros, Kenyan	
Weight:	120 to 140 pounds			
Build:	Unknown			
Languages:	French, Swahili, Arabic, English, Comoran			
Scars and Marks:	None known			
Remarks:	Mohammed likes to wear baseball caps and tends to dress casually. He is very good with computers.			

CAUTION

FAZUL ABDULLAH MOHAMMED WAS INDICTED ON SEPTEMBER 17, 1998, IN THE SOUTHERN DISTRICT OF NEW YORK, FOR HIS ALLEGED INVOLVEMENT IN THE BOMBINGS OF THE UNITED STATES EMBASSIES IN DAR ES SALAAM, TANZANIA, AND NAIROBI, KENYA, ON AUGUST 7, 1998.

REWARD

The Rewards For Justice Program, United States Department of State, is offering a reward of up to $25 million for information leading directly to the apprehension or conviction of Fazul Abdullah Mohammed.

SHOULD BE CONSIDERED ARMED AND DANGEROUS

IF YOU HAVE ANY INFORMATION CONCERNING THIS PERSON, PLEASE CONTACT YOUR LOCAL FBI OFFICE OR THE NEAREST AMERICAN EMBASSY OR CONSULATE.

www.fbi.gov

Poster Revised November 2001

FIGURE 10-17 Fazul Abdullah Mohammed—A key al Qaeda operative and the mastermind of the 1998 U.S. Embassy bombings in Kenya and Tanzania. *Source:* FBI Photo via CNP/Newscom.

military checkpoint in June 2011 should have a negative impact on al Qaeda in the region. The United States had placed a "bounty" of $5 million on Mohammed and had attempted to assassinate him at least six times since 2006 (Figure 10-17). The most recent attempts were in 2008 and 2009, when U.S. military used its satellite tracking and eavesdropping capability to track cell phone conversations between al Qaeda operatives and launched a series of cruise missiles at a specific Somali house, killing and wounding several militants but not Mohammed. Again in 2009, a U.S. Special Forces unit targeted another al Qaeda commander Saleh Ali Nabhan—his vehicle was attacked by a helicopter gunship, killing Nabhan and several other al Qaeda members (Figure 10-18).

FIGURE 10-18 Ayman al-Zawahiri—One of FBI's ten most wanted terrorists. *Source:* Ropi/ZUMA Press/Newscom.

Politically Expedient Response

The Nairobi attack caught the Clinton administration almost totally unprepared for a problem of such magnitude, at a time when the president was facing serious personal and legal problems of his own. The attack prompted the same political and military response as the 1986 Libyan attack on U.S. servicemen in Germany. That incident resulted in then president Reagan ordering an attack on Libya, even though there was no verifiable evidence that the Libyans were, in fact, responsible.

If retribution or retaliation is to be meted out, and it seems to have been in this case, governments must be cautious about the levels of violence and the message that they are sending, not only to a small group of determined terrorists but also to whole nations that become the target.

The effectiveness of retaliatory attacks against Sudan and Pakistan has been determined to be marginal at best.

FIGURE 10-19 Westgate Shopping Mall attackers, Nairobi. *Source:* Kenya Defence Force via Citizen TV/AP Images.

Westgate Shopping Mall Attack

At around midday on Saturday September 21, 2013, al-Shabaab terrorists attacked the Westgate Shopping Mall in an upscale Nairobi neighborhood often frequent by expatriates, tourists, and westerners. The attack was a commando-style attack on unsuspecting shoppers enjoying a day out at the exclusive shopping center. Four men armed with AK-47 assault weapons and a stash of hand grenades entered the mall and systematically went through the mall shooting dead as many people they could find—when, three days later the mall was finally declared secure it was found that a total of sixty-seven had been killed and a further one hundred and seventy-five wounded. There has been no conclusive evidence that the four attackers were killed and it seems probable that all four may have escaped. The response to the attack has caused the Kenyan government much criticism for the way the response was handled and how long it took the Kenyan Defense Force to reach the mall—allegedly three hours after the attack. Police arrived on scene about thirty minutes after the start of the gunfire. In the confusion and the evacuation of around one thousand shoppers it seems some if not all the assailants may have escaped that way. The conduct of the Kenyan military was captured on mall CCTV allegedly looting stores as they went through the building. Al-Shabaab claimed responsibility for this assault claiming it was in retaliation for Kenya's offensive in Somalia (Figure 10-19).

ANGOLA

Angola had been Portugal's prize jewel in Africa for more than five hundred years. Portuguese navigator Diego Cam landed in Angola in 1482 and left his mark in the traditional Portuguese shape of the cross. Over the centuries, the Portuguese exploited little, if any, of the natural wealth of the country, which was rich in mineral deposits. With colonial development happening throughout other regions of Africa, Angola continued to languish in quiet slumber (Figure 10-20). Holden Alvaro Roberto founded Angola's first nationalist movement in 1956 and five years later led the first attack on colonial settlers in Angola. His Union of Angolan Peoples (UPA) drew its main support from his Bakongo ethnic group. In 1962, he transformed the UPA into the National Liberation Front of Angola (FNLA), which operated mainly from Zaire (later the Democratic Republic of the Congo). In 1975, Roberto and the leaders of the other two independence movements in Angola reached an agreement with Portugal and signed a peace treaty that led to the country's independence. Fighting immediately broke out between the three factions, however, and the FNLA, backed by several

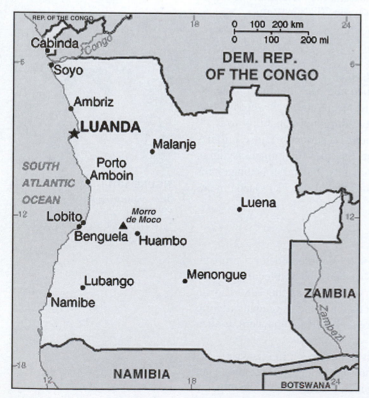

FIGURE 10-20 Map of Angola. *Source:* Central Intelligence Agency, *The World Factbook, 2008.*

Western countries, was decisively defeated in 1976 by the Popular Movement for the Liberation of Angola (MPLA), which was supported by the Soviet Union and Cuba. Roberto spent the next fifteen years in exile, returning to Angola in 1991.[21]

They killed many villagers and committed atrocities on both the living and the dead. At one location, the victims were put through a sawmill while they were still alive.[22] They attacked men, women, and children, hacking limbs from bodies and heads from torsos. Roberto died in Luanda in August 2007.

Popular Movement for the Liberation of Angola

The Popular Movement for the Liberation of Angola (MPLA) started in the late 1950s in the Angolan capital of Luanda and, by 1961, had begun to fester into a civil war throughout the country. In the northern region of Angola, the **Front for the Liberation of Angola (FNLA)** was formed, and, in 1966, the National Union for the Total Independence of Angola (UNITA) appeared. The warring factions continued sporadic fighting over the years. However, the Angola military's overthrow of the Colonial Portuguese government in 1974 led to Angola's eventual independence a year later. With the guerrilla army's spread throughout the country, neither of the sides could agree as to which would eventually lead the new government, and fighting resumed. The MPLA was receiving considerable aid from the USSR, as well as Cuba. The Russians supplied weapons, training, and support, while Cuba supplied the fighters to help with the guerrilla war.

By 1976, the battles were over, and the Marxists dominated and influenced the MPLA. With a Marxist government so close to the northern border of Namibia, formerly Southwest Africa, the South African government continued to provide support and weapons to the UNITA rebels fighting against the Marxist government forces of the MPLA. Many of those fighting with the UNITA were South African mercenaries as well as former British soldiers. A cease-fire eventually came into effect in May 1991 and lasted until October 1992.

At that time, UNITA refused to accept the election results and fighting resumed between UNITA and the MPLA government. Sporadic fighting continued over the next two years, and, finally, in 1994, it was agreed that UNITA guerrillas would merge with the Angolan army. All of this took place under the watchful eye of UN peacekeepers, and although the transition was slow, the new government of National Unity came into office in April 1997. Since that time, UN forces have pulled out of Angola.

However, the ongoing decades of violence since Angola's independence from Portugal have now seen a dramatic shift in the fortunes of one of the main protagonist groups, namely the ongoing battle with the National UNITA. In February 2002, government troops engaged in a fierce firefight with UNITA rebels led by their patriarchal leader, Jonas Savimbi. During this single action, Savimbi was killed when troops attacked his stronghold in the southern region of the country. The short- and long-term effects of his death will likely mean that there will be a vacuum and those insiders will likely concentrate on a power struggle, thus fracturing UNITA. Whether this means the end of UNITA, it is still too early to say. Much of the funding support for UNITA came from its illegal trade in diamonds. It is probable that the illegal trade will continue and arms will still be traded for them. Savimbi's movement has not benefited from the end of the Cold War when much of its support network came from the Democratic Republic of the Congo, headed up by Mobutu Sese Seko.

MOZAMBIQUE

Sandwiched between Tanzania and South Africa, this legacy of Portuguese colonialism bears the ravages of civil war. Many of Mozambique's problems stem from its nearby neighbors, South Africa and Zimbabwe, the former Rhodesia (Figure 10-21). Organized along the lines of a one-party state, the current Mozambique government moved out of the realm of a guerrilla/terrorist organization and became a political party. In the early 1960s, many inhabitants were becoming increasingly frustrated with the Portuguese rule, and the **Front for the Liberation of Mozambique (FRELIMO)** was formed.

FRELIMO carried out operations against the Portuguese until 1974, when the country was finally granted independence. FRELIMO was a strong Marxist regime,

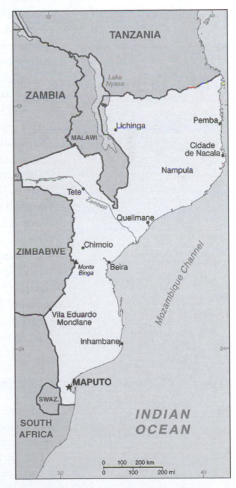

FIGURE 10-21 Map of Mozambique.
Source: Central Intelligence Agency, *The World Factbook, 2008.*

opposed to the white minority rule (apartheid) of South Africa in the 1980s and also of the Ian Smith minority independence government of Rhodesia (Zimbabwe). When independence was declared, FRELIMO closed its western border with Rhodesia and many dissidents from Rhodesia set up bases in Mozambique to attack the Smith government, assisted by the Russian-supported FRELIMO. As the ideological focuses of the surrounding states changed, so did Mozambique. The Samora Machel government in Maputo supported the banned ANC movement in South Africa and supplied weapons, training, and support to terrorists fighting cross-border battles with the South African security forces. Mozambique also had its own internal strife at this time, and South Africa supported the Mozambique National Resistance Movement (RENAMO) in its guerrilla war with the Marxist government. By 1984, South Africa and Mozambique reached an agreement to stop supporting terrorists and guerrillas in each other's country. However, this did not stop RENAMO from continuing its war against apartheid with the FRELIMO. RENAMO's tactics were aimed at totally destabilizing the country, and it began to destroy even schools and medical facilities with over eighteen hundred schools and five hundred health centers destroyed. Close to one hundred thousand people were killed in countryside villages.

Death of Samora Machel

In 1986, then President Samora Machel was killed when his Russian-made Tupolev aircraft (with a Russian crew) crashed into a hillside on the South African side of the border. What is uncertain about this crash is the manner in which it occurred. Was it an accident or a planned assassination? There has been speculation since the crash that there was a high-level South African plot to eliminate Machel. Evidence from the crash suggests that external influences somehow tampered with the directional systems of the Tupolev 134A-3 aircraft. Because it was so far off course, it is suspected that a decoy navigational beacon was activated to misdirect the aircraft onto a crash course. South Africa covertly supported the increasing number of RENAMO raids into Mozambique and had increasingly angered Machel. Whether South Africa was involved or not, it is known that there were raised tensions in the previous weeks before the crash, including threatening signals from the SA Defense Ministry. This led to extreme tension between the two countries and continuing distrust on both sides.

By 1992, the two sides reached an uneasy peace and called for an election process that would include RENAMO on the ballot. When voting took place in 1994, FRELIMO had forty-four percent of the vote and RENAMO thirty-three percent. There is no special antiterrorism legislation in Mozambique. Despite the Penal Code of 1886, which is the basis of criminal law in Mozambique, the only existing legislative act, which criminalizes terrorism, is Law No. 19/91 (the Law of Crimes against State Security).

Threat from jihadists in Mozambique is relatively small. As the country is a one-party state and all sides have had a hand in developing the state to what it is today and as many Muslims would be members of FRELIMO, any outside influences from jihadist cells would likely become known to the political leadership. FRELIMO party members rely on the party for their commercial, economic, and political interests and success. As a country situated on the east coast several other landlocked countries use Mozambique to transit to the coast; trade goods as well as people need to transit Mozambique to reach the Indian Ocean. In October 2013, RENAMO declared that the peace deal of 1992 between itself and FRELIMO was at an end. Currently tensions still exist between the two groups RENAMO and FELIMO. RENAMO on the defensive and not aligned with the political scene the opportunities for civil war are never far away. What characterize the issues between the two are the extra judicial killings and shootings of politicians, activists, and journalists.

RWANDA

A small, landlocked African state, Rwanda had become infamous with the unexplained murder of Diane Fossey, the famed naturalist and expert on silverback gorillas. In the 1960s, others knew of Rwanda for its fabulous pictorial postage stamps that graced many a philatelist's collection. But, in 1994, it became a killing field for the native Hutus, who eventually massacred well over half a million Tutsis (Figure 10-22).

Rwanda had for centuries been a land of farmers occupied by the Hutu tribesmen and Pygmy hunters. In the thirteenth century, the warrior Tutsis invaded and took control over the Hutus. To the casual onlooker, it might seem logical to assume that the Hutus and Tutsis were sworn enemies.

That could not be further from the truth; in fact, Hutus and Tutsis had lived side by side and intermarried for hundreds of years.

There are few differences in the physical characteristics of the two tribes. They look the same, pray to the same Gods, and had peacefully coexisted for centuries. So what happened to cause the genocide that took place in 1994? One must first look at the role played by the colonial forces of Belgium that ruled up to the early 1960s. The Belgian authoritarian control in Rwanda organized and institutionalized the ethnic stereotypes in the country. As it was impossible to physically distinguish between Hutu and Tutsi, the Belgians decreed a system that sounds like it came out of the Dark Ages in order to define in which ethnic group a person belonged. Amazingly, it used these following criteria: If a farmer owned nine cows or less, he was issued an identity card stating he was a Hutu; if he owned ten or more cows, he was a Tutsi. The Belgians had overnight created a class structure dependent on the details of an identity card, and this had been the basis for a social division of the two tribes since the 1930s.

The Belgians had created minority elite; they gave privileges and positions on the Belgian colonial administration structure. The Belgians ruled by the grace of the Tutsi minority in Rwanda, who had been schooled and educated by the Belgians. As they grew more powerful, they sought to throw off the mantle of colonialism and demanded independence. To counter the Tutsis' demands, the Belgians began to switch their allegiance to the Hutu majority, producing enough hatred against the

FIGURE 10-22 Map of Rwanda. *Source:* Central Intelligence Agency, *The World Factbook, 2008.*

Tutsis to start a popular uprising. The uprising brought the Hutu into government and over one hundred thousand Tutsis were killed. A similar number of Tutsis, fearing further atrocities, fled to neighboring Uganda in the north, where they remained in exile. It was this exiled group and their descendants who returned to begin the civil war in 1990. In exile, the group formed the Rwandan Patriotic Front (RPF), which was made up of displaced Tutsis and Hutus. The RPF aimed to replace the oppressive and repressive government with a new democratically elected government.

The Hutu-dominated government of President Habyarimana was determined to remain in power. The Hutu planned to eradicate the Tutsis in methods not dissimilar to the Nazi extermination of the Jews. The tool of the trade, in this instance, was propaganda. As most of the Hutus were illiterate farmers, the government began to systematically bombard the population with radio announcements that were deliberately and openly anti-Tutsi. It went beyond just denouncements of the Tutsis, but actively demanded that civilian Hutus kill any and all Tutsis they came across. Terror and threat were repeated over and over in efforts to sow the seeds of total annihilation of the Tutsis. In a format reminiscent of South American death squads, the Hutu government set up civilian militia, training them in weaponry, hand-to-hand combat, and methods to quickly kill their enemy, the Tutsis. This organization was called the Interahamwe, meaning "those who attack together." The Hutu militias began killing Tutsis wherever they found them, and soon it became apparent that to kill a Tutsi would not be considered a crime in that country . . . it was just eliminating a form of vermin. However, after three years of the civil war and slaughter, a cease-fire was finally reached between the two sides in 1993. Then, under the auspices of the United Nations in 1994, the devastated country prepared to set up some form of transitional government. However, the Hutus continued to arm and train its civilian militia openly, right under the noses of UN observers. It is still not clear to the international community as to why the United Nations made no effort to report these facts or to seek any clarification on how to handle the issues.

Death of a President

Uprisings often need to have a "trigger mechanism" to set them off. In April 1994, the plane carrying then President Habyarimana was shot down as it approached Kigali, the Rwandan Capital, killing the president. This single incident became the "green light" for the genocide to begin once more in earnest. Within hours of his death, the attacks and killings of Tutsis commenced, and within a single month nearly half a million Tutsis lay dead and the rest were scattered throughout the country. Those who were able to escape fled to neighboring countries. The United Nations stood by and observed the genocide and has been criticized for failing to intervene and stop the massacres.

Two months into the killings, the United Nations passed a resolution to send in a UN peace-keeping force of around five thousand troops. With the killings all but over, and the RPF advancing from the north, many of the Hutu militia escaped across the border to Tanzania and to refugee camps set up inside the border. The point may have been missed in newspaper articles in regard to the genocide in Rwanda and the need for urgent humanitarian aid for the refugees. But most of the refugee camps held only the murderous members of the Hutu, as nearly all the Tutsis had been caught and killed in the preceding six-week period. The country's demand that the Hutus and Tutsis reintegrate within Rwanda is unique in world history. Genocide, civil war, refugee flight, abundant hate propaganda, a culture of impunity, and ongoing insurgency and atrocities—this is Rwanda. The most telling and difficult question is whether the people of Rwanda can rewrite a social contract that will be acceptable to any functioning society. Can they overcome their mutual suspicion and live as neighbors and fellow countrymen again? The Hutus returning to Rwanda must fear retaliatory actions being meted out against them, the same as to the Tutsis in 1994.

In recent history, such a reintegration has never happened. It certainly did not take place in Germany, causing the international community to create Israel, a sovereign Jewish state. Fleeing from the killing fields, the people of Cambodia resettled in other countries. Rwanda today is still a dangerous and suspicious place.

DEMOCRATIC REPUBLIC OF CONGO, FORMERLY ZAIRE

The Democratic Republic of Congo (DRC) is located in Central Africa and straddles both the equator and the Congo River. With a population of 40 million and rich with mineral resources of gold, copper, zinc, and diamonds, to name but a few. Henry Stanley discovered the region in the 1870s and was asked to set up Belgian trading posts along the Congo River in 1878 by King Leopold of Belgium. The king ruled this African country as his own private fiefdom, and it only fell under the control of the Belgian government in 1908. At that time, it was called the Congo Free State.

By the 1960s, colonial Belgian rule was coming to an end, and, on June 30, 1960, the Belgian Congo became the independent Republic of Congo. The first president of the new Central African Republic was Joseph Kasavubu, with the legendary Patrice Lumumba as his prime minister. Unluckily, for the young, Communist-inspired Lumumba, his position was extremely tenuous in the eyes of the West, particularly the United States.

The 1960s was the height of the Cold War, and the CIA was intent on eliminating Soviet involvement in mineral-rich central Africa. The CIA conspired with factions that were anti-Communist to overthrow the Lumumba government and install a pro-West regime. This was achieved by infiltrating mercenary elements into the country. The CIA had planned to poison Lumumba; however, prior to his assassination, the army mutinied. The army at this time was led by a young Zairian officer Joseph Desire Mobutu. In July and again in September 1960, Mobutu, an army colonel, announced the suspension of all political parties and took control of the country. In November 1960, Lumumba was arrested and handed over to rebel forces and was executed on January 17, 1961. For the next four years the government was in turmoil, until the military coup of Desire Mobutu. The next thirty-two years saw Desire Mobutu rule the country with an iron fist and in a somewhat African tradition plundered the country's central bank for his own personal use and gains, buying homes, villas, and castles in Europe. His leadership was violently anti-Communist and strongly pro-West, which suited the world situation in the Cold War years, and the particular interests of the United States, Mobutu received vast sums of "development" aid, aimed at preventing the spread of any Communist influences. In the 1970s, he began a period of "Africanization" and changed his name to Mobutu Sese Seko, meaning "He the all-powerful warrior." Names of cities were changed; Leopoldville changed to Kinshasa, and the country to the Democratic Republic of Zaire, from Congo. Mobutu has plundered his country to such a state of deprivation that when the Hutu and Tutsi fighting in neighboring Rwanda spilled over into Zaire, he had no military to stop the incursions. The Rwandans were led by an old friend of Patrice Lumumba, namely Laurant Kabila.

Mobutu Sese Seko

Mobutu's tyrannical reign was all about ancient methods of pillage and plunder in a twentieth-century format. He was estimated to be one of the five richest men in the world and was president of one of the poorest nations and lowest standard of living in Africa.

In a country of such enormous mineral wealth, it was not difficult to establish where the wealth had gone. Mobutu lived a lavish lifestyle in Africa and had villas throughout Europe. One of the earliest uprisings against his regime came in 1964, in the area of the eastern Congo. It was led by a young Marxist rebel, Laurent-Desire Kabila, who would later return to lead the civil war against the Mobutu regime. Much of what took place in the Congo was a result of outside influences and internal disputes between the many ethnically diverse tribes that had settled in the region. Refugees from rebel actions and atrocities in neighboring countries also were factors.

Hutu and Tutsi differences in Rwanda played a significant part in the eventual rebellion and civil war that overtook the DRC. Insurgent rebellion was prevalent throughout the long dictatorial reign of Mobutu, but he had always managed to put down the uprisings, either by force or by proclaiming presidential or legislative reforms. The country existed as a one-party state under Mobutu, so challenges to his rule were frequent. Citizenship issues and land rights also added to the tensions of the DRC. The complications of the various regions of the DRC are interwoven within the ethnic groups, who vie for power. The principal groups are located in the province of Kivu, which has a long history of ethnic violence; these groups are the Hunde, Nande, and Banyarwanda.

Banyarwandans are a collection of displaced Rwandans who arrived in the region to work the land, courtesy of their colonial Belgian masters; they comprise both Hutus and Tutsis. Members of this group were not considered to be citizens of Zaire under Mobutu's rule, and that has not changed with the transition to Kabila's government in 1997. The local chiefs in Northern-Kivu Province had rented to the Banyarwandans most of the land they occupied. By 1993, the Banyarwandans were pushing for reforms and an end to the injustices carried out against them. What was to complicate the situation in Zaire was the massive and sudden exodus of Hutus from Rwanda. Included in this exodus was the local Militia Interahamwe, which had been involved in the genocide in Rwanda after the death of the Rwandan president.

An uprising in 1993 escalated into yet another, full-scale ethnic battle. Most of those killed were Banyarwandans. The situation was not improved by the arrival of the Hutu refugees from the fighting and killing in Rwanda. The uprising spread and soon became a national movement to overthrow Mobutu. The rebel forces consisted mainly of Tutsi warriors, and soon Laurent Kabila became their revolutionary leader.

Widespread disillusionment in the Zairian army led to the eventual capitulation of the Mobutu government. On May 16, 1997, with only his personal bodyguard remaining in Kinshasa and the rebel forces on the doorstep, Mobutu left quietly for the safety of Morocco, where he lived in exile until his death in September 1997 from prostate cancer. However, since Kabila came to power, the ethnic violence between the factions has not ceased, and with unprotected borders, the DRC has seen an increase in rebel attacks from outside. From within, the fighting and massacres have continued, particularly in the North and South Kivu provinces. Hutu and Tutsi continue to kill each other. Much of Kabila's support comes from the army, which has been dominated by Rwandan Tutsis.

The Congo can be viewed in much the same vein as Somalia as it, too, is defined as a failed state. Since the start of the ceasefire in 1999, the most contentious issues are still unresolved. The country is variously occupied by six foreign armies and roving bands of militia. Hundreds of thousands have been displaced in the war years and have not yet been repatriated.

The Congo is home to many non-Congolese groups and one, in particular, is the Hutu-dominated Liberation Army of Rwanda (ALiR), which fled from that country after the genocide it perpetrated in Rwanda in 1994. The ALiR continues to be supported by the government in Kinshasa, as the Congo has no effective military force to deal with the occupying forces of Rwanda and Uganda. The Tutsi-dominated regime in Rwanda, afraid of renewed Hutu attacks, maintains its own occupying forces in eastern Congo, refusing to withdraw until the Hutu groups are disarmed. And, for reasons of their own, Angola, Zimbabwe, Namibia, Uganda, and Burundi all maintain a strong military presence in the Congo as well. President Joseph Kabila and his backers, Angola and Zimbabwe, refuse to consider power sharing through dialogue with anti-government rebels without guarantees of Rwanda and Uganda's full withdrawal. The rebels and their sponsors, on the other hand, refuse to consider withdrawal until a transitional government is established through dialogue and Rwanda's border security is guaranteed. These external demands have to be addressed as part of the Congo's political transition. In total, these challenges appear to present a near-impossible "catch-22." But they can be resolved if the international community, and especially the United Nations, is prepared to make a greater commitment to completing all three parts of the peace process.[23]

NIGERIA

The rise of Islam in Nigeria is not something that should necessarily be a surprise, particularly to the Nigerian public. The country has been subjected to years of government squandering and corruption, so much so that Muslim regions have turned to the strict Sharia to enforce laws (Figure 10-23). After 9-11, there were sporadic outbreaks of violence between Muslims and Christians, including burning and looting of Christian-owned shops and restaurants that served alcohol in retaliation for a Christian attack on a mosque. In the many decades since the retreat of colonial powers, Africa has been an unsettled and volatile land. So, it is not surprising that radical Islamic fundamentalism would have a significant foothold in areas of Nigeria as well as other underdeveloped nations in Africa. Does the rise of Islam also mean that there is likely to be an increase in fundamentalist attitudes toward Western democracies and values? Certainly, a minority would seek to use religion as a cover for subversive operations against either the host state or to assist in propagating the fundamentalist movement.

Lawlessness and crime are an everyday problem for most nations of the world; however, the activities noted in Nigeria lend a new twist to the meaning of crime fighting. The Bakassi Boys are a group of young men who have taken some measure of control over the lawless southern city of Onitsha. The Bakassi Boys operate a terror subculture working outside of the established law. The Boys' brand of terror is to snatch victims, usually suspects in some crime or wrongdoing, and subject them to interrogation and, in many cases, summary execution. The Anambra state governor, Chinwoke Mbadinuju, has financed the group and provided it with weapons and even police vehicles. Quite clearly, law and order has broken down, and regional southern states have turned to vigilante operations to suppress crime. This can quickly lead to wider regional implications for the formation of private armies to do the bidding of their financial backers. Nigeria is Africa's most populous nation, with more than one hundred and twenty-five million people and over two hundred distinct ethnic groups, so it is not unusual to have clashes on religious, ethnic, and communal grounds. The violent outbreaks have claimed thousands of lives since the election in 1999 of then president Olusegun Obasanjo, following sixteen years of military rule. That period of military rule was able to contain ethnic and religious violence. More than nine hundred people died in 2004, and there are many claims that the Nigerian police and military did nothing to prevent the killings from taking place.

In a report on two waves of killings in Plateau and Kano state in February and May 2004, Human Rights Watch said the government's failure to punish the killers was feeding the cycle of violence. Central Nigeria lies on a religious fault line, dividing the mainly Christian south and the predominantly Muslim north. Tension has been heightened by the adoption of the strict Islamic law, or Sharia, by several state governments elected with the ending of military rule in 1999.

In rural areas, the divide between Muslims and Christians often coincides with a conflict over land use. Violence in Plateau dates back to 2001 when around one thousand people were killed in less than a week in September during religious riots in the state capital, Jos. Over the next two years, there followed a series of tit-for-tat attacks by Muslim and Christian communities in the hinterland that escalated into large-scale violence again in 2004.[24]

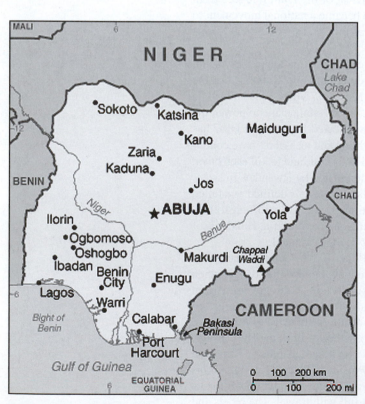

FIGURE 10-23 Map of Nigeria. *Source:* Central Intelligence Agency, *The World Factbook, 2008.*

Nigeria is oil rich and has seen such companies as Shell Petroleum Development take an almost fifty percent stake in the oil reserves of the country. Most of the pipeline and development activity is centered on the Niger delta, and it's in this area that a shadowy and violent group has emerged to attack pipelines, kidnap workers, and generally harass and disrupt the supply of crude oil. The Movement for the Emancipation of the Niger Delta (MEND) operates in fast inflatable boats along the Niger and began operating in late 2005 with attacks on the oil infrastructure. The Nigerian then president Olusegun Obasanjo had attempted to make electoral reforms that would allow him to preside for a third term; a vote in the Senate supported by then Vice President Atiku Abubakar rejected his attempt to make the necessary amendments. Oil wealth and government corruption continue to be the order of things in Nigeria and with oil at $100-plus per barrel and with production set at around three million barrels per day, the country would see revenue of around $100 billion. Controls being as weak as they are in Nigeria, it was not surprising that Abubakar would want Obasanjo out of power, and it was he who helped set up the MEND militia organization.[25] Attacks against the oil infrastructure have gone on for several decades; however, the activities of MEND were somewhat different as they focused on political change rather than an all-out assault on the oil patch. Their systematic approach had the desired effect and the third term in office for Obasanjo failed to materialize. May 2007, as part of a new crackdown on the mismanagement and corruption in Nigeria's oil industry, saw a new president in office; Umaru Yar'Adua took office pledging drastic changes and reforms. His vice president was Goodluck Jonathan, an ethnic Ijaw from the Niger Delta Province, who turned out to be an official spokesman for MEND. President Yar'Adua died in May 2010 and Vice President Goodluck Jonathan was sworn in as president.

MEND immediately had concerns that revenues would not be flowing in the manner that they demanded and set about disrupting the pipeline operations and the flow of crude. Many attacks are committed against oil interests and many are attributed to MEND, but in fact are carried out by other like-minded militants operating under MEND's umbrella. As the years have passed, MEND has become more of a loose affiliation of gangs—some operating independently of MEND's authority. To combat MEND, the Nigerian government has used the country's counterinsurgency troops from the Nigerian Joint Military Task Force. MEND continues to be a force in the area despite the heavy military presence to counter their activities.

Boko Haram (BK)

Objective

- Create an Islamic State (caliphate) governed by Islamic law (Sharia)
- Create the caliphate in northern Nigeria and the border areas of Chad, Niger, and Cameroon
- Removal of all western influences
- Total exclusion of western education

The group is prepared to enter into dialogue with the government but only when the following conditions have been met:

- Unconditional release of all imprisoned members of Boko Haram.
- The immediate prosecution of all those involved in the killing of Boko Haram leader Malam Muhammad Yusuf after he was taken into police custody in July 2009.
- An investigation into the alleged poisoning of Boko Haram suspects awaiting trial.
- Implementation of Sharia in the twelve northern states of Nigeria. These states adopted Sharia codes in 1999, but their current application is not strict enough to meet Boko Haram's standards.[26]

Size and Strength

This will be a variable as **Boko Haram** forcibly recruits young children as child soldiers in the areas it attacks. Overall strength could be 20,000–25,000.

Modus Operandi

- Creates cells that infiltrate regions, towns, and villages.
- Uses suicide bombers in major cities—creating the fear that the Nigerian military cannot protect the people.
- Attacks villages and kills hundreds and burns down buildings.
- Uses children as suicide bombers.

FIGURE 10-24 Abubakar Shekau—Leader of Boko Haram. *Source:* AP Images.

Approximately fifty percent of Nigerians are Muslims and the remainder Christians, and like many other African states Nigeria is blighted by corruption and sectarian and tribal fighting. The Boko Haram is located in the northern reaches of the country and has embarked on a Taliban-style campaign to force their brand of extreme ideology of Islam on the northern states. This has led to outright confrontation with the government and numerous attacks against the civilian population, including Christian churches and Muslims who do not follow their brand of Islam and also targeted assassination of imams. The police have often been targets for indiscriminate attacks. Several campaigns to neutralize by force have always led to resurgence by Boko Haram. In June 2011, the group targeted the police HQ in the capital Abuja with a powerful car bomb.

BK continues to be the major cause for concern in Nigeria and the possible influence of the Islamic State is fairly clear in light of events in 2015 and 2016. Boko Haram's original leader and founder Muhammad Yusuf was captured by Nigerian security forces and died in custody in 2009—the circumstances of his death are unclear. He was succeeded by Abubakar Shekau who has been ruthless in his control of the group and purging any and all opposition to his rule. He has established a Shura Council of his selected supporters and all actions are approved through the Shura which in effect is a rubber stamp for Shekau to wage jihad in the manner he thinks fit (Figure 10-24).

Funding of Boko Haram

Like many terror groups this one uses many of the usual tactics, including robberies, theft and resale of oil, kidnapping, Internet scams, foreign charities as well as external financial support from al Qaeda. The group has been sustained in its operations from the funding trickling in through **Zakat Hawala**—Zakat funding is a principle where Islamic banks or institutions pay a tithing, or contribution to those who are needy or deserving.[27] Hawala means "money transfer without money movement" this is the practice of remitting funds without the traditional use of a bank.[28] This allows for the transfer of money from one individual to another through the connection of a Hawala dealer. Though there are circumstances where Hawala can be used legitimately, through the transfer of funds purely for familial support, money laundering is a frequent occurrence in the case of narcotics trafficking, fraud, or terrorism funding.[29]

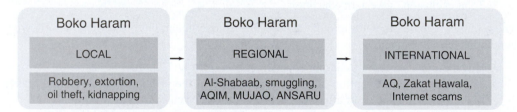

While the Nigerian government has put a watch on charities and banks for their possible Boko Haram financing, preventing, detecting, and stopping Hawala has proven more difficult, as tracking the transactions is far more dubious. Zakat and Hawala funding essentially allows any institution or individual in the world to outsource support for the rapidly expanding terrorist group. Kidnapping for ransom remains a central part of the BK funding strategy which buys for them weapons and ammunition. A declassified 2013 British government report estimated that at least $70 million USD in ransom payments had been paid to Islamist kidnappers since 2009, of which AQIM received an estimated $45 million. Funding for this group can be broken down into three areas: local, regional, and international. The most open and visible is the kidnapping that it has been successfully carrying out. It is also financially supported by AQ affiliates such as The Movement for Unity and Jihad in West Africa (MUJAO), a splinter group of the Organization of al Qaeda in the Islamic Maghreb (AQIM) and The Vanguard for the Protection of Muslims in Black Africa (ANSARU) which is a faction that split from Boko Haram in 2012 objecting to the indiscriminate killing of Muslims. Like its counterpart Boko Haram, it engages in kidnappings particularly of westerners—it was responsible for the kidnapping of foreign workers from the United Kingdom and Italy in 2011. The following year they were both killed in a failed rescue mission supported by the British Special Boat Squadron (special force) regiment. The ANSARU group is more internationally aligned than Boko Haram and its leadership has been trained by AQIM. How close or how distant apart are the two groups Boko Haram and ANSARU is difficult to determine. While they have been active, they go for long periods without mention so it seems likely that they are either rejoined with Boko Haram or operating as a proxy for them in the north.

Boko Haram rejects the notion of western education and democracy, and uses the colonization and western influence as a rallying cry against Allah. It is clear that the sole use of force is not what can combat this form of terrorism. There has been a shift in their ideology since inception but their beliefs remain the same; the establishment of Sharia and the removal of western influence. However, the methods now in use to reach their objectives are far from the fundamentalist movement initiated in 2002. Their methods now resemble those of al Qaeda and their affiliates. The biggest challenge with tackling the elimination of Boko Haram is not the removal of the group's leaders, but the fact that they have allegiances with Islamic extremist factions across Africa and the Middle East. These groups thrive in impoverished areas, frequently where there are already underlying ethnic or religious conflicts. Nigeria has found itself in the predicament of combating a force that only grows stronger in retaliation to government and military force. BK has also pledged allegiance to Islamic State and although it is not moving along the same lines as we see happening in Libya, as BK is not claiming and securing territory to control. Its hit-and-run activities, bombings and suicide bombings, and kidnappings are fueling the sectarian divide in Nigeria and neighboring countries. The Nigerian military is fully occupied in handling this threat and so far has been unable to diminish BK's activities.

Kidnapping for Ransom

The group has been very successful in using kidnapping for ransom:

- On February 19, 2013, Boko Haram kidnapped a French family from the town of Dabanga. Shekau claimed responsibility for the abduction and demanded that the Cameroonian government release all detained Boko Haram members in exchange for the French hostages. The family of seven was released during April 2013 amid speculation that France had paid a ransom of $3 million, the biggest payment to date received by Boko Haram.
- On November 13, 2013, Boko Haram kidnapped a French priest, Georges Vandenbeusch, from the northern town of Koza. Boko Haram again claimed credit for the kidnapping in a statement provided to the *Agence France-Presse*. Vandenbeusch was released a month after his capture amid claims that French authorities paid a cash ransom to the group. Both France and Boko Haram denied that a ransom was paid.
- On April 24, 2014, Boko Haram kidnapped 270 schoolgirls from the government school in Chibok, North East Nigeria. Pledges by the international community to get them back have been so far unsuccessful. BK has said that they will be married off to BK fighters or sold as slaves. Few have been repatriated so far. When recruiting a new member Boko Haram offers recruits a choice of how he wants to be paid: he can have a payment of $3,000, or a virgin. Thus, the kidnapped girls potentially represent over $600,000 that Boko Haram does not have to pay to its new recruits. In addition, if the negotiation process turns out to be successful in obtaining the girls' release, ransom paid by the Nigerian or other governments could add millions of U.S. dollars to Shekau's war chest.[30]

BK has been able to intensify its attacks as a result of training provided by al Qaeda aligned groups AQIM and AQAP. The group has been credited with causing more than four thousand deaths during 2014.

A further disturbing activity associated with BK kidnappings is their use of children as suicide bombers—a UN report disclosed that in 2015, the number of children used in suicide missions had jumped ten-fold. The UN Children's Agency UNICEF estimated forty-four children, some as young as eight years old, were made to carry out attacks across Nigeria, Cameroon, and Chad in 2015. This was up from just four in 2014.[31]

Summary

The rise of Islamic extremism and strict ideology is spreading through northern and central Africa and threatens to destabilize vulnerable and corrupt governments. Although mineral resource and oil exploration continues unabated, it is in most countries to the detriment of the economy and the population at large, with often only corrupt governments and their supporters benefiting. The establishment of an apartheid-free South African nation under the presidency of Nelson Mandela had its share of violence perpetrated by both sides. South Africa is still considered one of the richest and most powerful nations in Africa, and its influence over its neighbors over the coming years will be of considerable interest worldwide.

The troubles plaguing the regime of Robert Mugabe and the struggle that brought him to power in Rhodesia/Zimbabwe were all typical of states gaining nationhood in southern Africa. Many of the fledgling countries that fought for independence have suffered under the hammer of tyrannical dictators, whose only real interests were to use capital and foreign investment in their respective countries for bankrolling their personal lifestyles. The influences of Communist involvement in the region over the past fifty years have been considerable and destabilization seems to continue in one form or another.

Review Questions

1. Describe the tactics used by al-Shabaab in countering both Somali and Kenyan forces.
2. Analyze the success of Operation Jonathan.
3. List and explain the reasons behind the spread of Islamic State in central Africa.
4. Describe the external forces influencing PAGAD and why does it pose a threat to the stability of RSA?
5. Explain why kidnapping has become such a growth industry in the arsenal of African terror organizations.
6. List and explain the use of child abductees by Boko Haram.

End Notes

1. Stephanie Hanson. *Al-Shabaab*, Leadership and Division (August 10, 2011), http://www.cfr.org/somalia/al-shabaab/p18650.
2. Omar Shafik Hammami. Added to the FBI's Most Wanted Terrorists List https://www.fbi.gov/mobile/press-releases/2012/omar-shafik-hammami-added-to-the-fbis-most-wanted-terrorists-list.
3. The Jamestown Foundation Terrorism Monitor. http://www.jamestown.org/uploads/media/TerrorismMonitorVol13Issue8_03.pdf.
4. Bruce Quarrie. *The World's Secret Police* (London: Octopus Books Ltd., 1986, p. 104).
5. J. Carter Johnson, from Kitgum. "Deliver Us from Kony." *Why the children of Uganda are killing one another in the name of the Lord* (Uganda, January 2006). http://www.christianitytoday.com.
6. Richard Buteera. "The Reach of Terrorist Financing and Combating It–The Links between Terrorism and Ordinary Crime." (Washington, DC: International Society of Prosecutors, August 12, 2003).
7. Coalition for Human Rights and Justice Institute for Northern Uganda.
8. Institute for war and peace reporting (AR No. 121, July 12, 2007), http://www.iwpr.net/.
9. Beacham Publishing's TRAC (Terrorism Research & Analysis Consortium); *Uganda's Rising Threat: The Allied Democratic Forces (ADF)*; http://www.trackingterrorism.org/article/ugandas-rising-threat-allied-democratic-forces-adf; accessed Sunday, May 8th, 2016.
10. Douglas Reed. *The Siege of Southern Africa* (Johannesburg, South Africa: Macmillan, 1974, p. 45).
11. Richard Buteera. "The Reach of Terrorist Financing and Combating It—The Links between Terrorism and Ordinary Crime." Telegraph.co.uk. (Washington, DC: International Society of Prosecutors, August 12, 2003).
12. "Breaking the Silence, Building True Peace." *A Report on the Disturbances in Matabeleland and the Midlands 1980–1989*. (1997), http://www.hrforumzim.com/members_reports/matrep/matreppart1a.htm.
13. Reed. *The Siege of Southern Africa*, p. 95.
14. Peter Hawthorn. "Mugger of the Nation." *Time, Canada Limited* (December 8, 1997, p. 37).
15. Bill Dixon and Lisa-Marie Johns. "Gangs, Pagad & the State: Vigilantism and Revenge Violence in the Western Cape." *Violence and Transition Series*, vol. 2 (May 2001). Bill Dixon is a Senior Lecturer in the Department of Criminal Justice, University of Cape Town, and a researcher at the Institute of Criminology.
16. http://en.wikipedia.org/wiki/People_Against_Gangsterism_and_Drugs.
17. http://www.pagad.co.za/aims.htm.
18. *SCG International Risk*. Terrorist Group Profiles. http://www.scgonline.net/index.htm.
19. Anneli Botha. "PAGAD: A Case Study of Radical Islam in South Africa." *Publication: Terrorism Monitor*, vol. 3, no. 17 (September 14, 2005), http://www.jamestown.org.
20. Kenya, Capsule History. http://www.africanet.com.
21. Holden Alvaro Roberto. http://www.britannica.com/EBchecked/topic/505518/Holden-Alvaro-Roberto.
22. Reed. *The Siege of Southern Africa*, p. 25.
23. "Disarmament in the Congo: Preventing Further War." *International Crisis Group Report* http://www.intl-crisis-group.org/projects/showreport.cfm?reportid=519.
24. Ibid. UN Office for the Coordination of Humanitarian Affairs, NIGERIA: Rights Group Accuses Government of Letting Religious Killers Off Hook.

25. *Global Market Brief* (May 10, 2007). Stratfor.com.

26. "Nigeria's Boko Haram Issues Conditions amongst wave of Islamist Violence." *The Jamestown Foundations Terrorism Monitor*, vol. 9, no. 25 (June 23, 2011), http://www.jamestown.org/programs/gta/.

27. "London's Drive to Become the Sharia Finance Capitol of the World" Gorka, Katie. The Counter Jihad Report. May 29, 2014. http://counterjihadreport.com/tag/zakat-2/.

28. Patrick Jost and Harjit Sandhu. "The Hawala Alternative Remittance System and its Role in Money Laundering." Financial Crimes Enforcement Network. Page 1 of 27. http://www.treasury.gov/resource-center/terrorist-illicit-finance/Documents/FinCEN-Hawala-rpt.pdf.

29. Patrick Jost and Harjit Sandhu. "The Hawala Alternative Remittance System and its Role in Money Laundering." Financial Crimes Enforcement Network. Page 12 of 27. http://www.treasury.gov/resource-center/terrorist-illicit-finance/Documents/FinCEN-Hawala-rpt.

30. Beacham Publishing's TRAC (Terrorism Research & Analysis Consortium); *Boko Haram: Coffers and Coffins; A Pandora's Box - the Vast Financing Options for Boko Haram*; Kidnappings; http://www.trackingterrorism.org/article/new-financing-options-boko-haram/kidnappings; accessed Saturday, May 7th, 2016.

31. UNICEF Report. "Beyond Chibok." http://files.unicef.org/media/files/Beyond_Chibok.pdf.

Southern and Southeast Asia

LEARNING OUTCOMES

After studying this chapter, students should be able to:

1. Summarize how Partition in India fuels current day events and terrorist activity.

2. Describe how the fight for control of Kashmir fuels unrest and violence between India and Pakistan.

3. List the Sri Lankan terrorist front organizations and the methods used by them to garner both financial and political support.

4. Describe the role played by the Pakistani ISI and its involvement over several decades as a supporter to terror organizations.

5. Describe the close relationship between the Taliban and al Qaeda.

KEY WORDS TO NOTE

Haqqani Network—Afghan insurgent group closely aligned to al Qaeda and sponsored by the Pakistani ISI

Harakat-ul-Ansar (HUA)—Sunni Islamic militant group based in Pakistan and operating mainly in Kashmir

Inter-Services Intelligence (ISI)—Pakistan's intelligence agency established by the British Army in 1948

Khmer Rouge—A Cambodian Communist movement came to power in 1975 and was one of the most violent regimes of the twentieth century; responsible for the deaths of approximately 1.7 million people by execution, starvation, and hard labor

Lashkar-e-Taiba (LeT)—Army of the Pure—one of the largest Islamist terror organizations in Southern Asia—attacks both civilian and military targets

Liberation Tigers of Tamil Eelam (LTTE)—A separatist group seeking an independent state for ethnic Tamils in Sri Lanka

Madrassas—Islamic religious schools—many found in Pakistan

Mullah Omar—Leader of the Afghan Taliban and leader of the Afghan Government 1996–2001

Naxalites—Maoist group formed by student bodies in the 1960s

Pol Pot—Cambodia's leader of the Khmer Rouge

OVERVIEW

India until 1947 had for the prior two hundred years been the jewel in the British Crown of colonialism. The independence movement began in the early part of the century and would lead to full independence and the creation of India and Pakistan on August 15, 1947. It would also inaugurate a long period of religious turmoil and sectarian violence that continues today (Figure 11-1). In 1945, India was over four hundred million people: two hundred and fifty million Hindus, ninety million Muslims, six million Sikhs, millions of sectarians, Buddhists, Christians;

five hundred independent princes and maharajahs; twenty-three main languages, two hundred dialects; three thousand castes.[1] The situation is further exacerbated by both India and Pakistan having nuclear weapons programs. The chapter discusses ongoing battles for autonomy and freedom, fought largely by terrorism and insurrection and shows how difficult it is to separate the problems into neatly defined categories. The ongoing Islamist attacks in India, the simmering problems between Pakistan and India over Kashmir, and charting the rise and fall and the resurgence of the Taliban in Afghanistan will be the aim. In addition, we will take a critical look at the potential threat of the Islamic efforts to unite into a global power stretching from the Persian Gulf to the eastern states of the Russian Republic (Figures 11-2 and 11-3).

INDIA

Islamic influences spread across the subcontinent over a period of five hundred years, starting in the tenth and eleventh centuries. Turks and Afghans invaded India and established sultanates in the areas around and near Delhi. Then descendants of Genghis Khan swept across the Khyber Pass in

General Statistics—Suicide attacks 2000–2015	
Total Attacks	1,464
Total Deaths	9,854
Total Wounded	23,935
Average Deaths per Attack	6.7
Average Wounded per Attack	16.3

FIGURE 11-1 General Suicide statistics—Suicide attacks have been part of terror attack campaigns in the region. Statistics compiled here indicate the severity of these suicide attacks. *Courtesy:* Chicago Project on Security and Terrorism, http://cpost.uchicago.edu/

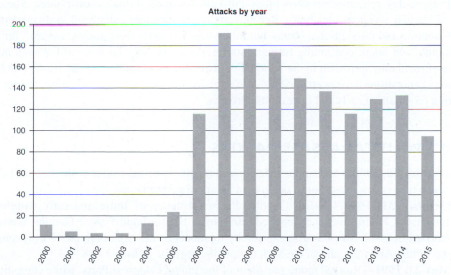

FIGURE 11-2 Suicide attacks by year 2000–2015. *Courtesy:* Chicago Project on Security and Terrorism, http://cpost.uchicago.edu/

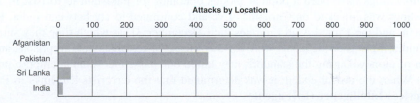

FIGURE 11-3 Suicide attacks by country/location 2000–2015. *Courtesy:* Chicago Project on Security and Terrorism, http://cpost.uchicago.edu/

FIGURE 11-4   Map of India.   *Source:* Central Intelligence Agency, *The World Factbook, 2008.*

the eleventh century and established the Mughal Dynasty, which lasted from the eleventh to the fifteenth centuries (Figure 11-4). During this period, there were two major cultural and religious systems—those of the Hindus and the Muslims. These cultures had centuries of mutual contact, trade, and lasting influences on each other. The British appeared on the subcontinent in 1619 and, by the middle of the 1800s, controlled most of present-day India, Pakistan, and Bangladesh. In 1857, a rebellion in north India was led by mutinous Indian soldiers, resulting in the transfer of all political power to the British Crown, which then began administering most of India directly and controlled the rest through treaties with local rulers. By the late 1800s, India had taken its first steps toward self-government. The British viceroy established provisional councils comprised of Indian members to advise the Crown. By 1920, India's Mahatma Gandhi had transformed the Indian National Congress political party into a powerful movement against British colonial rule.

Following Gandhi's concepts of nonviolent resistance, the party used both parliamentary means and noncooperation to compel the British to give India its independence. In 1947, India was awarded Commonwealth status and Jawaharlal Nehru became India's first prime minister. A period of continuing and escalating bloody conflicts between the Hindus and Muslims finally led to the British partition of India. This division, created on the basis of incompatible religions, resulted in the formation of East and West Pakistan, where there were Muslim majorities. These groups were forcibly moved—Muslims to the north and Hindus to the south—creating anger and animosity that still pervades to this day. After partition, India became a full member of the Commonwealth, and a republic, on January 26, 1950.

Present-day relations between India and Pakistan took a downward plunge when both acquired nuclear weapons capability. Recent tests seem not more calculated to divert attention from economic and international issues, but rather than to "rattle their nuclear sabers." India has long complained about continuing foreign interference from Afghanistan and Pakistan and the menace of escalating terrorism in the region. For years, the most ruthless of the Islamic and other terrorist organizations have been known to use Afghanistan as a base for recruiting, training, and harboring terrorists to carry out operations abroad.

INDIA'S POLITICAL ASSASSINATIONS

January 30, 1948—Mohandas (Mahatma) Gandhi, spiritual leader of the Indian independence movement, was shot to death by a fanatical young Hindu.

October 31, 1984—Indira Gandhi, Prime Minister of India and only daughter of Jawaharlal Nehru, took her married name from her husband Feroze Gandhi, whom she married in 1942. She was assassinated by members of her Sikh bodyguard as revenge for the Indian Army assault on the Sikh temple in Amritsar in June 1984.

May 21, 1991—Rajiv Gandhi, president of the Indian Congress Party, while campaigning, was assassinated by an LTTE female suicide bomber.

Aircraft hijackings have been a popular modus operandi for Pakistani terrorists. In 1999, an Indian airliner was hijacked on Christmas Eve and continued to fly between India, Pakistan, Afghanistan, and the United Arab Emirates until December 31, at which time they surrendered to UAE authorities. Their demands were for the release of terrorists held in prisons and also a large sum of money. During the standoff, they killed one passenger in an attempt to press their demands. When the ordeal ended, it was determined that the terrorists had links to Pakistan's **Inter-Services Intelligence (ISI) agency**.

On many occasions, India has drawn attention to the presence of training camps in neighboring Kashmir and Afghanistan. Terrorists are trained and equipped to carry out operations in

India, particularly in the states of Jammu and Kashmir. Many hundreds of thousands of refugees from Afghanistan's war against the Russians were readily recruited by their protectors in Pakistan and used to foment terrorism and to pressure India into granting even more territory in the Kashmir region. In many instances, the ISI is believed to be behind any number of terror attacks in India.

SPECIAL ECONOMIC ZONE

Although fighting between Muslims and Hindus within the country is not uncommon, the Indian government has considerable exposure to internal troubles due to rapid business expansion in its special economic zone—a swath of land stretching almost across the country that has seen phenomenal growth and wealth to the booming IT industry. Land grabs by many unscrupulous politicians have led to large numbers of displaced tribesmen in these areas. India faces militant threats primarily from three sources:

1. Maoist rebels known as Naxalites
2. Tribal-based ethnic separatists
3. Islamist militants fighting in the name of Kashmir

Most militant activity is in the Jammu and Kashmir regions and the northeastern part of the country. The **Naxalites** have their origins in the student movements of the 1960s who wanted to help India's peasantry. They grew quickly as a Maoist group and conducted isolated acts of banditry. The Maoists were suppressed by Indian Police and between 1967 and 1972 over forty thousand Naxalites were imprisoned. The Naxalites made a comeback after several decades of inactivity. In 2012 alone they carried out over one thousand attacks aimed primarily at police and infrastructure. They have made direct threats against multinational corporations, though they primarily focus their attacks on police stations, locally owned factories, and Indian government officials. The Naxalite movement has created a single command center for the revolution, which clearly means more attacks are to come.

The Naxalites still have a host of problems to deal with, however. India has at least ten Naxalite splinter groups that have broken away from the main movement due to differences over ideology and militant strategy, along with general disillusionment with the movement and war fatigue. Indian media also report Naxalite defections on a nearly daily basis, though these incidents often are exaggerated and in some cases stage-managed by the police. This was most recently illustrated in January 2008, when reports came out that as many as seventy-nine Naxalites in Chhattisgarh had defected. Soon enough, allegations emerged that innocent tribal people were forced to "surrender" as Maoist rebels.

ISLAM AND INDIA

Most Islamist attacks have centered in India, and militants have traditionally not been exported from India, and those operating within the country have likely come from and been sponsored by Pakistani-based groups. Al Qaeda seems to have paid scant attention to India as a center for targeting attacks, but India's internal security apparatus and lack of security infrastructure would make certain sectors and particularly the affluent special economic zone a prime, "soft," target for Islamist militant attacks. Osama bin Laden made mention of India in proclamations, and in 2006, he called on the Kashmiri Muslims to rise up against India. Al Qaeda appears to have no Indian base as such and would most likely depend on Kashmiri jihadists to do its bidding in India. Successful attacks have been carried out by Kashmiri militants, and the devastating railway bombings in Mumbai in 2006 and the Mumbai massacre in November 2008 are good examples of the spread of the jihadist threat.

The threat to India from Islamic State is also now a Prevent one—there have been reports of several Indian fighters traveling to both Syria and Iraq to join IS. For its part IS has made recruiting inroads to India using online chat rooms, Twitter, and Facebook to spread the jihad and encourage recruitment.

The oft repeated exhortations of IS are based on the supposition that all "true Muslims" should be part of its brand of jihad and serve the Caliphate. This has resonated relatively well across South Asia, including India with its 170 million-strong Muslim population.[2] Indian authorities have had some success particularly in early 2016 with the arrest of the Islamic State purported leader in India, Muddabir Mushtaq Sheikh (alias Abu Musab). The IS in India uses the name Junud-al-Khalifa-e-Hind (JKH, or Soldiers of the Caliph in India). The group was in the early planning stages for multiple attacks on infrastructure across India.

The discovery of JKH and the arrests of its members in January have brought to light the threat of IS-inspired extremism in India. While the bulk of the Indian Muslim population has rejected the group's ideals, a small number of extremists were able to organize themselves to a worrying degree simply by using the Internet and social media to tap into existing indigenous militant networks. Despite cracking down successfully on the Indian Mujahideen in 2008, the Indian authorities cannot afford to be complacent.[3]

MUMBAI ATTACKS, NOVEMBER 2008

India's version of 9-11 took place in the heart of India's economically rich city of Mumbai, formerly Bombay. As we have witnessed elsewhere in the world, well-planned and coordinated attacks by well-armed and determined individuals or groups can and will succeed in most cases if security is not vigilant; in the Mumbai attacks, the government had intelligence several weeks' prior that an attack was probable. However, it is clear that public gathering places, train stations, restaurants, hotels, and the like were totally unprepared for an attack such as this one. At the attack locations, there was little evidence of any security presence established to deter this onslaught.

The terrorist group responsible for the Mumbai attacks has been identified as **Lashkar-e-Taiba (LeT)**, or Army of the Pure. They have targeted Hindus in India and brought India and Pakistan to the brink of all-out war. In 2000, a LeT attack on India's Parliament in New Delhi prompted the Indian government to mobilize 700,000 troops to India's border with Pakistan. Whether the Mumbai attack was intended to have the same effect, we do not know, but the rhetoric between Pakistan and India was ramped up. Strategically, the attack may also have been designed to divert Pakistani forces from the western border where the Pakistani Army is fighting Taliban insurgent forces.

LeT was designated by the United States as a Foreign Terrorist Organization, forcing the Pakistan government to similarly ban it. In the past, LeT is believed to have been trained and supported by the Pakistani ISI agency in exchange for a pledge to target Hindus in Jammu and Kashmir and train Muslim extremists in India. Experts also indicate that LeT is supported by Saudi Arabia as well as Pakistani citizens. It has a network of terrorist training centers and religious schools in Pakistan and has its headquarters in Lahore.

Attack Time Line

The attack in Mumbai lasted from November 26 to 28, 2008, and also reminds us of the need for a greater control of the media. The trend for reporting every last detail on every guest or hostage, and every developing issue related to the security presence, greatly assisted the attackers who were able to monitor a vast array of media reports on their own success and progress at the locations they had attacked.

The LeT terrorists left the sanctuary of Pakistan on November 22 and traveled by boat into India's territorial waters and transferred to a larger vessel; the following day they are believed to have sent a distress call that was picked up and responded to by an Indian fishing vessel. The crewmembers of this vessel were all killed with the exception of the captain, who navigated them to their destination near the entrance to Mumbai harbor where they transferred to rubber dinghies. The ten terrorists landed in the fishing area and then spread out in five teams of two—all were equipped with AK-47 assault weapons, ammunition, hand grenades, and other types of explosives.

TARGETS   The five teams had a set of priority targets to attack:

- The Leopold Café, a popular restaurant in south Mumbai frequented by foreign businessmen and tourists;
- The Mumbai Central Railway Station and Terminus, always packed with travelers and commuters;
- The Taj Mahal Hotel, visited by foreign businessmen, tourists, and government officials;

- The Oberoi-Trident Hotel, also in South Mumbai and similarly popular with tourists and foreign businessmen;
- Nariman House, a Jewish Outreach Center, also in South Mumbai, owned and operated by a Jewish couple from New York.

The first team attacked the railway station at around 9.30 P.M., firing indiscriminately into the packed station and killing fifty-six and wounding over a hundred. The two-man team then fled the railway station and made for a secondary target to cause maximum disruption—the nearby Cama Hospital, where they began to fire at hospital staff and patients. As they left, they were challenged by Indian Police officers whom they shot and killed or injured and hijacked their vehicle and drove away. They were intercepted at a police roadblock; one was killed in the ensuing shootout and the other apprehended.

While the first team began its attack on the railway terminus, the second team attacked the Leopold Café near the Taj Mahal Hotel. They shot and killed ten diners and staff and then headed to the Taj Mahal Hotel, where a third team had already begun to attack staff and diners in the front lobby and the restaurant area. The two teams began rounding up hostages believed to be either British or Americans. The fourth team began a similar attack on the Oberoi Hotel and the fifth attacked the Jewish Center. The government response was to send a team of Naval commandos from Delhi, who arrived on November 27. The siege of the hotels and the Jewish Center lasted for nearly forty hours. The hotels were both badly damaged by fire, and the Rabbi and the other hostages including his wife were all killed by the terrorists. There were a total of one hundred and seventy-four deaths and three hundred and eleven injuries, with the majority of those killed being Indians.

The attackers were all Pakistani nationals, nine were killed and one was captured. The security services also noted that the terrorists carried satellite phones and had been communicating with handlers back in Pakistan during the assault on the five targets.

Motives

Previous terror attacks have pushed these two nuclear powers to the brink of all-out war, and it may be that this was the intention again due to the long-running and simmering dispute over Kashmir. Another more probable motive was the targeting of Westerners and in particular U.S. and British citizens as part of the global jihad and the even-more significant target—the Jewish Center. The terrorists also killed specific groups and not indiscriminately—the Jewish Center was a specific killing zone, whereas in the hotels Muslim hostages were set free and those of other nationalities and religions were executed.

Pakistan's ISI has used several organizations in its strategy to destabilize India:

1. Lashkar-e-Taiba (LeT)
2. Harkat-ul-Mujahideen (HuM)
3. Harkat-ul-jihad-e-Islami (HuJI)
4. Jaish-e-Mohammed (JeM)

THE PUNJAB AND SIKHISM

The northern Indian state of the Punjab has seen politics and religion mix with deadly results. In 1984, it led to the assassination of then Prime Minister Indira Gandhi by her own Sikh bodyguards who believed she had used the politics of religion for her own political gains and to the benefit of the Congress Party in the Punjab. Violence continued in Punjab for years after her assassination. In May 2007, there were clashes between mainstream Sikhs and followers of the Dera Sacha Sauda. The Dera had openly supported the Congress Party in the state assembly elections in 2007; however, Akali Dal, the main Sikh political party, won and since then has encouraged open protests against Dera. The flash point for violence was the heretical behavior of the Dera leader, one Ram Rahim Singh, who dressed up as Gobind Singh, the Sikh's most revered "guru." The weak apology by Singh did little to tone down the acts of violence that followed. A Dera is a temple that conducts educational and social activities, and there are thousands of Deras in Punjab; however, it appears that Mr. Singh may have outgrown the organization with nearly half a million followers, both Sikhs and lower-caste Hindus. As the Akali Dal and Congress continue to play religion and politics, the likelihood of sectarian attacks is very real. This is also exacerbated by the economic hardship in the Punjab due to over-farming and the falling water table.[4]

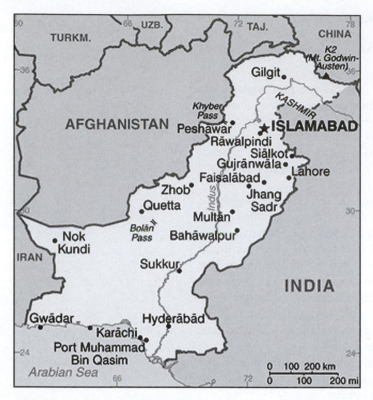

FIGURE 11-5 Map of Pakistan. *Source:* Central Intelligence Agency, *The World Factbook, 2008.*

PAKISTAN

Tensions between the United States and Pakistan continued through 2011, and though a supporter of the War on Terror, the killing of Osama bin Laden and the implications that he was being protected by Pakistan's spy agency, the ISI, or elite members of Pakistan's military have done little to help Pakistan's fragile political machine (Figure 11-5). Pakistan has opposed secret CIA operations within Pakistan including the use of unmanned drones inside its territory. From the U.S. perspective, Pakistan is considered a key ally despite the obvious concerns about ISI and the tracking of bin Laden to a military town inside the country.

U.S. NAVY SEALS KILL OSAMA BIN LADEN—MAY 2011

Osama bin Laden has been the U.S. Number One Most Wanted Terrorist since the September 11 attacks on the United States (Figure 11-6). It took the United States ten years to track down the mastermind behind 9-11 to Abbottabad, not far from the Pakistani capital Islamabad, where he was killed by U.S. Navy SEALS on May 1, 2011. Special Forces units the world over celebrated this successful operation, which is believed to have taken not more than forty minutes to complete and was done without the knowledge or permission of the Pakistan government. Aside from killing bin Laden, the SEALs netted a treasure trove of intelligence, including laptop computers, hard drives, and cell phones. Britain, the United States, and their allies steadfastly attempted to track him and his cohort following the invasion of Afghanistan, but bin Laden along with Ayman-al-Zawahiri and Taliban leader Mullah Omar had always managed to either hide out in the rugged mountains or escape into Pakistan. Bin Laden, through his own magnetism, was able to spawn a global movement of al Qaeda spreading through the Middle East to Northern and Central Africa and Europe; while loosely affiliated, these groups held true to his ideology of attacking the West. Many of bin Laden's family fled to the border region with Iran, but the exact location of bin Laden had never been discovered. Intelligence reports suggest that he had been almost housebound in Abbottabad for the five years preceding his death (Figure 11-7). Although bin Laden has been replaced, the fact of his death will likely have little impact on the spread of Islamic extremism or the attacks on Western targets. Other organizations have lost their leaders; the Taliban leadership has been decimated but still continues to operate and is probably now more extreme than it was prior to the military invasion of Afghanistan. Dead too are Yasser Arafat, Sheikh Yassin, and others, but all their movements continue to operate in spite of their losses. In Pakistan, the leader of the pro-Taliban Red Mosque, Abdul Rashid Ghazi, is dead, as is the Pakistani Taliban leader Baitullah Mehsud, but their deaths have had no noticeable effect on Islamists across Pakistan.

Pakistan's reputation as a terrorist haven has seen many Westerners targeted for kidnapping or assassination.

In November 1997, four U.S. employees of Union Texas Petroleum and their Pakistani driver were murdered in Karachi when their vehicle was attacked near the U.S. Consulate. Shortly after the incident, two separate groups claimed responsibility for the killings, the Aimal Khufia Action Committee, a previously unknown group; and the Islami Inqilabi Mahaz, a Lahore-based group of Afghan war veterans. Both groups cited the motive for the attack as being the conviction of Mir Aimal Kansi, a Pakistani National, tried in the United States for the 1993 murder of two CIA employees and the wounding of three others. Kansi was found guilty and sentenced to death. Ramzi Ahmed Yousef, who was extradited from Pakistan to the United States in 1995, was convicted in New York in November 1997 for his role in the 1993 World Trade Center bombing in New York City.

FIGURE 11-6 Photo of Osama bin Laden. *Source:* World History Archive/Alamy Stock Photo.

BENAZIR BHUTTO

Benazir Bhutto was portrayed as Pakistan's last great hope to bring a level of democracy to Pakistan. Unfortunately, any hope of that died with her assassination in December 2007, when a gunman and suicide bomber attacked her, killing her instantly. Ms. Bhutto had only recently returned to Pakistan from a self-imposed exile of eight years, following President Pervez Musharraf's dropping of corruption charges against her.

Before her return to Pakistan, she had clearly criticized the government of Pervez Musharraf for failing to reign-in and defeat the Islamic militants of al Qaeda and the Taliban. "Pakistan is in a crisis and it's a crisis that threatens not only my nation and region, but could possibly have repercussions on the entire world."[5] Benazir Bhutto was returning to Pakistan as a symbol of hope for the country. She had previously been elected prime minister in 1988 and had immediately run afoul of the powerful military machine and the ISI Agency, both of which have significant control and influence. Within two years of taking office, she was dismissed by the military on charges of corruption and misrule. She regained power in the 1993 general election at about the same time as the Taliban regimes were coming into power in Afghanistan. Her party, the Pakistan Peoples' Party, is left-leaning and eschews religious extremism but had recognized in the Taliban the opportunity to secure trade routes across southern Afghanistan. Her difficulty with confronting her own military was also a problem, and she agreed to provide covert aid to the Taliban regime, but denied to the United States that Pakistan was funding or arming the Taliban. In 1996, she was again removed from power by the military and sought exile in London and then Dubai, where from a distance she remained involved in Pakistani politics.

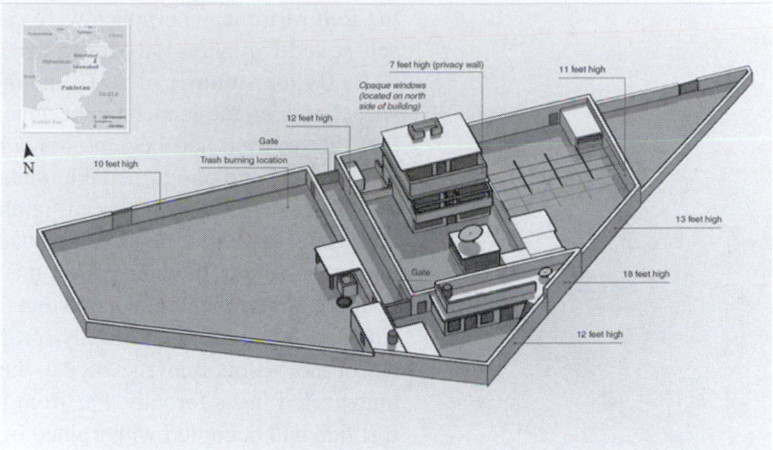

On October 18, 2007, Bhutto returned to Pakistan, and the first attempt on her life took place just after midnight on October 19, 2007. Her entourage was en route from Karachi International Airport to the tomb of Muhammad Ali Jinnah, the country's founder, when it was attacked by suicide bombers in the dense crowd around Bhutto's armored bus. Reports indicated that there were two explosions shortly after one another and that around one hundred and forty people were killed—how many were killed by the bombings and how many by the stampeding masses as they escaped the carnage has not been determined. What was clear was that the moment she set foot in Pakistan she would become a target of either the Musharraf supporters or Islamist militants. Prior to her return, she had pledged to take on the Islamists and went so far as to say that if she were prime minister, she would permit the United States to send troops into Pakistan if the situations in the tribal areas were to further deteriorate. Musharraf ordered troops to storm Islamabad's Red Mosque, and Ms. Bhutto came out in strong support of the action.

There has been speculation that the attack on Bhutto was in fact a government conspiracy; however, on December 27, 2007, after attending a political rally in Rawalpindi, she was shot by an assailant as she stood in the well of her vehicle, her head and shoulders exposed through the sun roof, when the assailant then detonated an explosive vest, killing twenty people including Benazir Bhutto.

Pakistan's military is coming under continuous attacks from Islamist militants in the rugged Northwest Frontier Provinces (NWFP). Pakistan's military is a very formidable force and most certainly one to be reckoned with. In the past where assassination attempts against government officials have taken place, swift and violent retribution has been meted out by the military.

FIGURE 11-7 Aerial photo of Abbottabad Compound in Pakistan where Osama bin Laden was killed by Special Forces. *Courtesy:* U.S. Central Intelligence Agency.

The Lal Masjid (Red Mosque)

The Red Mosque in the Pakistani capital Islamabad has been in place since 1965 and is home to fundamentalist teachers with links to global terrorism and jihad in the intervening decades. The mosque leadership had been openly opposed to the government, and after the London bombings in 2005, Pakistani police investigated links between one of the bombers, Shehzad Tanweer, and the Red Mosque. The police were confronted and repulsed by baton-wielding women from the self-styled vigilante, Lal Masjid Brigade.

By the summer of 2007, the mosque leadership had become more and more extreme and speeches from the leadership became far more menacing. Pakistani authorities were of the belief that the mosque had become home to jihadists from the tribal region bordering Pakistan and Afghanistan and had turned the fundamentalist religious institution into an armed military camp. The Chinese government was a significant supporter of Musharraf and his regime and had a large number of its nationals in Islamabad. When the Lal Masjid brigade kidnapped seven Chinese nationals from a massage parlor, this raised the stakes for the mosque to a significant level. The Chinese government demanded that the Pakistani authorities take action to release the kidnapped Chinese. Islamabad is a heavily fortified city, so when President Musharraf proclaimed "surrender or die" as his final message to the inhabitants of the mosque, the ensuing daylong battle was unexpected in its ferocity. Far from being a bastion of education, the Red Mosque was heavily fortified and occupied with trained fighters and militants from banned religious groups and fighters linked to both the Taliban and al Qaeda militias operating in the tribal regions. The weeklong standoff at the mosque was followed up by 200 commandos storming the enclave resulting in more than one hundred deaths, including another dozen soldiers and the extremist leader Abdul Rashid (Figure 11-8).

Pervez Musharraf

As chief of the Army, General Musharraf had been in power since the military seized control of Pakistan in 1999 and was a supporter of the U.S. "War on Terror." This has made him a target for Muslim fundamentalists as well as opposition parties. In November 2007, there were challenges to the validity of his re-election as president. His suspension of the Pakistani Constitution did nothing to curry favor with the powerful state judiciary, and his jailing of several key ministers including the Chief Justice Minister would cause a political backlash amid attempts to impeach him. It was with this backdrop that Musharraf resigned as president in August 2008 rather than face impeachment. In September 2008, Asif Ali Zardari—the widower of Benazir Bhutto—who was until his wife's assassination not in the political limelight and in fact was better known for his conviction and imprisonment for corruption—was sworn in as president. In May 2011, he had to cope with the fall-out in Pakistan because of the killing by U.S. Special Forces of al-Qaeda leader Osama bin Laden in the town of Abbottabad. The fall-out from Bin Laden's death exposed the uneasy relationship between the Pakistan People's Party (PPP) and Pakistan's military and intelligence services in the governance of

TERRORIST ATTACK BRIEF

Terror Group—Pakistani Taliban
Attack Target—School in Peshawar, Pakistan—operated by the military
Date—December 16, 2014
Attack Method—full assault with weapons, explosives, and suicide vests
Casualties—Dead Nine teaching staff and one hundred and thirty-two children

A total of seven attackers wearing suicide vests entered the school compound by scaling the walls and initially setting off explosions. The terrorists began to shoot indiscriminately targeting children and teachers as they went from classroom to classroom. The school is located close to a Pakistani military compound not far from the border with Afghanistan, and many of the children were sons and daughters of military personnel. The Taliban claimed the attack was carried out in response and retaliation for military actions against the Taliban that had been launched in June 2014 in the North Waziristan region as the Pakistani government had vowed to go after all terrorist/militant in the region that borders Afghanistan.

FIGURE 11-8   Terrorist Attack Brief—Attack on a school in Peshawar, Pakistan.   *Source:* http://www. telegraph.co.uk/news/worldnews/asia/pakistan/6305970/Boy-13-kills-41-in-Taliban-suicide-bombing-in-Pakistan.html

the country. Recriminations over the killings reflected the traditionally poor relations between his PPP and the army as well as tenser relations with Washington, already strained because of continued U.S. drone strikes against militant targets in the north-west of his country. He served as Pakistan's 11th President from 2008–2013.

Pakistan, Afghanistan, and Islam

Religious differences and a long history of violence and hatred among former brothers and fellow countrymen still separate India and Pakistan. Sponsoring international terrorism, separatist subversion, and insurgency are not new to either side. Since the 1970s, Pakistan has also trained Sikh and Indian separatist movements. The Shiromani Gurudwara Prabandhak Committee (SGPC) is the major Sikh terrorist organization in India. It established tight control over the culture and economy of the Indian state of Punjab in the early 1980s and forced Sikh traditionalism and conservatism on Punjabi society. Pakistan was quick to recognize this as an opportunity to exploit further divisions in India. The Sikh struggle for an independent state attracted Pakistan's attention. Pakistan had long held its own claims to Kashmir and saw some possible benefit from encouraging the formation of a Sikh state, Khalistan, located in the Punjab, as this would weaken India's defense of the remaining portion of Kashmir. Pakistan hoped to exploit the tensions in Kashmir in order to destabilize India and began to provide support and training as terrorist activities of the Sikh militants increased. The Sikhs began to represent such a potential threat that India, in July 1984, launched an assault on the Golden Temple at Amritsar, one of the holiest places for Sikhs. Ultimately the escalation of Sikh separatist terrorism resulted in the assassination of Indira Gandhi the same year. The Sikhs' armed insurrection escalated as high-quality weapons became available. The arsenal included sophisticated bomb-making materials and better training for Sikh separatists in the Afghanistan mujahideen camps. The long reach of Sikh terrorism further resulted in the bombing of the Air India jet from Toronto that blew up over the coast of Ireland, killing three hundred and twenty-nine passengers.

A corresponding ideological development in Indian Kashmir then occurred. Almost overnight, the prevailing popular sentiment in Indian Kashmir was the belief that because the targets of Indian security forces were Muslims, Islam was in danger. This had a galvanizing effect on the fanatical Islamic youth of the Kashmir region, who formed new cadres of terrorists. The extent of Pakistani and Afghan influence on the Islamist transformation of the Kashmir insurgency was profound and deadly.

Pakistan's ISI began to assume quite a different role from its behind-the-scenes maneuvers. It seemed to be taking over direct control of the Sikh movement. The ISI made the city of Darra, Pakistan, the primary source of weapons for the Sikh, Tamil, and Kashmiri liberation movements. Darra became the storefront for the regional illegal arms market.

Having witnessed the initial impact of the Islamist message in Indian Kashmir, Pakistan began to broaden its horizons and set its sights higher. During the Soviet occupation of Afghanistan, the U.S. and its regional allies funneled cash and material support to the Afghan mujahedeen during the war period from 1980-1990. The logistics for much of this was handled by the Pakistani ISI which under President Zia al-Haq exercised almost supreme authority. ISI acted not only as a distributor but also a sponsor and trainer for the mujahedeen fighting the Russian occupation. A significant proportion of aid received by the ISI from the Americans for the Afghan jihad, aid which continued for a further two years after the end of the jihad and the Soviet withdrawal managed to use it against Pakistan's main regional enemy, India.[6]

The Harakat-ul-Ansar

An Islamic militant group based in Pakistan and operating primarily in Kashmir, **Harakat-ul-Ansar (HUA)** was formed in October 1993 when two Pakistani political activist groups, Harakat ul-Jihad al-Islami and Harakat ul-Mujahideen, merged. Faroogi Kashmiri is currently leading this group. His predecessor, Fazlur Khalil, supports the al Qaeda doctrine of attacks against the West and the United States. Khalil is the secretary general of the organization.

The HUA has carried out a number of operations against Indian troops and civilian targets in Kashmir and has been linked to the Kashmiri militant group, Al-Faran, which kidnapped five

Western tourists in Kashmir in July 1995; one was killed in August 1995 and the other four reportedly were killed in December of the same year. The HUA has several thousand armed supporters located in Azad Kashmir, Pakistan and in southern Kashmir and the Doda regions of India. These areas are composed of mostly Pakistanis and Kashmiris, but include Afghans and Arab veterans of the Afghan war. The HUA uses light and heavy machine guns, assault rifles, mortars, explosives, and rockets.

Based in Muzaffarabad, Pakistan, its members have participated in insurgent and terrorist activities primarily in Kashmir. The HUA trained its militants in Pakistan and in Afghanistan during the Taliban regime, prior to the U.S. airborne attacks of 2001. They collect donations from Saudi Arabia and other Gulf and Islamic states and from Pakistanis and Kashmiris. The source and amount of its military funding are unknown. Khalil was detained by Pakistani forces in 2004 but released later that year. One of HUA's associates is Ahmed Omar Sheik, who was convicted for the abduction and murder of the *Wall Street Journal* journalist Daniel Pearl. HUA began to use a different name in 2003, calling itself Jamiat ul-Ansar (JUA).[7]

The head of Pakistan's ISI political section developed a long-term program called K-2, aimed at castigating the Kashmiri and Sikh subversive efforts by making them appear to be under one umbrella of Sikh and Kashmiri extremists and Muslim fundamentalists. These groups would clearly not become allied with each other because of long-held hatred among them. This program would then intensify acts of violence in Punjab, Jammu, Kashmir, and the Terai region of Uttar Pradesh. Escalation of terrorism and subversion since the early 1990s is widely believed to have been a direct outgrowth of the ISI's implementation of the K-2.

Sikh terrorists were increasingly smuggling weapons from the Jammu and Kashmir areas or from Ganganagar in Rajasthan, where the ISI had its own bases. Clandestine ISI support for the Sikh terrorists continued to improve. By 1992, the ISI was operating thirteen permanent, eighteen temporary, and eight joint training camps for Kashmiris in Pakistan and Kashmir alone. Thus, while these Kashmiris failed to incite or stir up a popular war, they did establish enough popular support to embark on the second phase: a direct and violent confrontation with the Indian security forces, whom they consider to be occupiers. That would not have been possible without Pakistani and other Islamist support.

Many of the factions involved in the Afghanistan civil war included large numbers of Egyptians, Algerians, Palestinians, and Saudis. Many of these factions continue to provide haven to terrorists by facilitating the operation of training camps in areas under their control. The factions remain engaged in a struggle for political and military supremacy over India. The Indian and Pakistani governments both claim that the intelligence service of the other country sponsors bombings on its territory. The government of Pakistan acknowledges that it continues to provide moral, political, and diplomatic support to Kashmiri militants, but denies allegations of providing any other assistance.

Lashkar-e-Taiba (Army of the Pure) (aka Lashkar e-Tayyiba; Lashkar e-Toiba; Lashkar-i-Taiba)

This Islamist group has been active since the mid-1990s and formed the military wing of the Markaz-ad-Dawa-wal-Irshad, which was founded in 1989 and recruited volunteers to fight alongside the Taliban. During the 1990s, experts say LeT received instruction and funding from Pakistan's intelligence agency, the ISI, in exchange for a pledge to target Hindus in Jammu and Kashmir and to train Muslim extremists on Indian soil.

Ideology

Islamist organization seeks to bring about a union of all Muslim majority regions in countries that surround Pakistan. They also challenge India's sovereignty over Jammu and Kashmir.

The LeT is based near Lahore, Pakistan and is led by a former Islamic Studies Professor Hafiz Muhammad Saeed. LeT is able to operate quite freely from Pakistan with little interference from the Pakistani Security Services.

It came to notice in 1997 during Nawaz Sharif's second term as Pakistan's prime minister. LeT uses "suicide attacks" where small groups of fidayeen (suicide squads) would storm a security force camp and kill as many personnel as possible. They reportedly changed the name to Pasban-e-Ahle Hadith following their inclusion in the U.S. State Department's Foreign Terrorist

Organization list. One of its main goals is the destruction of India and the establishment of an Islamic state. LeT was launched during the last days of Afghan resistance against Soviet occupation. Though LeT's entry into Jammu and Kashmir was first recorded in 1993, it came into the picture of Kashmir militancy only in 1997. Its induction to Kashmir is believed to be the result of deteriorating Harakat–ISI relations.

Lashkar's militant activities soon outshone those of Harakat. The group would first use local Kashmiri militants only as helpers and guides, keeping both the armed operations and leadership with nonlocal cadre, generally Punjabis from Pakistan. Today, the outfit is the largest group active in the Valley with a dedicated *Fidayeen* unit (suicide squad) that changed the landscape of militancy in Kashmir (Figure 11-9).

LeT has twenty-two hundred offices across Pakistan and an estimated two dozen camps along the Line of Control, an unmarked border between India and Pakistan in Jammu and Kashmir. Two LeT

FIGURE 11-9 Suicide vest displayed in Peshawar by Pakistan security official. *Courtesy:* Mohammad Sajjad/AP Images.

training camps are located at Muzaffarabad, the capital of Pakistan-held Kashmir. The training is divided into two phases—Daura Aam (basic phase) and Daura Khaas (special phase). During the first phase, a twenty-one-day period, students are motivated to internalize jihad as an exclusive life-long mission, mainly through intensive exposure to semi-mythical stories glorifying the lives and exploits of Islam's historical martyrs. The second phase lasts for three months and involves weapons training, ambush, and survival techniques.[8]

However, what really drives the organization's ideological indoctrination and the rigors of its jihadist training is a concept evolved by Hafiz Saeed. His unique approach has been to merge Islamic education with modern curricula, thus ensuring a balance between religious and secular training.[9]

LeT has also become a focus for the Pakistan ISI to use it in its campaign against India. LeT played a major role in the planning and execution of the bomb attacks on a train station in the Mumbai financial district in July 2006, when powerful bombs ripped through seven commuter trains killing one hundred and seventy-four and wounding nearly five hundred others. Like HUA, the LeT is used to pit Muslims against Hindus, and by placing bombs and targeting either of the religious groups they hope to succeed in their objective (Figures 11-10 and 11-11).

SIKH TERRORISM

Sikh terrorism is mainly sponsored by expatriate and Indian Sikh groups, with designs to create an independent Sikh state called Khalistan (Land of the Pure) from Indian territory. Active groups include Babbar Khalsa, International Sikh Youth Federation, Dal Khalsa, and the Bhindranwale Tiger Force. A previously unknown group, the Shaheed Khalsa Force, claimed credit for the New Delhi marketplace bombings in 1997. Sikh attacks in India are usually against Indian officials and facilities, other Sikhs, and Hindus. They include assassinations, bombings, and kidnappings. These attacks have dropped markedly since 1992. Indian security forces

Attackers, Attacks, and Casualties by Religion 2000–2015				
Religion	**Attackers**	**Attacks**	**Killed**	**Wounded**
Hindu	28	28	198	665
Muslim (NA)	13	13	64	172
Muslim (Sunni)	7	7	61	264
Unknown	1,447	1,417	9,531	22,834

FIGURE 11-10 Suicide attacks and attackers by religion 2000–2015. *Courtesy:* Chicago Project on Security and Terrorism, http://cpost.uchicago.edu/

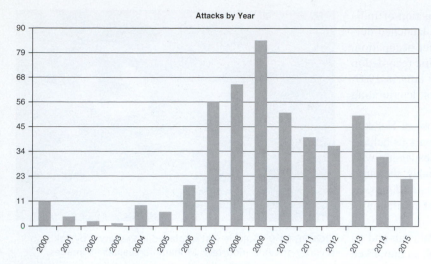

Attacks by Year

FIGURE 11-11   Suicide attacks by year India, Pakistan, and Sri Lanka 2000–2015.   *Courtesy:* Chicago Project on Security and Terrorism, http://cpost.uchicago.edu/

killed or captured many of the senior Sikh militant leaders and disrupted extremist groups. Many low-intensity bombings that might have been credited to Sikh extremists occur without subsequent claims of credit. Sikh militant cells are active internationally, and extremists gather funds from overseas Sikh communities. The Sikh expatriates have formed a variety of international organizations that lobby for the Sikh cause overseas. Most prominent are the World Sikh Organization and the International Sikh Youth Federation.[10] The International Sikh Youth Federation was first established in the mid-1980s in the United Kingdom and opened chapters in Europe, the U.S.A, and Canada.

Pakistan's ISI has supported this organization for a long time. It provides training camps, funds, arms, and ammunition to the members of ISYF along with other Khalistani groups.[11] Pakistan-based chief of the Babbar Khalsa International Wadhava Singh and chief of the ISYF Lakhbir Singh Rode are said to be among the top Punjab militants who, in league with the ISI, have been assigned the task of carrying out militant activities. The ISI also wants to create a common front between Khalistan and Kashmiri terrorist groups.

KASHMIR

Over the decades, there has been a continuous cycle of declared and undeclared wars between India and Pakistan, with an ever-increasing enmity between the two countries. Protagonists of each country are emphatic about their separate claims to Kashmir and stubbornly proclaim that they will never give up that claim.

The Kashmir problem was created toward the end of British rule in India and still lies at the heart of the instability between Pakistan and India. This issue even affects Afghanistan. In the last years of British rule, all parties agreed to divide India into a Hindu-majority country called India and a Muslim-majority country called Pakistan. Pakistan took its first form as East Pakistan (now Bangladesh) and West Pakistan, about eleven hundred miles apart on either side of India.

The state of Kashmir was close to the heart of Jawaharlal Nehru, the first prime minister of independent India; he did not wish to give it up to Pakistan, in spite of its Muslim majority. The departing British, under Lord Mountbatten, made no secret of their dislike for the nascent state of Pakistan and for its leader, Mohammed Ali Jinnah. Britain's Viceroy, Lord Mountbatten joined Nehru in persuading the Hindu Raja of Jammu and Kashmir to accede to India. To afford India with a contiguous connection to Kashmir and make it defensible, the British granted the adjoining Gurdaspur district to India, instead of Pakistan as was originally planned.

The Muslim majority of Kashmir has been unwilling to accede to Indian rule over Kashmir and has been involved in a steady escalation of resistance to India since independence in 1947. As a result, India has had more troops and other security forces per capita in Kashmir than any other nation has had anywhere. The George W. Bush administration referred to all Kashmiri resistance fighters as "Terrorists." Had it not been so tragic, it would have been considered funny that Bush and Russian President Putin stood side by side as they jointly told Pakistan's President Musharraf to stop aiding terrorists in crossing the ceasefire line into Indian Kashmir. George Bush was obviously ignoring the record of his companion, Putin—a man responsible for the killing of almost one hundred thousand Chechens. In Kashmir, the fact is that Indian forces have long prevented a reign of terror. Kashmiri Muslims disappear after being "detained" by Indian security forces. If they are lucky enough to ever return, it is only after suffering severe torture. Many are killed either "while resisting arrest" or "while attempting to escape"—euphemisms applied with impunity by the occupying forces.

No sooner had India and Pakistan become independent than hostilities began for the possession of Kashmir. It is said that the Kashmir dispute has been the cause of two wars between

India and Pakistan. The two nuclear-armed nations have hardly ever had a week without an exchange of some kind of deadly weapons fire along the ceasefire line that exists between Indian Kashmir and Pakistani Kashmir. Huge numbers of soldiers have been killed and wounded in this game of "keep-away," but each side carefully keeps their losses a closely held secret. Billions of dollars have been spent in pursuit of continuing warfare between the two nations attempting to get an upper hand in the battle for Kashmir. At the same time, millions of people constantly face death by starvation and preventable diseases (or even nuclear war!).

India regards Kashmir as a part of India and, therefore, pride and honor are involved; for Pakistan, it is also a matter of "survival" because the only major river in Pakistan now originates in Kashmir.

At the time of independence, there were six major rivers flowing through Pakistan. All, except for the Indus River, flowed through the province of Punjab ("five waters") in North Eastern Pakistan. The Ravi, Sutlej, Beas, and Chenab rivers all flow from Indian East Punjab, and the Jhelum flows from Kashmir. In the 1950s, India drew up plans to divert the flow of some of the rivers that passed through Pakistan. After over nine years of negotiations, an agreement was then made that resulted in the "Indus Waters Treaty" of 1960. This treaty gave up three of the rivers, the Ravi, Beas, and Sutlej, for India's exclusive use, while the Indus, Jhelum, and Chenab were determined to be shared with Pakistan.

Currently, Pakistan is accused of supporting the "terrorists" in Kashmir. These are all largely Kashmiris supported by Pakistanis who are struggling to remove Indian rule from Kashmir. Pakistan supports them by providing protection, shelter, and military support. This is no different from Indian support of rebels in areas of Pakistan like Baluchistan, the North-West Frontier Province, and so on. In fact, the largest support India gave to any rebel movement in Pakistan (which pales in comparison with anything Pakistan has done in India) was to the Bangladesh Freedom Fighters. This support first began in 1971, when India began providing shelter to the Mukti Bahini, the Bangladesh Liberation Army, until war was declared between India and Pakistan, resulting in Bangladesh independence. In hindsight, this was a just war for India to be involved in, as the Bengalis were oppressed and near-genocidal action was being taken against them by the (Western) Pakistani Army. One could make a similar argument for the Kashmiris of today and for support of their liberation movements.

Since independence, India has dissolved at least three popularly elected state governments of Kashmir. The Muslim governments of Kashmir failed to toe the Indian line by demanding more and more autonomy, so India imposed presidential rule over them, each time lasting for years. During the last sixty years of war and terror between India and Pakistan, only a few voices have been heard demanding Kashmir for Kashmiris—and both sides ignored them. Why did they not vacate Kashmir and leave it for the Kashmiris to rule? Such a step would have led to the first rapprochement between the two warring nations. It would also have allowed the beleaguered Kashmiris their first opportunity to attempt to live and prosper in peace.

A Kashmir with open borders would give people from India and Pakistan opportunities to meet, promote mutual understanding, and invest there in joint ventures. With the elimination of tensions in Kashmir would come a scaling back of arms and, perhaps, demilitarized borders. All three nations spring from the same source; families have been split among the three sides and even culturally the similarities far outweigh the differences.

Resolving the Kashmir issue may be the first and greatest step in preventing many future wars and separatist movements in South and Central Asia.

Nuclear Proliferation Threats

There has been much worldwide commentary on whether or not Islamic terror groups such as al Qaeda are searching for the means to develop weapons of mass destruction (WMD). Pakistan has had a thriving nuclear program since the 1970s, and its leading scientist Dr. Abdul Qadeer Khan has also provided much-needed assistance to the Iranian nuclear program. Through the support and financing of the Pakistan government, Khan was in control of the Khan Research Laboratories. The U.S. CIA is of the belief that Khan may have been peddling nuclear technology to unfriendly countries and terrorist groups like al Qaeda. A vast majority of Pakistanis view Khan as a celebrity figure who donated money to charities throughout the country. According to the 2015 *Nuclear Notebook Report* by Bulletin of the Atomic Scientists, Pakistan now has a stockpile of 110–130 warheads, compared with 90–110 in 2011. The Nuclear Notebook, one of the most authoritative sources of information on Pakistan's nuclear capabilities, also said that Pakistan continues to expand its nuclear arsenal and production of fissile material.

ISLAMIC MILITANCY

Since 9-11 and up until his resignation in August 2008, President Pervez Musharraf had pledged support to the War on Terror and had gone on record that he would deal with Islamic terrorists who reside within Pakistan's borders. Most of the arrests of al Qaeda-linked suspects have occurred in Karachi. Official reports target Karachi as being home to more than four hundred and seventeen well-known terror cells and operatives from differing sectarian and militant organizations. Karachi has a population in excess of fourteen million with more than a thousand religious schools and ten thousand mosques. Many former Taliban fighters fled from the Afghan war to the border towns of Pakistan's northwest frontier and spread into Karachi, a fertile recruiting ground for misguided youths for jihad. When the Taliban controlled Afghanistan, a large number of Pakistanis trained for jihad in Taliban-supported training camps and the numbers, which cannot be confirmed, are thought to be over thirty thousand such fighters over the years. Following 9-11, the Pakistani government cracked down on militant fund-raising and focused more specifically on those groups supporting jihad in Kashmir. One such terror organization is the Lashkar-e-Jhangvi (LJ), an extreme Sunni group that has its roots in a sectarian movement calling itself Sipah-e-Sahaba Pakistan. With sectarian violence the group's goal, its main subjects for attack have been mostly those from the Shia religious sect. The group had ties with the Taliban regime in Afghanistan and aided many fighters returning through the northwest frontier cities of Peshawar and Rawalpindi. It was this terror group that had made attempts on former President Musharraf's life.

The Jaish-e-Mohammed (JeM, the Army of Mohammed), an Islamic extremist group based in Pakistan, was formed by Masood Azhar upon his release from prison in India in 2000. Azhar's release resulted from the hijacking of an Indian Airlines flight, which had similar modus operandi to the attacks that took place on 9-11. In the Indian Airlines hijacking, the terrorists slit passengers' throats with knives smuggled onto the flight and then stormed the cockpit. Masood Azhar was released from prison in India in exchange for the one hundred and fifty-five passengers on board the flight.

JeM's aim is to unite Kashmir with Pakistan. It is politically aligned with the radical political party, Jamiat Ulema-e-Islam Fazlur Rehman faction (JUI-F). In October 2001, the United States announced the addition of JeM to the Treasury Department's Office of Foreign Asset Control's (OFAC) list, which includes organizations that are believed to support terrorist groups and have assets in U.S. jurisdiction that can be frozen or controlled. In 2001, JeM was added to the U.S. list of Foreign Terrorist Organizations. The group is located primarily in Peshawar and has its operations in Kashmir. Most of its support members come from Pakistani or are former Taliban/Afghan fighters. The leadership of JeM has threatened to kill India's prime minister in its bid to rid Jammu and Kashmir of Indian forces. JeM's extensive organization in Pakistan has set up schools for jihad at its offices throughout the country, and with its external links to the former Taliban regime in Afghanistan as well as Sunni terror cells in Pakistan, JeM will continue to be a threat in the region. JeM uses suicide attacks as well as more conventional attacks with light weapons and improvised explosive devices (IEDs). Although banned in Pakistan since 2002, the group appears to operate openly in many areas of Pakistan.

NEPAL

Nepal is a region probably most famously known for Sir Edmund Hillary's conquering of Mount Everest, rather than a hotbed for political violence and insurgency (Figure 11-12). The insurgency in this poverty-ridden kingdom came from a Maoist movement looking to replace the monarchy with a Communist state. Democratic reforms seemed unlikely and King Gyanendra announced a state of emergency in February 2005, following his dismissal of the government, and has become increasingly reliant on the Royal Army, which had been less than effective in fighting the rebel insurgents. The king had also relied on political collaboration with India, which feared that the insurgency could spread there with support from left-wing groups. In May 2008, the end finally came to the two hundred and forty year reign of the Nepal Royal family, following which the Nepalese government reached a peace accord with the Maoist rebels, in a country desperate for peace.

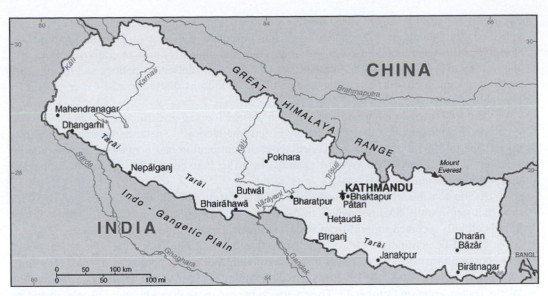

FIGURE 11-12 Map of Nepal. *Source:* Central Intelligence Agency, *The World Factbook, 2008*.

Nepal was declared a republic by the Constitutional Assembly, which voted to abolish the Hindu monarchy, which had been in control of the country for over two centuries. King Gyanendra came to the throne soon after a large number of the Royal family was massacred in 2001. Conspiracy theories abounded about his involvement, which would only sour his relationship with his subjects. His sacking of the government and his embarking on a period of autocratic rule can have only hastened his demise. In 2011, most insurgent and terrorist activity faded away and most Maoists laid down their weapons. Elections were held in November 2013 in which the Nepali Congress won the majority of seats but in early 2014 formed a coalition government with the second placed Communist Party and a new Constitution came into effect in 2015.

SRI LANKA

The Democratic Socialist Republic of Sri Lanka is an island in the Indian Ocean, south of India. It is slightly larger than West Virginia and was known as Ceylon until 1972 (Figure 11-13). Sri Lanka was the center of Buddhist civilization in the third century B.C. and still has a strong Buddhist majority (sixty-nine percent), with minority representation by Hindus (fifteen percent), Christians (eight percent), and Muslims (eight percent), distributed among an estimated population of more than 18,700,000. As of 2001, the Sinhalese constitute seventy-four percent of Sri Lanka's population, Tamils are eighteen percent, Muslims seven percent and Burghers comprise most of the rest of the population.

The Portuguese first settled on this island in 1505, followed by the Dutch in 1658. The British arrived in 1796 and made it a colony of the British Empire in 1853. Sri Lanka was granted independence in 1948. The Ceylonese government resisted an insurrection by terrorists attempting its overthrow in 1971.

LIBERATION TIGERS OF TAMIL EELAM—LTTE

The Tamils of Sri Lanka constitute a distinct nation and form a social entity with their own history, tradition, culture, language, and traditional homeland. The Tamil people call their nation "Tamil Eelam." Founded in 1976, the **Liberation Tigers of Tamil Eelam (LTTE)** was the most powerful Tamil group in

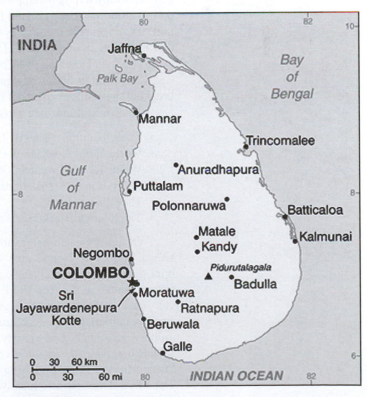

FIGURE 11-13 Map of Sri Lanka. *Source:* Central Intelligence Agency, *The World Factbook, 2008*.

Sri Lanka and used overt and illegal methods to raise funds, acquire weapons, and publicize its cause of establishing an independent Tamil state. Frequent episodes of Sinhalese nationalism during this time also limited the ability of many Tamils to find education or employment according to their expectations and the international climate of revolutionary politics and national liberation movements had its attractions. Some of the conditions that generated the conflict have changed, some never will.[12]

The LTTE began its armed conflict with the Sri Lankan government in 1983 and relied on a guerrilla strategy that included the use of terrorist tactics.[13] The armed uprisings began to take shape in 1983 as Tamils complained about discrimination and demanded an autonomous state for Tamils and so began a quarter century of conflict between the Tamils and the Sinhalese-dominated government of Sri Lanka.

As the conflict worsened, Tamils fled to India and further afield with more than two hundred thousand Tamils having sought political asylum in the West, many in Canada. The Sri Lanka Tamils initially received support from India and Indian Tamil groups in South India.

The LTTE continued its terrorist activities through the 1990s, attacking government troops and economic infrastructure targets and assassinating political opponents. The LTTE's most spectacular terrorist attack in 1997 was a truck bombing directed at the newly opened Colombo World Trade Center on October 15. The explosion injured more than a hundred people, including many foreigners, and caused significant damage to nearby buildings. Eighteen people, including LTTE suicide bombers, hotel security guards, and Sri Lankan security forces, died in the explosion. Sri Lankan authorities shot two of the terrorists as they tried to escape, and another three killed themselves to avoid capture. One of the bombers lobbed a grenade into a monastery as he fled the scene, killing one monk. In two separate incidents in June, in the Trincomalee area, the LTTE assassinated two legislators and nine other civilians.

During the summer months of 1997, naval elements of the LTTE conducted several attacks on commercial shipping, including the abduction of the crew of an empty passenger ferry and setting it on fire. The captain and a crewmember, both Indonesian, were released after only three days. The LTTE stormed a North Korean cargo ship after it delivered a shipment of food and other goods for civilians on the Jaffna Peninsula, killing one of the vessel's thirty-eight North Korean crewmembers in the process. The ship's North Korean captives were freed five days later and eventually returned to the vessel. The LTTE also hijacked a shipment of more than thirty two thousand mortar rounds bound for delivery to the Sri Lankan military. In September, the LTTE used rocket-propelled grenades to attack a Panamanian-flagged, Chinese-owned merchant ship that had been chartered by a U.S. chemical company to load minerals for export. As many as twenty people, including five Chinese crewmembers, were reported killed, wounded, or missing.

The United States designated LTTE a Foreign Terrorist Organization, pursuant to the orders of the Antiterrorism and Effective Death Penalty Act of 1996.[14]

Known Sri Lankan terrorist front organizations included the following:

- The Liberation Tigers of Tamil Eelam (LTTE)
- World Tamil Association (WTA)
- World Tamil Movement (WTM)
- Federation of Associations of Canadian Tamils (FACT)
- The Ellalan Force
- The Internet Black Tigers (IBT)[15]

Of all of these organizations, the LTTE was by far the most powerful Tamil group in Sri Lanka. The LTTE group's elite "Black Tiger Squad" conducted suicide bombings against many important targets, and all rank-and-file members carried a cyanide capsule to kill themselves rather than be caught. The LTTE was insular and highly organized, with its own intelligence service, naval element (the Sea Tigers), and women's political and military wings. The LTTE integrated a battlefield insurgent strategy with a terrorist program that targeted key government and military personnel, the economy, and public infrastructure. Political assassinations included the suicide bombing attacks against Sri Lankan President Ranasinghe Premadasa in 1993 and Indian Prime Minister Rajiv Gandhi in 1991 (the group's only known terrorist act outside Sri Lanka). The LTTE detonated two massive truck bombs directed against the Sri Lankan economy, one at the Colombo Central Bank in January 1996 and another at the Colombo World Trade Center, as mentioned previously. The LTTE also attacked infrastructure targets such as commuter trains, buses, oil tanks, and power stations. Its preference was to attack vulnerable government facilities and then withdraw before reinforcements arrive, or to time its attacks to take best advantage of security lapses on holidays, at night, or in the early morning. The LTTE is also known to have recruited approximately ten thousand-armed combatants in Sri Lanka, with approximately three to six thousand members that formed a trained cadre of fighters. The group also had a significant overseas support structure for fund-raising, weapons procurement, and propaganda activities.

The Tigers controlled most of the northern and eastern coastal areas of Sri Lanka but conducted operations throughout the island. Headquartered in the Wanni region, LTTE leader Velupillai Prabhakaran established an extensive network of checkpoints and informants to keep track of any outsiders who entered the group's area of control. The LTTE's overt organizations supported Tamil separatism by lobbying foreign governments and the United Nations. They also used international contacts to procure weapons, communications, and bomb-making equipment. The LTTE exploited large Tamil communities in North America, Europe, and Asia to fund its fighters in Sri Lanka. Information obtained since the mid-1980s indicates that some Tamil communities in Europe were also involved in narcotics smuggling. The LTTE learned well from the tactics employed by the IRA in Northern Ireland.

Throughout 2006 and 2007, fighting escalated between elements of the LTTE and the Sri Lankan military in spite of an agreed ceasefire. The Tamil leader, Velupillai Prabhakaran, announced the commencement of the Fourth Eelam War in November 2006, while the Sri Lankan government only made the announcement in January 2008 that the ceasefire was at an end.

Actions by the Sri Lankan military throughout 2007 did little to cause the LTTE to waiver in their demands for a Tamil homeland. The Sri Lankan military gained the upper hand in the Eastern Province and overran rebel positions at Sampur, just south of the port of Trincomalee, plus gaining control of two key coastal towns, greatly restricting the LTTE's ability to resupply its eastern forces from the north. The military launched Operation Definite Victory, clearing the LTTE from the Ampara district before moving on to other rebel controlled towns. The LTTE seemed powerless to respond after their camps were overrun one after the other.[16]

The ebb and flow of success in insurgent operations was reality in this theater of war, and the Tamils continued to attack government forces and use new methods of attack to undermine the government as much as to publicize their presence (Figure 11-14). In March 2007, the LTTE launched its first aerial attack using light passenger aircraft to carry bombs and successfully attacked an air force base outside the capital Colombo. The same year they launched a commando raid on an air base north of Colombo, and while all the commandos were killed, they managed to destroy a large number of Sri Lankan Air Force aircraft on the ground, including two attack helicopters.

More than seventy thousand have died since the conflict started in 1983.

The success of the Tigers was in many ways due to their fund-raising abilities abroad, with a flourishing and loyal Tamil diaspora in Western countries, including Canada, the United States, Australia, and Great Britain. Vast numbers of Tamils have fled as refugees to the West and are "taxed" by the LTTE, who also engage in criminal activities for fund-raising including widespread credit card fraud. Most weapons brought into the area originated from dealers in Southeast Asia and then were smuggled in by a small flotilla of LTTE-operated ships.

TERRORIST ATTACK BRIEF

Terrorist Group—LTTE (Tamil Tigers)

Case Facts—In a nighttime attack mounted by members of LTTE, a small craft had mingled with fishing boats near Trincomalee and silently approached a Sri Lankan Naval fast-attack vessel, ramming it and setting off explosives. The Sri Lankan vessel was severely damaged and thirteen seamen were killed in the blast.

Investigation—The incident came at the end of almost four years of ceasefire between LTTE and government forces. The Sri Lankan FAV sank shortly after the explosion and only two seamen were rescued alive. Tamil tigers use not only conventional bombs to target government forces but also their own version of Navy and Air Force to target shipping and Air Force targets. The tigers are known to frequently use suicide bombers both male and female.

FIGURE 11-14 Terrorist Attack Brief—Naval attack Trincomalee, Sri Lanka—January 7, 2005. *Source:* Ethnic Conflict History of LLTE attacks, http://sricolama.com/ethnic-conflict.html?start=3.

Defections from the LTTE leadership and successes on the military side enabled a military campaign in the spring of 2009 to overrun almost all but a small enclave of Tamils in the coastal region. Two Army divisions trapped the Tamils fighters, and their leader, Velupillai Prabhakaran, was killed by the military. On May 17, 2009, the Tigers formally laid down their weapons and twenty-six years of conflict were at an end. Unfortunately for this small country, the spectre of Islamic State has appeared with several Sri Lankans from the minority population of Muslims migrating to Iraq and Syria to fight with Islamic State. The Sri Lankans were likely recruited through online forums as IS continues to spread its propaganda machine. While several moved to Syria in 2015, they are being portrayed in IS propaganda as heroes of the Caliphate in the hope that this becomes a recruiting and rallying call to Sri Lankan Muslims. In Sri Lanka itself, several prominent Muslim associations have denounced Islamic State and any Sri Lankan Muslims planning to join IS.

AFGHANISTAN

The Taliban

The Taliban ("Students of Islamic Knowledge Movement") ruled Afghanistan from 1996 until 2001. They came to power during Afghanistan's long civil war. Although they managed to hold ninety percent of the country's territory, their policies—including their treatment of women and support of terrorists—ostracized them from the world community. Put into context of Afghan history, the rise of the Taliban, though not their extremism is unsurprising. Afghanistan is a devoutly Muslim nation; ninety percent of its population is Sunni Muslims (Figure 11-15). Religious schools were established in Afghanistan after Islam arrived in the seventh century, and *Taliban* became an important part of the social fabric: running schools, mosques, shrines, and various religious and social services and serving as mujahideen when necessary.

After the 9-11 attacks, the U.S. government pressed the Taliban government of Afghanistan to turn over bin Laden and the al Qaeda leadership who had sought sanctuary in the mountainous regions of the country. To no one's surprise, the Taliban refused to give him to the United States. Their refusal was the signal for the aerial bombing of Taliban military sites. By November 21, the Taliban had lost control of Kabul, and by early December, had been completely routed. In 2008, more than five years as Afghanistan's leader, President Hamid Karzai came to power; he still had only marginal control over large swaths of the country. The Taliban continues to fund its insurgency through the drug trade. An August 2007 report by the United Nations found that Afghanistan's opium production doubled in two years and that the country supplies ninety-three percent of the world's heroin.

Islamic extremists from around the world, including Egyptians, Algerians, Palestinians, and Saudis used Afghanistan as a training base from which to operate. The Taliban, as well as many of the other combatants in the Afghan civil war, facilitated the operation of training and indoctrination facilities for non-Afghans in the territories they controlled. Several Afghani factions provided logistic support, free passage, and sometimes passports, to members of various terrorist organizations. Many of these individuals, in turn, were involved in fighting in Bosnia and Herzegovina, Chechnya, Tajikistan, Kashmir, the Philippines, and parts of the Middle East. That the Taliban is a ruthless organization is beyond question, and the tribal warlords on the other hand were often as equally vicious. One such leader was Mullah Dadullah, who was described in intelligence reports as being the military mastermind of the Taliban insurgency. Dadullah had, until his death in 2007, been front and center of the military activities of the Taliban. Dadullah traveled to Pakistan to

FIGURE 11-15 Map of Afghanistan. *Source:* Central Intelligence Agency, *The World Factbook, 2008.*

raise money and arms for the insurgency and focused his attention on the **Madrassas** in Karachi to recruit his fighters. In 2003, Mullah Omar released a tape naming him as a member of the new ten-man leadership council that would "confront the occupation." He led the Taliban's day-to-day operations in the south and southwestern Afghanistan, but, more importantly, he was one of the closest links between the Taliban insurgency and al Qaeda. As part of his fund-raising efforts, he was responsible for the increase in kidnappings in the region, which provided a good level of income for the Taliban. He was also the Taliban's spokesman for the progress of the insurgency and was at ease dealing with the news media, especially when it came to detailing his involvement in training suicide bombers, executing suspected collaborators, and beheading hostages. On many occasions in 2006, he was listed as killed in actions against the U.S. and Afghan forces. He was a ruthless fighter and particularly so in battles against the Northern Alliance when the U.S. war to remove the Taliban started in 2001. He had been sentenced to life in prison in absentia by a Pakistani Court for attempting to assassinate Maulana Shirani, then a member of the Pakistan Parliament. Mullah Dadullah lost a leg when he trod on a landmine in 1994; however, this did not deter him from his personal involvement in the fighting with the then Afghan government forces and also against the Northern Alliance. He was killed in a clash with British and U.S. Special Forces in Helmand Province on May 13, 2007. He was a close friend and ally of the Taliban leader Mullah Omar and his loss was at the time a serious blow to the Taliban.

The realities of the War on Terror and the Afghanistan campaign that filtered out after the ousting of the Taliban may have punctured the mood that prevailed in October 2001. The idea that the Afghanistan campaign was a possible new strategy for warfare, based on the employment of massive, precision-guided airpower with little commitment of ground troops, has obviously been revisited. Large numbers of Afghan civilians died, owing to less-than-precise bombing, and scores of people allied to the United States were targeted and killed by U.S. forces, acting on sometime faulty intelligence. Relying on Afghan mercenaries to do the fighting on the ground resulted in Osama bin Laden's escape from the Tora Bora Mountains. And when U.S. troops did engage in close-quarters fighting with the Taliban/al Qaeda forces in the Gardez area near Pakistan in early March 2002, an enemy that was assumed to be on the run bloodied them.

NATO formally ceased military operations on December 28, 2014, and handed control of military ops to the Afghan government and military. This would usher in a period of dramatic change as we now witness a resurgent Taliban in the north and the presence of Islamic State in the country. These two factors and the fall of the strategically important city of Kunduz in September 2015, along with the U.S. and NATO forces in very steep decline, the country will fall prey to both Taliban and IS attacks and land grabs. Attacks on government facilities by both sides continued into 2016 and while reports emerged of some IS insurgents being killed by Afghan forces it has not stemmed the tide of insurgent activity. In the meantime, the Taliban will continue. Perhaps it is not just coincidence that Kunduz was the first city to fall at the hands of Afghan Mujahideen after the Soviet withdrawal of Afghanistan in 1979.

AL QAEDA (THE BASE)

Al Qaeda was established in the 1980s by Osama bin Laden, originally recruited by the CIA in its efforts against the Soviet occupation of Afghanistan. Al Qaeda was bin Laden's creation from fighters who had been recruited to confront the Soviet forces in Afghanistan. Assisted by the Palestinian cleric Abdullah Azzam, they recruited thousands of fighters for the mujahideen. Once the Soviets withdrew, these fighters were dispersed to follow bin Laden's wider goals of a holy war against Western democracies that were invading Muslim lands. Throughout the 1990s, few in the United States or elsewhere knew of bin Laden, but with attacks on U.S. embassies in Africa, the bombing of the USS *Cole* in Yemen, and ultimately the 9-11 attacks on New York and Washington, bin Laden became the most hunted man on earth. The United States attacked his bases in Afghanistan and invaded the country; at every turn bin Laden was able to escape to the lawless tribal areas bordering Pakistan and even into Pakistan itself. The United States considers al Qaeda to be the biggest terrorist threat that it faces and almost every terrorist attack since 9-11 bears the hallmarks of al Qaeda involvement. Al Qaeda is believed to have terror cells in more than 100 countries with many thousands of sympathizers and supporters in Western countries. It has also inspired al Qaeda affiliates to take up the cause of jihad and adopt the al Qaeda name. It also maintains close ties with the following terror organizations that follow the same Sunni dominated ideology:

- Egyptian Islamic Jihad
- The Libyan Islamic Fighting Group
- Islamic Army of Aden (Yemen)
- Jama'at al-Tawhid wal Jihad (Iraq)
- Lashkar-e-Taiba and Jaish-e-Mohammed (Kashmir)
- Islamic Movement of Uzbekistan
- Al Qaeda in the Islamic Maghreb (Algeria) (formerly Salafist Group for Call and Combat)
- Armed Islamic Group (Algeria)
- Abu Sayyaf Group (Malaysia, Philippines)
- Jemaah Islamiyah (Southeast Asia)

On May 1, 2011, a team of U.S. Navy SEALs tracked bin Laden to a house in Abbottabad in Pakistan, where he was shot and killed; the value of this killing has yet to be felt. Many young and impressionable followers of bin Laden held the view that their inspirational leader was invincible, and having slipped out of reach of the United States for more than ten years, his death will certainly be a blow to many of his followers. His replacement and long-time deputy, Ayman al-Zawahiri, does not have the same charisma as bin Laden, but the global movement may well be capable of overcoming this difficulty. Bin Laden will undoubtedly be considered a martyr, and many more attacks on the West will be carried out in his name. What is clear is that al Qaeda has been able to adapt when faced with adversity and remains a dangerous and adaptive organization. Al Qaeda promotes an ideology that unites a variety of grievances including that there is a global conspiracy led by the United States and Israel against Muslims and Islam. The terrorists draw their inspiration from a global message that has been articulated by figures such as Osama bin Laden. The message is uncompromising and asserts that the West represents a threat to Islam, that loyalty to religion and loyalty to democratic institutions and values are incompatible, and that violence is the only proper response. Al Qaeda members adopt an extreme interpretation of Islamic teaching, which they believe places an obligation on believers to fight and kill to achieve their aims. Most Muslims and the world's leading Islamic scholars reject this position. The terrorists point to the depravations suffered by Muslims and label the United States and Israel (Crusaders and Zionists) responsible for those depravations.[17] They assert that the solution to this problem is to eradicate Western influences from the Muslim world, replace existing governments with a supranational "Caliphate" and impose a strict and exclusive form of government based on their particular interpretation of Sunni Islam. The governments of many Muslim states are branded as "apostates" who do not adhere to its definition of "true Islam." Secular republics and religion-based monarchies alike are attacked on this basis. By branding them as guilty of apostasy—an offense for which Islamic law prescribes a death sentence—the terrorists justify taking violent action against the governments and citizens of those states, even though they are coreligionists.

Al Qaeda strongly objects to democratic elections in Muslim lands and in particular in Afghanistan, Iraq, and Palestine. It claims that democracy is a rival "religion" and that principles such as freedom of speech and freedom of religion are equivalent to apostasy, punishable by death. In al Qaida's view, the only acceptable form of government is a "Caliphate" based exclusively on Sharia law.

Al Qaeda is not a monolithic organization, nor is it merely a "brand name." It is, instead, a movement consisting of a "network of networks." The al Qaeda movement can be characterized as comprising three elements:

Al Qaeda core: consists of the surviving members of al Qaeda's senior leadership and other operatives under their direct control. This is essentially the remnant of the original pre-9-11 al Qaeda organization. It has been badly disrupted by the worldwide campaign against terrorism, but it remains active in planning attacks and recruiting operatives.

Al Qaeda-linked networks: consisting of terrorist networks that share al Qaeda's ideology and are in occasional contact with the al Qaeda core. The "fertilizer plot" terrorist cell convicted in April 2007 is an example of such a network; one of its members had travelled to Pakistan for terrorist training and is believed to have had direct contact with al Qaeda figures.

Al Qaeda-inspired networks and cells: consists of groups that share al Qaeda's ideology but do not have current contacts or links with al Qaeda. One such terrorist network carried out the 2004 Madrid train bombings; another such network, the Indonesian terrorist group Jemaah Islamiyah, carried out the Bali bombings of 2002 and 2005.[18]

Al Qaeda Operations

A large number of attacks carried out by al Qaeda have been both spectacular and unforgettable for the impact they have created:

- **1998**—simultaneous bombings of U.S. embassies in Nairobi and Dar es Salaam
- **2000**—suicide bombing of USS *Cole*—Yemen
- **2001**—airline hijackings in the United States—aircraft flown into World Trade Center and the Pentagon in Washington
- **2002**—attempt to shoot down passenger airliner in Kenya with surface to air missile
- **2003**—car bomb attacks in Riyadh, Saudi Arabia
- **2005**—simultaneous suicide bomb attacks on London, U.K. subway system
- **2006**—attack on Saudi oil refining facility
- **2007**—failed bomb attack on Pakistan's prime minister, Benazir Bhutto
- **2007**—car bomb attacks in London, the United Kingdom, and Glasgow International Airport
- **2009**—attempted and failed suicide bomb attack on Northwest Airliner en route to Detroit

Bin Laden will be remembered by history as the man who revived the idea of pan Islam. This had long been derailed in the Arab world by national self-interest and the great flirtation with socialism. From socialism came secularism and the one-party state where democracy failed. Al Qaeda exemplified bin Laden's jihadist version of Islam and for a while appealed to the poor and disenfranchised. Across the globe, local and regional groups found common cause in the mantra of global jihad. Bin Laden's appeal also rested on the fact that he had brought down one superpower in Afghanistan and could do so again with the United States.[19] While al Qaeda as a core organization centered in Afghanistan may be on the wane—bin Laden's death has done little if anything to deter jihad. In fact, since his death the rise of jihad and a proclaimed Caliphate in the Middle East has brought Muslims to the gathering call of al-Baghdadi. When the United States invaded Iraq in 2003, a country considered the Muslim historical heartland—bin Laden had always viewed his long-term strategy as fighting a defensive long war against the West— here was the opportunity being afforded to not just al Qaeda but all jihad-minded groups and individuals. Iraq would quickly become a magnet for jihad and as money poured in, the number of foreign fighters traveling there rapidly surpassed the number that were in Afghanistan. The Arab Spring that characterized 2011 and saw regimes fall did not inspire the growing acceptance of jihadi ideology as much as the failure of democratic reform efforts and the government counteractions that threw many into the arms of the jihadists. When nonviolent protests are met with violence, civil protesters respond, and that is what happened in Syria, Libya, Yemen, and Iraq, where Shiite authority violently put down Sunni protests. This spiral of violence provides a recruiting bonanza for jihadist groups.

TALIBAN-LINKED INSURGENTS—HAQQANI NETWORK

Groups confronting NATO coalition forces are primarily either al Qaeda or aligned with the Taliban, and one of the most daring and confrontational groups is the **Haqqani Network**, which is based in North Waziristan but within close proximity to the Afghan border. Haqqani is led by Jalaluddin Haqqani and his son, Sirajuddin Haqqani. Jalaluddin fought with the Taliban against the Soviets and rose high up in the Taliban movement after the Soviet withdrawal and is believed to have had close ties with **Mullah Omar**. While the father is believed to be either seriously ill or possibly dead, his son has taken over as operational commander of the Haqqani Network. The methods of attack have been suicide bombings, truck and car bombings, and raids on government and police buildings dressed as either police or military—these raids have also targeted banks and prominent hotels occupied by Westerners. Most always their actions leave a trail of bodies in their wake and appear more concerned about a large body count of civilians than military. It is believed the group through the father has support from Arab countries in the Persian Gulf and members travel to those regions. There are concerns also that this group has influence with the Pakistan ISI, which may be providing strategic information to Haqqani. The Haqqani commanders have been targeted and have always managed to avoid capture.

ISLAMIC EMIRATE OF AFGHANISTAN

When the Soviet Union was forced out of Afghanistan in the late 1980s, the country was at the mercy of the tribal warlords. From 1930 to 1978 was likely the most peaceful period in Afghanistan' modern history but that would end with a pro-Soviet communist coup, and their inability to maintain any control, cohesion, or administrative responsibility ultimately led to the Soviet invasion. This, in turn, inspired an American-led counter interventionist strategy, implemented through Pakistan as the "frontline state," in support of the Afghan Islamic resistance forces (the *Mujahideen*). The Soviets were forced to leave Afghanistan by the end of the 1980s, and their protégé regime collapsed in Kabul in April 1992.[20] A country that had suffered over a decade of deprivation welcomed the control and discipline that the Taliban offered. Mullah Omar with the support of Pakistan's ISI set the Taliban up almost as its proxy militia in Afghanistan. The Taliban imposed its extreme religious doctrine including sharia on the population. When Osama bin Laden fled to Taliban-controlled Afghanistan in 2006, he was welcomed along with his money and Arab influence. During the 1990s, the United States was more preoccupied with accessing oil and gas rights and deny them to Iran, and if it had not been for the bin Laden-sponsored attacks on embassies in East Africa, the Taliban may have continued unabated for many more years to come. However, the subsequent missile attacks on Afghan targets in attempts to kill bin Laden did little to persuade the Taliban from dominating Afghanistan. The Taliban also offered training and support to Chechens seeking independence and even offered to open a diplomatic mission in Kabul. In 1999, Pakistan's General Pervez Musharraf overthrew the government in a bloodless coup. Musharraf originally agreed to help arrest bin Laden, but his influence failed to make that materialize. General Musharraf urged the international community to recognize the Taliban as the legitimate government of Afghanistan. As the threats against the West mounted, the United States had sanctions imposed by the UN—none of which had the slightest effect on the Taliban.

In early 2008, Mullah Omar still reigned supreme over the Taliban, who had changed their official name to the "Islamic Emirate of Afghanistan" in communiqués. He managed to avoid capture, but has found a way to appear in videos released to the Middle East media. In December 2007, rifts in the al Qaeda organization started to become public when Mullah Omar sacked Mansour Dadullah, the brother of Mullah Dadullah. Mansour was commander of the southern area of Afghanistan. Although it is unclear why he was removed, his references to "worldwide jihad" reflect an ideology akin to that of al Qaeda, rather than the more traditional Taliban focus on Afghanistan. He also was an advocate of extreme and controversial tactics seen as unpopular in Afghanistan. Dadullah was captured by Pakistan security forces as he and five others attempted to cross into Pakistan's southwestern Province of Baluchistan.

Washington's continued tilt toward Israel has not helped in shoring up the legitimacy of its Arab allies among their people. Israel is the great spoiler of the U.S. effort to manage the Middle East, and Israel can get away with it because it can rely on massive support in the U.S. Congress to blunt pressure from the U.S. Executive Branch. Indeed, the Afghan fiasco and Israel's continued intransigence, it can be argued, have combined to make Washington's strategic situation in the Middle East and the Persian Gulf worse rather than better. There have been no political or military gains in Southeast Asia, with Indonesia maintaining its distance from Washington and the U.S. buildup in the Philippines becoming more controversial by the day. The introduction of U.S. forces in some of the Central Asian republics—the so-called Stans—may, on the surface, seem to be a strategic plus, especially when one takes into consideration the energy reserves of the area. However, with the failure to achieve decisive military or political victory on any front, Washington's Central Asian deployment may actually be a case of overextension.

The impressions (real or imagined) that the United States is now actually working to undermine Islam is being strengthened by U.S. support of regimes in Uzbekistan and Turkmenistan. These regimes, like America's other ally, Turkey, are brutal in their suppression of Muslims and any practice of Islam. As the negative image of the United States grows throughout non-extremist Islam, so do acts of terrorism against Americans and U.S. facilities in Islamic regions.[21]

Drugs and the Taliban

The big question surrounding opium production in Afghanistan, in terms of international drug control efforts, was how to prevent the massive opium poppy harvest in Afghanistan from reaching global drug markets. And the more important question that follows is one of how to end decades of Afghanistan's dependency on opium growing at all. To fully understand the importance of the issue, one only needs to know that as recently as 2004 Afghanistan accounted for a huge proportion of the global production of opiates as well as for most of the heroin found in European markets.

Taliban authorities finally issued a ban on opium poppy cultivation, declaring it "non-Islamic." This ban resulted in a considerable decrease of opium production in 2001. There are plenty of theories as to the motivation of that oppressive regime's decision. Some believe that the Taliban wanted to escape a threat of new sanctions, while others speculate that it wanted to please the international community and relax its isolation. Many have said that the reason for the ban was that the Taliban simply wanted to increase the price of existing stockpiles from the record harvest in 1999, which was forty-six hundred metric tons and "next-to-the-best harvest" in 2000 of thirty-three hundred metric tons. Whatever its motivation, the Taliban's ban was effective. In 2001, the areas under opium poppy cultivation were reduced by ninety-one percent. If the ban had been maintained for another year, the existing stockpiles (estimated to amount to two or three years of production) would have melted down with all the predictable consequences: a gradual shortage of heroin in European markets; increase in prices and decrease in purity of the heroin offered; and even a higher demand for treatment. That historic opportunity in international drug control efforts is now in danger of being missed or, at least, delayed.

The period following the events of 9-11, and the subsequent fall of the Taliban regime, coincided with the opium poppy planting season in southern and eastern Afghanistan. Since the Taliban has been removed from power, the amount of land now used for opium production is larger than the corresponding total for coca cultivation in Latin America (Colombia, Peru, and Bolivia combined). In 2007, Afghanistan produced eighty-two hundred tons of opium, thirty-four percent more than was produced in 2006, thus accounting for ninety-three percent of the global opiates market! No other country has previously produced narcotics on such a massive and deadly scale. Quite clearly, opium production in Helmand and Kandahar provinces is being fuelled by the ongoing insurgency, with Helmand accounting for almost fifty percent of the production. In 2007, the Taliban controlled large swathes of Helmand and Kandahar provinces as well as along the border with Pakistan.[22]

Present and Future Challenges

In terms of the country's drug trade, some believe Afghanistan would be better off if the Taliban were still in power. The answer is clearly "no!" It was the Taliban regime that profited from the drug business for years and made Afghanistan a safe haven for international terrorist masterminds and created conditions for drug trafficking in the first place.

The Taliban regime seized control of the major opium producing areas of Afghanistan in 1996 and regularly collected taxes from the drug business (ten percent from producers and twenty percent from traders). It is difficult to imagine that in such a tightly controlled society, producing, selling, and stockpiling of literally thousands of tons of opium could have gone on throughout the 1990s without the complicity of the Taliban. Further proof of the regime's involvement in the growth of opium production is the fact that there were no recorded drug seizures in that country, while ninety percent of global seizures of heroin took place in neighboring Iran.

On January 17, 2001, Afghanistan's new interim authority head, Dr. Hamid Karzai, issued a ban that was even more comprehensive than the one issued by the Taliban. His decree banned not only cultivation but also processing and illicit use, smuggling, and trafficking of opium. At the time of the ban, most opium poppy fields had already been sown.

The illicit trade in opium is likely centered along the border with Pakistan and also involves trafficking in weapons and manpower. The presence of state-of-the-art weapons has not been as evident in Afghanistan as in Iraq. There is little use of missiles or surface-to-air missiles (SAMs) in the volatile Helmand province or around Kandahar. In addition, the numbers of fighters facing NATO troops has not increased, and British military estimates the Taliban insurgents to number between five and six thousand.

The Taliban and al Qaeda groups have mounted military attacks against U.S., Canadian, and British troops using varied tactics from hit-and-run assaults to suicide attacks, car and truck bombs, and the more sophisticated IED attacks. There has been little let up in the ongoing battles, and regular surges by U.S. troops serve to move Taliban elements from area to area. During 2011, there were hints and rumors of willingness on the part of the United States to talk terms with the Taliban. With over a decade of military operations failing to remove or dissuade the Taliban, Americans have grown war weary. In a speech from the White House in June 2011, President Obama made the following announcement:

> Al Qaeda is under more pressure than at any time since 9/11. Together with the Pakistanis, we have taken out more than half of al Qaeda's leadership. And thanks to our intelligence professionals and Special Forces, we killed Osama bin Laden, the only leader that al Qaeda had ever known. This was a victory for all who have served since 9/11 . . . . We do know that peace cannot come to a land that has known so much war without a political settlement. So as we strengthen the Afghan government and security forces, America will join initiatives that reconcile the Afghan people, including the Taliban. Our position on these talks is clear: They must be led by the Afghan government, and those who want to be a part of a peaceful Afghanistan must break from al Qaeda, abandon violence, and abide by the Afghan constitution. But, in part because of our military effort, we have reason to believe that progress can be made.

In spite of the above there is still hope that there may be reconciliation with the Taliban and the existing government, however, the Taliban announced in 2015, that its leader and founder Mullah Mohammad Omar was dead and had probably died in hospital in 2013. He was succeeded by his deputy Mullah Akhtar Mohammad Mansour who had served as the Taliban's aviation minister when they ruled Afghanistan from 1996–2001. 2016 was no less lethal for the Taliban when Mullah Akhtar Mohammad Mansour was killed by a U.S. drone strike in the Pakistan state of Baluchistan on May 21. Mansour likely gained his power base with the Taliban through his personal and high level links to Pakistan's ISI. Mansour's leadership was not without its own problems and challenges came from within the group. In March 2016, up to a hundred Taliban militants were reported to have been killed in Herat during clashes between rival Taliban factions. Reports of his own personal wealth have surfaced in Pakistan and he is purported to have holdings in Dubai and it is assumed the wealth he was able to generate came from drug dealing. No doubt that his targeted death at the hands of a U.S. drone was not communicated in advance with Pakistan. The relationship with the U.S. administration and Pakistan will remain tenuous as a result. This will remain a problem country for the foreseeable future with both the Taliban/al Qaeda and IS as front runners in what could be a long period of further internal destabilization for Afghanistan. As we look forward, al Qaeda has begun to move back into the region since the U.S. pullout in 2014 and with a resurgent Taliban and an emboldened al Qaeda needing to show it has still the power and ability to carry out attacks we may be asking ourselves what fifteen years of military presence has done to eradicate both the Taliban and al Qaeda in Afghanistan.

BURMA (MYANMAR)

Burma is a mysterious Southeast Asian nation that most people know very little about. Veterans of World War II will recall the Burma Road and the Flying Tigers, but most of us probably know little or nothing of today's Burma (Figure 11-16). Images of shining pagodas, elephants, and flying fish at play along the mighty Irrawaddy River, from Rudyard Kipling's famous poem "Road to Mandalay," may come to mind. But Burma's reality today has little in common with such romantic legends. For most of its modern history, following independence from Britain in 1948, Burma has been run by a military-controlled socialist regime that has isolated the country, wrecked its economy, and totally repressed its many diverse ethnic populations.

A massive and peaceful "people's power" demonstration movement demanded an end to the military dictatorship in 1988 and again in 2008. The army leadership reacted violently and swiftly to repress and quell this movement. To maintain the status quo, a new military junta, the State Law and Order Restoration Council (SLORC), seized direct power to quell any kind of movement toward democracy. Crowds of peaceful protesters were machine-gunned down by SLORC troops, and thousands were killed. For a few days, events in Burma captured world headlines but were soon replaced by sound bites about other world events in some more familiar locales. Global attention briefly picked up again, however, in December 1991, when Daw Aung San Suu Kyi, the long-detained democracy advocate and leading voice of freedom for Burma, was awarded the Nobel Peace Prize.

Still, most of the world has little interest in Burma. To further confuse the situation, the SLORC generals changed the country's long-standing official name (by decree and without public consultation) to Myanmar, a transliteration of the country's Burmese language name. And Burma's democratic opposition and powerful generals outright rejected the name and refused to recognize it. More confusion came in November 1997, when the generals renamed their own junta the State Peace and Development Council (SPDC) in hopes of improving their rapidly deteriorating and well-earned bad international image.

People who argue that trade and tourism can help promote respect for human rights are pressing for increased international involvement with the Burmese military regime. Some claimed that "constructive engagement" might convince the junta to fight drug trafficking and to reduce its reliance on China.[23] A few simply declared that business and human rights are separate issues that should not be mixed. The junta itself, backed by a few Asian autocrats, asserts that it respects human rights in an "Asian" or "Burmese" context and such internationally recognized standards do not apply in Burma. Among these critical human rights issues is the SPDC's continuing detention of opposition figures.

Ethnic Cleansing of Minority Groups—Muslims

Rohingya which is a Muslim minority in the Burmese state of Arakan State have been persecuted and ethnically cleansed over the past four years. Buddhist monks have helped fuel the unrest by urging attacks against the Rohingya.

FIGURE 11-16 Map of Burma. *Source:* Central Intelligence Agency, *The World Factbook, 2008.*

In 2012, following a bout of sectarian violence, the Burmese government destroyed mosques and conducted mass violent arrest and blocked all aid to displaced Muslim communities. On October 23, 2012, after months of meetings and public statements promoting ethnic cleansing, Arakanese mobs attacked Muslim communities in nine townships, razing villages, and killing residents while security forces stood aside or assisted the assailants.[24]

In the deadliest incident, on October 23, at least seventy Rohingya were killed in a daylong massacre in Yan Thai village in Mrauk-U Township. Despite advance warning of the attack, only a small number of riot police, local police, and army soldiers were on duty to provide security, but they assisted the killings by disarming the Rohingya of their sticks and other rudimentary weapons they carried to defend themselves. Included in the death toll were twenty-eight children who were hacked to death, including thirteen under age five.[25] It is estimated that there remain around one hundred and fifty thousand displaced Muslims.

Central to the persecution of the Rohingya is the 1982 Citizenship Law, which effectively denies Burmese citizenship to Rohingya on discriminatory ethnic grounds. Because the law does not consider the Rohingya to be one of the eight recognized "national races," which would entitle them to full citizenship, they must provide "conclusive evidence" that their ancestors settled in Burma before independence in 1948, a difficult if not impossible task for most Rohingya families.

Resolution of the political impasse in Burma will eventually require real, substantive dialogue with the democratic opposition, including Aung San Suu Kyi and representatives of the ethnic groups. Arbitrary detentions are unjustifiable and will only worsen rather than solve the political crisis.

The United States has protested the policies of the Burmese government through its embassy in Rangoon and will continue to work with like-minded countries to press the Burmese government to take positive action, including the release of political prisoners and the initiation of a genuine dialogue with Aung San Suu Kyi and other NLD leaders.

The 1997 explosion of a parcel bomb at the house of a senior official in Burma's military-led government was the country's most significant terrorist event. On his visit to Burma, Bishop Tutu spoke of the blast that killed the adult daughter of Lieutenant-General Tin Oo, second-secretary of the ruling State Law and Order Restoration Council. No group or individual claimed responsibility for the attack, but the government of Burma attributes the act to Burmese antigovernment activists in Japan. The package containing the bomb bore Japanese stamps and postmarks. The Burmese expatriate and student community living in Japan denies any involvement in the incident.[26]

Burma is a poor country, with an average per capita GDP of approximately $406, at a weighted exchange rate, perhaps double that in terms of purchasing power parity. Progress on market reforms has been mixed and uneven. Beginning in 1988, the Burmese government partly opened the economy to permit expansion of the private sector and to attract foreign investment. Though modest economic improvement ensued, since 1993 the pace of economic reform has slowed and major obstacles to further reform persist. These include disproportionate military spending, extensive overt and covert state involvement in economic activity, state monopolization of leading exports, a bloated bureaucracy prone to arbitrary and opaque governance, and a poor education and physical infrastructure. In addition, due to international opposition and to the SPDC's unwillingness to cooperate fully with the International Monetary Fund (IMF), SPDC access to external credit from the IMF, World Bank, and Asian Development Bank continues to be blocked by sanctions. In September 1998, the World Bank announced that Burma had defaulted on its loan repayments. Some analysts think the laundering of drug profits in Burma's legitimate economy is extensive.

At the ASEAN meetings in Manila in July 1998, then U.S. secretary of state Albright, with Foreign Minister McKinnon of New Zealand, led a discussion of the political impasse in Burma. The meetings included representatives from Austria, Australia, Canada, Germany, Korea, Japan, and Great Britain and Burmese Foreign Minister Ohn Gyaw. The ministers expressed their concerns over the deteriorating conditions in Burma and demanded a speedy, peaceful resolution to the situation. They pressed for the immediate commencement of an SPDC dialogue with the democratic opposition, to include Aung San Suu Kyi. Secretary Albright continued to actively promote international constructive engagement with the SPDC toward an improved human rights climate.

It is clear that the SPDC is not eager to release its chokehold on the Burmese people, and the world's attention is often drawn away from such remote areas. In 2010, the military rule formally ended and has since then seen a slow but gradual move toward political reform culminating in Aung San Suu Kyi being elected to parliament in March 2012. A large number of pro-democracy parties took part in the elections, which have been described by observers as relatively transparent and without interference. Nonetheless, the military still retains significant power and presence within the country.

CAMBODIA

Cambodia is located on the Gulf of Thailand, between Thailand and Vietnam. It is a tiny country, slightly smaller than Oklahoma. The country is a land of rice paddies and forests and is dominated by the Mekong River (Figure 11-17). It has a population of about

FIGURE 11-17 Map of Cambodia. *Source:* Central Intelligence Agency, *The World Factbook, 2008.*

eleven million, ethnically composed of Khmer (ninety percent), Vietnamese (five percent), Chinese (one percent), and other (four percent). The religious preference is overwhelmingly Theravada Buddhist (ninety-five percent). Cambodia was called "Kampuchea" under the disastrous dictatorship of the **Khmer Rouge**.

The economy has been destroyed by decades of war, but it is slowly recovering. Government leaders are moving toward restoring fiscal and monetary discipline and have established good working relations with international financial institutions. Growth, starting from a low base, was strong between 1991 and 1996. Despite such positive developments, the reconstruction effort faces many tough challenges because of internal political divisions and the related lack of confidence of foreign investors.

Rural Cambodia, where ninety percent of about 9.5 million of the Khmer live, remains mired in poverty. The almost total lack of basic infrastructure in the countryside hinders development and contributes to a growing imbalance in growth between urban and rural areas over the near term. Moreover, the government's lack of experience in administering economic and technical assistance programs and rampant corruption among officials slow the growth of critical public sector investment. The decline of inflation from the 1992 rate of more than fifty percent is one of the bright spots in Cambodia's return to a peacetime period. In a somewhat interesting and unusual move, the Khmer Royal Armed Forces (KRAF) was created in 1993 by the merger of the Cambodian People's Armed Forces and the two non-Communist resistance armies (KRAF is also known as the Royal Cambodian Armed Forces, or RCAF).

Offshore islands and sections of the boundary with Vietnam remain in dispute and the maritime boundary with Vietnam is not clearly defined. Also, parts of the border with Thailand are now in dispute, as its boundaries are also not clearly defined. In the Golden Triangle, where Cambodia, Thailand, and Vietnam have mutual borders, heroin is being routed to the West, giving Cambodia the possibility of becoming a major money-laundering center. High-level, narcotics-related corruption reportedly involves the government, military, and police. There are small-scale opium, heroin, and amphetamine production operations in Cambodia and a larger production system of high-grade marijuana for the international market.

Hard-liners based in the Khmer Rouge stronghold at Anlong Veng regularly launched guerrilla-style attacks on government troops. Guerrillas are also suspected in two deadly attacks against ethnic Vietnamese civilians in Cambodia, but they have denied playing a role in the disappearance of two Filipino and two Malaysian employees of a logging company in 1997.

The death of former Khmer Rouge leader **Pol Pot** (Saloth Sar), in 1998, in the Thai-Cambodian border area, brought an end to one of the most chilling and bloody chapters of the twentieth century. During Pol Pot's four years of rule over Cambodia, from 1975 to 1978, the Khmer Rouge was suspected of killing as many as two million people through mass executions, starvation, and slave labor.

The genocide in Cambodia was the outcome of a complex historical development in which the pernicious ideological influence of Stalinism came together with the military bloodbath carried out against the people of Indochina. Pol Pot will be little mourned by the people of Cambodia.

The fate of British mine-clearing expert Christopher Howes, allegedly kidnapped by the Khmer Rouge in March 1996, remains unresolved. Unconfirmed reporting suggested Howes was with forces loyal to Pol Pot, and some Cambodian officials expressed fears publicly that he had been killed. In May 1996, Khmer Rouge leader Khieu Samphan denied any knowledge of Howes' whereabouts.

Incidents of terrorism in East Asia continue to increase. Continuing defections from the Khmer Rouge to Cambodian forces reduced the threat from the terrorist group, but guerrillas in the Cambodian provinces have been responsible for deadly attacks on foreigners. The unstable political situation in Cambodia has led to marked political violence. In October 1997, the secretary of state designated the Khmer Rouge as a Foreign Terrorist Organization pursuant to the Antiterrorism and Effective Death Penalty Act of 1996.

Pol Pot

The political activity of Pol Pot (Saloth Sar) began in post–World War II France, when Cambodia was part of its Indochina colony. The son of a relatively well-off peasant family, Pol Pot received a government scholarship in 1949 to study in Paris, where he gravitated with a number of his friends to the Stalinist circles around the French Communist Party. He returned to Phnom Penh in 1953, worked as a teacher, and was involved in the start of the embryonic Communist Party in Cambodia. Police repression under the government of Prince Norodom Sihanouk, the country's first postcolonial ruler, forced the party leaders to flee the capital in 1963 and seek sanctuary in the remote rural areas of the country.

It was only after the American intervention in Cambodia during the Vietnam War that Pol Pot and the Khmer Rouge began to get wider support. From a badly organized force of less than five thousand men in 1970, the Khmer Rouge expanded to an army of around seventy thousand. In April 1975, the Lon Nol dictatorship collapsed and Pol Pot came to power. The peasant-based army and Khmer Rouge leaders carried out policies of an anti-working-class character, which had far more in common with fascism than socialism. With an economy in shambles, Pol Pot was unable and unwilling to organize the feeding of the cities; he ordered the evacuation of Phnom Penh and other towns. The entire urban population of workers, intellectuals, civil servants, small shopkeepers, and others was driven into the countryside to harsh labor on irrigation schemes and other grandiose projects aimed at elevating agricultural production.

Under Pol Pot's leadership, the Khmer Rouge conducted a campaign of genocide in which an estimated two million people were killed during its four years in power in the late 1970s.[27]

The Khmer Rouge is a Communist insurgency that is trying to destabilize the Cambodian government. It is still engaged in a low-level insurgency against the Cambodian government. Although its victims are mainly Cambodian villagers, the Khmer Rouge has occasionally kidnapped and killed foreigners traveling in remote rural areas. One to two thousand members of the Khmer Rouge operate in outlying provinces in Cambodia, particularly in pockets along the Thailand border.

The Khmer Rouge may not be considered as a serious threat to the destabilization of Cambodia, but, some twenty years and three Cambodian regimes later, the National Army of Democratic Kampuchea, as the Khmer Rouge military is known, continues to wage warfare and terrorism from scattered jungle bases of operation in an attempt to regain control of Cambodia and resume its utopian experiment. Although there have been large-scale defections from the Khmer Rouge to Cambodian government forces since 1996, and the group suffered a significant split in 1997, it still may be considered dangerous.

THAILAND

The ancient Kingdom of Thailand sometimes referred to as "Siam" lies southeast of Burma and borders the Andaman Sea and the Gulf of Thailand. It is slightly more than twice the size of Wyoming. This country has a population of almost sixty million; the ethnic groupings are Thai (seventy-five percent), Chinese (fourteen percent), and other (eleven percent). Religious affiliations are Buddhism (ninety-five percent), Islam (3.8 percent), Christianity (0.5 percent), Hinduism (0.1 percent), and other (0.6 percent). Thailand is independent since 1238 A.D., and has never been colonized. A new constitution was approved in 1991 and amended in 1992 (Figure 11-18).

History Timeline—Thailand

Some significant dates:

- **June 24, 1932**—King Prajadhipok falls in a bloodless coup, and a constitutional monarchy and parliament are introduced. A succession of military dictators retains power for most of the period until 1973.
- **October 14, 1973**—four hundred thousand student-led protesters topple the military rulers, leading to a brief period of unstable democracy.

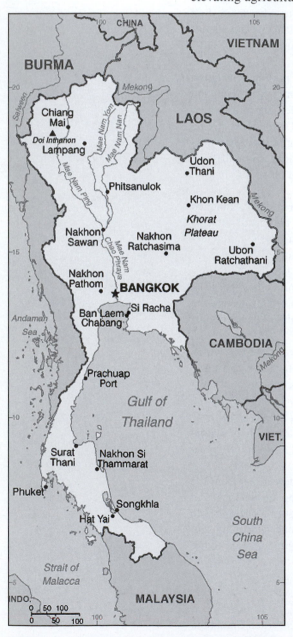

FIGURE 11-18 Map of Thailand. *Source:* Central Intelligence Agency, *The World Factbook, 2008.*

- **October 6, 1976**—A bloody crackdown on student protesters ends with the military returning to power.
- **March 1980**—Moderate military ruler Prem Tinsulanonda survives several coup attempts.
- **July 1988**—General Chatichai Choonhavan wins general elections.
- **February 1991**—General Sunthorn Kongsompong stages a coup and topples Chatichai's civilian government.
- **May 1992**—Junta member General Suchinda Kraprayoon assumes the prime minister's post, drawing hundreds of thousands of protesters into the streets of Bangkok demanding a return to civilian rule. The king intervenes and General Suchinda agrees to resign.
- **September 23, 1992**—Democrat party leader Chuan Leekpai is elected prime minister.
- **October 11, 1997**—The king signs the country's sixteenth "People's Constitution" into law, in a major development for political reform and democracy.
- **March 4, 2000**—The first senate elections are held under the new constitution.
- **January 6, 2001**—Telecommunications magnate Thaksin Shinawatra wins elections in a landslide to become the twenty-third prime minister.[28]
- **September 19, 2006**—Thaksin Shinawatra is accused of corruption and is ousted in a bloodless military coup and goes into exile in Dubai.

Thailand is one of the more advanced developing countries in Asia. It depends on exports of manufactured goods, including high-technology goods, and the development of the service sector to fuel the country's rapid growth, averaging nine percent since 1989. Most of Thailand's recent imports have been for capital equipment and raw materials, although imports of consumer goods are beginning to rise. Thailand's thirty-five percent domestic savings rate is a key source of capital for the economy, and the country is also benefiting from rising investment from abroad.

THAILAND'S INSURGENCY

Since 2001, the level and intensity of Thailand's insurgency has started to increase, with the main problem areas being the southern Thai Provinces of Pattani, Yala, and Narathiwat, home to the majority of the country's Malay Muslims. Statistics from the Thai Ministry of the Interior show that in 2001 there were fifty terrorist-related incidents across the three affected Provinces, with nineteen police officers killed. In 2002, guerrillas attacked several police stations, seizing huge quantities of arms and ammunition. Between January and November 2004, some five hundred and seventy-three people were killed and five hundred and twenty-four injured.[29] There are no indications that Thailand's insurgents are being exported to other conflicts around the globe and their focus is purely on domestic political grievances. However, as Malay Muslims are known to practice a more moderate form of Islam, but Wahhabi teachings and the increase in religious schools in the south being sponsored and supported by states in the Middle East is a cause for concern to the Buddhist government. The sharp rise in insurgent attacks in 2007 and the types of attack being carried out point to a level of expertise that was not previously evident. This leads analysts to believe that the increased insurgency may be due to the presence of foreign fighters. Thailand has been ruled by a Buddhist-dominated government for decades and is kept in power by a powerful military with unwavering support for the Thai monarchy. The south is home to the poorest of the population, and the Malay Muslim grievances go back decades stemming from discrimination and attempts at forced assimilation by successive ethnic Thai Buddhist governments. The presence of insurgent groups date back to the late 1960s and early 1970s, created to defend against Communist influences spreading across Thailand's borders. In 1971, the Thai Royal family sponsored the Village Scouts, a right-wing ultra-nationalist group established not to be involved in politics but as a group to do the bidding of the Royals. Today they continue to have the support of the Thai Royal family as well as the Royal Thai police and military. In the 1970s and 1980s, the most effective of the groups operating was the Pattani United Liberation Organization (PULO), calling for an independent Islamic state in Thailand.

The government stemmed the unrest with political and economic reforms that undercut support for armed struggle, and hundreds of fighters accepted a broad amnesty. The insurgency looked to be all but over by the mid-1990s.

But new strains then appeared, with four particularly significant groups emerging or re-emerging, with violence erupting early in 2004. The major groups active today include the following:

- BRN-C (Barisan Revolusi Nasional-Coordinate, National Revolutionary Front-Coordinate), the only active faction of BRN, first established in the early 1960s to fight for an independent Pattani state. Thought to be the largest and best organized of the armed groups, it is focused on political organizing and recruitment within Islamic schools.
- Pemuda, a separatist youth movement (part of which is controlled by BRN-C), is believed to be responsible for a large proportion of day-to-day sabotage, shooting, and bombing attacks.
- GMIP (Gerakan Mujahidin Islam Pattani, Pattani Islamic Mujahidin Group), established by Afghanistan veterans in 1995, is committed to an independent Islamic state.
- New PULO, established in 1995 as an offshoot of PULO and the smallest of the active armed groups, is fighting for an independent state.

FIGURE 11-19 Map of Vietnam. *Source:* Central Intelligence Agency, *The World Factbook, 2008.*

Major attacks started in January 2004, involved carefully coordinated attacks in which militants raided an army arsenal, torched schools and police posts, and the following day, set off several bombs.

The second, on April 28, 2004, involved synchronized attacks on eleven police posts and army checkpoints across Pattani, Yala, and Songkhla and ended in a bloody showdown at the Krue Se Mosque, when the Thai army gunned down thirty-two men inside. By the end of the day, one hundred and five militants, one civilian, and five members of the security forces were dead.

The third, on October 25, 2004, began with a demonstration outside a police station and ended with the deaths of at least eighty-five Muslim men and boys, most from suffocation after arrest as a result of being stacked five and six deep in army trucks for transport to an army base.

There are several explanations, none mutually exclusive, for why violence has escalated. Two of the most plausible are the disbanding of key government institutions, and the fear and resentment created by arbitrary arrests and police brutality, compounded by government failure to provide justice to victims and families. Rapid social change has also contributed to insecurity and frustration in Malay Muslim communities and a feeling that their way of life, values, and culture are threatened.[30]

Separatists have continued to wage an insurgency and by 2012 more than six thousand had died. The government has had little success in putting down or negotiating a peaceful settlement with the insurgents.

The simmering differences between the Thai military and the government will do nothing to resolve the situation in the south. On the contrary, while politicians and generals continue their infighting and political power struggles, it will give the insurgents more opportunity to attack and destabilize the government. The heavy-handed response to the insurgents by both the military and police is fueling the current insurgent attacks.

VIETNAM

The Socialist Republic of Vietnam is a Communist state made up of the former North and South Vietnams, after ten years of the Vietnam War. This country, war torn for many decades, is in Southeastern Asia, bordering the Gulf of Thailand, the Gulf of Tonkin, and the South China Sea, between China and Cambodia (Figure 11-19). It is slightly larger than New Mexico. After consolidation at the war's end, Vietnam has a population of over seventy-five million. The ethnic population distribution is Vietnamese (eighty-five percent to ninety percent) and Chinese (three percent), with Muong Tai, Meo, Khmer, Man, and Cham making up the ethnic balance. Religious affiliations are (in descending order) Buddhist, Taoist, Roman Catholic, indigenous beliefs,

Islam, Protestant, Cao Dai, and Hoa Hao. Vietnam won its independence from France in 1945 when the French colonial forces were defeated. Its new constitution was approved in 1992.

Vietnam is a poor, densely populated country that has had to recover from the ravages of decades of war, the loss of financial support from the former USSR, and the rigidities of a centrally planned economy. Substantial progress has been achieved over the past ten years in moving forward from an extremely low starting point. Economic growth continued at a strong pace with industrial output rising by fourteen percent during 1996; real GDP expanded by 9.4 percent. Foreign direct investment rose to an estimated $2.3 billion for the year. These positive numbers, however, mask some major difficulties that are emerging in economic performance. Many domestic industries, including coal, cement, steel, and paper, reported large stockpiles of inventory and tough competition from more efficient foreign producers. While disbursements of aid and foreign direct investment have risen, they are not large enough to finance the rapid increase in imports. It is widely believed that Vietnam may be using short-term trade credits to bridge the gap. That is a risky strategy, one that could result in a foreign exchange crunch in the near term.

Vietnamese authorities continue to move very slowly toward implementing the structural reforms needed to revitalize the economy and produce more competitive, export-driven industries. Privatization of state enterprise remains bogged down in political controversy, while the country's dynamic private sector is denied both financing and access to markets. Reform of the banking sector is proceeding slowly, raising concerns that the country will be unable to tap sufficient domestic savings to maintain current high levels of growth. Administrative and legal barriers are also causing costly delays for foreign investors and are raising similar doubts about Vietnam's ability to maintain the inflow of foreign capital. Ideological bias in favor of state intervention and control of the economy is slowing progress toward a more liberalized investment environment.

Vietnam has disputes over maritime boundaries with Cambodia and is involved in complex negotiations over the Spratly Islands in the South China Sea. These are ongoing with China, Malaysia, the Philippines, Taiwan, and possibly Brunei. There are also unresolved maritime boundaries with Thailand and with China in the Gulf of Tonkin, and disputed ownership of the Paracel Islands in the South China Sea, which are occupied by China but claimed by Vietnam and Taiwan. Offshore islands and sections of boundary with Cambodia are in dispute as well. Key growing areas in Vietnam cultivated over three thousand hectares of poppy in 1996, producing twenty-five tons of opium, making it a major opium producer and an increasingly important transit point for Southeast Asian heroin destined for the United States and Europe. Vietnam has a growing opium addiction problem, plus possible small-scale heroin production in country. While there is little known terrorism in Vietnam, a Vietnamese court sentenced two persons to death and three others to life in prison for carrying out a grenade attack on the waterfront in Ho Chi Minh City in 1994, in which twenty persons, including ten foreigners, were injured. The five were part of the Vietnam Front for Regime Restoration, an antigovernment exile group based in the United States (Figure 11-20).

Ho Chi Minh

The affectionate name given to him by his countrymen, "Uncle Ho," gives rise to an image as a kindly, humble man. Yet Ho was a lifelong revolutionary, who first led an insurrection against Japanese occupiers. In 1945, Ho's commandos took Hanoi, the Vietnamese capital. In one of

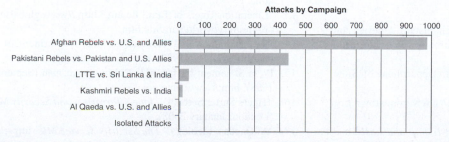

FIGURE 11-20 Suicide attacks by campaign 2000–2015. *Courtesy:* Chicago Project on Security and Terrorism,

the ironies of history, Ho Chi Minh paraphrased a future enemy's benchmark of freedom—the U.S. Declaration of Independence—while addressing an enormous crowd after the success against the Japanese. Ho proclaimed: "All men are born equal. The Creator has given us inviolable rights: life, liberty, and happiness!"

Ho again led revolutionary forces against outside control, fighting an eight-year war that led to the division of Vietnam into two countries, North and South Vietnam. An election that was meant to be held in 1956 to reunite the country under a democratically elected leader was never held. South Vietnam, backed by the United States, refused to participate in the elections, fearful Ho would win.

Ho's regime in the North became rigidly totalitarian. After the defeated French exited, the United States escalated its involvement, supporting a series of weak governments in South Vietnam.

Vietnamese independence was finally achieved, just six years after Ho's death in 1969. The victory came at a staggering price: An estimated three million North and South Vietnamese were killed in the struggle.[31]

Summary

We have seen how politics of the British Empire went a long way to create the ongoing issues and border and ethnic problems between India and Pakistan. Thousands of terrorist attacks plus numerous assassinations (assassination of two prime ministers named Gandhi), religious hatred (Hindus, Muslims, and Sikhs), political genocide (Khmer Rouge), and state terrorism (Burma) up to conventional and nuclear war possibilities define this region. Kashmir remains an unresolved region and a focal point for unrest. Murder and mayhem has been stemmed in Sri Lanka and Thailand alone stood somewhat calm until 2001, but increasing insurgent problems in the south and an influx of Islamic extremists is giving rise to concerns. The situation between India and Pakistan, the involvement of Pakistan's ISI in support of terrorism, and the U.S. killing of Osama bin Laden in Pakistan has not stopped the rise of jihad. Added to that mix is the significant presence of Islamic fighters in the Northwest Frontier Provinces and the flow of fighters either entering or leaving Afghanistan. The incredibly long histories of most of the nations in the region have created long memories and simmering hatreds.

Review Questions

1. Describe how terrorist organizations are allowed to flourish in Pakistan.
2. Explain why Kashmir remains an ongoing flashpoint between nuclear India and Pakistan.
3. List and explain the tactics used by the Sri Lankan terrorist movements.
4. Describe the role played by the Taliban in the development of Afghanistan after the Soviet invasion.
5. Explain why the death of Osama bin Laden did not lead to the end of global jihad.

End Notes

1. Paul Johnson. *Modern Times.* (New York: HarperCollins Publishers, Inc, 1991, pp. 469–474).
2. Animesh Roul. "How Islamic State Gained Ground in India Using Indigenous Militant Networks." *Terrorism Monitor,* vol. 14, no. 9, (Jamestown Foundation, April 29, 2016).
3. Ibid.
4. The Economist. "India's Sikhs: Heresy and History." (July 7, 2007).
5. Macleans. (December 3, 2007, p. 30).
6. John K Cooley. "Unholy Wars, Afghanistan, America and International Terrorism," Second Edition, pp. 57, 225, Pluto Press 2000.
7. "Patterns of Global Terrorism." U.S. Department of State. (2005).
8. The Jamestown Foundation. http://www.jamestown.org/publications_details.php.
9. Saeed Shafqat. *The Rise of Dawat ul-Irshad and Lashkar-e-Taiba in Pakistan: Nationalism without a Nation.* Christopher Jaffrelot, Ed. (New Delhi: Manohar Publications, 2002).
10. "Patterns of Global Terrorism." U.S. Department of State. (1998).
11. SATP—ISYF. http://www.satp.org/satporgtp/countries/india/states/punjab/terrorist_outfits/ISYF.htm.
12. John Thompson. "The Liberation Tigers of Tamil Eelam: Essential Points." *Mackenzie Institute Briefing Note #25* (2009). http://www.mackenzieinstitute.com/2009/tamil-tigers-040609.htm.
13. "Liberation Tigers of Tamil Eelam." http://www.globalsecurity.org/military/world/para/ltte.htm.
14. "Patterns of Global Terrorism." U.S. Department of State. (Washington, DC, 1997). http://www.state.gov.
15. Press Statement by James P. Rubin, spokesman (September 8, 1998). http://www.state.gov.
16. "Tigers Suffer Setback." *Jane's Terrorism and Security Monitor* (London: January 2008).
17. "Al Qaeda's Ideology." *The Security Service MI5.* https://www.mi5.gov.uk/output/al-qaidas-ideology.html.
18. Ibid.

19. Anthony Tucker Jones. "The Fall of Osama bin Laden." *The Journal of International Security* (Chertsey, UK: Albany Media Ltd., May 2011, pp. 6–8).

20. Amin Saikal. "The Taliban, Pakistan's Geopolitical Instrument, America's Problem." South Asia Terrorism Portal. http://www.satp.org/satporgtp/publication/books/global/aminsaikal.htm.

21. Walden Bello. (April 29, 2002). http://www.state.gov.

22. UN Office on Drugs and Crime. Afghanistan Opium Survey, 2007 Report.

23. Editors. "Afghanistan's 2002 Opium Harvest." *Intersec.* (March 3, 2002, pp. 78–81).

24. Human Rights Watch. "Burma: End ethnic cleansing of Rohingya Muslims." https://www.hrw.org/news/2013/04/22/burma-end-ethnic-cleansing-rohingya-muslims.

25. Ibid.

26. Irrawaddy News Magazine Interactive (Archives). http://www.Irrawaddy.org.

27. The Death of Pol Pot. (2008). http://www.wsws.org/news/1998/apr1998/plpt-a18.shtml.

28. http://australianetwork.com/news/infocus/s1745603.htm.

29. *Jane's Intelligence Review.* (May 1, 2005).

30. "Southern Thailand: Insurgency Not Jihad." *Asia Report #98* (May 18, 2005). http://www.crisisgroup.org/home/index.cfm?id=3436.

31. PBS. www.pbs.org .

The Pacific Rim

LEARNING OUTCOMES

After studying this chapter, students should be able to:

1. Summarize the supposed threat to China posed by the Falun Gong.
2. Demonstrate how the use of nerve agents can be effective in terror campaigns.
3. Describe how Afghan veterans are continuing to shape the Abu Sayyaf organization.
4. Illustrate the rise of extreme Islam in Indonesia.

KEY WORDS TO NOTE

Abu Sayyaf Group (ASG)—A small but effective Islamic terror group that seeks an independent Islamic state along the Sulu archipelago

ETIM—East Turkestan Islamic Movement—a separatist group demanding independence from China

Falun Gong—A spiritual discipline originating in China—the movement is categorized by China as terrorist in nature

Japanese Red Army (JRA)—Formed in 1970 to foment a global revolution—responsible for airline hijackings and massacre at Lod Airport in 1972

Jemaah Islamiyah (JI)—Indonesian-based Sunni Islamic extremist organization, the stated goal of which is to create an Islamic state encompassing Indonesia, Malaysia, Thailand, and Mindanao in the Southern Philippines

Moro Islamic Liberation Front (MILF)—Formed in 1977, it is an Islamic movement fighting for an independent homeland in the Southern Philippines

Sarin—Nerve agent used in the 1995 Tokyo subway attack

Shoko Asahara—In 1987, founded Aum Shinrikyo as a religious cult

OVERVIEW

The Pacific Rim contains those countries that sweep in a long arc from Australia to Japan. Many have been suffering serious financial crises. As major trading partners to the United States and the European Economic Community, many have brought the world great turmoil; through wars, insurgencies, corrupt governments, and from right- and left-wing terrorism. These problems have a major impact on the other countries of this region. Their financial and political chaos creates opportunities for terrorist groups to take advantage of the turmoil to advance their agendas. This chapter builds upon the previous analysis of Southern and Southeast Asia and discusses how individual countries are reacting in terms of their backgrounds and histories of terrorist actions. We will study the resurgence of the Abu Sayyaf group and its allegiance to Islamic State and the threat that poses to the largest Muslim population, Indonesia.

CHINA

Our examination of the Far East and the Pacific Rim cannot begin without first discussing the People's Republic of China (PRC). Following the fall of the Soviet Union, the PRC has now become the world's second-greatest superpower (Figure 12-1).

China is bordered by a coastline of over ten thousand miles that includes the East China Sea, Korea Bay, Yellow Sea, and the South China Sea. The country is only slightly smaller than the United States. Its land borders are over fourteen thousand seven hundred miles long and include the countries of Afghanistan, Bhutan, India, Kazakhstan, North Korea, Kyrgyzstan, Laos, Macau, Mongolia, Nepal, Pakistan, Russia (Northeast), Russia (Northwest), Tajikistan, and Vietnam. China is the world's fourth-largest country (after Russia, Canada, and the United States), with a population of approximately 1.3 billion. The ethnic makeup of this world giant is as follows: Han Chinese, 91.9 percent; Zhuang, Uighur, Hui, Yi, Tibetan, Miao, Manchu, Mongol, Buyi, Korean, and "other" make up the remainder. While China is officially atheist, it is traditionally pragmatic and eclectic. Daoism (Taoism), Buddhism, and Muslim religions are unofficially practiced by two to three percent of their population, and Chinese Christians number only about 1 percent. But, remember, these are percentages of 1.3 billion people—and one percent still represents a very large number!

China was an ancient, and widely scattered, society until it was unified under the Qin, or Ch'ing, Dynasty in 221 B.C. The Ch'ing Dynasty, the last of the dynasties, was replaced by the Chinese Republic in 1912. PRC was later established in 1949. Beginning in late 1978, the Chinese leadership began moving the economy from a sluggish, Soviet-style, and centrally planned economy to more market-oriented economy, but still one that is within a rigid political framework and firmly under Communist Party control. The authorities switched to a system of household responsibility in agriculture in place of the older collectivization. It increased the authority of local officials and plant managers in industry, permitted a wide variety of small-scale enterprises in services and light manufacturing, and opened the economy to increased foreign trade and investment. The result has been a quadrupling of China's GDP since 1978. Agricultural output doubled in the 1980s, and industry also posted major gains, especially in coastal areas near Hong Kong and across the Strait in Taiwan, where foreign investment helped spur output of both domestic and export goods. On the darker side, the leadership often experienced in its hybrid system the worst results of socialism (bureaucracy, lassitude, and corruption) as well as those of capitalism (windfall gains and stepped-up inflation). Beijing has periodically had to backtrack, retightening central controls at intervals. From 1992 to 1996, annual growth of GDP accelerated, particularly in the coastal areas, averaging more than 10 percent annually, according to official Chinese figures. From 1995 to 1996, inflation dropped sharply, reflecting tighter

FIGURE 12-1   Map of China.   *Source:* Central Intelligence Agency, *The World Factbook, 2008.*

monetary policies and stronger measures to control food prices. At the same time, the government struggled to

- collect revenues from provinces, businesses, and individuals.
- reduce corruption and other economic crimes.
- keep afloat the large, state-owned enterprises, most of which had not participated in the vigorous expansion of the economy and many of which have been losing the ability to pay full wages and pensions.

It is estimated that from sixty to one hundred million surplus rural workers were then adrift, between the villages and the cities, many subsisting on part-time, low-paying jobs. Another long-term threat to continued economic growth was the deterioration of the environment—notably, air pollution, soil erosion, and the steady dropping of the water table, especially in the north. China still continues to lose arable land, because of erosion and economic development. Furthermore, the Chinese government gives insufficient priority to serious agricultural research. The next few years might see increasing tensions between a highly centralized political system and an increasingly decentralized economic system.[1]

China is also a major transshipment point for heroin produced in the Golden Triangle and is beginning to experience a rapidly growing domestic drug abuse problem.

PAN-TURKIC MOVEMENT—UIGHURS

Terrorism in China had matured long before the 9-11 tragedy, with February 5, 1997, marking the beginning of active terrorism in the country. Terrorist activities have three separate yet inter-related dimensions. First, the insurgent movement has a well-defined political program, aimed at achieving independence through ethnic struggle. More concretely, this program contains a mixture of ideas including the Pan-Turkic movement that spread to Xinjiang at the beginning of the last century. In the 1930s, when Xinjiang was at the height of turmoil, the Uighurs established an East Turkestan Islamic Republic. Although it existed for only three months, its legacy died hard. In the early 1980s, the spirit of independence based on Turkish ethnicity was rekindled, inspiring many Uighurs who resented Chinese domination of local affairs. Ethnic self-determination works in tandem with Pan-Turkism as another motivating factor. Under the banner of human rights and equality, the dissidents use both peaceful means of lobbying in the international arena and violent means by way of protest within China. The movement has generated sympathy from a range of Uighur communities in remote Xinjiang. Second, Jiangdu activists have built base networks both at home and abroad, with extensive foreign connections revolving around three centers of activity, each of them interconnected. Activists launch anti-China campaigns under the name of promoting human rights and ethnic equality in the West. Dozens of Islamic organizations comprising Chinese exiles were legally registered in Central Asia during the mid-1990s, such as the East Turkestan Liberation Movement in Kazakhstan. Although most of them were later outlawed, they continued to engage in covert operations that pose a security threat to Beijing. The third center used to be in Afghanistan, where Xinjiang insurgents received indoctrination and military training from al Qaeda. One Chinese source revealed that more than fifty known terrorist organizations existed in Central Asia and that more than 500 Xinjiang insurgents had been trained in Afghanistan.[2]

Reports from China on terrorist events have been limited, and most events since 1997 have been attributed to separatist attacks by Uighur who continue to wage a campaign of violence. The Uighur, a Chinese-Muslim ethnic minority group, is concentrated in the Xinjiang autonomous region in far-western China. Xinjiang is a resource-rich and strategically important region bordering Afghanistan, Pakistan, and Kazakhstan among other nations. Beijing is intensely sensitive to threats to its territorial integrity both there and in Tibet. Beijing claims that the World Uighur Congress is the front organization for East Turkestan Islamic Movement (**ETIM**).

In February 1997, Uighur separatists conducted a series of bus bombings in Urumqi, which killed nine persons and wounded seventy-four. Earlier Uighur rioting in the city of Yining resulted in as many as two hundred deaths. Uighur exiles in Turkey claimed responsibility for a small pipe bomb that exploded on a bus in Beijing, killing three persons and injuring eight. In another incident, Uighur separatists were blamed for killing five persons, including two policemen. The Chinese government quickly executed several individuals who were involved in both the rioting and the bombings. Beijing claims that support for the Uighurs is coming from neighboring Muslim countries, an accusation that has been strongly denied.

The government has tightly controlled the practice of Islam and most all religions, and official repression in the Xinjiang Uighur Autonomous Region (XUAR) targeted at Uighur Muslims tightened in some areas. Regulations restricting Muslims' religious activity, teaching, and places of worship continued to be implemented forcefully in the XUAR. The government continued to repress Uighur Muslims, sometimes citing counterterrorism as the basis for taking action that was repressive. Chinese authorities detained and arrested persons engaged in unauthorized religious activities. The government reportedly continued to limit access to mosques, to detain citizens for possession of unauthorized religious texts, imprison citizens for religious activities determined to be "extremist," and force Muslims who were fasting, to eat during Ramadan, and confiscating Muslims' passports in an effort to strengthen control over Muslim pilgrimages. In addition, the Uighur government maintained the most severe legal restrictions in China on children's right to practice religion. In recent years, Uighur authorities detained and arrested persons engaged in unauthorized religious activities and charged them with a range of offenses, including state security crimes. Xinjiang authorities often charged religious believers with committing the "three evils": terrorism, separatism, and extremism. Uighur authorities prohibited women, children, Chinese Communist Party (CCP) members, and government workers from entering mosques.[3]

The East Turkestan Islamic Movement

The Uighurs are an ethnic minority group of approximately eight million. Their ethnicity, language, and culture are more similar to the Turkic peoples of neighboring Central Asian republics. Although the East Turkestan Islamic Movement (ETIM) seeks to establish an independent Islamic regime, the majority of Uighurs are Sunni and do not necessarily support the idea of a separate Islamic state. ETIM is a small but extreme group founded by the Uighurs, whose mandate is an independent state called "East Turkestan." From the Chinese government perspective, it is quite convenient to have this group operating here as it is close to the center of Islamic extremism in Afghanistan and Pakistan and allows the Chinese to claim that they are fighting the "War on Terror" in their own backyard. This allows them to put pressure on the U.S. Administration to "ignore" Chinese human rights issues. In 2002, the U.S. State Department deported two ETIM members to China from Kyrgyzstan for allegedly plotting attacks on the U.S. embassy in the Kyrgyz capital of Bishkek, as well as other U.S. interests.[4]

In January 2007, the government announced that it had conducted raids on a suspected ETIM training base in the Pamir Mountains in Xinjiang Province, an area of rugged mountains bordering Afghanistan and Tajikistan. China claims that ETIM members were being trained, funded, and supported at the base by al Qaeda.

Former president George W. Bush met with the then president of China in October 2001 in Shanghai. During an exchange of views and mutual support on matters confronting the global threat of terrorism, George Bush stated, "… the government of China responded immediately to the attacks of September 11th. There was no hesitation, there was no doubt that they would stand with the United States and our people during this terrible time. There is a firm commitment by this government to cooperate in intelligence matters, to help interdict financing of terrorist organizations. President Jiang and the government stand side by side with the American people as we fight this evil force."[5] The meeting between the two heads of state in October 2001 signaled that China would make the most of controlling those groups that were considered subversive and internal enemies of the state. China's communist regime, which fears that China could splinter if regional separatist movements gain ground, has long called the ETIM a terrorist group. On January 21, 2002, the Information Office of the State Council (China's cabinet) issued a report arguing that terrorist forces from Xinjiang "jeopardized…social stability in China, and even threatened the security and stability of related countries and regions." The report cited four waves of terrorism during which Uighur activists were allegedly responsible for explosions, assassinations, attacks on police and government institutions, and poison and arson attacks both inside China and abroad. From 1990 to 2001, the combined efforts resulted in over two hundred incidents, one hundred and sixty-two deaths, and more than four hundred and forty injuries. During those years, Xinjiang police reportedly broke up four hundred and eighty-seven terrorist groups and identified two hundred and fifty-three major violent terrorist crimes. The most serious threat purportedly came from organizations operating from neighboring countries, such as Afghanistan and Uzbekistan, but the report also alleged that other groups, operating from bases in Turkey, Germany, and the United States also sponsored terrorist activities.

Much of the State Council's report and a subsequent one in September 2002 focused on the ETIM, dozens of whose members allegedly trained in Afghanistan.[6] China continues to state that ETIM is sponsored by al Qaeda, and there maybe some truth to this as at least twenty-two were captured by U.S. forces in Afghanistan and sent to Guantanamo, where they were interrogated and most all were released but not deported to China. It seems likely that although these fighters had received training at Afghan camps, it does not necessarily make them adherents to al Qaeda. From China's perspective, it would make sense to cast ETIM as linked with al Qaeda and global jihad to allow them a freer hand in dealing with internal disputes in that region. As the Chinese press is state controlled it is extremely difficult to get any accurate data relative to activities involving ETIM that can be independently verified. Up to 2011 the group has conducted relatively unsophisticated attacks by using improvised explosives, ramming pedestrians with vehicles, and armed attacks on government buildings.

Falun Gong

While there has been limited reporting on terrorism in China, members of the "**Falun Gong**" spiritual group have created cracks in the tight controls of mainland China's leadership. The government's anti-Falun Gong propaganda—a new phase in the battle between this group and the government—could possibly pose a bigger threat to the Communist Party, if that country's rate of urban unemployed were to rise up in support of the Falun Gong. The Falun Gong has hacked into Chinese government television broadcasts in Yantai, Shandong Province, and briefly aired a message saying, "Falun Gong is good." The incident was one of a string of broadcast station hackings that hit six cities in six months, primarily in the country's northeastern "rust belt," where unemployment and labor unrest are growing. The group was trying to counter the government's massive anti-Falun Gong propaganda campaign, which centers on the January 2001 self-immolation attempt by a group of Falun Gong followers in which two had died. These new tactics revealed the Falun Gong is technological savvy and may even have pointed to a shift in focus. Since most of the Falun Gong broadcasts were focused on China's northeast, the government fears groundwork may be underway for a new showdown with the group, one that could draw on the urban unemployed. By hacking into state television, taking its case directly to the Chinese people, the Falun Gong is also confronting China's central leadership, a strategy that has thus far used peaceful demonstrations, appeals for dialogue, and attention from foreign media to try to convince Beijing to lift its ban of the movement. The government's inability to crush the group has only reinforced Beijing's perception that the Falun Gong is a serious threat to its authority. Although the group could simply have gone underground after the government outlawed it in 1999, it chose to fight for its rights, which has led it down the path toward confrontation.

The Falun Gong emerged as a semi-religious exercise group in the early 1990s and grew rapidly, crossing all socioeconomic classes, and filled a spiritual void in China at a time of rapid change. Falun Dafa (also called Falun Gong) is an advanced practice of Buddha school self-cultivation, founded by Mr. Li Hongzhi, the practice's master. It is a discipline in which "assimilation to the highest qualities of the universe—Zhen, Shan, Ren (Truthfulness, Compassion, Forbearance)—is the foundation of practice. Practice is guided by these supreme qualities, and based on the very laws which underlie the development of the cosmos." Master Li's teachings are set forth in a number of texts, among which are included Falun Gong, Zhuan Falun, The Great Perfection Way of Falun Dafa, Essentials for Further Advancement, and Hong Yin (The Grand Verses). These and other works have been translated into thirty-eight languages, and are published and distributed worldwide.[7]

In April 1999, after a run-in with a local government, the Falun Gong then confronted Beijing directly in perhaps one of the most impressive displays of civil action in China since the 1989 incident in Tiananmen Square, when more than ten thousand followers and students, converged along the street outside the government compound in Beijing, in a daylong silent vigil. This Gandhi-inspired peaceful demonstration, which faded quietly into the night, unfortunately had precisely the opposite effect on the Chinese Government. Rather than persuading China's leaders to legitimize the Falun Gong, it sparked confusion among the country's elite. The protest showed the Falun Gong's well-developed command and communications structure could be pervasive across Chinese society. After a brief respite, Beijing banned the group, and began a crackdown, rounding up and detaining thousands of Falun Gong's members. Falun Gong quickly appealed for international help. It turned to and drew international media attention at a time when China was petitioning for entry into the World Trade Organization (WTO), and bidding seriously to host the 2008 Summer Olympic Games. Falun Gong then began appearing in Tiananmen Square in peaceful protest. The heavy-handed crackdown by Chinese security forces that followed was captured on foreign media and broadcast worldwide.

In January 2001, the group's strategy fell apart after a group of alleged Falun Gong practitioners arrived in Tiananmen Square and set themselves on fire! Whether these were simply overzealous members of the Falun Gong, or a group of people misled by government infiltrators to take extreme measures, the self-immolation proved a propaganda coup for the Chinese Government.

Whereas previous government claims that the Falun Gong was evil and dangerous were more often brushed aside by many Chinese who felt Beijing was overreacting, the pictures of half-burnt young girls on national television gave credence to the government's argument. Once again, the Falun Gong altered its strategy. Foreigners, rather than Chinese followers in Tiananmen Square, increasingly carried out protests and wherever the Chinese leaders traveled in Europe or Asia, supporters of the Falun Gong were there. In January 2002, they began a new tactic of pirate attacks on government television. The first incident took place in Chongqing, Sichuan Province, and was followed on February 16, in Anshan, Liaoning. In Anshan, three Falun Gong activists tapped into the local cable line but were caught in the process, and security forces shot at least one.

On March 5, Falun Gong activists managed to hack into eight channels in Changchun, Jilin Province, the hometown of Falun Gong Founder, Li Hongzhi. They broadcast two twenty-minute films contradicting the self-immolation story and extolling the virtues of the Falun Gong. On April 21, they struck in Harbin, Heilongjiang Province, reportedly airing pro-Falun Gong material for more than an hour.

Two recent cases, in Laiyang and Yantai, both in Shandong Province, were shorter broadcasts, simply relaying the message that "Falun Gong is good." But, in these cases, rather than hacking into cable lines, the Falun Gong managed to hijack the government satellite broadcasts, according to Chinese security officials, cited by the *South China Morning Post*, something quite a bit more sophisticated than splicing a VCR into cable lines.

The most recent Falun Gong activities have three key characteristics: First, they all suggest that what appeared to be a headless organism does have a centralized planning and organization structure. Second, the attacks indicate sophisticated technological savvy, particularly if the group managed to pirate into the state's satellite system. The similarity of the attacks and their dispersal also suggest there is an active training network inside the Falun Gong. Finally, the TV hijackings took place in China's northeast rust belt. Heilongjiang, Jilin, and Liaoning Provinces have been the sites of active labor protests for months, and large-scale demonstrations have rocked Daqing and Liaoyang and broken out in Fushun and Anshan. Although this could be a coincidence, the area is the traditional support base of Falun Gong; it also could be an attempt to bridge the gap between the group and the large pool of unemployed state workers there.

There appears now to be a realization among the Falun Gong leadership that the Chinese government will not change its position on the group particularly after a three-year nationwide campaign denouncing it as an evil cult and a socially destabilizing element. The following is a brief chronology of the reported manner in which China treated a Falun Gong practitioner. A brief chronology of Ms. Gao's suffering under the Chinese government's persecution:

- **July–December, 1999**—Arrested five times in Shenyang and Beijing for petitioning the government to stop persecuting Falun Gong. Suffered beating and force-feeding in jail.
- **February 2000–January 2001**—Arrested and detained in Masanjia Labor Camp. Suffered various tortures.
- **June 20–July 7, 2003**—Arrested and detained in Shenyang Detention Center. Suffered electric baton shock, beating, and forced feeding.
- **July 8, 2003**—Sentenced to three years of forced labor in Longshan Labor Camp. Suffered various tortures.
- **May 7, 2004**—Handcuffed to a steel pipe and shocked on the face by two policemen with three electric batons for seven hours. Face was disfigured.
- **July 7, 2004**—Ms. Gao's photos published on a Falun Gong website (http://www.minghui.ca/).

- **May 8–October 4, 2004**—In police custody at a hospital.
- **October 5, 2004**—Escaped police custody.
- **March 6, 2005**—Re-arrested.
- **June 6, 2005**—Sent to a hospital's emergency room.
- **June 12, 2005**—Parents informed to come to the hospital.
- **June 16, 2005**—Died in the hospital.[8]
- **70–100 million**—Number of Falun Gong adherents practicing in China before the ban in 1999.
- **450,000–1 million**—Estimated number of Falun Gong practitioners held in labor camps, prison camps, and other long-term detention facilities at any given time.
- **87,000**—Number of reports of torture against Falun Gong adherents to emerge from China since 1999.[9]

HONG KONG

Hong Kong returned to its former status as a province of China on July 1, 1997. High-flying Hong Kong businesspersons and others fled from the island in droves when this move was first announced several years ago. Many are now returning back to be, "where the action is," in Asia. In a joint declaration, China promised to respect Hong Kong's existing social and economic systems and lifestyle. Hong Kong borders the South China Sea and mainland China, about six times the size of Washington DC, and is scattered over more than two hundred islands. The six and a half-million people are an unbalanced ethnic mix of ninety-five percent Chinese and five percent other. They practice religion in an eclectic mix of ninety percent local religions and ten percent Christians (Figure 12-2).

Hong Kong has long been the major and most dynamic business and financial center of mainland Asia and a bustling free market with few tariffs or nontariff barriers. Natural resources are severely limited, and food and raw materials must be imported. Manufacturing and construction account for about eighteen percent of GDP. Goods and services exports account for about fifty percent of GDP. Real GDP growth averaged a remarkable eight percent. A shortage of labor continues to place upward pressure on prices and the cost of living. Prospects remain bright but only as long as major trading partners continue to be reasonably prosperous, and they probably will, as long as investors feel China will continue to support free market practices. While terrorism has been virtually nonexistent there, Hong Kong is a major hub for the Southeast Asian heroin trade and is involved with transshipment of drugs and money laundering. There is also an increasing problem with the indigenous population's amphetamine abuse.

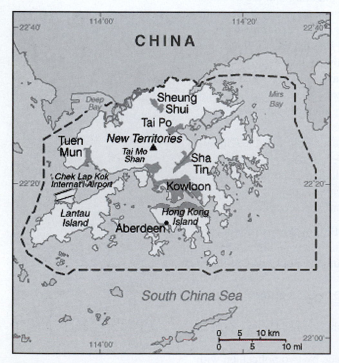

FIGURE 12-2 Map of Hong Kong. *Source: Central Intelligence Agency, The World Factbook, 2008.*

TAIWAN (REPUBLIC OF CHINA)

The Republic of China (usually referred to as Taiwan since the 1970s) on the island of Taiwan has experienced at least twenty terrorist events since 1979, including thirteen aircraft hijackings and five bombings. Factors responsible for the relatively small burden of terrorism on Taiwan in the past include tight military control over political dissent until 1987, a warming relationship with the PRC in the 1990s, political inclusion of major internal cultural groups, geographic isolation, and a lack of other significant international enemies.

The Republic of China borders the East China Sea, the Philippine Sea, the South China Sea, and the Taiwan Strait. It is north of the Philippines, on a large island off the southeastern coast of China, and is slightly smaller than Maryland and Delaware combined. The population of approximately 21,699,776 is composed of Taiwanese (eighty-four percent), mainland Chinese (fourteen percent), and aborigine (two percent). Religion in Taiwan is based on a mixture of Buddhist, Confucian, and Taoist (ninety-three percent), Christian (four and a half percent), and "other" (two and a half percent). Political pressure groups include the Taiwan independence movement and various environmental groups. Debate on Taiwan independence has now become acceptable within the mainstream of domestic politics in Taiwan. Political liberalization and the increased representation of the opposition Democratic Progressive Party (DPP) in Taiwan's legislature have opened public debate on the island's national identity. Advocates of Taiwan independence, including those within the DPP, oppose the ruling party's longtime traditional stand that the island will still eventually be reunited with mainland China. Goals of the Taiwan Independence Movement include establishing a sovereign nation of Taiwan and entering the United Nations. Other organizations supporting Taiwan independence include the World United Formosans for Independence and Organization for a Taiwan Nation.

Taiwan has a dynamic and capitalist economy, with considerable guidance of investment and foreign trade by government officials, and partial government ownership of some large banks and industrial firms. Real growth in GDP has averaged about nine percent a year over the past three decades. Export growth has been even faster and has provided the impetus for industrialization. Inflation and unemployment are very low. Agriculture contributes less than four percent to GDP, down from thirty-five percent back in 1952. Traditional labor-intensive industries are steadily being moved offshore and replaced with more capital and technology-intensive industries. Taiwan has become an active major investor in China, Thailand, Indonesia, the Philippines, Malaysia, and Vietnam. Tightening of labor markets has led to an influx of foreign workers, both legal and illegal.

Taiwan is involved in long-standing and complex territorial disputes with China, Malaysia, the Philippines, Vietnam, and (possibly) Brunei over the Spratly Islands. The Parcel Islands are occupied by China, but are claimed by both Vietnam and Taiwan. China and Taiwan also dispute claims over the Japanese-administered Senkaku-shoto (Senkaku Islands/Diaoyu Tai). The island nation is tightly controlled, and there is no discernible terrorist activity. Taiwan is considered an important heroin transit point, and there seems to be a fast-growing problem with domestic consumption of methamphetamine and heroin.

JAPAN

Japan is a constitutional monarchy that became an independent state in 660 B.C., through the efforts of Emperor Jimmu. Located in Eastern Asia it is an island chain between the North Pacific Ocean and the Sea of Japan, east of the Korean Peninsula. Japan is slightly smaller than California and has a population of over one hundred and twenty-five million (Figure 12-3). The appetite of the Japanese for fish is contributing to the depletion of this resource in Asia and elsewhere. Ethnic diversity is literally unknown in Japan, where 99.4 percent of the population is Japanese, and about half a percent is Korean. Religions are also similarly broken out: Those who observe both Shintoism and Buddhism comprise eighty-four percent, and other comprises sixteen percent.

Japanese government–industry cooperation, a strong work ethic, their mastery of high technology, and a comparatively small defense allocation (roughly one percent of GDP) have helped Japan's economy advance with extraordinary rapidity to become one of the most powerful in the world. One notable characteristic of the Japanese economy is the working together of manufacturers, suppliers, and distributors in closely knit groups called keiretsu. A second basic feature has been the guarantee of lifetime employment for a substantially large portion of the urban labor force. But, sad to say, this guarantee has been slowly eroded. Industry, the most important sector of their economy, is heavily dependent on importing raw materials and fuels. The much smaller agricultural sector is highly subsidized and protected, with crop yields that rank among the very highest in the world. Usually self-sufficient in rice, Japan must import about fifty percent of their requirements of other grain and fodder crops. Japan maintains one of the world's largest fishing fleets and accounts for nearly fifteen percent of the global catch.

FIGURE 12-3 Map of Japan. *Source:* Central Intelligence Agency, *The World Factbook, 2008.*

Aum Shinrikyo

Doomsday Cult—originated in 1984

Founded by—Shoko Asahara

Membership—the elite within Japan's University system

Numbers—1500–2000 members

Doctrine—followed its own interpretations of Buddhist beliefs and doctrines—believed that the world would end with nuclear Armageddon instigated by the United States. Only those that came to Aum could be saved.

Aum Shinrikyo is fanatical cult that is obsessed with the apocalypse. It was responsible for the Sarin gas attack on the Tokyo subway system in 1995 but since then has not been credited with any further attacks. According to the U.S. Department of State, Country Reports on Terrorism **Shoko Asahara** established Aum in 1987 and the cult received legal status as a religious entity in 1989. Initially, Aum aimed to take over Japan and then the world, but over time it began to emphasize the coming of the end of the world. Asahara predicted in the late 1990s that the United States would initiate Armageddon by starting World War III with Japan.

Aum Shinrikyo began its public campaign of terror on June 27, 1994, in Matsumoto, a city of three hundred thousand and approximately three hundred and twenty-two kilometers northwest of Tokyo when a group of cult members drove a converted refrigerator truck into a nondescript residential neighborhood. Parking in a secluded parking lot behind a stand of trees, they activated a computer-controlled system to release a cloud of Sarin. The nerve agent floated toward a cluster of private homes, a mid-rise apartment building, town homes, and a small dormitory. This neighborhood was targeted for a specific reason. The dormitory was the residence of all three judges sitting on a panel hearing a lawsuit over a real-estate dispute in which Aum Shinrikyo was the defendant. Cult lawyers had advised the sect's leadership that the decision was likely to go against them. Unwilling to accept a costly reversal, Aum responded by sending a team to Matsumoto to guarantee that the judges did not hand down an adverse judgment. A light breeze (3–5 knots) gently pushed the deadly aerosol cloud of Sarin into a courtyard formed by the buildings. The deadly agent affected the inhabitants of many of the buildings, entering through windows and doorways left open to the warm night air. Within a short time, seven people were dead. Five hundred others were transported to local hospitals, where approximately two hundred would require at least one night's hospitalization.

Their next major act of violence would serve as a wake-up call to the world regarding the prospects of weapons of mass destruction and terrorism. On March 20, 1995, packages were placed on five different trains in the Tokyo subway system. The packages consisted of plastic bags filled with a chemical mix and wrapped inside newspapers. Once placed on the floor of the subway car, each bag was punctured with a sharpened umbrella tip, and the material was allowed to spill onto the floor of the subway car. As the liquid spread out and evaporated, the vaporous agent spread throughout the car. Tokyo was experiencing a coordinated, simultaneous, and multi-point assault. The attack was carried out at virtually the same moment at five different locations in the world's largest city: five trains, many kilometers apart, all converging on the center of Tokyo. The resulting deaths and injuries were spread throughout central Tokyo. First reports came from the inner suburbs and then, very quickly, cries for help began to flow in from one station after another, forming a rapidly tightening ring around the station at Kasumigaseki. This station serves the buildings that house most of the key agencies of the Japanese government. Most of the major ministries, as well as the national police agency, have their headquarters at Kasumigaseki.

By the end of that day, fifteen subway stations in the world's busiest subway system had been affected. Of these, stations along the Hibiya line were the most heavily affected some with as many as three to four hundred persons involved. The number injured in the attacks was just under three thousand eight hundred; of those, nearly a thousand required hospitalization—some for no more than a few hours, some for many days; and twelve people died.[10] Aum dabbled in many different biological agents. They cultured and experimented with botulin toxin, anthrax, cholera, and Q fever. In 1993, Asahara led a group of sixteen cult doctors and nurses to Zaire, on a supposed medical mission. The purpose of the trip to Central Africa was to learn as much as possible about and, ideally, to bring back samples of Ebola virus. In early 1994, cult doctors were quoted on Russian radio as discussing the possibility of using Ebola as a biological weapon.

The U.S. Secretary of State designated Aum Shinrikyo as a "Foreign Terrorist Organization," pursuant to the "Antiterrorism and Effective Death Penalty Act of 1996." In addition to the murder charges stemming from the Sarin nerve gas attack, Aum's leader Shoko Asahara faced sixteen other charges, ranging from kidnapping and murder to illegal production of drugs and weapons. Nine former Aum Shinrikyo members pleaded guilty or received sentences from twenty-two months to seventeen years for crimes they committed on behalf of Asahara. One Aum Shinrikyo member was acquitted of forcibly confining other cult members. Shoko Asahara claims to be a reincarnation of the Hindu god Shiva, who promised to lead his followers to salvation when impending Armageddon arrived. Asahara was arrested on Mount Fuji in 1995 and was eventually convicted and sentenced to death in 2004. His final appeal was dismissed in 2006, and he waits execution. He was succeeded by Fumihiro Joyu, a former engineer who was the head of Aum's Moscow operation and Aum was recast as Aleph with the aim of convincing authorities that the remade group posed no threat to Japan. In late 2003, however, Joyu stepped down under pressure from members who wanted to return fully to the worship of Asahara. A growing divide between members supporting Joyu and Asahara emerged. In 2007, Joyu officially left the group and in May established a splinter group called Hikari No Wa, which is translated as "Circle of Light" or "Ring of Light." Japanese authorities continued to monitor both Aum (now called Aleph) and Hikari No Wa. Could Aum Shinrikyo ever again develop the potential to give this so-called catastrophe a nudge? In 1999, Japanese police had unearthed "Sarin precursor chemicals," hidden by Aum Shinrikyo in mountains north of Tokyo, then raising the question, "What else was the cult hiding?" A few months before that, a self-declared Aum Shinrikyo member threatened to release gas at eleven Moscow subway stations.

In its continuing crackdown, police have confiscated more than half a million leaflets. Aum Shinrikyo has never apologized or expressed remorse for its past actions. An apology is vital if the cult expects any chance of normal relationships with Japanese society, but the cult's six leaders have not come to the same conclusion. The Japanese authorities could have outlawed Aum Shinrikyo using a draconian 1952 law against subversive activities, but it decided that the sect did not pose an "immediate and obvious threat" to public safety. And, meanwhile, clumsy policing and political paralysis may continue to provide the conditions for Aum Shinrikyo to rise and thrive once more.

JAPANESE RED ARMY

> Founded—1971 by Fusako Shigenobu
>
> Ideology—Marxist-Leninist, anti-imperialist, and anti-Zionist
>
> Goals—To create a proletarian revolution in Japan
>
> Dates of Operation—1971–2001

Small and extremely violent they received their training in the Palestinian camps of the Middle East and were responsible for deadly attacks such as the Lod Airport massacre in Israel in 1972, which it carried out on behalf of the Popular Front for the Liberation of Palestine (Figure 12-4). In 1974, they attacked the French Embassy in The Hague, taking several hostages until the French government released one of their colleagues. Five members were convicted in Lebanon on various charges related to forgery and even illegal residency and sentenced to three years in prison. Another member, Jun Nishikawa, was captured in Bolivia and deported to Japan, where he was indicted for his role in the 1977 hijacking of a Japanese Airliner flight. Four of the five **Japanese Red Army (JRA)** members arrested remain in custody in Lebanon. Tsutomu Shirosaki was captured in 1996 and brought to the United States to stand trial for the offenses arising from a rocket attack against the U.S. Embassy in Jakarta, Indonesia, in 1986. He was convicted in Washington DC, of assault with the intent to kill, attempted first-degree murder of internationally protected persons, and attempted destruction of buildings and property in the special maritime and territorial jurisdiction of the United States. He was also convicted of committing a violent attack on the official premises of internationally protected persons. In February 1998, he was sentenced to thirty years in prison. Fusako Shigenobu was arrested in Japan in 2000 and in February 2006 was sentenced to twenty years' prison for planning the Lod Airport massacre in 1972. Seven hardcore JRA members remain at large. Since the late 1970s, the group has been inactive and not operating as a distinct terror group and it is believed that some JRA members have been operating under the umbrella of a group calling itself the Anti-Imperialist International Brigade.

TERRORIST ATTACK BRIEF

Terrorist Group—Japanese Red Army (obo. PFLP)

Case Facts—The JRA carried out a machine gun attack inside the terminal of LOD airport. In the ensuing mayhem the terrorists were able to kill twenty-five and wound a further seventy-six passengers and staff. Two of the terrorists were killed in a shootout with Israeli security and the third was arrested.

Investigation—Cooperation between two terrorist groups was at play in this attack, carried out by the JRA on behalf of the Popular Front for the Liberation of Palestine. All three Japanese members were previously trained in terror tactics in Lebanon. The three terrorists had arrived on an Air France flight carrying slim musical cases. Once inside the terminal they opened the case and using the hidden weapons opened fire. The assault was claimed by the PFLP as revenge for the DeirYassin attack by Jewish Irgun forces in 1948. Tsuyoshi Okudaira and Yasuyuki Yasuda died in the terminal and Kozo Okamato was seriously injured—he survived and was sentenced to life in prison but was later released in a prisoner exchange in 1985 with other Palestinian prisoners. He remained in Lebanon but was arrested along with four Palestinians by the Lebanese in 1997. After serving three years in prison he was freed in 2000.

FIGURE 12-4   Assault/shooting—Lod airport Tel Aviv Israel—May 30, 1972.   *Source:* Gus Martin— *Understanding Terrorism, Challenges, Perspectives, and Issues.* 5th Edition (Sage Publishing, 2016, p. 223).

THE TWO KOREAS

The Democratic People's Republic of North Korea

Following World War II, Korea was split into two and its northern half had come under Soviet-sponsored Communist domination. North Korea tried to conquer the U.S.-backed Republic of South Korea in the Korean War (1950–1953), but failed. North Korea's president, Kim Il-sung, then adopted a policy of diplomatic and economic "self-reliance" as a check against excessive Soviet or Communist Chinese influences. Kim Il-sung set out to mold North Korea's political, economic, and military policies around his eventual objective of reunifying the two Koreas under his control (Figure 12-5).

Kim Jong-Il was officially designated as his father's future successor in 1980. He assumed a growing political and managerial role until his father's death in 1994, when he assumed full power without opposition. After decades of sad economic mismanagement and resource misallocation, the North, since the mid-1990s, has relied heavily on international food aid to feed its population while continuing to expend resources to maintain an army of about 1 million. North Korea's long-range missile development and research into nuclear, chemical, and biological weapons, and massive conventional armed forces are still a major concern to the international community. In 1994, North Korea signed an agreement with the United States to freeze and ultimately dismantle its existing plutonium-based nuclear program. The International Atomic Energy Agency (IAEA) was monitoring North Korea to assure its compliance with the agreement. North Korea later was found to be in violation of that agreement, when the world learned that it was pursuing a nuclear weapons program based on enriched uranium. In 2002, North Korea expelled the IAEA monitors and, in 2003, declared its withdrawal from the International Non-proliferation Treaty. In mid-2003, Pyongyang announced it had now completed their reprocessing of spent nuclear fuel rods (to extract weapons-grade plutonium) and was now developing a "nuclear deterrent." Since August 2003, North Korea has participated in six-party talks with the United States, China, South Korea, Japan, and Russia to try to resolve the stalemate over its nuclear programs. Kim Jong-Il died of a heart attack in December 2011 and like his father before him power was passed by him to his youngest son Kim Jong-un. Since coming to power Kim has ruthlessly cemented his power base by purging his ruling party of all that would seek to oppose him. He still manages to have a stranglehold on every facet of daily life.

FIGURE 12-5   Map of North Korea.   *Source:* Central Intelligence Agency, *The World Factbook, 2008.*

What makes the West have grave concerns is North Korea's capability in the areas of nuclear and biological/chemical weapons. Pyongyang unilaterally withdrew from the Treaty on the Non-Proliferation of Nuclear Weapons (NPT) in January 2003 and is not a party to the Comprehensive Nuclear-Test-Ban Treaty (CTBT) or a member of the Missile Technology Control Regime (MTCR). The DPRK (Democratic People's Republic of North Korea) is not a party to the Chemical Weapons Convention (CWC), and is believed to possess a large chemical weapons program. North Korea has an active nuclear testing program and conducted tests in both 2013 and 2016. Added to this is its capability of enriching uranium and producing weapons-grade plutonium. It has both short and long range ballistic missiles capability.[11]

Kidnapping for Political Ransom

Hostage taking and kidnapping are nothing new but it is a well-practiced art in North Korea. The "arrest" of a foreign national on trumped up charges so that the individual(s) can be used as international bargaining chips for the benefit of the North. On April 30, 2016, North Korea sentenced a U.S. citizen to fifteen years' hard labor for "hostile acts" against the state. The American Kenneth Bae was legally in North Korea in November 2015 as the owner of a North Korean Travel company when he was arrested. This arrest is just one of many thousands of cases where North Korea has abducted people, a practice that has continued since WWII and the Korean War. Abductees until recently were never acknowledged by the North as existing. From South Korean fishermen to movie actresses, the North used them for its nefarious activities. Most were trained in the art of spying so that they could infiltrate back to their countries. A 2011 U.S. Committee for Human Rights report in North Korea found that North Korea has abducted more than a hundred and eighty thousand people from twelve countries. The committee called on the United States to re-list North Korea as a state sponsor of terrorism because of the abductions, which are categorized under 18 U.S.C. Section 2331 as acts of terrorism.[12] In October 1983, DPRK agents brought explosives from a North Korean diplomatic mission and placed three bombs in the roof of the Martyr's Mausoleum in Rangoon, Burma, coinciding with South Korean President Chun Doo-hwan's official visit. The explosion killed twenty-one people and wounded forty-six others, including the South Korean foreign minister, deputy prime minister, and several members of the South Korean Cabinet. The attack was carried out by three members of the North Korean military; however, Pyongyang denied any involvement with the bombing and adroitly avoided accountability.[13]

In 1987, two North Korean spies posing as Japanese father and daughter boarded Korean Airlines flight 858 to Abu Dhabi—during the flight they secreted a bomb inside the aircraft, they departed from the flight in Abu Dhabi which then took off—the aircraft exploded killing all one hundred and fifteen passengers and crew.

The Republic of South Korea

South Korea has experienced thirty suspected terrorism-related events since 1958, including attacks against South Korean citizens in foreign countries (Figure 12-6). The most common types of terrorism used have included bombings, shootings, hijackings, and kidnappings. Prior to 1990, North Korea was responsible for almost all terrorism-related events inside of South Korea, including multiple assassination attempts on its presidents, regular kidnappings of South Korean fisherman, and several high-profile bombings. Since 1990, most of the terrorist attacks against South Korean citizens have occurred abroad and have been related to the emerging worldwide pattern of terrorism by international terrorist organizations or deranged individuals. The September 11, 2001, World Trade Center and Pentagon attacks and the 2001 U.S. anthrax letter attacks prompted South Korea to organize a new national system of emergency response for terrorism-related events.

Korea was an independent kingdom under Chinese Suzerainty for most of the past millennium. Following its victory in the Russo–Japanese War in 1905, Japan occupied Korea; five years later it formally annexed the entire peninsula. After World War II, a Republic was set up in the southern half of the Korean Peninsula, while a Communist-style

FIGURE 12-6 Map of South Korea. *Source:* Central Intelligence Agency, *The World Factbook, 2008.*

government was installed in the north. During the Korean War (1950–1953), U.S. and UN forces intervened to defend South Korea from North Korean attacks supported by the Chinese. An armistice was signed in 1953, splitting the peninsula along a demilitarized zone at about the thirty-eighth parallel. Thereafter, South Korea achieved rapid economic growth, with per capita income rising to roughly "eighteen-times" the level of North Korea. In 1987, South Korean voters elected Roh Tae-woo to the Presidency, ending twenty-six years of military dictatorship. South Korea today is a fully functioning, modern democracy. In June 2000, a historic, first North–South summit took place between the South's president Kim Tae-chung and the North's leader Kim Jong-II.

The United States planned to withdraw one-third of its thirty-seven thousand troops from South Korea by the end of 2005, according to a South Korean government official. The withdrawal the first pullback since 1992, included thirty-six hundred American soldiers scheduled to deploy from South Korea to Iraq in summer 2005, stated Kim Sook, head of the North American Division at South Korea's Foreign Ministry, at a press briefing in Seoul. He said the South Korean government was informed of the plan. The American decision to cut troops in South Korea—the only major American military presence in the Asian mainland—caught South Koreans by surprise.

The cutback appears to be part of a wider-planned rearrangement of American troops to be in the Pacific. With Washington's concern growing about monitoring and patrolling international sea lanes in the region, the United States is already investing tens of millions of dollars in expanding Air Force and Navy facilities on Guam, in the Western Pacific.

"The South Korea lobby in Washington is dying," a conservative American lawyer, John E. Carbaugh, said, referring to the fact that there are no longer any Korean War veterans in the U.S. Congress. On the peninsula, Communist North Korea has 1.1 million soldiers, and South Korea has 690,000. The American contingent of 37,500 troops, about one-tenth the size of the U.S. forces at the peak of the Korean War, is largely symbolic.

THE PHILIPPINES

The Republic of the Philippines is situated in Southeastern Asia, on a long archipelago between the Philippine Sea, and the South China Sea. It is east of Vietnam and is slightly larger than the State of Arizona (Figure 12-7). The scattered population of more than seventy-six million has an ethnic mix of Christian Malay (ninety-one and a half percent), Muslim Malay (four percent), Chinese (one and a half percent), and other (three percent). The major religions are Roman Catholic (eighty-three percent), Protestant (nine percent), Muslim (five percent), Buddhist and other (three percent).

The Philippines has broadly defined terrorism as "the premeditated use or threatened use of violence or means of destruction perpetuated against innocent civilians or non-combatants, or against civilian and government properties, usually intended to influence an audience" with the purpose of creating a state of fear to extort, coerce, intimidate, or cause persons or groups to change their behavior. Terrorist methods are hostage taking, piracy, sabotage, assassination, arson, armed attacks, threats, hoaxes, bombings, and shootings. It is a signatory to eleven of the twelve international counterterrorism instruments and supports the adoption of a Comprehensive Convention on International Terrorism that would supplement the Declaration on Measures to Eliminate International Terrorism. Threats to the stability of the Philippines come from a triangular attack from communist-inspired terrorism (New People's Army) and the Islamic groups of Abu Sayyaf group (ASG), **Jemaah Islamiyah (JI)**, and the Moro Islamic Liberation Front. The three Islamic groups are not all aligned but do use one or other as proxy organizations to front their attacks; were they all to be aligned with a singular goal, the threat would be considered far more extreme.

Abu Sayyaf

Abu Sayyaf Group (ASG) means "bearer of the sword" in Arabic—its roots can be traced back to the Soviet invasion of Afghanistan and the global jihad movement that was created. The group's ideology is to form an Islamic state in the Philippines, and much of that is derived from its leadership that met with al Qaeda leaders in Afghanistan back in the 1980s. ASG was formed by Abdurajak Janjalani, a veteran of the Afghan

FIGURE 12-7 Map of The Philippines.
Source: Central Intelligence Agency, *The World Factbook, 2008.*

Mujahideen and originally financed by a Saudi businessman living in the Philippines. Janjalani met members of the al Qaeda hierarchy including bin Laden's brother-in-law Jamal Khalifa who was the director of the Saudi-based charity Islamic International Relief Organization, and in 1991, set up a number of reputable charities in the Philippines that constructed schools and clinics that also supplied fighters for the ASG. In the early 1980s, between three and five hundred Moro fundamentalists arrived in Peshawar, Pakistan, to fight with the mujahideen fighting the Soviets in Afghanistan; one of them, Ustadz Abdurajak Janjalani, emerged as a leader. Janjalani was the son of a Basilan ulama and became a fiery Islamic orator himself. He attended an Islamic university in Saudi Arabia, graduating in 1981 before studying Islamic jurisprudence at Ummu I-Qura in Mecca for three years.

He returned to Basilan and Zamboanga to preach in 1984. In 1987, he traveled to Libya and then continued on to join the mujahideen and fought the Soviets for several years in Afghanistan. In Peshawar, Janjalani befriended a wealthy Saudi supporter of the mujahideen, Osama bin Laden. Janjalani, and later his younger brother, Khadaffy Janjalani, received training in the late 1980s and early 1990s at a training camp near Khost, Afghanistan, that was run by a professor of Islam, Abdul Rab Rasul Sayyaf, whose belief in the strict Wahhabi interpretation of Islam found him in favor with many wealthy Saudis, including Osama bin Laden.[14] ASG and the Islamist **Moro Islamic Liberation Front (MILF)** have their centers of operation in the same geographic region of the Sulu archipelago and easternmost island of Mindanao, where a rugged terrain has made it difficult for the government to root them out. ASG has become well known for its kidnappings, mainly of foreign tourists, usually for ransom, bombings, and extortion (Figure 12-8). ASG's trail of terror stretches back to its first bombing attack in 1995, when it carried out an attack on a small town in Mindanao Province. It's most prominent attacks came in 2000, when an armed group of ASG members attacked an upscale resort complex in Malaysia and kidnapped twenty-one tourists. The following year, it continued its campaign of striking high-profile locations and targeting foreign tourists. In 2001, ASG again kidnapped more Westerners from a Philippines' resort complex and subsequently murdered several hostages, including an American citizen, when security forces attempted a rescue operation. A similar fate occurred during a rescue attempt of U.S. hostages in June 2002, which also resulted in the death of another U.S. citizen.

Continued attacks in 2004 included the bomb attack on a ferry in Manila Bay that killed 132 passengers and is believed to have been the work of a faction loyal to ASG. The group's successes were limited when the United States and Australia sent troops to the Philippines to train the army in counterinsurgency techniques. The military onslaught against the ASG reduced its numbers to around four hundred and fifty by early 2005. However, like so many other insurgent terror groups, ASG managed in February 2005 to launch simultaneous bomb attacks in Manila, General Santos City, and Davao, killing eleven people and wounding more than one hundred. Janjalani was killed

TERRORIST ATTACK BRIEF

Terrorist Group—ABU SAYYAF

Case Facts—Boat loads of Abu Sayyaf terrorist attacked the upscale Palawan Island Resort in May 2001and without encountering any resistance took a large number of hostages and returned with them to safe territory on Mindanao. The number of hostages including several American missionaries fluctuated as Abu Sayyaf continued to take and release hostages over the next twelve months. During this period, several of the hostages were killed by beheading.

Investigation—The kidnappers had demanded $1 million for the safe return of the American hostages, and a smaller ransom was paid. However, they were not released. In June 2002, U.S.-trained Philippine commandos attempted a rescue operation for the two U.S. captives and a Filipino nurse being held with them. Two of the hostages including an American were killed in the shootout, and the American missionary Garcia Burnham, although injured, was freed. The Philippine government following the 9-11 attacks in the United States received significant support for counterterror operations and its special forces have been successful in countering Abu Sayyaf. However, the group remains resilient and the government has blamed Abu Sayyaf for the February 2004 bombing of car ferry in Manila Bay killing one hundred and thirty-two people.

FIGURE 12-8 Kidnapping for ransom—Tourist resort, Palawan Island, Philippines—May 27, 2001.
Source: Gus Martin—Understanding Terrorism, Challenges, Perspectives, and Issues. 5th Edition (Sage Publishing, 2016, p.152).

TERRORIST ATTACK BRIEF

Abu Sayyaf Executes Two Canadians—May and June 2016

The Abu Sayyaf group funds most of its terrorist operations through kidnapping for ransom and extortion so the kidnapping of Canadians made monetary sense to the organization. Canada's stated and repeated stand on paying ransom is well known. Canada will not and does not pay ransom for hostages. However, Abu Sayyaf who had seized John Ridsdel and three others in September 2015 executed Ridsdel in May 2016, and when no ransom was surrendered for the second Canadian, Robert Hall was also executed by beheading in June 2016. The terror group had demanded that the Canadian government pay $12.9 million for Hall's release.

FIGURE 12-9   Terrorist Attack Brief—Two Canadians executed by Abu Sayyaf.   *Source:* https://www. stratfor.com/analysis/hostages-countries-face-impossible-choice.

in a clash with Philippine police in December 1998, and his younger brother, Khadaffy Janjalani led the group into the new millennium. With the peace agreement between the government and the Islamist Moro Islamic Liberation Front gaining pace, it seems highly likely that the smaller ASG would want to create a level of instability and try to attract hard-line, dissident members of MILF who have little sympathy for the peace deal. The regional extremist group, JI, whose strongest ally until the 2003 peace deal was MILF, has possibly the most to lose in this probable outbreak of peace. The MILF rebels handed over an Italian priest, Luciano Benedetti, to Philippine government officials several hours after he was kidnapped by MILF forces.

The ASG continues to be a serious threat to security and the group is as of 2014 pledging its allegiance to Islamic State. In September 2015, the group raided a resort on Samal Island and took four hostages, Kjartan Sekkingstad, a Norwegian national, Canadians Robert Hall and John Ridsdel, and Filipina Marites Flor. The group had demanded $6 million for each hostage in ransom and threatened to execute a hostage if it was not paid. In late April 2016, news reports and a video of Canadian hostage John Ridsdel being beheaded was posted by ASG. The Canadian government has refused to pay ransom to terrorists. The ASG then released ten Indonesian sailors whom it had held captive since March 25, 2015 (Figure 12-9).

ASG uses kidnapping as a major tool in its fundraising. It is also using the notoriety and propaganda machine of Islamic State which is happy to extol the work being carried out by ASG. ASG will come under more intense pressure from newly elected Philippine President Rodrigo Duterte who has been nicknamed "The Punisher". Kidnappings for ransom by the group have gone almost unchecked since 2015 – Duterte is pledging to rid the region of the jihadist group and launched a military campaign in August 2016 specifically targeting the group. ASG has kidnapped both foreigners as well as locals over the past twenty months. Its aggression has increased substantially since it openly pledged support for Islamic State in 2016. The 2016 beheading of two Canadian hostages, suggests that its kidnappings are now driven by more than financial concerns. The mission conducted by the Philippine military in late summer 2016 yielded some results in that they believe they killed the man who masterminded the beheading of the Canadian hostages, one Mohammad Said. ASG continues to hold foreign hostages for ransom but with some of the local captives escaping the clutches of ASG during the summer of 2016 they have will have provided much needed intelligence on the ASG to Duterte's military. The escapes may be an indication of security issues within ASG camps is slipping and the hostages will be more desperate to escape when the alternative is beheading.

ASG received several million dollars from its kidnapping for ransom operations in the first half of 2016. Only time will tell on the success rate of Duterte's military offensive but with the group changing from one that has primarily focused on its criminal activities to one that is openly stating allegiance to Islamic State may mean a shift in how they conduct operations as a possible proxy of the IS.

New Peoples Army (NPA)

The NPA was formed in 1969 and was inspired by the Cultural Revolution in China—the group is left-wing Maoist in its ideology. The NPA is the guerrilla arm of the Communist Party of the Philippines (CPP). It aims to overthrow the government through protracted guerrilla warfare. It is the longest running Communist insurrection in the world and is still the most active conflict in the Philippines. Although primarily a rural group, the NPA has an active urban infrastructure to carry out terrorism, and it uses city-based assassination squads called sparrow units. It derives most of its funding from contributions of supporters and so-called revolutionary taxes extorted from local businesses. NPA is in disarray because of a split in the CPP, a lack of money, and successful government operations. With the U.S. military gone from the country, NPA has engaged in urban terrorism against the police, corrupt politicians, and drug traffickers. The NPA has an estimated strength of several thousand members who operate throughout the Philippines. It is unknown whether it receives any external aid. The CPP-NPA remains a designated terrorist organization by both the United States and Europe. In an interview between The Communist Party of the Philippines spokesman Ka Roger and *Jane's Terrorism and the Security Monitor*, it was evident that the CPP had no intention of laying down arms or coming to any deal with the government, and its posture is still to replace the existing government with a Leninist style peoples' revolutionary government. It views the current ruling system as semi-colonial, semi-feudal, and dominated by foreign capitalist countries. The CPP also accused former President Arroyo of "fixing" the 2004 vote. Ka Roger also went on to explain how the CPP would set up a mass people's militia, reorganize the military, set up a pro-people program, complete the land reform, and nationalize strategic industries and fast track a national industrialization program. Over forty thousand people have died as a result of the Communist-inspired insurgency.[15]

INDONESIA

Indonesia, the former Dutch East Indies, is situated in Southeastern Asia on an archipelago in between the Indian Ocean and the Pacific Ocean. It has a varied population of almost two hundred and ten million in a land area slightly less than three times the size of Texas. Independence from the Netherlands came in 1949. The combined islands of Indonesia have the largest Muslim population in the world (Figure 12-10).

Indonesia enjoyed a decade and a half of peace in the 1950–1960-time frame, but its political fortunes shifted significantly in 1965, following a leftist coup attempt against President Sukarno, the republic's first leader. Within days, the army executed the leaders of the coup, but its aftermath brought a wave of violence. Rightist gangs, encouraged by their military commanders, killed tens of thousands of alleged Communists. By 1966, an estimated half million people had been killed in the violent unrest. The events of 1965 and 1966 left the then president Sukarno severely weakened. In 1966, he was forced to transfer key political and military powers to General Suharto, who led the military defeat of the coup. In 1967, the legislative assembly named Suharto acting president, removing Sukarno from power.

With the backing of the military, Suharto quickly proclaimed a "New Order" in Indonesian politics, concentrating on policies of economic rehabilitation and development. Using advice from Western-educated economists, Indonesia grew steadily, transforming itself from an agricultural backwater to a highly diversified manufacturing and export-driven state. Per capita income

FIGURE 12-10 Map of Indonesia. *Source:* Central Intelligence Agency, *The World Factbook, 2008.*

levels rose from $70 in 1966 to $900 in 1996, while the proportion of the population living below the poverty line declined from sixty percent to an estimated eleven percent over roughly the same period. The government instituted further economic reforms in the early 1980s, liberalizing trade and finance and expanding foreign investment and deregulation. Trade and investment boomed as a result; Indonesia's economy grew more than seven percent annually from 1985 to 1996.

In the mid-1970s, Suharto moved quickly to stop what he saw as a leftist move, to then force the colony of East Timor to be independent, after Portugal abandoned the territory. Fearing creation of a state that could destabilize surrounding provinces, Suharto sent in troops to crush that movement and annexed East Timor. Thousands of people died during the fighting, or later starved to death.

The United States cut off some military assistance to Indonesia in response to a November 1991 shooting incident in East Timor involving security forces and peaceful demonstrators. In 1996, government forces swept through East Timor again, this time after a series of guerrilla attacks on security personnel. The government takeover of the Indonesian Democratic Party's East Timor headquarters in July of that year triggered serious rioting in Jakarta. Human rights officials say that five died and one hundred and forty-nine were injured in the attack. Twenty-three other people were reported missing.

Despite the corruption and human rights abuses, Suharto continued to stay in power into 1998. His grip on power started deteriorating the year before, however, when Thailand announced the devaluation of the Baht in July 1997. This move caused the value of Indonesia's currency, the Rupiah, to drop as much as eighty percent at one point. Foreign investors fled and many companies that were adversely affected by the currency devaluation went bankrupt. Like other Asian countries, Indonesia's banks were hit especially hard; by January 1998, sixteen banks had their operations suspended. As the country negotiated with the International Monetary Fund over the terms of its $43 billion bailout package in early 1998, riots began to erupt over rising food prices, gradually intensifying despite violent police efforts to put them down.

The People's Consultative Assembly, a legislative body that was largely appointed by the president himself, re-elected Suharto to a seventh term. Student protests broke out amid calls for him to step down. In May, riots and looting turned violent as tens of thousands of students demonstrated in Jakarta and other parts of the country. Hundreds perished in clashes with security forces in Jakarta. In a show of resistance, students then began to occupy the country's Parliament grounds, demanding the president's resignation. On May 21, Suharto bowed to the pressure and resigned from his office, naming Vice President B.J. Habibie as his successor. There were attempts to charge Suharto with corruption after his resignation but none succeeded and he died in January 2008.

Within days, Habibie pledged to lift restrictions on political parties and hold open elections as part of a package of reform measures intended to liberalize life in Indonesia and revive political activity that had been stifled for more than four decades. The moves, however, did little to quell the unrest. Throughout the summer of 1998, student demonstrators continued to demand the resignation of then President Habibie as well, claiming that the government had done little or nothing to stem the country's economic crisis or spiraling high prices.

In November 1998, student-led protests for greater democracy in Jakarta turned violent after a crackdown on demonstrators killed at least five students and two others. As rioting ensued, demonstrators burned shops across the city and set cars ablaze. At least sixteen were killed over a period of several days.[16]

The United States welcomed the Indonesian government's newly established broad-based fact-finding team in 1999 to investigate the causes of the May riots and the rapes of ethnic Chinese women. In November, the team, which included representatives from the government, the Indonesian military (ABRI), the police, and nongovernment organizations, released its report. Despite the "reservations" of some members, and the fact that investigators, victims, witnesses, and family members faced anonymous death threats and other forms of intimidation, the fact-finding team issued a credible, balanced report under difficult circumstances.

The report determined there were three types of riots: (1) some were local and spontaneous, (2) some were aggravated by provocateurs, and (3) others were obviously deliberate, to include an involvement by elements of the military. The report called for further investigations and even had recommended that Lt. Gen. Prabowo and all others involved in cases of kidnappings of political activists be brought up before a military court. The report also verified that eighty-five acts of violence targeted against women occurred during the riots, including rapes, tortures, sexual assaults, and sexual harassment, mostly being against ethnic Chinese.

To restore confidence, it was crucial that the Indonesian government implement the team's recommendations, including further investigation of military leaders and others alleged to be involved in fomenting or participating in the violence. It was further strongly urged that the Indonesian government take steps to prevent intimidation and threats of violence against investigators, witnesses, and their families and that those responsible for these acts should be held accountable.[17]

Portugal and Indonesia are now in a dispute over the sovereignty of Timor (East Timor Province). The United Nations does not recognize Portugal's claim. Those two small islands are in ownership dispute with Malaysia. Indonesia continues to be an illicit producer of cannabis, largely for domestic use, but has a possible growing role as a transshipment point for Golden Triangle heroin. Separatist groups in East Timor apparently continued to target non-combatants and were involved in several bomb-making activities in 1997. In Irian Jaya, a former province of Indonesia, in April 1997, an alleged attack by the separatist Free Papua Organization against a road surveying crew left two civilians dead. If Indonesia cannot get its economic situation straightened out, it is a powder keg for escalating violence and terrorism between the state and opposition groups.

Indonesia has a population of two hundred and forty million most of whom practice a moderate form of Islam that condemns violence. Islamic terrorism has been extensive throughout the region and was led primarily by an al Qaeda "proxy organization," JI. This shadowy Islamist terrorist organization had developed economic and military assets through the use of cells (fiahs), operating throughout Southeast Asia. Guided by its objective of creating an Islamic state ruled by Sharia (Islamic law), JI wants to create an Islamist theocracy (JI's conception of Dawlah Islamiyah, or Islamic state), which would unify Muslims in Thailand, Malaysia, Indonesia, Brunei, and the Southern Philippines. JI shares a common philosophy with, and has links to, the al Qaeda network. JI emerged as the most extensive transnational radical Islamist group in Southeast Asia.

It became synonymous with attacks planned against not only Western interests but also Christian churches in Indonesia. The government of Singapore had discovered in 2001 that JI was planning to attack the British and U.S. embassies, as well as Australian interests in Singapore (Figure 12-11).

De-Radicalization

Indonesia has developed a radicalization program which although not centrally administered or well-resourced, it was Indonesia's response to the growth of radical Islam in the most populous Muslim region of the world. The program was administered by Indonesia's Detachment 88 which is the country's Special Operations response unit. The unit was responsible for intelligence gathering and searching out terror cells and networks and it achieved remarkable success—having

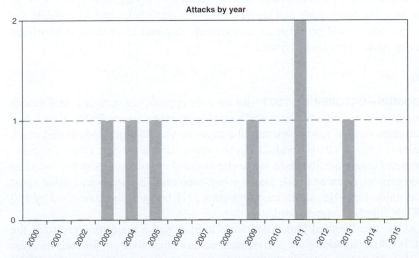

FIGURE 12-11 General statistics on suicide attacks in Indonesia 2000–2015. *Courtesy:* Chicago Project on Security and Terrorism, http://cpost.uchicago.edu.

only been formed after the 2002 Bali bombing. The program leverages the trust developed with extremist prisoners or uses former militants in a culturally sensitive manner to engage in de-radicalization and disengagement. The program supports family visits to the prisons where militants are held and even funds the visits of family members and also helps to make their prison "experience" more culturally comfortable. They believe that this soft approach encourages the prisoners' support networks and encourages positive attitudes.

Indonesian authorities have reported that its program has been highly successful in gaining intelligence from extremist prisoners, while anecdotal evidence suggests some success in encouraging prisoners to disengage from violence.

The numbers of fighters going to IS locations to fight probably amounts to around seven or eight hundred—the de-radicalization strategy needs to also focus on the number of websites and as of 2016 there were over three thousand pro-Islamic State websites in operation. The number of returning fighters to Indonesia is unknown but if and when they do, they most certainly pose a threat to the region as well as to U.S. regional interests. Stabilizing the political region, as well as eradicating extremist rhetoric in the area is more crucial than ever, since local and extremist sentiment tends to thrive in areas that are politically and economically unstable. Moving extremist rhetoric away from populations that are vulnerable to radicalization, as well as proactive and aggressive actions from countries within the area will very quickly change the dynamic of ISIS in the region.[18]

JEMAAH ISLAMIYAH (JI)

Leadership

Although there is no firm timing for the start of JI it is fair to say that it originated with Yemeni-born Indonesian clerics Abdullah Sungkar and Abu Bakar Bashir. Both fled from the Middle East to Malaysia in the 1980s to avoid prison sentences.[19] JI has its ideological origins in the Darul Islam (DI) movement of the 1950s and 1960s, in which insurgents of West Javanese descent carried out a violent campaign that attempted to establish an Islamic state in Indonesia that would encompass Thailand, Singapore, Malaysia, Brunei, Indonesia and the southern Philippines.

Abu Bakar Bashir was JI's spiritual leader following Sungkar's death from natural causes in 1998. It is thought that Bashir split from JI around 2008 and set up Jamaah Ansharut Tauhid (JAT).

The group's activities were certainly enhanced by links to al Qaeda and its leadership calling for the destruction of the United States, the United Kingdom, Australia, and the Philippines. JI has been led by Abu Bakar Bashir, the Indonesian cleric since the mid-1990s. In 1994, JI set up a training camp to replace its Afghanistan locations, setting up Camp Hudaibiyah, which became its headquarters for the Philippines. JI was linked through Ramzi Yousef to the now infamous Bojinka plot to blow up international flights in 2005. Yousef was based in Manila, and the plot was foiled by British authorities. Yousef had targeted a dozen aircraft flying across the Pacific to the United States by bringing bomb parts and liquid explosives into planes and assembling the bombs in flight. The bombers would get off at an intermediate stop and leave the bombs primed and timed to explode en route to the United States.

Western Targets

BALI NIGHT CLUB BOMBS—OCTOBER 12, 2002   As the time approached midnight on October 12, two separate bombings occurred—the first was a suicide bombing inside Paddy's Irish Bar and in the ensuing mayhem patrons ran outside into the street at which point a second and much larger explosion occurred when a VBIED exploded in the street outside the Sari Club. The powerful VBIED was secreted inside a Mitsubishi van and estimated at two thousand five hundred pounds of improvised explosive placed inside plastic filing cabinets. The bomb was made up of potassium chlorate, aluminum powder, sulfur mixture with a TNT booster, and connected by 150 meters (490 ft) of PETN-filled detonating cord.

The majority of the two hundred plus killed were tourists and a majority were from the Australian mainland. In 2003, an Indonesian court sentenced three men to death for their involvement in the Bali bombings; on November 9, 2008, Imam Samudra, Amrozi Nurhasyim, and Ali Ghufron were executed by firing squad.

Who is Abu Bakar Bashir?

An elderly Indonesian cleric of Yemeni descent, stately, if frail, in appearance, Abu Bakar Bashir (also spelled Ba'asyir), hardly comes across as one of the world's most fearsome men. His inflammatory rhetoric, however, has commanded widespread concern. Bashir was released from Indonesian prison on June 14, 2006, after serving out a twenty-five-month sentence. He was found guilty by Indonesian courts in 2003 of being part of an "evil conspiracy" to commit the 2002 Bali suicide bombings, though all charges directly linking him to the attacks were subsequently dropped. He was arrested again in 2011 for facilitating and operating a terrorist training camp near Aceh and was sentenced to fifteen years in prison, and from his prison cell he declared his allegiance to Islamic State in 2014. Although he has pledged support the same cannot be said of the JI organization he once commanded as it has not sided with Islamic State and has in fact taken an anti-IS stance.

If Bashir's involvement in coordinating the Bali bombing is debatable, as many experts have said, it is also somewhat beside the point. Indonesian officials say a striking number of the more than two hundred Jemaah Islamiyah militants arrested in the aftermath of the Bali attacks cited Bashir as their inspiration, the ideological general of their "holy war." Bashir has accordingly been labeled the "spiritual leader" of JI by a number of news sources.[20]

The following attacks are attributed to the JI network:

1. **Christian Churches attacked**—December 24, 2000: JI bombed a series of Christian churches across Indonesia killing fourteen and wounding twelve.
2. **Bali Night Club Bombing**—October 12, 2002: Two hundred and two, mainly foreign tourists, killed in bombing of Bali nightclub, eighty-eight of those killed were Australians. JI planned and executed the bombings.
3. **Ferry Terminal Bombing**—March 4, 2003: JI planted a bomb near a ferry terminal in the southern Philippines where the government was fighting Muslim separatist rebels, sixteen were killed.
4. **JW Marriott**—August 5, 2003: JI was responsible for bombing the JW Marriot in Jakarta, killing twelve and wounding one hundred and fifty.
5. **Australian Embassy Bomb**—September 9, 2004: JI detonated a bomb near the Australian Embassy in Jakarta killing ten people.
6. **Jimbaran Bay, Kuta Bombing**—October 2, 2005: JI responsible for bombings in Jimbaran Bay and Kuta, tourist destinations in Bali, Indonesia. Twenty-six dead and over a hundred wounded.
7. **Ritz-Carlton and JW Marriott Hotel Bombing**—July 17, 2009: JI again targets the same Marriott Hotel in Jakarta as in the 2003 attack, killing nine people.

Since the last major attack against Western targets in 2009, the JI have been somewhat silent on the international front but have continued attacks of a more localized nature and somewhat less sophisticated. Of more concern and particularly to Australia has been the early release of many of those convicted in the Bali bombings. Close to fifty people, most of them members of Jemaah Islamiyah, were involved in planning and executing the 2002 Bali attacks. Most served sentences ranging six years or less to eighteen years. Those released included terrorists who were peripherally involved in logistics and financing and procurement of explosives and suicide bombers.

Southeast Asians comprise only a small fraction of the estimated sixteen thousand foreigners in ISIS. They include Malaysia's first suicide bomber and members who have been featured in ISIS beheading videos. Importantly, their ability to recruit through social media has broadened their base and sped up the process of radicalization and recruitment. While some have ties to the former network of JI, many have no ties; ISIS is reaching entirely new demographics, including women. Recruits represent the entire socioeconomic spectrum; there is no single profile of recruits. While JI's splinters have debated the utility of targeting the "near enemy" or "far enemy," ISIS has focused on violent sectarianism and attacks what it deems "apostate" regimes; many JI splinters have come to the conclusion that targeting the "far enemy" was very counterproductive. ISIS has reinvigorated social welfare organizations and transnational networks across Southeast Asia. While most JI attacks had organizational backing, ISIS has inspired "lone wolf" attacks that perhaps are less lethal but almost impossible to prevent (Figures 12-12 and 12-13).

Attacks and Casualties by Year			
Year	Attacks	Killed	Wounded
2000	0	0	0
2001	0	0	0
2002	0	0	0
2003	1	12	149
2004	1	10	180
2005	1	6	41
2006	0	0	0
2007	0	0	0
2008	0	0	0
2009	1	2	25
2010	0	0	0
2011	2	0	52
2012	0	0	0
2013	1	0	1
2014	0	0	0
2015	0	0	0

FIGURE 12-12   Suicide attacks and casualties by year 2000–2015.   *Courtesy:* Chicago Project on Security and Terrorism, http://cpost.uchicago.edu.

Attacks and Casualties by Weapon			
Weapon	Attacks	Killed	Wounded
Airplane	0	0	0
Belt Bomb	4	8	118
Car Bomb	2	22	329
Other	1	0	1
Unknown	0	0	0

FIGURE 12-13   Suicide attacks and casualties by weapon 2000–2015.   *Courtesy:* Chicago Project on Security and Terrorism, http://cpost.uchicago.edu

ISIS has successfully rekindled terrorism in Southeast Asia after years of decline. In the years following the October 2002 Bali bombing, over five hundred members of JI, including many of its leaders, were arrested across Southeast Asia. Attacks since then have been relatively small scale. JI was riddled with factionalism and was seriously divided over strategy and tactics. There were two chief camps: There were advocates of the al Qaeda line who established a new organization, al Qaeda in Indonesia, under the leadership of Noordin Mohammad Top. On the other side were people who argued that targeting the West had little impact on the movement's objectives and led to government crackdowns, and who articulated a strategy based on waging sectarian conflict in Sulawesi, the outer islands, in order to create pure communities governed by Shariah from which JI could emanate without provoking heavy-handed government responses.

The pro-al Qaeda group did stage suicide bombings in Jakarta in 2009, but that was it. Elite Indonesian counterterrorism forces replaced the clumsy and thuggish Brimob forces in Central Sulawesi, helping to neutralize the advocates of sectarian violence. Other members of JI threw in the towel and established nominally nonviolent organizations such as JAT. In 2009–2010, there was an attempt to reunify these divisions: JI leaders who had been hiding in Mindanao returned to Indonesia and established a large training camp in Aceh. This cell, which called itself "al Qaeda on the Veranda of Mecca" (a Koranic reference to Aceh), was influenced by Lashkar-e-Taiba's 2008 takeover of the hotel in Mumbai and wanted to replicate that bold but low cost operation in Jakarta. This cell was broken up and more than 125 members were found. A senior member of this cell, Umar Patek, was arrested in Abottabad, Pakistan, shortly before Osama bin Laden was killed by U.S. Navy Seals.[21]

AUSTRALIA

Six separate statements issued by bin Laden or his deputy Ayman al-Zawahiri specifically threatened Australia:

- On November 3, 2001, bin Laden said, "The Crusader Australian forces were on the Indonesia shores…they landed to separate East Timor, which is part of the Islamic world."
- In an interview released in mid-November 2001 concerning the war in Afghanistan, bin Laden said, "In this fighting between Islam and the Crusaders, we will now continue our Jihad. We will incite the nation for Jihad until we meet God and get his blessing. Any country that supports the Jews can only blame itself…what do Japan or Australia or Germany have to do with this war? They just support the infidels and the Crusaders."
- Bin Laden made further reference to Australia in a videotape released in the United Kingdom in May 2002 in which he said, "What has Australia in the extreme south got to do with the oppression of our brothers in Afghanistan and Palestine?"
- On November 12, 2002, bin Laden made a statement that gave much more prominence to Australia than any other non-U.S. Western country and reaffirmed Australia to be a terrorist target: "We warned Australia before not to join in [the war], in Afghanistan, and [against] its despicable effort to separate East Timor. It ignored that warning until it woke up to the sounds of explosions in Bali. Its government falsely claimed that they were not targeted."
- On May 21, 2003, in an audiotape, Ayman al-Zawahiri said: "O Muslims take matters firmly against the embassies of America, England, Australia, Norway and their interests, companies and employees."
- On October 18, 2003, in an audio message addressed to the American people concerning the war in Iraq, bin Laden stated that, "We maintain our right to reply, at the appropriate time and place, to all the states that are taking part in this unjust war, particularly Britain, Spain, Australia, Poland, Japan and Italy."[22]

In May 2004, an Australian citizen Jack Roche pleaded guilty to charges of conspiracy to commit offenses against the Crimes (Internationally Protected Persons) Act 1976. Roche was sentenced to nine years' imprisonment. Roche was associated with Jemaah Islamiyah in Australia, trained in Afghanistan, and met with and took direction from Hambali and other extremist identities, including Khalid Sheikh Mohammed. Roche videotaped the Israeli embassy in Canberra and the Israeli consulate in Sydney in June 2000 as a preliminary measure to support a possible future terrorist attack in Australia (Figure 12-14).

Australia is considered a safe country. Only a few terrorist acts have been carried out over the past sixty years:

1975—A letter bomb that originated in the Middle East injured a press secretary at the Queensland State Premier's office.

1978—A bomb explodes outside the Hilton Hotel in Sydney where the Commonwealth heads of government were staying.

FIGURE 12-14 Map of Australia. *Source:* Central Intelligence Agency, *The World Factbook, 2008.*

1980—Turkish Consul General, Sarik Ariyak, was assassinated in Sydney by two members of the "Justice Commando of the Armenian Genocide."

1990—Gasoline bomb attack on a Jewish College in Sydney.

1996—A premature explosion of a parcel bomb in a Melbourne mailroom was believed to be intended for a major pro-Yugoslav supporter.

2002—Jack Roche, a British-born convert to Islam, was charged with plotting bomb attacks on the Israeli embassy in Canberra and the Israeli consulate in Sydney. Roche claimed to have been al Qaeda-trained in Afghanistan. In May 2004, he pleaded guilty to charges of conspiracy to commit offenses against the Crimes (Internationally Protected Persons) Act 1976 and was sentenced to nine years' imprisonment.

2010—three Islamists were sentenced in Sydney for plotting an armed attack on an Australian Army camp. All were of Australians of Somali or Lebanese descent and with links to al-Shabaab. The planned suicide attack was in retaliation for Australia's military involvement in Afghanistan.

2014—Lone gunman takes hostages at Lindt Café in Sydney, NSW

INTERNATIONAL TERRORISM

Australia has been a staunch ally in the War on Terror and is an outspoken supporter of both the United States and Great Britain. Regionally, its proximity to Indonesia makes it a target for Islamic extremists. Australian nationals were targeted in the Bali attack, so the threat remains a serious one for Australia. Indications are that Australia must reckon on a sustained campaign over many years to diminish that threat. Regionally, terrorist groups like JI show themselves to be capable of adapting to the setbacks following the arrest and prosecution of most of those responsible for the Bali bombing.

JI, al Qaeda affiliates, and Islamic State retain a potent capacity to inflict harm on Australian interests in Southeast Asia. The Australians cannot discount the possibility of a threat emerging from splinter groups inspired by the jihadist ideology of IS, al Qaeda, and JI. The very anti-Western nature of these groups will focus more likely on locations outside the country, where Australians travel for vacations. Areas such as Bali and Bangkok, Thailand, are havens for not only Western tourists but also Australians.

Australia has made specific amendments to its legal frameworks to specifically target terrorist organizations and the membership of such organizations. Under Australian Law there are two ways for an organization to be identified as a "terrorist organization." Either an organization may be found to be such an organization by a court as part of the prosecution for a terrorist offense or it may be specified in Regulations, known as "listing." Before an organization can be listed, the attorney general must be satisfied on reasonable grounds that the organization is directly or indirectly engaged in preparing, planning, assisting in, or fostering the doing of a terrorist act.

The listing of an organization ceases to have effect two years after its commencement, or if the minister ceases to be satisfied that the organization is directly or indirectly engaged in, preparing, planning, assisting in, or fostering the doing of a terrorist act, whichever occurs first. When a court has determined, or by regulation it is determined, that an organization is a "terrorist organization," it is an offense to

- direct the activities of the organization;
- recruit persons to the organization;
- receive training from or provide training to the organization;
- receive funds from or make available funds to the organization; and
- provide support or resources to the organization.

It is also an offense to be a member of any listed terrorist organization and to intentionally associate with a person who is a member or who promotes or directs the activities of a listed terrorist organization where that association provides support that would help the terrorist organization to continue to exist or to expand. Australia has officially listed twenty such terrorist groups:

- **Abu Sayyaf Group**
  Listed November 14, 2002, re-listed November 5, 2004, November 3, 2006, November 1, 2008, October 29, 2010, and July 12, 2013.

- **Al-Murabitun**
  Listed November 5, 2014.
- **Al Qaeda (AQ)**
  Listed October 21, 2002, re-listed September 1, 2004, August 26, 2006, August 8, 2008, July 22, 2010, and July 12, 2013.
- **Al Qaeda in the Arabian Peninsula (AQAP)**
  Listed November 26, 2010, re-listed November 26, 2013.
- **Al Qaeda in the Islamic Maghreb (AQIM)**
  Listed November 14, 2002, re-listed November 5, 2004, November 3, 2006, August 9, 2008, July 22, 2010, and July 12, 2013.
- **Al-Shabaab**
  Listed August 22, 2009, re-listed August 18, 2012, and August 11, 2015.
- **Ansar al-Islam**
  Formerly known as Ansar al-Sunna—Listed March 27, 2003, re-listed March 27, 2005, March 24, 2007, March 14, 2009, March 9, 2012, and March 3, 2015.
- **Boko Haram**
  Listed June 26, 2014.
- **Hamas'Izzad-Din al-Qassam Brigades**
  Listed November 9, 2003, re-listed June 5, 2005, October 7, 2005, September 10, 2007, September 8, 2009, August 18, 2012, and August 11, 2015.
- **Hizballah's External Security Organisation (ESO)**
  Listed June 5, 2003, re-listed June 5, 2005, May 25, 2007, May 16, 2009, May 10, 2012, and May 2, 2015.
- **Islamic Movement of Uzbekistan**
  Listed April 11, 2003, re-listed April 11, 2005, March 31, 2007, March 14, 2009, March 9, 2012, and March 15, 2015.
- **Islamic State**
  Formerly listed as al Qaeda in Iraq—Listed March 2, 2005, re-listed February 17, 2007, November 1, 2008, October 29, 2010, July 12, 2013, listed as Islamic State of Iraq and the Levant on December 14, 2013, listed July 11, 2014 as Islamic State.
- **Jabhat al-Nusra**
  Listed June 28, 2013.
- **Jaish-e-Mohammed**
  Listed April 11, 2003, re-listed April 11, 2005, March 31, 2007, March 14, 2009, March 9, 2012, and March 3, 2015.
- **Jamiatul-Ansar**
  Formerly known as Harakat Ul-Mujahideen—Listed November 14, 2002, re-listed November 5, 2004, November 3, 2006, November 1, 2008, October 29, 2010, and July 12, 2013.
- **Jemaah Islamiyah (JI)**
  Listed October 27, 2002, re-listed September 1, 2004, August 26, 2006, August 9, 2008, July 22, 2010, and July 12, 2013.
- **Kurdistan Workers' Party (PKK)**
  Listed December 17, 2005, re-listed September 28, 2007, September 8, 2009, August 18, 2012, and August 11, 2015.
- **Lashkar-e-Jhangvi**
  Listed April 11, 2003, re-listed April 11, 2005, March 31, 2007, March 14, 2009, March 9, 2012, and 3 March 2015.
- **Lashkar-e-Tayyiba**
  Listed November 9, 2003, re-listed June 5, 2005, October 7, 2005, September 8, 2007, September 8, 2009, August 18, 2012, and August 11, 2015.
- **Palestinian Islamic Jihad**
  Listed May 3, 2004, re-listed June 5, 2005, October 7, 2005, September 8, 2007, September 8, 2009, August 18, 2012, and August 11, 2015.[23]

Australia has been exposed to terrorism and is increasingly witnessing the advent of Islamic terrorism. By 2016, the government of Australia believed that nearly 200 Australian citizens were actively participating in the fighting with Islamic State in Syria and Iraq. In addition, there have been incidents in Australia that have the hallmarks of "lone wolf" jihadists.

Since the Bali bombings in 2002 and 2005, there have been a number of attempted or planned attacks on Australian soil. There have been thirty-five prosecutions and twenty-six convictions and the review of the Government's counterterrorism arrangements contains the following list of "terrorist plots" disrupted since 2001:

- **2003**: Faheem Lodhi convicted on terrorism charges for plotting to bomb the national electricity grid or defense sites.
- **2005**: Nine individuals were convicted on terrorism charges for attempting to procure chemicals and materials to build explosive devices as well as being in possession of a large quantity of extremist material.
- **2005**: Nine arrested in Melbourne and charged with plotting mass casualty attacks, with the intention of coercing the Australian Government to withdraw from Iraq. All nine were convicted of terrorism offenses.
- **2009**: Holsworthy Army Barracks, Sydney—Five men charged with conspiracy for preparation for an attack using firearms. Three were convicted.
- **2014–2015**: The Australian security service and Federal Police conducted numerous raids to counter Islamic State.
- **2015**: Australia's Prime Minister announced tough new legislation around citizenship and to clamp down on those citizens fighting for Islamic State.

Lone Wolf Attacks

As we have seen in previous chapters, the lone wolf attack is a low cost opportunist attack which requires minimal funding and is extremely difficult to prevent or detect in advance. Australia has succumbed to this type of event.

Lindt Chocolate Café attack—Martin Place, Sydney, NSW

At 09:45 on December 15, 2014, a lone gunman walked into the popular café in downtown Sydney and took patrons and staff as hostage. In the days leading up to the attack, an anonymous call was made to the police in regard to the nature of Man Haron Monis' website. The matter was investigated by the Australian Security and Intelligence Service and there were no indicators to confirm that this person was either in the planning stages or ready to execute any attack. Early on in the siege hostages were seen holding a black flag with Arabic script—the attacker was also noted to be wearing a black headband with an Arabic inscription. Both the flag and the inscription have been seen as Islamic State paraphernalia.

Little, if any, negotiations were conducted during the sixteen-plus hours of the siege which ended around 2 A.M. the following morning. The hostage-taker Man Haron Monis killed one of the hostages at which time the New South Wales Police stormed the building. In the ensuing gunfire Monis and one of the hostages were killed by the police.

In the aftermath of this attack it has been revealed that Monis had a long history of sexual assaults on women and was no stranger to authorities. He may well have been psychologically unbalanced and had become obsessed with extremism. He was not connected to any radical Islamist group and there are no indicators that he was being handled or directed by external terror groups. It seems likely that his unbalanced mind and infatuation with extreme Islam lead him to this attack. There were no preplanning indicators and this is now being viewed as a completely random attack of an insane individual—unfortunately in the age of Islamist terror attacks we become wiser after the event. This attack is similar to other ones designated as "lone wolf" attacks, for example, the Parliament Hill, Ottawa shootings in 2014, where Michael Zehaf-Bibeau shot a soldier on guard duty at the National War Memorial and then rampaged into the parliament buildings.

According to psychologists who study radicalization, propaganda, jihad, and calls to kill infidels in the name of "God" can push mentally ill individuals to act even in the absence of any direct contact with Islamists.[24]

Seventeen hostages were seized by Monis and during the siege five managed to escape. No direct contact was made with Monis who had made his hostages post You Tube videos about his demands on their respective Facebook pages.

Australians Targeted

On May 6, 2016, the Attorney General for Australia provided the following press release:

NEIL PRAKASH   The Australian Government has been advised by the United States Government that Australian citizen and member of Islamic State of Iraq and the Levant (ISIL), Neil Christopher Prakash, was killed by a U.S. airstrike in Mosul, Iraq, on April 29, 2016.

Neil Prakash was a prominent ISIL member and a senior terrorist recruiter and attack facilitator. Prakash has been linked to several Australia-based attack plans and calls for lone wolf attacks against the United States. He has appeared in ISIL propaganda videos and magazines and has actively recruited Australian men, women, and children and encouraged acts of terrorism. He is considered to be Australia's most prominent ISIL recruiter. His death disrupts and degrades ISIL's ability to recruit vulnerable people in our community to conduct terrorist acts.

SHADI JABAR KHALIL MOHAMMAD   We have also been advised by the United States Government that Shadi Jabar Khalil Mohammad was killed in a U.S. airstrike near Al Bab, Syria, on April 22, 2016 along with her Sudanese husband.

Mohammad and her husband, Abu Sa'ad al-Sudani, were both active recruiters of foreign fighters on behalf of ISIL, and had been inspiring attacks against Western interests.

Mohammad is the sister of Farhad Mohammad, who shot dead an employee (Mr Curtis Cheng) of the New South Wales Police Force in Parramatta on October 2, 2015.

These incidents remind us that Australians who engage in terrorist activity and move into overseas conflict zones are placing themselves and others at significant risk.

The Australian Defence Force, intelligence and security agencies work closely with the United States and other allies in the fight against ISIL.[25]

Summary

The threat from Islamic extreme terrorism is a continuing threat in Southeast Asia and the Pacific. Although Islamic State does not appear to have a strong foothold in the region, its attempts to recruit like-minded fanatics will continue through its online propaganda program. Abu Sayyaf has continued to be a thorn in the side of the Philippines government and has announced its allegiance to Islamic State. This may have little effect other than to make it appear a more dangerous entity in the region as it continues to behead Western hostages. Australia is also in the forefront of Islamic extremism and has seen its citizens taking part in jihad and dying in Syria and Iraq.

Review Questions

1. Explain the methods adopted by the Chinese to control Falun Gong.
2. Describe how Abu Sayyaf continues to pose a threat to the Philippines.
3. Describe how Islamic State has managed to rekindle terrorism and recruiting in the region.
4. Describe how de-radicalization programs can help deny extremist recruiting.

End Notes

1. Secretary Madeleine K Albright. "Meeting the Far East Crisis: What Should Governments Do?" U.S. Department of State. http://www.state.gov.
2. Dr. You Li. "China's Post 9/11 terrorism Strategy." *China Brief*, http://www.asianresearch.org/article/2047.htm.
3. Country Report on Human Rights Practices.U.S. Department of State. (2007). http://www.state.gov/g/drl/rls/hrrpt/2007/100518. htm. "The White House: U.S., China Stand Against Terrorism: Remarks by President Bush and President Jiang Zemin." in Press Availability Western Suburb Guest House (October 2001).
4. Council on Foreign Relations. (July 2008). http://www.cfr. org/publication/9179/east_turkestan_islamic_movement_etim. html_terrorist_organizat-ions.
5. "U.S., China Stand Against Terrorism, Remarks by President Bush and President Jiang Zemin" in Press Availability Western Suburb Guest House (Shanghai, People's Republic of China), White House Press Release (October 19, 2001).
6. A Human Rights Watch Briefing Paper for the 59th Session of the United Nations Commission on Human Rights. "In the Name of Counter-Terrorism: Human Rights Abuses Worldwide" (March 25, 2003). http://www.hrw.org/un/chr59/ counter-terrorism.
7. Brief Introduction to Falun Dafa. http://en.falundafa.org/introduction.html.
8. Falun Gong Human Rights Working Group. http://www. flghrwg.net/index.php?option=content&task=view&Itemid= 50&id=1272.

9. The Falun Data Information Center. *Annual Report* (2010), http://faluninfo.net.

10. Kyle B. Olson. Research Planning Inc., "Arlington, Virginia, USA." *Emerging Infectious Diseases*, vol. 5, no. 4 (1999). U.S. Center for Disease Control. www.cdc.gov.

11. Nuclear Threat Initiative. http://www.nti.org/learn/countries/north-korea/

12. "North Korea's Legacy of Terrorism."*World Affairs.* http://www.worldaffairsjournal.org/article/north-korea%E2%80%99s-legacy-terrorism.

13. Ibid.

14. Zachary Abuza Balik. "Terrorism: The Return of Abu Sayyaf." *Strategic Studies Institute Paper* (2005, p. 2).

15. Jane's Terrorism and Security Monitor. (October 2007).

16. Tim Ito. (October, 1998). Washingtonpost.com.

17. George Wehrfritz. *Newsweek* (April 13, 1998, pp. 24–30).

18. Hasan Abdul-Karim. "ISIS in the Pacific and the Threat to the Homeland." http://www.hstoday.us/single-article/isis-in-the-pacific-and-the-threat-to-the-homeland/3d880acbab68768b3ef9316c1f3e2e48.html.

19. "Mapping Militant Organizations." http://web.stanford.edu/group/mappingmilitants/cgi-bin/groups/view/251.

20. Council on Foreign Relations. (June 2009). http://www.cfr.org/publications/10219.

21. Dr. Zachary Abuza. "Joining the New Caravan: ISIS and the Regeneration of Terrorism in Southeast Asia." *Strategic Studies Institute* (United States Army War College: June 25, 2015).

22. Australian Government Department of Foreign Affairs and Trade. (2004)." Transnational Terrorism:The Threat to Australia." http://www.dfat.gov.au/publications/terrorism/

23. Commonwealth of Australia. Australian National Security: Listed Terrorist Organizations. Accessed May 17, 2016. https://www.nationalsecurity.gov.au/Listedterroristorganisations/Pages/default.aspx.

24. "Global Terrorist groups exploit mentally ill people to carry out attacks." *Strait Times.* http://www.straitstimes.com/world/global-terrorist-groups-exploit-mentally-ill-people-to-carry-out-attacks-experts. Retrieved May 17, 2016.

25. "Death of Australian citizens Neil Christopher Prakash and ShadiJabar Khalil Mohammad." Joint Media Release, Government of Australia. Attorney General for Australia, Senator the Hon George Brandis QC. https://www.attorneygeneral.gov.au/Mediareleases/Pages/2016/SecondQuarter/5-May-2016-Death-of-Australian-citizens-Neil-Christopher-Prakash-and-Shadi-Jabar-Khalil-Mohammad.aspx.

Latin America and South America

LEARNING OUTCOMES

After studying this chapter, students should be able to:

1. Describe how death squads have been employed to control peasant revolutions in both historical and modern day Central America.

2. Summarize how land seizure in rural regions led to the rise of terrorist groups.

3. Explain the nature and importance of the drugs trade in fueling terrorist activity in Central America.

4. Explain how the gang problems in Central and Latin America affect the United States.

5. Describe how FARC and other Marxist groups have been countered by the Colombian Government.

6. Explain why international terrorists may find a safe haven in Colombia to plan attacks elsewhere.

KEY WORDS TO NOTE

Cali cartel—Drug cartel founded in 1977 in southern Colombia around the city of Cali

Che Guevara—Marxist revolutionary born in Argentina and a key figure in the Cuban Revolution

Chiapas—Southeast Mexican State where a peasant uprising led by the Zapatista National Liberation Army continues to press for greater autonomy

Death Squad—An armed group that conducts extrajudicial killings or forced disappearances of persons for the purposes of political repression, genocide, or revolutionary terror

Emiliano Zapata—The leader of the peasant revolution in the state of Chiapas

Genocide—The deliberate killing of a large group of people, especially those of a particular ethnic group or nation

Monsignor Juan Gerardi Conedera—Guatemalan Catholic priest and human rights activist beaten to death after compiling a report on human rights abuses in 1998

Morazanist Patriotic Front (FPM)—A radical, leftist Honduran terrorist group that first appeared in the late 1980s; its attacks were in protest of U.S. intervention in Honduran economic and political affairs

Popular Revolutionary Army (EPR)—A leftist guerrilla movement that advocates armed struggle in order to overthrow the Mexican government

Revolutionary Armed Forces of Colombia (FARC)—Established in 1964 as the military wing of the Colombian Communist Party and is a large well-organized Marxist movement

Sandinista National Liberation Front (FSLN)—(*Frente Sandinista de Liberación Nacional*), a socialist political party in Nicaragua, named after Augusto César Sandino, leader of the Nicaraguan resistance against the U.S. occupation of Nicaragua in the 1930s. Party members are called **Sandinistas** in both English and Spanish

Shining Path (Sendero Luminoso)—A left-wing Maoist group that seeks to overthrow the Peruvian government

United Self-Defense Forces of Colombia (AUC)—An umbrella organization for paramilitary groups in Colombia

Zapatista National Liberation Army (ELZN)—A revolutionary leftist group based in Chiapas, the southernmost state of Mexico

OVERVIEW

Geographically, Latin America includes the landmass extending from the Rio Grande border between Texas and Mexico to the southern tip of South America, plus some Caribbean islands. The total landmass is two and one-half times the size of the United States. Brazil alone is larger than the continental United States.

The physical features of this vast expanse present sharp differences: the Andean mountain range, which stretches the full length of South America and has peaks as high as twenty thousand feet; the dense, tropical forest of the Amazon basin; the arid desert plains of Northern Mexico; and the fertile, deep grasslands of the Argentine pampas.

Latin America has three primary racial groups: native indigenous Indians, white Europeans, and black Africans. Spanish is generally spoken everywhere, except for Brazil (Portuguese), the Andes (Quechua and other uniquely Indian languages), Guatemala (over twenty Indian languages), the Caribbean (French, English, and Dutch), and Mexico (scattered pockets of Indian languages). By early 2005, the total population of this vast area came to 365,384,570 compared with 295,267,054 million in the United States.[1] Latin American society displays startling contrasts between rich and poor, city and country, learned and illiterate, powerful lords of the hacienda and the deferential peasants, and the wealthy entrepreneurs and desperate street urchins. Politically, Latin America includes twenty-six nations, whose recent experiences range from military dictatorships to electoral democracy. Economically, Latin America belongs to the "developing" world, having been beset upon, and battered by, historical and contemporary obstacles to rapid economic growth. Here, too, there is diversity: from the one-crop dependency of tiny Honduras to the industrial promise of Brazil, Chile, and Mexico.

Throughout modern history, Latin Americans have sought to achieve political and economic independence from colonial, imperial, and neo-imperial powers with only one goal: wealth for the winners. It is a bitter irony that the name "Latin America" was coined by mid-nineteenth-century French, who thought that since their culture, like that of Spanish and Portuguese America, was "Latin" in context (i.e., Romance language speaking), it was destined to assume leadership throughout the continent. As these observations suggest, Latin America resists easy categorization. It is a region rich in paradoxes:

1. Beginning in 1492, its conquest by the Spanish and Portuguese created a new social order based on domination, hierarchy, and intermingling of European, African, and indigenous Indian elements. The European intrusion profoundly altered the Indian communities. Compared with the ancient civilizations of Africa and Asia, these Latin American societies are relatively young. Most nations of Latin America obtained political independence from Spain and Portugal in the early nineteenth century, more than a hundred years before successful anticolonial movements in other Third World countries.

2. Throughout its history, Latin America has been both tumultuous and stable. Its tradition of political violence has erupted in coups, assassinations, armed movements, military interventions, and (more rarely) social revolutions. Ideological encounters of liberalism, positivism, corporatism, anarchism, socialism, communism, fascism, and strong religious teachings of every doctrinal hue have sharpened the intensity of struggle. Despite the differing forms of political conflict, old social and economic structures have persisted.

3. Latin America has been independent and dependent and autonomous and subordinate. The achievement of nationhood by 1830 in all but parts of the Caribbean basin represented significant growth and achievement. Yet, this nationhood continued to be affected by colonization originating from Britain and France, and ultimately, the United States.

4. Latin America is both prosperous and poor. Ever since being conquered by the Europeans, the region has been described as rich in natural resources: first, the lust for silver and gold

and, today, for petroleum, gas, copper, iron ore, coffee, sugar, soybeans, or for expanded trade in general. But the image of endless wealth lingers. In startling contrast, there is also the picture of great poverty: peasants without tools, workers without jobs, children without food, and mothers without hope.

To understand Latin American history and its many experiences with terrorism, political violence, and insurgency requires a flexible, broad-based approach.

LATIN AMERICAN TERRORISM

Terrorism that has occurred in Central and South American countries tends to be significantly different than terrorism that has taken place in Western Europe, Asia, and the Middle East. Many Latin American countries have suffered from "state terrorism," including the use of **death squads** by extreme right-wing, authoritarian governments. People employ terrorist violence in the name of many causes. Insurgency, freedom fighting, or just plain terrorism from both the left and the right continues unabated in Colombia. The tendency to label as terrorism any violent act of which we do not approve is erroneous. Terrorism is a specific kind of violence. It therefore begs the question: Is state involvement in systematic abuse of human rights and a government's tacit support of military junta and the use of unofficial death squads in many Central and South American countries terrorism? The so-called banana Republics, joked about in the early part of the twentieth century, became serious problems when they experienced revolutions and insurgencies in the 1970s and 1980s. The former Soviet Union and other Communist causes often backed efforts to destabilize the area and break the U.S. support of dictators.

We begin with the most prominent terror movements in Central America, from their developmental stages after the Mexican Revolution of 1910 to the changes in typical terror tactics in South America. Drug dealings by Colombian, Mexican, and other drug cartels (referred to as narco-terrorism), and the oppressive regimes in Uruguay, El Salvador, Argentina, and others will be discussed. The horrors associated with Latin American death squads will be explored, along with the conditions, tactics, and distinctive characteristics of Latin American terrorism.

MEXICO

For several decades after independence, Mexico's political life was a prototype of chronic political instability. National governments came and went at gunpoint, threatening the new nation's territorial integrity (Figure 13-1). By the mid-nineteenth century, Mexico was heading toward a liberal government that would have greatly reduced the power of the church and the corresponding burden of its colonial legacy. Political liberalism, however, gave way to the dictatorship of Porfirio Diaz from 1876 to 1880 and again from 1884 to 1911 and, thus, was confronted by the Mexican

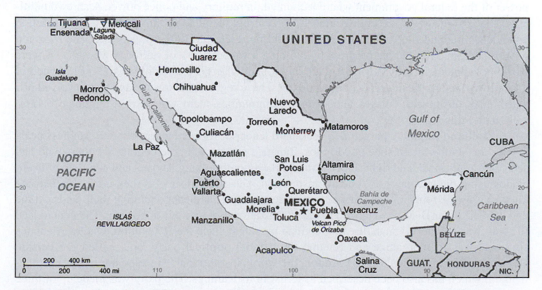

FIGURE 13-1 Map of Mexico. *Source:* Central Intelligence Agency, *The World Factbook, 2008.*

Revolution . . . the first of the world's great twentieth-century revolutions. Out of that revolution, a stable political system arose that has been unmatched anywhere in Latin America. The Wars for Independence left Mexico in abject decay. Actual fighting was widespread and protracted, leaving a severely disrupted economy. Gold and silver mines, once the pride of Spain's overseas Mexican empire, had fallen into disrepair. Insurgents and royalists had made it a point of killing technicians, while thousands of miners had gone off to war, leaving the mines to fall into ruins. Roads had been neglected as well, so the country lacked a workable system of transportation and/ or strong communication capability. Travel by stagecoach was difficult and hazardous, and transport, often by pack saddle, was costly and slow. This was a serious obstacle to economic progress. It was estimated that over thirty percent of the entire adult male population in Mexico was unemployed, often angry, and usually well-armed. They posed not only an economic problem, but a social and criminal threat as well. Some of these veterans did find work while others turned to crime (highway robbery being a particular favorite). Some stayed on in the military while others drifted into unofficial, quasi-military police units that provided support for local political bosses, generally known as *caudillos*, who were soon to play a dominant role in Mexico's political scene.

There were two institutional power bases in Mexico after independence—the Catholic Church and the Mexican military. The church had come through the independence wars with most of its wealth intact. The second power base was the military, which dominated national politics during the forty-year period from 1821 to 1860. Mexico had at least fifty separate presidencies, each lasting an average of less than one year! Army officers led thirty-five of these ill-starred regimes. The usual means of winning the presidential office was through a military coup to get rid of the sitting president. Looming through this period was the powerful figure of General Antonio López de Santa Ana, who held the presidency on nine separate occasions and who installed figureheads at other times. Santa Ana was one of Mexico's most famous caudillos. These strongmen assembled their armed followers (miniature armies), who were primarily seeking wealth. Once they fought their way into national power, they participated in the further draining of national reserves, until the next reigning caudillo, armed with new followers, fought his way into power. The caudillos themselves did not bother too much with the job of governance. That was left up to a cadre of lawyers and professional advisors, many who described themselves as *licenciados*, meaning licensed, degreed, or in some way considered to be certified individuals.

General Porfirio Diaz assumed power after the death of Benito Juarez in 1872, who had himself overthrown Maximilian von Habsburg of Austria (1863–1867). The Diaz Era (1876–1911) signaled progress, but at a stiff price. For the thirty years of his reign, Diaz proved himself to be a master of political intrigue. He began by creating a broad coalition of his military colleagues and followers. Building his army was one of his major goals, and he forged ahead while maintaining control of a vast countryside, where the large majority of Mexicans lived. Diaz relied heavily on a force of *guardias rurales*, or rural police. In short, Diaz patiently built up the power of the federal government where it counted, in military and police power. A shrewd politician, Diaz avoided ever presenting himself as a corrupt dictator. He simply had the constitution amended, time and time again, so that he could be re-elected to the presidency. The Mexican government made economic progress by building a vast network of railroads whose costs were partially supplemented by private foreign investment. The government took to seizing much of the railway land in the interest of nationalizing. These regular seizures of land also involved private homes, businesses, villages, and farming communities, many who were struggling economically under this regime.

Emiliano Zapata emerged as a rock-hard leader of former landowners and landless peasants in the southwestern state of Morelos. Zapata's groups were the country dwellers who had seen their traditional land rights taken away by the smooth-talking lawyers and a myriad of licenciados using the new laws of "liberal" inspiration. These Zapatistas (as they inevitably became known), saw the rebellion as a chance to restore justice. That meant regaining their lands. At the end of World War II, Mexico looked to industrialization as a way out of poverty. The man to lead the way was Miguel Aleman, the first civilian president since the Revolution. One of Aleman's first acts was to reorganize and rename the official political party, now called the Partido Revolutionario Institutional (PRI). Adding the word "institutional" signaled a turn toward pragmatism, which has also been described as leftist in its leanings. The party was made up of three sectors: peasant, worker, and popular. The format is still retained. PRI emerged as a dominant official party, different from any other in Latin America. This era signaled a start of what became Mexico's legacy of political dominance through a one-party system. In 1964, Mexico's other political party, known as Partido Autonomista Nacional (PAN, a right-wing-oriented party), began to win seats in the Mexican congress, although it was still overwhelmingly outweighed by PRI representation. In 1971, guerrillas appeared on the scene, calling for violent action against the PRI. They staged a series of bank robberies and kidnappings. The latter reached into the diplomatic corps, and their victims included the U.S. Consul General in Guadalajara and the daughter of the Belgian ambassador. In 1974, the father-in-law of the president was seized and held for ransom by militant guerrillas. In the state of Guerrero, an ex-school teacher, Lucio Cabanas, led a guerrilla army that began to strike at will. Cabanas had turned revolutionary soon after his 1962 election as general secretary of the Federation of Socialist Peasant Students in Mexico. He fled the city for the Guerrero mountain region where he led his Army of the Poor and Peasant's Brigade against Injustice. It kidnapped the official PRI candidate for governor and defied the army by direct attacks on isolated outposts. It took a ten thousand-man army more than a year to hunt down and kill the rebels and their leader. Despite predictions on the left, Cabanas had no successor in Guerrero or elsewhere, as the guerrilla threat soon faded. To avoid capture, Cabanas committed suicide.

In the late 1960s, student-initiated protests in Mexico shook the Western world. The precipitating factor was Mexico's hosting of the summer Olympic Games in 1968. The Mexican government went all out to "sell" Mexico to the world. The Mexican Left, always strong among students, was upset that the government might succeed in this public relations venture. There began a test of wills. A secondary school clash in Mexico City in 1968 was met by brutal force from the riot police. Protest spread to the national university in August, culminating in a strike. The government thought it was a "subversive conspiracy" bent on disrupting the Olympic Games. President Diaz Ordaz responded by sending army troops onto the campus, thereby violating its historic sanctuary status. The battle was quickly joined. Could the student left stop the Olympic Games? The tragic pattern of confrontation between students and troops continued. On October 2, 1968, a rally of students in the Mexico City section of Tlatelolco drew an unusually heavy contingent of security forces. An order to disperse was not observed and the police and paramilitary forces moved in. Later they claimed to have taken sniper fire from surrounding buildings. They began shooting, and the crowd was caught in a murderous crossfire, as hundreds fell dead and many more wounded. The massacre at Tlatelolco sent a shudder throughout Mexico. There was no inquiry and no convincing explanation from the military or civilian authorities responsible for the slaughter. Many critics said the massacre proved the bankruptcy of the PRI monopoly on power. By the same token, the brutal show of force convinced everyone that mass challenges to authority would only bring more death and destruction. The effect was then very chilling.

On January 13, 2005, Special Prosecutor Ignacio Carillo announced that Mexico would be bringing charges of **genocide** against two dozen former officials for the 1968 leftist dissident student massacre at Mexico City's Tlatelolco Plaza, just days before the Olympic Games opened. Former president Luis Echeverría, who was interior minister at the time, was under investigation for his role in the tragedy. In July 2004, the prosecutor sought to bring genocide charges against Echeverría and twelve others in a different case, a 1971 attack on students that left at least a dozen dead. The charges were dismissed based on the statute of limitations, and the Supreme Court is reviewing Carillo's appeal. He pledged to file charges in the Tlatelolco case even if the Supreme Court has not ruled in the 1971 killings, though the High Court's decision is seen as crucial to establishing a framework for prosecuting similar cases.

In June 2006, eighty-four-year-old Echeverría was charged with genocide in connection with the massacre. He was placed under house arrest pending trial. The following month he was cleared of genocide charges, as the judge found that Echeverría could not be put on trial because the statute of limitations had expired.

President Vicente Fox, of the Partido de Accion Nacional (PAN), took office in 2000, ending seventy-one years of single-party rule by the PRI party. He pledged to expose Mexico's repressive, secret past. From the 1960s to the 1980s, a hundred or more Mexicans are reported to have died at the hands of government security forces in a so-called dirty war against dissidents. Rights groups hailed Fox's appointment of Carillo in 2002 as an unprecedented step toward ending official impunity. But limited resources, court maneuvers, and resistance by police and military have hampered the prosecutor. Of eleven "dirty war arrest warrants," just three suspects have been arrested and face trial. Genocide, normally associated with slaughters like the Nazi killing of the Jews, is increasingly being used in human rights cases around the world. In Mexico, genocide can apply if victims were targeted as members of a group, such as a student movement.[2]

North American Free Trade Agreement

Mexico's emergence from a colonial past has been conditioned by one factor that no other Latin American nation shares: a two thousand-mile border with the United States. That proximity has produced benefits and liabilities. Harvard-educated economist Carlos Salinas de Gortari, at the age of thirty-nine, was elected president of Mexico in 1988. He quickly moved toward an economy based more on free market principles than on state control and toward better economic relations with the United States. He is, perhaps, best known for his role in negotiating the North American Free Trade Agreement (NAFTA). Salinas was a técnico, a competent technocrat with little, or no, grassroots political experience. Technically, he was highly qualified to deal with the nation's problems. Politically, however, he had to define himself on the campaign trail. Salinas won with only 50.4 percent of the vote—his victory marred by allegations of fraud. As president, he worked to revive Mexico's economy by curbing inflation and reducing government regulations. He became the major promoter of NAFTA, and in signing the accord (in 1992), reversed Mexico's historical resistance to foreign investment and to U.S. involvement in its affairs. Although Salinas's administration was praised for its economic reforms, it lost some of its luster when his brother, Raúl, was arrested in 1995 for the 1994 murder of a PRI official and was later (1996) accused of massive financial misappropriations. After Carlos Salinas responded by criticizing the Mexican government, he was pressured into de facto exile, only returning to Mexico in 2000. All the optimism resulting from the NAFTA accord promptly came under assault. On January 1, 1994 (the day after NAFTA came into effect), a guerrilla movement in the poverty-stricken state of **Chiapas** rose up to denounce the free trade accord, the Salinista economic model, and the undemocratic character of the political regime.

Zapatista National Liberation Army

A major issue facing the Mexican government has been the land dispute surrounding the Chiapas region in southern Mexico. Mexico has experienced almost unprecedented economic growth in the past few decades, but there has been a clear failure to equitably distribute that wealth due to a lack of social reform. As a result, Mexico remains a country of "haves and have-nots." In addition to Chiapas, other regions have experienced guerrilla warfare. These are located in the regions of Oaxaca, Hidalgo, Veracruz, and Puebla. Immortalized from the days of the revolution, Emiliano Zapata who had been conscripted into the army and served for seven years fought passionately for restoration of confiscated land; his Plan of Ayala, called for the seizure of all foreign-owned land, all land taken from villages, confiscation of one-third of all land held by "friendly" hacendados, and full confiscation of land owned by persons opposed to the Plan of Ayala. Zapata, who was killed in an ambush in 1919, is still lauded by the peasants of southern Mexico as their true hero. Using Zapata as a symbol of revolutionary righteousness, the Zapatista movement continues to wage an armed struggle for land rights in the Chiapas region. This group, called the **Zapatista National Liberation Army (ELZN)**, appeared violently on the world scene in 1994, when it fomented an armed uprising against the Mexican government, to protest the distribution of land in the region. This movement better fits the definition of a guerrilla group than a subversive terror organization. The group uses many different terror tactics to achieve notoriety and influence political aims.

As we have seen in so many other conflicts, land was the primary issue that influenced the uprising. Mexicans who farmed and eked out their living had long been granted land for their families. This ended with NAFTA, when the Mexican government stopped its Land Distribution Program. Angry and well-armed men from Chiapas then came out of the hills and attacked the cities. The Mexican government responded by sending in the military. Chiapas became a region controlled by the Mexican army. Many of Mexico's problems revolved around the failing economy in 1994 and the slow rate of recovery. The erosion of the ruling Institutional Revolutionary Party's (PRI) power has not helped and continues to contribute to the unrest. In 1995, thirty thousand Mexican soldiers, intent on the destruction of the ELZN guerrillas, invaded the Chiapas region. The exercise was an abject failure, and ELZN simply disappeared into the hills of

Chiapas, much like the Viet Cong did in Vietnam. The soldiers continued to surround Realidad, believed to be the center of Zapatista operations. To appeal for the farmers' rights to the land and a cessation of the violence, Bishop Samuel Louis Garcia acted as a mediator for the ELZN, the people of Chiapas, and Mexican authorities. Chiapas remains a region of ongoing conflict and one of the main reasons for the fall of the long-ruling PRI in Mexico. The PRI lost both the presidency and the governorship in the province of Chiapas in 2000. Vincente Fox began his term with the intention of bringing an end to the ELZN rebellion in that region. The talks between Fox and the ELZN foundered, and the zones controlled by the Zapatista rebels, although much quieter now, continue to remain off-limits to government control.[3]

The Zapatistas, relying on the classic tactic of surprise attacks, and with considerable communications skills, initiated a public relations extravaganza. As the premier online guerrilla group, it carefully disseminated many of its official documents and communiqués to a global online audience. While the group enjoyed some crucial successes, it has also been saddled with considerable political and military limitations. This predicament stands in sharp contrast to the context of the group's famous hero, Emilo Zapata, who also marched to the rhythm of global politics and, subsequently, achieved broad revolutionary goals.

The Chiapas regional conflict gets little press, but the issues of land grabs and unchecked violent attacks continue. Massacres of farm workers are not uncommon and the police do little to prevent such actions.

Right-Wing Violence

An extreme right-wing movement called "Peace and Justice" has been carrying out attacks against the ELZN and its supporters. This group pledges its support to the Institutional Revolutionary Party and operates as a death squad in the Chiapas region. The viciousness of the attacks seems to have the support of the military, as well as the local police authorities, and this has led to beatings, murders, and the mass evacuation of entire villages. Active units, pledging support for the government and finding support from the police, appear to have the same goals seen in state-sponsored terrorism: "the systemic and purposeful creation, by a political regime, of fear by violent means, and/or by the threat of such violence." The purpose of the systematic exercise of such publicly visible violence is to maintain, legitimize, or strengthen the social and administrative control of the state. The activities of the Peace and Justice Group seem destined to be part of the fabric of Mexican society for this region. By generating significant fear, this right-wing group is able to influence the predominantly Mayan Indian population of Chiapas.

Popular Revolutionary Army

The **Popular Revolutionary Army (EPR)** ranks second in strength to the Zapatista movement. With its base and origins in the southern states of Oaxaca and Guerrero, it gains support from the poverty-stricken villages of those regions. The topography of the regions . . . forested mountains and rugged terrain . . . makes an ideal home base for a guerrilla force. The EPR is a left-wing group, considered by the Mexicans to actually be several different movements operating under a single banner. EPR attacks have been sporadic and often without defining a clearly understood objective. Ambushes of federal police and military convoys are EPR's primary tactics. Their strength and size have yet to be determined, but the group claims to have over twenty thousand guerrillas operating in the southern states. Support for the group has also come from an unknown outside source that may well be responsible for arming it with modern, Russian-made weaponry. In response to the logistics and training it has received from Peru's Marxist-oriented Shining Path, the EPR set up a Mexican support committee for the popular war in Peru. Sustained operations have been difficult, and it is questionable if the group has the ability to employ any effective tactics to disrupt or alter government policy. Some EPR attacks on the outskirts of Mexico City have occurred and communiqués have been issued to its members to target the "fat cat" capitalist businesses located there.

Other movements are surfacing in the poorer regions of Mexico as a result of the country's economic woes and the perception that the poor are getting poorer and the rich are getting richer. Such groups as the Revolutionary Army of Popular Insurgence and the Armed Front for the Liberation of the Marginalized People of Guerrero may be following the Zapatista uprising as a means for gaining concessions from the government. It is unclear whether the Mexican military can contain more than one guerrilla army at a time. Currently, it is fully occupied with the Chiapas region and it would seem incapable of handling yet another battlefront.

Narco-Terrorism

Drug trafficking, organized crime, human rights violations, disappearances, arms trafficking, and state abuse are familiar. But what is narco-terrorism and where does the term originate. The first mention and use of the term we believe dates back to the Sendero Luminoso (Shining Path) in Peru during the campaign against them in the 1980s. The term was coined to describe attacks by Shining Path against counternarcotics police in Peru. The term gathered more attention following the 9-11 attacks on the United States. The Department of Defence has defined narco-terrorism as: *"Terrorism conducted to further the aims of drug traffickers. It may include assassinations, extortion, hijackings, bombings and kidnappings directed against judges, prosecutors, elected officials, or law enforcement agents, and general disruption of a legitimate government to divert attention from drug operations."* The global War on Terror announced by President Bush in 2001 also encompassed the war on drugs. Making the link between drug trafficking and terrorism maybe over simplistic; however, there is evidence of terrorist groups such as FARC (Colombia) and Shining Path (Peru) using the proceeds of drugs to carry out attacks. If we look at Mexico we see organized crime families controlling the lucrative drug trade. Mexico is the main supplier to the U.S. market of heroin, methamphetamine, and marijuana and a major transit country for cocaine sold in the United States. In April 2011, Michael McCaul, U.S. Republican Representative of Texas and Chairman of the Homeland Security Oversight and Investigations Subcommittee, introduced a bill to add Mexico's six main 'cartels' (then listed as Arellano Felix, Los Zetas, Beltran Leyva, Familia Michoacana, Sinaloa Cartel, and the Gulf Cartel) to the U.S. State Department's Foreign Terrorist Organizations list, arguing that "the [Mexican] cartels use violence to gain political and economic influence." The unsuccessful bill would have increased U.S. law enforcement powers in Mexico, including easier access to the cartels' finances and tougher sanctions against organizations and individuals providing them support.

That drug cartels excel in the use of violence and commit them in such a way as to create terror in the community. Many examples are available—beheadings are not just restricted to Islamic State but are used by cartels to send messages and to control turf. In 2011, members of Los Zetas burnt down a casino in Monterrey, in the northeast state of Nuevo León, and fifty-two people, including a majority of women, died as a result. It was later revealed that the attack was meant to scare the owners of the casino, who had refused to pay the "cartel" a weekly extortion fee, and the situation escalated.[4] Los Zetas have been particularly brutal in their tactics, often publicly displaying bodies or body parts.

Disappearances and Human Rights Abuse

Mexico is seen as being very forceful in its crackdown on the drug cartels but there is a broader story when it comes to police and military actions. The police/military are accused of extra judicial killings and to all intents and purposes act with almost impunity. In 2014, the disappearance of forty-three student teachers in Iguala remains a black mark against the police and the government. Mexico's National Register of Missing and Disappeared People recorded five thousand and ninety-eight cases between January and October 2014. One hundred and sixty-two of these cases are being investigated at the federal level. The forty-three students were en route to a demonstration at the time they "disappeared" in September 2014, the students commandeered several buses to travel to Mexico City to commemorate the anniversary of the 1968 Tlatelolco massacre. They were intercepted by local police and a confrontation ensued. Details of what happened during and after the confrontation remain unclear, but the official investigation concluded that once the students were in custody, they were handed over to the local "United Warriors" crime syndicate and presumably killed. Mexican authorities claimed Iguala's mayor, Jose Abraca and his wife María de los Ángeles Pineda Villa, masterminded the abduction. Since the incident more than eighty arrests have been made and of that number forty-four are police officers.

The UN special rapporteur on extrajudicial, summary, or arbitrary executions conducted a fact-finding mission to Mexico in April–May 2013, and stated that extrajudicial executions by security forces were widespread and often occurred without accountability.

GUATEMALA

Outside Communist influences in Guatemala during the last fifty years have done much to further human rights violations through the dictatorships and juntas that have to come to power. During the Cold War years, this influence was particularly strong (Figure 13-2). The United States assisted in the military overthrow of Guatemala's Communist regime in 1954, but the series of extreme right-wing military governments that followed did nothing to initiate reforms. Rather, they focused on campaigns against Communist infiltration. With so much oppression in the country, the peasantry began to retaliate by establishing the Rebel Armed Forces (FAR), which began to take shape in the early 1960s and was the precursor to the Guatemalan National Unity (URNG), established in 1982. The military had little success in repressing such movements and, with the arrival of URNG, embarked on a campaign of state-sponsored terror.

The military was unleashed and clandestine death squads formed, while military and security police openly committed murder and torture. The resulting exodus from the region gradually gained international attention. Military leaders in Guatemala, however, were becoming desperate to remain in power, so they increased the tactics of state-sponsored terror and murder against their people. A "scorched earth" policy was employed in many instances and whole villages, as well as lands and crops, were destroyed. Torture of suspected Communists was commonplace, and the methods of torture were grotesque and usually fatal. Human rights in Guatemala, and past U.S. support for the regime, are issues to ponder, as are questions regarding the level of involvement of the U.S. government in political murders, torture, and human rights abuses.

FIGURE 13-2   Map of Guatemala.   *Source:* Central Intelligence Agency, *The World Factbook, 2008.*

The Bishop of Guatemala—Monsignor Juan Gerardi Conedera

Guatemala and its rebels signed a peace deal in 1996, which did little to eradicate the violence that permeated the country. In April 1998, **Monsignor Juan Gerardi Conedera** released his report "Guatemala Never Again," concerning human rights abuses and violations mainly perpetrated by the Guatemalan Army, and two days later was beaten to death as he returned to his home. Conedera was the coordinator of the Archbishop's Human Rights Office (ODHA) and was the driving force behind the project for the Recovery of Historical Memory (REMHI), which had been created to shed light on the war's human rights violations. It seemed likely that his death was the work of a Guatemalan death squad. Death squads had killed with impunity during the thirty-six-year conflict.[5]

Impunity

The abuses and atrocities perpetrated by the Guatemalan state had relied on a system of impunity defined as "freedom from accountability for criminal wrongdoing, or freedom from other legal sanctions." The impunity system in Guatemala was conducted by several simple mechanisms. First, the state denies any state-sponsored violence, and second, those who would have made claims of torture and rights abuse had simply "disappeared." Such disappearances made it difficult to bring any judicial action against Guatemala. In the sixteen years leading up to 1990, it is estimated that over a hundred thousand Guatemalans were killed, and possibly another forty thousand disappeared without a trace! The government has a very thin veneer of democracy, and its ability to control the powerful military is doubtful, especially when it comes to human rights abuses. The peace accord, finalized in 1996, brought an end to thirty-six years of internal fighting, and Guatemalans began returning to their villages from neighboring countries. One such village that will likely never recover from atrocities committed by the military is the remote mountain hamlet of Plan de Sanchez where the army slaughtered more than two hundred people, mostly Mayan women and children. On July 18, 1982, soldiers on anti-insurgency duties overran the hamlet, then raped and tortured villagers, herded them into a building and blew it up. No one has been prosecuted for the Plan de Sanchez massacre and few have faced justice for other rights abuses. In 2005, the Inter-American Court of Human Rights in Costa Rica awarded three hundred and seventeen family members close to $25,000 each to be paid by the Guatemalan government.[6]

State-sponsored terrorism in Guatemala has fostered a populace with a shared set of experiences of systemic human rights violations. It is a populace not only cynical of the formal, institutional applications of justice but also one that has experienced extralegal "justice" in the fight for social control and social transformation of Guatemalan society.[7]

The Civil War

The first thorn in the side of successive oppressive military governments was the Rebel Armed Forces (FAR), which began limited guerrilla operations as far back as 1962. Over the years, the movement grew among the indigenous groups and expanded to include the Guerrilla Army of the Poor (EGP) in 1972 and the Organization of People in Arms (OPRA). With the merging of these three guerrilla movements, all with the same causes and complaints, the Guatemalan National Unity Group (URNG) was formed. The military conducted operations in which they destroyed villages and killed entire populations. In some of these operations, their actions, which were collectively called "pacification," typified those used in the Vietnam War. They employed a scorched earth policy. By targeting the civilian population in the countryside, the military assumed it would stop support of the guerrilla army.

At the end of Guatemala's civil war, four hundred and forty villages had been burned off the face of the planet.[8] The Guatemalan state had conducted approximately six hundred and sixty massacres, displaced one and a half million people, and murdered between one hundred and fifty and two hundred thousand individuals. Tens of thousands of civilians remain documented as "disappeared."[9] Parents witnessed their children's heads smashed into trees and husbands were forced to watch their pregnant wives violently gang raped and hacked to death by soldiers.[10]

Since the 1996 Peace Accords, there have been many attempts to bring justice to Guatemala. Amnesty International has been prominent in detailing human rights abuses believed to be perpetrated by the military and the death squads. This has led to attacks against prominent Catholic Church leaders in Guatemala to try to silence their criticism.

By the end of 1998, climatic changes in the region prompted the government to suspend parts of its Constitution. Following the distinctive impact of Hurricane Mitch, which decimated several Central American countries, including Guatemala, the government of Alvaro Arzu suspended two articles of the country's Constitution: Articles Six and Twenty-Six. This is believed to be a direct result of the looting and violence in the cities following the hurricane and the government's fear of a resurgence of terrorism.[11] Article Six protects Guatemalans from detention or imprisonment without cause or in the absence of a court order, while Article Twenty-Six guarantees the right of freedom of travel. Such severe measures threaten to return Guatemala to a repressive government. The likelihood that Guatemala will experience noticeable progress with regard to the overall quality of democratic governance, reforms, and human rights due to high levels of corruption is definitely not on the near horizon. Guatemala remains a country where the privileged and elite manipulate the legislative, executive, and judiciary branches in order to ensure that their past and present unlawful actions are not subject to public scrutiny or even the rule of law.

HONDURAS

Honduras has undergone the least turmoil of all the Central American republics. Rivalries between the Liberal and Conservative parties persisted to the mid-twentieth century, popular agitation has been minimal, and power has rested in the hands of a triangular alliance—landowners, foreign investors (mainly United Fruit), and the military (Figure 13-3). Because of its economic and political weakness, Honduras has been especially vulnerable to outside influence. Honduran history reveals a fundamental fact of Central American political life—the emergence of the military as an autonomous caste and as a supreme arbiter in national affairs. A career in the Honduran

Armed Forces offers chances of upward mobility to middle-class young men. The aristocracy controls land, universities are restrictive, and there is hardly any industrial development. An ambitious person of middling origin has almost no alternative. As a result, recruits and cadets take immense pride in the honor and dignity of the military as an institution, and officers tend to look down on politicians and civilians.

Strife with neighboring countries has played an important part in Honduran history. During the 1960s, tensions with El Salvador mounted steadily. There have been long-standing, although minor, territorial disputes. El Salvador is a densely populated country; Honduras is just the opposite. Consequently, people from El Salvador looking for jobs in Honduras create resentment. A 1963 law prohibited companies from employing more than ten percent foreigners (read Salvadorans), and a 1968 decree prevented Salvadorans from gaining title to Honduran land.

As has been evidenced throughout most of Central America, the paranoia that gripped the United States during the Cold War years was played out in its support of countries ripe for Communist influence. Honduras has benefited from decades of military support from the United States and was involved, throughout the 1980s, in fighting the invading Sandinistas and in hunting down rebel Contra bases. Geography made it inevitable that Honduras would be drawn into the U.S.-sponsored war against the Sandinistas. The United States rapidly transformed Honduras into a launching pad for Contra attacks against neighboring Nicaragua. Thousands of regular U.S. military and National Guard units rotated duty in Honduras, inundating the economy with hundreds of millions of U.S. dollars. All of these activities just reinforced the power of the Honduran military.

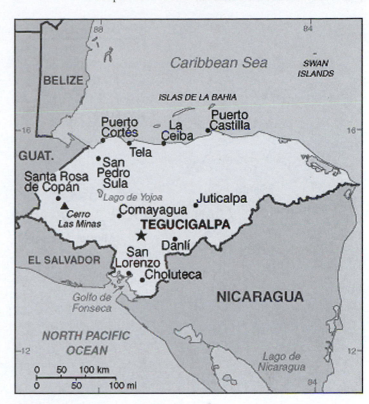

FIGURE 13-3 Map of Honduras. *Source:* Central Intelligence Agency, *The World Factbook, 2008.*

Morazanist Patriotic Front

The **Morazanist Patriotic Front (FPM)** is a small, extreme left-wing terror group that was violently opposed to U.S. intervention and support of the right-wing political government in Honduras. It first appeared in the late 1980s, and its attacks were aimed mostly at U.S. military personnel. It carried out bomb attacks on military buses carrying U.S. service personnel and, in 1989, claimed responsibility for just such an incident, in which three U.S. servicemen were wounded. Since then, FPM attacks have been sporadic and ineffectively executed.[12] Currently, there have been no known incidents arising from this organization and in the past had ties to the government of both Cuba and Nicaragua.

EL SALVADOR

As in Mexico, Salvadorians have been engaged in an ongoing demand for land reform and rights, dating back nearly seventy years. Much of El Salvador's economy was based on its coffee production and export, which was controlled by an influential group of families (Figure 13-4). The first protests date back to the first quarter of the twentieth century and to a campaigner from the Central American Communist Party, Augustin Farabundo Marti. His goal, like that of the Chiapas of Mexico, was not the overthrow of the government, but the redistribution of wealth from the land on an equitable basis. By 1930, the country was under military control of General Martinez, who sided with the society elite and coffee growers. Augustin Farabundo Marti was arrested in a military crackdown on his movement and was subsequently executed by a firing squad. The peasants were not organized in sufficient numbers to mount any sort of insurgent response. The military sought to purge the country of peasant "subversives" and went on a killing spree, accounting for more than thirty thousand deaths. In 1981 alone, there were twelve thousand five hundred and one murders reported in El Salvador.

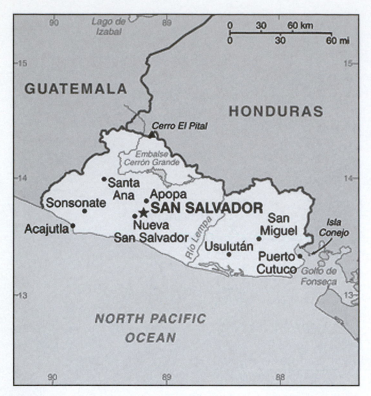

FIGURE 13-4   Map of El Salvador.   *Source:* Central Intelligence Agency, *The World Factbook, 2008.*

FIGURE 13-5   Map of Nicaragua.   *Source:* Central Intelligence Agency, *The World Factbook, 2008.*

In the late 1960s and 1970s, El Salvador provided further example of extreme right-wing terror used as a governmental tool to eradicate opposition. Again, death squads were utilized and two specific groups were formed, one covert and the other overt, to protect wealthy landowners and to spread fear among the peasants. In 1968, the commander of the El Salvador National Guard[13] formed the ORDEN. This was an intelligence-gathering organization that went beyond information gathering, and included kidnapping and murdering peasants. In attempting to analyze and define terrorism, some scholars believe that the actions of death squads are not terroristic in nature. However, the subversive actions of a terrorist or guerrilla organization spread fear, disorder, and uncertainty within the ruling government and the country as a whole. Repression by death squads or paramilitary groups has the identical impact. Periods of relative peace were interrupted by violence perpetrated by the death squads both clandestinely and openly. The violence ended in 1992 with a peace agreement. Liberal views made anyone a target for death squads, including priests and nuns who were murdered. Also targeted were outspoken labor leaders and politicians. Throughout the 1980s, fear was pervasive throughout El Salvador.

NICARAGUA

This small Central American country of four and a half million has been embroiled in what can best be described as a struggle between superpowers. Nicaragua has had a leadership that boasts close ties to the United States and its military training institutions (Figure 13-5). Nicaragua has been supported by the United States since the mid-1930s, and its repressive National Guard was built and modeled on the U.S. National Guard and that is as close as the comparison can be. In power since 1937, the National Guard was separate from the military and operated as a private army and bodyguard for the Somoza family. It was allowed and encouraged to infiltrate and control all state operations and big business and ensured the Somoza family were fabulously wealthy. A very young but aggressive Anastasio Somoza García took over control of the National Guard when responsibility was turned over by U.S. marines in 1934. In the following years, Somoza consolidated his control over the Guard, purging any opposition from within, to his power base. On February 21, 1934, he ordered and approved the capture and murder of Augusto César Sandino. Sandino's execution was followed by the persecution and execution of hundreds of men, women, and children living in the semiautonomous region previously set aside for the former guerrillas. Sandino had led a peasant revolt against the U.S. presence in Nicaragua and its support for the regime through the 1920s and 1930s. He was at the point of making a deal with the government when he was assassinated. By 1937, Somoza had enough control to overthrow the president and have himself installed in office. He remained in power until his assassination in 1956, but by then, he had secured the country for his family to rule with impunity and support from the United States. He was succeeded by his son Luis Somoza.

SANDINISTA NATIONAL LIBERATION FRONT

The **Sandinista National Liberation Front (FSLN)** was formally organized in Nicaragua in 1961. Founded by José Carlos Fonseca Amador, Silvio Mayorga, and Tomás Borge Martínez, the FSLN began in the late 1950s as a group of student activists at the National Autonomous University of Nicaragua in Managua. Many of the early members were imprisoned. Borge spent several years in jail, and Fonseca spent several years in exile in Mexico, Cuba, and Costa Rica. Beginning with approximately twenty members in the early 1960s, the FSLN continued to struggle and grow in numbers. By the early 1970s, the group had gained enough support from peasants and students groups to launch limited military initiatives.

On December 27, 1974, a group of FSLN guerrillas seized the home of a former government official and took as hostages a handful of leading Nicaraguan officials, many of whom were Somoza relatives. With the mediation of Archbishop Obando y Bravo, the government and the guerrillas reached an agreement on December 30 that humiliated and further debilitated the Somoza regime. The guerrillas received US$1 million ransom, had a government declaration read over the radio and printed in *La Prensa*, and succeeded in getting fourteen Sandinista prisoners released from jail and flown to Cuba along with the kidnappers. The guerrilla movement's prestige soared because of this successful operation. The act also established the FSLN strategy of revolution as an effective alternative to a policy of promoting change peacefully. The Somoza government responded to the increased opposition with further censorship, intimidation, torture, and murder.

That the Somoza regime was continually propped up by successive U.S. governments is no surprise. Nicaragua was an outspoken opponent of the Cuban revolution and provided support for the Bay of Pigs in 1961. The Cold War was not a distant memory for the United States, and military assistance was provided to the Anastasio government to fight the Sandinistas. Anastasio Somoza had succeeded his dead brother through rigged elections in 1967 and continued in the family tradition—he was president of the country and also in personal charge of the National Guard so exercised total military and political power over the country. By now both middle class and peasants alike flocked to the Sandinista National Liberation Front.

Countering terrorism in El Salvador has recently been more focused on gang activity and their targeting attacks against the police. The state has a weakly worded definition of terrorism: "evidence of intent to provoke states of alarm, fear or terror in the population, place in imminent danger or affect the life or physical or mental integrity of people." To this end, the state has decided to employ its anti-terror legislation to combat the gangs in El Salvador which will only serve to blur the lines between organized crime syndicates and terrorism.

CONTRAS

The United States was willing to work with the FSLN, but by 1981, and with the arrival of President Ronald Reagan, the United States believed that the Sandinistas that were now the official government of Nicaragua were being actively supported by both the Soviet Union and Cuba and were arming the rebels in El Salvador. All support for Nicaragua was suspended, and the United States began providing support to Nicaraguan groups willing to overthrow the Sandinista government. The Contras is the name given to these groups, which included members of the now-defunct National Guard only too eager to return to the Somoza style of extreme right-wing government. The Contra leadership was represented mostly by former members of the National Guard; this fact made the movement highly unpopular among most Nicaraguans.

The Contras established operational bases in Honduras from which they launched hit-and-run raids throughout northern Nicaragua. The charismatic Edén Pastora abandoned the Sandinista revolution in July 1981 and formed his own guerrilla group, which operated in the southern part of Nicaragua from bases in Costa Rica. The United Nicaraguan Opposition operated in the northwest, the Opposition Block of the South operated in the southeast, and the Nicaraguan Coast Indian Unity operated in the northwest. Although the Sandinista army was larger and better equipped than the Contras, the antigovernment campaign became a serious threat to the FLSN government, largely through damage to the economy.

As the Contra war intensified, the Sandinistas' tolerance of political pluralism waned. The Sandinistas imposed emergency laws to ban criticism and organization of political opposition.

Most social programs suffered as a result of the war because the Sandinista regime was forced to increase military spending until half of its budget went for defense. Agricultural production also declined sharply as refugees fled areas of conflict.[14]

For the United States, a far more significant political bombshell was about to detonate at the Pentagon. Questions arose concerning the level of U.S. involvement in drug trafficking in exchange for weapons to the Contras. There have been many sensational journalistic pieces that pointed a finger at the CIA and the Reagan administration. The 1995 Kerry Committee Report holds some interesting facts in its findings. The subcommittee found that the Contra drug links included the following:

- Involvement in narcotics trafficking by individuals associated with the Contra movement.
- Participation of narcotics traffickers in Contra supply operations through business relationships with Contra organizations.
- Provision of assistance to the Contras by narcotics traffickers, including cash, weapons, planes, pilots, air supply services, and other materials, on a voluntary basis.
- Payment to drug traffickers with U.S. Department of State funds authorized by the Congress for humanitarian assistance to the Contras, in some cases after the traffickers had been indicted by federal law enforcement agencies on drug charges, in others while traffickers were under active investigation by these same agencies.[15]

There is no doubt that those involved in these drug schemes on the U.S. side hoped to expunge any pending legal indictments in return for assistance to the rebel Contras. The level of exploitation by the drug traffickers was purely self-serving and certainly not ideologically driven.

When examining the infrastructure that was in place in the 1970s for the movement of illegal narcotics through Central America to the United States, it was a simple shift of purpose to include weapons into this mix. This was a method the Sandinistas used to bring Cuban weapons into Nicaragua. Supply and staging areas abounded along the Nicaraguan border with Costa Rica, and most of the neighboring governments, which supported the actions of the Sandinistas, offered them safe haven and the opportunity to transfer drugs and weapons for their cause. When the Sandinistas finally gained power, the gunrunning did not cease. In fact, all that changed was the end user. The suppliers now had El Salvadoran rebels as customers, and not the Sandinistas.

One name has become synonymous with the Contras in the 1980s: U.S. Lt. Col. Oliver North, who at the time "managed" Contra operations on the southern front. Evidence in the Kerry findings relates also to a U.S. national living in Costa Rica, John Hull, an Indiana farmer who moved to Costa Rica and bought up large tracts of land. The area, known as Hull's Ranch, happened to include six airstrips, ideal for drugs and weapons smuggling. Hull helped the CIA with military shipments to the Contras and was also heavily involved in transshipment of drugs from Colombia. Added to this was the fact that the U.S. State Department was actively signing contracts with companies and their principals—companies that were either under investigation or had been indicted on narcotics-smuggling charges. These companies were used to make military hardware drops to the Contra rebels.

PANAMA

Formerly under Spanish rule, this tiny strip of land between the Pacific and the Atlantic first became a province of Colombia, before gaining its independence in 1903. Famous for the Panama Canal, which was under the control of the United States until the late 1970s, Panama has been a largely rural nation (Figure 13-6). The country has seen many varied forms of military governments over the past century or so, but the most notorious was that of General Manuel Noriega, who became president in 1983. From the time he came to power, he ran a corrupt government, made millions of dollars from drug trafficking to the United States and from diverting aid funds. Noriega controlled the public with strong-arm tactics and death squads. In 1988, a Florida grand jury indicted him on charges of racketeering and drug running. Up until 1989, Noriega continued to act with impunity. However, after the death of a U.S. Marine officer and Noriega's overturning the results of a democratic election, former President George H. Bush gave the almost unprecedented order for U.S. troops to invade Panama and restore the elected president. The marines seized Noriega and handed him over to U.S. marshals. He then stood trial and was sentenced

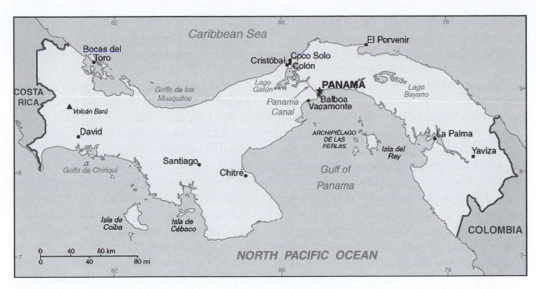

FIGURE 13-6 Map of Panama. *Source:* Central Intelligence Agency, *The World Factbook, 2008.*

to forty years in federal prison, he was granted conditional release in September 2011 and in December 2011 was extradited to Panama to serve a twenty-year prison term. Some think the effort to restore democracy in Panama was more about trying to stem the endless flow of drugs into the United States than to bring Noriega to trial for his drug trafficking.

CENTRAL AMERICAN GANG PROBLEMS

Gangs are Central America's number one crime problem. Violent young men experienced in gunplay and in evading law enforcement efforts are being sent back to countries they haven't seen since they were children. Some are dropouts; many can barely speak Spanish. Gangs enlist teenagers who are abandoned, unemployed, and devoid of hope and teach them what they know best, that is, robbing, stealing cars, selling drugs, and killing. In the mid-1990s, the United States stepped up deportations of Central American criminals; many of them gang members from the 18th Street, or Mara 18, and its chief rival, Mara Salvatrucha 13 (MS-13).

An estimated one hundred and fifty thousand gang members, or Mareros, control the streets of Central America, at times outgunning local police in El Salvador, Honduras, and Guatemala. Salvadoran officials say gangs are responsible for eighty percent of the homicides in that country. According to regional leaders, gangs are becoming the most destabilizing threat since the civil wars in Central America ended, over two decades ago. Some have been involved in extortion and mass murder, others linked to organized crime. As a whole, they threaten not only their rivals and public safety in general, but they even threaten the success of the Central American Free Trade Agreement (CAFTA). It is a fact that better economic and political conditions did not deter the explosion in the number of gangs throughout the 1990s. Across the board, Central America experienced economic growth after decades of internal conflicts. Yet, gangs grew in number, in part because of U.S. deportation policies that returned to the region thousands of gang members convicted of crimes, but primarily because of inaction or impotence of regional governments. In December 1994, leaders of the thirty-four democracies, meeting in Miami during the first Summit of the Americas, recognized the threat of youth marginalization and the need to take practical steps to counter it. As yet, however, no unified regional strategy has been adopted.

Former U.S. Secretary of Defense Donald Rumsfeld warned of an "antisocial combination" of terrorists, drug traffickers, and gangs that is increasingly seeking "to destabilize civil societies" in the region. When it comes down to figuring out who in the U.S. government will take the lead to address this security threat, however, most security officials seem averse to even recognize that they are discussing it. Perhaps the reason for this is obvious. All security threats, and gang violence in particular, cannot be met by force alone. Addressing this issue will require a mix of law enforcement, prevention, rehabilitation, parental involvement, and after-school programs—a whole web of social initiatives that developing countries generally lack. Helping

Central America get a grip on its gang problem would require a significant investment of time and resources from different agencies in the U.S. government. The Department of Justice and the U.S. Agency for International Development would have much larger roles than would the Pentagon or other security agencies.

U.S. officials failed to anticipate how other countries would be affected by the deportation of unwanted gang members: "The world is too global to export a problem and not expect it to come back," said David Brotherton, a professor at the John Jay College of Criminal Justice in New York, who has written two books on gangs. "In El Salvador, Guatemala, Honduras, and Mexico, there's a whole new inner-city youth subculture that originated in the First World. We've created an insoluble problem, and these countries just can't respond. There's no social work infrastructure. There's no rehabilitation. There's no money. They have enough trouble just providing basics for their own people." The U.S. Immigration and Customs Enforcement (ICE) launched a nationwide gang enforcement program in 2005 and began Operation Community Shield, a national law enforcement initiative that targets violent transnational street gangs through the use of ICE's broad law enforcement powers, including the unique and powerful authority to remove (deport) criminal aliens, including illegal aliens and legal permanent resident aliens.

In May 2005, it expanded Operation Community Shield to include all transnational criminal street gangs and prison gangs. Since the launch of Operation Community Shield, ICE's Homeland Security Investigations (HSI) and its partners have arrested more than thirty-two thousand gang members and associates, representing more than twenty-four hundred different gangs and cliques.

These apprehensions include more than twenty thousand criminal arrests and over thirteen thousand administrative immigration arrests. Of these, four hundred and fifty-one arrests were of gang leaders, and almost fifteen thousand of the arrested suspects had violent criminal histories. Through this initiative, HSI has also seized more than fifty-eight hundred firearms.[16]

Results

Under Operation Community Shield, ICE:

- Partners with federal, state, and local law enforcement agencies, in the United States and abroad, to develop a comprehensive and integrated approach in conducting criminal investigations and other law enforcement operations against violent street gangs and others who pose a threat to public safety.
- Identifies violent street gangs and develops intelligence on their membership, associates, criminal activities, and international movements.
- Deters, disrupts, and dismantles gang operations by tracing and seizing cash, weapons, and other assets derived from criminal activities.
- Seeks prosecution and/or removal of alien gang members from the United States.
- Works closely with our attaché offices throughout Latin America and foreign law enforcement counterparts in gathering intelligence, sharing information, and conducting coordinated enforcement operations.
- Conducts outreach efforts to increase public awareness about the fight against violent street gangs.[17]

Central American governments are searching for strategies to combat gangs. The Honduran Congress unanimously passed one of the hemisphere's toughest anti-gang laws in 2003, setting a maximum twelve-year prison sentence for gang members. El Salvador followed with its own version of what has become known as the *mano dura*, or firm hand, which locks up any young man who bears gang tattoos. In May 2004, Mexico's southernmost state of Chiapas approved five-year prison sentences for anyone who simply belongs to a gang. Human rights activists complain that gang members are being hunted down and killed by police, but the crackdowns continue, especially against the Mara 18 and Mara Salvatrucha 13, which are Central America's largest and most violent gangs. The gangs have proven to be resilient. Every time they're uprooted, they resurface in another neighborhood, another city, and another country. They move with the assurance that no matter where they go, fellow gang members will feed them, house them, orient them, and provide them with weapons. The MS-13 gang had its origins in the 1980s in the United States and is a national and international criminal organization whose members conduct gang activities in the United States and Central America. According to the indictment, the term "Mara" is used in El Salvador for gang, while the phrase "Salvatrucha" is a combination of the words "Salva"—an abbreviation for Salvadoran—and "trucha," which is a slang term for the warning "fear us," "look out," or "heads up." Male gang members are required to complete an initiation process, often referred to as "jumped in," where the new member is beaten by other members until the count of 13. Female gang members are initiated by either being "jumped in" or submitting to sexual activity with gang members. MS-13 gang members often display their membership through tattoos reading "MS" or "MS-13" in gothic lettering and/or by wearing the gang's colors—blue and white—or clothing bearing the number "13" or numbers when added together total 13. MS-13 members pay dues that are used for the benefit of and provided to MS-13 members who are imprisoned in the United States, El Salvador, and Panama as well as to buy firearms to be used to conduct the enterprise's illegal activities.[18]

A variety of U.S. reports from federal agencies estimated gang membership at ten thousand in El Salvador, thirty-six thousand in Honduras, and fourteen thousand in Guatemala, while criminal organizations were becoming increasingly active in neighboring Belize, Costa Rica, and Panama. Central American gangs are increasingly transnational, noting that Salvadoran-based Mara Salvatrucha 13 is believed to have up-to twenty thousand active members operating in thirty-eight U.S. states and with between eighty to one hundred thousand international members. The violence in Mexico has reached epic proportions with several thousands of people killed, including journalists, police, lawyers, and judges as well as tourists caught in the middle of shootouts.[19] The southern border with Guatemala also poses significant risks for locals as a result of Mexican drug gangs infiltrating inaccessible areas such as the Petén region. The Mexican Zetas, an organized crime syndicate, use this area for drug smuggling activities and as a transshipment point for northerly routes. In May 2011, twenty-seven farmworkers were massacred and of those twenty-six had been decapitated; this method of execution is increasingly popular to demonstrate to locals the need for complete compliance with the drug gangs.[20]

COLOMBIA

Colombia's geography has had a significant effect on its history and on the evolution and development of what is often described as a fragmented and divided society. Colombia is bordered on the northwest by Panama, on the east by Venezuela and Brazil, and on the southwest by Peru and Ecuador (Figure 13-7). The eastern half is a low, jungle-covered plain, drained by spurs of the Amazon and Orinoco rivers and inhabited mostly by isolated, tropical forest Indian tribes. The fertile plateau and valley of the eastern range are the most densely populated parts of the country. Historically, the most populated areas have been divided by its three mountain ranges. The dispersion of much of the population into isolated mountain pockets has long delayed the development of transportation, adequate means of communication, and the formation of integrated national markets. Due to these geographic and spatial limitations, Colombia has developed local and regional cultures. Politically, this dispersion has created regional antagonism and local rivalries that were expressed in the nineteenth century in civil war and in the latter part of the twentieth century in intercommunity violence.

Over the last two centuries, Colombia has suffered through virtually continuous warfare. Colombia has been characterized by a pronounced fractured dispersion of power, further manifested by extreme levels of localism and regionalism. It is not surprising that all of this contributes to disproportionately high levels of violence in Colombia. One of the most severe challenges to U.S. policy toward Colombia derives from issues involving human rights. Political and extrajudicial actions involving government security forces, paramilitary groups, and

FIGURE 13-7 Map of Colombia. *Source:* Central Intelligence Agency, *The World Factbook, 2008.*

members of the guerrilla forces result in the deaths of thousands of civilians. Paramilitary forces are responsible for the great majority of these deaths. Many others are displaced by rampant and uncontrolled violence. The homicide rate is considered to be one of the highest per capita in the world. Government security forces are frequently involved in many of the abuses, including extrajudicial killings, and they sometimes collaborate directly and indirectly with paramilitary forces. And, although the government has worked to strengthen its human rights policy, the measures adopted to punish officials accused of committing violations, and to prevent paramilitary attacks, are insufficient. In the meantime, paramilitary forces have increased their social and political support among the civilian population in many parts of the country.

Marijuana, cocaine, and kidnappings have been products of Colombia for more than forty years, but the market for drugs did not take off until the wealthy and middle classes in the United States began abusing them.

Cocaine became the drug of choice, and the opportunity for expansion into a North American market was huge. Drugs in Colombia are controlled in two regions of the country: Medellin and Cali. The Medellin and **Cali cartels** control nearly eighty percent of Colombia's distribution of drugs. Terrorist groups in Colombia have been fully involved in the sale and supply of narcotics for financial support in their bitter fight against successive Colombian governments. Terrorism has become a by-product of the drug trade and a means of control and power. Extortion, kidnapping, and murder are all hallmarks of the drug cartels. It is difficult to appreciate the enormous wealth that comes from the machinations of the drug trade. Drug barons are known to have utilized outside "sources" to assist their own internal security services. Colombia also has to contend with an insurgent group of left-wing rebels, revolutionaries, and terrorists that have plagued the state for the last five decades.

A fifty-year insurgent campaign to overthrow the Colombian government escalated during the 1990s, fueled in part by funds from the drug trade. Although the violence is deadly and large swaths of the countryside are under guerrilla influence, the movement lacks the military strength and popular support necessary to overthrow the government. An anti-insurgent army of paramilitaries has grown to over several thousand strong in recent years, challenging the insurgents for control of territory and illicit industries such as the drug trade and the government's ability to exert its dominion over rural areas. While Bogotá steps up efforts to reassert government control throughout the country, neighboring countries worry about the violence spilling over their borders. In August 2000, the U.S. government approved "Plan Colombia," pledging $1.3 billion to fight drug trafficking. President Andres Pastrana, elected in 1988, used the plan to undercut drug production and prevent guerrilla groups from benefiting from drug sales. In August 2001, Pastrana signed "war legislation," which expanded the rights of the military in dealing with rebels. Alvaro Uribe of the Liberal Party won the presidential election in May 2002 and took office in August, pledging to get tough on the rebels and drug traffickers by increasing military spending and U.S. military cooperation. An upsurge in violence accompanied his inauguration, and Uribe declared a state of emergency within a week. In his first year, Uribe beefed up Colombia's security forces, with help from U.S. Special Forces, launched an aggressive campaign against the drug trade, and passed several economic reform bills.

In May 2004, the United Nations announced that Colombia's thirty-nine-year-long drug war had created the worst humanitarian crisis in the Western Hemisphere. More than 2 million people had been forced to leave their homes, and several Indian tribes are now close to extinction. Colombia now has the third-largest displaced population in the world, with only Sudan and the Congo having more. Uribe has produced some impressive results in fixing his country's ills, however. According to his defense minister, during 2003, more than 16,000 suspected leftist guerrillas and right-wing paramilitary vigilantes had surrendered, were apprehended, or were killed. The U.S. Office of National Drug Control Policy has announced that coca production has declined by 30 percent, but Colombia still continues to produce 75 percent of the world's cocaine.

Terrorism in Colombia

Colombia's democracy and its forty-plus million inhabitants have been under assault since the early 1960s and 1970s by three Marxist "narco-terrorist" groups: The **Revolutionary Armed Forces of Colombia (FARC)**, the National Liberation Army (ELN), and the **United Self-Defense Forces of Colombia (AUC)**. These three groups were capable of providing over twenty-five thousand well-trained combatants. FARC and AUC have had a pronounced involvement at all levels of the drug trade and derive a considerable income from it—some estimates run as high as $300 million annually. In 2001, the AUC killed two Colombian legislators and FARC kidnapped six; and the three groups accounted for the assassinations of twelve mayors.[21]

FARC is a Marxist terrorist group that was established in 1964 by the Communist Party of Colombia to defend what was at that time communist-controlled autonomous regions. By any standards FARC is on record as being one of the best-equipped and best-funded terrorist organizations in Latin America. FARC has militia groups in the cities and special forces units that operate where "most needed"; the group also has a "vast support network full of logistical experts in bombing, transportation, kidnapping, arms trafficking, food storage, FARC's current structure is the same as the structure established in 1982, and the group's structure is centralized to an "extremely high" degree and described as follows:

Its basic military unit is the column, composed of twenty to forty fighters; it is an operational unit in charge of the control of a certain territory, of collecting taxes and rackets and of military actions. A plurality of columns makes up a Front. The Fronts sometimes congregate in Blocks. Front and Block commanders respond directly, both militarily and financially, to the secretariat, which operationally is the supreme direction of the group.[22] FARC gains drug revenues from the production, manufacture, sale, and distribution of narcotics. The numbers of kidnappings according to the Colombian government dropped dramatically from the peak year in 2000 when thirty-five hundred people were taken, down to five hundred and twenty-one in 2007. As part of the U.S. government's Plan Colombia, which was focused on reduction of the flow of cocaine, the United States has provided some $5 billion worth of aid and a fraction of that amount has gone toward the Antiterrorism Assistance (ATA) program. The Colombian government gives credit to a little-known program, run by the U.S. State Department's Bureau of Diplomatic Security, which has trained more than six hundred GAULA members. (GAULA is the Spanish acronym for Unified Action Groups for Personal Liberty.) The DS training, offered under its Antiterrorism Assistance program, has focused in particular on rescuing hostages.[23]

An extreme left-wing, Communist-inspired movement, FARC aspires to the overthrow of the Colombian government, and little else. In a country where kidnapping is commonplace, the FARC targets the government, military, locally elected municipal mayors, police, and civilians. Much of FARC's income is derived from not only drug trafficking but also robbery, kidnapping, and extortion. FARC is rabidly anti-United States and its campaign resembles that of Cuban-style revolution. FARC's membership of active terrorists was believed to number around sixteen thousand at its peak in the 1990s, which dwindled down to approximately nine thousand in 2008, but still managed to gain some support in rural areas from the indigenous population.

Most observers do not consider FARC's central demands as realistic, that is, their demands for the ending of privatization and reduction of the twenty percent unemployment rate and other reforms seem hopelessly futile. On the political front, the Colombian government of President Andreas Pastrana had made slow headway in negotiating a peace deal with FARC. In 2001, the year leading up to the elections, negotiations became bogged down and the Pastrana government threatened to end the deal that had created a demilitarized zone (DMZ) in southern Colombia, an area approximately the size of Switzerland, which had long been occupied by FARC. Since the events of 9-11, the Colombian government has been fortified with U.S. aid and military hardware for the express purpose of combating the drug trade in Colombia. This aid has given significant impetus to the Colombian military to go on the offensive against FARC, something of a novelty for Colombia's military, which has traditionally fought in defensive mode against FARC. Operation "Black Cat" commenced in February 2002. This military offensive was directed against FARC with the use of aircraft and helicopters. At the same time, Pastrana annulled the FARC's political status and issued arrest warrants for its leaders. In the February 2002 campaign, the Colombian military struck so far into FARC territory that the group was taken totally by surprise. The area attacked was the town of Barrancomina in eastern Colombia, an area where the sixteenth Front of FARC had been able to operate with complete impunity. The significance of the attack showed that the Colombian military had the skill and the intelligence support, as well as the military know-how, to attack FARC. In future campaigns, this will no doubt be a deciding factor in peace talks, if they ever resume. FARC's resilience has never really been in question and the organization has been a proven survivor. FARC cannot be called a truly Communist-inspired movement, even though committed Communists are included in its membership. FARC is also involved in the drug trade; although it cannot be considered a drug cartel, it is definitely involved in narco-terrorism. Because FARC flourishes in the deep rural and jungle regions of the state, it could be considered a peasant army. In some respects, this may be true but, because of its wide-ranging terror attacks, it cannot be termed as the vanguard of the peasant populace. FARC's appeal to the peasantry could be rationalized, as it offers a level of employment when there is no prospect elsewhere. The failures of the group's participation in government representation may spawn an organization that will feed off the lucrative trade in drugs, kidnappings, and extortion. However, in the spring of 2011 FARC released a number of kidnapped military personnel who they had held for over ten years. At the same time they renounced the further use of kidnapping.

FARC will likely continue to become even more marginalized as it sees itself up against the U.S.-backed Colombian military and an ever-growing number of paramilitary forces. In this context, it is expected that now that it has been hit systemically in areas where it once operated with complete freedom, it will have to reconsider its actions and adapt to survive in this new environment. It has lost its founder Manuel "Sureshot" Marulanda to a heart attack in 2008 and in 2010, its military head Jorge Briceno Suarez was killed when his jungle camp was raided. Guillermo Saenz, the group's leader since 2008 was killed in 2011. The FARC membership has also dwindled in recent years down to around eight thousand. A peace accord has been in the planning phase since 2014 and the Colombian government hopes that the deal when implemented will lead to the demobilization of FARC. The peace deal calls for an amnesty for FARC members but how that will be progressed is uncertain. In September 2015, the agreement reflected the understanding between Bogota and the FARC that the government will guarantee that an unspecified number of rebels will not face prison if they agree to confess to their crimes before the transitional court. It seems that the question of whether militants will receive similar amnesty deals for crimes related to drug trafficking—the biggest factor impeding the group's demobilization thus far—has been answered sufficiently enough to convince the rebels to remain in negotiations. Indeed, Colombian President Juan Manuel Santos has already publicly said his government will try to prevent the extradition of FARC members for such crimes.[24]

NATIONAL LIBERATION ARMY

The National Liberation Army (ELN), formed in 1963, is a smaller and less organized operation than FARC and has carried on a long-term campaign against the Colombian government. It is predominately a Marxist-inspired group and has a membership of about three thousand fighters. Similar to FARC, the ELN is anti-United States and frequently engages in the profitable tactic of kidnapping. The target is usually a businessman from a foreign company working in Colombia. In addition, ELN targets U.S. and foreign installations for bomb attacks. ELN's operations are focused on Colombia's northwestern border with Venezuela—regions that produce cannabis and poppy opium. ELN and FARC have both systematically targeted Colombia's oil facilities and, in 2001, the government suffered nearly $500 million in lost revenues. To this end, the United States has supplied $6 million in foreign military funds (FMF) to train Colombian military units to protect the Cano Limon pipeline, which has been repeatedly bombed by both groups. ELN continues the practice of kidnappings for ransom.

RIGHT-WING DEATH SQUADS

The right-wing death squads, which rose to prominence in Colombia, appear to have had the tacit support of both the government and the military. Many of these defense groups sprang up in the 1960s and 1970s in response to FARC's terrorist activities against wealthy landowners. Over the years, the groups, which tended to operate in select areas, moved from defensive to offensive strategies. They began to attack suspected members of FARC and intimidated peasant villagers believed to be helping the FARC.[25]

In central Magdalena, drug cartels began buying up rich tracts of land and were directly responsible for transforming the self-defense units into right-wing death squads.[26]

For the Colombian drug lords, the end justifies the means. This is the real issue in the rise of death squads and the necessity for terrorist actions in this country. In a country so heavily dependent on the production and export of drugs, the methods used to terrorize the populace are not intended as means to overthrow or replace a political system. These efforts are aimed at maintaining the status quo and fear, for the groups' own benefit, and for dissuading police, judges, and politicians from strict legal approaches in dealing with drug cartels. The rise of the right-wing death squads and paramilitaries dates back over thirty years, when rich landowners, farmers, and the drug cartels adopted their own small and very private protection forces. These have grown into a sort of loose coalition known as the AUC. AUC and FARC have been responsible for more than five thousand kidnappings and the deaths of more than four thousand Colombians. AUC has publicly stated that it gains most of its support and income from the lucrative drug trade. Allegations of human rights abuses by the AUC abound. It has been linked on more than one occasion to senior members of Colombia's military elite. The AUC's methods of intimidation have resulted in more than three hundred and forty thousand Colombians being forcibly evicted from their homes, bringing the total number of displaced persons to more than two million in just the last decade.

Alvaro Uribe, who swept to a landslide victory in the 2002 elections, was unable to exert much control outside the large urban centers. Uribe had ongoing talks with AUC, which was formed in 1997, but the group continued to indiscriminately slaughter leftist guerrillas, politicians, activists, union leaders, as well as civilians until 2003. Information from the Colombian National Police states that between January and October 2000, the AUC carried out eight hundred and four assassinations, two hundred and three kidnappings, and seventy-five massacres in which five hundred and seven people died. Uribe's decommissioning of AUC began in earnest in 2003, and the number of attacks and assassinations dropped considerably and allowed the Uribe government to continue pursuing FARC and ELN. One of the major problems facing the Colombian government is AUC's deepening involvement with drugs. Since 2003, some thirty thousand paramilitaries have been disbanded; however, this does not mean that they have been arrested but have more likely become involved in the lucrative drugs trade.

As for international links, one of bin Laden's close associates, Mohammed Abed Abel, a member of Egypt's largest militant group, Jamaat al-Islamiyah, was arrested in Bogotá, Colombia, in early November 1998. He was subsequently released by the Colombian authorities and deported back to Ecuador, his country of origin. Why would such a high-ranking and high-profile terrorist be in Latin America? It may be assumed that he was either studying the U.S. Embassy as a potential target or negotiating meetings with FARC or ELN to set up trade deals involving drugs for weapons. FARC and its connections to Irish paramilitary groups came dramatically to a head when the Colombian authorities arrested several senior IRA members in 2001. Prior to their arrest, Colombian authorities revealed that the IRA men had been involved in training members of FARC in military tactics, the use of explosives, and the manufacture of arms. General Tapias, chairman of the Joint Chiefs of Staff for the Armed Forces of Colombia, made these claims in testimony before the U.S. House of Representatives International Relations Committee in April 2002. The types of attacks the FARC mounted in 2002 showed a higher level of sophistication than had previously been the case. The attacks' level of sophistication was similar to those of the IRA. The reason and background for IRA involvement is not yet clear but, of course, there is plenty of speculation from the various security organizations. In Britain, the suggestion is that the FARC paid the IRA $2 million for the training in explosives, and, of course, the U.S. concern is that it may be a hint of a much broader coalition of international terror relationships, but there is no hard evidence for this. The official response to the arrests from the IRA came from Gerry Adams, the leader of Sinn Féin. While Adams refused to testify before the U.S. House International Relations Committee, he did respond in writing to the chairman of the committee, Henry Hyde. Adams wrote: "Let me state again that neither I, nor anyone else, in the Sinn Féin leadership was aware that the three men were traveling to Colombia."[27]

Of course, the careful wording in this statement cannot be construed that Sinn Féin was not aware of their involvement, no doubt a good enough reason not to testify. It seems highly probable that FARC was delving deeper into drug trafficking in exchange for military hardware and much-needed cash reserves for its continuing fight.

From Counter-Narcotics to Narco-Terrorism

During the past several years, U.S. foreign policy toward Colombia has undergone significant changes. The events of 9-11, combined with the definitive rupture of the Colombian government's peace process with the rebels in February 2002, have converted this country into the primary training theater for U.S. counterterrorism operations in the Western Hemisphere today. Washington's traditional counter narcotics policies have been based on repressive, prohibition-ist, and hard-line language. The manner in which Colombia has addressed the drug problem derives substantially from the U.S. approach, with most of Bogotá's measures to fight the drug trade the result of bilateral agreements or the unilateral imposition of specific strategies designed in Washington DC. It has been theorized that these approaches have produced countless nega-tive consequences for Colombia, aggravating the armed conflicts that continue to escalate and forcing urgent national problems such as the strengthening of democracy, the defense of human rights, the reduction of poverty, and the preservation of the environment to become secondary to countering the drug trade.[28]

Between 1996 and 2001, U.S. aid to Colombia (in the form of military and other government assistance) increased approximately fifteen fold, from $67 million to over $1 billion.[29]

At conceptual and practical levels, it is difficult for the United States to separate the war on drugs from its counterinsurgency efforts. Given that the global War on Terror has targeted the links that exist among terrorism, arms, and drugs, a new term "narco-terrorism" has been coined to describe players such as the FARC, former AUC, al Qaeda, and others that fund terrorist-related activities with drug money.[30]

In 2003, President Bush asked the Congress for an additional $600 million for Colombia, with the majority being in the form of military aid to rebuild and train the stag-nating Colombian military. The request included line items to train and equip two new Colombian army brigades to protect the Cano Limon-Covenas oil pipeline, in which the American firm, Occidental Petroleum, is a large shareholder. Dubbed "Plan Colombia," the infusion of millions of dollars aimed at destroying the coca crops that so easily pro-duce the cocaine for the cartels and FARC. FARC's significant control of the drug industry in Colombia is how it derives most of its financial support—estimated to be $1.3 billion per year. FARC has also been implicated in providing training to the kidnappers of for-mer Paraguayan President Raul Cuba's daughter, Cecilia, who was abducted in September 2004 and found dead in February 2005. FARC was also responsible for the kidnapping of Colombian presidential candidate Ingrid Betancourt who remained a captive from 2002 through 2008 when she was rescued along with three U.S. employees of Northrop Grumman by Colombian Special Forces. Betancourt had been kidnapped while campaign-ing in the DMZ.

The drug trade drives Colombian terrorism from both the left and the right, and there is little evidence to suggest that the price of cocaine or its demand in the United States has declined as a result of around $8 billion being spent on trying to eradicate the problem. The Colombian cocaine trade was estimated at $35 billion in 2000.

The assistance given to the Colombian military by the United States has been rewarded by the death of one of their most wanted—Raul Reyes had been, until his death, the one and only spokesman for the FARC.

Luis Edgar Devia Silva aka Raul Reyes (September 30, 1948—March 1, 2008)

Raul Reyes, the central figure and spokesman for the FARC in almost all communications was killed on March 1, 2008, when the Colombian Air Force launched a bombing raid on a FARC camp about 2 miles from the Colombian border just inside Ecuador. Reyes had been sentenced in absentia for the deaths of thirteen policemen and eighteen soldiers, eighteen kidnappings, and the deaths of a judge, a physician, three judicial auxiliaries, the ex-minister of Culture Consuelo Araújo, congressman Diego Turbay and his mother, Catholic monsignor Isaías Duarte, governor of Antioquia Guillermo Gaviria, the Colombian ex-minister Gilberto Echeverri, eleven members of the Valle del Cauca Assembly, and at least four other persons. Most of these persons were kidnapped before their deaths.[31]

FARC had also sought support from Venezuela and reports after the death of Raul Reyes that the Colombian military had found a number of files on his computer indicating that the for-mer government of Hugo Chavez was prepared to back FARC did nothing for regional stability. The claims were swiftly denied by the Venezuelan leader.

PERU

Peru is the second largest cocaine producing country in the world and a major exporter of cocaine and cocaine base to markets in South America, Mexico, the United States, and Europe (Figure 13-8). The U.S. Crime and Narcotics Center estimated that in 2008, forty-one thousand hectares of coca were under cultivation in Peru. In 2009, the Government of Peru manually eradicated ten thousand and twenty-five hectares of illicit coca. Eradication, linked closely to alternative development programs, has led to dramatic reductions of coca cultivation in the Upper Huallaga Valley where eradication efforts are focused; this is particularly evident in San Martin department. However, challenges remain in other parts of the country where State presence is limited, and where increased coca cultivation and trafficking have been reported, such as in the Apurimac and Ene River Valley. Peru is a key U.S. partner in the region, and the United States, is committed to working with the Peru to effectively address illicit coca cultivation, narcotics trafficking, and the related transnational criminal challenges that follow.[32] Peru is often remembered only for its fabulous Inca villages, Machu Picchu, and the high Andes Mountains. History informs us that an Inca chief, Tupac Amaru and his followers overcame their colonial Spanish masters in the latter half of the seventeenth century. The country has been under the control of military juntas throughout much of the twentieth century, but civilian rule returned to Peru in the 1980s. Peru suffers from two sources of indigenous terrorism: The **Shining Path (Sendero Luminoso)** and the Tupac Amaru Revolutionary Movement (MRTA).

FIGURE 13-8 Map of Peru. *Source:* Central Intelligence Agency, *The World Factbook, 2008.*

Sendero Luminoso (The Shining Path)

Shining Path has its origins in the university city of Aucayacu, in the upper Huallaga region. Abimael Guzman, who received his indoctrination and training in China in 1965, at the start of the Chinese Cultural Revolution, created and led The Shining Path. His trips to, and training in, China, taught him to set up and organize clandestine political and terrorist activities against the democratic state. On his return he became the leader of the pro-Maoist faction of the Peruvian Communist Party. Guzman was working high in the Andes Mountains as a university lecturer studying the exploitation suffered by Peru's Indians. He had no trouble drawing parallels with the Chinese peasants who had fought for Mao Zedong three decades earlier. He recruited his students into the Maoist Party and sent them to agitate in the Indian villages.[33]

Students comprised the bulk of the organization, a reflection of the leadership's organizational strategy of tapping into the existing state-organized network of education to recruit Sendero devotees. His movement went underground in 1976 and began preparations for its campaign of terror and insurgency in 1980. Sendero derived much of its power by relying on ethnic factors and by resurrecting the feeling of historical greatness associated with the Inca civilization. A second and related story, from Peruvian history since the Spanish conquest in the early 1500s, concerned the effects of its subjugation, first to Spain, then to England, and most recently to the United States. It describes a legacy of exploitation, debt, and generally bad development that provided ready-made fuel for Sendero Luminoso to create and promote a radical and isolationist ideology.

Sendero burst onto the scene by assassinating any village leaders who resisted the group's call to smash authority and establish an egalitarian utopia. Many local police crumbled before the group, which issued no manifestos and maintained absolute silence about its structure and leadership. Mounting Sendero violence in the highlands forced the Peruvian government to authorize a military offensive, which left its own wake of repression. Peruvian military tactics failed to eliminate Sendero. On the contrary, the movement spread to other highland provinces and to Lima. More massacres in the Sierra and blackouts (from dynamited power lines) in greater Lima demonstrated growing Sendero strength. Sendero forced the government into greater reliance on the police and the military. Government forces killed indiscriminately, prompting the firing of numerous commanders for atrocities in the field and for the slaughter of numerous prisoners who had surrendered after a massive prison riot.

In 1976, while the Peruvian government was trying to restore the democratic processes and the economy of the country, Guzman and his Sendero Luminoso followers were training with automatic weapons. They were of the belief that Peruvian society had to be torn down, and a classless society designed to replace it. Guzman and his followers started out as the saviors of the poor of Peru. That was to quickly change as Guzman's Marxist style became similar, in his approach to the natives, to that of the Khmer Rouge in dealing with the Cambodians. In merging the extreme teachings of Chairman Mao with the philosophy of **Che Guevara**,[34] a dangerously violent hybrid emerged. Like the Khmer Rouge, Guzman and his guerrillas set about the destruction of the country by intimidating villagers into either joining the movement or die. Those who refused were promptly killed. The group quickly became a cult of mass murderers, feared for their savagery throughout Peru. Guzman's aim was to overthrow the Peruvian democratic government and replace it with a Marxist dictatorship, built in his own image. Over the next fourteen years, the group's reign of terror took the lives of twenty-five thousand Peruvians and resulted in over $20 billion in damage to the country's infrastructure. Sendero terrorists included a number of female operatives who have been known to use small children to deliver suicide bombs to public buildings and police stations. Guzman's philosophy and ideals spread farther than just Peru; he had goals of resurrecting the old Inca Empire; his terrorists threatened not only Peru but also Ecuador, Colombia, and Bolivia. Guzman's supporters believed him to be invincible, and they called him the "Fourth Sword of Marxism."[35]

Fortunately for Peru, this belief was to be rudely upset by his capture in September 1992. During the 1980s, terrorist activity had been so prevalent that villagers were fleeing to the urban slums of big cities, such as Lima, to escape the ravages of the Shining Path. International observers feared that the democratic government in Peru would not be able to deal with the onslaught from Guzman's Shining Path. After his capture in 1992, the movement staggered, lost direction, and began to disintegrate. President Fujimori was determined to overcome both narcotics trafficking and terrorism in Peru and seemed to have the overwhelming support of the people. Prior to Guzman's capture, several other key members of the Shining Path were behind bars. No doubt, information gathered during their interrogations assisted in Guzman's apprehension. Fujimori's democratic administration and revival of the country's economy had done much to defeat the terrorist threat, which, considering the meager level of counterinsurgency training available to the poorly equipped security police, is quite surprising. Following Guzman's capture, the void was temporarily filled by Oscar Durand, the group's strategist on military matters until he himself was captured by the Peruvian authorities in 1999.[36]

The Shining Path, in spite of the setbacks of the late 1990s, is still a credible and deadly force and a problem for Peruvian authorities. Shining Path was weakened as a consequence of an August 2013 operation conducted by Peruvian security forces that resulted in the deaths of two of the terrorist organization's top four commanders, Orlando Borda (Comrade Alipio) and Martin Quispe Palomino (Comrade Gabriel). In March, the then-chief of the VRAEM Special Command, Army General Leonardo Longa, claimed that the Shining Path only had around 100 armed fighters left in the emergency zone, concentrating more on criminal activities, primarily drug-related. The group has indicated its willingness to negotiate a peace deal with the government; however, President Humala has insisted his government will not negotiate with terrorists.

Tupac Amaru: Movimiento Revolucionario Tupac Amaru

The second of Peru's terrorist movements takes its name from the previously mentioned legendary Inca leader, Tupac Amaru II, a revered Indian rebel who led an uprising during the late-eighteenth century against Spanish colonial arrangements. Movimiento Revolucionario Tupac Amaru (MRTA), considered in part a rival to Sendero, was actually less powerful, but still a very deadly Peruvian guerrilla organization during the late 1980s and early 1990s. The original rebellion by the Inca leader, Tupac Amaru II, was ultimately suppressed, but it remained a symbol of ethnic-political unity and hinted at prospects for more successful uprisings in the future. The greatness of the Inca Empire has remained alive in the hearts of many of Peru's indigenous population.

With the country heading toward elections in 1993, the levels of terrorism began to pick up and, by 1996, both MRTA and Sendero were resorting to campaigns of terror once again. Sendero was not able to deliver the same number of guerrillas to the campaign as it had previously, however, and the numbers of combatants were also significantly lower.

Victor Polay formed the Tupac Amaru in 1985. A traditional Marxist-Leninist movement, its goal was the overthrow of perceived imperialism in Peru. The group had no external support, and its membership was considerably less than that of Sendero. Polay was captured in 1992 and sentenced to life in prison. In a spectacular display of support and solidarity for Polay, Tupac Amaru stormed the Japanese ambassador's residence in Lima during a diplomatic Christmas celebration in December 1996. They took hundreds of guests, mainly diplomats, as hostages. In front of the world's press and television corps assembled outside, Tupac Amaru demanded the release of Polay. With the strong support of the Peruvian population, Fujimori stood his ground and did not give way to the threats from the terrorists. The assault on the ambassador's residence took place when about four hundred guests were seated for a meal. The celebration was short lived, as more than a dozen heavily armed guerrillas stormed the grounds, firing weapons into the air. The attackers were calling themselves the Edgar Sanchez Special Forces, commanded by Comrade Edigirio Huerta. The assault began at about 8:00 P.M. on December 17, 1996. The situation was delicate, as a large number of foreign dignitaries and ambassadors were being held hostage, including the ambassadors of Austria, Brazil, Bulgaria, Cuba, Guatemala, Panama, Poland, Romania, South Korea, Spain, and Venezuela. The government of President Fujimori steadfastly refused to negotiate with the terrorists. Both political and economic implications would rest on the outcome.

The Tupac Amaru demands were as follows:

1. They would shoot hostages unless their demands were met.
2. Release of their imprisoned comrades, totaling up to five hundred.
3. Transfer of freed prisoners and hostages to a jungle hideout, with the last hostage to be released at the final destination.
4. Payment by the Peruvian government of a "war tax" of an unspecified amount.
5. An economic program to aid the Peruvian poor.[37]

The End of the Crisis

After dragging on for four months, the drama was eventually brought to its climax when Peruvian special security forces tunneled into the compound and rescued the hostages. Up until the middle of March, negotiations had been proceeding well, and the numbers of hostages had dwindled down to seventy-one, as concessions and counter-concessions were made. However, Fujimori would not budge on the terrorists' main demand, which was for the release of the imprisoned members of Tupac Amaru. At 3:20 P.M., April 22, 1997, the rescue began. The Peruvian government had authorized a rescue mission: tunneling, which had taken weeks, was now completed, allowing security forces to gain entry for a surprise strike. Explosions and gunfire were heard from inside the compound and plumes of smoke curled up from the residence windows. Within forty minutes, the 140-man rescue team had secured the residence, all fourteen Tupac Amaru guerrillas were dead, and twenty-five hostages were injured. Two members of the rescue team died in the operation. This incident brought worldwide congratulations to Fujimori for his stance against terrorism. But the attack was also a harsh reminder of the vulnerability of political leaders to terrorist attacks.[38]

In overall terms, the Peruvian authorities have seen some considerable success go their way in the war on domestic terrorism. In 2001, they had captured more than two hundred and fifty-nine suspected terrorists, and since the 9-11 attacks, Peru presented itself as a strong regional leader in the fight against terrorism and has participated in the U.S. State Department Antiterrorism Training Assistance program.

BOLIVIA

Bolivia, named after independence fighter Simon Bolivar, broke away from Spanish rule in 1825; much of its subsequent history has consisted of a series of nearly two hundred coups and countercoups. It has been a land-locked country ever since the war of 1879–1884 when Chile seized

FIGURE 13-9 Map of Bolivia. *Source:* Central Intelligence Agency, *The World Factbook, 2008.*

the Port of Antofagasta and the surrounding area (Figure 13-9). As a result, Bolivia's relations with Chile have been troublesome throughout its history. Comparatively democratic civilian rule was established in 1982, but leaders have faced difficult problems of deep-seated poverty, social unrest, and drug production. During the last months of 2001, the country witnessed several corruption scandals involving government officials, growing crime rates, and evidence of a criminal network that had infiltrated national police authorities. Current goals include attracting foreign investment, strengthening the educational system, resolving disputes with coca growers over Bolivia's counter-drug efforts, and waging an anticorruption campaign. Bolivia is the world's third-largest cultivator of coca (after Colombia and Peru), with an estimated eighty-four hundred hectares under cultivation in 2003, a twenty-three percent increase from 2002. Intermediate coca products and cocaine exports go mostly to or through Brazil, Argentina, and Chile to European and U.S. drug markets. Eradication and alternative crop programs have not been able to keep up the pace with farmers' attempts to increase cultivation. Money-laundering activities related to narcotics trade, especially along the borders with Brazil and Paraguay, have flourished.[39]

In August 1971, Colonel Hugo Banzer overthrew the leftist popular regime of Juan Jose Torres. The majority of the military, and the business class, supported the new regime. The Banzer administration could best be described as a return to an openly authoritarian state. He repressed all social groups opposed to his regime, especially workers and peasants. Between 1971 and 1978, around nineteen thousand Bolivians were exiled, including Juan Lechin, head of the Bolivian Workers Union and four ex-presidents.[40]

Thousands were detained at different times and were subjected to numerous kinds of torture. However, the number of persons actually killed by the state was relatively low. The universities were frequently closed and all union activity was forbidden. One particularly grisly event gained special notoriety: the so-called massacre in the Cochabamba Valley in January 1975. In protest against the prices fixed by the government, the peasants in that central region blocked the roads. In retaliation, the military harshly repressed them. Many died or disappeared.[41]

When a military coup toppled the Bolivian government in 1980, the usual array of journalists, opposition politicians, and trade unionists were detained by the secret police, the Servicio Especial Seguridad (SES). However, most detainees were only held for a short period of time. Politically motivated assassinations have also been a hallmark of political unrest in the region. An outspoken member of the Socialist Workers Party was kidnapped in January 2002, and his tortured and bullet-riddled body was found two days later. Many of the violent gang activities are laid at the door of former groups involved in urban guerrilla activities in Chile. One of the main protagonists in Brazil's gang problems is Mauricio Norambuena, a leading figure in the Manual Rodriguez Patriotic Front (FPMR), which is now believed to have its base in Montevideo, Uruguay. The FPMR was as the armed wing of the Chilean Communist Party in 1983 and was named after Manual Rodriguez, hero of Chile's war of independence from Spain. FPMR splintered in the late 1980s, and one faction became a political party in 1991. The dissident wing FPMR/D is Chile's only remaining active terrorist group with less than thirty members.

BRAZIL

Brazil has become a seething hotbed for kidnappings and extortion. Although Brazil has a subversive and anti-Western group called the Tupac Katari Guerrilla Army (EGTK), the group's actions have been extremely limited (Figure 13-10). Brazil is famous in international terrorist circles for the pamphlet, *Mini-Manual of the Urban Guerrilla*, written by Carlos Marighella in 1969. On Tuesday, November 4, 1969, Carlos Marighella was assassinated in São Paulo. On that day, two missions were simultaneously interrupted. The first was the life of a man who, for nearly forty years, had been shaping theories in the struggle against the dominant system. The second was that of a determined urban guerrilla. Marighella was killed in an ambush as he was about to begin rural guerrilla warfare, the next step in his liberation cycle. He had the unique position of having made valuable contributions to the revolutionary cause in both theory and practice. During the last year of his life, as a parallel to the action he undertook, he wrote intensively to support his theories about the liberation of Brazil.

The *Mini-Manual of the Urban Guerrilla* has special importance. The work examines the conditions, characteristics, necessities, and methods of guerrilla warfare by the urban guerrilla, and demonstrates Marighella's sense of detail, organization, and mental clarity. It also shows, in passing, that Marighella was endowed with inexhaustible confidence and a youthfulness that belied his fifty-eight years. The manual became one of the principal books for every man who, in the inevitable battle against the bourgeoisie and imperialism, takes the road of armed rebellion.[42]

The Mini-Manual of the Urban Guerrilla

The chronic structural crisis characteristic of Brazil today, and its resultant political instability, is what has brought about the upsurge of revolutionary war in the country. The urban guerrilla is a man who fights the military dictatorship with arms, using unconventional methods. A political revolutionary and an ardent patriot, he is a fighter for his country's liberation, a friend of the people and of freedom. The guerrilla areas of operation are in the large Brazilian cities. There are also bandits, commonly known as outlaws, who work in the big cities. Many times, assaults by outlaws are taken as actions by urban guerrillas. The urban guerrilla, however, differs radically from the outlaw. The outlaw benefits personally from the action, and attacks indiscriminately without distinguishing between the exploited and the exploiters, which is why there are so many ordinary men and women among his victims. The urban guerrilla follows a political goal and only attacks the government, the big capitalists, and the foreign imperialists, particularly North Americans.

Another element just as prejudicial as the outlaw and also operating in the urban area is the right-wing counterrevolutionary who creates confusion, assaults banks, hurls bombs, kidnaps, assassinates, and commits crimes against urban guerrillas, revolutionary priests, students, and citizens who oppose fascism and seek democracy. The urban guerrilla is an implacable enemy of the government and systematically inflicts damage on the authorities that exercise power. The principal task of the urban guerrilla is to distract, to wear out, to demoralize the militarists, the military dictatorship and its repressive forces, and also to attack and destroy the wealth and property of the North Americans, and the Brazilian upper class.

The urban guerrilla is not afraid of dismantling and destroying the present Brazilian economic, political, and social system, for his aim is to help the rural guerrilla and to collaborate in the creation of a totally new and revolutionary social and political structure, with the armed people in power. He must have a certain minimal political understanding, and to gain that, he must read certain printed or mimeographed works such as follows:

- *Guerrilla Warfare* by Che Guevara
- *Memories of a Terrorist*
- *Some Questions about the Brazilian*
- *Guerrilla Operations and Tactics on Strategic Problems and Principles*
- *Certain Tactical Principles for Comrades Undertaking Guerrilla Operations*
- *Organizational Questions*
- *O Guerrilheiro*, newspaper of the Brazilian revolutionary groups

FIGURE 13-10 Map of Brazil. *Source:* Central Intelligence Agency, *The World Factbook, 2008.*

Personal Qualities of the Urban Guerrilla

His bravery and decisive nature characterize the urban guerrilla. He must be a good tactician and a good shot. The urban guerrilla must be a "person of great astuteness to compensate for the fact that he is not sufficiently strong in arms, ammunition, and equipment." The career militarists or the government police have modern arms and transport, and can go about anywhere freely, using the force of their power. The urban guerrilla does not have such resources at his disposal and leads a clandestine existence. Sometimes he is a convicted person or is out on parole and is obliged to use false documents.

Nevertheless, the urban guerrilla has a certain advantage over the conventional military or the police. It is that, while the military and the police act on behalf of the enemy, whom the people hate, the urban guerrilla defends a just cause, which is the people's cause.

The urban guerrilla's arms are inferior to the enemy's, but from a moral point of view, the urban guerrilla has an undeniable superiority. This moral superiority is what sustains the urban guerrilla. Thanks to it, the urban guerrilla can accomplish his principal duty, which is to attack and to survive. The urban guerrilla has to capture or divert arms from the enemy to be able to fight. Because his arms are not uniform, since what he has are expropriated or have fallen into hands in different ways, the urban guerrilla faces the problem of a variety of arms and a shortage of ammunition. Moreover, he has no place to practice shooting and marksmanship. These difficulties have to be surmounted, forcing the urban guerrilla to be imaginative and creative, qualities without which it would be impossible for him to carry out his role as a revolutionary.

The urban guerrilla must possess initiative, mobility, and flexibility, as well as versatility and a command of any situation. Initiative, especially, is an indispensable quality. It is not always possible to foresee everything. And the urban guerrilla cannot let himself become confused, or wait for orders. His duty is to act, to find adequate solutions for each problem he faces, and not to retreat. It is better to err acting than to do nothing for fear of erring. Without initiative there is no urban guerrilla warfare.[43]

FIGURE 13-11 Map of Uruguay. *Source:* Central Intelligence Agency, *The World Factbook, 2008.*

URUGUAY AND PARAGUAY

In comparison to other Latin American states, Uruguay seemed to have an advantage with a prosperous economy built upon its sugar crop and its large export market. However, as has been evidenced in other regions of the world, the onset of severe economic downturns has led to the rise of worker parties, student revolts, and general unrest. This was the scenario in Uruguay when its economy crashed in the late 1950s (Figure 13-11). With the collapse came unrest, high unemployment, and inflation. The sugar workers had already organized labor unions, and by the end of the 1950s, the union was being led and influenced by extreme elements demanding social reforms and justice. Confrontation was the ultimate result.

National Liberation Movement: The Tupamaros

The Tupamaros movement grew out of the disillusionment of unionists, who marched on Montevideo, Uruguay's capital, in 1962. The name for the group is taken from Tupac Amaru II, the leader of an eighteenth-century revolt over Spanish rule in Peru. The confrontations with police ended in numerous arrests. The government, unsympathetic to union demands, and rather than listen to its claims, portrayed the unionists as insurgents and guerrillas. Raul Sendic, a law student arrested during the clashes, rose to form the National Liberation Movement (MLN) in 1963. Sendic emerged from a brief spell in prison, bitter and determined to fight back. The government imposed more restrictions on rights and freedoms, which forged the beginnings of terrorism in Uruguay. Largely an agricultural country, to mount an effective campaign, the group decided that its base and battleground would be the streets of Montevideo. The aim of the MLN was not to replace the government, but to force issues and change policy for the redistribution of wealth. Although the MLN espoused Marxist theories, it did not engage in rhetoric at the expense of public support. By the end of the 1960s, the Tupamaros had grown significantly and were believed to number more than two thousand. The combatants had no doubt studied the *Mini-Manual of the Urban Guerrilla* as their activities and tactics mirrored Marighella's teachings. They used bank robberies and kidnapping to fund their operations. Their methods became an example for other terror groups operating in urban centers of the world. The police in Uruguay were unable to stop the growing surge of the Tupamaros. With the democratic fabric in tatters, the police resorted to torture to extract information and to deter would-be Tupamaros. Many suspected members of the MLN ended up in the country's top-security prison, the Penal de Libertad, under the control of the country's secret police, the *Organismo Coordinador de Actividades Anti-Subversivas*.[44]

Methods of torture were cruel, inhuman, but effective and included rapes, sensory deprivation beatings, burning, electrical shocks, and sleep deprivation.

The end for the Tupamaros came about unexpectedly. The chaos they had brought to the cities forced the government into a more vigorous application of repressive measures. In classic fashion, the Tupamaros' brand of terror forced the government to respond with its own brand of terror. However, they sought respectability and began to align with left-wing political movements to replace the government at the polling booth. This was a disaster, as left-wing constituents did not favor terrorism, and the bid for a socialist ticket failed. As socialists, they should have expected support from the working classes, but MLN was made up mainly of middle-class Uruguayans. With the failure of the political movement, a strong right-wing military government came into power. The populace endorsed its draconian measures in curbing the Tupamaros. The result was mass arrests and the end of MLN. The kidnapping of the British Ambassador, Sir Geoffrey Jackson, in Montevideo in 1972 ultimately shattered the myth that the Tupamaros were invincible. Shortly after Jackson's release from captivity, a general election was held, and the *Frente Amplio* (Broad Front), a strong political supporter of the Tupamaros, was decimated at the polls. The government was returned to office with a clear mandate to try to end terrorism.

The Tupamaros serve as an example of how to organize an effective strike force of terrorists in an urban environment, using the city for cover and following the advice of the *Mini-Manual of the Urban Guerrilla*. Other terror groups have profited from this example in Northern Ireland and in West Germany. The tactics employed by these middle-class terrorists, as saviors of the poor of Montevideo, did not translate into popular support for the movement. To some extent, this organization was built on small independent units and a cell-like structure, also a hallmark of the Irish Republican Army.

Internationally, South American countries could become havens for Middle East and North African terrorist groups: not just a sanctuary but also a fertile recruiting, logistical, and financing region. Uruguay does not figure on the world map of terrorism but is an outspoken supporter of antiterrorism conventions in the region. Al-Said Hassan Mokhles, a suspected Armed Islamic Group (GIA) member, was discovered in Uruguay, and his presence immediately brought a request for extradition to Egypt where he was wanted on terrorist offenses. GIA does have links with al Qaeda, and many Algerians have migrated to North America, in particular Canada, over the last two decades. Uruguay has also become a home base for the Chilean Urban Marxist Guerrilla movement, the Manuel Rodriguez Patriotic Front.

The terrorist organization Hezbollah has been active in the tri-border region where Argentina, Paraguay, and Brazil converge (Figure 13-12). Little has been done about

FIGURE 13-12 Map of Paraguay. *Source:* Central Intelligence Agency, *The World Factbook, 2008.*

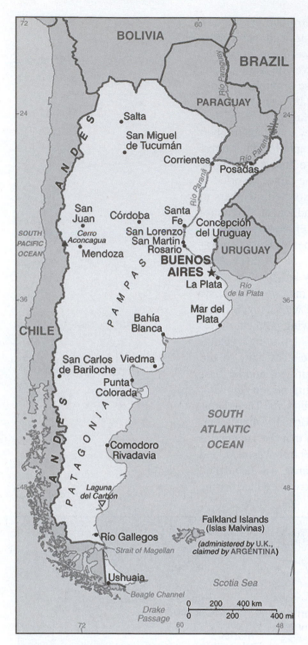

FIGURE 13-13   Map of Argentina.   *Source:* Central Intelligence Agency, *The World Factbook, 2008.*

Hezbollah's presence particularly in Brazil as that country does not recognize any issues with Hezbollah and appears unwilling or unable to confront the problem. The main issue here is that the Hezbollah are actively raising funds for terrorism activity elsewhere. Tracking terrorist fund-raising and financing is not a finite art, and Brazil has not had any success in this area. In addition, most South American countries with the exception of Argentina have not suffered from any Middle Eastern-influenced violence and are thus not motivated enough to go after Hezbollah. Hezbollah would certainly like to gain a foothold in Latin America and get closer to the United States to conduct intelligence operations. How extensive and well supported they are is still not known.

ARGENTINA

Argentina has suffered through systematic human rights violations under strict military juntas since the mid-1970s. To escape those domestic problems, the military government called up their historic claims to the Falkland Islands in the South Atlantic (Figure 13-13). Argentina had claimed title to the islands, which are populated by British families. Before the battle for the Falklands (1982), Argentine's military had attempted to "remove" all political opponents to its regime. This was achieved by clandestine arrests, which were followed by the disappearance of those arrested. Brutalized and tortured bodies, dumped in the ocean, were pulled up in fishing nets.

Before World War II, Argentina had close ties to Germany. However, in 1945 the government of General Farrell severed its links and joined the allies in the defeat of Germany. Two of the most celebrated names associated with South American politics are Colonel Juan Domingo Peron and his equally famous wife, Eva. Peron was certainly responsible for initiating the use of what is now termed "death squads." His vision on coming to power as president in 1946 was to industrialize at the expense of the agricultural industry, which had been Argentina's economic mainstay for most of the century. With industrialization and heavy government spending came staggering inflation never before seen in Argentina. Left-wing political opposition to Peron's activities mounted, and as the 1950s dawned, Argentina was sliding down a dangerous slope, where food shortages and protests were the order of the day. In response, Peron nationalized the press and took total control over what was printed in the media. In 1949, he had created his own secret police force known as the CERT. CERT and its later version, the Division de Informacion Politicas Antidemocratic (DIPA), hid within its ranks a group designed for torture and repression called the Triple A, or the Argentine Anti-Communist Alliance. Peron was deposed in 1955, three years after the death of his wife, Eva.

The Triple A

The Triple A (AAA) was an extreme right-wing death squad that functioned clandestinely at the beginning of the 1970s and consisted of members of the Argentine military and police. Many people suspected of being left-wing sympathizers were abducted, usually in the very early hours of the morning. The captors would explain that they were government agents. Death camps were set up apart from the normal prison structures of the country, making it almost impossible for relatives to locate those taken, let alone establish what kind of agency had detained them. There were forty-seven of these secret camps, which were similar to the concentration camps built by the Nazis, in World War II.[45]

As the years of unceasing military repression grew, so did the pressure from the Red Cross and Amnesty International who accused the military junta as accountable for those missing. In a remarkable piece of legislation passed by the Argentine government in 1979, those who were missing were presumed to be "legally dead" unless it could be proven otherwise!

International Terrorism in the Tri-Border Area

The relatively lawless Tri-Border Area (TBA) region, the area where the borders of Paraguay, Brazil, and Argentina meet has been an area that has seen the development of international terrorist activity and which first came to notice with two bombings in Buenos Aires by Hezbollah in the early 1990s, the first attack was a bombing of the Israeli Embassy which killed twenty-nine people, and this attack it is believed was aided by Iranian diplomats. The second attack was on a Jewish Community Center where eighty-five people were killed. In both instances, the finger is clearly pointed at Hezbollah who may well have been acting on behalf of Iran (Figure 13-14).

Fund-raising and recruitment for terrorist activities has gone relatively unchecked in the TBA and has for years drawn attention as a center for contraband smuggling, drug trafficking, and large-scale money laundering, in part because all of the countries whose borders are involved profit from the illicit trade. It is also an easy place to hide and move money. Estimates of the amount of drug money alone laundered through the two main urban centers in the TBA, Foz do Iguacu and Ciudad del Este, range as high as $12 billion a year. Hezbollah is not the only extreme Islamist group believed to operate in the Central American region as Intelligence Services have documented the presence of Hamas and al Qaeda.[46] Despite the presence of Islamists in the region, there have been no specific attacks in the last decade from them. It is likely that this area is used as a source of fund-raising for the various Islamists organization planning and coordination for operations elsewhere.

Montoneros

One of the military junta's main targets was the Montoneros (Movimiento Peronista Montonero) and its supporters. Set up as a left-wing Peronista movement after the death of Juan Peron, this group was active from 1975 to 1979. The Montoneros were violently opposed to the military takeover of the Argentine government. They attempted to organize the union movement as a cohort in their activities, but a brutal crackdown by the junta prevented any effective action in the cities, and the group had to settle for actions in the countryside. Their tactics were hit-and-run, using bombings and shootings. By 1979, the group had been totally destroyed.[47]

This is yet another example of how an extreme right-wing military government resorted to terrorism of its own to remain in control . . . by using torture, murder, and widespread intimidation.

CHILE

Chile had minor problems with terrorism from the FPMR, which was formed in 1983. As the armed wing of the Chilean Communist Party, it split into a faction, calling itself the Lautaro Youth Movement, which was a mixed bag of leftist elements and criminals that remained active through the early 1990s with the unlikely goal of overthrowing the government. The group

TERRORIST ATTACK BRIEF

Terrorist Group—Islamic Jihad

Case Facts—Five are killed and 106 wounded when a bomb destroys the Israeli Embassy building in Buenos Aires.

Investigation—Responsibility was claimed by Middle East terror group Islamic Jihad. The investigation was slow to proceed, and in 1994, a second bomb went off at a Jewish Community Center, also in Buenos Aires. The Argentine government did little to progress any investigation, and in 1998, evidence of Iranian government involvement was uncovered. The Argentine government expelled several diplomats, but since then no individual has been charged with any crime in relation to the embassy attack.

FIGURE 13-14 Bombing—Israeli Embassy—Buenos Aires—March 17, 1992. *Source:* Israeli Ministry of Foreign Affairs.

FIGURE 13-15 Map of Chile. *Source:* Central Intelligence Agency, *The World Factbook, 2008.*

targeted police and government officials and carried out bank robberies to fund its operations (Figure 13-15).

MILITARY DICTATORSHIP

General Augusto Pinochet, a military dictator of strong Fascist principles was one of the most significant influences in Chile over the past twenty-five years. He is considered by many as Chile's elder statesman. Few dictators ever successfully reach happy retirement, but Pinochet is an example of one who has "gone the distance," despite the appalling acts during his rule. Pinochet swept to power in 1973 during a bloody military coup that removed the Marxist regime responsible for the mismanagement of the country and its economy over a three-year period.

The Marxist leader Salvador Allende was the first democratically elected Marxist president to head any nation in the Western Hemisphere. Allende came to power in 1970 on a ticket promising social programs for Chileans. His government took immediate control of the country's copper mines and banking system. His huge increase in the minimum wage structure and attempts to keep the cost of consumer products at a low level fueled runaway inflation. Between 1971 and 1973, inflation rose by nearly four hundred percent! The government was besieged on all sides. Violent protests began in the streets of Santiago. The military, assisted by the CIA, overthrew the Allende government on September 11, 1973. Allende was arrested and died in custody. Reports on the circumstances of his death vary from torture, execution, to suicide.

The Pinochet Years

The military coup, followed by yet another junta, was not widely popular. Fighting broke out between right-wing supporters of Pinochet and the extreme-left Communist elements. The junta cracked down hard on opposition by dissolving congress, restricting the freedom of the press, and privatizing nationalized industries. Pinochet banned all political opposition parties and ran the country as a dictatorship. The trigger point for the attempted coup was not a momentary aberration on the part of Pinochet; in fact, many of the high-ranking military generals actually served in the Allende cabinet. What caused the problems for the military was the inclusion of left-wing extremism into the fabric of Chile's society. Allende had placed Communist reactionaries in the armed forces to incite rebellion, and over fourteen thousand foreign agitators moved into Chile. These included Cuban DGI agents, who were in Chile to reorganize internal security for Allende, as well as Soviet, Czech, and North Korean military instructors and arms suppliers, and hard-line Spanish Communist Party members. Their intent was to organize revolutionary brigades to take on the established military. The 1970s were a decade of change for Central and South America, and insurgent terror groups and guerrilla movements were on the move from Montevideo to Managua.[48]

To stem the left-wing subversives, the Pinochet junta carried out mass arrests and used torture to gain both information and confessions. They arrested not only Chileans but also foreign subversive elements. These are the actions for which the international community wanted Pinochet held accountable. Executions were commonplace in Chile, and the targets were leftist politicians, trade unionists, and other activists. Many simply disappeared, never to be heard from again. The junta engaged semi-official death squad organizations to do some of its dirty work. The Avengers of the Martyrs was a fascist paramilitary movement comprised mainly of military and police/security personnel. To ensure the security and paramilitary groups could conduct business in an unfettered manner, the military passed a decree to effectively denude the legal process and protection of the public. The Decree Law on Amnesty gave security forces total immunity from prosecution.

The Pinochet regime laid the foundation for a vibrant South American economy and passed it on to a democratic government that followed. Pinochet had turned Chile from a second-rate, Third World country into a strong market economy. Military dictators usually leave in the same violent manner by which they arrived in power, but Pinochet is considered by many in Chile to be a hero of the people, and to a great many others, a murderer.

In 1998, on a visit to Britain for back surgery, General Pinochet was arrested in his hospital bed and there were requests for his extradition. The highest court in Britain dealt a stunning blow to Pinochet, and in a stand for international law and justice, the British have hammered a nail into a portion of his coffin. Pinochet and the democratic government of Chile claimed he had diplomatic immunity as a former head of state and was therefore not subject to arrest and extradition. In the majority decision handed down in November 1998, Britain's Lord Nicholls commented: "The Vienna Convention on diplomatic relations may confer immunity in respect of acts performed in the exercise of functions, which international law recognizes as functions of a head of state, irrespective of the terms of his domestic constitution." Lord Nicholls further commented: "It hardly needs saying that the torture of his own subjects, or of aliens, would not be regarded by international law as a function of a head of state."[49]

Santiago's reactions to the decision led to waves of protest, as well as outpourings of relief. Pinochet subsequently returned to Chile and stood trial in what was termed the "Caravan of Death." Pinochet orchestrated political killings soon after he swept into power in 1973 and unleashed death squads to systematically execute political prisoners and subversives throughout the country. A ruling came down in March 2001, which was then appealed to the Chilean Supreme Court, which, in July 2002, accepted the earlier ruling that the former dictator was mentally unfit to stand trial. To many, his death on December 10, 2006, was a fitting end to his regime's horrendous abuse of civil liberties. On the international terror front, Chile experienced two terror-related incidents. In the wake of the 9-11 attacks, the U.S. embassy received a functional letter bomb, and an anthrax-laced letter was sent to a doctor's office. However, the composition of the anthrax did not match with those strains used in the U.S. attacks. In a wider investigation, the government of Chile began to take a serious interest in the activities of Lebanese businessman Assad Ahmed Mohamed Barakat. It is suspected that Barakat was involved in financial holdings and money transfers for the Lebanese Hezbollah terror group.

Links to Lebanon and Hezbollah

Muhammad Yusif Abdallah is a senior Hizballah leader in the TBA and an important contributor of funds to Hizballah, notably hosting a fundraiser for the terrorist group in the TBA in 2004. Abdallah has personally carried money for Hizballah, serving as a courier of Hizballah funds from the TBA to Lebanon. He has traveled to Lebanon to maintain connections to the Hizballah hierarchy and has met with members of Hizballah's security division. Likewise, Abdallah has also received money from Hizballah to support the Hizballah network in the TBA.

Abdallah is an owner and manager of the Galeria Page building in Ciudad del Este, Paraguay, a shopping center with several businesses owned by Hizballah members. He reportedly pays a percentage of his income to Hizballah based on profits he receives from Galeria Page. In addition to his Hizballah-related activities, Abdallah has also been involved in the import of contraband electronics, passport falsification, credit card fraud, and trafficking counterfeit U.S. dollars.

Muhammad Tarabain Chamas is a member of Hizballah in the TBA, specifically Hizballah's counterintelligence element in the TBA and provides Hizballah with security information on residents there. Muhammad Tarabain Chamas is the private secretary for senior TBA Hizballah leader Muhammad Yusif Abdallah and the principal administrator of the Galeria Page building in Ciudad del Este, Paraguay. In addition to maintaining close contacts with TBA Hizballah members, Muhammad Tarabain Chamas maintains daily contact with Hizballah members in Lebanon and Iran and has transported funds from Hizballah members in the TBA to Hizballah in Lebanon.[50]

FIGURE 13-16 Map of Venezuela. *Source:* Central Intelligence Agency, *The World Factbook, 2008.*

VENEZUELA

Venezuela was once considered a democratic oasis in a desert of military dictatorship, but not anymore. Unlike much of Latin America, Venezuela has had a history of democratic government since 1958, with lessening interference by the military. Venezuela suffers incursions by Colombian terrorists in the border villages and towns. Kidnapping and extortion are the main activities of both the ELN and the Colombian People's Liberation Army (EPL) (Figure 13-16).

Since the independence movement led by Venezuela's favorite son, Simon Bolivar, in the early 1800s, the country had been the home to a succession of military dictators. Venezuela began to prosper with the discovery of oil, becoming its main source of revenue. Mismanagement and corruption ended the military dictatorship of General Gomez in 1935, when the democratic movement, supported by the army, overthrew him and established a democratic government. The country has been ruled by two parties since 1958: the Accion Democratica (AD) and the Christian Democratic Party (COPIE). Each has had its share of periods in office. However, economic downturns have stalled government action on behalf of the many poverty-stricken Venezuelans. Although there is no active terror movement in the country, there are definite signs that reforms will be needed if democracy is to endure. The government has utilized severe measures to control the country in tough economic times. Hugo Chavez, President since 1999, seeks to implement his "Twenty-first Century Socialism," which purports to alleviate social ills while at the same time attacking capitalist globalization and existing democratic institutions. Current concerns include a weakening of democratic institutions, political polarization, a politicized military, drug-related violence along the Colombian border, overdependence on the petroleum industry with its price fluctuations, and irresponsible mining operations that are endangering the rain forest and indigenous peoples.[51]

There are also problems associated with cross-border incursions from Colombia and the probability that the Venezuelan government has been turning a blind eye to such actions. For the landowners and ranchers in the border regions, this has meant reliance on vigilante squads and support from AUC in Colombia to combat the FARC incursions into Venezuela. Hugo Chavez had to contend with a coup attempt in April 2002, which briefly saw him ousted from power. A general strike in November 2002 shut down Venezuela's oil industry. Noticeably, the U.S. television news coverage had failed to note that this strike was not being led by the working-class masses but by the middle-class management population! In its attempt to unseat Chavez, the opposition party had attempted to illicit support for a coup from the United States; however, the Bush government was more concerned with global issues involving Iraq and North Korea and paid little attention to Venezuela. Chavez became rabidly anti-American with every speech he made. Before 2006, Chavez was little known to the U.S. public, but in his outburst at the UN General Assembly in September 2006, speaking the day after former President George W. Bush, he stated, "Yesterday the devil came here. Right here and it smells of sulfur still today." He made many odorous comments and called the U.S. President a drunkard and a terrorist and Condoleezza Rice (Secretary of State), a sexually frustrated and illiterate female; his goals were a direct challenge to the United States. Chavez sought alliances with most of the world's more extreme leaders, that is, Mahmoud Ahmadinejad of Iran, Bashar al-Assad of Syria, and Kim Jong-II of North Korea. Iranian factories are being constructed in Venezuela, and there are direct flights between Caracas and Tehran. He had been outspoken for his support of Hezbollah and been openly hostile to Israel for its Lebanon attacks in 2006. Clearly, he thought he was a force to be reckoned with. During the first decade of this century Venezuela was oil rich and the climb in oil prices emboldened him, as his government reaped the riches from the soaring price of a barrel of oil. He had often threatened to cut off the supply of oil to the United States; however, this was not be a reality in the short term as Venezuela exports approximately fifty percent of its oil to the United States.

Chavez had also been involved in indirect talks with the FARC in an effort to have some of the numerous hostages released. In February 2008, the FARC released three hostages who had been held for more than six years. President Chavez caused considerable displeasure to the Colombian government by speaking directly with FARC, an action not sanctioned by the Colombians. He was re-elected for another six-year term in October of 2012, but finally succumbed to cancer in 2013.

ECUADOR

Ecuador is not a region well known for terrorism and insurgency. In the past decade, it has remained relatively calm with the exception of the October 12, 2000, kidnapping of eight oil rig workers by armed men that lasted into early 2001. The hostage takers executed Ron Sander, one of the U.S. hostages. A little-known group calling itself the Revolutionary Armed Forces of Ecuador (FARE) has taken credit for two bombs that exploded in the coastal city of Guayaquil (Figure 13-17). The FARE could be a front for the FARC or a stand-alone group. Either way, its emergence suggests that the Colombian conflict soon will affect U.S. personnel and assets outside Colombia. In August 2002, a bomb attack on a McDonald's restaurant was claimed to be the work of an unknown terror group calling itself the FARE. FARE states that it is a prodigy of the

FIGURE 13-17 Map of Ecuador. *Source:* Central Intelligence Agency, *The World Factbook, 2008.*

FARC, and it threatened more violence and assassination. At this juncture, very little is known about the group, its makeup, or its aims. However, there is a probability that it could actually be a breakaway faction of the FARC and could be setting up in Ecuador to make the politicians wary of being aligned with the U.S. war on narcotics in the region. Elections held in October 2002, were a focal point for the FARE in its wish to influence any political outcome. Authorities have previously reported the presence of FARE, but no terror attacks have been previously attributed to the group, which authorities say may number several hundred members from both Ecuador and Colombia. The FARE does not appear to be linked to drug trafficking; however, if it is actually FARC by another name, narcotics trafficking may soon be on its agenda. The leftist governments of both Venezuela and Ecuador continue to lash out at their neighbor Colombia mainly for its pro-U.S. stance. In March 2008, Colombian aircraft crossed into Ecuador and killed Raul Reyes, raising the possibility of a military confrontation between the three. Ecuador has been tolerant of the presence of FARC rebels residing inside its territory and the March 2008 raid was roundly condemned by the main leftist governments in South America and this has fuelled Latin America's ideological divisions. Colombian President Alvaro Uribe had received vast sums for his campaign against the drug trade and FARC terrorists, and what was originally hailed as a major victory for the Uribe government became the focus of open hostility from Ecuador and Venezuela. Both countries view Colombia as a pawn of the United States. On the other hand, the Colombian military claimed to have discovered evidence that FARC was attempting to obtain materials to build a dirty bomb.

Summary

Central and South America have been mostly under strong right-wing military rule for many decades of the twentieth century, and into the twenty-first. They have also suffered the ravages of death squads. In studying the causes of terrorism and guerrilla activity throughout Latin America, there are trends that become apparent. In Mexico, El Salvador, Chile, and Uruguay, much of the activity was related to land claims, where the few wealthy landowners had immense influence on the ruling political and military governments. In protecting those interests, the extreme-right death squads operated with impunity. Violations of human rights and the prosecution of those responsible continue to the present. The loss of loved ones to death squads will continue to plague the citizens of new democracies as they strive to move forward. After four decades, Colombia and the threats from FARC would appear to be diminished significantly—the presence of foreign-supported terror groups present in the region will continue to cause problems for global security as will the Hezbollah presence in the tri-border regions. Kidnappings, murder, drug trafficking, disappearances, corruption, human rights abuses are all a part of the fabric that makes Latin America a region for continued concern. The presence of Lebanese Hezbollah and Hamas members as well as the GIA will prompt U.S. power brokers to keep close watch on developments to ensure that international terrorism, with aims of attacking the United States and its interests, is not played out in the region.

Review Questions

1. Explain how a strong right-wing government manages to hold onto power in Guatemala.
2. Describe how narco-terrorism is a confusing term in the overall definition of terrorism.

3. List the gangs and countries they originate from that cause major issues in U.S. society.
4. Describe the rise and fall in popularity of the Shining Path in Peru.
5. Describe the goals of foreign terrorist groups that have been able to get a foothold in South America.

End Notes

1. U.S. Census Bureau. http://www.census.gov/main/www/popclock.html.
2. "Mexico, Post Rebellion Pains." *The Economist* (January 12, 2002, p. 35).
3. *Reuters News Service*. http://www.reuters.com/.
4. Daniel Hernandez. "Who is responsible for the casino tragedy in Mexico?" *Los Angeles Times*. (August 29, 2011). http://latimesblogs.latimes.com/laplaza/2011/08/monterrey-casinoattack-mexico-debate-terrorism-ownerresponsibility.html.
5. Piet van Lier. *War called Peace, Death of a Bishop* (1997). http:zena.securforum.com/znet/LAM/zGuatemala.html.
6. Mica Rosenberg. (February 9, 2006). www.Boston.com/news.
7. Frank M. Afflitto. Abstract from a paper presented at the Conference of the American Society of Criminology (San Diego, CA, November 20, 1997).
8. Victoria Sanford. *Buried Secrets: Truth and Human Rights In Guatemala* (New York: Palgrave Macmillan, 2003, pp. 14–270).
9. Ibid.
10. Ibid.
11. Global Intelligence Update. http://www.stratfor.com/standard/analysis.
12. "Patterns of Global Terrorism." *U.S. Department of State, Publication* 10321 (2008). http://www.strafor.com.
13. Jonathan R. White. *Terrorism: An Introduction* (Belmont, CA: Brooks Cole Publishing, August 2002, p. 157).
14. "Federal Research Division: Library of Congress Country Reports." *Nicaragua* (1996). http://coun-trystudies.us/nicaragua/
15. The Kerry Committee Report. (April 19, 1995).
16. Operation Community Shield Overview. U.S. Immigration and Customs Enforcement (ICE). https://www.ice.gov/national-gang-unit.
17. U.S. Immigration and Customs Enforcement. www.ice.gov/pi//investigations/comshield/index.htm.
18. "Anti-Gang Effort Leads to Indictment of MS-13 Gang Members." U.S. Attorney's Office: Southern District of Texas (August 11, 2011). http://www.justice.gov.
19. *Mexican Drug Wars*. www.global security.org.
20. "Guatemalan Massacre Leaves 27 Dead." *Jane's Intelligence Review Country Risk Watch*, vol. 23, no. 6 (Coulsdon Surrey: IHS Jane's Sentinel House, June 2011, p. 5).
21. U.S. State Department's International Information Programs. "Grossman Outlines Terrorist Threat to Colombia." Testimony by Ambassador Marc Grossman, Undersecretary of State for Political Affairs before the Senate Committee on Foreign Relations Sub-Committee for Western Hemisphere Affairs (April 24, 2003). http:///usinfo.state.gov/topical/pol/terror.htm.
22. Immigration and Refugee Board of Canada. *Colombia: Revolutionary Armed Forces of Colombia (Fuerzas Armadas Revolucionarias de Colombia, FARC), including information on criminal activities, such as drug trafficking and kidnapping; state response to criminal activity (2009–February 2011)*, COL103709.E (April 5, 2011). http://www.unhcr.org/refworld/docid/4dbfcc952.html, extracted April 6, 2012.
23. Kevin Whitelaw. "The State Department is Helping Train Elite Police Units to go After Kidnappers and Rescue Hostages." (February 27, 2008). www.USNews.com—Inside Colombia's War on Kidnapping.
24. Stratfor. "Colombia Nears a Final Peace Deal." (October 9, 2015). https://www.stratfor.com/analysis/colombia-nears-final-peace-deal.
25. Stan Yarbro. *The Christian Science Monitor* (November 18, 1998).
26. Ibid.
27. U.S. Department of State's International Information Programs. "U.S., Colombia Investigate Expansion of Terrorist Alliances." Charlene Porter Washington, File Staff Writer (April 25, 2002). http://usinfo.state.gov/topical/pol/terror02042500.htm.
28. Colombia: Basic Information. http://www.info-please.com/ipa/A0107419.html.
29. Noam Chomsky. "On the War on Drugs." Interviewed by Week Online *DRCNet* (February 8, 2002). http://www.chomsky.info/interviews/20020208.htm.
30. Mike Gray. *Drugs & Terrorism* (2001). http://www.narcoterror.org/mike_oped.htm.
31. U.S. Department of State. Briefing Note. (2008).
32. "Bureau of International Narcotics and Law Enforcement Affairs." *Program and Budget Guide, Fiscal Year 2011* (U.S. State Department, 2011).
33. Sam Dillon. "As Peru Votes, Insurgents Mystique Casts Shadow." *Miami Herald* (June 10, 1990, pp. A1, A26).
34. Jonathan R. White. *Terrorism: An Introduction*. (p. 82).

35. "The Shining Path Comes Back." *The Economist* (August 17, 1996, p. 35).

36. *Armed Conflict Reports*. (Peru, 1980). http://www.ploughshares.ca/libraries/ACRText/ACR-Peru.html.

37. Gabriel Escobar. "Peruvian Guerrillas Hold Hundreds Hostage." *Washington Post*, Foreign Service (December 19, 1996).

38. CNN Interactive World News. "One Hostage Killed in Daring Peru Rescue." *CNN* (April 22, 1997). http://www.cnn/world19704/22/peru.update.late.

39. *CIA World Factbook*. Country Reports. (2008). http://www.cia.gov/cia/publications/factbook/geos/bl.html.

40. San Jose State University, Economics Department. http://www2.sjsu.edu/faculty/watkiins/bolivia.htm.

41. Justicia Y Paz. "La Massacre del Valle de Cochabamba." *La Paz Cadernos* (1975).

42. N. A. Keck. CPP. ASIS Presentation Paper (May 16, 1996).

43. Carlos Marighella. *Mini-Manual of the Urban Guerrilla* (Pamphlet, 1969, pp. 1–2).

44. Bruce Quarrie. *The World's Secret Police* (London: Octobus Books Ltd., 1986, p. 48).

45. Bruce Quarrie. *The World's Secret Police*.

46. Douglas Farah. "Hezbollah's External Support Network in West Africa and Latin America." (International Assessment and Strategy Center, August 4, 2006). www.strategycenter.net/research/pubID.118/pub_detail.asp.

47. Jonathan R. White. *Terrorism: An Introduction*, pp. 48, 49.

48. Arnaud de Borchgrave. "Demonized for Killing a Left-Wing Plot." *The Washington Times* (October 1998, p. A15).

49. International News. *The Globe and Mail* (Canada, November 26, 1998).

50. U.S. Department of the Treasury. "Treasury Targets Hizballah Fundraising Network in the Triple Frontier of Argentina, Brazil, and Paraguay." (June 6, 2006). https://www.treasury.gov/press-center/press-releases/Pages/hp190.aspx.

51. Country Reports. "Venezuela." *CIA World Factbook*. https://www.cia.gov/library/publications/the-world-factbook/geos/ve.html#top.

PART THREE

The War on Terror

Countering Terrorism

LEARNING OUTCOMES

After studying this chapter, students should be able to:

1. Describe the evolution of aviation security and the major events that promulgated policy changes.

2. Recount how police and military forces had to evolve to combat and counterterrorism in the last thirty years of the twentieth century.

3. Explain why aviation and aviation facilities remain attractive targets for terrorists.

4. Cite the international conventions established against terrorist acts over the last sixty-plus years.

5. Describe the post 9-11 initiatives, programs, and improvements to airport passenger screening.

6. Describe the nature of dirty bombs and the threat they pose to the West in the hands of terrorists.

KEY WORDS TO NOTE

Emergency Provisions—Northern Ireland (Emergency Provisions) Act 1973—Established the Diplock Courts in which terrorist offenses could be tried by a judge without a jury

General Staff Reconnaissance Unit Number 69—Formed in 1957; also known as Sayeret Mat'kal, the leading unit in Israel's counterterrorism arsenal

Grenzschutzgruppe 9 (GSG-9)—German Police unit formed as a direct result of the Munich Olympic Games massacre

Groupmentd'intervention de la Gendarmerie Nationale (GIGN)—France's national police anti-terror strike force

Interpol—International Criminal Police Organization created in 1923, it facilitates cross-border police cooperation and supports and assists all organizations, authorities, and services whose mission is to prevent or combat international crime

Joint Task Force 2 (JTF-2)—Canadian Forces special operations unit

MANPADS—Man-portable Air Defense Systems

Major Criminal Hijack (MCHJ)—International Maritime Organization definition of major transnational organized crimes at sea

Nazer Hindawi—April 17, 1986, placed a bomb in his pregnant girlfriend's carry-on bag attempting to blow up an El Al flight at London's Heathrow Airport

Nerve Agents—A class of phosphorus-containing organic chemicals

Operation Bojinka—Islamist plot to blow up eleven commercial airliners between Asia and the United States

Radiological Dispersal Device (RDD)—A weapon designed to spread radiological materials

Special Air Service (SAS) Regiment—Elite British military unit formed in North Africa during World War II

Vesicants—Blistering agent used in chemical weapons

OVERVIEW

Since September 11, 2001, the world has had to take stock of the way it counters what has evolved into a global threat. The threats emanate not only from al Qaeda and Islamic State as global actors on the stage of terrorism but also from religiously motivated "lone wolf" Islamists. During the last four decades of the twentieth century, the emphasis for countering terrorist attacks was focused upon the specific terrorist groups, targeting specific areas within many defined regions or countries. Urban terrorism, particularly in Western democracies, was unfamiliar to the security forces of most countries until the 1970s. Terrorist attacks such as the 1972 Munich Olympic Games massacre of Israeli athletes showed the world how unprepared security/police forces were at handling such situations. Individual countries had thus established elite counterterror units for both domestic and foreign deployment. Not a day passes without mention of terrorism or an insurgent atrocity or bombing in some area of the world. The United States has enacted legislation that is considered draconian in application and also many will argue, attacks U.S. civil liberties and fundamental rights and freedoms—laws that are barely raising a whimper from the public. The structure of U.S. security has been radically transformed, as a result of the attacks on September 11, 2001. The emphasis now is on protecting vital areas of national infrastructure, food sources, the material supply chain, roads, railways, aviation, bridges, dams, and computer systems. The government and its intelligence services are looking to the future on how to hopefully protect, prevent, deter, and detect the next major terror attack.

This chapter looks at the unconventional forces that have been established to counterterror and discusses what may have changed since 9-11, particularly in the United States and Europe. We discuss attitudes aimed toward countering the scourge of terrorism. We will review the most effective and recognized response units for countering terrorism from around the world, some well known, and others less so.

Aviation still continues to present itself as a prime target for terrorists, so we will look at the protection of aviation to both facilities and aircraft in flight.

There is no single type of violent extremist; no single method of recruitment; no single source of motivation or support. There is no single story, no easy synonym for one region, religious tradition, or culture. Some violent extremists believe that they are pious. Others are not. Some are misinformed and misled. Others are educated and knowledgeable. Some are beyond reach. Others will still listen. Some are more focused on what they're running *to*; others more driven by what they're running *from*. Some become disillusioned. Others become very, very dangerous.[1]

In short, the nature and range of possible drivers of violent extremism can vary greatly—from individual psychological factors to community, sectarian, and religious divisions—and these persist across different ethnicities and cultures. But while there is no single cause, we do see common denominators—common factors that breed or help accelerate violent extremism, including feelings of alienation and exclusion, exposure to vile and rampant propaganda, a lack of critical thinking skills, and experiences with state-sanctioned violence, heavy-handed tactics by security services, and the systematic denial of opportunity. Of course, there is no grievance so bitter, no disadvantage so deep that it ever justifies murder, rape, and slavery.[2]

THE ROLES FOR COUNTERTERRORISM

Are the actions of subversive groups, insurgents, and terrorists considered criminal behavior? Throughout this text the issue continues to surface, whether the issue of terrorism is in the Far East, Near East, Middle East, Europe, or North America and how best to legislate against those bent on terrorism. In many countries, legislation has been enacted not only to ban membership in terror organizations but also to sometimes allow for certain suspensions of civil rights to facilitate law enforcement and intelligence activities. To implement successfully in a democratic society requires that the government ensure that such legislation requires review and renewal on a regular basis. In the United Kingdom, the legislation restricting the Irish Republican Army and other terrorist groups required the government to regularly justify its need for such drastic powers because, without such justification, it would automatically lapse.

The terrorist tactics that strike fear in the public for political gain are well documented. Terror and insurgent groups particularly Islamic State (IS) utilize a myriad of internet protocols for fund raising, advertising, recruiting, and communications via websites, chat rooms etc. Live streaming and videos of beheadings and other atrocities has added to the global call for jihad. In these instances, terrorist and insurgents inflict enormous pressure on governments to respond in a specific manner—to either act or react in a determined manner. In the same manner, the events of 9-11 allowed a frantic American public to then think that every Muslim or Arab was a terrorist in waiting. The way we regarded our ethnically and religiously different neighbors suddenly changed. It would be incorrect to cast a suspicious eye at every "Muslim-looking" person. Government intelligence and security forces have been criticized for "racially profiling" specific ethnic and religious groups. On 9-11, the attackers were of Middle East and North African origin, but does the color of the skin determine a person's political and ideological status in society? Intelligence, of course, is not the sole domain of their governments; in nearly all instances, the planning for any major assault, or a terrorist attack, has involvement in the gathering of intelligence by the terrorist group, individual, or organization. In the case of 9-11, there was ample time and opportunity for the terrorist groups to openly view and study the methods used at security checkpoints of the targeted airports, and, no doubt, they conducted dummy runs. In the theater of Northern Ireland, the Provisional Irish Republican Army (PIRA) has always used intelligence gathering successfully to execute operations and has used tactics designed to strike at security forces as they respond to a bomb attack. We have seen insurgents in Iraq and Afghanistan using this same tactic as they detonate one car bomb, and then a second when rescue workers and security personnel arrive on scene.

In the same way, we cannot characterize any group purely by their religious beliefs. Not every Catholic is, by any stretch of the imagination, a supporter of the PIRA and neither must one now make the mistake that every swarthy skinned person is therefore an Islamic extremist. Immigration must come under specific scrutiny in the United States and Canada, as well as review method and process by which students and visitors visas are issued and how checks are made.

The problem for Americans, if, in fact it is considered a problem, is that they enjoy a free and open democracy and value their freedom of speech, their freedom of association, and an ability to travel without undue hindrance. This concept is in stark contrast to many countries, where such liberties are not accepted. The events of 9-11 were perpetrated by people who took advantage of those freedoms and liberties, and they will continue to attempt to destroy those values and freedoms wherever they can.

Maintaining Order

The past examples of the "Irish Troubles" have been remarkable in many respects. In Britain and Northern Ireland, the role of the policeman had always been very public, and the typical British "Bobby" was always on hand to assist. During the terrorist bombing campaigns of mainland Britain, from the late 1960 to 2000, the police had not resorted to a system of rigid rules and control. As has been evidenced in many Latin American countries, terrorist threats and very harsh intimidation have too often been met by even harsher measures inflicted by military and paramilitary police. For the British, terror against the public, in general, reached epidemic proportions in the 1970s. But order and calm prevailed, and public outrage was contained. Rather than form vigilante groups to hunt down suspected terrorists, the British public and media were fully supportive of police actions. TV news showed the police as the front-line troops, always the first on the scene of whatever new atrocity the PIRA or others had perpetrated. In the 1970s, London became a virtual battleground, but sound police tactics and investigative techniques did far more to bring the terrorists to justice than the suspension of any civil liberties might have done.

In many countries, armed and aggressive police forces are a reality. That was not the case in Great Britain, where police were predominately unarmed throughout the PIRA crisis. The police adhered to their role of identifying, tracking down, and apprehending the terrorists, just as they would to any criminal. Police investigations are all about the necessity to gather information, intelligence, and, ultimately, solid evidence. Britain's Special Branch, which deals with terrorists, took the lead in gathering intelligence on subversive Irish groups operating in Northern Ireland and Great Britain. Success for such efforts, however, must be as a result of cooperation among police, the public, and the media. As evident in the United States, such cooperation among agencies can often be strained. Some police agencies jealously guard not only sources but information as well. The public is usually the last to know the true story. There is no simple right or wrong answers with the tactics in combating terrorism. There are, however, many examples of (how and how not) to deal with terrorist situations.

The most open display of police weaponry up until the terrorist attacks in 2005 was at London's Heathrow Airport, which has been the site of numerous false alarms, as well as actual terrorist bombings and mortar attacks carried out by Irish terrorists. The message is clearly sent that the police are ready to respond with overwhelming force. Sadly, since the London subway attack, the sight of armed police in the capital is now as common as it is in the United States.

Racial Profiling

In a world where we not only have to be seen to be politically correct but also to actually apply that correctness to such issues as national security is a considerable challenge. Clearly, the overall reliance on race as the predetermining factor when there are many other avenues or tools for law enforcement to use is incorrect. However, the mere mention of the word "profiling" gets politicians and rights groups in an uproar. The ultimate solution, one that would most effectively strike a balance between the preservation of civil liberties and the need for heightened security, has been elusive. Increased polarization about the effectiveness of racial profiling and its application by law enforcement toward terrorism will continue to be hotly debated. There are two kinds of glaring mistakes we could potentially make in regard to terrorism: One is failing to identify terrorists because we don't want to offend anyone, and two, investigating someone who resembles the profile of a terrorist and therefore upsetting them as a result if the person is not a terrorist.[3] An extreme example of what can go wrong relates to the London Underground bombing threat in 2005 where police had a suspect under surveillance at an apartment block in the capital. A male, who was seen leaving the premises, was challenged by police but did not stop. The police had a new "shoot to kill" policy if they "suspected" a suicide bomber. The unfortunate man was wearing a backpack and ran down into the Stockwell underground station, at which point he was shot five times in the head at point blank range. It turned out that Jean Charles de Menezes, twenty-seven, was not involved in terrorism but was a migrant worker possibly working illegally in the country.

Repression

To determine whether a state's repressive actions against terror are effective, one only has to examine the Soviet Union—before the fall of the Communist regime. Very few, if any, kinds of terrorist attacks were either recorded or reported in the former Soviet Union, which had a thriving community of secret police and thousands of informers permeating both business and society. This made it almost impossible for subversive ideas to become reality. The KGB would almost always snuff out such plots before they could be executed. With the breakup of the Soviet Union, we have witnessed a significant increase in both criminal and terrorist activities. The fall of the Soviet Union was so sudden and the Russian Federation of States underwent such rapid change that it eventually brought about the collapse of the state and of the well-structured and supported police service. In a vast empire that had relied on the state police for all forms of investigations and tactics, both overt and covert, there was now only chaos and a vacuum. The vacuum was filled by criminal and subversive elements that filled the void vacated by established authority.

The drastic reduction in the need for nuclear weapons capability created a ready market in which rogue governments could acquire nuclear technology and even create devices, especially if they could afford to bid at the highest prices. While no terror group has actually used a nuclear device so far, there is an obvious concern that the ingredients to make a "dirty bomb" could well come out of the former Soviet states where controls have been weak and the tracking of such materials is suspect.

Great Britain, since the 1990s, is a very different battleground altogether. With ever-increasing demands on civilian police forces, they have adopted a significant "Big Brother" approach to their duties, maintaining a watchful eye on the communities they serve. Closed-circuit television cameras that monitor the heart of the major cities, as well as the network of the major motorway systems, have aided in the search for serious criminals and terrorists. Civil libertarians and the extreme left-wing agitators may argue that it is an invasion of privacy, but the London Metropolitan Police have had indisputable success in tracking down terrorists who abandon vehicles packed with explosives.

To observers, it would have been an acceptable solution in the wake of the PIRA bombing campaign to unleash the army against what were perceived to be vicious and callous terrorists. One must keep in mind that an army's main role is that of national defense, not policing. In Northern Ireland, when the Royal Ulster Constabulary was unable to protect Catholics from Protestant violence, the army was called in to "assist." That assistance to the Catholic community became the rallying call for the under-equipped Irish Republican Army of the day. As matters further deteriorated at the end of the 1960s, the army was brought into a policing role that involved searches of houses for weapons. At the very least, the army's actions were heavy handed and the soldiers became the objects of hatred and scorn for the local Catholics they were attempting to protect.

Military responses to terror events have also been graphically emphasized by the Israeli use of heavy armor, helicopters, and fighter aircraft to attack elements of Hamas in the West Bank and Gaza regions. Winning the war in Iraq is a point in question; winning the peace has been something else altogether. While military tactics have been used in attempts to "pacify" large areas of Iraq, little consideration was given to the ethnic, religious, clan, and social structures that fuel the counterinsurgency campaigns. Israel mounted a campaign in 2002 to identify locations where suspected terrorist leaders were and then hit them with extreme force. The problem was that Israel was actually targeting areas where civilians lived. Collateral damage can always occur where terrorists are concerned; however, firing rockets into densely packed apartment buildings with the express intent to kill one suspected terrorist will invariably result in the deaths of innocent civilians. We have seen and heard how many American soldiers are killed and injured in Iraq or Afghanistan but little or no figures are available on the significant casualty figures for the Iraqi or Afghan population when troops target a civilian area where insurgents are hiding. The international community questions Israel's actions but has not done so of the United States in regard to Iraq. Of note here is that Israel's military actions have not been successful in curtailing the never-ending cycle of violence in Israeli cities and in the Palestinian areas of the West Bank and Gaza Strip, nor has U.S. policy in Iraq or Afghanistan quelled the insurgency there. From Israel's perspective, its intelligence network has become so efficient in targeting suspected terror elements that it will continue targeting civilian areas as a means of routing out terrorists.

NORTHERN IRELAND

Without imposing martial law in Northern Ireland, the British government used a statutory instrument to control the lawlessness of the terror groups operating against security forces in the province. Special powers to deal with "The Troubles" came into effect in 1973. The Northern Ireland (**Emergency Provisions**) Act empowered the military to have a greater impact in dealing with the terrorists. "No go" areas sprang up in Belfast and Londonderry during the Troubles, allowing terrorists to remain in their "safe houses" within the communities they were fighting to protect. The emergency provisions gave sweeping powers to the military to search houses at any time without the necessity of search warrants. The security forces could detain and question anyone for up to four hours. These methods allowed the military to build up a significant database of information about the people of Northern Ireland. From 1972 to 1976, the army searched nearly 250,000 houses and uncovered 5,800 weapons and 661,000 rounds of ammunition. Added to these powers was the internment of active members of terrorist organizations. Hundreds of Irishmen were interned in the 1970s and, in hindsight, brought the Provisional IRA to the brink of defeat. Nearly all its executive and operations groups were either serving prison sentences or interned.[4] The IRA's call for a Christmas truce in 1974 was made from a position of extreme weakness. After all, there was no way IRA demands for the swift total withdrawal of the British from Northern Ireland and general amnesty for all convicted terrorists would be met. It would be another twenty-four years before the IRA terrorists would walk out of prison as part of the Good Friday Agreement of 1998.

Legislation

Many operational methods and legislated practices can be put into place, but it must ensure that civil liberties are not abrogated to such an extent that the public is duly affected by their restrictive nature. Over the past forty years, there have been significant pieces of legislation and internationally recognized conventions aimed at curbing and countering terrorist activities. The first major terror attacks that attracted global attention involved PLO hijackings of commercial airliners. Those hijackings coupled with the ineptitude of most governments in handling such crises, prompted international anti-hijacking legislation to be drafted. It also prompted a more fundamental approach by one of the target states, Israel.

Israel was one of the first states to provide trained and armed "sky marshals" on all of its aircraft. For all El Al flights, specially trained staff conducts stringent physical and profile security checks on every passenger. So effective was the El Al approach that the terrorists had to find a "soft underbelly" to attack. This, in several instances, was a ground-level attack at airport check-in counters and attempts to shoot down aircraft by means of RPG-7 rockets, as was the case with the failed attack by Black September terrorists at Orly Airport in France. The RPG-7 is a reloadable, shoulder-fired, muzzle-loaded, recoilless antitank and antipersonnel rocket-propelled grenade launcher that launches fin-stabilized, oversized rocket-assisted HEAT grenade from a smoothbore 40-mm tube. The launcher with optical sights weighs 15.9 pounds and has a maximum, effective range of three hundred meters against moving point targets and five hundred meters against stationary point targets and therefore ideal for use in and around airports and airfields (Figure 14-1).

The fundamental principle of international legislative instruments, such as the Chicago Convention and, in particular, Annex 17, was that they required member states to safeguard global air transportation from acts of unlawful interference. The convention applied a common set of standards for the security of international civil aviation.

TERRORISM AND AVIATION

Attacks against civil aviation has long been a choice target for terrorists dating back to the 1970s, and remains so today; however, 9-11 laid bare the blatant incompetence of airport security that Americans had become used to prior to that fateful date. The inadequacy of the Airline Security Program to protect passengers flying out of international airports in the United States was totally exposed. Although aviation security was thrust to the forefront in 2001, the problem of lax airport security had been around for decades. In 1968, there were twenty-seven hijackings and attempts to hijack commercial airliners to Cuba. In 1969, Palestinian terrorists were responsible for a large majority of the eighty-two hijackings worldwide as they attempted to publicize their cause and to put pressure on the Israeli government to release Palestinian prisoners. It would be grossly unfair to be critical of only U.S. aviation when the problem is systemic across all countries, with the possible exception of Israel. The Federal Aviation Administration (FAA) has the responsibility

FIGURE 14-1 Surface-to-air Stinger Missile. *Courtesy:* US Army.

for the safety of U.S. civil aviation. Although it has an excellent staff with immense expertise, it was severely hampered in its ability to implement the changes needed to protect civil aviation from terror attacks inside the United States. This was, in part, because the FAA lacked the funding for research and development of new technology. Also, a powerful aviation lobby had been successful in blocking some of the necessary changes. There are international conventions that cover protocols for dealing with hijackings, aside from the criminal statutes that nation-states have promulgated to deal with individual criminal acts. The enacting of international treaties covers the issue of international terrorism and the hijacking of aircraft. Twelve significant conventions, developed over the last sixty years and related to terrorism, are as follows:

1. Convention on Offenses and Certain Other Acts Committed on Board Aircraft ("Tokyo Convention," 1963—safety of aviation)
2. Convention for the Suppression of Unlawful Seizure of Aircraft ("Hague Convention," 1970—aircraft hijackings)
3. Convention for the Suppression of Unlawful Acts against the Safety of Civil Aviation ("Montreal Convention," 1971—applies to acts of aviation sabotage such as bombings aboard aircraft in flight)
4. Convention on the Prevention and Punishment of Crimes against Internationally Protected Persons (1973—outlaws attacks on senior government officials and diplomats)
5. International Convention against the Taking of Hostages ("Hostages Convention," 1979)
6. Convention on the Physical Protection of Nuclear Material ("Nuclear Materials Convention," 1980—combats unlawful taking and use of nuclear material)
7. Protocol for the Suppression of Unlawful Acts of Violence at Airports Serving International Civil Aviation, Supplementary to the Convention for the Suppression of Unlawful Acts against the Safety of Civil Aviation (extends and supplements the Montreal Convention on Air Safety, 1988)
8. Convention for the Suppression of Unlawful Acts against the Safety of Maritime Navigation (1988—applies to terrorist activities on ships)
9. Protocol for the Suppression of Unlawful Acts against the Safety of Fixed Platforms Located on the Continental Shelf (1988—applies to the terrorist activities on fixed offshore platforms)
10. Convention on the Marking of Plastic Explosives for the Purpose of Detection (1991—provides for chemical marking to facilitate detection of plastic explosives [e.g., to combat aircraft sabotage])
11. International Convention for the Suppression of Terrorist Bombing (1997, UN General Assembly Resolution)
12. International Convention for the Suppression of the Financing of Terrorism (1999)[5]

The application of an acceptable level of aviation security is well documented and was graphically detailed in a statement before the House of Representatives, Government Activities and Transportation Subcommittee in September 1989 by Homer Boynton, one year after the Pan Am disaster over Lockerbie, Scotland. Homer Boynton, security director of American Airlines, stated to the subcommittee that "In 1988, ICAO estimated that worldwide, 1.1 billion passengers flew on board eleven hundred commercial aircraft, on nearly forty thousand flight segments. During this period one explosive device caused the awful aviation disaster over Lockerbie, Scotland. If one looks at these statistics in their totality, security personnel were seeking one explosive device carried by one passenger among 1.1 billion passengers."[6]

Taking Boynton's comments in the context of the 9-11 events seems to underscore the point that even though security agents are on the job, they are not necessarily going to find everything. Unfortunately, the U.S. system had been so deplorable for the previous two decades; it is surprising that such an event had not happened earlier. Boynton's comments would seem to point the finger at security screeners missing a bomb in baggage, when, in fact, that was not the specific case in Pan Am 103; there were more factors to the inherent risk that passengers were taking by flying Pan Am in 1988. The President's Commission on Aviation and Terrorism concluded in 1990 that Pan Am was basically an accident waiting to happen and the Lockerbie disaster was preventable. What are the undisputed facts in this case? A terrorist was able to place a bomb in a suitcase that went on board Pan Am 103. The bomb detonated at 31,000 feet, killing two hundred and fifty-nine persons on the aircraft and eleven on the ground. If this was preventable, perhaps it is important to understand how easy it was in 1988 for human elements to come into play. After the FAA inspected Pan Am's operation at Frankfurt, West Germany, it was concerned with the airline's lack of a verifiable tracking system for interline bags (i.e., bags transferring from other airlines) and the confused state of its passenger screening process. The FAA inspector wrote, "The system, trying to control approximately forty-five hundred passengers and twenty-eight flights per day, is being held together only by a very labor-intensive operation and the tenuous threads of luck." The inspector went on to condone the actions by adding: "It appears the minimum FAA requirements are being met." Luck, however, was not on the side of passengers of Pan Am 103 in 1988. Among the many questions being asked after the Lockerbie bombing was, "How did the interline bag get onto the flight?" The answer to that is "with ease," given the vagaries of the systems at that time. Reconciliation of passengers with their baggage is a central issue—the requirement being that an aircraft on an international flight will only carry bags for the passengers it has checked in for the flight. Having stated that, there is obviously a weak link that is ready to be exposed by the current Islamic extremist terrorists prepared to die for their beliefs. The strategy for 9-11 was to identify the weaknesses of aviation security and exploit them in order to carry out the suicide mission. Purely ensuring that passengers fly with their baggage will not prevent a suicide attack.

Looking ahead, the old ways of doing things are gone forever. The U.S. Department of Homeland Security is implementing next-generation technology to identify many multifaceted threats, not only to aviation but also to a whole gambit of possible targets, in the fields of mass transit, ports, airports, and railways. Looking back at Pan American Airlines in 1988, one of the main problems was that the screening process for interline bags was by X-ray detection. Even with the X-ray technology in place, the system was incapable of detecting the trace elements of the Semtex explosive used in the Lockerbie explosion. What could have been detected were the sources used to detonate the explosive. As is so often the case, human error played a part in the bombings, as well as a lack of sufficient technology to detect the specific explosive. In Pan Am's defense, it informed the President's Commission that the FAA director of Aviation had given the airline verbal approval to X-ray interline bags rather than searching or reconciling them with passengers, which, not surprisingly, the FAA denied.

There are some eerie similarities between the intelligence failings in 1988 and what went wrong, thirteen years later, on 9-11. Prior to the bombing of Pan Am 103, the intelligence community had received warnings that trouble was brewing in Europe. A total of nine security bulletins that could have had relevance to the Pan Am tragedy were issued between June and December 1988. One bulletin described how a Toshiba radio cassette player, containing a fully primed bomb with a barometric trigger, was found by the West German police in a vehicle belonging to a member of the PFLP-GC. The FAA cautioned airlines that the device found by the West German authorities "would be very difficult to detect via normal X-ray" and informed U.S. airlines that passenger/baggage reconciliation procedures "should be rigorously applied." That specific threat was received by the U.S. embassy in Helsinki on December 5, 1988, detailing a threat that a woman would carry a bomb on board a Pan Am flight from Frankfurt in the following two weeks, was released by the FAA and then redistributed by the U.S. State Department to U.S. embassies around the globe. The U.S. embassy in Moscow made the information public to the country's two thousand-member community of U.S. citizens, including alerting Moscow news media.[7]

It seems surprising that Pan Am management and security were then not paying specific attention to baggage reconciliation at this juncture. In view of the FAA's threat assessment, there were significant lapses in adherence to the careful application of the reconciliation process at Frankfurt on that fateful day in 1988. It is also important to appreciate just how impotent the FAA was in dealing with Pan Am's security problems. Even after the Lockerbie disaster, the FAA found numerous security discrepancies with Pan Am, at both Frankfurt Airport and London's Heathrow Airport. Only six months after Lockerbie, an FAA inspector's report on June 9, 1989, stated, "The posture of Pan Am is considered unsafe; all passengers flying out of Frankfurt on Pan Am are at great risk."[8]

Concerning the attacks on the World Trade Center and the Pentagon, an awakened and anxious public is fully aware the plot to attack aviation was brought to the attention of the FBI from flight-training academies inside the United States and from reports from its own agents. The clear failure of any resource to follow up on such intelligence is but one issue that led to the tragic destruction on 9-11.

Security improvements in the 1990s, particularly in the light of the aforementioned President's Commission, fell woefully short. The viewpoint of the FAA was basically that "it won't happen here." Hijacking aircraft was not yet a North American problem as it was seen by U.S. authorities to be a European and Eastern European issue. After all is said and done, no one had been injured by an act of terrorism against airliners flying within or from the United States. Admiral Cathal Flynn stated that in the decade since (Pan Am 103) amid attacks on other carriers, no U.S. aircraft had been successfully attacked and not one person harmed on U.S. flag flights anywhere in the world, despite terrorist's determined efforts. He also said, "This owes a great deal to strengthened intelligence and law enforcement efforts and to international cooperation in fighting terrorism, both airport and carrier programs have been key factors."[9] Since these comments were made, it was clear that the intelligence process had failed and both airport and air carrier programs were shown to be completely inadequate to protect the traveling public and aviation facilities from terrorist attacks.

Passenger Screening at Airports

There are many issues surrounding passenger screening, and the related training of the security operatives. In the United States and Canada, in the decades leading to 9-11, aviation regulations had made the airlines responsible for security of passengers and baggage screening. In many other regions of the world, governments have made the airports responsible. As was shown after 9-11, passengers were able to board aircraft with small-bladed knives that were used to gruesome effect to disable pilots and eventually crash aircraft into the World Trade Center and the Pentagon. The need to apply screening processes developed as a result of hijackings by Middle East and European terror groups in the late 1960s and early 1970s. At that time, the threat posed was from gun and explosive-toting terrorists who were gaining access to aircraft. Their intent was not specifically to kill, but to use hostages as bargaining chips for the release of prisoners held in jails, in Israel and Europe. By 2001, the training and equipment for passenger screening had not changed that much since those early days. The message was clear to terrorists in the past and still is today: As long as aviation security measures are not in place, aviation is a lucrative, media-grabbing, and sensational target.

Tombstone Technology

When the body count becomes too much for an administration to bear, the cost of fixing most existing problems gets the necessary funding it should have had in the first place. We like to refer to this a, "tombstone technology." The fact remains that 9-11 could have been—and most probably should have been—detected in advance and therefore prevented. This may be a very bold assertion, but it is an assertion we are definitely not alone in making. In North America, all the airlines were tasked (up until 2002) with the security of passengers. Costs are always an issue for airlines, and, in the United States, security companies were required to bid on security-screening contracts. The successful bid was almost always given to the lowest bidder. Our security was entrusted to low-paid, low-skilled, often untrained, poorly motivated individuals and, in many instances, new immigrants. Not only were they poorly paid, but a proportion of them were, in fact, illegal immigrants. This was the case in the United States in the last two decades of the twentieth century. The level of training and the types of test items that the staff used for training were totally out of context with the types of weapons and cutting devices available on the market. So, there were significant holes in the screening process, both in the United States and elsewhere. Inconsistency is also another issue. Different items attract attention at one airport, but perhaps not at another, and this problem continues.

A major flaw in the process, and one most noticeable in the United States, had been that passengers and the general public could go through security screening, but all this did was raise the obvious prospect of breaches and banned items getting through the security screening process. The security screeners, working at minimum wage and having been poorly trained, had only about seven seconds to determine what they were viewing on the X-ray monitor. Added to this, most passengers (before 9-11) took the view that security was a hindrance. The abuse suffered by low-paid screeners from irate passengers and airline staff is legend. In many cases, the decision on whether a passenger could take a specific item on board was referred to an airline supervisor for a decision. Most of the decisions were made in favor of the fare-paying passenger. This did little for the morale of the screeners and even less for security. The problem is underscored in such documents as the 1994 U.S. Government Accountability report to Congressional Committees on Aviation Security. In that report, which disseminated the President's Commission Report, the commission raised concerns about screeners' efficiency, mail and cargo, and the coordination of security between law enforcement and airport personnel. Little changed in the intervening years; "shutting the barn door after the horse has bolted" adequately describes what has taken place since 9-11. Responsibility for airport security was passed to the Department of Homeland Security's Transportation Security Administration (TSA). Now all airport security screeners are federalized, creating a long-awaited, consistent level of training, for all those employees. Added to this is the requirement to screen all hold baggage. The one hundred percent screening of hold baggage has been a reality in the United Kingdom since 1998, but North America and some European countries were far behind. Since 9-11, funds have been budgeted and are being provided to support the security functions at U.S. airports and seaports; however, this may be too little, too late. Prior to 9-11, the opportunity existed for terrorists to openly observe the screening processes at U.S. airports, to assess where the weakest points were, to see how the screeners searched and what items they took from passengers. It is not improbable to suggest that they had done dummy runs with similar objects, and even if they had been detected, the outcome would not have brought them to the attention of the authorities.

El Al Hijacking—July 23, 1968

To date, this is the only ever successful hijacking of an Israeli commercial flight.

The flight originated in Rome and was destined for Tel Aviv. It was seized by members of the Popular Front for the Liberation of Palestine and forced to fly to Algiers in North Africa the hostages were held until the end of August. This assault had the immediate effect of changing Israeli policy around aviation security and has led them to the highest standard security measures, including intensive questioning and profiling of passengers prior to boarding, conducting physical searches of passengers and aircraft, and placing armed guards on board every flight. As we see from the next example, eighteen years later their program paid off.

Proxy Suicide—El AL (Israeli Airlines)

An early attempt at a proxy suicide bombing involves the case of **Nazer Hindawi**, a Jordanian-Palestinian who with the support of Syria had spent a considerable amount of time in Ireland and befriended a young Irish girl whom he managed to get pregnant. On August 17, 1986, he sent her back to the Middle East to meet his family and the route he chose for her was via an Israeli Airlines flight from London's Heathrow Airport. By the spring of 1986, the world was well accustomed to airport delays caused by security checks, with Heathrow being no exception. The traveling public was subjected to waiting in monotonous lines for hand luggage to be searched, blissfully ignorant that the suicide or mule bomber even existed. There had, at this juncture, been no recorded attempts to destroy an aircraft by suicide bombing. This was to change on that April day. Terminal One at Heathrow International was the hub for British Airways European and domestic arrivals and departures. However, on several days of the week, it was also the terminal used by Israel's El Al Airlines for its Boeing 747 flight to Tel Aviv, Israel. At mid-morning, with the El Al 747 at departure Gate 23, passengers for that flight began to come through the pre-boarding security checks. All passengers leaving the United Kingdom in 1986, and specifically those with checked baggage, were asked a series of questions:

- Is this your baggage?
- Did you pack it yourself and are you taking any packages for somebody else?
- Have you left your baggage unattended at any time?

After answering the questions, the passengers would proceed to an immigration desk for passport inspection, not far from the watching eye of Metropolitan Police Special Branch officers.

On this day, the young woman from the Republic of Ireland answered all the questions. Her passport was checked and her hand luggage and hold baggage were screened by X-ray. The girl proceeded to the El Al boarding gate with her single piece of carry-on baggage. The bag was of nylon construction with an expanding compartment at the base, a type of bag used by millions of travelers. El Al prides itself on being one of the most secure airlines in the world (with good reason); it always conducts its own secondary security check and questioning of every passenger. The pregnant girl was going to visit her boyfriend's family in the Middle East; he, however, was not traveling. The El Al security staff thought this was an unusual story, and while doing the physical check on the bag, noticed that even when empty it seemed overly heavy for its construction. At that point, a police explosive search dog reacted to the bag. Further inspection revealed several sheets of plastic explosive wired to a calculator and battery. The bomb was in a false bottom of the bag. The boyfriend, Nazer Hindawi, had befriended the young woman, gotten her pregnant, and was sending her to her death. He had gone to remarkable lengths and considerable planning to pull this attack off. He was sentenced to forty-five years in prison. The plan was for the bomb to detonate approximately two hours after departure. After the failed bombing, Hindawi sought refuge at the residence of a Syrian diplomat in the United Kingdom.

The Global Threat to Civil Aviation

The 1970s and 1980s were the decades of hijackings—preferred mode of attack for terrorists at that time. As effective security was moved against that threat, the terrorists shifted their attention to other areas of aviation they considered to be weak. Pan Am 103 is one example. The attacks against civil aviation tend to get lost in the mists of time. Few remember the specific threats and attacks, particularly when they occur in far-away countries. We list here some specific examples where the threat is from explosive devices, either placed in the hold or as cabin baggage. A Pan Am 747 had a bomb explode on board on a flight from Tokyo to Honolulu in August 1982, and also the same year an improvised explosive device (IED) was discovered on a Pan Am 747 at Rio de Janeiro airport. In December of the same year, a piece of checked luggage was removed from an Alitalia (Italian Airlines) flight when the passenger who checked the luggage did not board the aircraft. The passenger was checking the bag through to a Pan Am flight to New York. Police discovered a bomb inside the bag.[10]

The terrorist hijackings by Palestinian groups in the late 1960s and 1970s changed the face of aviation for the next thirty years. For the terrorists, a hijacked aircraft became a way to attract the worldwide media coverage that the group craved, allowing them to present an agenda or message about their cause instantly and universally. For respective governments and the public, the horror became too much to deal with. Measures to counteract these depredations were hastily drawn up and passenger screening for hand-carried baggage was born. Security is, in many ways, a reactive function, and this has been clearly demonstrated in the aviation industry.

OPERATION BOJINKA

Six years prior to 9-11, al Qaeda planned an attack targeting U.S. flights from Manila in the Philippines. **Operation Bojinka** was planned in 1995 and was uncovered by Philippine authorities—they stumbled by accident on a bomb-making factory in an apartment block that had caught fire and discovered sulfuric acid, nitric acid, sodium trichlorate, ammonia, silver nitrates, and nitrobenzoyl, and a document written in Arabic that detailed how to construct liquid bombs. They also found twelve forged Norwegian, Saudi, and Afghan passports. The apartment was rented by Ramzi Yousef, and details of the Bojinka plot were found on the hard drive of his laptop detailing flight schedules and detonation information. Yousef is currently serving 240 years in prison for the 1993 World Trade Center bombing. The plan was to attack eleven passenger aircraft operating between Asia and the western United States by planting bombs. Bojinka is believed to have been directly funded by Osama bin Laden. Ramzi Yousef and Khalid Sheikh Mohammed (KSM), the alleged mastermind of those attacks, told his U.S. interrogators that planning for the attacks on New York and Washington began in 1994 in the Philippine capital. Mohammed stated that he and his nephew Ramzi Yousef, who is serving a life sentence for his role in the 1993 World Trade Center bombing, began plotting the September 11 attacks seven years earlier. In 1994, the two tested airport security—Mohammed on a flight from Manila to Seoul, South Korea; Yousef on a flight from Hong Kong to Taipei, Taiwan. Mohammed stated that the two men converted fourteen bottles of contact lens solution into bombs by replacing their contents with an inexpensive liquid explosive readily available in the Philippines.[11]

LIQUID BOMB PLOT

London, UK—August 10, 2006

The reason why we are no longer able to bring liquids through passenger screening points throughout the world is due to the plot uncovered by UK authorities in 2006.

A group of British Muslims allegedly planned suicide missions on at least seven international flights from London's Heathrow to North America. On this occasion, intelligence work was able to prevent the attacks being carried out (Figure 14-2). The attackers planned to use items that could be legally carried on board an aircraft, hidden inside containers of liquid. The bombs were constructed by removing liquid from a sealed drinks container and replacing it using a syringe to insert the explosive substance made up of a mixture of hydrogen peroxide and other organic compounds including a sugar additive to produce a hotter and more powerful explosion.

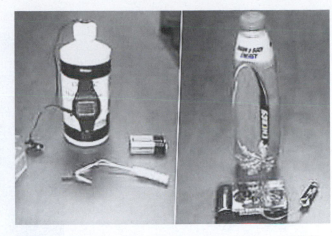

FIGURE 14-2   Transatlantic airlines plot.   *Courtesy:* DHS/TSA.

The team of eight planned their suicide mission detonating their IEDs using a hexamethylenetriperoxidediamine (HMTD) detonator rigged to some sort of electric spark trigger from an electronic device, such as a disposable camera flash bulb, while the airliners were cruising at altitude above the Atlantic Ocean.[12] Scientists at the Sandia National Laboratory, working in cooperation with the DHS, conducted testing of the liquid explosive and detonation methods the terrorists planned to use and found the improvised explosive to be extremely powerful.[13]

Airports are busy and often cramped locations designed and built in the decades before security of passengers and aircraft became such a significant issue. Even newly built facilities in the United States over the last five years of the twentieth century failed to factor in hardening of the facility for security purposes, especially the screening areas, or incorporating sophisticated detection devices into the baggage sorting/conveyor systems. A demand had now added an additional layer of baggage security to an already overburdened system. The problem facing the airlines was, "Who is going to pay for all this added security?" In the long run, it would, of course, be the traveling public, as it always is. After the bombing of Pan Am 103 in 1988, it was important to develop effective explosive detection equipment that could handle the heavy volume of baggage. Throughput was also part of the immediate challenge for airports and aviation security experts. Screening hold baggage had not been a priority for North America in spite of the President's Commission Report in 1990. Since 9-11 and the advent of the TSA in the United States, 100 percent screening of checked baggage at long last became a reality. As we move forward, the government (TSA) intends to continue research into more effective ways to scan baggage for explosive substances and devices by funding programs to efficiently inculcate the airport/airlines' baggage systems with state-of-the-art technology to screen checked baggage. The remaining gap in screening now reverts to the cargo hold and the amount of unchecked mail and freight. So as governments continue to find ever more sophisticated methods to prevent the next unthinkable attack, the very sobering message we now get from the terrorists is that they want nothing from us except our destruction! Hussein Mussawi, former Hezbollah leader, stated, "We are not fighting so that the enemy may offer us something. We are fighting to wipe out the enemy."

Airport Facilities

Airports are, by their very nature, open and public places and in March 2016, the Zaventem International Airport in Brussels was shown to be just such a place where terrorists would exploit that openness. As a result, the opportunity for terrorists to leave bombs in such public places is always present. Only awareness, vigilance, and response by the public and police can help to avert disasters (Figure 14-3). What about security in the other sectors of the aviation industry? What about mail and airfreight carriers? How secure are they? Airlines move millions of tons of freight throughout the world and a large percentage travels without any serious screening in the holds of passenger aircraft. At the present time, this area of airline operation is open to attack. Furthermore, access to the aircraft by catering facilities, airport workers, and so on must receive serious attention if the sterility of the aircraft is to be maintained. It is of little benefit to any operation if the passengers are fully screened for weapons, but airport workers

FIGURE 14-3   Bomb-Making Awareness Program.   *Courtesy:* https://www.dhs.gov/bomb-making-materials-awareness-program.

are allowed almost unrestricted access without checks. Without stating the obvious, the opportunity exists for airport workers to secrete weapons or even bombs on an aircraft. A comprehensive system must be employed to assure the integrity of all those persons who have access to restricted areas of the airport and also the bags and items that they carry in with them. Although measures are in place to verify freight by known shipper, this is a far cry from a totally secure cargo hold, inserting heavy-duty screening equipment and bomb detection dogs into this mix will delay freight operations, but will it deter a would-be terrorist? In 2010, we saw terrorists in Yemen placing explosives in printer cartridges and having them shipped through Europe to the United States (Figure 14-4). In the 2010 incident, the cargo flights and the packages were subsequently intercepted in Dubai and at Britain's East Midlands Airport, but the door is still open. On October 31, 2015, a Russian airliner belonging to Metrojet was brought down over the Sinai Peninsula with an onboard bomb. The flight had originated at Sharm el-Sheikh and the crash killed all on board. How did they get a bomb on the aircraft? Airport workers, security staff, contract and agency staff working at the airport, baggage handlers and loaders—the finger would certainly point in that direction. We look at airports such as our major centers, Paris, New York, and London and expect superior security but what happens at the lowly regional airports and how is the threat of possible security breaches handled and managed? Terrorists will always seek the soft target and if they can't attack JFK, LHR, or Charles De Gaulle airport then any other without the overtly powerful security mantel will do.

PASSENGER TERMINAL ATTACKS

As already evidenced in Europe, threats also extend to passengers waiting at check-in counters. For airports and security, these areas require consideration and attention. Attacks can

FIGURE 14-4   Cargo Planes Bomb plot—printer cartridge bomb.   *Courtesy:* TSA.

occur even at times of heightened security, and the United States most certainly was on guard on Independence Day in 2002, when a man of Middle East origin opened fire at the El Al check-in desks at Los Angeles International Airport. The June 2007 vehicular attack on Scotland's Glasgow Airport by two men driving a bomb-laden vehicle are prime examples of how easy it is for the determined terrorist in these cases to launch an attack. In January 2011, a suicide bomber attacked passengers in the arrivals area at Moscow's Domodedovo Airport, killing thirty-five. What do we learn from such events? El Al, the Israeli national airline, is a model for all other airlines. El Al prides itself on its stringent security systems and passenger profiling. El Al does not restrict its security activities solely to the airport and the perimeter areas of airport facilities but also includes hotels where its crew stays on international flights. The June 2008 information that was being gathered by a group from Hezbollah in Toronto, Canada, was specific to the location where the El Al crew was staying. El Al immediately changed its security procedures as a result, fearing an imminent attack against its personnel and operations.

Attacks on airports have been relatively few but have always taken authorities by surprise. The attacks on Heathrow Airport in 1994, the Scottish attack in 2007, the attack in Moscow in 2011, and the Brussels airport attack in 2016 are good examples of the lengths to which a group of committed individuals will go to in order to cause death and destruction.

Heathrow Airport Attacked by Irish Terrorists—1994

FIRST ATTACK On Wednesday March 9, 1994, between 5:00 P.M. and 5:30 P.M., using a recognized code word, telephone calls were received by various news organizations warning of the following:

- Bombs at Heathrow and
- In terminals and runways in one hour.

Just before 6:00 P.M., there was an explosion in a car in the parking lot of the Excelsior Hotel, on the north side of the airport. Several cars were engulfed in flames, and four mortars were found near the northern runway.

- None had exploded on impact.
- No damage or injury occurred.
- The hotel parking lot had in the past been utilized as an evacuation point.

SECOND ATTACK On the following day between 5:30 P.M. and 9:45 P.M., a number of similar calls were received. At midnight, four more bombs were fired from wasteland beyond the perimeter on the southern side of the airport near Terminal Four. Again there was no explosion, damage, or injury. The launcher was a freestanding, purposely built apparatus, placed in undergrowth and concealed with plastic sheeting and branches.

THIRD ATTACK Three days later on Sunday, March 13, 1994, there were again a series of similar calls between 6:00 A.M. and 6:40 A.M. Flights were diverted from the southern runway, and just after 8.00 A.M., rockets were again fired toward Terminal Four, from the opposite direction. One landed on the terminal without causing damage.

FOURTH ATTACK Between 6:45 P.M. and 7:30 P.M. the same day, coded calls were received, giving the same unspecific information, stating that bombs had been placed at Heathrow and Gatwick. Contingency plans were implemented at both airports, but this was found to be a hoax. It is properly described as an attack because the disruptive effect was equal to that at earlier incidents.[14]

While the type of device used by the PIRA in this attack was crude and unsophisticated, had they had the opportunity to use Man-Portable Air Defense Systems (MANPADS), they would surely have hit targets that they chose. There are an estimated half a million **MANPADS** currently in existence. Some of the simpler systems are available for as little as $1,000 on the open market. The MANPADS used thus far in terrorist attacks, such as the Russian-made SA-7, suggest that terrorist groups currently do not have access to more sophisticated systems, although general small-arms proliferation trends suggest that it is only a matter of time before they acquire more advanced systems. Many MANPADS are unaccounted for, including at least forty Stinger missile systems missing after the 1991 Gulf War, as well as hundreds of U.S.-made MANPADS shipped to foreign nations and then left untracked, with thousands of systems built by France, China, and Russia.[15]

In the Heathrow Airport attack, this was the first time police and intelligence had to not only be concerned with the airport facility and its protection but also evaluate the threat from areas surrounding the airport. The better use of closed-circuit television systems (CCTV) and better intelligence on who owns the lands and buildings in close proximity to airport facilities now had to be viewed in the overall risk assessment for an airport. Following 9-11, there was considerable concern about the use of and the availability of Stinger missiles against U.S. and UN targets. While there is no evidence to suggest that any Stinger missiles are in the United States, it is important to note that a U.S. military factsheet details the Stinger in this manner: "The missiles' complexity can be accommodated by almost any potential user nation or group."

The "Stinger missile" is 5 feet long and weighs thirty-four pounds. It was and is manufactured by Raytheon and can be fired from a distance of five miles and has a vertical range of ten thousand feet. A Stinger would be a lethal weapon when used against a conventional civilian airliner. Stingers were originally sent to Afghanistan as part of the campaign to arm the local mujahedeen against the Soviet invasion. At the time of the transfer, there were advocates against such a move, with the outright fear that the Islamic fundamentalist who dominated the Afghan mujahedeen had about as much love of the West as they did for the Soviets. The opportunity for some to be traded to terrorist organizations was a genuine and highly conceivable proposition. Other countries that have Stinger missiles include Somalia, Iraq, the United Arab Emirates, Qatar, Zambia, and North Korea.[16] Attacks by shoulder-fired missiles have been an ongoing concern since the November 2002 attack in Kenya against an El Al flight taking off from Mombasa. There are earlier recorded attacks, but the underlying worry is the existence of these systems in such large numbers.

Glasgow International Airport (UK)—Facility Attack

In June 2007, a full frontal attack using a vehicle as a means to deliver an incendiary bomb took place at Glasgow International Airport in Scotland when two men of Middle East appearance drove a Range Rover SUV loaded with propane tanks and soaked in gasoline at the main doors of the terminal. The attack was thwarted by the reinforced doors to the building to prevent such attacks; the vehicle and its two occupants caught fire and both were arrested by members of the public and airport police. This is an example of the vulnerability of public locations to this type of uncoordinated but nevertheless deadly style of attack. Had they succeeded in breaching the doors, the resulting mayhem and death would have been considerable.

Karachi, Pakistan—Jinnah International Airport—Facility Attack

On the evening of June 9, 2014, a heavily armed and well-trained group of members of the Pakistan Taliban carried out a commando style assault on the cargo and VIP area of Jinnah International. They were well equipped with AK-47s, grenades, rocket launchers, and suicide vests. The attack resulted in twenty-one deaths, including all ten attackers. It took Pakistani forces nearly eight hours to regain control and end the assault.

A People Issue

Prior to the events of 9-11, a problem in U.S. and European airports had been the vast number of people having access to the restricted areas of airports. What measures can be taken to ensure that airport workers, baggage loaders, re-fuelers, aircraft cleaners, and the like have undergone sufficient background checks to assure authorities of their integrity? News reports out of the United Kingdom in early September 2002 indicated that at least fifteen illegal aliens were employed cleaning aircraft at London's Heathrow Airport.

The FAA studied weapon detection rates at the twenty-five largest airports in the United States and found that the lowest rates were at Boston's Logan International; Newark, New Jersey; and Dulles Airport in Washington, DC. After the loss of TWA 800 off Long Island, New York, in 1996, the Gore Commission made many recommendations in regard to airport security, including positive bag matching for passengers on domestic flights. The airlines insisted that the resulting cost in delays was unacceptable and came up with a proposal to use Computer-Assisted Passenger Profiling. This would permit the airlines to identify from a set of parameters those passengers who might pose a threat. The four hijackings of 9-11 showed how devoid of any value that system turned out to be. Since 9-11, we have been led down a path; Americans falsely believe that the TSA has tightened airline security by federalizing all security screeners. However, as we approached the one-year anniversary of 9-11 in 2002, the new TSA reported that all was not well. It revealed that screeners at thirty-two of the largest U.S. airports failed to detect weapons and explosive devices in approximately twenty-five percent of the tests it carried out in June 2002. Granted tests are designed to show weakness in the system; however, twenty-five percent is higher than expected, and in airports such as Cincinnati, Jacksonville, and Las Vegas, the newly monitored screeners failed to detect at least half of the tests, and at Los Angeles International, the failure rate was forty-one percent.[17]

The following Statistical Information Was Provided by the U.S. Transportation Security Administration:

In 2014, TSA screened more than 653 million passengers (about 1.8 million per day), which is 14.8 million more passengers than 2013. TSA screened more than 443 million checked bags and nearly 1.7 billion carry-on bags.

2,212 firearms were discovered in carry-on bags at checkpoints across the United States, averaging more than six firearms per day. Of those, 1,835 (83 percent) were loaded. Firearms were intercepted at a total of 224 airports; 19 more airports than 2013.

There was a 22 percent increase in firearm discoveries from 2013's total of 1,813.

The top five airports for firearm discoveries in 2014 were:

- Dallas/Fort Worth International: 120
- Hartsfield-Jackson Atlanta International Airport: 109
- Phoenix Sky Harbor International Airport: 78
- Houston George Bush Intercontinental Airport: 77
- Denver International Airport: 70 (Figures 14-5 and 14-6).

FIGURE 14-5 Firearms discovered at TSA checkpoints in 2014. *Courtesy:* TSA.gov

Passenger Profiling

Most civil liberty groups have denounced the practice of "profiling" airline passengers. The concept behind profiling is to utilize skilled practitioners to identify passengers who warrant more in-depth security screening before they board an aircraft. The screeners are trained in security-related issues and human behavior. El Al uses profiling and, of course, its safety and security record is second to none.

In November 2004, the U.S. TSA began testing a new form of passenger pre-screening called "Secure Flight." This program was intended to replace the now-defunct Computer-Assisted Passenger Pre-screening System (CAPPS II). CAPPS II was a very controversial and expensive U.S. government experiment that had been slow to get off the ground.

Under Secure Flight, TSA receives information for each passenger (from the airline). TSA then determines any matches of information with government watch lists and transmit matching results back to aircraft operators. To this end, the TSA has issued the *Secure Flight Notice of*

FIGURE 14-6 Inert C4 found in a passenger's checked baggage Tampa, Florida. *Courtesy:* DHS/TSA.

Proposed Rule Making (NPRM), which lays out the Department of Homeland Security's plans to assume watch list matching.

Secure Flight, the TSA's behind-the-scenes watch list matching program, fulfills a key recommendation of the 9-11 Commission by assuming responsibility of watch list matching from individual airlines. By establishing a consistent watch list matching system, Secure Flight enhances aviation security and more effectively facilitates air travel for passengers. Secure Flight requires airlines to collect a passenger's full name (as it appears on government-issued ID), date of birth, gender, and Redress Number (if applicable). By providing complete information, passengers can significantly decrease the likelihood of watch list misidentification. Secure Flight watch list matching takes a matter of seconds to complete, and providing these data enables passengers to print their boarding passes at home or at an airline kiosk. Secure Flight does not conduct watch list matching or approve the issuance of a boarding pass by an airline if complete passenger data are not submitted.[18]

Secure Flight matches limited passenger information against government watch lists to do the following:

- Identify known and suspected terrorists.
- Prevent individuals on the No-Fly list from boarding an aircraft.
- Identify individuals on the Selectee list for enhanced screening.
- Facilitate passenger air travel by providing fair, equitable, and consistent matching process across all aircraft operators.
- Protect individuals' privacy.

Secure Flight compares passenger records to expanded "selectee" and "no-fly" lists already in use. Passengers whose records match names on the lists will be subject to commercial background checks to verify their identities.[19]

The TSA began Secure Flight by compiling a "Terrorist No-Fly Watch List." The entire program became fully operational in late 2010 for all flights operating to, from, and within the United States.

One problem with the program is the number of people who have been falsely identified as "terrorists" because their name matches, or closely resembles, names on the No-Fly list. Once a name is on the list, it is impossible to remove it and then some "innocent" travelers are detained every time they fly and they can't do anything to get their name off the list.

Screening Passengers by Observation Technique

The Israel's El Al has been profiling passengers for its flights for the past thirty-plus years with considerable success. Passengers and the public are monitored for behavior traits as they enter the airport and the observations extend to the airport perimeters and parking areas. In Canada in February 2008, the Chair of the International Pilots Association called for the Canadian authorities to adopt Screening Passengers by Observation Technique (SPOT), claiming that it was already in use by the TSA in the United States. Under the U.S. SPOT program, TSA stopped seventy thousand passengers between January and December 2006 for questioning, and although no terrorists were arrested, they did arrest more than seven hundred individuals. But that 1 in 100 hit rate involved alleged money laundering, drugs, and weapons possession to immigration violations to outstanding warrants. A U.S. GAO Report reviewed the use of SPOT in 2013 and there was clear indication that SPOT was not providing the expected results. According to the GAO, available evidence does not support whether behavioral indicators, which are used in the TSA's SPOT program, can be used to identify persons who may pose a risk to aviation security. GAO reviewed four meta-analyses that included over four hundred studies from the past sixty years and found that the human ability to accurately identify deceptive behavior based on behavioral indicators is the same as or slightly better than chance. Further, the Department of Homeland Security's (DHS) April 2011 study conducted to validate SPOT's behavioral indicators did not demonstrate their effectiveness because of study limitations, including the use of unreliable data. Twenty-one of the twenty-five behavior detection officers (BDO) GAO interviewed at four airports said that some behavioral indicators are subjective. TSA officials agree, and said they are working to better define them. GAO analyzed data from fiscal years 2011 and 2012 on the rates at which BDOs referred passengers for additional screening based on behavioral indicators and found that BDOs' referral rates varied significantly across airports, raising questions about the use

FIGURE 14-7 The author displaying items seized at an International Airport Passenger Screening location – these items continue to be brought to airports throughout the world. TSA figures of weapons seizures at airports seem not to be decreasing.

of behavioral indicators by BDOs. To help ensure consistency, TSA officials said they deployed teams nationally to verify compliance with SPOT procedures in August 2013. However, these teams are not designed to help ensure BDOs consistently interpret SPOT indicators.[20]

Following the Glasgow Airport attack in 2007, the British have installed the technology version of the same process by funneling images from CCTV cameras to a computer system that will detect ten thousand separate facial "micro expressions," including signs of fear and deception and, reportedly, even an individual's skin temperature.

The TSA and DHS use layers of security to ensure the security of the traveling public and the Nation's transportation system. TSA checkpoints constitute only one security layer of the many in place to protect aviation. Others include intelligence gathering and analysis, checking passenger manifests against watch lists, random canine team searches at airports, federal air marshals, federal flight deck officers, and more security measures both visible and invisible to the public.

Each one of these layers alone is capable of stopping a terrorist attack. In combination, their security value is multiplied, creating a much stronger, formidable system. A terrorist who has to overcome multiple security layers in order to carry out an attack is more likely to be preempted, deterred, or to fail during the attempt (Figure 14-7).

European Civil Aviation Conference

Nations are responsible for implementing effective aviation security systems for flights leaving their country. Terrorism is an international issue as modern air travel allows terrorists to strike anywhere within hours. Therefore, it is necessary to have an international body to work with governments to develop measures, standards, and recommended practices . . . that body is the European Civil Aviation Conference (ECAC). The ECAC operates with the active support of the International Civil Aviation Organization (ICAO). ECAC, formed more than twenty years ago, has the following three principles in the area of aviation security:

1. The threat of unlawful interference with civil aviation in its many forms of violence is likely to persist.
2. The ICAO Standards and Recommended Practices in aviation security have to take into account the widely varying provisions available for their implementation in more than 180 contracting states of ICAO.
3. Mutual understanding and close and constant cooperation between all state authorities concerned are necessary to achieve and maintain a high standard of aviation security.[21]

COMBATING TERRORISTS

One of the first considerations any would-be hijacker would have looked for during the last two decades of the twentieth century was the amount of mass media publicity he or she could hope to achieve for the "cause." Hijacking an aircraft and demanding it be flown to JFK Airport in New

York, or to London's Heathrow Airport, would gain worldwide media attention. Because of the size and complexity of these airports, the ensuing chaos and disruption to the traveling public would be horrendous. In combating a hijacking, it is imperative that authorities have the option to "direct" the hijacked aircraft to an airport of their choice. Authorities must be able to handle the incident without disrupting the major airports and airline systems of the world.

U.S. Sky Marshals (Federal Air Marshal Service—FAM)

In response to the hijacking of TWA Flight 847 in 1985, President Ronald Reagan directed the secretary of transportation, in cooperation with the secretary of state, to explore expansion of the armed Sky Marshal program aboard international flights for U.S. air carriers. Congress responded by passing the International Security and Development Cooperation Act (Public Law 99–83), which provided the statutes that supported the Federal Air Marshal Service.

The "Sky Marshal" program has in fact been around since the late 1960s, when armed U.S. customs agents operated in plain clothes on U.S.-flagged international flights. At the time of the 9-11 attacks, there were around fifty operational U.S. Sky Marshals. That was to rapidly change, and the U.S. government announced an immediate increase in the numbers required to protect U.S. civil aviation from future terrorist attack. Currently, air marshals staff several positions at different organizations such as the National Counterterrorism Center (NCTC), the National Targeting Center, and the FBI's Joint Terrorism Task Forces. They are also distributed among other law enforcement and homeland security liaison assignments during times of heightened alert or special national events.

Aircraft Hijack Response Location—Stansted Airport, UK

London's third airport is little known to the international traveler, who will normally arrive at the gateway airports of Heathrow, on the outskirts of London, or Gatwick, about one-hour south of London. Stansted, located to the east of London, has become the venue of choice for authorities in dealing with a hijacked aircraft. This supposes, of course, that they are able to hoodwink the terrorist into believing the plane is actually landing at Heathrow. The airport was first used to receive a hijacked aircraft in 1975, when a BAC 1-11 was hijacked on a domestic flight between Manchester in the north of England and London. The hijacking took place as the aircraft was approaching Heathrow. The pilot managed to divert, without the hijackers' knowledge, to Stansted. The hijacker then demanded money and to be flown to France. By the time the pilot had flown around and landed at Stansted, the hijacker was convinced he was in France. Few police were available in those days to cover Stansted Airport and, as a result of inadequate police power, some valuable lessons were learned. These lessons were incorporated into the training of the **Special Air Service (SAS) Regiment** for dealing with terrorist hijackings in the future. Security operations were lacking in the following:

- Numbers of police on hand to deal with an emergency of this magnitude.
- Designated emergency rendezvous points for emergency services.
- Communications between pilot and ground.
- A designated command post for the operation.

The requirement to train and maintain a level of response became of great importance. A second hijacking, originating in central Africa in 1982, ended up with an Air Tanzania Boeing 727 landing, after a circuitous route around Europe, at Stansted. On this occasion, the response was a combined police and military operation with the elite SAS in attendance to mount a hostage rescue if police negotiations failed. While police negotiated, a team of SAS members embarked on similarly configured British Airways 737 and flew directly from Heathrow to Stansted. As a result of protracted negotiations involving the Tanzanian high commissioner, the siege was brought to a peaceful conclusion some twenty-four hours later. Also apparent in this incident was the media's role and their release of sensational and news-breaking pictures. Images of armed police lying in wait near the aircraft could have been a considerable problem for the negotiators had the pictures reached the hijackers. In any democratic society, the value of the press and its principal focus of newsgathering must be weighed against the impact on the situation at hand. Close cooperation between the media and authorities is an issue that must be addressed in terror and hijacking incidents.

FIGURE 14-8   Disassembled .22 calibre firearm found in a passenger's carry-on baggage at JFK Airport, New York in 2014.   *Courtesy:* DHS/TSA.

In August 1996, a Sudan Airways A310 Airbus, originating in Khartoum, was hijacked by an Iraqi group demanding that the plane be flown to Italy. Because of insufficient fuel, the aircraft landed in Cyprus, refueled, and then took off for London. Stansted, as a result of the valuable lessons of the last twenty years, was ready and waiting to receive the aircraft. This particular hijacking was to end peacefully. Stansted remains the airport of choice for receiving terrorist-controlled flights into the United Kingdom.[22] On February 7, 2000, an Afghan Airlines Boeing 727 was hijacked during a flight to the Afghan city of Mazar-i-Sharif and was then flown to the Uzbek capital of Tashkent. It eventually landed at Stansted. It has been the scene of international hijacking dramas three times in the past thirty years—all of which ended in the surrender of the hijackers without loss of life (Figure 14-8).

Policy

Western governments react to terrorist activity by responding to them as swiftly and effectively as possible. The use of advanced military spy satellites and unmanned aerial drones to track down terrorists has enhanced this effort. Is the problem of defining and dealing with terrorism a police or a military problem? By example, the bombing of U.S. embassies in Nairobi and Dar es Salaam in the summer of 1998 was very difficult for the local police to deal with. In trying to come to terms with an enemy not residing within its own borders, the United States responded with a pre-emptive military strike at the bases of suspected terrorists in both Sudan and Pakistan. Was the United States violating sovereign territory of these two countries? The primary target was Osama bin Laden and his al Qaeda network, who were suspected of being behind the two bombings, as well as the subsequent attacks against the USS *Cole* in Yemen. As a result of the two bombings, and the U.S. retaliatory strikes, we wondered who would fire the next shot in anger. The next shot was from the Islamic extremists of bin Laden's al Qaeda on September 11, 2001.

International cooperation in dealing with global terrorism was addressed at the Lyon Summit Conference in 1996. Ministers responsible for state security agreed on a framework of some twenty-five measures. The agreement focused on the following main points:

1. Adopt internal measures to prevent terrorism by improving counterterrorism cooperation and capabilities. By adopting this strategy, governments could focus on training of counterterrorism personnel to prevent all kinds of terrorism actions including the use of chemical, biological, and toxic substance attacks.
2. Accelerate the research and development of methods to detect explosives and other harmful substances that cause death or injury and also to develop standards for marking explosives in order to identify their origin in post blast investigations.
3. In respect to prosecution and deterrence, the agreement noted that where sufficient justification existed according to national laws, that states must investigate organizations, groups, and associations, including those with charitable social or cultural goals, used by terrorists as a cover for their operations. (An example of such a group would be the Irish Northern Aid Committee or NORAID, which supports and collects funds for the IRA in the United States.)

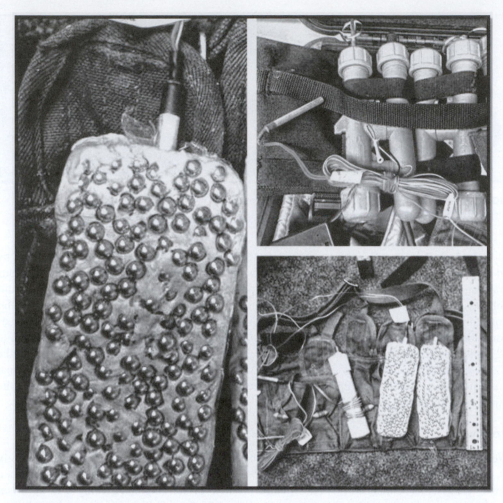

FIGURE 14-9   Training to detect explosives and IEDs is critical but leaving them behind for passengers and airline staff to find causes major issues for security.   *Courtesy:* DHS/TSA.

4. Adopt laws for the restriction and control of weapons and explosives including export controls, to prevent their use by terrorist organizations.
5. Review and amend all current anti-terror legislation.
6. In dealing with political asylum issues, states must ensure that the rights and freedoms of a country are not taken advantage of by terrorists who seek to fund, plan, and then commit terrorist acts.
7. Facilitate the exchange of information through central authorities to provide speedy coordination of requests. Direct exchange of information between competent agencies should be encouraged.
8. The exchange of information should specifically identify the following:

  • The actions and movement of persons or groups suspected of belonging to or being connected with terrorist networks.
  • Travel documents suspected of being forgeries.
  • Trafficking in arms, explosives, or sensitive materials.
  • The use of communications technologies by terrorist groups.
  • The threat of new types of terrorist activities including those using chemical, biological, or nuclear materials and toxic substances (Figure 14-9).[23]

UN SECURITY COUNCIL RESOLUTION 1373

After 9-11, the General Assembly of the United Nations, by consensus of the one hundred and eighty-nine member states, called for international cooperation to prevent and eradicate acts of terrorism. The United Nations also held accountable the perpetrators and those states that harbor and support them. UN Security Council Resolution 1373 was unanimously adopted on September 28, 2001, under Chapter VII of the UN Charter. Resolution 1373 is a legally binding resolution on all member states. It defined the new international campaign to deal with terrorism. It required, among other things, that all member states prevent the financing of terrorism and deny safe haven for terrorists. Resolution 1373 makes it imperative for all states to review and strengthen their border security operations, banking practices, customs and immigration procedures, law enforcement and intelligence cooperation, and share pertinent information with respect to these efforts. The full implementation of 1373 will require each member state to take specific measures to combat terrorism; most will have to make changes to laws, regulations, and practices.

The United States took the following steps:

- **September 23, 2001**—Executive Order 13224 froze all the assets of twenty-seven foreign individuals, groups, and entities linked to terrorist acts or supporting terrorism and authorized the freezing of assets of those who commit or pose a significant threat of committing acts of terrorism.
- **September 28, 2001**—The United States sponsored the UN Security Council Resolution 1373, calling on all UN members to criminalize the provision of funds to all terrorists, effectively denying terrorists' safe financial haven anywhere.
- **October 5, 2001**—The U.S. attorney general redesignated twenty-five terrorist organizations, to include al Qaeda, as foreign terrorist organizations pursuant to the Antiterrorism and Effective Death Penalty Act 1996. Giving material support or resources to any of these foreign organizations is a felony under U.S. law.
- **October 12, 2001**—Under Executive Order 13224, thirty-nine names were added to the list of individuals and organizations linked to terrorism or terrorist financing.
- **October 26, 2001**—The United States enacted the USA Patriot Act, which significantly expanded the capability of U.S. law enforcement to investigate and prosecute persons who engage in terrorist acts.
- **October 29, 2001**—The Foreign Terrorist Tracking Task Force was created and aimed at denying entry into the United States of persons suspected of being terrorists and locating, detaining, prosecuting, and deporting terrorists already in the United States.
- **November 2, 2001**—The United States designated twenty-two terrorist organizations located throughout the world under Executive Order 13224, thus highlighting the need to focus on terrorist organizations worldwide.
- **November 7, 2001**—The United States added sixty-two new organizations and individuals, all of whom were either linked to the Al Barakaat conglomerate or to the Al Taqwa Bank, which have been identified as supplying funds to terrorists.
- **December 4, 2001**—The United States froze the assets of the Holy Land Foundation in Richardson, Texas, whose funds are used to support the Hamas terrorist organization, and two other entities, bringing the total to 153.
- **December 5, 2001**—The secretary of state designated thirty-nine groups as terrorist organizations under the Immigration and Nationality Act, as amended by the USA Patriot Act.[24]

THE PATRIOT ACT

This hastily formed act was the congressional response to the events of 9-11; however, like other timed legislations, the Bush administration sought to have this act reinvigorated and the provisions in it made permanent. The act has allowed for expanded surveillance of terrorist suspects and increased the use of material witness warrants, which allow suspects to be held incommunicado.

1. **The Patriot Act allows investigators to use the tools that were already available to investigate organized crime and drug trafficking.** Many of the tools the Act provides to law enforcement to fight terrorism have been used for decades to fight organized crime and drug dealers, and have been reviewed and approved by the courts. As Sen. Joe Biden (D-DE) explained during the floor debate about the Act, "the FBI could get a wiretap to investigate the mafia, but they could not get one to investigate terrorists. To put it bluntly, that was crazy! What's good for the mob should be good for terrorists." (Cong. Rec., 10/25/01).

- **Allows law enforcement to use surveillance against more crimes of terror.** Before the Patriot Act, courts could permit law enforcement to conduct electronic surveillance to investigate many ordinary, non-terrorism crimes, such as drug crimes, mail fraud, and passport fraud. Agents also could obtain wiretaps to investigate some, but not all, of the crimes that terrorists often commit. The Act enabled investigators to gather information when looking into the full range of terrorism-related crimes, including: chemical-weapons offenses, the use of weapons of mass destruction, killing Americans abroad, and terrorism financing.

- **Allows federal agents to follow sophisticated terrorists trained to evade detection.** For years, law enforcement has been able to use "roving wiretaps" to investigate ordinary crimes, including drug offenses and racketeering. A roving wiretap can be authorized by a federal judge to apply to a particular suspect, rather than a particular phone or communications device. Because international terrorists are sophisticated and trained to thwart surveillance by rapidly changing locations and communication devices such as cell phones, the Act authorized agents to seek court permission to use the same techniques in national security investigations to track terrorists.

- **Allows law enforcement to conduct investigations without tipping off terrorists.** In some cases if criminals are tipped off too early to an investigation, they might flee, destroy evidence, intimidate or kill witnesses, cut off contact with associates, or take other action to evade arrest. Therefore, federal courts in narrow circumstances long have allowed law enforcement to delay for a limited time when the subject is told that a judicially-approved search warrant has been executed. Notice is always provided, but the reasonable delay gives law enforcement time to identify the criminal's associates, eliminate immediate threats to our communities, and coordinate the arrests of multiple individuals without tipping them off beforehand. These delayed notification search warrants have been used for decades, have proven crucial in drug and organized crime cases, and have been upheld by courts as fully constitutional.

- **Allows federal agents to ask a court for an order to obtain business records in national security terrorism cases.** Examining business records often provides the key that investigators are looking for to solve a wide range of crimes. Investigators might seek select records from hardware stores or chemical plants, for example, to find out who bought materials to make a bomb, or bank records to see who is sending money to terrorists. Law enforcement authorities have always been able to obtain business records in criminal cases through grand jury subpoenas, and continue to do so in national security cases where appropriate. These records were sought in criminal cases such as the investigation of the Zodiac gunman, where police suspected the gunman was inspired by a Scottish occult poet, and wanted to learn who had checked the poet's books out of the library. In national security cases where use of the grand jury process was not appropriate, investigators previously had limited tools at their disposal to obtain certain business records. Under the Patriot Act, the government can now ask a federal court (the Foreign Intelligence Surveillance Court), if needed to aid an investigation, to order production of the same type of records available through grand jury subpoenas. This federal court, however, can issue these orders only after the government demonstrates the records concerned are sought for an authorized investigation to obtain foreign intelligence information not concerning a U.S. person or to protect against international terrorism or clandestine intelligence activities, provided that such investigation of a U.S. person is not conducted solely on the basis of activities protected by the First Amendment.

2. **The Patriot Act facilitated information sharing and cooperation among government agencies so that they can better "connect the dots."** The Act removed the major legal barriers that prevented the law enforcement, intelligence, and national defense communities from talking and coordinating their work to protect the American people and our national security. The government's prevention efforts should not be restricted by boxes on an organizational chart. Now police officers, FBI agents, federal prosecutors, and intelligence officials can protect our communities by "connecting the dots" to uncover terrorist plots before they are completed. As Sen. John Edwards (D-N.C.) said about the Patriot Act, "we simply cannot prevail in the battle against terrorism if the right hand of our government has no idea what the left hand is doing" (Press release, 10/26/01).

- Prosecutors and investigators used information shared pursuant to section 218 in investigating the defendants in the so-called "Virginia Jihad" case. This prosecution involved members of the Dar al-Arqam Islamic Center, who trained for jihad in Northern Virginia by participating in paintball and paramilitary training, including eight individuals who traveled to terrorist training camps in Pakistan or Afghanistan between 1999 and 2001. These individuals are associates of a violent Islamic extremist group known as Lashkar-e-Taiba (LET), which operates in Pakistan and Kashmir, and that has ties to the al Qaeda terrorist network. As the result of an investigation that included the use of information obtained through FISA, prosecutors were able to bring charges against these individuals. Six of the defendants have pleaded guilty, and three were convicted in March 2004 of charges including conspiracy to levy war against the United States and conspiracy to provide material support to the Taliban. These nine defendants received sentences ranging from a prison term of four years to life imprisonment.

3. **The Patriot Act updated the law to reflect new technologies and new threats.** The Act brought the law up to date with current technology, so we no longer have to fight a digital-age battle with antique weapons-legal authorities leftover from the era of rotary telephones. When investigating the murder of *Wall Street Journal* reporter Daniel Pearl, for example, law enforcement used one of the Act's new authorities to use high-tech means to identify and locate some of the killers.

   - **Allows law enforcement officials to obtain a search warrant anywhere a terrorist-related activity occurred.** Before the Patriot Act, law enforcement personnel were required to obtain a search warrant in the district where they intended to conduct a search. However, modern terrorism investigations often span a number of districts, and officers therefore had to obtain multiple warrants in multiple jurisdictions, creating unnecessary delays. The Act provides that warrants can be obtained in any district in which terrorism-related activities occurred, regardless of where they will be executed. This provision does not change the standards governing the availability of a search warrant, but streamlines the search-warrant process.
   - **Allows victims of computer hacking to request law enforcement assistance in monitoring the "trespassers" on their computers.** This change made the law technology-neutral; it placed electronic trespassers on the same footing as physical trespassers. Now, hacking victims can seek law enforcement assistance to combat hackers, just as burglary victims have been able to invite officers into their homes to catch burglars.

4. **The Patriot Act increased the penalties for those who commit terrorist crimes.** Americans are threatened as much by the terrorist who pays for a bomb as by the one who pushes the button. That's why the Patriot Act imposed tough new penalties on those who commit and support terrorist operations, both at home and abroad. In particular, the Act:

   - **Prohibits the harboring of terrorists.** The Act created a new offense that prohibits knowingly harboring persons who have committed or are about to commit a variety of terrorist offenses, such as destruction of aircraft; use of nuclear, chemical, or biological weapons; use of weapons of mass destruction; bombing of government property; sabotage of nuclear facilities; and aircraft piracy.
   - **Enhanced the inadequate maximum penalties for various crimes likely to be committed by terrorists:** including arson, destruction of energy facilities, material support to terrorists and terrorist organizations, and destruction of national-defense materials.
   - **Enhanced a number of conspiracy penalties:** including for arson, killings in federal facilities, attacking communications systems, material support to terrorists, sabotage of nuclear facilities, and interference with flight crew members. Under previous law, many terrorism statutes did not specifically prohibit engaging in conspiracies to commit the underlying offenses. In such cases, the government could only bring prosecutions under the general federal conspiracy provision, which carries a maximum penalty of only five years in prison.
   - **Punishes terrorist attacks on mass transit systems.**
   - **Punishes bioterrorists.**

Eliminates the statutes of limitations for certain terrorism crimes and lengthens them for other terrorist crimes.[25]

U.S. NAVAL STATION—GUANTÁNAMO BAY—CUBA

U.S. Naval Station Guantanamo Bay is the oldest U.S. base overseas and the only one in a Communist country. Located in the Oriente province on the southeast corner of Cuba, the base is about four hundred miles from Miami. The United States leased the forty-five-square-mile parcel of land in 1903 to use as a coaling station. The U.S. Department of Defense (DOD) has been holding "detainees" at GITMO since the invasion of Afghanistan in 2002. The base is under a strict military rule and the majority of "detainees" are suspected Islamist militants who have been handed over to the DOD by both military and CIA.

The Joint Task Force is tasked with observing, interviewing, and interrogating the detainees. No doubt a certain amount of intelligence has been gathered in regard to bomb making activities and many have been identified as having studied at U.S. universities before embarking on their jihad with Osama bin Laden's al Qaeda movement. Unclassified reports from the DOD in 2005 indicate that one detainee identified eleven fellow detainees as Osama bin Laden's bodyguards, who all received their terrorist training at al Farouq, a known terrorist training camp. Another detainee, the probable twentieth 9-11 hijacker, confirmed more than twenty detainees as bin Laden's bodyguards. The detainees in many cases when captured were wearing a type of watch that has been linked to al Qaeda and radical Islamist IEDs. The particular watch is favored by al Qaeda bomb makers because it allows alarm settings and therefore detonations more than twenty-four hours in advance.

Methods of interrogation have been surfacing and one of the more popular claims from released detainees and detainee lawyers is that some have been subjected to a form of torture termed "water boarding," an interrogation technique in which the detainee is put in fear of drowning. The use of this practice has been denied at GITMO; however, the CIA admitted to using the technique on al Qaeda detainee KSM. Under the Obama presidency, there has been significant pressure to close secret prisons, Guantánamo Bay in Cuba in particular; the president issued an Executive Order to that effect in January 2009:

EXECUTIVE ORDER—REVIEW AND DISPOSITION OF INDIVIDUALS DETAINED AT THE GUANTÁNAMO BAY NAVAL BASE AND CLOSURE OF DETENTION FACILITIES

Over the past 7 years, approximately 800 individuals whom the Department of Defense has ever determined to be, or treated as, enemy combatants have been detained at Guantánamo. The Federal Government has moved more than 500 such detainees from Guantánamo, either by returning them to their home country or by releasing or transferring them to a third country. The Department of Defense has determined that a number of the individuals currently detained at Guantánamo are eligible for such transfer or release . . . The individuals currently detained at Guantánamo have the constitutional privilege of the writ of habeas corpus. Most of those individuals have filed petitions for a writ of habeas corpus in Federal court challenging the lawfulness of their detention . . . It is in the interests of the United States that the executive branch undertake a prompt and thorough review of the factual and legal bases for the continued detention of all individuals currently held at Guantánamo, and of whether their continued detention is in the national security and foreign policy interests of the United States and in the interests of justice. The unusual circumstances associated with detentions at Guantánamo require a comprehensive interagency review . . . The detention facilities at Guantánamo for individuals covered by this order shall be closed as soon as practicable, and no later than 1 year from the date of this order. If any individuals covered by this order remain in detention at Guantánamo at the time of closure of those detention facilities, they shall be returned to their home country, released, transferred to a third country, or transferred to another United States detention facility in a manner consistent with law and the national security and foreign policy interests of the United States.[26]

President Obama stated in 2009 that the prison would close—that has not happened and as of 2016 approximately ninety-one detainees remain in Guantanamo. The Obama plan is to remove detainees to U.S. mainland prisons and close Guantanamo entirely—this is now something that Congress has agreed to. The exact timing of the closure is still to be determined and those remaining detainees can expect an appearance in a Military Tribunal or in a civilian court in the United States.

Military Commissions (Tribunals)

Military tribunals are not a new concept and have historically been used to prosecute enemy combatants who violate the laws of war. The last time they were used by the U.S. military was during World War II. The concept and goal of the commission is to provide the accused with a full and fair trial and at the same time provide protection for classified and sensitive information and the protection and safety of all personnel participating in the process and that would include the accused.

The tribunals came in to force with the 2006 Military Commissions Act to try "unlawful enemy combatants" and sought to limit the ability of detainees to challenge their detention via habeas corpus petitions (a ruling later overturned) and allow hearsay evidence into trial. It was also intended to keep the death penalty as an option. President Obama amended this law with the Military Commissions Act of 2009, which placed greater restrictions on the use of hearsay and "coerced" evidence, and afforded detainees greater due process.[27] Under the George W. Bush government, it was necessary to establish the following in order to proceed with a military tribunal and determine that a detainee

- is or was an al Qaeda member;
- has engaged in, aided or abetted, or conspired to commit acts of international terrorism against the United States; or
- knowingly harbored one or more of the individuals described above; and
- it is in the interest of the United States that such individual be subject to this order.

Once charges had been determined and laid by the chief prosecutor, a Military Commission Panel is appointed, and this panel will consist of a presiding officer who must be a judge advocate and at least three other military officers as members. Questions of law are ruled on by the presiding officer. Unlike a civil court, the panel members vote and, if necessary, on a sentence; however, the presiding officer does not have a vote in this process. The accused is entitled to hire a civilian defense counsel at no cost to the government as long as that counsel is a U.S. citizen and is admitted to practice in a U.S. jurisdiction, has not been sanctioned to disciplinary action, is eligible for and can obtain SECRET clearance, and will agree to follow the rules of the commission. In the modern era, these commissions have come in for a considerable amount of press and civil liberty scrutiny. Military tribunals continue but with the long-term goal of the Obama administration to have the case tried in civilian court.

INTERNATIONAL POLICING

International police cooperation has existed for several decades through the **International Criminal Police Organization (Interpol)**. Interpol considers terrorism to be "a crime, characterized by violence or intimidation, usually against innocent victims in order to obtain a political or social objective." Interpol distinguishes between terrorism and organized crime: Organized crime has a profit motive, whereas terrorism's goals are not primarily for financial but rather for ideological gains. Interpol considers terrorism to be its number-one focus. The international organization supports the one hundred and eighty-two member countries with a multipronged approach in providing intelligence on terrorist groups and identifying terrorist suspects. Due to its European location, Interpol has lent support to the member states for training assistance in building counterterrorism capability. Interpol also fashions itself as the authority that is ready, able, and willing to facilitate liaisons among the agencies of law enforcement, immigration, and customs as well as military intelligence organizations.

INTELLIGENCE GATHERING

Intelligence gathering for terrorist offenses is primarily the domain of police forces, many of which grudgingly share information. When IRA attacks occurred in London in the early 1990s, the intelligence-gathering operations were transferred from the police to the arm of British intelligence known as MI5. MI5's analysis encompassed not only IRA terrorists, but all groups that could pose a threat. In March 1996, the British government published a report by the Parliamentary Committee on Security and Intelligence, which detailed that about 39 percent of the government's resources went toward compiling data on terror group membership, infrastructure, and methods. When cases of terrorism are brought to trial on evidence painstakingly gathered by both police and MI5, it would be counterproductive for a spy to appear on the witness stand to give testimony. Cooperation between these agencies is essential, and there has been successful cooperation between the British police and the intelligence community.

In the United States following 9-11, much was made of intelligence failings on the part of the U.S. intelligence community. It is, of course, easy to be critical after the event has taken place. However, there were indicators that were missed and relevant reports that were not followed up on. In order to determine the problems, we should first make an analysis of the current and historic state of the U.S. intelligence services. It has been said that the United States has the greatest intelligence gathering apparatus in the world. However, if the right people do not listen and react to the information, it just becomes another secret file to be uncovered in future decades. Many U.S. intelligence agencies have been focused on preventing large-scale conflicts. And there is a serious need for such intelligence; however, the risk from modern terrorism and unconventional attacks appears to warrant the same level of resources. The Cold War era of intelligence, by comparison, is viewed as a simpler mode. It was easier to train covert operators to operate in the former Soviet Union than it is to train operatives to go native and assimilate into Arabic cultures and communities, mainly due to the constraints of culture, religion, and self-identification.

Budget constraints on human intelligence (HUMINT) can be traced back to the 1970s, when the United States began spending huge sums on improving the eyes and ears of the intelligence community with modern technology and satellite programs. On the other hand, the field operative has the capability to make judgments that are specific to a designated target country or culture that an analyst located thousands of miles distant would be unable to achieve. A very good example of such a failing in a military context was the inability of the U.S. administration to have adequate intelligence about what Iraq's intentions were prior to its invasion of Kuwait. Similarly, it may also have been important to have intelligence targeting the activities of the Pakistan's Inter Service Intelligence (ISI) agency and its support of the Taliban and Osama bin Laden's mujahedeen.

In addition to the lack of HUMINT resources, there is a balance in signals intelligence (SIGINT), in developing new systems and technologies to penetrate more sophisticated communications without forgetting how to decode the old systems of encryption. Since 9-11, the fear of "sleeper cells" has become a threat to the nation's security and this becomes a challenge for the forces charged with protecting domestic security. Quite obviously, any Islamic extremist elements would likely conceal themselves in regions where other members of the same religious ethnicity reside. The ability of the sleeper to elude possible detection relates to the likely communications gap among the U.S. State Department, which controls and issues visas; the Immigration and Naturalization Service (INS), which has responsibility for investigating and deporting illegal immigrants; and the Federal Bureau of Investigation (FBI), the organization tasked with domestic counterintelligence. The bureaucracies that have developed have also been the impeding factor in creating an effective means of performing counterterrorism operations and investigations within the United States. Harry S. Truman, for this very reason, combined the country's intelligence efforts under the Central Intelligence Group, the forerunner to the CIA, more than fifty years ago. However, with the speed in the development of technology and the vying for political influence and budgetary constraints, the notion of a synergistic approach to the development of intelligence has been overlooked.[28] The Department of Homeland Security, which was designed to be the all-encompassing body that would meld the intelligence communities together, runs the serious risk of continuing to be a bureaucratic behemoth that will fail. With control and oversight in so many areas of enforcement, it is natural to think that with its huge budget and vast array of departments; it is set up to fail. Although it is easy to be critical, we believe that protecting the homeland is the priority, but whether the amalgamation of so many diverse operations will be a long-term success story is yet to be established.

As the planning for terrorist attacks often spans countries and regions, fighting terrorism requires the same level of effort and cooperation among nations. Spearheading the International Police (INTERPOL) agency's antiterrorism efforts is the Fusion Task Force (FTF), created in September 2002 in the wake of the alarming rise in the scale and sophistication of international terrorist attacks.

FTF's primary objectives are to

- Identify active terrorist groups and their membership.
- Solicit, collect, and share information and intelligence.
- Provide analytical support.
- Enhance the capacity of member countries to address the threats from terrorism and organized crime.

As terrorist organizations' far-reaching activities are inextricably linked, the task force investigates not only attacks but also organizational hierarchies, training, financing, methods, and motives. INTERPOL has identified public safety and terrorism as a priority crime area, and countries can benefit from INTERPOL's unique position in the international law enforcement community in the fight against terrorism. The INTERPOL officials involved with the FTF are all terrorism specialists seconded from their home countries.

Regional and Global Efforts

Six regional task forces have been created in regions considered to be particularly susceptible to terrorist activity: Project Pacific (Southeast Asia), Project Kalkan (Central Asia), Project Amazon (South America), Project Baobab (Africa), Project Europe, and Project Middle East. An immediate goal is to increase the number of officers from the above regions to develop region-specific initiatives and enhance the effectiveness of the task force in these areas. In January 2008, 119 member states were contributing to terrorism-related matters.

Fusion Task Force in Action

INTERPOL works closely with organizations such as the United Nations al Qaeda and Taliban monitoring teams and the International Criminal Tribunal for the former Yugoslavia to maintain its lists of suspected terrorists. FTF also maintains a secure website for member countries, which includes all information on the Fusion Task Working Group Meetings, including presentations and analytical reports; photo boards of suspected terrorists; and notices and diffusion lists. In January 2008, 545 users were accessing the FTF-restricted website.[29]

INTELLIGENCE SERVICES

MI5 (Secret Intelligence Service)—United Kingdom

The origins of the British Secret Intelligence Service (SIS) are to be found in the foreign section of the Secret Service Bureau, established by the Committee of Imperial Defense in October 1909. The Secret Service Bureau was soon abbreviated to "Secret Service," "SS Bureau," or even "SS." The first head of the foreign section, Captain Sir Mansfield Cumming RN, signed himself "MC" or "C" in green ink. Thus began the long tradition of the head of the Service adopting the initial "C" as his symbol.

Cumming sought to ensure that the foreign section of the Secret Service Bureau maintained a degree of autonomy, but the War Office managed to exercise extensive control over his actions. The outbreak of the World War I in 1914 brought a need for even closer cooperation with military intelligence organizations within the War Office. The most significant manifestation of this was the virtual integration of the foreign section within the military intelligence directorate. Thus, for much of the war, Cumming's organization was known as MI1(c). The debate over the future structure of British intelligence continued at length post–World War I, but Cumming managed to engineer the return of the service to foreign office control. It was known in Whitehall by a variety of titles, including the "Foreign Intelligence Service," the "Secret Service," "MI1(c)," the "Special Intelligence Service," and even "C's organization." Around 1920, it began to be referred to as the SIS, a title that it has continued to use and which was enshrined in statute in the Intelligence Services Act 1994.

"MI6" has become an almost interchangeable title for SIS, at least in the minds of those outside the service. The origins of the use of this other title are to be found in the late 1930s when it was adopted as a flag of convenience for SIS. It was used extensively during the World War II, especially if an organizational link needed to be made with MI5 (the Security Service). Although "MI6" fell into official disuse years ago, many writers and journalists continue to use it to describe SIS.[30]

Joint Terrorism Analysis Centre (JTAC)—United Kingdom

The Joint Terrorism Analysis Centre, or JTAC, was created as the United Kingdom's center for the analysis and assessment of international terrorism. It has been in existence since June 2003 and is based in Thames House. Although the head of JTAC is responsible to the director general of the Security Service, JTAC operates as a self-standing organization comprising representatives from eleven government departments and agencies. JTAC analyzes and assesses all intelligence relating to international terrorism, at home in the United Kingdom and overseas, and produces assessments of threats and other terrorist-related subjects for customers from a wide range of government departments and agencies. Within the Security Service, JTAC works especially closely with the International Counter Terrorism branch, which manages investigations into terrorist activity in the United Kingdom, in order to assess the nature and extent of the threat there. JTAC is also the agency that sets threat levels pertaining to threats from international terrorism.

National Counterterrorism Center

NCTC serves as the primary organization in the U.S. government for integrating and analyzing all intelligence pertaining to terrorism possessed or acquired by the U.S. government (except purely domestic terrorism); serves as the central and shared knowledge bank on terrorism information; provides all-source intelligence support to government-wide counterterrorism activities; establishes the information technology (IT) systems and architectures within the NCTC and between the NCTC and other agencies that enable access to, as well as integration, dissemination, and use of, terrorism information.

NCTC serves as the principal advisor to the DNI on intelligence operations and analysis relating to counterterrorism, advising the DNI on how well U.S. intelligence activities, programs, and budget proposals for counterterrorism conform to priorities established by the president.

Unique among U.S. agencies, NCTC also serves as the primary organization for strategic operational planning for counterterrorism. Operating under the policy direction of the president of the United States and the National Security Council NCTC provides a full-time interagency forum and process to plan, integrate, assign lead operational roles and responsibilities, and measure the effectiveness of strategic operational counterterrorism activities of the U.S. government, applying all instruments of national power to the counterterrorism mission.[31]

CIA and FBI

Following the 9-11 attacks, two major pieces of U.S. legislation, the U.S. Patriot Act and the Intelligence Reform and Prevention of Terrorism Act, were designed to provide a cohesive level of coordination for intelligence and information sharing between the CIA and FBI. Prior to 9-11, each agency jealously guarded the information it gathered. The FBI intelligence program was built on the following core principles:

- Independent Requirements and Collection Management: While intelligence collection, operations, analysis, and reporting are integrated at headquarters divisions and in the field, the Office of Intelligence manages the requirements and collection management process. This ensures that the FBI focuses intelligence collection and production on priority intelligence requirements and on filling key gaps in its knowledge.
- Centralized Management and Distributed Execution: The power of the FBI intelligence capability is in its fifty-six field offices, four hundred resident agencies, and fifty-six legal attaché offices around the world. The Office of Intelligence must provide those entities with sufficient guidance to drive intelligence production effectively and efficiently, but not micromanage field intelligence operations.
- Focused Strategic Analysis: The Office of Intelligence sets strategic analysis priorities and ensures they are carried out both at headquarters and in the field.
- Integration of Analysis with Operations: Intelligence analysis is best when collectors and analysts work side by side in integrated operations.

Concepts of operations (CONOPs) guide FBI intelligence processes and detailed implementation plans drive specific actions to implement them. CONOPs describe the Intelligence Requirements and Collection Management system and are supported by lower-level collection and collection support processes and procedures defined in the FBI's *Intelligence Requirements and Collection Management Handbook*. These concepts and processes complement FBI operations and are enhanced by the commission's recommendations.[32]

COUNTERTERRORISM UNITS

Great Britain

In the world of counterterrorism operations, few are as effective as the British Special Air Service Regiment. Terrorism in the twentieth century has taken place primarily in the fifty-year period after World War II; therefore, counterterror and counterinsurgency units have also developed since the war. An eccentric Scot, David Stirling, formed the SAS during World War II. A commando officer, Captain Robert Laycock, ably assisted him. During the war, conventional army theoreticians frowned upon the activities being proposed by the unconventional Stirling. At 6′5″, he was an impressive figure, and he believed passionately that there was an important role for "special operations" behind enemy lines. In Egypt, Stirling teamed up with a Welsh Guardsman and an Australian, Jock Lewes and formed the SAS. Protocol was the order of the day, and for Second Lieutenant Stirling to communicate his ideas to the general commanding Middle East operations would require going through a long chain of command. Stirling thought the war would be over before his ideas reached the general. By fortuitous accident, he met with the deputy commander, General Ritchie, who was so impressed with the lieutenant's ideas that they were soon put into practice for operations behind German lines in North Africa. This first unit was named "L' Detachment, Special Air Service Brigade," and the SAS was born.

The SAS of the 1990s is a far cry from that of the war years and has developed into what is arguably one of the best counterterror units in the world. Many counterterrorism organizations around the world have been modeled after the SAS. The regiment is headquartered in Hereford in the west of England, but with government spending cuts, it was destined for a new home at Royal Air Force base at Creedenhill. The SAS is made up of a Special Projects Team, and it is from this team that the Counter Revolutionary Warfare Squadron was formed to handle both foreign and domestic terrorism issues. Training for the SAS is constant, with one squadron always on standby to leave at a moment's notice to deal with a terrorist situation. An Operations Research Unit supports all SAS projects and has developed weaponry specific to the needs of the Regiment. This unit developed the stun grenade, which is widely used by counterterrorism units around the world. The unit also developed night-vision goggles and special ladders for aircraft and train assaults.

As a peacetime unit, the SAS has been primarily involved in dealing with Irish terrorists. The Provisional IRA referred to the British application of the SAS in Northern Ireland as death squads sent to terminate Irishmen. Unfortunately, for the Provisional IRA, the SAS was extremely effective in the urban warfare of Northern Ireland. The speed and efficiency with which the unit carried out operations stunned the Irish terrorist community.

SAS activity is not restricted to the United Kingdom, however, and it is believed that the regiment has been involved in operations against Libya. Adding to their mystique is the anonymity of its members. A plethora of news cameras from around the world covered the hostage drama at the Iranian Embassy in London (April 30, 1980) and captured live the dramatic rescue by armed men dressed in black fatigues. The success of that raid, which led to the death of all but one of the terrorists, placed Britain firmly in the spotlight as a country that did not deal lightly with terrorists and was prepared to use whatever force was necessary to end a crisis. This operation had been under the control of the civil police authorities until the Home Secretary William Whitelaw gave the authority for the military (SAS) to advance an assault on the embassy. This was the first time the public saw the SAS in action, and although there was an outpouring of indignation from extremists, the vast majority of Britons supported the actions of the SAS team.

Their success has to be coupled with a highly competent intelligence network and through a variety of ways the security services in Northern Ireland became adept at infiltrating as well as coercing information from informants. In 1987, the SAS carried out one of its most successful operations in Northern Ireland when it ambushed a team of PIRA terrorists about to attack a police station in Loughgall. Their intelligence was so precise that they knew all the details of the attack right down to the equipment to be used and the exact time date and location for the attack.

Several RUC and SAS men stayed in the police station acting as decoys. Outside, the SAS set up ambush positions, alongside the road past Loughgall Police Station. Apart from the main ambush force, several cutoff groups were put in place to cover possible escape routes.

The attack began at 7 P.M., a stolen blue Toyota van was seen driving past the police station, presumably scouting the area ahead of the main attack group. A few minutes later, it returned, followed by a stolen JCB (digger), with three hooded men in its cab, and a large oil drum in its front bucket. The JCB crashed through the wire fence around the police station. The SAS watched as the three hooded men jumped from the cab, one of them lighting the fuse on the oil drum. As the three IRA men ran from the JCB, five armed men leaped out of the Toyota van and started firing at the station. The SAS immediately opened fire and within seconds all eight PIRA men were dead.

It had been the most significant firefight between the SAS and the PIRA and had a decidedly one-sided result. The incident seemed, at least temporarily, to rattle the PIRA, who were troubled by the breach of security that led to the ambush.[33]

Gibraltar—March 7, 1988

At the height of the "Troubles," intelligence reports indicated that a Provisional IRA active service unit was planning to place a large bomb in the centre of Gibraltar to coincide with the military "changing of the guard" ceremony. An SAS unit tracked the Irish team and gunned them down in broad daylight. Those killed were Daniel McCann aged 30, Sean Savage aged 24 and Mairead Farrell aged 31, all three were known Provisional IRA members with Farrell having served 10 years for her part in the bombing of a hotel in Belfast in 1976. The SAS team attacked the three PIRA members and, according to witness reports, gunned them down in cold blood. The subsequent outcry over claims of the government's "shoot-to-kill" policy seemed too much for a democracy to handle. The PIRA now had its "martyrs" and an opportunity to haul the British government before the European Court of Justice, which condemned the assault. The resulting court decision showed that caution was required, lest the counterterrorist forces go too far. For the PIRA, it meant the group had the right to not only shoot first but to kill as well!

The SAS is on good terms with numerous countries and has actively assisted training many counterterror units. It is believed that the SAS is present, either officially or unofficially, at every terror incident to view how it was handled and to determine what went well and what went wrong. Thorough debriefs are held, and every minute detail of the operation is analyzed. The SAS was present and provided assistance to the Peruvian government when terrorists took control of the Japanese Ambassador's residence in Lima in 1996.

The British Royal Navy has its own counterterrorism unit to rival the SAS: the Special Boat Squadron (SBS). This unit is highly trained to respond to maritime acts of terrorism, though it has not been widely used. Most notably, the unit responded with the SAS to the bomb threat on the ocean liner, Queen Elizabeth II, in the North Atlantic. Specifically designed for naval operations, the unit was deployed prior to the arrival of the Naval Task Force off the Falkland Islands in 1982 at the outbreak of war between Great Britain and Argentina.

SAS associates: Because of the proven effectiveness of the SAS regiment and its legendary exploits since World War II, other Commonwealth countries have modeled their counterterrorism units on the SAS. The Australian SAS and the New Zealand SAS have adopted the same name.

On the international stage, special force units teamed up in Iraq. The year 2006 was one of the bloodiest years for suicide and car bombings, particularly in Baghdad. The environment would be uniquely suited to the expertise of the British SAS and the U.S. Delta Force. It is not by coincidence that the number of daily bomb attacks had all but dried up in Baghdad in 2007 and 2008, and this was not from a lack of will on the part of groups like al Qaeda in Iraq who have been responsible for a vast majority of the suicide and car bombings. British military sources indicated in late 2008 that over three thousand terrorists had been either killed or captured by Special Operations units and this had reduced the number of attacks down from over one hundred and fifty a month to around three or four.

Australia

The Tactical Assault Group (TAG) and the Special Air Service Regiment (SASR) were originally formed in 1957 and comprise Australia's response to any outbreak of domestic terror. The Australian SAS was originally a single company. By 1964, two additional companies had been added and the unit was renamed the SASR. The regiment saw military action in Borneo, and with the outbreak of the Vietnam War, was instrumental in training the Australian army for its role in Southeast Asia. By the time the Vietnam War ended, the SASR had achieved some impressive results in the area of "special operations." Since the Vietnam War, Australia has not seen terrorist activity at home and the unit has been scaled down. Like its British counterpart, SASR engages in training and assists other units in the West. SASR has staff based at Fort Bragg and Little Creek in the United States. A specialist unit, the Offshore Installations Assault Group (OAG), is also available for seaborne counterterror response. Since its creation, the SASR has lost a total of seventeen men: Six were killed on active duty in Vietnam, three in operations in Borneo, and eight during a training exercise near Townsville in 1996.

Rhodesian SAS

The Rhodesian SAS is part of the original regiment that was disbanded at the end of World War II. Rhodesians have a long and proud history of engagements on foreign soil. One World War II Rhodesian, Mike Sadler, served with the SAS in North Africa and was considered to be the best navigator in the Western Desert.[34] When the war was over, members of the SAS were returned to their respective countries. The regiment was almost disbanded, but survived as a territorial unit.

After World War II, the next problem facing the allied powers was the rise of Communism in the Far East. It was the Malayan crisis of 1951 that established the reasons for retaining a Rhodesian SAS regiment for actions at home and abroad. The Commonwealth countries were asked to supply volunteers for a force in Malaya to handle the entrenched Communist terrorists. It was commanded by Major "Mad Mike" Calvert, who had been given the go-ahead to form a self-sustaining warfare unit, trained in jungle conditions to operate for long periods of time. Its mission was to continually harass and disrupt Communist terrorist activity. Major Calvert flew to Rhodesia to meet with the contingent of one hundred men and briefed them on the Malayan operation. The unit from Rhodesia would become C Squadron 22 SAS (Malayan Scouts).[35]

The Malayan emergency was to last until the end of that decade, and the Rhodesian SAS remained on station for two years. On returning to Africa, the unit was disbanded and the men returned to their civilian lives. The lessons learned in that Far East operation were of value in the country's development as it struggled for its identity and independence in the 1960s. Rhodesia's army was in need of specialized expansion and development. Following an assessment, it was decided that the SAS Squadron would be established as a branch of the Rhodesian army. Training would be conducted under the auspices of the British SAS at Sterling Lines in Hereford, England. The Rhodesian military had a long and successful history of graduates at the Sandhurst Military Academy in England. Among those selected to join the newly formed Rhodesian SAS were remnants of the old Malayan task force of C Squadron.[36]

The Rhodesian SAS was exceptionally well trained and schooled in jungle warfare and were accomplished paratroopers. The squadron assisted the 22 SAS Regiment in operations with the British army in the Crater District of Aden (now Yemen) during that crisis. The 1960s were a time of rationalization and decolonization. The breakup of parts of Rhodesia began: The northern part became Zambia, and Nyasaland became independent Malawi. In 1964, Ian Smith, a Rhodesian-born former World War II fighter pilot, became prime minister of the country, determined to take Rhodesia to full independence from Britain. Politics would play a major role in the gradual demise of the SAS in Rhodesia. When Ian Smith was unable to convince the British government to grant independence to Rhodesia, he declared a Unilateral Declaration of Independence (UDI). This resulted in sanctions by Britain and a full trade embargo by the United Nations. The following fourteen years of turmoil in the region would end with a black national-ist government in power and the dissolution of the SAS. On December 31, 1980, the Rhodesian SAS disbanded and its members fled south to South Africa, taking with them the memorial to their war dead.

Republic of Ireland

The Army Ranger Wing (ARW) is classified as an elite counterterror force and Ireland's front line against terrorism. Not as well known as its British counterparts, the SAS, the ARW has an impeccable reputation. The unit is made up of approximately 100 members and is subordinate to the chief of staff of the army. Like the SAS it has some of the same basic responsibilities, including the following:

- Hostage rescue in extreme situations such as hijackings, both maritime and aircraft.
- Search and rescue operations.
- Close protection security to VIPs and selected government officials.
- Ongoing maintenance of contingency planning for terrorist attacks.

Although there are no current details of actions undertaken by the group, the unit has maintained close ties with European counterterrorism units, including the French GIGN and the German GSG-9. ARW has been involved in peacekeeping operations through the United Nations in Somalia, Bosnia, and Lebanon.

Spain

Grupo Especial De Operaciones (GEO) Spain, which has had problems with the ETA terrorist group, and also GRAPO, was late in establishing an effective counterterrorism unit. In 1978, following the successes of the German GSG-9, Spain sought help from Germany in setting up GEO. One of Spain's difficulties was finding fiscal and political resources with which to staff the unit. Spain has both left-wing and right-wing terrorist problems, so there was a desperate need for apolitical members of any elite unit for this type of activity. Spain's GEO is not well known outside that country, but is a highly trained and effective force. Although Spain has a thriving munitions industry of its own, the GEO uses the same assault weapons as their counterparts in GSG-9, favoring the Heckler and Koch MP5. As secretive as their comrades in the SAS and GSG-9, GEO has had some unsung successes in dealing with terrorists. In May 1981, twenty-four right-wing terrorists occupied the Central Bank of Barcelona, taking over 200 hostages. GEO stormed the bank, killing one terrorist, freeing all hostages, and capturing ten terrorists.[37]

Guarda Civil: Spain's second unit, the Unidad Especial de Intervencion (UEI), handles hostage taking and terrorist activity and operates within the structure of the Guarda Civil (National Police). UEI is responsible to the ministries of the interior and defense and forms part of Spain's national police force. Like the GEO, it is deployed across the country and has had notable successes in rescuing kidnapping and hostage victims from both ETA and GRAPO.

The Persian Gulf

Cobras (Sultan of Oman Special Forces, SSF): Britain continued its tradition of providing training and logistical support for friendly Middle East countries with close ties to the Royal Military Academy at Sandhurst. The Sultanate of Oman has seen very little terrorist activity but, when the region started to destabilize with pro-Communist guerrillas under the Popular Front for the Liberation of Oman (PFLO), the sultan requested assistance from Britain. The Oman rebellion lasted thirteen years between 1962 and 1975. During that time, the British SAS was actively involved in counterterrorism operations with the Sultan's army. However, the Sultan was not prepared for the kind of terror and insurgent tactics the guerrillas would use. The SAS assisted and was instrumental in bringing down the opposition forces. When the fighting was over, Sultan Qaboos decided that his country would never again be without a response unit for insurgency and terrorism.

The British SAS provided training and guidance in setting up the Sultan's Special Forces (SSF), the Cobras. Based in Dhofar and Muscat, they are considered the most elite force in the Persian Gulf region. Cobra teams are set up along the same military lines as the SAS and are on constant, fifteen-minute standby. From their bases in Dhofar and Muscat, they have provided assistance to neighboring Kuwait. The Cobras are seconded to the Omani police, who are less well equipped and trained and retain jurisdictional control of incidents. Jealousy and interservice rivalry have not helped efforts to maintain this effective force in the Gulf.

France

Groupmentd'intervention de la Gendarmerie Nationale (GIGN): Unlike the SAS, the GIGN was formed following the terrorist attacks at the Munich Olympic Games and the takeover of the Saudi Embassy in Paris. The GIGN is a police unit, not military, and recruits to this unit come from the ranks of the paramilitary police service, the Gendarmerie Nationale (National Police). All members undergo eight months of rigorous training similar to that of the SAS, to include parachute qualification. On successful completion, they are based at the Maisons-Alfort near Paris. As a police unit, the GIGN is called on to deal with criminal incidents as well as terrorist attacks. The unit is heavily armed with Heckler and Koch MP5 submachine guns, as well as an assortment of sophisticated handguns. The GIGN is also trained in negotiating skills and recognizing psychological weaknesses and changes in the state of mind of the terrorist. Like the SAS, GIGN shuns publicity. It has had remarkable success in rescuing kidnapping victims. GIGN's most spectacular action was the 1994 storming of an Air France airbus at Marseilles, which resulted in the death of all thirteen hijackers, members of the Armed Islamic Group (GIA) from Algiers.

The Research, Assistance, Intervention, and Dissuasion (RAID) unit is currently the lead counterterror unit in France and has been leading the fight against radical Islamists in France. This special tactical unit was the result of the rapid rise in terror attacks in France during the 1970s and 1980s at a time when the French National Police were unable to handle rising numbers of terror attacks. Headquartered outside Paris in Bievres and consisting of around 100 members, this elite organization reports to the director general of French Police. It gathers and selects its members from the French National Police, and like other Western-style elite units, its organizational structure includes sections for intervention, negotiation, and tactical support units that flex to the threat being dealt with. RAID was first seen in action during a hostage standoff in Nantes in 1985—the same year it was officially launched. RAID was developed by Robert Broussard, a police/special operations expert who had been given the task of tackling rising criminal networks and terrorism.

Netherlands

Bijondere Bijstands Eenheid (BBE): "Qua Patet Orbis" (The Whole World Over) is the motto of the Netherlands Marine Corps. "Send in the marines" has always been an option for Western governments and is an often-used phrase. In the case of the Netherlands, that is exactly what takes place in response to hostage-taking and terrorist actions. The Netherlands has one of the oldest military organizations in the world (the Dutch Marine Corps), which was founded on December 10, 1665. Today's Royal Netherlands Marine Corps numbers about twenty-eight hundred. The corps is split into two separate areas for operational purposes: one group in the Netherlands for NATO duties and the other stationed in Aruba in the Dutch Antilles. The Marines represent a strike force that can respond to any terrorist situation. A section of the Marine Corps handles counterterrorism operations and is called the BBE. Translated, this has the literal meaning "different circumstances unit." The Dutch government states that it does not negotiate with terrorists, although the country is not beset with severe terrorist problems. One incident that resulted in conflict relates to Dutch colonialism in Indonesia. In 1975, a group from South Molucca hijacked a train hoping to bring pressure to the Dutch government. The hijackers were members of the Free South Moluccans Youth Organization (VZJ) demanding an independent homeland.

The Netherlands' response was to send in the Marines (BBE). On this occasion, as with others involving the South Moluccans, the siege was ended by force, resulting in the death of the terrorists and minor injuries to the rescuers and the rescued. Each attack unit of the BBE consists of two, thirty-three-man platoons, each comprising four assault teams. They are further broken down into five-man units. The unit's functions are similar to those of the British SAS and are assisted with maritime operations from the 7th SBS, another elite unit made up of four, six-man intervention teams.

Norway

Forsvarets Spesial kommando (FSK, Special Defense Commando): Norway's elite military response unit was formed in 1982, primarily as a defensive unit to deal with terrorist attacks against its many North Sea oil rigs. It is also responsible for the close protection of the Norwegian Royal Family, the national assembly, and other government officials. The FSK is a branch unit of the Norwegian Army Jegerkommando. This is another unit that has used the example of the SAS, and the start-up of the unit involved five years of close involvement between the two. FSK and SAS have maintained close ties and often train together on exercises. The close nature of the two units brought the FSK some unwanted publicity when it was reported in the Norwegian press that it had been involved in SAS operations against the IRA in Northern Ireland in 1994, a report that both governments strenuously denied. FSK has also seen service overseas when it was dispatched to Kashmir to help locate a Norwegian being held captive by Al-Faran guerrillas.

Germany

Grenzschutzgruppe 9 (GSG-9) is considered one of the elite terrorist response units of modern time. It was formed following the disaster at the 1972 Munich Olympic Games. After the horrendous events, the Germans were not prepared to allow such atrocities to happen again. In the case of the Olympics, it was the soft target with worldwide media coverage that the Black September movement was after. In the two decades after the end of World War II, Germany had taken pains not to produce any elitist forces for any purpose. GSG-9 was formed and was fully operational by April 1973, six months after the Munich massacre. Unlike the SAS, GSG-9 would form part of the Federal Border Police service and not part of the German military. Each member must be a volunteer and a member of the Border Police. The iconic leader and founding leader of GSG-9 was Colonel Ulrich Wegener who joined Germany's Federal Border Police in 1958. His training with both the FBI and the Israeli Secret Service gave him expert knowledge on terrorism and was the logical choice to lead the group. He is believed to have been involved with the Israeli raid at Entebbe in 1976. Wegener's orders had been to create a small and highly flexible antiterrorist unit that could be used and deployed at a moment's notice. Following his success at Mogadishu, he was promoted to brigadier and given ultimate control over the whole of the Federal Border Police.[38]

The group is split into three definable units, each with fifty members: GSG-9/1 is responsible for counterterrorism; GSG-9/2 handles maritime counterterrorism; and GSG-9/3 deals with airborne issues. The federal government supplies GSG-9 with the best and most advanced equipment available. The group operates in five-man units and is outfitted with two sets of combat gear: one for day and the other for nighttime operations.

Israel

SAYERET MAT'KAL: Sayeret Mat'kal is also known as the **General Staff Reconnaissance Unit #69** and was founded in 1957. This unit has been in the forefront of every Israeli anti- and counterterrorism strategy since its inception. It is the unit that is also dedicated to handling hostage-taking incidents. In wartime, this unit takes on the role of intelligence gathering. The Sayeret Mat'kal actively does the bidding of the Israeli government and has hunted down and executed known terrorists. After the Munich massacre, it was mandated to track down and kill those involved. Operation Spring Youth was an offensive strike carried out by the Sayeret Mat'kal in 1973. It has carried out actions that for nearly every other Western power would be unacceptable; however, to the embattled Israelis, the group's actions are accepted as a requirement in the protection of the state. On April 9 and 10, 1973, Sayeret infiltrated Beirut, which had to be considered extremely hostile territory, and assassinated the leaders of the Black September organization. This action was carried out successfully at three separate locations in West Beirut.

Egypt

Unit 777 was created by former President Anwar Sadat in 1978 following the increase in attacks particularly by Palestinian terror groups. Earlier the same year Egyptian military personnel were dispatched to Cyprus following the hijacking by members of the PFLP of a Cyprus Airways flight. The Egyptian operation to Cyprus was hastily planned and very poorly executed. When the Egyptians came on to the island airport they were mistaken by Cypriot troops as more terrorists—this resulted in a firefight between the two forces and resulted in numerous deaths of Egyptian soldiers. The Egyptian authorities had failed to consult with Cyprus and never notified them in advance of the troop arrival.

Czech Republic

Utvar Rychleho Nasazeni (URNA) is the Czech Republic's rapid response counterterrorist police and crime-busting force. URNA is modeled to be similar to its elite counterparts in the German GSG-9 and the French GIGN. It has specific responsibilities and as such is tasked directly from the ministry of the interior to protect foreign heads of state, secure major sporting events against sabotage, and assist the police in drugs and serious crime interdiction. By far, its most important role is its intervention in extreme terrorist situations, including hostage taking and hijackings. Although not as well known as other Western European counterterror units, URNA is considered one of the elite reaction units and is held in very high regard.

Indonesia

After the 2002 Bali bombings, Indonesia recognized that the main threat to national security came from regional terrorist networks whose leaders returned to Indonesia after Suharto fell from power in 1998. An elite counterterrorism unit, Densus 88 (Detasemen Khusus 88, or Special Detachment 88), was Indonesia's answer to the terrorists who exploited the country's weakened security environment. Among the terrorists were many former Afghan jihadist as well as Abu Bakar Ba'asyir and the late Abdullah Sungkar—the duo that founded Jemaah Islamiyah (JI) while in exile in Malaysia between 1985 and 1998.[39] Detachment 88 was formed within the Indonesian Police Service and is based outside Jakarta and has been funded by the U.S. government with training from the CIA and FBI as well as the U.S. Secret Service. The unit has over 400 members and became operational in 2005 and like many other anti-terror units mirrors those already operating successfully in Western Europe.

HOSTAGE RESCUE UNITS

Most countries designate, train, and equip teams to deal with hostage-taking crises and the protection of VIPs and government officials. These units in the Philippines are called the Aviation Security Commando (AVESCOM) Unit. In Thailand, Hostage Rescue Units (HRUs) functions are the responsibility of the Royal Thai Air Force. In India, the highly trained Special Counterterrorist Unit (SCU) is considered to be the best in Asia. Malaysia uses the Special Strike Unit of the Royal Malay Police, and Sri Lanka has the Army Commando Squadron. In the Middle East, Bahrain and Saudi Arabia have units trained by the British SAS and the French GIGN, respectively. The Hashemite Kingdom of Jordan maintains the 101st Special Forces Battalion, which also provides sky marshals for Alia, Jordan's national airline. Egypt has had a colorful history of failures in hostage rescue in recent decades. Both of the incidents occurred in the Mediterranean. Egypt uses the Saiqa unit for counterterrorism operations, as well as Force 777, created in 1978. The countries of Latin and South America use sections of the military and federal police services for HRU functions in most cases.

The United States of America

Hostage rescue, kidnapping, and their negotiations have long been the province of the FBI, assisted by special police squads that are formed in almost every jurisdiction in the United States. These units are termed "Special Weapons and Tactical (SWAT) units." The FBI is the U.S. federal agency responsible for information and intelligence gathering at home, which is not, as many believe, the domain of the Central Intelligence Agency. The CIA is mandated for intelligence and field operations outside the United States and for protecting U.S. interests. With varying gun laws throughout the United States, weapons offenses are a daily diet for the state police, with SWAT teams regularly called upon to deal with many criminal activities, particularly bank holdups. With the hostage crisis in Tehran in the 1970s, the need arose to have dedicated and well-trained tactical teams to deal with subversive activities both at home and abroad.

Hostage rescue is a risky business, and usually when rescues go wrong they go wrong very quickly and often with disastrous results. In 1985, Egypt Air 648 was hijacked to the island of Malta in the Mediterranean. The Egyptian government dispatched its counterterrorism strike force, Force 777, to the island to assist with the hostage rescue operations. The Maltese government gave the go-ahead for Force 777 to take action against the terrorists. The assault began at about 8:00 P.M., lasting for more than a minute and a half, which is nearly four times longer than most anti-terror groups will take to storm aircraft and release hostages. The series of mistakes, miscalculations, lack of intelligence, and planning resulted in the death of the passengers, some of whom were shot by snipers, who mistook escaping passengers for terrorists and gunned some of them down.[40]

"Delta Force" was the 1970s' brainchild of Charles Beckwith. Beckwith realized that the United States did not have the same capability for hostage rescue and counterterrorism response as the Europeans and proposed establishing an elite unit from the ranks of the U.S. Special Forces. Selection began, using the same disciplined methods as used by the SAS, which Beckwith himself had experienced with the SAS in the 1960s. After the seizure of the U.S. embassy in Tehran, in November 1979, the Delta Force was placed on standby to handle the rescue and evacuation of the hostages. Considerable intelligence gathering and logistical planning went into the plans to rescue the hostages, and the Delta team was front and center. The mission was to fail due to dust storms. One of the mission's helicopters crashed into a C-130 that was carrying munitions, resulting in the deaths of eight members of the U.S. Marine Corps.

The members of Delta Force managed to escape injury and returned to the United States without completing their mission. After the abortive mission to Iran, a Special Operations Group was initiated, and from that came the creation of SEAL Team Six in 1980. SEAL Team Six is the Navy's equivalent to the Delta Force and is responsible for handling counterterrorism in any maritime environment. Its beginnings relate directly to the failure of the Tehran operation, which had been designated by the code words, "Eagle Claw." The name SEAL Team Six was chosen as a ploy to confuse the Soviets as to exactly how many SEAL units the United States then had available at that time. All of the SEAL platoons were trained in counterterrorism. SEAL Team Six went through an extensive training regimen that involved training overseas with members of the SAS, GSG-9, GIGN, and other counterterrorism organizations. SEAL Team Six would undergo further changes to its structure, including a name change due to its poor reputation within the Navy. SEAL Team Six was embarrassed by its founding member, Commander Richard Marcinko, who was charged with an assortment of offenses, ranging from fraud to bribery, and was sentenced to a brief term of imprisonment. Following this fiasco, the unit designation was changed to the Naval Special Warfare Development Group (NSWDG). Structured on the same lines as the SAS and numbering approximately 200 men, the NSWDG covers a wide spectrum of abilities, much the same as the SAS and the SBS. Unlike their European counterparts, they have not had the opportunity to prove themselves, as the SAS had at Prince's Gate or the GSG-9 had at Mogadishu, although they have been in both covert and overt operations since the 1980s.

In 1985, NSWDG was on standby in the Mediterranean during the *Achille Lauro* hijacking, which claimed the life of Leon Klinghoffer, but it was not called into action. In the same year, the unit was used during the U.S. invasion of Grenada to rescue the governor of the island, Sir Paul Scoon. During that operation, four SEALs drowned during the helicopter insertion offshore. The SEALs were used for the initial landings in Somalia in 1992, when they came ashore in scuba gear to a media throng with video cameras and floodlights who broadcast their invasion, live, around the world. This was a prime example of poor understanding between operational forces and the media. The SEALs have their place in history with their most notable action, the attack on Osama bin Laden's Pakistan compound, the seizure of masses of intelligence, and the death of the U.S. Most Wanted Terrorist himself in May 2011.

In domestic situations, the United States uses the Alcohol Tobacco and Firearms (ATF) unit for dealing with criminals who are stockpiling illegal weapons. For weeks, the news media covered a major ATF operation in Waco, Texas. The ATF went to execute a warrant against the Branch Davidians, led by David Koresh. An ensuing gun battle and a long standoff later resulted in an ATF assault. A fire erupted and all inside the compound were incinerated. It was discovered after the event, however, that many had been killed or committed suicide before flames overtook the buildings.

CANADA

Joint Task Force Two

From 1993 onward, responsibility for counterterror operations in Canada changed from a Royal Canadian Mounted Police (RCMP) role to a military function. A rather secretive military force known as **Joint Task Force 2 (JTF-2)** functions much in the same way as its SAS British counterparts. The unit is known to have operated in Eastern Europe, particularly in Bosnia and in regions of Afghanistan in pursuit of al Qaeda leader Osama bin Laden. JTF-2 arrived in Afghanistan in December 2001 and joined other Special Ops forces from the United States, Britain, and Australia, based at the former Taliban stronghold of Kandahar. The Canadians were assigned to Task Force K-Bar, a multinational special operations group led by U.S. Navy SEAL Captain Robert Harward.

K-Bar consisted of some twenty-eight hundred personnel, including support and air staff, and under Harward's command were Special Forces units from the U.S. Navy, Army, and Air Force, as well as forces from Denmark, Germany, Norway, Australia, Canada, New Zealand, and Turkey. U.S. Marine helicopters provided air transport.[41]

PIRACY

The Oxford English Dictionary defines "piracy" as "Robbery, kidnapping, or violence committed at sea or from the sea without lawful authority, especially by one vessel against another." The International Maritime Bureau Piracy Center provides a more recent definition of piracy: "The act of boarding any vessel with the intent to commit theft or other crime and with the capability to use force in the furtherance of the act." Article 101 of the United Nations Convention of the Law of the Sea defines piracy as follows:

Piracy consists of any of the following acts:

   a. Any illegal acts of violence or detention, or any act of depredation, committed for private ends by the crew or the passengers of a private ship or a private aircraft and directed
      i. on the high seas, against another ship or aircraft, or against persons or property on board such ship or aircraft;
      ii. against a ship, aircraft, persons or property in a place outside the jurisdiction of any State.
   b. Any act of voluntary participation in the operation of a ship or of an aircraft with knowledge of facts making it a pirate ship or aircraft;
   c. Any act of inciting or of intentionally facilitating an act described in subparagraph (a) or (b).

Although sea piracy has been in existence for centuries and, to many, it will conjure up an almost romantic or exotic event, the truth is far different. Sea piracy remains a major economic and security threat. Areas of the globe most affected by sea piracy are located in the waters of the Horn of Africa, the Far East, the South China Sea, and the waters surrounding Indonesia and the Philippines. Frequent attacks on shipping go virtually unnoticed in the news media; however, crew deaths are not an uncommon result of piracy. In earlier days, almost all trade around the globe went via ships, and the lucrative routes between the Middle East and the Far East were the hunting grounds for myriads of pirates. The well-known, sixteenth-century English sea Captain Sir Francis Drake could also be likened to a pirate. His ships' targets were invariably those belonging to Spain. Britain had been on and off at war with Spain and the seizing of Spain's ships was not considered to be piracy, at least not by the British. Drake was deemed to be a "privateer," and his many countrymen operated under the same royal protection. However, the Spanish government considered Drake and Walter Raleigh to be dyed-in-the-wool pirates. Piracy on the high seas has developed and become more sophisticated with the passage of time and with obviously higher risks and greater rewards for the pirates. The International Maritime Organization has defined three types and levels of piracy:

   1. An attack on a ship operating close to shore, often an opportunist attack, by pirates in small, high-speed, seagoing craft, with the intent to steal cash and personal valuables from the crew and the ship's safe. This is defined as a Low-Level Armed Robbery (LLAR).
   2. Medium-Level Armed Robbery and Assault (MLAAR). This level of attack is invariably a deadly assault on the ship's crew and/or passengers, often by well-armed and equipped pirates. This type of attack has often been coordinated with the aid of a mother ship, enabling the attack to take place in international waters.
   3. The most serious level defined by the organization, **Major Criminal Hijack (MCHJ)**, invariably involves international criminals who are well-equipped and trained. These groups will either take total control of the vessel, stealing the vessel's entire cargo and off loading it to another ship, or casting the crew adrift and re-naming the ship.

What makes piracy so lucrative and accomplishable in the twenty-first century? A large number of states have depleted their navies, thus leaving them unable to have a presence to deter pirate attacks on ships, both in international and territorial waters. Add to this a dimension of high technology in which many vessels are now dependent on much smaller operating crews, creating an opportunity for pirates to operate unhindered. Shipping in international waters is protected by the "flag" of the country in which it is registered. Many countries adopt a "flag of convenience" for their vessel, which means that a vessel owned in one country (such as the United States or Great Britain) can be registered in another country (Panama, Liberia, or Cyprus, for example), thus avoiding international safety and taxation regulations. Nearly 90 percent of ocean-going cargo ships entering U.S. ports are operating under foreign flags. Many of these ships, such as Greek-flagged and flag-of-convenience ships (officially called "open-registry ships"), operating out of Piraeus employ low-wage seamen from the developing countries of Pakistan and the Philippines. Flag-of-convenience countries are often unwilling to take any significant diplomatic action against countries from which pirates are operating. The International Maritime Bureau has a piracy center located in Kuala Lumpur, Malaysia, that has responsibility to provide information around the clock on piracy activities in all the regions of the globe.

The 2014 report from the IMB shows a total of two hundred and forty-five incidents of Armed Robbery and Piracy have been reported to the IMB Piracy Reporting Centre (PRC). The 2014 incidents are broken down as follows:

- 183 vessels boarded
- 28 attempted attacks
- 21 hijackings and
- 13 vessels fired upon.

Some four hundred and forty-two crew members have been taken hostage, thirteen injured, nine kidnapped from their vessels and four crew fatalities.

Whilst the number of overall incidents has decreased year on year, there has been a noticeable upward trend in the number of vessels successfully hijacked, with twenty-one in 2014 compared to twelve in 2013. This increase is attributed entirely to the rise in small coastal tanker hijackings in Southeast Asian waters in 2014.[42]

The legal aspects of piracy are somewhat convoluted, if not complex. The international community recognizes that an act of piracy can only be committed in international waters and must therefore be dealt with under international law. Should the commission of a seaborne attack on a maritime vessel occur inside territorial waters, the responsibility for pursuing and prosecuting the incident as robbery falls to the state that claims the territorial right over that region. International law requires any warship or government vessel to "repress piracy on the high seas" and to come to the aid of any vessel under attack. The rules of engagement for sea piracy, as it affects government vessels, are that force should only be used as a means of self-defense against piracy. There are, in fact, no listed rules of engagement for sea piracy. The action of individual member state's navies is governed, therefore, by each state.

Historical data on piracy do not go farther back than 1980. In the early 1980s, private groups targeted ships at anchor and waiting to berth in the Nigerian ports of Lagos and Bonny. They would attack after dark and break into containers on board. The eventual outcome was a concerted crackdown by Nigerian police and customs to root out the pirates and their bases of operation. Piracy has also been highly prevalent in the Far East in the Straits of Malacca, one of the busiest shipping lanes in the world. In efforts to contain and minimize the attacks against commercial and other shipping, the International Maritime Organization established a working group to study the problem and come up with a methodology and recommendations. The results of the study were that the underreporting of acts of piracy should be discouraged and that masters should immediately report acts and attempted acts of piracy. Probably the most significant effort was the assistance of technology through the International Telecommunications Union and the International Mobile Satellite Organization (Inmarsat). This technology enabled the inclusion of "piracy/armed robbery attack" as a category of distress message that ships are now able to transmit through Digital Selective Calling (DSC) or by using Inmarsat.[43] The message will be received automatically by ships and shore stations in the area. Maritime piracy continues in many regions of the world and particularly in areas where it is easy for pirates to escape without detection. The vastness of the South China Sea is testament to that, and there are attacks on fishing vessels around the many islands of the Philippines. In these attacks, pirates take the fish and any other valuables on board or take the entire vessel.

The Piracy Reporting Center in Kuala Lumpur operates around the clock providing daily bulletins on pirate activity. The center is supported by voluntary contributions from shipping lines and insurance companies. Technology such as global positioning and tracking systems allows shipping companies to adopt such innovations as the SHIPLOC system, an inexpensive method of using satellite technology and the Internet to track individual ships. Irrespective of technology piracy is likely to continue as the pirates become more sophisticated in their modus operandi. Whether a ship will be used in a terrorist attack, such as the destruction of a passenger cruise liner, with massive loss of life, is no doubt on the list of scenarios being looked at by the security and intelligence communities. As of July 2004, ships above 500 tons had to be equipped with alarm systems that silently transmit security alerts containing tracking information in case of emergency. Vessels were required to emboss their International Maritime Organization (IMO) number on their hulls. Since 2003, ship owners have been able to install high-voltage electric fencing to discourage intruders, although ships carrying highly volatile cargo (including oil) cannot use such fencing.[44]

The UN Convention of the Law of the Sea, Article 105

The seizure of a pirate ship or aircraft: On the high seas, or in any other place outside the jurisdiction of any state, every state may seize a pirate ship or aircraft, or a ship or aircraft taken by piracy and under the control of pirates, and arrest the persons and seize the property on board. The courts of the state that carried out the seizure may decide on the penalties to be imposed and may also determine the action to be taken with regard to the ships, aircraft, or property, subject to the rights of the third parties acting in good faith.[45]

Countering the Threats from the Sea

Terrorist groups such as Hezbollah, JI, the Popular Front for the Liberation of Palestine-General Command, and Sri Lanka's Tamil Tigers have all at one time sought to develop a maritime capability. Intelligence agencies estimate that al Qaeda affiliates now operate dozens of phantom ships—pirated, repainted, renamed, and operating under false documentation, manned by crews with fake passports and forged competency certificates. Security experts have long warned that terrorists might try to ram a ship loaded with explosive cargo, perhaps even a dirty bomb, into a major port or terminal. Such an attack could bring international trade to a halt, inflicting multibillion-dollar damage on the world economy.[46] In 2004, Panama and Liberia agreed to allow countries that formed part of the Proliferation Security Initiative (PSI) to board ships sailing under both Liberian and Panamanian flags. The obvious value of this agreement was that any ships owned and operated by al Qaeda would likely be registered and flagged as either Panamanian or Liberian. More than half the ships that traverse the globe are covered by the so-called flags of convenience. Intelligence gathered on al Qaeda suggests that the group has had the opportunity to operate more than three hundred vessels of varying sizes, posing a serious threat to ports, particularly in the United States and Europe. To complement the ability of the major navies of the world to board "suspect" ships on the high seas, additional measures have been established to protect the integrity of cargo—not just at the port of final destination but also at the port of export. Stringent global strategies came into force on June 1, 2004, including the International Code for the Security of Ships and Port Facilities (ISPS) and amendments to the International Convention for the Safety of Life at Sea (SOLAS). The new ISPS code and the amendments to SOLAS adopted by the 162-member International Maritime Organization (IMO) require all companies operating ships of more than 500 tons on international voyages to designate security officers, prepare contingency plans, and be fitted with new security alert systems.

Human Rights and Piracy

Two European states have recently been ordered to pay thousands of Euros in compensation to Somali pirates as their human rights had been disregarded at the time of their arrest. On December 4, 2014, the European Court of Human Rights (ECHR) ordered France to pay compensation ranging from USD 2,500 to USD 6,100 to nine Somali pirates involved in incidents against two French flagged vessels. At the time of the attacks in 2008, Somali pirates were acting with almost total impunity. The robust action of the French Authorities in retrieving the ransom and arresting the pirates, on the ground in Somalia should once again be commended. The compensation order was made as France failed to present the pirates "without delay" after transferring them 4,000 miles to French territory in order to hear the charges before a judge. In this case, the pirates were held for an additional forty-eight hours prior to being presented before a judge, a period of detention which constituted a "violation of their rights to freedom and security." The ECHR also ordered France to pay the pirates' legal cost of between USD 3,750 and USD 11,250.

There then followed on December 8, a similar ruling from the Danish High Court over the detention of a pirate gang involved in the unsuccessful hijacking of a Danish Product Tanker in November 2013. On November 10, 2013, the Danish Navy intercepted a suspected mother ship in the vicinity of an aborted piracy attack and arrested nine suspected Somali pirates. The pirates who claimed to be fishermen who had unfortunately lost their equipment were kept on the vessel and presented before a Danish magistrate on November 23, 2013, via a video link. In comparison with the conditions the pirates were used to in Somalia, no doubt the Dames were splendid hosts during the period of incarceration on board the naval ship. Nevertheless, this thirteen-day ordeal was considered deplorable by the Danish attorney general, who awarded each of the pirates USD 3,270 for false imprisonment as the Danish Constitution dictates that "you cannot be held for more than twenty-four hours without charges being brought."

The context of these crimes should not be forgotten. These criminals were responsible for unacceptable high levels of unprovoked violence, kidnappings, sometimes torture and murder against seafarers simply going about their lawful business upon the high seas.[47]

Achille Lauro—1985

There is one act of piracy/hijacking in the last quarter of a century that stands out not just for its boldness but for the callous actions of the terrorists involved. In 1985, the Italian cruise ship *Achille Lauro* was taken over by the Palestine Liberation Front terrorists at the exact same time as Palestinian–Jordanian talks were being conducted in London. The PLF demanded the release of fifty Palestinians held in Israeli prisons in exchange for the safe return of the cruise ship. Among the passengers were American Jews, and one an elderly U.S. citizen Leon Klinghoffer, who was confined to a wheelchair, was tossed overboard and drowned.

The hijackers eventually surrendered to Egyptian authorities, including the leader of the PLF Abu Abbas. As they began their flight from Tunis to Egypt, the aircraft was intercepted by U.S. Navy fighters and forced to fly to a NATO base in Sicily. Italian police arrested the hijackers, but not before diplomatic wrangling between the United States and Italy was eventually resolved with the intervention of President Reagan. It is believed the intended target was not the cruise liner, and in fact, the terrorists were planning a raid in Egypt when they were discovered on the *Achille Lauro* with weapons and explosives.

While piracy is an ongoing problem for shipping in the South China Sea and Horn of Africa, particularly Somalia, the concern is also generated by the vast numbers of containers and container ships that circumnavigate the oceans. The potential that just one of these containers could contain a nuclear, chemical, or biological weapon for detonation at a U.S. port is of obvious concern. Prior to 9-11, the numbers of containers being screened entering the United States amounted to less than half of 1 percent of all container traffic. Reporting requirements are now placed on shipping lines prior to a ship's arrival; security officers are required on board ships; and stringent security protocols are in place at originating ports. The threat to the food chain and controls on imports of foods is the domain of the U.S. Food and Drug Administration (FDA), an agency not under the umbrella of Homeland Security. The FDA has oversight in areas of biodefense when it comes to contamination of foods. The FDA is responsible for about eighty percent of the U.S. food supply and its oversight includes safe production, processing, storage, and holding of domestic imported food. Past concerns related to food safety have revolved around individual attempts to contaminate a specific food or food service location. In 2002, a restaurant owner in China added chemicals to a competitor's food, killing dozens and sending several hundreds to hospitals. A more serious threat emanated from the United Kingdom in January 2003, when police arrested a group attempting to place "Ricin" into the food supply of a British military base. The FDA has formulated four major regulations under the authority of the Public

Health Security and Bioterrorism Preparedness and Response Act of 2002. Owners and operators of foreign or domestic food facilities that manufacture, process, pack, or hold food products for human or animal consumption in the United States must submit information to the agency about their facility and emergency contact information.

Container Security Initiative

In January 2002, the U.S. Customs and Border Patrol (CBP) announced the introduction of the Container Security Initiative. This measure is intended to ensure that maritime containers posing a risk for terrorism are identified and examined at foreign ports before they are shipped to the United States. The initiative is founded on four core principles:

1. Using intelligence and automated information to identify and target containers that pose a risk for terrorism.
2. Pre-screening those containers that pose a risk at the port of departure before they arrive at U.S. ports.
3. Using detection technology to quickly pre-screen containers that pose a risk.
4. Using smarter, tamper-evident containers.

The three core elements of CSI are:

- Identify high-risk containers. CBP uses automated targeting tools to identify containers that pose a potential risk for terrorism, based on advance information and strategic intelligence.
- Prescreen and evaluate containers before they are shipped. Containers are screened as early in the supply chain as possible, generally at the port of departure.
- Use technology to prescreen high-risk containers to ensure that screening can be done rapidly without slowing down the movement of trade. This technology includes large-scale X-ray and gamma ray machines and radiation detection devices.

CSI is now operational at ports in North America, Europe, Asia, Africa, the Middle East, and Latin and Central America. CBP's fifty-eight operational CSI ports now pre-screen over eighty percent of all maritime containerized cargo imported into the United States.[48]

CHEMICAL AND BIOLOGICAL WEAPONS

Understanding Chemical, Biological, and Nuclear U.S. Food and Drug Administration Strategies

Prior Notification of Food Shipments: This regulation became effective in December 2003 and requires the FDA to receive prior notice of imported food shipments before the food arrives at a U.S. port. This would amount to more than twenty-five thousand notifications about incoming shipments every day.

Establishment and Maintenance of Records: Manufacturers, processors and packers, importers, and others are required to keep records that identify the source from which they receive food and where they send it.

Administrative Detention: The FDA has authority to detain any food for up to thirty hours for which there is credible evidence that the food poses a threat to humans or animals.

Combating the Proliferation of Weapons of Mass Destruction

The threat from WMD may be overstated or, depending on your viewpoint, the threat may be understated. Since the end of the Cold War, the world is awash with nuclear products, waste, and material. There has been debate about nuclear stockpiles and their accessibility in the former Soviet republics, and accounting for those stockpiles has not been an exact science. At a Global Threat Reduction Initiative conference in Vienna in 2004, the head of the UN Atomic Energy Agency (AEA) stated that there are about three hundred and fifty sites in fifty-eight countries that possess highly enriched uranium (HEU) and approximately two dozen have enough material to build a nuclear weapon. The director general believed it was just a matter of time before terrorists deployed a nuclear device. There are tens of thousands of unprotected, suitable radioactive sources available to terrorists, even in wealthy and well-ordered societies. There were fifty cases of illicit traffic in radioactive materials in 2003, and the smugglers often target materials used in the medical and science industries.[49] A 1991 official report by the UN Special Commission to Iraq (UNSCOM) stated that inspectors had found 46,000 chemical munitions in Iraq. From that, 20,000 were 120-mm CS-filled bombs; 14,000 contained mustard gas; and a further 11,000 were filled with the nerve agent sarin. UNSCOM later discovered hidden stockpiles of 200 anthrax bombs and eighty Scud rockets at Salah ad Din near Tikrit. The invasion of Iraq was predicated on the existence of Iraq's nuclear weapons capability and to date that appears to be somewhat of a fallacy.

Chemical Weapons

Chemical agents used in warfare dates back to World War I, with the first known use of a chemical agent. The German army began dispersing chlorine gas against British and allied troops on the battlefields of Europe in 1915. Mustard gas was first used during the trench wars of World War I two years later. Records show the Italians also used mustard gas against the Ethiopians when they invaded Ethiopia in 1935, and the Japanese used mustard gas and also chlorine gas during their invasion of China in 1930. The Germans made further developments in the production of nerve agents in the late 1930s. Both the Germans and the allied armies had significant stockpiles of chemical weapons but neither side used them during World War II (1939–1945). Mustard gas was used by the Soviets and the Egyptians in Yemen between 1963 and 1967. The United States used chemical defoliant agents such as Agent Orange, Agent Blue, and Agents Purple and White in the Vietnam War. Agent Orange, a herbicide made of two common weed killers, was used frequently—over fifty million pounds were dropped over Vietnam during the war. The Soviets used nerve agents and mustard gas against the mujahedeen in Afghanistan between 1977 and 1989. Both Iran and Iraq used mustard gas in their war from 1979 to 1989.

History of Chemical Terrorism

There has been a long history of terrorists and criminals using poisons and toxins for political assassination and other crimes with political motivation:

- **1976**—the Arab Revolutionary Army injected mercury into citrus food products.
- **1979**—the West German police raided a safe house of the Red Army Brigade and seized 400 kilograms of chemical precursors used to make nerve agents.
- **1985**—an Israeli military base discovered that its supply of coffee had been contaminated with a nerve agent.
- **1984**—several people died from arsenic poisoning after the drug Tylenol was contaminated with arsenic poison.
- **1994**—in Tokyo, the Aum Shinrikyo sect released sarin gas into the subway system, killing twelve people and injuring more than five thousand.
- **September 2004**—in the Ukraine, Viktor Yushchenko, President of Ukraine, was poisoned by dioxin, probably orally administered, and some suggest it may have been "Yellow Rain," a chemical agent used by the Soviets in the Afghan War.
- **August 2013**—sarin gas used in suburbs of Damascus.
- **March 2016**—Islamic State used chlorine bombs against the civilian population in Kirkuk, North Eastern Iraq.

There are a large number of chemical agents in existence today that could cause serious disruption if released into a general population:

- **Nerve agents:**

  GA—Tabun

  GB—Sarin

  GD—Soman

  VX—V agents

- **Vesicants or blistering agents:**

  H—mustard

  HD—distilled mustard

  HN—nitrogen mustard

  CX—phosgene oxime

  L—lewisite

- **Blood agents:**

  AC—hydrogen cyanide

  CK—cyanogen chloride

- **Choking agents:**

  Chlorine

  Phosgene

  Chloropicrin

- **Irritating agents:**

  CN—standard tear gas

  CS—stronger tear gas; induces vomiting

  DM—adamsite vomiting agent

Nerve Agents

These chemicals are designed to attack the body's nervous system in such a way as to cause convulsions or death. **Nerve agents** are liquid at ambient temperatures and are some of the most dangerous of all the chemical agents. Looking at Aum's attack on the Tokyo subway, all the symptoms of a nerve gas attack were prevalent: pinpoint pupils, blurred vision, eyes aggravated by light, excessive sweating, runny nose and nasal congestion, coughing and difficulty with breathing, nausea and vomiting, anxiety, and giddiness.

Some of the outward warning signs that could indicate a nerve agent attack include the following:

- Explosions that dispense gas, mists, or liquids
- Unscheduled or unusual spraying activities
- Localized explosion that destroys only a package or parcel
- Abandoned spray equipment
- Presence of large numbers of dead fish or animals and bird life
- Mass casualties without obvious trauma
- Definite pattern of casualties and symptom commonality
- Casualties located in possible obvious target locations, such as government and military establishment buildings, mass-transport systems, and so on

Vesicants

These chemicals are blistering agents. They were first produced for use in World War I. The vesicant used in the war was called mustard gas because it smells like mustard. These agents cause severe skin burns and damage to the eyes and respiratory system, if inhaled. If a large area of skin is exposed to the gas, absorption into the blood stream is usually inevitable. **Vesicants** are heavy, oily liquids and, in pure state, are almost colorless and odorless. They have a high propensity for penetration into layers of clothing and quickly absorb into the skin. They are extremely powerful but are far less lethal than nerve agents. A few drops of mustard gas on the skin can cause severe injury and three grams absorbed through the skin will likely be fatal.

Symptoms of vesicant poisoning include reddening of the eyes; congestion, tearing, a burning, gritty feeling in the eyes, followed by pain and spasm of the eyelids. The skin will blister depending on the level of exposure and initial itching and redness, followed by pain and tenderness. Blisters will appear and likely be fluid filled and are most common in warm, moist areas of the body, such as in the groin area and under the armpits. There will also be a burning sensation in the nose and throat, coughing, and shortness of breath.

Blood Agents

Most blood agents are derivatives of cyanide compounds and, therefore, packages of cyanide salt and acid precursors may be present in any attack scenario. Blood agents produce casualties by interfering with the blood's ability to transfer oxygen to the cells, which can lead to death by asphyxiation. These agents are common industrial chemicals and information is publicly available on them. The outward warning signs include large numbers of casualties displaying common symptoms; the strong smell of peaches or bitter almonds is also a good indicator of blood agents.

Choking Agents

These chemical agents attack the respiratory system and cause acute distress. They also produce copious amounts of fluid, which can result in death by asphyxiation which resembles drowning. The most common symptoms are choking and coughing. Outward signs are the obvious chemical odor, such as the strong smell of chlorine, while phosgene has the odor of freshly cut hay.

Irritating Agents

These are the most common agents and are found in products such as tear gas, designed to cause respiratory distress and copious tearing. They have the irritating smell of pepper but are generally nonlethal. Chemical agents are relatively easy to manufacture and just as easy to disperse. They are easier to control than a biological agent and, although not contagious, may contaminate by persistence. Chemical agents can be mass produced and are easier to hide and disguise, rather than a conventional weapon. The mere mention of the words "chemical weapons" will spread terror.

BIOLOGICAL WEAPONS

Biological weapons are, by their very nature, indiscriminate and difficult to contain and control. The delivery system for such a "weapon" continues to pose significant problems for a terrorist group. While a chemical attack would be the simpler attack to mount, the bio-attack weapon remains an ultimate weapon for the twenty-first-century terrorist.

History of Biological Weapons

- **1346**—the Tartar Army, led by Khan Janiberg, attacked the city of Kaffa and catapulted plague-infested bodies of their own men over the city walls.
- **Fifteenth century**—the Spanish conquistador Pizarro gave clothing contaminated with smallpox to natives in South America.
- **1940**—the Japanese dropped "plague" on China.
- **1972**—103 countries signed the Biological Weapons Convention, which prohibited the development of both biological and chemical weapons, as well as their use.
- **1980**—the German Red Army Faction was found in a Paris safe house making botulin toxin.
- **1984**—Cuba reportedly was stockpiling toxins.
- **1991**—the Iraqi government admitted research in the use of anthrax, botulinum, and clostridium toxins.
- **1994**—the Aum Shinrikyo sect in Japan attempted an aerial drop of anthrax over Tokyo.
- **1995**—an Aryan nation's member was arrested in Ohio with a container of plague.
- **October 2001**—envelopes containing spores of anthrax were sent to U.S. news media and government offices, causing nationwide panic.[50]

Soon after 9-11, letters laced with anthrax began appearing in the U.S. mail. Five Americans were killed and seventeen were sickened in what became the worst biological attack in U.S. history.[51] In August 2008, Department of Justice and FBI officials announced a breakthrough in the case and released documents and information showing that charges were about to be brought against Dr. Bruce Ivins, who took his own life before those charges could be filed. On February 19, 2010, the Justice Department, the FBI, and the U.S. Postal Inspection Service formally concluded the investigation into the 2001 anthrax attacks and issued an Investigative Summary. The case involved the issuance of more than 5,750 grand jury subpoenas and the collection of 5,730 environmental samples from sixty site locations. In addition, new scientific methods were developed that ultimately led to the break in the case—methods that could have a far-reaching impact on future investigations.[52] This involved the anthrax bacterium, which produces shell-like spores that allow the bacterium to live in a dormant state in the soil. However, when anthrax is used as a weapon, the spores can become airborne and enter the lungs, where they become active. If enough of the spores are inhaled, the results can often be fatal. Anthrax is a serious infectious disease caused by the bacterium *Bacillus anthracis*. Anthrax is a disease that is common in cows, sheep, horses, and goats. The occasions of human contamination have been as a result of infection by persons coming into close contact with an infected animal.

Inhalational Anthrax

This is the most dangerous form of anthrax. It results when a person inhales anthrax spores into the lungs. Symptoms do not appear immediately, but usually within two to six days after being infected. It is possible that symptoms will occur as late as sixty days after initial infection. Symptoms included headache, fever, coughing, and difficulty in breathing, chills, weakness, and chest pain. This disease can be controlled by antibiotics if diagnosed promptly. Inhalation anthrax is not contagious and does not spread from person to person.

Cutaneous Anthrax

This form of anthrax occurs when the anthrax spores come into direct contact with a cut or break in the skin. Evidence of infection will become apparent within one to seven days of contamination with an itchy bump reminiscent of a small insect bite. The bump will develop blisters and then turn to a painless sore with a black center. Lymph glands in the area or near the affected area may begin to swell. This form is not as dangerous as the inhaled anthrax, but if not treated, this anthrax has a twenty percent mortality rate. This form is also not contagious and responds well to antibiotics.

Intestinal Anthrax

This form of anthrax occurs when a person eats meat from an infected animal that has died from anthrax, or drinks water or other liquids contaminated with anthrax spores. This form will cause vomiting, fever, pain in the abdomen, and diarrhea. Symptoms appear within seven days of infection. If left untreated, the form has a sixty percent mortality rate and, like the two previous forms, is also noncontagious.

Smallpox

This is a highly infectious, viral disease. The last recorded naturally occurring cases of smallpox were prior to 1977, when it was eradicated following a worldwide vaccination campaign. Smallpox comes with influenza-type symptoms and a rash spreading over the body. Pus-filled blisters develop and serious complications can result in blindness, pneumonia, and kidney damage. Infected persons who have not been vaccinated have a 30 percent mortality rate.

Toxins

The poisonous by-products of microorganisms, plants, and animals are called toxins. They tend to be stable because they are not living; however, toxins such as ricin and botulin have the advantage of being relatively simple to manufacture and are extremely lethal. Toxins can cause almost immediate paralysis of the cardio respiratory system in humans. Ricin is probably the deadliest known plant toxin and is a protein extracted from the castor bean seed. Ricin poisoning will result in nausea, muscle spasms, convulsions, and vomiting. There is no antitoxin or vaccine currently available and death from ricin poisoning can occur in three days.

Botulism

This neurotoxin is released by the bacterium *Clostridium botulinum* and is associated with rotting food. It is a very poisonous substance. If a person ingests or breathes in the toxin, symptoms of nerve disruption will occur. Cold and flu-like symptoms, with a trace of numbness in the lips and fingertips, double vision, and chest paralysis are its many symptoms. Death occurs from respiratory failure. With the quick administration of an antitoxin, the mortality rate for botulism is twenty-five percent; however, if left untreated the mortality rate is one hundred percent.

Pneumonic Plague

This condition is a rare result of *bubonic* plague and is caused by bites from an infected flea. It turns into pneumonic plague and then becomes a highly contagious and virulent form of pneumonia. Symptoms include fever, chills, coughing, difficulty breathing, and rapid shock. There is a fifty to ninety percent mortality rate if left untreated and fifteen percent when diagnosed and treated with antibiotics.

Tularemia

Tularemia is also known as "rabbit fever" or "deer fly fever." Tularemia is extremely infectious. Relatively few bacteria are required to cause the disease, which is why it is an attractive weapon for use in bioterrorism.[53]

Avian Flu

Avian flu, or the "bird flu," is a highly contagious disease of animals caused by viruses that normally infect only birds, and less commonly, pigs. There have been recent incidents starting in Southeast Asia in 2003 and throughout 2004 and 2005, where the virus has crossed the species barrier and infected humans. The highly pathogenic bird flu is extremely virulent. It spreads very rapidly through poultry flocks, causing disease and affecting multiple internal organs, and has a mortality that can approach one hundred percent, often within forty-eight hours. The causative agent, the H5N1 virus, has proved to be especially tenacious. Despite the death or destruction of an estimated 150 million birds, the virus is now considered endemic in many parts of Indonesia and Vietnam and in some parts of Cambodia, China, Thailand, and possibly also the Lao People's Democratic Republic. Control of the disease in poultry is expected to take several years. The widespread persistence of H5N1 in poultry populations poses risks for human health. Of the few avian influenza viruses that have crossed the species barrier to infect humans, H5N1 has caused the largest number of cases of severe disease and death in humans. Unlike normal seasonal influenza, where infection causes only mild respiratory symptoms in most people, the disease caused by H5N1 follows an unusually aggressive clinical course, with rapid deterioration and high fatality.

Of greater concern is that the virus, if given enough opportunities, will change into a form that is highly infectious for humans and spreads easily from person to person. Such a change could mark the start of a global outbreak (a pandemic). A pandemic can start when three conditions have been met: a new influenza virus subtype emerges; it infects humans, causing serious illness; and it spreads easily and sustainably among humans. The H5N1 virus amply meets the first two conditions: It is a new virus for humans and has infected more than a hundred humans, killing over half of them. No one will have immunity should an H5N1-like pandemic virus emerge. All prerequisites for the start of a pandemic have therefore been met save one: the establishment of efficient and sustained human-to-human transmission of the virus. The risk that the H5N1 virus will acquire this ability will persist as long as opportunities for human infections occur. These opportunities, in turn, will persist as long as the virus continues to circulate in birds, and this situation could endure for some years to come.

Contingency planning to meet and counter the threat of WMD since 9-11 has taken on monumental proportions. The U.S. government is spending in excess of $2 billion per annum to counter these threats.

Developing an effective response plan is critical not only to community and governments but also in the private business sector. While the likelihood of a terrorist attack having a sudden and direct impact on a particular business is relatively low, there is always the need to act prudently and prepare Business Resumption and Interruption Plans, as well as Disaster Planning and Critical Incident Command procedures. Although these plans are more likely to have been part of the planning process for national and state governments, there is every reason for individual companies to consider plans for disaster events, which should include flood, tornado, earthquake, major fire, chemical accident, and terror attack. Although the terror attack is the one significant incident that comes to most people's attention, the likelihood of the preceding five events occurring is much higher. It has been suggested that up to seventy percent of small- to medium-size businesses fail to recover from a disaster. For a national- or state-level plan to be implemented, it should include the following components:

- Information-gathering system
- Threat awareness—be able to determine what threats the organization must be aware of
- An effective communications plan and early-warning system coupled with evacuation procedures
- Particularly in the United States, interagency agreements on command and control in disaster situations
- Detailed procedures on how to identify the release of chemical or bio agents and equipment needed to respond to such a threat or incident
- An appropriate disposal capability
- Procedures for setting up and deploying decontamination stations and personnel to man them

Practical training either in a real-life setting, or a "table top" setting, should be conducted on a regular basis to determine the capability of responders to a specific incident involving mass casualties. This will involve having all the significant players represented at a "table-top" exercise to ensure that each group or organization is fully conversant with the role it has to play. The attacks of 9-11 were an example of the flaws in the emergency communications coordination, which seriously contributed to the high number of emergency responder losses on that fateful day.

DIRTY BOMBS

To better inform the public on what a dirty bomb is, and what terrorists might intend to try to accomplish in setting off such a weapon, the following information from the U.S. Regulatory Commission is provided.

A dirty bomb is in no way similar to a nuclear weapon or nuclear bomb. A nuclear bomb creates an explosion that is millions of times more powerful than that of a dirty bomb. The cloud of radiation from a nuclear bomb could spread tens to hundreds of square miles, whereas a dirty bomb's radiation could be dispersed within a few blocks or miles of the explosion. A dirty bomb is not a "Weapon of Mass Destruction" but a "Weapon of Mass *Disruption*," where contamination and anxiety are the terrorists' major objectives.

Basically, the principal type of dirty bomb, or **radiological dispersal device (RDD)**, combines a conventional explosive, such as dynamite, with radioactive material. In most instances, the conventional explosive itself would have more immediate lethality than the radioactive material. At the levels created by most probable sources, not enough radiation would be present in a dirty bomb to kill people or cause severe illness. For example, most radioactive material employed in hospitals for diagnosis or treatment of cancer is sufficiently benign that about a hundred thousand patients a day are released with this material in their bodies.

However, certain other radioactive materials, dispersed in the air, could contaminate up to several city blocks, creating fear and possibly panic and requiring potentially costly cleanup. Prompt, accurate, non-emotional public information might prevent the panic sought by terrorists.

A second type of RDD might involve a powerful radioactive source hidden in a public place, such as a trash receptacle in a busy train or subway station, where people passing close to the source might get a significant dose of radiation. A dirty bomb is in no way similar to a nuclear weapon. The presumed purpose of its use would be, therefore, not as a weapon of mass destruction, but rather as a weapon of mass disruption.

Terrorists have been interested in acquiring radioactive and nuclear material for use in attacks. For example, in 1995, Chechen extremists threatened to bundle radioactive material with explosives to use against Russia in order to force the Russian military to withdraw from

Chechnya. While no explosives were used, officials later retrieved a package of cesium-137 the rebels had buried in a Moscow park.

Since September 11, 2001, terrorist arrests and prosecutions overseas have revealed that individuals associated with al Qaeda planned to acquire materials for a RDD. In 2004, British authorities arrested a British national, Dhiren Barot, and several associates on various charges, including conspiring to commit public nuisance by the use of radioactive materials. In 2006, Barot was found guilty and sentenced to life. British authorities disclosed that Barot developed a document known as the "Final Presentation." The document outlined his research on the production of "dirty bombs," which he characterized as designed to "cause injury, fear, terror and chaos" rather than to kill. U.S. federal prosecutors indicted Barot and two associates for conspiracy to use weapons of mass destruction against persons within the United States, in conjunction with the alleged surveillance of several landmarks and office complexes in Washington, D.C., New York City, and Newark, N.J. In a separate British police operation in 2004, authorities arrested British national, Salahuddin Amin, and six others on terrorism-related charges. Amin is accused of making inquiries about buying a "radioisotope bomb" from the Russian mafia in Belgium; and the group is alleged to have linkages to al Qaeda. Nothing appeared to have come from his inquiries, according to British prosecutors. While neither Barot nor Amin had the opportunity to carry their plans forward to an operational stage, these arrests demonstrate the continued interest of terrorists in acquiring and using radioactive material for malicious purposes.

Sources of Radioactive Material

Radioactive materials are widely used at hospitals, research facilities, and industrial and construction sites. Radioactive materials are used for diagnosing and treating illnesses, sterilizing equipment, and inspecting welding seams. The Nuclear Regulatory Commission, together with thirty-two states, which regulate radioactive material, has over twenty-one thousand organizations licensed to use such materials. The vast majority of these sources are not useful for constructing an RDD.[54]

Control of Radioactive Material

NRC and state regulations require licensees to secure radioactive material from theft and unauthorized access. These measures have been stiffened since the attacks of September 11, 2001. Licensees must promptly report lost or stolen material. Local authorities make a determined effort to find and retrieve such sources. Most reports of lost or stolen material involve small or short-lived radioactive sources not useful for an RDD. Past experience suggests there has not been a pattern of collecting such sources for the purpose of assembling a dirty bomb. Only one high-risk radioactive source has not been recovered in the last five years in the United States. However, this source (Iridium-192) would no longer be considered a high-risk source because much of the radioactivity would have decayed away since it was reported stolen in 1999. In fact, the combined total of all unrecovered sources over a five-year time span would barely reach the threshold for one high-risk radioactive source. Unfortunately, the same cannot be said worldwide. The U.S. government is working to strengthen controls on high-risk radioactive sources both at home and abroad.

Summary

Not a day goes by without some form of atrocity in the name of terrorism perpetrated on an unsuspecting public. Protecting the public at large has been the main consideration of the United States and many Western governments. U.S. efforts have been centered on protecting the homeland and the rapid rejuvenation of its intelligence services and apparatus. While the tragic events of 9-11 recede somewhat from our memories, new terror events are taking shape daily such as the ongoing insurgency in Iraq and Syria—the continuing rise of global jihad centered in Syria. Islamic State and al Qaeda are still present and pose a threat to nations in Europe, the Middle East, Africa, Asia, and North America. Will we see an attack using chemical, biological, or radiological weapons against cities in the West? While governments attempt to make national security a front-line topic, how far do we go in this respect? How vulnerable are we to an attack against our infrastructure? The Internet is a tool we have all come to rely on, so will the hacking of systems and the insertion of worms and viruses become serious enough as to affect our daily lives? We are at war against an enemy who wants nothing less than the seeming destruction of democratic societies. Where is the middle ground? Is there any middle ground? Wars have a beginning and an end, although we see no end to global terrorism.

Specialized counterterrorism units have been used as a response mechanism and may be viewed as a well-advertised deterrent by governments unwilling to deal with terrorists. As can be seen with Northern Ireland, both police and specialized units have been deployed in the common cause of fighting terrorism. Special military powers to restrict, control, search, and intern suspected members of illegal or proscribed organizations have also been instituted. In democracy, specialist units like the SAS, GIGN, and GSG-9 can operate effectively and have the support of the government and the public they serve. It is also necessary and prudent to have strict guidelines and controls for the use of such counterterrorism units. In Northern Ireland, the accusations of a "shoot-to-kill" policy and "death squads" were hurled by the IRA in a desperate attempt by that subversive group to halt the activities of a response mechanism that was too effective for their purposes. Piracy on the seas shows that there are regions of the globe susceptible to this type of rabid activity and the dangers it poses to the international community. Many ships containing extremely hazardous cargoes circumnavigate the globe, and the risks to nation-states and the opportunity for terrorists to take advantage must not be discounted.

Review Questions

1. Describe the reasons why El Al would be the most secure airline to fly.
2. List the major attacks against aviation that have changed airport security procedures for the travelling public.
3. Explain the meaning of "tombstone technology."
4. Describe how intelligence gathering has been improved since 9-11.
5. Explain what methods the British employed to counter Provisional IRA active service units.
6. Describe how a nerve agent differs from a vesicant.

End Notes

1. Antony J. Blinken. Deputy Secretary of State. "New Frameworks for Countering Terrorism and Violent Extremism." http://www.state.gov/s/d/2016d/252547.htm.
2. Ibid.
3. "Is Racial Profiling a Non Issue in the Age of Terrorism?" (2008). http://www.racerealtions.about.com.
4. Paul Wilkinson. *Terrorism and the Liberal State* (p. 155).
5. United Nations Conventions against Terrorism. (2011). http://www.un.org/terrorism/
6. Homer Boynton. Government Activities and Transportation Subcommittee (Taylor and Francis, 1990). "Aviation Terrorism Air Carrier Security Programs: Statement before the U.S. House of Representatives." *Terrorism*, vol. 13, no. 4–5 (July–October 1990, pp. 353–357).
7. Report to the President's Commission on Aviation Security and Terrorism. (1990). www.frac.com.
8. Ibid.
9. Cathal Flynn. "Aviation Security Is Tight." *USA Today* (March 19, 1999, p. A14).
10. Billie Vincent. "Aviation Security and Terrorism." *Terrorism: An International Journal*, vol. 13, no. 6 (December 1990, p. 404).
11. Maria Ressa. "Philippines: U.S. missed 9/11 clues years ago." http://www.cnn.com/2003/WORLD/asiapcf/southeast/07/26/khalid.confession/index.html.
12. Bartholomew Elias. "Airport and Aviation Security: U.S. Policy and Strategy in the Age of Global Terrorism." (CRC Press: Taylor and Francis, 2010, p. 84).
13. "Plot Would Have Killed Thousands." *ABC News* (August 6, 2007).
14. Commander David Tucker. London Metropolitan Police, Avsec World 94 Proceedings Chicago (October 23–26, 1994).
15. "Protect Airliners from Missiles." *The Post and Courier*, Charleston, SC (December 31, 2002, p. A10).
16. Alan J. Kuperman. "Stinger Missiles and U.S. Intervention in Afghanistan." *Political Science Quarterly*, vol. 114, no. 2 (1999). http://www.jstor.org.
17. Ed. Stephen Ulph. *Jane's Terrorism and Security Monitor* (London: Jane's Information Group, 2002).
18. TSA Secure Flight Program Overview. http://www.tsa.gov/what_we_do/layers/secureflight/index.shtm.
19. Electronic Privacy Information Center. www.epic.org/privacy/airtravel/profiling.html.
20. "TSA Should Limit Future Funding for Behavior Detection Activities." GAO-14-159: Published: Nov 8, 2013. Publicly Released: Nov 13, 2013.
21. Alan Pangborn. "How Far Has Europe Come Since Pan Am 103?" *Intersec*, vol. 6 (Three Bridges Publishing, May 5, 1996, p. 195).
22. Gerry Edwards. "Hijackers' Gateway." *Intersec*, vol. 8, no. 14 (Three Bridges Publishing, April 1998, p. 168).
23. Summary of the Ministerial Conference on Terrorism, Paris. (July 30, 1996). www.efc.ca/pages/doc/g7.html.
24. Report to the United Nations Security Council Counterterrorism Committee. (December 19, 2001). www.fas.org/irp/threat/unsc.html.
25. U.S. Department of Justice. https://www.justice.gov/archive/ll/highlights.htm.
26. "Closure of Guantanamo Detention Facilities."—*The White House* (January 22, 2009). http://www.whitehouse.gov/the_press_office/ClosureOfGuantanamoDetentionFacilities/
27. Jonathan Masters. Closing Guantanamo—Council on Foreign Relations. http://www.cfr.org/terrorism-and-the-law/closing-guantanamo/p18525.

28. Sean Hill. "The Complexity of Intelligence Gathering." *Sam Houston University Crime and Justice International*, vol. 17, no. 56 (October/November 2001, p. 5).

29. "Fusion Task Force, Operational Support." *Interpol.* www.interpol.int/Public.

30. MI5. https://www.mi5.gov.uk/output/Page57.html.

31. National Counterterrorism Center. https://www.nctc.gov/index.html.

32. "Creating a National Intelligence Director." Statement of John S. Pistole, Executive Assistant Director, Counterterrorism/Counterintelligence, Federal Bureau of Investigation, before the House Judiciary Committee Subcommittee on Crime, Terrorism and Homeland Security (August 23, 2004).

33. Elite Forces. http://www.eliteukforces.info/special-air-service/sas-operations/loughgall/

34. Barbara Cole. *The Elite: The Story of the Rhodesian Special Air Service* (Transkei: Three Knights Publishing, 1984, p. 6).

35. Ibid.

36. Ibid. (p. 15).

37. Leroy Thompson. *The Rescue* (Bolder, CO: Paladin Press, 1986, p. 84).

38. Ibid. (p. 64).

39. Jacob Zenn. "Indonesia's 'Ghost Birds' Tackle Islamist Terrorists: A Profile of Densus 88." *Terrorism Monitor*, vol. 9, no. 32 (Jane's Terrorism Monitor, August 2011).

40. Ibid. (p. 20).

41. David Pugliese is author of *Shadow Wars: Special Forces in the New Battle against Terrorism* as well as *Canada's Secret Commandos: The Unauthorized Story of Joint Task Force Two.*

42. "ICC IMB Piracy and Armed Robbery Against Ships." Annual Report. (2014). http://www.hellenicshippingnews.com/wp-content/uploads/2015/01/2014-Annual-IMB-Piracy-Report-ABRIDGED.pdf.

43. "The Maritime Safety Division, International Maritime Organization." www.imo.org/home.asp.

44. Gal Luft and Anne Korin. "Terrorism Goes to Sea." *Foreign Affairs*, vol. 83, no. 6 (November/December 2004). http://www.iags.org/fa2004.html.

45. United Nations. http://www.un.org/Depts/Cos/Conventies.agreements.htm.

46. Luft and Korin. "Terrorism Goes to Sea."

47. ICC International Maritime Bureau. "Piracy and Armed Robbery Against Ships." Report for the period January 1–December 31, 2014. *Piracy News* (p. 31).

48. "CSI: Container Security Initiative." U.S. Customs and Border Protection. https://www.cbp.gov/border-security/ports-entry/cargo-security/csi/csi-brief.

49. Anthony A. Lukin, Ph.D. "Understanding Nuclear, Biological and Chemical Weapons." A presentation at the Justice Institute of British Columbia Provincial Emergency Program Academy (April 7–8, 1997).

50. Centers for Disease Control (CDC). (2011). www.cdc.org.

51. "The FBI: Famous Cases and Criminals." (February 2011). http://www.fbi.gov/about-us/history/famous-cases/anthrax-amerithrax/amerithrax-investigation.

52. Ibid.

53. "Basic Information about Sars." Centers for Disease Control and Prevention. http://www.cdc.gov/ncidod/sars/factsheet.htm.

54. U.S. Nuclear Regulatory Commission. Fact Sheet on Dirty Bombs. (December 12, 2014).

The Future—What Next for Terrorism?

THE PAST AND THE FUTURE

Looking to the future and predicting what may or may not happen will always be a challenge so we base predictions on what is currently prevailing in the world and what the world may look like in the next ten to twenty years. Of course, to look forward, it is necessary to look back at what significant events that have taken place and how they have shaped or are changing the dynamics of the world we live in. Many of us may never have heard of the Sykes-Picot Agreement and what it meant a hundred years ago when it was secretly put into being by the empires of Great Britain and France (Figure 15-1).

Much of what is happening today and likely in the next decade in the area of the Middle East and beyond has a direct correlation to an agreement developed by the British and French, the Sykes-Picot Agreement. They would conspire to redraw the geography of the Middle East from Persia to the Mediterranean and out of the Levantine region they would create new countries, namely Lebanon, Syria, Jordan, Iraq, and the Palestine Mandate. Some, if not all, of these states are in sectarian turmoil today. The current crisis in Syria and Iraq is hard to distinguish with competing players and foreign nations vying for control and that is before any mention of an Islamic Caliphate. Turkey and the Ottoman Empire have historically been powers in the region.

Even though the Ottoman Empire was crumbling in 1916, the seeds of Turkish nationalism had already been planted. The Committee of Union and Progress, a predecessor to the Republican People's Party that espoused Turkish nationalism, was established before the decline of the empire. The party grew and adjusted its direction as Mustafa Kemal Ataturk ignited nationalist sentiment for the creation of a new Turkish Republic. Underestimating Turkish power was perhaps among the greatest mistakes that the Allied powers made between 1916 and 1922. In 1911, Britain refused the offer of an Ottoman alliance, and in 1915, Turkey accomplished one of its greatest military victories at the Dardanelles, the eight-month-long naval campaign that repelled British, French, and Russian forces.[1]

Now in 2016, a pragmatic Turkey has emerged and is active across the Middle East. Despite the stress it might cause its relationships with some of its allies, Turkey seeks to carve out a safe zone in northern Syria both to help combat the Islamic State and support Syrian rebels and to contain Kurdish attempts at sovereignty. (The Kurds represent an ethnic majority in southeast Turkey.) In addition, Turkey is trying to rebuild ties with Israel, to bolster relationships in the Gulf and to preserve its selective links with Iraqi Kurdistan.

As we marked hundred years in May 2016 since the Sykes-Picot Agreement, we can see that for the best part of the last fifty years, Iraq has passed from decades of Sunni minority dominance with Saddam Hussein through a war with Iran, a war with the United States and years of UN sanctions followed by yet another war with the United States, followed by a Shiite dominant government, corruption, and misrule and a virulent Sunni insurgency.

Before the civil war started in Syria, the state was home to twenty-two million and by 2016, more than half have fled their homes and their country. More than 470,000 have been killed, 4.8 million have actually fled the country and 6.5 million are internally displaced.[2] With 30 million Kurds living in the Levantine region they remain the world's largest stateless minority. As the Kurds make the concerted push for their own autonomous state in the region of Northern Iraq, the creation of borders remains a major hurdle for so many ethnic, religious, and linguistic

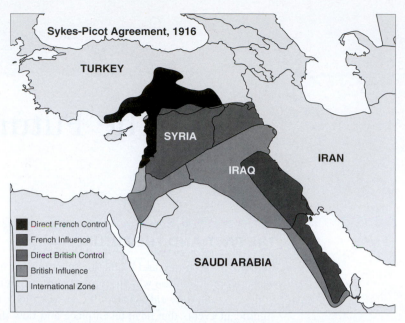

FIGURE 15-1   Sykes-Picot Agreement.   *Courtesy:* www.stratfor.com.

groups. Defining the borders may have seemed more simplistic under Sykes-Picot but in today's Middle East as yet there is no strong force able to impose its force to create new borders. No doubt in time, these will be reformed along different lines and the weak states such as Iraq and Syria may become different state entities based no doubt on the influence of the global players and ideologies from Saudi Arabia, Iran, the United States, and Russia, but this will not happen without further short-term pain and problems in the region.

AL QAEDA AND ISLAMIC STATE

The future threat from global terror entities has to focus on these two groups which at the moment are not in any sort of alliance. In fact, they are fighting each other in the Syrian conflict. But what is the probability that there could be a merger of the two groups? It is possible—the current leaderships are both currently engaged in trying to be the ruler supreme of the jihadi world. However, a merger should not be discounted—both groups are followers of Sunni–Salafist faith and both see Islam as being the target of the West and in particular the United States of America. While IS is a relatively new phenomenon and al Qaeda has been around for nearly thirty years both wield significant influence in the field of jihad—both have affiliates, particularly in Africa and Southeast Asia. Al Qaeda is supported by the Taliban, both have a central leadership and both aim to create a caliphate, IS has already declared a caliphate in Iraq and parts of Syria and that was a more distant vision under bin Laden and the current leadership. Individual fighters may have differing agendas, and their loyalties may shift according to which group is perceived as dominant. In addition, both organizations appeal to self-radicalized individuals, who help the groups build their respective brands through terrorist acts carried out in other regions, including in the United States and Europe.

Some of the areas where the two groups are not in confluence remain problematic for an early merger. A vast majority of Islamic scholars do not support the IS declaration of a Caliphate in the Levant. Unlike al Qaeda, IS has taken a harsh approach to the Shia religion by not only destroying Shia mosques but also killing Muslims not aligned to their brand of religious fervor. Al Qaeda has always professed to a far war by attacking the West first (9-11) and then driving out their influence from Muslim lands; it has not been their practice to gain and hold territory as IS has done since 2013. Into this mix is also their need to rid the region not only of Western influence but also the removal of the crusaders and Zionists from Palestine.

For any substantial changes in attitude between the two organizations would likely come with a change in leadership on both sides. More moderate leaders, if that is the correct term to use, may decide that an IS–al Qaeda alliance could pose a potent regional and global threat. In terms of appeal, IS would appear to have the upper hand with its polished and slick use of online media channels for recruiting and advertising. Al Qaeda appears to lag behind in this regard and the younger generation of jihadists may be drawn to the rebranded version of jihad under IS. However, both have been successful in plotting and carrying out overseas attacks against the West. The 2015 Charlie Hebdo attack in Paris was carried out by brothers who had pledged allegiance to al Qaeda and the November attacks the same year targeting restaurants and a concert hall was the work of Islamic State followers.

IS has managed to attract perhaps twenty-five thousand-plus foreign fighters with around five thousand from the West, including the United States—the attraction being the draw of the Caliphate where Abu Bakr al-Baghdadi is preaching jihad and claiming that this is where the civilizational struggle for Islam is being fought and it being every Muslim's duty to come to the Caliphate and take up the fight.

Thousands of aerial bombings by United States and other Western nations have been carried out against IS in Syria and Iraq to considerable affect but they are not defeated. Coupled with this, we see the Iraqi Army and an assortment of Shia militias plus Iranian militias taking the fight to IS. This has to be sustained and IS has to be denied territory for the Caliphate to fail. A March 2015 report commissioned by the United Nations Security Council found that the number of foreign fighters for Islamist causes worldwide was higher than it has ever been and had soared by seventy-one percent between mid-2014 and March 2015. The United States will need to exploit the differences and rivalries between IS and al Qaeda to have a measure of success and ultimately to deny territorial gains to IS.

So, for the next few years, we will watch how these two play along—it would be a frightening outcome if the two merged to form a united jihad front but we believe although they have some significant differences in their operational mandates, there are enough plus points that they are agreed upon that they could well merge.

We have discussed radicalization in previous chapters but to emphasize the issue which will not go away and Europe will continue to have a radicalization problem and not just from the influx of migrants from the Syrian conflict. Socioeconomic factors, often named as a source of radicalization, do not explain the radicalization of Muslims in Europe. In the United Kingdom, forty-two percent of Islamist-related offenses were perpetrated by employed individuals or full-time students. Almost one-third had attended college. Umar Farouk Abdulmutallab, for example, the Nigerian student who tried to blow up an airplane flying from the United Kingdom to the United States with explosives in his underwear on Christmas Day 2009, was the wealthy son of a banker and had graduated from the prestigious University College London.[3]

Future spectaculars by either al Qaeda or IS must be anticipated, for example, incidents such as the detection of a Frenchman attempting to cross into Poland with a large arsenal of weapons and explosives. That he was linked to an extreme right wing group and was not al Qaeda or IS is indicative of the possibilities of attacks against major sporting events with the Euro 2016 just days away and the upcoming Tour de France cycle race in July 2016. In this instance, Ukrainian authorities spotted the Frenchman as he attempted to purchase weapons. He was stopped by Polish border security in possession of three rocket launchers, one hundred detonators, 100 kilos (210 lbs) of TNT, and half a dozen Kalashnikov assault weapons.[4] As the backlash against Islam is continuing to rise in Europe, security will be focused on the extreme right as they seek to attack symbols of Islam in the West.

In the near future, as the ongoing battles in Syria and Iraq are destabilizing Islamic State, they may engage in an outside spectacular event to re-establish their international terror credibility with their followers. An all-out attack by the Islamic State could involve the assassination of Syrian President Bashar al-Assad, or an attempt on a figure head in the West, a campaign of terrorism in Baghdad or Damascus, or a spectacular attack designed to draw the United States or Europe further into the war, thereby changing the dynamics of the conflict.

AVIATION

Possibly the very first aircraft hijacking dates back to Peru in 1931, and then again between 1948 and 1958, there was approximately one hijacking per year—of course, air travel was in those decades for the rich almost exclusively. With the advances made in air travel, the decade of the 1960s saw a huge surge in attacks on aviation. In 1968 alone, there were thirty-eight hijackings which surpassed the following year with eighty-two. Airport security and passenger screening were aimed at preventing a hijacking primarily, and airline crews were taught how to respond to terrorists by following their instructions. Until 2001, the understanding was that the terrorist did not want to die. Fast-forward that ingrained thought to September 11, 2001, and we see the ease with which determined suicide hijackers were able to complete their missions. While the airline industry remains a constant target for terrorists, it has become extremely difficult to get explosives onto an aircraft. Modern technology and better training have made it almost impossible to get the items on board an airliner. To assemble the needed elements from household liquids would be almost impossible to manage. After 9-11, there have been two unsuccessful attempts at downing an airliner with a homemade bomb, Richard Reid the shoe bomber in December 2001 and the attempt to down Northwest Airlines flight 253 over Detroit on Christmas Day 2009. In both instances, there was a very small amount of TATP involved; however, the use of and acquiring and mixing the correct quantities while maintaining a very cool environment (otherwise the TATP significantly degrades) may lead to the handler blowing himself up even before he reaches the airport! No doubt the unskilled terrorists are trying methods to conceal, mix, blend, and hide the ingredients before attempting further attacks.

TERRORISM LARGER STAGE

Osama bin Laden is believed to have controlled a personal fortune estimated at over $300 million and spent it freely on his war against the United States and Western democracies. He combined financial muscle with religious extremism—a deadly cocktail! Bin Laden and a coalition of Islamic extremist groups issued a fatwa (similar to that issued against Salman Rushdie in Iran); Rushdie's novel *"The Satanic Verses,"* which was published in 1988, provoked controversy throughout the Muslim world. Bin Laden's wording was chilling: "To kill the Americans and their allies, civilian and military, is an individual duty for every Muslim who can do it, in any country in which it is possible to be done." In spite of his death, we expect his jihad to continue on a global scale. One fear is that the next attack could involve weapons of mass destruction (WMD). The use of chemical or biological weapons is an obvious concern for intelligence analysts and national security organizations.

Prior to 9-11, our fears were focused on terrorism committed in other countries like Tanzania and Kenya—of course, we are referring to the bin Laden-sponsored attacks on the two U.S. embassies in Africa. The U.S. response to such terror attacks was defined and targeted, limited to bombing attacks on bases in the Sudan and Afghanistan. Predicting the future is difficult and analyzing the past is obviously a lot easier. The al Qaeda as we now know is probably more predictable than we might have imagined. Over the last decade, it has responded to every U.S. operation mounted against it. The passage of time between attacks by extreme Islamic groups purporting to represent al Qaeda seems due, in part, to the planning that goes into each mission/assault. They plan their attacks carefully and leave little to chance. If the attack plan is put at risk, the perpetrators retreat until the timing is correct. Intelligence sources indicate that on 9-11, there were other terrorists in the air who could not or did not follow through with their missions. More recently, the attacks on the London subway system were well planned and coordinated. In Spain, the Madrid train station bombings went off during the morning rush hour; 9-11 also took place in the morning; and both the Madrid and London attacks occurred on a Thursday. As time and events unfold, it is this kind of information that will be used to identify trends and bring the full weight of the intelligence and counterterrorism apparatus to bear. London's attack on July 7, 2005, came on the opening day of the G8's Economic Summit in Scotland. The media and British security were focused primarily on this event. A distracting bonus for the terrorists, in this case, was that on the previous evening, Londoners were celebrating the city's selection as host of the 2012 Olympic Games and were in celebratory mood.

It is over a decade since the 9-11 attacks and the world is just as dangerous today, perhaps more so, than in the last years of the twentieth century. The threat is real—as real as it was in 2001. In fact, it is a permanent condition to which we all must adapt.

We already know what the terrorists want to do to us. We have it from their late leader, Osama bin Laden, in his own words, from a December 2001 videotape broadcast by the Arabic television news station Al Jazeera:

- "Our terrorism is against America. Our terrorism is a blessed terrorism…"
- "It is very important to hit the U.S. economy with every available means …[It] is the base of its military power."
- "If their economy ends, they will busy themselves away from the enslavement of oppressed people … it is important to concentrate on the destruction of the American economy."

To his second point, in 2010, we saw the economies of European nations collapsing and the crisis with the trillions of dollars of debt facing the United States. No doubt, bin Laden, if he were still alive, would like to lay claim to bringing the United States to its "financial knees," but as we know, there were a multitude of financial failings that had nothing to do with the War on Terror.

WEAPONS OF MASS DESTRUCTION

The United States is making alliances around the world, not just to track down Islamic extremist networks but also to identify those countries that are trying to acquire the materials to develop and construct such WMD.

A U.S. Government Accountability Office (GAO) report to the Senate Intelligence Committee in February 2002 reports then CIA Director George Tenet's comments in a detailed briefing on national security threats. Tenet outlined the key dangers:

1. The al Qaeda is working on "multiple-attack plans" and putting cells in place to carry them out.
2. Iran continues to support terrorist groups and has sent arms to Palestinian terrorists and the group Hezbollah. Tenet said: "Tehran also has failed to move decisively against al Qaeda members who have relocated to Iran from Afghanistan."
3. Terrorists could attack U.S. nuclear plants or chemical industry sites using conventional means "to cause panic and widespread toxic or radiological damage."
4. Al Qaeda cells in major European and Middle Eastern cities could launch attacks, and al Qaeda is connected with groups in Syria, Somalia, Yemen, Indonesia, and the Philippines.
5. There are fears that al Qaeda and other terrorists will attack using nuclear, chemical, or biological weapons. Director Tenet said, "Terrorist groups worldwide have ready access to information on chemical, biological, and even nuclear weapons via the Internet, and we know that al Qaeda was working to acquire some of the most dangerous chemical agents and toxins."
6. Tensions between India and Pakistan continue to remain high over a December 13, 2001, terrorist attack on the Indian parliament, and the two nations could resort to nuclear weapons. Tenet said: "We are deeply concerned that a conventional war, once begun, could escalate into a nuclear confrontation."
7. Terrorists could attempt to attack the United States by conducting cyber-strikes designed to cripple U.S. electronic-based infrastructures. Countering the terrorist threat and determining the response will present the biggest challenge for the coming months, and for years to come.

This 2002 report may seem dated, however, it's valuable to look back and comment on the past as we predict the future.

Al Qaeda and latterly Islamic State have spread into a global movement and multiple attack plans have been launched and fortunately not many with success, and we have seen the presence of trained fighters engaged in the Iraq insurgency, supported by Iran. Item number 3 in the above-mentioned list has not taken place; item number 4—we have observed the presence of more al Qaeda-affiliated and IS-affiliated factions across Europe and North Africa as al Qaeda reorganizes, reinvents, and rejuvenates itself while IS continues to attempt to build its Caliphate; item number 5—we have seen in the United Kingdom incidents of potential attacks using ricin being disrupted by police as well as planned attacks of similar nature in Italy and Germany; item number 6—India remains the fastest-growing economy, but there are considerable tensions between Muslims and Hindus that could erupt in violence at any time. The brink of war with neighboring Pakistan has been averted but not helped by the bombings and killings in Mumbai in 2008.

Even more dated is the following extract from a 1997 Congressional Record on WMD and nuclear materials:

> At its peak in 1992, the Soviet Union possessed approximately forty-five thousand nuclear warheads and weapons grade nuclear material to fabricate thousands more. The Soviet Union also produced an unknown amount of highly enriched uranium for reactors and for their nuclear navy. That material is also weapons usable.

While we will never know for certain how much of this material exists, the number 1,200 metric tons of weapons-usable material is frequently used.

If one considers that a simple nuclear weapon requires fifteen kilograms of highly enriched uranium and four kilograms of plutonium, there is enough weapons usable nuclear material in Russia to build more than sixty-three thousand nuclear weapons, each of which could fit in a briefcase.

Even when the material is in dedicated storage facilities, it represents a threat. At Chelyabinsk-65, bulk plutonium is stored in a warehouse with glass windows and a padlock on the door. Inside the facility are over ten thousand ingots of separated plutonium stored in thermos-sized containers—perfect for picking up and walking out.

If the terrorists who tried to blow up the World Trade Center had used a nuclear weapon made of that weapons usable nuclear material, Manhattan—all the way up to Gramercy Park, would have disappeared. If such a device had been set off in Oklahoma City, most of Oklahoma City would have disappeared.

The examples I have given are using a simple weapon design that is available over the Internet. If a rogue nation were to hire a Russian weapons designer and have access to the necessary material, that designer could build a sophisticated, multiple-stage weapon many times more powerful.[5]

THE FUTURE THREATS FROM WMD

There is broad discussion about the countries that have the desire and capacity to build components for WMD. In fact, there are more than twenty-eight countries with the ability to build chemical agents, and some of them are not considered "friendly states." The United Nations Special Commission to Iraq found over forty-six thousand munitions filled with chemical agents; of these, twenty thousand were 120-mm CS-filled bombs, fourteen thousand contained mustard gas, and eleven thousand contained sarin. Later discoveries were made near Saddam Hussein's Tikrit base, including two hundred anthrax bombs. The fears for the future are real. UN inspectors were kept out of Iraq for years, and there is little doubt that development and production of chemical agents continued in secret, unabated. The key question is whether the Iraqi regime passed on any of its deadly technology or hardware to Islamic extremists with desires to continue attacks against the West—the United States in particular.

North Korea, according to a 1996 U.S. DOD report, "has the ability to produce limited quantities of traditional infectious biological-weapon agents or toxins." A 1988 comment by Iran's parliamentary speaker Hashemi Rafsanjani stated, "Chemical and biological weapons are a poor man's atomic bombs and can easily be produced. We should at least consider them for our national defense." Syria is also considered to have one of the largest chemical warfare capabilities in the Middle East. So, is the threat of an attack by chemical or biological agents a credible threat? In the context of the 9-11 attacks, the future scenario seems just right for such an attack. If the aim of terror groups like al Qaeda is mass destruction, it behooves all of us to be cognizant of the risk of such an attack in the future.

Nuclear Threats

The threat of a terrorist attack with nuclear weapons may be the least likely, although there has been international concern about security of facilities in the former Soviet states and the rumors of accessibility of materials for arming nuclear weapons. Preparing and constructing a nuclear device is no small feat—it is hard to achieve and requires massive investment and considerable technical expertise. Osama bin Laden certainly had the wealth to achieve that goal, but his next problem would have been the method of delivery. The main constituent of a nuclear weapon is highly enriched uranium (HEU) or plutonium. The quantities of HEU estimated around the globe amount to around two thousand tons, plus an additional three hundred tons of plutonium. Building a nuclear warhead can be achieved with as little as twenty-five pounds of HEU. Without the sophisticated machine tools, electronic circuitry, and triggering devices needed to make a proper nuclear weapon, merely blowing up a lump of plutonium or HEU with conventional high explosives could still cause widespread and deadly radioactive pollution.[6]

Chemical and Biological Threats

In 1972, one hundred and three countries signed the "Biological Weapons Convention," which prohibited the development of biological and chemical weapons and their use. We now know that the risks of biological and chemical attacks are very real. The anthrax attacks against U.S. public officials and their offices after 9-11 showed how easy it was for a relatively insignificant amount of "white powder" to stampede a public into mass panic and hysteria—presumably one of the aims of that specific act. The anthrax attacks of 2001 made whole governments sit up and take notice of the threat and also made governments realize how unprepared they were to respond.

Biological weapons are created in naturally occurring organisms that cause diseases. Two of the most common examples are the bacterium *Bacillus anthracis*, which produces a toxin, and smallpox, a viral disease that is highly infectious. Chemical weapons are poisons, such as the nerve gas sarin used in Japan's subways and mustard gas, which was used in trench warfare in World War I. Smallpox, on the other hand, was virtually eradicated worldwide by the end of the 1970s after an aggressive two-decade-long worldwide vaccination campaign. This highly infectious viral disease could now be used against a generation that has not been so vaccinated, and the unvaccinated death rate would likely be about 30 percent. The only known remaining smallpox cultures being kept under tight security are in Kosovo, Russia, and Atlanta. Starting up a biological weapons laboratory merely requires a person with full knowledge of microbiology and a few thousand dollars' worth of equipment. Development may be one issue, but maintaining control over the culture could pose a very significant problem for the would-be terrorist. Probably one of the most significant reasons why we have not witnessed broad attempts at biological terror is the issue of containing the culture. Bacteria and viruses do not discriminate between terrorist and target and the person who releases the bio-weapon can easily suffer its effects.

On the chemical front, sarin gas, which was used by the Japanese Aum Shinrikyo terror group to attack a Tokyo subway, has a devastating effect. The gas is odorless, colorless, and attacks the central nervous system. Death can occur within two to fifteen minutes. Cyanide, a more commonly known chemical agent, is a gas that can be produced in massive quantities with apparent ease. Cyanide acts almost instantly and the target that ingests it usually dies within seconds. Tabun is a nerve agent that has been around since the 1930s and has been used as a pesticide in many regions of the world. Like many other nerve agents, it is absorbed via the skin. Tabun is resistant to heat and can be delivered in aerosol format, which would make it capable of delivery by artillery shell.[7]

A 1991 audit by the U.S. General Accounting Office indicated that nine chemical sites in the United States were potentially vulnerable to aerial attack, and that four of these sites may be susceptible and vulnerable to ground attack. Since 9-11, Homeland Security has focused resources on many of such sites in the United States. The use of chemical and biological agents may be restricted to those organizations bent purely on destroying democracy, rather than those that are using terrorism as a "bargaining chip" for their own styles of democracy.

HOLY TERROR

Terrorism motivated by religious imperatives is growing rapidly. So great is this change, according to Bruce Hoffman, we may have to consider revising our notions of the stereotypical terrorist organization. Hoffman explained that traditional terrorist groups could be characterized as those that engage in conspiracy as a full-time avocation, living underground and constantly planning and plotting terrorist attacks, perhaps even under the direct control or at the behest of a foreign government. What we viewed as an amateurish attack on the World Trade Center in 1993 reveals to us the kind of individual/terrorist groups that we must contend with in the future. From that investigation, it became evident that the Islamic extremists had not fully completed the attack. It was, however, completed eight years later by their brothers-in-arms in the suicide attacks of 9-11.

"Holy terror" and the purely so-called secular terror have radically different value systems, mechanisms for justifying their acts, and concepts of morality. For the religious terrorist, violence is a divine duty and divine writ. Secular terrorists generally regard indiscriminate violence as immoral and counterproductive; on the other hand, religious terrorists view such violence as both morally justified and necessary. Also, whereas secular terrorists will attempt to appeal to a constituency composed of sympathizers and the aggrieved people they claim to speak for, religious terrorists act for no audience but themselves and their faith. This absence of a constituency, combined with an extreme sense of alienation, means that such "holy" terrorists can justify almost limitless violence against virtually any target or group of people that are not considered adherents to their religious beliefs.

Religious or ethnic extremism could more easily allow terrorists to overcome the psychological barriers to committing mass murder than a radical political agenda has provided in the past. Many white supremacists actually welcome the prospect of a nuclear war or all kinds of terrorism. They see it as an opportunity to eliminate their avowed "enemies" and permit the fulfillment of their objectives—to create a "new world order" peopled exclusively by the white race. Any doubts about the seriousness of such hate groups were dispelled when police and federal agents raided a white supremacist compound in rural Arkansas in April 1984 and discovered a stockpile of some thirty gallons of cyanide to be used to poison municipal water supplies. The targets and tactics of "holy terror" operations that have occurred or been attempted during the past decade clearly lead to a conclusion that a possibility exists for far more destructive acts. Ominous examples already abound:

- Poisoning of water supplies of major urban centers—not only American white supremacists but also terrorists in India are alleged to have made such plans.
- Dispersal of toxic chemicals through internal building ventilation systems, which has been attempted by white supremacist "skinheads" in Arizona.
- Indiscriminate, wanton attacks on busy urban centers' transportation systems, as in Madrid, Spain, London, Paris, Brussels, and Orlando.
- Attacks on power grids to disrupt electrical service to large population areas, conducted by a black Muslim sect in Colorado.
- Poisoning of food, undertaken in Oregon by followers of the Bhagwan Rajneesh to influence a local election.

As the new millennium approached, the somewhat superstitious fears of a nation became real, when Ahmed Ressam was intercepted entering the United States from Canada with a bomb planned for use on the Los Angeles International airport. Ressam was convicted in July 2005 and sentenced to twenty-two years in prison. While our attention is now fully averted toward terrorist cells at large, we should not discount other threats that could still pose significant danger. If we simply ignore the right-wing militias and the network they have stitched together across the nation, we will do so at our own peril. It is clear that militia movements are continuing to grow rapidly. We need only type in the word "militia" on any Internet browser and we will find dozens of examples.

SUICIDE AND RELIGIOUS TERRORISM

Suicide as a means to attack an enemy is not a new tactic; it dates back in the modern era to 1881, when a group of Nihilists wielding homemade bombs assassinated Tsar Alexander II in St. Petersburg, Russia, as he rode in his armored carriage near the Winter Palace. During World War II, the Japanese used Kamikaze pilots to dive bomb into the United States and allied shipping with devastating results. First used intentionally during the October 1944 Battle of Leyte Gulf, the kamikaze attackers succeeded in damaging allied warships, most notably the USS *St. Lo*, USS *Intrepid*, USS *Franklin*, USS *Bunker Hill*, and the Australian HMAS *Australia*. In addition, the Japanese developed weapons designed to carry out suicide attacks, including the Kaiten-manned torpedo, the Ki-115 purpose-built kamikaze plane, and the Ohka rocket-powered kamikaze plane.

U.S. Air Force intelligence has reported that the use of suicide bombers has spread worldwide since 1990. Between 1980 and 1990, suicide bombings occurred in three countries: Lebanon, Sri Lanka, and Kuwait. From 1991 to 2002, however, the tactic had spread to fifteen countries, from Algeria and Chechnya to Argentina and Croatia and to the United States,[8] and of course in 2005, it spread to the United Kingdom as well.

Terrorism associated with suicide attacks had been the signature style of the Palestinian bombers in Israel and the occupied territories and of the Tamil Tigers in Sri Lanka. In the Iraq insurgency and in Afghanistan, suicide attacks have been regular occurrences. Suicide had been an alien form of attack in the West until the terrorist suicides and hijackings on 9-11 and the suicide bombing attacks in London. Britain was prepared and had consistently warned of an attack by Islamic militants. The British alert level had been high during the run-up to the spring 2005 general election, which returned Tony Blair to his post as prime minister. The security posture was somewhat heightened when the world leaders attended the G8 Economic Summit in Edinburgh, Scotland, with opening ceremonies slated for July 7, 2005. The attack on the London Underground transport system for all its planning and audaciousness shook British politicians and the public to the core—this was not the work of external groups but second-generation immigrants born, raised, and educated in England to mainly middle-class families!

In 2004–2005, there were over four hundred suicide attacks, mostly in Iraq, and 2007 saw a total of six hundred and fifty-eight globally with five hundred and forty-three being in the Iraq–Afghanistan theater. The bombings have spread to dozens of countries on five continents, killed more than twenty-one thousand people, and injured some fifty thousand since 1983, when a suicide attack blew up the U.S. embassy in Beirut. In addressing the root causes of terrorism, we believe that comments presented by the former British Prime Minister Tony Blair in the days after the London attack in 2005 were overstated and not germane. He stated to a BBC interviewer that the underlying causes of these attacks were lack of democracy, the Middle East conflict, and poverty. Blair's belief that these are the root causes of terrorism is fundamentally flawed; if he believes that by creating democracy or removing poverty, terrorism will be eliminated, he is incorrect. The poorest nations of the world are not the ones producing the terrorist phenomenon. In discussing democracy, it is certainly not clear-cut that this is an important goal for the terrorists' agenda. The terrorists who perpetrated the 9-11 attacks, the Madrid train bombings, the London Underground attacks, and the attack on Glasgow airport in 2007 have been described as foot soldiers who had little frontline involvement in terrorist activities prior to the attacks. In all of these attacks, none of the perpetrators lived in abject poverty—in fact, the British attackers could be described as middle class and reasonably well educated, and in the Glasgow attacks, the perpetrators were medical doctors. We need to focus on the root cause of international terrorism. The terrorist ideology supports a system of beliefs that allows for the devaluation of the lives of innocent victims, in most cases civilian victims of so-called targeted enemy societies; and encourages and promotes extreme violence, including suicide, as a method of responding to grievances. Why do extreme promoters of the Islamic faith use such an ideology to make use of poverty, repression, and conflict to aid in recruitment? Terrorist organizations are fundamentally organizations or businesses. While they may have been founded as a response to some grievance either real or perceived, they soon become focused on their own continuity and perpetuation; otherwise they sooner or later would just disappear. A successful terror organization does what is necessary for its own survival. To that end, it requires resources and recruits, so it produces ideology, propaganda, and terror attacks to compete for these inputs. We clearly need to understand that terrorism is an industry and terrorist organizations are not about to go out of business because of any social or political improvements we can bring about. We need to attack these organizations directly, reducing their ability to motivate, raise funds, recruit, and organize attacks.[9]

Because suicide attacks are dramatic and often effective for a relatively small economic cost, suicide bombings will continue to increase. There are approximately 1.6 million Muslims in Britain, according to the British Home Office. A 2004 report by the Home Office detailed that thirteen percent of British Muslims believed that suicide attacks against Western targets were justified. Respondents linked this attitude to anger over foreign policies and the presence of British and U.S. troops in the Middle East. In the United States, a 2009 Pew Report showed a total of almost 2.5 million Muslims residing there. If radicalization of even one percent were to take place, that would pose a significant problem for Homeland Security.

Children as Suicide Bombers

As ghastly as the heading may appear, this will be a reality in certain areas of the globe. That suicide bombers were traditionally young males has also changed as now we see more female and elderly suicide attackers and in Iraq, we have witnessed the use of the mentally challenged to deliver suicide bombs. As for child bombers, we have already seen photographs of Palestinian children in combat fatigues and mock suicide belts in training for missions. In 2005, we saw a mixed gender suicide attack on the Jordanian capital—although the target of the 2005 attack was not unusual, the make-up of the suicide bombers was. Both were from al Qaeda in Iraq and were a married couple. In 2004, an Israeli soldier manning a checkpoint near the city of Nablus discovered a thirteen-pound explosive device in the backpack of a twelve-year-old Palestinian boy. The schoolboy had been tricked into carrying the bag by members of a Palestinian terrorist group. The soldier was alerted by the cell phone ring tone in the backpack. In 2006, a Palestinian mother of nine and grandmother of twenty-six was killed by Israeli security as she attempted to detonate a suicide vest. Currently, this lady is the oldest suicide bomber recorded to have successfully carried out a mission. In 2011, we saw jihadist websites showing children training in jihadist training camps using weapons and explosives. For the future, we will need to be wary of attempts by terrorist groups, particularly al Qaeda attempting to get body bombs onto aircraft.

TECHNOLOGY AND COUNTERING TERRORISM

Technology and counterterrorism have grown exponentially in the past twenty years—technology that was commercially available to security forces was adapted to their requirements, but that was twentieth century; in the twenty-first century, technology needs to be invented that will combat the terrorist enemy who is far more proactive as opposed to reactive. We will need to develop technology in an environment that is several steps ahead of the terrorists and their planning and execution of attacks. At the present time, technology is gathering information that is so extensive and so vast that the capacity to hold the information and disseminate it to various security networks is problematic. Our first step should be to leverage the existing technology by creating a technology breakthrough that integrates all the resources under one cohesive system. We cannot hope to succeed if we do not get the best return on our investment. In other words, we must channel resources for development into specific targeted areas rather than spending a little on a whole host of different technologies hoping to find the silver bullet. We need to be assured that we have the advanced technology to do battle with the terrorists—they are swift to adapt to changes but they have limited resources for technology. Our experts need to be super innovative in this regard. Areas such as Biometrics and its associated technology should be increased in its use for counterterrorism. It already has the following uses which can and should be further expanded to include such areas as the pattern recognition and walking gait, ear shape definition, facial thermography:

- *Fingerprint recognition:* the most widely used and well-known biometric technology. It relies on features found in the impressions made by distinct ridges on the fingertips.
- *Voice recognition:* this technology identifies a person based on the differences in the voice resulting from physiological differences and learned speaking habits.
- *Iris recognition:* this technology relies on the distinctly colored ring that surrounds the pupil of the eye.
- *Face recognition:* this technology identifies individuals by analyzing certain facial features such as the upper outlines of the eye sockets or sides of the mouth.
- *Hand geometry:* this measures the width, height, and length of the fingers; distances between joints; and the shape of knuckles.

NON-LETHAL WEAPONS   One of the most significant challenges in the war on terrorism is that its battlefields are often the everyday world, where civilians and terrorists often stand side-by-side, where as much attention must be given to safeguarding lives and property as to disrupting, apprehending, or incapacitating terrorists. Non-lethal weapons may offer the military and law enforcement a new range of options for taking the battle to the terrorist without endangering others.

Non-lethal weapons are discriminate, explicitly designed and employed to incapacitate personnel or materiel while minimizing fatalities and undesired damage to property and environment. These weapons are actually a set of capabilities which have approximately three functions:

1. *Counterpersonnel*, which involves controlling crowds, incapacitating people, preventing access to specific areas, and removing people from facilities, buildings, or areas of operation;
2. *Countermaterial*, which may involve preventing vehicles, vessels, or aircraft from entering an area or disabling or neutralizing these means of transportation; and
3. *Countercapabilities*, which focuses on disabling or neutralizing facilities and systems, including those for WMD.[10]

New Technologies

NANO-TECHNOLOGY   The work being conducted on Nanotechnology is far reaching and it needs to be adapted to the counterterror industry as well as the medical and life safety industries. Nanotechnology involves developing or working with materials and complete systems at the atomic, molecular, or macromolecular levels where at least one dimension falls with the range of 1–100 nanometers.[11] Nanoscale sensors are generally designed to form a weak chemical bond to the substance of whatever is to be sensed, and then to change their properties in response (that might be a color change or a change in conductivity, fluorescence, or weight.[12] Nanodevices offer the opportunity for fast, cheap, and accurate sensors and detectors, and markers that can be used for a wide range of forensic activities.

Directed Energy Weapons

These are weapons that have been designed to inflict casualties and damage equipment and infrastructure by depositing energy on their intended target. Active defenses such as directed-energy weapons could provide counterterrorism protection for critical infrastructure.[13] The potential for these weapons as part of an organizational response to critical infrastructure may become invaluable.

Harnessing these various future technologies to our global needs in counterterrorism will come at a price and will likely only be developed in the West. This will come over time but we need to have such an arsenal of counterterror weapons at our disposal. If we look back at the dawn of this century, the use of unmanned aerial vehicles or drones was something more akin to science fiction movies but with the speed of technology advancement aerial drones is a reality in the fight against terror. However, these drones are also commercially available which means they are in the hands of terrorists also to plan their next operation.

Summary

It may take next generation technology to combat and counter terrorism. We know that, worldwide, we have failed to gather all the available intelligence and accurately analyze and spot the signs to interpret it. This will change, and the wheel will turn.

As we attempt to look toward the future and what may lie ahead in the world of terrorist acts, we anticipate that terror networks and affiliates that attack in the name of Islam will concentrate on spectacular events, but likely not on the dramatic scale of 9-11, which required a considerable amount of planning and training. The suicide bomber is able to strike at will and without warning and cause a large number of casualties. There is currently an almost unending supply of young fanatics willing to become suicide operatives in what might best be described as the poor man's smart bomb. In terms of modern-day terrorism, military occupation of Muslim lands by foreign armies' has been a contributing factor in the creation of the suicide bomber. From a broad perspective, suicide bombers are usually from outside the country they are attacking but that trend has changed somewhat. The U.S. military noted that a significant number of attacks by suicide bombers in Afghanistan are carried out by foreign Arabs, while the suicide attacks in London were carried out by young British men of Pakistani and Jamaican descent. The ideology of al Qaeda and Islamic State has not become extinct through the War on Terror; rather, it has become entrenched at the grassroots level. IS has also been able to establish a presence in at least nineteen different countries between 2014 and 2016, even in areas where its competitor, al Qaeda, has been operating for years. There is no doubt that suicide attacks and attempts at spectacular terror events will continue in the foreseeable future as will low cost "lone wolf" style attacks with high impact results.

End Notes

1. Stratfor. "Marking a Century of the Modern Middle East." Analysis (May 15, 2016). https://www.stratfor.com/analysis/marking-century-modern-middle-east.
2. Ian Brenner. "The Toxic Legacy of a Middle East Map." *TIME Magazine* (May 30, 2016).
3. Robin Simcox. "We Will Conquer Your Rome: A Study of Islamic State Terror Plots in the West." The Henry Jackson Society (2015). http://henryjacksonsociety.org/wp-content/uploads/2015/09/ISIS-brochure-Web.pdf.
4. Telegraph on line. Arrest of Frenchman with three rocket launchers and 100 kilos of TNT raises fresh Euro 2016 security fears. http://www.telegraph.co.uk/news/2016/06/05/arrest-of-frenchman-with-three-rocket-launchers-and-100-kilos-of/
5. U.S. Congressional Record. *National Defense Authorization Act for Fiscal Year 1997* (1997).
6. Paul Cornish. "Sabotage by Sarin." *Intersec: The Journal of International Security*, vol. 7, no. 9 (Surrey, UK: Three Bridges Publishing, September 1997).

7. www.milnet.com.

8. Strategic Forecasting Inc. (2011). http://www.stratfor.com/

9. Dan Radlauer. "The London Bombings and the Root Causes of Terrorism." Paper to the International Policy Institute for Counterterrorism (July 10, 2005).

10. James Jay Carafano, Ph.D. "The Future of Anti-Terrorism Technologies." *Future Technologies*, Homeland Security Lecture #885.

11. Daniel Ratner and Mark A. Ratner. *Nanotechnology and Homeland Security* (Upper Saddle River, N.J.: Prentice Hall Professional and Technical Reference, 2004, p. 13).

12. Ibid. (p.21).

13. Jack Spencer and James Jay Carafano. "The Use of Directed-Energy Weapons to Protect Critical Infrastructure." *Heritage Foundation*, Backgrounder No. 1783, August 2, 2004. www.heritage.org/Research/NationalSecurity/bg1783.cfm.

Risk Management, Incident Management, and Business Continuity Management

OVERVIEW

In the last fifteen chapters, we have focused on historical events related to countries and terrorist groups and in each of those chapters there have been a multitude of targets, some military, many civilian and government. What does this all mean for the practitioner who has studied terrorism and needs now to understand how risk is managed and mitigated in a corporate structure and environment. In this chapter, we will discuss the methodology for conducting a security risk assessment in general terms that can be applied to almost any company structure or organization. Having completed the risk assessment, it is then important to have in place a tried and tested Business Continuity Management (BCM) Program.

The statistics below published in 2016 by the U.S. Department of State clearly indicate the targets for terrorism are not exclusive to police and military targets—so it becomes even more crucial for companies to be prepared for an emergency or disaster scenario. The damage to a business can be catastrophic and its ability to recover by applying risk management, incident management (IM), and a business continuity plan will go a long way to insure the health of the company or organization in the recovery process.

More than half of all targets attacked in 2015 (fifty-five percent) were classified either as private citizens and property or police, as shown in Figure 16-1. In 2015, a total of eleven thousand seven hundred and seventy-four terrorist attacks occurred worldwide, resulting in more than twenty eight thousand three hundred total deaths and more than thirty five thousand three hundred people injured. In addition, more than twelve thousand one hundred people were kidnapped or taken hostage (Figure 16-2).

Attacks targeting police were most frequently aimed at police buildings, checkpoints, and officers or security forces, and were most prevalent in Bahrain (seventy-three percent), Turkey (forty-eight percent), and Saudi Arabia (forty-six percent). The most ubiquitous targets of terrorist attacks in 2015 were private citizens and property (attacked in sixty-three countries), police (attacked in fifty-eight countries), and general (non-diplomatic) government targets (attacked in fifty countries).On average, there were nine hundred and eighty-one terrorist attacks, causing two thousand three hundred and sixty-one deaths, and injuring two thousand nine hundred and forty-three people per month worldwide in 2015. There were 2.5 deaths and 3.3 people injured per attack, including perpetrator casualties[1] (Figure 16-3).

Attacks on airports and aircraft decreased by sixty percent; twenty-three airports or aircraft were targeted in 2015, down from fifty-eight in 2014. However, other types of transportation were targeted more frequently in 2015, increasing to three hundred and eighty-one from three hundred and fifty-six in 2014.[2]

WHAT IS A RISK ASSESSMENT?

A risk assessment is a systematic examination of a task, job or process that you carry out at work for the purpose of

- identifying the significant hazards that are present (a hazard is something that has the potential to cause someone harm or ill health).

Target Type	Number of Targets
Private Citizens & Property	4,514
Police	2,159
Business	1,149
Government (General)	1,136
Military	715
Terrorists/Non-State Militia	447
Religious Figures/Institutions	394
Transportation	381
Educational Institution	297
Utilities	255
Violent Political Party	161
Government (Diplomatic)	148
Journalists & Media	146
Other	145
NGO	53
Telecommunication	46
Airports & Airlines	23
Food or Water Supply	17
Tourists	7
Maritime	6
Abortion Related	5
Total	**12,204**

FIGURE 16-1   Targets of terrorist attacks worldwide 2015.   *Courtesy:* U.S. Department of State.

Month	Total Attacks	Total Deaths*	Total Injured*	Total Kidnapped/ Hostages
January	1,270	2,340	2,781	1,726
February	1,078	2,127	2,713	894
March	903	2,378	2,829	1,214
April	928	2,919	2,650	1,155
May	1,017	2,676	2,705	1,725
June	929	2,727	3,407	535
July	986	2,946	3,645	1,204
August	993	2,400	3,349	1,260
September	881	2,266	3,491	543
October	1,040	2,300	2,722	877
November	928	1,610	2,581	769
December	821	1,639	2,447	287
Total	**11,774**	**28,328**	**35,320**	**12,189**

*Includes perpetrators.

FIGURE 16-2   Terrorist attacks and casualties worldwide by month, 2015.   *Source:* Bureau of Counterterrorism and Countering Violent Extremism. Country Reports on Terrorism 2015. http://www.state.gov/j/ct/rls/crt/2015/257526.htm.

	Total Attacks		Total Deaths*		Deaths per Attack*		Total Injured*		Injured per Attack*		Total Kidnapped/ Hostages	
	2015	2014	2015	2014	2015	2014	2015	2014	2015	2014	2015	2014
Iraq	**2,418**	3,370	6,932	9,926	2.99	3.07	**11,856**	15,137	5.23	4.79	**3,982**	2,658
Afghanistan	**1,708**	1,594	5,292	4,507	3.24	2.91	**6,246**	4,700	4.00	3.15	**1,112**	719
Pakistan	**1,009**	1,823	1,081	1,761	1.10	0.99	**1,325**	2,836	1.36	1.61	**269**	879
India	**791**	764	289	418	0.38	0.57	**508**	639	0.68	0.89	**862**	305
Nigeria	**589**	663	4,886	7,531	9.29	12.81	**2,777**	2,251	7.67	6.31	**1,341**	1,298
Egypt	**494**	292	656	184	1.34	0.63	**844**	452	1.73	1.55	**24**	29
Philippines	**485**	378	258	240	0.54	0.65	**548**	367	1.16	1.00	**119**	145
Bangladesh	**459**	124	75	30	0.16	0.24	**691**	107	1.52	0.87	**4**	7
Libya	**428**	554	462	435	1.24	0.90	**657**	567	1.85	1.21	**764**	336
Syria	**382**	232	2,748	1,698	7.99	8.24	**2,818**	1,473	9.78	9.32	**1,453**	872
Worldwide	**11,774**	**13,482**	**28,328**	**32,763**	**2.53**	**2.57**	**35,320**	**34,785**	**3.30**	**2.86**	**12,189**	**9,461**

*Includes perpetrators

FIGURE 16-3   Ten countries with the most terrorist attacks in 2015.   *Source:* Bureau of Counterterrorism and Countering Violent Extremism. Country Reports on Terrorism 2015. http://www.state.gov/j/ct/rls/crt/2015/257526.htm.

- deciding if what you have already done reduces the risk of someone being harmed to an acceptable level, and if not;
- deciding what further control measures you must take to reduce the risk to an acceptable level.

Risk assessments should also be carried out to satisfy the requirements of legislation but above all to ensure the health and safety of employees.

PURPOSE

The intent of the risk assessment document is to outline the elements of the corporate security program and associated standards that should be implemented by all operations and facilities in order to mitigate the identified risks and to provide a safe and secure work environment for their employees, contractors, visitors, and the general public. The program will support proper planning, good management, and smooth transitioning consistent with the overall future direction of the Company.

EXECUTIVE SUMMARY (SAMPLE DOCUMENT)

A risk assessment MUST include an executive summary to cover the overall aspects of the assessment.

"The primary objective of this Security Corporate Program is to support the safety and security of employees, contractors, visitors, facilities, and assets. It is important to make a distinction between 'deter' and 'eliminate'. No security measures, regardless of how involved or sophisticated, can ensure absolute protection against every possible threat. It is the sole intent of any security program to provide such obstacles and observation methods that demonstrate to a potential perpetrator that the risks of exposure, failure or capture are greater than the potential for success in perpetrating the incident.

The plan calls for all employees, contractors, and visitors to come under some form of control and monitoring (electronic or natural), as they enter the facilities, the storage areas, and other exterior areas where high-value assets and hazards are located.

Under the direction of the Risk/Security group all facets of the organization will be required to adopt these security standards and measures for current and future facilities and operations."

SAMPLE RISK ASSESSMENT

Listed below is a typical Threat Risk Assessment contents page:

CONTENTS

1 Executive Summary 4
2 Methodology 5
    2.1 Threat Risk Assessment Process 5
    2.2 CPTED 7
    2.3 Zoning 9
    2.4 Zone Physical Security Standards 10
3 Threat Analysis 13
    3.1 Violence from Persons Suffering from Substance Abuse and/or Mental illness 13
    3.2 Disgruntled Employee 13
    3.3 General Theft and Vandalism 13
    3.4 Disgruntled members of Public 14
4 Findings and Recommendations 15
    4.1 Basement Level 15
        4.1.1 Internal Offices 15
        4.1.2 Human Resources Department 17
    4.2 1st Floor 18
        4.2.1 Foyer 18
        4.2.2 Finance Department 19
        4.2.3 Building IT/Server Room 20
        4.2.4 General Offices 22
        4.2.5 Windowed offices 23

4.3 2nd Floor..23
4.4 3rd Floor..24
    4.4.1 President's Office..24
    4.4.2 CFO Offfice...25
    4.4.3 Community Affairs Offices 26
    4.4.5 Server Room 27
4.5 4th Floor..27
4.6 Public Areas...28
4.7 Interaction Points..28
4.8 Building Exterior 29
4.9 Logistical Security...31
    4.9.1 Security Organization..31
    4.9.2 Security Policies and Procedures 31
    4.9.4 Security Awareness and Training 32

1. Executive Summary—EXAMPLE

During October to December 2015, David Smith and Dennis Thompson of Corporate Risk Managed Solutions were contracted by the Company to carry out a threat risk assessment and *Crime Prevention through Environmental Design* (CPTED) review of the Company doing business in Dallas TX. The purpose of this review was to: (1) identify the threats to the Company, its employees, contractors, and visitors; (2) assess the level of associated risk, identify vulnerabilities in the current security measures; and (3) provide recommendations for risk mitigation measures adopting security best practices and CPTED principles.

The review was carried out through detailed examination of the Company Main Building, interviews with departmental and organizational stakeholders and review of all relevant background information.

The primary threat to the Company is workplace violence from persons visiting the building. Types of persons include mentally disturbed persons, substance abusers, and disgruntled members of the public and employees.

There are a number of measures currently in place within the Company including electronic access control and duress reporting systems. It was identified that these systems provide a level of protection but require expansion and correct specification to maximize the overall effectiveness. It was also identified that CCTV should be included to provide the correct level of monitoring of the building. As a part of this review we have provided classification of the areas in the building and provided standards for the protection of each classification level to provide a template process for the design of physical security measures.

It was identified that there is a lack of security policies and procedures and associated training for the employees of Company. An example of this is the use of duress buttons at the reception desks in the main foyer and President's office. There are currently no policies and procedures for the use of and required response to this system.

There is inherent risk with the public's level of accessibility to sensitive areas in the building and the ability to move around the building unmonitored and uncontrolled. The main areas of concern are the Basement level and 3rd floor areas as the access to the 2nd and 4th floor offices are controlled by the electronic access control system. It is recommended that the public areas be terminated at the entrances to these sensitive areas and access be controlled with physical and procedural measures. This added layer of protection will cost effectively mitigate the risk while maintaining the open door concept within the spaces.

2 Methodology

2.1 THREAT RISK ASSESSMENT PROCESS (Figure 16-4)   As part of conducting a threat risk assessment for the Corporation's facility, hazards to people, property, and information were reviewed. Examples of these elements include:

- Verbal/physical aggression/attack to employees, contractors, or visitors.
- Damage to personal and company property.

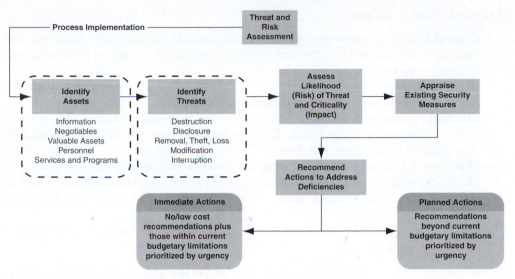

FIGURE 16-4   Threat and risk assessment.   *Courtesy:* Dave Loban.

- Theft of company assets (both physical and information).
- Access to personal/privileged, sensitive, and confidential information.

The next step of the assessment was to determine potential impacts, including frequency, probability, and severity:

- **Could it happen?** Exposure: Probable frequency values are assigned as follows:

Rare	**1**—less than one per year
Annual	**2**—one to five times per year
Monthly	**3**—six to twenty times per year
Daily	**4**—more than twenty times per year
Continuous	**5**—e.g., inadequate ventilation

- **Is it going to happen?** Probability measures the likelihood of an event linked to the identified hazard occurring or being realized.

Inconceivable	Is practically impossible and has never occurred
Rare	Has not been known to occur after many years of exposure
Possible	Can be envisaged to occur after many years of exposure
Moderate	Has a good chance of occurring and is not unusual
Conceivable	The most likely result of the hazard/event being realized
Almost Certain	High degree of certainty event will occur

- **How bad could it be?** Potential severity values are assigned as follows:

Low	1—No injury, minor financial loss
Moderate	2—Minor injuries, medium financial loss
Elevated	3—Major injury, high sociological and economic impact
High	4—Fatality, major sociological and economic impact
Critical	5—Multiple fatalities, catastrophic sociological and economic impact (Figure 16-5).

Probability						
	5 Almost Certain					Critical
	4 Conceivable				High	
	3 Moderate			Elevated		
	2 Possible		Moderate			
	1 Rare	Low				
		1 Low	2 Moderate	3 Elevated	4 High	5 Critical
				Severity		

FIGURE 16-5   Risk assessment matrix.   *Courtesy:* Dave Loban.

The resulting risk levels are:

- **Critical** A security deficiency is identified with potential for material financial loss, serious injury, physical damage, or adverse publicity and there is no current protocol in place to detect or mitigate the occurrence.
- **High** The same as critical, there is a security protocol in place; however, the protocol is assessed as insufficient to detect or mitigate the occurrence.
- **Elevated** A security deficiency is identified with potential for financial loss, personal injury, damage, or adverse publicity. There is a security protocol in place but it is assessed as insufficient relative to the risk level.
- **Moderate** A security deficiency is identified with potential for a financial or safety risk. There is an effective security protocol in place to prevent such occurrences provided the protocol is adhered to. However, there is insufficient evidence that the protocol is followed effectively at all times.
- **Low** A security deficiency is identified with potential for minor financial, safety, physical damage, or publicity.

The final steps of the assessment determine what is already being done, and what further action is necessary. After prioritizing the recommendations below, the Company will be in a position to evaluate the availability of funding and determine the associated implementation plan.

2.2 CRIME PREVENTION THROUGH ENVIRONMENTAL DESIGN (CPTED) CPTED is an approach to planning and development that reduces opportunities for crime. Research has shown that the proper design and effective use of the built environment can lead to a reduction in both the opportunity for crime and fear of crime. CPTED uses the physical environment as protection against attack by creating a defensive environment from both the physical and the psychological aspects at the same time.

The goal of CPTED is the reduction of opportunities for crime or undesirable behavior to occur. This reduction is achieved by employing physical design features that discourage undesirable behavior, while at the same time encouraging legitimate use of the environment.

Communities, neighborhoods, buildings, streets, and parks can all be made safer through the application of design principles that make it more difficult to carry out inappropriate activities.

CPTED can reduce crime, undesirable behavior, and fear of crime through:

- *Territoriality:* fostering occupant's, visitor's, and employees' interaction, vigilance, and control over their environment.
- *Surveillance:* maximizing the ability to spot suspicious people and activities using three types of surveillance:
  - ○ *Natural surveillance.* Opportunities for natural surveillance occur as a direct result of architectural design (designs that minimize visual obstacles and eliminate places of concealment). These open designs also encourage use of the environment, as people feel safer when they can easily see and be seen.
  - ○ *Mechanical surveillance.* Mechanical surveillance methods, such as CCTV and electronic monitoring, are normally used only when natural surveillance alone cannot sufficiently protect an area. Public and semi-private zones that are concealed from view or that experience regular periods of isolation or inactivity can benefit from some type of formal surveillance.
  - ○ *Organized surveillance.* This uses fixed guard posts and security patrols along with employees and other capable guardians performing functions similar to "Neighborhood Watch" programs.
- *Defensible Space:* identifying ownership by delineating private space from public space through real or symbolic boundaries:
  - ○ To provide maximum control, an environment is first divided into smaller, clearly defined areas or zones. Under the defensible space guidelines, all areas are designated as either public, semi-private, or private. This designation defines the acceptable use of each zone and determines who has a right to occupy it under certain circumstances.

- *Public zones.* These areas are generally open to anyone and are the least secure of the three zones. This is particularly true when the zone is located within a building or in an area with uncontrolled access and little or no opportunity for close surveillance.
- *Semi-private zones.* These areas create a buffer between public and private zones and/or serve as common use spaces, such as interior/exterior courtyards. They are accessible to the public, but are set off from the public zone. This separation is accomplished with design features that establish definite transitional boundaries between the zones.
- *Private zones.* These are areas of restricted entry. Access is controlled and limited to specific individuals or groups. A private residence is a good example of a private zone.
  - Division between zones is generally accomplished with some type of barrier. These can be either physical or symbolic.
    - Physical barriers, as the name implies, are substantial in nature and physically prevent movement. Fencing, some forms of landscaping, locked doors, and the like are examples of physical barriers.
    - Symbolic barriers are less tangible. Nearly anything could serve as a symbolic barrier. The only requirement is that it defines the boundary between zones. This type of barrier does not prevent physical movement. All that is required is that it leaves no doubt that a transition between zones has taken place. Low decorative fences, flower beds, changes in sidewalk patterns or materials, and signs are examples of symbolic barriers.
- *Access control/target hardening:* using physical barriers, security devices, and tamper-resistant materials to restrict entrance:
  - *Natural access control.* Occurs as a direct result of architectural design (designs that control the flow of traffic and encourage or discourage access). Hallways, directional signs, lighting, and landscaping all have a role to play toward directing pedestrian and vehicular traffic.
  - *Mechanical access control.* This is the card access, readers, doors, locks, and generally the hardware, which controls access to spaces.
  - *Organized access control.* This uses fixed guard posts and security patrols along with employee awareness and other capable guardians performing functions similar to "Wal-Mart Greeters" and subtly monitors and controls personal access.
- *Maintenance:* ensuring that a building or area is clean and well-maintained. This also relates to maintaining policies and employee capabilities.

2.3 ZONING For the purposes of standardizing the physical security standards across the organization's facilities, it is important to use a system which adopts a series of security levels that are clearly defined along with the appropriate security measures for each level on a graduating scale. Each area is assessed and evaluated using threat, risk, and operational and logistical parameters to ascertain the appropriate security level for the space. The areas are then examined and compared to the standards described in this plan. A gap analysis can then be developed to provide the physical measures required to meet the requirements directed by the security level.

This physical security design should be coupled with the appropriate operational and logistical measures required to capitalize on the improved design. This approach will provide a clear and concise security design and operation that will increase the level of protection for the occupants of the building.

There are four security levels in the buildings.

Public This level applies to areas that the general public have unrestricted access to during normal working hours. There are no specific security measures in place.

Administration This level applies to areas on the building floors which interface with visitors, deliveries, and couriers. Persons entering these areas have undergone a first level of screening and are granted access due to the proof of having legitimate business with the building tenants. The measures in place in these areas are based upon first level screening and control such as recording of credentials and escort.

Operations   This level applies to areas within the building that contain sensitive material and the main body of employees. Unescorted access is restricted to authorized persons only. The measures for this level include structural perimeter protection and electronic access control.

Restricted   This is the highest level of security and applies to areas to which if compromised would have a catastrophic impact on the business or to which an extraordinary risk exists. These areas contain critical infrastructure, highly sensitive information, and high risk members of staff. The measures for this level include enhanced perimeter protection and increased access control.

2.4   ZONE PHYSICAL SECURITY STANDARDS   The following are the physical security standards to be adopted for each security zone level.

Zone Level 1—Public

This level applies to areas that the general public have unrestricted access to during normal working hours.

- Lighting
  - Lighting installed on building exterior
    - General around building (0.5 to 2.0 foot candles)
    - Covering entrances (10 foot candles)

Zone Level 2—Administration

This level applies to areas on the building floors which interface with visitors, deliveries, and couriers. Persons entering these areas have undergone a first level of screening and are granted access due to the proof of having legitimate business with the building tenants.

The measures in place in these areas are based upon first level screening and control such as recording of credentials and escort.

- Access Control
  - Intercom and remote entry controlled by Company employee
  - Electronic access control readers for all authorized persons

- Door and window security
  - All access and exterior doors locked and monitored
  - All accessible windows secured and hardened

- Intrusion detection and alarms
  - Doors installed with contact sensors
  - Windows monitored with glass break sensors
  - Panic device at employee desk

- CCTV
  - Fixed camera installed behind employee desk covering interaction point
  - Video installed in intercom when clear line of sight from desk to intercom not available

- Lighting
  - To provide sufficient light for subject identification
- Other
  - Subject escorted at all times

Zone Level 3—Operations

This level applies to areas within the building that contain sensitive material and the main body of employees. Unescorted access is restricted to authorized persons only. The measures for this level include structural perimeter protection and electronic access control.

- Access Control
  - Electronic access control on all zone perimeter entrances

- Door and window security
  - All access and exterior doors locked and monitored
  - All accessible windows secured and hardened

- Intrusion detection and alarms
  - Doors installed with contact sensors
  - All accessible windows monitored with glass break sensors

- CCTV
  - Fixed camera installed covering all access points

- Lighting
  - To provide sufficient light for subject identification

Zone Level 4—Restricted

This is the highest level of security and applies to areas to which if compromised would have a catastrophic impact on the business or to which an extraordinary risk exists. These areas contain critical infrastructure, highly sensitive information, and high risk members of staff. The measures for this level include enhanced perimeter protection and increased access control.

- Access Control
  - Electronic access control on all zone perimeter entrances

- Door and window security
  - All access and exterior doors locked and monitored
  - All accessible windows removed
  - All walls to be slab to slab construction

- Intrusion detection and alarms
  - Doors installed with contact sensors
  - All accessible windows monitored with glass break sensors
  - Panic alarms installed inside space or carried by person

- CCTV
  - Fixed camera installed covering all access points
  - Fixed camera inside restricted space

- Lighting
  - To provide sufficient light for subject identification

3 Threat Analysis

3.1 VIOLENCE FROM PERSONS SUFFERING FROM SUBSTANCE ABUSE AND OR MENTAL ILLNESS The company offices are a focal point for persons demonstrating abnormal behavior caused by mental illness or substance abuse. During the review it was stated that dealing with disturbed persons was common occurrence.

Examples of persons that can be met while interacting with the public:

- All cases of schizophrenia (a psychotic disorder)
- Severe cases of major depression and bipolar disorder (mood disorders)
- Severe cases of panic disorder, obsessive-compulsive disorder, and post-traumatic stress disorder (anxiety disorders)
- Severe cases of attention deficit/ hyperactivity disorder (typically, a childhood disorder)
- Severe cases of anorexia nervosa (an eating disorder).

3.2 DISGRUNTLED EMPLOYEE A disgruntled employee is any person with such knowledge of the production facility that if dissatisfied could affect business continuity through damage or negative publicity.

There are many reasons why employees may become disgruntled in the workplace. The core reasons are typically broken down to the employee being overworked, underpaid, unappreciated, or passed up for a promotion. Once an employee has become disgruntled, they often enter into an adversarial relationship with their employer. This can often be a one sided situation, as the employee will typically try to hide their level of displeasure to not put their employment at risk.

The threat from a disgruntled employee can manifest in a number of ways:

1. Theft of property
2. Leakage of information
3. Damage to infrastructure
4. Workplace violence

3.3 GENERAL THEFT AND VANDALISM Theft from the Company site will be occurring whether it is accountable or not. It is the loss prevention methods in place that will deter and manage the cost implications derived from the theft of equipment, money, stationary, and supplies. All items are subject to theft from employees, contractors, and visitors to the Company.

3.4 DISGRUNTLED MEMBERS OF PUBLIC There are reasons members of the public can become disgruntled with the Company. These persons may wish to express their frustrations directly within the building. The level of anger will be dependent upon a number of factors and there is a significant threat of workplace violence.

4 Findings and Recommendations

4.1 BASEMENT LEVEL

4.1.1 Internal Offices The corridor on this level is open to the public. Offices and areas off this corridor are not open to the public and are categorized as Operations level areas.

- Operations
- Maintenance
- Human Resources
- Procurement

Threats to these areas include:

1. Compromise of building infrastructure
2. Compromise of Company operations
3. Injury of staff from disgruntled employees
4. Injury of staff from mentally disturbed or persons under the influence of drugs or alcohol

Risk Assessment

Exposure: 2

Probability: Moderate

Severity: Elevated

Risk Level: Elevated

Type	Reason	Number
Internal	Inter-departmental	82
External	Appointment	6
	Visitor for staff	4
	Pick up documents	2
	Drop off documents	3
	Drop in General enquiries	21
	Cold call	6
	Total	**124**

FIGURE 16-6 Summary of visitors to building. *Courtesy:* Dave Loban.

Following the zoning standards, the offices off this corridor must be secured at all times and controlled with access control readers. This will result in the installation of twelve access control readers.

It was presumed that public access to the Procurement Department was required for the delivery of contract documents. It has been stated that due to the increased use of online processing of contracts there is a small number that require members of the public accessing the Procurement Department. This number is expected to increase during specific times such as the delivery times of major tenders.

As a part of this study the Procurement department logged the number and type of visitors over a period of approximately four weeks from the 5th to the 30th of November 2015.

In summary, the results of this study are as follows (Figure 16-6)

Recommendation 1—The corridor itself can be segregated from the public by installing a wall and electronically controlled access door adjacent to the employee washrooms on the basement level. This would provide the ability to categorize the corridor as an Operations level area and negate the requirement for the access to the individual offices to be electronically controlled. This would be a more cost effective solution which meets the security requirements while allowing free movement of the employees within the area.

Recommendation 2—A fixed high resolution CCTV camera should also be installed within this corridor to cover all activity.

Recommendation 3—There is an IT switch room in a closet directly off this corridor. This is categorized as a restricted level area. This area requires a fire proof door with electronic access control.

Recommendation 4—The Access Control office is categorized as a Restricted level area as it houses the main control terminal for the building access control system. Therefore, this office requires electronic access control to be installed on the entrance door.

There are a number of offices on this floor that have exterior windows. These windows are at or below ground level and due to the design of the building are used as refuge points for persons to sleep and/or use drugs. These windows are vulnerability points for the building.

Recommendation 5—Anti-break window film should be installed on the windows of these offices. A tinted or mirrored variety would also provide protection by deterring view inside the offices from the exterior.

Intrusion detection sensors linked into the building intrusion alarms system should be installed inside all offices that have windows that can be accessed from the ground level. These sensors should either be (a) acoustic glass break sensors such as the DSC Acuity Series or (b) Passive Infra Red motion detection sensors such as the DSC LC 171 Series.

4.1.2 Human Resources Department   The Human Resources department is located on the Basement level. The location of the entrance is such that there is no line of site to any other department. The reception is manned by two members of staff and leads to offices and interview rooms.

If a disturbed person was to enter this area and cause a problem the staff would only have the telephone as a means to raising an alarm.

Exposure: 3

Probability: Moderate

Severity: Elevated

Risk Level: Elevated

Recommendation 6—The reception desk should be expanded so as to create a physical barrier and segregation between the public and administration areas. CCTV should be installed to record the interaction between members of public and the employees.

Recommendation 7—Duress devices should be installed on both desks. Correct policies and procedures for the use of the duress system should be developed and implemented. Appropriate security training should be given to all members of staff that man the reception desks.

The HR employees carry out termination and disciplinary meetings. These meetings have the potential of causing threatening situations involving workplace violence.

Exposure: 1

Probability: Possible

Severity: Elevated

Risk Level: Moderate

Recommendation 8—Duress devices should be installed on all desks within rooms in which interviews and meetings take place. Correct policies and procedures for the use of the duress system should be developed and implemented. Appropriate security training should be given to all members of staff that man the reception desks.

4.2   1ST FLOOR

4.2.1   Foyer   The Foyer is an open area with good lighting and layout for the adoption of CPTED principles. There are two reception desks off the Foyer; into the Finance department and one main central reception desk. These reception desks are at risk from members of the public with negative purposes as covered in Section 3.

Risk Assessment

Exposure: 3

Probability: Moderate

Severity: Moderate

Risk Level: Moderate

The main reception desk has good line of sight to the south and west entrances as well as the stairwells to the basement and 2nd floor levels. However, this reception desk is also the internal mail area and the receptionist is also responsible for the sorting and processing of this mail. It was noticed during the review that during times when the mail is being processed the receptionist has his/her back to the foyer.

The reception desk is fitted with duress devices and lights connected to the President's office reception desk. It was stated during the review that there are no policies and procedures for the use and response to this duress system.

Recommendation 9—Correct policies and procedures for the use of the duress system should be developed and implemented. Appropriate security training should be given to all members of staff that man the reception desk.

Recommendation 10—It is recommended that CCTV cameras be installed in the foyer to provide an electronic record of all persons entering Company and moving through the foyer area. Specific locations will be covered on Section 4.6—Public Spaces.

4.2.2   Accounts Payable and Receivable Department   The Finance department is located on the ground floor of the building. Money and sensitive documents are stored in this area in a safe at the rear of the department. There are a number of teller stations in which Company related transactions are made with the public.

The risk related issues present in this area are the following:

- Security of money and sensitive materials
- Workplace violence
- Fraudulent transactions

There are fixed cameras installed in the department monitoring the entrances and teller stations. There are also electronic card access readers installed on entrance doors.

Risk Assessment

Exposure: 3

Probability: Moderate

Severity: Moderate

Risk Level: Moderate

Recommendation 11—It is recommended that adjustments of the existing CCTV cameras be carried out to provide the most effective coverage as shown in the table below (Figure 16-7).

4.2.3   Building Server Room   The Server room contains critical IT infrastructure vital to building and Company operations. The room is located directly off the main foyer and adjacent to the Finance department.

The main access to the room is controlled by electronic access control access door. The fire suppression system uses Halon which is a hazardous material and use of this type of system requires effective exits

Type	Target	Adjustment
Fixed	Safe door	Camera angle too sharp. Move camera back minimum of 6 feet to provide coverage of safe door and corridor
Fixed	Door to Chamber	Camera too close to door. Move camera back minimum of 4 feet
Fixed	Teller stations	The camera angle is directly behind the teller. This results in the recording of the transaction being blocked by the teller's body. Each camera should be moved to the correct angle to cover the teller, patron, and transaction

FIGURE 16-7   CCTV recommendations. *Courtesy:* Dave Loban.

to be provided. The rear entrances lead into the Finance department; these doors are emergency exit doors but neither is fitted with the correct door hardware in compliance with the Fire Code.

There is a single pane window in the rear wall which does not provide any protection and could be easily compromised.

Risk Assessment

Exposure: 1

Probability: Moderate

Severity: High

Risk Level: Elevated

Recommendation 12—It is recommended that the following mitigation measures are taken:

1. Install CCTV inside the main access door from the foyer
2. Install CCTV inside the main Server room area
3. Install an electronic access card reader to the Server room inner door
4. Install the correct emergency door hardware and signage to the two rear doors and the main access door
5. Remove the window on the rear wall

4.2.4 Corporate Meeting Rooms   The Company Committees Rooms are a focal point for debate and public interaction on Company issues, policies, and programs. There is an inherent threat from disturbance by disgruntled members of the public. Also many of the meetings are carried out during hours when the Company on the whole is unoccupied. These types of meetings have been the stage for violence including incidents involving firearms.

The main access is controlled by lock and key and there has been instance when this door has been left insecure. The rear access from the main building foyer is controlled by electronic access control. Access to the Accounts Payable and Receivable department is also controlled by electronic access control.

From the foyer of the committee rooms unmonitored access can be gained to the Company Corporate offices on the 3rd floor.

Risk Assessment

Exposure: 2

Probability: Moderate

Severity: High

Risk Level: Elevated

Recommendation 13—It is recommended that CCTV be installed covering the Corporate Meeting Rooms as follows (Figure 16-8)

Recommendation 14—It is recommended that electronic duress devices linked to the building intrusion alarms system coupled with effective response policies and procedures be installed.

Recommendation 15—Installation of electronic access control on the door to the stairwell to the Administrator's office on the 3rd floor and the main entrance to the Administration Foyer.

Type	Target	Note
PTZ	Committee Meeting Rooms–Foyer	Pre-sets programmed into access control system to activate camera pre-sets when doors compromised
Fixed	Main access	Dedicated electronic record of all persons entering the Foyer
PTZ	Committee Rooms	Electronic record of all activity within the chamber

FIGURE 16-8 CCTV locations. *Courtesy:* Dave Loban.

4.2.5 Windowed offices There are a number of offices on this floor that have exterior windows. These windows are at ground level and instance of undetected breakage of these windows has occurred. These windows are vulnerability points for the building.

> **Recommendation 16**—Anti-break window film should be installed on the windows of these offices. A tinted or mirrored variety would also provide protection by deterring view inside the offices from the exterior.

Intrusion detection sensors linked into the building intrusion alarms system should be installed inside all offices that have windows that can be accessed from the ground level. These sensors should either be (a) acoustic glass break sensors such as the DSC Acuity Series or (b) Passive Infra Red motion detection sensors such as the DSC LC 171 Series.

4.3 2ND FLOOR Referring to the zoning plan, the 2nd floor is categorized as an administrative level area. There are six booths for public interaction. All interaction points are under threat from disgruntled and unstable members of the public. There is electronic access control from this area into the internal offices.

> **Recommendation 17**—Fixed CCTV cameras should be installed to cover the booths and the interaction between staff and the public. Duress devices should be installed under all desks within the booths. Effective operation and response policies and procedures should be developed for the use of these duress devices.

Within the office space there is a closet containing IT infrastructure. Due to its criticality as part of the building infrastructure this area is categorized as Restricted.

> **Recommendation 18**—Electronic access control should be installed on the entrance door to this area.

4.4 3RD FLOOR The 3rd floor of the Company is a particular point of vulnerability due to the personnel and operations carried out in the departments on this floor. This floor is a primary focal point for all types of negative action from the public. The risk and vulnerability assessments for this floor have been carried out for the departments and areas and are described below. However, at this point, it has been determined that the threats and risk present for the occupants of this floor is significant.

> **Recommendation 19**—It is recommended that the public level area be restricted at the entrance to the floor. A manned reception area should be designed and constructed with a seating area for visitors. This measure will greatly reduce the risk to the entire floor.

The location of this desk will give good viewpoints to the stairwells from the 2nd floor and to the 4th floor. The reception desk should be fitted with an electronically controlled turnstile with access control readers to gain access with a remote release controlled by the member of staff at the desk.

The desk should be fitted with a duress button linked to the building intrusion alarm system. Effective operation and response policies and procedures should be developed for the use of the duress button. A fixed CCTV camera should be installed behind the desk to record all interactions with the public at the desk.

4.4.1 Offices of the President and CEO Due to VIP status the President and CEO offices including the Chief Financial Officer offices are categorized as Restricted level areas.

There is a reception area with an Executive Assistant whose desk is fitted with a duress reporting system linked to the main reception desk on the 1st floor. It was stated that there are no formal policies and procedures for the operation and response of this duress system.

There have been numerous instances of persons entering the reception area wishing to talk to the corporate leaders without appointment and who have become agitated and may have been mentally disturbed or under the influence of drugs or alcohol. This presents a significant threat to the occupants of this area. In these instances, it has been a member of staff that has dealt with the individual including the President himself. Compliance was achieved through force of presence as opposed to formal conflict resolution training.

Risk Assessment

Exposure: 4

Probability: Conceivable

Severity: High

Risk Level: High

Recommendation 20—The doors to the Restricted level offices should be monitored with electronic access control. The access door to the reception area should be fitted with electronic access control to allow electronic control from the Executive Assistant's desk and capability to lock down the whole area if a threat exists. Remote release for the Executive Assistant's desk duress system should be linked to the building intrusion alarm system. Effective operation and response policies and procedures should be developed for the use of the duress button.

CCTV should be installed to monitor the Reception area.

4.4.2 Company Seismology Department The Company Seismology department contains sensitive material that by its nature could be targeted and if compromised will have a negative impact on Company operations. Therefore, the offices have been categorized as Operations level areas with the central area categorized as an Administrative level area.

Risk Assessment

Exposure: 1

Probability: Moderate

Severity: Moderate

Risk Level: Moderate

Recommendation 21—The Operations level offices should be monitored with electronic access control. The reception desk should be fitted with a duress button. Effective operation and response policies and procedures should be developed for the use of the duress button.

Recommendation 22—CCTV cameras should be installed in the following locations (Figure 16-9)

4.4.3 Public Relations Offices The Public Relations department is the public "face" of the Company. Employees of this department are often in the media representing the Company's standpoint on contentious issues. Therefore, employees of this department are under threat of workplace violence from disgruntled members of public.

There is a reception desk at the entrance of this department. There are currently no security measures present in this department.

Risk Assessment

Exposure: 1

Probability: Moderate

Severity: High

Risk Level: Elevated

Recommendation 23—Electronic access control should be installed on the entrance door to the department with remote release at the reception desk. The desk should be fitted with a duress button linked to the building intrusion alarm system. Effective operation and response policies and procedures should be developed for the use of the duress button.

4.4.5 Server Room There is a large server room adjacent to the washrooms in the Public Relations department. This room contains critical IT and security system infrastructure and therefore is categorized as a Restricted level area.

Type	Target	Note
Fixed	Main access	Record of all persons entering the department
Fixed	Rear access	Surveillance of rear door from stairwell

FIGURE 16-9 CCTV locations. *Courtesy:* Dave Loban.

The door of this room swings out into the corridor which is a safety hazard.

Recommendation 24—The door to this room should be monitored by electronic access control and monitored by a fixed CCTV camera installed in the corridor.

Recommendation 25—The entrance door should be adjusted to swing inwards into the room.

4.5   4TH FLOOR   Referring to the zoning plan the 4th floor is categorized as an Operations level area. This is due to the fact that the offices on this floor are primarily Company department managers. There is an unmanned reception desk and there is electronic access control from this area into the internal offices.

Recommendation 26—A fixed CCTV camera should be installed behind this desk covering the desk and the top of the stairs from the 3rd floor. The desk should be fitted with a duress button in case it is ever manned. Fixed CCTV cameras should also be installed inside each entrance door to provide and electronic record of all persons entering the Operations area. Within the office space there is a closet containing IT infrastructure. Due to its criticality as part of the building infrastructure this area is categorized as Restricted.

Recommendation 27—Electronic access control should be installed on the entrance door to this area.

Recommendation 28—There is a rooftop access hatch at the top of the south stairwell. This hatch should be fitted with an intrusion sensor linked to the building alarms system.

4.6   PUBLIC AREAS   Due to the general threat to the building there is a requirement for general surveillance of the areas throughout the building accessible by the public. This will be achieved by CCTV cameras installed in the following locations. Please note that some of these cameras may have been mentioned in previous sections (Figure 16-10)

4.7   INTERACTION POINTS   During this report it has been described that all points of interaction with the public be fitted with duress devices and fixed cameras.

Recommendation 29—The use of this duress system should be integrated into a building wide set of policies and procedures which includes the response from external agencies, such as the Armed Response Agencies, Law enforcement agencies etc. Specific training should be given to all persons interacting with the public including conflict resolution training. At no point should an untrained and unqualified member of staff be put at risk by dealing with disturbed and possibly violent persons.

The standpoint of the policies and procedures should be report (activate the system), retreat (to a safe area), minimize exposure (Inter-departmental communication and lock down) and wait (for a qualified response).

Type	Location	Description
PTZ	Basement base of stairs from 1st floor	General surveillance of stairwell and washrooms access
Fixed	Main entrance	Surveillance of all persons entering the building
Fixed	South entrance	Surveillance of all persons entering the building
PTZ	Main foyer	Surveillance of main foyer and line up area for Collections
PTZ	2nd floor top of stairs from 1st floor	General surveillance of stairwells and 2nd floor booths

FIGURE 16-10   CCTV locations.   *Courtesy:* Dave Loban.

4.8   BUILDING EXTERIOR   The building exterior is open and provides adequate natural surveillance during daylight hours. Excessive foliage and treed refuge areas have been removed.

However, during darkness, the light levels around the building are not to adequate standards. The current light levels around the building and walkways are insufficient as measured as a part of this review and the minimum foot candles at ground level for the areas around the building need adjusting.

Recommendation 30—It is recommended that the lighting around the perimeter of the building and parking lot be reviewed and brought up to current standards.

The design of the building provides a number of refuge areas at the basement level. It is recommended that lighting be installed in the eaves of these areas to discourage people taking refuge. This will also remove the dark spots around the building making the use of walkways safer and provide Security patrols advanced warning and identification of persons in these areas.

4.8.1 CCTV Coverage As described during the 2015 CCTV review, there are a number of areas around the building requiring CCTV surveillance. The perimeter of the building and windows at ground level should be covered as well as walkways to the parking lot and areas in which vagrancy and drug use occur such as the loading dock and lower office windows area (Figure 16-11).

4.9 LOGISTICAL SECURITY

4.9.1 Security Organization Currently there is no security department within the Company's organization. This has resulted in separate departments assuming the responsibility for definition of security measures in their individual areas. This has created the fragmented and limited system currently in place.

Type	Location	Description
Fixed	Building SW	General surveillance building south
Fixed	Building SE	General surveillance building east
Fixed	Building NW	General surveillance building north
Fixed	Building NW	General surveillance building west
Fixed	Loading dock	General surveillance of loading dock area and refuges
Fixed	Building NE	Surveillance of refuge area outside basement offices windows
PTZ	North	General surveillance of north building, refuge areas, and access to parking lot

FIGURE 16-11 CCTV coverage–external. *Courtesy:* Dave Loban.

Recommendation 31—It is recommended that a Security Manager position be created within the organization as a part of the Risk Management group. This position will provide the leadership and direction for the development of all aspects of the Company's security needs and be responsible for the management and control of security related issues and programs.

The qualifications for the position should include but not be limited to the following:

- Certified Protection Professional designation from the American Society of Industrial Security
- Knowledge and experience in risk mitigation practices
- Knowledge of physical security systems
- Knowledge and experience in the development and implementation of corporation level security programs
- Experience in police and procedure development

4.9.2 Security Policies and Procedures There is an apparent lack of security policies and procedures in place within the Company organization. Policies and procedures are the backbone of the security program. They provide a guide for all members of the site community about all security operations and responsibilities for all levels of the organization.

The adoption of security policies and procedures will ensure that security will become an integral part of the site operations and management. This education, adoption, and engagement methodology has been proven to be the most beneficial way of increasing the security profile of any organization.

Recommendation 32—The following list summarizes the policies and procedures not identified by the Company during the review and therefore, should be developed and implemented:

- Equipment security
  - Storage of equipment and vehicles
- Security Assistance Involving Disturbed People
- Internal Investigations Policy
- Security Organization Policy, including Security Records Management
- Human Resources Security
- Workplace Threats and Violence Policy, including Incident Assessment / Resolution Process
- Communications
- Public Information Program / External Communications
- Information Technology

- Security Systems Management and Computer Security
- Employee Protection of Computer Hardware, Software, and Data

4.9.4 Security Awareness and Training   Security awareness and training of the employees and contractors within the organization is low. Security awareness is an effective tool when implemented throughout an organization because it brings to bear the entire population of the site in providing a secure environment and mitigating security related risk.

> **Recommendation 33**—The Company would benefit by basing its Corporate Security Program on the principle "Security is Everyone's Responsibility." Effective implementation of this concept requires the adoption of a corporate culture based on this philosophy. Changing the present culture towards this objective requires the development of a security awareness program for management, employees, and contractors to ensure a full understanding of the security philosophies and mandates of the Company. This includes educating the same regarding the policies and procedures in place to ensure the security of the organization, assets, business, and safety of its employees, contractors, and stakeholders.

1. A security awareness program should be developed for management, employees, and contractors to ensure a full understanding of the security philosophies and mandates of the Company, and the policies and procedures in place to ensure the security of the organization, assets, business, and safety of its employees, contractors, and stakeholders. This adoption of security would provide a cultural change for risk mitigation into the organization and would provide a corporate model of "Security is Everyone's Responsibility."
2. The training should be developed in two categories:
   - **General**—covering topics applicable to all stakeholders and employees.
   - **Specific**—developed based on the type and level to meet the requirements of each business and organizational level.
3. Topics covered in the Security Awareness Program should include:
   - The threats and risks faced by the industry and organization.
   - Security policies and procedures:
     - General
     - Department and job specific
   - The nature of sensitive material and physical assets.
   - Employee and contractor security responsibilities.
   - Security of operations, including requirements for proper handling of sensitive material in physical form, marking, transmission, storage, and destruction.
   - Consequences of failure to properly employ security practices in the workplace, including the consequences to the organization as detailed in the Severity section of the Risk Management Process.
   - The training is to be given to all members of the Company organization and be a part of the orientation process for employees and contractors.
   - The medium and delivery of the training program is to be determined by Company's departments based on operational and geographical suitability.
   - Following the implementation security awareness should be included into the Company business operations and communications and be maintained by regular meeting and discussions and refresher and/or increased security related training.
4. Security awareness training should also form part of the job orientation process for all new employees and contractors.[3]

SECURITY MANAGEMENT PLAN (SAMPLE)

Standards Document Layout

The document is split into six sections:

- Section 1—Background
  - Security Program Development
  - Zoning
  - Zone Physical Security Standards

- Section 2—Physical Security Standards
  - Access Control
  - Electronic Access Control
  - Door Security
  - Windows
  - Lighting
  - Intrusion Detection
  - Panic Alarms
  - CCTV
- Section 3—Logistical Security
  - Information Security
  - Security Awareness
  - Security Intelligence
  - Electronic Device Sweeps
- Section 4—Administrative Security
  - Human Resources Security
  - Employee and Contractor Screening
  - Executive and Employee Protection
  - Security Policies and Procedures
- Section 5—Operational Security
  - Key Control
  - Monitoring and Response
  - Incident and Crisis Management
  - Liaison with External Resources
- Section 6—Quality Management
  - Incident Management Debrief
  - Drills and Exercises
  - Intelligence Management
  - Systems Maintenance

OVERVIEW

Section 1—Security Program Overview

The purpose of this document is to provide an overview of the Security Program. This program provides a systematic approach to the development of site security throughout the organization in accordance with the corporate security philosophy. Adoption of this process will ensure a standardized security program for all operations which will in turn support safety and leadership mandates and enhance the protection of personnel, assets, facilities, and core business.

Development Process

The development process follows a step by step approach which addresses all aspects of a comprehensive and integrated security program:

- Technical
- Operations
- Logistics
- Administration

Development of each component of the program is required to provide the correct level of security and the ability to manage risk and counter threats to the operations and organization. The development process is designed to factor in all operational, administrative, and geographical aspects of the operations with corporate standards for risk mitigation. The development of this program requires interaction and effort at the site and operations levels with support from the Corporate Risk and IS groups in order to ensure its suitability at the local and organizational level and ensure the success of the program. The program will provide all levels of the organization a working system for the management of security and the countering of threats and the mitigation of risk[4] (Figure 16-12).

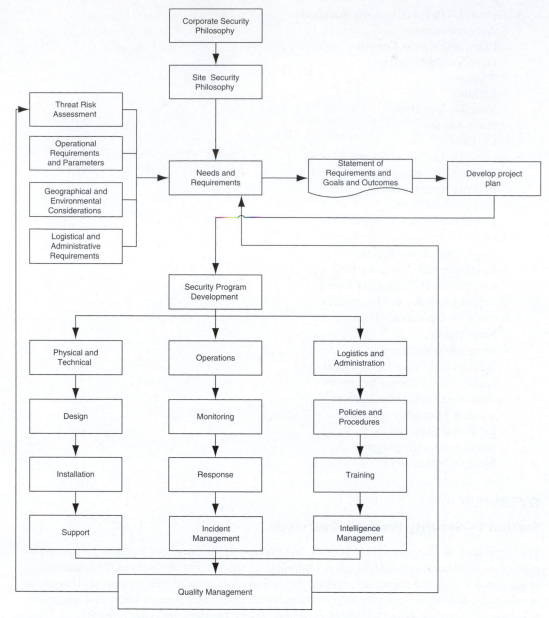

FIGURE 16-12 Flow chart for developing the security plan.   *Courtesy:* Dave Loban.

The above information is designed to assist practitioners in developing a sound Risk Management protocol and procedure together with physical security standards.

A sound organization will also need to have a Business Continuity Program and a tried and tested IM protocol in place which is tested on a regular basis either by practical exercising of the plan components or in a table top environment.

BUSINESS CONTINUITY MANAGEMENT AND INCIDENT MANAGEMENT

What is BCM?

Business Continuity Management (BCM) is a business-owned, and driven process that establishes a fit-for-purpose strategic and operational framework that

- will proactively improve corporate resilience against the disruption of a business or organization's ability to achieve its key objectives;

- will provide a practiced methodology of restoring the corporation's ability to supply its key products and/or services to an agreed level within an agreed time frame after a disruption; and
- will deliver a proven capability to manage a business disruption and protect the corporation or organization reputation.

Why should organizations create a BCM?

Primarily BCM is an important element and strategy of good business management, service provision, and entrepreneurial prudence. Operational personnel are responsible for maintaining the ability for the operation/business to function without short or long term disruption. All activities are subject to disruptions, such as fire, flooding, and power failure. A BCM provides a corporation the capability to adequately react to any operational disruptions while protecting welfare, safety, and business integrity.

BCM must be regarded as a value solution for business and should not be regarded as a costly planning process. Some of the important benefits of a BCM are the ability to proactively identify the impacts of an operational disruption; the corporation has in place an effective response to disruptions which minimizes the impact on the overall health of the organization; it maintains an ability to manage unsuitable risks and encourages cross-team functioning; the corporation is able to demonstrate a credible response through a process of exercising. By adopting and adapting a BCM and a response plan could enhance its business reputation as well as being able to demonstrate its ability to manage and recover from a serious disruption may well gain a competitive advantage.

When business is disrupted, it can cost money. Lost revenues plus extra expenses means reduced profits. Insurance does not cover all costs and cannot replace customers that defect to the competition. A business continuity plan to continue business is essential. Development of a business continuity plan includes four steps:

- Conduct a business impact analysis to identify time sensitive or critical business functions and processes and the resources that support them.
- Identify, document, and implement to recover critical business functions and processes.
- Organize a business continuity team and compile a business continuity plan to manage a business disruption.
- Conduct training for the business continuity team and testing and exercises to evaluate recovery strategies and the plan.

Information technology (IT) includes many components, such as networks, servers, desktop and laptop computers, and wireless devices. The ability to run both office productivity and enterprise software is critical. Therefore, recovery strategies for information technology should be developed so technology can be restored in time to meet the needs of the business. Manual workarounds should be part of the IT plan so business can continue while computer systems are being restored.[5]

What are the outcomes of an effective BCM program?

The outcomes of an effective BCM program are:

- that key products and services are identified and protected, ensuring their continuity;
- that an incident management (IM) capability is enabled to provide an effective response;
- that staff are trained to respond effectively to an incident or disruption through appropriate exercising;
- that stakeholder requirements are understood and able to be delivered;
- that staff receive adequate support and communications in the event of a disruption;
- that the company's reputation is protected; and
- that legal and regulatory standards and obligations are in compliance.

There are three key components to a successful Business Continuity Program:

Physical Component—PROACTIVE	Crisis Management Component—REACTIVE
Physical Security	Business Continuance
Environmental	Damage Control
Power	Incident Management
HVAC	Life/Safety

Physical Component—PROACTIVE	Crisis Management Component—REACTIVE
Water	Public Relations
Voice/Data Circuits	
Data Security	
Data Backup/Vaulting	
Risk Management	
Business Impact Analysis	
Alternate Site Strategy	
Business IT	

Recovery Component—REACTIVE
Business Recovery Plans
IT Disaster Recovery Plan

The Business Continuity Plan Structure (Figure 16-13)

Training

Training is essential to ensure that everyone knows what to do when there is an emergency, or disruption of business operations. Everyone needs training to become familiar with protective actions for life safety (e.g., evacuation, shelter, shelter-in-place, and lockdown). Review protective actions for life safety and conduct evacuation drills ("fire drills") as required by local regulations. Sheltering and lockdown drills should also be conducted. Employees should receive training to become familiar with safety, building security, information security, and other loss prevention programs.

Members of emergency response, business continuity, and crisis communications teams should be trained so they are familiar with their role and responsibilities as defined within the plans. Team leaders should receive a higher level of training, including incident command system training, so they can lead their teams. Review applicable regulations to determine training requirements. Records documenting the scope of training, participants, instructor, and duration should be maintained.[6]

INCIDENT MANAGEMENT

One of the most important steps to take is developing an incident/crisis management team that is available to handle a crisis based on unfolding events. There are four key elements or components in this regard:

1. Scope
2. Objective
3. Plan Considerations
4. Key elements of the plan

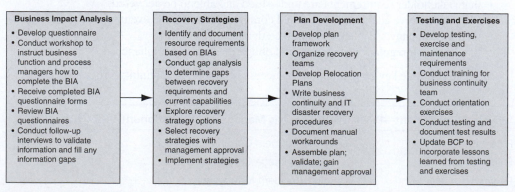

FIGURE 16-13   BCM process chart.   *Courtesy:* Department of Homeland Security.

Scope	Objective
• Emergency Response • Crisis Management • Resumption of Operations • Expanded Recover • Complete Restoration	• Ensure the safety of all employees and the general public • Meet the customers requirements through continuity of server • Maintain a strong financial position and acceptable levels of cash flow & profit. • Protect and perpetuate a positive corporate image • Comply with legal and regulatory directives • Minimize losses and liabilities • Achieve a full recovery of business operations
Plan considerations	**Key elements of the plan**
• Fire • Natural Disaster • Sabotage and Bomb Threat • Civil Disturbance • Operational Mishaps • Workplace Violence with serious injuries or death	• Site emergency action plan • Hazardous material control and response • Notification process (internal & external) • Damage assessment • Cleanup and salvage • Resumption of time sensitive operations • Recovery of temporary operations • Process for permanent recovery

FIGURE 16-14   Management plan components.   *Courtesy:* J. Spindlove.

Emergency Response/Crisis Management/Incident Management Plan Components (Figure 16-14)

WORLD HEALTH ORGANIZATION

In 2009, the WHO declared a Global Pandemic from Swine Flu, (since then we have the threat of Ebola). It was the first time in forty-one years that the WHO had declared a pandemic. Many organizations at the time tried to assess their capability and capacity to handle this sudden crisis and everyone wanted to know how companies were planning to manage the risk.

Many companies and public organizations likely found the following at that time:

- They had no formal/consistent approach to BCM.
- There was fragmented ownership of the BCM topic.
- No common language/terminology across the business i.e., Crisis Management, Disaster Management, Incident Management, Disaster Recovery, etc.
- Poor visibility of how robust these BCM plans were and when they were last updated and tested.
- No national level plans to deal with Country/Global incidents like Pandemics.

In summary, a large proportion of companies were not organized or prepared to handle the Pandemic crisis.

There are many terms to describe an IM Plan as we see above—for our purposes, we will refer to the Crisis/Incident Management Team (IMT).

There are key factors developing a response mechanism to a crisis or MI and I have shown that in this diagram (Figure 16-15)

"Invocation" is the act of declaring that an organization's response plans and/or capabilities such as IM are to be put into effect. Invocation is one of the five elements of incident response (see diagram above) and

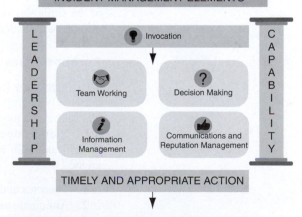

FIGURE 16-15   Incident management pillars.
Courtesy: J. Spindlove.

if clearly defined can lead to timely and appropriate action supported by the critical pillars of leadership and capability. Leadership is considered a major factor in the success of a response to a crisis.

An incident, if well managed does not need to turn into a CRISIS.

Incident Definition

An incident is a situation that might be, or could lead to, business disruption, loss, emergency, or crisis. Remember that an incident if well managed does not have to turn into a crisis! The key is incident awareness and recognizing an incident then thinking about trigger points, escalation and Incident Management Team (IMT) call-out. Although in most cases an incident may be obvious, look out for the creeping crisis, in most cases they can be mitigated if recognized early enough.

An example of a poorly managed incident that was watched around the globe was the sinking of the Italian cruise ship Costa Concordia in 2012, off Giglio Island resulting in the death of twenty-three people. Yes, running aground was a disaster and it was further compounded by a crew that were left leaderless as the captain was one of the first to leave the sinking ship.

A court in Italy convicted five people of manslaughter over the Costa Concordia shipwreck. The ship's crisis coordinator for the Italian cruise company Costa Cruises, Roberto Ferranini, was given the lengthiest sentence of two years and ten months.

Concordia's hotel director was sentenced to two years and six months while two bridge officers and a helmsman sentences ranged from one year and eight months to one year and eleven months.[7]

Recognizing the Incident

- Is it obvious?
- Is it a creeping crisis?
- Do you think worst case?
- Do you understand your vulnerabilities?
- How to avoid starting on the "back foot"?

At this point you will need to decide if you will call out the IMT and should be reviewing your criteria for invoking the Crisis Plan.

The Incident Management Team

- How is the team called out?
- Who is on the team?
- Where will the team meet under different circumstances?

When it comes to team working, it is important to consider who is on the IMT and what are their roles and responsibilities. Failure to understand roles and responsibilities often leads to confusion and misunderstandings and false expectations. Team leaders will have many if not all of the skills shown below. What is important is that the group operates as a team for a common purpose with a clear strategy and objectives.

Competencies

The Emergency Planning Society (UK) has a developed Core Competencies Framework that lists twelve competences that are considered necessary to be a "Competent Practitioner" for emergency management. They include knowledge, judgment skills, energy, experience, and motivation required to respond adequately to the demands of managing a crisis. A competent practitioner will be able to demonstrate achievements and experience across the following areas:

1. Theories and concepts in emergency management
2. Anticipate and assess the risk of emergencies
3. Plan for emergencies
4. Plan for business continuity

5. Validate emergency and business continuity plans
6. Communicate to enhance resilience
7. Manage the response to emergencies
8. Manage the recovery from emergencies
9. Act effectively across your organization
10. Co-operate with other organizations
11. Debrief after an incident, exercise, or other activity
12. Manage computer generated data to enhance decision making[8]

Your company should have in place a major incident reporting procedure. The procedure must be a corporate requirement and does not replace the need to report certain incidents under local, State, and Federal legal requirements. A Major Incident (MI) may either cause or have the potential to cause:

- fatality, multiple serious injuries, cause of ill health (either immediate or delayed) to a visitor, contractor, or a member of the public;
- serious business disruptions or extensive damage to property, inside or outside the establishment;
- the attendance of external emergency services;
- the company to be involved in prosecution or serious financial loss.

Decisions in advance need to determine exactly where the IMT will work from and determine the needs of the Team and the facility being provided. At a minimum the following is a sample list:

- Functioning phone system
- Headsets
- Direct lines, video and teleconferencing
- Radios, Computers, Fax Machines, Printers
- Incident Boards, Maps and Reference Manuals
- Stationary, Shredders
- Communications links (Wi-Fi, Cellular etc.)

Formal meetings within the IMT are important. They allow for a set-agenda to be followed and for team members to provide situational reports from their respective areas of responsibility. They also allow for objectives to be set, actions to be allocated and reviewed at subsequent meetings to ensure that the response is in accordance with the plan of action.

Action Management Process

There also needs to be a thorough action management process that not only records actions as they are agreed but also monitors their progress between meetings, and when difficulties are identified refers back to the IM in a timely manner. The progress of actions should be an integral part of subsequent meetings as should the referencing back to the aims and objectives to ascertain that they always remain current. An action management process will:

- Compare all actions against the current aim and objectives and report any inconsistencies.
- Chase any outstanding actions; receive the responses and update the master record.
- Identify the outstanding actions prior to the next meeting.

Create new actions if the updates identify a need to without referring to the IM (if appropriate).

Conducting Team Meetings

- What other organizations do you interface with?
- When do their meetings take place?
- How do you dovetail your meetings with those of other interested parties as well as other levels of management within your corporate hierarchy?

Where meetings are taking place at various levels of management within an organization and/or with external partners it is important to establish a cohesive rhythm. This process therefore enables one meeting to feed to the next and for decisions to be briefed at subsequent meetings. As an example, an IMT meeting may precede a meeting of the Board thereby enabling the Board to base strategic decision-making upon the latest information from the IMT. Board decisions will then be discussed at the next IMT meeting and so on.

Team meetings:

- Set an agenda
- Meeting should last no longer than 20–40 minutes
- Hold meetings once or twice a day and likely more frequently in early emergency phase of the incident
Think about need for 24/7 working shifts and long days

It takes twenty years to build a reputation and five minutes to ruin it!
A tarnished reputation and the way an incident is handled can either make or break an organization. Failure to plan is planning to fail.

There are many instances one can point to where the actions or deficiencies of those tasked with being the face of the company cause more reputation damage than was ever anticipated.

Two significant events are available that adequately describe the company's failure to plan and respond accordingly.

On July 6, 2013, a runaway train in the Canadian province of Quebec loaded with oil crashed and exploded in the center of the small town of Lac-Megantic, destroying a large area of the town center and killing forty-seven residents. The train was operated by a U.S. company Montreal Maine and Atlantic. Its founder and CEO took four days to get to the town in Quebec and when he did so was heard to say that he had suffered too. He provided a misleading statement on the cause of the crash before any determination as to its cause was uncovered by investigators. It did not help that he could not speak French and the vast majority of his audience did not understand or speak English. The resulting fallout from this incident which was headline news around the world was that the company filed for bankruptcy within the following four weeks and ceased to operate.

Don't become the news story—BP Oil Spill, Gulf of Mexico—April 2012
On April 20, 2010, the Deep Water Horizon oil rig in the Gulf of Mexico operated by British Petroleum (BP) erupted in a ball of fire and sent millions of gallons of oil into the Gulf of Mexico. The explosion killed eleven oil rig workers and supposedly caused the worst environmental disaster in U.S. history. Tony Hayward was at the time the CEO of BP and based in the BP HQ in London. He became the face of the disaster. He was in front of the cameras when he made the off the cuff remark that "he wanted his life back"—offhand comments to the media will always backfire and this one reverberated throughout the United States. Most Americans perceived him as an offensive buffoon and President Obama stated that he would fire him.[9]

The above are two examples of being ill-prepared to respond in the public arena to a crisis regardless of the actions being taken to mitigate the incident. The media focused on Tony Hayward's comments and he became the news. Very few news channels covered the overall story or focused on the dead oil rig crew, but Tony Hayward became the center of attention by his seemingly idiotic and offhand comments.

INCIDENT AWARENESS

Gaining incident awareness is a key element of a logical decision making process. Incident awareness is the process of **perceiving**, **comprehending, interpreting, and evaluating** what is happening in a crisis combined with the ability to identify and model foreseeable future developments. Incident awareness and decision-making should not be considered stages on their own; they are strands that flow throughout all stages of an incident including the assessing of trigger points and whether they have been reached.

It is crucially important to identify all sources of information, however, the most important source will be your trusted team whether they are at the front end or part of the IMT. Accurate and tested information will enable good decision-making.

Difficulties with decision making:

- Incident awareness?
- Competence?
- Information overload!
  - Use of the decision-making tools
  - Developing incident objectives
  - Logging information during incidents
  - Ensuring decisions are justifiable and defensible

Defensive versus Defensible

Don't become a defensive decision-maker:

When it comes to decision-making, it's really important to understand and recognize the difference between being defensive and defensible. Defensive decision-making is based on self-protection with associated misguided risk aversion and using an overly narrow frame of incident awareness.

A defensible decision maker will be rooted in an appreciation of the information available with a thorough understanding and assessment of that information to determine what is the right thing to do under the circumstances.

Defensive decisions result from:

- being self-protective
- misguided risk aversion
- overly narrow frame of reference

Defensible decisions will be rooted in:

- Assessed, analyzed, and critically evaluated evidence
- Appreciation and understanding of that evidence
- That understanding suggests the right thing to do under the circumstances.

So, why do we worry about the above elements and what is the value to any organization of a defensible decision maker. One example clearly is the BP disaster—Tony Hayward was being defensive.

With sound decision-making will flow sound results.

Outcomes—Good Decision Making

- Protection of life
- Risk of injury mitigated
- Reputation protected
- Achieve overall strategy and objectives
- Possible protection from future litigation and prosecution
- A confident and professional response
- Reduces risk aversion
- Should receive support of organization if decisions were assessed for given circumstances—even if harm results!

Consider the following **Three W's** as a Decision-Making Tool:

- *What* is the information?
- *What* does the information mean to us as a group, organization, or business?
- *What* do we do now we have the relevant information?

The tool itself for decision making is broken down into five stages:

Stage One: Define the incident or crisis, what is happening, what has happened, and seek clarification of matters that have come to your attention.

Stage Two: The next stage is assessing the situation, including any specific threat, the risk of harm, and the potential for benefits.

Stage Three: What, if any, are the legal and contractual obligations— review applicable policies and procedures.

Stage Four: Identify the different ways to make a particular decision or resolve the situation with the least risk of harm.

When developing response options, outcomes should be assessed against potential consequences and risks such as:

Political (e.g., food and fuel shortages will attract Government action)

Environmental (e.g., pollution will involve EPA or OSHA on enforcement)

Social (e.g., loss of access to homes by adjacent communities due to fire)

Technological (e.g., decision to shut down mainframe may have wider implications)

Economic (e.g., effect on customers to sustain their businesses)

Ethical (e.g., effects on health and wellbeing of staff etc.)

Legal/Regulatory (e.g., required to act or failure to recognize right to life)

Organizational (e.g., wider impact upon organization from loss of assets)

Stage Five: The final stage is making and implementing decisions. Remember to monitor the outcomes and ensure that the decisions are proportionate to the circumstances, that they are legitimate, you are actually authorized to make such decisions and that they are ethical.

This process does not end, in fact constant information flow is highly valued; the cycle must be continued as further information is received (constant incident awareness) and following the monitoring of the decision making outcomes. Finally, decisions are not valid unless they can be justified under post incident review and scrutiny, so remember it is vital to keep records that include:

- Sequential numbering
- Dates and Times
- Information and Assessment
- Options available
- Decision and reasoning
- Reason why other options were dismissed
- Recorders details
- Capability to have sign off by principal decision maker

MANAGING INFORMATION

Sound information management leads to good incident awareness that in turn leads to good decision-making. The key asset in managing an incident is high quality, accurate and assessed information. Management of information is therefore crucial. Information needs to be actively sought and channels need to be monitored. Processing information from all channels needs really good team working and sharing of data. It also needs exceptional horizon scanning and assessment tools and may require a dedicated team role. The speed of twenty-first century media is now in split seconds rather than tomorrows newspapers.

An example of speed of communication in twenty-first century

ASIANA Airlines Flight 214—July 2013

Incident—On July 6, 2013, the ASIANA Boeing 777-200 crashed on final approach to San Francisco International Airport. The speed with which this crash was publicized defines how fast information is disseminated in the modern era and not coming from any credible news source:

Timeline:

- Boeing 777 crashes onto runway at 11.27 A.M.
- 11.28 A.M. within 30 seconds a photo of the crash was posted on Twitter by a Google employee boarding another flight (on Twitter before passengers have even evacuated the aircraft)

- 11.30 A.M. aircrafts emergency shuts deployed
- 11.45 A.M. a passenger on the flight posts a Facebook photo of the accident
- 1.20 P.M. Boeing issues a statement on its Twitter account
- 3.00 P.M. National Transportation Safety Board holds press conference
- 3.39 P.M. The airline involved releases a statement

Communication

In any major incident or event, there will always be a need to communicate and getting the timing of that correct is often a challenge.

The important points to remember:

- *Who*—which impacted or interested parties need to be communicated to and with
- *What*—assess what message or information needs to be disseminated
- *When*—determine the timing and frequency of information communication

The message and the messaging are important—you or the team need to tell the story, be honest in the communication, avoid placing blame and be compassionate. The message should be concise and consistent with the event in question. Sign off from the communication.

Those receiving the message expect you to provide a level of reassurance, while acknowledging the impact the incident is having on those concerned. The message should if needed provide timelines for updates relative to progress and/or recovery.

TESTING YOUR ORGANIZATIONAL RESPONSE

If you have established a Business Continuity Plan and set up response teams to handle a crisis it is critical that the plans are tested to make sure that all involved know what their particular role is during an incident or crisis.

Consider a recovery strategy that requires relocating to another facility and configuring equipment at that facility. Can equipment at the alternate facility be configured in time to meet the planned recovery time objective? Can alarm systems be heard and understood throughout the building to warn all employees to take protective action? Can members of emergency response or business continuity teams be alerted to respond in the middle of the night? Testing is necessary to determine whether or not the various parts of the preparedness program will work.[10] Depending on the type of business the exercise can be done in a real life setting or in a tabletop-style exercise. The following is an example of how to run a Tabletop Exercise Scenario.

EXERCISE OBJECTIVES

- Understanding why we have Continuity and Disaster Recovery Planning
- Understanding the purpose of the exercise
- Outline the exercise
- The scenario of self-assessment exercise
- What did we find out?
- Actions to take away
- Any other questions?

WHY CONTINUITY AND DISASTER RECOVERY PLANNING?

Definitions

- **Business Continuity:**
  - Managing the risks to business operations from disruptions.
- **Business Continuity Planning:**
  - How a company prepares for future incidents that could jeopardize the organization and its short- and long-term health. (Incidents include local incidents like building fires, regional incidents like earthquakes, national incidents like pandemic illnesses, and terrorist attacks)

- **Business Continuity Plan:**
  - Documents how the company will recover and restore, partially or completely, interrupted critical function(s) within a predetermined time after a disaster or extended disruption.
- **Continuity Management:**
  - The management process to help the development of Business Continuity Plans and Disaster Recovery Plans and ensuring that plans are matched, effective, and tested.
- **Disaster Recovery Planning:**
  - The process of regaining access to the data, hardware/software, and services necessary to resume critical business operations after a natural, accidental, or human induced disaster.
- **Disaster Recovery Plan:**
  - Documents how access to data, hardware/software, and services necessary to resume critical business operations, after a disaster, will be undertaken to achieve the requirements of the Business (as defined in the Business Continuity Plan).

INCIDENT MANAGEMENT EXERCISE

The Purpose of the Exercise

- When something happens it will not be planned!
- If we exercise we become fit
- By working together, we have more strength
  - in knowledge
  - in experience
- Communication and basic requirements is the key
  - Who do I contact?
  - How do I contact?
  - What do they need to know?
  - What do I need to know?
- Are there alternative actions I should consider?
- Does my plan need updating or changing?

For the purpose of this exercise we will have events spanning a 72-hour period

- The scenario is based on incidents that have actually happened
- Timeframes will be adjusted to fit the time available for the test:
  - First 24 hours—**Each 2hrs** will be about **10 minutes** (2 hour)
  - 24 to 48 Hours—**Each 4hrs** will be about **10 minutes** (1 hour)
  - 48 to 72 hours—**Each 6 hrs** will be about **10 minutes** (40 minutes)
- The Disaster Recovery Plan and any other supporting documentation may be referred to at any time
- Ask as many questions as you wish
- The Self-Assessment Exercise will finish with short sessions on:
  - **Lessons Learned**
  - **Actions to take away**

The objective of this section is to provide a scenario for the testing of plans, as your business or organization develops its Continuity Management capability and experience. The severity of the event and the complexity of the test is identified as 1 (Low) to 3 (High). Severity 3 tests would relate to loss of a major part of the business and loss of life. The following is just an example template to utilize for a Tabletop Exercise.

The Scenario Self-Assessment Exercise Test Set	Severity (1 Low to 3 High)
1. Terrorist / Criminal activity resulting in complete loss of building	3
2. Access to premises lost due to chemical spillage in access road	1
3. Loss of network services due to an intermittent fault	1
4. Fire in a Server Room resulting in its loss, complication of network failure	2

5. Power Failure to computer room   1
6. Pandemic Medical Emergency   2

The required test Scenario should be identified based on discussions with your organizational or business leaders to determine the correct type of scenario. As our text in the last 15 chapters has focused on terrorism the scenario chosen will be a terrorist event.

Scenario Test 1.1

Phase 1: First 24 Hours (2 hours = 10 minutes)

1. **6 A.M. Wednesday**: You receive the information from your operations manager that external landline communications to your premises have failed. On the news and Twitter, you hear that an explosion has occurred at or very near your premises.
2. **8 A.M. (2 hours) Wednesday**: You are unable to reach your office and there is much congestion on the roads and some roads are blocked by police; you are informed that there has been an incident but that it is apparently under control. Operations at the premises have been directly affected and communications are severely affected. There are no network or voice communications by landline outside of the premises.
   Applications have been unavailable for 2 hours.
   Email is unavailable from or to the premises.
   Your Management Board is asking for a status update.
3. **10 A.M. (4 hours) Wednesday**: Some key staff are able to get to the premises location, but access is restricted.
4. **12 P.M. (6 Hours) Wednesday**: News is broadcast on the TV that a Terrorist incident has occurred and that some communications in the City have also been cut.
5. **2 P.M. (8 hours) Wednesday**: Alternative means of communications are assessed.

As mentioned earlier, one of the main problems in an incident is information is incorrect or lacking. Do not think ahead for the team and provide them with any additional information. If they are floundering help them think logically through the problem. If information is lacking they should assume the worse and plan accordingly. It is easier to step back than to react when it is too late.

1. *Key actions: When to declare an emergency? Who to contact? What activities to start? Engage intraday processes, are copies of the plan available? Does the Team have stationery, cell phones, laptops, and other equipment? Do they have a prearranged place to meet?*

Key staff will often not be available

2. *Key Actions: What should the staff available do? How does the plan help? What communications to the Board are necessary? What communications with the Client (if any)?*

See 2 above

News Broadcast—some communications cut

3. *Key Actions: Information will come from various sources. It is important to make an assessment of its credibility and likely impact.*

Alternative means of communications

4. *Key Actions: Plans should have included this as a basic requirement. In an emergency it will be necessary to assess methods of communications the need and the reliability.*

Scenario Test 1.2

Phase 1. First 24 hours (4 hours = 10 minutes)

1. **4 P.M. (10 hours) Wednesday:** No additional information has come in.
2. **6 P.M. (12 hours) Wednesday:** Announced on the radio that two other bombs have been found and a third device has exploded close to the premises. Staff are concerned about their safety.
3. **8 P.M. (14 hours) Wednesday:** An alternative means of external communications is considered viable using wireless technology.

4. **10 P.M. (16 hours) Wednesday**: A device explodes at the perimeter of the premises, it is close to power lines. Damage is minor but there is broken glass in the buildings as some windows are broken.
5. **12 A.M. (18 hours) Wednesday:** Contractors on site to repair board up windows. Staff reports some equipment missing from their offices.
6. **2 A.M. (20 hours) Thursday:** No additional information.
7. **4 A.M. (22 hours) Thursday:** No additional information.
8. **6 A.M. (24 hours) Thursday:** Board asks for another status update.

Information is lacking what should the team do?

- *Key Actions: Is there enough information to proceed? If not what do the Team do?*

Two devices found staff concerns

- *Key Actions: At this stage the information is still that publicly broadcast valid if the information is correct. (with the Authorities) Take best advice. Are HR informed and fully involved? What communications to Staff and to the Board?*

Wireless communications alternative to be implemented

- *Key Actions: How will the team manage implementation? Not Micro Manage? Consider: How ordered? How resourced? How paid for? Implications of other possible events?*

9. **Explosion at Perimeter**
   - *Key Actions: Need for delegation of tasks. Liaison with authorities, security of the site, damage to site and utilities, danger to staff from debris.*
10. **Contractors on Site**
    - *Key Actions: Where did the contractors come from? Who is managing them? If equipment is missing whom is the loss reported to? What additional security measures are taken? Who needs to be informed?*
11. **No additional information**
    - *Key Actions: What actions should the team be taking?*
12. **No additional information**
    - *Key Actions: What actions should the team be taking? Suggest they should be reviewing current status. Asking for updates from staff under their control. Seeking information from authorities. Considering what may happen next.*
13. **Board asks for an update**
    - **Key Actions:** Plans should include how information is provided and who it is provided to.

Scenario Test 1.3
Phase 2: 24 hours—48 hours (4 hours = 10 minutes)

1. **10 A.M. (28 hours) Thursday:** Work on an alternative Communications service begins. The external telecoms company has indicated that repairs to the landlines will take two days as a significant section of copper cabling has been removed and will have to be replaced.
2. **2 P.M. (32 hours) Thursday:** Civil Authorities report on TV that the incident is down to terrorist activities. The loss of communications is a separate criminal event.
3. **6 P.M. (36 hours) Thursday:** Senior Board Management is asking for an update and assessment of the situation.
4. **10 P.M. (40 hours) Thursday:** Technician advises that alternative communications channels are operational but at a reduced band width.
5. **2 A.M. (44 hours) Friday:** No additional information.
6. **6 A.M. (48 hours) Friday:** No additional information.

This is the 2nd 24-hour period. How is the team resourced to cover 48 hours?

1. **The unexpected happens copper cabling is missing; external utility supplier gives estimate of two days to recover**
   - *Key Actions: On this information are the alternative arrangements considered adequate? What if the repair takes more than two days? Are the explosions and the thefts related?*

2. **Terrorist activities confirmed for the bombings**
   - *Key Actions: Are we dealing with two incidents, one of terrorist activities and other of criminal damage and theft?*

3. **The Board is asking for an update**
   - *Key Actions: Is the communications team involved? What sort of message are we going to give to the Board, the clients, and the public?*
   - *Is the team going to check on previous actions and clean-up from the explosion of the previous day?*

4. **Alternative Communications but reduced Bandwidth**
   - *Key Actions: What bandwidth is needed to maintain operations? What are the priorities? How can the bandwidth be managed to reduce unnecessary communications?*

5. **No additional information**
   - *Key Actions: update and review of current actions.*

6. **No additional information**
   - *Key Actions: What additional actions are necessary? What monitoring needs to take place?*

Phase 3: 48 hours--72 hours (6 hours = 10 minutes)

1. **12 P.M. (54 hours) Friday:** Investigation into the missing equipment identifies that it has been taken by people pretending to be contractors. The police have recovered some property.

2. **6 P.M. (60 hours) Friday:** No additional information.

3. **12 A.M. (66 hours) Saturday:** The authorities announce that although there is still a state of alert, the situation has stabilized and appears under control.

The utility company confirm a completion time for cable repairs at 4 P.M. Saturday

1. **6 A.M. (72 hours) Saturday:** The employees at the site are shaken by the events and want to know what can be done to protect them on the site.

Your Board asks for an update.

End of Test

Phase 3 This stage is getting to the end of the incident (6 hours = 10 minutes).
This is the 3rd 24-hour period. How is the team resourced to cover 48 hours?

1. **Information on loss of equipment**
   - *Key Actions: This shows the importance of record keeping during an emergency. Information records may be needed for legal and review purposes. Who is liaising with the authorities?*

2. **No Additional information**
   - *Key Actions: No information does not mean it is time for a rest. What review is the team undertaking?*

3. **Situation stabilized. Confirmation of cable repair completion time**
   - *Key Actions: Staff will still be concerned what actions should be taken? Given the confirmation on cable repairs what action is necessary? (Change over to normal operation. What is to happen to backup communications [short term and long term])?*

4. **Staff Shaken**
   - *Key Actions: Is HR fully involved to deal with staff concerns regarding advice, counselling arrangements for unsocial hours that have occurred.*
   - *What communication should go to the Board, clients, and the general public, are the communications team involved?*
   - *What has happened to site security? Has this all been resolved?*
   - *What is to happen to review the events and update plans and intraday procedures?*
   - *Are any additional backup services or equipment considered necessary?*

End of Test

Exercise Review Self Assessment

✓ Are there improvements/ additions possible to our plans?

✓ Does this make us think of other scenarios I should be planning for?

✓ How can my plans be adapted to help the organization?

✓ Our plans are well defined, but we must make them available and known to more staff?

✓ What should we do next?

It is important to record the actions and decisions taken during the recovery reprocess. This should include timing of actions. It will help to improve future plans and will give a reference point for actions during the recovery process.

Example self-assessment questions above are provided and should be asked of the team at the end of the exercise. **These should be asked one at a time.** The results should be recorded in thc Report on the Exercise.

Summary

While fifteen chapters have been dedicated to global terrorism this chapter has discussed how to prepare in a business environment to respond to disasters and incidents and then to recover from them. Since 9-11 the world has undergone significant change, particularly in the areas of cultural differences and attitudes towards immigration and refugees; one only has to look at the problems of migration and refugees in the European Union to get a glimpse of what problems may lie ahead. The vast majority of migrants are on the move purely for economic reasons. This becomes exacerbated when terror groups such as IS and al Qaeda are waging a global jihad and hiding in plain sight among migrants. Fear and prejudice remain rampant and will not go away and neither will perceptions about different religious beliefs and customs. The threat to businesses either directly or indirectly from terrorist activity must be addressed in a formal manner and we hope that by providing some small guidance on risk and risk management protocols will assist the reader to better prepare for disaster response and recovery.

Being prepared to handle events such as a terror attack on a facility whether it be a public or private concern there is always going to be a requirement to have plans in place to respond, manage, and to recover from such an event. While terrorism may not be focused on your facility specifically, the facility or organization may receive collateral damage from such acts, including fire and blast damage, water or flood damage, and significant power outages. This chapter has provided some examples of programs that can be used as templates for Risk Assessment, Security Plans, and Business Continuity. In conclusion, planning for a disaster and insuring that your organization has plans in place and teams trained and regularly tested will be a powerful value added to your organization's operational fitness.

End Notes

1. Bureau of Counterterrorism and Countering Violent Extremism -Global Terrorism Statistics for 2015 U.S. Department of State Country Reports on Terrorism - May 2016 http://www.state.gov/j/ct/rls/crt/2015/257526.htm.
2. Ibid.
3. David Loban.
4. David Loban.
5. U.S. Department of Homeland Security. https://www.ready.gov/business/implementation/training.
6. Ibid.
7. Costa Concordia. "Five jailed for average of two years each after being found guilty of manslaughter." http://metro.co.uk/2013/07/20/costa-concordia-five-jailed-for-average-of-two-years-each-after-being-found-guilty-of-manslaughter-3890910/#ixzz4AuqzotRQ. Downloaded June 7, 2016.
8. https://www.the-eps.org/
9. "Tony Hayward gets his life back." *New York Times*, Sept 1, 2012. http://www.nytimes.com/2012/09/02/business/tony-hayward-former-bp-chief-returns-to-oil.html?_r=0
10. U.S. Department of Homeland Security. https://www.ready.gov/business/implementation/training.

GLOSSARY

Abu Bakr al-Baghdadi—Leader of the Islamic State—proclaimed the first emir of the Islamic Sate of Iraq and Levant in 2014.

Abu Hamza al-Masri—Former imam of London's Finsbury Park Mosque.

Abu Musab al-Zarqawi—Jordanian militant who ran terror training camps in Iraq and formed al Qaeda in Iraq—was killed by U.S. forces in 2006.

Abu Sayyaf Group (ASG)—A Philippine Islamic terror group that seeks an independent Islamic state along the Sulu archipelago.

Accion Nacional Espanola (ANE)—Spanish National Action, right-wing terror movement that targets Basque separatists.

Active service unit (ASU)—A term used by the Provisional IRA to describe one of its active terror units or cells.

Aden Protectorate—An area of southern Arabia that, by treaty, was under British Protectorate rule during the early to mid-twentieth century; now part of the Republic of Yemen.

Adherents—Individuals who have formed collaborative relationships with, act on behalf of, or are otherwise inspired to take action in furtherance of the goals of al Qaeda—the organization and the ideology—including by engaging in violence regardless of whether such violence is targeted at the United States, its citizens, or its interests.

Affiliates—Groups that have aligned with al Qaeda.

African National Congress (ANC)—Center left political party dates back to the early-twentieth century. In 1944, the ANC youth wing was formed by Oliver Tembo and Nelson Mandela. Established to defend the rights of the black majority in South Africa and has been in power in South Africa since 1994.

Afrikaner Weerstandsbeweging (AWB)—The Afrikaner Resistance Movement; an extreme left-wing group comprising white South Africans.

Ahmed Ressam—Migrant caught crossing into the United States with bomb making equipment aimed at bombing Los Angeles International Airport—known as the Millennium Plot.

Air India Flight 182—Flight originating in Vancouver was destroyed off the coast of Ireland by a bomb placed in a bag in the hold of the aircraft.

Algerian Salafist Group for Preaching and Combat (GSPC)—An Islamic terrorist organization that has gained much support from disenfranchised Muslim youth in Europe and has emerged as a major source of recruiting and support for al Qaeda operations. A splinter faction of the Algerian Armed Islamic Group (GIA), the GSPC, is engaged in efforts to overthrow the secular government of Algeria and to organize high-profile attacks against Western interests.

Ali Hassan al-Majid—"Chemical Ali," first cousin to Saddam Hussein; the head of the Iraqi chemical weapons program through the 1980s and 1990s.

Al-Fatah—A left-wing nationalist Palestinian political party and largest member of the PLO. It has supported a wide variety of European terrorist groups through the 1960s and 1970s.

Al Ja zeera—Qatar-based Arabic TV station; since the 9-11 attacks, it has aired many video messages from Osama bin Laden. Literal translation from Arabic means "an island."

Al Qaeda—An international terrorist movement first heard of in the late 1980s. Founded by Mohammad Atef and Osama bin Laden. Based in Afghanistan and supported by the Taliban government throughout the 1990s. Its aims are the destruction of non-Islamic governments. It is now spread throughout the world with many fighters in the mountains of Pakistan.

Al-Sabah dynasty—Succession of rulers in Kuwait; Sabah al-Ahmad al-Jabir al-Sabah is the current prime minister of Kuwait and was appointed to this position by his brother, the emir of Kuwait, Jabir al-Sabah in 2003.

Al-Shabaab—Islamic militant group based in Somalia seeking to create an Islamic caliphate in the region.

Amn al-Kharji—The little known foreign intelligence department for the Islamic State.

Anders Behring Breivik—A Norwegian citizen and far right Fascist responsible for the 2011 massacre in Oslo.

Anti-Fascist Resistance Group of October First (GRAPO)—Formed in 1975 as the armed wing of the illegal Communist Party of Spain during the Franco era. GRAPO advocates the overthrow of the Spanish government and its replacement with a Marxist-Leninist regime. The group is anti-United States and seeks the removal of all U.S. military forces from Spanish territory. The group issued a communiqué following the attacks of September 11 in the United States, expressing its satisfaction that "symbols of imperialist power" were decimated and affirming that "the war" has only just begun.

Antiterrorism and Effective Death Penalty Act of 1996—Laws enacted by the United States to combat terrorism and provide justice for victims of terrorism.

Anti-Terrorism Crime and Security Act 2001 (ATCSA)—Counterterrorism bill introduced into law by the government of the United Kingdom.

Anwar al-Awlaki—An American born imam who later became the most influential English-language recruiter for the cause of violent jihad. Killed in a U.S. drone strike in 2011.

Apartheid—Policy of segregation along racial lines; once practiced in South Africa.

Arab Spring—A series of antigovernment protests, uprisings, and armed rebellions that spread across the Middle East in early 2011.

Arafat, Yasser—(August 24, 1929–November 11, 2004) Awarded the Nobel Peace Prize in 1994. Symbolically portrayed as the leader of the Palestinian struggle for an independent Palestinian state; often viewed by outsiders as a corrupt politician and a stumbling block to peace in the Middle East; considered a terrorist by Israel.

Ariel Sharon—Joined the Haganah in 1942, became Israel's prime minister in 2001. Suffered a massive stroke in March 2006.

Armata Corsa—An underground separatist movement established in 1999 opposing the links between nationalists and the Corsican Mafia.

Armed Islamic Group (GIA)—Islamic terrorist group operating in Algeria.

Armed Proletarian Nuclei (NAP)—Left-wing movement originating in the Italian prison system.

Armee Republicaine Bretonne (ARB)—Breton Liberation Army; a small nationalist antiglobalization movement with its roots in the Breton region of France.

Armenian Secret Army for the Liberation of Armenia (ASALA)—A Marxist-Leninist extremist organization that operated from 1975 to 1986; led by Hagop Hagopian until he was assassinated in Athens in April 1988.

Army of God—U.S. domestic terror group that engages in violence; targets abortion clinics and medical practitioners.

Army Ranger Wing (ARW)—Republic of Ireland's elite counterterror unit.

Assassination—Targeted killing of an important person for political or ideological reasons.

Aum Shinrikyo—Japanese terror group known for the sarin gas attack on the Tokyo subway in 1995.

Autodeterminaziorako Bilgunea (AuB)—Formed in February 13, 2003. Comprises prominent representatives from the Basque left-wing pro-independence movement, as well as those from other political backgrounds. Political agenda to demand the right of the Basque people to make decisions regarding their future and supporting a democratic solution to the Basque political conflict.

Aviation Security Commando (AVESCOM)—Philippines hostage rescue unit.

Ayatollah Khomeini—Iranian Grand Ayatollah, leader of the Iranian revolution against the Shah of Iran in 1979.

Ba'athist Regime—Pan-Arabic socialist party that was prominent in Iraq and continues in Syria; party of Saddam Hussein.

Babbar Khalsa International (BKI)—A Sikh terrorist group sponsored by expatriate Indian Sikhs demanding an independent Sikh state called Khalistan (Land of the Pure) from Indian territory.

Badr Brigade—Shiite militia group composed of Iraqi military officers who escaped, defected, or were captured during and after the Iran–Iraq war, 1980–1988.

Bahraini Hezbollah—Organization believed to be supported by Iran; seeks to overthrow the Bahrain government and replace it with a fundamentalist Islamic regime.

Bakassi Boys—A violent vigilante group that operates with almost impunity as supposed anticrime vigilantes.

Balfour Declaration—Lord Balfour's 1917 declaration pledging British support to a Jewish homeland in Palestine.

Basque Region—Area in northern Spain and southwest France (Pyrenees); the Basque people (approximately 2 million) inhabit the region.

Basque Socialist Coalition—Known as the Herri Batasuna (People's Unity) Party; led by Arnoldo Ortiz.

Batasuna, Herri—The People's Unity Party; Spanish organization led by Arnoldo Ortiz; officially denies any links or involvement with the ETA terrorist organization; also known as The Basque Socialist Coalition.

Black September—Palestinian fighters who attempted to seize power in Jordan; subsequently, the Jordanian military expelled thousands of Palestinians from Jordan in September 1970. Black September gained notoriety for the killing of eleven Israeli athletes at the Munich Olympic Games in 1972.

Boevaya Oranisatsia (BO)—"The Fighting Organization"—terror suborganization within the Social Revolutionary Party; given autonomy under the party.

Boko Haram—Nigeria-based Islamist terror group demanding imposition of Islamic Law throughout the region.

Bolsheviks—Extreme left-wing radicals, who favored revolution; led by Lenin.

Bojinka plot—Serbian word meaning "big bang" was a plot hatched by Ramzi Yousef to smuggle bomb making materials in liquid form on to a number of aircraft and detonate them in mid-air.

Bureau of State Security (BOSS)—The South African state security service.

Cali cartel—A powerful drug cartel operating in Colombia.

Canadian Security Intelligence Service (CSIS)—A relatively young organization that tracks threats to national security within Canada.

Charlie Hebdo—French weekly satirical magazine, published in Paris.

Che Guevara—Marxist revolutionary born in Argentina and a key figure in the Cuban Revolution.

Cheka—Communist secret police organization established during the Russian Revolution in 1917.

Chiapas—A state in Southeast Mexico where a peasant uprising led by the Zapatista National Liberation Army continues to press for greater autonomy.

Cobras—Sultanate of Oman elite Special Forces unit.

Communist Combatant Cells (CCC)—A Belgian terror group.

Contras—Terrorist organization and armed opponents of Nicaragua's Sandinista Junta of National Reconstruction following the July 1979 overthrow of Anastasio Somoza Debayle and the ending of the Somoza family's forty-three-year rule.

CPTED—Crime prevention through environmental design.

CSI—U.S. Container Security Initiative—global security initiative established by U.S. Customs and Border Protection in 2002 to target and screen container traffic.

Customs and Border Patrol (CBP)—The U.S. Border Patrol; the mobile uniformed law enforcement arm of the Department of Homeland Security (DHS). Originally established on May 28, 1924, by an act of Congress passed in response to increasing illegal immigration.

Dada, Idi Amin—Self-declared president for life of Uganda who came to power following a coup in 1971; he purged the military and the country of most of his opponents and exiled 70,000 Ugandan Asians with British passports. He died in exile in Saudi Arabia in 2003.

Dal Khalsa—Sikh terrorist organization supported by ex-patriot Sikhs; their aim is to establish the independent Sikh state of Khalistan.

Death Squad—An armed group that conducts extrajudicial killings or forced disappearances of persons for the purposes of political repression, genocide, or revolutionary terror.

Decommissioning—Provision in the Northern Ireland Peace Agreement that puts weapons beyond the use of Irish terror organizations.

Democratic Front for the Liberation of Palestine (DFLP)—Marxist-Leninist organization founded in 1969 when it split from the Popular Front for the Liberation of Palestine (PFLP). The DFLP believes Palestinian national goals can be achieved only through revolution. Joined other rejectionist groups to oppose the Declaration of Principles signed in 1993. In the 1970s, the DFLP conducted numerous small bombings and minor assaults and some more spectacular operations in Israel and the occupied territories, concentrating on Israeli targets. They have only been involved in border raids since 1988, but they continue to oppose the Israel-PLO peace agreement.

Democratic People's Republic of Korea (DPRK)—A communist state dominated by a one-man dictatorship. North Korea's long-range missile development and research into nuclear, chemical, and biological weapons and massive conventional armed forces are of major concern to the international community. The current ruler of North Korea is Kim Jong-un.

Democratic Progressive Party (DPP)—Taiwanese opposition party.

Department of Homeland Security (DHS)—U.S. government agency created after the attacks of 9-11.

Dev Sol—Revolutionary People's Liberation Front, formed in 1978 following a split with the Turkish People's Liberation Front, is a Marxist organization that is violently anti-NATO and anti-USA.

Diplock Commission—Commission set up in 1972 to consider legal measures against terrorism in Northern Ireland, which led to the establishment of courts without jury; named after Kenneth Diplock.

Doku Umarov—Islamist leader described as the Chechen bin Laden.

Domestic Terrorism—Groups of individuals who are based and operate entirely in the United States and Puerto Rico without foreign direction and whose acts are directed at elements of the U.S. government or population.

Emergency Provisions—Powers given to the military by the Northern Ireland Emergency Provisions to combat urban terror in Northern Ireland.

Emiliano Zapata—The leader of the peasant revolution in the state of Chiapas.

ETA-Military—Military branch of the Basque terrorist organization.

Ethnic cleansing—Depopulation or deporting (war crime) often during wartime and associated with genocide (crime against humanity).

ETIM—East Turkestan Islamic Movement—a separatist group demanding independence from China.

European Civil Aviation Conference (ECAC)—European organization responsible for developing policies and standards for civil aviation.

Euskadi Ta Askatasuna (ETA)—Founded by young nationalists in 1952, it is a Basque separatist group fighting for independence from Spain.

Executive Order 13224—An executive order signed into law by U.S. President George W. Bush on September 23, 2001, in response to the September 11, 2001, attacks.

Extraordinary rendition—The extrajudicial transfer of a person from one country to another—a practice of the U.S. government to transfer suspected terrorists to countries known to practice torture.

Falun Gong—Spiritual movement that came to prominence in the People's Republic of China and is widely repressed in that country.

Fatwa—An Islamic pronouncement or ruling—considered a scholarly opinion on Islamic law.

Fedayeen—An Arab commando or guerilla unit.

Federal Air Marshal Service (FAMS)—Federal Sky Marshall program designed to place armed guards on U.S. aircraft in flight.

Ferdinand, Archduke Franz—His assassination in Sarajevo in 1914 triggered the start of World War I.

Fiahs—Indonesian term for terrorist cellular structures; for fundraising, religious work, security, and operations.

Frankincense—Aromatic resin widely used in religious rites.

Freedom of Access to Clinic Entrances (FACE) Act—Activities by pro-life activists in the United States attempted to block free access to abortion clinics by surrounding clinics with picketers attempting to shut them down. This activity was prohibited by the FACE Act.

Frente Revolucionario Anti-Fascista Y Patriotico (FRAP)—Left-wing Maoist group.

Front de la Liberation Nationale de la Corse (FLNC)—A group of Corsican separatists.

Front de Liberation du Quebec (FLQ)—Canadian extreme separatist movement active in the 1960s and 1970s.

Front for the Liberation of Angola (FNLA)—The FNLA was founded in 1954 as the Union of Peoples of Northern Angola to advance the interests of the Bakongo rather than to promote independence.

Front for the Liberation of Mozambique (FRELIMO)—Movement against Portuguese rule; originated in the early 1960s.

G8—A group of eight countries—the United States, Canada, Great Britain, Russia, France, Germany, Italy, and Japan—that meet as a world economic forum.

GAO—United Sates Government Accountability Office.

Gastarbeiter Program—Program that brought Turkish workers to Germany to help rebuild the country after World War II.

General Staff Reconnaissance Unit Number 69—Formed in 1957; also known as Sayeret Mat'kal, the leading unit in Israel's counterterrorism arsenal.

Genocide—The systematic and planned extermination of an ethnic, religious, political, or national group.

God Father of Jihad—Nickname for the Palestinian cleric, Abdullah Yusuf Azzam who was the central figure in the global development of the militant Islamist movement.

Good Friday Agreement—Plan for devolved government in Northern Ireland signed on April 10, 1998; includes terms of early release of prisoners and decommissioning of weapons.

Grand Mufti of Jerusalem—The Muslim cleric in Jerusalem responsible for Muslim Holy sites including the Al Aqsa Mosque.

Great Trek—1835–1843 journey by Afrikaner farmers from Cape colony of South Africa to escape British domination.

Grenzschutzgruppe 9 (GSG-9)—German counterterrorist group founded after the Munich Olympic Games attack by Palestinian terrorists.

Groupment d'intervention de la Gendarmerie Nationale (GIGN)—A French counterterror unit with a ninety-men-strong unit designed to antiterrorism and police operations similar to U.S. police SWATs. It is organized in four 15-men groups. The GIGN have conducted counterterror actions outside France in Djibouti, Lebanon, and the Comoros Islands.

Grupo Especial De Operaciones (GEO)—Belgium's Para-commando Regiment contains two small units that are special operations capable. The first, ESR (Equips Speciales de Reconnaissance Compagnie) dates back to 1960, when it was formed to give the I Belgium Corps a long-range reconnaissance capacity. This unit is company sized and uses the standard weapons of the Belgium Army. Two similar units exist within the reserve structure. The second unit is a small frogman section. It is a highly secretive unit, but is known to be about platoon sized and is similar to the British Special Boat Squadron (SBS).

Guantanamo Bay—U.S. military base in Cuba where "detainees" and suspected Islamic militants from Iraq and Afghanistan are being held.

Gulags—Forced labor camps set up by the Soviet internal police for dissidents and politicians.

Gulf Cooperation Council (GCC)—Council comprising Qatar, Oman, the UAE, Saudi Arabia, Kuwait, and Bahrain; set up in 1981 to address common economic and social issues within the region.

Hague Conventions—International treaties first negotiated at The Hague in the Netherlands pronouncing formal statements on the laws of war.

Hajj—Muslim pilgrimage to the Holy City of Mecca.

Hamas—An offshoot of the Islamic Brotherhood and an acronym for the Islamic Resistance Movement.

Harakat-ul-Ansar (HUA)—Pakistani Islamic militant group that operates primarily in Kashmir.

Hashemite Kingdom—The official name for the Middle East kingdom of Jordan.

Hashish eater—Origin of the word "assassin" in ancient times.

Haqqani Network—Afghan insurgent group closely aligned to al Qaeda and sponsored by the Pakistani ISI.

HEU—Highly enriched uranium.

Hezbollah—Radical Arabic organization that established itself following the Israeli invasion of Lebanon; the group is often linked with terror attacks in the Middle East.

Hizb ut-Tahrir—A global Islamic political party whose goal is to unite all Muslim countries to unify as an Islamic Caliphate.

Holocaust—Mass extermination of mainly European Jews during World War II by Nazi Germany.

Home Rule—The principle of self-government.

Human Intelligence (HUMINT)—An intelligence gathering by tracking suspects, interviews, and interrogations; primarily under the domain CIA in the United States.

Ian Paisley—Protestant minister who became the public face of opposition to the Republican movement.

IED—An improvised explosive device or homemade bomb sometimes using military munitions.

IICD—Independent International Commission to oversee the decommissioning of paramilitary weapons under the provisions of the Northern Ireland Peace Accord.

Ilich Ramirez Sanchez—"Carlos, the Jackal"—led the 1975 assault on the OPEC HQ in Vienna.

Immigration and Customs Enforcement (ICE)—Is the largest investigative arm of the Department of Homeland Security. As part of its homeland security mission, ICE seeks to maintain the integrity of the immigration system through effective enforcement of U.S. immigration laws.

IMU—Islamic Movement of Uzbekistan—militant Islamist group formed in 1991.

Indian National Congress—Created in 1885, the Indian party that led the drive for an independent India from British rule; its iconic leader after World War I was Mahatma Gandhi.

Information Analysis and Infrastructure Protection (IAFP)—The Department of Homeland Security would merge under one roof the capability to identify and assess current and future threats to the homeland, map those threats against current vulnerabilities, inform the president, issue timely warnings, and immediately take or effect appropriate preventive and protective action.

Inspire—An English online magazine published by al Qaeda in the Arabian Peninsula aimed at influencing jihad and targeting young men and women to take action.

International Atomic Energy Agency—Agency responsible for monitoring nuclear stock piles.

International Criminal Tribunal for the Former Yugoslavia (ICTY)—United Nations court of law handling war crimes.

Internment—Confinement, often used in wartime; in this case, used in Northern Ireland during the 1980s to combat Irish republican terrorism.

Interpol—International Criminal Police Organization created in 1923 to assist with international police cooperation; headquartered in Lyons, France; has 184 member countries making it second in size to the United Nations.

Inter-Services Intelligence (ISI)—Pakistani intelligence organization founded in 1948 and has more than 10,000 members; it collects foreign and domestic intelligence and coordinates intelligence functions of the three military services.

Irgun—Hebrew term for the National Military Organization, a Zionist group that operated between 1931 and 1948 in British-mandated Palestine.

Irish Free State—Established by treaty with Great Britain as a dominion within the Commonwealth of Nations in 1922 and become a sovereign state in 1937 (Eire).

Irish National Liberation Army (INLA)—Irish Republican paramilitary organization was founded in 1974. Its terrorist activities have spread to mainland Britain, and it was responsible for the assassination of Airey Neave, a close political friend of British Prime Minister Margaret Thatcher.

Irish Republican Army (IRA)—A Catholic paramilitary organization.

Islamic Jihad—An umbrella organization of Palestinian terrorist groups operating from the Middle East; many terrorist groups add the word "jihad" to their title.

Islamic Revolutionary Guard Corps (IRGC)—Army of the Guardians of the Islamic Revolution—formed in Iran following the revolution to protect the Islamic regime.

Islamic State—An extreme Sunni Islamic insurgent group formed in Iraq. The group declared a Caliphate had been established in 2014.

Islamism—Islamic ideology demanding total adherence to Islamic laws.

Izz ad-Din al-Qassam Brigades—The military functioning wing of Hamas in Gaza.

Jabhat al-Nusra—Islamist group fighting against the Syrian regime—established in 2012 as al Qaeda's proxy in Syria.

Jaish-e-Mohammed (JEM)—The Army of Mohammed; an Islamic extremist group based in Pakistan formed by Masood Azhar upon his release from prison in India.

Jamaat ul-Fuqra—Terrorist group established in Pakistan and with operations inside the United States—considered a probable al Qaeda affiliate.

Janjaweed—Armed militia group operating in Darfur, western Sudan.

Japanese Red Army (JRA)—Marxist revolutionary terror group active in Europe during the 1970s.

Jemaah Islamiyaah (JI)—Shadowy Islamic terror group that has spread throughout southern Asia.

Jihad—Islamic term used to describe a holy war against religious or political oppression.

Joint Task Force-2 (JTF-2)—Canadian Special Forces unit established in 1993 when the Canadian armed forces took responsibility for counterterrorism operations within Canada; very secretive unit about which little is known.

Joint Terrorism Analysis Center (JTAC)—Organization that analyzes and assesses international terrorism in the United Kingdom; established in 2003.

JTTF—Joint Terrorism Task Force established in July 2002 to serve as a coordinating mechanism with the FBI's partners. Some 40 agencies are now represented in the National JTTF, a focal point for information sharing.

Justice and Equality Movement (JEM)—Organization in Darfur challenging the administration in Khartoum.

Jyllands-Posten—Danish morning newspaper that published cartoons of the Prophet Muhammad.

Keiretsu—Japanese term used to describe a close-knit group of manufacturers, suppliers, and distributors.

KGB—The Committee for State Security; Soviet secret police, founded by Felix Edmundovich Dzerzhinsky in 1954; lasted until the collapse of the Soviet Union and was dissolved in 1991.

Khalid Sheikh Mohammed—Al Qaeda's Number 3 man who claimed responsibility for Daniel Pearl's death.

Khalistan—Country formed on October 7, 1987, where the Sikh nation declared its independence from India.

Khmer Rouge—The Communist Party of Cambodia; during its reign of power from 1975 to 1979, it was responsible for the execution of several million Cambodians.

Khmer Royal Armed Forces (KRAF)—The 1993 merger of the Cambodian People's Armed Forces and the two non-Communist resistance armies; also known as the Royal Cambodian Armed Forces, or RCAF.

Killer College—A major training facility for terrorists in Russia.

Killer instinct—Predilection to kill, not in anger, not in the heat of the moment, but in cold blood.

KINTEX—Bulgarian weapons producing company.

Kirov, Sergei—Bolshevik who took part in the 1905 Russian Revolution and the Russian Civil War of 1920. He was a popular and loyal supporter of Josef Stalin and was assassinated in December 1934.

Kosovo Liberation Army (KLA)—A Kosovar Albanian group that sought to break away from the Federal Republic of Yugoslavia in the 1990s.

Kurdistan—Region of the Middle East inhabited by Kurds and covering areas of Turkey, Iraq, Syria, and Armenia. The region is not recognized demographically; however, it accounts for approximately 25 million Kurds.

Kurdistan Freedom and Democracy Congress (KADEK)—Also known as Kurdistan Workers' Party; was established in 1974; is a Marxist-Leninist insurgent group, which aims to create a democratic Kurdish state.

Kurdistan Workers' Party (PKK)—Marxist-Leninist insurgent group made up of Turkish Kurds; founded in 1978. The group's goal has been to establish an independent, democratic Kurdish state in the Middle East.

Lashkar-e-Taiba (LeT)—Army of the Righteous—one of the largest Islamist terror organizations in Southern Asia—attacks both civilian and military targets.

Lashkar-i-Jhangvi (LJ)—Extreme Sunni Muslim group that has its roots in a sectarian movement calling itself Sipah-i-Sahaba Pakistan; its main targets for attack are from the Shia religious sect. The group had ties to the Taliban in Afghanistan.

Laws—Rules established for the orderly operation of a society.

Lee Rigby—Unarmed soldier from 2nd Battalion Royal Regiment of Fusiliers, run down and beheaded in London by jihadists.

Letter bomb—Small, improvised explosive device hidden inside an envelope or a package mailed to a targeted person or organization.

Liberation Tigers of Tamil Eelam (LTTE)—Sri Lankan terrorist movement seeking an autonomous homeland.

Lockerbie—Small village in southern Scotland where Pan Am 103 crashed, destroying many homes and taking the lives of all on board as well as many on the ground.

Lynch Law—The process of condemning and punishing a person by mob rule without any trial—dates back to the eighteenth century, when William Lynch self-instituted tribunals.

MI5—British intelligence organization.

Macheteros—Armed Forces of Puerto Rican National Liberation, also known as the Popular Boricua Army (Ejercito Popular Boricua), commonly known as the Macheteros, claimed responsibility for numerous bombings and robberies, causing a reign of terror in Puerto Rico. The goals of the Macheteros were complete autonomy and sovereignty for Puerto Rico.

Madrassas—Islamic religious schools that teach and preach strict adherence to Islamic codes—found widely in Pakistan.

Mahdi Army—Formed in 2003, the Mahdi Army is an armed group loyal to Muqtada al-Sadr, a Shia leader from a family line of revered clerics persecuted under Saddam Hussein.

Major Criminal Hijack (MCHJ)—International Maritime Organization definition as major transnational organized crimes at sea.

Mancino Law—Italian law aimed at hate crimes.

Mandela United Football Club—Name given to the bodyguards of Winnie Madikizela-Mandela, wife of former president of South Africa, Nelson Mandela.

Mandela, Nelson Rolihlahla—The first black president of South Africa.

Man-Portable Air Defense System (MANPADS)—Systems as the Russian (SA-7 and SA-14, Igla SA-16 and SA-18) and the U.S.-manufactured FIM-92 Stinger; easy to use and readily available on the black market; pose an acute threat to military aircraft and civilian airliners.

Mau Mau—Insurgent movement in Kenya that attacked Europeans in the 1950s; comprising mainly Kikuyu tribesmen.

McVeigh, Timothy James—American who was convicted for the bombing of the Federal Building in Oklahoma City on April 19, 1995, killing 167 people; he was executed on June 11, 2001.

Mehmet Ali Agca—Turkish nationalist who attempted the assassination of Pope John Paul II in St. Peter's Square, Rome, on May 13, 1981.

MEND—Movement for the Emancipation of the Niger Delta-a militant group operating in the Niger Delta and claim to be fighting corrupt government practices.

Middle East—A region of the world comprising Israel, Lebanon, Syria, Jordan, the Gulf states, and Saudi Arabia.

Militia—A militia is a group of citizens organized to provide paramilitary service.

Milli Görüs—Largest Muslim organization in Germany with over 27,000 members; its influence is felt within the tight-knit Muslim communities particularly in the Turkish Muslim areas; also known as National Vision.

Monsignor Juan Gerardi Conedera—Bishop of Guatemala was beaten to death two days after releasing a human rights report on April 26, 1998.

Mohammed, Khaled Sheikh—Al Qaeda's Number 3 man who claimed responsibility for Daniel Pearl's death.

Montoneros (Movimiento Peronista Montonero)—Argentinean leftist guerrilla group active during the 1970s. *Montonero* was a local name for nineteenth-century guerrillas. The group formed around 1970 from the socialist supporters of Juan Domingo Perón.

Morazanist Patriotic Front (FPM)—A radical, leftist Honduran terrorist group that first appeared in the late 1980s; its attacks were in protest of U.S. intervention in Honduran economic and political affairs.

Mores—Accepted behaviors and customs within a social group.

Moro Islamic Liberation Front (MILF)—An Islamic terrorist group fighting for an independent Islamic state in the southern Philippines.

Mossad—Institute for Intelligence and Special Assignments; Israeli intelligence organization, founded in 1949 by David Ben Gurion.

Movimiento Revolucionario Tupac Amaru (MRTA)—Peruvian guerrilla organization during the late 1980s and early 1990s; smaller than The Shining Path but equally as dangerous and ruthless.

Movimento Politico Occidentale (MPO)—(Political Movement of the West)—Italian Skinhead organization.

Mujahideen—An Arabic term for an Islamic guerilla fighter.

Mujahedin-e Khalq (MEK)—Formed in the 1960s, the organization was expelled from Iran after the Islamic Revolution in 1979, its primary support came from the former Iraqi regime of Saddam Hussein starting in the late 1980s. They conducted anti-Western attacks prior to the Islamic Revolution. Since then, it has conducted terrorist attacks against the interests of the clerical regime in Iran and abroad. The MEK advocates the overthrow of the Iranian regime and its replacement with the group's own leadership.

Mullah Omar—Leader of the Afghan Taliban and leader of the Afghan Government 1996–2001.

Muslim Council of Britain—Established in 1997 with membership from more than 250 Muslim organizations in Great Britain—its first secretary general was Iqbal Sacranie who received Knighthood from Queen Elizabeth II in 2006.

Multiculturalism—Official Canadian government policy since its introduction in the 1970s on the social importance of immigrants and their integration.

Myanmar—Originally Burma; the country was renamed in 1989.

Narodnaya Volya (NV)—A nineteenth-century Russian terrorist organization; translation means "The People's Will."

National Liberation Army—A terminology often adapted by a terrorist group in a fight against legitimate authority.

National Organization of Cypriot Combatants (EOKA)—Was a Greek Cypriot military resistance organization that fought for self-determination and for union with Greece in the mid- to late 1950s.

National Targeting Center (NTC)—Part of the U.S. Department of Homeland Security; provides tactical targeting and analytical research in support of customs antiterrorism efforts.

National Union for the Total Independence of Angola (UNITA)—Formed in 1966 by Jonas Savimbi, its charismatic leader. The group was formed from the politicized split in the Angolan independence movement. Until 2002, the group was largely a military force and had been fighting a civil war since 1975. Jonas Savimbi headed the group from its formation until his death in 2002.

Naxalites—Maoist group formed by student bodies in the 1960s.

Nazer Hindawi—April 17 1986 placed a bomb in his pregnant girlfriend carryon bag attempting to blow up an El Al flight at London's Heathrow Airport.

Nerve agents—Chemical agents used to attack and disable the human central nervous system.

New People's Army (NPA)—Maoist group formed in December 1969 with the aim of overthrowing the Philippine government through protracted guerrilla warfare; the military wing of the Communist Party of the Philippines (CPP).

New World Order—Term used to describe what some extreme believers think the U.S. government is determined to create; often referenced by U.S. militia organizations.

Nidal, Abu—Born in 1937 Sabri al Banna; prior to Osama bin Laden, Nidal was considered one of the most dangerous terrorists. He spent many years in Syria, Libya, and Iraq, where he died under mysterious circumstances in 2002.

NORAID—Irish republican organization that (Irish Northern Aid Committee) actively collected funds in the United States to support republican activities in Northern Ireland.

North Atlantic Treaty Organization (NATO)—Alliance of twenty-six countries from North America and Europe committed to fulfilling the goals of the North Atlantic Treaty signed in April 4, 1949.

November 17—Greek terrorist revolutionary organization; is Marxist-Leninist, anti-imperialist, anti-United States, anti-Europe, and anti-NATO.

Ocalan, Abdullah—Imprisoned leader of the Kurdish Workers' Party in Turkey.

Ogaden National Liberation Front (ONLF)—Separatist group fighting for an independent state in the Ogaden region.

Oklahoma City Federal Building—Building destroyed by a truck bomb placed by Timothy McVeigh.

Operation Bojinka—Islamist plot to blow up eleven commercial airliners between Asia and the United States.

Operation Crevice—UK Police operation in 2004 to uncover Islamist terror cells operating in England.

Operation Desert Storm—The first Gulf War of 1991; led by the United States and a coalition of countries to remove Iraqi forces from Kuwait.

Omar Khadr—A Canadian of Pakistani origin captured in Afghanistan and detained in Guantanamo; tried, convicted, and sentenced under U.S. Military Commissions Act 2009 after pleading guilty to killing U.S. serviceman Christopher Speer.

Omar Shafik Hammami—U.S. citizen who migrated to Africa and joined the al-Shabaab terrorist group.

Orange Order—Originating in the seventeenth century, this is the largest Protestant organization in Northern Ireland and regards itself as defending civil and religious liberties of Protestants and seeks to uphold the rule and ascendancy of a Protestant monarch in the United Kingdom.

Organization of Petroleum Exporting Countries (OPEC)—Headquartered in Vienna, Austria, the principal aim of the organization is the determination of petroleum policies of its member countries and the determination of the best means for safeguarding their interests, individually and collectively. The member states are Algeria, Iran, Indonesia, Kuwait, Iraq, Libya, Nigeria, Qatar, Saudi Arabia, Venezuela, and the United Arab Emirates.

Palestine—Region of the eastern Mediterranean coast from the Red Sea to the Jordan valley and from the southern Negev desert to the Galilee Lake region in the north. The word itself derives from "Plesheth," a name that appears frequently in the Bible and translated to English is "Philistine."

Palestine Liberation Front (PLF)—Small breakaway group from the PFLP based in the West Bank and Lebanon.

Palestine Liberation Organization (PLO)—Established in 1964 as a political body representing the Palestinian people. It is also a paramilitary organization that has dedicated itself to the establishment of a Palestinian state in former Palestine. Yasser Arafat became chairman of the PLO in 1969 until his death in 2004.

Palestinian Islamic Jihad (PIJ)—Formed by militant Palestinians in the Gaza Strip during the 1970s; committed to the creation of an Islamic Palestinian state and the destruction of Israel.

Palestinian National Liberation Movement (Fatah)—Founded in 1959 by Yasser Arafat—Fatah joined the PLO in 1967 and Arafat took over as leader.

Papa Doc—Francois Papa Doc Duvalier—notorious ruler of Haiti throughout the 1960s.

Partisans—An irregular army evading and attacking an invading or occupying force.

People's Consultative Assembly—Indonesian legislative body largely appointed by the president himself; reelected Suharto to a seventh term.

People's Republic of China (PRC)—Often referred to as Red China, a Communist country in Asia with a population of 1.3 billion.

PETN—Explosive pentaerythritol tetranitrate—difficult to detect—explosive used by Richard Reid the Shoe Bomber.

Police Service of Northern Ireland (PSNI)—Predominantly Protestant police force formally known as the Royal Ulster Constabulary; name changed under the terms of the Northern Ireland Peace Agreement.

Pol Pot—Leader of Communist regime in Cambodia, which he renamed Kampuchea; in 1976, he unveiled a "4-Year Plan" that detailed the collectivization of agriculture, the nationalization of industry, and the financing of the economy through increased agricultural exports. Thousands starved to death as a result.

Popular Front for the Liberation of Palestine (PFLP)—Terrorist group under the umbrella of the PLO.

Popular Revolutionary Army (EPR)—Left-wing Mexican group; ranks second in strength to the Zapatista movement based in the southern states of Oaxaca and Guerrero; considered by Mexicans to actually be several different movements operating under one banner.

Prescribe—To establish rules, laws, and direction.

Proscribe—To outlaw and ban terror organizations.

Provisional Irish Republican Army (PIRA)—A splinter from the original IRA movement that has waged a terror campaign in the United Kingdom and Northern Ireland.

Pushkin Square—Locality in the center of Moscow; renamed after Alexander Pushkin in 1937.

Qods Force—Part of the Islamic Revolutionary Guard Corps (IRGC) responsible for extraterritorial operations, including terrorist operations. A primary focus is training Islamic fundamentalist terrorist groups.

Racial Profiling—The inclusion of race as a specific indicator as to whether that person is likely to commit a crime—used widely in the United States and challenged by human rights organizations as racism at worst.

Radicalization—Process by which an individual or group adopt increasingly extreme political, social, or religious ideals.

Radiological Dispersal Device (RDD)—A weapon designed to spread radiological materials.

Radovan Karadzic—Bosnian Serb leader convicted in 2016 by ICTY of genocide.

RAF—Red Army Faction—left-wing German militant group that morphed from the Baader-Meinhof gang in the 1960s.

Rebel Armed Forces (FAR)—Leftist Guatemalan terror group. Formed in 1962 by junior officers of the Guatemalan military who had previously led an unsuccessful coup attempt against the conservative Guatemalan government; the officers created the FAR to continue their antigovernment attacks. The FAR allied with several leftist terrorist organizations in 1982 to form the Guatemalan National Revolutionary Unity (URNG).

Reign of Terror—The period between 1793 and 1794 during the French Revolution when thousands were executed.

Rejectionist—A Middle East political term meaning the unilateral refusal of any peaceful settlement with Israel.

Revolutionary Armed Forces of Colombia (FARC)—Established in 1964 as the military wing of the Colombian Communist Party, FARC is Latin America's oldest and best-equipped insurgency of Marxist origin.

Revolutionary People's Struggle (ELA)—A Greek, violent Marxist-Leninist organization.

Robben (Island) University—Prison situated off the coast of South Africa prison for members of the previously banned ANC; where many prisoners learned the art of political debate.

Rogue states—Term applied to countries or states deemed as a threat to global security and/or supporters or sponsors of terrorism.

Royal Ulster Constabulary (RUC)—Paramilitary police force of Northern Ireland; the removal of the word "Royal" came about during the Northern Ireland Peace Agreement. The force is now the Police Service of Northern Ireland.

Russian Federation—The current government structure of the former USSR.

Sandinista National Liberation Front (FSLN)—(*Frente Sandinista de Liberación Nacional*), a socialist political party in Nicaragua, named after Augusto César Sandino leader of the Nicaraguan resistance against the U.S. occupation of Nicaragua in the 1930s. Party members are called "Sandinistas" in both English and Spanish.

Sarin—Nerve agent used in the 1995 Tokyo subway attack.

SAS—Special Air Service—British Army Regiment heavily involved in counterterror operations.

Satanic Verses—Novel written by British author Salman Rushdie in 1989, contained some unflattering references to Islamic history, which resulted in Iran's Ayotollah Khomeini calling for Rushdie's death.

SAVAK—Ministry of State Security during the reign of the Shah of Iran.

Sayeret Mat'kal—Also known as General Staff Reconnaissance Unit Number 69—is the Israeli elite counterterrorist organization.

Sayyid Qutb—Egyptian and member of the Muslim Brotherhood.

Scheduled Offenses—Offenses such as terrorism tried in "Special Courts."

Schengen Agreement—Treaty of 1985 that laid the foundation for a Europe free of borders.

Sectarian—Strict or rigid adherence to a particular religion; where two or more religions come into conflict, extreme actions and violence often occur, as seen in Northern Ireland.

Selassie, Emperor Haile—Born in July 23, 1892; was emperor of Ethiopia from 1930 to 1936 and 1941 to 1974. He was an Ethiopian Orthodox Christian his entire life. He was removed from power in 1974 and died in suspicious circumstances under house arrest in 1975.

Sharia (Islamic Law)—Arabic term for Islamic law, most often stemming from the Quran.

Sheikh Ahmed Yassin—Muslim cleric and founder of Hamas—assassinated by Israel.

Shining Path (Sendero Luminoso)—Peruvian radical, Marxist group that grew out of the Communist movement in the 1960s. Its radical Marxist ideology was shaped by its founder, Abimael Guzmán Reynoso. Guzmán, a former university professor, was able to use his position within academia to gain credibility and entice students to his fledgling Communist movement. He was captured in 1991 and remains in prison.

Shiromani Gurudwara Prabandhak Committee (SGPC)—Is the major Sikh terrorist organization in India.

Shoko Asahara—In 1987, founded Aum Shinrikyo as a religious cult.

Shumukh al-Islam—A jihadist forum that posts information related to jihadist ideology.

Signals Intelligence (SIGINT)—The discipline of intelligence gathering through electronic intercepts of messages by varied means.

Sinn Féin—Led by Gerry Adams—left-wing Irish republican political party that seeks an end to British rule in Northern Ireland.

Sithole, Ndabaningi—Leader of the Ndonga faction of Zimbabwe African Union (ZANU).

Special Air Service (SAS) Regiment—The elite British military unit used for counterrevolutionary warfare operations—established in North Africa during World War II and based in the west of England.

Special Boat Squadron (SBS)—British special forces unit; waterborne counterpart of the Special Air Service Regiment; employed in waterborne special ops for the British Royal Navy.

Special Category Status—A de facto prisoner-of-war status for Irish prisoners convicted during the Troubles.

Special Immigration Appeal Commission (SIAC)—U.K. Act established in 1997 providing a method of appeal for immigrants ordered to deport from the United Kingdom.

SPOT—A method employed to screen passengers by observation techniques.

Stalin, Joseph—Russian leader from 1928 to 1953; summarily executed millions of his opponents. "Stalin" means "Man of Steel."

Stansted Airport—A UK airport situated to the east of the capital and used as a hijack response location for aircraft hijackings.

Stammheim Prison—Prison where members of Germany's Baader-Meinhof Gang were imprisoned.

State Law and Order Restoration Council (SLORC)—Burmese military junta that controlled the region in 1988.

State Peace and Development Council (SPDC)—Burmese military renaming itself from SLORC in 1997.

State-Sponsored Terrorism—Term to describe governments that support terrorist groups either by ideology or through material support and training.

Sudan Liberation Movement/Army (SLA)—Group originating in the region of Darfur to challenge the administration in Khartoum.

Sunni—The largest division of Islam; Sunni Muslims range from Indonesia through the Middle East and Africa.

SWAT—U.S. Special Weapons and Tactical units—established as hostage rescue units by most U.S. police forces.

Sykes-Picot Agreement—A secret agreement reached during World War I between the British and French governments pertaining to the partition of the Ottoman Empire among the Allied Powers. Russia was also privy to the discussions.

Symbionese Liberation Army (SLA)—U.S. group made prominent by the kidnapping of Patty Hearst in 1974.

Sympathizers—Someone or a group that shares and understand the same common goals.

Talwinder Singh Parmar—Considered part of the plot group that bombed Air India Flight 182 in 1985, killing over 300—also leader of the Babbar Khalsa terrorist organization. Killed by Indian police while in custody in 1992.

Tabun—Used as a nerve gas in chemical warfare.

Task Force on Violence against Abortion Providers (TFVAAP)—An investigative arm of the Department of Justice, the Civil Rights Division of the Department of Justice. The TFVAAP investigates any instance in which customers or providers of reproductive health services are criminally threatened, obstructed, or injured while seeking or providing services.

TATP—Tri-acetone Tri-peroxide (TATP)—Ingredient for IED that acts as a high explosive. It is highly susceptible to heat, friction, and shock. For its instability, it has been called the "Mother of Satan."

Terrorist incident—An attack or threat of an attack carried out by terrorists.

Terrorist No-Fly Watch List—A compilation of suspicious names gathered from airline passenger manifests.

Terry Waite—Special Envoy to Britain's Arch Bishop of Canterbury—captured and held hostage by Hezbollah from 1987 to 1991.

Theo Van Gough—Dutch filmmaker murdered on the street in Amsterdam.

Tonton Macoutes—Haitian Secret Police—used to spread fear and terror among the populace.

Transportation Security Agency (TSA)—U.S. agency created after 9-11 to replace low-paid, poorly trained airport screeners.

Troubles—Generally describes the period of conflict (Catholic vs. Protestant) in Northern Ireland between 1968 and the Belfast Agreement of 1998.

Turkish Revenge Brigade—A little-known, ultranationalist, extreme right-wing group operating in Turkey.

Uighur—Separatist movement in Turkistan.

Umar Farouk Abdulmutallab—aka the Underwear Bomber—with explosives in his underwear attempted to blow up a flight to the United States on Christmas Day 2009.

UN Security Council Resolution 1373—Resolution that called for international cooperation to prevent and eradicate acts of terrorism worldwide; unanimously adopted on September 28, 2001, under Chapter VII of the UN General Assembly by consensus of the 189 member states.

Unilateral Declaration of Independence (UDI)—Declared on November 11, 1965, by Ian Smith of Rhodesia.

Union of Islamic Communities and Organizations in Italy (UCOII)—The largest Muslim group in Italy. UCOII has a network of more than fifty mosques throughout the country. It has a network throughout Europe and supports an International Muslim Brotherhood.

United Self-Defense Forces of Colombia (AUC)—Group formed to combat the leftist terrorist organizations operating in Colombia, primarily the FARC and ELN. The AUC grew out of the paramilitary and self-defense groups formed in the 1980s.

URNA—Utvar Rychleho Nasazeni (URNA) is the Czech Republic's rapid response counterterrorist police and crime-busting force.

U.S. Marine barracks in West Beirut—October 1983—A Hezbollah suicide bomber drove an explosive laden truck into the barracks killing 241 U.S. Marines.

U.S. Patriot Act—Law passed in 2001 following the 9-11 attacks in the United States; uniting and strengthening America by providing appropriate tools required to intercept and obstruct terrorism.

VBIED—Vehicle-borne improvised explosive device.

Vesicants—Blistering agent developed for use in chemical warfare. A chemical weapon used in World War I and by Saddam Hussein against the Kurds.

Waco Massacre—Armed raid by members of the FBI and ATF on the Branch Davidian base in Waco, Texas.

Wahhabism—Islamic religious movement within Islam founded by Muhammad ibn Abd al-Wahhab (1703–1992).

War on Terror—Phrase established after the attacks on the World Trade Center and the Pentagon in September 2001 to detail the coming "war" against terrorism on worldwide scale led primarily by the United States.

Water Boarding—A form of water torture where a captive is restrained and water poured over a cloth on the face forcing a gagging reflex—has the sensation of being drowned.

World Trade Center—Group of buildings in New York City destroyed on September 11, 2001, by two hijacked aircraft that were flown into two of the towers.

Zakat Hawala—Islamic funding principle used to move vast sums of money undetected.

Zapatista National Liberation Army (ELZN)—Violent Mexican organization that opposes NAPTA.

Zealots—A person(s) who is uncompromising and fanatical in pursuit of their religious, political or other ideals.

Zimbabwe African National Union (ZANU)—Robert Mugabe's ruling political party.

Zimbabwe African People's Union (ZANPU)—Opposition group opposed to ZANU.

Zimbabwe People's Revolutionary Army (ZIPRA)—Opposition group opposed to ZANU.

INDEX

Abbas, Abu, 229, 287, 478
Abbas, Mahmoud (a.k.a. Abu Mazen), 218, 228
Abdellah Azzam Brigades, 55
Abdul Aziz, King, 264–265
Abdul-Hamid II, Sultan, 173
Abdullah, Bilal, 132
Abdullah, Crown Prince, 265
Abdullah, King, 233
Abubakar, Atiku, 333
Abu Dujana Al Afgani (Ansar Group, Al Qaeda in Europe), 148
Abu Ghraib prison, 64, 273
Abu Marzuq, Musa, 36
Abu Nidal organization (for Sabri al- Banna), 219–220, 248, 255
  aviation targets, successful attacks on, 220
Abu Sayyaf, 248
Abu Sayyaf Group (ASG), 358, 385, 394
"Acceptable enemies," 6
Accion Democratica (AD), 432
Accion Nacional Espanola (ANE), 145
Acebes, Angel, 146
Achille Lauro, 229, 230, 287, 474, 478–479
Acholi Pii Camp, 311
Acholi tribe, 312
Action Direct (AD), 150
Action management process, 525
Active service unit (ASU), 101
Adams, Gerry, 36, 97, 98, 419
Aden Protectorate, 297
Aden (South Yemen), 297
Adherents, 376. *See also* Al Qaeda
AEG-Telefunken, 181
Afghan Airlines Boeing, 457
Afghanistan
  Islamic Emirate of, 360–361
  Mullah Omar, 360
  present/future challenges, 361–362
  Taliban, 356–357
African National Congress (ANC), 320–321
Afrikaner nationalism, 318
Afrikaner Resistance Movement, 319
Afrikaner Weerstandsbeweging (AWB), 319
Agca, Mehmet Ali, 207
"Agreement," the
  decommissioning, 115–116
  prisoners, 116–117
  security, 117–118
Ahmadinejad, Mahmoud, 29, 294, 432
Ahmed, Abdullahi Yusuf, 304
Ahmed, Kafeel, 132
Ahmed, Mahmud, 56
Ahmed Jibril, 225
Ahtisaari, Martti, 115
Aidid, Mohamed, 304
Aimal Khufia Action Committee, 344
Aircraft hijacking, combating
  Aircraft Hijack Response Location, 456–457
  Federal Air Marshal Service—FAM, 456
  overview, 455–456
  policy, 457–458
Aircraft Hijack Response Location, 456–457
Air-India Flight, 74, 83–84
Airport facilities, 449–450
Air Tanzania Boeing, 456
Akali Dal (AD), 80
Akbar, Jawad, 131
Al-Abdaly, Taimour Abdulwahab, 184
Al-Aqsa, 221–222

Al-Assad, Bashar, 240, 241, 432
Al-Assad, Hafez, 238, 240
al-Awlaki Anwar, 299
Al-Bakr, Ahmed Hassan, 276
Al-Bakri, Mukhtar, 60
Albanian National Army (AKSh), 205–206
Al Banna, Sheik, 245
Albright, Madeleine, 364
Al Dosari, Juma, 60
Aleman, Miguel, 402
Alexander II, Tsar, 496
Al-Faqih, Abdelrahman, 249
Al-Fatah (or Al-Asifa), 219
Alfred P Murrah Federal Building, 49, 50
Algeria
  Al- Qaeda in the Land of The Islamic Maghreb-formerly GSPC, 260
  Armed Islamic Group (GIA), 259
  December 1991 elections, 258–259
  economic crisis, 257
  October 1988 riots, 257–258
  overview, 256–257
  Rais Massacre, 259–260
Algerian Islamic Salvation Front, 243
Al-Husseini, Mohammed Amin, 27
Ali (Rightful Prophet of Islam), 32
Ali Jinnah, Mohammed, 350
Ali Jinnah, Muhammad, 345
Al-Ittihad, 306
Ali Zardari, Asif, 346
Al-Jazeera, 36
Al-Juweir, Fahd bin Faraj, 267
Al Khalifa, Hamad bins Isa, 288
Al Khalifa, Isa bin Salman, 287
Al Khalifa, Khalifi bin Salman, 287
Al-Khawarizmi, Abu Ja'far Muhammad ibn Musa, 275
Al-Kifah Refugee Center, Brooklyn, New York, 66
Alleanza Nazionale (National Alliance), 168
Allende, Salvador, 430
Allied Democratic Forces (ADF), 313
All India Sikh Students Federation, 81
Al-Majid, Ali Hassan ("Chemical Ali"), 275, 276
Al-Majid, Hussein Kamil Hassan, 277
Al-Manar TV network, 238
Al-Masri, Abu Ayyub, 279
Al-Masri, Abu Hamza, 56, 60, 93, 125, 126
Al-Megrahi, Abdel Basset, 121
Al-Muhajiroun, 125–126
Al-Murabitoon ala Ard al-Isra (The Steadfast on the Land of al-Isra), 225
Al Qaeda
  base of, 357–359
  Belgium, 179
  characteristic elements of, 358–359
  France, 152–153
  Germany, 156–163
  India, 341
  in the Land of the Islamic Maghreb (AQIM), 260
  Iran and, 296–297
  and Islamic State, 490–491
  Morocco, 243–244
  operations, 359
  Somalia, 304
  Sunni ideology of, 358
  Turkey, 177–178
  United States of America, 55
  WMD, possible links to, 286
Al- Qaeda in the Arabian Peninsula (AQAP), 299–300

Al- Qaeda in the Land of the Islamic Maghreb-formerly GSPC, 260
Al- Qaeda Jihad Organization in the Land of Two Rivers (Mesopotamia—Iraq), 279
Al Qaeda sponsor, 295–296
Al-Qassam, Izz al-Din, 229
Al-Rahman, Omar Abdel (the Blind Sheikh), 66
Al-Rashadi, Walid Mutlaq, 268
Al-Sabah, Amir Sheikh Saad Al-Abdullah, 272
Al-Sabah, Sheikh Abdullah Al-Salem, 272
Al-Sabah dynasty, 272
Al Shabaab, 305–307
Al-Shehhi, Marwan, 55, 162
Al-Shifa Pharmaceutical Factory in Khartoum, 255
Alwan, Sahim, 60
Al-Zarqawi, Abu Musab, 148, 149, 235, 279, 280, 281, 282
Al-Zawahiri, Ayman, 393
Amin, Salahuddin, 131
Amnesty International, 64
Amn al-Kharji, 286
Angola
  Diego Cam, 326
  Front for the Liberation of Angola (FNLA), 327
  historical overview, 326–327
  Holden Roberto, 326
  Jonas Savimbi, 327
  National Union for the Total Independence of Angola (UNITA), 327
  The Popular Movement for the Liberation of Angola (MPLA), 327
Angry Brigade, the, 123
Animal Liberation Front, 124
Animal Rights Militia, 52
Antiabortionists, 52
Anti-Fascist Resistance Group of October First (GRAPO), 146
Antiterrorism, Crime and security Act 2001 (UK) ATCSA, 127
Antiterrorism and Effective Death Penalty Act of 1996, 354, 365, 381, 459
Anti-Terrorism Assistance Program (ATA), 417
Antiterrorism Crime and Security Act of 2001, 110, 127
Anzar, Jose Maria, 147
Apalategui, Miguel, 143
Apartheid, 318–319
Apprentice Boys, 105, 112
"Arab Revolution," 158
Arab Spring
  Egypt, 246–247
  Fatah and Hamas, 229
  North Africa, 248
  Syrian unrest and, 241–242
Arafat, Yasser, 27, 212, 215, 217
Arar, Maher, 64
Araújo, Consuelo, 420
Archbishop's Human Rights Office (ODHA), 407
Argentina
  Al-Qaeda, 429
  CERT, 428
  death squads, 428
  Division de Informacion Politicas Antidemocratic (DIPA), 428
  drug trafficking, 429
  Eva Peron, 428
  Falklands, battle for, 428
  Hamas, 429
  Hezbollah, 429

historical overview, 428–430
Juan Domingo Peron, 428
Montoneros (Movimiento Peronista Montonero), 429
Tri-Border Area (TBA), international terrorism in, 429
Triple A (AAA), 428
Argov, Shlomo, 220
Arguello, Patrick, 234
Aristide, Jean-Bertrand, 90
Armata Corsa, 150
Armed Front for the Liberation of the Marginalized People of Guerrero, 405
Armed Islamic Group (GIA), 151, 258, 259
Armed Islamic Movement Group, 258
Armed Proletarian Nuclei (NAP), 167
Armee Republicaine Bretonne (ARB), 150
Armenian Secret Army for the Liberation of Armenia (ASALA), 177
Armenian terrorism, 177
Armitage, Richard, 56
Army for the Liberation of Armenia (ASALA), 150–151
Army of God, 51
Army of Islam, 228
Army of the Poor and Peasant's Brigade against Injustice, 403
Army Ranger Wing (ARW), 469
Article 101 of the United Nations Convention of the Law of the Sea, 475
Article 3 of the United Nations Convention Against Torture, 64
Arzalluz, Xavier, 144
Arzu, Alvaro, 408
Asahara, Shoko, 380
Ashraq al-Awsat, 222
Asian Development Bank, 364
ASIANA Boeing 777-200 crash, 528–529
Assad, Bashar, 240
Assassin (hashish-eater), 26
Assassination, 16–17
Atomic Energy Agency (AEA), 479
Atta, Mohammed, 55, 147
Aum Shinrikyo, 380–381
Australia
    counter-terrorism units, 468–469
    Crimes (Internationally Protected Persons) Act 1976, 393
    international terrorism, 394–396
    Jack Roche, 393
    terrorist acts (past sixty years), 393
    threats to (Bin Laden, al-Zawahiri), 393
Australian Embassy bombing, 391
Autodeterminaziorako Bilgunea (AuB), 144
Autonomous Active Service Units (ASU), 102
Autonomous jihad, 59
Avian Flu, 484
Aviation, 491–492
    airport facilities, 449–450
    civil aviation, global threat to, 448
    Computer-Assisted Passenger Prescreening System (CAPPS II), 453
    Computer-Assisted Passenger Profiling, 452
    conventions related to terrorism. *See* Conventions, related to terrorism
    El Al airlines Boeing 747, 447
    European Civil Aviation Conference (ECAC), 455
    Gore Commission, 452
    Heathrow Airport attacks, 451
    hijacking, combating
        Aircraft Hijack Response Location, 456–457
        Federal Air Marshal Service—FAM, 456
        overview, 455–456
        policy, 457–458

improvised explosive device (IED), 448
intelligence failings, 445
Lyon Summit Conference in 1996, 457
Man Portable Air Defense Systems (MANPADS), 451
"No fly" lists, 454
Operation Bojinka, 448
Pan Am 103, 448
passenger profiling, 453–454
passenger screening, 446
a people issue, 452
President's Commission on Aviation and Terrorism, 444–445
Screening Passengers by Observation Technique (SPOT), 454
"Secure Flight," 454
Secure Flight Notice of Proposed Rule Making (NPRM), 453–454
security improvements 1990s, woefully short, 446
Stinger missile, 452
tombstone technology, 446–447
Transportation Security Administration (TSA), 447
trolley bag bomb, 122
TSA statistical information, 453
U.S. General Accounting Office report to Congressional Committees on Aviation Security, 447
weapon-detection rates, 452
Aviation Security Commando (AVESCOM), 473
"Axis of Evil," 248
Axis Rule in Occupied Europe (Lemkin), 39
Ayro, Aden Hashi, 304
Azad Babbar Khalsa (Independent Babbar Khalsa), 81
Azzam, Abdullah Yusuf, 55
Azzouz, Samir, 182

Baader, Andreas, 158
Baader-Meinhof Gang, 158
Babbar Khalsa International (BKI), 79
Babbar, Sukhdev Singh, 82
Babbar Khalsa (BK), 81–82, 349–350
Babbar Khalsa International (BKI), 79, 81
BAC1–11, 456
Bacillus anthracis, 483, 495
Bagri, Ajab Singh, 83
Bahrain, 287–288
Bahraini Hezbollah, 288
Bakassi Boys, The, 332
Baker, Abdul Haqq, 152
Bakri, Omar, 124
Bakunin, Mikhail, 40, 190
Balcombe Street siege, 102
Balfour, Sir Arthur James, 213
Balfour Declaration, 213
Bali Night Club bombing, 390, 391
Bangladesh Liberation Army, 351
Banyarwandans, 331
Banzer, Hugo, 424
Barak, Ehud, 215
Barakat, Assad Ahmed Mohamed, 431
Bardo National Museum, Tunis, 254
Bargouti, Marwan, 228
Barisan Revolusi Nasional-Coordinate, National Revolutionary Front-Coordinate (BRN-C), 368
Barot, Dhiren, 129
Barre, Said, 304
Basayev, Shamil, 199
Basayev, Shamil Salmanovich, 199
Bashir, Abu Bakar (also Ba'asyir), 390, 391
Bashkortostan, 197
Basque Nationalist Party (PNV), 143

Basque region, 141
Basques
    Basque separatism, 142
    Spanish nationalism and, 141
Basque Socialist Coalition, 144
Basque Youth Movement, 143
Bataclan Theater attacks, 153–156
Ba'athist regime, 274
"Battle of the Diamond," 112
Beckwith, Charles, 474
Beghal, Djamel, 151
Begin, Menachem, 216, 244
Belgium
    Al- Qaeda in, 171
    Communist Combatant Cells (CCC), 181
    DARE, 178
    New Force Party, 178
    overview, 178–179
    Revolutionary Front for Proletarian Action (FRAP), 181
    West New Post, 178
Believing Youth Movement, 298
Ben Bella, Ahmed, 257
Benedetti, Luciano, 386
Ben-Gurion, David, 213, 214
Benhammedi, Mohammed, 249
Benito, Eustakio Mendizabel, 143
Bendjedid, Chadli, 257, 258
Benghazi attack, 250–251
Bernadotte, Count Folke, 214
Berriew, Lord, 110
Beslan school attack, 199
"Beyond the pale," 14
Bhindranwale Tiger Force, 349
Bhindranwale, Jarnail Singh, 81, 82
Bhutto, Benazir, 345, 359
Bin Laden, Osama
    media and, 36
    Sudan, expelled from, 249
    U.S. Embassy (Nairobi, Kenya), attack on, 324
Bin said, Qaboos, 290
Bin Suleiman, Salah Fathi, 249
Bin Taimur, Sultan Said, 289
Biological and chemical attacks, 495
Biological weapons
    Avian Flu, 484–485
    Bacillus anthracis, 483
    Botulism, 484
    bubonic plague, 484
    contingency planning, 484
    Cutaneous Anthrax, 483
    history of, 482–483
    Inhalational Anthrax, 483
    Intestinal Anthrax, 483
    Pneumonic Plague, 484
    practical training, 485
    response plan, developing, 484–485
    Ricin, 493
    Smallpox, 483
    Toxins, 483
    Tularemia, 484
Biological Weapons Convention, 495
Birdal, Akin, 177
Black and Tans, 95, 97
Black June, 219
Black Panthers, 50, 53
Black September, 17, 160, 178, 219
Black Tiger Squad, 354
Blair, Sir Ian, 132
Blair, Tony, 34, 94, 98, 497
Blanco, Luis Carrero, 143
Block, Dora, 310
Bloody Sunday (first), 95
Boeremag (Boer Force), 322

Boers, 318
Boevaya Oranisatsia (BO), or the Fighting
    Organization, 190
Boko Haram, 333–334
    funding of, 334–335
    kidnapping for ransom, 335
    modus operandi, 333–334
    objective, 333
    size and strength, 333
Boko Haram-Nigeria-May 2011, 17
Bolivar, Simon, 423, 432
Bolivia
    Cochabamba Valley massacre, 424
    drug trade, 424
    Manual Rodriguez Patriotic Front (FPMR), 424
    overview, 423–424
    political changes, 424
    Servicio Especial Seguridad (SES), 424
Bolshevik Revolution, 189
Bolsheviks, 190–191
Bond, Julian, 54
Border security
    Israel, ongoing issue on, 212
    in Rwanda, 331
    U.S. troop security within Iraq, 241
Boriken, or Borinquen, 75
Bosnia-Herzegovina, 205
Botha, Louis, 318
"Bottom-line" considerations, 6
Botulism, 484
Bouyeri, Mohammed, 182
Boynton, Homer, 444
BP Oil Spill, Gulf of Mexico, 526
Brabourne, Lady, 101
"Brandwag," 319
Brazil
    Carlos Marighella, 424
    Hamas and Hezbollah, 427, 429
    Mini-Manual of the Urban Guerrilla
        (Marighella), 424, 425
    overview, 424–425
    Tupac Katari Guerrilla Army (EGTK), 424
    urban guerrilla, personal qualities of, 424–425
Brigades of Martyr Yasser Arafat, 221
British Broadcasting Corporation (BBC), 115, 227
British Secret Intelligence Service (SIS), 465
Brotherhood of Assassins, 26
Broussard, Robert, 471
Brown, Gordon, 132, 133
Brussels attack, 179
    timeline, 180
Buback, Seigfried, 160
Bulgaria, 207–208
Bureau of Alcohol, Tobacco and Firearms (ATF),
    50, 474
Bureau of State Security (BOSS), 319
Burma (Myanmar), 362–364
    "constructive engagement," 363
    Daw Aung San Suu Kyi, 363
    drug trafficking, 363
    human rights and, 363
    market reforms, 364
    parliament election (2012), 364
    State Law and Order Restoration Council
        (SLORC), 364
    State Peace and Development Council (SPDC), 363
    Thura Tin Oo, 364
Bush, George Herbert, 29
Bush, George W., 2, 193, 265, 277, 350, 375
Bushnell, Prudence, 48
Business continuity, 529
Business Continuity Management (BCM)
    defined, 520–521
    need for, 521
    outcomes of, 521–522

plan components, 523
process chart, 522
Business continuity planning, 529
Business Resumption and Interruption Plans, 485
"Butcher of Kurdistan," 275
Byrne, Pat, 102

Cabanas, Lucio, 403
The Cabinet Home Affairs Committee, 125
Caesar, Julius, 26
Cagol, Margherita, 166
Cairo Gang, 95
Cali cartel, 416
Callaghan, James, 96
Calvert, "Mad Mike," 469
Cam, Diego, 326
Cambodia
    historical overview, 364–366
    Khmer Rouge, 365, 422
    Khmer Royal Armed Forces (KRAF), 365
    Pol Pot (Saloth), 365
Cameron, David, 128, 129
Canada
    Air-India Flight 182, bombing of, 83–84
    Bill C-36 of Canada's Anti-terrorism Act, 76
    Front de Liberation du Quebec (FLQ), 80
    illegal drug trade, 78
    immigration and, 78–79
    Islamist threat to, 85
    Joint Task Force 2 (JTF-2), 474–475
    list of entities, 76
    overview, 74–75, 76–79
    refugee claimant system, 88
    refugees, liberalism toward
        Omar Khadr, case of, 87–88
        overview, 84
    Sikh terrorism
        Babbar Khalsa (BK), 81–82
        overview, 80–81
        speaking out against, 82
        Talwinder Singh Parmar, 82–83
Canada's Anti-terrorism Act, Bill C-36, 76–77
Canada's Security and Intelligence Service
    (CSIS), 78, 82
Canadian Broadcast Corporation (CBC), 125
Canadian Immigration Service, 84
Canadian Security Intelligence Service, 83
Carbaugh, John E., 384
Card, Francis, 98
Carette, Pierre, 181
Carillo, Ignacio, 403
Carlos the Jackal, 158, 190
Carter, Jimmy, 216, 244
Castro, Fidel, 88–89
Catholic Reaction Force (CRF). *See* Irish National
    Liberation Army (INLA)
Caucasus dissidents (Ingushetia), 193
Caudillos, 402
Celik, Oral, 207
Cellular structure, 12, 102
Central American Free Trade Agreement
    (CAFTA), 413
Central American gang problems
    18th Street, or Mara 18, 413, 414
    Central American Free Trade Agreement
        (CAFTA), 413
    Mara Salvatrucha 13, 413, 414, 415
    overview, 413–414
    results, 414–415
Central Intelligence Group, 464
Charlie Hebdo, 153–154
Charter of Rights and Freedoms (Canada), 88
Chavez, Hugo, 420, 432
Chebli, Driss, 147
Chechnya

assassinations, 198–201
Caucasus, problems in, 197
current situation, 198
historical overview, 197
Russian forces in, 193
Cheka, 191
"Chemical Ali," 275
Chemical weapons
    blood agents, 482
    chemical agents, 480
    chemical terrorism, history of, 480–481
    choking agents, 482
    irritating agents, 482
    nerve agents, 481
    overview, 480
    vesicants, 481–482
Chernomirdin, Viktor. S., 199
Chiapas region, 404–405
Chicago Convention, Annex 17, 443
Chile
    Augusto Pinochet, 430
    Avengers of the Martyrs, 430
    "Caravan of Death," 431
    death squads, 431
    foreign agitators, 430
    international terrorism, 431
    Manuel Rodriguez Patriotic Front (FPMR), 424
    Pinochet years, 430–431
    Salvador Allende, 430
China
    drug trafficking, 374
    East Turkestan Islamic Movement (ETIM),
        375–376
    East Turkestan Islamic Republic, 374
    East Turkestan Liberation Movement, 374
    Falun Gong, 376–378
    George W. Bush, October 2001 meeting, 375
    Hong Kong, 378
    Islam, 374
    Islamic organizations, 374
    Jiangdu activists, 374
    Kazakhstan, 374
    overview, 373–374
    Pan-Turkic movement, 374–375
    Taiwan (Republic of China), 378–379
    terrorism in, 377–378
    Uighur Muslims, 375
    Uighurs, 374–378
    Xinjiang Uighur Autonomous Region
        (XUAR), 375
Chretien, Jean, 87
Christian Democratic Party (COPIE), 432
CIA Predator Drone, 60
Claudia (freighter), 101
Civil liberty, and human rights, 108–111
Closed-circuit television (CCTV) cameras, 130,
    441, 452
Cobras (Sultan of Oman Special Forces, SSF), 470
Coco, Francesco, 166
Code of Hammurabi, 275
Codified law, 22
Collective blame, 40
Collett, Peter, 239
Collins, Michael, 94–95
Collinson, Paul, 113
Colombia
    Alvaro Uribe, 416, 419, 433
    Anti-Terrorism Assistance Program (ATA), 417
    demilitarized zone (DMZ), 417
    drug trafficking, 416
    historical overview, 415–416
    Hugo Chavez, assisting FARC, 420, 432
    human rights and, 415
    insurgent campaign, 416
    Jamaat al-Islamiya, 419

Mohammed Abed Abel, 419
National Liberation Army (ELN), 416, 418
peace talks, 417
"Plan Colombia," 420
Raul Reyes (a.k.a. Luis Edgar Devia Silva), 420
Revolutionary Armed Forces of Colombia
    (FARC), 416–417
right-wing death squads, 418–419
terrorism in, 416–418
Unified Action Groups for Personal Liberty
    (GAULA), 417
United Self-Defense Forces of Colombia
    (AUC), 416–417
U.S. foreign policy, 419
Colombian People's Liberation Army (EPL), 432
Colombo World Trade Center bombing
    (October 15, 1997), 354
Colon, Hernandez, 75
"Colons," 257
Coltan, 316
Combat Methamphetamine Epidemic Act of 2005, 66
Commission on the Intelligence Capabilities of
    the United States regarding Weapons of
    Mass Destruction, 65
Communist Combatant Cells (CCC), 150, 181
Communist Party of the Philippines (CPP), 386
Computer-Assisted Passenger Prescreening
    System (CAPPS II), 453
Computer-Assisted Passenger Profiling, 452
Concepts of operations (CONOPs), 466
Condera, Monsignor Juan Gerardi, 407
Connolly, Nial, 101
"Constitutionalist" groups, 50
Constitutional rights, 17–18
Container security initiative (CSI)
    CBPs domestic process, 479
    chemical, biological, and nuclear FDA
        strategies, understanding, 479
    core principles, 479
    CSI overseas process, 479
    ports operating under, 479
Continuity IRA (CIRA), 98
Continuity management, defined, 530
Contras, 411–412
Control Orders, 127
Convention against Torture, 64
Convention for the Prevention and the Punishment
    of the Crime of Genocide, 39, 256
Conventions, related to terrorism
    Convention for the Suppression of Unlawful Acts
        against the Safety of Civil Aviation, 444
    Convention for the Suppression of Unlawful
        Acts against the Safety of Maritime
        Navigation, 444
    Convention for the Suppression of Unlawful
        Seizure of Aircraft, 444
    Convention on Offenses and Certain Other Acts
        Committed on Board Aircraft, 444
    Convention on the Marking of Plastic
        Explosives for the Purpose of Detection
        (1991), 444
    Convention on the Physical Protection of
        Nuclear Material, 444
    Convention on the Prevention and Punishment
        of Crimes against Internationally Protected
        Persons, 444
    International Convention against the Taking of
        Hostages, 444
    International Convention for the Suppression of
        Terrorist Bombing, 444
    International Convention for the Suppression of
        the Financing of Terrorism, 444
    Protocol for the Suppression of Unlawful Acts
        against the Safety of Fixed Platforms
        Located on the Continental Shelf, 444

Protocol for the Suppression of Unlawful
    Acts of Violence at Airports Serving
    International Civil Aviation,
    supplementary to the Convention for the
    Suppression of Unlawful Acts against the
    Safety of Civil Aviation, 444
Core Competencies Framework, 524–525
Corsican Army (Armata Corsa), 150
Cosa Nostra ("our thing"), 54
Cosgrave, William, 96
Countering terrorism. *See* Terrorism, countering
Counter-man-portable air defense system
    (MANPADS) program, 451
Counterterrorism, and Security Bill, 136–137
Counterterrorism units
    Australia
        Offshore Installations Assault Group
            (OAG), 469
        Special Air Service Regiment (SASR), 468
        Tactical Assault Group, 468
    Czech Republic, Utvar Rychleho Nasazeni
        (URNA), 472
    France
        Groupment d'intervention de la Gendarmerie
            Nationale (GIGN), 470–471
        Research, Assistance, Intervention, and
            Dissuasion (RAID), 470
    Germany
        Federal Border Police, 472
        Grenzschutzgruppe 9 (GSG-9), 472
        GSG-9/1, 472
        GSG-9/2, 472
        GSG-9/3, 472
    Great Britain
        British SAS, 467–468
        Counter Revolutionary Warfare
            Squadron, 467
        L Detachment, Special Air Service
            Brigade, 467
        Operations Research Unit, 467
        Special Boat Squadron (SBS), 468
        Special Projects Team, 467
    Ireland, Army Ranger Wing (ARW), 469
    Israel, Sayeret Mat'kal (General Staff
        Reconnaissance Unit #69), 472
    Netherlands
        7th Special Boat Squadron, 468
        Bijondere Bijstands Eenheid (BBE), 471
        Marines (BBE), 471
        Royal Netherlands Marine Corps, 471
    Norway
        Forsvarets Spesialkommando (FSK, Special
            Defense Commando), 471
        Norwegian Army Jegercommand, 471
    Oman, Cobras (Sultan of Oman Special
        Forces, SSF), 470
    Rhodesia (Zimbabwe)
        C Squadron 22 SAS (Malayan Scouts), 469
        Rhodesian SAS, 469
        Special Air Service Squadron, 468
    Spain
        Grupo Especial De Operaciones
            (GEO), 470
        Guarda Civil, 470
        Unidad Especial de Intervencion (UEI), 470
Courtailler, David, 152
Courtailler, Jerome, 152
Crimes (Internationally Protected Persons) Act
    1976, 394
Crime Prevention Through Environmental Design
    (CPTED), 506–507
Cross, James, 80
Cross-border terrorism, 438
Crusades, 30
Cuba

Fidel Castro, 88–89
Gallego, 88
overview, 88
Cumann na mBan, 103
Cumming, Sir Mansfield, 465
Cuomo, Mario, 47
Curcio, Renato, 166
Customs and Border Patrol (CBP), 479
Cutaneous Anthrax, 483
Cyanide, 495
Cycle of violence, 39
Cyprus
    National Organization of Cypriot Combatants
        (EOKA), 172
    overview, 172
    Turkish invasion–July 20, 1974, 172
Cyprus Broadcasting Station, April 1, 1955
    bombing of, 172
Czar Alexander II, 188, 189
Czech Republic, 208–209
    counter-terrorism unit, 472

Dada, Idi Amin, 302, 309
Dadullah, Mansour, 360
Dadullah, Mullah, 356
Dahdah, Abu, 146
Dal Khalsa, 349
Dal Khalsa (party of the pure), 81
Darfur, 255–256
Dark Ages, 329
Dasuwal, Sukhdev Singh, 81
Dawson Field, 234
Death squads, 410, 418–419
De Chastelain, John, 116
Decommissioning, weapons, 115–116
De Gaulle, Charles, 80
Deir Yassin massacre, 214
Delgado de Codex, Juan Carlos, 146
Delta Force commandos, 474
De Menezes, Jean Charles, 132, 441
Demilitarized zone (DMZ), 417
Democratic Front for the Liberation of Palestine
    (DFLP), 231
Democratic Front for the Liberation of Palestine-
    Hawatmeh (DFLPH), 217
Democratic Opposition of Serbia (DOS), 205
Democratic People's Republic of North Korea
    (DPRK), 282–283
Democratic Progressive Party (DPP), 379
Democratic Republic of Congo (DRC), 330
    Banyarwandans, 331
    historical overview, 330
    Joseph Desire Mobutu, 330
    Joseph Kabila, 331
    Joseph Kasavubu, 330
    King Leopold, 330
    Laurant Kabila, 330
    Liberation Army of Rwanda (ALiR), 331
    Mobutu Sese Seko, 331–332
    Ugandan troops in, 310
Department of Defense, terrorism,
    definition of, 8
Department of Homeland Security (DHS)
    creation of, 19
    Homeland Security Presidential Directive-6, 63
    intelligence gathering, 463–465
Department of Treasury, 142
Dera Sacha Sauda, 343
Derwish, Kamal, 60
De Valera, Eamon, 95
Dev Sol, 174
Digital Selective Calling (DSC), 476
Diplock Commission, the, 109
Diplock Courts, 109
Diplomatic immunity, 120–121

Direct Action Against Drugs (DAAD), 103
Directed-energy weapons, 499
Directorate of Inter-Services Intelligence (ISI).
　　See Inter Service Intelligence agency (ISI)
Dirty bombs (radiological dispersal device, RDD)
　　impact of, 485
　　overview, 485–486
Disaster Planning and Critical Incident Command
　　procedures, 485
Disaster recovery plan/planning, 530
Division de Informacion Politicas Antidemocratic
　　(DIPA), 428
Doc, Papa, 90
Doctor Zhivago, 190
Domestic terrorist acts, 50
Dominican Republic, 89–90
Dosanjh, Ujjal, 83
Douglas Leigh, 239
Dozier, James, 167, 208
Drake, Sir Francis, 475
Drive-by shootings, 54
Driver, Aaron, 86–87
Duarte, Isaías, 420
Dudayev, Dzhokhar, 197
Dumont, Lionel, 152
Durand, Oscar, 422
Duvalier, François "Papa Doc," 90
Duvalier, Jean-Claude "Baby Doc," 90
Dzerzhinsky, Feliks, 191
Dzhugashvili, Josef Vissarionovich, 190.
　　See Stalin, Joseph

Easter Rebellion, 101
Easter Uprising, 97
East Turkestan Islamic Movement (ETIM),
　　375–376
East Turkestan Islamic Republic, 374
Ebrahim, Abdus Salaam, 322
Echeverri, Gilberto, 420
Echeverria, Luis, 403
Ecuador, 433
　　Revolutionary Armed Forces of Colombia
　　　　(FARC), 433
　　Revolutionary Armed Forces of Ecuador, 433
Egypt, 472
　　Anwar Sadat, 1919–1981, 245
　　Arab Spring, 246–247
　　Islamic extremists and, 245–246
　　Muslim Brotherhood, 245
　　overview, 244
　　twentieth-century politics, 244–245
Egypt Air 648, 473
Egyptian Islamic Jihad, 245
18th Street, or Mara 18, 413, 414
El Al Airlines Boeing 747 flight to Tel Aviv,
　　Israel, 447
El Al Airlines hijacking, 447–448
Elbaneh, Jaber, 60
El Baradei, Mohamed, 195
Eldad, Israel, 214
El-Qaddafi, Muammar, 247–248
El-Sadr, Mousa, 237
El Salvador
　　Augustin Farabundo Marti, 409
　　Central American Communist Party, 409
　　death squads, 410
　　historical overview, 409–410
　　ORDEN, 410
El-Sambouli, Lieutenant, 245
El Sayed, Omar, 88
Emergency Planning Society (UK), 524
Emergency Provisions, 442. See also The Northern
　　Ireland Act
Enemy combatants, 462
Ensslin, Gudrun, 158
Entity, defined, 76

Erbakan, Necmettin, 163
Espanastatikos Laikos Agonas (ELA,
　　Revolutionary Peoples Struggle), 171
Essid, Sami Ben Khemais, 168
Essig, Christopher G., 8
Estonian Guerrilla Movement, 1944–1955, 192
ETA-5, 142
ETA-6, 142
ETA-Berri (or young ETA), 142
ETA-Military, 142
ETA-Politico Military, 142
ETA-Zarra (or old ETA), 142
Ethiopia, 303–304
Ethiopian People's Revolutionary Democratic
　　Front (EPRDF), 303
Ethnic cleansing, 30, 34, 203–204, 256
Europe, Muslim population in, 180–181
European Civil Aviation Conference (ECAC), 455
European Convention on Human Rights, 109
European Court of Human Rights, 128
European Economic Community (EEC), 142
European Union (EU), 172, 315
Euskera, 141
Euskadi Ta Askatasuna (ETA)
　　development of, 143
　　historical overview, 142–143
　　history timeline, 145–146
　　new century—new campaign, 143–145
　　opposition to, 145
　　terrorists, definition of, 5
Eva Peron, 428
Executive Order 13224—September 23, 2001, 142
Executive summary, risk assessments, 503
Extraordinary rendition, 64
"Extreme sanction," 16

"Fair game" for terrorists/dissenters, 6
Faisal, King, 265
Falklands, battle for, 428
Falun Gong, 376–378
Fardoust, Hossein, 292
Fatah, 218
Fatwa, 54
Fedayeen, 217
Fedayeen Saddam, 277
Federal Air Marshal Service—FAM, 456
Federal Bureau of Investigation (FBI), 464
　　domestic terrorism, defined, 50
　　FBI construct, 8
　　Joint Terrorism Task Forces, 456
　　terrorism, definition of, 8
Federalnaya Sluzhba Bezopasnosti Rossiyskoy
　　Federatsii (FSB), 194
Federal Republic of Yugoslavia (FRY), 205
Ferdinand, Archduke Franz, 5, 203
Fernandez, Ronald, 76
Ferry terminal bombing, 391
"Fertilizer bomb," 126
Fiahs, 389
Fidayeen unit (suicide squad), 349
Fighting Communist Cells. See Communist
　　Combatant Cells (CCC)
FIM-92 Stinger man-portable, surface-to-air
　　missiles, 55
Finsbury Park Mosque, 125
Flag-of-convenience ships (officially "open-
　　registry" ships), 476
Fleischer, Ari, 277
Fletcher, Yvonne, 121, 249
Flynn, Harry, 104
"Foraging Arabs," 213
Ford, Terry, 315
"Forest brethren," 192
Formation of intent, 25
Fort Dix Army camp, planned attack on, 70
Fortuyn Pim, 182

Fossey, Diane, 328
Fourteenth Amendment of the U.S. Constitution, 17
Fourth Geneva Convention, Article 49, 214
"Fourth Sword of Marxism," 422
Fox, Vicente, 403
France
　　Action Direct (AD), 150
　　Al- Qaeda in, 152–153
　　Armed Islamic Group (GIA), 151
　　Armee Republicaine Bretonne (ARB), 150
　　Army for the Liberation of Armenia (ASALA),
　　　　150–151
　　Corsican Army (Armata Corsa), 150
　　counterterrorism units, 470–471
　　Front de la Liberation Nationale de la Corse
　　　　(FLNC), 150
　　Groupe d' Intervention de la Gendarmerie
　　　　Nationale (GIGN), 151
　　Japanese Red Army, 149–150
　　overview, 141, 148–149
　　Palestine Liberation organization (PLO), 149
　　Popular Front for the Liberation of Palestine
　　　　(PFLP), 149
Franco, Francisco, 141
Frankincense, 289
Freedom fighters, 6
Free South Moluccan Youth Organization
　　(VZJ), 471
Frente Revolucionario Anti-Fascista Y Patriotico
　　(FRAP), 146
Friedman, Thomas, 266
Friends of/Sinn Fein, 98
Front de la Liberation Nationale de la Corse
　　(FLNC), 150
Front de Liberation du Quebec (FLQ), 80
Front de Liberation Nationale (FLN), 256
Front for National Salvation (FRONASA), 310
Front for the Liberation of Angola (FNLA), 327
Front for the Liberation of Mozambique
　　(FRELIMO), 327
Front Islamic du Salah (FIS), 257
Fujimori, Alberto, 422–423
Fundamentalists, 33–34, 245, 346, 348
Fusion Task Force (FTF), 464, 465

G-8 Summit, 151
Galaid, Ali Khalif, 304
Gallego, 88
Gandhi, Indira, 80, 81, 340, 347
Gandhi, Mohandas (Mahatma), 34, 340
Gandhi, Rajiv, 42, 340
Gang of Roubaix, 152
Garang, John, 255
Garcia, Anthony, 131
Garzon, Baltazar, 144
Gastarbeiter program, 160
Gaviria, Guillermo, 420
Gaza-Jericho agreement (1993), 226
Gaza Strip, 223
Gemayel, Pierre, 237
General Staff Reconnaissance Unit Number 69,
　　438. See also Sayeret Mat'Kal
Geneva Conventions, 64
Genocide, 30, 39, 204, 255
Georgia, 202–203
Gerakan Mujahidin Islam Pattani, Pattani Islamic
　　Mujahidin Group (GMIP), 368
Gerena, Victor M., 52
German Alternative (Frank Huebner), 161
Germany
　　Al- Qaeda in, 161–163
　　counterterrorism units, 472
　　historical overview, 156–157
　　neo-Nazi factions, 160
　　new order, 157
　　Olympic Games movement, terrorism and, 160

overview, 140–141
post-World War II terrorism and, 157–158
reawaking of the past, 160–161
Red Army Faction (RAF), 158–159
Skinheads, 160
in the twenty-first century, 161
Gestapo, 156
Ghasoubun, 147
Ghazi I, King, 275
Gilani, Sheik Mubarak Ali, 66
Gill, Surjan Singh, 83
GITMO. *See* U.S. Naval Station Guantanamo Bay
Glasgow International Airport (UK), 452
Gligorov, Kiro, 205
Goba, Yahya, 60
Golden Temple, 80–83, 347
Golden Triangle, 374, 389
Goldstein, Baruch, 232
Good Friday Agreement, or Belfast Agreement, 94, 97, 99
Gore Commission, 452
Goulding, Cathal, 97
Government Accountability Office (GAO), 493
Government of Ireland Act of 1920, 95
Gozzoli, Sergio, 168
Great Trek, 318
Great War of 1914–1918, 10
Greece
    Anarchist Street Patrol, 172
    Children of November, 172
    Conscientious Arsonists, 172
    Cyprus, 172
    Espanastatikos Laikos Agonas (ELA, Revolutionary Peoples Struggle), 171
    New Group of Satanists, 172
    November 17 group, 169
    overview, 140–141, 169–171
    Revolutionary Cells/Revolutionary Nuclei (RN), 171
Grenzschutzgruppe-9 (GSG-9), 159, 160
Groenewald, Jan, 319
Groupement d' Intervention de la Gendarmerie Nationale (GIGN), 151, 470–471
Grupa De Resistencia Antifascista Primo Octobre (GRAPO), 146
Grupo Especial De Operaciones (GEO), 470
Guantanamo Bay, 60
Guatemala
    Archbishop's Human Rights Office (ODHA), 407
    civil war, 408
    historical overview, 407
    impunity, 407–408
    Monsignor Juan Gerardi Condera, 407
    Organization of People in Arms (OPRA), 408
    Plan de Sanchez massacre, 408
    Rebel Armed Forces (FAR), 407, 408
    Recovery of Historical Memory (REMHI), 407
"Guatemala Never Again" (Condera), 407
Guatemalan National Unity Group (URNG), 407, 408
Guerilla Army of the Poor (EGP), 408
Guevara, Che, 89
Gulags, 191
Gulf Cooperation Council (GCC), 272
Gulf war (first), 451
Guzman, Abimael, 421

Habash, George, 221
Habibie B.J., 338
Habyarimana, Juvénal, 329
Haddad, Gregoire, 237
Haddad, Wadi, 221
Haganah (Hebrew defence), 215–216
Hagopian, Hagop, 177
Hague Conventions, 2

Haig, Alexander, 160
Haile-Mariam, Mengistu, 303
Haiti, 90–91
Hajj, 269, 294
Hamas, 218
    Hamas– Fatah Disunity, 227–228
    military wing of, 55
    organization and structure of, 225–226
    overview, 223–225
    weaponry, 229
Hammami, Omar Shafik, 305
Hammurabi, King, 275
Hanbali School of Law, 266
Hanjour, Hani, 55
Haouari, Mokhtar, 79
Haqqani Network, 359
Haqqani, Sirajuddin, 359
Harakat al-Kifah al-Musallah (Armed Struggle Movement), 225
Harakat al-Muqawama al-Islamiyya (Islamic Resistance Movement, IRM), 225–226
Harakat-ul-Ansar (HUA), 338, 347–348
Haraket el-Mahroumeen, or Movement of the Deprived (AMAL), 237
Haram al-Sharif (The Noble Sanctuary), 215
Hariri, Rafki, 236, 238
Harkat, Mohamed, 88
Harkatul-Mujahideen, 343
Harward, Robert, 475
Hashemite Kingdom of Jordan, 233
Hashish eater, 26
Hate crimes, 52, 138, 160, 168
Haut Comite d'Etat (HEC), 258
Hawalas (informal money transfer networks), 66
Hawatmeh, Nayef, 228, 231
Hawi, George, 236
Hayer, Tara Singh, 82
H-Blocks, 99
Heathrow Airport attacks, 451–452
Herri Batasuna (Peoples Unity) Party, 144
Herstigte Nasionale Party (HNP), 319
Hertzog, Albert, 319
Hertzog, J., 318
Hezbollah, 28
    Algeria, 258
    also known as, 237
    goal of, 237
    Israel, at war with, 239–240
    kidnapping, 238
    structure and development, 239
    suicide bombers, 239
    Syria and, 240–241
    targets, 238
    in Turkey, 176–177
    war with Israel, 239–240
Highly enriched uranium (HEU), 195, 479, 494
Hinckley, John, 26
Hindawi, Nazer, 447
Hitler, Adolf, 309, 319
Hizb ut-Tahrir (HT), 125–126
HMAS *Australia*, 496
Hobeika, Elie, 236
Ho Chi Minh, 369–370
Hoffman, Bruce, 5, 495
Holocaust, 157
Holy terror, 495–496
Holy War, translation of, 33
Holy Warriors, 35, 58
Homeland Security Act of 2002, terrorism, definition of, 7
Homeland Security Presidential Directive-6, 63
Home Rule Bill for Ireland, 105
Honduras
    Morazanist Patriotic Front (FPM), 409
    overview, 408–409
Hong Kong, 378

China, territorial dispute with, 379
drug trafficking, 378
economy, 378
overview, 378
Hostage crises, examples of
    Black September—March 1973, 178
    Boko Haram—Nigeria, 17
    Front de Liberation du Quebec (FLQ)—October 3, 1970, 80
    Japanese Ambassador's Residence, 17
    Lebanese Hostage Crisis, 16
    Red Army Faction September (RAF) 1977—Hanns-Martin Schleyer, 158
Hostage rescue units (HRUs)
    Bahrain, units British SAS trained, 473
    Egypt
        Force 777, 473
        Saiqa unit, 473
    India, Special Counterterrorist Unit (SCU), 473
    Jordan, 101st Special Forces Battalion, 473
    Malaysia, Special Strike Unit of the Royal Malay Police, 473
    overview, 473
    Philippines, Aviation Security Commando (AVESCOM), 473
    Saudi Arabia, units French GIGN trained, 473
    Sri Lanka, Army Commando Squadron, 473
    Thailand, Special Counterterrorist Unit (SCU), 473
    United States
        Alcohol Tobacco and Firearms (ATF), 474
        Delta Force, 474
        Federal Bureau of Investigation (FBI), 473
        Naval Special Warfare Development Group (NSWDG), 474
        SEAL Team Six, 474
        Special Operations Group, 474
        Special Weapons and Tactical (SWAT), 473
        U.S. Special Forces, 474
Hostage taking, 15–16
    defined, 15
    legal issues in, 16
    U.S. policy toward, 16
House of Deputies (or Dáil Eireann), 95
Howard, John, 315
Howes, Christopher, 365
Huebner, Frank, 161
Huerta, Edigirio, 423
Hull, John, 412
Hull's Ranch, 412
Human intelligence (HUMINT), 464
Human rights
    civil liberty and, 108–111
    and piracy, 477–478
Hume, Alec Douglas, 123
Hussein, Qusay, 277
Hussein, Saddam, 274–277
Hussein, Uday, 277
Hutus, 328–329
Hyde, Henry, 419

IBEX, 292
Ibrhiam, Mukhtar Said, 130
Immigration and Customs Enforcement (ICE), 414
Improvised Explosive Devices (IEDs), 448
Impunity, 407–408
Incident
    awareness, 526–528
    defined, 524
    recognizing, 524
Incident management (IM), 522
    action management process, 525
    exercise, 530–534
    IMT meeting, 525–526
Incident Management Team (IMT), 524
    meeting, 525–526

information management, 528–529
Independent Commission on Policing for
    Northern Ireland (Patten Report), 96
Independent Commission on Policing in Northern
    Ireland, 112, 118
Independent International Commission on
    Decommissioning (IICD), 107, 115
India
    aircraft hijacking, 340
    Al- Qaeda, 341
    Dera Sacha Sauda, 343
    Gandhi family assassinations 1948–1991, 340
    historical overview, 339–340
    Indira Gandhi, 340
    "Indus Waters Treaty" of 1960, 351
    Islam and, 341–342
    Kashmiri Muslims, 341
    militant threats, sources of, 341
    Mohandas (Mahatma) Gandhi, 340
    Naxalites, 341
    nuclear weapons capability, 340
    political assassination in, 340–341
    Punjab and Sikhism, 343
    Rajiv Gandhi, 340
    Ram Rahim Singh, 343
    Special Economic Zone, 341
    Tamil Tigers (LTTE), 340
    See also Mumbai attacks
Indian National Congress, 340
Indo-Canadian Times, 82
Indonesia
    B.J. Habibie, 388
    de-radicalization, 389–390
    historical overview, 387
    Indonesian military (ABRI), 388
    Islamic extremism, 389
    Jemaah Islamiyaah (JI), 390
    May riots and rapes, 388
    "New Order," 387
    People's Consultative Assembly, 388
    political freedom, 388
    Suharto, 387–389
    Sukarno, 387
    Timor Timur (East Timor Province), 389
Indonesian military (ABRI), 388
"Indus Waters Treaty" of 1960, 351
Inhalational Anthrax, 483
Inmarsat, 476
Inside Terrorism (Hoffman), 5–6
Institutional Revolutionary Party (PRI), 404
Insurrection in Euskadi, 143
Intelligence Reform and Prevention of Terrorism
    Act, 466
Intelligence Requirements and Collection
    Management Handbook (FBI), 466–467
Intelligence services
    CIA and FBI
        Concepts of operations (CONOPs), 466
        FBI intelligence program core principles,
            466–467
        Intelligence Reform and Prevention of
            Terrorism Act, 466
        Intelligence Requirements and Collection
            Management Handbook (FBI), 467
        overview, 466
        U.S. Patriot Act, 466
    Joint Terrorism Analysis Centre (JTAC)—UK, 466
    MI5 (Secret Intelligence Service), 463
    MI6, 465
    successes, 467
Interahamwe, 331
Inter-American Court of Human Rights, 408
Internment, 99–100
Internal terrorism, 27
International Airport in Glasgow, Scotland, 132

International Atomic Energy Agency (IAEA),
    195, 382
International Civil Aviation Organization (ICAO),
    455
International Code for the Security of Ships and
    Port Facilities (ISPS), 477
International Convention for the Safety of Life at
    Sea (SOLAS), 477
International Convention for the Suppression of
    Terrorist Bombings, 444
International Criminal Police Organization
    (INTERPOL), 194, 463, 464–465
International Criminal Tribunal for the Former
    Yugoslavia (ICTY), 205, 206
International Maritime Bureau Piracy Center, 475
International Maritime Organization (IMO), 475,
    476, 477
International Mobile Satellite Organization
    (Inmarsat), 476
International Monetary Fund (IMF), 364
International Rescue Committee (IRC), 311
International Security and Development
    Cooperation Act (Public Law 99–83), 456
International Sikh Youth Federation, 349–350
International Telecommunications Union, 476
Internet
    control orders, 127
    Ku Klux Klan and, 53–54
    Patriot Act, 65
    techno terrorism, 498
    terrorism and, 39
    terrorists/insurgents use of, 439
Internet Black Tigers (IBT), 354
Internment, 99–100
INTERPOL, 118, 194, 463, 464–465
Inter Service Intelligence agency (ISI), 340, 464
Intestinal Anthrax, 483
Iran
    and Al Qaeda, 296–297
    as Al Qaeda sponsor, 295–296
    Assembly of Experts, 293
    class structure, 293
    drug trade, 291
    IBEX, 292
    Islamic foreign policy, 294
    Kurdish Democratic Party, 293
    Mohammad Reza Pahlavi (Shah of Iran),
        291–294
    Mujahedin-e Khalq (People's Mojahedin of
        Iran), 291
    Mujahedin-E Khalq Organization (MEK), 291
    Muslim Iranian Student's Society, 291
    National Liberation Army of Iran (NLA), 291
    nuclear weapons and, 294–295
    overview, 290
    People's Fedayeen, 293
    piracy issue, 308
    political pressure groups, 287
    SAVAK, 291–292
    Special Intelligence Bureau, 292
    White Revolution, 292
Iran-Iraq war, 26, 272, 276, 281
Iraq
    Badr Brigade/Corps, 281
    Ba'thist regime, 274
    international terrorism, support for, 287
    Iran, restoration of relations with, 275
    Islamic Supreme Council of Iraq, 281
    Mahdi army, 280–281
    Mujahideen Shura Council, 280
    Operation Iraqi Freedom, 277
    overview, 273
    Qusay Hussein, death of, 277–278
    Saddam Hussein (1937-2006), 274–277
    Sunni insurgent groups

Al Qaeda in Iraq, 279
    Ansar al-Islam, 279
    Ansar al-Sunnah Movement, 279
    Imam Ali Bin-Abi-Talib Jihadi Brigades,
        278–279
    Iraqi National Islamic Resistance, 278
    Iraqi Resistance Islamic Front (JAMI), 278
    Islamic Army in Iraq, 279
    National Front for the Liberation of Iraq, 278
    Uday Hussein, death of, 277–278
    UN Special Commission to Iraq (UNSCOM), 480
    weapons of mass destruction (WMD), 286
Ireland
    "Agreement," the, 116–117
    civil liberty issues, 108–111
    Continuity IRA (CIRA), 102–103
    counter-terrorism unit, 469–470
    Diplock Commission, the, 109
    Direct Action Against Drugs (DAAD), 103
    Independent Monitoring Commission, 106
    internment, 99–100
    Irish Free State, 95–96
    Irish National Liberation Army (INLA),
        104–105, 107
    Irish Republican Army (IRA), or Provisional
        Republican Army (PIRA), 5, 94, 101–102,
        113–114
    Irish terrorism, countering, 119–120
    Loyalist groups proscribed, 106
    Loyalist Volunteer Force (LVF), 106, 107
    Northern Ireland, 96
    Northern Ireland Peace Process, 114–118
    Orange Volunteers (OV), 108
    overview, 94
    political objectives, 97–100
    power-sharing executive, 118–119
    Prevention of Terrorism Act, 109
    Progressive Unionist Party (PUP), 106
    Protestant Marching Season, 111–113
    Real Irish Republican Army (RIRA), 104
    Red Hand Commando, 106
    Red Hand Defenders (RHD), 107–108
    Republican groups proscribed, 106
    Republican Sinn Fein (RSF), 103–104
    Royal Ulster Constabulary (RUC), 118
    sectarian violence, 112
    Southern Ireland, 97
    terror, logistics and financing of, 100–101
    "The Troubles" 1968–1998, 96–97
    turf wars, 108
    Ulster, 96–97
    Ulster Defence Association (UDA), 106–107
    Ulster Defense Association (UDA)/Ulster
        Freedom Fighters (UFF), 107
    Ulster Democratic Party (UDP), 106–107
    Ulster Loyalist Democratic Party (ULDP), 107
    Ulster Volunteer Force (UVF), 105–106
    Ulster Volunteers, original, 106
    War of independence, 1919–1921, 95–96
Irgun, 214–215, 216
Irgun Zvaileumi, National Military Organization
    (NMO), 215–216
Irish Free State, 95–96
Irish National Liberation Army (INLA), 98,
    104–105, 106, 107
Irish Northern Aid Committee (NORAID), 457
Irish Republican Army (IRA), or Provisional
    Republican Army (PIRA), 5, 94, 101–102,
    113–114
Irish Republican Brotherhood (IRB), 94
Irurkos, 143
Islam
    brief history, 31–32
    India, 341–342
    Pakistan, 347

radicalization, specific phases
  indoctrination, 60
  jihadization, 35
  pre-radicalization, 59
  self-identification, 59
4UK, 125–126
Islamic State, 175–176
  al Qaeda and, 490–491
  fundraising, 285–286
  persecution, 285
  propaganda, 285
  strength of, 253–254
  threat to Libya, 251–254
  threat to Saudi Arabia, 271–272
  and use of children, 284
  weapons and munitions, 285
Islamic Center in Gaza, 225
Islamic Concern Project (Islamic Committee for Palestine), 231
Islamic Group (Al-Gamaa al-Islamiyya), 245
Islamic Jihad, 237, 245
Islamic Jihad Brigade, 280
Islamic Movement of Uzbekistan (IMU), 395
Islamic Organization, 225
Islamic Republican Party (IRP), 293
Islamic Resistance Movement (IRM), 225, 226
Islamic Revolutionary Guard Corps (IRGC), 295
Islamic Salvation Front (FIS), 257
Islamic sharia, 10
Islamic Supreme Council of Iraq, 281
Islami Inqilabi Mahaz, 344
Islamism, 32
Islamist Militants, 198
Islamiyah, Jemaah, 384
Israel
  Abu Nidal organization (for Sabri al-Banna), 219–220
  Al-Aqsa, 221–222
  Al-Fatah (or Al-Asifa), 246
  Ariel Sharon, 241
  counter-terrorism unit, 522
  disengagement plan, 244–246
  early history, 237
  Gaza Strip, 223
  Hamas, 223–229
  Hezbollah, 239
  Hezbollah war with, 239–240
  Irgun Zevaileumi, National Military Organization (NMO), 215–216
  LOD (Israel) airport attack May 30, 1972, 234–235
  Mossad targeted assassination, 241
  National Military Organization (NMO), 215–216
  1993 Declaration of Principles, 232
  Operation Bayonet, 219
  Operation Spring Youth, 472
  overview, 212
  Palestinian Liberation Organization (PLO), 217–218
  political considerations, 212–213
  Popular Front for the Liberation of Palestine (PFLP), 221
  settlements and terror, 213
  Six-Day War, 212
  Stern Gang, 214–215
  terrorism, threat from, 216
  weaponry
    Democratic Front for the Liberation of Palestine (DFLP), 231
    Kach, 232–233
    Kahane Chai, 232–233
    Palestinian Islamic Jihad (PIJ), 231
    Palestinian Liberation Front (PLF), 229–230
    Qassam Rockets, 229
Israeli Defense Force (IDF), 213
Italy

Alleanza Nazionale (National Alliance), 168
Armed Proletarian Nuclei (NAP), 167
Financing Security Committee, 168
hate crimes, 168
international terrorism, 168
Law No. 205 (Mancino Law), 168
Movement of Proletarian Prisoners, 167
Movimento Politico Occidentale (MPO), 168
Movimento Sociale Italiano (MSI), 168
Ongoing Struggle (Lotta Continua), 167
overview, 140–141, 165
Partisan Action Group (GAP), 167
Red Brigade (RB), 166–167
Skinhead ideology, 168
Skinhead organizations, 168
terrorism and, 165
Ivins, Dr. Bruce, 483
Izetbegovic, Alija, 205
Izz ad-Din al-Qassam Brigades, 227
Izz al Din Al Qassam Brigades, 28, 226–227

Jabarah, Abdul, 88
Jabhat al Nusra, 242
Jackson, Sir Geoffrey, 427
Jacobin dissenters, 4
Jaish-e-Mohammed (JEM) (the Army of Mohammed), 352
Jamaat ul-Fuqra, 38, 66
Jamaat al-Islamiyya, 245
Jamiat-I Ulema-i Islam Fazlur Rehman faction (JUI-F), 352
Jamaat Islamiyah, 419
Jane's Intelligence Digest, 209
Janes Terrorism, 387
Janjaweed, 256
Japan, 379
  Aum Shinrikyo, 380–381
  government-industry cooperation, 379
  Japanese Red Army (JRA), 381
  keiretsu, 379
  nuclear program, 382
  overview, 379
  Sarin, 380–381
Japanese ambassador's residence (Peru), attack on, 422–423
Japanese Red Army (JRA), 149–150, 381, 381
Jarrah, Ziad Zamir, 55, 162
Jemaah Islamiyah (JI), 384, 395
  leadership, 390
  Western targets, 390
Jenkins, Brian, 8
Jewish Defense League (JDL), 232
Jihad, 30, 33–34
Jihadi-Salafi ideology, 59
Jihadization, 35
  U.S. targets, 35
  See also Bin Laden, Osama
Jimbaran Bay, Kuta bombing, 391
Jinnah International Airport attack, 452
Johal, Hardial Singh, 83
John Paul II, Pope, 207
Johnson, Alan, 228
Join the Caravan (Azzam), 55
Joint Task Force Two (JTF-2), 474–475
Joint Terrorism Analysis Centre (JTAC)—UK, 466
Joint Terrorism Task Force (JTTF), 66
Jordan
  airline hijacking, 234
  LOD (Israel) airport attack May 30, 1972, 234–235
  Middle Eastern affairs, role in, 235
  overview, 33
Josephson, Ian, 84
Juan Carlos, King, 145
Juarez, Benito, 402

June Second Movement, 160
Justice and Equality Movement (JEM), 256
Justice Commandos of the Armenian Genocide, 177
JW Marriott bombing, 391
Jyllands Posten, 183

Kabardino-Balkaria, 197
Kabila, Joseph, 331
Kabila, Laurent, 316, 330
Kach, 232
Kach organization, 232
Kadyrov, Akhmad, 198
Kahane, Binyamin, 232
Kahane Chai, 232
Kahane Chai organization, 232
Kaiten manned torpedo, 496
Kamikaze pilots, 496
Kampuchea. See Cambodia
Kansi, Mir Aimal, 344
Kaplan, Muhammed Metin, 181
Karamanlis, Costas, 169
Karzai, Hamid, 356
Ka Roger, 387
Kasavubu, Joseph, 330
Kashmir, 347–348, 350–352
Kashmiri, Faroogi, 347
Kazakhstan, 192, 197, 373
Kaczynski, Theodore, 41
Keenan, Brian, 239
Keiretsu, 379
Kemal, Fateh, 151
Kemal, Mustafa, 173
Kenya
  historical overview, 323
  Kenyan African Union (KANU), 323
  Mau Mau, 323
  U.S. Embassy, attack on, 324
Kenyan African Union (KANU), 323
Kenyatta, Jomo, 323
Kerry Committee Report of April 1995, 412
KGB, 192, 194, 208, 441
Khadr, Omar, 87–88
Khaled, Leila, 35, 233, 234
Khalid, King, 265
Khalil, Fazlur, 347
Khalistan (Land of the Pure), 349
Khamenei, Ali, 293
Khan, Abdul Qadeer, 351
Khan, Mohammed Sidique, 59, 126, 131
Khawaja, Mohammad Momin, 131
Khmer Rouge, 365, 422
Khmer Royal Armed Forces (KRAF), 365
Khomeini, Ayatollah Ruhollah, 26, 237, 293
Khrushchev, Nikita, 192
Khyam, Omar, 131
Ki-115 purpose-built kamikaze plane, 496
Kidnapping, 335, 383
Kilburn, Peter, 239
Killer College (Patrice Lumumba University), 192
Killer instinct, 12
Kimathi, Dedan, 323
Kim II-Sung, 382
Kim Jong-II, 382, 432
Kim Sook, 384
King, Martin Luther, Jr., 54, 96
KINTEX, 207
Kirov, Sergei, 213
Kitab (al-jabr) w'al-muqabalah (Al-Khawarizmi), 275
Kitab hisab al'adad al-hindi (Al-Khawarizmi), 275
Klein, Hans-Joachim, 158
Klinghoffer, Leon, 229, 230, 287, 474, 478
Knights of Europe, 29
Konkert, 158
Kony, Joseph, 312

Koresh, David, 50
Korody, Amanda, 85
Kosovo, 205, 495
Kosovo Liberation Army (KLA), 205
Krayem, Nayef, 238
Kristallnacht (night of the broken glass), 157
Kurdish Democratic Party, 293
Kurdistan, 174–175
Kurdistan Freedom and Democracy Congress
    (KADEK), 175
Kurdistan Freedom Falcons (TAK), 175
Kurdistan Workers Party (PKK), 174–175, 242
Kurds, 276
Kuwait
    Al- Qaeda influence, 272
    Al-Sabah dynasty, 272
    ethnic mix, 272
    Gulf Cooperation Council (GCC), 272
    Iranian influence, 273
    Iraqi occupation, 273
    oil industry, 272
    overview, 272
    Shiite political influence, 273
Kyrgyzstan, 195–196, 201, 375

Lackawanna Group, 60
Lahoud, Emil, 238
Langi tribe, 309
Laporte, Pierre, 80
Laqueur, Walter, 8, 18
Lashkar-e-Toiba (Army of the Pure) (LeT), 348
Lashkar-e-Jhangvi (LJ), 352
Latin America and South America
    overview, 400–401
    terrorism, 401
    See also individual countries
Laws, 3, 15, 19
Laycock, Robert, 467
The League of Nations
    member states, 11
    terrorism, definition of, 9
"Lebanese for a Free and Independent Lebanon," 236
Lebanon
    Hezbollah, 237–239
    overview, 235–236
    Palestinians come to, 236
    political assassinations, 236–237
    Shia sect in, 237
Lechin, Juan, 424
"Legitimate" target, 6
Leizaola, Jose Maria, 143
Lemkin, Raphael, 39
Lenin, Vladimir, 189, 190
Leopold, King, 330
Letter bomb, 41
Lewes, Jock, 467
Lewis, John, 54
Liberation Army of Rwanda (ALiR), 331
Liberation Tigers of Tamil Eelam (LTTE), 84,
    353–356
    "Black Tiger Squad," 354
    suicide bombers, 354
    terrorist activities of, 354
Libya
    Libyan Islamic Fighting Group (LIFG),
        249–250
    Muammar el-Qaddafi, 247–248
    Northern, establishing base in, 252
    Operation El-Dorado Canyon, 248–249
    overview, 247
    Pan Am 103, 121
    territorial methodology, 253
    threat to, 251–252
    United States, diplomatic relations and, 121
Libyan Islamic Fighting Group (LIFG), 249–250

Libyan People's Bureau, St. James's Park,
    London, 248
Libyan Revolutionary Committees, 248
Li Hongzhi, 377
Lindt Chocolate Café attack, 396
Liquid bomb, 449
List of entities, 76
Litvinenko, Alexander, 137
Lockerbie, Scotland, 84, 121, 444
Lodhi, Maleeha, 56
London—July 21, 2005, 130–131
London—July 7, 2005
    closed-circuit television (CCTV) cameras, 130
    overview, 129
    terror attack timeline, 129–130
"Lone Wolf" attack, 41–42, 85, 396
    in Quebec and Ottawa, 86
Long Kesh, 99
Long Kesh (renamed Maze Prison), 99
Lord's Resistance Army (LRA), 311, 312–313
Lorenz, Peter, 160
Los Macheteros, 52, 76
*Los Macheteros: The Violent Struggle for Puerto
    Rican Independence* (Fernandez), 76
Louis Garcia, Samuel, 405
Low-Level Armed Robbery (LLAR), 475
Loyalist Volunteer Force (LVF), 106, 107
Loyal Orange Institution, or Orange Order, 112
Lugbara tribe, 309
Lugovoi, Andrei, 137
Lukwiya, Raska, 313
Lumumba, Patrice, 330
Luminoso, Sendero, 421–422
Lynch, Charles, 54
Lynch Law, 54
Lyon Summit Conference in 1996, 457

Macheteros, 76
Madani, Abbassi, 258
Made, Joseph, 316
Madikizela-Mandela, Winnie, 321
Madrassas, 357
Mafia, 54
Magloire, Paul, 90
Mahdi army, 279
Mahjoub, Mohamed Zeki, 79
Mahler, Horst, 158
Mahmood, Waheed, 131
Major Criminal Hijack (MCHJ), 475
Major Incident (MI), 525
Makarios, Archbishop, 172
Malan, D.F., 318
Malcolm X, 53
Malik, Ripudaman Singh, 83
Mancino, Boccacci, 168
Mancino Law, 168
Mandela, Nelson, 34
Mandela, Nelson Rolihlahla, 320
Mandela United Football Club, 321
Man Portable Air Defense Systems
    (MANPADS), 451
Manson, Charles, 26
Manuel Rodriguez Patriotic Front (FPMR), 424,
    429–430
Mao Tse-tung, 143
Mara 18 or 18th Street, 413
Mara Salvatrucha 13, 413, 414–415
Marcinko, Richard, 474
Marighella, Carlos, 166, 424
Maritime piracy, 476
Marsh Arabs, 275
Marti, Augustin Farabundo, 409
Martin, Leo, 98
Marx, Karl, 190
Maskhadov, Aslan, 199

Mass murder, 39
Mau Mau, 323
Mauritania, 243
Maze Prison, 99
Mbadinuju, Chinwoke, 332
Mbeki, Thabo, 315
McCarthy, John, 239
McCauley, Martin, 102
McConville, Michael, 111
McGee, Patrick, 100
McGlinchey, Dominic, 105
McGuiness, Martin, 98, 112, 116, 118
Mckee, Billy, 98
McMichael, John, 106, 107
McStiofain, Sean, 98
McVeigh, Timothy, 48, 49, 52
McWhirter, Ross, 98, 102
Meadowbank Investment Limited, 249
Mecca Agreement, 227
Medellin cartel, 416
Media, 505–506
Medium-Level Armed Robbery and Assault
    (MLAAR), 475
Medium to Close Range (MTCR) class missile
    programs, 123
Meinhof, Ulrike, 158
Meir, Golda, 219
Mejadi, Tahar, 79
Mesopotamia, 279
Metropolitan Political Collective, 165
Metsavennad, 192
Mexico
    Antonio Lopez de Santa Ana, 402
    Armed Front for the Liberation of the
        Marginalized People of Guerrero, 405
    Army of the Poor and Peasant's Brigade against
        Injustice, 403
    Chiapas region, 404–405
    drug trade, 406
    historical overview, 401–404
    Institutional Revolutionary Party (PRI), 404
    North American Free Trade Agreement
        (NAFTA), 404
    Partido Autonomista Nacional (PAN), 403
    Partido de Accion Nacional (PAN), 403
    Partido Revolutionario Institucional
        (PRI), 402
    Peace and Justice group, 405
    Plan of Ayala, 404
    Popular Revolutionary Army (EPR), 405–406
    Porfirio Diaz, 401–402
    Revolutionary Army of Popular Insurgence, 405
    right-wing violence, 405
    student-initiated protests, 403
    Zapatista National Liberation Army (ELZN),
        404–405
MI1(c), 465
MI5 (Secret Intelligence Service), 463–464, 465
MI6, 465
"Miami Cubans," 89
Michael VIII, 29
"Micro expressions," 455
Middle East, 211–261. *See also individual
    countries*
    U.S. foreign policy, 61–62
"Middle East Crisis," 212
Mike's Place (Israel), 223
Military Commission Panel, 463
Military Commissions (Tribunals), 463
"Military Front of ETA," 143
Military Order, 463
Military Tribunals. *See* Military Commissions
    (Tribunals)
Militias, 48, 51
Milli Görüs, 163
Milosevic, Slobodan, 205–206

Mini-Manual of the Urban Guerrilla (Marighella), 424, 425
Mobutu, Joseph Desire, 330
Mobutu Sese Seko, 331–332
Mohammad, Mahmoud, 84
Mohammad V, 173
Muhammad V, Sultan, 243
Mohammed, Khalid Sheikh, (KSM), 38, 58, 462
Mohammed, Ramzi, 130–131
Mohammad, Shadi Jabar Khalil, 397
Mohammed VI, King, 243
Mujahedin-e Khalq (People's Mojahedin of Iran), 291
Mokhles, al-Said Hassan, 427
Monaghan, James "Mortar," 102
Monotheism and Jihad Group, 279
Montoneros (Movimiento Peronista Montonero), 429
Morazanist Patriotic Front (FPM), 409
Mores, 3, 22
Moro, Aldo, 167
Morocco, 243–244
Moro Islamic Liberation Front (MILF), 384, 385
Mosed, Shafal, 60
Mossad, 216
Mossadegh, Mohammad, 291
Mountbatten, Lord Louis, 101, 350
Moussaoui, Zacarias, 125, 151
Movement for Democracy and Justice in Chad (MDJT), 260
Movement for the Emancipation of the Niger Delta (MEND), 333
Movement of Proletarian Prisoners, 167
Movimento Politico Occidentale (MPO), 168
Movimento Sociale Italiano (MSI), 168
Movimiento Revolucionario Tupac Amaru (MRTA), 422–423
Moyo, Jonathan, 316
Mozambique
    Front for the Liberation of Mozambique (FRELIMO), 327
    historical overview, 327–328
    Mozambique National Resistance Movement (RENAMO), 328
    Samora Machel, death of, 328
Mozambique National Resistance Movement (RENAMO), 328
Msika, Joseph, 317
Mubarak, Hosni, 216
Mugabe, Robert, 314, 317
Mugniyah, Imad, 240, 296
Muhammad Ali Jinnah, 345
Mujahedin-E Khalq Organization (MEK), 291
Mujahideen, 360
Mujahideen Shura Council, 280
Mukti Bahini, 351
Multiculturalism, 84
Mumbai attacks, 342–343
    motives, 343
    targets, 342–343
    time line, 342
Murphy, Lenny (The Master Butcher), 108
Musawi, Abu, 239
Museveni, Yoweri Kaguta, 310, 311
Musharraf, Pervez, 346–347
Muslims
    demographics, 300
    ethnic cleansing of, 363–364
    in Europe, 180–181
Muslim Association of Britain, 34
Muslim Brotherhood, 224, 241, 244, 245, 246
Muslim Councils in Great Britain, 34
Muslim Iranian Student's Society, 291
Muslims of America, 66
Mussawi, Hussein, 449
Mussolini, 165

Mustard gas, 275
Mutesa, Sir Edward, 309
Muzenda, Simon, 317

Narodnaya Volya (NV) (1878–1881), 189–190
Naseem, Mohammed, 34
Nasrallah, Hassan, 239
National Army of Democratic Kampuchea, 366
National Catechism (Bakunin), 40
National Counterterrorism Center, 466
National Islamic Front (Sudan), 255
National Liberation Army (ELN), 416, 418, 432
National Liberation Army of Iran (NLA), 291
National Liberation Army or Workers Army, 5
National Liberation Movement (MLN), 426–428
National List (Christian Worch), 161
National Military Organization (NMO), 215–216
National Offensive (Michael Swierczek), 161
National Organization of Cypriot Combatants (EOKA), 172
National Resistance Army (NRA), 310
National Resistance Movement (NRM), 310
National Security Presidential Directive 9: Defeating the Terrorist Threat to the United States, 58
National Strategy for Combating Terrorism document, 58
National Targeting Center (NTC), 456
National Union for the Total Independence of Angola (UNITA), 327
Nation of Islam, 53
NATO Peacekeeping Force (KFOR), 205
Nanotechnology, 499
Narco-terrorism, 406
Nasrallah, Sheikh Hassan, 240
Naxalites, 341
Nechaev, Sergei, 40
Neeve, Airey, 105
Nehru, Jawaharlal, 340, 350
Neo-Nazis, 53
Nepal, 352–353
Nerve agents, 481
Netanyahu, Jonathan, 310
Netherlands
    counterterrorism units, 470
    Dutch cartoon—freedom of the press, 183
    Free South Moluccan Youth Organization (VZJ), 471
    Hofstadgroep, 182
    overpopulation issue, 182
    Pim Fortuyn, assassination of, 182
    Samir Azzouz, 182
    Theo Van Gough, assassination of, 182
New Black Panther Party for Self-Defense, 53
New People's Army (NPA), 384, 386–387
New PULO, 368
Newton, Huey, 53
New Ulster Political Research Group (NUPRG), 107
New World Order, 52, 496
New York Police Department (NYPD), 59
New York Times, 223, 266
Nicaragua
    Contras, 411
    fund-raising, 411
    Hull's Ranch, 412
    National Guard of Nicaragua, 411
    overview, 410
    Somoza Anastasio, 410
    Sandinistas, 411
    Sandinistas National Liberation Front (FLSN), 411
    U.S. Central Intelligence Agency (CIA), 412
Nicholls, Lord, 431
Nichols, Terry, 48, 52

Nigeria
    Atiku Abubakar, 333
    Bakassi Boys, The, 332
    Chinwoke Mbadinuju, 332
    Goodluck Jonathan, 333
    Islam, rise of, 333
    Movement for the Emancipation of the Niger Delta (MEND), 333
    Muslims and Christians, conflict between, 332
    oil wealth/government corruption, 333
    Olusegun Obasanjo, 332, 333
    Umaru Yar'Adua, 333
"Night commuters," 312
Nihilists, 496
9-11 attacks
    aftermath of, 57–58
    Commission Report, 56, 161
    preparations for, 55–57
1993 Declaration of Principles, 231, 232
1967 Six-Day War, 214, 219
Nishikawa, Jun, 381
Nizar, Ben Muhammed, 88
Nkomo, John, 316
Nkomo, Joshua, 314–315
"No fly" lists, 45
Non-lethal weapons, 498
Nongovernmental organizations (NGOs), 36
Norambuena, Mauricio, 424
Noriega, Manuel, 412
Noris, Benni, 79
North, Oliver, 238, 412
North American Free Trade Agreement (NAFTA), 404
North Atlantic Assembly (NAA), 181
North Atlantic Treaty Organization (NATO), 150, 205
North Caucasus, 197
Northern Aid Committee (NORAID), 457
Northern Ireland
    Protestant Marching Season, 111–112
The Northern Ireland Act, 112
Northern Ireland Civil Rights Association, 96
Northern Ireland Emergency Provisions Act (1973), 109, 442
Northern Ireland Peace Process
    decommissioning, 115
    overview, 114–118
Northwest Frontier Provinces (NWFP), 345
Norway, counterterrorism units, 183–186, 471–472
November 17 group, 169
Nuttall, John, 85

Obama, Barack, 16, 362, 462, 463, 526
Obasanjo, Olusegun, 315, 332–333
Obote, Milton, 309, 310
O'Brady, Rory, 98
Ocalan, Abdullah, 174, 175, 241
Ó Conaill, Dáithí, 103
Odhiambo, Okot, 313
Office for the Protection of the Constitution (BFV), 163
Office of International Criminal Justice, 194
"Officials," 101
Ogaden National Liberation Front (ONLF), 303
Ohka rocket-powered kamikaze plane, 496
Ohnesorg, Benno, 160
Ojeda Rios, Filiberto, 52, 76
Okamoto, Kozo, 382
Okello, Tito, 310–311
Oklahoma City Federal Building, 13
Okomato, Kozo, 234
Okhrana (the Tsarist secret police), 40
Olmert, Ehud, 216, 228
Omagh bombing, 104
Oman, 288–290
    counter-terrorism unit, 470

Omar, Mullah, 357, 359
Omar, Yassin Hassan, 130
O'Neill, Anthony, 111
O'Neill, Juliet, 77
O'Neill, Terrence, 96
Ongoing Struggle (Lotta Continua), 167
Ongwen, Dominic, 313
Ontario Consultants on Religious Tolerance, 33
"Open-registry" ships, 476
Operation Bayonet, 219
Operation Blue Star, 81, 82
Operation Bojinka, 448
Operation Crevice, 131
Operation Desert Storm, 276
Operation El-Dorado Canyon, 248–249
Operation Iraqi Freedom, 277
Operation Iron Fist, 312
Operation Jonathan, 310
Operation Peace for Galilee, 220
Orange Lodges, 112
Orange Order, 108, 112
Orange Volunteers (OV), 108
ORDEN, 410
Ordine Nuove (New Order), 165
Organisation Armee Secrete (OAS), 257
Organismo Coordinador de Actividades Anti-Subversivas, 427
Organization of People in Arms (OPRA), 408
Organization of Petroleum Exporting Countries (OPEC), 149
Ortiz, Arnoldo, 144
Oslo Peace Accords, 214
Ottawa Citizen, 77
Ottawa, Lone Wolf attacks in, 86
Otti, Vincent, 313
Oyite-Ojok, David, 310
Ozlam Properties Limited, 249

Pacification, 408
Pacific Rim, 372–397. *See also individual countries*
Padfield, Phillip, 239
Padilla, Jose, 57
Pahlavi, Mohammad Reza (Shah of Iran), 291–294
Pais, Frank, 89
Paisley, Ian, 111–112, 115, 116, 118
Pakistan
    Abdul Qadeer Khan, 351
    Aimal Khufia Action Committee, 344
    Asif Ali Zardari, 346
    Benazir Bhutto, 345–349
    Harakat-ul-Ansar (HUA), 347–348
    Inter Services Intelligence (ISI), 340
    Inter Services Intelligence Agency, 340
    Islami Inqilabi Mahaz, 344
    Islam militancy, 352
    Kashmir, 350–352
    Lal Masjid Brigade, 346
    Lashkar-e-Taiba (Army of the Pure) (LeT), 342, 348
    Muhammad Ali Jinnah, 345
    Northwest Frontier Provinces (NWFP), 345
    nuclear proliferation threats, 351–352
    overview, 344
    Pakistan Peoples Party, 345
    Pervez Musharraf, 346–347
    Ramzi Ahmed Yousef, 344
    Red Mosque, the, 345–346
    The Shiromani Gurudwara Prabandhak Committee (SGPC), 347
Palestine, 34, 172, 212, 213, 215, 224–225
    See also Al-Aqsa; Palestine Liberation Organization (PLO); Popular Front for the Liberation of Palestine (PFLP)

Palestinian authority, 218
Palestine Liberation Front (PLF), 230
Palestine Liberation Organization (PLO), 5, 149, 217
Palestinian Islamic Jihad (PIJ), 28, 231, 294
Palestine Liberation Front (PLF), 230
Palestinian Muslim Brotherhood, 225
Palestinian National Liberation Movement, 218
Palestinian State, question of, 212
Pan Am 103, 121, 444
Panama, 412–413
Panama Canal, 412
Pan Arab Movement, 275
Pankisi Gorge, 202
Pan-Turkic movement, 374–375
Paraguay, 424, 426–428, 429
Paris, attacks on, 153–156
Parmar, Talwinder Singh, 74, 81, 82–83
Partido Autonomista Nacional (PAN), 403
Partido de Accion Nacional (PAN), 403
Partido Revolucionario Institutional (PRI), 402
Parti Quebecois, 80
Partisan Action Group (GAP), 167
Partisans, Yugoslavia, 203
Pasban-e-Ahle Hadith, 348
Passenger profiling, 453–454
Passenger terminal attacks
    "Stinger missile," use of, 451–452
    at Heathrow airport, 451–452
Paster, Stephen Paul, 66
Pastrana, Andres, 416, 417
Patrice Lumumba University (Killer College), 192
Patriot Act, 459
Patriot movement, 49
Pattani United Liberatioin Organization (PULO), 367–368
Patten, Chris, 118
Pearl, Daniel, 38, 66, 348
Pearse, Padraic, 94
Peel, Sir Robert, 119
"peep-o-day boys," 112
Pemuda, 368
Pentaerythritol Tetranitrate (PETN), 299
People against Gangsterism and Drugs (PAGAD), 321–322
People of the Book, 33
People's Commissariat for Internal Affairs (NKVD), 191
People's Congress of Kurdistan (KONGRAGEL), 175
People's Consultative Assembly, 388
People's Democratic Republic of Yemen, or PDRY, 297
People's Fedayeen, 293
People's Liberation Army (PLA). *See Irish National Liberation Army (INLA)*
People's Republican Army (PRA). *See Irish National Liberation Army (INLA)*
People's Republic of China (PRC). *See China*
Peron, Juan Domingo, 428
Perovskaya, Sophia, 189
Persian Gulf, 263–264. *See also individual countries*
Peru
    Edgar Sanchez Special Forces, 423
    Japanese ambassador's residence, attack on, 423
    Movimiento Revolucionario Tupac Amaru (MRTA), 422–423
    overview, 421
    Sendero Luminoso (The Shining Path), 421–422
    Tupac Amaru Revolutionary Movement (MRTA). *See Movimiento Revolucionario Tupac Amaru (MRTA)*
PFLP-GC, 241, 445

Phalanges, 216
Philippines
    Abu Sayyaf Group (ASG), 394
    Communist Party of the Philippines (CPP), 386–387
    CPP-NPA, 387
    Jemaah Islamiyaah (JI), 390–393
    Moro Islamic Liberation Front (MILF), 385, 386
    New People's Army (NPA), 384
    overview, 384
Physical security standards, zone level, 508–509
Pinochet, Augusto, 430
    dictatorship of, 430–431
Piracy
    Article 101 of the United Nations Convention of the Law of the Sea, 475
    definitions of, 475
    human rights and, 477–478
    International Maritime Bureau Piracy Center, 475
    See also Sea piracy
Piracy Reporting Center (Kuala Lumpur, Indonesia), 477
PKK (Kurdistan Workers' Party), 175
"Plan Colombia," 101, 416
Plan de Sanchez massacre, 408
Pneumonic Plague, 484
Poland, James M., 8
Polay, Victor, 423
Police (Northern Ireland) Bill of May 2000, 96
Police Service of Northern Ireland (PSNI), 96
Polisario Front, 243
Political Terrorism (Schmid), 5
Polo, Marco, 26
Polonium-210, 137
Pol Pot (Saloth), 365–366
Popular Front for the Liberation of Palestine (PFLP)
    Declaration of Principles (September 13, 1993, Oslo), 217
    in France, 149
    history of, 221
Popular Front for the Liberation of Palestine (PLO), 84
Popular Movement for the Liberation of Angola (MPLA), 327
Popular Revolutionary Army (EPR), 405
"Poqo," 321
Porfirio Diaz, José de la Cruz, 401–402
Powell, Colin, 29, 199
Power, Thomas, 105
Prabhakaran, Velupillai, 355–356
Prakash, Neil, 397
Pravda, 190–191
Prescribed behaviors, 3, 22
President's Commission on Aviation and Terrorism, 444
Preval, Rene, 90
Prevention of Terrorism Act, 109
Prevention of Terrorism Act 2005, 127
Prevention of Terrorism Act of 1989, terrorism, definition of, 7
Princip, Gavrilo, 203
Progressive Unionist Party (PUP), 106
Project Souvenir, 85
Proliferation Security Initiative (PSI), 477
Proscribed behavior, 3
Protestant Action Force. *See Ulster Volunteer Force (UVF)*
Protestant Action Group. *See Ulster Volunteer Force (UVF)*
Protestant Marching Season, 111–113
Provincial Legislature Building bombing, 85

Provisional IRA (PIRA). *See* Irish Republican Army (IRA), or Provisional Republican Army (PIRA)
"Provisionals," 101
Public Health Security and Bioterrorism Preparedness and Response Act of 2002, 478–479
Puerto Rico, 50, 52, 75–76
Punjab and Sikhism, 343
"Puppet" terrorist organizations, 27
Pushkin Square bombing, 198
Putin, Vladimir, 137, 193, 206, 350

Qaeda in Iraq, or AQ-I, 279
Qassam Rockets, 229
Qatada, Abu, 153
Qibla movement, 322–323
Qods Force, 295
Quebec, Lone Wolf attacks in, 86
Qur'an, 33
Qurei, Ahmed, 222
Qureshi, Mohammed Yousef, 183
Qutb, Sayyid, 267, 268

Rabin, Yitzhak, 214
Racial profiling, 441
Radicalized jihadist, 59
Radiological dispersal device (RDD), 485
Rafizadeh, Mansur, 292
Rafsanjani, Ali Akbar Hashemi, 293
Rahanwein Resistance Army, 306
Rahman, Omar Abdel, 66
Raleigh, Walter, 475
Ramaphosa, Cyril, 115
Rashad, Ahmad, 225
Rashid, Abdul, 344
Reagan, Ronald, 26, 76, 101, 248, 255, 325, 411–412, 456, 478
Real IRA (or New IRA), 97
Real IRA 2008 New Years Statement, 104
Real Irish Republican Army (RIRA), 104
Rebel Armed Forces (FAR), 407, 408
Recovery of Historical Memory (REMHI), 407
Red Army Faction (RAF), 158–159, 166
Red Brigade (RB), 166–167
    kidnapping, 167
    overview, 166
    structure of, 167
Red Cells, 160
Red Hand Commando, 106
Red Hand Defenders (RHD), 107–108
Red Mosque, the, 345–346
Rees, Merlyn, 99
Regina v. Singh, 88
Reid, Richard, 56, 66, 125, 152
Reign of Terror, 4
Reinsurance (Acts of Terrorism) Act, 1993, section 2(2), 7
Repentance and Emigration (al-Takfir wa'l Hijra), 258
Republican Guard, 276, 277
Republican Sinn Fein (RSF), 103
Republic of South Korea, 383–384
Ressam, Ahmed, 79, 125, 259
Revolutionary Armed Forces of Colombia (FARC), 101, 416, 417–418, 433
Revolutionary Army of Popular Insurgence, 405
Revolutionary Catechism (Nechaev), 40
Revolutionary Cells/Revolutionary Nuclei (RN), 171
Revolutionary Front for Proletarian Action (FRAP), 181
Revolutionary Guard Corps, 273
Revolutionary Guards, 28, 293
Revolutionary Movement for National Liberation, 143
Revolutionary People's Struggle (ELA), 171
    See also Espanastatikos Laikos

Agonas (ELA, Revolutionary Peoples Struggle)
Reyat, Inderjit Singh, 82, 83
Reyes, Raul (a.k.a. Luis Edgar Devia Silva), 420, 433. *See also* Revolutionary Armed Forces of Colombia (FARC)
Reyna, Leonel Fernandez, 90
Rhodesia. *See* Zimbabwe
Rice, Condoleezza, 432
Richardson, Jerry, 321
Richard the Lion-Hearted, 30
Ricin, 478
Rigby, Lee, 133–134
Risk assessments
    defined, 501, 503
    executive summary, 503
    methodology, 504–509
    purpose of, 503
    sample, 503–518
Riyadus Salikhin group, 199
Robben Island University (Isle of Purgatory), 321
Robespierre, 4
Roche, Jack, 393
Rogue states, 27, 32, 58, 100
Roh Tae-woo, 384
Rosello, Pedro J., 75
Rosie, George, 7
Royal Cambodian Armed Forces, or RCAF. *See* Khmer Royal Armed Forces (KRAF)
Royal Canadian Mounted Police (RCMP), 80
Royal Engineers Bomb Disposal, 113
Royal Irish Constabulary (RIC), 95
Royal Ulster Constabulary (RUC), 96
RPG-7, 443
Rumsfeld, Donald H., 413
Rushdie, Salman, 237, 294
Russia and the Soviet Union
    Beslan school massacre, 199
    Boevaya Oranisatsia (BO), or the Fighting Organization., 190
    Bolshevik Revolution, 189
    Bolsheviks, 190–191
    Chechnya, 197–201
    Chechnya, Russian forces in, 193
    church, the, 190
    Federalnaya Sluzhba Bezopasnosti Rossiyskoy Federatsii (FSB), 194
    free-market economy and the Russian mafya, 194–195
    Galina Starovoitova, 194
    International Atomic Energy Agency (IAEA), 195
    Joseph Stalin, 190–191
    KGB, 192, 194, 208
    into the millennium, 192–193
    Narodnaya Volya (NV) (1878-1881), 189–190
    organized crime, 194
    overview, 188–189
    Patrice Lumumba University (Killer College), 192
    People's Commissariat for Internal Affairs (NKVD), 191
    Pushkin Square bombing, 198
    Russian Federation, 192
    Russian Revolution, 190–191
    Russian Theater siege, 199
    school for terrorism, 192
    secret police, 191
    Social Democratic Labor Party, 189
    Ukraine, 201–202
    Vladimir V. Putin, 193
Russian anarchists, 40
Russian Federation, 192
Russian Kalashnikov (AK-47 assault rifle), 158
Russian-made SA-7, 451
Russian Orthodox Church, 190
Russian Revolution

Estonian Guerrilla Movement, 1944–1955, 192
great terror, the, 191–192
Rwanda
    Belgium rule, 329
    historical overview, 329
    Hutus, 328–329
    Interahamwe, 329
    Juvénal Habyarimana, 329
    Juvénal Habyarimana, death of, 329–330
    Rwandan Patriotic Front (RPF), 329
    Tutsis, 328–329
Rwandan Patriotic Front (RPF), 329

Saadi, Luay, 232
Sabra massacre, 216
Sacranie, Sir Iqbal, 34
Sadat, Anwar, 245
Sadler, Mike, 469
Sadr, Muqtada, 263
Saeed, Hafiz, 349
Safire, William, 223
Saifi, Amari, 260
Saladin, General, 30
Salafist Group for Preaching and Combat (GSPC), 260
Salah, Ali Abdullah, 298
Salah-al-Din, 278
Salameh, Ali Hassan (a.k.a. Abu Hassan), the "Red Prince," 217
Salinas de Gortari, Carlos, 404
Samphan, Khieu, 365
Sanabal Relief Agency, 249
Sanchez, Ilich Ramirez ("Carlos the Jackal"), 149, 158
Sanchez, Ricardo, 277
Sander, Ron, 433
Sandinista National Liberation Front (FSLN), 411
Sandinistas, 411
Sands, Bobby, 98
Santa Ana, Antonio Lopez de, 402
"San Tribes" (bushmen), 318
Sara Properties Limited, 249
Sarin, 41, 380, 381, 480, 495
Sarin gas, 495
Sarin toxin, 41
Satanic Verses, The (Rushdie), 237, 294
Saud, King, 265
Saudi Arabia
    Abdul Aziz, King, 264–265
    Abdullah, Crown Prince, 265, 266
    Abdullah, King, 233
    Al-Qaeda and, 266
    Consultative Council, 265
    Faisal, King, 265
    Khalid, King, 265
    overview, 264
    Saud, King, 265
    Sayyid Qutb, 267
    Sharia (Islamic law), 268
    threat to, 271–272
    U.S. Middle East policy, 266
    Wahhabi Islam, 266–267
SAVAK, 292–293
Savasta, Antonio, 208
Savimbi, Jonas, 327
Sayeret Mat'Kal, 472
Saygili, Aynur, 79
Scheduled offenses, 109
Schengen Agreement, 180–181
Schlayer, Hanns-Martin, 158
Schmid, Alex, 5
Schumann, Jurgen, 159
Scoon, Sir Paul, 474
Scranton, William W., 214
Screening Passengers by Observation Technique (SPOT), 454–455

Seale, Bobby, 53
Sea piracy
    container security initiative, 479
    container traffic, 478
    daily commentary and bulletins on, 477
    food safety, 478
    historical data on, 476
    historical overview, 475
    lucrative and accomplishable, 476
    rules of engagement, 476
    threats from the sea, countering, 477
    types and levels of, 475
Second Intifada, 215
Sectarian violence, 112
"Secular terror," 495
Secular terrorists, 495–496
"Secure Flight," 453–454
Secure Flight Notice of Proposed Rule Making
    (NPRM), 453–454
Security Bill, counterterrorism, 136–137
Security Council Resolutions 687 (1991) and 883
    (1993), 275
Security management Plan, 518–520
Security Monitor, 387
Selassie, Haile (Lion of Africa), 303
Sendero Luminoso (The Shining Path), 421–422
Sendic, Raul, 426
"Sentinels," 319
Serno-Solovevich, Alexander, 40
Servicio Especial Seguridad (SES), 424
Sese Seko, Mobutu, 316
Shah of Iran. See Pahlavi, Mohammad Reza (Shah
    of Iran)
Shaimiev, Mintimir, 197
Shakhrai, Sergei, 197
Shallah, Ramadan Abdullah, 231–232
Shamir, Yitzhak, 214
"Shankill Butchers," 108
Shaqaqi, Fathi, 231
Sharia (Islamic law), 268, 389
Sharia Law, imposition of, 253
Sharif, Omar, 126
Sharon, Ariel, 213, 215, 216, 236
Shatila massacre, 215
Sheik, Ahmed Omar, 348
Shevardnadze, Eduard, 202
Shia Muslims, 32
Shia sect in, 237
Shiites, 237, 239, 274, 287
Shiloah, Reuven, 216
Shining Path (Sendero Luminoso), 421–422
SHIPLOC system, 477
Shipping attacks, 475
Shiromani Gurdawara Pradbandhk Committee
    (SGPC), 80–81, 347
Shirosaki, Tsutomu, 381
Shoot-to-kill policy, 119, 132, 309, 468, 487
Shumukh al-Islam, 184
Siam. See Thailand
Sidqi, Bakr, 275
Sieff, Edward, 149
Signals intelligence (SIGINT), 464
Sikh Babbar Khalsa movement, 91
Sikh extremism, 82
Sikh extremists (Khalistan), 83
Sikh terrorism
    Babbar Khalsa (BK), 81–82
    overview, 80–81
    Pakistan, 347
    Shiromani Gurudwara Pradbandhk Committee
        (SGPC), 347
    speaking out against, 82
    Talwinder Singh Parmar, 82–83
Simón Bolívar, 76
Simple continuum, 3

Singh, Gobind, 343
Singh, Iqbal, 79
Singh, Manmohan, 83
Singh, Ram Rahim, 343
Sinai Province (SP), 247
Sinn Féin
    founding of, 94–95
    media and, 36
    provisionals, adopted by, 98
Sinn Fein Ard Fheis (party conference), 102–103
Sipah-e-Sahaba Pakistan, 352
Sithole, Ndabaningi, 315
Skinheads, 53, 138, 160, 168
Sky marshals, 456, 473
"Sleeping Commandos," 143
Sloan, James, 112
Smallpox, 483, 495
Smith, Ian, 314, 469
Smuts, Jan, 318
Social Democratic Labor Party (Russia), 189
Social Democratic Labour Party (SDLP), 114
Socialist Revolutionary Party, 40
Somalia
    Al- Qaeda in, 304
    clan infighting, 305
    Ethiopia, relationship with, 305
    historical overview, 304
    maritime piracy, 476
    9-11, changes since, 478
    piracy issue, 308
    Somali Revolutionary Socialist Party, 304
    United Somali Congress (USC), 304
    United States and, 304
Somali Islamic Movement, 306
Somali Revolutionary Socialist Party, 304
Somali Supreme Islamic Courts Council
    (SICC), 303
Somoza, Anastasio, 410
Sossi, Mario, 166
Sousse Beach Resort, Tunisia, 254
South Africa
    African National Congress (ANC), 317,
        320–321
    Afrikaner Nationalism, 318
    Afrikaner Resistance Movement, 318
    Afrikaner Weerstandsbeweging (AWB), 318
    Apartheid, 318
    Boeremag (Boer Force), 322
    Boers, 318
    Bureau of State Security (BOSS), 319
    extreme right-wing Afrikaner movement,
        319–320
    future, 320
    Great Trek, 318
    Herstigte Nasionale Party (HNP), 319
    historical overview, 317–318
    Islam in, 321–322
    Mandela United Football Club, 321
    Nelson Rolihlahla Mandela, 320
    People against Gangsterism and Drugs
        (PAGAD), 321–322
    Robben Island University (Isle of Purgatory), 321
    Robben University, 321
    "San Tribes" (bushmen), 318
    Umkhonto We Sizwe (Spear of the Nation), 319
    Winnie Madikizela-Mandela, 321
    Zulus, 318
South China Morning Post, 377
Southern and Southeast Asia
    overview, 338–339. See also individual countries
Sovereign Nation newspaper, 104
Soviet MI-24 helicopters, 55
Spain, 147
    Basque separatism, 142
    counterterrorism units, 467–468

11M, 148
ETA history timeline, 145–146
Euzkadi Ta Azkatasuna (ETA), 142–147
Frente Revolucionario Anti-Fascista Y
    Patriotico (FRAP), 146
Grupa De Resistencia Antifascista Primo
    Octobre (GRAPO), 146
Islamic extremists' attack on, 146–147
March 11, 2004, Madrid station bombings, 148
overview, 147
Spanish nationalism and the Basques, 147
Special Air Service Regiment (SAS), 119, 456
Special Boat Squadron (SBS), 468
"Special Category Status," 99
Special Economic Zone, 341
Specially Designated Global Terrorist (SDGT),
    142, 249
"Special Night Squads," 215
Special Powers Act (1922), 99
Special Weapons and Tactical (SWAT) units, 473
Spence, Augustus (Gusty), 105
Spiritual sanctioner, 60
Sri Lanka
    Colombo World Trade Center bombing
        (October 15, 1997), 354
    Fourth Eelam War, 355
    historical overview, 353
    Liberation Tigers of Tamil Elam (LTTE),
        353–356
    terrorist front organizations, 354
Staggie, Rashaad, 322
Stalin, Joseph, 190–191
Stammheim Prison, 159
Stanford Technology Corp. (STC), 292
Stansted Airport, UK, 456–457
Starovoitova, Galina, 194
State Law and Order Restoration Council
    (SLORC), 363
State Peace and Development Council
    (SPDC), 363
State-sponsored terrorism, 27–29
    advantages of, 28–29
    overview, 27–28
    state sponsor: implications, 28–29
    as warfare in the twenty-first century, 27
Steenson, Gerard, 104
Stern, Avraham, 214
Stern Gang, 214–215
Stinger missile, 451–452
Stirling, David, 467
Stoke Newington Eight, 123
Stone, Michael, 108
Students for Democratic Society, 52
Sudan
    Darfur, 255–256
    Osama bin Laden, 255
    U.S. strike on, 255
Sudan Airways A310 Airbus, 475
Sudan Liberation Movement/Army (SLA), 256
Sudan People's Liberation Movement/Army
    (SPLM), 255
Sufism, 126
Suharto, 387–388
Sukarno, 387
Summer Olympic Games, 129, 492
Sunni Muslims, 32, 237, 247, 300, 356
"Supergrass" trials, 105
Surface to air missiles (SAMs), 362
Suu Kyi, Aung San, 363, 364
Sweden, 183–186
Swierczek, Michael, 161
Symbionese Liberation Army (SLA), 50
Sympathizers, 12
Syria
    civil war components, 242

Hezbollah and, 237–238
  Mossad targeted assassination, 241
  opposition groups in, 242–243
  overview, 240–241
Syrian intelligence operation, 122
Syrian Unrest-Arab Spring, 241–242

"Table-top" exercise, 485
"Table-top" setting, 485
Tablighi Jamaat, 126–127
Tabun, 495
Tabun (nerve gas), 275
Taher, Yasein, 60
Taiwan (Republic of China), 378–379
Takfir wal Hirja, 152
Takushi, Okudeira, 234
Taliban, 346
  Afghanistan and, 356–357
  drugs and, 361
  Osama bin Laden, 357
Taliban-Linked Insurgents, 359–360
  See also Haqqani Network
Tamil Tigers. See Liberation Tigers of Tamil
    Eelam (LTTE)
Tamimi, Azzam, 34
Tanweer, Shehzad, 131
Task Force K-Bar, 475
Taymiyyah, Ibn, 266
Tenet, George, 493
Terre'Blanche, Eugene, 319
Terrorism
  past and future of, 489–490
Terrorism, as criminal behavior, 15
Terrorism, brief history of
  contemporary events: historical roots, 40–41
  cyclical nature of, 40
  Islam, 31–32
  jihad, 33–34
  media and
    government leaders, what they want, 37–38
    overview, 35–36
    terrorists needs and the media, 36–37
  overview, 24–25
  religious, 30–31
  state-sponsored
    advantages of, 28–29
    overview, 27
    state sponsor: implications, 28–29
    as warfare in the twenty-first century, 27–28
  state sponsors of terrorism (U.S. Dept. of
    State), 27–28
  Turks and the First Crusade, 29–30
  violence and, 24–26
  violence becoming terrorism, 26–27
Terrorism, countering
  aviation. See Aviation
  biological weapons, 482–485
  Business Resumption and Interruption Plans, 485
  chemical weapons, 480–482
  container security initiative, 479
  counterterrorism, roles for, 439–440
  counterterrorism units. See Counterterrorism units
  dirty bombs, 485–486
  Disaster Planning and Critical Incident
    Command procedures, 485
  hostage rescue units (HRUs), 473
  intelligence gathering, 463–465
  intelligence services, 465–467
  International Criminal Police Organization
    (Interpol), 463
  Internet, 439–440
  introduction, 439
  legislation, 442–443
  maintaining order, 440–441

Military Commissions (Tribunals), 463
Northern Ireland (Emergency Provisions) Act, 442
  overview, 439
Patriot Act, 459
piracy. See Piracy; Sea piracy
racial profiling, 441
regional/global efforts, 465
repression, 441–442
threats from the sea, 477
U.N. Security Council Resolution 1373,
    458–459
U.S. Naval Station Guantanamo Bay, 462
Terrorism, definition of
  approaches to defining, 5–8
  Brian Jenkins, 8
  constitutional rights, 17–19
  continuum of behavior, 3
  Department of Defense definition, 8
  FBI construct, 8
  FBI definition, 8
  George Rosie, 7
  Homeland Security Act of 2002, 7
  James M. Poland, 8
  overview, 2–3
  Prescribed behaviors, 22
  Prevention of Terrorism Act of 1989, 7
  Proscribed acts, 3
  The Reinsurance (Acts of Terrorism) Act, 1993,
    section 2(2), 7
  searching for, 2–3
  simple continuum, 3
  Terrorism Act, 2000, 7
  terrorist incident, 3
  United Nations, 10
  U.S. Army Training Manual (1984), 18
  U.S. Code of Federal Regulations, 18
  U.S. Department of Defense, 18
  U.S. Department of Defense (DOD) constructs,
    8–9
  U.S. National Security Strategy, current, 18
  Vice President's Task Force, 8
  Walter Laqueur, 8
Terrorism Act of 1989, 8
Terrorism Act 2005, Section 3, 127
Terrorism Act 2006, 127–128
  content of, 128
  law enforcement, 128
Terrorism Act of 2000, 109
Terrorism: Is It a Criminal Act or an Act of War?
    (Essig), 8
Terrorist attack, 501
  Abu Sayyaf, 385
  casualties, 502
  Caucasus dissidents (Ingushetia), 193
  countries with most, in 2015, 502
  Islamic Jihad, 429
  Islamist Militants, 198
  Japanese Red Army (obo. PFLP), 382
  "Lone Wolf" attack, 41–42, 85, 86–87
  LTTE (Tamil Tigers), 355
  Muslim Brotherhood, 245
  Palestine Liberation Front (PLF), 230
  PKK (Kurdistan Workers' Party), 176
  Revolutionary Guards and Students, 293
  Sikh extremists (Khalistan), 83
  Syrian intelligence operation, 122
  targets worldwide, 502
  Taliban, 346
Terrorist groups, structure of, 12
Terrorist incident, 3
Terrorist No-Fly Watch List, 454
Terrorist qualities, 12
Terrorists
  definition of, 5
  motivations for, 13–15

qualities, 12–13
War on Terror, 14
Terrorist Screening Centers (TSCs), 63
Thailand
  Barisan Revolusi Nasional-Coordinate,
    National Revolutionary Front-Coordinate
    (BRN-C), 368
  economy, 367
  Gerakan Mujahidin Islam Patani, Patani Islamic
    Mujahidin Group (GMIP), 368
  history timeline, 367–368
  insurgency, 367–368
  New PULO, 368
  overview, 366
  Pattani United Liberatioin Organization
    (PULO), 367
  Pemuda, 368
  Village Scouts, 367
Thatcher, Margaret, 35, 99, 100, 101, 119, 120
"The Islamic State of Iraq," 279, 282
The New York Times, 223
"The Troubles" 1968-1998, 96–97, 98, 105, 116, 442
The Wall Street Journal, 66
"Third Reich," 156
Thompson, John, 40
Threat analysis, 509–510
Threat risk assessment process, 504–506
Tiedemann, Gabrielle, 158
Timor Timur (East Timor Province), 389
Tin Oo, Thura, 364
Tonton Macoutes (secret police), 90
Torres, Juan Jose, 424
Tovex high explosive, 49
Toxins, 483
Trabelsi, Nizar, 147, 179
Transjordan, 212
Transportation Security Administration (TSA),
    447, 453
Treaty, reduction of nuclear stockpiles, 277
Treaty of Lausanne, 173
Tri-acetone Tri-peroxide (TATP), 180, 299
Troubles, Northern Ireland, 39
Trolley bag bomb, 122
Trudeau, Pierre, 80
Truman, Harry S., 212, 464
Tse-tung, Mao, 143
Tsvangirai, Morgan, 315
Tudjman, Franjo, 205
Tularemia, 484
Tunisia, 254
Tunisian Presidential Guard, 254
Tupac Amaru II, 426
Tupac Amaru Revolutionary Movement
    (MRTA), 421
Tupac Katari Guerrilla Army (EGTK), 424
Tupamaros movement, 426–428
Turbay, Diego, 420
Turkey
  Al- Qaeda in, 177–178
  Armenian terrorism, 177
  Dev Sol, 174
  Hezbollah, 176–177
  Kurdistan Freedom and Democracy Congress
    (KADEK), 175
  Kurdistan Workers Party (PKK), 174–175
  Mustafa Kemal, 173
  nationalist threat, 177
  overview, 169, 173
  Peoples Congress of Kurdistan
    (KONGRA-GEL), 175
Turkish Revenge Brigade, 177
Turkmenistan ("Land of the Turks"), 29
Tutsis, 328–329
TWA 800, 452
Twomey, Seamus, 98

Ufundi Cooperative Bank, 48
Uganda
    Acholi Pii Camp, 311
    AIDS crisis, 311
    Asian exodus, 310
    Bureau of State Research, 309
    cannibalism, 310
    David Oyite-Ojok, 310
    Democratic Republic of Congo (DRC), 312
    Entebbe, airline hijacking to, 310
    ethnic cleansing, 309
    Front for National Salvation (FRONASA), 310
    historical overview, 309–310
    Idi Amin Dada, 309
    International Rescue Committee (IRC), 311
    Lord's Resistance Army (LRA), 312–313
    Milton Obote, 309, 310
    National Resistance Army (NRA), 310
    National Resistance Movement (NRM), 310
    Northern Tanzania, invasion of, 310
    Operation Jonathan, 310
    Public Safety Unit, 309
    state-sponsored genocide, 309
Uganda National Liberation Army (UNLA), 310
Uganda National Liberation Front (UNLF), 310
Ugandan People's Defense Forces (UPDF), 312
Uganda Patriotic Movement (UPM), 310
UN High Commissioner for Refugees
        (UNHCR), 311
Uighurs, 374, 375
Ukraine, 201–202
Ulster, 96
Ulster Defence Association (UDA), 100, 106
Ulster Democratic Party (UDP), 106
Ulster Freedom Fighters (UFF), 107
Ulster Loyalist Democratic Party (ULDP), 107
Ulster Volunteer Force (UVF), 105–106, 107
Umarov, Doku, 198
Umkhonto We Sizwe (Spear of the Nation), 319
Unabomber, 41, 50
UN Convention of the Law of the Sea, Article
        105, 477
UN High Commissioner for Refugees
        (UNHCR), 311
Unified Action Groups for Personal Liberty
        (GAULA), 417
Unilateral Declaration of Independence (UDI),
        314–316, 469
Union of Russian Men, 40
Unit 101, 213
United Kingdom
    Alexander Litvinenko, 137
    Angry Brigade, the, 123
    Animal Liberation Front, 124
    Animal Rights Militia, 124
    counter-terrorism units, 467–468
    extreme right-wing groups, 138
    Finsbury Park Mosque, 125
    initial decisions, 124–125
    Islamic extremist threats
        Control Orders, 127
        International Airport in Glasgow,
            Scotland, 132
        laws to accommodate terrorist acts, 128–129
        overview, 124–125
        Prevention of Terrorism Act 2005, 127
        Tablighi Jamaat, 126–127
        Terrorism Act 2006, 127–128
        London—July 21, 2005, 130
    London—July 7, 2005, 129–131
    Operation Crevice, 131
    overview, 94
    shoot-to-kill policy, 119
United Nations
    Arab Convention, English translation, 10–11

counter terrorism actions, 10
crimes against humanity, defined, 204
2005 September summit, 10
terrorism, definition of, 9
United Nations Convention Against Torture,
        Article 3, 64
United Nations General Assembly
    Ad Hoc Committee (AHC), 10
    Comprehensive Convention on International
        Terrorism (CCIT), 10
    terrorism, definition of, 99
United Nation's Global Counterterrorism Strategy, 10
United Nations Human Development Agency, 77
United Nations Security Council Resolutions
        (UNSCR), 121
United Self-Defense Forces of Colombia (AUC),
        400, 416–417
United Somali Congress (USC), 304
United States of America
    Black Panthers, 53
    connect the dots, failure to
        Dot #1—1993: World Trade Center Bombing
            in New York City, 47–48
        Dot #2—1995: The Oklahoma City
            Bombing, 48
        Dot #3—1998: U.S. Embassies Targeted in
            Africa, 48–49
        Dot #4—2000: The Suicide Bombing of the
            U.S.S. Cole, 49
        Dot #5—2009: The Underwear Bomber—
            Detroit, 49
    domestic terrorism
        defined (FBI), 50
        foreign groups, 50
        Ku Klux Klan, 50
        left-wing aggression, 52
        left-wing terrorism, 51
        Puerto Rican terrorists groups, 51
        religious extremist groups, 50
        revolutionary nationalists groups, 52
        right-wing terrorism, 52
    domestic terrorists, 48
    extraordinary rendition
        Maher Arar—Canadian citizen, 64
        overview, 64
        USA PATRIOT Improvement and
            Reauthorization Act of 2005, 65
    flight training, 9-11 attacks, 55–57
    homegrown terrorists (1990s), 49
    hostage taking, policy toward, 15–16
    Ku Klux Klan (KKK)
        historical overview, 53–54
        victims of, 54
    Nation of Islam, 53
    neo-Nazis, 53
    New Black Panther Party for Self-Defense, 53
    9-11 and aftermath
        chronology of events, 57
        overview, 55–57
    Osama bin Laden and al Qaeda threat, 54–55
    radical Islam and
        indoctrination, 60
        jihadization, 59
        overview, 59
        pre-radicalization, 59
        self-identification, 59
    religious extremism
        Jamaat ul-Fuqra, 66
    skinheads, 53
    state sponsors of terrorism, list of, 89
    USA PATRIOT Improvement and
        Reauthorization Act of 2005 Combat
        Methamphetamine Epidemic Act of
        2005, 65
    specifics of, 82–83

watch lists, 63
Uniting against Terrorism: Recommendations for
    a Global Counterterrorism Strategy, 10
Unity Government
    Fatah and Hamas, 229. See also Arab Spring
UN-led mission to Kosovo (UNMIK), 205
Unmanned aerial vehicles (UAVs), 229
UN Resolution 598, 276
UN Resolution 678, 276
U.N. Security Council Resolution 1373, 458–459
UN Special Commission to Iraq (UNSCOM),
        277, 480
Urban guerrilla, personal qualities of, 425
Urban II, Pope, 29
Uribe, Alvaro, 416, 419, 433
Uruguay
    Armed Islamic Group (GIA), 427
    Frente Amplio (Broad Front), 427
    National Liberation Movement (MLN), 426–428
    Organismo Coordinador de Actividades Anti-
        Subversivas, 427
    overview, 426
    Penal de Libertad, 427
    Raul Sendic, 426
    Tupamaros movement, 426–427
USA Patriot Act 2001, 19–22
USA PATRIOT Improvement and Reauthorization
        Act of 2005, 65
U.S. Central Intelligence Agency (CIA), 410
    FARC–PIRA link, 102
U.S. Customs and Border Patrol (CBP), 479
U.S. Department of Defense (DOD)
    constructs, 8–9
    terrorism, definition of, 401
U.S. Department of Homeland Security, 445
    See also Department of Homeland Security
        (DHS)
U.S. Department of Justice (DOJ), 65
U.S. Food and Drug Administration (FDA), 478
    biological, chemical and nuclear weapons, 479
U.S. foreign policy, 61–62
U.S. Government Accountability report to
        Congressional Committees on Aviation
        Security, 447
U.S. Government Accountability Office
        (GAO), 493
U.S. House of Representatives International
        Relations Committee, 114
U.S. law 18 USC 1203, Act for the Prevention
        and Punishment of the Crime of Hostage-
        Taking, 16
U.S. Navy SEALs
    bin Laden, killing of, 344, 357
U.S. Naval Station Guantanamo Bay, 462
U.S.S Bunker Hill, 496
U.S.S. Cole, suicide bombing of, 49, 299
U.S.S. Franklin, 496
U.S.S. Intrepid, 496
U.S. sky marshals. See Federal Air Marshal
        Service—FAM
U.S.S. St. Lo, 496
U.S. State Department's Bureau of Diplomatic
        Security, 417
U.S. Treasury Department's Office of Foreign
        Asset Control's (OFAC), 352
U.S. Visa waiver program (VWP), 59
Utvar Rychleho Nasazeni (URNA), 472
Uzbekistan, 195

Van der Graaf, Volkert, 182
Van Gough, Theo, 182
Vehicle borne explosive devices (VBIEDs), 6
Venezuela, 432–433
    Accion Democratica (AD), 432

Christian Democratic Party (COPIE), 432
Colombian People's Liberation Army
(EPL), 432
corruption, 432
cross-border incursions, 432
FARC, indirect talks with, 432
Hugo Chavez, 432
National Liberation Army (ELN), 432
Venezuelan Communist Party, 192
Vesicants, 481–482
Victorious Sect Army, 280
Vidal, Victor, 27
Vienna Convention on Diplomatic Relation,
1961, 120
Vietnam
Ho Chi Minh, 370
overview, 369–370
Villeneuve, Raymond, 80
Violence
described, 26
terrorism and, 24–26
Volante Rosse, 166
"Volunteers," the, 101
Von Hindenburg, Paul, 156

Waco compound of the Branch Davidians, 50
Waco Massacre, 50
Wahhabi Islam, 266–267
Wahhabis, 266
Wahhabism, 60
Waite, Terry, 238
Wakkas, Sallah, 207
Wales, 112
War against terrorism
biological and chemical attacks, 495
children, as suicide bombers, 497–498
future threats and possible trends, 494
holy terror, 495–496
nuclear threats, 494
overview, 489–490
suicide and religious terrorism, 496–497
suicide bombers, children as, 497–498
technology and counterterrorism, 498–499
terrorism gets a larger stage, 492–493
weapons of mass destruction (WMD), 492
WMD, future threats from, 494
War Graves Commission Cemetery, 248
"War of the Cross," or Crusade, 29
War on Terror
declaration of, 58
description of, 49
9-11 attacks and, 14
Water boarding, 462
Weapons of mass destruction (WMD)
biological weapons, 482–485
Business Resumption and Interruption
Plans, 485
chemical weapons, 480
combating the proliferation of, 479–480

dirty bombs, 485–486
Disaster Planning and Critical Incident
Command procedures, 485
Iraq, 276
Libya, 248
Weather Underground Organization
(Weathermen), 52
Web sites
American Society for Industrial Security, 517
Army of God, 51
Benazir Bhutto, 345
Canadian Security and Intelligence Service, 78
Constitutional Rights Foundation, 17–19
Danish Cartoons, 183
International Crisis Group, 336
The Jamestown Foundation, 187
Jane's Information Group, 262
Liberation Tigers of Tamil Eelam, 370
The Mackenzie Institute, 92
Militant Islam, 195
The Security Service MI5, 370
U.S. Department of Defense, 301
Washington Institute, 262
"Weeping mother" stories, 37
Wegener, Ulrich, 472
Welsh, Richard, 170
Westgate Shopping Mall Attack, 326
Whitelaw, William, 99
White Revolution, 292
Wingate, Orde, 215
WMD, future threats, 494–495
biological weapons, 495
chemical weapons, 495
nuclear weapons, 494
Woolwich attack timeline, 134–135
Worch, Christian, 161
World and Islam Studies Enterprise, 36
World Bank, 364
World Health Organization (WHO), 523
World Sikh Organization, 350
World Trade Center bombing, 47–48
Wright, Billy King Rat, 105, 107

Xinjiang Uighur Autonomous Region
(XUAR), 375
Xiros, Savas, 171

Yallop, David, 187
Yanukovych, Viktor, 201
Yar'Adua, Umaru, 333
Yarkas, Imad Barakat, 146
Yassin, Sheikh Ahmed, 34, 223
Yasuki, Yasuda, 234
Yellin-Mor, Natan, 214
Yeltsin, Boris, 192, 197
Yemen
Aden (South Yemen), 297
Believing Youth Movement, 298

British domination, 246
Hamas in, 298
overview, 297
People's Democratic Republic of Yemen, or
PDRY, 297
PIJ in, 298
separate states and unification, 297–299
U.S.S. Cole, 298
Yemen Arab Republic (YAR; Yemen Sanaa or
North Yemen), 297
Yemen Arab Republic (YAR; Yemen Sanaa or
North Yemen), 297
Young, Andrew, 54
Young Turks, the, 173
Yousef, Ramzi Ahmed, 344, 448
Yugoslavia
international criminal tribunal for the former
Yugoslavia, 205
modern-day problems, 203–206
World War I to ethnic cleansing, 203
Yushchenko, Victor, 201

Zaire. See Democratic Republic of Congo (DRC)
Zakat Hawala, 334
Zapata, Emiliano, 402
Zapatista National Liberation Army (ELZN),
404–405
Zealots, 27
Zenawi, Meles, 303
Zeroual, Liamine, 259
Zimbabwe, 315
Access to Information Act, 316
AIDS, 317
coltan, 316
Commonwealth Observer Group, 315
communist involvement, 314
counter-terrorism units, 469
DRC, actions in, 316
Ian Smith, 314
Joshua Nkomo, 315
land-redistribution program, 317
Movement for Democratic Change, 317
National Heroes' Day in 2002, 315
overview, 314
Public Order and Security Act, 316
Rhodesian Special Air Service Regiment, 314
Robert Mugabe, 314
suspension from the Commonwealth, 315
Unilateral Declaration of Independence (UDI),
314–316
Zanu-PF 5 Brigade, 316–317
ZAPU movement, 31
Zimbabwe African National Union (ZANU), 314
Zimbabwe African People's Union (ZANPU), 314
Zimbabwe People's Revolutionary Army
(ZIPRA), 314
Zoning, 507–508
Zulus, 318